In memory of three people who died in the period covered by this volume:
My wonderful mum, Betty Campbell, 1926–2014
My best friend and colleague, Philip Gould, 1950–2011
My assistant who became a friend, Mark Bennett, 1969–2014

And of three who have died since:
Charles Kennedy, 1959–2015, whose death came
not long after defeat in the 2015 election
Tessa Jowell, 1947–2018, symbol and driver of the Olympic Spirit
Syd Young, 1937–2020, friend, mentor, great man

DIARIES: VOLUME 8

Rise and Fall of the Olympic Spirit, 2010–2015

RISE AND FALL OF THE OLYMPIC SPIRIT

ALASTAIR CAMPBELL

DIARIES: VOLUME 8, 2010–2015

Biteback Publishing

First published in Great Britain in 2021 by
Biteback Publishing Ltd, London
Copyright © Alastair Campbell 2021

ISBN 978-1-78590-086-0

10 9 8 7 6 5 4 3 2 1

A CIP catalogue record for this book is available from the British Library.

Set in Palatino and Gotham

Printed and bound in Great Britain by
CPI Group (UK) Ltd, Croydon CR0 4YY

MIX
Paper from
responsible sources
FSC® C020471
FSC
www.fsc.org

Contents

Introduction

Once upon a time, not so very long ago, Labour seemed invincible. I can remember my fellow diarist Alan Clark giving me his considered assessment, some time between Tony Blair's first election win in 1997 and the Tory MP's sudden death in 1999, that 'you boys have put paid to us for good. It's all over.'

He was, as those who knew the man or his diaries will confirm, prone to exaggeration, and fond of colourful analysis leading to dramatic conclusions. But he genuinely struggled to see a way back for the Conservatives, thrashing around in the wake of our parliamentary majority of 179, failing to dent TB's standing or popularity as New Labour strolled to a second three-figure majority in 2001. And when we won again in 2005, even after the Iraq War, it was perhaps easy to imagine that 'the other AC', as he used to announce himself when calling my office for a grumble and a gossip, had had a point.

Our disappointment at a third-term majority reduced to sixty-six was driven in the main by the comparison with those of four and eight years earlier, and by the knowledge that the shrunken majority would also shrink TB's authority, and so make him more vulnerable to the pressures that finally saw him leave Downing Street a decade after he had arrived there. He had seen off four Conservative Party leaders and the fifth, David Cameron, led the Commons in a standing ovation for TB after his final session at the despatch box.

It is odd, today, writing this as 2020 turns to 2021, to hear Boris Johnson's majority of eighty constantly described as 'enormous', given it is not much bigger than one which, a decade and a half ago, created in the New Labour team a sense of disappointment and alarm. But whereas Clark saw an existential threat to the Tories as a party of power, as the Blair juggernaut rolled over its territory into the new century, TB himself did not. 'The Tory Party is slumbering,' he would occasionally say if he ever felt those around him were beginning to get a little presumptive about Labour's right to rule, 'but it will be back.' It perhaps explains, as much as any basic politics or ideology, why he never liked to stray from the political centre ground.

Today, it is the Labour Party that is wondering whether it will ever see power again. Two interesting historical statistics to mull amid any pondering that that observation may have triggered. Stat 1: Labour's record in the past eleven general elections – lost, lost, lost, lost, won, won, won, lost, lost, lost, lost. Stat 2 is one I pointed out in Volume 7 but has even greater relevance today: Eton College has produced three times as many Prime Ministers as the Labour Party in its entire 120-year history. One of those Etonians, David Cameron, is Prime Minister for the period covered by this volume. Another, Boris Johnson, is Prime Minister now.

Of those eight Labour defeats, the one that ended Volume 7 and saw Gordon Brown leave Downing Street after Labour's longest ever sustained period in office – thirteen years – at least prevented the Tory majority many had expected. Nonetheless, Volume 8 begins with Cameron installed as Prime Minister, albeit as the head of a rare UK government coalition, with Liberal Democrat leader Nick Clegg as Deputy Prime Minister.

Looking back at the years leading up to this moment, perhaps it was inevitable, given the mood in the country appeared to be one of fatigue with Labour, but people were not wholly sure about Cameron and the Tories, so they threw in Clegg as someone to keep an eye on him and help to curb Tory excesses. Cameron, who in opposition had often looked as if he lacked a coherent driving purpose beyond winning power, was accidentally gifted one – to make coalition government work.

But he and his Chancellor, George Osborne, also had, from the moment they entered No. 10 and No. 11, two major political objectives: to build enough support to be able to dispense with the Lib Dems by the time of the next election, an endeavour in which Clegg was perhaps overly helpful, given he often became the defender of some of the Tories' most damaging and regressive policies; and to attach blame for the ravages of the global financial crisis to Labour. On that, I felt strongly that there was far too little pushback from Gordon Brown's successor, Ed Miliband, an argument he tired of hearing from me, and which you may tire of reading in the pages that follow. I was, however, interested to hear former Bank of England Governor Mark Carney, delivering the Reith Lectures of 2020, point to the pivotal role Brown and Chancellor Alistair Darling paid in rescuing the global economy during the crisis of 2008. Yet Cameron and Osborne hammered home 'the mess we inherited', not merely to pin the blame for a global crisis on Labour, but also to justify the policies of austerity, the effects of which we are still living with. They were a lot better at politics than they were at economics.

The volume ends with Cameron winning a majority that on the morning of the 2015 election neither he nor Ed Miliband seemed to expect, and though Theresa May let that majority slip when she called the 2017 election, and subsequently had to rely on Northern Ireland's Democratic Unionists, the Tories have now been in power for a decade. Assuming the current term runs its course, the Conservatives' Cameron–May–Johnson tenure of Downing Street will be longer than that of Labour's Blair and Brown.

So Cameron's two elections act as starting point and end point of this volume. In between came a decision that more than any other will define his, and Johnson's, place in history. How Cameron *wanted* to be defined could perhaps be seen in one of his more memorable speeches, in 2005, when he said, 'Everyone is welcome in the modern compassionate Conservative Party,' which he urged to 'stop banging on about Europe'. How he *will* be defined is as the man who decided that the only way to stop them banging on about Europe was to promise an in/out referendum that no one but a tiny minority of the most passionate Eurosceptics had been asking for. And now here we are, two referendums later (Scotland figures fairly large in this volume too), with Cameron and May both gone, Brexit 'done' (though with nobody entirely clear what that means), and 'compassionate Conservatism' has Priti Patel as Home Secretary and no room on the candidates list for people like Ken Clarke, Dominic Grieve or Anna Soubry – nor for anyone else unwilling to stand on a platform that Brexit means whatever Johnson decides it means at any time now or in the future.

Cameron is adamant he had no option but to call the referendum. I profoundly disagree. It was a tactic replacing a strategy. It did indeed quieten his Eurosceptic wing for a while, and help him win back some support being lost to UKIP. That was its purpose. He could reasonably argue that it helped him win the election. Fine. But then he had to deliver what he promised, and we all know where that ended: for him, out of power, and, more importantly, for the country, out of Europe. That is for another day, but of all the events that unfold in the following pages, Cameron's referendum decision is the one of the greatest import, because of what, where and who it has led to.

As for the referendum on Scottish independence, I suspect I am not alone in feeling that English nationalism and global populism are a big part of what fuelled both Brexit and Johnson, which in turn has helped the SNP's cause too. It is not at all fanciful to imagine that in 'taking back control' through Brexit, Johnson will break the union in at least two parts, Scotland and Northern Ireland. It was interesting to be reminded when editing this volume that then SNP leader Alex Salmond sounded me out to be part of any transition team, should his cause have been won. The proposition feels both more realistic and more attractive than it did. From being a full-on 'No' campaigner in 2014, it's fair to say I am now less certain.

The other startling moment from that meeting with Salmond was his response when I asked how he had managed to see off any suggestion from Cameron that Scots outside Scotland, or even everyone in the UK, should have had a vote on such an important constitutional change. His reply was that the Prime Minister never made the suggestion. It would suggest that David Cameron was somewhat cavalier with regard to both referendums that took place on his watch.

There is another David in this story, however, and who knows how different our history might have been had David and not Ed Miliband become the other David's opponent in 2010. It is of course impossible to prove the counterfactual, but that 'Labour picked the wrong brother' became one of the defining drumbeats of this period. Ed had, and continues to have, many qualities, and if Labour do get back into power under Keir Starmer, there is no doubt he will be an important figure in that government. But if it was a surprise that he stood against his older brother, who had been Foreign Secretary under Gordon and was a clear favourite when the post-GB leadership election began, it was perhaps an even bigger surprise that he won. It also felt, to those of us who had lived through one Shakespearean drama, the TB–GBs, that Labour was forcing itself to live through another, this time with real brothers. It tested loyalties and friendships to the limit.

You may remember from Volume 7 my regular pangs of guilt at not feeling wholly enthusiastic about being dragged back into the political and electoral arena by GB, as I sought to build a different kind of life to the one I had lived for a decade with TB. You will see in this one guilt at not doing more to help David win the leadership election, and then subsequently guilt at not helping Ed more, mixed perhaps with guilt with regard to David that I was helping him at all. You will see that I did, as with GB, and despite the best efforts of my psychiatrist, David Sturgeon, get 'sucked in'. So many Davids! David S thinks politics, and the need to be needed by people in power, is my 'demon'. He thinks I am relentlessly torn between a life devoted to myself and my family and my own interests, and a life fighting and winning political arguments and battles and being needed by others to fight them.

Perhaps that struggle explains why, despite regularly being told that I *must* get a seat, and that I could become leader – even TB said so at times – it never seemed like that to me. Maybe I knew too much, about the job, and myself.

So why the guilt? Well, David M and I had worked closely in TB's team for years, in opposition and government. Fiona and I were his and his wife Louise's referees in their application to adopt children. We had been on holiday together. We were good friends, and friends should always be there for each other. We remain good friends, but David and Louise definitely felt I could have done more to help, and they have a point. Indeed, though I helped a little behind the scenes, I think my only public statement in the campaign was one that was not intended to be public at all, when I told a Labour fundraiser that I worried Ed 'would make the party feel good about losing', which someone immediately briefed to a Sunday newspaper.

Also, a little like the subsequent EU referendum that so many of us misread until it was too late, perhaps I went along with the conventional wisdom that David was bound to win, which, among members and MPs, he did. But Ed managed to win sufficient support in the union section of the electoral college to win overall, to the evident shock of his brother – and the delight, it has to be said, of the other David, the Tory one. There is even a half-decent Cameron joke in this volume, when my friend Edi Rama, the Prime Minister of Albania, is teasing him, passing on my view that he will lose the next election. 'Alastair is wrong,' said Cameron, 'because he has got the right Edi in Albania and the wrong Edi in Britain.'

I do feel – and it partly explains why I wrote a book called *Winners: And How They Succeed* during this period – that both Britain and Labour were losing winning ways and winning mindsets. It certainly has felt odd at times that the one leader who led Labour to the only three wins out of those eleven efforts is someone successive leaders have rarely asked for advice and support. Against Theresa May, Jeremy Corbyn campaigned well and won more support than expected. But he lost. Yet his supporters behaved as though it was a great win. When he lost to Boris Johnson two years later, he proclaimed: 'We won the argument.' That sounded a lot like what feeling good about losing might look like. But of course Corbyn did not exist in a vacuum. Politics is a continuum, and I have said before that Tony begat Gordon, begat Ed, begat Jeremy. By that I do not mean that they created them, but that perhaps each was created as something of a counterpoint to what went before. But I do feel we moved step by step away from winning ways towards losing ways, and it will not be easy for Starmer, even against a government as venal and useless as Johnson's, to reverse the losses next time around.

There are plenty of low points in this volume, not least the death of my mother, and also that of Philip Gould. Iraq continues to be a big part of events, as the Chilcot Inquiry heads slowly to its conclusion, and the Leveson Inquiry into media standards also ensures there is no escaping events of the past.

Many of the low points relate to something very personal, and very difficult for both Fiona and me, namely the descent of our son Calum into alcoholism, and all the difficulties and sleepless nights that brought with it. Eventually, he found the rehab place that worked for him, in Scotland, and he has not touched alcohol since. A high point. I found it harder to deal with his problems than I had with my own when I faced similar difficulties with alcohol at around the same age. Calum's experience, our daughter Grace's anxiety, which led to her cutting short her university education in Paris, and my two older brothers' continuing struggles, further fuelled my interest in and involvement with mental health campaigns and causes.

Many of the high points came from the London 2012 Olympic and Paralympic Games. How sad that we have since lost Tessa Jowell, who did so much to make them happen, and was so happy during those wonderful weeks. And how sad that we have also lost so much of that Olympic spirit that was so pervasive, making it surely one of the best times ever to be British and alive. I tried, and failed, to persuade Cameron through Cabinet Secretary Jeremy Heywood – another great guy sadly gone – to use the legacy of the Olympics for a wholesale change in the way we view sport and use it across a whole range of government responsibilities. Jeremy was keen. Cameron, sadly, was not.

During the Games, it was as though everyone had swallowed some kind of happiness pill that made them smile more, talk on the Tube more, and for once look for the good in people and events rather than the bad. Optimism ruled.

Even our newspapers, which so often yearn for things to fail, which had articulated the narrative first that we wouldn't land the Games in the face of competition from Paris, then, when that hurdle was crossed, that we wouldn't get things ready on time and that everything would go wrong, had to get with the happy pill programme and join in the fun and celebration.

The eyes of the world were on us, and from Danny Boyle's breathtaking opening ceremony to IOC president Jacques Rogge's formal closing of what he called the 'happy and glorious' Games, they saw a country that was modern, vibrant, dynamic, outward-looking, multicultural, confident, welcoming, successful, united. Athletes and fans landed from every corner of the planet, and the smiles of wonder on their faces suggested they had taken the happy pill too. As they all headed home, their views of the UK almost certainly enhanced, it was possible to see London 2012 as a model in the art of what has become known as soft power. The UK has since been replaced by France at the top of the Soft Power Index.

The London 2012 project itself, started under one government and completed under another, showed what can happen when a sense of unity develops around major challenges, the short-, medium- and long-term benefits of which most can sense, even amid all the risks that such projects inevitably carry.

Yet it is impossible to escape the feeling that Britain is communicating a very different sense of itself to the world today. Back then, Britain and the world could revel in London Mayor Boris Johnson's unique mix of zipwire wit and manicured buffoonery. London 2012 took his profile and popularity home and abroad to a new giddy level.

But how is this for an unintended consequence? The Olympics made Johnson the force that he became. And it is in large part the force that he became that delivered Brexit. And how is this for a hideous irony? If the face that Brexit Britain presents to the world today had been the face we had presented when going for the Games... no chance. What was I saying about Britain at the time of London 2012? '... modern, vibrant, dynamic, outward-looking, multicultural, confident, welcoming, successful, united.' Would any of those adjectives be applied to the Brexit Britain Johnson now leads?

We are less modern, less vibrant, less dynamic, less outward-looking, less multicultural, less confident, less welcoming, less successful. And we are less united than at any time I can ever remember. In less than a decade it feels as if we have taken that Olympic spirit, the mood of London 2012, and created a Britain that represents the very opposite of all it represented, and felt like, at the time. I find it very hard not to be very sad about that.

It is why Tessa Jowell, without whom there would have been no London 2012, and who sadly died in 2018, is one of the six people to whose memory this volume is dedicated. It is dedicated also to a friend who was clearly ill during this period and died not long after losing the 2015 election, Charles Kennedy; to my friend and mentor Syd Young, who died shortly before the first Covid lockdown, and to whom we have not yet been able to say a proper farewell; and to three people who died between 2010 and 2015, and who in very different ways gave me and my family wonderful love and support – my best friend in politics, Philip Gould; my assistant who became a friend, Mark Bennett; and above all my mum, whose presence I still feel, not least because of the message she left to us on her deathbed:

'Those you love don't go away,
They walk beside you every day.'

Neither Tessa, nor any of them, would be able to fathom how Britain has gone from what it was in 2012 to what it is less than a decade later.

Finally, a few thanks. This is the eighth full volume, and the tenth book in all, of my diaries. I would like to thank the team at Biteback, who have published the last four of the eight full volumes. They are unfailingly enthusiastic and professional, and in particular I would like to thank Olivia Beattie, Lucy Stewardson, Namkwan Cho, Suzanne Sangster, Vicky Jessop and James Stephens.

Bill Hagerty has been my editor on the diaries for all eight volumes, ever since Richard Stott, editor of *The Blair Years*, died shortly before that first of the ten books was published. Bill has carried out that task with diligence and dedication, and I thank him for it. I also thank all who continue to take an interest, and hope you enjoy reading *The Rise and Fall of the Olympic Spirit*.

Who's Who

May 2010 – June 2015

David Cameron	Prime Minister 2010–16 (DC)
George Osborne	Chancellor of the Exchequer 2010–16 (GO)
Ed Miliband	Leader of the Labour Party 2010–15 (EM, Ed M)
Nick Clegg	Leader of the Liberal Democrats 2007–15, Deputy Prime Minister 2010–15
Tony Blair	Prime Minister 1997–2007 (TB)
Gordon Brown	Former Labour Chancellor, Prime Minister 2007–10 (GB)
Alastair Campbell	Writer, campaigner, adviser to TB and Ed M (AC)
Fiona Millar	AC's partner (Fiona, FM)
David Miliband	Labour MP, Foreign Secretary 2007–10 (DM, David M)
Harriet Harman	Deputy leader of the Labour Party 2007–15
Ed Balls	Shadow Home Secretary 2010–11, shadow Chancellor 2011–15 (EB)
Alan Johnson	Secretary for Health 2007–09, Home Secretary 2009–10
(Lord) Charlie Falconer	Former Labour Cabinet minister, shadow Cabinet member
(Lord) Peter Mandelson	Former Labour Cabinet minister
Douglas Alexander	Shadow Foreign Secretary 2011–15
Cherie Blair	Wife of TB (CB)
(Baroness) Tessa Jowell	Minister for Olympics 2005–10, member London 2012 Olympics Organising Committee
Jack Straw	Former Labour Cabinet minister
Andy Burnham	Former Labour Cabinet minister, shadow Cabinet member
(Lord) Paddy Ashdown	Former leader of the Liberal Democrats, peerage 2001

Charles Kennedy	Former leader of the Liberal Democrats
William Hague	Foreign Secretary 2010–14, Leader of the Commons 2014–15
Michael Gove	Secretary of State for Education 2010–14, Chief Whip 2014–15
Jeremy Hunt	Culture Secretary 2010–12, Health Secretary 2012–18
Vince Cable	Liberal Democrat, Business, Innovation and Skills Secretary and president of the Board of Trade 2010–15
Alex Salmond	Leader of the Scottish National Party 2004–14, First Minister of Scotland 2007–14
Nicola Sturgeon	First Minister of Scotland 2014–
John Bercow	House of Commons Speaker 2009–19
Boris Johnson	Mayor of London 2008–16
Jeremy Heywood	Cabinet Secretary 2012–18
Jonathan Powell	TB's former chief of staff
Catherine Rimmer	CEO of the Tony Blair Institute
David Axelrod	Barack Obama strategist, adviser to Ed M
Justine Thornton	Lawyer, wife of Ed M
Louise Shackleton	Musician, wife of David M
(Baroness) Margaret Thatcher	Former Prime Minister
(Lord) Sebastian Coe	President of 2012 Olympics organising committee and former athlete
Godric Smith	Head of comms, Olympic Delivery Authority
Greg Nugent	London Olympics director of marketing
Anji Hunter	Formerly Tony Blair's director of government relations
Tom Baldwin	Labour head of communications
Andy Coulson	Downing Street director of communications 2010–11
Tim Livesey	Ed Miliband's chief of staff
Tim Allan	Public relations consultant, former adviser to TB
Mark Bennett	Labour activist, Mayor of Lambeth, AC's assistant
(Lord) Philip Gould	Political pollster and strategist, peerage 2004 (PG, Philip)
Gail Rebuck	Wife of Philip, publisher
(Lord) Neil Kinnock	Leader of the Labour Party 1983–92 (NK)

(Baroness) Glenys Kinnock	Former minister, wife of NK, AC family friend
Rachel Kinnock	Daughter of Neil and Glenys, adviser to Ed M
Edi Rama	Albanian politician, Prime Minister 2013–
Hashim Thaçi	Prime Minister of Kosovo 2008–14
Endri Fuga	Rama's communications director
(Sir) Alex Ferguson	Manchester United manager 1986–2013 (AF)
David Moyes	Manchester United manager 2013–14
Sean Dyche	Burnley FC manager 2012–
Anne Robinson	TV personality, friend of AC
David Sturgeon	AC's psychiatrist (DS)
Dave Brailsford	Manager, Team Sky cycling
Chris Froome	Cyclist, Team Sky
Brendan Foster	Businessman and commentator, former athlete
Jamie Oliver	Celebrity chef and restaurateur
Ed Victor	AC's literary agent (Ed V)
Andrew Marr	Television and radio presenter
Paul Dacre	Editor, *Daily Mail*
Piers Morgan	Journalist, broadcaster and television personality
Andrew Neil	Journalist and broadcaster
Matthew Freud	PR executive
Rupert Murdoch	Chairman, News Corp
Rebekah Brooks	CEO of News International 2009–11 and News UK 2015–
Sir Brian Leveson	Judge, chairman of the public inquiry into culture, practices and ethics of the British press 2011–12
Sir John Chilcot	Chairman of Iraq inquiry
Hugh Grant	Actor, press reform advocate
Gerald Shamash	AC lawyer
Nick Robinson	BBC News political editor
(Sir) David Frost	Broadcaster, TV host
Bill Clinton	42nd President of the United States (BC)
Hillary Clinton	US Secretary of State 2009–13
George W. Bush	43rd President of the United States (GWB)
Barack Obama	44th President of the United States
Nicolas Sarkozy	President of France
Angela Merkel	Chancellor of Germany
François Hollande	President of France 2012–17
Vladimir Putin	President or Prime Minister of Russia 1999–

Betty Campbell	Mother of AC
Donald and Graeme Campbell	Brothers of AC
Liz Naish	Sister of AC
Rory, Calum and Grace Campbell	Children of AC and FM
Audrey Millar	Mother of FM
Gavin Millar	Brother of FM

The Diaries

Wednesday 12 May 2010

I hadn't seen much of the Cameron stuff last night so caught up with it this morning.* I felt he did OK, but no better. There was already a total change of media tone. I did a few interviews, the best with Richard Bacon [BBC] asking me about the last hours with GB, Martin Argles [*Guardian*] having put some of his behind the scenes pictures online. Really moving. Message from GB in Scotland to say thanks. [Lord] Paddy Ashdown [former Lib Dem leader] called, said that he was really sad we had not been able to pull off a Lib–Lab deal, but Nick Clegg [Lib Dem leader, now Deputy Prime Minister] had decided early on. TB had felt the Tory–Lib coalition was inevitable once the results were clear. He said we had to help David [Miliband, outgoing Foreign Secretary], though we agreed he had to hone his basic political skills. Mark Bennett [AC assistant] had sent a message volunteering to help and got a rather impersonal 'Someone may be in touch' message. David M launched his leadership campaign as I was on the radio and it felt a bit rushed. I was getting lots of exhortations to stand myself – not sure how that would work, but GB had hinted at that yesterday when he said I should look for a seat, and go for it. Piers Morgan [broadcaster] was on saying the same.

Into Random House for a meeting on *Prelude to Power* [first full volume of AC diaries]. The Adam Boulton [Sky News political editor] row [heated exchange live on TV] had cut through big time, people asking me about it everywhere I went. I was sending a letter of complaint to Sky. I took legal advice and the feeling was that if I wanted to, I had a legitimate complaint with Ofcom. [Friend, former Justice Secretary and former Lord Chancellor] Charlie Falconer's view, though, was that I was the clear winner of it, so what was the point? But there were others telling me I had a case for defamation over him suggesting that [Lord] Peter Mandelson [outgoing Lord President of the Council] and I were involved in an unconstitutional stitch-up, that we were compulsive liars and that I was unpatriotic. Even

---

* The general election on 7 May had failed to produce an overall majority for any party. Conservative leader David Cameron then began negotiations with Liberal Democrat leader Nick Clegg to form the first UK coalition government since the Second World War.

the *Daily Mail*, which libels me on close to a daily basis, seemed to accept he had gone over the top.

My blog was getting more reaction than ever, and there was a thing on *The Guardian* that I was 'most popular twitterer in UK'. Grace [AC daughter] saying everyone at school was talking about it. I watched a bit of the Cameron–Clegg press conference in the No. 10 garden, but once the Beeb started saying there was birdsong in the garden I had had enough. I was worrying depression was going to set in pretty soon. It almost certainly would. I fixed *The Late Late Show* [Irish TV talk show] for Friday to get out of the country.

Thursday 13 May

Fuck me, a week since the election. It felt like months. The hard reality settling in. Burnley down [relegated from the Premier League], Labour out. Horrible to see those fuckers in there, with the media of course giving them a total blow job. GB called early on from Fife. He sounded pretty feisty again. On Clegg, he said it wasn't true that he [GB] had rejected demands for more time for coalition talks with us. They had stopped them, Clegg had decided and that was that. He had said there were no policy differences between us. It was about workability. GB said that he felt I should maybe do a big piece for someone on the background. He said he really didn't mind if I went through what went on, what he said. He reckoned Clegg was quite a weak figure who had been pushed hard by his team. GB was convinced he was genuinely torn. Our view had been that he was always going to go to the Tories. He realised it now. There was no place in the inner circle for Paddy or any of the others who were helping us. But the Libs were going to remain divided. They were trying to make out we were to blame for everything coming to an end, which was, he said, bollocks.

He said he had warned him that he was going to have real difficulty on Europe. Clegg then went off and said he was going to get them to change their line on Europe. It was all a bit naïve. But the reality is a lot of people voted Lib Dem to stop the Tories so would not be happy to see them in government together. PG sent through a note of focus groups showing that Clegg was fading – they think he has a bit of a nerve being there to prop up a Tory government. GB said Clegg obviously hoped he could temper Tory policy a bit but it was still a Tory government and he was convinced they would 'eat them up, spit them out and then go for their own mandate'. His main point of attack was that 'When it came to big issues they went Tory. That was their choice.' Even at lunchtime on resignation day Clegg said he had not made up his mind, he was worried about Europe, would decide by 5 p.m. Then he kept asking for more time. GB kept telling him why he felt the Tories could never deliver for him. 'I said if you go with the Tories you are going with the old politics. With us you could have gone progressive.' He has gone conservative.

GB said he had sent him a letter with all the issues he felt we could work together on and they couldn't. More and more bloody time. GB was almost reliving it, so much so I said you just need to take a break now. I know, he said, but you guys need to make sure they don't manage to position this against us. He said he apologised for dragging me back to No. 10 when he knew I hadn't really wanted that full-on role. But he was grateful. Never forget we stopped them winning a majority. There was definitely a feeling he had saved his best for last, when it was too late. There was a nobility in the end.

He felt Vince Cable [Lib Dem MP, Business, Innovation and Skills Secretary] would be the first to walk. He said he had virtually said to him he wouldn't serve in a Tory Cabinet. Clegg had also said to GB that he wished they had known each other better before, that he felt there was not much to build on there. We chatted for half-hour or so and he sounded very up and down. I went to collect Fergie [Alex Ferguson, manager Manchester United] at Euston then to Camden Brasserie to meet Fiona and the boys. He said GB was brilliant and clever but didn't have the TB roundedness. Calum [AC son] was telling us why he felt David M wouldn't win the leadership, that he thought the party would look for something different. I sent a note to TB on some of the dangers. He wanted us to be involved but not open about support. He said afterwards he felt I should move on, just let go, put politics behind me.

Out to collect Alex at the Landmark then head to Battersea for the Sport Industry Awards where he was getting a lifetime achievement award. At my table there was Alex, Brendan [former athlete, commentator] and Sue [Foster], Kelly Holmes [athlete], Paul Deighton [CEO London Olympics organising committee], [Baroness] Tanni Grey-Thompson [former Paralympian, politician] and Haile Gebrselassie [Ethiopian long-distance running star]. Lovely bloke. Invited me out to his resort in Ethiopia. I was presenting one of the awards and had a little pop at Clegg, which seemed to go down OK though one or two complained afterwards it was not appropriate. Will Greenwood [former rugby player] said something quite nice – you lost, but everyone knows you made a difference and nobody is going to think it was down to you that you lost.

Friday 14 May ·
Rayan [Benjamin, driver] took me to City [airport], tiredness really creeping

in. Cameron off to Scotland. How happy did Danny Alexander [Lib Dem MP, Secretary of State for Scotland] look to be with him? Tessa [Jowell, shadow minister for London] called to say she had been asked to go and see Jeremy Hunt [Culture, Media and Sport Secretary] at four. She had decided she would do something with the Olympics but not appointed by the Tories. We talked about the leadership scene. She felt it had to be DM, but that Ed [Miliband, David's brother] was motoring in the parts of the party David was maybe losing. [Shadow Education Secretary] Ed Balls's intentions not clear. She said David was not great at relating to people he might deem to be beneath him. Ed's problems were judgement and decision-making. Dublin looking great. Gym, kip, early dinner with Paul Allen [Irish PR friend] at Bentleys, then out to *The Late Late Show*. Bertie [Ahern, former Taoiseach of Ireland] called for a chat. He was a bit PNG [*persona non grata*] at the moment so I was determined to say something nice about him. Wide-ranging interview and with a nice enough tone. I admitted I had turned down a peerage.

Got away about 11. Really tired. Long chat with David M when I got back to the hotel. He said Ed had called him and was definitely standing. When he asked why, he said because he felt he had something to say and he could win. David said Louise was really upset – more than David in a way. He said Ed would be a great Lib Dem leader. He would go for the war, all the left-leaning stuff and pick up the leftist votes and try to show DM as a Blairite, as though that was a weakness, while David would want to get past the Blair–Brown era. I said he needed to improve message and organisation. I said his launch could have been a lot better and he needs better people. We agreed to meet up soon. I said the last thing you need is the idea of it being a TB team takeover but you do need more rigour and professionalism. Ed would do the comfort zone stuff. He wouldn't give you real leadership. He would pamper not lead. I think it could become a real mess, all this. After all the TG–GB stuff, now this, this time real brothers. Nightmare.

Saturday 15 May

Bob Crow [general secretary, Rail Maritime and Transport Workers' Union] was on the same plane back. He said he couldn't believe the Tories and the Libs had got into bed together. I spoke to TB in the car from the airport. He felt David had to win because he was alone among them in being a possible PM. Cameron would beat Ed. When Labour loses you go for a leader or a therapist. The therapist makes you feel better about defeat but doesn't do the things that need doing to win. He takes you to the comfort zone, says lie down, make yourself comfortable, don't think too deeply. A leader slaps you on the face a bit and says what needs to be done. I could hear on the radio in the car Ken Livingstone saying it should be Balls and if not Balls Ed M.

TB said the Cameron thing was ludicrous but they could make it work for quite a long time if they had to. The Tories were ruthless but the Libs would get a taste and quite like it. Later he sent me a note saying I had to help David. I said I was happy to help, but not happy to get too sucked in. I said I can't keep doing the same things for a succession of different people and be expected to lift so much of it. David needed to get a strong team that is not the old TB team but something new and fresh. Part of leadership is finding the right people, not going for the obvious.

Sunday 16 May
Charlie Kennedy [former Lib Dem leader] was out, critical of the coalition, which was running fairly big. We had a quick text exchange and I tweeted that he and Paddy were Lib Dems with principles. 'I think you're being quite generous to Paddy', he texted. But although there were clearly going to be fault lines, it was extraordinary how quickly the idea of the coalition being quite a normal thing was taking hold. Cameron was on *Marr* [Andrew Marr's morning programme]. It seemed to me he had almost accidentally been given a clear purpose. It wasn't clear during the election and that was one reason he didn't get a majority, despite his positives. He was adapting to it though. How he continued to adapt to it would decide politics for the next generation. Ed Miliband [shadow Energy and Climate Change Secretary] was also on *Marr*. He had a nice manner but I couldn't help thinking the public would see him as weak. My worry was that he could well appeal to the party without reference to the public. David called about some speeches he had planned. He was pretty shell-shocked by Ed standing. He couldn't really see what Ed offered that he didn't, and so concluded it was as much about stopping him as having a really new and different vision.

Off to The Belfry [Sutton Coldfield Hotel] with Rayan for a cancer charity fundraiser. I enjoyed chatting to Martin O'Neill [Aston Villa manager], who was interesting on how agents had changed the game for the worse, how much harder it was to build real relationships with players, and how the money was now crazy. Even young players felt little loyalty.

Monday 17 May
Cab to the Royal Throat, Nose and Ear Hospital in Gray's Inn Road for a nasal polyps removal. I had a draft of TB's book and read another hundred

or so pages before the anaesthetist and doctor came in to talk me through what was going to happen. The anaesthetic worked really quickly, next I knew I was being wheeled back in with two guys looking over me. Rory came in p.m. with books for me to sign for all the doctors and nurses. Ten in all. Turned out we needed more. Amazing how many people involved for a relatively minor op. I did a couple of blogs re. the NHS and how brilliant they had all been. Fiona couldn't believe how quickly I was out and how well I seemed, despite the bandages stuffed up the nose which made me look like my nose had broken in dozens of places.

Tuesday 18 May

David Laws [Lib Dem minister, Treasury Chief Secretary] had done a press conference with George Osborne [Chancellor] at which they had set out some of the areas for cuts, with more detail to come next week. Laws had also revealed Liam Byrne [last Labour Chief Secretary] had left him a letter – 'There's no money left, good luck'. It was a silly thing to do, but Laws was pretty humourless in the way he took it on. It indicated they were really going to go for us as having screwed the economy. Heaven knows what Liam had been thinking, unless he knew him and felt he could trust him to take it as a joke. [Lord] David Triesman [chairman] had been forced to quit the Football Association after some kind of *Mail on Sunday* sting, and I was getting a few calls about whether I should go for it.* I was feeling a bit groggy, but it might be that it was as much about post-defeat depression as about the anaesthetic. Who knows? I certainly didn't feel great though.

Wednesday 19 May

Clegg did his big political reform speech but it wasn't really as big as he was making out. 'Bigger than anything since the Great Reform Act'. Hardly. What about women's votes? They were getting a nice easy ride though, that's for sure. I finished TB's book and sent through eleven pages of detailed comments. Agreed to do *Question Time* next week. Greg [Nugent, friend and marketing executive London 2012] was doing a great job hyping the 2012 Olympics mascots which were launched on *The One Show*. Not feeling right. I need a lift from somewhere. I was working on a depression piece for the *Mirror* to hit back at some crap written by Janet Street-Porter

---

* The newspaper revealed that Lord Triesman had made allegations of Spain and Russia attempting to bribe referees in the 2010 World Cup.

May '10: 'There's no money left' joke backfires

[journalist] in the *Mail*. Silly piece saying depression the latest must-have accessory.

Thursday 20 May

Andrew Adonis [former Labour Cabinet minister] came round to talk about his future. He wanted to do a book on the talks that led to the coalition. He was going to see GB about it tomorrow. I said for it to work he would have to get on to the Clegg and Cameron side of the story too. We reminisced a bit, chatted about the campaign, what he might do, what others might do. He felt the coalition would not go beyond a couple of years. Tory MPs were getting agitated at Cameron. Today was the coalition government document launch, showing where the manifestos had met. I caught a bit of it and they did pretty well. It didn't look or sound ridiculous when Cameron was described as PM.

Then he went off to Belfast, then Paris to meet [Nicolas] Sarkozy [President of France]. He was seeing [Angela] Merkel [Chancellor of Germany] in Berlin tomorrow. He was certainly motoring. I felt he had been handed a real strategy on a plate – showing that a coalition government could work and in so doing he could show the Tories had really changed. I watched *Question Time*. There was a little frisson in the audience when they announced Piers [Morgan] and I would be on next week. They were bound to do Iraq and they were bound to get people turned against me. On the other hand we were out of power and I could get myself up there in a different way.

Friday 21 May

Round to Gail's [Rebuck, chair, Random House] for a meeting on TB's book positioning. Gail, Philip [Lord Gould, pollster, husband of Gail], Charlotte Bush [RH publicity]. TB had decided no to serial which was good news. I felt his big problem with the British public was money. I felt strongly that TB needed to do some pre-entry work, possibly a series of events and speeches, maybe even make the launch of the book related to people who had been involved or felt involved in his premiership. Gail said in Australia recently someone said, 'You have to remember that here at least the gloss has not come off.' How do we get that feeling back?

PG felt it required honesty about his relationship with the British people, that he had to be honest about what worked and what didn't. He had to accept some of the criticisms. There was maybe more reflection in the book but there was still a lot of defiance. He was maybe too defensive re. Iraq. And two fingers to those who expected a predictable memoir by a former PM. The *Mirror* ran my riposte to Janet Street-Porter on depression which I then put up as a blog and it got a huge response. I was worried the anaesthetic had slowed me down too much. Chilled out a bit but I could feel the mix of physical lethargy and mental grief only kept at bay by the pills.

Saturday 22 May

I was watching *Soccer AM* [Sky Sports football talk show] with Calum when the phone went. It was the one I normally never answer, but this time I did. Royal Free A and E. 'Are you Rory Campbell's dad?' Yes. 'There has been an accident. He was in getting his jabs for a trip to Asia, he fainted and has cut open his head.' And then – 'We are not sure about the extent of the damage.' Jesus. Heart-stopping moment. I ran up there, and as I arrived was saying 'must not faint, must not faint' to myself. I found him after a few minutes, in the A and E blue zone, acute cases. Pale as death. Oxygen mask. Monitors everywhere. Blood. Really hot. I stroked his arm for a bit then felt myself going. I knew I would. I told the nurse I was a bit squeamish, 'so warn me if you're going to use needles'. It made no difference. I went to get a stool to sit down but found myself moving to a bed and by the time I got there I crashed. Doctor came over, then Rory's nurses. Oxygen, heart ECG, wires, the works. Pulse down to twenty-nine. Doctor said later they were a bit worried for a while. At one point all I could hear was Rory saying, 'Dad, Dad, you OK?' Then he was off for a head scan while I saw a cardiologist, a consultant, X-rays, tests, lots. They even got their heart specialist in on his day off. We couldn't get hold of Fiona – at the hairdresser's – but Calum eventually found her.

Fiona laughed at my usual wimpishness when I first told her I had fainted. I was hoping to get out tonight but they said the blood pressure variability was a bit alarming and they would like me to stay. At first I was in an open ward, cordoned off, but who should I hear visiting his dad at the bed opposite but John Kampfner [political journalist]? I had to lie there and listen to him burbling on, not least about his next book. I got moved to a side room. Really nice staff. Grace went and got loads of books from home to leave as presents. The doctor was a big Labour supporter. People seemed genuinely perplexed about the new government and some scared. He gave me a knockout drop and I slept OK.

Sunday 23 May

Seen by Michael Beckles, the consultant. I was OK to go but he was a bit worried about my blood pressure dipping when standing up. I went round to see Rory who seemed better. After a few hours we both felt well enough and headed home. Word had spread about us being in hospital. TB. Fergie. Peter M, all called, all found my fainting quite funny. GB called. Really nice and warm. He said they had been worried for us. He said he was feeling OK but it didn't sound it. He was not sure what he would do. He had to come down to London for a day to take his seat. He had plenty of things he could do but he would take a bit of time. I said I felt he had left with great dignity and nobility but it was going to hurt for a long time and he needed to take his time, but not atrophy. There wasn't much chance of that but he did sound a bit down. He was still raging about the media. He genuinely felt that if the media was not changed in some way then politics and government could not function as it should. But Cameron would now cash in his chips and he would let the [Rupert] Murdoch [media magnate] agenda hold sway.

Monday 24 May

I watched the Osborne–Laws press conference, setting out the first £6.2 billion cuts. Laws looking like he was enjoying it a bit too much. Osborne handing over a lot of the tricky stuff. Osborne had the Lib Dems where he wanted them. They were going to use them to do the hard stuff, then blame them in some way. Mum was down for a few days. Looking pretty good but her feet were giving her hell. I saw David Sturgeon [psychiatrist]. We talked through recent weeks, and the general sense of mid-downness. He felt I had to take a holiday before not too long and then think things through from my perspective.

Tuesday 25 May

Birthday. Pottering. Trying to help Grace revise but I was so useless at this science stuff. Queen's Speech day so all the usual build-up. Lovely day for it. Cameron and Clegg walking together, as TB and CB had done. Not a bad package in terms of reach and spread but lots of intellectual inconsistency in it. Schools Bill getting the most attention. Also rolling back a lot of our security agenda from a civil liberties angle. Welfare reform. Harriet [Harman, Labour deputy leader] did OK in the debate. Cameron a bit shrill. Popped out for a nice lunch in Belsize Park with Nikki Turner, [celebrity footballer] David Beckham's right-hand woman on the sponsorship side. Liked her. Proper person. I was mugging up on Laws because *Question Time* had indicated he was going to be the minister on the panel. In the afternoon John Harris from *The Guardian* round to do the main interview on *Prelude to Power*.

He wanted to do off-book stories. But on the diaries it was a bit alarming how much it was about GB and his impossible-ness. I did my best but he said I was being evasive, that there was a disjunction between what I said in the diaries and what I was saying now. I was too much back in team and rebuttal mode, trying to see the good side in everyone. I sensed even though he was a bit anti-TB he was fine re. me and the piece ought to be OK. PG and Tessa came round with cakes and birthday presents and we later went out to the Vine for dinner. PG was not looking well. Losing weight and lacking his usual sparkle. Nice evening though. F and I getting on OK.

Wednesday 26 May

Andy Burnham [shadow Health Secretary] launched his leadership campaign. He was very good on the radio. The mood in the PLP was definitely moving to Ed M. I was talking to Ed Victor [agent] and *The Guardian* about possible extracts in the book serial. I was also starting to alert people and feeling stressed out about the whole thing. I took a daytime Diazepam for the first time in a while. My main worry was GB and also reaction in the PLP. There was still no clarity about which minister was going to be on *Question Time*. They were now only 'hopeful not definite' re. Laws. Gove had launched the new education plans today so I was following all that and getting notes from Fiona on it. She was terrific on the detail.

Thursday 27 May

I finally got the panel for tonight – no minister. I asked why no minister and answer came there are none. Out to speak to a Euromoney conference. Bit edgy but did OK. In and out in an hour then to Labour HQ to see the briefing team for QT. The place was really quiet compared with last time. But they were good people and needed continuing support. Lots of nice little chats and a good briefing, then home. I couldn't believe they had no minister on and tweeted a few insulting thoughts. I set off with Rayan and Mark after first framing a picture of David Laws, thinking I would put it on the desk as a way of illustrating that he was meant to be there. Arrived as Piers did and we were bantering away. It was in a theatre in Gravesend. Taken to the green room. [Sir] Max Hastings [former editor and author] looking older and redder than I expected him to. Susan Kramer [former Lib Dem MP] being told by everyone they wished she had beaten Zac Goldsmith [Tory, victorious over Kramer to become MP for Richmond Park]. John Redwood [Tory MP, former minister] and I had quite a good chat on what the new politics meant. He seemed genuinely to think it would lead to improved debate because people could be more open about differences. Popped another Diazepam. Quite nice reception for me and Piers, which neither of us expected.

I was seated next to [David] Dimbleby [presenter] and just before the start I could see his script and there was something about me at the top beyond the usual name-check. Turned out to be something about Downing St refusing to put a minister up against me if I was the Labour voice. He then read it out at the start. I was quite taken aback. I had already been intending to go at them over failing to field a minister. But this was doubly pathetic. It would also run as a story. I said something at the top of one of my early answers and pulled out the Laws photo. I was thinking welfare reform would go early but in fact they did cuts, schools, rebellions, a long one on Iraq in the context of the Eds distancing themselves, and then one on entrapment. I was on form on cuts and education, got most of the lines I wanted to – though not the one on all editors using private schools for their own kids. Redwood was more mellow than usual but did quite well. Apparently schools got more questions than anything else and there was major hostility to the government plans. Iraq went on a bit long and I felt a bit pissed off at some of it but the audience were definitely listening.

The audience was not really hostile at any point. I got lots of applause on most of the answers. Seemed to be quite a lot of Labour people in there and generally not a bad mood. The only time I almost rose to a bait was Piers asking me to apologise re. WMD. I pushed back OK. Also when an audience member asked if I would be happy for my own kids to die in Iraq, I think I had audience support in how I dealt with it. At the end all but Hastings stayed for dinner. Everyone seemed to think Andy Coulson [Downing Street director of communications] had made a mistake trying to get me off.

Quite enjoyable dinner. Piers regaling with stories of my stitching him up. He was also reading Twitter obsessively, and saying there were lots asking why he and I did not have a double-act programme. There were very mixed views on how long the coalition would last. Piers thought weeks and was taking bets re. the same. I spoke to Tom Price [Labour press officer] to give him some quotes and get Ben Bradshaw [shadow Culture, Media and Sport Secretary] up re. the Laws boycott story. Piers was saying again he seriously thought I should run for office, that I was head and shoulders above the contenders. He had torn into Balls and Ed M as gutless cowards for turning against TB and he hoped they didn't win because of it. He reckoned I could become leader if I somehow got in soon. Seemed fanciful but he was adamant. 'The Tories are scared shitless of you, as they showed again tonight.' Earlier I had sent a note to GB, copied to TB and Peter M, on the diaries. Peter seemed pretty dubious about it all. He said he had not read *The Blair Years* [condensed diaries, already published] and would not read these. GB did not reply.

Friday 28 May

Feedback from last night pretty overwhelmingly good. Massive reaction online to the Tories trying to keep me off. I did Nicky Campbell [radio presenter] early on and though he tried to give me a bit of a hard time he was not really pushing it. Don't think he really believed they had a leg to stand on. Nice calls from Alex and Charlie F. Both felt last night went well. Alex said why didn't you hit Morgan and Hastings. Charlie felt the Iraq bit was fine though I looked strained. Out to NW10 to record *Politics Show* on the Beeb extracts on the diaries. Then starting to manage the *Guardian* coverage for tomorrow. Then came news that the *Telegraph* had a big one – Laws having to give back £40k taken as rent he paid to a guy he lived with. Sounded at first blush pretty tough for him.

Saturday 29 May

I did a blog on Laws saying part of me hoped he was not scalped but that the Tories would jettison him if they felt he would damage them. *The Guardian* OK on the book but news-wise blown out by Laws. I was dealing with the *Sunday Mirror* who were doing second serial. Trying to get them to pull back from too much CB and personality stuff. Later the word started to emerge that Laws was going to quit and indeed he did, followed by Clegg saying how brave and principled he was etc. I tweeted that it was sad on a personal level but that I felt no sympathy for Clegg or Cameron who had milked it for all it was worth.

Sunday 30 May

Out to do the *Politics Show* with Jon Sopel [presenter]. Danny Alexander had replaced Laws – five years after being a national park press officer – and now there were questions about HIS expenses and tax affairs. To Millbank to do a couple of diaries interviews, then home to watch England v Japan [2–1]. I did a couple of tweets – Frank Lampard never missed two successive penalties under Labour and Bangladesh never scored more than 140 in opening a partnership v England under Labour. Someone persuaded me to do my first hashtag – #neverhappenedunderLabour and within no time it really took off.

Monday 31 May

Long chat with David M. I said the problem with the whole contest was the sense that we were all beating our chests and not really looking forward. He wanted to signal a break with the past which was fine but he needed a better pivot to the future. He needed to be clear how his agenda would differ from the others. Ed M was going to go round trying to make everyone feel better about losing. David felt there did have to be a proper understanding of how badly we did before the forward agenda could be met. He was clearly stung by the way his brother was trying to position it all as DM was Blair, Balls was Brown and he was in the middle. I was trying to recall some of those early days when TB was energetically scoping out the future. The truth is that the coalition was motoring and we lacked message or clarity or power going forward. We agreed to meet up soon. I did a blog offering prizes for the best #neverhappenedunderLabour tweet. Some great ones coming in.

Monday 31 May

Out for a walk with Fiona, then to see my new GP [Dr Horton]. Reviewed medication. Told him all the various ailments. Blood pressure fine. I got Random House to cancel the *Telegraph* interview with Mary Riddell [journalist and friend] because they had broken the embargo on the book. Mary said it was nothing to do with her, and she was mortified but I felt we had to make a bit of a stand. Bank Holiday so mainly pottering around but later out to *The One Show*. Nice chat with Christine Bleakley [presenter] who was thinking of leaving for ITV to do a breakfast show with Adrian Chiles [former *One Show* co-presenter]. Liked her. Lovely smile and very friendly.

Tuesday 1 June

The #neverhappenedunderLabour thing really worked well. Sorting out prizes for the best tweets. The winner said his local library couldn't afford my book because of cuts, which never happened under Labour. Lots of people saying they could not find the book. Really annoying. It turned out Waterstones had the wrong [publishing] date. Also that Amazon underordered. I was starting to rant a lot. Ed weighing in for me. To CNN [Cable News Network]. Did half-hour or so with Becky Anderson. She was less edgy than last time, quite a good interview. The best though later was with Philip Dodd of Radio 3 *Night Waves*. He had read the book and had also thought up some interesting lines of questioning, not least on my love–hate relationship with journalism. Good interview. Tough but fair. Proper chat.

Wednesday 2 June

To Great Ormond Street to film the LLR [leukaemia research charity]

Lifeline Appeal for the Beeb. Some of the filming back where Ellie [Merritt]* died. I only had to do five pieces to camera in different parts of the hospital but it took quite a while because of people moving around, trolleys, couriers, etc. I missed DC's first PMQs. Round-robin email later from Peter M, saying he was doing his autobiography in the autumn, calling it 'The Third Man'. PG saying it was going up against TB and with a bit of vengeance attached to it. Gail was a bit worried about it.

Thursday 3 June
Out early for Breakfast TV and nineteen local and regional radio interviews with BBC GNS [regional news network]. The Radio Guernsey interviewer said would I please put him in my diary. There you go. Quite a few had read *All in the Mind* [AC novel]. Then to Richard Bacon, excellent as ever. Friendly and good questions. Good online response too. Calum off back to Manchester for last two exams.

Friday 4 June
Out for a quick spin on the bike before John Rentoul [political commentator] came round for an *IoS* [*Independent on Sunday*] interview. 'I have to ask a few *Indy* peacenik questions.' It was fine though, and I don't think any bollocks dropped. Then *Daily Politics*. Programme fine. Did a bit on books, also re. Cumbria and whether Cameron was right to visit – he was – and general coalition stuff.† Off to Hay [Hay-on-Wye festival], had a rather uncomfortable kip in the car before arriving at Moccas Court, lovely Georgian house ten miles outside Hay. CB there last year. They said she was quite charming. Lovely scenery. View on to the river. To the festival, far bigger than I had expected. Also not quite as Guardianista. Ed V [Ed Victor, AC's literary agent] in his element. Through to the event which was packed with a waiting list. Pretty warm response on arrival. Perfectly fair interview with Francine Stock, Q&A with the audience ranging over devolution, TB and money, the coalition, legacy, depression, all sorts really. Felt fine. Best response to a defence of record ended with 'You'll miss it you know' (meaning Labour in power) and best laugh probably when I was taking the piss out of *Guardian* for backing Lib Dems and so helping Cameron into power. Old schoolfriend, Tim Finney, there.

* Daughter of Lindsay Nicholson and John Merritt, AC's close friend, who also died of leukaemia.
† The Prime Minister had visited the Cumbria location of a shooting spree by a lone gunman who killed twelve and left eleven more injured before killing himself.

Saturday 5 June

Up early, just after six. Did Ken Livingstone at LBC. He had just had Andrew Gilligan on so we both had a pop at him.* OK chat, around an hour, though it was extraordinary how much Ken made the whole thing about himself. I was amazed they let him get away with it. Out for [singer and friend] Mick Hucknall's 50th at a lovely rented house near Thatcham in Berks. Drinks in the garden, mainly talking to Peter Schmeichel [former footballer] and Kate Garvey [former TB aide]. Ronnie Wood [Rolling Stones guitarist] was the only music figure I recognised. [Lord] Alan West [former First Sea Lord] was there because he took Mick and his dad on a submarine. Nice do. Dinner in a giant tepee. Good food. Noddy Holder [musician] and wife Susan who wanted me to try to persuade her back after she voted Lib Dem for first time. Mick made a good speech and emphasised how important Labour was to him. Checked the *Indy on Sunday* and there was an annoying misleading headline saying I was attacking Ed M. Contacted Ed to make clear I had not said what I was quoted as saying, namely that he was not up to leading the party, and would 'only make people feel good about losing'.

Sunday 6 June

Alex called from 'absolutely roasting' France. Chilling out but finding the heat OTT, he said. He wanted to hear about Mick's do. I did a blog on the subtle changes in the *IoS* editing that made it look harsher on Ed than it was. I watched Soccer Aid [UNICEF charity celebrity event] from Old Trafford. Really missing it. There looked to be an even better atmosphere than the two times I did it. Nicky Byrne [Irish singer, celebrity player] texted to say the Hollywood guys were good fun but shite players! Good enough game [England v Rest of World]. 2–2 then RoW won after mammoth penalty shoot-out.

Monday 7 June

Start the Week [BBC Radio 4 show] with novelist Yann Martel, playwright Joy Wilkinson who had done a little play for the Tricycle Theatre's Women, Power and Politics season on [former Labour Cabinet minister] Margaret Beckett's leadership challenge and was running the thesis that women were not pushy enough and vain and ambitious enough to get to the top. The

* Gilligan was the journalist who in 2003 on BBC Radio 4's *Today* programme described a British government dossier paper on Iraq and weapons of mass destruction as having been 'sexed up'.

fourth person was Thea Sharrock, who was directing a little-known war-time Terence Rattigan play [*After the Dance*]. We all gathered in the dingy BH [Broadcasting House] foyer, then taken up to join Andrew Marr and his team for really bad coffee and a few sad croissants. He ran through the themes and the order – me, Joy, Yann, Thea. Yann Martel a tiny bit up himself but I guess with a novel [*Life of Pi*] that sold 7 million behind him he could afford to be. Joy comes from Burnley so we yacked about that and she said she wished I had stood. I liked her play and was chuffed she had got some of the detail about Margaret B – e.g. the pens and pencils in a runner band – from the diaries. She referred to the diaries even more than I did.

Marr concentrated a bit too much on the dysfunctional soap opera side of things from the diaries but I guess that was inevitable. Again he was too prone to refer back to himself and I played into that a bit. 'My two favourite stories in the book about you…' He glowed! Said to me afterwards he was writing a book about the Queen and that all the courtiers had spoken very well of my role in the Diana funeral week. Round to another studio to do Stephen Nolan [Northern Ireland presenter]. Lots on Martin McGuinness [former provisional IRA leader, Deputy First Minister]. I was saying how impressive I found him. Then home to meet Edi Rama, leader of the Albanian socialists, and his team Endri Fuga and Erion Veliaj. They were trying to generate international support for the line that the 2009 parliamentary election was stolen. They had been badgering me on social media for ages to see them and help them. They were a nice bunch of guys. Wanted to get my books translated out there, and also get me out on a visit. First leadership hustings at the GMB [trade union]. Ed M had a dig at Peter M, suggesting he should go for 'dignified retirement'. DM was not looking comfortable.

Tuesday 8 June

I did a blog on Cameron using the 'oldest trick in book' – things are worse than we feared – and the cover of Lib Dems to do what they always wanted to. The leadership debate was taking people out of the real game of going for the Tories. Instead they were going for each other. The Tories were going to use this period to hammer the line that we caused the need for [public spending] cuts. I sent David M, Ed M, Ed B and Andy B a text to that effect. Osborne statement on cuts. They were peddling the line that they had discovered all these terrible new things. In fact they had been on the same lines through the election. Danny Alexander did interviews afterwards and was poor. Too much umming and erring and repeating himself. He was not really clear or convincing. At least Osborne looked like he believed it.

Wednesday 9 June

Out on the bike before heading for the train to Leeds. Addison Lee driver was another black guy saying I had something the others didn't and I should think about a political career started afresh. Then PG called with bad news. Localised return of cancer cells but also a largish tumour on the throat. More chemo and radiation, possibly more surgery. He was doing his usual brave face and fighting talk but he admitted it would be harder and I detected a little less confidence in his voice. I spoke to Gail who sounded not too bad, in that the shock was not as great as first time around. But it was all a bit grim. Georgia [Gould's daughter] taking it badly. Got the boneshaker to Harrogate and arrived in OK time to sign a few books and get ready for the Standard Life dinner. I picked up a fair bit of both angst and irritation re. the coalition.

Thursday 10 June

Home by mid to late morning. Meeting up with Donald [brother] and his Scots Guards Association pals who were playing at Beating Retreat later. Calum [AC son] and Audrey [Millar, FM's mother] arrived and we had a little mingle before heading to the ceremony [Horse Guards Parade]. Donald did the lone piper bit. Did a proud tweet.

Friday 11 June

Did a long stint on the bike then went off to meet Calum in Marylebone. Arranged to meet him at Pret behind Gt Portland Street. A guy called Glenn from the Special Olympics campaign spotted me and came over asking me to stand for Parliament and get the leadership. He said you'd kill Cameron and the more the press say you're a liar the more people like me think you're one of the few who tell the truth. Then off to Queen's [Club] tennis with Calum. [Lord] Tony Giddens [sociologist and author] also there, very pessimistic about the future. Politically, economically, the lot. First Andy Murray then Rafa Nadal went out. World Cup starting, in South Africa, so back to watch France v Uruguay. Really dull.

Saturday 12 June

I spoke to TB. First chatted on the party leadership stuff. He said it was extraordinary that the people who had delivered three wins were deemed surplus to the debate and those who had lost were being seen as great seers. He felt that Ed M would not beat Cameron but equally that David M had not quite clicked, though at least he was standing up for difficult choices and a proper message. He said he was minded to intervene at some stage. He knew that Douglas Alexander was advising David to keep him out but someone needed to shake the whole thing up pretty quickly or else it was a disaster area. Diane Abbott [Labour MP] would pitch the thing to the left and allow Ed more room to manoeuvre. That being said he felt DM ought to win.

He said the problem was we were being presented as having been in for thirteen years of consistent government. There were ten years of us and then three very different years of GB. He felt that if we pitched too far away from a clearly centrist path, the public would keep Cameron in for a while. Earlier I had a perfectly pleasant chat with Cherie. She was asking about Philip, said TB was incurably optimistic but he was being unrealistic. I told them both I felt it was not going to be good. CB quizzing me re. GB, also what was Peter up to with his book? 'Was he intending to be spiteful and if so against whom?' She said she and TB were fine but he was up to his eyes in MEPP [Middle East Peace Process]. Loads of meetings with Bibi [Benjamin Netanyahu, Prime Minister of Israel] and he felt he was getting both the Israelis and Hamas to shift a little. *On verra.*

Then a long chat with PG re. his illness. For him, he sounded pretty down. Fiona was out to see Ed M on education then to Compass [centreleft think tank]. She said she found them all a bit underwhelming. I said the party risked making the wrong decision and we would be out for as long as we had been in.

Sunday 13 June

The Tories were also starting to crank up for tomorrow's 'the books are worse than we thought' announcement by the new Office for Budget Responsibility [independent economic forecasting body]. Verity Harding [adviser to Lib Dems] came round for a chat. She said the party was being left to atrophy. People really pissed off that they were basically just propping up the Tories. She was shocked that Clegg and others had been so keen on the coalition idea and also how readily they were going for it. She said there were plenty more people who felt like her. Her big thing was civil liberties, but they were going to be so desperate for power that they would do pretty much anything the Tories wanted.

Monday 14 June

News dominated by the government's well-orchestrated 'things worse than we expected' OBR report and Osborne's statement. Then a Clegg speech. Cameron later. Pretty well concerted. I was off to Weybridge to do some fast driving at the Mercedes track, sneaky preparation for doing *Top Gear*. I did the driving with a young guy called Ollie. Nice guy, good fun. He said by the end I was pretty much on the limit. I was surprised how tiring it was, and how high the heartrate seemed to go, which he said was a mix of adrenaline and the G-force of acceleration. He reckoned the top guys would be several hours a day in the gym because fitness was so much a part of the modern driver.

Tuesday 15 June

To King's Cross to head for Leeds. I had to collect my tickets from the counter where one of the rail guys said they should rename *Question Time* the Piers and Alastair show and have us on every week. Piers meanwhile was really hitting it big now. He was being lined up as the next Larry King [US TV host] for CNN. I sent him a well-done message. No keeping him down. Biggest Twitter response in ages when I did a tweet saying the annoyance at the vuvuzela [plastic horn instrument used by South African football fans] was now greater than the annoyance caused by it. David M called as the train was pulling out. He sounded OK but the thing with Ed felt all wrong. He said while he was trying to hold up for the record and the importance of leaders taking tough positions, Ed was just tacking left the whole time. He felt he just wasn't ready but he was conscious of the fact that Ed was motoring and exploiting perceived weaknesses in David's armoury.

He was worried about the *Newsnight* debate tonight and how to handle the Tory onslaught on our record. I said he should defend it but also always be focused on the future. The one who seized the future would and should win. I didn't think Ed was coming over well and I said also he needed to get stuck into the economy and the cuts debate with a few big speeches and interventions. I said a few people who had seen the hustings said he was slightly playing into the technocratic caricature. He said Ed was trying to say it was all values. I said you say fine but we don't disagree on that. Where there is disagreement is in leadership and policy. Ed is basically saying he will be led by the party rather than lead it. I also think they were all underestimating Cameron.

To Yorkshire TV for a pre-record with a new and very nice presenter – Christine Talbot. Almost all on the book and afterwards she tweeted how nice and funny I had been. They asked me to sign the wall and I did it between [William] Hague [former Tory leader] and Cameron. Car to Grassington through some terrific scenery. Booked into the Devonshire Inn then went for a run. Tough hills. Fiona called to say Calum had been taken to A and E having fallen playing tennis. He had broken his nose and cut his face badly. I had to try to put it out of my mind when I was speaking but I felt the whole time I should get back, especially when Fiona was telling me how bad the treatment was. She had to fight to get a scan and he had clearly got memory problems. She said he was asking the same questions repeatedly including about things that happened several years ago. They didn't clean him up properly and he was there for hours without really getting the treatment he needed. We spoke to Iain Hutchinson [surgeon] who saw him then got him seen at the UCH who put a load of stitches in his lip. I felt sick.

I turned on the news to see the reaction to the Bloody Sunday inquiry. Pretty amazing scenes in Derry. Pretty irritating to see Cameron lording it. But he did well to be fair and caught the mood well. Up to the Devonshire Hall. Nice venue and lovely crowd.

Someone asked me whether I was secretly flattered by the idea that Malcolm Tucker [fictional spin doctor, *The Thick of It*] was based on me. I asked the audience if they all knew who Malcolm Tucker was. A gentle 'no' murmur could be heard. I asked for those who had never heard of *The Thick of It* to raise their hands. I reckon between a fifth and a quarter went up. If you add in a few for people who don't like to admit ignorance to anything, or don't like being asked to raise their hands by some bloke on the stage, that means a fair proportion of educated, informed, middle-class opinion had no idea who he was. The questions ranged far and wide, we must have got through a few dozen, including who was the best PM we never had from the past thirty years. I put that to the audience too and from a choice of Denis Healey [former Labour deputy leader], Ken Clarke [Justice Secretary and Lord Chancellor], [Lord] Michael Heseltine [former Tory Deputy Prime Minister] and John Smith [former Labour leader], John won by a landslide. The media is still doing the honeymoon bit for Clegg, but the feeling is out there that the Lib Dems are being used pretty ruthlessly by the Tories and that a lot of what Lib Dem voters (there were plenty of them) voted for is not what the MPs they sought to elect are now promoting.

At these kind of events I give out prizes for the best questions as a way of encouraging people to ask questions I am unlikely to have been asked before. In third place – have you ever accidentally left on a microphone and what did you say? In second place – what will you say about Grassington in your diary tonight? (I can definitely say I have never been asked that before.) But the winner of a signed *Prelude to Power* came from a lady who asked: 'Which was the greatest act of betrayal – Owen Coyle's or Nick Clegg's?' [Coyle left Burnley for Bolton.] Given we were not that far from Burnley, Owen Coyle may be a little hurt to know that more hands went up than for Malcolm Tucker. Still, I guess for people to come out to hear me on a night Brazil are entering the World Cup suggests they were not massive football fans. As for the answer, I went for Coyle in that his leaving Burnley was in some ways a bigger shock and affected me more personally at the time. But the mood of the audience, if I read it right, seemed to think Clegg won the betrayal game by a mile. Bed late and Calum still not been seen properly. F said the treatment was shocking.

Wednesday 16 June

When finally I got home Calum was a lot worse than I had feared or expected. Nose bashed and bloody. Cuts and stitches on lips. He was going to take a knock over this. He was putting on a brave face but it wasn't nice to see. Dave Brailsford [manager, GB and Sky cycle racing teams] popped round and was really nice to him. Showed him some pictures of bad facial injuries, to show how quickly they could heal. He was not ruling out Bradley Wiggins [Sky road racer] winning the Tour de France. They were doing a lot of new-kid-on-the-block stuff. He was describing some of the new stuff he was doing with them, including super-sophisticated morning briefings for the team on the bus. Lovely guy.

Out to the Tower Hotel for the Coutts reception. Signed a few more books and then we headed off to Greenwich. Almost totally white male audience. Usual mix of big and small talk en route to the venue which was one of the most beautiful rooms I had ever spoken in. A dining room at Greenwich naval college where Nelson had lain in state. Fabulous wall and ceiling paintings which had seemingly taken decades to complete. I was sitting next to the chief exec. Osborne was at the Mansion House axing the FSA [Financial Services Authority] so they were all pretty busy on that. Despite problems with my voice it went really well and they all seemed happy. All got *Prelude to Power* as they left which seemed to go down well.

Thursday 17 June

I got a cab over to [former diplomat, journalist, friend] Jamie Rubin's, as we were off to play golf at Queenwood. Had a brief chat with Christiane Amanpour [broadcaster, friend, wife of Jamie], still pushing for a chat with TB for ABC and her new show (which was stressing her out, said Jamie) and bemoaning Piers becoming the new big star at CNN. Jamie set to be a consultant with Hillary [Clinton, US Secretary of State] to 'socialise' him with the [Barack] Obama [US President] people who seemingly hated him because of stuff he did during the HC–BO [Democratic presidential nomination] campaign.

Lovely day. Met at the course by the guy who looked after Jamie when he played there with Bill Clinton [former President], and he set us up with a couple of caddies. Nightmare tee shot across the practice green. Then another howler. Picked up though, made a few good shots, two out of this world, including a 130-yard bunker shot to the pin. I was down most of the game, then took the lead on the 17th, but blew the 18th. The news dominated by Tony Hayward of BP at the Congress inquiry into the oil spill, where he was dire. Arrogance, incompetence, God knows what, but he was dire.

Friday 18 June
Bill [Hagerty, AC's co-editor of diaries] had been round with some of Volume 3 which I worked on in the car on the way to TB's place in the country. David Mellor had been pressing me to see TB re. a Libyan business issue and he and his son were bringing their Kuwaiti friend to brief TB. TB was just back from the States and despite the tan he was looking pretty tired. The house was even more impressive with a stack of new paintings in there. We chatted re. GB. TB asked what I thought he would do. I said the opposite of him, though if a big financial job came up I am sure he would take it. TB again saying he had never worked so hard. He was up to his eyes in MEPP but was also still doing major rounds on the speeches etc.

When Mellor arrived it was small talk then down to business. TB very clear what he could do and what he couldn't do. I set off and was home to do a bit of work before heading out for a dinner at the Park Lane Hilton. European Institute of Internal Comms. Annoying that it was the same time as England v Algeria [0–0] but they had a screen outside. I was surprised how few of the people at the dinner came out to watch. England poor.

Saturday 19 June
Rory [son] back from Vietnam. Calum's face healing OK but he still seemed down. I did another Lib Dem blog based on [political editor] George Parker's line in the *FT* that Cable never believed what they said at the election re. cuts. They were becoming a much bigger target.

Sunday 20 June
Georgia and I swapping notes for tomorrow's PG–Grace Gould party. DM and family came round p.m. He felt things were going OK, but the situation with Ed was clearly difficult. He said he had to put the family thing out of his mind, or else it would spook him even more. So Ed M had to

be just another contender. It was the only way he could deal with it. If he thought about it too much, it just occupied his mind. Ed was really difficult to handle because his basic message was that he would never leave the party behind and it was a clever way of playing in Iraq and making DM the voice of that. He said the hustings had been OK but it was clearly between the two of them. He was worried. Louise [DM's wife] looked pretty stressed. I sensed they had both been spooked and hurt by what Ed did, and it made campaigning really difficult. He did not look or sound like a guy with momentum.

Monday 21 June

I did a quick blog on the leadership election, saying the contenders really had to pile in with impact on the back of the Budget. Popped out for lunch with Gloria De Piero [Labour MP] at Camden Brasserie. She was all at sea and in need of some very basic advice about how to build her career and profile. She felt the party was in a bit of a state and though backing DM was worried a lot of the new ones were falling for the Ed empathy. I worked on the PG [party] speech. Had a few jokey whacks in there. Peter M would be doing readings from his book, *How I Was Right All Along*. And there would then be a musical put on by some of the leadership contenders, entitled 'Blair and his has-beens only won three elections, what the fuck do they know about politics?'

Good atmosphere. Philip seemed pretty tired. Peter M there briefly but I missed him. Ed and DM missed the speeches. Kicked off with video which included nice tributes from TB and GB. PG spoke in his usual somewhat stilted way. My speech re. them both seemed to go down well though the microphone kept cutting out and maybe I went on a bit long but there were a few people in tears by the end so at the emotional level it clicked. PG later jumped into the pool with Grace. Said it was a great moment.

Tuesday 22 June

Missed the start of the Budget. Osborne did it pretty well, but Harriet's [Harman, acting leader] response was good. Dropped her a line. Clegg's nodding dog routine was worth a quick instant blog. The pundits were giving Osborne marks for courage of convictions but once the cuts started to bite the progressive claims were going to ring hollow. It was tough and the consequences were going to be severe. Big hike in VAT, big cuts, not as tough on banks as people expected. He did look the part though, that much could not be taken away from him.

Thursday 24 June

Off to Berlin. Good display of *P2P* in Smith's at [Heathrow] Terminal 1. Finally got into editing Volume 2. Met by a driver and taken to the Adlon. The build-up to Germany v England not nearly as hysterical as in London. I was there ostensibly for a speech to a financial conference. Got better during the Q&A but not one of my best. Feedback pretty positive though. More banks people asking if I would do stuff for them on the strategy side of things. Did another little run then watched the football.

Friday 25 June

Out for a run by the waterside near the Reichstag. Berlin so clean compared with London. Out to the airport. Home and out to Brent Cross with Grace to get some clothes for *Top Gear*. Conference call with Ed V, Gail and Susan. Ed laid our complaints. TB late with his final chapter. Peter M sent over a Danny Finkelstein blog saying how the diaries showed the real tensions between me and Peter. He was clearly gearing up I think for a bit of a whack.

Monday 28 June

With Grace to Weybridge for another session at Mercedes Benz. Grace having a starter driving lesson. Was OK. Researched Jeremy Clarkson [controversial presenter] a bit. Certainly said some crazy stuff, but probably best to play along with him a bit.

Tuesday 29 June

Off to Birmingham, traffic out of London a nightmare. Interview with Ed Doolan [BBC local radio]. Kind of *Desert Island Discs*. Mix of political and personal. In the Mailbox, a new Birmingham shopping centre and people could wander up to the window and look in. Off to the heritage collection at the British Museum [Gaydon, Warwickshire] where, much to TB's amusement when I told him, I was speaking to the Automotive Leaseplan conference – car fleets – under the banner 'The future of fleet.' Did my best to make it relevant. I was getting an OK response tweeting to ask for advice re. how to handle Clarkson on *Top Gear*. Mix of kill him and play with him. It was a tricky one though, for both of us.

Wednesday 30 June

Grace chose my clothes and off I set for Dunsfold aerodrome in Surrey where *Top Gear* was recorded. Fairly large crew, many wearing 'I am the Stig' T-shirts. Eventually out to the track to meet the Stig [anonymous *Top Gear* character], fully dressed and helmeted. Nice enough guy, middle-class, possibly military I would say. Quite softly spoken but a good, patient teacher. Went round a couple of times with him, taking in the track, first slowly, then at speed. It was impossible to imagine going as fast as he did but within a few laps I wasn't far off it. There was a lot to take in, and I made loads of mistakes, not least constantly going into fifth gear when I wanted third, and it took me ages to get the hang of the final bends. My last ride was the best and I reckoned I would be inside Nick Robinson [BBC political editor] if not all of the ones who did it [celebrity 'test track' competition] last week. Definitely worth having done the pre-training.

I met Clarkson and we had a little pre-chat during which he slagged off Mark Thompson [BBC Director-General] a fair bit. He had told him I was coming on the show. 'That man is never off the BBC,' said MT. 'I told him if it wasn't for you getting rid of [Greg] Dyke he wouldn't have a job.'*

I was taken in, up through the audience, a few boos and jeers but mainly in good humour. He said Simon Cowell [reality TV producer] was the only other person to be booed like that. Good light-hearted interviewing style, e.g. starting with 'What is your favourite colour, favourite dog, favourite Girls Aloud member?' He was winning the best laugh lines but I got in a few OK lines. We also had a decent argument or two on the environment and TV debates. It was neither great nor terrible. He did to be fair mention the diaries a couple of times albeit comically, e.g. Why is there not more about the ludicrous M4 bus lane? I said Volume 2 was all about that. The lap edit had been done pretty quickly. Didn't look as good as I thought it would but the time was OK and I was second on the board. Ahead of Nick Robinson so texted him to say I was feeling smug. Whizzed by, little chat after then home. It was all fairly low-key faff and Clarkson was very friendly and trying not to be obnoxious though he came out with a couple of real anti-PC belters e.g. when I said he was not sound on gay rights. 'Yes I am,' he said. 'I demand the right not to be bummed.'

Thursday 1 July

Early Eurostar to Brussels. Very quiet. Worked on the speech for the European Comms summit. Hot day. Cab to the Cube and in for the event. Around 500 comms people. Quite Germanic feel to it. I did a basic strat

---

* Former Director-General who resigned after criticism of BBC news reporting by the Hutton Inquiry into the circumstances surrounding the death of David Kelly, former weapons inspector in Iraq.

comms piece which seemed to go OK, ditto the Q&A, then a book signing. Went for lunch with Phil Townsend [Manchester United comms director] who was speaking at a seminar on sponsorship tomorrow. He was planning to stay till Fergie went, or David Gill [Man United CEO], whichever was first. Did RTÉ [national broadcaster] *Drivetime* then a run and a visit to the Jacques Brel museum. Bought a new 5CD compilation. Out to the airport and saw a massive front-page Danish paper headline and pictures of Steve [Stephen Kinnock, Neil's and Glenys's son] and Helle [his wife, Helle Thorning-Schmidt, Danish politician]. Seven pages inside. Turned out to be about him paying tax in Switzerland not Denmark.

I texted them all and eventually spoke to Rachel [Stephen's sister], Steve and Helle and text exchanges with Neil and Glenys [Lord and Lady Kinnock, former Labour leader and his former European Parliament member wife]. Rach said it had been going on for ages and had been massive in the Danish press. She said Steve was at the end of his tether. Also, she had stopped working for Ed M because Grace [Rachel's daughter] had cut her leg and she had been away, never saw them enough and it was getting ridiculous. I spoke to Steve who was at a conference in Kazakhstan. He sounded pretty fed up and though he felt they could have toughed it out as he lived and worked a lot of the time in Switzerland, Helle's people felt they had to give something and so had agreed to an inquiry to show it was all above board, a pledge to pay in Denmark and an agreement to backdate and pay any advantage he had accrued by not paying tax in Denmark. Sounded a nightmare.

Rach said Neil was raging about it. He texted me to say why would anyone ever want to go into politics at all? He was really hacked off. Helle called and was her usual amazingly chirpy and resilient self. She said it had definitely damaged her in the polls and that it was not over yet. She still felt she could win though and that was what mattered. As we landed in Dublin, the woman behind me said she was going to see me at the Trim festival. The man behind her said he was going to see me at IBEC [Irish Business and Employers Confederation]. And the woman next to him said she was reading my book. So it was a bit of a love-in, but a very nice welcome.

Friday 2 July
Up earlyish to begin a fairly long round of interviews, then to IBEC, the Irish equivalent of the CBI. First a session with the comms team, trying to get ideas going for marketing Irish business, then a session with some of their biggest members. Nice bunch. Very open and honest about how reputationally damaged they were by the crash and its aftermath. A couple

more interviews, then driven down to Trim. Smallish place in nice country-side, and I was booked into a big golf course hotel. Lovely people again.

The event was being compèred by Senator David Norris, a gay and very English-sounding guy who was standing for Irish President. He was a big character. I was sitting with minister Noel Dempsey, one of [Taoiseach of Ireland] Brian Cowen's key people, his daughters and Barbara Nestor [Trim festival comms director], who had got me over there. Plenty of MPs from all parties there and there were a total of fifteen mini-speeches before my thing, which was an interview by journalist John Waters. Norris had a fair few digs in his linking bits so I quite enjoyed saying later that I couldn't imagine Ireland voting for someone who sounded like a minor member of the British royal family, and they may as well go for the Queen! The interview was fine, though Waters was a bit heavy, for example when he said that journalists would expect him to press me on Iraq, I said, 'Are you here for journalists who aren't present or the audience that is?'

Also pushed back hard, and got a good response, on TB's record and legacy. Barbara was good fun, as was her fiancé Shane, and I hung around doing pictures and chat till gone half-one. Late for me, though I later learned some of them were at it till six. I sensed a lot of support for my anti-media line, including from journalists. Quite a few mentioned my depression stuff too. Really nice event, enjoyed it. Good chat with Leo Varadkar [TD].

Saturday 3 July
The papers were full of [rugby player] Brian O'Driscoll's wedding. Akin to a royal event. I was page 3 *Irish Times*, and in *The Independent* a nice picture of me and Barbara. I had an hour-long very personal interview with TV3. Childhood, family, beliefs stuff. Went OK though I was a bit tired. Another packed flight, home for the second half of Argentina's 4–0 battering by Germany.

Sunday 4 July
Swim in lido, which was fabulous, and also later did a bike ride. I watched *Top Gear* with Rory, Fiona and Tessa who had popped round for dinner. They felt it was pretty good and I could tell Rory was pretty impressed by the driving. Tessa just kept going on about how young I looked. I thought the banter with Clarkson was pretty good, though they edited out loads of the good stuff, and I spent the evening tweeting about a lot of the cuts which got a big response, both people wanting me to do more on the same theme, and others saying shut the fuck up. Tessa seemed OK, though she said the leadership election was deadening and whoever decided it should be so long was crazy.

She worried the party was not clear about the lines of attack against the government. The Lib Dems were being whacked but in a way that was letting the Tories off the hook a fair bit. She said Alistair Darling [former Chancellor] was the only one really standing up against the mauling we were taking on the economy. She felt Ed was motoring but would be a disaster, the other three [Andy Burnham, Ed Balls, Diane Abbott] knew they had no chance. It was David's to lose, Tessa felt, and at the moment he was losing it.

Monday 5 July

Set off for Newcastle for the ICT [Information and Communications Technology] conference. Good to meet Brendan [Foster] and have a chat. He had read Volume 1 of diaries and was amazed how difficult GB had been from the word go. Mainly teachers at the conference and a few kids who interviewed me. Calum called to say he had got a 2.1 which was great news, a fantastic achievement after all the ups and downs. I'd been worrying more and more about his drinking but he seemed to buckle down and pull it out at the end. For the speech I used a terrific blog by Mike Baker, ex-education correspondent of the Beeb, who warned teachers were fearful of being taken back to the dark ages. Audrey was round to celebrate Calum's result when he and Fiona got back from Manchester [University].

Tuesday 6 July

Blog on Gove and Clegg's slavish support for any cuts that were suggested. Another chat with TB on the leadership election. He said he had more work than he could cope with.

Thursday 8 July

Up at Mum's, out for a longish run, then with Mum to see Robert Templeton [bed-ridden relative]. Home on the 4.33. Bimbo-looking blonde doing her nails in my seat as I got on the train. I sat opposite her and after she'd said, 'You're AC, aren't you?' I learned she had two first-class degrees, had just got a distinction in her master's on the legal implications of the international financial order. Really bright. We had a good chat on the way down. She called her mum and dad and said, quietly but loudly enough for anyone to hear, that she was with me and I was nice etc. Better than your average train stranger. Popped in to see PG on the way home. He was still trying to work out his best way forward health-wise. The US doctor had admitted doing the wrong op but he intended to stick with him if the chemo didn't work and they were able to operate. To RIBA [Royal Association of British Architects] for the Mind [mental health charity] awards. I was presenting the champion award. Some good winners and some great speeches. I was sitting next to [constitutional and political reform minister] Mark Harper's private secretary trying to entice her into talking about what the new lot were like. 'Sue Gray [Cabinet Office civil servant] would have my guts,' she said. Fiona had got her honorary degree from Middlesex and had really enjoyed it.

Friday 9 July

Did a blog re. Gove – second apology yesterday – having to watch the word 'hapless' didn't stick to him. Up to a lovely house in Hampstead, Admiral's Walk, to do an interview with Nick Robinson for his documentary on the five days after the election. I had gone through my diaries for the time and read out the stuff on the final call from Clegg. Also clear he was getting different versions from different places. The media were currently obsessed with the hunt for Raoul Moat.* Great tweet from someone who said Moat had been given his own TV show – 'the news'. It was one of those media frenzies which was wiping out pretty much anything else, though the hype for Peter's book was swinging in.

Saturday 10 July

TB had been to Kosovo yesterday and had been given a hero's welcome. Did a blog on the therefore inevitable news blackout. The media are determined that when it comes to foreign policy they see him purely in terms of Iraq. Peter was running big in *The Times*, added to which he was doing some cringey ads in a velvet jacket and cravat and 'let me tell you a story'. Set off for Sussex with Rayan to head for Piers's wedding party. Far posher house than I expected. Fewer photographers and celebs. Piers enjoying himself, as was Celia [Walden, PM's new wife]. Sarah Brown [Gordon's wife] was talking to me when [CEO News International] Rebekah Wade's husband [former racehorse trainer Charlie Brooks] came over and said Rebekah was over there if she wanted to talk to her. Sarah took evident delight in saying she was already talking to other people but if Rebekah wanted to come over, fine. Either RW behaving too grandly, or nervous.

---

* A major police operation was launched in Tyne and Wear and Northumberland to apprehend Moat, who was at large after shooting three people in two days. After six days avoiding capture, Moat shot himself.

Anyway she came over and they had a little chat, the first since *The Sun* turned against GB.

I talked to Andy Coulson who said he was re-reading *TBY* and finding it useful. He seemed fairly on top of things but looked tired and a bit wan. I said I thought the public service cuts plus reforms would be the thing that risked sending the Lib Dems offside. Nice enough chat. Piers's brothers had a pretty clear view on him, not least the Army one who told me Piers always took his name in vain, but he supported the Iraq War. Paul Dacre [editor, *Daily Mail*] there but did a runner when he came to the food queue and found me at the end of it. Nice enough do. There till about twelve. Mainly talked to his family towards the end. He had still not signed his CNN deal but it was getting closer, he said.

Sunday 11 July

World Cup final a big disappointment. Holland were awful, resorting mainly to clogging and Spain found it hard to play their usual game. Poor old Howard Webb [referee] ended up giving fourteen yellow cards and a red and being blamed by the Dutch for costing them the game [0–1]. I started the game wanting Holland to win and was very pleased when they didn't.

Monday 12 July

Peter's book serial started on 'Clegg the executioner', on the talks post 6 May. It was clear his whole strategy was to present himself as the main man for TB and then GB. I got a few bids but decided not to do them. I had bad vibes. It was looking very bitchy and gossipy. Out to Fifteen for lunch with Danielle Roet [TV programme maker] and colleagues about their idea for me to teach politics in [celebrity chef] Jamie Oliver's *Dream School* idea [second-chance education]. I gave them my reservations re. celeb bollocks and the thing just being used to run down state schools, but I felt by the end of it their hearts were almost in the right place. Fiona was convinced I was heading for one of my turns, said I was becoming narky and difficult.

Tuesday 13 July

A longish run, then did a blog on yesterday's NHS white paper. Andrew Lansley [Health Secretary] was trying to present it as all about more power to GPs but it was really about cuts and more private sector. Added to schools it could be a real problem for them but they were getting away with a lot because we were leaderless, nobody was really defending the record – which they were trashing – and the leadership contest was not taking off. The *Telegraph* called and asked me to do a notebook, which I decided to do as a way of sending a warning shot to Peter about what he was up to. I wrote about how some of my diary extracts contradicted some of Peter M's versions of events.

I said diaries are but one form of historical documentation. Memoirs are another. The benefit of the diary over the memoir though is the immediacy and the lack of hindsight. The benefit of the memoir over the diary is, hopefully, a broader perspective. But in getting out his version of the election aftermath, he could have done worse than ask to see my diaries of the time.

To the World Service where I did an hour-plus interview with Matthew Bannister for the *Outlook* programme [BBC World Service]. Then to Fern Britton who had a C4 show. It was a mix of light and heavy and when she got on to Iraq I felt my heart racing suddenly – the first time in ages. And when she got on to David Kelly I just said I wasn't going to talk about it. I recovered OK but it wasn't great. Out for dinner with Neil and Glenys, Hugh Hudson [film-maker] and Sue Birtwistle [Lady Eyre, drama producer, wife of Sir Richard] at Sheekey's. Neil and Glenys on the rampage re. Peter's book, and also said she had not enjoyed working for David M at the FCO.

Wednesday 14 July

The Peter stuff was on to Day 3 and worse than ever. 'Mad, bad and dangerous' – all the worst things TB said about GB, plus some nonsense about a so-called Operation Teddy Bear – a Peter and John Birt [former BBC Director-General] paper on how to demolish the GB empire. Neil was spitting with fury last night, and others would be now. Tessa said it was so different to how I had handled my diaries and people would note that. I texted TB to say today was even worse. He said his own book would provide the context re. GB. 'Brilliant but difficult' was the formulation I had used about him yesterday. TB's was 'brilliant but impossible'. Peter had quoted TB as saying re. the Peter Foster flats drama that I had made it all about me and twisted the facts to make a stand – and that I had done the same re. the Hindujas.[*]

I texted Peter to say one day you will learn to accept that TB, not I, sacked you, and did he realise his book so far damaged him and everyone

---

[*] In 2002 career criminal Foster had assisted Cherie Blair with the purchase of two flats in Bristol at a 'discount'. The resultant scandal – 'Cheriegate' – prompted Mrs Blair to make a public apology. In 2001 Peter Mandelson had resigned as Northern Ireland Secretary after allegations of lobbying the Home Office on behalf of the wealthy Hinduja brothers, who were seeking British passports.

else and helped nobody but *The Times* and the Tories? 'Very sour,' came the reply. 'Don't be so crabby.' David M called later, on his way back from another hustings. He sounded a bit down. When I said that he had to find a way of saying not just that the Blair–Brown era was over, but showing it in ideas and policy, he said it was a good idea, as though he had not thought of it. I know he had, but he had not really cut through. He said Ed had moved from empathy to a message that basically said he was the one who could move beyond TB–GB. He said he found it astonishing how easily Ed had slipped from the GB shadow. He felt the others had no chance at all and that it really was between the two of them. So we were set for another personal psychodrama to dominate the party's politics.

Thursday 15 July

Met up with Dick Caborn [former minister for sport] at Lord's [cricket ground]. I was there as Mrs Caborn! Hosted by the ECB [England and Wales Cricket Board], usual good food and hospitality and not bad cricket once the weather cleared. Matthew Doyle [TB political adviser] called and said *The Times* were saying I was responsible for the 'Blair livid at Peter' stories. I said I certainly made clear I was livid and that I had spoken to others. Matthew said they didn't want to feed the idea as it would 'thrill Peter's publishers to think he was livid'. So whatever the truth he intended to play it right down. Peter would be half loving it and half hating it all. Loving the focus on the book. Hating the sense of the party hating it. Dick's view was that he liked to be seen as the friend of the rich and gilded and they liked to see him as the Labour person they could relate to.

Peter Chittick and Carolyn Fairbairn [personal friends] round for dinner so at least I had a genuine excuse to miss Peter's launch. Charlie F went and later filled me in. He said there were not many politicians – Pat [McFadden, former Labour minister], Rosie [Winterton, shadow Leader of the House], him and [Baroness] Sally [Morgan] from TB's Lords circle – Robert Harris [novelist], lots of journos. His sense was that Peter was really enjoying it, and loving the idea that yet again he had taken people by surprise. First he had gone backroom to front of house. Then GB hater to GB saver. Now Mr Discretion to Mr Indiscretion. He felt he was immune to the criticism.

Friday 16 July

JP [[Lord] John Prescott, former Labour deputy leader] came round p.m. The usual JP madness accompanying him. David [son] came with him on the Tube but they got lost walking to our place. Eventually, half an hour after saying they were at Kentish Town – I thought they were in a car – JP called to say he had broken down. Have you called the AA? No. Not a car. My foot. I had to go and collect him outside the school. Meanwhile David had gone off somewhere else. Anyway we had a good chat about Iraq and the Chilcot Inquiry [into the Iraq War]. He felt they were going to try to get him to say he was not happy about the level of Cabinet discussion. He agreed with my analysis that in part the whole thing risked being the revenge of the establishment. He said [Lord] Robin Butler and [Lord] Richard Wilson [former Cabinet Secretaries] had both recently made speeches to the effect that if only there had been a more traditional Whitehall approach it might have been better. We agreed he needed to get to a place that said, for all the advice given, ultimately ministers had to decide.

He was fine on most points though he would have to watch out for detail. He said in reality it was a lot more presidential under TB but he felt on this there had been all the discussion anyone could have wanted. He intended to have a pop at Clare [Short, former Labour Cabinet minister who resigned in protest over UK's involvement in the Iraq War] and also 'red socks' as he called [Sir] Chris Meyer [former UK ambassador to the United States]. He was convinced all Meyer's protestations about being in or out of meetings was all about status and thinking about his memoirs. On Peter he was reasonably relaxed, if only because he said he couldn't understand why anyone would be surprised. There for a couple of hours then I drove him to the Jubilee Line as he told me why he wanted to be Treasurer of the party, and how Tony Woodley [joint general secretary of Unite Trade Union] was trying to block him. 'I've got the black spot'. Good to see him but also something a bit sad about watching him limp off. He had been pretty defensive about the Lords but his main points were that it gave him a platform, there were some really clever people in there who would help take the Tories apart.

Saturday 17 July

Blog on public services. They are moving from possibly needed cuts to totally macho approach. Later nine plays at the Tricycle Theatre under the banner 'Women, Power and Politics'. Sounded heavy but enjoyed it. Highlights were a very funny play, *Handbagged*, on the relationship between the Queen and Mrs Thatcher, and *Acting Leader* which featured [former Cabinet minister] Margaret Beckett's attempt to follow John Smith as Labour leader. Then John Hollingworth [actor] with a Nick Clegg soliloquy. I cannot remember much of what was said. But I do remember laughing, and I remember the audience laughing at this as much as at anything else the evening had to offer. It confirmed me in my view that as the comedians and satirists mourn the political passing of New Labour's most satirised figures, among whom I would have to include myself, Clegg is being fattened up to help replace us.

Tuesday 20 July

Read TB's final chapter. I didn't much like it. Too speechy, a bit rushed. Did a note on it with a lot of suggestions for change. But he came back and said it was deliberately different. He wanted to put over a world view and he wanted something that would respond to what he saw as the soft dominant politics of the time. He felt the Iraq inquiry would be grim because they would be too weak to resist the clamour, not least from establishment people now turning their backs. He was on pretty good form but said he hated being in Britain just now because of the endless trashing of the record, partly by the Tories and the media but helped by some of our own. And of course he felt GB had sanctioned some of that down the years.

He was fairly balanced about GB in the final chapter but he was saying directly that we lost because we were not New Labour any more. He was fairly relaxed about Peter, said life was too short but he did feel his book had damaged him in the eyes of serious people. Gail was spitting mad. She felt he had effectively trashed everyone and all for a few *Times* headlines. PG had seen him at the weekend and he had not really gone for him but he felt angry and betrayed. If Peter had one thing he could do it was to stand up for New Labour and he didn't.

Wednesday 21 July

Round to see PG. Chemo not working as it should but he was still amazingly up about things. He was very heavy about Peter's book, said he clearly saw the whole era as Blair–Brown–Mandelson, when there were whole periods he was barely involved. We were both sadder than we were angry, though, that Peter had become more distant, including from the families. Home to meet Fiona, Calum, Grace and Sissy [Bridge, neighbour] then off to Heathrow. Worked flat out on the plane on Volume 2. Much more interesting than Volume 1. Landed in Boston, lovely day. Out to Doug and Suzanne's [Kahn, family friends] in Beacon Hill, near [Senator, former US presidential candidate] John Kerry's house.

Friday 23 July

In Maine, at Doug and Suzanne's place on Lake Megunticook. Tragedy over the other side of the lake. A boy was missing after some kids had been daring each other to jump from the cliff. Doug said it was the first death like that. Devon Stewart, seventeen. Grace and Sissy among the last to see him alive. David M called a couple of times. He felt he was winning but was a bit alarmed to learn TB's book was out on the day the leadership ballot papers went out. It would have TB up in lights, and he still felt he was being pinned as TB's man in a way Ed was not seen as GB's. I was getting into the habit of a daily seven-mile run with Suzanne. Working through Volume 2 and there was an irony in Peter constantly complaining he was not fully involved. C.f. his own book.

Monday 26 July

Really sad mood around the place as a result of the kid's death. People were still jumping though. I felt there was something a bit odd though. Four boys. Three ended up swimming over the lake. One said he was turning back. Died thirty yards short. The girls felt he – or one of them – had been put under pressure to leap. He was terrified. Anyway all a bit sad. Nice day apart from that. We ran a reverse route. Suzanne thrashing me though. Real pain in hips and lower back. Maybe time to call it a day.

The week had gone really quickly. But I had managed to work my way through the whole book and worked out what I thought was the right strategy. I had also managed to switch out of UK politics for a while. Cameron had not made that much of an impression here though PG felt he had generated a fair bit of interest among informed opinion with his deficit plan. He was also making some pretty bold statements on foreign policy e.g. pro-Turkey, a big whack at Israel. What I couldn't work out was whether they were all thought through or a bit off the cuff. He was also making a big trip to India taking stacks of ministers, business people, sports and culture. But meanwhile the cuts were starting in earnest. He was winning on boldness and style but maybe storing up a lot of problems.

Tuesday 27 July

Out water skiing with the girls but my back wasn't up to it. We set off for Boston at 3. We had had a good week. F and I got on well. Two lovely paintings to take home. Calum had had a bit of space. Grace loved it. And I had broken the back of Volume 2.

Wednesday 28 July

Home then round to see PG. He had had a massive dose of chemo yesterday. The cancer was down a bit but not enough to operate. He was on a bit of a twin-track strategy. Talking the talk about fighting and staring it down, but also saying he was talking to Gail about life after death and the girls were thinking about it all too. He looked OK and seemed fairly energetic. He had played tennis with Calum and Georgia the other day and said it was one of the happiest days of his life because he thought he would never play again. He was angry about Peter but didn't want to break off completely, especially not now. GB had called the other day and they had had a long chat. GB was livid with Peter, felt he had given him the chance to rehabilitate himself in the eyes of the party by bringing him back to the centre, he had taken it, done it well, and now blown it again. He felt hurt by it.

PG felt it was largely down to TB and GB, and to me, to fight for the record and the legacy. He said TB and GB were in very different positions politically but both could make an OK defence of the other and they should do it. It was in their mutual interest. He was keen to write a book defending Tony but he didn't have the energy. He felt DC was doing well on boldness but badly on some of the stuff that would come back to haunt. He had seen David M and felt he was in OK shape.

Thursday 29 July to end August

Between Maine and France I did a fun event in Munich, a conference of US lawyers and their families. I knew as soon as I met Deb Kuchler [lawyer], the organiser and some of her associates that it would go well. It was hard to imagine a UK lawyers' event like this. Families, kids, day trips here there and everywhere, but above all just a really positive and warm bunch of people. I managed to catch the Nick Robinson documentary on the five days between election and coalition formation, and he was pretty fair. Told the story well. On the way back I got chatting to a guy at the airport about Peter. He said he was loving it because it stood up the Tory analysis of New Labour. That was the real unpardonable bit of what he had done. Nice enough dinner for Calum's 21st at the Vine. We all made little speeches and then he did one and it was really moving and, as David [Mills, Tessa Jowell's husband] pointed out, incredibly emotionally intelligent. The evening ended with [Sir] Ian Kennedy [lawyer, head of new Independent Parliamentary Standards Authority] popping in and having a very bad row with David, who was laying into him re. MPs' expenses regulation.

The holiday started out OK despite F and I being a bit snarly at first. Out on the bike with Rory most days, between two and four hours. On the Thursday a horrific ride in the Mistral. Five hours. At times virtually going backwards. From Séderon to Buis-les-Baronnies the wind was of mind-blowingly tough, character-forming horror. Rory said it was the worst hour of his life. TB wanted a conference call on the first day on his book and the positioning, and the idea of giving the money [royalties] away. Catherine [Rimmer, TB aide] had raised it with me and I was in favour. It would have been good to give some to the party too I think but he had gone for giving all of it to the RBL [Royal British Legion]. The haters would still go for him, but reasonable people would appreciate it. He sounded OK but a bit nervy. The problem was he hated the UK media and loved being out of it and this would put him back right in there.

Alan Milburn [former Labour Health Secretary] agreed to advise the new government on social mobility which set off a little flurry. Nina [Parker, friend] came running in to say Grace had fallen and hurt herself. Bloody nightmare. At the foot of the swing, screaming in pain, her ankle facing two ways. It looked like one of those awful football injuries that have players out for months. Impossible to console her, screaming in pain, F panicking. I called Zizi [friend] at the bar to find out how to get the sapeurs-pompiers. Call 18. They were there in half an hour, and superb. She was screaming in agony a lot of the time but they managed to calm her and then get her strapped up, in the ambulance and we set off for Vaison.

She was in real pain. They got her in quickly for an X-ray which showed a double fracture. They didn't have the capacity to operate there so we were moved onto Orange by another ambulance. Grace was veering between calm and hysteria. Crying lots and lots – about an operation, plates and screws, ruining the holiday, all the consequences etc. I stayed over with her, and had a really uncomfortable bed next to hers. Neither of us slept at all well. The doctor came in about 9 the next morning and said it would require surgery and the whole process began. She was not in great shape psychologically. The boys came over with a few things, then Fiona, by which time she was already under the anaesthetic while we sorted out finances and insurance etc. Terrific level of care, Fiona sorting insurance.

It was a pretty grim thing for her though and a crap way to spend a holiday for all of us. Very few of the staff spoke English, including the doctors, so I was pretty much having to stay the whole time to translate. Catherine called during one interlude. She was seeing the MoD re. TB's decision to give all of the proceeds from the book to a military rehabilitation programme via the RBL. Cherie and now Matthew Doyle were worried there would be something of a 'blood money' attack. I felt he should ignore it, that most people would see it as a very generous gesture. It was important it was not seen as tactical or, even worse, as a response to a campaign. My ideal was for there to be mention of it in the book, maybe on the dedication page or in the main body of the text. Might be too late for that but it would show it had been thought through.

We agreed GB and especially TB saying we lost because we stopped being New Labour, plus Iraq, were the likeliest main stories. I asked if it was possible to make a part donation to the party too but Catherine seemed to think he wanted it all to go to military rehabilitation. He also needed a narrative that explained his admiration and gratitude without this being an admission of guilt or error. She said pretty much everyone was appalled at Peter's book. Also said no way would TB have said all the stuff re. me being too big for my boots, a liability etc., because he had constantly been trying to get me to stay. Neil and Glenys were sending funny texts re. Peter, e.g. why oh why didn't the Welsh FA hire him after he had brought down the Berlin Wall and freed Mandela – they would have won the World Cup by now? PG was out for a week only, on not-bad form, not as energetic and doing the usual permanent commentary, but good to see him there.

Grace's accident meant less of a holiday than we would have liked. For the first week or so, Fiona or I slept at the hospital. When she finally got out, we had daily nurse visits and daily trips to the physio. Plus another trip to Orange to see a surgeon to check all was well. She was pretty amazing once she accepted it, which took a few days. But it meant going out was a bit more of a hassle. The treatment was first class. The physio, Patrick, operated out of an office in the car park. He was eccentric. Danced with the bandages, pulled funny faces. Once he knew I liked Jacques Brel, he played Brel music as he dealt with Grace.

Gail was reasonably relaxed but worrying a lot re. the TB book. He had not yet told her of the plan to give away the proceeds to the British Legion. I felt I had to tell her and in any event it was going to leak fairly soon as people inside the MoD and the Legion started to know. It came out and ran OK on the news but a lot of the papers ran with 'blood money' needless to say. He really was damned either way. He was getting one-way traffic on his reputation at the moment. Also some authors protesting at Water-stones letting him do a signing. Rory read the manuscript, and loved it. TB and I had a couple of exchanges while he was in Malaysia. He knew there would be questions re. guilt etc. but he clearly felt it was the right thing to do. He sounded very defensive about the whole thing. He needed to get to a different mindset on it. The *Mail* and others were pushing for a full Kelly inquest and Dominic Grieve [Attorney General] seemed unsure what to do. I was just reading the bit in TB's book re. Howard's weakness being opportunism and up popped the slimeball to call for a full inquest.

The pathologist popped up to say it was textbook suicide. Seven years on it was still part of our holiday. Fiona drove back on her own and I took Grace by train, the journey OK despite lack of air con, lack of wheelchairs at London. Couple of nice charity surprises when we were away. Yes from

Kevin Spacey to re. LLR night. Also got a call from John Bercow [Commons' Speaker] who was reading, and said he was loving, *P2P*, and wanted to offer Speaker's House for a dinner for LLR. He said he found the diaries riveting. He was genuinely surprised how bad the tensions had been, felt we had kept a lid on it all pretty well. He was also wanting me to go in for a chat any time in September. The Aussie election looking like a hung parliament. Got an approach from the ALP [Australian Labour Party] re. how best to handle in the coming days.

Rory off to ride Alpe d'Huez and had another bloody accident, knocked off by a lorry on the descent. There was a list of media influencers via Twitter and I came fourth after the Beeb, *Guardian* and Reuters, which suggested I was spending far too much time doing it. The worst thing about coming back was the drop in standard of healthcare for Grace. We went from what felt like a cocoon to something Kafkaesque. Fiona driven to the end of her tether just trying to fix an appointment with a specialist orthopaedic surgeon, the French having said we must do so as soon as we got back. Grace GCSEs good. She got a bit upset that she couldn't enjoy it the same as the others because of the crutches but she did go out with the girls. When finally we saw the specialist at the Royal Free, they rather upset the apple cart by pretty much wanting to reverse everything the French had been doing, e.g. plaster instead of the half thing she had, no physio yet, no daily injections. But we went with it.

Tuesday 24 August
Meeting first thing with the researcher on the Jamie Oliver *Dream School* programme. I just wasn't sure this telly thing was what I really wanted or needed. Most of the stuff I ever saw was crap and I couldn't see I would get the enthusiasm to make the change needed to make stuff I would feel I could live with. TB and Gail were getting more fretful as publication date neared, though to some extent the scale of coverage had been low since the donation story.

Thursday 26 August
I was feeling a bit listless and not really sure what I needed to be doing. No big project on the horizon apart from the diaries and that was all a bit backward-looking and same old same old. Fiona was convinced I was feeling edgy because whenever I felt I was almost escaping I got drawn back in for something, e.g. TB's book stirred it all up again. She felt I was probably more upset by Peter's book than I was letting on. I was certainly pissed off with it. Out for dinner with Neil and Glenys. Felt I had to stay

off the politics with them. I couldn't be bothered listening to how good Ed M was. I felt he was too tactical and too soft left ever to be able to win, and that taking on David was just a bit odd.

Friday 27 August
Gail getting frazzled by TB office constantly changing their plans. Mind you, part of the change was driven by the fact that he was going to the White House for talks early next week. Gail asked me to stiffen TB a bit as they were talking of changing timetables and not putting out extracts as planned on the day before publication.

Saturday 28 August
Off first thing to Swansea. Met up with Paul Fletcher [CEO, Burnley FC] to chat over the idea of a University of Football Business at Burnley. News leading with Tory plans to scrap NHS Direct [health advice and information service]. Off to Gail and Philip's place in Burford [Cotswolds]. PG looking pretty tired. Gail just fretting re. the TB book. Ditto TB. He asked for a conference call tomorrow before he did his interviews. I sent through a long note about the need not to be defensive and just get above all the nastiness and pettiness. The most important thing was the sense of a big personality, a big event, and his voice filling the political space again so that the book could lead to some reassessment.

It was unfortunate that it was going out at the same time as the ballot papers, but there was nothing he could do about that. David M was not keen for a direct endorsement because Ed was basically running the line that he was change and David was continuity. TB sounded a bit hurt but did say he understood. Both of us felt that a joint thing with JP could work well. David just wanted JP. JP wanted it done as a joint thing. We were pretty clear that we were going to try to separate out the book from the election. But it wouldn't be easy.

Sunday 29 August
Call with TB and his office, later joined by David Hill [former No. 10 director of communications for TB]. TB was sounding a bit nervous. He had Martin Kettle [*Guardian*] and Andrew Marr to do in the next twenty-four hours. Went over difficult questions. Re. money, I said he needed to emphasise he was still doing public service but funding it himself. Re. GB to go with brilliant but impossible. Get over big picture and legacy. Longish walk to pub lunch at the Carpenters. Georgia talking about how

nice people were and how pleased they were to see me when we walked around the place. PG talking a fair bit about his illness and seemed very tired. Gail just anxious. She asked me to have another call with TB before his interviews to try to break him out of the defensive mindset.

He was getting worried that his pretty clear allegation that GB was behind a cash for honours push and implicated in the Tom Watson 'coup' unless TB backed down over pension reforms would go majorly neuralgic. I said he just needed to get above the noise and not be defensive. Blogged on the Milibands after reading Cameron wanted Ed and feared David. JP called. He had seen TB yesterday and wanted to come out for David together. He felt that would carry a fair bit of weight. But David – and this was a sign of how crazy things were now – had said to him he would prefer JP endorsement alone. Kind of weird that the guy who won three elections was thought to be hors de combat. JP said he felt angry that the record was being undermined. He didn't want Ed because he felt he would not be able to lead. He was already way too much in hock to the unions. Paul Kenny of the GMB had basically said if Ed didn't win there would be no money for the party.

JP wanted my take on how the media would play a joint endorsement. I felt a net positive, though with risk attached. I was beginning to get a blizzard of bids. Feeling a bit anxious about the whole thing. David M called late on. He said he still felt confident. After a lot of beating around the bush he asked if I would help write his speech for a win on the Saturday. 800 words. The buzz was still that it was all a bit close to call but I kind of felt he would win. The thing was none of them had really struck out in a bold direction. Ed had got noticed more and in a way that was heavily tactical. But it was definitely winning new support.

Monday 30 August

The Marr interview seemed to go OK for TB when he did the pre-record for Wednesday. He said it had helped to talk it through because he had not been in a good place. He just hated being back in the British media swim. Did a slow two-hour run. Blogged, pottered, long chat with Richard Bacon, who was doing a pre-record with TB tomorrow. Political news dominated by a self-indulgent intervention in the leadership debate from Peter. It played totally into Ed's hands, as he was able to get up David as Peter–TB and the whole thing a referendum on New Labour which had become toxic. Long chat with David about his victory speech for the Saturday. He was still confident. He said the situation with Ed was 'cold'. He felt he had been running quite a nasty campaign, trying to pin Iraq and other deemed TB failings on David and himself as the only change. It was not going to be easy to get over it, whatever the result.

Peter was right factually to say Ed would take the party backwards, but he was not the person to be saying it. 'Root canal treatment would be preferable to this,' David said. He was really hacked off with him. 'This was about him and his book, not me and the election.' He sounded OK but my worry was it was now becoming very much David as continuity and Ed as change.

Tuesday 31 August

Good piece in the *FT* by Gideon Rachman on the hatred of TB being over the top. TB said Bacon was tough but good. He was now in the States. He said David M was worried about his backing. He said he understood, but it must be pretty galling. I decided to do Tony Livesey [presenter] on 5 Live late on, partly because he was a Burnley fan, partly just to get a voice out there and calibrate a bit re. the GB stuff. We heard *The Guardian* were splashing – tendentiously – on a headline saying TB said he always knew GB would be a disaster. *The Times* on GB departing from New Labour. It was all fairly inevitable but TB wanted a bit of pullback from it. Livesey also had the *Telegraph* which had got hold of a foreign version of the book so it was all pretty big out there and would be huge tomorrow.

Wednesday 1 September

TB book and the *Marr* interview were being trailed on the Beeb and dominated pretty much all day. I did a blog on the back of *Marr* talking about the book and being fairly reasonable about it. I sensed a kind of reassessment beginning with those who had read it. There was also a lot of surprise at the freshness and the candour. And it was flying off the shelves. Lots of the usual suspects out there attacking but the overall sense was of a big figure back on the stage with a big voice and a lot of interest in what he had to say. I was getting tons of bids but stayed out until later. Decided to do *News at Ten* live and *Newsnight* with JP and Chris Mullin [former Labour MP]. Most of the focus through the day was his stuff re. GB, also Iraq but the scale of the thing was getting through.

Out to see John Bercow and his wife Sally at Speaker's House. Tea and chocolate cake. Bercow really liked the diaries. He was picking my brain on various things past and present. Really interested in the mechanics of how we worked. He chatted over how he had decided to become Speaker. Felt it unlikely he would be a minister. Interested in reform etc. Portraits of past Speakers all around us, Betty [Boothroyd] looking quite mellow, stood by the bed, Michael Martin in all his finery but looking a bit sad. Bernard Wetherill, Selwyn Lloyd. Bercow seemed to love the place. He'd only taken four days' holiday and most of that, it seemed, spent reading my book. Sally came in. Real livewire and said I was one of her heroes.

He was unsure about Cameron. Didn't dislike Clegg but felt he had been too discursive at the despatch box when he stood in. He felt none of the Labour candidates really had it but that David M was best in the House. She was backing Ed Balls and trying to persuade me in that direction, fairly unsuccessfully. Talked over the LLR event he was offering – on her birthday. He asked if I would take another big job. It was a good question. It entirely depended on what. The TB–GB story was raging away all day but funnily enough not as neuralgic as I thought it would be. Later to *News at Ten*. Both the reports by Tom Bradby and Lucy Manning were good for the book and good for TB. There's no doubt it is going to be a massive seller, and worldwide. I did my best to recalibrate for GB. Earlier, at TB's request, I had sent an email to GB saying TB had not said, either in the book or the interview, the line used by *The Guardian* as their headline, namely that TB 'knew he would be a disaster as PM'.

Quick car to *Newsnight*, where we were all probably too much in agreement. Again I tried to separate TB from DM and leadership elections. JP pushed back a bit on the idea that TB did not really let down GB on his promises to go. I made the point that TB said he would go provided GB supported him on reform. GB only heard the first bit, TB was only interested in the second bit. We had a bit of a laugh about the line about TB worrying how much he drank. John Reid [former Labour Home Secretary] had used a great line, that where he came from in Scotland, budgies drank more than TB did. David P there too and showed me a *New York Times* story [phone hacking] on Coulson they were running tomorrow.* That one was not going to go away. I was glad I had done a couple of interviews but equally glad I had done no more.

Thursday 2 September

TB called first thing after getting back from America. He'd sent an email overnight saying thanks for the help, and thanks for being a calming voice yesterday in a 'mad axeman' kind of way. He felt a little troubled about the impact on GB, and also worried if it was going to create problems for David M. But I felt what yesterday did was simply remind people he was a big figure making big waves still and that his voice was out there for the first time in three years. I was not sure he needed to do much more by way

---

* In a story about phone hacking by *News of the World* journalists, the *NYT* alleged that Coulson, the then editor, had imposed 'a hypercompetitive ethos, even by tabloid standards' and that he had been present during discussions about hacking mobile telephones.

of media. It was set. It outsold Peter eight to one at Waterstones on Day 1, according to Susan Sandon [Random House]. TB asked if I was through with Peter. I said there was a nastiness in the way he rewrote history. I told him of the note I sent to Peter at the end of the last campaign on how I hoped we did not drift so far apart again. No reply. Just the round-robin email to say the book was being announced.

TB had not read the book but said he had told Peter he worried the fall-out damaged him not just with the party but with the business world too. I told him what Chris Mullin had said, that he looked tired and drawn, and he said he really was tired. Another overnight flight wouldn't help. He was intending to do more on the MEPP now and delegate more of the TBO [headquarters office] and charity stuff. He said it had been weird being back in the White House. He'd been there for the ME talks and had been at a dinner for Obama, Hillary, Netanyahu and [Mahmoud] Abbas [President of Palestine]. He felt there was a small chance of things starting to move. Also felt that Obama was in need of a fair bit of help. The right were on the march and Fox [US TV channel] was rampant in terms of dominating the media landscape. He wanted to put together a few ideas and people to help. Back on GB, I said there had been no reply to the note I sent on his behalf yesterday, telling him that TB had not said he knew he would be a disaster. He said the problem was people kind of knew how he felt and also knew that GB *had* been a bit of a disaster by comparison. But whatever was in the book he felt we had to keep saying there was this other more productive and more positive side.

I did a blog on the William Hague [Foreign Secretary] situation, basically defending him and saying that this situation said more about the media than Hague.* Of course if his statement of yesterday was not true – and he had had gay relationships with this man or anyone else – he would be finished. But I sensed he was telling the truth and said so. Got a call from the Beeb straight away re. doing clips which I did later after doing the Richard Bacon show on the back of the TB interview. TB was OK and there was an interesting reaction, which I picked up on, from comedian Dom Joly who said he knew you were meant to be anti-TB but he liked him. I said that was a pretty common response. Also weaved in a couple of mentions of the media blackout on the *NYT* probe into Coulson.

Friday 3 September
Nice lunch with Nicola Howson [PR executive] at Elena's Etoile. She felt

---

* Hague released a personal statement to refute 'untrue and deeply distressing' rumours of an affair with a young special adviser who had resigned his job following press speculation.

I should be doing big telly stuff, that I was 'unemployable' in a conventional sense because of the name, the fame and the baggage. But she felt the name could be put to 'change the world' use in a different way. She felt major serious telly was the way to go. She thought I had done well new media-wise but that sometimes it came over like there were certain things I couldn't let go. So while I complained I was not allowed to escape my past, sometimes I played into it. E.g. ranting at Dacre and others. I loved her frankness. Re. TB book she agreed with me, as per an email I had sent to Gail and PG, that the launch had gone well, but now maybe pull back a bit. No need for breakfast or daytime telly, or signings where there would only be coverage if there was trouble.

To SW1 to do an interview on TB's book for German telly. I was a bit on autopilot but it was OK. The producer said they were glad to have Blair back in the news. They could never get the station interested in Brown and though there was a bit of interest in the coalition early on, it had faded. TB book on for record-breaking sales. He called a couple of times from Dublin where he was on *The Late Late Show*. Paul Allen [Irish PR executive] keeping me up to speed with the security and all the protests being planned.

Saturday 4 September

Two-hour run. Longest in ages. Slow but OK. Definitely up for the GNR. The worst thing was the sore hips and the slight limp afterwards. Not that many years ago that I could do twenty miles and not feel too bad. No more. Worked on Volume 2 intro, further toning down the attack on Peter M. The TB story today was the trouble at the book signing in Dublin. Heavy security and it did make you wonder if it was worth it. He was going to have to think carefully about Waterstones on Wednesday. The Coulson story was picking up. JP really going for it on the angle of the cops not properly investigating or informing people who had been targeted. Piers texting from LA to say he was enjoying TB's book though he couldn't believe he didn't mention him once. 'I love the fact Peter barely figures while you are all over it.' He said it reminded him why he had liked him. His Larry King replacement show being announced Wednesday. He really wanted Obama first show but would also like to do TB and me together. Funny old world.

Sunday 5 September

I did a blog on Coulson, saying there were questions for No. 10, *News of the World*, the media generally and the cops. Denis MacShane [Labour MP] reckoned the cops were holding back because they were worried their own links to Murdoch would be exposed. Most other papers were just willing it away by silence but JP was out there now. Also Tessa saying she was told she had been hacked twenty-eight times. Alan Johnson [former Labour Home Secretary] calling for review etc. Good piece by Will Hutton [*Observer*] on what it all said about Murdoch. TB called and emailed, saying he was moving towards cancelling the book signing in Waterstones on Wednesday. The protesters would claim it as a big victory but I agreed it was probably better than a mini-riot in London. There was, however, a danger that they then turned their attention to the launch do at Tate Modern.

Monday 6 September
The Coulson story was finally taking off, with MPs back and Tom Watson [MP former Labour Whip] getting a PNQ [private notice question]. I hoped MPs didn't confuse wood for trees. I feared they would. I tweeted that Coulson was trees. The media culture more generally was the wood and the cops were somewhere in the forest. Led to a big response including lots of punning on cops-copse. JP was out there. Chris Bryant [Labour MP] pushing quite hard. *The Times* did a bit. Sky were finally doing. The Beeb going pretty big. But Theresa May [Home Secretary] basically parked on a line that ministers didn't interfere in police operational issues. It was going to need more pressure to keep it going. My worry was that Coulson would go but the broader questions would then die. Tessa said the same. MPs did OK. But Tories were mainly saying it was all just politicking. There was a real sense that several of the papers were not pushing because they probably got up to the same and worse, and also that the cops had not pursued because they were too close to Murdoch.

Meanwhile TB finally went snap on cancelling the signing, so that went fairly big and led to loads of online activity about the launch. Book was still selling like crazy. I was meanwhile feeling edgy the whole time. I did a run and had an instant energy crash. Bollocks to this. Got to rediscover drive and energy and focus.

Tuesday 7 September
Email early from TB. He said he and GB were due to be seated next to each other at a do for the Pope [Benedict XVI] next week. 'Should we speak?' I couldn't work out if he meant should he and I speak or he and GB at the event. He asked me to scout out how GB was feeling. Word came back sad not angry, blamed himself a lot, knew he had not always behaved well but felt TB was not straight with him. Loads on Twitter re. the Tate

Modern launch. Quite a few re. out to get me and 'other war criminals' if they can't get TB. *Bookseller* confirming TB book best seller ever re. politics, mine second since BookScan [publishing data provider] began. Blog on Coulson again making the point that Labour needed to stay focused on bigger picture re. media and cops. [Assistant commissioner John] Yates at a select committee today and said he would interview Coulson. That would keep it running a bit. A few pieces around suggesting leadership contenders should listen a bit more to TB.

TB had decided to call off the launch party and wanted to know if I agreed? The problem was that the protesters would be right alongside people queuing to go in and the cops couldn't guarantee safe access to anyone but TB. He was worried some of his friends and family would get hit. There had been a lot on the internet re. me, Jack Straw, Geoff Hoon [former Labour Cabinet minister] going. I said we needed one or two unexpected voices out there saying it had now gone too far. He was pretty angry about it. Meanwhile he was emailing me the whole time about whether I had spoken to GB to ascertain his state of mind. He was really quite worried about how they would be with each other at the event for the Pope's visit next week. I said he should just cold-call him. See it like a cold swimming pool. Once you're both over the initial shock it will be easy. Yeah right, he said. I agreed to speak to David Muir [GB strategist] again. He said GB felt he had a lot of shit poured over his head, from Peter's and Tony's books. He was feeling pretty down. The Pope visit was going to be fraught enough even without all that.

Wednesday 8 September

Breakfast with Ed [Victor] to go over where we were on the diaries. He felt TB's book good for me, not just reputationally but also vis-à-vis the diaries. Alex called re. voting in the leadership and other elections. He was going for David but didn't want to get into doing public stuff. He had written to him. Had also written to Balls wishing him luck but saying he was voting for someone else. We chatted about [Wayne] Rooney [Man United and England player]. He sounded a bit down about him. The papers had been full since the weekend of Rooney and prostitutes. I said what are you going to do about him? 'What can I do? There is something in him that means he will always do stuff like this. He is also the last guy on earth who should take a drink.' I asked if Colleen [wife] was going to stay with him. He said the other players said there was no way she would leave him.

TB doing *This Morning* on which he trailed the idea of cancelling the party. He said he didn't want all the hassle it would cause. Cameron's dad was taken ill in France and later died. Clegg did PMQs v Jack Straw. Coulson dominated again. It felt pretty bad for him. I was blogging on and off on it. Mainly making the point that nobody really believed he didn't know but also that this had to be about more than Coulson. It had to be about the media culture.

Thursday 9 September

Coulson still dominating, with Yates at the select committee leading to [Keith] Vaz [Labour MP, chairman home affairs select committee] reopening inquiries. Bryant had successfully pushed for a Commons debate, and more and more voices were piling in. I had an interesting chat with Matthew Freud at the Saatchi & Saatchi [advertising agency] bash. He had seen Coulson yesterday. He felt the whole thing was going to get very nasty. There was a chance this would now lead to fresh police and parliamentary inquiries. He reckoned there was a chance Murdoch, Rebekah [Brooks] and Coulson would all end up having to give evidence on oath. 'They either have to admit to illegal activity, have Alzheimer's or perjure themselves. None of these are attractive options.' Grace and I had a little outing to see Philip. There was a chance of an operation within a few weeks but it was not certain it would work. He was getting more and more philosophical about it.

Tessa came round for a chat. She had decided not to stand for the shadow Cabinet. She wanted to focus on 2012 [Olympics] but maybe hold out the prospect of doing it again in a couple of years. She seemed really down for her. Sixty-three. I said if her heart was not in the shadow Cabinet idea, just say no. She obviously still felt a need to be needed but maybe it really was time to make way for a new generation. Out later to the Saatchis' 40th anniversary party at the Saatchi Gallery. Maggie Thatcher there looking quite frail. John Major [former Prime Minister] looking tanned. Lots of the old Tories there. I sensed that they felt Coulson was toast. Also interesting the extent to which they felt the issue had to go more broadly than Coulson, to press standards. Really nice chat with Dominic Lawson [journalist] and Rosa Monckton [wife]. She wanted to start a Mumsnet-type website for parents of mentally disabled kids. Hundreds and hundreds of people there. Too hot. Saw Douglas [Alexander] and Philip G but not many Labour people. It really felt like the Tories were back as masters of the universe. Nick Soames [Tory MP] said he loved Peter's book 'because it's so bitchy'.

Maurice Saatchi made a not-bad speech on the history of the company. Charles [brother] not there of course, all adding to the mystique. Maurice modest enough to say they would have been nothing without Maggie. He was happy to be a footnote in her history.

Friday 10 September

Osborne had done an interview with Nick Robinson last night and had said there would be £4 billion welfare cuts on top of what had been announced in the Budget. PG said yesterday he felt that the Tories and the press had successfully painted Britain as a terrible place to live. It wasn't. Anything but. And when the cuts fell people would realise what they missed and the political problems would mount.

Saturday 11 September

Looking forward to a real football day, Everton v Man U, then over to our game. Set off with Rory and Rayan. Got to Everton about an hour before kick-off and met up with AF. Said he wasn't playing Rooney [former Everton player]. I thought he was winding me up. But he said he wasn't going to put him through the abuse he would get there. Bill Kenwright [theatre producer, Everton chairman] on great form. Took me up to the boardroom for brunch. Great match. Alex livid at the end of it. 3–1 up, drew 3–3 thanks to two late goals. Everton fans jubilant.

Off to Burnley v Preston. First I did *Football Focus* [football preview TV show] predictions in the boardroom, up against Mark Lawrenson [pundit, former player]. Another amazing match. 3–1 down with four minutes to go and won 4–3. Alex there because of Darren [son, manager of Preston]. Left at 3–1 to avoid the traffic. He texted me later, 'Not my day.' I was working on DM's acceptance speech. Peter Hyman [TB strategist and teacher] had done a good draft and I was working on that as the basis. David asked me how he could best use me. He took my email as a 'Let's meet' kind of thing, as though I was going to be part of the team. Back for *Match of the Day*. Losing 8–5 to Lawrenson with two to go. In three games late goals cost me points. All on the Sunday and Monday games.

Sunday 12 September

Watched Birmingham v Liverpool. 0–0, bang on. Three points brought me level with Lawrenson. All on tomorrow now.

Monday 13 September

TUC [Trades Union Congress] kicking off. Getting more attention than at any time in years. Media trying to push them into a really militant position but in the bits I saw they were doing pretty well at pushing a genuine line of argument about the deficit. Also starting build-up to Lib Dem conference and things not great for Clegg. Off to see Ian Kennedy and his IPSA chief executive and a couple of outside advisers. We went through their plans for the next stages. I said I felt they were too focused on their own role and image rather than the job they had to do. The MPs complaining can't all be wrong. They were also too worried about what the press said. They should deliver on expenses and then try to get to the issue of pay pretty quickly. He should be in the lead on that. Stoke scored in last minute v Aston Villa to put me ahead in the prediction battle v Lawrenson.

Tuesday 14 September

Out to Camden Labour v Camden New Journal football match. Richard Osley of the *Camden New Journal* had been tweeting to get me to do it. Took the boys and we won 10–4. Scored a couple. Rory man of the match. Raised over a grand. TB getting his US Liberty medal finally, from Bill [Clinton, previous winner]. David Muir called to say TB and GB were going to speak pre the Pope visit so their first chat was not live on TV.

Thursday 16 September

OK run. Nice day. Baroness [Sayeeda] Warsi [Tory peer, chair of the Conservative Party] had done a really silly interview on God, saying we had been wrong not to do God and they did because faith was so important.* Totally missing the point. Did a few tweets and later a blog on what I had actually said and meant. Off to the NHS conference in Lincoln. Some good exhibits of innovative mental health stuff being done. Sat through the conference then did my bit which went fine. Lots of people saying what a help it had been for me to be open re. mental health. Lots of worries about cuts as well. *Newsnight* chasing me to do a turn on 'We don't do God' in the context of the Pope's visit. Pope visit going well. TB was bizarrely spooked about having a chat with GB. When finally he did he said it had not been easy, that GB was back in victim mode.

Friday 17 September

The Pope got terrific coverage from his visit to Scotland yesterday. I was getting some nice comments and reaction on the web – even from the *Telegraph* – at my suggestion that it was possible to be a pro-faith atheist. Re. Warsi, Fiona made the point that TB converted to Catholicism and that GB was a religious son of the Manse. The aptly named Will Heaven [comment

---

* In 2003 AC had intervened in an interview in which TB was asked about his Christianity. 'We don't do God,' he interrupted.

editor] said on his *Telegraph* blog that I showed deeper understanding than those protesting against the visit. The Pope was in London today so I got the Tube to Random House rather than risk getting caught up in the road closures etc. Meeting with Martin Soames [lawyer], Bill Hagerty [co-editor] and Joanna Taylor. Took us a couple of hours to go through it all. Joanna was of the view that I should do much less on TB book in the intro and no mention in flap copy. Fiona meanwhile seeing Cherie for the first time in ages. We met at the Wallace Collection restaurant afterwards because Alan Seymour [Gospel Oak Primary School head] wanted to take her out to recognise her eighteen years as governor.

She said CB had been friendly enough but it was all a bit tense. TB was there briefly and she said he was very friendly – he later sent me an email saying she was looking fabulous – but she found it all a bit bizarre. There was no discussion with CB of anything that might be termed remotely risky. And when she did get on to Labour leadership for example, F moved her on, saying we had moved on and were trying not to get too involved. I watched a lot of the Pope coverage. TB and GB perfectly friendly in front of the cameras at the Westminster Hall event. TB said afterwards it was all a bit strained.

David Muir told me GB was feeling pretty put upon by the whole books thing. But quite a few people commented on how close they seemed compared with the non-speaking down the Tory end of the front row. The Pope had an unusual accent and a very understated delivery. But it forced you almost to strain to listen and the more I listened the more I heard and enjoyed what he was saying. The visit was going better than anyone had really expected. I got a big response to a tweet I did on a BBC reporter who said there were at least four ex-PMs there. I said it would be a miracle if there were more. Maggie looking a bit out of it. The hair was still magnificent but the face was weak. Good speech by Bercow.

Saturday 18 September

The makers of the crapola *Special Relationship* [TV dramatisation of TB's relationship with Bill Clinton and George W. Bush] were probably getting a bit out of my slagging it off in the *Radio Times* but even so I decided to have another pop on the blog this morning. There were the inevitable 'If he hates it, it must be good' but I will be very surprised if it connects or succeeds in anything like the same way as *The Queen*. Michael Sheen [actor, portraying Blair] was in *The Guardian* saying he didn't care if it was accurate or not because he had no way of knowing. Interestingly Aaronovitch [*Times* columnist] thought I should welcome it because it reminded people TB did Kosovo and did it well. *Football Focus* was on just before Calum and I left for Palace v Burnley. They did it OK, then Lawrenson saying it was obvious why I won – I had nothing to do and so just studied stats all the time. Fabulous match even though it was 0–0. We should have won it. Lift to Gatwick then up to Newcastle for the Great North Run tomorrow.

Sunday 19 September

Dick Caborn taking the mick and saying I was too much in the comfort zone. I probably was. But when he said we needed to do another sports fundraising dinner I just said no. There was a bit of light rain at the start so lots of us gathered under the bridge at the bottom of the first hill. Usual nice mood. Haile Gebrselassie there, which added a certain something. I had a different pacer this time, Ashley. We did OK. Couple of bad miles in the middle and one a bit later on but I felt OK on the last one. 1.53. Way worse than my best but close to last year so not bad. I had said I would give up if I went over 2h so I would have to do it again. Got a helicopter away with Haile, who almost beat the world record. We had an interesting chat about the price of cows!

He confirmed he would fancy going for President. Maybe I could help him? But they were worried about the security situation if he went for it. Later out for a dinner I was speaking to the Voluntary Organisations' Network North East. Nice bunch and we had a good and very strategic chat about how to handle the cuts agenda. Good argument, and as we discussed it I started to feel the beginnings of the strategy I thought Labour should adapt. I recommended they take Big Society at face value and really go for it. Show that their services will help save money in the long term. They were mainly Labour I think and I enjoyed talking to them.

Monday 20 September

Bumped into [Sir] Stuart Bell [Middlesbrough Labour MP] on the train. Asked him what he was up to. 'Really just wrestling with the future of social democracy.' Conference call re. a speech then to see David Sturgeon [psychiatrist]. I was finally off medication again which was great but I was worried. Later out to meet Fiona and Tanya Byron [psychologist] for dinner. They had been speaking at the Ham and High book festival. Now they were trying to get me to do a film on 'new feminism' which would involve me admitting I had got things wrong.

Tuesday 21 September

Up at six-ish and off to Leeds. Two main events, speech and panel discussion for the Leeds Foundation Trust mental health members' day and later

'Dine to Change', at which Sue Baker of Time to Change [mental health campaign group] and I tried to persuade business of the problem of stigma and discrimination. Really pissed off to be missing Burnley v Bolton. But it was a good event. Also sold loads more books. And attitudes definitely changed as the evening wore on. Some openly admitted ignorance and discriminatory attitudes. But they then agreed to do something about it.

Thursday 23 September

Charlie Enstone-Watts [trainer, friend of Calum] came round and we did an hour's boxing training. Very different but he pushed me pretty hard and was really good at what he did. I worked a bit on David M's acceptance speech before heading to Gatwick to meet up with Kate White [LLR charity] to fly to Jersey for the golf day tomorrow. Met by [Sir] Bob Murray [chairman of Sunderland FC]. To his interesting art deco house then out for dinner with him and Sue [wife]. Lovely couple. Both really rooting for David. I said I had a nagging feeling that he would not get it. That there had been enough doubts for people to hold back and go for Ed. Talked about life in Jersey which clearly they loved but which was all a bit slow for my tastes, not to mention money-centric.

Friday 24 September

Out early and met up with my team for golf at Le Moye. Stableford four-ball. I played atrociously but they were quite a good bunch. Introduced themselves as probably the only three Labour voters there today. Nice guys but God the golf was poor. We ended up coming last! Worst I had played in yonks. Also got soaked. Nice enough do though two days out quite a lot to raise £16k among a land of multi-millionaires. Flew back late p.m. The odds had shifted on the leadership with Ed now replacing David as favourite. I texted David to ask what was going on. Hopefully nothing, he said.

Saturday 25 September

Woke to blood all over carpets downstairs, Molly [pet dog] clearly ill and F took her off to the vet. Turned out she had the same as me – colitis! I did a pretty desultory and bog-standard blog on the leadership situation, saying it was a big day for the party, that I still hoped and thought DM would win but with the caveat that the bookies did not get much wrong. And as TB had warned right at the start, the party was always capable of making the wrong decision. Audrey came round and we watched the leadership election result. The candidates knew the result. We didn't. It was hard to tell from the body language. DM smiling, Ed not. That said Ed to me. David was ahead in every round until the very end when Ed took it with a lot of union support. David first to his feet to go and hug him. Then Ed got up to speak. He looked a bit scared and slightly shell-shocked. He spoke OK without it being great. New generation. 'I get it'. But even from home I could tell – and Gavin [Millar, Fiona's lawyer brother] among others later confirmed it – that the mood in the hall was not fantastic.

I felt it was a disaster. The wrong choice in the wrong way. I'd be very surprised if David stayed in these circumstances. Neil was all over the airwaves, jubilant, over the top. I was glad I wasn't there. Gav texted to say Neil had said he hoped this showed me the error of my New Labour ways. Of course everyone would rally round Ed, but to be frank I couldn't even bring myself to tweet about it. I was glad to be out of it. I texted DM to say he should now do what is in his interests and not listen to all the noise. He texted to say he wanted to have a proper chat tomorrow.

Sunday 26 September

People were beginning to notice I had said nothing so I did a blog basically saying Ed should not worry about all the labels being applied to him. He should be his own man and take his time to paint his own picture. It was bollocks really though. I could be wrong but I just couldn't see this working. I watched Ed on *Marr* and to be fair he was OK but not much more than that. David called. Louise had sent me a text saying she felt like she had been through a car crash and it would take a while to get over it. David said at the moment he still felt very proud of his team and the campaign they fought. He knew that feeling gutted and angry would follow. What made him angriest, he said, was that he just knew we would have less of a chance and the Tories were going to get away with murder. He said he would say all the nice things about Ed but he had fought a pretty negative campaign. He had learned at the feet of GB and everything was 'for me or against me'.

He dreaded to think what Cameron would do with him. He would need good people around. His current staff were not going to be up to it. As for himself he had decided he wouldn't stand for the shadow Cabinet. He had spent three years saying GB was the right man to be PM and he didn't want another few years pretending to believe in something he didn't. He would stay as MP, be loyal, make a contribution but away from the soap opera. It would be hard for Ed to get his own space if he was still around. He sounded OK but said the whole thing had been very difficult. He had won almost 90 per cent of the local parties, including Sadiq Khan's. The Tories would milk it, Ed as the unions' man.

He said he and Louise had moved out of Manchester to get a bit of breathing space and lots of people at the hotel were being very nice. A woman said she would vote for him but not his brother. Ed would do his best to seem centrist and sensible. But his politics really were those of GB. He [David] was not going to rock the boat in any way. Soap-operisation had become a real problem. But it may be that just being there would allow our opponents to talk of boat-rocking and interpret it all as such the whole time. He sounded pretty down by the end of it. He was scathing about Neil saying 'we've got our party back'. It was all about Tony really. I said it was quite weird that our most electorally successful leader was PNG in parts of the party. He ended with 'OK, Allypally,' and off he went. I was getting loads of bids on the situation but turned them all down. Tessa called. She was going to see Ed. She said she was under pressure to stand for shadow Cabinet. I thought she was mad. There really did need to be sense of change now. I also felt she would find it really hard in there.

Monday 27 September

I set off for Manchester for *A Question of Sport*. An Irish guy at Euston said I was his hero and could he have a picture? Then a few others gathered round. It was nice when people said nice things but I hated it when you then had a bit of a circle thing going on and people watching. I was met by a driver and taken to Granada studios. Saw Labour conference delegates around the place but had no desire to get involved. Matt Dawson [former rugby player] said, 'Isn't there some Labour thing going on in town?' I was on his team with Joe Hart [footballer], against Kevin Day [comedian] and Jess Ennis [heptathlete] on [former cricketer] Phil Tufnell's team. Jess was truly stunning and really nice with it. All a bit surreal being there. All the rooms where we had put the finishing touches to GB's pre-election rally. And the set was where he made the speech. Nice atmosphere but I didn't do well. It sort of whizzed by but without the enjoyment I thought there would be. I was not on form. Gracie was right that these light entertainment shows didn't suit my humour. It overran so I missed the last train and got a car back.

Tuesday 28 September

I was worried yesterday hearing that tickets for Kevin Spacey [actor] charity event were stuck in the 300s so I asked LLR to fix up some media. Did Nick Ferrari [LBC radio presenter] who was great at letting me plug the phoneline and also Nicky Campbell. I did a tweet asking Nicky would he let me plug the event or just ask about Ed M? He raised it first off and said plug away. My basic line on Ed was that people would unite around him, that it was silly to see it as a death knell for New Labour, that it was a moment to move on and adapt to that. I can't say my heart was in it. I refused to do telly because truth be told I was only interested in selling tickets for the event. Audrey and I were watching Labour coverage. She felt it was too bland, and also didn't like all the dumping on the past.

Brendan Foster called. He said, 'Can you imagine five years after he's gone Man U fans saying "God that Alex Ferguson was a shit manager, wasn't he?" That's what these guys are doing with you lot, the most successful electoral team Labour had ever built.' Ed's conference delivery was OK but no better. Odd stance. Odd hand movement. Eyes closed for too long at the end of sentences. The cameras cut to David when Ed said the Iraq War was wrong. David leaned over to Harriet and said, 'Are you clapping, because you voted for it?', which was picked up by the media hiring a lip reader – another sign he wouldn't be able to escape it. He had one or two nice touches but too much 'new generation' and way too much 'let's be honest'.

Helle [Thorning-Schmidt] sent me a text saying I had to give him a chance. I would. But he was now surrounded by people deluding them-selves it was a success. I was struck too by people outside saying it hadn't worked. I was talking to Jamie Redknapp and he said he, Graeme Souness, Ruud Gullit and Richard Keys [Sky Sports pundits/presenters] had all been watching and all thought, 'You've picked the wrong one.'

David called me on his way back from Manchester, travelling with Ben Evans and Amanda Levete [friends]. He had made up his mind he couldn't stay around. He had gone along with my idea of doing it as a letter to his local party. He was totally decided. 3.45 tomorrow. Let Ed have his day but then he had to get it done before nominations for the shadow Cabinet closed. We chatted away about the arguments and then about what he might do. He said he wanted to focus on foreign affairs, education and community organising. He was clear he had done the right thing, but still smarting at what had happened. It was a big blow but he seemed to be bearing it pretty well.

Wednesday 29 September

Did a talkSPORT radio interview from the lounge at Heathrow about Ed and David. Again dropping a strong hint re. him not standing for shadow Cabinet. Flew to Prague on Czech Airlines. Strangely comforting that they go under flight numbers beginning with OK. Worked on crisis speech, landed, off to the Hilton where all the KPMG [financial services] guys were gathered. Got a good response when I said the public were fed up with the way the media did not do serious issues in detail any more. There was a film before the interview in which someone said it was all very well to punish the banks but the banks were central to financing the recovery. I said they had to get out there and make that argument. Said too many business leaders were scared to get their head above the parapet.

Out for a nice run through a lovely park on the far side of the river. It really was a great city and in far better nick since joining the EU. Getting through Prague airport was superb. Modern, comfortable, efficient. Joseph Harker had asked for a piece on DM for *The Guardian* so I worked on that and also a smaller piece for the *Mirror* and then a blog on the soap-operisation of politics, in part based on the discussion at KPMG. I had rewritten Helle's speech to [Labour] conference and she texted me to say she got a standing ovation so thanks. We got into an exchange re. Ed. I said he was so clearly the wrong choice it was a disaster. Helle said the mood had been a bit odd and I had to try to help Ed. Everything I was hearing about his team was not good. Worked on the plane to Rome, then met some of the Confindustria people who had organised the conference. It was the Italian equivalent of the CBI, but bigger. Nice enough bunch.

Thursday 30 September

Pretty Italian all round. Didn't start on time. Several speakers who were given between three and ten minutes and all went on far longer, and hardly any of them addressed the theme of crisis communications. The audience – mainly business people, including some comms guys – seemed to enjoy it OK. It was quite a weird set-up though. Three speeches then I had to give a mini one saying what I was going to say when I gave my grand-sounding *lectio magistralis* no less. Then a Q&A including one of [Prime Minister of Italy] Berlusconi's staff – Silvio was seeing off another vote of confidence – who was complaining the internet was stopping true information getting out there. I said Berlusconi showed even if you controlled the media you couldn't always control the message.

The Moroccan ambassador had a bit of a whack at TB. Nice atmos though. Back to the hotel. Loads of emails and calls coming in and driving me a bit crazy. Then a sudden blitz from the Ed M camp. Stewart Wood [adviser] asked if I could see him to talk over one or two comms issues. I said the problem was deeper than comms. If the speech and interviews were anything to go by, it was about deep strategy – lack of – and he needed a major outreach to the public PDQ. Then Ed texted me – maybe coincidence. He said it was a lovely piece on David in *The Guardian*, this was all very difficult but could we meet up for a chat? I said of course.

TB sent a hilarious email about a dream he'd had. He was hosting a leaving do for me. I interrupted his speech and launched into an all-out attack on his record. He hit back but as he spoke I literally grew a beard in front of his eyes. And we both ended up weeping ... now that is weird. I said my dreams were usually about him and Gordon trying to kill each other with axes, though I had one recently when he and Arsène Wenger [Arsenal FC manager] were having a shouting match about the Middle East.

I was feeling a bit nervous about the *Dream School* thing. Partly the fact it was reality TV, and the worry it would be crap. Also that I wouldn't be able to hold the class. Tony Curtis [actor] had died and there was a picture of him on the front of *The Guardian*. He looked like Peter Hyman. It made me think of calling Pete and getting a few tips now he was teaching. He was brilliant. Name badges so you learn and use their names quickly. Find a way to praise early. Be firm. Insist from the off that when you speak nobody else speaks. If it feels wrong, move on. If you sense they're bored, do something different in the middle. Exercise maybe. We chatted too about Ed and David. He was pretty gutted. Said if Ed asked for help he would probably not give it to him. He felt they had run a stupid and also dishonest campaign.

The car came for me and I set off for Mill Hill and *Dream School*. Brilliantly set up. A real head, fairly tough character. He had had troubles at school himself but also had a teacher who turned him on to learning. I texted Daley Thompson [former decathlete, *Dream School* fitness volunteer] who was out doing PE. He said, 'Go home before they get back. They're a nightmare.' I chatted to him when he got back. Really hard to control, he said, and from some tough backgrounds. They were nice when you got to them but hard to get to. I went through the lessons schedule with the TV people. They said David Starkey [historian] had been a bit of a disaster. They had just about run him out. Rory and Grace had both said I needed to get their attention straight away, be firm, loads of praise, show no fear. Rory said he was worried. Grace said I would be fine. But never talk down to them. That was Starkey's problem. He had probably never met kids like that.

Mary Beard [basic Latin] had had a rough time. She and I were exchanging emails. She had found it tough. She was in academia and this was frontline tough teaching. The kids all trooped in in dribs and drabs and before long I could tell I would be OK. I gave out name badges, said something to all of them, introduced myself, then asked them to say what they thought about politics, almost all indifferent or negative. Then I showed the films I had made – on women's rights, Martin Luther King and Obama, gay rights and so on. They started to engage. By the end I felt several were really up for it. Several came and asked for specific help. One or two tried it on. Nana Kwame with baseball cap and iPod. Two or three of the girls with shouting in class. But I felt I did OK and really enjoyed it. I tweeted a bit on how good they had been. Also got into Twitter exchanges with some of them. Took Grace and Rory out for dinner. They loved some of the stories about the kids' attitude especially Harlem showing me her mum on Facebook and saying, 'Ain't she fit, sir?' Jourdelle with his crutch – 'I fell off a government pavement, sir, and I intend to sue.' There were some bright kids in there for sure. I asked what they cared about and they got going pretty well. Fair few equality issues. Lots of them said they hated the government. They had all got through school without qualifications yet some of them were clearly bright. We had called my subject 'politics, media and campaigns'. None had heard of George Osborne. Four knew of Nick Clegg. All recognised Thatcher and TB from photos. All but a couple recognised Cameron and GB. None recognised Major, or had heard of him. They all recognised Obama and [Osama] Bin Laden. Most recognised Katie Price [model, previously known as Jordan], Simon Cowell, Jay-Z [rapper] and Mahatma Gandhi. They had sat pretty rapt watching the short films on the fight of the Pankhursts to get votes for women, the US civil rights movement, Nelson Mandela's long walk to freedom, and on how Labour legislated on gay rights. They were quickly pretty passionate about campaign ideas of their own.

Saturday 2 October
I called Andy Coulson to ask whether we could get the *Dream School* kids into Downing Street. He seemed pretty up for it. The situation with Calum had taken another turn for the worse. He was drinking way more than was good for him, and I had said last night I was not going to the football with him if he came in worse for wear. F and I were also disagreeing about how best to address it and ended up having a dreadful row, a total shouting match, all the usual stuff we had grown tired of saying down the years. Then when Calum came back, he was on the edge now, his eyes odd, noises odd, and a lot of angry talk, mostly aimed at me. Fiona called a doctor and he refused to speak to them. I got them to come out. Nice guy came and he talked to him for a fair while. He was quite young though, and I sensed he was a bit nervous both about the situation and also seeing me there. 'You'd better ask the big man,' Calum kept saying, nodding at me, whenever the guy asked him how he was, or whether he felt OK. It was a bad scene.

Eventually he suggested we go to A and E. By now the TV match was underway and Calum said he wanted to wait to the end. I wanted to get on with it. We went to A and E. Now he was saying he needed to say goodbye to the staff at the White Horse [pub]. I had deprived him of the football and now this. It meant he did a runner while I was checking him in. Went to the pub to get him back, got him in to see a nurse and eventually a very nice Italian psychiatrist who talked to him for a while. I called Jack and Charlie [Calum friends] and broke down talking to Charlie. I just didn't know what to do. Fiona in and out. She was out when finally we saw the crisis team and then moved to the Grove [Royal Free mental health crisis unit]. It was a pretty tough environment. Some hard cases in there. His room too hot. But I felt better he was there and deep down I think he did too. I barely slept again and when I did I woke up crying.

Sunday 3 October

We went to see Calum, who was still on edge, and we talked a bit to the nurses. I got the sense they were just about coping, but working under a lot of pressure. I felt a bit cheered up he was being cared for. But it was going to be a long haul, and I didn't feel he was anywhere near the point of thinking he had to change his ways. Fiona was convinced he was punishing us for something. I was booked to do the Henley Festival which I could really do without. A very nice guy drove me down and just talking about this that and the other made me feel a bit better. I met Anna Botting [TV presenter] pre the interview [with her] in the town hall. Nice chat, and Q&A, with one wanker who I used pretty mercilessly thereafter. Joe Hemani [businessman] said it was brilliant and immediately shelled out five grand for charity for a few signed books. Gave out free tickets for tonight's Kevin Spacey [charity] event for best question. Ended up with two – who are the most courageous people you met? I did a mix of political and military courage. Then: 'If you had to put together a strategy to ensure David not Ed led Labour at the next election, what would it entail?' I ducked it but it was a good question.

Home, then out to see Calum again, then out to the Criterion for the Spacey event. Fabulous. The best of the four we had done for the charity so far, I think. He threw himself into it and Melvyn Bragg [broadcaster and author] was superb as interviewer. Kevin arrived with his little pork pie hat. Nice atmosphere at the reception. Kevin was brilliant. He was funny, inspiring, did some great voices, mixed serious and less so. Then out for dinner at The Wolseley with Ed [Victor] and family and John and Sally Bercow. They were a good laugh and they had a great time. He was pretty funny on some of the wackier or more pompous MPs. She was just a volcano of fun and ideas. Home and had a long chat with Alex re. Calum. He said he saw nothing worrying in him last time he saw him. He suggested

I drop everything and just look after him. He was in the States. I fixed for him to get a private tour of the White House visit. Good to talk to him.

Monday 4 October

First I saw the psychiatrist and his team of five and explained what had happened. I broke down a few times along the way. Ended saying we all needed to change a bit, but also that I couldn't see how we could look after him as things were. Calum came in and the psychiatrist was pretty clear he had to stay for a while. He really wanted out but it was going to be a long haul.

Headed to Mill Hill for a *Dream School* session. They had just had Simon Callow and Dominic West [actors], and they'd had an OK time. I had a one-on-one with Harlem who wanted to talk about the importance of the benefits her mum received. She lived in a hostel because she and her mum couldn't get on, yet they were still close. Had a really nice and gentle chat with her. She was definitely bright and like a lot of them more political than she realised. The lesson itself was about the ideas for a manifesto or pledge card. They had some great ideas – e.g. Jake with a car-sharing scheme via Facebook. They cared a lot about equality and fairness. They got into some of the ideas big time. But they couldn't stop bloody talking. We did OK though. Rowdier than lesson one. Thinking up ideas for votes too after the vote on who did the best speech. Harlem won. She had done benefits.

I did a few interviews then off to the hospital again. I was angry with Calum because he went out for a walk having said that Jack [friend] was his brother, and they had let him out on that basis. Philip and the Hutchinson boys went, then I went back with Grace later. He was really cross with me that I told them about Jack not being his brother. Led to another bloody row with F later.

Tuesday 5 October

Osborne was getting a lot of flak over child benefit, having announced it would not go to higher-rate taxpayers. It was clear from interviews with ministers that the first they heard was via the radio or TV. And there was a pretty immediate backlash starting up. I did a blog drawing in Harlem's speech on benefits yesterday and suggested the kids knew more about the impact of these cuts than the Tories. I wondered if Cameron and Osborne had ever met people like these. I went to see Calum who was getting pretty angry about being there, though I think enjoying meeting some of the other patients.

Out in the evening to the Waverley [paddle steamer] on the Thames. Jim Pettigrew had hired me to speak and mingle a bit and help them promote it as a conference, charity and corporate venue. Nice event. Andy Robinson [rugby coach] and Sam [wife] there. Spent most of the evening talking to them, reminiscing about the Lions [AC had toured New Zealand as Lions media adviser] and also telling them re. *Dream School*. They were a great couple and good fun to spend the evening with. I probably didn't mingle as much as I should have done but it had been a while. Dixie Ingram, ex-Guards pipe major who knew Donald, was there and I had a blow on his pipes. Played OK. Calum was convinced he was getting out Thursday. We would see.

Wednesday 6 October

I had been watching *Newsnight* last couple of nights and I got the sense of the Tories making it up as they went along. For sure there was a lack of grip. Cameron had gone out yesterday to brush up after Osborne but had only succeeded in opening up more problems. I was going to miss his conference speech live, or so I thought because of *Dream School*. I went out there early. Chat with Mary Beard, who was going to offer the kids the chance to skip the lesson – translating a Latin poem – if they wanted. Half left and the rest were great, she said. Long chat with Nana Kwame about his housing problems and agreed to try to help. He behaved a lot better in the class, presumably because I gave him some attention. In the class we were doing interviews. Me interviewing them and them interviewing each other. They got into it.

Off to see Calum at the hospital. Some of the patients really getting drawn to him. A headteacher who was mid-manic breakdown. A guy there full of really odd conspiracy theories. Calum not engaging much with the medics, though they said he was better when we were not there. He was definitely directing his anger my way. Off for Liverpool. I was feeling tired, a mix of the angst and stress re. Calum and also the sense of doing too many things not well enough. Met off the train by a nice copper and driver, off to Knowsley Hall. Lovely venue. The event was mainly for pensions analysts and thank God they said don't talk about pensions.

I had managed to catch a fair bit of Cameron. It struck me as underwhelming. The Big Society was not really taken forward policy-wise. 'Your country needs you' and 'It takes two' were weak without a bigger and more original argument. I didn't get the impression he had stormed it. Considering this was his first post election, it was weak. But he could do well if he could show future economic success was related to cuts strategy. If it became ideological he could be in trouble though. Clegg could be toast or do well. Ed – all depended on how he did. If he made a shift too far leftwards or just campaigned as an opposition leader, he helped Cameron.

With Calum and Fiona to the psychiatrist. First us, then him. The guy felt there was a downside to being in with worse cases who were gravitating to him. Also his anger was becoming counterproductive. I was anxious about it but we agreed he could leave later today and, though still technically an inpatient, he could come and go as he, we and the docs thought sensible. He seemed better but still tense and anxious. The doc, who had been at Caius and had been looking us all up, seemed to know what he was doing but I was still worried. Fiona saying we had to trust Calum more. Rory was at a sports conference at Stamford Bridge and I set off and made it in time for Arsène Wenger and Billy Beane [US baseball executive], interviewed by Damien Comolli [technical director St-Étienne]. Wenger was superb. A touch of genius. He had some wonderful observations about people, how to spot and deal with players, team psychology, bringing on kids etc. He spotted me and kept looking over when he said anything that might apply to politics, and nodding or raising his eyes as though to say, 'Is that right?' I found myself nodding on to a lot of it.

Billy Beane was also fascinating, on the detail of his *Moneyball* [film about sabermetric analysis of baseball statistics] approach. Massive soccer fan. Together they were fascinating. But what really struck me about Wenger was that he was a deep thinker and someone who worked at understanding people. We ended up having lunch together. He was very open and warm. Mainly chatting about management techniques but ranging far and wide. I told him Alex F was going to the White House tomorrow. He said he loved the way that when United lost a home game in Europe last year Alex went to a race meeting the next day and clearly loved it. He was fascinating on how he studied players, the data, the assessing of every goal to see who made mistakes, the getting rid of players a year early not a year late, and so on. Lovely interesting stuff. I texted AF to say I was with him. 'Let me know what he's up to'.

I did a blog suggesting there was a lot DC and EM could learn from Wenger and his management of people. AW accepted that it was easier to manage difficult members of the team in sport – you got rid of them – than in politics, where even if you sacked them, they were still hanging around the pitch and the changing room. I pointed out that Ed Miliband cannot even pick his top team, which may seem like it is healthily democratic, but in leadership and team-building terms is a dreadful model. Yet so many of the principles of leadership and team building are the same in both arenas, and I worried politics was lagging behind again. Clarity of purpose and objective. (Still a bit woolly from DC, and too early to see from EM.) The requirement of an obsession about winning matched by a hatred of losing, requiring attention to every detail, and the margin of every detail that may have an impact upon outcome and performance. Honest and ongoing analysis of strengths and weaknesses, of your own and of your opponents. Special attention for the special players. Never underestimating your opponents, or devising strategy according to what you want to be the truth, rather than what in reality it may be. (Labour activists have a habit of imagining everyone thinks like they do – to be avoided.)

I loved Wenger's quote, 'The comfort zone is the enemy of top-level sport ... every day is a battle between the comfort zone and "Can I be the best?"' Billy Beane put it another way: if your team wins eight in a row, you still have to make sure there is a 'level of discomfort' in the ranks, that they do not assume they are now invincible. What came over from Wenger, much more than in his interviews, was a real understanding of humanity and human nature, and that too is one of the keys to leadership. He said people are lost in their dreams ... they say they want to be the greatest player, or the greatest actress, or they want to stop drinking ... 'I say what is your plan? Your plan *right now*, in this moment, to make the dream come true?' With data analysis now so much a part of elite sport, he was asked if he would like to see the day when managers could hire players without even meeting them, because so much information was available. He pulled a face, and said, No, certainly not. 'The value of the human being,' he said, 'is to see, and to love.'

Then I prepared for my interview with Johan Bruyneel [cycling team sporting director]. Rory had done a great job on the research and it was easy to go through it. He was a good talker, clever, good storyteller. Did a fair bit on drugs. Alberto Contador and Lance Armstrong the biggest egos. And they had to be. Resented structure of the sport. Tour de France the main event. The teams got no TV rights. Crazy. He was looking into a breakaway G-14-type thing based on Formula One. Then off to Cliveden [country house hotel]. Another fundraiser. I was really tired at the moment though. Doing too much and being utterly drained by Calum. Discussed it all with a woman whose daughter was struggling with heroin addiction. Sounded horrific.

Friday 8 October
Lily Carter [communications director] came round with a few dozen books for me to sign for Rethink [mental health charity] and then we chatted a

bit about the renaming ideas for the charity. Like a lot of people I had met in recent days she was down about David M and felt we were in trouble even with the cuts coming. Calum had a hospital appointment and went on his own. I didn't feel he was really facing up to the need for change but we'd see. I went round to Rory's new flat in Belsize Park Gardens. Nice. Calum had a beer with him which really worried me. He's home, but still not engaging with me at all about his drinking.

Saturday 9 October

I set off fairly early for Cheltenham [Literature Festival], reading diaries Volume 2 copy-edit. It read pretty well and the richness was vastly superior to Volume 1. I got there, did a little TimesOnline interview, flirted with Jilly Cooper [author], who later said on the Sky books programme that I was the sexiest man around, and then waited for Harlem and Nana Kwame [*Dream School* pupils]. Nana Kwame was wearing a tie and seemed to be quite into it. Libby Purves was interviewing me. She said she felt she had been stuck inside a tent with me, TB, JP, GB etc. I said but had you enjoyed the holiday? Yes, she said, but it was nice to get home. In the Q&A a question about David Kelly and whether there should be a new inquest, also whether I would ever work for the coalition, and what strategy for Ed. I said I thought it had been a good move to put Alan Johnson in as shadow Chancellor. But I said if they just went on cuts without a proper economic narrative, the Tories would be happy.

I had teed up Libby to ask about youth engagement and I got Harlem to speak from the front row. She did her benefits spiel but did it a lot harder than in the class and warned there would be war if they went for all the benefits without there being jobs. It was quite an impressive culture shock. One or two heckled but a few came to me at the signing and said they really enjoyed it. It was like a political awakening. We had a chat backstage after the signing and Harlem and Nana Kwame were trying to persuade me to stand for Parliament and run for PM. I was saying I was too old. She said no way. You're better than these other people. And if you want us to get engaged you need to do it all over again too. She said her heart had been pounding, that she couldn't believe how cool I was when people had a go, that her nan said none of the working-class people ever had a bad word for me. She liked TB too. So glad they came and they were buzzing with it. I introduced Nana Kwame to Salman Rushdie [author]. NK said: 'Mmmm, I know the name, not the face, remind me.'

Out to the Centaur [racecourse venue] for the session on Obama. James Harding [editor, *The Times*] chairing me, Bonnie Greer [author], Peter Hennessy [historian] and Justin Webb [broadcaster]. We had a good session, again over a thousand people. I was basically sticking up for Obama. Also warned against any further Foxisation of the news. I had had a long chat on the way down with Tom Fletcher [UK foreign policy adviser, diplomat], who said Obama had started out a bit slow, constantly saying he could not do too much at once. He was now motoring a bit more. He was going to need to up a few more gears though. He had been pretty cool and aloof and a lot of the Europeans felt he couldn't really give a shit. Generally, Tom said, working for Cameron was OK. A lot calmer than working for GB. Fergie texted from the States having had a great trip to the White House and lunch with [Sir] Nigel Sheinwald [UK ambassador]. I called Nigel. He said Obama was doing OK but not much better. There were going to be more changes. I felt I had stuck up for him pretty well. Found myself always sticking up for the politician v the media. I said the politicians had a lot more power than they realised but too many kowtowed and they needed to be tougher. But who knows if it was true.

A short signing then Ben Wegg-Prosser [formerly TB's director of strategic communications] and his wife arrived. Ben was friendly enough, Peter M less so when he arrived a few minutes later. No warmth there at all.

Sunday 10 October

I did a blog on Cheltenham, partly on Harlem but also focusing on Obama. I was struck by something both Tom and Nigel said, that he needed to open out on more fronts. It was World Mental Health Day so I did a bit of media on that which got a pretty good response. Rory O'Connor [psychiatrist] round p.m. Nice Irish guy recommended to us by David S. Alcohol expert, dealing a lot with doctors and dentists. Saw Calum at length, then us, then him again. Definite problem and best addressed by giving up all alcohol, but he didn't want to, and didn't think he needed to.

David M called a couple of times from a weekend away in Lyme Regis. He said I was the expert at rebuilding lives after a car crash. How do I do it? He said he was staring at a corpse and it was his career. Pretty clear he would not be getting involved with Ed. He felt that even though Alan J better than Ed B as shadow Chancellor it was all a bit of a mess and he just couldn't see Ed doing it. I took him through how I had tried to work out fairly systematically what I needed to do and then did it. But always have to be adaptable. He sounded OK but this had been life-changing stuff. Melissa [Benn, writer] heard part of the conversation because we were out for dinner, including some of the things I said re. Ed, but she felt he had shown quite a lot of toughness and ruthlessness and that while he was from the GB school he was not necessarily of it. She said I should help him. I could really make a difference.

Monday 11 October

Out on the bike and met Philip in the park. He was on good form, very warm and encouraging about Calum and the family more generally. He was clear the operation was a risk. He reckoned 5 to 10 per cent chance of death in the operation itself. Also a chance they would open him up and find they couldn't do it. Then it was just a question of managing it. He was worried about Georgia. Also Gail panicking a bit about being on her own. He had had a long session with Andrew Cooper [Conservative strategist], who said the Tories had a very clear strategy – exaggerate the need for cuts, blame Labour, then cut not quite so bad, see the economy come good, then take credit. They had done loads of focus groups on Ed and David, and Ed was without doubt the one the Tories wanted. Philip had seen a fair bit of TB and felt the book had lifted his reputation a fair bit. But a way to go. He felt Peter was in a bad place.

I did a blog about Harlem at Cheltenham after receiving an email from someone in the audience who had seen it as a political awakening. Up to *Dream School* for a session with Jamie, [Sir] Andrew Motion [poet and novelist] and for part of the time [Lord] Robert Winston [scientist, Labour peer]. We sat with the head and just chatted. Andrew Motion said he was really struggling. He just couldn't control them. We all agreed it made us think more highly of teachers. We also realised the major limitations. But we all felt it was possible to make some progress with some of them. They all felt Harlem had a real temper which I had not really seen. Motion and Beard were maybe the ones least used to kids like this. Anyway it was an OK chat. I think Jamie's heart was in the right place but inevitably a lot was about himself really.

Ben WP called. He said he felt Peter and I ought to meet up and get to a better place. Felt it was bad and a bit demeaning that we were sniping at each other the whole time. I agreed but said in my mind it had gone beyond. His book was an outrage. It showed he was not a team player. Ben said he thought he had not been rude at Cheltenham. I said maybe he had grown immune to it all. But I had moved on and was not sure I could be bothered trying to go back. I said I agreed the sniping was silly but mine was a fraction of what I felt. Chat with Gail re. Calum then off to Barclays Capital [investment banking advisory services] dinner. God, I hated the 'How do you spend your time these days?' question. But it was an OK evening. Really wealthy Swiss guy there who said Peter was smart but had damaged himself.

Tuesday 12 October

Dream School. Some of the parents were in for the day and I had a nice chat with Harlem's mum, who said she was really enjoying it and felt I was listening to her in a way most people did not. The lesson was one of the best. We had the team from Saatchi's helping design stuff as we went. They had done some really good work and the kids liked seeing their stuff. Wayne Rooney earning ten times more than entire school teaching staff. When is a benefit not a benefit? When it's a necessity. Some of the kids really into it, and enjoying the creative flow. Probably the best lesson yet I would say. Also looking good for a visit to No. 10.

Earlier had a session with Alvin Hall [financial adviser], who was doing maths, and Cherie [Blair], who had just finished a lesson on human rights. She had a bit of a barney with Nana Kwame who ended up walking out. Cherie on best behaviour with me, a couple of little jokey snaps re. alpha males but by and large OK. She was really into the idea of the school and felt some of them had been doing OK. After the lesson – which was double the usual length with a break in the middle – we went to Nana Kwame's house. One-bedroomed ground-floor flat in Southwark. Kept it fairly tidy. The only books were the ones various *Dream School* teachers had given him. Chatted over his background and his housing issue and what he wanted to do about it. He was bright but needed direction. He was also in a bad place re. hating all his social workers.

Wednesday 13 October

Early start, off with Rayan to the Nottingham Belfry. Conference of managers and bid process people. Did a blog on the way re. the nodding dogs of the coalition, Cable and Clegg having stood on their heads once more, this time on student tuition fees. I did a pretty good speech on teamwork which seemed to go down well. Used a lot of Wenger and Fergie and Lance [Armstrong] as well as the usual political stuff. Talked a bit about *Dream School* too. Rayan had collected Mum so we drove back while I was trying to sort next *Dream School* lessons. Yes to Downing Street from Andy Coulson. Home then out for a meeting with Hugo Bague [human resources director] re. the possibility of working with Tom Albanese, the Rio Tinto Zinc chief exec. We had a very frank chat about what I could or could not do for them.

Later out to Random House for meeting with Sue Gray [Cabinet Office] re. Volume 2. She said she had loved it, lots of laugh-out-loud moments. As expected she wanted a few royal and intelligence bits taken out. It was all fairly straightforward. Nice to see her. She said she didn't really like TB's book. She liked JoP's and she liked mine. Didn't like Peter's but felt it was what you would expect. She said Cameron was OK to work with, Clegg a bit at sea. I missed PMQs but Ed seemed by all accounts to have done pretty well.

Thursday 14 October

Off with Rayan to Ironbridge, home of the industrial revolution, for the Brammer Manufacturing Awards. Then off to Telford, Labour fundraiser at a theatre in town. Interviewed by Mike Ion [parliamentary candidate]. Nice event. Had a session with premium ticket holders then book signing and then the event. Really nice reception. As so often at these events, being asked why I didn't stand myself. I said it was the one thing I might regret but I wondered if fifty-seven at next election was not too old. But it was interesting how many people were saying it these days.

Friday 15 October

Out for a really crap run. Hillary Clinton had taken a pop at us and other NATO countries over cuts in defence spending. My sense was the Tories were doing a lot of expectation management. It would not be so bad, and they would wait for the economy to pick up, and take the credit. Off to Liverpool, working on my speech on the way. One of my favourite venues – BT convention centre – and they were a good bunch, the Chartered Society of Physiotherapy. Mainly about mental illness but also bigging up what they do and a few tips on dealing with the cuts strategy and media negativity. Then a signing which went on for ages. Picking up a lot of bad vibes about the coalition. On the way home chatting to *Dream School* people re. whether to take all the kids to Downing Street. Worried some of them would misbehave and embarrass me. They felt strongly I was crazy to try to take them all. I felt instinctively it would be OK and that we would look a bit elitist and exclusive if we narrowed it down. Home – Calum out, but seemed to have got on OK with Rory O'C.

Saturday 16 October

Rayan waiting for me in the street when some twat chased Michael the postman. Rayan stepped in because he was convinced he was going to hit him. Bastard. Michael going through a lot at the moment what with the 7/7 [London bombing] inquest. His son had been killed and he had that haunted look I often see in parents who have lost children. The papers were packed with the build-up to the spending review. The government were probably overcranking a bit. Also a piece in *The Guardian* trailing Hannah Rothschild [writer and philanthropist] documentary about Peter M. Off to Sheffield. Met at Bramall Lane [Sheffield United football ground] by Dick Caborn and had lunch with him and his dad. Paul Fletcher joined us for a bit to talk over the football university idea. Dick had seen Ed M yesterday when he had been up visiting Sheffield Forgemasters. He said he was desperate to see me and he needed help. Ed had called me a couple of times but I had missed the calls. He asked me to pop round over the weekend but I couldn't. I suppose I should help a bit but I don't want to get sucked in as I was by GB. Dick felt he was OK, that he would learn but he did need a lot of help. And he needed good people. He needed heavyweights. He also needed to be out of Neil K's shadow. Nil–nil halftime. We [Burnley] went two up. Two–all. 3–2 up, 3–3 in injury time. Fiona called halfway through to say Calum was refusing to go to his appointment. Had to get heavy and get Rory O'C on the case.

Off to Ilkley Festival. Christine Talbot [broadcaster] chaired it nicely. Twice I got a bit panicky about Iraq and just about held it together but I could feel my voice weakening. Maybe need to see DS again. I think it was Calum and the pressure of that, plus maybe there was something in the sustained stuff re. Iraq that got to me more than I realised. Best question was about China and what I felt about the Chinese Communist Party basing their comms model on New Labour. The audience laughed. I played for time, with a bit of eye movement to roll with the laughter, then said I thought I knew what the question was based on – a story by *The Guardian*'s Beijing correspondent a while back that Chinese government spin doctors had been given a copy of *The Blair Years* to help them in their work. But no, said the man… He was an academic specialising in Chinese communications and the New Labour modelling had been revealed in a book by a renowned fellow academic, whose name I didn't catch. More laughter from the audience, as they realised I couldn't dance around this one… I was going to have to answer directly, and say how I felt that the Chinese Communist Party based its comms model on the one we had devised.

After a few seconds thinking about it, I admitted to a certain pride. It was, after all, a command and control comms structure, so to have a command and control country as big as China reckon that the model worked was moderately flattering. And no, that does not mean I support the Chinese approach to media control and human rights. A few questions later I was asked to reflect on how the observation that 'power corrupts and absolute power corrupts absolutely' related to the New Labour era. I pointed out that compared with our Chinese friends, democratically elected leaders have a lot less power. I said that perhaps one of the reasons the Chinese economy had been advancing so rapidly of late was precisely because the government had far greater power to take and implement decisions, not held back by the views and rights of their people… and no, this is not an argument to kick out democracy, just an observation worth thinking about every time an infrastructure project is held up by a decade-long public inquiry.

I suggested the Chinese give my diaries out to all the citizens as well as the spin doctors. *Big Al's not-so-little Red Book*. Wouldn't harm sales at all, and I'm sure my publishers, Random House, would do a nice special sales deal if the government opted to get one for all 1.3 billion citizens. I did a blog on the way home, suggesting to Wen Jiabao [Premier of China's State Council] this has to be a two-way relationship, and if you've taken our comms model, I think there should be a bit of payback in the direction of those who designed it.

Sunday 17 October
Had to talk to Rory O'C again to get his sense of how we dealt with the Calum situation. Nightmare goes on. *On n'est jamais plus content que le moins content de ses enfants.* Went to collect Mum from the station and then to King's Cross before heading home to watch a lot of football. Rooney the talking point – not picked – and AF had just about had enough of him.

Monday 18 October
Sue Gray called to say the spooks had hit the roof about a line in Volume 2, re. who we spied on. Met Sue later and took it out. Also the royals were 'asking nicely' if I could take out the reference to someone saying 'the di(e) is cast' on the last day before the funeral. It was all a bit random but Sue was great about it all. She said you know we will have to send you a pompous letter, don't you? She liked Coulson, which surprised me. Also felt DC had real confidence and more depth than she expected.

Tuesday 19 October
Did a quick blog on the defence review and how the press would have killed us if we had said we were building aircraft carriers without planes on them.* We would never, ever, ever, ever have heard the end of it. The cartoonists would live off it for months; the headline writers would go into orgiastic delight; *The Sun* would dig out the old front pages of Neil Kinnock announcing his 'Surrender' to whatever enemy wanted to come in and take over; every retired general in the land would wander on to the telly sofas to say their fears about Labour not being trustworthy on defence had been borne out. And a few serving ones would be wining, whining

---

* Defence Secretary Liam Fox announced that the first of two new carriers would be configured to carry only helicopters and then 'mothballed' or sold before a second would enter service using American or French aircraft.

and dining the country's massed ranks of defence correspondents to make sure the views of 'senior military sources' were bombarding the front pages and the airwaves. It would be one of the defining moments of our time.

Off to *Dream School* and easily my worst session. Long discussions in which some of the team tried to persuade me not to take the lot of them to No. 10. I said I knew best blah and I trusted them. But by the end of the lesson I was beginning to wonder if I could. I had to throw out Angelique because she was so rude and obnoxious. A few of the others not much better. Some seemed quite excited by the idea of going to No. 10. But they did not behave well in general. By the end of it I was a bit frazzled. Two more legged it halfway through but came back later to apologise. They said they were worried they were going to lose it.

Earlier chat with Cherie who had lost her voice but seemed to have had an OK lesson. She was joshing like the old days but also seemed to have got something out of it. Liked the kids. I was worried about some of them though. Nana Kwame made his crack about wanting to assassinate Cameron again. I said if he said it once more he was out. Absolutely knackered at the end of it. Then they wanted me to sit and talk to some of the relatives too. Interesting how the camera guys were getting pissed off with a fair few of the kids. Alex did his press conference and after the silence of yesterday confirmed Rooney wanted a move. Handled it well.

Wednesday 20 October

Big day. After all the build-up, the spending review. And a sign of my new life that I was likely to miss it if my golf round went on a bit – which it did. Jamie Redknapp [footballer turned TV pundit] had to pull out because of a knee problem which required a scan so went ahead with me and Jamie Rubin's better-ball v David Mills's ball. Plus he gave one of us – us to choose – a shot per hole. But I ended up playing better than I had ever done virtually and won fairly easily. Lovely cold sunny day. David a bit down not least because Matthew [son] was clearly moving to the view that he wouldn't make it as a golf pro and a job he had lined up had been withdrawn. Nice time though. Got the end of Alan Johnson's response to the spending review on the drive home. Quickly caught up on what the main points were, and did a blog on how the ones who caused the crisis which led to the cuts were laughing all the way from the bank. It was a big day and a lot to digest. They were presenting it as fair and progressive but the IFS [Institute for Fiscal Studies] were quickly coming out with the line that it was regressive. Did a phone call to Jamie Oliver re. the Angelique situation. I was moving to the view that we were going to have to take a smaller number, though I would prefer still to be able to take them all.

Lunch with Calum. A bit better but hard grind. I felt he had to accept he had a problem and should just stop drinking. He didn't. PG went to see Ed and found him a bit bereft. Asking what he should be doing. Not clear re. what he needed staff-wise. I missed PMQs but PG said it was a bit terrifying – you could see DC looking through Ed and feeling confident there was not much there. Also that Ed had been Old Labour for the campaign and reverted unconvincingly. Ed told PG he really needed me and TB to help with advice and personnel etc.

Thursday 21 October

Early start to head for Brighton and the Chartered Institute of Public Relations conference. I did a fairly standard comms speech with a bit of new stuff thrown in re. the coalition e.g. Cameron should have won the election but lacked strategy. Now they have purpose – make the coalition work. Objective – get the deficit down. Strategy – slash the deficit, say there is no alternative and blame Labour. One of the women at the Q&A said why the hell were Labour not rebutting better? Fair point. The coalition were doing pretty well in pushing the line that the economic tough stuff was all needed because of the Labour record. I was on OK form though had a bit of an asthma attack after a few minutes. Long chat with Alex who called as I was leaving. Chatted about Calum for a bit then re. Rooney.

The fans had been great last night. They knew what was going on. Rooney was trying to get older players on his side but not much there. Gary Neville [club captain] had had a go, told him he was a prick. He and David Gill [Man United CEO] were due to do a conference call with Glazers [American owners] at two. They were minded to keep him to his contract. If they sold and got 100 million, people would say it would go on debt anyway. Hiding to nothing. He would be happy to tough it out and show them no player dictates what happens. He sounded like he really had had it with him. Rooney would not win the support of the fans or the players. It was not going to help the mood around the place but it would work itself out. Out for a very nice dinner with PG, Gail and Georgia. He gave me a lovely leather-bound memento of his birthday party with pictures and copies of speeches. All our family there and only Grace [Gould] missing. I kind of felt he would get through the op next week but there was no way of being certain.

Friday 22 October

To my last full lesson at *Dream School*. I was taken in to see Simon Callow doing a scene from *Romeo and Juliet* with them. Angelique was there dressed in Shakespeare garb and asking me if I had received her letter. She sent me a really nice email yesterday saying she was so sorry about being rude and was desperate to go to Downing Street. She seemed sincere. But I gave her a tough line, said I had been clear that who went in part depended on how they behaved and her behaviour had been appalling. So I had to make a stand. The TV people were urging me to relent but I said no. Then John D'Abbro, the real head teacher, changed my mind. He said if this was a mainstream school, there would be no question. But how brilliant would it be if we could go from 'Lord of the Flies' to 'polite and sensible with the PM' in four weeks? He got quite emotional about it, said he would back me whatever but maybe have a think dependent on her behaviour in the class today.

It did make an impression and when she stayed quiet I realised she was trying. I actually had no fear about her behaving badly at Downing Street but I did feel I had to back down a bit but so what? Coming together pretty well now. The kids had come on a fair bit and I sensed some would really make something of themselves. Meanwhile news came through that Rooney was staying at United. So God knows what had gone on there to change things overnight.

Saturday 23 October

Off to Oxford with Fiona and Rayan for Rory's graduation. He was looking smart in his white tie bollocks. The Vice-Chancellor spoke well. Nice manner. Had some nice lines. My favourite, 'It is not what you know but what you do with what you know that counts.' We were seated with hundreds of other parents to the side of the main group of Oxford top brass. The 'graduands' were directly in front of them. Lots of bowing and cap-doffing and most of it done in Latin, which the V-C defended on the basis of a link back to excellence down the ages. They did the whole thing pretty well considering how many they had to get through. I tweeted that I had no memory whatever of my graduation and that drink may have been a factor. Nice atmosphere outside. We met up with Rory's mates. He was the first to take off the white tie, which was an echo of my picture at Cambridge as the only one without a tie. Quite a nice lunch at Balliol afterwards. I was moaning about missing the Reading game but given we lost 4–0 hey-ho.

Sunday 24 October

Ed Miliband had been pressing me for a while to go and see him for a chat. I drove round to his street and met him walking along with a very pregnant Justine and their son. We went in and settled down in the front room. He was keen to get my take on things. As before, he was maybe more questions than answers. He knew he needed a strong chief of staff – Lucy Powell [leadership campaign manager] was doing it at the moment but was probably a No. 2. He needed a comms strategy person and he needed a media person. He was fine with Greg Beales [adviser] heading policy. Stewart Wood [adviser] was doing media but he was not sure he was right for it. As for general direction he was probably saying what he thought I wanted to hear so was clearly aware of the difficulties of being painted too distant from the centre ground. Peter M had been making approaches and being 'nice'.

Ed seemed to be thinking of Ben WP, Patrick Loughran [senior adviser to GB] as possibles. He asked if I thought Peter Hyman would be interested. I said probably not. Would he have worked for David? he asked. Probably. He asked me how that was. I said I think people felt surprised he had gone for it and also that quite a few of David's people felt Ed fought a pretty underhand campaign. I said how was it with David? I got the impression they hadn't talked much. He needs space, he says, though he added, 'I wish he would have stayed but I understand why he didn't.' I said I thought the Tories had failed to win because of lack of clear strategy, but now they had one and we needed to counter it bit by bit. He had played into their strategy in my view by doing too much distancing from the record. We had to take them apart on trying to blame everything on Labour, rather than big global factors. He was relaxed but fairly defensive, denying that he had been negative, and saying he understood what he needed to do. I said re. hirings it was not just about individuals but also the team and he said he had got someone looking at that, someone who worked with big business organisations. He felt he had a bit of time.

I said he needed more energy from the team. I asked whether Balls was onside and he gave me an unsure look. He said, 'You are not as opposed to Balls as some of the Blairites?' I said I had doubts about his public appeal but he was good at going for the Tories. However, we must not just become the anti-cuts people. We have to have an argument for the country and the economy. I suggested that he set up a number of groups on renewal. He needed a team that had the right to range over the economy. He needed to use some of the younger ones to do more re. students and kids. We agreed on votes at sixteen. He felt the Libs were finished but accepted if the Tories sorted the economy they were in good shape.

We talked about PG, who was about to go to hospital. He then asked me how best he could use me. 'I don't mean I'm asking you to come and work for me, because I know you won't, but I'd like to think I can call on you.' I said I would be happy to do that but I am phobic about Westminster.

Told him I was seeing Cameron tomorrow. I said he had been damaged by the sense of the left owning him. Neil saying 'We've got our party back' connected at a certain level and it was damaging. It was a perfectly nice meeting. He seemed to like some of the suggestions I made about how to broaden the base of his profile. He looked and sounded a bit nervy. But I said his advantage was the fact he could paint his own picture but he needed to start soon.

Monday 25 October

Dream School to Downing Street day. Andy Coulson called and also sent a couple of nervy emails. I felt it would be OK in the end. They would be boisterous at the start but calm down. Coulson was paranoid about it all being about me, or about him, or that I would take over the grilling of DC. I assured him on all fronts and also said I thought the kids would be fine. I had sent over a couple of lines on each and he said, 'The last thing any of us want is a haranguing.' Indeed!! Into town and to No. 10. The kids arrived on a bus and I got on at the end of Downing St to give them a little pep talk and get a final assurance they would behave. Henry and Charlotte snogging to the last. Angelique now with Jake. She said thanks for letting her come. Conor assured me he would not let me down. They were quite buzzy about the whole thing as they went through the security and the cops were good with them. I had tipped off Harry Page [photographer] to be there to get some snaps and he was all over it.

The kids were milling around, then we were taken in and given a tour, up the stairs, then the State rooms. Coulson's staff watching on a bit nervously. Down to the Cabinet room to check the seating plan. Coulson asking if I minded not being at the Cabinet table. 'We want it to be about the kids'. Yeah right. No problem though. I said I was happy to sit out of Cameron's eyeline and only intervene if any of the kids kicked off. Osborne popped his head round. Had a little chat with him. Asked if he wanted to meet the kids. 'No, let Cameron get the glory!' Cameron indeed! We had arrived fairly early so they moved Cameron's diary around to bring us forward. The kids came in and sat down and I had a last word with those who would definitely be speaking.

I stood by the door and waited for DC to bound in. All shiny and chirpy. Seemed a bit bigger than last time I saw him. Sat down and said, 'So how we gonna do this?' Jourdelle started off. Harlem did benefits but she was so on her best behaviour that she lost a lot of the passion. And as I expected he was able to generalise re. the deficit, the legacy, the blah. Aysha also got a bit muddled re. public and private schools and DC blathered on about his own kids at state schools. He was hopeless on tuition fees but the kids didn't really come back. Henry was OK on legalising cannabis but he repeated himself a fair bit. Conor OK on pay. Then Nana Kwame was probably best, on youth services. Cameron was trying to give the impression any cuts were local but Nana Kwame came back at him. Jourdelle did an excellent bit on how they felt they had got more out of the teachers at *Dream School* because we were passionate and free to teach as we saw fit. He said they had sixteen GCSEs between them. But they're not thick. Cameron managed them perfectly well. I would love to have come back at him on various points but he was OK manner-wise. He hung around and chatted a bit more, signed autographs, then as he left said to me, 'Sorry to see Burnley's result at the weekend.' Coulson looked relieved.

We headed out to the street, did more interviews and then Osborne appeared again. He was signing autographs too so they had him, DC and me, and Harlem and others were telling him I was the best out of all of them. Henry had another go at him re. legalising cannabis and also took the mick re. his dandruff. Harlem was really warm in her interviews, said I was fair and I cared whereas she didn't think the government did. Angelique good too. Lots of photos on the door. Aysha saying she wished she could have gone at him more. Nana Kwame the same. We went out and I was immediately being asked by people at the end of the street for pictures, which made the kids laugh. They were all saying they were my kids. Jourdelle saying he wanted to be an MP. Lots of farewells then off they went back on the bus. I got a cab home, relieved it had gone OK, and quite proud of them too.

Tuesday 26 October

PG's operation in Newcastle. Ten hours. Alive at the end of it and Gail said that the doctors seemed quite happy. Going to be a long haul though. Mervyn King [Governor, Bank of England] had had a right old go at the banks so did a blog on that pointing out that the government needed to do a bit more too. Conor had yesterday used the line that 7 billion – bankers' bonuses – was the same figure as the extra welfare cuts. Off to Paris for a dinner, interrupted by Fiona drama at home. Steve [plumber] had been fixing radiators in Grace's old room and something went wrong so the bloody kitchen flooded.

Thursday 28 October

Boris Johnson came out with a really strong line on the housing benefit cap, saying on the radio that there would be no Kosovo-style social cleansing on his watch. Heavy line. I did a blog saying that if it was an accident, fine, but if it was deliberate, Cameron had a real problem. It was hard to tell sometimes with Johnson what he was up to. Within a few hours he had done a 'taken out of context' which, given he had done a big 'not on my watch' statement on the radio, was unconvincing. Tweeted re. him bottling it. Then re. Tebbit accusing Cameron of Vichy-style surrender at the EU summit on future financing. *Plus ça change.* Gail called to fill me in on PG. He was OK. The op had been gruelling but he was conscious, and had been rude to Gail a couple of times which she saw as a good sign. Ran home but had energy crash. Up to 15–7 [stones] and back on the crap. Chocolate, biscuits etc.

Calum a bit better yesterday, buoyed by the chance of a job with the party. Off to Sheffield. Met at the station then off to the Students' Union. Nice venue. Being interviewed by a local council guy, Paul Billington. Went fine. Inevitably a couple of questions re. Iraq but generally it was all fairly friendly and a good reaction, especially from a lot of the students at the signing afterwards. Good rapid-fire session at the end, with good mix of serious and less so, football and the rest. Also a woman reminiscing re. me meeting her at Wimbledon three years ago, saying how 'gallant' I was and did I get free tickets? Made that a running theme. Interesting to test the water on Clegg as this was his seat and we were right at the heart of the university. My sense was that some felt he was between a rock and a hard place, but a lot felt really badly let down, especially about the tuition fee pledge. I was developing a line that if people felt he was being used as an ideological human shield for Tory cuts, then he had a real problem.

Friday 29 October

Out for a not-bad run round Sheffield. Back to do a blog on Cleggland, incorporating some of the things said last night including the possibility of defection to the Tories. I was asked last night what advice I would give if I was Clegg's PR man. I said stop bleating, start doing your own big picture and start wising up to how the Tories were using you. Got a pretty big response. One of the weaknesses of focusing on Clegg, from Labour's perspective, was that it gave Cameron more space to get away with things. Picked up at 10.15 by a very nice guy called Arshad and we set off for Chester. He felt Clegg was actually stronger in Sheffield for being DPM. Arrived in Chester and could not believe how busy and also how fantastic the centre was. Heaving. Staying at a little hotel, the Coach House. Cameron claiming triumph at Brussels for keeping EU budget rise to 2.9 per cent after initially saying he would get a freeze. Media buying it. Off over the border to Wales for the launch of the Welsh Assembly Government and Mind Cymru youth mental health first aid scheme. At a school in Saltley. David Hanson and the local Labour MP there, with Mind people and schoolkids and a few others. I spoke a bit about my own experience and the work of Time to Change, then we did an interactive exercise on anxiety. Mind were thrilled that Welsh radio and telly covered it. Back to Chester, later out to the Racecourse for the Literature Festival. I did forty minutes just talking, a mix of funny stories, then a bit about diaries and novels, then a thing about the media. Got through about thirty-plus Qs and got fantastic reception.

Sunday 31 October

I was judging cupcakes of all things, and signing books, at a Camden Cupcake charity event at Camden Market. [Journalist] Alix Coole's daughter Daisy was doing it in memory of her dad [Bob Coole, journalist] and raising money for the hospice where he died. Raised a few bob.

Monday 1 November

PG called, sounded OK considering everything. He said the op had been over ten hours. He was still in intensive care, had four nurses there pretty much full-time and was fairly confident. Didn't know the analysis post op yet and I sensed he didn't want to. Not yet. Just getting through a day at a time.

Wednesday 3 November

Midterms pretty grim for Obama. Bike out to Bill Hagerty's to go over the changes for 2000. Fairly painless. Later to Kevin Spacey's CBE award party in his flat on Westminster Bridge Rd. Nice do and he was enjoying wearing his gong plus a jokey version of it. Fiona due but she was feeling rough and we went home fairly early.

Thursday 4 November

In for a meeting with Tim Allan, Steve Morris and Martin Sheehan [former No. 10 advisers] to agree a plan of action for involvement with Portland [consultancy and PR agency]. Ought to be reasonably interesting. They were keen to use me to get into bigger deals and seal some of them, also get new government work overseas. Fairly buzzy little company Tim had built up.

Friday 5 November

Ill all night. Up to Mill Hill for last *Dream School*. Jamie Oliver and I chatting in the caravan. Then we all got together for a bit of a wrap chat. I had enjoyed it on the whole and so had the kids. Some of them had seized it. Calum and Rayan arrived and we set off for Norwich, Delia Smith [TV chef, joint owner Norwich FC] having asked me to do an event at the ground. Chatted to Phil Webster [journalist], settled down to the dinner with Delia and Michael [Wynn-Jones, husband], Kevin Piper [TV presenter] who was doing the Q&A with me, and Henry Sutton [writer] and his wife Rachel. Delia on form. As ever raging about the financing of football. Agreeing with me that the Championship was in many ways better than the Premier League. Lovely venue with the pitch behind us.

Talked to Phil about the possibility of *The Times* taking on the next book. Signed up Delia as an ambassador for the University of Football idea. 'Do you take your holidays in Iraq?' the only hostile question in the Q&A. Lots of interest in my analysis of the coalition which was that if the public sensed ideology driving the cuts then both parts would take the hit. For now Clegg was getting hit hardest. Yet another audience that seemed underwhelmed by Ed M I'm afraid, including Delia. Lovely chat with Henry, a writer, academic and *Mirror* books editor, and his wife re. the block I currently had on fiction. Sort of felt I did need to get going with another one though. Calum seemed to be enjoying it OK.

Saturday 6 November

Tuition fees cranking up as a problem with the protest march a few days away. Breakfast with Calum and later lunch with Delia, Michael, her mum and usual gathering of friends. The match was odd. Played well in the first half, went two up, then dreadfully in the second half and ended up drawing 2–2. Home and Calum straight out on a big bender. Big story of the day was Coulson having been interviewed by cops [over *News of the World* phone hacking]. Stayed out of it.

Sunday 7 November

Suddenly really cold. Quite big build-up to Cameron's China trip and he was clearly going through the same contortions as we did re. human rights and how much to raise it. Business the big pitch. F and I anxious all day re. Calum.

Monday 8 November

Long and quite good chat with Calum. At least the beginnings of acceptance that he needed to change things. Did a bit of work then out to the

Michael Foot [former Labour leader] celebration at the Lyric. Nice enough do though too long and too many speeches. Cherie read a message from TB which was fine but there wasn't much warmth for TB from the audience. The event was compèred superbly by Jo Brand [comedian], with a Welsh choir and band, and singer Lesley Garrett. Tributes and poems from GB and Neil Kinnock. Roy Hattersley [former Labour deputy leader] focused on Michael's love of books (many of which are currently in our house because Fiona helped the family clear the house when he died), Geoffrey Goodman [former *Daily Mirror* industrial editor] on his journalism, Kate Hudson [Campaign for Nuclear Disarmament] on his commitment to nuclear disarmament, Rodney Bickerstaffe [former trade union leader] on the changes he made as a minister, [Baroness] Helena Kennedy [Labour peer] on his commitment to liberty, Geoffrey Robertston [QC] on the damages he took from Rupert Murdoch over allegations that Michael was a KGB agent, Francis Wheen [journalist] on the absurdity of said allegations, Peter Jones [former Argyle director] on Michael's love of Plymouth Argyle. There were contributions from his great nephew Matt, Michael Cashman [actor, member of European Parliament] and historian Brian Brivati who was one of those echoing the comments above, not least by reminding us of Michael's sheer niceness and his optimism.

There was a mention of the so-called donkey jacket when [Lord] David Steel [former Lib Dem leader] told the story of how he had tried to alert Michael to the dangers of the coat he was wearing shortly before all the politicians walked out into Whitehall for the Remembrance Day ceremony.* Michael was having none of it. His lovely wife Jill had bought it for him, it was a lovely coat and that was that. Steel also told of the best put-down he ever received – and it came from Michael – who said in one debate that DS had gone from rising hope to elder statesman with nothing much happening in the intervening period. And Rodney Bickerstaffe had dug out Michael's first speech from the front bench where he protested at the horror of fat men asking all the thin people to tighten their belt. Could come in handy as the cuts programme rolls out. First time I had seen Neil since Ed M win. We were friendly enough but I think we both sensed a bit of edge. Avoided 'we got our party back'. Good turnout for Michael though and the family would be happy it was over.

Tuesday 9 November
David Muir round for a cup of tea. Said he had voted for Ed but really

* When Labour leader Foot had been criticised and caricatured for wearing a short clark coat in contrast to the long black overcoats worn by other men at the Cenotaph.

felt for David. We all felt EM was moving too slowly and of course now he was on paternity leave. David [Muir] said GB had in a way reacted worse to TB's book than Peter's even though Peter's was so much worse. He said it was like a delayed shock. But he felt he was OK and was going to be out and about a bit more.

Wednesday 10 November

Out with Rayan to Stanstead to the Chartered Institute of Housing. Like a lot of bodies they felt pretty beleaguered but were engaging pretty well in the debate I thought. I sensed I was seen in quite a different way now. Half player, half commentator. Into town and to the Association of Corporate Treasurers dinner at the Grosvenor House. Nice do. Was on form. Lot of serious money there. Home really late. Unfortunately, I missed the *Dream School* party. Bush's memoir arrived [*Decision Points*]. He was doing quite a good job of rehabilitation.

Thursday 11 November

Did a blog bringing together the two events I did yesterday. Mainly focused on the idea that housing ought to be higher up the political agenda. Why it wasn't was beyond me but maybe the woman from the National Housing Federation was right in that people saw their housing as totally personal whereas they saw the communal aspects of, say, health and education. I set off for Bill's and did the last few months of the Volume 3 edit. I had still not heard from Sue about any more demands from the Palace, which was all getting a bit tricky time-wise. Wild and windy day, plane eventually took off an hour late and I arrived in Aberdeen just in time for the dinner, an annual business event hosted by Northsound [radio station]. Really good bunch at the top table. I did a mix of funny and serious, weaving as I went and all OK. Really enjoyed Scottish dinners like this. Good bunch. Definite shift in mood towards me since we lost power I think. And someone said that maybe the fact I went back to help GB when I probably knew it was lost had endeared me to some. There was very little of the hostility there used to be.

Friday 12 November

Up at six, out for a run, a hill session, then out to a restaurant in the docks for a Labour Party breakfast fundraiser organised by Anne Begg [MP]. I detected a fair bit of retreat to the left in the questions and I did a big number on learning the lessons of success as well as failure. We cannot just become a repository for protest against the cuts. Lovely reception and a very warm tribute from Richard Baker [Member of Scottish Parliament] in the vote of thanks but the fully paid-up Blairites sounded a bit embarrassed and there was definitely a real desire to tilt to the left. Books sold out. Sarah Duncan [Labour councillor] took me out to the airport telling me how Anne had tripled her majority against a trend in a region that was mainly Lib and Nat. She was pretty clear in her view of [Alex] Salmond [Scottish National Party leader] as a Tartan Tory. The problem was that he really was popular and clever enough to avoid the flak caused by the cuts. Flew down to Newcastle. Got a cab to the Royal Victoria Infirmary and was thrilled to see PG looking so well. His hair had thinned and he was a little more stooped but given I had been expecting tubes and bandages and all the rest I was pretty amazed at how back to how he used to be he was.

Nice little walk down by a duckpond in the shadow of St James's Park, chatting about the kids, and a little about politics. He was fulsome in praise of the nurses, who did seem terrific. Brendan came round to pick me up. Mike Griffin the surgeon popped in. Fairly fond of himself but given he basically saved lives why shouldn't he be? Philip said he didn't think we would get on but I liked him. Very direct type. Took Grace [Gould] to the station – she seemed to think he was a lot better – and then to the Copthorne [hotel] for a late lunch. Brendan going on about parts of my book, especially GB and the nightmares he gave us. Felt the coalition was getting away with murder not least because Ed was not up to it. Too many people just felt he did not look like, sound like or seem like a Prime Minister. Train back, really nice woman from Montserrat serving tea. Said she loved TB and what Labour did.

Saturday 13 November

Decided at last minute to head to Burnley v Watford, picking up Steve [Loraine, relative] on the way, and reading Bush's book, as I was reviewing it for *The Guardian*. I was enjoying it. More reflective and analytical than I expected. Or than he would get credit for. He had basically taken a number of key decisions, political and personal, and used them as staging posts in his life story. Weird match, poor for an hour, 2–1 down, Ross Wallace on as sub and turned it round for 3–2 win. Finished the Bush book. I decided I would do a totally positive review, not least to wind up the Guardianistas.

Monday 15 November

Blogged on the government wanting to put a happiness index into analysis of government policy. Fairly supportive, but pointed out the need to include mental health in there. I filed the Bush review which *The Guardian* liked (probably because they knew they would get the avalanche of online vitriol I predicted). I started to write the 'happiness speech' for next year, an annual Birmingham University thing [Baggs memorial lecture] they had asked me to do. Fiona was stunned they had asked me 'as the least happy person available'. Out in the evening to Fiona's farewell from Gospel Oak [primary school]. Eighteen years as governor and chair. Nice do. Good speeches. Out for dinner to the Italian with Andrea Kennedy [family friend]. She texted me later to ask why I was so quiet. Don't know. Just feeling a bit down I guess.

Tuesday 16 November

Good piece in *The Guardian* on Gove's cuts to school sport. Bloody scandalous and as with so many of these cuts they did not really have a mandate. The news was totally wiped out by the announcement of Prince William and Kate Middleton's engagement. Wall to wall and totally fawning. Time for a telly-free day. Ironically, as that was going on without stop, Queen's private secretary [Sir] Christopher Geidt was reading my book with Sue Gray at the Palace. Sue called around six – just as Joanna was getting really panicky about deadlines – and said he was very reasonable, it had gone well and there were just a few changes he would like. They didn't like me saying Prince Philip was sounding old and frail and life at Balmoral was like being in the trenches. They didn't like me saying the Queen was 'pissed off' at one point. Sue said he liked and respected me, thought it was nicely written and he didn't want to be difficult. He had laughed out loud at points. She sounded really pleased. 'But wait a bit before the next one, would you?'

Wednesday 17 November

Over to Random House to go over the final changes from the Palace. Went to the canteen with Joanna to have a real feed-up before my 24-hour fast pre my colonoscopy. I started to get calls and tweets about Cameron having a pop at me in PMQs when Harriet had had a go at his vanity photographer (who had gone back on the Central office payroll). He said, 'We won't be employing Alastair Campbell to sex up dossiers to make the case for war'. I tweeted that he had voted for the war, his leaders having had access to the same intelligence. Emailed Coulson a couple of times to ask what DC was on about and whether he was retreating from his position on Iraq. I ran home and did a bit of work before starting the first round of laxatives. Didn't seem to be as dramatic as last time. Still bloody unpleasant.

November '10: AC complains at Cameron attack

Thursday 18 November

To the Royal Free [Hospital]. A nice nurse called Kirsty got me settled, changed and registered. Consultant Mark Hamilton seemed OK. He knew somehow about my fear of needles – they had probably all got to hear about my fainting spell a while back. The sedatives were strong and I remember a lot less than when I first had it done. I saw a bit of it on film but I think I must have been fairly well gone most of the time. Anyway the good news – and he seemed really surprised – was that the colitis seemed to have gone. He had taken a few biopsies to check everything but he reckoned it was in good shape. Felt a bit groggy but Rory came to collect me and take me home. Twitter all atwitter with my inclusion as a nominee in the Bad Sex in Literature Awards again. Ate two dinners to satisfy the hunger that had built up.

Friday 19 November

The Bush book review went on Guardian Online with the predictable reaction. One or two in there positive though. Word came through later that the Jordanian PM could see me there next weekend. Finished piece for *Scotland on Sunday* re. Labour v SNP [Scottish National Party]. Ed Miliband called. He wanted to pick my brains re. comms director. He had seen someone he thought might be good, but wanted me to see him too, to check him out. Chatted to Catherine MacLeod [special adviser] later. She had finally left Alistair D but said a part of her felt she would never leave. Not sure what she wanted to do or what she could do. New peers announced. Mainly Tories and some real rum names in there.

Saturday 20 November

On the train up to Edinburgh, for another [Lennoxlove] book festival, working on future speeches. Fiona working on a piece on her experience as school governor. We moved carriages after a while as the one we were in was freezing cold. Fairly long journey but on time and met by a jubilant chatty driver – Scotland had just beaten South Africa 21–17 [rugby] – who took us to Lennoxlove House [historic house]. Nice enough place but a lot of Scots establishment types around and with my cold getting worse I wasn't really in the mood. I had a bath and tried to get in better shape. Dinner downstairs with some of the other authors – Jim Naughtie [broadcaster] and Simon Hoggart [*Guardian*] the ones I recognised – but as arranged I met up with Iain Gray [Labour leader in Scotland] and his wife Gill to chat about the Labour campaign in Scotland. He felt fairly confident. Salmond was not as popular as before and there was a feeling

– as I had said in the piece I did for tomorrow's *Scotland on Sunday* – that they had ducked genuine decisions that had to be taken when John Swinney [SNP Finance Secretary] did the Budget last week. Iain said he and Salmond really didn't get on. Salmond found it impossible to look him in the eye. He was not a man who reached out to other people. Iain was not exactly charismatic but he had a nice manner and he would be quite a tough campaigner I think. He was very keen for me to go up and see the MSPs and also get involved in the campaign. He was not exactly OTT re. the quality of his MSPs. When I suggested some of the tasks they needed to be set he smiled and shook his head. I thought the thing he said about Salmond not being able to look him in the eye was quite interesting. He should build on that, re. him not being straight with the Scottish people.

Nice enough chat then Mum arrived with some of the Gullane crowd [home to family of AC's father's sister Flora] so we went upstairs for a drink with them in the blue room. Alistair Moffat [writer and journalist] doing the interview, but my voice was beginning to go which was a bit of a nightmare. Q&A fine. A fair few Tories in there. One said he would like to shoot me. Got a laugh or two out of slapping down a guy who asked if I could live in the present tense. Said I was being asked about a book about the past. Could skip to talking about 2012 but it would be rude to the festival – though not as rude as your question. Or as fatuous. Went down well. His wife said afterwards he was a bit of a dick. Someone asked if Fiona forgave me for doing the job. I asked her and she said a rather sharp 'No comment.' Drinks after the book signing and I was amazed that Aunt Jean [Caldwell], Susan, Sheena and Anne [cousins] were also there. Had a good natter with them all before heading to bed. Susan [Law] really grateful. She was unbelievably passionate about her charity work. And pretty strong for Labour too.

Sunday 21 November

Had a rough night, but despite the cold and the rain went for a long walk with Fiona and didn't feel too bad. We got a lift with Alistair Moffat to the station. He had seen GB a few times, felt at first that he seemed a lot better but was now less so. Alistair was clearly as fond of him as ever. His line of questioning last night suggested he really felt that GB's Scottishness had been held against him when he didn't get the leadership in '94. Working on the (delayed) train. As we pulled out of Doncaster Ed M emerged with an assistant. He had just been to a memorial service in his constituency [Doncaster North]. I had been tweeting and as a result was being chased by *Channel 4 News*, re. the *Observer* splash on an alleged Cabinet split over the axe on school sport.* Arranged to do a clip on arrival. Ed seemed OK, was conscious of the fact that there were a few stirrings about his leadership. He called it noises off, but there was definitely a need to spell out a clear direction and make a few key appointments. I said he really should try to ignore the noises off and the media. He should set out a series of processes that allowed him to put in place policy development and party change plans. I said last night I wasn't very satisfied with my answer on the party's direction because I didn't sense where he was heading. I said I had explained that 'learn the lessons' sounded like we were saying everything was a failure. But we needed to learn lessons of success i.e. why we had won three times – by understanding people live in the centre and in the real world. He had only really come off his paternity leave to comment on [former Tory minister] Lord [David] Young's 'never had it so good' [claim about 'vast majority' of people, *Daily Telegraph*]. I thought that was not needed. He had just about managed to stay out of the royal wedding fandango and clearly wasn't really looking forward to it. Home, did C4 clip, then had an early night. Calum out on the razz again and came back with a cut face.

Monday 22 November

Out to Portland to speak to the staff. Later out with F (after another row about Calum) to the Commons for the dinner John Bercow was throwing for LLR. Mix of our people and Durrants [media monitoring firm]. They had bought a whole load of new companies and some of them were there along with some of their top clients. Nice chat with John and Sally and their kids who came down to see everyone. I was trying to save my voice but there was as ever quite a lot of small talk. John did a little speech, on how this event came about. He said some very nice things about me and the way I did the job. He told a funny story about how it was not true he was the shortest-ever Speaker, that three were shorter after being beheaded.

I did a fairly standard opener with jokes, political assessment and a plug for the charity then John and I mixed up a Q&A. All fairly easy. Gave signed books to Sally for her birthday. John saying he would love to do another event in the future. He really was a good support. Nice evening but I was feeling rougher and rougher.

---

* The government announced it would end Labour's £162 million annual funding for school sport in England.

Tuesday 23 November

I went to the instant access GP and he confirmed I had a chest infection and needed antibiotics. Lift with Rayan to the airport for the flight to Glasgow. Scottish media still full of the threatened referees' strike on Saturday. Also the build-up to Rangers v Man U tomorrow. [Sir] Kenneth Calman [Chancellor University of Glasgow] collected me and he and his wife Anne took me to the university. He was not just very intelligent, well-read and experienced but he had a lot of bows and most of them in public service. University Chancellor most obviously but Boys' Brigade, National Trust, several other things. He was also passionate about education as being a liberator for the poor as well as all about elitist universities.

There was a nice reception downstairs. A lot of very nice people there. Great to see [Baroness] Meta Ramsay [former MI6 officer] and we reminisced a bit about John Smith, for whom she was an adviser. David Whitton, still doing well as an MSP. [BBC chief political correspondent] Laura Kuenssberg's dad came over and introduced himself. Nice guy, tall and handsome and after a while I could see and hear a bit of Laura in there. The dinner was in the fabulous Bute Hall where Dad had probably taken a few exams. Sir Ken made a big fuss of Mum and of Donald who played well. [Sir] Muir Russell [former civil servant] was also at my table and he reminded me it was twenty years this week that Maggie left office. He had taken the notes for her last Cabinet meeting. Speech fine. There definitely seemed to be a feeling that Salmond was not in good shape. Tories still pretty much nowhere. Mum had a really nice time and despite the cold I enjoyed it. Book signing went on past 11 but I was in bed before 12.

Wednesday 24 November

Home, chest still nowhere near right, then had to head out to RTZ. Meeting with Tom Albanese. We went over what he felt his problems were and what others felt they might be. They saw it as being about charisma. He saw it as getting to a different strategic space where he could start to lead people better, bring people on and maybe prepare the succession for three years hence. He said he had always been a workaholic. He did a lot more speeches and media than I expected. I went through my ten points on strategy and he seemed to buy most of them. He said he was someone who finished other people's sentences. He said he liked my reputation and what I had done for myself and for others. I said what we needed to do was package and re-message around major speeches and modus operandi to deliver more of an elder statesman feel to where he was. I said I was happy to work with him but he needed to be clear he thought I could add something.

Went to meet Paul Fletcher and Philip Wilson [executive] re. the setting up of UCFB (University College of Football Business). They wanted me to be Chancellor. The usual thing of saying it would be only a few days work. Still it was tempting. We went to the house for a cup of tea with the boys who both said I should do it. Fletch, who is a Beatles fanatic, loved the Lennon picture I had got for Fiona. Also got out of the cab to take a photo of Abbey Road recording studios. He really was a great laugh. Had the boys in hysterics with his description of the old groundsman at Blackpool who used to stand where the team-sheet was posted and say how useless they all were (as they stood there seeing if they were playing). I took them to the station and agreed to get more involved. Fletch was impossible to resist.

TB called later. He had been with the Qatari PM who was trying to get the FA rep to back their 2022 WC bid. The problem was they weren't supporting us for 2018 but I said I would talk to Geoff Thompson [head of England bid]. He was in Paris, though unaware that Sarko had called the French press a bunch of paedophiles at last week's Lisbon NATO summit!! He sounded a bit down, or a bit distant. He was off to Canada tomorrow, somewhere else the next day. I said slow down. He said it was all coming together really well but it was hard work. I said I was about to watch the Peter M documentary. The programme was odd. In the end I felt a bit sorry for him. He came over as clever but over-preening and ultimately quite lonely. Hannah Rothschild had used pretty much all of the bits of me, which was not a lot because I had avoided her. She used the 'gay tie' exchange when Peter said my tie was gay and I said he gave it to me.

One of the London papers had run a piece on Ed M's Dartmouth Park [home] set which said though I was unlikely to be welcomed back, when GB said farewell to everyone at No. 10 he was fairly perfunctory with Peter M, but said 'You're a bloody genius' to me. In fact Ed had called twice in the past twenty-four hours to get advice re. his PMQs on school sport. He did fine. I'd watched it earlier with Fiona and I sensed he was starting to get under Cameron's skin. There had been more protests against tuition fees and EMA [Education Maintenance Allowance] abolition. Grace and her mates had gone on the march in London and ended up being kettled as the cops stopped anyone getting to Lib Dem HQ. She missed her physio appointment – but kept texting me to say 'People hate the Tories even more now.'

Thursday 25 November

The Royal Free called to say all the bowel biopsies were perfect. Read up on Jordan on the plane [to Amman] while listening to a fabulous history of classical music. Also watched a nice film on Johan Cruyff and listened to a Justin Bieber CD to see what the fuss was about. Interesting guy on the plane who introduced himself, said he really liked the way I operated and thinks I should go back into full-time politics. He was [former Palestine President Yasser] Arafat's ex-development adviser. There to do a peace and prosperity through music project. American guy opposite me had twelve large glasses of red wine. Arrived, met, taken to the Hyatt to meet Steve Morris and two of his team, Noha El Nabawy, a very nice Egyptian educated in the US, and Dawn Rennie, who comes from Sale.

Friday 26 November

Breakfast with Portland team plus Ghalia who had been hired as comms director and who was a good friend of Rania Atalla [adviser to Jordanian government]. I'd had a chat with Rania who was pleased I was there but said this region was harder than I imagined. I was getting a clear message re. what needed to be done. The plan was for me to have one meeting with the PM [Samir Rifai]. Went at Rania's suggestion to the Wild Jordan, a US-funded eco restaurant overlooking the Citadel. Nice place, great view, then to an old house cum museum overlooking the street market. Back for a run, bit of work at the hotel, and a kip before meeting and dinner with the PM's private secretary who was currently doubling as chief of staff. It was pretty clear they had a really thin operation.

I did a phone interview with *The Observer* re. the bad sex in fiction awards, again saying I wanted to win, which was likely to make me lose it, which is what I wanted. One of those awards best to be nominated for, but not win!

The Cabinet reshuffle and new Parliament and Senate was potentially a big moment for the Jordanians. The private secretary seemed seized of it. Good chat and then dinner with a wider group at Levant. Did a little spiel. They seemed to like the PM. We talked about Twitter and I drafted a few tweets for the PM, largely as a joke. Ghalia sent them through to him and within a minute two of them were up there. She said, 'Why can't I write like that?' I said it's easy but it has to feel authentic. PM emailed to say can he do one in Arabic? So good banter even before meeting. I got them to email back in Arabic – Chelsea will get all they deserve which is nothing. Nice evening though I was wheezing even more with all the smoking going on.

Saturday 27 November

They were all very deferential re. 'his majesty' but I sensed he and the PM recognised what needed to be done. So hopefully it would get done. I had a little run, got myself a four-quid haircut in one of the back-street barbers then back to change before heading to the PM's office. He popped out to say hello. Bigger than I expected. Big smile. Seemed genuinely embarrassed about how late he was running. I said no problem, let's do a longer dinner. Good meeting with the oddly named minister for mega-projects – Dead Sea, nuclear power and transport. He said we had met before when he came to have a look round No. 10 in 2003. He was a bright and lively guy and totally got what needed to be done message-wise. He was exasperated with some of his colleagues who seemed to care more about their profiles. 'We don't even get elected so why don't they just do their jobs?' He was pretty clear about the scale of the problems.

Out to the PM's fabulous house about half an hour out of town. We had an hour or so in the lounge, just chatting, fairly informally, very friendly. He admitted that part of him could have lived with not being reappointed, but you cannot say no, when asked. The country faced a lot of challenges, everyone had to do what they could. It was clear it is a tough place to be a leader. It was not easy to balance truth and problems. I said honesty and openness better. The public had to feel they were in a leader's confidence. People do not mind being confronted with problems so long as you are honest about it, take them into your confidence genuinely, let them know how you are thinking and why. He said he had developed a thick skin, but his team told me the criticism was tough, and it was hard not to take it to heart.

We talked a lot about principles for strategy and leadership. He seemed fascinated by some of the Clinton stories, his ability to focus even at the toughest of times personally. And once I talked through the kind of operation we had had in No. 10, he was keen to get more and more detail. He had had a situation recently which led to the sacking of a minister, and it seemed to be hanging over him. But he said when you thought about what Clinton went through, and survived, it helped give you perspective. I said it was not possible to have a strategy for the future if you were obsessing with decisions of the past. We had a funny chat about worrying. I said worrying about being worried was a sign of stress. He liked my line about my problem being that I worry about being worried. We talked about the difference between stress (bad) and pressure (good). There till gone midnight.

Really beautiful terrace. On a clear day, he said, you can see the whole of the Dead Sea. There's Jerusalem. It was so beautiful, yet he said he had very little time to be out there. I said TB always managed to get rest, but it was perhaps easier if you had proper systems of support. It was good to meet him, really nice chat, and I left hoping it had been of some use.

Sunday 28 November
Up at six, tired, and out to the airport. Had been an OK visit, and I had enjoyed the session with the PM and got a better feel for the place. I'd done a talk for the team and they asked for notes. I felt the PM needed to follow his instincts more. That does not mean always ignore advice or be blind to the obvious,

but if something feels like it fits the strategy, it's important to go for it. And if something feels wrong, 'where there is doubt, there is no doubt'. Don't do it.

OST. Be clear about Objective. Work hardest on Strategy. Only then go Tactical. The appointment of a new government was the opportunity to visit afresh core strategy, to refine and harden it. The new Cabinet, new Parliament, new Senate had to produce fresh political energy, signal the direction of travel. They ought to be going for brutal honesty regarding some of the difficult decisions. They needed to build respect for candour and leadership. It cannot be easy with the growing sense of media negativity. I told them not to worry too much about it, trust the public to see and hear beyond headlines, most importantly into the reality of their own lives but also into a deeper understanding that leaders have difficult jobs and difficult decisions to take. They should have in mind the idea of being in a permanent dialogue with them, take them into confidence about the nature of the work, the choices, the consequences of making the wrong choices.

It was similar to what I had been saying to Ed M, that every hard question, every criticism, every complaint is an opportunity to explain. He needed to think of all the difficult questions before questioners have. He needed to understand he was communicating all the time, even with body language. I really hammered home the need for rest and fitness. Mental and physical fitness related. Feel better, and therefore perform better, if in good physical shape. Use exercise to clear thoughts and help the decision-making process. Do something non-work-related every day. Read a book. Go for a walk. Don't just think about the job all the time.

On the plane I worked on a speech based on my ten acronyms: OST. Objective, strategy, tactics; TLTP. Best team leaders are best team players; BB. Be bold; BA. Be adaptable; CC. Stay calm in crisis; LBL. Listen BUT lead. Not listen AND lead; PCBV. Patience can be a virtue; YSTA. You set the agenda; HAP. Head above parapet (when things are difficult); NBC. No blame culture. And then I did another shorter version which I turned into a note for Ed too. The strategy piece was where I sensed he was wanting most support. On the flight I watched a fantastic documentary on Sumo wrestling. The stars were treated like gods. Amazing footage not just of the fights but the eating they had to do.

Monday 29 November

WikiLeaks was dominating the media with their 250,000 US cables.[*] I did

---

[*] WikiLeaks, a non-profit organisation that published material from whistleblowers, released classified cables that had been sent by US embassies and consulates to the State department. The largest set of confidential documents ever to be released into the public domain soon became known as 'Cablegate'.

a blog saying [Julian] Assange [WikiLeaks editor-in-chief] was a creep, journos way too sanctimonious about this, and the most worrying stuff Arab leaders and the scale of hatred of Iran. Osborne was doing new growth forecasts and starting to gloat a bit. *Panorama* doing FIFA corruption. Nick Watt [political journalist] called, having read the book for *The Guardian*. He said the thing that struck him most in a way was the negativity to Peter M. News-wise he felt it was GB, and also stuff re. the royals.

Tuesday 30 November

The weather was playing havoc with transport but British Midland to Belfast was OK. Did a 5 Live pre-record on the World Cup bid and what Cameron could realistically do when he went to Zurich [FIFA HQ]. The buzz was all pointing to Russia and the *Panorama* programme will not have helped. If there is one thing the corrupt don't like it is being found out. The plane sat for ages on the tarmac but eventually we got away and though late I managed to get into the Merchant Hotel to change, meet up with Barbara Nestor [PR] and head to the fabulous City Hall. Carolyn McCall [CEO] was the pre-dinner speaker. Nice chat with her re. just how different easyJet was to *The Guardian* [as CEO of Guardian Media Group]. She was glad to be out of the papers. She said even something like WikiLeaks did not do much for her these days. EasyJet was now carrying more people than BA and Virgin. That really did surprise me. Nice crowd at the top table. Mix of business and politics. Graham Sutherland from BT who was the first of many to ask if we had picked the wrong Miliband. They all clearly thought we had. I'd talked to Ed earlier and he is still thinking of going down the route of hiring someone from broadcast for the top media job and has asked me to check one telly candidate out, who had expressed an interest. People in his team seem sure Allegra Stratton [*Guardian*] is also in the frame for something. Quite good friends with him apparently, and she had almost worked for him when he was Climate Change Secretary. Thinks it would be good to have a woman, which it would, provided good at the job. Always assumed she is fairly classic *Guardian*, if more New Labour than most, but seemingly has been courting, or been courted by, Maurice Glasman [founder, Blue Labour] and they had seen Ed together.

Mark Simpson of the Beeb [Ireland correspondent] was hosting it and was incredibly nice about me and about TB in the intro, and what we did for the north. I did a mix of jokes and serious, past and future, trying out a few NI stories, Q&A had good, mix of past and commentary on now. There was a good response to my line about banks dragging down the whole of business, and needing to explain more. On the political front, the feeling from politicians and civil servants was that the DUP [Democratic Unionist Party] were well placed for the May elections.

Wednesday 1 December

I did a quick blog on how much Belfast had changed, then breakfast with Barbara and off to the airport. Jason Donovan [entertainer] was on the same flight and we got talking at the security check. I didn't recognise him at first and was on the point of asking if he was Aussie when I realised who he was. I made it in time for the Sky *Book Show*. Mariella [Frostrup, presenter] had a bad back and was a bit lacking her usual sparkle. I didn't feel terribly on form and Emma [publicist] felt I was too much on the 'people can buy or not buy, am not much bothered' tone. Mariella was inviting us to her house in Scotland en route to the Highlands when we went up for Christmas. She was very tactile and flirtatious and that voice was just too sexy. Back to the airport, lunch with Emma [Mitchell, publicist] then another delayed flight. It looked like I was going to miss the Rome–Bari connection but that flight was delayed too so I just made it.

Got to Bari around midnight, finally got to bed around one. Knackered. Flying really was no fun at all and today had been particularly tiring. Mariella was texting asking me to do her *Desert Island Discs*-type book show on radio and pressing to visit them in Scotland.

Thursday 2 December

Nice run along the beachfront. Interesting town. Fabulous old part which was like a different country. Very clean. Nice-looking people. I did a half-hearted blog calling for Single European Directive on showers and shampoos in hotels after failing to work the shower or read the labelling on the bottles in the shower. The event itself was organised by the Puglia region and was a lot bigger than I had been expecting. Fifty speakers. Eighty workshops. I was one of the '*lectio magistralis*' speakers which was a grand way of saying keynote. The boys were texting to keep me in touch with events in Zurich where FIFA were about to announce the venues for the 2018 and 2022 World Cup finals. Then to a meeting with the interpreters who wanted to read through my notes and begged me to read slowly. They said that Italian required about 50 per cent more words to say the same thing so please go easy. It meant I was less natural and less fluent than usual but they seemed happy enough.

I sensed real hostility to Berlusconi. Not one person speaking pro. His relationship with [Vladimir] Putin [Prime Minister of Russia] – odd and possibly corrupt it was being suggested – was the latest WikiLeaks thing. By now the World Cup odds had shortened on England but then Calum texted to say that 'unconfirmed rumours' were saying England out on the first round. That turned out to be the case. Russia 2018 and Qatar 2022.

Huge celebrations in Doha. Yet another late plane but made connection in Milan. Andriy Shevchenko [Ukrainian footballer] sitting in front of me playing blackjack on his phone. Finally home by half-ten and caught up on the World Cup story. Two bloody votes and one of those was Geoff Thompson [FA]. Pretty humiliating for DC, Prince William and Becks [David Beckham]. But the feeling overwhelmingly was of FIFA madness.

Friday 3 December
Ed M called, to say the guy he had fancied for comms had said no. He was now planning on maybe Bob Roberts [political editor, *Daily Mirror*]. The Allegra Stratton thing had fizzled out. Apparently she has landed a column. I said what about Tom Baldwin [*The Times*] who had called me in Italy and sent through rather an intelligent note on how Ed might broaden and deepen his media profile. He said there was no sense of him being out there on his terms. It was all a bit listless and directionless at the moment.

Sunday 5 December
Rory and I had been at the Chelsea game yesterday, and I texted Alex to say there was something seriously wrong there. He called and we ended up having a long natter re. the World Cup bid. We talked a lot about Calum, my worries about his drinking.

Monday 6 December
Miranda Green, ex-press secretary at Paddy Ashdown's office, was round to do an interview for a books website. She was pretty scathing about Clegg for the mess he had landed himself in. But she said Paddy, having first been keenest on a Lib–Lab pact, now felt totally on board for the coalition. He was out and about today as part of the operation to win support for trebled tuition fees. I started to look at post-'03 diaries. Brought back a lot of memories. I was surprised at just how much TB and I spoke, and how much I went in there, post my departure. On serial of Volume 2, we had agreed to go with *The Guardian*, who were currently totally obsessed with WikiLeaks of course.

Tuesday 7 December
David M round first thing. Looking OK. Very slim, even thinner than before I thought. He was very down on Ed, said he would not say anything to undermine him in public or to MPs and journos but he worried it was hopeless. Ed had run a negative campaign, saying what he was not

– namely New Labour – and now it wasn't clear what he was for. Added to which there was the GB victimhood thing in there. They really persuaded themselves they were being done in and briefed against and all the rest and it was bollocks. He felt the other key people in the shadow Cabinet were either opportunist, invisible or going backwards.

For himself he intended to stay as an MP, do some foreign policy stuff, environmental stuff, continue to build Movement for Change, make some money speaking. He wanted to learn a lot of new things. He wanted to be in a new big job or placed to get one within three years. He felt TB was busy but not learning new things. He seemed to define a lot of things in terms of jobs. I said one thing I had learned was that it was possible to make a difference in different ways. He said he hated the Commons, full of self-important people running around thinking they were making a big difference and very few of them were. He said he didn't want Ed to fail but he could not see how he would succeed.

We had a nice enough chat but I said I felt he ought to think of a way of doing more in and for the party but he felt it would only be used to create problems. I wasn't sure about that. Home to do a bit of work, then out with the boys for lunch to talk about Calum's interview at the party tomorrow. Bought myself a plant. Another first. Also got an Amazon purchase without asking Fiona for help. Another advance! Julian Assange was arrested [in London for alleged sexual assault in Sweden] and then kept in custody.

Wednesday 8 December

I did a blog on WikiLeaks, pointing out that they can spin with the best of them. I had quite an interesting Facebook exchange with Mark Stephens, Julian Assange's lawyer. I asked if Assange was as odd as he seems. No, he said, just principled, which some people found odd. But it was such a narrow view of principle. I also suggested Mark change his FB photo – of himself engulfed by cameras yesterday – because it looked too much like he was enjoying it. Assange was in the Scrubs which cannot have been nice but I still reckoned there was a part of him that liked it. As I said on the blog, if all these dark forces were operating against him, the last place they wanted him right now was in jail. But it had become one of those frenzies where only one side was being presented – he was a hero freedom fighter and of course a few in the States were saying such stupid things that they helped him a fair bit. There was a much bigger response to the blog than usual, mainly negative so obviously there was quite an operation going on, but also quite a few echoing my point that people like Pilger [journalist] and Ken Loach [film-maker] were in no position to know if he was innocent of the sex charges in Sweden or not.

Calum got the job he went for at the Labour Party. Later out to Gauthier restaurant for the annual James Purnell [former Cabinet minister]–Liz Lloyd [former TB deputy chief of staff] organised Blairites' dinner. TB had to pull out because of a trip to Israel. It was also announced today that he was going back to the Iraq inquiry on 18 January, in the week diary Volume 2 came out. Bloody nightmare. PG had said he was glad he couldn't go because he felt there was always something a bit un-Labour about it, that they all just bitched – before about GB, now about Ed.

I decided not to engage with Peter M and he seemed to be in similar mode about me. Sarah Hunter [former TB policy adviser] seemed a little shocked by it but I had decided that I had spent too long too often dealing with it and that the book, film and general manner post election was the last straw. I had a nice chat with Liz Lloyd, still enjoying the bank, and Sarah who was really enjoying her work at Google and explained a bit about how it all worked. David [Hill] and Hilary [Coffman, his partner and former TB press officer] in good form. James working in TV now. Peter H in many ways the most settled, really loved his job and clearly did it well. There wasn't too much politics, just a sense that Ed wasn't cutting it, which was certainly flavour of the month in the media. Anji [Hunter, former TB director of government relations] felt the reason people were angry with TB was about money more than Iraq. Nice enough evening though. PG missed. He had had some bad histology reports which were not as good as they had been hoping for. Basically the cancer was almost certain to return. He sounded, for him, pretty down.

Thursday 9 December
I did another blog praising Ken Clarke [Justice Secretary] even though he had taken in vain my support on mental health issues to say in the House I supported the whole package.* But I did think he was doing the right thing and I also thought Cameron would move towards another U-turn quite soon. Today was all about the tuition fees vote, though by the end of the day the story was less the government winning the vote than the security of the royals after Charles and Camilla got attacked in their car on the way to the theatre. There was on-and-off violence all day and some pretty bad scenes with police horses charging into [students' fees] protesters near Parliament. Clegg was probably close to being shot to pieces and it was amazing the extent to which Cameron was avoiding the heat on all this. I walked through Covent Garden to meet Natascha [McElhone,

---

* Clarke's proposed prison reforms included thousands of offenders with mental health, alcohol or drug abuse problems being diverted into treatment programmes.

actress, friend] for lunch. She was on good form, full of the usual good advice re. some of my situations and also thinking about accepting an offer to write a series.

Grace parents' evening. Obviously the usual concentration and chattering with friends issue but in general doing well.

Friday 10 December

Off to Newcastle via Mum's with the boys. Still really snowy and as we got nearer to Wheatley, very icy. Stayed for lunch then set off for Newcastle. Philip texted to say he was feeling nauseous so could we hold off for a bit. He was clearly not in as good shape as he wanted to be but after Rory and I had a little run in the freezing cold PG texted us to go round. Lovely flat up near [nineteenth-century Prime Minister] Earl Grey's statue. Nice lively area and he was in OK spirits. Calum was withdrawn which was getting me down. PG was lively of mind as ever and full of stuff re. Ed, David (who was coming to see him tomorrow and like me, PG felt he should think about getting back into the policy and political frontline).

He was talking more though about where it might all end, how he had to accept now the chances were the cancer would come back and it gets harder to survive every time. Grace [Gould] was on good form and Gail, who arrived late having been in London for a TB office book signing, was reasonably stress-free. I had done a blog on the universities fees revolt, saying that Labour needed to get more of the focus on the Tories. The Lib Dems were providing pretty extraordinary cover for them. We left them around nine and the three of us went to dinner but Calum was totally disengaged.

Saturday 11 December

Brendan [Foster] came to the Vermont Hotel for breakfast. He was not keen on Ed yet though the boys had both felt he was not too bad at PMQs recently. The media were trying to create a sense of crisis but he seemed quite cool. I had a couple of calls over the weekend with Tom Baldwin who was moving towards the idea of working for Ed. He asked if I knew who else Ed had seen about the job. I said I did, but I didn't think it was fair to say, because the guy worked in telly and in the end it hadn't worked out, and he would not be happy if his name got out there. 'So will we have to wait for your diaries Volume 25?' Tom can be a bit wild, but he is bloody hard-working, knows a story, gets strategy more than most hacks do, and won't take any crap.

We drove over to Burnley and I was re-reading *Madame Bovary* to see if I wanted to take up the documentary idea that had been proposed about it. Fletch [Paul Fletcher] practical joke time. He had had the huge airbrushed photo of me framed and put in the gents which he said had been renamed Campbell's Craphouse. Funny. Clive Holt [director] was urging me to stand for Burnley. He said we were going to be left behind unless we got a high-profile figure campaigning for us. The match was extraordinary. Brilliant first half. Two up. Then totally abject second half. Lost 3–2. Home by nine. Classic text from Fiona when I told her what had happened, 'That must have been exciting.'

Monday 13 December
Calum saw Rory O'Connor first thing who felt he was playing games, not really engaging. Fiona was interviewing for the William Ellis [school] headship and not feeling at all well. I think both of us were being hit health-wise by the stress of worrying about Calum. Another sleepless night. I spent the whole morning on a conference call plugged into a meeting at Burnley which the new director John Banaszkiewicz had called on his 'new ideas' to create Burnley as a global brand. It was a bit ragged but a few half-decent ideas in there. [Eric] Pickles [Local Government Secretary] set out the council cuts which was pretty big on the news. Fiona and Grace out to the ballet.

Tuesday 14 December
I did a blog on Cameron avoiding the shit, for example getting Clegg to take the flak on fees and now councils on cuts. Then out with Grace to Ed Victor's Christmas party. Nice enough do and Ed made a nice fuss of Grace. Celia [Walden, journalist, wife of Piers Morgan] very funny about living apart from Piers. I texted him to say she looked great. She said you looked really rough, he said. Grace and I out for dinner as F tried to rest, really not feeling well.

Wednesday 15 December
Fiona really rough. Lunch at St Pancras Grand with Jacques Séguéla [French publicist] and an assistant. They were writing a book on recent campaigns and wanted an interview plus maybe for me to do a preface. Also asking if I fancied working on Sarko's campaign. He told me he had introduced Carla [Bruni, wife] to Sarko and that Sarko was taking it really badly that

she had been reported in the French press as having been unfaithful.[*] '*Il n'aime pas être cocu.*' Keen to know what the UK thought of Sarko. The impression had weakened. He felt in so far as Cameron was known it was as Thatcher '*en pantalon*'. Talked a fair bit about how both Obama and Sarko had communicated better as candidates than as presidents. Home to meet [Sir] John Holmes [former diplomat] and chat over possibilities. He was director at Ditchley Foundation [promoting international relations]. He felt we overreacted to 11 September and that we exaggerated terrorism and ultimately had to do a lot more talking to the bad guys. He worried TB's legacy for the foreseeable future was totally defined by Iraq. Nice to see him. Good guy and it was amazing how much he did in the early years.

I set off for City and only just made the Dublin flight. Alex called re. arrangements for the weekend and vented his spleen again about Wenger, who had blamed their defeat at the weekend on the pitch, and not gone up for a drink, though AF had asked him to. He went off at one about Cameron. Said the Nazis only wanted Aryans. These guys only want the rich at university. He had watched PMQs and thought Ed did OK. Good chat and he was clearly in good shape going into the Christmas period. I met a nice guy on the flight to Dublin, a *Racing Post* guy called Donal who was quizzing me non-stop but also giving me quite a good take on Ireland and the upcoming elections.

Landed, met by a guy from Ghana with an Irish accent – he had been there twenty-two years and married an Irish woman. Dinner with Paul Allen and Barbara Nestor [Irish business people] picking brains for the speech and taking the temperature re. the elections. The economic back-drop was grim, but the place was heaving.

Thursday 16 December

Out for a little run. Back to work on today's speech. *Irish Times* poll showed Fianna Fáil in dire straits. But the others' favourability ratings weren't that good. Jimmy Murphy from the Marketing Society came up to chat through things. My main message was stop the spiral of negativity and it's amazing what you can endure. Awards, then lunch, then my speech and a really good Q&A. Lots of serious but also lots of jokey. I was nice about Brian [Cowen, Taoiseach] and about Bertie [Ahern] but with very little support. They had clearly had it with them. The bookies were offering 20–1 on a Fine Gael–Labour coalition. One tough question on Iraq but dealt with it fine. A woman saying she loved hearing me get out of tight spots.

---

[*] Reports in the French press and on the internet alleged that the French President and his wife had both been having affairs.

Saturday 18 December

Snow falling really quickly. I texted Alex, who we were due to meet for dinner, when the Arsenal game was called off. He texted back to say his was off too so not travelling. I worked a bit then round to see Philip who had come back yesterday. He was even thinner than last week but still, despite Mike Griffin's fairly gloomy prognosis, determined to keep going and beat it. Gail seemed pretty down though she perked up a bit. On the political scene, PG felt Ed was still in question-asking not answering mode. Tom Baldwin called halfway through, wanting to meet up. He had started with Ed and said he was finding it tough. There was no functionality to the operation and he wanted guidance on how to bring it. Big piece in the *Mail* on me and him. Tweeted that Dacre's homoeroticism was alive and kicking. Tom felt he was yet to work out what he wanted to do. They had put a note round re. not saying coalition, but Conservative-led government.

Fiona popped round and we went over more of the health stuff. PG certainly putting up a fight. Georgia appalled I 'had a driver' (though Gail booked him for Christmas for her mum and dad).

Sunday 19 December

Weather still grim. Fiona finally, after weeks of trying, got me to go with her to Halfords to get a bike rack. Hendon central. Cold. Took ages. I moaned the whole time. She said this is how normal people live. They go to shops and buy things together. I said I didn't want to be normal. I hate shops. Grace was having all her friends round for 'Christmas dinner' so I popped round to Rory's then out for dinner with him and Fiona. The WikiLeaks stuff rumbled on and the leftist media loved Assange to bits. Interesting though that Mariella, Lindsay [Nicholson, journalist friend], Tessa, Fiona all absolutely loathed him.

Christmas holiday

We couldn't get the house in Scotland at Easter so Fiona had booked it for Christmas and we headed off there on the 22nd, the kids and Audrey by train, Fiona, Molly and I by car. We stopped on the way at Mariella [Frostrup]'s place near Barr in Ayrshire. The whole country seemed to be covered in snow, but apart from getting slowed up by an accident at Luton we had a good run. Their house was a good hour from the motorway and the last few miles through tiny villages and over tracks but it was worth it for the views and the walk in the morning. We had a good time and my sense is Mariella is a genuinely nice person. We talked a bit about GB and how lost he seemed. His book had been reasonably well received by serious folk but even on that he seemed determined just to do the opposite of whatever TB did. So TB does a bestseller focused on the whole story. He does a heavy number on economics.

The house was an old derelict bothy which they had converted into something quite special. There was no phone or mobile signal and it was quite nice being totally out of touch. On the drive up I thought a bit about whether I was being unreasonable re. Peter M. Anji had texted me after the TB team dinner and said: 'Did you and Peter really not speak? How has it come to this?' But I felt I had spent a lot of time and used a lot of energy defending him and supporting him and his book and film were just final straws. He was now setting himself up as a global consultant. Good luck to him but he really had annoyed me with the way he projected the story of New Labour.

By the time we got to Conaglen it was absolutely freezing and Fiona was worrying how Audrey would take to it. But though the snow stayed for a few days the temperature lifted a bit. The scenery was fantastic, different to Easter but just as stunning in a different way. Rory and I managed to use the bikes most days. Calum was still a bit down and withdrawn even when Mum arrived though he was better by the end. It worked better with fewer people. Us, Audrey, Lindsay, Mark [husband] and Hope [daughter]. Lots of long walks. The usual overeating. Brian Laws was sacked after we lost at home to Scunthorpe. I was talking to Alex about it when he got news Darren [manager, Ferguson son] was sacked at Preston too, shortly afterwards. I was feeding in ideas to Barry Kilby and Brendan Flood [directors] about successor.

Christmas Day was good. Fiona liked her necklace. The kids seemed happy enough. Tessa and David came after Christmas and so did Mum. She and Audrey had a good time together. I felt Aud was declining a bit whereas Mum seemed to be improving. Few visitors and fewer people staying which was good. Charlie Kennedy came for dinner one night. He seemed more relaxed than last time. Perhaps the strain of the marriage had been a real problem.[*] Also politically he seemed more liberated. He clearly didn't much rate Clegg or hold out much hopes for the party in the long term. He was hysterical about Simon Hughes [Lib Dem deputy leader] who had been bought off with a Rt Hon. title and appointment as 'access advocate' on further education. Totally bound to end in tears. He said he intended to encourage Simon to become more and more high profile.

We ended up agreeing we should scrap leaders' debates and have the deputies do it so Simon could be seen at his squirming and agonising best.

---

* Charles Kennedy and his wife, Sarah Gurling, had announced their separation the previous August.

Charles did not have that much good to say for many of his colleagues, though he rated Laws highly. Alexander less so. He wasn't drinking, though that may just have been because he was driving. He had a hell of a gut on him. But of all the times he had been this was the most relaxed I had seen him and things seemed OK with Donald [his son], who was still obsessed with our Donald's piping. I asked if he was drinking too much and he said no, he felt OK about it just now. But I wondered if he was overdoing it a bit, not drinking because driving. The weather dominated the news. England retained the Ashes. Chelsea continued to stumble. The honours [New Year's] were pretty dull.

Vince Cable's appearance on *Strictly Come Dancing* special got more play than it otherwise would have done following his stitch-up by the *Telegraph*.* Fascinating story. *Telegraph* did him over generally slagging the Tories but then [Robert] Peston [BBC business editor] revealed they had withheld a section where he said he was going to beat Murdoch re. BSkyB takeover. If he had been a Tory he would have been sacked but they kept him on but took his media regulation role and gave that to Jeremy Hunt. Big win for Murdoch. When Tessa was up she said they had seen Cameron at Rebekah's party. David said he heard him saying he didn't mind helping the Liberals because they had to be seen to get something out of the coalition. I had a few phone chats with Tom Baldwin who was beginning, with Bob Roberts, to make a difference. E.g. briefing that they would stop saying coalition and call it the Conservative-led government. Also in terms of trailing Ed words etc. But they still lacked the big economic message and there was not enough pushback on the 'all Labour's fault' attack by the Tories. Ed sent me a few messages including one thanking me for recommending Tom and asking me to stay in touch with him.

We were gone over a week in total but I wasn't sleeping too well. I was re-reading diary Volume 2 to get my head in the zone for that and there was too much CB–Anji which troubled me. Tessa read it and felt there was a danger the stuff about me and Peter would be the main thing. She had some good ideas for how to position it. 24-hour media. Lack of talent development one of our weaknesses. Big beasts not a good basis for team politics. The general feeling developing was that Ed was not cutting it. But he had time I guess and the cuts and the VAT rise were yet to kick in in a way that affected people's lives. Calum and Tessa discussing ideas for development work and fundraising for the party. On New Year's Eve I decided as Calum and I had to leave at 6 a.m. for the football that

---

* In a conversation with *Telegraph* reporters Cable claimed to have 'declared war' on Murdoch, boss of News Corporation, who was bidding to take full control of BSkyB, of which his company owned 39 per cent.

we should bring it forward three hours and pretend we were in central Europe. So I was in bed by ten.

Saturday 1 January 2011

Off next morning via Burnley and a terrific 4–2 win v Sheffield United. Brendan keen on Paul Lambert as next manager. Fergie was sure he wouldn't come. Mum off to Edinburgh with David and Tessa, Fiona got a lift with Mark to Glasgow then train home. We left the car and bikes at Stan [Ternent, former Burnley manager] and Kath's and Kath took us to the ground and picked us up. Really nice people and on the list for future Conaglen visits, definitely. Stan was off to Maine Road scouting. He was still desperate to get back into management. We were home by nine.

Sunday 2 January

Fiona's birthday. We had been getting on well, only a bit snarly and she liked the paintings I had got her. I was getting a little bit back into the swing, regular blogging again, planning speeches and visits. TB went to see PG and said he had the right attitude which was to enjoy every moment. PG was worried that TB's reputation was still tanking. He didn't seem to care but deep down he must do. In fact I know he did. Also his going back to the inquiry was bound to be hanging over him a bit. It was hanging over me and I wasn't even going. Out for dinner with the Bridges and the Watts [friends]. We had a good chat about Boris and Ken. It was pretty clear to me Boris would win again not least by distancing himself from Cameron.

Monday 3 January

I sensed the Tories' 'all Labour's fault' line was weakening. I had a couple of chats with Tom Baldwin about how Ed might reframe this. With the VAT [tax] rise coming in tomorrow Ed was already on the case with that but we still needed a bigger argument about the past and the reality of the crisis to get over the fact the Tories were using a false set of economic and political arguments to justify the cuts and reforms. Ed had called a couple of times to say Tom was making a difference. Off to Reading v Burnley. Lunch with John Madejski [Reading owner]. John clued up as ever. Had some interesting insights. He felt Russia would follow the World Cup with a new league to rival ours. He felt [Roman] Abramovich [Chelsea owner] would do a runner soon. Chelsea really dipping in form. He thought TB's reputation had fallen whereas mine had risen. With TB there was no sense of a reassessment, even with the book. He felt I had been battered and

January '11: PG worries re. TB reputation

came out stronger. Nice chat. Liked him. Also reminded him he was the one who told me last year to spend time with your mum because you'd miss her when she was gone. In part why we took her to Scotland.

We lost 2–1 after missing four really good chances. We took Calum to the station because he and Rory were going to the darts' final at Ally Pally [Alexandra Palace]. They loved it. Then to Zizzi for the Labour fundraiser. Mainly an Ed crowd, quite a few anti-Tony. Others very warm but I sensed some of it was for me still being out there flying the flag rather than for TB. But I did my thing about the need to learn lessons of what went right as well as what went wrong. I also said we had to defend the record better and we had to get back into this bigger argument about the past. The Tories were determined to blame us for the crash, and we had to rebut it, because it was their justification for cuts they wanted to make anyway. One or two Iraq questions. I still felt edgy when I got into that. One or two were asking about mental health and also about religion. I got asked about 'we don't do God' a lot these days. Worked on a piece for *The Times* on depression on the way home.

Tuesday 4 January

Tessa was having some useful thoughts about the book. She felt I should make big political points to get above the noise. She had spoken to TB who was a bit jumpy about it. I spoke to him and his worry was that after his and in particular Peter's book, it would just be seen as more f***ing psychodrama. I said I was working on a bigger narrative. Some big themes and also a week in Ireland to emphasise the NI stuff. Lunch with Ed V to review where we were.

We were at the Townhouse in Dean Street. Nice enough place. Had to get home for a bit of work and a few conference calls. Not yet back in the swing though. Ed M had had a couple of good days on the economy. I blogged on the need to keep going with this big economic attack. Veronica Simpson [Burnley Former Players Association] called asking if I could go to [former Burnley player] Ralph Coates's funeral tomorrow.

Wednesday 5 January

Olli Issakeinen [AC follower] had done another terrific posting on my blog yesterday so I blogged about him and appointed him economics adviser to the website! There were people saying they were following me to follow him. It was pretty extraordinary for a Finn to be so well informed about our politics. I felt the economic argument turning a little. Then off to Enfield to Ralph Coates's funeral. St Stephen's Church. It was a nice service though the electronic organ was out of tune. His family asked me to go to the do afterwards at White Hart Lane [Tottenham Hotspur football ground]. His son Paul made a fabulous speech. He cried a couple of times in the middle which set me off a bit too. Father–son stuff inevitably had me thinking, and worrying, about Calum. There were two big pictures up against big grey pillars, one in Burnley gear, one in Spurs. Good turnout from Spurs and Burnley.

Chatted with a few of the players outside. I wonder what funerals for the current generation will be like, whether players would stay as friendly as this generation seemed to. So many of the players will settle in different countries. I liked his first wife and we had a good chat about how the world of footballers has changed. Out to Royal China with F, Calum and Grace to see PG, Gail and Georgia. Philip not in bad shape considering. Gail seemed more relaxed but it was all pretty stressful. He said that the latest doctor had said it could all happen quite quickly. More scans tomorrow. He was if anything even thinner and eating remained a real problem. He just couldn't swallow without pain. Ed M called while we were there to say Tom was doing a good job and to say he was reading *Prelude to Power*. 'God, any of the personality clashes I have are as nothing,' he said. He wanted to meet up again. We were all a bit lifted by PG seeming OK. Calum also in good form.

Thursday 6 January

Blogged on Cameron–Coulson and the way the media were still following their line. The *NoW* news editor had been suspended before Christmas and that only emerged yesterday. How big a story would that have been if that had been me in No. 10, but it did not really fly apart from the usuals like *The Guardian*. Off to Surrey for a conference of lawyers hosted by law firm Pinsent Masons. Sat through a couple of OK sessions on law and then the economy – really interesting stuff on how the emerging markets were growing at our expense – then did my session on rules of strategy. Nice people including some who were passionately anti-private schools. They were all very negative about Ed.

Friday 7 January

Went out for a run first thing with Mary, one of the lawyers at the do, who was training for her first triathlon. Back for breakfast and I did a blog on the Coulson situation, Cameron having been very dismissive again yesterday. The truth was being dragged kicking and screaming but they would be better off getting it all out there. The behaviour of the cops was extraordinary compared with the way they went after us over so-called cash for honours. Then I did my crisis management session. Fifteen rules of crisis management followed by teamwork role-play around a few imagined crises. They were pretty good at it and got better as it went on. The boss, Alastair Morrison, a really nice guy.

Then off to Random House. We went over the media schedule. Also chatted to Nick Watt [*Guardian*] about the serial. They were thinking royals and inside the world of TB for part one, psych flaws and other breakouts for part 2. I emphasised I wanted to avoid the Peter M feel around the book, wanted it on substance and big themes not just all the tittle-tattle and obvious headline material.

Saturday 8 January

Fabulous piece by John Lloyd in the *FT* on how the media did not think through what they did e.g. in Vince Cable, WikiLeaks. Rory called and asked if I wanted to go to Arsenal v Leeds. I called Kate Laurens to sort tickets. OK match, one–all, amazed how many home fans left at one–nil down with a few minutes to go. Then out with F to Ben and Amanda's extraordinary new house in Islington. Nice time. Really like them. The main room was vast, high ceiling, rolling roof, big sofas in the middle, kitchen against a wall, big dining table. All very modern and minimalist but nice, really well done. She is such a terrific architect and both of them genuinely nice people. They felt we were screwed with Ed.

Sunday 9 January

Bit of a stand-off with Calum who had been majorly on the piss last night. It was really getting me down. Neither Fiona nor I slept much at all. Worked in a half-hearted way upstairs then did two hours on the exercise bike while watching Man U v Liverpool. Poor game but good result [one–nil] for Alex who was really up for it. Out for dinner then a long call with TB. He was preparing for the Iraq inquiry. He said that they were asking for half a day but basically saying that unless he gave the Cabinet Secretary permission to release the private letters between him and Bush, they would want a full day. He said he sensed they were going to go for him for being 'mind made up too easily' and Jack [Straw] for not doing enough to slow down the rush to war. He said if they were critical he was going to go for them. They were totally missing the point about the nature of the problem we were dealing with. On the diaries he said it was not my fault but after Peter's book and to a lesser extent his own there was a danger that it was all presented as more tittle-tattle and psychodrama. He was keen for me to think through the story that I wanted and really try to get it. I didn't think the storification was going to be dreadful, but it was probably TB–GB and he said any policy story – even a bad one – is better. He said over time the diaries would be good for the historical record, but for now the media just wanted bad stories. He felt I should get out and do a big defence of New Labour. He said the political and media scene made him despair.

Monday 10 January

Gave Calum a lift to Euston as he headed off to Oldham for the by-election. Looked like we were going to win but later he reported back that it was not the best organised of teams up there. I did a blog on the shooting of Gabrielle Giffords headlined 'time for right-wing prophets of hate to calm the rhetoric'.* Sarah Palin was getting it in the neck for ads they had run with Democrats – including Giffords – in the crosshairs of a gunsight. There is no doubt the right-wing media and some politicians had created a vile and violent atmosphere. The same was developing here, though thankfully not over guns, but the all-round nastiness on a lot of social media was pretty grim.

I went to see David Sturgeon. I said that I was really worried about Calum, worried he was developing a real problem with the booze, but also that he was blaming me for his problems. DS said it was a case of him wanting my approval, feeling he couldn't have it because of the way he was behaving, so he pushed me away. I also felt I was anxious about all the interviews when the book came out. He said that was a clash between anger and fear. I needed to ask myself what was the worst thing that could happen. It would not be that bad. And if it felt like it might be, take valium. My *Question of Sport* appearance was on. Watched it. Not my finest hour.

Tuesday 11 January

Going through the second half of the diaries to give a run-through of possible themes and stories for the serial. I was starting to get properly in the zone, coming up with ideas and themes and the like. I did a blog on men and depression, *The Times* having run my piece as part of their special today. Also planning media stuff in advance of the speech I was doing tomorrow for Mental Health Research UK at Nottingham University. The

---

* On 8 January Democrat Giffords, a House of Representatives member, narrowly survived an assassination attempt in a supermarket near Tucson, Arizona. Six died and many others were wounded by gunman Jared Lee Loughner.

January '11: AC seeing psychiatrist re. Calum's drinking

figures on mental health research were puny compared with e.g. cancer research. Iain Gray [Scottish Labour leader] emailed asking if I could do an event for his shadow Cabinet at the end of the month.

Wednesday 12 January

Did Radio Nottingham on mental health research then watched PMQs which was OK but Ed has a few habits that need ironing out. I called Tom Baldwin to go over some – e.g. odd hand movement, sitting down sideways, and speaking out of the side of his mouth. However, Cameron's thin skin was becoming a problem for him, and an opportunity for Ed. Tom said Allegra Stratton, who sounds like she is still keen to get in there, had been on to him and anyone else who will listen, saying that 'the real Ed' was warm, funny and clever, but that was not coming over. There were lots of 'real Ed' chats going on. Tom said he was worried that 'if it carries on like this, Lucy Powell will convene a meeting where we all have to bring in our best "Real Ed" ideas'.

PG was doing a note on the diaries. He said he was loving them but feeling there were all sorts of different problems in there. Nice do at Nottingham University. Lots of Notts great and good there and they were almost all women – the main ones anyway – police constable, prison governor, probation service, sheriff, high sheriff. Nice atmosphere. Spoke well and sold lots of books and in the end raised about £17k for them. Home about one. Wrote a blog on all these top jobs being done by women. Impressive.

Friday 14 January

Really trying to get my head in gear for the launch. Usual anxiety. Working on *The Guardian*'s final cut. They went on foreign mainly and pulled out TB reading the Bible before Iraq bombing in '98. Also Piers being described as a slug by TB. Got pretty big reaction so far.

Saturday 15 January

Eddie Howe [AFC Bournemouth manager and former player] confirmed as Burnley manager. Working flat out on the book. Went to get Alex from the Landmark and brought him round for dinner. He was on great form, though hungover after a night out in Aberdeen. Lots of talk with the boys about the players. Mellowed re. Becks. Felt Gary Neville would be a coach. It was comic how much he loathed Cameron. Absolutely raging any time his name came up.

Sunday 16 January

Finished the read-through on Volume 3 and started to work on an intro. With Grace to United at Spurs. Becks was there and Grace got herself a picture with him. Amazing to see the effect he had on people. Nice chat with Bobby Charlton [former Man United and England star]. Quite an exciting 0–0.

Monday 17 January

Out for breakfast with [Lord] Paul Myners [former Financial Services Secretary] and Tim Allan. Paul interesting on how he was cast aside by GB when he started to disagree with him about spending too much. Interesting guy and I liked him more than I thought I would. Well connected too. He had been chilling but was now looking to do more work. Tim was stuck in a train station and half-hour late so Paul and I yacked away. He had read all the Labour books and felt the story really was that GB was not fit to do the top job. Home to do PA interview – Hannah Stephenson said she preferred the novel [*All in the Mind*]. Going a bit on the Anji–CB stuff. GB. Then an hour with Roland Watson [political editor, *The Times*] and Anushka [Asthana], new colleague. Tried to be more reflective. [George] Galloway [former Labour MP] was confirmed for *Question Time*. Yuk. Also Clarke Carlisle [Burnley player, chairman, Professional Footballers' Association]. He and I had a chat about things and agreed to do so again. [Lord] Peter Goldsmith's extra evidence [to Iraq inquiry] was put out and taken as a distancing from TB, and his feeling that TB had not been straight at various times.

Tuesday 18 January

Out to lunch at Mossiman's to advise the Association of Corporate Treasurers. Real problem with them not being clear about what they were about. Home to work on *Question Time*. They had put out the panel and there was a lot of Twitter excitement about me and Galloway. Also [Sir John] Chilcot [chairman, Iraq inquiry] released letters between him and Gus O'Donnell in which Gus revealed they were refusing to publish the papers from TB to Bush. Watched Piers interviewing Oprah [Winfrey, talk show host] on the first of his CNN shows. Boy he had landed on his feet again. Spoke to Matthew Doyle re. TB. He was pretty pissed off and convinced the inquiry was going to go for him big-style.

Wednesday 19 January

Another bad night on the sleep front. It always seemed to be like this when I had a big media round coming up. Fiona felt it was because I was angry still having to defend everything. I could hardly complain though about being asked about the past if I was publishing volumes of diaries. I spent most of the morning getting on top of Iraq. Charlie F called and as ever was superb in getting to the point of the Goldsmith additional evidence that had gone to the inquiry. The headlines all dwelt on his line that he was uncomfortable with some of TB's statements on legality. But the document as a whole showed that 1, he was giving provisional advice at a time he was unaware of the negotiating history and 2, he came to the conclusion it was lawful. JoP [Jonathan Powell, formerly TB's chief of staff] also did a good note saying do not get drawn into discussion of unacceptable veto. I spent an hour on the exercise bike going through my own Chilcot folder, as I had done when I gave evidence myself.

The BBC were starting to ramp up *Question Time*, putting out clips online of 'other titanic shows'. Galloway also putting stuff on his website. So it was certainly going to get hyped. They were up against a new comedy news show on C4 – which I was due to do next week – and so hoping the two of us, plus Clarke Carlisle as their first ever footballer, would drive up ratings. Stephen Wall [diplomat, former EU adviser to TB] was at the inquiry and had a pop, saying that after Chirac's '*quelles que soient les circonstances*' TB had sent me out to play the anti-French card and that we misrepresented what Chirac said. I spoke to Matthew Doyle and we agreed a line that we did not need an interview to know Chirac was opposed and would not support military action. TB was now thinking of allowing them to declassify the notes to Bush. I felt – and was planning to say – that despite the 'I'll be with you whatever' tone to Bush, publication would not harm TB. I spoke to him and he said the system had let him down. He thought they agreed that it would be a bad precedent for them to be published, the President having received them In Confidence, but now both Cameron and Gus [O'Donnell] seemed to be saying it was up to TB. There is no doubt – as per Wall the latest evidence – that there is a bit of revenge of the mandarinate going on.

I went to party HQ to get their briefing for *QT* from Peter Morton [head of press] and Simon Jackson [director of policy]. Fairly obvious what would come up – health reforms which had been raging all week, Iraq, EMAs [Education Maintenance Allowances] and maybe something economic more generally. I was a bit wired and not totally concentrating. But once I got the Charlie point embedded in my head and memorised bits of Goldsmith's note, it was fine. Or at least I felt better. Paul Allen and the guys from the *Sunday Independent* arrived. We went over to the South Bank to do some pictures then back to do the interview and a radio ad. Nice guys. Felt it would set up the Irish trip well. It was funny going round the party and everyone going 'Oh no' when they heard Galloway was on. It was the same at Michael Cashman–Paul Cottingham's party fund-raiser event for celebs at their flat. Nice event. I talked mainly to [Sir] Ian McKellen [actor]. Ian was a lovely guy, talked a bit about Burnley, where he came from. Everyone said stay calm with Galloway. David Mitchell [comedian, writer] arrived and we had a chat about his new show. He said he had never voted Tory but had voted Lab and Lib before. 'Never again on Libs,' he said.

Ed M arrived, did the rounds then made a nice little speech after being introduced by a very funny Jo Brand. He spoke well, made his big point that in politics every generation tried to make life better for the next but with EMAs and tuition fees and cuts this lot were doing the opposite and they were worse than Thatcher. It went down well. I gave Rachel a lift home. She said Ed might call me in the morning because Alan Johnson was about to resign. His marriage had broken up and he had had enough. I said it should be Balls [as Chancellor]. But it should be exaggeratedly clear from the start that he is not in the undermining game. Balls had done well at home affairs and was opposing well. He was also strong on economics even if he did not always have good judgement. Poor old Alan though. This was going to be wretched for him. He was such a nice guy, but it seemed his wife had run off with one of his protection guys. That is fucking grim.

Thursday 20 January
TB texted at half-six to say he was up if I wanted a chat. He was still mulling publication of the notes. He was also still going over when and how to say he regretted the false impression he gave when he first gave evidence, when it might have sounded like he was dismissive of regrets. We talked about each at length. I felt the notes were fine. Only the tone was embarrassing. But the substance was him trying to get the US down a different track. He was really angry with the way the inquiry had handled it but I said he had to put that to one side. He said re. *QT* I should be calm and forensic. It was a good thing Galloway was on because he would rant and I could be factual. I felt a lot stronger after talking to him, partly because the advice was good and also because as we went over what the main problems were I felt I had the answers. The conspiracy theorists would not be happy but reasonable people would see.

He also had some great facts about the state of Iraq today and had read the evidence of the head of the FCO [Foreign and Commonwealth Office] team at the UN who was happy with UNSCR [Security Council Resolution] 1441 legality throughout. The *Times* interview came out well plus an online interview. Then on to the media rounds. I spoke to DS and we agreed I should take half a Valium before *QT*. When it came to it I started to feel a bit edgy at *This Morning* on ITV even though I knew it would be fairly soft. It was with Ben Shephard and Holly Willoughby and went fine. Couple of questions on TB and the inquiry where I said I thought it would be fine to publish the notes. One down two big ones to go.

To RH to go over more Iraq briefing. TB had sent me his 10k-word statement to the inquiry yesterday and I read it carefully. Again he had gone through it all so forensically it was a real help. At Sky we got plenty of diaries in but also covered all the tricky Iraq questions. Also did a few lines on *QT* including Galloway ramping up and some facts on Iraq today. Good response. Set off with Mark B and Rayan for Burnley, where *QT* was being recorded, just reading and rereading and working out lines. Mark was helpful because he kept me calm and pretty good judgement on lines that worked or didn't. We met up with Clarke Carlisle at the Oaks Hotel. We went through what was likely to come up and on Iraq it was immediately clear he was nearer to Galloway than me. I didn't push too hard just took him through some of the arguments. Then on health and EMAs he was a bit all over the place but had a couple of simple points he wanted to say. I felt he could either be OK or absolute disasterville.

The Alan J news had broken as we were in Osborne's seat and I tweeted both sadness for him and also saying Balls was the one Osborne feared. It was running as a news foot on Sky as we walked into the hotel. Ditto my words on Sky re. TB and Chilcot. We set off for Unity College, a new-build school in Towneley. Gordon Birtwistle [local Lib Dem MP] the first person I met in the Green Room, then Galloway, who grunted, later Simon Hughes and Caroline Spelman [Environment Secretary]. Nice chat with David Dimbleby about Alan J and I sensed it was first question, Iraq second, health third. That was how it panned out, with EMAs and unemployment fourth and Oldham fallout fifth. I got a really warm welcome walking out and George got a few boos. I had taken another pill and felt OK in the warm-up question – on footballers' wages where I stayed close to Clarke C's pro-footballer line, tactically it has to be said in that I hoped it might soften his view on other stuff. I sensed he was a Liberal Democrat (as indeed during the final question on the by-election fallout it turned out he was).

When Iraq came up it went pretty much according to plan – to George for a rant, then Dimbleby reminded him of his 'morally acceptable to kill Blair in suicide bomb attack', then to me. I did my impersonation of him grovelling at Saddam's 'courage, strength and indefatigability' then went into argument.[*] I ended up doing as well as I could I felt and though

* In 1994 Galloway had visited Saddam Hussein, complimenting him on having these qualities after greeting him 'in the name of the many thousands of people in Britain who stood against the tide and opposed the war and aggression against Iraq'.

Galloway called me every name under the sun I didn't rise and then we moved on. I wasn't brilliant on the rest but OK and between us George and I got the audience on our side against the coalition on the reforms and had some fun at Simon's expense re. his abstaining habits. Caroline was pretty weak, but I probably interrupted her too much, as Dimbleby – and later Fiona and plenty of twitterers – pointed out.

Clarke went down well. I got in a few of the points I wanted – e.g. the fact we were in a new school the likes of which will not be built now that the BSF [Building Schools for the Future] programme is scrapped. The impersonation of Galloway seemed to go down pretty well. Did OK on challenging Hughes re. EMAs. AF said later Spelman seemed intimidated by me and George. Dimbleby was pretty fair and he and I had some OK banter going. I got mildly mobbed on the way out, including people asking me to stand for the seat. Massive response on Twitter and broadly positive. Fucking glad it was over.

Friday 21 January

Did a blog first thing on Balls and Ed, making the point that they really had to work together and be seen to and not allow anyone to portray them as a new TB–GB. Ed B sent me a message thanking me for the Good Luck message I sent him yesterday and for what I said on *QT*. I said they really needed to show there was no division and it required an exaggerated sense of their shared approach. I was getting a lot of bids on TB and Iraq but I decided to stay out of it for now, till we see how it went. As of last night he was thinking both of doing regret up front and saying OK to publication of the Bush notes. In the end he did neither. He was doing fine. They seemed to be slightly more aggressive but not much. He was calm, a bit too much 'everyone knew what I thought' but on top of detail and good on big picture, especially later on Iran when he said we had to get out of the 'wretched' sense of apology that what they were doing was our fault. The demos were a bit smaller and more low-key and though it was wall to wall on the media there was less venom maybe.

I had to leave to go in for a Steve Wright pre-record. His team wanted to do today so that they could carry my first comments on Andy Coulson who had announced he was leaving Downing Street. But Steve W insisted on leaving it as a pre-record for next week. I tweeted that Cameron's judgement would become the issue. If they thought Coulson going would bring the *NotW* issue to an end they were wrong. This was going to make the BSkyB [ownership] decision even more sensitive. Plus put the police issue centre stage. Plus get more focus on all the civil cases now being brought. So it was not going away. I was getting inundated with bids re. Coulson but after discussing around I decided against, partly because I was so tired and worried I would make a mistake. Also I didn't like the feel of grave-dancing. Godric [Smith, Olympics director of communications] made the very good point that it would make it all about spin doctors rather than about the real issues. I ended up doing a blog saying why I wasn't doing it and making a few points. *Guardian* asked to run it. All a bit odd. Coulson saying it was so high profile he couldn't really do his job but that was balls. It had not been that high profile. Nothing like the stuff I had endured. There was definitely something else behind this.

TB called after getting away from the inquiry. He felt Chilcot was basically a decent man but it would be hard not to be influenced by the media agenda. He was not sure but he felt we might be in Hutton territory, namely he would put us through our paces but ultimately be reasonable. I had sent him Psalm 56, the one Liz sent to me, and he said he did feel he was being pursued by slanderers. He had felt OK in the arguments and his note was strong. There had been a few heckles and jeers when he expressed regret but he felt it was more important that he had said what he did. He was heading off to Abu Dhabi and was not unhappy to be leaving. The general sense had been that TB had been strong and authoritative, yes, gave no ground, but did give a proper explanation. He obviously thought that it was wrong for them to publish the really sensitive stuff, but on his exchanges with Bush, I think reasonable people would have found it hard not to understand his logic, even if they disagreed with it. Of course the haters were out hating, but all in all he did well. Filled him in on last night. I was getting mainly good feedback. Also getting written into the Coulson stuff as an example of someone who did that job well.

Saturday 22 January

I decided to do media on the fallout from Coulson today and did a blog to set the framework for it – the issues were Cameron's judgement, the extent of industrial phone hacking at the *News of the World*, the BSkyB decision and the role of the police. In to do *Loose Ends* [radio show] – Lenny Henry [comedian] and Andrew Neil [journalist] and a Bristol comic who had done a film on Japanese men and love dolls. Clive Anderson [presenter] a bit antsy re. me being devious but it was OK. Nice music. Andrew interesting on public schoolboys being back in power. Then did a stack of media – Beeb, Sky, ITV – which ran on bulletins pretty much all day. Fergie felt Clarke Carlisle had been poor on *QT* but he was getting a terrific write-up.

Sunday 23 January

Snotty book review in *The Observer*. Seemed to criticise lack of context and hindsight. It was a fucking diary. Also Craig Brown having loved *TBY* for the Mail on Scumday now hated this one. Ho-hummery. Out on the bike with Rory. He had been at John Banaszkiewicz's when they had a call with Eddie Howe who had gone through what he thought of all the players. Some definitely on the way out. He thought I should sue Galloway for saying I was a murderer and a Nazi. Back to work on *Radio Times* piece on plain speaking. TB spoke to Sheikh Mansour [Deputy Prime Minister, United Arab Emirates, and football clubs owner] about getting [Manchester] City loan players for Burnley. TB said that he had pushed pretty hard.

Monday 24 January

Spent most of the morning working on various articles. Five favourite diarists for *The List* – Pepys, Harry Truman, Anne Frank, [Franz] Kafka and Alan Clark [former Tory MP]. Murdoch was in town and it was going to get bigger and bigger post Coulson. Also another News Corp story – Andy Gray and Richard Keys [Sky Sport football commentator] had been caught off-mic saying sexist comments about the lineswoman Sian Massey. Jamie [Redknapp] was on, asking for a bit of advice on how to handle it.

I wondered whether it wasn't all related to the fact that Gray was suing the *News of the World*. Tweeted so. It was being cranked up big time, including by Sky. Meanwhile I decided to go for the cops re. phone hacking. Spoke to Gerald Shamash [lawyer] and agreed a letter. The only media I did myself was Iain Dale's LBC show at nine. Nice guy and it was a good interview. One caller asked me to run for MP or mayor. When I said I wasn't a Londoner I got a fairly big response of people saying that it didn't matter. Nice emails afterwards. He was a genuinely interested kind of guy. He also talked a fair bit re. my emotionalism. I mentioned Audrey and her thing about if you want a friend in politics get a dog.

Tuesday 25 January

[Sir] Richard Lambert [outgoing Director-General] had attacked the government's no-growth strategy in his farewell CBI speech. News phone hacking was rumbling on. I posted reports from the information commissioner re. unlawful trade in private information. And the Sky Sports sexism row was raging on. By the end of the day Andy Gray had resigned. Fiona went out and saw the side door had been kicked in and two of the old racing bikes nicked. The cops took it pretty seriously. Two PCs, then two DCs and a scene of crimes guy. I was halfway through a live Spanish radio interview when the cops first arrived. Had an interesting chat with the cops about the phone-hacking issue. They shared my view the thing stank. The scene of crimes guy was there for ages, doing fingerprints and bootprints and also F and I had to do ours to get eliminated. I was sure it had been targeted because of the fact I – rarely for me – tried to put my bike into the shed on Sunday. So someone saw I couldn't get the bike in because there were so many others in there. Anyway, cops were good.

Into RH to sign some books for *The Times*, then off to 5 Live for Richard Bacon. Bacon friendly and informed as ever. He was loving the fact that Sky reporter Andy Burton had been suspended because he once beat him up.[*] Andy Gray on the way out, Keys hanging on. Bacon and I did a bit of that, loads on the book, and a bit post Iraq. He said at the end he always loved talking to me and would like me to do a two-hour special for the next book. He said they were getting good feedback. Stayed till four then off to meet up with Calum for Pompey v Burnley. Played really well, and won 2–1. Call from Endri Fuga [Albanian Socialist Party director of communications] re. Albania and the government out killing opposition protesters. The economy was even more centre stage with crap growth figures and Osborne out blaming the weather. Murdoch in town trying to get a grip of things.

Wednesday 26 January

Mervyn King had made a speech straying perilously close to political territory so I blogged on that. He was effectively endorsing the 'no alternative' strategy re. cuts. Ed B piling in but needed to do more. I was trying to agree Five Books – again – for the new Annie Robinson [journalist, friend] books programme. How many of these shows are there? They wanted different ones but I didn't want to drop *Madame Bovary* and *Team of Rivals*. Went to Daunts to get *A Very British Coup* and *This Sporting Life*. Lunch for Aud's birthday at The Gatehouse. Cab to Portland for advisory council meeting, Tim by video from New York plus all the partners. Tim did an overview then we kicked around a few issues, including how to develop the international side of things.

Meanwhile ten missed calls, all about new police probe on phone hacking because of Ian Edmondson [*News of the World* editor] emails being discovered showing that he knew. I agreed to do *Newsnight* on it with Mark Lewis [lawyer]. The whole thing was unravelling. I was also keen to push the idea of the contrast with the zeal with which the cops pursued the

---

[*] In 2007 Burton had pleaded guilty and been fined for punching Bacon during an argument in a pub lavatory.

so-called cash for honours investigation. I was conscious of totally burning bridges with News Corp but so what? They were pretty disgusting. Mark Lewis was quite odd. But he knew his stuff. He also agreed with me I needed to get the cops to go broader than a letter to me suggested they would – namely saying they would look at [private investigator Glenn] Mulcaire's notes. Got Gerald S to write back and say they should commit to investigating allegations of phone hacking.

Thursday 27 January

LBC on first thing wanting to do a chat re. phone hacking. I called Tessa and asked if she was OK about me saying it was her that I meant when I talked about a Cabinet minister being doorstepped at our house after we had fixed the meeting by phone. She also said she had been hacked again in recent days. I mentioned that and by the end of the day she was wall to wall leading the news. Yates of the Yard was at the London Assembly and said the police could not follow every piece of gossip, rumour and innuendo. Tweeted to compare and contrast cash for honours. I did an interview for *Dispatches* [Channel 4], who were doing a quick turnaround on the whole phone-hacking issue. They seemed to be heading on the right lines. The main thing today was the *10 O'Clock Live* [Channel 4 current affairs show] interview. Tim Hincks [Endemol production company CEO] was telling me they were thrilled and nervous. I imagined they would want to do Iraq so I mugged up again. Grace and Calum both keen to come, with Nina and Laura [friends], and I think they had a good enough time. The show had not had great reviews first time out so it did feel a bit nervy. David Mitchell came to say Hi in the dressing room and he really was quite nervous.

I had half an hour going over stuff and took a chill pill to calm down. Went fine. Almost all on Iraq. Finally got to use some of the facts about post-Saddam Iraq. I also had a gentle whack at the mandarins. Jimmy Carr [comedian] was trying to get a bit of clapping going at various points. He was easily the funniest and the friendliest and Grace and Nina had a great chat with him afterwards. I was a bit pissed off that it was all Iraq and that there was next to no mention of the book. But Tim H said he thought 'I nailed it' and got a great response from the audience who would not normally see me. I missed most of the programme because I was over at *The One Show* interviewing John Whittingdale [chair of the Culture, Media and Sport Committee] for the film I was doing. He was excellent – clear and concise and with good points to make e.g. re. how the committee appears to have been misled and he will want them back. He also said that TB had been lobbied by Dacre and [Les] Hinton [executive

January '11: AC making film on hacking

chairman News International and publisher *News of the World*] not to go with the information commissioner's recommendation of two years for illegal trade in information.

Friday 28 January
Mandela was in hospital and there were worries he was dying. Did a blog just adding to all the voices wishing him well. I was getting pretty good feedback from last night's interview and the general feeling was that Mitchell had been a bit out of his depth. Brian Stanley [producer] of the BBC came round and we did a few pieces to camera for the *One Show* film. Later to the High Court to do Max Clifford [publicist], Mark Lewis and Paul McMullan [journalist]. Max quite spivvy but articulate. Said he had planted false stories via phone to show he was hacked. Pretty clear on his own situation though Mark Lewis felt he had not settled for a million but getting work instead. Then *NotW* reporter Paul McMullan who admitted to breaking the law and said he had no problem with it. Also that there was no way Coulson didn't know and that broader illegality went on. Film coming together OK. Out later to Riverside Studios to do [TV presenter] Adrian Chiles's show [*The Sunday Night Show*]. Mix of comedy and the odd serious bit. Off-mic he asked what I thought of the coalition and I did my usual rant ending with 'They are twats' which went well.

Saturday 29 January
The phone hacking was still slow-burning away. I did a blog on it putting in main points from the interviews I did yesterday for *The One Show*. John Rentoul was interested in taking something but most of the other media letting it go. The only media I had for today was Robert Elms on BBC London, which was fine. Liked him. Having contacted him last week with the idea of the self-review, this week Fraser Nelson [editor] came on and asked if I would do the *Spectator* diary. Worked on it while watching the football p.m. I texted Jack Straw, who was due at Chilcot next week, to say someone needed to rebut the idea they were somehow now involved in the decision-making process. He was heading back to the Middle East and thought it was all moving to a big wave of change.

Sunday 30 January
Fascinating issues poll in one of the papers, which had the NHS at only 4 per cent saliency. Adrian Chiles's show was asking if they could use the 'twats' bit I did off-mic with him re. what I thought of the coalition. I

worked on a speech for Ireland next week, then watched the FA Cup draw. Burnley got West Ham away. Watched the Adrian Chiles show which was OK. But Grace was right that these comedy shows were not my best format. Piers was pressing me to try to persuade TB to do his show.

Monday 31 January

I was wheezy again and went to see the doctor. She said I was not infected but should up the dose of the Ventolin and Symbicourt. To MTV for a 'My life in books' [TV talk show] interview with Annie Robinson for the Beeb. It was a nice show, and a good format, with two people discussing five books to tell the story of their lives. I chose *This Sporting Life, Madame Bovary, Team of Rivals* and *Saturday*, with *The Broons* and *Oor Willie* [Scottish comic strips] as my guilty pleasure. It was made by BBC Scotland so there were lots of really nice Scots girls around the place. The other guest was Jeanette Winterson [novelist] who I didn't think I would like. I liked her a lot. Amazing backstory, brought up by adoptive parents including a hard-as-nails mum she could only bring herself to call Mrs Winterson. She chose the Bible because her 'mum' used to seek to make them ultra-religious. She loved the language if not the sentiment or the mother. She was also into Virginia Woolf and poetry and spoke really well about all of it. Annie was lovely and friendly as always. Lionel Barber [*FT* editor] made an excellent speech for the Cudlipp Lecture which I put on to my blog.

Out to the Beeb to record the voiceover for *The One Show*. Jeremy Irons [actor] was there and said Sinead [Cusack, actress wife] had wondered why I did the Chiles show. She had a point. Mum also said several of her friends had wondered why I had done it. Not sure I should be doing that kind of thing. Need to keep focused on bigger things. Beginning to resent as well all the media I was doing to promote the book which didn't seem to be translating into sales, certainly not on a par with *TBY*, but that was inevitable I guess.

Tuesday 1 February

The Egyptian situation was cranking up a lot, and there were rumours the Jordanian PM was about to resign.* When he did I was in a flurry of calls with the Portland guys, trying to get some strategic advice put in there. I had a session with [communications vice-president] D-J Collins's

---

* Activists in Cairo were calling for an uprising in protest against poverty and government corruption, while protesters in Jordan demanded Prime Minister Samir Rifai's resignation over his economic policies.

team at Google. Great offices. Really relaxed. D-J wanted me to educate the policy team on campaigns. Really bright bunch, from all around the world. Met Rachel Whetstone [Google senior vice-president] for a chat. I hadn't realised she was there during the speech. She was very open, not disguising the divisions between Coulson and [Steve] Hilton [David Cameron's strategy director, Whetstone's husband]. Or that Cameron had been really poor at decision-making during the election campaign. Popped into the party HQ to meet up with Calum for lunch and pick up some briefing on the bankers' debate I was to do later with Trevor Kavanagh [associate editor, *The Sun*].

I had a really annoying moment at Victoria. Someone wanted me to sign the book. They didn't have one. So went to WHS to get one. Had one copy paperback Volume 1 and none of Volume 2. I was getting really frustrated at the work I was doing to promote it, without knowing if it was driving sales or not. The Parliamentary bookshop tweeted to say they had lots so I went in and signed them. To the Lanesborough for a discussion with Trevor Kavanagh in front of RBS [Royal Bank of Scotland] and clients. Trevor and I were not that far apart on the banks. Trevor really pushing the idea Eds [Miliband and Balls] had always hated New Labour and would not be in the right place. The bankers were still pretty defensive. Earlier I chatted with Jack Straw in advance of his appearance at Chilcot tomorrow. He said he sensed there was a lot of 'revenge of the mandarins' going on. He felt they would be pretty heavy in the end. We chatted away and he was trying out some of the lines he was planning. As often with Jack he was in the right place but saying it in odd ways.

Wednesday 2 February

Clegg was making an announcement on a new mental health strategy and making a lot of the right noises, so I did a reasonably supportive blog. I caught PMQs at which Ed M, who had visited Afghanistan last week, did all six on Egypt and Afghanistan. He and Cameron went into major agreement mode and there was a fair bit of restlessness around.

Thursday 3 February

I had some group in Eritrea pressing me to do something on what a scumbag [President] Isaias Afwerki was. I did a bit of research around the place and it really was a pretty grim tale. Worst in the world for press freedom. Dire on education and malnourished kids. Dire on pretty much everything. I linked it to the idea that the revolution in Egypt might not lead where people think and hope. Hosni Mubarak [President] was hanging tough and things were turning nasty on the streets. Out for lunch at the Grosvenor House, a League Managers Association lunch to celebrate Alex's 2,000th match. Pretty extraordinary turnout. Dozens of managers past, present and unemployed. I was seated next to AF. Lots of his Aberdeen people there including Stuart Kennedy still complaining about being subbed against Bayern Munich in [Aberdeen's] the Cup Winners' Cup year.

Chatted for ages with Mark [Ferguson, son] re. the economy. His business was doing well but he was still worried more generally. Peter Schmeichel [former Man United goalkeeper] the only player there. Martin Edwards only board member I spotted. Hugh McIlvanney [journalist] made a good speech. So did Alex who was full of nice words for the people in the room. I was surprised and a bit flattered to be seated next to him. We nattered away mainly about football and a bit of politics. God he can't stand Cameron.

Popped round to see PG who was OK but all the treatment was beginning to take a toll. He was saying how well he thought the kids were doing. Also saying he really felt I should lean towards telly. He had seen Ed M at a meeting with a few others and PG said he really looked like he needed help. He said if I had been there I would have gone crazy. He didn't stake out positions, just asked for views. PG also felt the team was nothing like strong enough. Nice chat. He was worried about Gail, more relaxed about the girls than before and definitely thinking more about death. Dinner with Rory. PG had said he was really becoming a nice person to add to the brightness.

Friday 4 February

Out really early for the first flight to Dublin which was cancelled because of the winds last night. So endlessly hanging round waiting for the next one. Papers full of the [forthcoming Irish general] election. The Egyptian demonstrators had dubbed today Departure Day but Mubarak was not departing. The plane was absolutely heaving. A guy across from me said he had read the book and loved it. He dropped it into the hotel later to get it signed and left a lovely letter saying how much Ireland owed TB and how history would see him differently. I used it in several of the interviews I did at the Merrion and at the book launch reception. Bertie A came to that but everyone was telling me his name was absolute mud. People would give him the peace process but that was it. They gave him a lot of the blame for the economy.

The interviews were all a bit samey, all trying to get me into the election scene. All a bit conveyor-beltish. The election was the main thing for most of it. The turnout at the reception was smaller than the last time I was here but I spoke better. Mainly a defence of politics and a defence of TB and the other politicians who had been involved. Paul had sorted a video from Alex, who said he liked how he came over as Father Ted in the diaries, popping in and out for tea and dispensing advice. Out for a drink with some of Paul Allen's team, waiting for Rory and Charlie [Smith, friend] to arrive. Useful to go over a few lines for *The Late Late Show*. Fergal Keane [BBC foreign correspondent] on. Had a nice chat with him. He said it was bollocks that the Irish were rebels. There was not enough rebellion given how awful [economy] events had been. Rory and Charlie whacking back the Guinness. The interview itself went fine. Then through a few high spots of the book, including NIPP [Northern Ireland Peace Process] and Ian Paisley [former First Minister of NI], and a fair bit on depression. Seemed to go OK. The boys headed out to some clubs while I went to bed. Long day but got through it fine. I had been tweeting during the day re. politics and that led to an avalanche of anger, a lot of it against Bertie.

Saturday 5 February

Paul had fixed for me to do Newstalk sports show today and guest on Dunphy tomorrow. Then to 4FM. Gareth O'Callaghan. Really liked him. He loved the book and it showed. We were in the same building as the Labour campaign HQ so I popped down to see them and did a little pep talk about mindsets of campaigns. They seemed reasonably clued up. But definitely a bit more left than New Labour. They were trying to say they would renegotiate the ECB [European Central Bank]–IMF [International Monetary Fund bailout] deal but it was not clear they could. They were heading into power in some form.

Met the boys to watch United in a big city-centre pub. Lots of people chatting to me, mainly very friendly but one or two hostile. A lot of Brits there and likewise mainly nice but a couple got a bit gobby and it could have got nasty so I left. One was just spoiling for a fight. For a couple of others it was Iraq. Rory well on but sobered up over dinner. Popped to another pub and again lots of people wanting to talk to me. Charlie loving it.

Sunday 6 February

Popped down for breakfast. Picked up the *Sunday Tribune*. It turned out it was a four-page wraparound the *Mail on Sunday*. The *Tribune* was in receivership and it was a total marketing scam. I started to tweet about it. The *ST* editor Noírin Hegarty was one of the other guests on the Eamon Dunphy show so we discussed it and I got them to get Roy Greenslade [media commentator] on so we could give them a kicking. Editor Noírin

Hegarty not surprisingly really hacked off. Good lively chat. I was developing some good lines on the Irish elections re. this being a classic moment for different sort of politician to emerge – straight, level with people, honesty and leadership. Met the boys for lunch, took them to the airport then headed to Belfast with Paul, trying to catch up on the way. We were staying at the Europa and I was in the Titanic Suite, with a plaque outside to commemorate Hillary Clinton's visit. Dinner with the crowd from Queen's University. Nice crowd and we chatted away about education, NI politics and general chitchat. Bed late again and beginning to tire.

Monday 7 February

Up early and a packed-out day ahead. To the Beeb to pre-record Nolan who pushed me on whether Martin McGuinness would be an acceptable First Minister. That was unlikely but the DUP were stoking it as a way of squeezing the UUP [Ulster Unionist Party]. Owen Paterson [Northern Ireland Secretary] had got into hot water saying it would show how far the process had come if he did. I was much in the same position and ended up being pretty supportive. To Queen's where I had six or seven back-to-back interviews, all a bit same old same old but fine. Then to the first of two speeches with students, then another speech to guests and another signing. It went pretty well. [Lady] Daphne Trimble [wife of David Trimble, former First Minister] was there and I said to her face what I had been saying on the media – that the diaries risked being unfair to Trimble, and I was sorry about that. The speech was basically a run round the block on the peace process, including how my diaries made you wonder how it ever happened whereas TB's book and his ten principles of peace processes made you think it was obvious. Good mood to the whole thing and a fair few books sold at the second event. More media then off to Stormont.

Had a good session with McG who was a bit heavier but on really good form. He said the First Minister question would not arise. He thought he and [Peter] Robinson [First Minister] would be back. He was full of praise for him, not least at the way he had got through the problems with his wife.* Also said he found him easy to work with but the institutions were set up to make sure there was power-sharing so to some extent it was inevitable to have the frustrations. He also did not want to give the Unionists any more power. He felt Trimble had been his own worst enemy. They [UUP] had no

---

* In 2009 Robinson's wife, Iris, also a politician, withdrew from public life following periods of mental illness. It then became known that she had conducted an extra-marital affair with a nineteen-year-old, whereupon she resigned from all elected positions.

chance not least because they had a new useless leader. He was very generous to TB, JoP [Jonathan Powell] and me, said we all made a massive difference and he felt it was wrong TB did not get more credit. As for himself
he said he never got grief going around the place – including in Loyalist
areas – and whenever he was in the UK he just got people saying keep it
up. Gerry Kelly [minister] popped in. Much friendlier than usual and more
relaxed. They were both – and so was Robinson later – contemptuous of
Cameron. He took no interest. They had no regard for the special circumstances. It was impossible to get a meeting even with Paterson, he said.

   We chatted away for an hour or so, a mix of reminiscing and current
analysis. He shared my sadness re. Bertie but said he had made mistakes,
e.g. the ad he did for the Irish *News of the World*, hiding away in a cup-
board [to publicise his new career as a sports writer]. He said there was
a dissident threat but though they had desire they lacked capacity and
the vast majority knew there was no going back. Down to see Robinson.
He was with a couple of young advisers. Very relaxed and for him even
jokey. He was on the same pitch as McG re. the political situation and
was even more contemptuous of the government. Cameron wasn't interested. He said Paterson was the worst SoS [Secretary of State] they had
ever had and he was getting close to saying so. We chatted about Coulson
and he was delighted he was in trouble because he said his own problems
started with the *NotW*. Then to the dining room to speak to members and
staff. The place felt like a normal political assembly. They wanted me to
do some work with them re. Kosovo. Back to Dublin, a little run then
out to do RTÉ *Eleventh Hour*, panel discussion. I was really being struck
how negative they all were and how snide about pretty much all their
candidates. Heaven help who wins. We had been watching bits of the
finance ministers' debate which was OK but the election had not really
ignited yet.

Tuesday 8 February

Did Pat Kenny's RTÉ show, then to Trinity and a pretty packed History
Society. I was planning to do the Ireland speech but they wanted media and
politics so I ad-libbed. OK, good Q&A and at the end a standing ovation
which for students was pretty good. Nice atmosphere. Interesting that not
one asked on Iraq. Very different to London. Then I met up with Paul and
went to the Westin to meet Brian Cowen's press guy. He was clearly shell-
shocked by recent events but said Brian was ready for getting out. It had
taken time to get there but he got to the right place. Micheál Martin was
able to reinject a bit of energy into Fianna Fáil but nobody felt they could
win. I had more media to do. People were beginning to tweet whether I

had got citizenship, then back to hotel. I was tired. Long days, long trip. One more day. Three speeches then home.

Meanwhile Catherine Rimmer was on saying could I go to Kazakhstan. I wasn't sure. I got the argument that we had to try to help countries to reform, and TB and team had a lot to give on how to modernise government, but it was hard to get the balance right between pushing for reform while getting stick for being too close to regimes way different to ours. Barbara [Nestor] picked me up for the main paying gig of the trip, a Leviathan [political cabaret] event at which I was interviewed by David McWilliams, economist turned media performer and playwright-author, then be part of a panel on the economy. Good crowd and good atmosphere. A bit of Iraq but not much. As Denis Hickie and Shane Horgan [former rugby players] said, I was treated like a celeb in Ireland and it seemed nobody dared give me a hard time. We shifted a fair few books then left for Cork. Paul had asked a pal to drive us down there but he hadn't a bloody clue and I was going mental by the end of the night. Barbara very apologetic at the hotel when finally we got there but it was not really her fault, and she was so nice anyway I wouldn't blame her if it was.

Wednesday 9 February

The afternoon event was asking if I could wait and do something in the evening but I really was ready for home. It had been fine but a day or two too long. Out to UCC [University College Cork], another driver fuck-up, then taken to the very nice and airy hall where I was speaking. A couple of demonstrators handing out leaflets but in the main a really nice atmosphere. I did a mix of NI, social media, defence of politics, and it went down well. The Q&A was lively in a round-all-the-houses kind of way. No mention of Iraq though, very different to UK. A couple of presentations at the end then a book-signing which went really well. I was pretty shagged though and glad to get to the airport and off. Got the last seat on the plane and sat at the back, listening to two incessantly talking stewardesses. I knew everything about their shift patterns by the time we got home.

Thursday 10 February

All the talk was of Mubarak making a statement to go. He ended up staying, or at least trying to. I had just about called it in a blog a little before. It all seemed too easy and people had their hopes up too high. Cork airport was the other big story, a plane crash killing six people. Brian Cowen was there doing a doorstep.

Friday 11 February

Kazakhstan was definitely on so I had to head to South Kensington and sort a visa. All a bit old Soviet style down there. Early morning queue. Eventually we got sorted. I sent through a note to TB and JoP making clear that this was only going to work if we were able to say this was leading to genuine change. Our critics would be out fast and furious saying we were putting a positive gloss on an autocratic regime. Mubarak eventually fell. Amazing when it happened and there would be plenty of others worrying now. The Swiss froze his bank accounts there which would put pressure on us and the Yanks to do the same. I worked on a *Dream School* piece for *The Times*.

Saturday 12 February

Cameron was getting a lot of grief on Big Society [political ideology empowering communities] and was planning for a blitz on it next week. But it was not really flying for him. Off to Watford with Calum. Won 3–1 thanks in part to a freak own goal, the goalkeeper kicking the ball against a defender's back – it rebounded and rolled fifteen to twenty yards into the net.

Sunday 13 February

Quick blog on the stalling Big Society. Long chat with PG who was feeling pretty rough now. Radiation not fun. Out on the bike for an hour or so, then watching loads of sport. Round with Rory to PG's for a chat. He seemed better than I expected but not easy. Georgia said her friends were raving about my *QT* performance, and asking why can't our politicians do that?

Monday 14 February

Out at six-ish and off to Heathrow to meet Laura Kyrke-Smith [Portland], who had been in Kazakhstan last week with Jonathan. The flights via Frankfurt and then on to Astana were painless enough. Security guy at Heathrow really down on Cameron and saying I should go back and help Ed. 'The government are destroying the country'. We arrived 11 p.m.-ish, six hours ahead, very cold but remarkably clean. Astana not as I had expected. [Nursultan] Nazarbayev [President] had moved the capital from Almaty to here so everything was new-build. A lot of it quite flash. We were in the President Hotel which was all very bling bling. Unfortunately, my room had a noisy air conditioning I couldn't turn off and at 3 a.m. I finally gave up and moved room.

Pretty much wall-to-wall meetings including with the PM. First to the head of the National Analytical Centre, a lively woman who was fairly cynical about the whole exercise. Her view – that people were not ready for democracy as we saw it, and in any event most did not want it – was fairly widespread. Then to the presidential palace to see the main foreign policy guy. More old-style but as the meeting wore on he was buying in more to the idea of using the election to signal greater change. The only narrative I could see was to say they had been totally focused on the economy but now were moving to political reform. We gave them a few ideas – TV debates (non-starter), town hall meetings, help for opposition presidential candidates, more openness to observers, media tours etc. He started out quizzical but came out warmer.

The party [Democratic People's Party] first deputy chairman was more sceptical. He said we had to understand how strange it sounded when you are trying to win a campaign and people like us come in and advise them on how to help opponents. I got that, but I said you are going to win and win big. The question is whether you can meanwhile help the country put a better image to the outside world. Off to lunch but we were interrupted and called to the PM's office. Karim Massimov was the one pushing for this project. He asked me for impressions, I went through where we were, and the sense I was getting, then he said let's meet again tomorrow. He was obviously, like everyone, a bit scared of the President. But I sensed he definitely wanted this to work and he didn't push back on any of the ideas we were putting forward.

Then to meetings with a couple of ministers, economy and deputy. Their economic record was a good one, including their handling of the crash, and they felt they would not have been so successful without a strong President in charge of a political system aimed at keeping control over so many ethnic and religious groups and with such powerful neighbours in Russia and China. They also had Kyrgyzstan as a neighbour in chaos having embraced democracy. Then to a bar to meet the more political presidential adviser. He was strongly of the view that over-rapid change was dangerous and that it was madness to think of ways that diminished presidential power or helped the ragbag of candidates coming forward. He said several were rich exiles causing trouble from abroad and we had to challenge them.

He had just done an interview saying Nazarbayev would win big, even bigger than before. He was leaving later for London and Chatham House where he would say that the country needed a lot longer of the same rule. Of all the meetings today it was the one that showed how hard this would be – but also why they had good reasons to be nervous about change. He really felt the people wanted the powerful to rule, and to be strong. There was no history of democracy and people were not clamouring for it, other than from outside. As for the Kazakhs I don't think I had ever seen so many different racial and facial types in one day. From Chinese to Mongol to white to near-Japanese to central European to Slav. Really was noticeable and funny therefore when the second presidential adviser said there were too many immigrants in the UK. Kasimov asked me to work on a speech for him, which I did, and turned it into a strategy note for the Portland team coming next week.

Wednesday 16 February
The party first deputy chairman saw us again. Yesterday he thought we were a bit mad, and started today with a joke about us being the 'how to lose' advisers. But he also said he had thought about what we had said, he seemed to get the point and said he would propose all we were saying to the President. Then to another meeting with the PM. He clearly felt that TB would have to see the President again. They were all very conscious of the people power driving change in the Arab world but they genuinely seemed to think it wouldn't happen here. It was of course easy to believe your own propaganda, and the state control of the media ensured a good profile for the President.

He was very funny re. WikiLeaks, said it had reported how he had been seen in a nightclub – with his wife! And dancing with her too. He was looking to us for drive rather than the other way round. Back to the hotel and a meeting with the head of the tax commission. He was fascinating because he totally rejected the Westernising view. He felt democracy was bad for the established democracies let alone them [Kazakhstan]. He talked about how slow we were to make change happen. And when we got on to the media, he said that if I thought the US had a free media I was crazy. It was a fascinating glimpse into a totally different way of thinking from someone who was clearly very bright. It was as if democratisation would destroy not strengthen the country, and he believed a lot of our weaknesses flowed from an arrogance about our systems.

The plane out was delayed so we had a couple of hours hanging round the airport where I finished my note for the PM and did a longer and franker version for the TBO and Portland teams. We would have to be realistic about how much progress can be made during the election campaign itself; and about how much can be done without the clear imprimatur of the President felt throughout the system. The meetings with his two senior advisers were instructive. With the first (foreign policy), I got the impression he understood what we were trying to do – namely show during the election period an understanding of the things that can be done to signal serious intent with regard to reform on the political track in the medium and longer term. He was open to most of our ideas on this. Meeting the senior political adviser, however, I sensed that he thought this approach (or at least some of the ideas for signalling it) risked diminishing Nazarbayev's power, and helping his campaign opponents. This unsurprisingly struck him as eccentric.

In so far as they made any conclusions that might lead to action, they seemed to be saying that Nazarbayev should make clear that in addition to meeting their legal requirements to give equal space to opponents, the media should actually give them greater billing than to the President, as he is so well known; that as he will not take part in the official TV debate, he should consider taking part in a public speech and Q&A session, and that the other candidates should be allowed then to face the same audience in the same way. Also that the OSCE [Organization for Security and Co-operation in Europe] and/or other election monitors should be invited in advance of the campaign, and be encouraged to look at every part of the electoral process.

We were also pressing for an international media tour in which journalists from different parts of the world were brought in and that they get access to the President, the PM, opposition candidates and were taken to rarely visited parts of the country. They doubted he would go for all of it but felt he would go for some. We were getting a varying sense of how many other candidates would run, from eleven to three. Two had already been rejected because they failed the Kazakh language test. Three accepted. Six are being considered but the election authorities said they had been unable to contact three of those to invite them in for the language test.

Nobody seems to think he will get below 80 per cent and he will probably do even better than last time. Of course that made the need to signal further democratic reform even greater. But it was clear we should not expect them to go too far, because they won't. There is no history or culture of democracy. Some openly express the fear that if they move too fast the consequences will be disastrous. There is little or no thinking about life beyond the current President. One or two were very open in their belief that Western-style democracy was wrongheaded, not just for Kazakhstan but for Western democracies too! And it was pretty clear that even those who are in what we might deem to be the right place will be reluctant to loosen control on the media.

The President's political adviser said Nazarbayev believed Gorbachev caused his own downfall by granting TV more freedom. He also, I told TB later, said the President was clear he needed at least ten more years to complete his vision for the country.

One final point I made to TB: one of the things they are most proud of is their multi-faith record. There may be added value in involving his Faith

Foundation in some way. There are regular religious conferences here. I worked on Massimov's speech, essentially not apologising for relentless focus on the economy, now saying they could move into other areas of reform, including democracy.

Thursday 17 February

Home again, I did a quick blog re. the idea that time was running out on the Tories' 'all Labour's fault' line. The economy was back centre stage as inflation was stubbornly high. Balls was getting stuck into Mervyn King as being too political. Cameron had also done a total about-turn on the sell-off of forests. He was actually getting a bit of credit for it. Then to collect Sarah Ellison from *Vanity Fair* who was over doing a piece on phone hacking. I talked to her on the way to Hinckley where I was doing an event for the British Frozen Food Federation. Then to De Montfort Uni and 200-plus students. Really nice bunch. No hostility at all. The audience was basically pro-Labour I would say. Did a few questions with a lecturer, then about thirty from the floor and it was a nice, open and engaging event.

Friday 18 February

Bahrain and Libya now really going for it on the [anti-government] protest front. No media in Libya and a lot of reports of deaths coming out. To RH for a meeting with Martin Soames [lawyer] re. Volume 3. A lot fewer problems than Volume 2. I stayed and worked through a stack of Bill's edits on Volume 4. All fine but slow work. Did blog on the difference between the *Question Time* audience response on forests sell-off last night – they seemed to like the idea of a U-turn – and the students who seemed to support my view that it showed lack of grip and competence.

Saturday 19 February

The Times gave a good show to my *Dream School* piece, including interviews from Cherie, Simon Callow and Robert Winston.

Monday 21 February

Over to Steel and Shamash [law firm] to meet Gerald Shamash, and a young QC who was handling a lot of the civil cases re. phone hacking. We had two DCIs on the way over and they wanted to brief me in advance. The cops were perfectly open and friendly, admitted the case had at first maybe not been handled properly, that before someone had to go through a lot of hoops to find out if they may have been involved but now they were taking a different approach. They also felt there was now enough civil and political pressure to keep going on this. They showed me a log detailing dates and times when I received calls through the *NotW* 'hub' but of course that would not include calls from mobiles. I said I would check against my diary. When I did, later, two of them related to when the Tessa/David situation was raging. They explained that when there were two calls in quick succession it could be that one was to engage the phone while the other was then able to get into the voicemail.

As for the papers there were a small number with 'Alistair' written on, but nothing that really rang bells. On one 'Fiona' was written just below but again there was nothing there that really leapt out. The QC said that if I had been a main target there would have been a lot more. I guess they were there for an hour and I sensed Gerald and the lawyer were trying to tease out stuff for other clients. How many cops involved? Around thirty, he thought. How many other people now asking to be investigated? A lot. I asked them if they were aware of McMullan and told them what he had said when I interviewed him. They weren't. They were clearly not that impressed by the Yates investigation but unsurprisingly would not get drawn too much on it. Some of the calls were definitely around the time of the separation when Tessa and David had both been at the house to sort out the statement, and we had been amazed people found out she was there.

Off to West Ham with Rory. Met Calum there. We played well first half but ended up 5–1 down. I was apparently on the live TV coverage and later on Sky still singing and cheering when we were three down. Libya still kicking off big-style and [Colonel Muammar] Gaddafi [leader of Libya] going crazier by the day.* TB taking a bit of a hit because of the 'closer relations' [with Gaddafi] and no voice out there defending him.

Tuesday 22 February

Grace had been nagging to spend the week in Paris with Rory and a friend to look at language schools. In the end it was just me and her and a nice couple of days. Early start. Eurostar. Hotel Le Colbert near Notre Dame. We visited La Sorbonne first, later the Alliance Française. Walking everywhere on a lovely cold and sunny day. Paris looking great and Grace really up for it. Managed a run but I was feeling a bit overweight myself. Nice

---

* As political and population unrest threatened Gaddafi forty-one years since he first seized power, the leader urged loyalists to take to the streets and in an angry and sometimes incoherent speech denied repression and bloodshed and vowed to die in his homeland rather than flee abroad.

day. Grace pretty much on for it and thankfully off the US idea. I did a blog, drafted by Godric, on the Velodrome for 2012 Olympics which was completed, ahead of time, on budget and looking fabulous.

Wednesday 23 February

Out for a run while Gracie got up and pottered for a while, before heading back. We had had a nice time. Ought to do more little touristy things like this. Grace was always good fun. She was working a fair bit harder too. Out in the evening for the Energy Institute dinner. 1,200 black-tie job, oil execs from all over the world. There was an old-style top table and I was next to James Smith from Shell and Ian Taylor from Vitol, one of the big oil shifting companies. Also had John Watson of Chevron who was the other speaker. Nice enough bunch. We talked a bit about how the oil world was panicking a bit with all that was happening in North Africa. Watson was sure Gaddafi would go. But it did not look like he would go easily or quickly. Cameron was now in Qatar and was not at all clear on what his trip was about. Hague also struggling, not least with the organisation of extracting Brits from Tripoli. I dropped TB a mail to say I felt he should say something because he was getting hit hard re. us getting closer to Gaddafi. Yet there was a very good argument for it and if you think what he would have been like had we not got him to give up WMD.

I did a mix of jokes and then telling them to get their act together as an industry as a whole which went down pretty well, though I gave them a fair amount of criticism. With bankers top of the unpopularity league, and journos, politicos and estate agents not great, I said they were vying for the fourth Champions League slot. Ian Taylor seemed a really nice guy and both he and Smith actually seemed quite sympathetic to Labour. Said they hoped Ed did OK. Ian said I really ought to get back in there. He felt I should stand. He said the thing I have learned is that there are very few people who really know how to make change happen and you are one of them. Watson's speech was a tour of the industry and I said in mine the positives he laid out had to be understood beyond the industry. He and others said afterwards I said the right thing at the right time but I suspect like the bankers they would go back into competitive silo only-care-about-the-company mode.

Thursday 24 February

Hague was trending on Twitter very negatively after a morning interview. I did a piece kind of defending him, in so far as I pointed out the impossibility of meeting expectations when power in the situation was so limited. We were applying our own judgements to Gaddafi who was not behaving according to our own norms. Hague did look a bit out of it. I also mentioned that for those who criticise the policy of getting closer to Gaddafi he would have been even worse with WMD. Later a Labour London fundraiser. Jim Fitzpatrick [Labour MP] compèring. Did a fairly standard political spiel. One hostile Q re. Iraq in the Q&A and later the guy said they would get us for war crimes in the end so he got both barrels and it went down well.

TB called from Kuwait and we chatted over whether he should do media on Libya. I felt the need was not urgent but there was no harm in his voice being out there and making clear that even if Gaddafi had not come good it was better to have got him into a more co-operative international position. It was being seen largely negatively, though most of the UK coverage was in the area of Brits trapped and FCO fuck-ups for which Cameron apologised.

Friday 25 February

Clegg had apparently said he had 'forgotten' he was meant to be in charge when he went off skiing with his kids while the Prime Minister was away on a trade visit to the Middle East. Then DC said no he's not. Did a blog on how the media would have killed had this been us in charge of such a shambles. Hague getting hit a bit. Conference call with JoP and Portland re. Astana. They had a good framework but as JoP and I said none of this was going to happen without the President going for it and he was unlikely to think everything we were proposing was in his interest. David Davies round for a chat on phone hacking. He was seeing the cops Wednesday next and there was definitely more to his case.

Saturday 26 February

Off with Calum to Preston. Terrific match in some ways, not least our 5,500 away-end turnout and the result, coming from behind to win 2–1. Cam went back to London while I drove to meet Fiona at Tessa and David's. Got there about eight. We watched some of [Mills's daughter] Jess's pop videos and I tweeted out a thing about iTunes and pre-ordering her latest song. She was doing really well. They were also more dead set on pursuing the phone hacking. Tessa was still a bit too close to the News Corp set, and too worried what they thought. But David was adamant.

Sunday 27 February

Chatted a bit about what I should say to Ed. Tessa said he needed more authority with the shadow Cabinet, and they all needed more ideas and energy. He needed to use the empathetic side to develop into properly organised community politics. We left after lunch and got back for the Carling Cup final. Great win for Birmingham after Arsenal fucked up. Papers starting to give pretty big build-up to *Dream School*. Web trails too, including my first lesson, and posters all over town.

Monday 28 February

Worked a bit on post-'03 diaries then out for a meeting with Dragonfly re. new TV ideas. Sanjay the main guy was a good mate of Pete Hyman. It was so hard to get decent ideas that were not rubbish or trivial. But they seemed OK. Working towards something that got people inserted into the political process. Went to meet Fiona briefly at the Wells pub, then to Ed's. I had been expecting a one-on-one session. But despite Tom B's efforts, he, Polly Billington, Ayesha Hazarika [EM special advisers] and Rachel K all came. I was early, they were late and Justine didn't hear the bell so I was outside for a while. When they arrived it was all a bit shambolic. Tom said they should all be seen and not heard and just let Ed and me talk.

I went through issues of mindset. He had to think leadership all the time, remind himself he was. Doing it and speaking it was one thing. He also had to think it. Went through some of the mental tricks. Also talked a bit about his body language, particularly in the House, the way he stood, the way he used his hands, odd mannerisms. He laughed: 'I said, "Be blunt but not brutal."' He took it all fine though. He felt PMQs was going better – which it was – but he also felt we should not worry too much. I disagreed, said it was the key battleground for strategy. He said Hague was damaged by being good at it – jokes not judgement. I said that was the point. We did him via PMQs. I said the big thing though was lack of clarity re. strategy. He had four OK building blocks – the Promise of Britain (and the idea that this could be the first generation not making life better for the next), the idea that the gap was not between poor and rich but rich and everyone else, community politics, and also a new politics.

I said all fine but two problems – nothing to hang them together (that could come) and also I really believed we needed to re-engage in the argument about the economy. Revisit the election arguments. I felt until we regained lost ground and won some arguments about how we got to where we are, we would not get people to listen to us. They would hear our attacks but say who are you to talk, you wrecked things in the first place – we couldn't let that argument stand. He was very resistant. I think in part he didn't want to be seen to be defending GB. His default position did seem to be to go against the past. Don't forget the successes, I said.

People needed to remember what good we had done with power. The Tories were defining us negatively. Don't help them to do so. I also pushed on the need for more big speeches and a few shots up the backsides of his colleagues. Apart from Balls and to a lesser extent two or three others they just were not making an impact. He bemoaned the shadow Cabinet elections, said they had to change the system. He felt that things with the shadow Cabinet were OK. I said that was not what I heard.

Later, when the others had gone, he said he thought Balls would be a problem at some stage. Why? Because he will. He is much more GB-style than I am. He feels he has to take all policy towards him. He and Yvette operate as a team, not just a married couple, and are both ambitious. Ed still thinks he will be leader. If not, Yvette thinks she could be, or definitely deputy leader. He also said things with David M were only just out of the deep freeze. He felt empathy was his strongest suit, also that he was able to get under Cameron's skin. Tom B and Bob R had made a big difference but he still felt a gap on strategy. He wanted someone who was a mix of me, Peter H and PG. I thought his team were OK with him but a bit defensive about him. He asked if I wanted a seat. Why didn't I go for Burnley? What about Fiona in Hampstead? I said I wouldn't rule it out but we were both in different places now. He said he wanted to be able to continue to use me. Fine, but as GB did, not full-time. He had seen TB and found it helpful. Rachel sent me a message to say they found it really useful. Hope so, but it didn't feel great.

Tuesday 1 March

To Oval Road and then CBC to do a couple of Canadian telly interviews. Arrived a bit late at Wiltons for lunch with Hezza [Michael Heseltine]. He was on pretty good form and we covered a fair bit of ground. He felt DC was doing well. That IDS and Gove were exceptional in terms of vision for their areas and now they had to push it through. I said they may have a vision but it is hardly a modern one or a good one. He felt DC was a Eurosceptic at heart but also a pragmatist and he was sensible enough to know to park the issue and not rage it up. He was enjoying chairing the Regional Growth Fund [panel examining how to boost regional economies] work but it was a bit of a one-off. He said he was sometimes taken aback by how hated TB was in some of his circles. He said he always defended him as 'the man who saved Britain from the Labour Party'. Ha-ha. He was still against us on Iraq, but felt TB was being unfairly hit over having dealt with Gaddafi. Major had been on the media this morning kind of defending TB, not least re. Libya giving up WMD. Hezza said at one point that we had both lived at the top and the centre in fascinating periods of history and 'isn't it great?' He felt I had taken pressure that was 'super-human' and that whatever journalists actually said, they all thought I had done it incredibly well. 'You were too good for them.'

Anne [Lady Heseltine] called and said to say hello. I don't know why, he said, but she always rather liked you. He felt I had always been kind to him for the wrong reasons – it was all about undermining Mrs Thatcher. Indeed. He had read Peter's book, enjoyed it but said 'I wonder if he knows how badly he comes out of it'. He was thinking about doing another book himself, on the journey – his and the issue's – re. urban regeneration. He said he would like honestly to analyse what worked and what didn't. It was a nice lunch, catching up, going over most of the current stuff but also able to reflect a bit more. He said I was right to stay out of the Lords – 'There are good people in there but you wouldn't like it' – but he felt I should stay involved in some capacity. He was head and shoulders above most of the current lot. Home to do a couple of interviews, the *FT* then *The Observer*. Grace and I off to Stamford Bridge for the Chelsea–Man U match, collecting Otis [Kelly, son of Natascha McElhone] from Natascha's on the way, then dinner with Joe Hemani. Grace and I took Otis down to see Alex. His face a total picture. When Alex told him to go in the Chelsea dressing room and kick all their ankles, he thought he was being serious and headed that way before we pulled him back. Grace took him out on the pitch while Alex and I chatted a bit. It was a terrific match for the neutral but they lost 2–1 after going one up so he was going to be deeply pissed off. Took Otis home and chatted with Natascha re. Grace and acting.

Wednesday 2 March

Out first thing to Heathrow and off to Frankfurt. Whacked off a quick blog on the idea of Cameron having cannibalising policies – e.g. Big Society but cuts. Trade–foreign policy but let's have a quick no-fly zone. He was beginning to make a bit of a tit of himself foreign policy-wise and Hague looked like he was not enjoying himself at all. I had a bit of a nightmare on the flight, when my phone slipped under my seat and they had to part-dismantle it to get it out. On the bus in Frankfurt to get the Astana flight I was approached by an Italian guy. 'What is a man like you doing going to a country like that?' I was fairly vague but said I was interested in the elections and whether they were committed to change. He said he had been going there to do business – oil – for eighteen years. He was from Sicily. He said there was nothing Sicilians could teach these guys about 'how to do business'. He said from what I know of you, you are a high reputation kind of guy. 'These people are not.'

Thursday 3 March

Out to the office at the university where Tim's Portland team, Charles Maclean and David Osborn, had set themselves up. Mark Flanagan also there, over advising on a digital strategy. We did a bit of work on the overall narrative. I suggested re-ordering the main points so that they started with economy first, now political reform, rather than leading on 'Nazarbayev is genuinely popular'. We talked over some of the difficult questions and emphasised we needed to have some substance to the reform message, or else it could be counterproductive.

From there to see the PM. As before he was more wanting to listen than signal direction himself. We were still no nearer knowing what if any of the specific reform ideas they might announce during the election. He felt some were possible but he wasn't clear which. I felt the PM was just nervous and still unsure what if any plans the President would let him announce. There was a live issue today which we said could be used as an opportunity to signal a different direction – namely the alleged blocking of Radio Free Europe's website. I said if he were to say he was looking into it, then make clear this was not policy and those responsible had been dealt with, that would be a good thing to do. But it dragged on all day. We didn't really have time to do the digital strategy.

He left us with a pollster called Galina and an interpreter. It was fairly interesting though – a bit like PG – you sensed she took from focus groups what she wanted to take. E.g. when people were asked how they felt about the President having billions in the bank abroad – 'They said he deserved it.' When people were asked about their worries about succession – which were real – they trusted him to train someone. When I asked if they actively wanted democracy, it was a pretty clear *niet*. In so far as she would admit public criticism it was of the idea that foreign companies made so much money out of the country. I felt it would need Charles to go on the road with these guys to keep them properly bolstered. Nice restaurant though I wondered if there was anything else going on when a very good-looking woman with a short skirt and low-cut top told us there were rooms for 3k tenge an hour.

Friday 4 March

Good win for Dan Jarvis in the Barnsley by-election. Libs came sixth and UKIP beat the Tories. I slept through the alarm and had to rush to get out for a meeting with the PM. This time he was better tonally but still we did not have the real meat that could be set out as reform. He said he was sure we would get some but it could not all come quickly. Also with Libya still dominating everything, and TB being presented as the autocrats' friend, it was only a matter of time before his and our involvement became an issue and we

March '11: PG-style focus groups – in Kazakhstan

needed to be careful. I said I could defend the idea of helping advise on the transition to democratic reform, but not on putting a gloss on a bad electoral process. We then headed to a nice café, with a lovely manageress looking after us, to meet the youngest of the delegation going abroad, Marat Beketayev, who was a presidential adviser in his early thirties. Charles had warned me he was old-style and made the wrong impression but he grew on me.

I gave him my take on the best way to communicate and he seemed to get it. He said you are asking us to do the opposite of what we have always been told to do – be proactive not defensive, strategic not tactical, proud not apologetic, but from a position of explaining the future steps as a way of being able to tell the story of the past – and he quite liked it. Back to the hotel for a meeting on digital strategy. It showed how fast they could move if they wanted to. A really bright guy was there – good English, fabulous knowledge of history – and was putting in place instant Twitter, YouTube and website in days. We also discussed a few good documentary ideas.

Our narrative felt strong but there was a big hole in it which could only be filled by substance. I worked on a note on the plane which I sent through from Frankfurt, including the beginnings of an op-ed to set out the outlines of a strategy. Economy the focus for twenty years – here is what it has achieved – now for political reform with same zeal. I had a bit of fun at Frankfurt, covering the piles of *Daily Mail*s at the BA desks with the *Frankfurter Rundschau*. Got home and after dinner watched episode one of *Dream School*. It was OK though there was way too much Jamie in it.

Saturday 5 March

Did a blog on *Dream School*, debunking some of the stereotypes. My trailers on the website looked OK but there was a story in some of the papers that I provoked a fight after one of the lessons. Round to see PG who was in OK form. He was in real pain at times but had only a week to go on the radiation front. Gail there, looking stressed out.

Sunday 6 March

The news was leading on an SAS team getting arrested by Libyan rebels near Benghazi.* All a bit dire for Hague who was becoming accident prone. DC about to do a speech against the enemies of enterprise. I was due to be going to Kosovo but Michael Davenport, ambassador in Serbia, called and cautioned mildly against me going there. He said it might be OK but

---

* Seven armed SAS officers were appointed by suspicious anti-Gaddafi militia when escorting a diplomat to meet rebel Libyan forces.

Kosovo was still raw and if other things were going wrong at the time I was due – e.g. EU accession – it could become difficult. He said I am not saying don't come but I am saying it could resurrect old passions and arguments.

Monday 7 March

Peter M had a defence of the last government's approach to Libya and I did a blog supporting him and also Jack Straw who had a very good piece in *The Times* on Saturday saying Gaddafi made him glad we had removed Saddam. Jack also told me Chilcot had sent him a grovelling apology about the second evidence session. Off at 10.30 for the Defence Academy at Shrivenham. PFI [Private Finance Initiative] project. Fabulous facilities. 300 or so officers on an MA level course and I mainly talked about strat comms and crisis management then Q&A. Had a bit of an asthma panic attack halfway in, which was difficult but recovered and it went down well. They seemed to go along with my line that we were failing on the comms front re. Afghanistan. Then to a meeting with a colonel who was heading a strat comms review for CDS [chief of defence staff]. A bit same old same old but probably good to stay in with these guys.

Later than planned got away and was home by seven. Exchanging emails with Clare Francis, widow of Labour social media adviser Mark Hanson who had killed himself a few days ago. Calum told me he had *All in the Mind* on his website as his favourite book. It worried me that maybe it had had a role in pushing him there. Clare and I discussed ways of using it to raise funds and be part of a memorial for him.

Tuesday 8 March

Pottering mainly apart from a very long Kaz conference call. Tim and I both of the view that with the TB focus re. Libya, and the Prince Andrew focus re. Kazakhstan – he was in trouble both over connections with US sex offender billionaire Jeff Epstein who I met once with Ghislaine [Maxwell, daughter of late tycoon Robert] and over a Kazakh relative of Nazarbayev who had paid 3 million over the odds for Andrew's house in Surrey – it was only a matter of time before the TB thing became a real issue.

Wednesday 9 March

Out early to do *Daybreak* [ITV] on *Dream School*. Adrian Chiles was away on Champions League duty so it was the stand-in team who were in there. Celia Walden in the makeup room, sticking to the line that Piers's CNN show was going well. The interview was fine and they had John Webster, my old German teacher in Leicester, on as a surprise. I was perfectly posi-tive about the *Dream School* experience. Off to the Sport Industry Awards. I was sitting with Tanni GT and had a good laugh with her.

Thursday 10 March

Portland wanted me to do an article, partly in response to Phil Stephens's piece about London becoming the global centre for reputational PR for bad people, to defend PR in the case of steering people towards democracy. I called the *FT*, who were keen and ended up working on it straight away. It was a bit risky in terms of pushing me out there but I would rather get my defence in first. All a bit rushed as I had to go out to an event at the Royal College of Physicians. It went fine and I was on OK form. I was getting a bit ground down by all the talks though.

Friday 11 March

There was a massive earthquake followed by a tsunami in Japan. Utterly horrific and the pictures were almost beyond belief. Suddenly Gaddafi – who was getting worse – was knocked right down the agenda, though Cameron and Sarko were pushing for a tougher line. I went out on the bike before going to see PG. Still in a lot of pain. Also clear that Gail really needed her work to keep her going. He said she was the one taking it all hardest. Chatted away about me, him, politics, the kids. He was thin and often in pain but he still seemed up for the fight.

Saturday 12 March

The media was wall-to-wall earthquake. The *FT* ran a shortened version of my PR London article. I put the full version on the website. Off to Gains-borough for Aunt Jeanie's 80th. Mum pleased I went and it was a nice enough do, though the day somewhat extended by Rayan's car breaking down. I did manage to get a fair bit of work done on the diaries in the car though. Fiona and I having a laugh at her having said to Alison Farthing [Michael's wife], in response to 'What do you do these days?' 'I think.'

Sunday 13 March

Longish ride on the bike with Rory. Out for lunch with Grace then we went to see Kate [Garvey] and her baby, Ada. All her family there, lovely people. Kate loving *Dream School* but her dad had a good point – you wouldn't be allowed to do Dream Hospital!

Monday 14 March

The Guardian ran a big number on Germany and I blogged on the poll showing the Brits were least keen in Europe on the cuts and deficit reduction plan. Out to meet Ed V for breakfast and agree a plan for Volume 3 that would be less me out there and more a build-up to Volume 4. I wasn't sure how much more talking I could be bothered with on this. Then out to the Caledonian club to do #commschat, an interactive Twitter thing where PR people were putting in Qs as we went. Stayed there for the Labour fundraiser Calum had organised for the Scottish elections. GB and Iain Gray, Alistair D, Douglas A, Charlie F. I had shelled out ten grand for me and Fiona and took Clive Tyldesley [sports broadcaster] and his girlfriend Susan. GB spoke well. He had a good line about a school in his constituency saying you came to us on the way up and on the way down again. Iain spoke well too. Both on the theme of how this generation was not able to be as aspirational as previous ones because of the mood of cuts etc. but we had to get them that sense of hope. Nice enough evening and a lot of plaudits for Calum. GB very nice to him. Fiona was sitting with Alistair D who was writing a book and told her he was going to tell the truth re. GB.

Tuesday 15 March

Set off with Rayan for Burnley, finished Volume 4 in the car. Got to the ground at five for an event at which Fletch, Brendan, Philip the UCFB [University College of Football Business] chief executive, me and then Brian Barwick [UCFB chairman] were speaking. Telling school heads from the area what it was about. I did a big pitch about education as an exportable good, plus something new to put Burnley on the map. Nice little event. Over for dinner in the Bob Lord stand, then watched an odd match. 2–2 v Coventry. And we were lucky to get the point.

Wednesday 16 March

Sue Cameron had done her [*Daily Telegraph*] column on Jeremy Heywood [Downing Street permanent secretary] being unpopular in Whitehall because he failed to stop the 'enemies of enterprise' speech by Cameron and because Jeremy had been 'puffing himself up'.* I did a blog whacking her, whacking the mandarins for the way they used her, and defending Jeremy. Out to Fresh One [Jamie Oliver's TV production company]. They had produced a few good ideas and we chatted over them for an hour

---

* In a speech in Cardiff, the Prime Minister had promised to confront the 'enemies of enterprise' in the civil service.

or so. I suppose of all the things we had been chatting about, the one on helping youngsters get political was probably the best area. But I quite liked their idea of me doing a newsroom and at the end of the day having a live news bulletin. Roy Ackerman [managing director] said it was one of his crazier notions and would be expensive, but I quite liked it. I noticed there were no non-white people around and pictures of Jamie absolutely everywhere. I guess if they owed their job to him fair enough. We chatted over *Dream School*, some of the good bits and bad bits. I felt it was badly and oddly edited but Roy said it had been a nightmare because there was so much good stuff.

Then to Shoreditch House for a meeting with Michael Parkinson Jnr [TV director] who wanted me to think about a two-part series on the history of newspapers.

To Portland for a photo for their brochure, then to Knightsbridge to meet up with the Kazakhstan delegation on their roadshow. US had gone OK, they seemed to think. Nurian Yermekbayev [assistant to the President] the obvious leader of the delegation. Seeing the *FT* tomorrow so we talked a little on that.

Friday 18 March

At Natascha's charity dinner last night we met artist Tom Hammick, nice guy, Old Etonian who sends his kids to state schools. He wanted my books so I posted them off to him and family. He was sending woodcuts in return and – horrors – inviting us to Glyndebourne. The UN has pretty much agreed, with a few abstentions, a SCR [Security Council Resolution] re. Libya, really strong and pretty much as Cameron and Sarkozy had been pressing for. I watched Cameron's Commons statement and he was pretty impressive. Blogged to say so and got a fair few 'drops down in shock' tweets and comments at the straight support. It may be that Sarko is just doing it for domestic purposes – needing a good crisis etc. – but Cameron had a touch of the TB–Kosovo to him, even if he was stopping well short of ground troops. Long chat with Ed Balls on the Budget and coming on LBC when I guest-presented. He agreed to do it, said he liked engaging with callers. Said Ed M needed to be encouraged to take a few more risks and be less cautious.

We talked about how to tackle Osborne, who was getting himself a good profile on the right – big *FT* mag piece tomorrow seemingly really favourable for him. Ed said Osborne avoided debate and tried to keep his head down and build up a private following first. He sounded energetic and up for a fight. I made the point that most of his colleagues could walk down any street unrecognised. Douglas was doing pretty well on Libya, which was going to change the mood and dominate even Japan and the Budget for a while on the news and political agenda.

Saturday 19 March
Out on the bike then with Calum to Bristol, meet up with Syd [Young] and discussed Andrew [son] taking over publicity for the book. To the match. Poor. Lost 2–0. Syd laughing at people stopping to talk to me and sign programmes etc. Met a guy on the train who had come over from Seattle. Worked for the Washington State transportation department. Nice guy, married an American, fascinating on just how split the US was – e.g. Obama offers billions for high-speed rail and Republican states turn it down because it is from Obama (who was also not coming out of the Libya situation as well as Cameron). Maybe he didn't mind. There was a lot of 'this isn't Iraq' around. Later big row with Grace because some of her friends were smoking cannabis in the garden.

Sunday 20 March
In a bad mood all day because of the row with Grace, who wasn't speaking to me. Out on the bike, bit of work then blogged on the government not publishing an NHS poll which showed record satisfaction ratings, obviously because of the changes and investment made by us not them.

Monday 21 March
Worked on LBC programme planning while driving to Warwick for the Rethink staff conference. At the university – actually in Coventry not Warwick – fabulous setting. I was doing a session with a guy who was helping the Time to Change campaign advertising and Genevieve Edwards from Terence Higgins Trust who was excellent. The whole theme of the session was the impact of comms on charities. Lovely warm day. Fiona checking out a new car. Watched next *Dream School* with Grace and Nina. They were finding Jamie more and more irritating. Told some of his team their reaction but these guys get so defensive. Then I worked on a vlog for tomorrow re. mental health and HIV, charity comms and how Lansley was – according to anyone you talked to – refusing to engage on his reforms.

Tuesday 22 March
Out with Rayan to the FCO. Chris Greenwood was the mental health co-ordinator for their Disability Action Group and had asked me to speak

to staff there. Quite odd going back in. Spotted by a few journos who were asking if I was there to help out on Libya comms. They sort of needed it at the moment. Dissonant voices between military and political and between NATO countries. French reverting to type. Matthew Rycroft [diplomat] was chairing my session so we had a chat about Iraq memories, also how pressed they were now. He said he had never known so many emergency centres – NZ earthquake, Japan, AfPak [Afghanistan and Pakistan], Libya. Julian Braithwaite [former TB speechwriter] was about to do the Libya comms so at least he had the Kosovo experience behind him. Good turnout and I was on good form going over much the same ground as yesterday but much more personal and they engaged a lot. Quite a few came out as depressives.

Chris had a real hell story to tell, several lost days, suicide efforts etc. I signed him up for the LBC show tonight. Book signing then home for a bit before out for LBC. Matt Harris the producer said he was a bit alarmed how chilled I was. They were all asking if I was looking forward to it – a bit – and whether I was nervous – no. I liked radio but as I said to Nick Ferrari when he interviewed me this morning to promote the whole thing, I didn't wake up yearning to be on TV and radio. Maybe I had in earlier years. I watched the *Dream School* latest episode because I had Nana Kwame and Harlem coming on the show. Harlem had another tantrum in episode four. They did fine and one of the best calls of the night was a teacher coming on to say Harlem had a streak of brilliance but needed real anger management.

Ed Balls was on for the first hour and that was fine. OK calls and an OK chat but I still felt there was something missing in our economic narrative. Ed M had sent me his draft speech for tomorrow which was fine but still not strong enough. I worked on it a bit but I was not really in the zone. LBC were keen for me to do more, including a daily show, but I just did not want that level of commitment.

Wednesday 23 March

Budget Day. Out on the bike on a lovely sunny morning to deliver a letter to No. 10 for [government grid co-ordinator] Paul Brown's farewell. Then back to blog on mental health and watch the Budget. Osborne did OK with a bad hand but the truth is last year's Budget remains more important for the next year than this one. Ed M did OK but he has a few mannerisms he needs to iron out. Osborne was pushing growth but it was not good against a falling forecast background. That being said his side liked it well enough and media-wise they got enough out of the petrol cut even if it was just a penny. Out later to Paul Brown's farewell at Walkers. Lots of the old team there so nice to see them. I sensed they were not that happy with the new regime. Also met Craig Oliver [Downing Street director of communications]. Said I was always around if he wanted a chat.

Thursday 24 March

Blogged on the Budget and later re. [former England cricketer] Boycott's remarks re. Mike Yardy [Sussex and England spin bowler] leaving the World Cup because of depression.* Big response to the depression piece which was a tale of my involvement and hero worship of Boycs down the years then explaining how last-century he was in his attitudes to depression. Did a 5 Live interview on it in between doing a bit of writing. A lot of upcoming speeches. All afternoon at Random House working through Volume 3 with Sue Gray. Slightly fewer comments than last time. The Queen as ever her main worry, spooks second, civil service third. She said she found this one harder-going partly because it could be so repetitive. She said Richard Wilson was the only person to have complained so far. We took a couple of hours though she still had 200 pages to go.

Friday 25 March

Bike, blog, meeting with the bank and later to Southampton for a speech to 300 accountants. Speech went well and also a Q&A with advance questions which I whizzed through. But the auction was really tough. Got there in the end but not before giving them a real hard time for how tight they were.

Saturday 26 March

Fiona off on the anti-cuts protest march which alas later turned violent.† Ed M sent me his speech for Hyde Park which was OK but I warned him to be careful about all the references to the suffragettes and the civil rights marches. I saw from Twitter later that though he toned it down he kept in too much of the thought. Also said he had to be clear there would have been cuts under us too. To Heathrow Radisson for the Tigrent [property investment education company] conference. Nice crowd. Almost American and evangelical. I did twelve great people I knew and/or worked with – Bill

---

* Pundit Boycott had been highly critical of Yardy's performances for England without initially acknowledging that the player's depression had dictated his decision to return from Colombo.
† A violent minority attacked symbols of wealth including a luxury car dealer and upmarket food store Fortnum & Mason.

Clinton, TB, Mandela, Martin McGuinness, Bono/Bob Geldof [charity-supporting rock stars], Diana, Cathy Gilman, Tim Berners-Lee [inventor of world wide web], Jimmy Wales (none of them knew who he was but had heard of Wikipedia), Fergie, Lance [Armstrong] and Haile [Gebrselassie]. Really good Q&A as well, with a lot on development, breakdown, dealing with stress etc. Interesting event. Out in the evening with Fiona to [William Ellis School's] Old Elysians' dinner. Was dreading it but it turned out to be OK. I was the butt of a fair few cracks but all good-natured.

Sunday 27 March

There was a terrific atmosphere on the way to the Emirates, raucous Scots mixing with dancing Brazilians. The match was pretty good too. Neither side really played it like a friendly. Alex called at half-time, said he was watching it on ESPN in the States, but for some reason thought it was a recording and said: 'Who scored for us?' Someone had told him Brazil won 4–1. In fact they won 2–0, Neymar getting both. 'I tried to get him but they wanted 40 million.' Rayan picked me up after the match and we set off to Heathrow. Timings worked out pretty well, and once we had dinner, read a bit and took a pill, I was pretty much out for the night. SAA [South African Airways] not as bad as one or two had led me to believe, and I loved the tailfin camera which meant you got amazing views on the screens of the clouds as the plane flew.

Monday 28 March

I was met in Johannesburg by André Hübner, one of the CMO guys, and a close protection guy. André was tall, totally bald, and pretty switched on. His firm had been hired to help the SA GICS (government information and communication system) and the boss of that had gone and had been replaced by a black radical, from the black management forum, [Mzwanele] 'Jimmy' Manyi. The *Sowetan* front page had 'Dirty Tricks Boss' as its front-page headline, over a story on Jimmy planning for the government to publish its own monthly paper. He was saying it was needed because the press didn't report the truth about the government, also that he would brief ten things and they would focus on only one. I advised him to set it much more in the context of low internet access and the government's duty to communicate to its citizens.

I went to the hotel, a five-star place seemingly owned by the Gaddafi family, and the place I remembered from when we were here for the Sustainable Development Conference years ago.

Out to the conference centre for lunch with Jimmy and some of his team.

Also met André's partners, TK and a guy called Carlo. Over the visit we discussed ways of maybe getting Portland tied in with them. They were a small company but had some pretty big contracts and this was clearly one of them. They were clearly wrestling with some of the issues I had wrestled with in government – co-ordination, departmental silos, lack of professionalism, a demanding and largely negative media. There was also something of a clash between forces of change and forces of conservatism. I sat in for Jimmy's Q&A after his presentation and though there was a fair bit of support for him, there were a few spiky exchanges too. One woman from the Treasury called him condescending and said they knew how to do what they were doing. Then she stormed out when he called her 'young lady' and said the one thing worse than not knowing is not knowing that you don't know.

He was clearly not a guy to stand back. I said to him later, after he had a real pop at the hacks who attended the dinner, that he should not pick too many fights at once, something TB had once said to me. In fact the media guys at the dinner were pretty friendly, and though they were a bit alarmed about the idea for the paper, and about plans for a media tribunal, they seemed to understand the need for more professional comms. Neo, one of the Gics team, told the conference there was a trinity – policy, public service delivery and comms. They had done a presentation to the Cabinet who were signed up in the main to a more proactive strategy. Jimmy asked me to make an off-the-cuff reaction to what I had heard so I trailed some of the speech themes for tonight and tomorrow. Back to the hotel for a dire run (altitude and weight slowing me down). Egypt's footballers were there looking pretty sad after losing to SA. Then out again for the dinner. Chatted a lot with the guys from the Beeb, Al Jazeera, *The Guardian* and AP and they were pressing me to get the government to focus properly on plans for Mandela's death. It was un-African to talk about it too much but I did raise it in the context of the next really important step for the country to become 'normal', also the sheer media logistics were going to be enormous.

The problem was that nobody really knew who had responsibility – Presidency, GICS and the Mandela Foundation. They had been the ones saying nothing when he was hospitalised which had created a lot of problems. There had been a vacuum and nobody filled it. Nor was it clear how many foreign dignitaries were to be invited. But all would want to be there. It was an interesting challenge. I said I would be happy to advise on country branding post Mandela too. The dinner went well, though Jimmy and the deputy minister from the presidency did come at it a bit too much from the anti-press perspective. I pitched things very much in the context of major change, then did the ten-point leadership and strategy pitch. Went down well and Jimmy said he found it helpful. The Beeb and AP really bent my ear on the Mandela situation, and the need for someone to grip what happened when he died. Some lovely people there and as ever most people warm and friendly. The Libya situation was getting trickier and trickier. In but not clear how to get out.

Tuesday 29 March

Someone was clearly briefing against Jimmy. *The* [South African] *Times* had a front-page story saying lots of communicators had snubbed the event and it was 'poorly attended' (which it wasn't). But it was the backdrop and I could see they were a bit tense and defensive. I was doing a few interviews over the course of the two days and the general sense was that Jimmy had lost respect of the media, but I defended him, even defended his paper but put a different pitch on it to the one he had been putting. The interviews were broadly friendly but with the usual cynicism about government rather than media comms.

Breakfast with GICS and the PR team and I advised against defensiveness. Talked up team building. Then in for my session and a very long Q&A. Went fine. Good response. The British High Commission comms guy had been following my tweets and came down for a meeting to go over some of the issues. He felt the South Africans had screwed up the Mandela hospitalisation – everyone imagined he would die at home rather than go to hospital – and he was worried they would screw up the funeral too. They had got away with the World Cup but it was a close-run thing. Nice guy, also pushing for me to write stuff on the trip for some of the papers. They were trying to help push them in the same direction. He feared Jimmy was going to come under a lot of flak. André escorted me out to the airport on the Gautrain. I had enjoyed meeting and working with them and I was sure there would be plenty more opportunities to come from it. Meanwhile JoP was out in Astana again and the same old stuff was playing out really.

Wednesday 30 March

We arrived in the early hours. I had slept OK again thanks to the pills. Train and cab home and in between resting, catching up and writing a piece for the SA media, I got hooked on the India–Pakistan cricket World Cup semi-final. The word was more than a billion people were watching it. Brendan came round as the cricket was ending in a win for India and he, Fiona and I set off for PG's party. Good turnout and PG made a good speech, singling out Mike Griffin and the nurses, the Marsden guy, the girls and Gail. David M was there, looking a bit stressed I thought. He texted me afterwards to say we should meet, that he was busy doing things but politics was in the wrong place. Ed M not there – he and Justine had announced their wedding plans today.

Chatted to Ian McEwan re. his books and [his wife] Annalena's [McAfee]. He said he had heard I chose *Saturday* as one of my favourite books and had reviewed Annalena's *The Spoiler* favourably. 'Glad you spend all your time reading my family's books.' Nice chat with Andrew Cooper [Tory strategist]. He seemed fairly overwhelmed by the No. 10 job. He said Jeremy Heywood said to him the whole time 'No. 10 has not worked in a co-ordinated way since AC left'. He said the meetings were unwieldy and indecisive. I said at least your ministers seemed largely bound in. He rolled his eyes. He said that Cameron was energetic and lively but it was very hard to get strategy working. Tessa and David there – T was beginning her hacking case against the *NotW*. Matthew Freud and Liz M – she was the only Murdoch person I think. Nice do. PG looking happy.

Off for dinner with Brendan F. Richard Dearlove there with the ex-head of CIA clandestine operations and another CIA guy. Chatted a bit. Nice chat. Not sure what was happening re. Iraq inquiry. Richard said on Libya they could do with me going back in there to sort the co-ordination. Brendan on great form. He was pushing me to devise my own TV format and pilot it properly. He felt it was in the area of me speaking rather than interviewing. He also thought I should do stuff exposing the way the news works. He said hearing me talk about it had totally shifted his views of how the news bent the truth. He felt Ed had no chance at all and that even if the Tory cuts really bit, Cameron would get back. Ed didn't pass the threshold.

Thursday 31 March

Out first thing for Heathrow and the flight to Barcelona. Whacked off a blog re. Cameron cutting Lansley adrift. Obvious from the papers that he was going to take over and recast the whole NHS thing. Worked on the Barcelona speech on the plane. Arrived at a fabulous airport, lovely sunny day and as near as you'll get to a perfect day trip. To the W Hotel, lunch with Paul from Intel [American technology company] and Jennifer from Burson-Marsteller [global PR firm]. Helpful for the presentation which went well, as did the Q&A. They had warned me to expect a few tough questions but they didn't really come. James Carville [American political commentator] had done the speech last year and Paul said mine hit the mark better in terms of being able to touch all the nationalities, though I found myself weaving in a lot of American stories. Book signing then out for a run along the beach. Really wished I was staying over. Such a fabulous place. I had forgotten just how fabulous. But by half-five I was heading back to the airport for a delayed flight home. There were too few meals on the plane but a lovely half Scots-half Nepalese stewardess called Kishori sorted everyone out. I wrote a blog for tomorrow on how a day trip to Barcelona was better than any medication. Home by eleven.

Friday 1 April

Really tired. Too many planes this week and too much catching up to do on run-of-the-mill stuff. Dinner with Mick Hucknall and Gabriella at a packed Le Boudin Blanc. Mick noticed I had a couple of glasses of wine. Later he told AF who called me and warned against. Chatted a lot about *Dream School*. Also him saying rolling a joint for Keith Richards [Rolling Stones musician] was rock 'n' roll heaven. Nice food and nice enough time but I was too tired. Mick really down on Ed M – said he was unelectable and we had to make a move no matter what Cameron did.

Saturday 2 April

Donald in town for his bagpipe contest so after a bit of India v Sri Lanka World Cup final – India won later – I went to Horseferry Road [London Scottish Pipes and Drums HQ] and sat with him. He played well but didn't win anything and didn't seem on great form. Later out for dinner but he didn't seem in great shape.

Sunday 3 April

Grace had called in the middle of the night from the Royal Free having fallen off a wall. Fiona went and got her and neither of us were much in the mood for sympathy. I was livid with her, just the latest sign that all she really cared about was having a good time with her friends. I was out all morning filming on a BMX bike for a LLR video [to promote the bikeathon]. I was with a stunt man who was going to be doubling for me. He and I were dressed identically so they could pretend I was doing the stunts. Quite enjoyed it though it was really tough on the legs. No power to the bike at all. Filming by the London Eye where we did a start scene. Started to tweet out the idea that I was stunt riding which got a good pick-up. But the day was pretty grim for Mother's Day and as always F and I started out on the same pitch but ended way apart. By the time of what was meant to be a nice family dinner at the Camden Brasserie I was barely speaking to any of them. Calum was trying to jolly things along but without much success.

Not feeling good though. A mix of Donald clearly not in great shape and Grace messing around again cast me down.

Monday 4 April

Out early to do a pre-interview for the Piers Morgan *Life Stories* on JP. They had already done TB and family. Lansley was getting hung out to dry. Cameron effectively taking over and Lansley having to announce a 'pause' in the parliamentary process. All a bit silly but they were still getting away with way too much. The results came through from Kazakhstan. The majority was even bigger than ever and the OSCE were out pretty quickly saying the expected standards had not been met. They had not really taken our advice.

Tuesday 5 April

Clegg was going through another phase of being hammered. He was up and about on social mobility but got whacked when he admitted he got internships through his dad's connections, having said that kind of thing had to stop. He and Wayne Rooney were trending all day – Rooney because of the FA action against him swearing into a camera at West Ham. I worked a bit on the two speeches for the Royal Mail conference tomorrow. Out to see PG who had had a long chat with Calum at the weekend to see where we were on things. PG was in pretty good shape and was confident albeit realistic about his chances.

Wednesday 6 April

To ExCel [convention centre] in lovely sunshine for the Royal Mail conference. Blogged en route on Clegg subtly cutting across Cameron message but being united in out-of-touchness. I met the impressive newish chief exec, a Canadian, Moya Greene. She took me through the somewhat grim prognosis and also through the politics of it all, which I used for my first presentation to the top leadership team. Was on form both in speech and Q&A. Moya was raving about it and asked me to do the same speech when speaking to the bigger group – 800 or so – later. I stayed to watch her being interviewed by Jon Snow and she was pretty impressive. Out and about in the sun to work on the next speech. Left for Stamford Bridge. Dinner with Joe Hemani, his Icelandic friend Alex, a German, an Irish property guy and a couple of others. Greg [Nugent] my guest. Good game and good win for United. Home late to watch bits of it again. Good laugh with Godric re. my line at the conference – the postman is the medium, message and messenger coming together.

Thursday 7 April

Out on the bike to meet Molly Dineen [documentary film-maker], with her lovely daughter Maud, to discuss film ideas. Her daughter and friends were really into *Dream School*. Molly's youngest kids were at the same primary school as Cameron's and Gove's kids and she said it was like a form of apartheid round there. The only non-white kids were diplomats'. Nice to see Molly and maybe there was scope to do something with her on kids and politics. Home to work a bit on tonight's stuff where I was MCing the Transform rebranding awards. Too many awards. I had to whizz through them really sharpish. TB had seen Nazarbayev. He said it went fine. When we saw the presidential post-election address there was a lot of our message in there. But we would have to see if there was follow-through with detail. Massimov staying as PM.

Friday 8 April

Breakfast with Joe Cerrell from the Bill Gates Foundation. We talked about the need to change the prism on development issues from 'sick dying child – give us your wallet' – to something more rooted in values and a universal understanding on the need for change. Out to funeral of Gerry Mackenzie [switchboard operator from No. 10 who had died aged fifty-three] in W10. Not as many ex-colleagues as I expected. Cherie and Jonathan from our time. Nice service though the priest had a dreadful cough. Cherie singing lustily as ever. She and I had a very nice chat about the *Dream School* kids. She later asked us to a 'friends' dinner so she was definitely in a friendlier place. Out on the bike p.m., then started to get calls re. News International apologising over phone hacking, admitting liability in some cases, offering a compensation fund. I tweeted a few times re. why far from drawing a line it would mean the tough questions would be in even sharper relief.

Monday 11 April

Out first thing to do talkSPORT. Richard Keys and Andy Gray were doing a daily show and had asked me on to talk sport, depression, charity stuff. I guess talkSPORT is quite big in the football world but it is a big drop from Sky. They both seemed a bit down. We had a good chat on air, did Burnley, Fergie, mental health. Run home in searing heat.

Tuesday 12 April

Breakfast with Paul Hamann, independent TV producer. Another one keen to get me involved in stuff. Did a lot re. prisons and other public institutions. He had one or two half-decent ideas too. Later to Manchester U v Chelsea for the Champion's League match. United on form and did well [won 2–1, 3–1 on aggregate].

Wednesday 13 April

Up early and off to Liverpool for the RCN [Royal College of Nursing]. Going to be quite a big day because Lansley was due there later but was going to speak only to fifty or sixty, not the whole hall. I was invited to do mental illness but got into the general situation. Had some good lines on the reforms. Did my own story, campaigns, general attack. Got two standing ovations and a lot of people asking why I didn't stand for office. I think I should have done earlier. Maybe I still should. Am definitely drifting a bit again. Busy without being driven. Book signing went on for a good while, then did a few interviews including with Kay Burley [Sky News presenter]. Good response because I wouldn't take any bullshit. Back later to the news that Gareth Crockett, who was doing a big charity cycling-running event for LLR, had been killed in a road accident. I spoke to his dad in Belfast. Seems an old man had just ploughed into them and sent Gareth 60ft through the air. Dreadful. Did a blog in tribute.

Thursday 14 April

Mike White [*Guardian*] had a nice write-up of my speech yesterday. *Guardian* asked me to do a piece on the news that Catherine Zeta-Jones [actress] was being treated for bipolar. Did it and also did a bit of radio and telly through the day. I was in two minds about it. Good on one level but on another it kind of reinforced the idea that only special people not ordinary people got it. Did a blog on some of Cameron's recent utterances e.g. not enough blacks at Oxford, rules and regulations re. street parties, and he was sounding more and more like a cab driver, just spraying opinions around on different things. Slaven Marić trying to fix my Croatian media profile. Posters up in Zagreb but wanted me to do interview with Ana Muhar [Croatian journalist] who was recently in the papers [re. relationship] with Adrian Chiles. Met her at the Italian in South End Green. Really good laugh and liked her.

Friday 15 April to Friday 22 April

Set off with Fiona, Rory, Grace and Tyler [Chambers, friend] for Belgium.

Calum staying to work and also going to Scotland to help on the campaign. Good journey, nice house and we had fantastic weather all week. Rory and I out on the bike every day. Pretty tough hills. Grace working a bit but I still felt she needed to do more. I was proofreading Volume 3 which Fiona was convinced just set me back every time. Fergie on to me a couple of times, first to rant and rave about John Reid chairing a platform with Cameron on AV [alternative voting], then to say the cops had been in touch re. phone hacking. His QC was seeing them the day after the Newcastle match. Nice to be away for all the [Prince William–Catherine Middleton] wedding hype though there was a fair bit where we were. Slaven sent through funny pictures of the Croatia posters. Nice week. Unbelievable weather. Heatwave stuff. Back for the Friday.

Saturday 23 April

Off to Derby on my own. Calum in Scotland. Great match. 4–2 to us and the play-offs were back on after three wins in a row. Ed M called in the evening. He had done the media whack, calling for an independent media review. He was worried about Scotland and wanted me to talk to Iain Gray. The problem was we had neutralised each other on policy so it became about personality and Salmond was the bigger character. Ed sounding a bit more confident. He was keen to make it more about the economy and the idea that if Salmond got another mandate he would think he could go for independence.

Sunday 24 April

Bike with Rory. Blogged a spoof chat between Clegg and Cameron agreeing to attack each other to help Clegg. Cameron has him where he wants him. Emerged that TB and GB not going to the royal wedding 'because they're not members of the Order of the Garter' whereas Major is. Fucking ludicrous. Probably some kind of establishment revenge. But pretty petty and silly.

Monday 25 April

Calum was up in Scotland but Rory came with me to the Portsmouth match. Not a bad game but we dropped two points, which meant getting to the play-offs required us to win at Leeds and home to Cardiff and others to drop points. Rory was clearly making an impression with some of the Burnley guys. Brendan Flood asking for his number on the stuff he was doing with Opta [sports analytics company]. Gave Rory my credit card to book Olympic tickets. I was in for £6k worth by the end.

Tuesday 26 April

Out on the first train to Paris. A ludicrously hectic and voicebox-destroying schedule put together by left think tank Terra Nova. I worried about the organisation when we marched out to the Paris taxi queue – always a bad idea at Eurostar. I suggested the metro. To their offices on the Champs-Élysées. First up a meeting with bloggers. Quite helpful to get a feeling for the new media scene. Not as developed as ours I sensed. Of course the French media was so different anyway. Most media owners had other interests which relied on the state and so there was far less boat rocking. Then a rather hectic lunch with a dozen or so journos. More of the same. They felt Sarko could hardly go lower. And yet they felt he might win.

I was emphasising the need for the PS [Parti Socialiste] to unite behind whoever was chosen – it was looking like [Dominique] Strauss-Kahn [managing director International Monetary Fund] or [François] Hollande – and then get a proper disciplined campaign. Few of the journos seemed to think they would or could. Also DSK had a lot of private life baggage and nobody was sure if that would flare up. Meanwhile the buzz was that Carla was pregnant. Did a couple of interviews, one on Cameron, the other on France. My voice was going, and I slightly lost it when I saw they had put in more long interviews, including with France 24 who would need me to do it in both languages. Melissa Bell [international correspondent] made it rather more pleasant than most. Good-looking, good fun and her dad was Martin Bell [former MP and war correspondent] so we chatted a bit about that off camera while on camera it was the usual – TB, spin, Iraq and for the French-language version much more on their scene. My French held up fine.

I went to our Residence for a while and Tess from the media team asked me to go over and talk to them. Fair few French around though one was about to get the boot for a security breach. They too seemed to think Sarko was in real trouble but could win. Then out to the Mairie [city hall] in the 3eme, where I was doing a symposium. They had wanted a speech, but I asked to do interview and Q&A instead. Olivier Ferrand, president of Terra Nova, was doing the first Qs, with the mayor chipping in, not least re. 'les mensonges d'Iraq' [lies on Iraq]. Yet they still liked and rated TB and seemed to think I was talking sense on what the PS needed to do. To a dinner of major Terra Nova backers. Business, intellectuals, others. Nice enough. Short speech pre dinner, Q&A after. Knackered when I got back to the Residence around half-eleven. My sense was PS could win if they got their act together, but their instincts were all towards factionalism and backward-looking.

Wednesday 27 April

Slept badly for some reason. Breakfast with Peter Westmacott [UK ambassador]. He reckoned DSK would stand and Sarko would win. But it was too close to call. Le Pen was doing well. DSK was high in the polls because he was not there. If and when he announced he was going for it, most would fall in behind. But people were not sure he had the stomach or the skills for it. Sarko would fight hard. He thought Sarko had learned from some of his mistakes, but he did not do humility well. They were sure Carla was pregnant. He got on well with DC. When I asked whether he thought I should get engaged with the PS he said he was sure I had the right analysis but not sure I would have much effect. They are incapable of discipline. One of the points I had been making was that the French tended to have debates, vote to resolve, then start the same debate again. It was the same old faces, many of them around when I lived here in the '70s.

Peter was quite interesting on Cameron. Born to rule. Impetuous. Not warm and cuddly. Clegg a hard sell to the French. Osborne even less cuddly but determined. Hague – there had definitely been a time when people felt he was losing it but he was now a lot better. Chatted a bit re. TB, GB. He was due to leave soon for Washington. Peter very gossipy as ever. He was due to do lots of royal wedding interviews but rather at a loss what to say. Off to a meeting with Pierre Moscovici [assembly member] at the National Assembly. He seemed quite down. Looked tired. Agreed that Sarko not to be underestimated and DSK had weaknesses as well as strengths. He was adamant I had to get my diaries into French because he felt the PS needed to see what work and discipline really was. When I said he seemed more down than I expected he said it was his background. Outside these four walls he would say they would win. But he was very down on Martine Aubry [PS secretary]. Painted a picture of her sitting at party HQ talking to nobody and doing nothing. Worked on a blog on the way back, the carriage half full of drinking, fat, rich, noisy Russians.

Cameron has said 'Calm down, dear' to Angela Eagle [shadow Chief Secretary to the Treasury] in the Commons which was going big, alongside poor economic figures. Ed M was on again, asking me to help Iain Gray in Scotland. Iain was bright and nice but couldn't punch through the screen in the way Salmond could.

Thursday 28 April

Cameron's 'Calm down, dear' jibe at Angela Eagle was getting a lot of play. Did a blog pointing out that the real significance was that once again it showed how easily needled he is on the NHS. Went to collect Mum with

Rayan and send her on her way to Tunbridge Wells [to visit relatives]. We had our usual argument about the royals. I was feeling more anti than ever as a result of the TB–GB non-invitation. Lots of different theories – Charles because of hunting ban, William because TB revealed details of private conversations in his book, Camilla because she doesn't like us. Idiotic whatever. It wasn't getting big play but it was one of those things people would remember. To Camden Brasserie to see Slaven and plan next week's Croatia trip. He said my visit was going to be a big deal because people didn't go to Croatia for this kind of thing much. Alex called after getting back from Spain where he had watched the Madrid–Barcelona match. Ugly game. We chatted about the Scottish campaign which was definitely going backwards. Salmond had risen to the campaign whereas Iain Gray had fallen away.

Into town to meet Jeremy Heywood at the ICA which was a bit crowded so we found a hotel nearby and had a couple of hours chatting over stuff. On the wedding snub he said it was very much the royals. Cameron and Osborne both went ballistic, said it was a bad error, worried they would get the blame. They have little time for GB but respect TB – they call him 'the master' – and in any event it would reflect badly on everyone. Cameron was worried if people thought it was his decision they would see it as spiteful and petty. Jeremy had called the Palace and asked what was going on but once it was out there they had decided and that was it. He said the whole Cameron team were pretty much obsessed by the TB operation. They respected TB, Peter and me and learned a lot from what we did. Jeremy had even floated the idea of them asking me in to help on Libya comms. He said he had said I was the only person who had ever managed to get the integration needed for this kind of thing. They were interested but in the end still saw me as a tribal Labour person they couldn't really trust on the inside.

I had floated with Craig Oliver the idea of my 'grilling the coalition' TV series. Jeremy liked it. But Craig emailed saying he couldn't see it. He couldn't see the Tory ministers going for it. Jeremy was clearly enjoying himself. He felt Cameron was not warm or cuddly but he was straight to work for. He delegated a lot. He was comfortable in his own skin and not scared of decisions or challenges. He said he had been genuinely impressive in getting the US to move on Libya. He worked hard, did a couple of hours on his boxes before coming down to the office and he was good at getting his head around tricky issues. Clegg was a bit battered but had realised resilience was all he had now. The Lib Dems surely realised they had nowhere else to go. He was not sure what [Chris] Huhne [Energy and Climate Change Secretary] and Cable were up to. Huhne was not impressive but didn't realise it. Cable was always a bit miserable so hard to tell. Hague had definitely lost his mojo at one point but seemed to have got it back.

Cameron and Osborne – he talked of them as a couple a lot – did not really rate Ed M. They were also not convinced about Balls and even though he was a good attack politician, it wasn't enough. We chatted a bit re. TB–GB and what they were up to. He was thinking about whether to move on fairly soon. He didn't quite know to what. Good to see him. He was clearly feeling better used, but also less frantic, than under GB. But they still did not have the right systems. Also Coulson was clearly important to Cameron and it was not easy for [Craig] Oliver to slot in but he was doing pretty well. Stopped off at the ICA bookshop, picked up a royal wedding sick bag, which were apparently selling well.

Friday 29 April

Royal wedding day. It was a pretty amazing spectacle though the bad taste re. TB–GB was even worse when you saw e.g. Boris Johnson, Douglas Hurd [former Tory Foreign Secretary], Mr and Mrs Ken Clarke, [Jeremy] Hunt etc. Fiona and Grace, joined by the Bridges and the Lownes [family friends], were loving the people and the clothes watching. Becks looked like Brad Pitt [film actor]. The couple did fine. Pippa the sister stole the show. By the end of the day thousands had joined a Pippa Middleton Ass Appreciation Society on Facebook. I knocked off a quick blog on the NHS, Howard Stoate [Labour MP] having said Cameron misused his views when he was telling Angela Eagle to calm down.* The media were in full arse-lick mode on the wedding. How different would politics or other walks of life be if they had the same approach. Out on the bike then back for a little street party organised by Victoria [Bridge, next-door neighbour]. Nice enough do. The crowds for the wedding had been enormous. Nobody could say it was anything but a success but their true colours had been shown by the guest list.

Saturday 30 April

Grace's birthday but she let me off to go to Leeds v Burnley. Good crowd and atmosphere, but we lost one–nil which meant play-off hopes were over. Drove up with Calum and back with Rory. They both seemed a bit down at the moment. Calum was also badly back on the booze and yet seemed to

---

* Cameron had quoted a *Guardian* article by Stoate, a doctor, taking out of context remarks about GPs and the NHS, when Angela Eagle intervened. Stoate responded in print, telling the Prime Minister to 'stop using the health service as a political football'.

accept it wasn't great for him. Back for Grace's birthday and then she went out, all glammed up with her mates. Hard to believe she was seventeen.

Sunday 1 May

Someone had put an unpleasant piece of graffiti on the wall at the end of the road. 'The blood is on your hands Mr C' in large black letters. Fiona was pretty unfazed but Grace was quite upset by it. I called Theo Blackwell [local councillor] who reported it and they said they would get rid of it soon. Fiona convinced it must have been someone who saw me at the street party and hadn't known before that I lived there. It was just another little sign though that we were out and a new crowd was in. It was I think the first time anything like that had happened. Demos yes but direct graffiti references like that no.

Off to Banbury to the Heseltines at Thenford. He had invited us after our lunch and though we knew we would be out of the political comfort zone I always liked both of them and it would be interesting to see the house and the garden. Far grander than anything I expected. The house was visible from a fair distance, dominant. The garden was remarkable. Three thousand different trees and shrubs. Different styles of garden within garden. Some extraordinary sculptures including a huge one of Lenin. He had the Gummers [Lord [John] Gummer, former Tory Environment Secretary, and wife Penelope] and the Ryders [Lord [Richard] Ryder, former Tory minister and BBC vice-chairman, and wife Caroline] staying for the weekend. The Gummers, particularly the wife, were cold. The Ryders were warm and friendly. I had always got on with Richard when he was Chief Whip. He was now chairman of a Cancer Institute and invited me to see their leukaemia work. We all went for a walk after coffee and à view of the cartoons which lined a whole three-storey staircase. I so wish I had bought more over the years.

They had a butler, a fair few staff, a biggish team of gardeners, horses, pool, lake, lovely views, a bust of Hezza in the hall, paintings of them, lots of other top paintings, the butler calling him My Lord and her My Lady, dogs, and one clearly besotted with him. As Fiona said they behaved more aristocratic than the aristos. She asked to go for a pee and thought she had taken a wrong turn because the loo looked like a throne not a loo. Some fabulous artefacts everywhere. 'Oh, we got that from India... Malaysia... Wherever.' One statue of an elephant weighing twenty tons. Trees 50ft tall driven from India. There were some seriously posh people at the lunch. A couple real plums in mouth. [Lord] Bernard Donoughue [academic, former Labour politician] there with Sarah. Andrew Knight [journalist, businessman] who agreed Rebekah was in trouble over phone hacking.

An artist, but mainly country toffs. I chatted mainly to Anne [Heseltine] and to a woman called Sally who was totally into *Dream School*. Anne was really interested in Calum because they had a grandson with dyspraxia. Rupert [son] was running Haymarket [media company].

Hezza said it was all very odd having a pass and a government office again. He was doing a job for Cameron and Clegg at BIS [Department for Business, Innovation and Skills]. Anne interesting on his dyslexia. His family had always frowned on books. He was not a big reader because he saw words letter by letter. In government he had always asked officials for verbal explanations of written papers before reading them. Fiona was up with Hezza and Andrew for lunch. Lovely food, nice time even though it meant missing the Arsenal–Man U match. Hezza seventy-eight, wife seventy-seven. He said he wanted his legacy to be his trees and his garden. He said only PMs really got remembered, and not many of them, but he had his politics and this. When he was in the garden he forgot everything else.

He felt Cameron was doing OK. Ryder really didn't rate Clegg. They both thought it a really bad mistake by the royals to snub TB and GB. Nice day. Fiona enjoyed it. Molly [dog] had a good walk. One of the other guests asked me, 'Do you really think we're that bad?' In the main, yes, I said. Hezza said my problem was I believed things. He didn't want me to sign the visitors' book though and said, 'You won't tell anyone you came, will you?!' He couldn't remember Labour people there before. 'Someone who was married to someone called Myra. Bernard didn't count! Did Roy Jenkins?' And so on. Day trip to a different world.

Monday 2 May

I was woken by a call from the Beeb asking if I would do stuff on Bin Laden being dead. Obama had announced it in the early hours. He had been tracked down via intelligence about a courier to a compound near a military garrison. Seals in helicopters had stormed it, killed him and three others. The phone went again and again but it didn't really need me, they were just looking for anyone to fill space. Obama was pitch-perfect tone-wise when he announced it, and I did a blog to say so, but that didn't stop quite a lot of 'USA, USA' and even 'four more years' triumphalism in the States. It was a big coup for him. When they announced the body had been buried at sea the conspiracy theories started but there was no getting away from it as a big moment and a big success for Obama. Amazing pictures of him and his national security team watching the raid live in the situation room. What a thing to be involved in, especially for the servicemen.

The story unravelled a little as the day wore on but the basic topline was they had found where he was and had gone in and killed him. Cameron sounded half asleep when he did a little doorstep. It was one of those rare events that would dominate every media outlet in the world. Interestingly there was very little outpouring on the Arab street, presumably because the Arab spring had delivered change they were interested in – freedoms, democracy – and not violence. It would have been different even a little while back. Went to collect Mum who had had lovely time at Tunbridge Wells and was now staying with us for a bit. Took her and Audrey to see [AC nephew] Jamie Naish's flat over in Leyton and I went out on the bike to get a look at the Olympic site. Took a bad turning and ended up on the A12 which was like a motorway. The buzz now was that it was William who blocked TB because he had revealed confidences about the Diana death week. Rory and Jamie round for dinner then watched part 2 of *Exile*. Terrific TV. Jim Broadbent as a man with Alzheimer's was incredible. I said to the kids they must put me down if I am like that.

Tuesday 3 May

Wall to wall Bin Laden of course. A lot of questions for Pakistan and how much they knew about where he had been based. Cameron did a statement which was fine. But domestic politics quickly back in the frame after the Tories leaked that Huhne had really gone for Cameron and Osborne over the nature of the AV No campaign. I did a blog finally swinging round to Yes and saying I felt a bit sorry for Clegg who was taking all the hits. To Fleet St for a meeting with Maurice Duffy [businessman] and Liz Mellon [business educator] re. Rio Tinto Zinc. Maurice had set the whole thing up, rightly said he was worried I would get bored with consultancy. My problem was in my head I felt as big as or bigger than people I was advising. If you have done PMs and other top political people it is hard to get excited by this, he said.

I did get excited by the next task – going to Comic Relief's grants committee with Sue Baker from Time to Change and doing a pitch for continued funding for the campaign. We had a problem in that the money – £4 million-plus – was dependent on a £16 million government slab of cash going in too and it was not certain we would get it. I worked up my script and I think we did well. I made the point that they would probably find it easier to fund services and that seeing attitudes change was not easy. But I felt it was working and with tough times there was a risk it all went backwards. The questions were all pretty helpful and friendly. Kevin Cahill, clearly supportive, asked me to talk about my own mental health situation. We also said we should co-operate on programming re. mental illness. We were in there for twenty-five minutes and Sue quickly got feedback they would recommend to the trustees that they continue to fund it. A lot of them said they had noticed the campaign and were sure it was working. I felt on form and Sue was thrilled with it after.

Wednesday 4 May

Calum off to Edinburgh to help the last push in Scottish elections. It was not going to be good. We went round to Kalendar to have breakfast with Grace, Jessie [Mills] and Tessa. Jessie really motoring in her career now. Tessa still trying to be low profile on her connection. On for £100k in the phone hacking. She said of the News Corp people: 'The more I have seen the more I see how evil they are.' Lovely message from Emma Freud re. Comic Relief. She said she heard I had been brilliant which I took as a signal it had got the OK. The problem now was going to be the government because Comic Relief would only do it if it had the bigger Department of Health funding.

Cab to Paddington. A lovely Ghanaian driver who said I had inspired him when a journalist to get into politics and now he was active in the party etc. It was interesting how muted the street reaction to Bin Laden's death was. Marginalised by the Arab spring. Off to Croatia, Zagreb via Rijeka. Looked lovely from the air. I was working on the hours of speeches I was doing tomorrow. I don't think I had ever had an event with so much speaking in one day. Effectively going to be talking for eight hours. Met by Slaven Marić and Mario Krtalić [media producer], who was the conference organiser. They had certainly promoted it. Billboards and four big TV spots. First off to a bank to lobby for sponsorship for their Youth Sport Games. Then to the Westin, where I was staying, for a meeting with a couple of people from the embassy who gave me a good background briefing.

Interestingly the UK was felt to be anti-Croatian compared with e.g. Germany. Denis MacShane had come out recently saying that we had never been keen on their accession to the EU. Also, there was very little ministerial through traffic. Ken Clarke had been recently and that went well but on the political side there were problems. Domestically they had major issues of economic sluggishness, dreadful corruption – though with a former PM [Ivo Sanader] facing jail they were getting a strong message through – and lack of any clear strategy. We discussed what they might do to get the UK in a better place on it all. Then to a meeting with a group of economists from the opposition. The banker had complained at the lack of clear strategy from the government and yet these guys were scared to spell out a proper plan. I tried to persuade them the route was open to a party being straight about problems and challenges ahead, but they didn't buy it.

Then to a meeting with four women who said they were my groupies – a professor of politics who said she told all her students I was a genius. Two of her ex-students now in PR who were involved in promoting the event.

It was a bit odd the extent to which I was seen as a big thing here. Also, while there I was called by the Slovenian PM [Borut Pahor] who asked if I would go and help him. He said everyone in politics in this region liked my style and would love to have me onside. I agreed to go out there. Also got calls in from Hungary and Macedonia. Dinner at a nice fish restaurant. Joined by deputy mayor and his daughter and ex-Real Madrid footballer and director Predrag Mijatović. He had come for the conference and had a mind way beyond football, though we did talk a lot of sport. Had a huge suite complete with jacuzzi and sauna so not having been able to have a run I sweated it out for half an hour. The buzz from Scotland was really not good. AV was a clear No as well. The only silver lining for us in that was that the pressures on the coalition would grow.

Thursday 5 May

Out early for a run, first through town and then found a lovely hilly park and did a half-decent trot around. Beautifully clean and nice sculptures around. Met Marija, the TV anchor who was hosting the event, with Milica, one of the self-styled 'groupies' who had been doing the PR. Also had to do a few interviews and a meeting with a woman campaigning for the rights of 350 deaf-blind people in Croatia. She had two full-time sign translators with her. Impressive. She said they had no rights and little support from the government. The life of a guide must be extraordinary, especially as she travelled everywhere with two of them. The event was well organised and staffed by a host of stunning women. I was in for three long sessions – first off strategy for leaders, second winning over the media, then finally crisis management and then a Q&A. I was on form but the voice and body did tire through the day.

Also had a lunch with the sponsors so no respite from talking. Slaven kept slipping in quick meetings with sponsors, Mario slipped in interviews, so I was totally shagged by the end of it all. Then right at the end – two more interviews 'just five minutes' which turned out to be twenty, then a meeting. Out for dinner with some of the same guys as yesterday plus Ana Muhar, who had interviewed me in London and showed me the old town today. Ana had been at the conference and said she needed her own OST (objective, strategy, tactics) session. Didn't get back till late and with a 6 a.m. departure for the airport I was starting to worry re. tiredness. Pedraj really nice and invited me to take the boys to Real Madrid to see how things worked there.

Friday 6 May

Up at six, off to the airport, reading the media brief on elections. OK in

England, good in Wales, dire in Scotland and AV a big No on low turn-out. At Gatwick, I did a blog effectively praising Salmond as having won because he was the only one with a clear strategy. It was all about leadership and direction and he had both. Jack McConnell [former Labour First Minister of Scotland] was the first person I bumped into at the airport. 'What the fuck!' we both mouthed. As the results came through it was clear we were talking about an earthquake. The Nats were heading for a majority. Nice guy called John drove me to Inverness. He was asking me about my depression and then said he got it. His son had devised a new self-help method and written a book. Loved the scenery on the way. I was staying at a hotel just out of town and went for a not-bad run, including a wicked hill. There had been a cock-up with the publisher, so the books were stuck in Birmingham, but the event itself went really well. Nice crowd. Got an interesting briefing on the University of the Highlands and Islands and their use of teleconferencing. Did a speech setting Salmond against my ten points for leadership and scored him well.

Saturday 7 May
Out for a run, breakfast, then a blog on conventional wisdoms, and suggesting the latest one – that SNP win did not mean support for independence – might be wrong too. One commenter said I should go for MSP seat. Train down through amazing scenery to Edinburgh then Newcastle. Rayan met me at Newcastle then we set off for Hexham. Lovely little place and the festival event was OK. Sold out, lively, even the Iraq questions were quite friendly e.g. how did you prepare for Chilcot? It was a standard interview then Q&A and went pretty well. The journey back was a bit of a nightmare. Two diversions off the A1. Home by three.

Sunday 8 May
Out on the bike for the first time in a while. Felt good. I think the runs had helped. Did another blog on Scotland. Can Scots in England vote in a referendum? United beat Chelsea which virtually guaranteed the title. Dinner at Charlie F and Marianna's. Lovely as ever. Good to catch up – wedding blah, coalition, TB – Charlie felt he was not in great shape and travelling too much.

Monday 9 May
All day at the Cumberland Hotel chairing and speaking at a Blackswan conference on innovation. Nice buzz at the end. To a meeting with Paul

Hamann [TV producer] who had got *Panorama* interested in me doing a film on alcohol. Watched his Strangeways Prison doc on ITV which was excellent.

The coalition first anniversary was looming and there was a lot of talk of them really falling out. Did a blog warning them not to imagine people cared too much about the emotionalism of it all. Rory wasn't feeling great so took him to the GP before heading for LLR. Did a Bulgarian radio interview then an hour pep talk with Cathy's leadership team, then Beeb on disability benefit changes, then to Random House for a meeting on volumes 3 and 4. *TBY* was still outselling the full volumes. They seemed happy enough that they would become classics and tick over, but we agreed a change of covers to differentiate. Worked on [former cricketer Ian] Botham's Ashes event, having been asked to chair the discussion at a film premiere, then out for dinner with Calum before heading to the Curzon Mayfair. Good banter with Beefy [Botham] and a nice chat with David Gower [commentator, former England captain]. Really likeable guy. Bob Willis [former cricketer] seemed quite cold and unfriendly. Discovered later he was a real Tory and very anti-us so turned it into a fair bit of banter in the Q&A.

Interesting that two cricket films had come out in the same week – *Sachin* and *Fire of Babylon*. Great chat with Mike Atherton and Mike Selvey [journalists, former players]. Both good blokes. I chaired the Q&A with Botham, Gower, Willis and James Erskine who made the film. Out for dinner with Botham and family. His mother-in-law had voted Labour for the first time ever. Liam Botham's fiancée Emma Sayle was interesting – ran something called Killing Kittens – effectively orgnanised parties in which women decided the action. She called it parties for the sexual elite. Always more women than men. Men not allowed to approach women, always in nice venues with loads of beds. She said the name came from a legend that every time a woman masturbated a kitten died. In between all that we talked Pakistan, coalition, Bin Laden, and lots of other stuff. Botham said that it was odd how we disagreed on virtually everything but got on really well. Another late night.

Blogged on sport and leadership based on the film last night. Call from Macedonia opposition leader re. her upcoming election. Sounded tough environment. Suggested 'the courage to change' as her main thing. She wasn't totally sure. She sounded pretty clued up about how to go about it but the government had a fair amount of grip. Paul Allen round with a guy, Paddy, who runs an addiction treatment centre in Ireland and is trying to get UK firms to use it. Good chat. Out to the Emirates for a speech to a university venue marketing conference. To TBO for a meeting with some of King Abdullah's people in advance of a TB meeting with the King tomorrow. We emphasised they had to have a big strategy.

Out to the Sport Industry Awards with Ruth Turner [TBO]. Went on too long but some good people there. Clive [former rugby coach] and Jayne Woodward, Andrew Strauss [England cricket captain] smaller than I imagined, Jackie Stewart [former Formula One driver], Jimmy Anderson [Burnley-born England cricketer] – chatted about Burnley – Tanni GT, Denise Lewis [former athlete]. Almost 2k people there. Also had a good chat with [sports minister] Hugh Robertson. He lacked presence but had enthusiasm. Home late again. Need to watch tiredness. Read PG's cancer piece. Very powerful.

Thursday 12 May

More bad figures on the economy yesterday, and with the coalition also looking a bit fractious, I blogged on the notion that both economic and political planks of the strategy were weakening. The problem of course was that there was little sense of us filling the gap. I was getting a lot of negative comment on Ed pretty much wherever I went. There was a tone to the question 'Do you think he is doing a good job?' that left a negative answer in the air unsaid. Off to Blackburn with Rayan for the opening of a new Enterprise Centre at St Mary's College, and then a dinner at Ewood Park.

We were halfway there when first Nick Watt and then others started to call about new evidence published by the Iraq inquiry. John Muir at the Cabinet Office was pissed off they hadn't forewarned me and so was I. It was basically a letter from a former defence intelligence guy, Major General Michael Laurie, saying that contrary to my evidence they DID believe the dossier was the case for war. It would no doubt spark a frenzy but I decided to say nothing. Later I tweeted simply to say I had nothing to add to my evidence, that the dossier was not the case for war, but the case for why the government was more concerned re. WMD, and that I had never met Laurie.

The whole thing felt totally political. The Beeb of course were ramping it and so would the papers, left and right. If you read the transcript it was pretty clear he only had hearsay and pretty second hand at that. The worry was that having seen what happened to Hutton, who stuck to what he actually thought based on the evidence, Chilcot would feel he had to go with the media mood. I spoke to some of my usual people but they felt I should ignore. Some, however, notably Charlie F and PG, felt we made a mistake in vacating the field. Fiona said the *Mail* turned up at the house so they were clearly going to gear up for it.

The school was terrific. Sarah Flanagan [assistant principal] had got me there and was a real bundle of energy, and the head had a nice dry sense of humour. I did a Q&A with history students. Lots from Burnley, 60 per cent on EMAs [Education Maintenance Allowances]. Bright kids though. Then the formal opening and then to play a four-a-side football match with teachers. Played badly. Had a cup of tea with a guy who had brought in a big folder of Burnley memorabilia and was chatting to him before we headed to Ewood [Park, Blackburn Rovers stadium]. Nice crowd. Getting battered by Burnley fans for being there at all. My table had no Rovers fans. Laurie going pretty big on the news but Fiona's view was people would see it for what it was. It came up in the Q&A but I just batted it off. I was quite keen to engage but John Muir was strongly of the view it would backfire with the inquiry. Did OK with the books, auctioned a Rovers ball wearing rubber gloves, Q&A all the usual. Best question was 'Osama bin Laden or Owen Coyle?', which I played for laughs. I was reading PG's cancer book which was excellent, and making edit comments. Home by two.

Friday 13 May

Charlie was really strongly of the view I should engage, or get others to do so. The *Mail* was its usual, *Indy* and *Guardian* both did on the front and the problem with my tweet denial and no more was, he felt, that it looked like we were vacating the field and effectively accepting the story against us. It was also so annoying the extent to which, after TB, it was me rather than the politicians, spooks or military who was the most in the firing line. John Muir still felt best to stay out of it, though he did write to the inquiry asking why I had not been forewarned. They were supposed to tell any high-profile witnesses likely to be mentioned in papers put on the website. They were clearly becoming a law unto themselves.

John was clear TB was going to be criticised but he had not heard if I would be or not. Chilcot had announced he would not be publishing until the autumn, so the whole thing was just dragging on. I spoke to TB who felt the Laurie thing was irritating but not important. But I worried he was being a bit blind to things, vacating the field in a way that was dangerous to his reputation if he was not careful. I chatted to Charlie, Philip and Godric and eventually did a short blog, in which I posted my evidence. Looking at the press it was obvious if you read it that it wasn't that big a deal but my worry was whether these people would be as strong as Hutton.

To the ICA to meet Craig Oliver. He was pretty open and expansive, and seemed to welcome a chat with, as he put it, 'someone who knew what a nightmare it was'. He agreed that they got a fairly easy ride but that it might change. He felt Clegg had been the punchbag, but it would not last for ever. DC was not thinking about cutting him loose. I said I felt they were both making a mistake in concentrating too much on the mechanics and the emotionalism of the coalition. I sensed DC did not think much of Huhne or Cable. He also did not push back on the notion that Obama was less outward-looking than Clinton or even Bush. Libya had been a real struggle. Even just before it was announced they got UN backing it was looking very unlikely. Craig was enjoying it but said it was hard to get the right balance between strategy and co-ordination on one hand, and tactics and media management on the other. He had pretty quickly moved from seeing the broadcasters as a good thing to being a pretty major pain. It was the trivialising that got him down and the inability to think beyond the story of the day. E.g. when Cameron did one year on interviews all they cared about was that day's non-event flurry re. something David Willetts [universities and science minister] had said which was spun out of context.

He said Osborne was in Downing Street a lot and it was a genuinely close and positive relationship. He was quizzing re. TB–GB. He had read the diaries and felt what really came through was how it never stopped, that you occasionally got a bit of breathing space and then it went so quickly. He said Cameron was good at rest and staying calm but he accepted he was beginning to look like he could lose his cool in the Commons. They didn't seem to rate Ed though. Departmental co-ordination was another issue where we seemed on much the same page. Just hard to get the obvious done. I pressed him on the grilling the coalition idea but he felt DC would see it as too much like setting himself up. I made the case for doing it and he said he would try to find a moment when he wouldn't dismiss it out of hand. But I doubted it would happen. We agreed to meet up periodically and I said though I would always whack the Tories hard if he ever felt like picking my brains he could do so in total confidence.

Saturday 14 May

Big day on the football front with United needing – and getting – a point at Blackburn to win the title, then City v Stoke Cup final at Wembley. Pinsent Masons [law firm] had given me a box for use by LLR and I headed there with Emma and books and met a group of corporate lawyers etc.

All OK. I did the usual spiel and we raised a few grand. Terrific location. One tier up from the royal box with my seat directly behind Cameron who was there as guest of the FA. His Special Branch guys had a real laugh when they saw me, as did the young woman looking after him. They must have texted him I was right behind him because at one point he looked around and up, spotted me and did a little half wave which everyone in our box spotted. Emma laughing, saying she loved the way I waited for him to wave first. The match was OK and the better team won, one–nil to City, though the Stoke fans were terrific. Rare to see the losing fans wait for the presentation.

Out for dinner with Clive Tyldesley and Susan at Fratelli la Bufala. He was interesting on the Lawrie stuff. Felt everyone would see it for the bollocks it was. But he felt I was better off not being close to Labour any more. He felt Ed was not up to it, was not going to win and the good side of my reputation was about me, and the bad side was about my role with the party. He could see why I had gone back to help GB but he felt it was bad for me that I had been back in there right to the end. Perhaps he was right. I certainly didn't feel too much like getting more involved than I was, but it was so frustrating the whole bloody thing.

Sunday 15 May

Woke to news that Dominique Strauss-Kahn had been arrested in New York and was going to be charged with attempted rape. Even though it was a shock I had felt his sexual predatory instincts would be a problem. I had asked Pierre Moscovici and Olivier Ferrand if the sex stuff would become an issue and they had thought not. But now this was unignorable, and basically he was finished. Even if it turned out to be a set-up it was impossible to get back from this. I did a blog saying that the hugely unpredictable French elections just got more unpredictable. There was also of course the IMF angle which was just as significant. And there would no doubt be others who would come out of the woodwork against him. Set off up the M1 to meet Mum and Graeme Naish [AC nephew] and then on to Middlesbrough, where I was playing in a charity match. Good laugh on the way. Graeme can talk for ever. The match was to raise funds for ex-Burnley and Boro fullback Gary Parkinson who had 'locked-in syndrome'. We got to the Riverside and learned early on that the Boro XI was made up of former and even current pros. We only had four proper players.

Tony Mowbray [former Middlesbrough player] was our manager and his team talk was basically 'they're good, you're shit, don't humiliate yourselves'. Amazingly we held out for seventy minutes. I played left back for the whole of the first half and the second half of the second half and did

OK. Saw off Stuart Ripley who used to be bloody quick. Mowbray said at half-time I thought you'd be dire and you weren't. Nobody mentioned the inquiry stuff all day. There were a few boos but mainly of a panto villain nature. Nice nosh after then home. Texted Alex to ask if the scouts had been there to see me rip Ripley. Why do you always mark shit players? he asked. One really sad moment. Marlon Beresford [ex-Burnley player], who was brilliant in goal for us, told me his brother, whom I met so many times at matches, had died. Back to stay overnight at Mum's.

Monday 16 May

Up early and off to Loughton to do the *Football Focus* head-to-head play-off with [Lord] Alan Sugar [business magnate]. We had come joint top in their predictions game, and this was to be the decider. Dan Walker [presenter] and his team already there. I had got Rory and Cam on the case and we were pretty sorted. Sugar had a few predictions the same but I reckoned I was OK. Sugar quite mellow and we had a good laugh including when going over stuff like West Ham's relegation, Spurs' season and then re. Alex. Sugar asked what the prize was and Dan said a seat on the sofa in Manchester, to which he said he wasn't going to win then – I could have it. Good laugh and would make OK TV.

Dinner with Tom Baldwin at the Camden Brasserie. The Ed M operation all sounded a bit dysfunctional. Shadow Cabinet not really onside and not motoring. Balls and Cooper had slowed up. John Healey saw himself as a leadership contender. Douglas constantly offside. Ed lacking in confidence. The office team weak, still lacking a clear chief of staff figure. Meetings taking for ever not to decide things. I did a bit of basic strategy but he did seem a bit at the end of his tether. I asked the core strategy and it was all a bit vague, lacking in edge and clarity. The place he seemed most comfortable with was the future and also optimism which at least had the makings of something. I wondered, however, if the public had largely made its mind up and whether Ed might see that.

Tuesday 17 May

Off to Fowey. Long train journey so caught up on a fair bit of work. Picked up by Kate who was running the festival. Off to the Old Quay Hotel. Nice place, nice view. Out for a run. Charlie Falconer had been pressing me to get something done on the way the Laurie letter was covered last week so after chatting to John Muir, who in turn was chatting to the inquiry, I did a letter pointing out I had never met him, we had never been made aware of such concerns and that many others had said I had not put on pressure and that the dossier was not the case for war. The festival was well organised, and mine a nice event. Sally Dodd from our *Tavistock Times* days was there, as was husband Dave who said afterwards I should stand for election and push Ed aside. He was adamant I could do it and had to do it. Otherwise it was a nice enough do. I spoke for the first half then a stack of questions, largely friendly. I was tired at the end though and after a signing headed back to the hotel.

Wednesday 18 May

Nice run through the morning mist, breakfast then a chat with Charlie before finally sending the letter to Chilcot, then train home. Grace was in full revision mode and I was mainly helping with that, politics. It was odd for us to be done in political history but I suppose we were. The media were going into frenzy mode on Ken Clarke who had suggested though had not actually said that some rapes were less serious than others. I did a blog on Fowey, pointing out that though media interviewers almost always say '*obviously* I have to ask you about Iraq…' it came up just three times – twice raised by me in my opening remarks, once by a member of the audience in a Q&A covering maybe forty or so different subjects. The more of these events I do, the more convinced I am that one of the reasons people pay good money to go out and hear people in the flesh, and then quiz them while deciding whether to buy their books, is that despite the enormous amount of airtime in the media age, they don't really feel they get a true sense of people or events.

All very Middle England kind of audience. Interesting though that my description of the *Mail* as evil was met by a generous round of applause, as was the observation that it was wrong not to have invited TB and GB to the royal wedding. Good questions e.g. 'Is Fiona keeping a diary?', which got a good laugh. Lots about Labour past and present. The main point though was I was sure the public want variety, not a media-decided monotony of tone, subject and prism, which is what we tend to get on the 24-hour news channels, overly influenced by papers with their own agenda.

Thursday 19 May

The media had gone into full-on sanctimony mode re. Ken Clarke and I did a blog saying what he said was less serious than Theresa May getting the bum's rush at the Police Federation conference.* Ed had called for Clarke's

---

* A speech by the Home Secretary in which she defended cuts and reforms to the police service was met by highly critical questioning and then complete silence.

May '11: AC defending Ken Clarke mid-media frenzy

resignation yesterday which I think was a bit of an error. To Trinity House near the Tower for a lunch of the Heating and Ventilation Contractors' Association. 'High point of my career,' I texted TB. Off to Leeds with Don Macintyre [*Independent* journalist] in tow who was updating his Peter M book and also writing about the record of the Labour government. I tried to be objective about both but it was hard re. Peter. Don said Peter had got even grander. He was now having his name thrown into the mix for the IMF and WTO [World Trade Organization] which would really irritate GB. The Tories were really rubbishing the idea of GB getting it. Peter M was probably just being used as a bit of mischief making.

The Queen's Ireland visit was going well though without much regard to TB's contribution. It would not be happening but for the progress under him and yet he was being written out of the script. I sent him a note saying I felt he really needed to think about a reputational strategy for himself. This kind of thing was happening because of the desire to mark him down not up. The more I thought about it the more shocking it was that all those Tories got invited to the royal wedding and the two most recent former PMs did not, and now that the Queen was making such a historic visit without any reference to his contribution to that history. The event in Leeds was a superbly well organised dinner to publish a report on the future for Yorkshire's economy. Rayan drove me back and I was in bed by two.

Friday 20 May

The inquiry published my letter and Chilcot's neutral response. Rayan collected me and we set off for Cowbridge for the book festival, organised by the local LLR branch. It consisted of me being interviewed in a chapel by Jamie Owen [BBC Wales]. He basically went chronologically through my life, and did it well. Fabulous reception, including when I defended myself on Iraq. Good Q&A which again was very friendly and supportive and ditto the book signing which went on for a fair old while. Really good idea to do this kind of thing as a fundraiser. Slept on the way back and was in bed by two again. Stiff as a board though.

Saturday 21 May

Tom Baldwin was keen for me to blog on Ed M's speech having the makings of a strategy, which I did. It was OK but not brilliant. But at least it did have a bit of message in there. The response on the website, however, was pretty negative. He was finding it hard to get heard at the moment. Chris Lennie [Labour deputy general secretary] told me Anne Black [former party chair] had said to the NEC they should move heaven and earth to get me back in there. I started tweeting with Sugar about tomorrow, our *Football Focus* celebrity predictions play-off. I was a bit bored though. Needed a new project. Maybe film. Maybe third novel. Watched *Breaking Bad* with Fiona. At least she and I were getting on well at the moment.

Sunday 22 May

Blogged on [former Downing Street deputy chief of staff] Gavin Kelly's piece in *The Observer*. He was about to publish a report on the collapse in living standards for the squeezed middle. Major implications if the economy grew but only the rich benefited. I missed Obama on *Marr* but the build-up to his visit was growing. The Queen had had another big hit in Ireland [state visit]. The wedding had taken the media back to largely fawning coverage for the royals. Amazing how they rode the waves. Watched the Premier League denouement and thanks to a late Theo Walcott goal for Arsenal I was in a big lead against Sugar. Then Spurs scored late to give him the only three-pointer of the day but after a bit of confusion it emerged I had won. Good banter via Twitter till finally he conceded. Talking to Fiona re. whether to go further on the phone-hacking stuff. Gerald had been told by a cop involved in the Jonathan Rees [private investigator] case that Peter, F and I had had invoices for work against our names paid to Rees's agency – for the *Mirror* rather than for the *News of the World*.[*] I was minded to take it further.

Monday 23 May

Cameron's struggling with Big Society – another relaunch today. Joanna sent me through the index for Volume 3 and I worked on that to make changes to the Who's Who Mark [Bennett] had sent me. Mark had been AWOL most of last week, to the point I was actually worried about whether he had killed himself. I had gone out to Streatham and not found him. Georgia saw him at David Cairns's funeral and told him how worried I was. She said he really was not in good shape. I knew that but didn't really know what to do. Ryan Giggs [Manchester United footballer] had a super-injunction out on his private life but Lib Dem MP John Hemmings named Giggs in the Commons, so the floodgates opened. Sky went into meltdown, Beeb followed later, and by the end of the day it was everywhere. I did a

---

[*] Rees and two other men were acquitted of murder after the director of public prosecutions abandoned their Old Bailey trial. It was then revealed that Rees had earned £150,000 a year from the *News of the World* for supplying illegally obtained information about public figures.

few bits and bobs of radio including 5 Live following on Hemmings. My main point was that these stories were not in the public interest as opposed to being of interest to the public, and that the system depended on there being a rule of law which Parliament made and judges interpreted.

Later out to the LMA [League Managers Association] dinner at the Park Lane Hilton. Lots of little chats with different managers – Steve Cotterill still angry re. Burnley, ditto Brian Laws [both former managers], chatted a bit to Eddie Howe [new Burnley manager] re. next season, really nice chat with Roy Hodgson [West Bromwich Albion head coach] who wanted to meet up for a proper discussion about politics. Nice enough do but I always found it very different being a speaker and being a guest at these kinds of events.

Tuesday 24 May

I did a pretty strong blog on the Giggs situation, essentially making the point that it was all about the tabloids being able to cover the sex lives of celebrities. Cameron taking their side for his own political reasons. I sent it to Alan Rusbridger [editor] and *The Guardian* used online. Round to see Philip who was on very good form. I said I was feeling a bit under-powered at the moment, and drifting, but he felt I was in a good place reputation-wise and all sorts of good things lay ahead. Bumped into Matthew Freud who was looking at an £18 million house in Primrose Hill. We had our usual chat re. the media and how shit it was.

Wednesday 25 May

My birthday. Obama's visit was dominating the media and he was doing well with it. TB and GB were invited to the State banquet and to the speech in Westminster Hall so maybe there was a bit of recalibration on that after the wedding snub. Lunch with Evgeny Lebedev [owner *Evening Standard*, *Independent* and *i* newspapers] in a Japanese restaurant in St James's. Not totally sure why he wanted to see me. Picking my brains on editors for the *Indy* and the *i*. He was quite bright, quite interesting and charming. But I didn't feel that impressed. He was certainly well plugged into the media world. He had seen the Jonathan Rees invoices, knew I had been targeted, or at least Rees had been paid for services rendered re. me. But he said his info was the police were not bothering with it.

Out to do a *Guardian* Saturday conversation with Hemmings on super-injunctions and Giggs. I wasn't terribly impressed by him. Impressed by the new *Guardian* offices though. He was down the line in the Midlands. Not sure at the end if I should have bothered but hey-ho. Home to do presents etc. Through the day trying to sort *Question Time* who had bid for me and I had said yes-ish until I learned this meant they were going to bounce Hilary Benn [shadow Leader of the Commons]. Tom Baldwin and Peter Morton tried to make the case that I was not an official Labour figure and that they regularly had two coalition people on there. On this occasion they were planning two plus the ghastly Christopher Meyer who had been media-tarting himself all over the place on the back of the Obama visit. So in the end I said No. The new editor Nicolai Gentchev apologised for the fact they had not been straight re. Hilary but said they saw me in the same light as someone like Paddy Ashdown, not officially on the party payroll but to all intents and purposes. Fair enough I suppose.

Thursday 26 May

Some of the papers ran stories on me being Labour's biggest donor in the first quarter, as only two individual donations were recorded, and mine of £10k was one of them. All suggesting things were a bit desperate for Ed on that front. Out first thing to do an interview for a BBC documentary on resignations. Up in a little studio flat in Hampstead. Mainly going over my own, Peter M, Estelle Morris, Ron Davies, Robin Cook. All fine but I never really enjoyed these bits-and-pieces projects.

Friday 27 May

Out first thing for a rare Q&A at a private school, the one used by John Banaszkiewicz [Burnley director] for his kids. Primary, lots of Europeans among the Brits, fairly small, and fantastically inquisitive kids. I must have got through well over a hundred questions, from the 'Do you have pets? How many kids? Favourite colour?' variety to Bin Laden and 9/11. One of them asked me what single thing I would do if I was PM for a day and they gasped with shock when I said abolish private education. Some seemed to get it when I explained why.

To Grosvenor Square to see TB who was in with Stephan [Kriesel, TBO], JoP and Catherine R. Had a chat with Vic [Gould, senior adviser] about TB's need to get a bit more engaged on a strategy re. himself, especially pre Chilcot. We had an hour or so just chewing over things. TB still felt that the wedding snub was OTT protocol rather than a snub but I'm not sure he meant it. He said the Queen had made a real thing of coming over to see him at the Obama dinner. He said he and GB had struggled to chat much at the Obama Westminster Hall speech, but that Cameron and Clegg were very friendly. Cameron had invited him to Chequers. He had seen Ed and told him he had to get a clear strategy. It had almost reached the stage where the wrong strategy was better than none. He felt Ed was trying to be both left-centre and centre-left. Both were permissible positions and he had said we would help him implement either but he had to choose one and go for it. He said he felt he was a nice guy but not up to it. He had also seen David and felt that there was a part of him that was glad not to have got the top job. I guess he meant that sometimes it was better to be the prince over the water, but my sense of David was that he had really wanted it, and was struggling to adapt.

On his own profile he wondered why I was so worried about a bigger impact from Chilcot. I said my worry was that it would develop as a revenge of the establishment. That was already happening in other ways – the wedding was the highest profile but also the way he was written out of the Ireland script. As for the media they now only wrote about him negatively. He bought that in general but he felt that for example his interview with Jon Snow for Channel 4 last night on Ratko Mladić's arrest was a lot friendlier than it would have been a while back.* I said he needed more things out there that reminded people of the things he had done other than Iraq. Even on that though he wondered if the reason the inquiry was delayed was because the Arab spring had given them pause for thought. I doubted it. He was pleased with the way both his business and foundations were going but wanted me to do more with him. He had his paperback out soon and was doing some media around that, which he wanted some help with in terms of message and positioning. He did say that if Chilcot really went for him he would just have to come out and defend himself. Nice to see him but though he seemed more chilled on one level he was still all a bit too frantic.

Newsnight called and asked me on re. FIFA, Mohammed bin Hammam [president, Asian Football Federation] and Blatter both now being investigated by FIFA ethics committee. I checked it out a bit and did a quick blog to get my head round what I might say – suggested the winds of the Arab spring were swirling round the world but passing FIFA by, that if it was a country it would be autocracy not democracy. Ended up doing it with Mark Palios [former FA chief executive] who said he was trying to carve out a bit of a media cum speaking career. I did say that if I was a betting man I would say Blatter would still be there after the election next week. Ed M was getting married and a bit of light relief when Calum sent me a text about his Aquascutum suit and I ended up sending to Ed a message intended for Calum, about getting a Stone Island [menswear brand] tattoo on his bum. Rachel called later, worried someone had hacked my

---

* Former Bosnian Serb warlord Mladić was to be jailed for life after being convicted of genocide and crimes against humanity in The Hague.

phone until I checked and realised I had sent it to the wrong number. Ed came on for a chat, had enjoyed the day he said but was clearly still quite worried about the constant refrain about a lack of impact.

Saturday 28 May

Guardian ran the Hemmings conversation which I also put on the blog and amid the usual Guardianista stuff there were quite a few backing my view. Pottered a bit then met up with Rory and headed for Wembley [Champions League final] via Kilburn where the United fans were gathering. The pub where we were meeting Stuart Bentham [personal friend, husband of Rachel Kinnock] and co. was heaving and a group, drunk but friendly, broke into 'only one Ali Campbell' but it was too crowded to have a drink so we headed to a restaurant over the road for something to eat. There was a steady stream of United fans asking for pictures and I think Rory seemed really chuffed at the reception I was getting. I'd noticed more generally recently that the usual greeting tended to be quite warm these days.

Out to Wembley on my own, again with OK reception, as Rory went to meet his mates. Our seats were right behind the goal with a little gaggle of Alex's friends and relatives. The atmosphere was OK without being brilliant. The guy in front sat the whole time and disappeared after half an hour. United started well but then Barcelona took control and though Rooney equalised it was all one way in the second half and 3–1 was actually a bit flattering. Texted Alex who said, 'It was an annihilation. Hard to know what else you could do against them.'

Sunday 29 May

Out to Croydon to record *The Big Questions*, Nicky Campbell's ethics and religious show, for next week. Me, Max Clifford, Lindsay [Nicholson] and James O'Brien [broadcaster] were on the panel, with a collection of other contributors on the front row – Mr Loophole, the driving solicitor, Brian Cathcart, journalism professor, a guy from the PCC [Press Complaints Commission] to echo Lindsay's support for them, a *Daily Star* reporter who resigned because of the Islamaphobic-slanted and often fictitious reporting, Paul McMullan re. hacking, and also Helen Wood who was Wayne Rooney's three-in-a-bed call girl, and someone who claims to have been Gordon Ramsay's mistress. Quite a good debate, me and Max agreeing more than I thought we would. We both hammered the PCC. My main point was that the tabloids would go to the wall without kiss and tell but they had to pretend it was about freedom of the press. Both Wazza's girl and Ramsay's woman tweeted nice messages later. Nice Polish driver managed to get me to St Pancras for the train to Paris. Not sure where it was all heading. Strauss-Kahn had thrown the PS pretty much into turmoil. Hollande slight favourite ahead of Martine Aubry [PS First Secretary].

Monday 30 May

Got a fairly early train, did a blog arising out of the *Big Questions* debate yesterday, drawing on Max Clifford saying in the warm-up question that he couldn't stand Cameron, also a bit of economy. Both F and I trying to help Grace with revision but she was not really motoring.

Wednesday 1 June

Really bored. Feeling on the edges of a depression and not sure what it was about. Blatter survived. Revising with Grace and also working a bit on [British and Irish] Lions diaries.*

Thursday 2 June

Working on novel three but not really motoring. Blogging mainly on health and social care stuff at the moment, but wondering if it all stacked up. Ed M called about Tim Livesey [civil servant who had worked for AC in No. 10], who seemingly was interested in working for him. I said he had been terrific for me, but I wondered if he could step up to a No. 1 position, and was unsure he had the politics. But definitely worth thinking about.

Friday 3 June

Meeting with Portland on the plan for mentoring work with some of their rising stars. Then to Gerald Shamash's office to meet a copper in the Jonathan Rees case, David Cooper, who found he was targeted by him when he was investigating the recent murder case which collapsed. He was planning to go for them but was also hoping to spread the load a bit and was telling me and Peter M about the fact that a news agency had invoiced the *Mirror* over quite a lot of stuff to do with us at the time of Peter's first resignation. There were several invoices related to Peter's mortgage. Three on me named in full – one of them with Fiona – and several just 'Campbell' which may or may not have been mine. Cooper there

---

* Clive Woodward had recruited AC to handle media relations on the 2005 Lions tour to New Zealand.

with Mark Lewis – never off his BlackBerry – and Jeremy Reed the QC and an assistant. There for over an hour but not sure it took us much further.

Sunday 5 June

Laura [Murray] decided to come with Calum, Rory and me to Burnley to watch us in the Soccer Six tournament at Burnley. BMW sent a car and the guy arrived in time for us to be off by eight, picking up reports of worsening weather by the time we got there. It was raining a bit when we arrived and there were hundreds of screaming kids waiting for the various boybands and reality TV stars on show. All a bit celeb subculture. My team was Burnley Fans with us three, Chesney from *Coronation Street*, a guy from *Hollyoaks* who could not kick a ball and spent all day stretching, a couple of other guys I never really got to know and Bertie Bee the Burnley mascot. We got changed, warmed up in the drizzle, met the refs for a bit of banter and rule explanation. First game against Merlin (eventual winners). We were playing like what we were – a team of strangers – and lost 4–0.

Second game was against The Wanted [boy band] who had won their first game so we really had to win. Changed the system so that Calum and I stayed at the back, Rory midfield, the two best players from earlier with rolling subs. Rory scored and then we sat back and tried to hold the lead. It got fairly physical at times and we did do a bit of mutual winding up with one of their players. At one point he had a little lash at me after we had been niggling each other and when I went to remonstrate he squared up and Rory came piling in. It was all fairly easily calmed down but later went crazy online and with the media. Video team had it all. Anyway we won, then easily won the next game and we were through to the quarters. 6,500 crowd, not-bad atmosphere at times and apart from against The Wanted the crowd was on our side. The quarter final was against *Hollyoaks* who were young and fit and trained together twice a week. But we did OK. One down, one–all, we missed a chance and then eventually we went down 2–1.

I got given a Star Player trophy – later discovered so did lots of others – and then we got changed, did a bit of gladhanding and headed home. Then Laura got a message – did you know Alastair was the lead story on the *Mail* website (doubtless in part revenge for this morning's *The Big Questions* when I used the line re. Dacre in charge of the PCC ethics code committee being like [Dr Harold] Shipman [serial killer] in charge of the GMC). Anyway we got it up and there were several photos run to suggest I had piled in and then Rory piled in after. Also Tom Parker – till now I didn't know who it was – had been stretchered off in a later match and the editing made it appear like it was a result of our exchanges. Cue a mini-avalanche – at one point both of us were trending – on Twitter.

Lots of threatening tweets from teenage girls. He tweeted that he had been in a fight with AC 'the MP' and twisted his knee. I tweeted after a while that I was sorry to hear of his injury and that it had been a competitive match. Then Darren Bentley [Burnley FC media manager] called and said it was all going a bit crazy and maybe I should do a blog to calm it down a bit. Did so. Rory was loving it though later slightly changed his tune and thought it was a bit embarrassing. Fiona and Grace not happy though later Grace very funny about it. At least it made the journey fly by though we had to stop for several pee breaks because of all the water taken on board. Mike Phelan called and said he thought it was the funniest thing he had seen in years. Alex texted: 'All that matters is you win one–nil.' That was the predominant reaction apart from the real Wanted devotees. Then I started to get tweets of support from One Direction [rival boy band].

Monday 6 June

The Wanted 'fight' was still going a bit. Eamonn Holmes [TV and radio presenter] defending me on Sky. Loads on Twitter and several papers doing big pieces – *Telegraph* pages one and three with a total of five pictures and the use of the word 'rotund' in the copy. I worked a bit on the diaries through the day then later out to the Hilton Park Lane to do the Marketing Society awards. Nice if noisy crowd and got a good reception. Talked about yesterday being a bad Twitter day then by the end of the evening today a good Twitter day because of all the suggestive tweets from inside the room. The organisers were thrilled.

Tuesday 7 June

I was going through current TV bids. Yes to a documentary on bagpipes. Yes to *Panorama* on alcohol. Yes-ish to *Question Time*. Yes to *This Week*. I did a blog on Osborne who was getting a great press for the IMF report of yesterday saying no changes needed to his economic policy. But I focused on a piece by Steve Richards [*The Independent*] comparing GO's modus operandi with GB, which George would hate. Out of the blue I was contacted by Buchanan PR saying they had been asked by the Syrian leadership, via Gulfsands [petroleum company], to ask if I might advise the [Bashar al-] Assad [President] regime on how to improve their image. It was a pretty easy one to say no to but first I checked out Tim [Allan] – who agreed – and then told Jeremy and John Casson [foreign affairs private secretary] at No. 10 in case they felt that it might open a few channels or allow them to get someone to think about using it to push reform. They agreed that it was unlikely to work and so I dropped it. The Buchanan guy said he was not sure how serious it all was but he had been led to believe it came from Bashar himself.

I wrote to the PR people to say it was a non-starter. I could see that on the one hand, if they are to reform, they are going to need proper strategic, political and comms advice. However, the backdrop is a really bad one and it was difficult to take at face value any real commitment to reform of a kind that would be acceptable to us. So the inevitable reputational hit for whoever might take on something like this would only be justifiable on any level if a positive end product in terms of change was clear, and it is difficult to see the scenario which leads to that as things stand. I passed it all on to Jeremy, and got a reply from John Casson. He had contacted our ambassador in Damascus to check how credible Gulfsands would be as a regime channel.

It turned out Rami Makhlouf, Bashar's cousin who is on the EU sanctions list, has a minority shareholding. The ambassador had been in touch with Mehdi Sajjad from Gulfsands, who is a British Iraqi, and heard from him that Rami was in trouble in Syria after a *New York Times* interview three or four weeks ago, which embarrassed the regime by implying that Assad has in effect been the guarantor of Israel's security. Mehdi says he advised Rami to get some professional PR advice via Buchanan. So that part stacked up, but he said he thought I was right to be sceptical about the request. There are some in the Syrian system arguing for reform, he said, but there was no sign they are calling the shots. 'The Syrian impact on your brand is likely to outweigh yours on theirs (no offence meant!),' he said, which at least made me smile.

Jack Straw called saying he had been asked to review Volume 3. I thought that was OK. I went through the period. He asked if I had said anything disobliging. I said I didn't recall anything. We ended up chatting re. Chilcot. He agreed with me that TB really needed to start thinking about it and we needed to start strategising about it. He was worried. He felt that [Sir Roderic] Lyne [former diplomat] and [Baroness] Usha Prashar were determined to be critical and personal and that there was always a risk the other two had shifted from their pro-war, pro-TB view because of all the media and 'dinner party circuit' pressure. He said we had to think about all the people we could get onside on the day, also think about bigger arguments to deploy. My worry – which he shared – was that the revenge of the establishment would be powerful, that the Tories had done a good job burying the record on the domestic front and this was the key to doing it on the international front.

I had a session with David Sturgeon after my little wobble last week. He was on at me again to go away for a week of total solitude. He felt there was a conflict between my past persona and a more real me. It was a good and interesting chat and I thought maybe he had a point. I was getting on better with Fiona, worried a fair bit re. the kids and was also resenting having taken and still taking so much of the TB flak. He said maybe it is because they know you have broad shoulders. Maybe. I said and maybe they sagged when I 'collapsed' on *Marr* and sag when I feel under pressure I don't deserve, especially if depressed. He said he felt the me of back then was not the real me. It was the me created by the remarkable circumstances I found myself in. Could be right.

Didn't help my mood that Rosie called and put on [Baroness] Patricia Scotland [shadow Attorney General] to tell me that the Attorney General [Dominic Grieve] had told her he was doing a statement on David Kelly on Thursday. Set me back a bit. David felt I had got through so much and now what happened is that certain buttons got pressed by certain things. Even something as silly as the 'fight' with the guy from The Wanted would have pressed buttons because it led to the usual critics making the usual points. Out for dinner with Fiona to discuss whether and if so when and where to do a week away on my own. No music, no TV or radio. No other contact. No phones. Write and read. Walk and think. He felt I would hate it at first but then get into it and find I learned a lot about myself. But I was very resistant. Watched an interesting discussion on *Newsnight* where the Lib Dems and Tories both claimed the Cameron statement on health met their (totally different) interests, and the health professionals said they were more confused than ever.

Wednesday 8 June

To TB's office for a discussion on his *Times* interview pegged to the paperback publication. Catherine R, Vic [Gould], Matthew [Doyle] and Ciaran Ward [head of media] from his office, me, Sally [Morgan] and Pat [McFadden, Labour MP] from outside. It was a bit of a struggle to get him into anything other than quite a right-wing position. As we tried he was basically saying GB cocked up on policy, the Tories were in all probability right about the deficit, Ed Balls was pushing the party into a position that would lose several elections. He said he had read Ed B's GMB speech and it was a recipe for disaster. We kept saying he did not need to go into the detail of every policy but he did need to say that the Tories were not progressive or fair and he was, and so were Labour and he was still Labour. It was interesting how his default position would see him essentially defend Tory positions more easily than Labour's, certainly in terms of body language, though he was partly playing up to us. Matthew made the point that his profile in parts of the party was not great and this was an opportunity.

By the end I was trying to persuade him to focus more on the international agenda – and maybe do a bit of pre Chilcot by saying the Arab spring should give people cause to rethink Iraq, not least because the democracy they already had had meant less violence. He was kind of up for it. I also suggested he do a big defence of the record. He was in danger of having his legacy trashed domestically because of the Tories' hit on the economy – and I suggested he did some of that – and internationally re. Iraq. But even though I gave him the figures which showed how the deficit was all about the crash, he was still prone to go on more about the decisions GB took, for example on National Insurance, top-rate tax etc.

We had a good laugh on The Wanted scrap. They today meanwhile put a video up with some footage, and some quite funny action replay mixing to the song 'Are you glad you came?' [The Wanted's 'Glad You Came']. 'Dad, why are you trending on Twitter again?' Grace tweeted – it was because of the hashtag #gladyoucamemrcampbell? These teenage fans were something else. Grace meanwhile was so happy her exams were over and telling everyone she had not been sure whether to write 'my dad' in the question they got about me. Left TB to do his interview with James Harding [*Times* editor] and David Aaronovitch. Chatted to Pat on the way out. He said he felt underemployed. The party was in poor shape, and Ed was finding the going tough. That was definitely the mood.

Popped in to see PG on the way home. On good form. Pleased Grace G had got a job with Apple. Caught PMQs in a cab. Ed went on Cameron's recalibration of the NHS stuff yesterday, but he didn't really hit home. Cameron's speech yesterday had been a bit of a dog's dinner and seemed to have caused as much confusion as it was designed to settle, but Ed didn't really hurt him. The other moment in there was Tom Watson asking Cameron about Jonathan Rees which would give the phone-hacking thing a whole new lift. I was talking to Gerald Shamash about whether to push out the stuff re. invoices we knew about but in the end there was no need, as *The Guardian* had them all and were going big on it.

I started to get calls on it as I arrived at the University of Westminster for the *British Journalism Review* interview for their conference. Up and downer with Bill [Hagerty, editor] about the privacy debate. [Late BBC foreign correspondent, Sir] Charles Wheeler's widow [Pip] presented an award in his name to Lindsey Hilsum [international editor, *Channel 4 News*], then Bill and I did the chat, interrupted halfway through by Boris Johnson [husband of Wheeler's daughter Marina] walking in, so he and I did a bit of joshing. Later he asked me to do a session for City Hall staff and also suggested I stand for mayor instead of Ken. He said he felt almost sorry for Ken, that he was past it and couldn't see it. Nice enough event, no big drama in the Q&A.

To Portland's party at the Serpentine Gallery. Peter M was there and pretty much cut me dead on the two occasions I tried to break the ice a little. PG had said Peter was definitely limbering to go against TB on Iraq. He was cold. Catherine picked up on it. Kate G said I should make more of an effort. I said I couldn't be bothered. Life was too short. Ben W-P and I were talking perfectly well about the phone stuff but so far as Peter was concerned it really was a bit of a waste of time. Bumped into Eric Pickles [Tory minister] and we agreed the *Mail* had touched up my gut in the Wanted pictures to make me look fatter so they could call me 'rotund'. 'Which you're not,' he said. 'No, indeed.' 'And nor am I.' He laughed at his own joke. To be fair he had a good deadpan delivery.

Thursday 9 June
Rowan Williams [Archbishop of Canterbury] had done a big attack on the coalition in the *New Statesman* which was the lead in the *Telegraph* and running big on the news. No mandate, unfair, not understanding etc. Strong stuff. I did a quick blog saying he was right to do it and right on the substance. To Victoria St for a meeting with Peter Morton about tonight's *This Week*. They had told me they had got Toby Young [journalist, free school co-founder and CEO] on about the AC Grayling university – he and lots of celeb academics were planning a new university – so I needed to mug up on free schools etc. Party a bit moribund. Peter a lovely guy and we got through a fair bit. The Attorney General's statement on David Kelly said there would be no new inquest so that was fine even if it wouldn't stop the conspiracy theories. Lunch with Calum who seemed better, then to Brown's Hotel for a Reed Business event.

Home to prepare for *This Week*. As I left home news broke about the *Telegraph* having a load of memos written by Ed Balls, plus letters exchanged between TB and GB re. the succession, which was being done as evidence of a 'brutal' plot. Chatted with Matthew to work out a line that was not dismissive, said it was not terribly clever, but they achieved a lot together. Truth is it showed what a horrible operation they ran, and Balls would likewise be trying the same now. Andrew Neil [*This Week* presenter] very excited by it. The Young discussion went fine and I whacked him a couple of times without getting too personal. Olly Grender [former Lib Dem head of communications] was also on, re. Libs and the coalition. I used my line about us now being the third most interesting party, defended Ed, as TB had earlier – and then Sally Bercow on parents' responsibility re. sexualisation of kids.

Went fine, good response on Twitter, including several urging me to stand and one saying 'best PM we never had'. I was still so undecided on this stuff. Fiona and Melissa thought Toby Young looked petrified, especially when I asked how much he was getting. Fiona thought he was a really torn person. Wanted to be like us but had fallen in with that *Telegraph/Spectator* crowd.

Friday 10 June

Tired but off early with Rayan to Burnley. A rash of overnight calls on the Ed Balls stuff in the *Telegraph*, which they were presenting as a plot to do in TB at the time of the 7/7 bombings. I stayed out of it but did send a text to Ed M saying if Ed B had any sense he would not deny it – as he was doing in interviews it seems – but admit they did go OTT at times and say the lesson for now is that we always worked best when we worked together. Unfortunately I sent it to the wrong Ed!! Ed B replied, 'Easy mistake.' I then said it was my strong view they needed to admit something of the past or else people would feel they just had not changed. I was in Burnley for the launch of the University College of Football Business and did lots of interviews on that but also did Beeb, Sky and ITN on the Labour stuff, with that same message about teamwork. Also did a shortish blog pointing out that yes, as Ed B said on the airwaves, we worked together to try to get TB and GB working together but that he tended to do it from a very GB perspective.

Tessa called for a long rant about how evil and nasty the whole GB operation had been for so long and said this was a reminder. I remained ambivalent about the whole thing, but certainly didn't really want to get too involved. Tom Baldwin called and said we had to avoid factionalism on it. The launch went fine, all the tellies and all the local papers. It was amazing how quickly it had gone from Brendan Flood's brainchild to something actually happening. On the way home I was working on the speech about happiness I was doing, developing the line that happiness depended how you felt as you approached death. Only then can you judge. Maybe it was an atheist's way of staying roughly on the straight and narrow.

Saturday 11 June

The Guardian were asking if I could get Alex F for the interview thing they were doing with Cameron, getting outsiders to ask questions of him. Did a blog on [US Defence Secretary] Robert Gates's speech warning that NATO was unsustainable without EU defence reform and greater investment. Bike ride out to Chelsea and I met Ana Muhar for a cup of tea. I was just

complaining at how public it was – and what a high proportion of tossers there were – when Trinny [Woodall, TV fashion presenter] walked by,
pap in tow, so he got pictures of her, her bloke and me. Had a bit of an
Alzheimer's moment in that I forgot who she was until she moved on.

Sunday 12 June

Off to Queen's Club with Calum for the Andy Murray–Jo-Wilfried Tsonga
final. Rained all day so no tennis. Just stayed in the President's Room.
Roger Draper [CEO, Lawn Tennis Association] hosting our table – told
me 65 per cent of Queen's members are Old Etonians. Bercow at our table.
Had a nice chat with him. He couldn't understand why Ed was getting
so marked down for last week's PMQs. He felt it was not great but not
disastrous. Calum liked him. Amazing how he remembered details of
the diaries and turned them into very personal questions – 'Rory must be
twenty-three now…' kind of thing. Seb Coe and his son Harry there so we
had a nice natter. He had the idea of us doing joint speeches to talk about
the campaign from the two different sides. I sent a tweet to Piers asking
what stories he got from the thousands paid to Jonathan Rees. It really
kicked off with him getting into Iraq War crimes etc., lots of my followers coming back re. faked photos and he and I really tearing off lumps.[*] I
stayed factual while he did the rhetoric stuff.

Monday 13 June

Meeting with Stephen Abell of the PCC. He said he knew I was a critic but
wanted me to have a better feel for what they do. Sensed he was quite a
smooth operator. There was not that much he could say to persuade me,
but he made a good case for the idea that he shared a lot of my analysis.
He claimed Dacre had no influence at all which struck me as odd. He was
opposed to statutory regulation and felt the papers knew they had to shape
up. Talked me through how they had tried to handle the phone hacking
and the Rees stuff. He was not exactly apologetic but knew they had not
handled it well. He said the best work they did was in people contacting
them for help and them being able to speak to the papers and get them
to back off. I found him moderately convincing on some fronts but felt
the PCC was still by the press for the press. He felt that was inevitable as

---

[*] Morgan had been fired in 2004 from the editorship of the *Daily Mirror* for authorising
publication of photographs of Iraqi prisoners being apparently abused by British Army
soldiers, which proved to have been faked.

if not there would have to be government money and that then took it dangerously close in.

I was doing a bit of research on the happiness speech which was quite interesting. Lots of studies showing that once people were above a certain income level, more money made little difference to happiness. Also that our wealth levels had risen substantially but our happiness levels were static over the same period. Dinner with Geoff Holt and his wife Elaine at the Camden Brasserie. He really was an impressive guy, and she was impressive too. He was 6ft 4 quadriplegic, having had a terrible pool accident. She was 5ft tall but strong enough to throw him around. He saw his work as raising the profile to raise cash and clout for disabled sailing. He said he put out his own statements using Ernest Read PR which was actually him. We agreed we should create a Twitter account for him. He apologised later for talking so much but to be fair he had a lot worth listening to. Fiona had said his speech to the boys at William Ellis had been the best and most inspiring.

Tuesday 14 June

Out to Grange St Paul's Hotel for a meeting with President [Ellen Johnson] Sirleaf of Liberia's team about her second term. Her son Rob was meant to be the main man. But he was half an hour late so we (JoP and I) chatted to her comms director and her special adviser, and some of TB's team. Underlined how much developing country governments had to learn of a very basic nature. Tanya Joseph [former TB press officer] there, having been out to Liberia a couple of times. I was on a bit of a dip which had the feel of a potential biggie. Long time out on the bike but not really clearing the head. Thinking about the retreat idea. Not sure.

Wednesday 15 June

Definitely major dip time. Not mega plunge but on the cusp. Out on the bike to try for a lift but it didn't work. So spent the day pottering and generally fannying around. Watched PMQs – Ed went on cancer patients losing benefits and Cameron didn't seem to know what he was on about, so it was taken as a win. Tweeted something supportive. TB's *Sun* interview had come out very pro-coalition and Cameron had co-opted him as a supporter of reform as well. Ed and co. not happy with TB but as TB emailed me, 'They spend all their time running down our record (Ed's latest speech had been all about us having been for the bankers and benefit cheats) and yet ask me for advice, support and money.' Fiona picked up on my mood and even though I was trying I couldn't really get going.

We ended up going out for dinner with Calum and Grace but I just felt hollowed out.

Thursday 16 June

Still down. Blog re. Osborne's Mansion House speech last night and in particular the need for Labour to resume and win the argument on the deficit. Used the 42.2 to 36.6 per cent deficit figures. It was crazy we were not pushing back on this. To Millbank to do an interview with Matt Flinders from Sheffield University who was doing a radio series in defence of politics. He shared a lot of my analysis but both of us were unclear about how to get to a better place. Text from David M saying he felt my heart had not been in helping him and Louise in the last year and he wanted to meet because he didn't want a friendship just to be in abeyance. I sent back a message that it was less about him than my desire to escape it all. Lunch with Bruce G, still nagging me to get a big job. He felt re. Ed M that he was a nice guy but unelectable. He felt the party might for once decide to go for a change. But he wasn't sure about where DM was in the party.

Friday 17 June

Matt Flinders sent me a lecture he had done – In Defence of Politics – which I read and enjoyed. He had quoted from my Cudlipp Lecture and at other points taken a lot of my usual arguments re. the media. But it was a big argument about how the media and public were no longer in tune with politics because they didn't understand the good that was done and didn't appreciate its importance and usefulness. I decided to put it up on my website instead of a blog and got a good response. I had been feeling pretty crap for a few days and went to see DS, who felt it was a mix of depression and anxiety. I decided it was probably right to start taking medication. I did a really long session on the bike. Getting lots of emails re. various projects but was unable to make decisions, small or large, in this kind of mindset.

Saturday 18 June

The talk of strikes had been getting louder and louder and 30 June was going to be a big day of public sector strikes over pensions. I'd committed to doing *Question Time* in Northern Ireland that day but after some deliberation, as it emerged there would be a serious impact, the Beeb called it off. I blogged about how the unions' anger was being fuelled because of the sense that people really did not feel like we were all in this together.

It was a scaled down version of Greece where the people were out rioting because they were being expected to take another austerity package and the bankers were just getting away with it. The news was dominated by Greece and Cameron was saying the UK would play no part in the bailout. The other thing going on was Ken Clarke being set up for a reversal on his sentencing policies.* Cameron having started out saying he would leave detailed policy work to departments was now taking over more – health and crime the most obvious areas. Internal disputes were starting to get out to the press – Steve Hilton and Osborne, Hilton and Andrew Cooper, who was in the papers a fair bit re. his polling advice. I started taking the pills.

Monday 20 June

Nick Watt was in reading Volume 3 at Ed's office. Said he liked it but I was worried he was too keen on the anti-Prince Charles stuff. Emma had gone through it marking with a yellow pen all the bits that weren't in *TBY* and there was a lot more royal stuff than I imagined. Had to go to the dentist for a loose crown.

Tuesday 21 June

I don't know if it was the new pills, or rising anxiety, but I was waking up lots in the night, with rivers of sweat pouring down my chest. I was also, having not been worried when the summons first arrived, started to obsess and panic about the speeding offence on 15 May. I also realised I had sent it back without keeping a copy – stupid – and that I had wrongly assumed it was from the Monday when I was diverted off the A1. In fact it was the day before, and I had no memory at all of being off the M1. I decided to get a solicitor but Gerald's colleague said I was probably facing a ban for 60mph in a 30mph area and I should just take it. I found the whole thing weird – just could not remember being there and could not imagine I would drive that fast if I knew it was a 30 limit. But for some reason it had suddenly really knocked me and also got me unnerved over other things – Chilcot, the book, the kids.

Did a blog on mental health after the outgoing president of the Royal College of Psychiatrists had done an interview saying how bad mental health services were becoming. I wanted someone to raise it at Cameron's press conference but they went mainly on his new sentencing stuff. There

---

* Despite support from the Lib Dems, the Justice Secretary was forced to abandon his plans for 50 per cent sentence discounts for early guilty pleas and other sentencing reforms.

was also an extraordinary outburst from him when he said of the military who were complaining about cuts 'you do the fighting, I do the talking'. That showed unbelievable confidence or arrogance or both. And also he got away with it. If that had been TB, my God we would never have heard the end of it. I did a bit of work in the afternoon then took Grace out for a driving lesson – stressful – and then we went out for dinner at Lemonia. One of the best things about not having travelled much was that I had spent a lot of time with the kids recently.

TB meanwhile was on asking if I could go to Jordan in the next few days. He said both the King and Queen needed urgent advice. But it wasn't clear that it was set up properly. I also did a note to the Slovenian PM on getting out there. I watched the education select committee hearing of the *Dream School* kids and teachers. Angelique talked the most, but the rest did OK. The chair asked if she made me cry after she said she was sorry how rude she was to me. No, she said, to which he said, 'That is a matter of regret to some of us.'

Wednesday 22 June

To St Gregory's Catholic Science College in Harrow. Great kids. 82 per cent non-white. 23 per cent rise in good results over three years. I did a Q&A with the sixth form and others who were terrific. Quite a lot on Iraq but lots of other stuff. Did a bit of a class war tweet about how they were brighter than the kids at the other Harrow up the hill. Did a blog on just how good these kids were and how the Tories needed to stop running down schools like this. Home then out to Talacre [Kentish Town sports centre] to speak to Camden sports council. The local councillor first then me, arguing people had to fight now to get in place the arguments that would be needed for the future. Then a discussion which got quite heated both on the new development planned near Talacre and the council sackings.

Andy Burnham round for dinner. I ended up feeling quite sorry for him. He was finding it quite hard to adapt to opposition. Also, he was hankering after health and though he enjoyed the education brief he was finding it frustrating that Gove had such a network of media support. The problem was that we were now the third most interesting party and also that the Andy B generation had never known a losing environment. It was just very hard to get noticed at the moment. I advised him just to keep going as the defender of state schools but stop short of doing class war. The problem was trying to get a strategic line that carried. He and Fiona discussed Gove and the best way to deal with him. She felt there was a growing sense of incompetence. Also that the choice issue was skewed to those who already had it. He was due to go to the Wellington College conference we had been invited to and was now, as it neared, hacked off that he had to. The problem was the right had all the arguments at the moment in terms of the balance of opinion in the media.

On the general scene he felt Ed was a nice guy and he was trying to help him 'but if I'm being honest I can't see him doing it'. Too cautious and also still surrounded by too many GB people. He also felt that he was really torn as to what his general strategy should be. I told him that TB had said to Ed he could either go New Labour or left of it and which ever he decided we could help put together the strategy but at the moment he was trying to be a bit all things. It had to be clear and come from within. Andy said that shadow Cabinet meetings were a bit tired and that several of them did next to nothing. He felt Balls was plotting. Healey [shadow Health Secretary] worked the PLP incessantly. There are people in there you won't recognise, he said. Tessa had a go at Balls this week for his unilateral announcement about calling for a VAT cut. He said you could have heard a pin drop. If Balls had been next to her he'd have throttled her. He felt re. TB that he should have been more careful about the way that his book and his recent interviews came out.

He was very down about David M, said he had assumed it was going to be his. Everyone else could see at the hustings that things were moving to Ed, apart from David. Despite that, Andy voted for him second after himself – then Balls then Ed M – because he felt he probably would have been better and also because he hated the way the Eds had moved away on Iraq and other parts of the record. It was a nice evening but both Fiona and I ended up feeling quite sorry for him for the life he was leading. He had been having a tough life personally, his wife having had major surgery and raised three kids often without him up north.

Thursday 23 June

Another bad night, sleepless and anxious. I went out for a long run, then later popped in to see Audrey and we had a nice chat about things. Worked at home then out to the Hilton for the *Municipal Journal* local government awards. Interesting how down many of them – including Tories – were on Pickles. It was partly the fact he had relished settling for such big cuts in the spending round but also the weekly bins issue – Pickles having preached localism while telling everyone what to do. I made the theme of my speech the fact that not only were the media negative about everything but so was the government – they had to run everything down in the economy, health, schools and other public services to justify their cuts and changes. Went down pretty well apart from one shout of rubbish when I said Gove never praised state schools.

June '11: Burnham finding it hard to adapt to opposition

Judging by how long it took to do all the pictures people wanted at the end I think it went down OK. I called Nick Freeman [Mr Loophole] re. my speeding offence and he agreed to try to get back the photo summons. He felt a ban probable but not certain. Could maybe trade points for ban. Also said I could still drive in France if banned but he didn't think it would come up soon. Sounded very clued up so I agreed with F he should take it on.

Friday 24 June

Still feeling pretty shit. Went to see PG who was in great form. Also very excited at the scale of what *The Times* were planning for his cancer piece. Four days plus an interview. He felt re. me it was years of pressure and a lot of anxiety about Chilcot. The speeding thing had suddenly upped my anxiety levels – no doubt about that. But he felt I was in a good place generally and that I should not worry too much. He wanted a lot of help with the political book he was writing – amazing that he was finding the energy to do all this writing. But the truth is he had found new force within himself and was using it to great effect. He got very tired later but he was in better shape than for a while. He was even talking about coming down to France for a few days. As ever we yacked away re. where the public was with TB–GB Peter M. I did a blog reprising the theme of last night's speech, pointing out that the anti-public services strategy was now a political strategy as clear as cuts was an economic strategy.

Saturday 25 June

Our annual trip to Wimbledon courtesy of Roger Draper at the LTA. Me, Calum, Keir [Kennedy-Mitchell] and Roland [Hutchinson, friends]. There had been some kind of security scare in the morning so lots of queueing to get tickets and then get in. We had lunch, nattered a bit then out to see [Roger] Federer win easily, then [Novak] Djokovic have an amazing match with [Marcos] Baghdatis. Our seats were right in line for one of the main camera angles so throughout the day I was getting texted and tweeted about looking bored, working on my BlackBerry etc. In fact the second match was really high quality. I got a bit hacked off with Calum because he and Roland went on the piss for the second half of the match and stayed behind after I left.

Sunday 26 June

London Bikeathon. Up early and off with Rory to Battersea Park. A new venue, not as nice as Chelsea hospital. Also health and safety and the cops made the start a bit late. Did the 52-mile route. Really hot by the time we finished. Two punctures.

Monday 27 June
Really hot again. Starting to fret more re. the weekend and the *Guardian* serial. Nick Watt way too excited re. the royal stuff and in particular TB's differences with Prince Charles.

Tuesday 28 June
Wen Jiabao [President of China] had been in town yesterday and had given a bit of a whack over DC's human rights stance.[*] Did a blog reflecting the fact that DC definitely pointed more to human rights than TB did. There was some stuff around on the possibility that it was harming us on the trade front. Out to the Ladies University Club to be interviewed by David Frost for his programme on interviews. Often I said something and he didn't seem to pick up on it as quickly as he might. I didn't feel I was on great form either but he seemed happy enough. Later out to The Connection St Martin-in-the-Fields to see an exhibition of art by the homeless. Bought three.

Wednesday 29 June
The *FT* had a story re. the deals signed by Wen Jiabao in Germany which were seven times bigger than the ones he did with the UK. Did a blog on that, the rising costs of rising crime (*Times* splash) and some really bad consumer spending figures yesterday. Pottered around then out to the John Smith Institute in The Strand. Twenty-two 'fellows' (people in politics and government around the world, Iraq, Kurdistan, Armenia, Ukraine, Russia, Azerbaijan) – over here for quite a while, had been all over the country looking at various elements of the system. Charlie F was chairing my session. The Kurd loved me; the Iraqi was pretty quizzical.

The traffic was dire but we just made it for the start of *Richard III* at the Old Vic. Kevin [Spacey] was absolutely brilliant.

The after-party was a pretty grand affair at the Savoy. Kevin was obviously subsidising so much of this stuff. I was worrying about how Charles

---

[*] Announcing a trade agreement with China, the Prime Minister said that respect for human rights was 'the best guarantor' of prosperity and stability. Mr Jiabao responded by urging co-operation and dialogue over the issue, not 'finger-pointing'.

and the Palace would react to my serialisation in *The Guardian* on Saturday. *The Guardian* were way over-excited about it. Home by twelve. F and I getting on well but she was a bit fed up with Grace being rude to her.

Thursday 30 June

Charlie Enstone-Watts [trainer] was round just after seven for an hour's boxing. I was on pretty good form, partly I guess because I had lost a bit of weight having not had a drink or much chocolate for weeks. With *The Guardian* starting the serial on Saturday, I called Paddy Harverson [communications secretary to the Prince of Wales and Duchess of Cornwall] early on to alert him to the book and *The Guardian*'s interest in the Charles stuff. He sounded a bit worried about it. He had been getting a hard time from Charles over the coverage of his finances. I said I felt he had done rather well, also that he had handled the Kate–William stuff really well. But he was fairly downbeat about things. Perhaps he felt Charles, his real boss, was being eclipsed by Prince William. *The Guardian* were really into the 'meddlesome prince' theme, so they were going to 'jump all over it'. I said I would send him the copy when I got it and also, if it helped, give them today words making clear this was as much about Mark Bolland [former deputy private secretary to the Prince of Wales] and Charles's then media operation, as about TB–Charles. He didn't sound too bad about it.

I also sent the themes through to Matthew and he said 'for now' TB was fairly relaxed. I was asking Nick Watt maybe to take out one or two of the bad bits, so it was not quite so negative. His argument was that they were all in the book and better to get them out there in a context over which I had a modicum of control. There was something in that. We chatted about it on and off through the day.

Laura from Portland came round and we set off for Stansted, and off to Slovenia. Read up on the country and the PM [Borut Pahor] on the way. He was in a difficult position having lost his referendum on pensions reform, but was now under a fair amount of economic and political pressure. He had had three resignations from the government from the Zares Party and was now ruling with the help of the Liberals, led by an attractive interior minister. The easyJet experience was not quite as awful as it might have been, though there was a Moroccan family at the front of the so-called 'speedy boarding' queue who took half an hour to go through. But despite the strikes the queues were not too bad. We were through fairly quickly.

PG called though and once we had discussed his health – he was very bouncy at the moment despite a problem with his pee – he said he was saying in his new book intro that there was always a good side to GB, also that though I was often down I always brought laughter to meetings, including with GB. We arrived in Ljubljana which on first impressions was a really nice place. You could see the former Yugoslav influence but also Italian. Good roads, clean, lively city centre. OK hotel, The Union. We met Špela [Vovk], the PM's public relations assistant, and a while after the PM arrived with his foreign affairs guy. He was tieless, very white teeth, very tanned, fit-looking, hardly surprising given he regularly does 50k runs. I was surprised that he wanted to eat outside in a fairly public place as I assumed they would have wanted these discussions to be very private.

By the end of dinner, the opposition leader had gone by, I had been introduced to the mayor (a political opponent) and a 'yellow press' journalist had arrived at a nearby table. And at the end of the evening Borut decided he wanted to go for a walk with me down the canal, which was lined with packed restaurant terraces. Over dinner he laid out his problems – he was really worried about the election, though the opposition leader was not totally confident. He had lost the referendum, he was now focused on making other reforms – health, labour markets – and he was worried about a German press story to the effect that Slovenia could be the next Greece. He said it was nonsense but wanted advice on how to deal with it. I laid out a rough plan aimed at getting through September when he would be doing the Budget and a no confidence motion. He said even if he lost it he would not be forced out immediately. But he was already thinking about his next job, possibly with a financial institution in the US. He was a very straight-talking and likeable guy, good sense of humour. But he had a curious approach to comms.

He saw PR effectively as 'polishing' and he was not someone who believed in e.g. social media, websites, setting the agenda. He was addicted to doing long press conferences. We talked at length about messaging and I felt what worked best for him was leadership and teamwork to take the right decisions to steer the country through global crisis. He liked that. I said he needed to embark on a major campaign of explanation about past, present and then future. He said people were not interested in facts. Not true. They were.

He said people would not listen about achievements – he was particularly irked at the lack of credit he got for a major agreement with Croatia. I said they would listen if you explained over time, not fifty things you have done but two or three. And they would listen if you used them to signal what you now planned for the future. He was quite resistant at first but he started to buy in more as time went on. He talked a fair bit about European work and clearly liked the foreign policy stuff. He really rated Cameron. He said people expected someone quite distant and sceptical but he had really made an impression. He was likeable and charming and made clever interventions. Even though we were not in the euro he held his own in those discussions too and came up with sensible points.

He said Merkel was No. 1 but Cameron had replaced Sarko as No. 2. Silvio was nowhere, a bit of a busted flush. People rated and respected GB on the economy but they found Cameron much easier to deal with. He was asking a fair few questions about TB–GB and could not understand why TB tolerated him for so long. He was also surprised I never went into elected politics because he felt I would have gone far. He said [Baroness] Cathy Ashton [Labour peer, first vice-president of the European Commission] had been a poor appointment. David M should have done it but he clearly thought he would become leader. He was doubtful that Ed could win. He followed our politics closely. He seemed to judge leaders in part according to whether it was possible to laugh and joke with them. He marked Merkel down for that reason. [Jean-Claude] Juncker [Prime Minister of Luxembourg] was a friend. Silvio was a hoot.

They did not have much of a culture of using outside consultants and the last experience of Slovenian consultants – in the referendum – was a disaster because they did a terrible YouTube film which he never saw and which he believes lost them the campaign. Also they are not a rich country. But he wanted to try to make it work. His team were desperate for it because clearly they had been saying much the same thing to him as I was but he didn't listen to them. He felt if he was 'just himself' it would get through. He had been a leader until he became PM but they felt he had since stopped leading. All a bit odd. He also had a mischievous side. He said the reason he worried about Twitter was because he would not be able to stop himself from saying crazy things. I said you just have to do it. We were able to talk very frankly very quickly and he was absorbing it even if he was a bit suspicious. He definitely needed help in terms of overall strategy.

Friday 1 July

Awoke to news that the prosecution case against Strauss-Kahn was falling apart. I texted Pierre Moscovici and Olivier Ferrand. They were still not clear whether he would be able to come back because though the hotel maid's case alleging rape was falling apart he did have sex with her and the sex issue was still a problem for him. I was expecting an hour or so with Borut this morning to pin down what we discussed last night and work out how to take it forward. We ended up staying there all morning, then going for lunch with a friend of his and then for a tour of the old government buildings before we headed for the airport.

He brought in his interior minister, Katarina Kresal, so that I could take her through the same arguments. She had been billed as the best-looking politician in the world and she was certainly good-looking for a politician. She was a bit cold, but she was far closer to my assessment of comms than he was and after I did the same spiel she said she was totally up for it. She had an assistant who talked to him in a way that I did not think entirely appropriate.

We talked through an outline plan-diary for the next few weeks and then left for lunch. An odd affair. We went to an office to meet a friend of his, an ex-marketing guy who now ran a boat show and was in the 'very depressed' yacht world. He felt the PM was overly talking down his own chances. He totally bought our approach. Maybe that was the reason he wanted us to meet him.

Meanwhile I was in and out talking to Nick Watt re. serialisation. I gave him a quote making clear Bolland was the problem as much as Charles. TB was fine re. Charles but not fine about the line on Jerusalem, him saying the Israelis giving it to the Palestinians was like us giving Westminster to the Germans. I managed to get the copy changed to make it clear he was passing on the views of others, not saying his own. Paddy H was asking for the copy before deciding whether to say anything and when he got it decided against. 'Don't write any more bl**dy books,' one email said. I guess that with William and Kate now conquering Canada they would be getting more worried and the meddling Charles was not a good place for him to be.

Borut took us on a tour of his old offices, showed us the press centre, then got Špela down to say goodbye. Rayan met us and after dealing with TB's anxiety re. Jerusalem we set off for home. Ate in then bed, watching the Strauss-Kahn fallout and trying to work out if he could get back in the French presidential race. Knackered. The phone and email started once *The Guardian* put their stuff online.

Saturday 2 July

The *Guardian* stuff was OK, fair bit of pick-up in the other papers. TB seemed pretty relaxed about things whereas Paddy [Harverson] said Charles was feeling a bit bruised. He had worse to come during the day with news the *Mail on Sunday* were doing a big number on all Charles's contacts with Tory ministers. Rayan took me to Heathrow for the flight to Dublin, and just before going to the plane I got an email from Johann Hari of *The Independent*. He had been at the centre of a bizarre storm over accusations that he lifted quotes from interviewees' books and other material and used them as his own. All very odd. He sent me a draft speech he was planning to make, said he had always admired me and could I offer some advice. I said he should make the speech, try to explain honestly why he did what he did, including his own vanity, and say what he hoped to learn. He said he would certainly feel differently about ministers and others who get caught up in storms in the future.

The flight was on time, I was taken to the Merrion and met up with Paul Allen and the team from the Toranfield addiction treatment centre. They were struggling a bit and needed to get into UK markets. I had a few ideas of people and organisations they should approach on this. Out later to RTÉ and the Miriam O'Callaghan show. Grace was terribly excited because Whitney Port [American TV personality] of *The Hills* [reality TV show] was on and I got them on the phone together. It was a good interview, very personal, lots on mental health and what I liked was she had notes and just took it wherever it went. Great mood in the green room afterwards and they were pressing me to go clubbing but I was a good boy and in bed by twelve.

Sunday 3 July

The Merrion really does a terrific breakfast and for once I pigged out – fruit, eggs and black pudding, kippers. Paul picked me up and we headed to do a radio interview with Sam Smith. Like last night there was more focus on what *The Guardian* ran re. me admitting I sometimes fell off the wagon than there was on the royals. I did a blog on it, saying even as I talked about it I worried people with drink problems would think, well, if he can have the odd one, so can I. As ever I enjoyed Dublin and got a good reception. I flew into City airport just after lunch and was back liaising with Nick Watt for part 2. I watched [Novak] Djokovic win the Wimbledon final then took Rory and Grace to see Audrey. Calum was in the pub and didn't join us for dinner which was a bit depressing. The Huffington Post [news website] had asked me to do a guest blog for the launch of the UK version so I worked on that, taking in both the perils of diary writing and the way the media was changing. There was a bit of an issue about why so many of us were doing this for nothing but I felt that was OK. I did my own blogs for nothing so what was the difference?

Monday 4 July

David Miliband came round. He had texted me a while back saying he was worried about our friendship falling into abeyance and that he felt we had not been there for them so we wanted to clear the air. It didn't start well when Maria the cleaner asked him if he was 'the one with the brother'. Then she said we saw the brother recently with the new baby. We went to my office and had a long chat on the political scene before getting to the personal. He was pretty down about it all. He felt he was 'too big' to be around the Commons. He never went in for PMQs. There was 'some' relationship with Ed but it was cool to say the least and he felt Ed was taking the wrong course. Well no, he said he felt Ed was not sure what the course was. Balls of course knew exactly what he wanted to do – be in denial about the past, move left for the future.

He had seen TB at a dinner last night for Condi [Condoleezza] Rice [former Secretary of State] who was over for the unveiling of the new Ronald Reagan statue. He felt TB was a bit remote but he was right that Ed needed a clear strategy. Choose which one! I asked if there was any chance of him going back in and he thought not. Shadow Chancellor was the only maybe and Balls had it. I said what about an overarching policy role and he said it would not work with Balls there. The truth is the disagreement was fundamental. He felt the speech which had been leaked – the one he would have made had he won – was the right strategy but he didn't believe Ed could do it. He was desperate to get out, now wished he had gone for the Europe job – agreed with Pahor, Ashton was not the right person – but he had really believed he would have become leader and 'saved the party'. He didn't think Cameron was that great but did not think Ed had any chance of winning. And because we had not properly explained either the record or the economic causes of the crash the Tories only needed a bit of economic recovery to get political recovery.

On the personal side I said he had to understand I had not really been desperate to go back in 2010, I was not keen to get too involved in the leadership election and I thought he would win. I was still half-in half-out. He said Fiona and I were the referees for their adoptions and it was sad if we drifted apart. I said I would see Louise and explain why I had been as I had been. Mind you, Fiona said later she felt the whole thing had been one way. They had always been popping round, but it was all about getting advice from me. David and I walked to Queen's Crescent and down to the dentist where I was due to get a crown fitted. I was glad we had chatted. I felt he seemed down. It had been a good chat but not with the closeness we once had, which I agreed we should make an effort to get back. I think he had a better understanding, now he was in a not dissimilar position, of why I was so ambivalent about so much of what was going on.

Matthew Doyle called as I arrived at the dentist to say [Sir] Michael Peat [private secretary] had called TB from Charles's office this morning and had wondered if TB could make clear he had no trouble with the Prince making contributions to public debate and having meetings with ministers.

I thought there was a danger it would keep it running as it was dying down. But they were keen and in the end TB did a letter to *The Guardian* saying sometimes he got annoyed but he valued the discussions etc. Out for a run then to see DS, mainly talking about Calum, and how worried I was about him. Then I started to get calls about a story *The Guardian* were breaking to the effect that [murdered teenager] Milly Dowler's phone was hacked by the *News of the World*.* Jesus. This was going to take it to a whole new level. It was also going to put Rebekah in the frame because she was editor at the time.

Tuesday 5 July

Cameron was in Afghanistan but the Milly Dowler story was turning phone hacking into a major frenzy. Surely Rebekah would have to go. I thought about calling her, but it was over a year since we had spoken, maybe more. Also, she was clearly of the view from the messages when I did hacking interviews two years ago at [Burnley FC chairman] Barry Kilby's wedding that I was PNG. The thing was sick. And there was talk of the Soham murder victims, the McCanns [parents of missing daughter Madeleine], Sara Payne [mother of murdered schoolgirl Sarah] also being hacked. Did a few radio and TV interviews about Milly Dowler and really went for it. The public revulsion took it to a whole new level which meant police, NI and Cameron finally would have to act properly. They were all pretty much in denial. Ed Miliband called and I said this really was the time to go for this. He had to stand up for what the public were thinking. He said that pretty much puts us on the wrong side of all the media.

I said it didn't matter. It would give him strength and definition. He said he had been thinking the same ever since he had called for a general inquiry into media standards. They had kicked him hard but he was still standing. I said at PMQs he needed to get Cameron to a broader inquiry. He asked me to text lines, which I did through the day. I sent Matthew Freud an email asking what he thought of them. Bunch of cunts, he said, been saying it for ages. PG confirmed Matthew had been anti-Rupert, James and Rebekah for some time now. There was a real feeling Rebekah would have to go but Rupert seemed pretty determined to keep her. Later did 5 Live and also *Newsnight* with Paxo. First me and Paul McMullan who was still defending phone hacking, also saying Rebekah would have

---

* The thirteen-year-old schoolgirl was reported missing by her parents when she failed to return home from school in March 2002. Her remains were discovered that afternoon. In 2011 it became known that the *News of the World* had accessed Dowler's voicemail after she had been reported missing.

known, then Arianna Huffington [co-founder Huffington Post] and Chris Blackhurst [editor, *The Independent*].

I was on pretty good form but maybe a bit flip towards the end about Arianna's constant plugging. I hadn't realised the pictures behind me were the Soham victims. But in terms of general message about this being a broader story of lowered press standards amid huge media change I think it was OK. I had seen Philip earlier who showed me the terrific spreads *The Times* were doing with his cancer stuff.

Wednesday 6 July

Breakfast with TB, Catherine Rimmer, Pat McF and Ciaran, mainly to go over his Progress [New Labour pressure group] event on Friday. Re. Rebekah, he asked me what I thought she should do as she had been asking for his advice. I said she was toast and ought to go. She had no choice. Are you sure, he said. I said there were only three people in the world who think she should survive – Murdoch, James and Rebekah. 'And you're the fourth,' CR said to him. He said he didn't like to dump on people who had been good to him. I said that was plain wrong. We should judge this stuff on the merits and he should have done something when we had the chance. He said I just tell you that it is a bloody hard place for a politician to put himself, with every major paper against him. I said I was talking to Ed and he was planning to go for them today and call for Rebekah to go. He raised his eyebrows and said, 'Well, it is a big risk.'

I said I felt he had been slow to see the opportunities we had because of the way the media had changed and that there was no reason to be so beholden. He said Murdoch had been the only one who stayed onside. I said it was for his own reasons. I had argued for years that this was a genuine cultural issue which we should have addressed. He didn't seem to buy it, even now. On the Progress event he was in two minds about whether to make an opening speech or merely do a Q&A. I said he needed to frame the argument, and that the most important thing he could communicate was that he was Labour not Tory, that the 'heir to Blair' thing was a naked attempt by the Tories to force Labour to the left and that we were falling for it. He said there were some things the Tories were doing which he supported because they ran with the grain of what we did. There were other things that he disagreed with. Well concentrate on them, I said. He said he was pretty fed up with the way the party ran him down.

The question that was worrying him was whether he should state openly that we were New Labour for ten years and stopped for three and in his view that is why we lost. The economic response to the crash was Old Labour. I felt the thing to be careful about was playing into the current mood which was very down on Ed. He said he was happy to say he supported him. He was happy to point out where the Tories were not progressive. But he didn't intend to do a massive rant against the Tories. We also talked a bit about the nature of the debate in the party. We were still behaving as though we were in government, with everyone feeling we had to say the same thing. In truth there was now the scope for a real debate. I said he should say that we could afford to be less controlling, more open to outside ideas and so forth. He said 'Blair calls for a big debate' is quite a thing. I said well it was a good thing to do. We were now the third most interesting party still behaving like the first.

Pat said that a lot of the new MPs had bought the line that anyone who raised issues was part of some Blairite plot, also that they did not really get what New Labour was about. They saw it as a winning tactical thing not a political philosophy. They had also bought a lot into the Balls agenda. And they believed Ed could not win. If he did the right things and chose the right strategy, he could, I said. After the others left TB had another go at picking my brains about the *News* situation. On Kazakhstan, I said we had to be able to show that him being involved led to meaningful reform. I did a few interviews for radio from there then went to Millbank for the Andrew Neil show. They had replaced Caroline Flint [shadow Communications Secretary] for me so it was me and David Davis [Tory MP, former minister] and [Lord] Norman Fowler [former Tory minister] on for a chat about phone hacking.

Overnight the story had been the existence of emails being handed to the police which showed that Coulson had authorised payments to police officers. I tweeted that it was an over-transparent attempt to shift it to Coulson and therefore Cameron on the day that we had PMQs and also the debate agreed to by John Bercow after Chris Bryant's emergency debate yesterday. I had done a blog saying if Cameron had any sense he would announce an inquiry – Clegg had said yesterday there wouldn't be one – and also set out a process to a new system of regulation. There was a little bit of 'You were too close to Murdoch too,' which I dealt with OK I think. At PMQs, Ed did well. We had had several chats through the day and he was clear about the approach. News International execs had told Tom Baldwin they were ready to throw Coulson overboard but wanted to protect Rebekah because she was 'family'. They've even started talking like the mafia. Ed showed a lot of balls today, went big and bold by demanding her head, knowing it meant they would absolutely go for him from now on in. Shifting focus to her and BSkyB is going to piss Murdoch off big time but leaves Cameron much more exposed. Cameron announced the inquiries but his manner was not good. He was also far too peevish once Ed made clear he was not really buying it.

Cameron would not go for Rebekah or move the line on BSkyB [satellite broadcaster].* Cameron did the right thing but didn't go far enough. There was also no clarity about whether it would be a judge in charge of it. Norman Fowler was totally in the right place on this. I said I felt if there was an inquiry he might be the man. But once Cameron announced it, the issue moved quickly to 'judge led' and we also got to the point of it being a dispute between Cameron and Clegg. I was tweeting every few minutes now. Social media was driving this a lot. At one point Rebekah, Coulson and Mulcaire were all trending. Ed sent through a Q&A lines to take document which wasn't bad but I didn't like the way he played along with the idea all parties were as bad as each other. He called about a speech he was due to make on Friday. He said you told me two months ago I would feel better and liberated if I did this, and I do. I know there is a price to pay in terms of media support but I am prepared to pay it. I said the more you find big bold strokes to make, that chime with the public and show Cameron as a tactical PR man, the better.

He sounded strong and up for it. He still had strategic and policy problems as my discussion with TB had shown up. But this was cutting through and would do him good, provided he also had policy solutions on things the public really cared about. I got a bit trapped in Millbank and did loads of interviews. Was getting bids from Oz, Holland, Germany but focused on the UK. 'Gobby', the fixer from the Beeb, told me that on the plane back from Afghanistan Cameron's people had been looking at my interviews and seeing what 'advice' I was giving. Andrew Neil made the same point, said they had obviously been reading your blog and maybe you should go on the payroll. But Cameron was still in a difficult position on Brooks, Coulson and BSkyB, and that was where Ed needed to press now.

Met up with Emma Mitchell [Random House] and headed to the launch of HuffPostUK. Odd event. Richard Bacon chairing. Arianna, me, Celia Walden, Jon Gaunt [former *Sun* columnist, broadcaster] (Kelvin MacKenzie bottled out it seems), Shami Chakrabarti [human rights and civil liberties campaigner] and Kelly Osbourne [singer–songwriter]. Lots of faffing around, lots of 'Arianna is five minutes away' and the discussion was a bit disjointed and the audience subdued. Gaunt and I tore into each other a bit. Kelly said in the lift afterwards, 'I just love the way you talk. Whatever anyone throws you come back with beautifully crafted answers so quickly.' I agreed with Shami more than either of us expected. We had to somehow manage the attack that in courting Murdoch we were as bad

* Rupert Murdoch's News Corporation, which already owned 39.1 per cent of BSkyB, had in 2010 made an offer to take full control of the company. This was rejected by BSkyB and the proposal was being reviewed by the government.

July '11: Ed M feels 'liberated' having attacked News

as the Tories. This was a different order of things. I was not on bookplug mode but at least the diaries had our differences in there, the arguments TB and I had over this. I was able to defend him while also attacking what the media had become.

[Lord] Charles Spencer [brother of Diana, Princess of Wales] was in the front row and was wildly clapping every attack I made. He also invited us back to Althorp [stately home] for the next festival. The last time was the day of Rebekah's wedding I seem to remember. David Prescott also reminded me it was two years this week that *The Guardian* first broke the story of the extent of the hacking. That was when I did interviews from Barry Kilby's wedding and effectively got myself PNG status with Rebekah et al. So glad I had given their party a miss last time. I was a bit pissed off with myself that when Bacon said 'You're a friend of Rebekah's,' I said 'was'. It was not quite what I meant and I tried but failed to correct it. What I meant was that we were friends but ultimately these are political and commercial friendships and when power shifted to the Tories that is where they went. After talking to Fiona and a 'terribly torn' Tessa – PG said she had been all over Rebekah at Matthew's party – I texted Rebekah.

I said we had not spoken for more than a year, I could not defend what *News* had done or how they had handled it, but I did feel for her personally and if ever she wanted to talk she could. She texted back straight away. 'I remember when Dr Kelly died you said it is at times like this you realise who your friends are – so thanks for nothing.' So that was that. She had indeed been supportive but she had also said I had done nothing wrong. The difference here was that what they did was indefensible, and it did happen on her watch. Anyway clearly bridges were burned. I said obviously there was little point me saying this but I felt if she had asked for counsel outside from time to time they might not be in this mess but they confused criticism with hostility and that was up to them. If she ever wanted to discuss now, then and all in between, that was up to her, I felt. They operate like the Mafia. I was glad it was now clear I had strong views and wanted no part of it.

Thursday 7 July

I did Nicky Campbell first thing and they sprung Peter Oborne [*Daily Telegraph* journalist] as a fellow guest. He had done a huge attack on Cameron and Brooks but couldn't resist having a pop at me too. Ludicrously said I was News International spokesman because I said I wanted to make sure this story now spread to other papers like the *Mail*. I got the upper hand, though quite a few on Twitter thought I was bullying a bit. Did a few others then set off for Burnley for the first board meeting of UCFB. I had Simon Kuper of the *FT* with me. He wanted to do a piece on me and sport. I wanted to do a piece on the university. He was a bit dry and dour. Hours of interview peppered with calls to interrupt. Lots of people on the media stuff including a few interviews. I did a little blog on the fact that today was publication day and I wanted to avoid the media rounds, then into another load of stuff on News International.

UCFB Board meeting was pretty good. I saw my role as asking a lot of fairly detailed questions about fees, financing plan – they were looking to be ahead by eighteen months. 100 students in first year, 300 per year by the end of the three years. So 900 by the end. Accommodation plans had 'expandability'. Couple of hours in all, going through loads of issues and it did have the feel of a plan that was working. Headed back off with Simon Kuper for home and it was as I was briefing Douglas Alexander for *Question Time* tonight that I learned – via him telling me from the Sky breaking news tickertape – that James Murdoch had announced the closure of the *News of the World*.

The phone went pretty mental straight away and for the next two hours I was on doing phoners for radio and TV. I went mainly on the line of serial mismanagement and also that it was likely to make matters worse. There were reports of mutiny at Wapping including from *The Sun*. I listened to Murdoch, to Ed M, to others as I was going from interview to interview. It really was a pretty mindblowing development. And even more mindblowing that Rebekah was going to stay. Home to do more stuff. Fiona was loving it all, really felt that they were getting what they deserved. And then rumours emanating from the police that Coulson was to be arrested tomorrow. He probably deserved it but I felt a bit for him.

The Guardian published Jack Straw's review of the book. It was broadly OK. As I expected he had a pop back at some of the things I said about the Home Office but it was in the main fair and insightful. I did a blog on the reports that Cameron and Clegg were at odds over whether there should be a judge in charge of the inquiry. Also did an interview for *La Repubblica* [Italian daily newspaper]. Got a call out of the blue from someone wanting me to do a big strategy job for Deutsche Bank. Sent a note through to Ed re. his media speech. Said he needed to stop putting us and the Tories in same boat. Also needed a few ideas re. nature of the inquiry and possible new regulation.

Friday 8 July
Worked on a long piece for the Daily Beast [American website], mainly focused on Cameron's judgement. Then heard Cameron was doing a press conference. I tweeted that he would signal judge review, end of PCC and

parking BSkyB takeover. He did the first two. His opening statement was pretty strong and he looked OK. But he got a bit peevish and arrogant in Q&A. He was still pretty weak re. Brooks and though I think he was right to say he was still Coulson's friend, he did not admit as he should have done that he had made an error of judgement in going for Coulson when so many advised that he shouldn't. The judgement issue was the one to push now. Worked on a diary for the *Evening Standard* magazine. TB was emailing to say it was time to resurrect the feral beast speech.[*] But I was saying that I had argued we should have done stuff about the press.

Coulson was arrested just before the press conference. Imagine the wankology if it had been me while TB was PM. Even when they were drowning in this stuff, they were actually getting quite an easy ride. Cameron had a dig at me re. [Iraq WMD] dossiers – which I used to have a pop back, and suggested he was still not showing the judgement and leadership he needed to. He tried to draw in TB and GB as in the same boat. I could see why but he was going to get hit on this all ways. Ed did a pretty good response. I went in to do [Adam] Boulton and one or two other interviews. I was pretty much into my stride. Off to CNN. Chatted to TB on the way. He had done his Progress event which went really well. Quite a lot of people tweeted that he needed to do more. He did his 'New Labour stopped when he stopped being leader', which would run a bit. Re. the media he said he thought Cameron did well at the start but then was poor. He felt Ed had got a bit of strength out of this.

CNN interview was pretty strong. I had definitely burned all bridges. Tweeted Piers that I wish it had been him doing the interview. He was not responding. Either keeping his head down because of the phone-hacking stuff getting nearer the *Mirror* or because of closeness to the *NotW* lot. I was getting tweets retweeted massively at the moment e.g. Cameron's line about giving Coulson a second chance made him sound like a probation service not the Prime Minister. Also on the terrific exchanges between Paul McMullan and [comedian and actor] Steve Coogan on *Newsnight*. Coogan went for Dacre which was good. Long chat with Alex. He sounded pretty rested but was fed up with agents he was having to deal with. The money was becoming totally ridiculous. He was totally seized of the media stuff and enjoying it. He said that it was now up to the public to dictate this. They had to decide if they wanted to keep buying all this shit. But ultimately it won't change if they don't change their habits. He was also still saying, 'Why didn't you do stuff to deal with these bastards before?' We should have done. It was

---

[*] In 2007 Blair had attacked the media for behaving 'like feral beasts' and eschewing balance or proportion. He said newspapers should and would be subject to some form of new external regulation.

annoying the way I was lumped in with the TB–GB strategy when I had been arguing against it. He said we had to stop tolerating the abuse that went towards anyone who disagreed with a paper's line.

Saturday 9 July

I was feeling a bit wired and probably doing too much. Good job I didn't have all the media rounds for the book to do. I had agreed to do a piece for the Irish *Sunday Independent* so I worked on that, alongside a piece for the *FT* for Monday. On the press, I probably had to admit we had got too close, as a way of opening the space to be heard about what I was saying on what needed to be done now. Then an hour or so working before we headed to Richard Bacon's party. Nice house and garden. Lovely bloke. Lots of chat on the *News* situation and nobody felt Rebekah could stay. But who knows what she would do. Home for dinner and in between watching the OTT coverage of the last day of the *NotW* – you'd have thought the Queen Mum had died – we watched the new *Brighton Rock*.

Sunday 10 July

Used the media brief to whack off a shortish blog on Murdoch losing the plot, Cameron's judgement and [John] Yates's apology in the *Sunday Telegraph*, saying phone-hacking investigation was a cock-up. Ed M had set up his *Marr* interview well overnight, saying they were going to have a Commons vote on stalling the BSkyB decision pending the criminal investigation. He did well, though I wish he would start to broaden out more specifically. He was fine though and cutting through in a way he had not thus far. He said he was grateful that I had said two or three months ago they only respect strength and that this could be the making of him. Long chat with Calum who had had a row with Laura. We worked on a letter together but ultimately this was about booze. I was in no doubt that until he accepted it was a problem and he resolved it this kind of thing would keep happening. I found myself though saying things I know used to wind me up when my drinking was out of control. Murdoch was flying in 'to tackle the crisis' but in the interviews I did I said the game had changed and they didn't seem to get it at all.

Out to the Freud-organised dinner for PG, hosted by James Harding to celebrate Philip's piece for them on cancer. It was a nice enough do but I was really baffled why initially we had not been invited, and was pretty sure because I was being so critical of News. He had said it was because he felt they couldn't ask me for money because of all the stuff I did already. Then that it was a *Times* guest list. All odd. I said I found it strange and eventually PG fixed for us to go. But Fiona wasn't keen anyway now and so I went on my own. It felt even more bizarre because there were very few money people there. His doctors Mike Griffin and David Cunningham. Cancer czar Mike Richards. Then it was Sally, Peter H, David M, Douglas, a few others. Elisabeth Murdoch was very warm and said she felt she ought to say sorry for everyone. Rupert Murdoch had arrived in London and done a little walk to the Stafford Hotel with Rebekah and when asked his priority said 'this one' i.e. her. Totally losing touch. The dinner was a discussion of cancer. PG spoke well though he faltered and paused a fair bit. The cancer guys spoke well. I said the new charity had to be clear if it was about research or awareness. Mike was enjoying it. Gail and the girls seemed happy.

Monday 11 July

The *FT* were happy with the piece I did on Murdoch. I started with Rebekah's wedding to Charlie Brooks, going through all the media and politicos who were there. GB arriving late. Cameron and Osborne. Murdoch of course, Dacre. Then told of the conversation with Cameron at the reception. I said that of course I hoped he did not win the election but if he did, and if he felt he should do something to try to improve the political debate and look into the standards and regulation of the press, I would be willing to support him and offer ideas. I said it was partly the journalist in me that knew things were in a bad place, and that the politics–media relationship did not serve the public well. He said it had got worse, hadn't it, but then as soon as Murdoch arrived at our shoulders, we changed the subject, showing the fundamental dishonesty about the whole debate.

In the piece, I praised Ed for making himself an enemy of much of the media. He was right that at times we got too close to News International. Right too that given the historic media bias against us he understood why we tried to level the playing field.

TB had shared my analysis that the press had become a problem not just for politicians but for the country, but also argued that with all our other priorities, people would not understand us taking on the press, which is how the media and the Tories would portray it. He also pointed out that it would look like revenge for the fact they had turned. But there were political considerations too – trying to govern, or win elections, is hard enough without all the press against you, and I accept that for all of us, at times media support was something we courted at the expense of positions of principle on media issues. That trap has now hopefully been sprung. The latest revelations have forced the police, News International and the government finally to act. The most important development for the long term was the announcement by Cameron of inquiries both into the practices of the press, and also the system of regulation that should replace the Press Complaints Commission. It means that we now have a once-in-a-generation opportunity for a new settlement between politics, the media and the public.

Nobody can seriously argue that the press we get is the press we deserve. A spiral of decline has led to the tipping point. It was all tricky for Cameron, who did not look comfortable announcing it. He has personal relationships at stake and, because of his hiring of Andy Coulson as his communications director, his judgement in question. Already the backlash from parts of the press has begun as they seek to maintain that anything but toothless self-regulation is an assault on a free press. I said parts of the media remind me of the trade unions before Margaret Thatcher came along. They felt they were untouchable. The press has considered itself untouchable. Today had the feeling of a dam bursting.

The police put out a statement saying that news were leaking details that could prejudice their inquiries. Then news that GB was hacked and blagged, including [son] Fraser's illness, about which he was phoned by Rebekah. After the GB stuff broke I got a few bids so went to Millbank. I stepped up the rhetoric even more. Amoral. Not fit and proper. It was also running that the royals were hacked. I did C4 with Simon Hughes and was using the *FT* piece as my argument – yes we got too close but now politics had a chance. Cameron had fucked up again, Ed facing [Jeremy] Hunt in the Commons when he announced BSkyB bid referral to the Competition Commission. Ed strong. Hunt weak. Cameron behind the curve.

I called Alex in the US and agreed maybe now was the time to do the story of his medical records being obtained by the *News of the World*. To the Fabians dinner. Chuka Umunna [former PPS to Ed M] was doing a fairly low-energy speech as I arrived. New MP Alison McGovern introduced me as a legend etc. I did stuff about today, and said like Westland this was not necessarily a vote changer. But it gave Ed the chance to show leadership and it gave all of us the chance to shape a new landscape and have a better debate upon it. The Murdoch trap was sprung. Good crowd and enjoyed it though I was knackered. Home and then Carl Bernstein [American investigative journalist and author] called to pick my brains and to tell me he was planning to come over and write a book on what was going on. He felt this was the end of Murdoch and possibly the end of Cameron.

Tuesday 12 July

5 Live sent a radio car and I was on with George Eustice, Cameron's ex-press guy and now an MP down in Cornwall. He and I had had a bit

of contact pre election via Steve Morris and were pretty much on the same page on the press. It was interesting that a fair few of the new intake of MPs were in the right place. He pointed out that Cameron had set out on the course of wanting not to be beholden to them but bit by bit had got drawn in. Rayan and I set off and were bang on time arriving at Birmingham University. The room where I was due to speak was the Cameron Room – because it was where DC prepared for the TV election debate. GB apparently broke the door handle. I went off to the Centre for Haematology to see the new place funded by LLR. Good place and nice people. They had got £2.5 million out of LLR and said it really made a difference. Nice introduction from the principal and nice welcome. A thousand people there and it went really well.

The basic thesis was a bit gloomy – we only know if we have had a happy life when it ends – but there was a lot of colour and character along the way. Book signing for half an hour or so, then a quick meeting with people from the Armed Forces Mental Illness charity Blurt, then to dinner at the Vice-Chancellor's residence. Lovely food. Nice crowd, mainly great and good. Did a bit of a Q&A and there was a lot of interest in the Murdoch stuff and where I thought it would go. Also on my breakdown which people were always interested in. Kitty Ussher [former Labour Party politician] there and I gave her a lift back to London. I told her I was thinking about standing for Burnley seat and would almost certainly get it. She was now working for Demos [cross-party think tank]. Jamie Redknapp called to chew the fat re. Murdoch and also to try to get work experience for [wife] Louise's brother Sammy. Fixed with TBO and also some work with me.

Wednesday 13 July

I called Ed to go through PMQs. He felt he had to get it to Coulson via getting Cameron to agree with various propositions – Rebekah had to go, the inquiry had to be far-reaching, and then three questions on Coulson. I felt that was too much and suggested max two. He was definitely finding his voice on this though. Train to Sutton then met Richard Ryder for a tour of the Institute of Cancer Research. The deputy director did a general presentation then Mel Greaves, world leader in childhood leukaemia, showed how Darwinism informed their understanding of the disease – essentially in the survival of the fittest the strongest cancerous cells got through. He explained it well, was nice about the charity, and said young adults and older people were still a problem. But they would get there.

As twelve approached Richard and I wanted to see PMQs, but nobody knew where there was a telly. We ended up watching it on a laptop. Cameron better than before but still behind the curve and Ed doing well. Cameron then did a statement on the hacking inquiry and there followed the debate which was dominated by GB picking up on his stuff from yesterday on *The Sun* allegedly getting Fraser's medical records by illegal means. We got the train back, nice chat with Richard who felt the government was a lot weaker than most people realised. Cameron and Osborne were the big figures but neither were strategic. He also felt it was a mistake to have Andrew Cooper as head of strategy. Polling is too short term and it will play to the worst of Cameron. He was totally on my side of the argument re. the media. Cameron ended up having to back Labour's motion pulling the plug on News International's bid for BSkyB. I sent Ed a message. He had done well on this, and today felt like a big, important parliamentary moment. Of course there was a danger that it would lead to the press going for him a lot harder, and fighting harder for the Tories, but he would also get marked up by a lot of people. He has set the agenda from opposition on this, which is no mean achievement in itself. And News International have now had to abandon the bid. All this is high risk for Ed. But he has made it a lot harder for people to say he is weak. And he looked a lot more comfortable in his skin today, and Cameron less comfortable in his.

The usual sudden flurry of bids so I went to the Beeb via Canadian TV. I bumped into Mike White at Millbank. He felt GB was OTT because we all knew he had tried to stay close to the Murdoch lot even after the stuff about Fraser. Mike felt we owed something of an apology to *The Guardian* because we had seen them as more of an enemy. I said in my defence that I had argued long and hard for changing tack on the right-wing media but neither TB nor GB were keen. Home via CNN, where I tweeted again about the way Piers had gone to ground. I was admitting we got too close, defending the fact I had tried to move things, and saying Murdoch was now in meltdown because they had not done the right thing re. phone hacking early when they should have done. A very interesting *Newsnight*. They had politicians and pundits but also the public who didn't seem too fussed. Tory MP Louise Mensch was excellent and I tweeted to say so.

Thursday 14 July

General blog focusing on Cameron–Coulson judgement and TB quizzing me when I took the job. As I said before – did Cameron and Coulson have the eyeball-to-eyeball conversation? I was taking a few hours out though with the Sky Arts team round to do the main interview for the bagpipes documentary. Nice crowd and all easy enough. Big drama mid-morning when Maria [cleaner] was hyperventilating because she thought she had won the 161 million Euro lottery. She had all the right numbers but when we called it was the wrong date on the ticket. What chance that? David Willetts called re. UCFB and sounded really keen so we were hoping for a visit. The Murdochs started the day refusing to go to the DCMS [Department for Digital, Culture, Media and Sport] select committee but did a volte face after getting a summons from the Commons Serjeant at Arms. So another round of bids which I stalled while doing my first mentor lesson with Finlay MacDonald [musician and composer] for bagpipes documentary. Then to St Stephens to meet the Hacked Off [press reform group] campaign team. They had just had a planning meeting with Hugh Grant [actor and media activist] and others. I arranged to meet some of them at PizzaExpress. I emphasised – and later said in blog and interviews – that it was important this did not look like a campaign against newspapers by the rich, the powerful and the famous, but a campaign to get good journalism to drive out the bad.

Finlay was a lovely guy – attached to the School of Piping and also with his own band – and it was amazing how much came back, even the ability to read the music. We did an hour on the chanter, then the pipes. Amazingly my own pipes were not far from being playable. I was definitely going to get on with him. He kept telling me he thought I was 'really good'. Good teacher more like. Then to Millbank and a stack more interviews. This was getting bigger and bigger in the States because of the suggestion 9/11 victims were hacked. PG called and said he thought I was getting the tone right but needed to watch I didn't do too much. Lots of tweets saying I needed a haircut.

Friday 15 July

There was a lot of interesting stuff from Clegg in the papers on the kind of system we needed for the press and also media ownership. I did a rare blog in praise of him. Out on the bike then to meet Louise [Shackleton, wife of David Miliband] at the Honest Sausage. David said they had both felt supported by their friends but not by us so it was important to clear the air a bit. She seemed quite stressed and clearly had found the whole thing with Ed really difficult. She had been totally shocked that he stood against David, and at the nature of his campaign. And needless to say, she felt the party made the wrong choice. It had felt at times like his campaign was out to destroy David. She worried that if David went back on the inside in some way, they would do it again. It was all so sad, I said, that we had all just about got through the whole TB–GB dramas intact, and now along comes another one, but this time with real brothers. I said that he had to be in or out, either get back into some major position – for example head of policy and manifesto preparation – or get right out. She wanted him out but equally she knew that for David it was an important part of his life and part of him wants to help the Labour Party get back to power. Even though the whole thing had been so awful, he still wanted to help. But she couldn't see it working. It had clearly been horrific, and she was clearly upset, on the verge of tears at times. She said she felt she had done her bit to hold the family together, that she and David had always been kind to Ed, so it was hard not to feel very hurt. There had been a ruthlessness about the campaign that would shock you, she said. 'What, even after TB–GB?' 'I guess he learned from that,' she said. She knew David and I had spoken, and I said I wanted her to understand why Fiona and I had not been perhaps as supportive as they would have liked. The first thing is that, in common with most people, we thought David was clear favourite. There was also a part of me hoping a new generation would come through on the strategy side. But most of all I said she had to realise we had wanted out of things. The last bit with GB had been difficult, and I had ended it feeling weighed down by the whole thing. I had left TB but never really left, and then Gordon had got me back in, or as in as I would let myself be drawn, and both Fiona and I felt suffocated by it all. Sufffocated by the feeling we would never come up for air. Fiona felt David had expected too much of us, they had expected us to be there on their terms, when it was clear we were trying to get away from it all. She also felt that once David was into leadership campaign mode, he only really bothered with us when he wanted or needed my advice. I got that maybe better than she did, because I knew he had to be totally focused, but it meant she just wanted us to be out of it all, truly escape. There had been so many moments of departure but no actual departure. David had an idea of what I could give him based on what he used to see, but I was no longer in that place, mentally. With TB, even when it was shit, I had the motor full on, but I had been ground down, and though obviously I wanted David to win, the idea of being right at the heart of another fight, another round of expectations, was hard. So I took the easy way out, to be honest, thinking David would win anyway. I said I really didn't want either of them to feel it was in any way a slight on them, and I hoped our friendship would stay strong. I got the feeling she completely got where I was coming from but felt maybe I underestimated just how hard it had been for them, and how much therefore they needed support from friends. Where she and Fiona were in agreement was in saying all of us – the Blairites – fucked things up by allowing GB to take over and by failing to strike when we could and should have done. I said it was never so blindingly obvious for me. I wanted to give GB the benefit of the doubt that he might grow once he got there, and I was never totally convinced David was totally up for it at the moment when the chance to strike came.

July '11: Heart-to-heart with David M wife, Louise

David was always worried about tearing the party apart. He also knew that Gordon was never to be underestimated in a fight.

As we chatted my phone started going with a rash of calls because it was announced Rebekah was resigning. So the meltdown continued.

It was a friendly chat but I could tell she was hurting, and said that if we had in any way contributed to that I was sorry. I said it was important she did not become bitter about the way the leadership panned out. I started to channel David S! I said she should try to forgive Ed. She said that was very hard. I said in which case they would need to get out, to move on. She said every day people approached David and said he was the right guy for the leadership but in a way it made it worse. I said I had exactly the same thing. If I had a pound for every time someone told me 'you picked the wrong brother...' But she was right, it made it worse, so it must be much, much harder for them.

Went for a haircut at Palushi's the Albanian and tweeted it out as there had been so many 'get a haircut' tweets yesterday. Then to Sky to do Boulton, where I was very measured about the need for regulation independent of government but free from media interests. I got the tone right. Did a few others then to the Gay Hussar for Geoffrey Goodman's 90th birthday. Chatted a lot to Glenys. Neil was perfectly friendly, but something had definitely changed since the leadership election. Tom Watson came in late and got a huge ovation.[*] Watson called me over at one point to show me something in a book about how he and Charlie Whelan had had a spat. Watson hadn't replied the other day when I texted him to say that I found it hard to forgive him for a previous campaign he was involved in – getting rid of TB – but he had done superbly well on this one, on phone hacking.

Geoffrey made a terrific speech about how he felt progressive voices were rising again and that the world was changing and coming back our way. He was as ever a bit over-sentimental re. Nye Bevan [late Labour minister for health], Neil, one or two others, but he spoke really well, both the content and also the voice which was remarkable for a ninety-year-old. Nice chat with Jill Palmer. John Jackson and Bill H the only other *Mirror* people there. Nice do. Off to do ITV then Al-Jazeera. Rebekah's resignation had been inevitable. I didn't particularly feel for her as they had been brought down by their own mistakes, their hubris and sense of untouchability. But as Grace said, it felt at one point like there had been a friendship of sorts there. Fiona's view was that all of them just used us as they needed us and they deserved what they got.

---

[*] As a member of the DCMS select committee, Watson had diligently questioned Rupert and James Murdoch and Rebekah Brooks in pursuance of the phone-hacking scandal.

Saturday 16 July

I was back over fifteen stone. Long bike ride. Round for dinner at David and Tessa's. I gave her a bit of a hard time on the fact we never did anything about the press, and she courted them all rather than challenged them.

Sunday 17 July

Out on the bike then to the airport and off to Nice for a LLR event. Tweeted. Bumped into a 'TB fan' at the desk who said history would be kind to us, and upgraded me for the flight out. Landed, cab to Golfe Juan, Hotel de la Mer. Out to the dinner at a beachside restaurant. Pretty wild weather though. There were a fair few rich people there but they were real tight arses. Charlie Metcalfe [businessman supporter of UK] and one or two of his friends rescued it but it was not as easy as it should have been when the auction got going. £10k for a dinner with Ian Botham, £17k for a statue, but otherwise hard pounding. Had the pipes with me and played a bit. They reckoned we would be close to £200k for the ride by the end. David Montgomery [media investor] was there with his wife Sophie and we had a bit of a chat about the Murdoch scene. Then came news Paul Stephenson [commissioner, Metropolitan Police] had quit as head of the Met.

Monday 18 July

The hotel was fairly low grade and the noise from a faulty cistern next door meant I hadn't slept well. Had breakfast then got a cab to the airport. Joe Hemani was sitting a few rows in front so spent a fair bit of the flight talking to him, the usual mix of football and politics. Richie Benaud [former Australian cricket captain] was on the flight too, looking pretty old. I did a blog headlined 'Cameron would have handled the crisis better if he had gone to a comprehensive.' He had still not got why this was damaging him, the judgement calls re. Coulson, the closeness to Rebekah, the Sky decision. I did get a feel from the public schoolboys doing the bike ride that they had so much advantage in life but they were not rounded. He didn't get how most people lived. Out on the bike in the rain then out to [head of sixth form] Malcolm Rose's farewell at William Ellis before collecting Grace from the station after her few days in Scotland helping out Susan [Law, AC cousin] at Riding for the Disabled. Yates finally quit from the Yard. Totally deserved all the opprobrium coming his way.

Tuesday 19 July

A bit of a media tarting day, with the circus of the Murdochs, then Rebekah, and earlier Stephenson and Yates at select committees. Did a round of pre-interviews, both commenting on the scandal generally, but also what they would expect and how I thought they should handle it. Lunch with Caroline Daniel [*FT*] after getting my phone mended in Hampstead. She had a new bloke, also loving her job, and wanting me to think of interesting interview pairings. To Millbank to do the *Daily Politics* special, from where I watched the hearings with David Davis and David Aaronovitch. Rupert seemed pretty out of it, James too management speak and false politeness, Wendi Deng [Rupert's wife] the star when she went for a protester who tried to get a plate of foam into Murdoch's face. The MPs did OK, though one or two were hopeless. Tom Watson not quite as forensic as I expected. Louise Mensch went for the *Mirror* and the *Mail* again. Tory press HQ were putting out stuff from my diaries following the questions about Murdoch visiting Cameron via the back door. There were no killer moments though I thought James might be in trouble for admitting that they had continued to pay Mulcaire's legal bills, and there were still a lot of unanswered questions about the payoff to Gordon Taylor [CEO, Professional Footballers' Association, whose phone had been hacked]. So it was not over even if the current storm was abating, and would probably reach the apex with Cameron recalling MPs tomorrow. My main point in post-event interviews was how divorced Rupert seemed from the detail, and how James should have been better briefed. They had not been allowed to make an opening statement but Rupert did a version of it at the end. Rebekah was much more poised and they didn't really land a blow.

To the new restaurant at the hotel at St Pancras for dinner with Delia Smith and Michael Wynn-Jones. Nice place, very buzzy, both on good form. She was desperate for us to do more to bring the Tories down. Not sure about Ed. Wanted me to fill them in on the hearings. Alex called from the States. Felt the Murdochs were poor, RW cool. Fred Michel [James Murdoch lobbyist] asked me my verdict. His was James did well, MPs badly! I asked Matthew Freud for his verdict. 'Marry an orphan,' he said.

Wednesday 20 July

Ed M called seven-ish about the Cameron statement and debate. He felt he had to keep pressing on Coulson but also try to get above it. I felt he should use the 'wilful blindness' line one of the MPs used yesterday. Also be cool and try not to let it turn into a bearpit. I did a blog saying Cameron ought to use today finally to admit an error of judgement – which he half did – and also for Osborne to get out there defending him and admitting his role. Bumped into Tom Kelly [former TB spokesman] who was now moving to another job with Network Rail. He felt Cameron would end up having to apologise. Obvious Coulson heading for jail. Then got the train to York. Was minding my own business when I saw on Twitter Cameron had mentioned my diaries – re. meetings with Murdoch – and I tweeted away merrily about that.

But then got a rash of messages that in a rant trying to put Labour spin doctors in the same boat as Coulson, Cameron referred to me 'falsifying' government documents. I consulted with TB and Sue Gray who agreed I should write to Gus O'Donnell pointing out I was cleared by three inquiries and asking for the evidence. Sent a letter while at Huntington School in York. Was asked about it – as at Harrogate later – in the context of what it said about Cameron that he ignored inquiries. Lots of twitterers suggesting I challenge him to say it outside Parliament and sue. It showed a very peevish under pressure side to him, and a nasty streak too. TB felt he did too much of that kind of thing when he was under pressure. That being said he felt that though Ed had got himself some breathing space, and shown leadership, Labour were in danger of diving down a cul-de-sac on this. There was also the possibility they would end up with the media even more offside, and with a real mission to kill.

TB was currently working on MEPP which he said was even more frustrating than usual. Good session at the school, mainly Q&A then book signing. Then to Harrogate and the festival event at the theatre. Interviewed by Henry Sutton [novelist] then Q&A and book signing. Real variety – from Palestine to did I have a Burnley tracksuit to where do I get my hair cut. Henry good in pushing the diaries and the novel, though we kicked off with the current stuff, including Cameron whack today.

Thursday 21 July

Really nice breakfast at the hotel, then headed for the station and off to King's Cross via York. Lunch with Nicola Howson [Freuds CEO]. Matthew Freud had said to Nicola that his strategy was to escape the idea he was a Murdoch. They had all been trying to tell Rebekah what the right approach would have been – investigate, fess up, sort out – but they went into denial mode early on. Nice chat, nice woman, really liked her. I was chasing Gus for a response to my letter about what Cameron had said about me, but despite being told it was coming yesterday I still didn't have it.

Friday 22 July

James Murdoch in a bit of bother because Colin Myler [*News of the World*'s last editor] and Tom Crone [*NotW* lawyer] had sent a letter to the select committee saying James Murdoch had been 'mistaken' in his evidence re.

not seeing the 'for Neville (Thurlbeck)' email which seemed to establish they knew this was not just a rogue reporter. Did a blog on that, on more questions re. Coulson, and on Cameron's whack at me, saying I was not going just to take it. Later out to TBO for a meeting with team from the King's office in Jordan.

Saturday 23 July

News totally dominated by a massacre by a lone wolf terrorist at a summer camp in Norway, seventy-seven dead. Then later Amy Winehouse [singer] dying. Email from Sue Gray with suggested Gus draft letter. One par OK – 'political knockabout that went too far' – and made clear it was about the February briefing paper not the September dossier. But it had a line about 'not casting any NEW aspersions' which neither Sue nor I liked. I did a rewrite and sent it over. She said she would try it on Gus. Radio Wiltshire then Ryan Tubridy on Radio 2, and this was his first of eight shows. Good interview, hacking, career, mental illness. I was tweeted by Emma Sayle who was listening on the way to the Test at Lord's and ended up joining her, Liam Botham, and later Beefy and Eric Clapton [musician] and his wife, in the box. Really good day's cricket. Liked Clapton. Bright. Felt DC was really damaged by the hacking stuff. Also sure that other papers were going to be dragged into it.

I was on Sky at one point and that led to Jonathan Agnew asking me to go on *Test Match Special* during tea. Had a good look around the press area. Met up with Boycott for his usual egotistical rant at politics, bankers, anything really. Nice day though. Eric clearly a close friend of Ian's. I gave him a sanitised version of the time I was suicidal at one of his concerts, but made sure he knew it was illness, not his music.

Sunday 24 July

Out on the bike for a bit, then to Holland Park for Maud [Millar, Fiona niece] singing in the opera *Albert Herring*. Alex texted from the US re. the *Sunday Telegraph* chasing re. the story of his medical records. He was trying to get it sorted quietly.

Tuesday 26 July

Phone hacking was dipping down the agenda and the economy coming centre stage again. Growth figures were being trailed as disappointing. To Random House to drop off the copy-edited Volume 4, Joanna worried about timings of legal and Cabinet Office vetting. Lunch with David Mellor at Sartoria. Not impressed by Cameron. Felt he lacked a project. Worried that the Murdochs would get away with it. Trying to persuade me to get into LBC. Thought I would enjoy it. Saying I was right to stay out of the Lords, that he felt I was bigger than most of the people in there.

Still chasing Gus. PG chasing me for help on the chapter he was writing as an epilogue to a new version of *The Unfinished Revolution* [1999 book by PG]. He sent me TB's intro, which was a bit heavy on the line of GB having run an Old Labour economic policy, but pretty good in terms of what you needed to fight a campaign. Donald called to say Mum had slipped outside the house in Scotland and was really badly bruised down the face. At one point she thought her eye had popped out.

Wednesday 27 July

One year to the Olympics. Blogged on that. Did a Q&A for an Albanian interview pre the trip there in October. Kosta Petrov [Macedonian businessman] said Albania and Macedonia were all systems go but Kosovo less so. Sam Nurding [Louise Redknapp brother] round in the morning, gave him a research project pre his meeting at TBO Friday. Nice kid.

Thursday 28 July

Really odd sleeping pattern at the moment. Bed early, fall asleep, wake up three-ish, awake till five or six, back to sleep then finding it hard to wake up. DS said stop the pills so did. Out on the bike, then to see PG and Georgia to go through his final chapter. Up to a hundred pages now. Some good stuff in there. He wanted me to help rewrite it so I took it home and did a fairly careful edit. In the morning I sent a fairly aggressive email to Gus O'Donnell on the lack of a response to my complaint and around 6 p.m. his letter finally came. It was as good as I was going to get so I put them on my website and said that was the end of the matter so far as I was concerned.

Friday 29 July

Ed M called. He was recovering from the operation to fix his nose. His voice if anything sounded worse, but it was early days after the anaesthetic. He was about to go on holiday and I was suggesting that he try to see Tim Livesey before going. He still didn't have a strong team and though I wasn't sure if Tim was a chief of staff, I felt he was worth seeing to work out if he might fit in somewhere. He was quizzing me about the fallout from phone hacking. He felt fine about how it had gone from his perspective. 'Maybe I should have gone for them three months earlier

when you suggested it'. But the worry now of course was that fundamentally nothing much changed and we end up with most of the media
against him and the Murdoch lot with a vengeance.

He felt fine about that, also felt that the Leveson Inquiry would have
to come up with some fairly strong recommendations. I said he needed to
get on to other issues quickly, ones where the public really felt resonance
and impact on their lives. I would still be hard-pressed to know what his
main political message was. Also there was a real lack of strength in depth
and he had to bring other people on. The American situation was grim,
with Obama trying to get a deal done with the Republicans on raising
the debt ceiling, but the new right-wingers were fucking crazy people.

Saturday 30 July

In to town to meet up with some guy on Twitter who wanted a book signed.
I got done for jumping red lights on the bike. The cop had followed me
through six lights so I didn't have a leg to stand on. He gave me a notice
that basically said if I was done for this again in the next year, all these
offences would come into play. Home then set off for Wheatley. Mum was
looking a little better but the bruising on her face had extended to her neck
so she was in quite a state. She had an amazing attitude to it all though.
Still smiling. Took her out to dinner and we had a nice chat. Matthew Doyle
emailed late on re. the *Mail on Sunday* splash which said Chilcot would
damn TB and also criticise me and Jack S. Not sure the extent to which
it was briefed or just made up but I agreed with Matthew he should put
out a strong line to the effect that it was a deliberate attempt to prejudge
a report which had not been written.

Sunday 31 July

A little bit of follow-up to the *MoS* stuff. Out for a run but I didn't have
my inhaler and something set off my asthma, so I walked back. Played the
pipes in [AC's sister] Liz's garden. Nice lunch there then set off with Jamie
[Naish, nephew] for home. He seemed to be doing pretty well work-wise.
Back to go out for dinner with Nick and Clio Blake [personal friends].
Nick felt Leveson would be pretty sound. Northern judge, probably not
keen on the metropolitan elite.

Monday 1 August

Spent most of the day pottering work-wise in between watching a lot of
the cricket. England way on top against India and ended winning to go

two-up. One more draw and they are world No. 1. I was also reading [former Zimbabwe Test cricketer] Henry Olonga's book. I had forgotten his and [coach, former Zimbabwe captain] Andy Flower's role in the anti-Mugabe protests.

Tuesday 2 August
Twitter valued at $8 billion. Did a tweet asking how much we all got. Off to Sussex with Fiona and Molly. Someone tweeted they saw me at Charing Cross 'with your gorgeous dog and lovely wife'! To Battle, met by Tom Hammick and his son Charlie and off to their charming, fairly ramshackle house in the countryside. Nice time. Tom's wife Martha a good laugh. Fiona got on well with Martha's mum Jill who was a big fan re. the education stuff. All very jolly and small-talky, nice kids, nice walk, then back.

Wednesday 3 August
To Portland for a long session with Steve's team and the top comms people from National Grid. They seemed keen on what we had to offer so hopefully it would work out OK. Joanna came round with Volume 4 MS p.m. to go through the legal report. Grace off to Greece.

Thursday 4 August
Heard that the Kosovo government trip was on for September. To Ron Marx to sort a calf and shoulder problem. Storms. Lots of coverage of the phone-hacking stuff getting closer to Piers. Fiona went to see [Jonathan Powell's wife] Sarah Helm's play, *Loyalty*, at the Hampstead Theatre, and came back deeply underwhelmed. She thought it was all a bit silly. She went for a drink with some of the actors later and seemed to think I had made the right decision to give it a miss.

Friday 5 August
The markets were all pretty much in meltdown. Cameron, Clegg and Osborne all away. Blogged on the economy blowing away any silly season. Lunch with Liz Lloyd. She had an interesting take on TB. He had not been the driving force behind New Labour – it was already happening. It was a force. He led something already underway, but since leaving – even more than when he was there – he defined himself against the party. It was detracting from what ought to be defined as a big success story, Iraq or no Iraq. Out for dinner with Melanne Verveer [Hillary Clinton

August '11: Markets in meltdown

adviser] and Phil. They were over for a week's holiday. She was enjoying her role – Hillary's ambassador for women's issues globally – but quite down on Obama, very down on US politics generally. Obama was likely to want Hillary to leave before her time to help campaign for him. She was looking to get out and join Bill in the 'Clinton PLC save the world in different ways' enterprise.

She had seen a fair bit of Cherie B and Sarah Brown, felt both were doing OK. She had a pretty good take on TB–GB – TB still had something special and Clintonesque, GB just lacked it. Obama was struggling though. I had seen his speech on the economy today, which he made to a military gathering, and he seemed lacking in mojo. The people in the audience behind him looked a bit underwhelmed. I felt he lacked a really clear sense of self. She felt that politics was taking such a hammering from the right. Also he tended to shy from fights rather than engage in them. She said he needed more sons of bitches like me who would not shy from a fight. They had stopped making the case properly. He was a good communicator but the overall communications was weak.

She felt – this in response to my saying so – that he could lose. The Tea Party though had a real grip now on the Republicans. The candidate would get the job by making crazy statements to get elected. That was his hope, the awfulness of the other side. But mainstream America had vanished. People felt the education system had failed. I said who'd have thought Bush was a moderate? We ended up swapping stories about how much we liked Bush on the personal front. Nice evening, at Vilandry. She felt we seemed on good form but I think wondered why we had no burning desire to stay involved. She was pleased I was speaking to Ed but felt he was weak. She got a lot of her UK politics from [Baroness] Mary Goudie [Labour peer] who said of the TB lot I was the only one really still banging the Labour drum. Not very loudly I said.

Saturday 6 August

Off to Burnley. Start of the season. The papers had a story about Sally Bercow doing *Big Brother*. I texted John to say I thought it was a really bad idea. He called me and said he was incandescent about it. He really was a feminist and believed spouses should be able to carve out independent lives. He felt it would be great if she could get a seat. But she was really pushing him with this. I asked if he thought I should text her and he felt yes, definitely, so long as she didn't think he put me up to it. He sounded quite down about it. He felt that they were only really interested because she was the Speaker's wife and it was inevitably going to damage his reputation as well as hers.

We chatted away for a while then I texted her to say my alarm bells were ringing loudly. It was bad for both of them. Please don't. She replied, 'Alastair you're a legend but it is 90 per cent done deal.' Richard Desmond [owner Channel 5] had promised £100k to her favourite charity and she couldn't sleep at night if she turned that down. Also Max Clifford would handle her PR when she was 'in the house' and make clear she and John were not the same thing. I replied that she should not fall for the charity thing. Desmond was interested in Desmond. Max was interested in Max. She could do real damage to herself and she could wave bye-bye to a seat. She felt she already had though. She kept saying she would not fuck up. I fear she would have no control of it. Got to Burnley early to do a meeting with some of the first intake of UCFB, mainly local, and a bit of media. Match [v Watford] OK but 2–2 felt like a couple of points dropped.

Sunday 7 August

Sally Bercow sent me a couple of texts in response to mine, advising her against *Big Brother*, saying she had already decided and she knew how to handle it. He had said yesterday that he felt this was a product of the alcoholic mindset, she was recovering, but now needed things like this. Riots overnight in different parts of London [following the police shooting to death of Mark Duggan, who they believed was carrying a handgun]. A sense developing that the government were all on holiday and not on top of it. Fiona, Molly and I set off early and drove to Burgundy. Stayed in an OK hotel which had a wonderful outdoor sculpture exhibition in the garden.

Monday 8 August

Set off early and arrived at Puymeras in the afternoon. Did a blog on the riots which were grim. They'd started over police handling of a suspect they ended up shooting but it went quickly to looting and wanton criminality. Cameron still away. Pressure building. There was a sense developing of where political dividing lines would go – Tories blaming us for failing on benefits and responsibility, us linking to cuts and economic austerity. People seemed to be saying Ed was striking the right tone.

Tuesday 9 August

Did a blog on this being a test as mayor now for Boris Johnson. Ed called and we agreed he should triangulate between what would be a hard Tory message and what would be a kneejerk reaction from the left. Tough on crime tough on the causes of crime was where people needed to be. Did a note. Then up to Merindol to see the house we were thinking of buying. Not quite right but they put us in touch with a Vaison estate agent who agreed to show us a few around the same price.

Wednesday 10 August

I was putting in some pretty long rides. Blogging most days but feeling off the pace. Maybe no point doing this stuff. Parliament was recalled for a debate tomorrow [on rioting and civil unrest]. Another chat with Ed who had cut short holiday ahead of DC. But now he was worried Cameron would really go hardline and be able to portray Labour as weak. We worked over the phone on his speech.

Thursday 11 August

Ed called several times. It all got a bit conference call/write by committee and in the end I said we should get a new draft of the speech and then speak again. The tone was fine but Cameron was bound to be able to have more substance. After I sent through a rewrite, Ed texted, 'Do you want a job?' I said no. I didn't mind doing the odd bit but was not keen to get back. We listened to the debate online. Both of them did pretty well. Tweeted and blogged that I felt Cameron was vulnerable at certain points.

Friday 12 August

Fiona and I having a nice time just the two of us, though the estate agentry was going to get complicated I think. Nice enough guy and seemed to know his stuff. Did a blog re. Cameron needing to show more respect and TLC for the police and military. Very helpful on the process. We saw half a dozen or so houses today. One OK, the rest not suitable.

Saturday 13 August

To Malaucène to get running repairs on the bike. To Avignon to collect the boys. Burnley lost at Palace [2–0].

Sunday 14 August

Out with some of [cycling aficionado] Craig Entwistle's guests [local, UK-born, cycling holiday, business] at Faucon for a five-hour ride round the base of Ventoux. I was easily the slowest, and not the oldest! Feeling it. Ed sent through a draft speech for tomorrow. Cameron on a very right-wing agenda now.

Monday 15 August

Text from Sue Gray saying the Detainees Inquiry [into alleged torture and mistreatment of UK terror suspects] wanted my details because they might want to see me. Annoying.

Tuesday 16 August

Another drama from Grace in Greece. Handbag nicked earlier in the holiday. Now she had got herself booked on the wrong flight on the wrong day. Had to get Maggie Draycott [British Airways] involved to sort. Rory not feeling great. Spent part of p.m. at the doctor's. Good service again. More phone-hacking stuff came out so did a bit on that.

Wednesday 17 August

As I feared from calls over the past couple of days, PG and Gail called to say they were not coming because he was not well again. He was going to have to go in for more tests. I could tell he was worried, more than the last time. He said that it was probably OK but it didn't sound great. Georgia and Grace arrived and were both on good form. I was going into a bit of a depressive dip though. Rowing a lot with Calum.

Thursday 18 August

Rode up Mont Ventoux from the Malaucène side, in two hours thirty. Rory did 1.13 from Bedoin. Elvis's 'Glory Glory, Allelulah' came on iPod shuffle as I did the last bend.

Friday 19 August

Arnaud [Bercker, estate agent] called and said there was a house he wanted us to see. At Faucon. We both loved it. Especially the view over Ventoux. Really nice. Definitely the one. Belgian retired couple selling. Out for dinner at Nyons. PG texted to say the results were not good. The cancer was back, this time in the lymph nodes. I spoke to both of them. Gail said it was a matter of months. PG as ever was refusing to accept it. He said they would not treat him if they didn't feel there was a chance but certainly grim news. We chatted about when, how and what he should say to the girls. We said nothing tonight and I felt a bit down about the fact their holiday was about to be ruined. PG said he would sleep on it. He sounded unusually down, not like the last time when he had been resolute at every moment. Of course they had said last time that if it came back he was a goner so he knew the girls would remember that.

Saturday 20 August

I had a long chat with Philip, going over what he should say to the girls, and then he called them. Georgia was crying a lot and then went for a long walk. Grace was more upbeat, or at least more ready to take the line that they would not put him through chemo again if they didn't think there was a chance. The boys supportive. Calum was great with them though he and I were not getting on well.

Sunday 21 August

Heatwave. We took the girls to Vaison then to Avignon station so they could head home. They would be going straight back and seeing PG in hospital. Calum went to Marseille for the football. Fiona, Rory and I to Craig's for dinner.

Monday 22 August

Another visit to the Boonens' [sellers] house in Faucon and this time we made an offer. Decided also to buy the piece of land that went with it. Fiona said is this mad? But it felt right. The view was out of this world, and the house felt very Fiona.

Friday 26 August

Out on the bike with Rory and Craig in howling wind. Horrible. Tweeted my hatred of bikes, heat, wind and being fifty-four. All afternoon with the estate agent and then the notaire. It all almost went belly-up, because they had misunderstood how the new tax laws would operate, so we went off for a cup of tea, worrying it might be off. But then they called and said as we were offering the asking price they would go for it. So all on again and we all trooped to the notaire to sign a contract. Fiona and I would have to have a French civil partnership. Also a French will. All getting more and more adminy. A storm broke out just as we left the office for Puymeras.

Out for dinner at Leonardo's and Calum and I had a bad scene when he said he wanted to try the Clan Campbell whisky. I didn't handle it well. Fiona was angry with me, Calum upset.

Saturday 27 August

I tried to speak to Calum but there had been a big and negative change in how he saw me. Basically I felt he was blaming all problems on me. There was a disrespect that went beyond what might be the usual father–son thing. And I was at a loss to know what to do about the drinking. Alex had said the other day that as I had been through the same thing I ought to be able to help but it didn't feel like that. I sensed it was all, or certainly a lot of it, about the feeling we forced him to go to Manchester. But when I think how much he used to enjoy time with me at Puymeras, and how close we were and how bad and angry things had got, it was heartbreaking. Alex was right that I ought to be in a good position to help, but it didn't feel like that. I felt I could not get through to him, and I felt a resentment that I didn't know how to deal with. The boys headed off around two.

Sunday 28 August

Craig changed my chainset ready for our departure for the coast. United beat Arsenal 8–2. Alex said he felt sorry for Wenger. Under pressure. He spoke to the Beeb for the first time since their row [over documentary film on football agent son Jason] began years ago. I went to the bike shop in Malaucène to buy a few bits and bobs, and they were majorly excited because Eddy Merckx [Belgian former champion cyclist] had been in and went for a ride with the mechanics at the shop.

Monday 29 August

Bike OK on bigger gears. Manningham-Buller out saying she had warned TB Iraq no risk to UK. The revenge of the establishment was definitely going to pick up. Off to the coast. Hotel Bailli de Suffren at Rayol-Canadel. Pretty luxurious. Grace and Sissy loved it. I was less keen. On another dip.

Wednesday 31 August

Bike to Lavandou Bormes village. Really tough hills in the area. St Tropez for the afternoon and evening. Not my cup of tea but F and the girls enjoyed it. Something horrible about the masses – mainly aspirational middle class – all down at the quayside watching these super-rich tossers partying on their yachts.

Friday 2 September

Breakfast then took the girls to Avignon and carried on for Crillon-Le-Brave for the weekend of Peter Chittick and Carolyn Fairbairn's anniversary festivities. They really pushed the boat out. The whole hotel was given over to their guests, split between family, Insead [business school], Winchester [where they lived] and a few others. Nice crowd but were definitely at the age where people talked mainly about their kids, their parents' proximity to death and their dog, though we were the only ones who actually had our dog with us. Good chat with the mother of the boy who had just got the worst GCSEs at Eton! At lunch with some of the Winchester friends, including a lawyer who had been to one of my speeches and was very friendly. Mark Byford [former BBC Deputy Director-General] the only person there I knew. Had a few chats with him. Nice people at our table at dinner. One or two others there keen to talk to me re. my mental health stuff.

Saturday 3 September

We had got the wrong day for the Ventoux ride – it was yesterday – so instead I went out with a couple of the guys round all my favourite routes, including Col de Madeleine [high mountain pass]. Perfect conditions. Lunch at a chateau where Peter and the hotel got their wine. Played the pipes in cycling gear to get the guests over to lunch. Mainly talking to a woman called Liz, an old friend of Carolyn's, re. mental illness. She was one of the people speaking at the main dinner tonight and got one of the best laughs later when she set out all the advice I had given her – just make one point – and followed it. Off to Vaison to get Molly sorted for the return at the vets, then buy some decent clothes for tonight, then back to pack. There was a mass going on in the little church in Crillon so I popped in. Pretty full. Nice mood and atmosphere. Mark Byford the only one of the UK guests in there. He told me he had gone in the opposite direction to TB – from Catholic to Church of England because he could not bear the Catholic Church's handling of the child abuse issue. A storm later so the dinner was moved inside. Tough work for the staff but they just about did it. I was next to Heather Rabbatts and a woman called Isobel who was advising me to take on another big job. Several of them over the weekend were urging me to get more active, possibly on the TV front. The speeches – seven in total – were all pretty good. Emily [daughter] made one and was really quite impressive for sixteen. Bed at two again.

Sunday 4 September

Breakfast with Peter and Carolyn and one or two of the other guests, then set off on the drive home. Didn't feel very rested, partly because of house hunting and Philip but mainly because of Calum. Fiona and I were getting on well when on our own though, which was good. The kids were all there when we got home but Calum was disengaged still.

Monday 5 September

Fixing the diary for the next few weeks then round to see PG. He looked better than I expected, but he couldn't eat and he said he was aware that he didn't have years to live. Months if lucky. He was actually surprised to have got out. He talked quite movingly of the chats he had had with Gail, and also his sense of a moment of reckoning in which he weighed up the good and bad in his life. He was so pleased to have had the new *Unfinished Revolution* delivered as he was there. It was like a birth.

The book looked great and I was looking forward to re-reading the old stuff from years ago, and seeing how it played out with the new. It was an upbeat and confident portrayal of the changes we [New Labour] had made, which was contrasting with the way Alistair Darling's book, currently being serialised, was coming over. Very harsh on GB, and angry. Lovely chat with Philip, usual TB, GB, current scene stuff, also re. our kids and how they were doing, then off on one of my book-signing bike rides. Hatchards, parliamentary bookshop and Waterstones NW3. Lots of admin and usual post-holiday bollocks to pick up on. Got into PG's book. Page 230 by bedtime.

Tuesday 6 September

Out to the Renaissance Hotel at St Pancras for a photo shoot with Cambridge Jones [celebrity photographer] and the portrait artist Alexander Talbot Rice. They were working together on combined painting/photos in a project for the Variety Club [children's charity]. Twenty-five photographers doing four people, all leading to a big auction. They were doing me, Jodie Kidd, an unknown and Charles, William and Harry together. All the pictures were to be auctioned so I was going to be small beer alongside three royals. ATR was majorly posh, had a military bearing, but warm and engaging. I showed him a photo of the Henry Mee portrait.* He said he made me look like the Duke of Edinburgh. He had done him, the Queen, Charles – who he found difficult, and he didn't like his short stubby fingers.

---

* Painted in 2009 for Mee's 'Thirty People Who Shaped the Age' exhibition.

He liked the Duke. He showed me his Thatcher which made her look a bit gruesome. 'Deliberate I should tell you,' he said. Cambridge was to take photos in a room upstairs and Alex would then draw from them, then want another session with me for the painting. It was quite a project. They seemed to get on well, worked together well and I was more relaxed than I normally am for a photo session.

We had breakfast to chat over the project and it was remarkable how they seemed to talk as though I was still living the life they identified me with. Painless enough and quite liked them. Wrote a little mail to Calum re. how hard things were and how we would always be there for him. On and off reading Philip's updated *Unfinished Revolution*. Re-read the original parts. Stands the test of time pretty well. Writes well. Good to be reminded of some of it, especially just how much we got done, how much change we drove.

Wednesday 7 September
Ed with a group of business guys tomorrow but didn't think there was much going on there. Later to Random House. Met up with Ed [Victor] first, chatted re. PG – both very down about it – and then re. the books stuff. I knew the future volumes would not sell like *TBY* but it didn't bother me. The point was for a real and complete record to be out there. Dinner at Claridge's – nice event for Accenture [management consultants] – them and some of their top clients for a chat re. social media. All very down on Ed. It was just becoming a given that he wouldn't win.

Thursday 8 September
Out first thing to see Nathalie Trousset, French lawyer, to go over what more needed to be done on the house front. She had a wonderful almost cartoon French accent. She was adamant as Brits we could not do a French civil partnership, but said that for tax reasons we were crazy not to be married. Down to RH and then a long meeting with Joanna and Sue Gray. Sue had a lot of comments from MoD and the spooks, the former worried about special forces references, the latter clearly not liking the sense of my closeness to the SIS. But the most important thing was Sue telling me the chances were Chilcot would not report until Easter. So much for the autumn. The nightmare goes on. It was not clear to me how much this was Chilcot himself, or his panel, or Margaret Aldred, the inquiry secretary. The vibe I got from Sue was that she sensed they were very hostile to TB and were really going to go for him. But it meant for the book we had a decision to make about timing. Sue felt I should discuss with TB,

who, incidentally, I was seeing later. Joanna and I agreed to keep to ourselves the Chilcot issue.

Off to see TB. Bumped into him carrying an enormous briefcase as he got out of the car. Doing his 'never been so busy' routine as we went up the stairs. Lots of piss-taking by me over the Murdoch godfather situation.[*] He said it was all Wendi – he'd be amazed if Rupert had even known. He was in 'fuck 'em' mode on that one. Very down on the political scene. Up re. his own operation and confident re. MEPP. Said finally he was in a position where he might make a difference. Re. Chilcot, Catherine and I tried to persuade him the delay meant he should try to put together a strategy for it, do some proper comms. He was fairly philosophical about it. Agreed in principle to do more.

He was instinctively strongly of the view I should delay the book. I would need a reason. But he felt the stakes were too high here to take any risk at all. Worst-case scenario, as Sue had suggested, was something in the book that they felt they hadn't been aware of, or my evidence hadn't covered, and then they decide to recall us. Wondered if they might get shipped a copy from someone in there. Apart from all that he seemed OK. Home then out to Melissa Benn's *School Wars* book launch. Nice speech in which she really praised Fiona. Her dad [Tony Benn, former Labour minister] was there, a bit more frail but still bright and chatting away. Nice do.

Friday 9 September
The court summons for my speeding arrived for 6 October. I sent it off to Nick Freeman. Bike with Rory then off with Rayan to Forest of Arden for a Denplan conference of dentists. I was on form. Really warm reception then off to Crewe. Regional party fundraiser at the football ground. Only about a hundred and the mood a bit flat. Got them going a bit with a message re. fighting for the record, stop conceding so much, and then with the pipes. Couple of Burnley fans on our table. It was fine but we really did feel like the third most interesting party.

Saturday 10 September
Out for a run. Did a blog on Gove having a whack at Fiona and Melissa as media elite. What? Him, Boris, Toby Young free school (launched this week)? Then met a young student from Leeds who was doing his dissertation on opposition leaders. Nice lad. Burnley were dire and we deservedly

---

* TB had become godfather to the Murdochs' nine-year-old daughter, Grace, which had just become public knowledge.

lost to Middlesbrough [2–0]. I managed to get through most of PG's book on the way home. Spoke to him too. Sounding weaker.

Sunday 11 September

I'd not really been getting back into blog mode. Kind of losing interest. Not sure if it was a bit of a depressive thing kicking back in, or maybe just the post-holiday blues. I filled in Gail re. the Sue Gray conversation and we agreed it might be best to delay. I was keen to press ahead but if TB and others felt it would be a problem maybe I should put on hold. Round to see PG and Georgia, with Rory. Philip was definitely getting thinner, and talking more about the end.

Monday 12 September

Off to Gatwick for the flight to Pristina [Kosovo]. I did my usual too-early thing and had ages hanging around in the lounge. I was met off the plane by Arjeta [Emra] from the British Council and we set off for Pristina. Still quite a lot of scars of war around the place, and Pristina itself was fairly drab and dusty. Lovely-looking women though, and friendly. I was booked into the Royal, which was not as grand as it sounds. First meeting was with Petrit Selimi [deputy foreign affairs minister], whose idea this had initially been and then to see the PM, Hashim Thaçi, his chief of staff and his European integration minister, Vlora Çitaku. Thaçi started with a big and warm personal thanks to me, and then went over some of the problems they faced – mainly the conflict with Serbia over the north, and the issue of recognition, including five EU countries refusing to recognise. I was mainly in listening mode, trying to get their own assessment of their problems before seeing if there was anything I could offer. They were certainly full of problems and it wasn't entirely clear if advice on comms and strategy was what they needed most. Anyway, we would see. Perfectly good opening meeting.

We touched on the accusations against him of organ trafficking but I felt that might be addressed better privately. Off to see our ambassador, a very thin guy called Ian Cliff who gave a very useful tour d'horizon. He felt I could help and so did Pieter Feith, the Dutch diplomat heading the EU bit of things. Met him for half an hour or so and he was very clear that what I did was exactly what they needed – strategy, co-ordination etc. Out for dinner with Vlora, Petrit, the chief of staff and an MP. Nice and incredibly cheap restaurant. They were fascinated by UK politics. Not impressed by Cameron or Ed M. Hopeful I could persuade Thaçi to have a bit of a change of modus operandi. E.g. he did not have a spokesman or a director of comms. Very little teamwork. To a Cuban bar where our ambassador from Albania, Fiona McIlwham, was arriving to meet her bloke, Daniel Korski, who was from the European Council on Foreign Relations and doing a workstream for Petrit. She was in her thirties, very smart and we chatted a bit about the problems in the region more generally.

Tuesday 13 September

Arjeta had told me there was a major nightlife and I slept badly because of it, with two nightclubs blaring away beneath my bedroom window. Off to a restaurant out of town for an all-day workshop with some of the young ministers, the President's staff and advisers to the government. Every single one of them smoked which was a bit of a nightmare. I went through my basic approach to comms, and they all seemed to take to it, but worried about their capacity to deliver. There were also clear tensions between the PM's team and the President's. But Petrit and Arjeta seemed to think it was worthwhile and that it got them thinking in different ways. My stuff was fairly basic, but they seemed to think it was pretty advanced. Then off to Kosovan TV for a half-hour interview which was a mix of the Kosovo war and what I was doing now. Dinner at the UK embassy with Ian hosting, me guest of honour, and several experts and opposition politicians. At the workshop I had asked them to list the three priorities for the government and there had been very little consistency. We got more at the dinner – economy, rule of law, recognition, the north the favourites.

Wednesday 14 September

I started to write a note for the government and after breakfast headed for a one-on-one with the PM. He was much franker about his problems – there was little teamwork and he had difficulties with colleagues. He was definitely up for a more strategic approach but worried about capacity. On organs he said he was totally confident. Interestingly when I saw the US ambassador Christopher Dell later he said he was very good at telling when Thaçi was uncomfortable or lying and he didn't feel he was on this. Organ transplants for selling was unbelievably complicated and they didn't even have dry ice at the time. Thaçi said he was not sure why Dick Marty [member, Council of Europe] went for him in the way he did but he was confident he could see it off.* His main thing was the north,

---

* In 2010 Marty published a Council of Europe report alleging inhuman treatment of people and killing of prisoners to remove human organs in Kosovo. The report alleged that the Prime Minister was implicated in illicit organ trafficking – claims rejected by the Kosovan government as 'baseless and defamatory'.

recognition and the economy. Ian Cliff had said to me they did have a bit of a blind spot on the rule of law, and that a lot of bad stuff went on.

I said to Thaçi he needed a strategy which explained constantly where they came from and where they were going. He didn't need to admit the trafficking, but he did need to say he came from a place of struggle and war. He also needed to have a clearer sense of priorities and he needed to get out there more. Dell later told me Thaçi had said he hoped I would go out more often. A meeting with Dell then off to the airport. Travelled with Daniel Korski but on the Budapest–London leg had a banker next to me who just didn't stop talking.

Thursday 15 September
Did a blog re. the banker on plane who had some pretty stark views on the economy. Catherine reading Volume 4 and TB jittery. To the InBev [brewing company] meeting at Portland, told them I might be making a film re. alcoholism and they were fine with that. Off to Cambridge for my speech on happiness and mental illness at Addenbrooke's Hospital. Did a load of interviews then to the main event. 400 people, nice crowd and the speech worked for them. Good Q&A. Terrific response as I left. Fiona called as I was driving home, having had another bad scene with Calum, and was really upset.

Friday 16 September
The Matt Parker [British Cycling coach] schedule was kicking in with me now. I kept saying to him it was ridiculous he was looking after me when he had so much else to do re. Olympics but he was adamant. He was texting and emailing and making sure I kept on the case.

Saturday 17 September
Two hours bike. Blog re. electoral registration, with the government saying it is no longer a requirement to co-operate in terms of getting your name on the electoral register. Bound to help the Tories. F and I went out to a surprise party for Michael [Delia Smith's husband]. About fifty people at a restaurant in east London. Tiny little Indian guy in charge, all over me and very funny. [Lord] David Owen [former Labour Foreign Secretary, former leader Social Democratic Party] was on our table, and we had a good chat. He was very persuaded – and almost persuasive – that Labour could win next time. I tweeted so and got a big response, a lot of it in disagreement. But he felt Cameron was not popular and lacked depth and that if Ed could cut through he would be fine. He was fairly impressed

with Ed Balls. Nice do, not at all celeb-y. Michael and Delia happy because Norwich had won at Bolton.

Sunday 18 September

PG on *Marr*. He did a fantastic interview, very moving and there was an enormous response. Most viewed on Beeb website. Alex texted to say What a man. I chatted to PG about it. He said he didn't know why he had said 'three months to live' because they had actually said months, not three. It gave us a new running gag, that he would be the British [Abdelbaset] al-Megrahi and we'd go from Unfinished Revolution to Unfinished Life to Miracle Survival.* He had *The Guardian* done as well which was running next week and had decided that was it. The girls had been a bit taken aback by three months but he felt they were OK. He said it was interesting how he wanted to see fewer people more often. Lots of people were wanting to see him but he was not really up for it.

Monday 19 September

Bike. Round to see PG. Usual stuff. Illness, the kids, death, TB–GB, whither politics. He had been with Gail to a burial spot in Highgate and felt happy about it. He had talked yesterday of 'the death zone' and he felt fine where he was. I had tweeted that even in the death zone he raised Labour spirits and he liked that. It was a lovely chat as we went through all the people close to us, also his assessment of who he still wanted to see and why. He said he felt I had been changing in the face of his illness, also that he was worried about how I would take it when he went. It was true that of all the political friends he was the one I had stayed closest to. He looked thin and a bit worn when I left and the jeans were hanging off him. But he was as interested in everyone else as himself.

To Gabriel's Wharf to meet up with Richard Keys who wanted some advice on how to rebuild his career. Clearly he still felt that he had been hard done by but I tried to explain he needed to reflect on it more deeply. Gave him a few ideas on things he needed to do and how he might do them.

Home to potter. Ed M and Douglas were sending me their speeches.

---

* The Libyan al-Megrahi was convicted in 2001 of 270 counts of murder in the bombing of Pan American flight 103 over Lockerbie, Scotland. Sentenced to life imprisonment, he launched a chain of appeals until in 2008 he was diagnosed with advanced prostate cancer and released on compassionate grounds the following year with a life expectancy of three months. He was returned to Libya and doubts were expressed whether he was as ill as claimed. He died in May 2012.

Ed's was OK but not much more than that. He had some nice lines but no compelling argument. The argument he did have was a bit overstated – all the systems we took for granted were letting people down. But it was weak on what he would put in its place. I did line-by-line track changes on it but by the end I was not sure I had helped much. I said to him he needed to get the argument straight in his head and then drive it through. He said his argument was we needed to change all these systems and show how they relate to our values. He said he liked the argument and now he needed to flesh it out. He asked if I would help more. I said yes but I am not going to get sucked in as I used to be. Meaning what, he said. Meaning I end up writing it and doing nothing else for days.

Went to meet Paul Hamann [former BBC head of documentaries] and Tom Anstiss [producer] to discuss the planned BBC *Panorama* on alcoholism among the middle classes. *Panorama* keen. Long chat with Nick Freeman who wanted to try to get me off the speeding charge. He had spotted that the notice of intended prosecution misrepresented the penalty and he felt that would be enough to get me off. He was really pushing me on it, said the whole argument gave him a hard on and he was really confident. I said it didn't get away from the fact I was speeding. Irrelevant, he said. He felt he could get it thrown out. I worried a combination of me and him and a magistrate would have a field day. They have to follow the law, he said. Chatted to Fiona and later Gav [Gavin Millar, Fiona's barrister brother] and my doubts were growing.

Tuesday 20 September

Long chat with AF re. [Labour Party] conference – he wasn't happy with a video he had done for it. He wanted to do it again. Got a letter from the Leveson Inquiry. Sometimes felt like a professional witness. They wanted me to write about the press ethics and culture. Sounded easy but would be a lot of work.

Thursday 22 September

To Random House to see Dan Franklin [digital publisher] re. the idea of an e-book on the media. I ended up agreeing to do one on happiness and depression instead. Sue Gray in with more comments mainly this time from MI5. Nothing terrible. Still not clear re. timing. I was not applying my mind to it. Drifting. Later for the first time in ages to Neil's and Glenys's for an Arts for Labour event. Nice chat with David Morrissey. Really nice guy, very Labour. Hadn't realised he was a Scouser. Glenys annoyed me a bit by saying the arts had been forgotten until now. Ed spoke well, went through some of the arguments for his speech and I said afterwards it sounded better than so far it read. Nice enough do. Calum had organised it but wasn't there.

Friday 23 September
Brian Williams from the Cabinet Office sent me an email to say Chilcot could be even later than we thought. Adding to the conundrum about book timing. The LLR event with Billy Connolly sold out in forty-eight hours. To Wild Pictures to meet the *Panorama* team. The doubts I was already having about using Nick Freeman's loophole increased and after talking to Fiona later I decided against. DS at six.

Saturday 24 September
Out on the bike then Grace and I went to the cemetery to see Philip's plot and tidy up John's and Ellie's graves [leukaemia victims John Merritt, AC's best friend, and daughter]. I was feeling low-level depression and anxiety all the time at the moment but it was lovely to be there with Grace and we went for lunch and had a fabulous chat. She was worried about PG I could tell. The Peter Oborne programme for *Dispatches* on TB's finances was getting a big build-up and the Channel 4 trailers were dire for him. They had sent over a question for me re. a visit to Kuwait, which I ignored, and forty questions to TB which they were not going to rebut one by one but generally and with a focus on the ones that were totally wrong.

Sunday 25 September
2 hour 40 mins bike with Rory out through Herts. The *Sunday Times* did a PG profile which was nice but a total cuttings job. I think the only person actually spoken to was me.

Monday 26 September
Did a blog pre Balls speech on the importance of Labour setting out an economic strategy this week. He actually did OK though he struggled with words at times. Worked on my Happiness e-book. Felt anything but happy at the moment. Depressed.

Tuesday 27 September
Fiona off to Liverpool for the Labour conference. It felt odd not being there

but I'm sure it's better I don't go. I would just get sucked into the speech and the media and sod it. Lunch with Steve Morris to review what I was doing for Portland. I watched Ed's speech there. The most interesting thing was how, even at a Portland-type place, there was so little interest in it. They livened up a bit when the live link went down. I thought Ed did OK but no more than that. The argument left too much ground for Cameron to attack which he surely would.

TB emailed later to say he didn't think it was too bad which surprised me. F said there were too many people up there who wanted Ed to fail. The reception in the hall had been flat. TB's name got booed by a few which would become a problem all round. It would help the Tories take the centre ground even more than they were. PG felt it opened too much space. We both felt we could have helped more than we did. I blogged on it, supportively, saying he had his argument and now had to flesh it out. Calum felt it was very much for the hall and would not cut through much. PG round with Grace later. Long chat re. the speech but also re. him. Looking frail and a bit more worried.

Wednesday 28 September

Another bad day on the head front. But managed to get out for 2.30 bike ride. I don't know why I couldn't get over this hump. Worried about Calum, Philip, the book, Chilcot. Maybe also feeling the France house meant I'd have to work too much and when I felt like this I didn't feel like working at all. Lovely sunny day but horrible dark mood.

Thursday 29 September

Hot. I walked to Baker St then got the Tube to South Ken and headed for lunch with Ana Muhar. Nice enough time but I was distracted and worrying I was lacking focus on things I should be focused on. Calum had decided he wanted to go to Spurs v Shamrock Rovers so I called Harry Redknapp to sort out tickets. Lovely bloke and we had a good chat. Ed sent me a message saying he was happy enough with the speech, that the press can't cope with an argument so they make it all about performance. Had a good time at the football. The Shamrock fans were brilliant. 3–1 Spurs.

Friday 30 September

Out to Borough to record an interview with Steve Hewlett for a programme on [Robert] Maxwell [media proprietor and former Labour MP] twenty years after his death. Also did a spot on Nicky Campbell re. Ricky

Hatton talking about depression. Then Ben Wright on PG. He was doing the BBC obit for radio and I had originally said no but changed my mind after talking to Philip who was fine about it. Then to Grosvenor Square to see TB, JoP, Catherine R, Matthew D and Ciaran. The meeting had originally been called to discuss Chilcot but Brian Williams told us he felt it was looking like Easter earliest and probably later than that. TB had just been to see PG so we talked a bit about that. At one point he was going on about how busy he was and how he had never worked so hard. I said 'You don't need to,' and he nodded and said, 'You mean time to focus on what really matters,' which was something PG was constantly saying. TB looked a bit worried about things and his team felt that the *Mail/Telegraph* were now engaged in a determined and relentless character assassination. We talked – again – about whether he should go for Dacre himself and – again – about whether he should do a blog. Other than that it was all a bit rambling and inconclusive.

The truth is there is nothing much we can do re. Chilcot but wait. I sensed it was not going to be good for any of us. Re. Volume 4, he said he was fine with it being published but with care. Catherine was reading it and worried about the sense of Bush being gung-ho for Iraq post 9/11. I felt all that reflected well on TB. I left more confused than ever about whether to press on or not. Lunch with Paddy Kielty [TV personality] to discuss the Cheltenham phone-hacking idea, where he would construct an interview with me around going through my phone contacts. Out later to see Fahad al-Attiya, head of the Qatari National Food Security Programme. He wanted a comms director and I agreed to think about finding someone, and also maybe help as an adviser. He was a smart guy and the project did sound pretty fascinating.

Saturday 1 October

Millwall v Burnley. Poor game but we won one–nil. Managed to avoid any hassle or trouble. The traffic coming back from Millwall was absolutely dire. Took me 1 hour 40. The *Sunday Times* called to say I was going to be playing the pipes with Bob Dylan and Mark Knopfler in my *First Love* performance. News to me, and it sounded very unlikely. I talked a bit about the programme in general to the reporter, Nicholas Hellen. He said he wouldn't quote me but actually quoted pretty much everything. Jane Gerber [producer] was a bit shocked they knew. She said yes, it was one of the approaches they had made but hardly anyone knew. In any event I doubted very much it would happen and we made that clear but they still went for a big P3 show on it. On one level they would think it was good publicity. But it was going to make it harder and harder to get anything Sky deemed worthy of the gig. It was also setting up the idea of anything I do being controversial.

For two or three days my neck had been getting more and more stiff and sore. I got Len [Finlayter, osteopath] to come round later and he said the neck muscles were in spasm. I was pretty sure it was the bike, doing the extra hours in a bad posture. Len really put me through my paces. I was screaming my head off at times. But it did feel a bit better later when I went to bed.

Sunday 2 October

A bit of follow-up to the Bob Dylan story. I had a long chat with Charlie F re. Volume 4 and Chilcot timing. He felt that I should think above all about the inquiry and if there was any risk of provoking them, or a recall, or making them feel they had another reason to criticise, I should avoid. That said wait, and it was probably the right advice. Out to Heathrow, signed stock at WHSmith with Tim the bookseller. Nice guy. PG called and we had another long chat. Even more than usual, he talked endlessly about his feelings and organisation of his death. Flew out to Frankfurt, then a reasonably quick transfer to the flight to Astana. Not exactly comfortable and my seat was broken. Managed to get a bit of sleep.

Monday 3 October

Michael Roberts met me at the airport and we drove in to the Peking Palace Hotel. The programme, after all Roberts's worries that the government had moved backwards in its desire for us to be plugged in, worked out fine. I grabbed a couple of hours sleep then went to the TBO team's offices on the 19th floor of the Diplomat Hotel for a team meeting. Seemed a good bunch. Half Western, half Kazakh. We talked through the programme and what we hoped to get out of it. Off to the presidential palace to see Nurlan Yermekbayev. He was friendly and welcoming as ever but a bit taken aback at our assessment that since the presidential elections they had gone back because of the criticisms of the new religious extremism law, prisons transferred from Ministry of Justice to Interior, and the treatment of striking oil workers. He asked for advice on how to deal with it which allowed us to press for a reform narrative.

Then to one of the city centre restaurants for lunch with Roman Vassilenko, chairman of the committee for international information. He was a bit old-school, but he warmed up a fair bit as we went on. Then to a meeting with Kairat Kelimbetov, minister for economic development and trade. Very bright and switched on and he was very keen to work with us.

He had asked for the meeting on hearing I was there and was very open and seemed genuinely bright and reformist.

To the MFA for a seminar with deputy ministers and senior officials. To our surprise the foreign minister turned up. I did my usual strat comms spiel but also gave them an honest assessment of how, if the international media coverage was anything to go by, the sense was they had gone a bit backwards. Then to a similar session with the Chartered Insurance Institute team. A lot younger, some sharper, and desperate for information about how we actually did the nuts and bolts. Nice bunch. At the end Roman just dictated a whole load of changes to how they were to work, based on the stuff I had been saying.

Tuesday 4 October

To Starcafe to see Yermukhamet Yertysbayev, one of the unofficial political advisers to the President. He had a very smart green suit and expensive shoes. He was very frank. Said that there was a feeling in the country a bit like in Russia before the collapse of the Soviet Union. We were advising to go for a late not early election, and build in time for the opposition to develop, as they had promised there would be opposition MPs. But even though in theory he saw the point, and said he once pushed for a ministry of democratisation, he clearly felt it best to go sooner not later. He said glasnost and perestroika ultimately lost the Soviet Union power.

Then to meet the foreign minister Yerzhan Kazykhanov. Doing note for Yermekbayev. He was a lot less hardline that I expected, and very open. He said their ambassador in the US had been told by the State department that the Bill had to make clear free religious worship, basic rights and the rule of law would be protected. He also wanted help on how to frame arguments. We were discussing the best way for TB to have an impact when he saw the President next week. I felt we should go for a shorter, clearer list of reforms, and make sure they did them. Perhaps we had over-reached with the length of the list before. He was a very bright guy, knew they had to reform but like all of them was worried about the timing and the pace. He said there were some within government who saw the scale of reform outsiders like us suggested, and it could feel overwhelming.

A quick lunch then back to the presidential palace to meet the President's press secretary, Baglan Mailybayev, and his helpful No. 2. As it happens, we later discovered he was being lined up for a promotion to the job of the next guy we were seeing, deputy head of the presidential administration, Maulen Ashimbayev. He was asking for help too, and we were by now well advanced with the note for Yermekbayev. It was possible to feel the tensions not just within the administration but within individuals.

Wednesday 5 October

Up at 4.20 a.m., which was 11.20 p.m. last night in the UK. The MFA workshops and seminars led to the head of comms (originally sceptical) issuing new instructions to staff on how their comms should be organised. They seemed to get the need for reform, but I suggested it was in part by getting buy-in for support on comms that we will hopefully get deeper into the system. They said they would show us an early draft of the President's 20th anniversary speech on 16 December. They also asked for help on specific reform ideas on the political front, including elections, civil society and local governance, and asked for more meetings in advance of TB's visit to flesh this out.

Rather dramatically, Yertysbayev had made comparisons with how the Soviet Union felt pre collapse. 'For reform and liberalisation, read glasnost and perestroika – and look where that ended!' He was full of talk of democratisation in theory – but when it came to how, it was difficult. They are concerned not just about extremism but also the readiness of exiled oligarchs to exploit openness. Another MFA adviser said he had seen a readout of a three-way conversation between Nazarbayev, Putin and Jiang Zemin [former general secretary of Chinese Communist Party] in which the President had been told in no uncertain terms where his real interests lay and that 'the West will never really engage with you'. They are sensitive too to the inevitable heightened interest in succession that the 20th anniversary may inspire, and they are conscious – though have to be reminded constantly – that the anniversary should not just be a celebration of the past and the President's status and longevity but an attempt to focus on next steps for the future.

I suggested TB present a small but concrete list of proposals rather than a vast shopping list of reforms at this stage. If we can get buy-in for those, and show how they can be properly implemented and communicated to their benefit domestically and internationally, the team on the ground will be able to accelerate the broader reform programme quite quickly, and turn the detailed workstreams into something quite significant and, more important, feasible. The President's speech can be the place where major steps forward are signalled, the period between now and then used to lay the groundwork.

The foreign minister in particular was very enthusiastic for this approach. But there is a 'turkeys voting for Christmas' element to their thinking, a feeling that only opponents will benefit from what we were suggesting. That was a constant tension, and understandable.

Another tension was between those who want to see NGOs develop genuinely, and those who see them largely as an extension of the state.

We had been pressing for them to amend the religious extremism law. Something else I suspected was not going to happen. 'We don't live near Norway and Switzerland but Pakistan, Afghanistan, Iran' was the attitude. Again, easier to see their point when you saw it through their eyes, not ours. They are adamant re. separation of church and state, but more important insist the threat is real.

Met by Rayan at LHR then home to do a bit of work.

Thursday 6 October

My driving case was in court today. Back into quandary mode re. the book. Worked on Leveson, then with F and PG to Highgate cemetery. It was clearly going to be a bit, or even a lot, over the top. 9ft by 4ft plot. Big statue. There were going to be half a dozen different events. Church. Cremation. Highgate. Wake. Memorial. He said he knew it was OTT but that was him. Lovely warm day and he really was talking about it all openly and positively. Met Victor the gravedigger. Fascinating guy. Followed his dad. Really cared about the work. So proud of how the place looked. I said to Philip is it not a bit weird thinking you are definitely going to be there? 'Yes, but I know I am going to die, so it is nice to know it is such a nice spot.' He said he was happy people would see the grave on their way down to Karl Marx, and he was going to have the words 'New Labour strategist' on it. We had a new running joke, as his statue would block the grave of a guy called 'Jimmy'.

Out on the bike. More Leveson. Sending it out for comments. Then to *Jersey Boys* with Grace. Loved it. Bit of a row leaving with that right-wing tit boxer trainer who supports Millwall. Can't remember his name. I was rather proud of the way Grace gave him a bit of a mouthful. Home via Matthew [Freud] and Liz's amazing house in Primrose Hill. Basically three big houses in one. Mainly talked to him re. PG and all the different events. He was a bit pissed but we had a good laugh.

Friday 7 October

Really getting there on Leveson. Help from Martin Sheehan on structure. The first Leveson seminar had happened yesterday and I took in stuff from Richard Peppiatt [former *Daily Star* journalist], who had been good, and hit back at some of the self-serving rubbish from the editors and Trevor Kavanagh. Another nice warm day so I walked through the parks to meet David Ginola [French former international footballer] for lunch at Galvin's in Baker St. He was on terrific form. The hair had been dyed a chestnut Paul McCartney colour. He was dressed like a man half his age but got away

October '11: Visiting PG's burial spot with him

with it. We had a really good time, a bit of football, lots on France and Britain and the difference. When we got on to politics he was adamant I had to run for office and go for the top. He said it was obvious when you saw the guys there now that they weren't very good. He reckoned I could do it. I understood power, he said. I explained it better than anyone he had ever heard. I was not old. I had energy and passion. It could work.

I felt not but the more I tried to explain the more determined he got that I should go for it. He almost persuaded me by the end. He was still keen to get a job in football but I reckoned his looks, image and maybe even his smartness counted against him. He had had a good chat with Alex at the United–OM [Olympique de Marseille] friendly charity match. He said the guy was different class to any other manager. It was about the depth of knowledge and the interest in other things. Really good lunch. I called the court but they didn't have the papers from the case yet.

Saturday 8 October

Out on the bike for two hours. Quick blog on Ed M's reshuffle of yesterday, saying now they had to do the hard stuff – defend better, attack better, win the arguments about the future better. It got a good response. Tom Watson and Michael Dugher [former shadow minister] both retweeted it. It was obvious but the shadow Cabinet had not been doing it. There was a terrific piece by Brian Cathcart in the *FT* mag about Christopher Jefferies* so I fed that into my Leveson paper. Off to Cheltenham for the 'phone hacked' interview with Patrick Kielty at the festival. Long chat with Ed re. Volume 4 on the way. I was moving, partly because of Charlie's arguments about the inquiry being more important to my reputation than the timing of the book, towards a fairly long delay. Ed seemed OK with that. The event went well. I played along with Paddy going through my phone and it was an OK mix of serious and light. Afterwards chatted to his girlfriend Olivia about depression. She got it bad. She wanted to get involved with charity and campaigns so we had a chat about how she might do it.

Sunday 9 October

To Bishop's Stortford for the fundraising match for the local football club. Chris Kamara [former player, Sky presenter], Dave Jones [Sky Sports

---

* In 2010 Christopher Jefferies was arrested on suspicion of murdering 25-year-old Joanna Yeates, who had gone missing in Bristol. Jefferies was released without charge but not before being subjected to savage press reporting that subsequently led to legal proceedings against several newspapers.

presenter] and Ben Shephard [ITV and Sky presenter] all there. Good fun. 3–3. I actually did OK and the lower weight was a big bonus. Great to see Marlon Beresford again, and to meet Jan Åge Fjørtoft [Norwegian ex-footballer, football pundit, adviser to Norwegian Football Association] who had brought his well-thumbed copy of *The Blair Years* to sign. Lovely guy, and bright. Home to work on the Leveson paper, taking in Charlie, Godric and PG comments. They all felt it was really strong but maybe tone down a bit. [Sir] Harry Evans [former editor *The Sunday Times* and *The Times*] was more on the 'harden it up' end of the argument. TB felt detone a bit and also add in more idea of what might follow the inquiry.

Monday 10 October

Walked to SW1 to meet [Lord] Dennis Stevenson [businessman]. He wanted to see me for a couple of things – first the Royal College of Psychiatrists had approached him to do a private members' Bill clearing up some of the mental history discriminations – jury service, MPs, company director etc. He had gone round all the relevant departments one by one. Felt it was doable. Wanted a bit of high horse heavy lifting. Also Wellcome Trust had asked him to use £20 million to set up a proper mental health charity for fundraising purposes, so he wanted me involved in that too. Chatted re. Peter M. He was surprised Peter and I had not spoken since the election. PG had seen him at the weekend and it was clear he had no desire for a rapprochement, that he had bought the line I did him in. Absolute tosh but hey-ho.

Off to see Matthew Freud at his office. Played table tennis then discussed all the PG 'death zone' events and the plans for memorial. He reckoned it was all about immortality and a wanting to be remembered as a big player. I thought it was more that he felt a bit like the fifth Beatle and wanted more recognition. But above all he was creating a sense of an event so that people didn't have to focus too much on the fact of dying. Carol Linforth [Labour director of events] called and said the party wanted to do something for PG but what? When she said maybe he comes in and they all sign something in a book, I said, 'What? A "get dead soon" book?'

Tuesday 11 October

TB called with some more thoughts on the Leveson paper. Some good, some less so. He was keen I take out the attack on Rebekah. He had the idea of an annual report which analysed how well they stuck to the code. Steve Morris did a good exec summary which I used almost word for word. Finally sent it off late p.m., with a covering note saying I would be happy to give oral evidence and that RH wanted to publish a version.

Wednesday 12 October

Early out for flight to Budapest then Skopje. I was met by Eris, one of the P World guys organising [communications and PR conference] the events, and taken to the Alexander Palace Hotel. Pictures of England and other football teams all over the place. Out for a run and later half an hour on the gym bike, surrounded by enormous body builders. I was working on tomorrow's seminar. Pressure on Liam Fox was growing.* It was clear he was going to end up going. Cameron hanging on again. Macedonian media interviews then dinner with key opposition people. It sounded a really hard environment. Papers shut down. TV shut down. Opposition getting next to no air time.

Thursday 13 October

Run. Did a quick blog whacking Dacre following his rant at Leveson seminar. Good place to do it from – him jerking off about media freedom FFS. BlackBerry had crashed which was really annoying and their handling of it – after two days now – had been woeful. Or woefuk as I typo'd, which took off a bit. Actually gave them good advice – explain while fixing, apologise when fixed, then think of recompense. The Skopje PRs were fairly bright, especially the ones who worked for UNDP [United Nations Development Programme]. Also a group of women who ran one of the biggest companies and wanted me to go into partnership with them. I did the morning on strategic comms. Lunch then crisis management and again they were pretty good though a couple actually based their entire strategies on lying. Spoke to some of them about mental health services which were apparently dire. One of the P World guys said the mental hospitals were worse than Auschwitz. Lots of rape and brutality. Long drive to Albania via Kosovo. We stopped for dinner at a nice restaurant in Kosovo, the White House. The waiter had family in Scotland. Finally got to Tirana for eleven. Tired.

Friday 14 October

Breakfast at the hotel with Edi Rama. He was looking fairly subdued. Went through all manner of things that had gone on – he was insistent the Tirana mayoral election had been stolen from him. Also told some

---

* There were calls for the Defence Secretary to resign following revelations about his relations with his best man, Adam Werritty. Fox had given Werritty access to the heart of government and British defence strategies while his activities were being funded by companies likely to benefit from government decisions.

amazing stories about Sali Berisha, the PM, and his unbelievably aggressive campaigning. Really went for Edi, family, health, you name it. So it was a tough environment. Edi ended up asking if I would run his strategy. I said I'd think about it. We talked over how it might work.

Blogged on Fox as the new Coulson in that Cameron was hanging on but Fox was clearly going to have to go. Later in the day he did. The all-day seminar with Albanian comms pros at the Rogner Hotel went well. More people than yesterday and probably higher quality in the main. They were interesting in that the men weren't handsome but the women were. They were particularly good on crises. Good mood in the breaks. Lots of photos at the end then off to see the PM. Real old-style building and he was pretty old-style too. I was a bit taken aback to find four TV crews there to record the meeting.

His press girl, Erla, seemed to find it amusing when I kept interrupting his overlong presentation on how well the country was doing – 'double-digit growth' (which Edi said was an invention and there were no independent stats) and low unemployment (Edi said they didn't count rural areas because they saw everyone as self-employed land workers) – to ask him why the EU assessment had not been good. Nearly all the Balkan countries fared pretty badly in recent reports. He had two tactics in response – blame Edi and say that because of Greece, Eurozone etc., people were less keen on Europe anyway. He was a very shrewd old sort, and part of me wondered if Edi was political enough to take him on. He kept coming back to the same points and I kept going back to the same questions. He kept telling me, 'This is your domain, this is about how we explain to the world' – but there was something of a reality problem with some of the issues in the EU analysis.

He saw himself as on the centre-right though he said Reagan was a hero. I asked where Edi was on the spectrum. Left, he said. And the President? More left. But he is from your party, I said. Yes, but the story of politics is treachery and betrayal. He is trying to start his own party and challenge me but he will fail. He struck me at the outset as not being impressive but as we walked out I felt there was a lot more to him and he would be hard to knock over. 'I saw Tony in America,' he said. We had a good chat. He said he had gone to UN General Assembly with three things in mind – media, business and politicians, in that order. He made a big thing of seeing us off then wandered off with Erla. Fiona McIlwham the ambassador had sent her car to collect me for a very nice dinner at her residence with four or five of the top TV people. Good bunch, one of whom was also an academic and publisher who wanted to translate the diaries. A couple of them presented long political programmes and had a good take on things.

They were very open about all the problems in their politics. Very pro-TB and what we did for Kosovo. They felt he should do more in the region for his reputation. They felt Cameron was OK, Ed M poor. Fiona was nice and bright and clearly enjoying the place though would be glad to get away too I sensed. I filled her in on the meetings I had had. She was not sure about the Edi offer. She felt he would get a lot out of it but that I would find it frustrating.

Back to the hotel where I went for a swim then out for a drink with some of the seminar people. One was a former transport minister who told me some mindblowing stories about the level of corruption. One senior minister had filmed secretly everyone he met and sent footage of some of them talking about bribes to the prosecutor. But he forgot to wipe all traces of footage of himself taking a bribe. He also told me I should campaign for mental health services there. 'They are barbaric.'

Saturday 15 October

Interview with Ilva Tare, one of the main TV interviewers, who had done her homework, then met Ralf Gjoni [director of communications] from the MFA. He knew London well. He advised against helping Edi. He didn't think he would win. Watched Wales lose 9–8 to France in the rugby World Cup semi-final, then went for a run before Endri Fuga collected me to take me to the airport. I was pretty level with him about my worries – was Edi strategic, would he take and act on advice, would I become a big issue, was corruption endemic in the whole system? He tried to assure me on all those things. He felt they could and would win. Nice guy. So was Edi. I was tempted. We agreed to look at all the polling and meet up in London. Back to news of Burnley losing to Reading [0–1] in the 9th minute of injury time.

Sunday 16 October

I planned on an hour bike ride but got the buzz and managed three hours around Herts. The weight was still off and I felt a lot better going up hills. Later to see David S with Fiona and Calum. Not a good scene. David shared my view Calum needed to see someone, but it would not work if he felt we had made him do it.

Monday 17 October

Out on the bike with Rory, then all day working on the Happiness e-book, though I was definitely heading for a down phase. It was weird to be writing about happiness while feeling anything but. Almost done and there was a lot of good stuff in it. I wrote to Steve Hilton to try to get a bit of government input, Cameron apparently taking an interest in the happiness agenda.

Tuesday 18 October

Finished Happiness and sent it to Dan Franklin and Ed. Then making plans for Norway. I spoke to Jane Owen the ambassador who gave me a very good brief on the political scene. Rich country feeling isolated from global crisis. Still reeling from the 22 July massacre. And in a hole with China who refused to accept the government had nothing to do with giving the Nobel Peace Prize to a dissident [Liu Xiaobo, writer, critic and human rights activist]. Also got briefed by the Labour Party who wanted me to go in and talk to party staff about how to win a third campaign. Out later for the Software Satisfaction Awards. Good crowd and I was on form. Did an OK speech mixing laughs and serious, whizzed through the awards, good Twitter feedback – did a special award for most sycophantic tweet of the night.

Wednesday 19 October

Round to see PG. He had seen the palliative care team and had decided he would die in a hospice. He was talking as matter-of-factly as ever but with less levity and a real sense of finality. The nurse had been brilliant, talked him through what happened, that basically you spent more time each day feeling sleepy and then, almost at a time of arrangement, you could go. 'There's no need to go to Switzerland.' He was wanting to spend more and more time with Gail, but needed to find time for the girls too. Also keen to see Calum. He said he was sure Calum would be fine, and I must be patient. I was very down about it all. Re. TB, we talked over why he didn't seem to have a strategy to repair his reputation. Joking re. how if I died now it would detract from his 'brilliant death zone media campaign'. A bit like with Dad, and with Richard [Stott, former editor], I was thinking every time I left if it was the last time I'd see him.

Jacques Séguéla's book had arrived. Dedicated to me. Out to LHR with Rayan and off to Norway. Met at Oslo airport by a tall blonde woman who drove me to town, talking a lot about 22 July and then also re. politics – she was a Conservative but liked [Jens] Stoltenberg [Prime Minister] for the way he had handled the massacre. My hotel was opposite the government buildings that had been bombed and in the same block as Labour HQ. Met the guy who was going to interview me tomorrow after my speech at the conference.

Thursday 20 October

Couldn't sleep because of noise from the ventilation system which was really irritating. Out for a run at 5.30. Totally dark but quite a nice way to see the place. Did a quick blog on impressions so far, and in particular the non-blame-game being played about the massacre. The difference was the media. Breakfast with Anne Gro Christiansen, reminiscing re. Cambridge etc. Amazing how she kept in touch with more people than I did. Over to the [Norway Labour Party] conference with Gro, who had put my trip together, and the host. 500–600 people at it. All kicked off with a brilliant dance group, then the mayor of Oslo being interviewed about 22 July. I did a forty-minute speech on the changed landscape, strategy, weaving in a fair bit on Norway. It was interesting how nobody mentioned [Anders Behring] Breivik [terrorist responsible for 22 July killings] and everyone mentioned the date – 22 July. Used it to show how sometimes communications could be collective and collectively strategic. Q&A afterwards which went fine, then interviews and book signing. Nice atmosphere. Lunch with the key people. Jan Åge Fjørtoft came along. More interviews.

Off to the Labour Party – the PM was in the States, so the foreign minister hosted the event for key party and government people. They asked me to talk about how to win the third election and also about how to do cross-government comms and how to integrate with the party. I think they found it helpful. They felt they had a problem in that nobody in Norway felt the economic situation was going to hit them. They had a massive sovereign wealth fund thanks to oil – they had pretty much run the whole thing as a state industry, which we should have done. I did team-ship, maximum openness for max trust, co-ordination and centralisation. But I emphasised the need for them to get ahead of the game on the social media front and make it part of a mainstream media strategy. I felt they were in OK shape but they were also worried that the Conservatives were positioning themselves more in the centre and getting away with it. I said they had to come up with policy positions that forced them back to their old positions. What they must not do is move off the centre ground.

Stoltenberg's big story (accidentally) out of the US pre Obama meeting was a row about some misunderstanding he and Bush had in the past. I said and tweeted that English was my mother tongue and I often misunderstood what he said. Foreign minister (tipped as next leader) said he saw a fair bit of TB in his Middle East role. Really liked him, loved his energy, felt sad his reputation was being hammered in the UK still. Interview with party magazine in the car to the embassy where I was meeting Jane Owen, our ambassador. Said most of her brief was energy. She was picking my brains on what the party guys were saying. She thought they were quite well placed. She asked if I would advise our government if asked. Had quite an interesting discussion re. my profile and how it still disabled me to some extent, though it also opened up huge new opportunities for me too. She said the China [Nobel Prize] problem for the Norwegians was one for everyone because it showed they could and would flex their muscles. She said oil was half of the Norwegian economy. They were conservative in their handling of the wealth fund and they reckoned it would be their saviour for generations.

Lovely building with a nice view down towards a fjord. She was quite pro-Chris Huhne, felt he was serious about the green agenda. Felt Cameron had leadership qualities. Felt Ed was making no impact at all. I told her what Rayan had said re. his friend saying, 'With Ed all I see is two lips wobbling and going blah blah blah.' She was quizzing whether I would advise the coalition, but I said there was probably too much mutual suspicion and also my baggage meant on the one hand I could command large speaking fees and still make a few waves, but on the other I was not considered for a lot of things I might be in an ideal world. Added to which I was too tribal. To a nice restaurant for an event with Hill and Knowlton [international PR agency] and some of their clients. Much the same stuff as earlier then a Q&A that was more anecdotes etc.

Friday 21 October

Up really early and off for the flight to Munich, where the plane to Marseille was delayed. Met Arnaud Bercker the estate agent then off to Faucon to meet the Boonens, link up with F and off to Vaison to sign all the papers with the notaire. Meanwhile I was in and out dealing with calls on Kazakhstan. The *FT* and the *Mail* were both chasing. Lots of email traffic to agree an overly defensive line. I felt they should be much more open and robust and confident, make the case they were helping develop, devise and implement change. I was worried though. I said to Fiona we could say that it was important to engage and try to get governments like this to reform but it was not easy to justify this one, not least because of the religious extremism law.*

Saturday 22 October

The house was lovely, and Fiona was happy, despite all the stuff she had to organise. The view of Ventoux was as good as ever, changing constantly,

---

* Religious freedom and human rights activists criticised President Nazarbayev's proposal to introduce a law on religious activity and associations in an alleged effort to curb religious extremism.

and the autumn colours were if anything more beautiful than summer. I had an extraordinary dream about Philip and John Merritt. I was at PG's funeral and was called on to speak by the vicar but suddenly froze. Then a head two rows in front turned round. It was John, really vivid, saying, 'Go on, it'll be fine.' The surroundings were all very fuzzy but he was as clear as a picture.

The papers were not as bad as they might have been re. Kaz. The *FT* made me look a bit defensive, suggesting I had avoided repeated efforts to contact me. Not entirely true. I had referred them to TBO as agreed. We were busy dealing with the pool man, then had a power cut. Boonen was driving us mad, clearly not wanting to leave. His wife was upset when she left, but he stayed even after that. The removal van arrived from London and we got all that installed fairly quickly. Out on the bike. Chatting to Endri [Fuga] re. him and Erion [Veliaj], Edi Rama advisers, coming over for a meeting re. strategy. I didn't want people to know where I was, so partly for that did a blog on the Eurozone crisis re. us being out of euro but also in it, because of the impact of the Eurozone debt crisis which was coming to a head.* Did the round of the neighbours. Nice enough people.

Sunday 23 October
Up early to watch the build-up to the rugby World Cup final. Ended up feeling very sorry for the French. 8–7. New Zealand would be unbearable. Out on the bike but got a puncture early on.

Monday 24 October
Woken by the most incredible wind, the *vent du sud* not the mistral. Really loud and powerful. Plants smashing. To the bike shop to get things fixed and went out for a ride, which was crazy. At one point, into the wind on a hill to St Leger, I was down to 3mph. Really getting blown all over the place. One or two follow-up stories re. Kaz but it seemed to be dying down. Susan Sandon emailed that she loved the happiness piece. Dinner at the Senes after they came to see the house. In a way they started the whole Provence thing as it was their house we came to first when Fiona spotted an ad in the *Sunday Times*.

---

* The Eurozone debt crisis started in 2009 and saw a number of EU member states, mainly Greece, Portugal, Ireland, Spain and Cyprus, unable to repay or finance their governments' debts without help from other Eurozone countries, the ECB [European Central Bank] and the IMF.

Tuesday 25 October

Out really early, drove in the dark to Nimes airport, for the full Ryanair experience. One person on check-in, one on bags, one on everything else. Also amazed at the hard sell on the plane – papers, food, SIM cards, duty frees etc. Rayan met me and drove me home. Lunch with the boys in Victoria, then to the Grosvenor House for a rehearsal of tonight's awards. Did an interview with a student then tried to have a kip, unsuccessfully. The awards dinner was fine – *PR Week* event and I was sitting with Danny Rogers, the editor, Paddy Harverson (PR of the Year) and Ian Holloway [Blackpool FC manager] (Communicator of the Year). Danny was worried people wouldn't understand why Holloway was getting it so I rejigged my script. Had a good chat with Holloway who said he almost came to Burnley – he was on the short list of two with Cotterill but they couldn't find a school near enough for their three deaf girls. He was clearly very close to his wife Kim, said she was a lot stronger than him, and also that his girls' deafness, and his dad's advice that the higher you went the more bullshit you confronted, were the reasons why he was such a good communicator.

Good chat with Paddy, who was telling me Prince Charles was in Burnley again today – 'he just loves the place'. We chatted a bit about what he might do next. I felt he was in some ways better placed than me because he did not have the controversy I did. Holloway pretty full on and very direct. Liked him. He was clearly a bit taken aback to be winning something like this but in part he was a response to the public desire for greater authenticity. Siobhan Kenny [*PR Week*] lecturing me, saying that I ought to stand for office or do some big media job. She said I know you are busy doing things but you need to do one big thing and really make a big difference. You are better than any of the people doing the top jobs right now. Awards – all thirty-one of them – whizzed by. Really swung through it. Managed to get away by eleven and was in bed at the Luton Ibis by twelve.

Wednesday 26 October

Up at five, walk to the airport ready for the 6.25 flight to Nimes. I was amazed at how busy the airport was and how many people were drinking at the bar. There was a Gerry Adams [Sinn Féin leader] lookalike boarding the plane with his wife and we had a little chat. He said things were really tough at the height of the IRA troubles. They lived half the year in France. I showed them pictures of the house then rather regretted it when he said I probably knew his daughter who worked for *The Guardian*. Home via Malaucène to collect the mountain bike after repairs. Kip then a three-hour bike ride with Philippe [Trouillot] the neighbour. He was seventy-two but bloody fit. The neighbours came round for a drink. All fine. Fiona saying she wished we were staying for longer.

Thursday 27 October

Out on the bike in unbelievable wind. Endri and Erion came over [from Albania]. Arrived late because when I sent instructions to come to Faucon, the iPad had 'corrected spelling' to Falcon which doesn't exist. Thankfully I emailed to ask where the hell they were. They had at least gone to Vaison as I had said it was the nearest big town. We had a good session going through their polling and then talking through their strategy. They were keen for me to get heavily involved. They felt I would become an issue but it wouldn't go on for long. They wanted me for strategy and also for coaching and inspiring the campaign team and showing them it was possible to be positive and to seize and drive an agenda. They felt they had technically good people, but they needed leadership and direction. Took them to the Girocedre [restaurant] which was very different in winter. Also bizarrely half the people in tonight were Brits. We discussed their plans for a manifesto process, and I talked through how I felt they could develop it into something that gave them strategic legs and a process that let them set the agenda. Had a brief chat with Edi [chairman, Albanian socialist party] on the phone. He was very keen.

Ed Miliband called for a final check on my take on Tim Livesey. His worry was that he was not hard enough. When Fiona said one of his qualities was that he didn't have a big ego, Ed said that was one of his worries. He felt that JoP never really ran our show, I did, and he felt he needed someone closer to me than JoP. But he liked him, felt he shared his politics and was sure he was technically up to the job. We chatted for a fair while and he talked to Fiona too. Ed said thanks for the work I had done on his HoC statement earlier in the week. Truth be told I didn't feel I made that much difference as I didn't feel very engaged in it.

Friday 28 October

We were up early and managed to get the house packed up and we were away by seven. Went via Paris so that Grace could take a look at the University of London college there. She wanted to go in on her own. She said I really don't want people to know you're my dad. Don't get me wrong she said. I think you're great but all my life people have said I am AC's daughter and I want to do things independent of you. Maybe Calum felt the same but had not felt able to do it. Maybe that was part of the issue.

Grace was more upfront. We got there in good time, she went in and had the tour, quite liked it. Then late lunch and off to Calais.

Saturday 29 October

Hour on the bike then, after a bit of a heart-to-heart with Cam, which I didn't handle well, off to Burnley with Rayan. Blogged re. Cameron's odd contributions from Perth – royal succession OK for a girl, women in boardrooms would lower pay, and bring back the British Empire medal. Oystons out in force at the Burnley boardroom. Good game. Won 3–1 v Blackpool. Home really late.

Monday 31 October

The morning taken up mainly with Kaz calls. More bad stuff on TB, this time the *Indy* focusing on the contrast between his faith foundation work and the Kazakh religious discrimination laws. I sensed someone inside the Kazakh government was stirring the issue as a way of disabling TB's operation. The fact that we spent most of these calls now talking about his reputational management issues suggested they were being successful. I felt we had been way too defensive the whole way through. So did he in theory but stopped short of doing much about it. He wasn't keen on the idea of an *FT* article by him. He said it was about making sure the Kaz government felt we were doing all this reputational management for them not us.

Good chat with David Halpern on happiness. He was the No. 10 point man on the issue, and he gave me a good sense of where things were inside the government. It was clearly very much Cameron's thing, but he was not getting much traction across government. Petrit came on saying our Kosovo proposal was accepted. Out to see *The Ides of March* [political film]. Robin van Persie [Arsenal footballer], baseball hat pulled low, and his wife were sitting behind us. 'Who's Robin van Persie?' Fiona said loudly when Grace said he was there.

Tuesday 1 November

George Papandreou [Prime Minister of Greece] had stunned his colleagues by announcing Greece would have a referendum on the latest bailout agreed at last week's Eurozone crisis summit. Took everyone by surprise. More market mayhem. With the G20 looming in Cannes, it was a total disaster area. Breakfast at the Mexican embassy with the ambassador and the President's new comms director, organised by Iain Bundred for Ogilvy and

Mather. She seemed quite defensive. Security the big thing for them. Did my usual stuff on the need for strategy and direction, worry less re. media and more re. public and self. Off to Burnley for a UCFB board meeting. Traffic disaster. Every motorway shut at some point. Missed the meeting. Met Brian Barwick to get briefed about it. Felt like it was going OK but with room for improvement. Some issues on behaviour at halls of residence.

Stayed up for the Leicester match. Lost 3–1. But also got message from Gail saying things were bad for PG. He had gone in for chemo but had a lung infection. Turned out to be pneumonia. They took him to intensive care. I was in tears a lot of the way back. He sent a message saying he was fighting on but he felt it might beat him this time. 'You have been the perfect friend and never ever let me down. Thanks for all your support now and always. Love to all. Take care of everyone.' I kept staring at it, feeling the finality of it, and crying. Told the kids and could sense how upset they were. I had a fair few friends but PG was the one who touched all the bases of my life – work, past, present, sport, family, holidays, books, kids, the lot. As with Dad, somehow the time spent thinking about it and preparing for it made no difference when it finally came. I told TB and said from the sound of things he wouldn't see the morning.

Wednesday 2 November

PG still with us. They had stabilised him and he said I should go in later. He was in bed ten on the intensive care unit. Gail and the girls there. A nice nurse called James who was a big Norwich fan. PG had his head inside a plastic bubble which was helping him to breathe. He had tubes galore into one hand and arm. Yet he was so much better than I had expected. Chatty, funny, and apart from when he moved, and lost his breath, generally OK. I said never do that to me again. What? Make me feel you're dead when you're not. But when the girls went to get a cup of tea, he said he was still looking at days not weeks. I stayed for an hour or so and it was at times almost as though he wasn't really dying. Like any other chat. But not for the first time when I left I wondered if it was the last time I would see him. I did a bit of work when I got home but I was feeling very down and anxious about him. I had to go out later and host the Portland pub quiz which was fine. Lifted me out of the gloom but I was straight back in on the way home.

Thursday 3 November

Breakfast with Keith Mills [Olympics organising committee] at Villandry. He seemed to think technically the Games were going fine. But they were worried about getting the tone right between austerity and celebration. More worried now about protests e.g. hijacking of the flame and transport. But his main thing was legacy. There wasn't one and he wanted to pick my brains on it. I felt one idea was for Cameron to elevate sport to the Cabinet and that minister then had to drive the post-Games strategy and show that the legacy would follow. I agreed to do a note as a draft letter to Jeremy Heywood and Steve Hilton. I felt they might go for it. Worked at home most of the day then had my first decent chat in ages with Cam. Barriers still up, but better. I asked him direct if he shared Grace's view that being my child was difficult, and he said no, unconvincingly. Out late for *This Week*. Nancy [Dell'Olio] one of the guests all over me, much to the amusement of the team. Portillo and I agreeing a fair bit. Papandreou was hanging on. But Sarko and Merkel had basically told him it was in or out of the euro, so now he was back in Greece beginning to backtrack on the referendum. The Chinese and the US were pretty united in looking aghast at the whole mess but not offering much by way of help.

Friday 4 November

Out to Cambridge with Rory and really nice ride with Godric. Forty-odd miles then lunch with him and Julia. Lovely people. He felt delay Volume 4. Even if there was only a slim chance of a recall to an inquiry, he felt it was not worth risking. Donald down for the night. On good form, but his chest wasn't good.

Saturday 5 November

Gail texted to say it could be Tuesday at the latest. I wrote to PG.

Dear Philip,

I hope, as do so many others, that somehow you find within you the strength to carry on. The courage you have shown since the day you were told you had cancer has been inspiring. If anyone can keep on defying the medical odds, you can.

But if this does defeat you this time, I don't want you to go without me saying what a wonderful person you are, and what an extraordinary friend you have been. Of all my friends, you are the one who touches virtually every point of my life – past, present, politics, work, leisure, sport and holidays, education, books, charity, and, more important than anything, family and friendship. I have been blessed to know you. So has Fiona. So have Rory, Calum and Grace. For so many of the happiest moments of our lives, you have been there, indeed often the cause of the happiness.

You've always been there in tough times too. You remember the Alex Ferguson quote – 'The true friend is the one who walks through the door when others are putting on their coats to leave.' You have displayed that brand of friendship so often, so consistently, and with such a force as to keep me going at the lowest of moments.

When I got your moving, lovely message on Tuesday, and was convinced you wouldn't see out the night, I felt like a limb had been wrenched from me. You know my crazy theory that we only know if we have lived a good life as we approach its end – perhaps we only know the real value of a friend when we lose him. The loss for Gail, Georgia and Grace will be enormous. But so many others were touched by you and will share that loss.

My favourite quote of our time in government came not from me or you, or any of the rest of the New Labour team. It came from the Queen in the aftermath of the 11 September attacks ten years ago. 'Grief is the price we pay for love.' You are much loved. There will be much grief. But it is a price worth paying for the joy of having known you, worked with you, laughed with you, cried with you, latterly watched you face death squarely in the eye with the same humility, conviction and concern for others which you have shown in life.

I will always remember you not for the guts in facing cancer, brave though you have been, but for the extraordinary life force you have been in the healthy times. Your enthusiasm, your passion for politics, and belief in its power to do good, your love of Labour, your dedication to the cause and the team – they all have their place in the history that we all wrote together. I loved the defiant tone of your revised Unfinished Revolution, your clear message that whatever the critics say, we changed politics and Britain for the better. So often, so many of our people weaken. You never did. You never have. You never would. That is the product of real values, strength of character, and above all integrity of spirit.

In a world divided between givers and takers, you are the ultimate giver. In a world where prima donnas often prosper, you are the ultimate team player. Perhaps alone among the key New Labour people, you have managed to do an amazing job without making enemies. That too is a product of your extraordinary personality, your love of people and your determination always to try to build and heal. It has been humbling to see you, even in these last days and weeks, trying to heal some of the wounds that came with the pressures of power. We can all take lessons from that, and we all should.

Of course I will miss the daily chats, the banter, the unsettled argument about whether QPR are a bigger club than Burnley. More, I'll miss your always being on hand to help me think something through, large or small. But what I will miss more than anything is the life force, the big voice. You have made our lives so much better. You are part of our lives and you will be for ever. Because in my life, Philip, you are a bigger force than the death that is about to take you.

I was in tears by the end of it, and when I pressed 'send' it felt so final.

Peter Hyman called to say PG had texted him to say '3–5 days' and wanted to know what that meant. So definitely moving to the end. Donald was down for a piping tournament and in between other stuff Calum and I went down to watch him play. He fluffed the piece and didn't make the prizes but he was pleased we went. Calum and I getting on a lot better. Later we went to the Ricky Burns title fight at Wembley,[*] Calum having said he fancied it. Rory took a girl from Preston who must have found it a baffling date. Frank Warren [promoter] very much the man in charge. Also a guy near us who had the most incredible gangster face and kept smiling across. Not as glamorous as I expected. No food or hospitality. But it was remarkable to be so close to the action, hear the grunts and body blows. Nice chat with Colin Hart from *The Sun*. I was worried about Philip though. I was keeping in touch with Gail and it was only a matter of time.

Sunday 6 November

I was torn about whether to go to Alex's 25th anniversary dinner up north because PG was clearly on the way out. Gail said all was calm and he was alive but unconscious. I felt I had to see him one last time so Fiona and I went in on the way to the station. Fiona said she didn't want to see him because she wanted to remember him as he had been when we went to the cemetery. But she was glad she came. We held his hand and Gail and the girls left us for a few minutes so we could just say our own farewell. They were talking about him in the past tense already and they seemed fairly calm. The girls had read my letter to him yesterday and as they finished it he said 'Funeral funeral' and had a big smile on his face. They said it may have been the last thing he heard because an hour later he was unconscious.

He was still breathing hard but he was not seeing or hearing and it was likely to be today. We'd known this was coming but it was still going to be hard. We hugged the girls and Gail walked us out, said she felt they would be OK for a day or two but when the shock set in she worried about the girls. I said we would be around. But she insisted we set off for Manchester. I did a blog on Alex's twenty-five years [as Manchester United manager], partly to take my mind off things.

---

[*] Burns beat Australian Michael Katsidis on points to win the World Boxing Association lightweight title.

Gordon [Brown] sent a really nice email, said Philip could not have had a better friend and this would be hard for me and Fiona. The do was at The Hilton and it was like a Campbell or Bob [Millar, Fiona's late father] family event. Mainly Scots. David Gill [Man Utd CEO] the only football person. Mick H, Ian McShane [actor] and Eamonn Holmes the only celebs. Lovely chat with Alex on the way in, telling me I would be strong to help Philip's family. We had a chat about Salmond. They were worried and felt we had nothing to answer with. We had David G at our table and he was filling us in on the incredible secrecy operation to unveil the AF stand yesterday without anyone knowing it was happening. Really nice guy. Good entertainment culminating in the Red Hot Chilli Pipers.

Don't know why but as they came on I texted Gail. Is all OK? Back came the message he had just died. She said it was a beautiful, blissful moment and I should not be sad. I went out to tell the kids and didn't really hold it together. Then spoke to Gail and the girls. Gail said the girls were holding a hand each, she had her hand on his back and he heaved a final breath and she said the Gregorian chant came to a climax and it was as though a light filled the room. Then Grace said, 'I think we'd better tell someone.' Georgia was hyper, talking ten to the dozen. I felt she would be fine short-term but a crash was coming. Grace wanted to speak to our Gracie. Our three were upset of course but really worrying about the girls and about me. All this was going on with the sound of the pipes behind me. Weird. Pipes.

Off to Tiree in a few days. With one great friend as another died. And then something really quite odd. An Italian friend of Alex's came over to me. I said I had just heard my friend died. It was as though he didn't hear. He said, 'Why are you wasting your life? You are a rare talent. Everyone knows you. You are clever, strong, experienced. Politics is fucked and you can fix it. Cameron. Miliband. Get in there. Knock them out. Do something. Don't just waste your talent. What are you doing – speaking, writing, OK, fine. It pays but it is not the same thing. Go for it.' TB sent me a lovely message saying I had been a great friend to PG, that he was so fond of me and the last time he spoke to him PG said I had taken him to new heights. The Scots were the most comforting of course but Mick was lovely too. The party went on till six but we pulled out about one. Felt like I was legless but not through drink.

Monday 7 November

I didn't sleep well. Up at six and wrote a tribute to PG. It had been a pretty amazing death, in that he had planned so much of the effect it would create. He was constantly asking himself not just how to make things easier for Gail, Georgia and Grace, but how in talking about his death he might help others, and what he might write and say now that could help the Labour Party in the future. He really was a team player. I did a couple of radio interviews but found it hard to hold it together. He was such a true friend, always loyal, but understanding that loyalty required honesty and frankness, and ideas about how to make things better. When we saw him for the last time yesterday morning, it was sad, but there was a magnificence to it all too.

Fiona read my tribute, and the piece I did for *The Guardian*, at breakfast and she was in tears, which set me off. I had cancelled pretty much everything so I could help Gail if needed and write and call people and stuff. But the day just went by in a kind of whir. Several times I was texting Philip only to remember he was gone. We all went round to Gail's in the evening. Susie [Figgis, casting director] already there. Nigella [Lawson, celebrity chef] popped in. Margaret McD. Tessa. Then Peter M arrived but didn't want to come up. Clearly because of me. Then twenty minutes later he reappeared and he did come up. It was a bit stilted at first but it warmed up OK. Then we sat down to watch TB's interview about Philip with Jon Snow. Really nice and Gail was sniffling a bit. Then back to the sitting room and all sat down and all of a sudden Peter looked at me, looked away, then started crying. Everyone stopped. Gail sat with him, he calmed down and the conversation carried on.

After he left I texted him to say Philip was really keen we try to get some kind of reconciliation. I'll try, came the reply. Nice message from Ed M. Ed V there briefly. Gail and the girls seemed as good as they were likely to be in the circumstances.

Tuesday 8 November

Out for a run and went to the cemetery. Lovely cold misty day. TB called as I was climbing a fence! We just chatted away, about Philip and all the other stuff and then a bit of work. He was going to miss him too. Gail texted me to say she had had a message on Philip's phone and thought what kind of idiot didn't know he was dead after all the publicity – and promptly leaned over the bed to tell Philip! To Random House to see Dan Franklin and work on the e-book on happiness. What a day to be doing it. Saw a few of Gail's people, chatting to them, then out to St Paul's Hotel for my speech to the Association of something or other financial.

Simon Lewis – ex-Buck House and GB, now working for this Association, said in the intro he had been standing next to me when GB said farewell to the Downing St staff and said, 'Alastair, you're a genius!' I had forgotten that. Off to Freuds and then up to see Matthew in Primrose Hill.

Nice chat, part logistics, part reminiscing, part what next. He was back on at me to do something big. [Baroness] Margaret [McDonagh, former Labour Party general secretary] was causing a bit of mayhem organising people for the funeral which was not going to be needed, but PG had told her he wanted a 'fucking big Labour funeral'.

Wednesday 9 November

Fog lifting a bit but not much. I had to go out to the Festival Hall for my second mentor session with Finlay MacDonald for the TV programme. Beautiful acoustics. He went through the event I would be doing – solo piper at a St Andrew's Day concert of the Scottish National Opera and National Youth Pipe Band. He wanted me to learn a new lament, 'Lest we forget', then the tune George McIntyre [former Queen's Own Highlanders Pipe Major] wrote for Dad, then a couple of new strathspeys and reels. Would be hard but I was pleased with the overall tone and range. Played OK but not great. Home briefly, then off for my four-day crazy trip. I would be sleeping three successive nights in airport hotels. Need a lifestyle review after this. On the other hand probably best to be busy. I was working the whole time on the PG tributes I was being asked to do. There were bits I would have to change a little to avoid hurt to one or two people. Then with Rayan to Pennyhill Park. Business audience. Theme of co-creation so talked about teamwork, lots re. PG. Was on terrific form at Q&A. Nice crowd. Nice event to get me out of myself. Slept at Gatwick Sofitel. Badly.

Thursday 10 November

Up at 5.10 and the inter-terminal shuttle was down. So a bloody replacement bus to the terminal. Did a quick blog on the Eurozone crisis which was really going belly-up. [George] Papandreou [Prime Minister] toast. Berlusconi following. But no world leadership worth the name. I suggested they call in GB and Alistair D. On the flight I worked on my speech for the Toranfield House [Enniskerry clinic] addiction conference. Met by Paul Allan who was chirpy as ever. Out to Co. Wicklow. Fabulous scenery. Did my usual mental health stigma story, Q&A, including some good stuff on the false economy of not tackling addiction, then media – including a really long and personal one for TV with Eamonn Keane [presenter] – and photos and a lovely run around Powerscourt Estate. Book signing. Chat with a woman from leukaemia charity. Visit to Toranfield House. Chatted to some of the addicts who had been there this morning. Mainly drugs and drink. Fabulous facility. Good chat with the guys running it.

3 Cs – control (have you lost it?), craving (do you?) and consequences. Into Dublin for a radio interview, dinner with Paul. Then Dublin airport hotel. Tired but couldn't sleep. Long chat with Georgia and Grace who were dipping, I think.

Friday 11 November

Up at six. The Ryanair experience not so bad. Not an empty seat on the flight to EMA [East Midlands Airport]. Met by Rayan at East Mids and off to [relative] Steve Loraine's. Call out of the blue from [Lord] Brian Mawhinney. Ostensibly to ask if I would speak to the Bible Society but he also said I really needed to get back into politics. He said you have a unique set of skills and politics needs them right now. Your perspective is important. It should be there. He said, 'I am a Tory. But politics cannot afford people like you to be on the sidelines.' Out for a run, then to Lichfield for two sessions talking to South Staffs college students. Dinner with the principal Graham Morley. The cathedral was lovely. We did a little run-through and then I asked if they minded if I went to the altar and read my PG speech. As I looked up the first thing I saw was a figurine of a piper. Don't know why but for the first time I felt I would be able to get through my speech on Tuesday OK.

Graham Morley said please give TB a message that he is liked and respected by millions. The ceremony was nice. Packed church. Seventy-seven graduates getting their scrolls. Did my 'believe you can and you're halfway there' speech. Off at 9.30. Slept in the car. Glasgow by 1.30. Gail a bit down when I spoke to her. Getting into Twitter row with Michael Fabricant [Tory MP, Lord Commissioner of the Treasury]. Young girl at the college had told me he had not replied to her letters re. granny's visa. He denied and off we went. But at least he would see them now.

Saturday 12 November

Another light sleep in another airport hotel. Fabulous haggis for breakfast though. Another interview for the documentary on the plane. Lovely scenery on the way in. George [Campbell, cousin] at the airport. Tiree [Inner Hebrides] car hire cars just waiting there with the keys in. Off to RockVale to meet Donald. Had to get him up. Then practised Finlay's picks. Off to Auntie Mairi's. Film crew loving it. She had been fierce on the phone but was great. Chatted away on camera re. Dad, Uncle Hector, our holidays, Papa chasing us when we kicked a ball through the kitchen window. The house felt smaller than I imagined it. No staircase from the kitchen. No scullery. We played the pipes out the back. Lovely pictures. Then back in to play some more and chat away. She was on great form now. To the beach at Ballevullin. More shots, more playing, another interview, all good stuff. Surfers in the water despite it being so cold.

Back to Corraraigh [croft where AC's father grew up]. Up to see John Neil [Brown, cousin] and Josie [his wife]. Then Coales to see the other Auntie Mairi, Dad's sister. Very frail but bright as a button. Lachie Mac-fadyen [cousin] there too. Crofter. Said it was tough financially but at least he was outdoors the whole time. Nice chat though Mairi was nearly blind and hard of hearing. Dinner at the Lodge. I showed Jane the producer my PG speech for the funeral, and she was in tears. So was I. Just had to cry myself out so I was OK on Tuesday. Donald on great form. We played in the bar till late and George and family came up, George dancing with the barmaid, one of the customers drumming. I was getting better. We did various options to see what 4 minutes would take – the time I would have in Glasgow. Bed late again. Glad to be here though. Auntie Mairi very tearful when talking about Lachie [AC cousin who took his own life in 2000]. She gave me a printed copy of Jessie Gray's eulogy from the funeral. 'I want you to keep this and remember him.'

Sunday 13 November

I couldn't sleep well so went out for a run around six when it was still dark. I spotted a sign for Balephetrish and remembered the beach there from childhood. Found my way to it just as it was beginning to get light. I ran up and down the beach a few times, then stopped to rehearse the speech for Tuesday. Pretty tearful at first, especially in the last bit of the letter. Then I spotted a black blob in the sea and realised it was a seal. Philip. Two more behind. Now it was Gail and the girls. Then two more. So now it was me, Fiona and our three. Then back to three and then three birds came flying down over the seals, did a little circle, then came back as five. Georgia had been talking about Bob Marley and 'Three Little Birds' last night. The sun now in the sky. Took a picture. Saying wow, unbelievable. Feeling some-thing very strongly. Sheep off to the right. More and more birdlife. Waves crashing gently right up to my feet. Feeling my dad's presence but also Philip's. I said to myself, 'Stay much longer and you'll get God.'

I sent a photo to Gail and Fiona, Matthew and Nicola, who all thought I was mad of course. But it was a powerful moment and would help me on Tuesday. Packed up and headed down to the ferry. Auntie Mairi and George to see me off. Lovely journey, smooth and beautiful scenery all the way. Couple from Keighley on the deck. Played a bit for them. Endlessly posting photos so that people ended up asking if I was working for the tourist board. Watched the Cenotaph Armistice Day ceremony, moving as ever, then did another interview. Felt the weekend had been worth it. Really enjoyable and the tunes were beginning to stick.

Arrived at Oban, new terminal, met by a driver and then discovered Alex was at Loch Lomond heading to the Hilton for an SFA [Scottish Football Association] dinner. So we arranged to meet for a cup of tea at the Hilton. With Cathy's brother-in-law as ever, and had a really nice time. Film crew loved him. A few interrupters but OK. Alex taking the piss re. the pipes. Saying he wanted to go to all the islands when he retired, especially Iona. Off to the airport, easyJet and home. Tired as hell. Glad to be back. Now Tuesday, which had been dominant anyway, all I was really thinking about. Chatted to Nicola and Matthew to work out seating plan for the funeral.

Monday 14 November

I was on the wattbike [exercise] when GB called to say Alan Keen [MP] had died. Ann [wife, also MP] wanted me to do something on my blog and maybe focus on football. I agreed to get some football quotes. They were obviously worried it would all be about expenses.* Nice chat. GB was effusive about my friendship for Philip, said it had been so strong and a real force for Labour when we were working together. He said he wanted to do what he could to help Georgia's political career. Into Freuds to see Gail, Georgia, Matthew and Nicola and go over all PG's last stuff. Where to seat Peter M a bit of an issue. We had him in the front at one point but Cherie wanted Leo and Kathryn [Blair children] nearby so we moved him back one with our kids. Nicola had everything else sussed fine.

I worked on a final version of Tuesday's letter-tribute, taking out bits some of them might take a bit personally, then to BBH [Bartle, Bogle, Hegarty, advertising agency] for a session with their staff on strategy. Good bunch and it went well. Sue Gray texted to say Chilcot was going to be majorly delayed so we had to go round the block on that again. Not slept well for a week now.

Tuesday 15 November

Georgia told us of an amazing dream... Her dad was packing and she was asking why he was there as he was supposed to be dead. He fussed on and then said everything would be all right. She woke up crying, went for a walk, and her iPod's first song was 'Three Little Birds' (like those in Tiree she said) and Bob Marley's line that every little thing's gonna be

---

* The Keens had been ordered to repay £1,500 after a Commons investigation found they had broken rules regarding second home expenses.

all right. I went out on the bike, up to the cemetery which wasn't open. Decided to go back later but when I did had a puncture. So maybe not meant to be. Meant to be celebration today. Letter from Leveson saying they wanted me for evidence 30 November. Exactly the kind of thing I needed PG for. Georgia, Grace [Gould], Rory and I went to the church for a rehearsal. Girls did fine. I did fine till the last sentence. But PG's sister, Jill the priest, was there, and said I'd be fine. I felt I would, partly because of pills, partly because of recent days and all the signals. Matthew pretty edgy, Nicola great. The girls doing OK though Grace said she felt pretty overwhelmed.

Home to get changed and sorted and then off we went with Rayan and another driver. Fiona and I were in the front row with TB, CB, Leo, Kathryn, GB, Sarah, with Aud and the kids behind. The three Gs opposite though a little behind. Packed church but I never really got to see all who were there. GB very warm. TB ditto. Mix of political, corporate and personal. Lovely service. Brilliant sermon by [Rev.] Alan Moses, including a dig at education policy with Gove there. It was lefty enough for me to say later maybe he should go for Alan Keen's seat. Beautiful choir, two good readings from TB and GB. I held it together pretty well. I had done my last rehearsals with our Grace upstairs and she made me do it again and again till I wasn't crying, and it helped get me through, especially as we had just sung 'Amazing Grace'. Relieved when I walked down the steps though the girls having done their poems so well I had to get through it. Then Jerusalem and then away.

PG would have loved it, without a doubt. Lots of milling outside, photographers snapping away. TB and GB both said what a great tribute it was. Peter and Neil both a bit chilly. Helle called later – she had been in town seeing Cameron – and said I just had to ignore it. Neil knew I was pissed off at 'We got our party back'. Off to the Mandarin Oriental. Huge ballroom plus side room set up with focus group settees etc. We named them central Scotland, Pennine belt, Edgware and Dudley. Freuds good at this stuff. I compèred speeches, first Georgia who spoke wonderfully, then Tony, then Matthew who read the email he sent to staff when PG died, then Prof Cunningham who said Philip gave others strength to fight cancer and face death.

I closed with the story of PG popping up on the marathon route, saying 'Come on you can do it' at several points and said that was the role he had played for so many in the room. Come on you can do it. Glad the kids were all there and I could break away a bit. Lovely reel of photos going including some from our best holidays. Georgia's playlist. All went well. Everyone saying great send-off. Nice emails from TB and GB re. how I handled it today. Lovely message from Alex saying the tribute was the most beautiful letter he had ever read. All still felt weird but he had had a great funeral and a great party and that was what he wanted.

Wednesday 16 November

Cremation day. Work backlog was piling up so tried to do a bit. Then we set off for Golders Green. Just Gail and the girls, her parents, us, Matthew, Pete Jones [old friend of PG], PG's sister doing the prayers and her husband and family, Suzy. East chapel waiting room all a bit cold. Reminded me of a football dressing room. Chapel nice and Jill did the service well. Off the coffin went and out we went and stood around all a bit unsure what to do. Off to Lemonia [restaurant], place at the back worked well. Nice time, mood lifting a little. Reminiscing. Bit more laughter than before.

Home and worked for a bit but fell asleep at my desk. Later chatted with the counsel to the Leveson Inquiry, Robert Jay. He said he liked my statement, said that would be evidence in chief, and he would take me through it, then take in questions others wanted to ask. I said I was worried they would try to resurrect Iraq. He said he wouldn't let that happen. Said he was determined to be neutral but he was basically a Hampstead liberal of the kind Dacre hated. He said he didn't let the *Mail* darken his home. Said he had been reading a lot about Murdoch. He felt I would probably have to give evidence twice – on media practices, and later on media and politics and what he called the unhealthy relationship with the Murdochs. Sounded OK.

Thursday 17 November

Out for a short run, really finding it hard to get my energy levels up at the moment. I was also looking to kick stuff out of the diary, feeling a bit under pressure. PG's death and funeral had taken more out of me than I was admitting maybe. Off at lunchtime with Rayan for Manchester for the *MEN* [*Manchester Evening News*] business awards at The Point, Old Trafford Cricket ground. Run-through, interview with Deborah Linton [*MEN* political reporter], found myself talking a lot about PG. The dinner itself was fine. We decided against a speech and instead just did questions from the floor, submitted on cards. Book signing then home. OK atmos. Back in the early hours. Too many of these late nights at the moment.

Friday 18 November

Lunch with James Erskine and AJ Riach [producers] re. a [Marco] Pantani [Italian racing cyclist] film. Maze restaurant. Not bad. Pitching to narrate but I think they wanted me more as a guide and judge on material. To TBO for meeting re. Kuwait. Then the Landmark for a fundraiser for the Jack and Ada Beattie foundation. Doing as a favour to Trevor B. Grace Gould and Rory came along as helpers and she really enjoyed. I was compèring. Lots of Normandy veterans there. Played the lament at the end which went down well. Good music, nice night, raised loads and Grace said she loved it. Trevor also gave me an amazing gift – a piece of 1920s memorabilia from BFC with £5k minimum price from Bonhams [auction house] on the back.

Saturday 19 November

Very early start to head for Burnley with Rayan. Collected my Football Focus [league predictions] award from Mark Lawrenson and Dan Walker. Played well first half then collapsed at end. Lost 2–1 [to Leeds United]. Fletch being ousted as chief exec. Off to Grantham to meet Fiona and then to Charlie F's 60th at Flintham Hall. Amazing old stately home. Lots of legal establishment there, including lots of Tories – Ken Clarke, Portillo, [Lord] Tristan Garel-Jones, who was mischievous as ever. Clarke looking pretty dreadful. Told me he was sticking to his guns on prisons and sentencing. Sat with Andrew Mitchell [International Development Secretary] and Tessa to one side, Maggie Rae [lawyer] to the other. Andrew reckoned despite the economy we were out for a long time.

He said the Cabinet was totally up for a media overhaul and Dacre was every bit as much in their sights as was Murdoch. We'll see. Nice do. Hamish [Falconer] made a terrific speech about his dad. Cherie read one from Tony which was quite funny. Charlie F spoke then I played happy birthday on the pipes and left to defy the fog on the way home. Cherie said a few nice words re. my speech re. PG then said, 'It almost made me like you.' At least we were still able to have a laugh. Bed by three.

Sunday 20 November

Chat Ed V in US re. various projects. Then Camden Brasserie to meet Edi Rama and Endri Fuga. I agreed to go ahead with helping the party prepare for the elections. There was something very likeable about them, and it could be fun, added to which I had always liked the Balkans work-wise.

Monday 21 November

Out to Woolwich to film with the Scots Guards. Freezing cold and I didn't play well. Good tips from Ross McCrindle though – down for tomorrow's

State banquet for the Turkish President – on pacing the strathspey and reel. Feeling fairly low on energy. Not playing well. Need to psyche up. Later out to LLR running and triathlon awards. Hugh Grant at Leveson. *Mail* saying 'mendacious smears' re. his claim *MoS* hacked him.

Tuesday 22 November

All morning doing local radio re. schizophrenia report on the most common myths. Too many but it was fine in the end. I had the flu jab without fainting. Then to the Hacked Off party for hacking victims. Steve Coogan, who had been at Leveson today, very warm and funny. Also said we shared an obsession – Dacre. Max Mosley [entrepreneur, sponsor of Hacked Off] on form and he was the one who seemed to be a bit more strategic. The rest rather caught up in it all. Chris Bryant, Tom Watson, Denis MacShane and Chris Huhne the only MPs. Not clear where it was all heading. Chatted around. Then met the lawyer for some of them, David Sherborne, who confirmed my fears the inquiry was unlikely to be forensic. It was groping around. He was trying to get at Dacre but was unlikely to be able to. He seemed to think Leveson had decided and was not really going to rock boats. He said there had been a lot of talk behind the scenes that my evidence was important. Odd event. Said to F afterwards I felt they were all getting into the bubble.

Wednesday 23 November

Two-speech day. An insurance event at St Pancras Hotel. Later engineering awards at the Dorchester. Good atmosphere. Mark Prisk, the minister for business and enterprise, was at my table. Pretty classic midranking Tory. Kept mentioning me in his speech. Did my usual few jokes then ra-ra against culture of negativity. Earlier I'd been to the cops to get my bike back. They have caught a guy nicking something else and found my bike in his house with tons and tons of other stuff. F and I discussing strategic review of life for both of us to decide what we really wanted to do on the work front. I needed to make some decisions. Doing too much and not a lot of it hyper-effectively.

Thursday 24 November

Walked to Waterloo to meet Matt Parker and have a chat. Nice guy. He had been really ill and had had depression after a virus. Really positive about the way I had tackled the diet and his programme. He was keen for me to do some kind of big event for Philip G, also maybe to do yoga with F! Interesting on the really big sums involved now in paying the top cyclists.

To [lawyer] Gerald Shamash's office to meet two cops from Operation Tuleta [phone-hacking investigation] and be shown the Jonathan Rees invoices I had already seen. They were really going through a lot of stuff but clearly felt that they would struggle to pin it all down. They said they had evidence of computer hacking, and that most phone hacking was industrial espionage rather than newspapers. I got an email from the inquiry saying I needed to see the Richard Desmond statement because it contained a response to something I had said. Tessa saying the *Mail* intended to show where I had said stories were untrue and yet were backed up by books. Through the week I was dipping in and out of some of the evidence sessions – Hugh Grant OK, but made the mistake of hinting the *Mail on Sunday* hacked him, without proof. Steve Coogan today. But the best were the 'real people' caught up in becoming newsworthy.

Sue Gray cancelled the meeting at 2.45 re. Volume 4, which was annoying. But she was dealing with a situation re. Cameron buying land from Lord [Peter] Chadlington [businessman, Tory donor].* I had dinner with Steve Hilton at Fratelli la Bufala. He said he was not working that hard because he was really demotivated. Clearly saw himself as one of the key triumvirate with Cameron and Osborne. But he was frustrated because there was no real agreed radical strategy and so far as there was one, there was no agreement. He clearly liked Cameron – 'Dave' – and felt he had lots of strengths, but he was too much of a compromiser. It wasn't just the coalition; it was his style. He liked to manage the gaps between people.

He was scathing about most of the Cabinet and a lot of the top civil service. E.g. said the Health perm sec was woeful. Can't believe she does that job. He had two young kids and did not allow the office to run his life. Not very up on Craig Oliver, loved Gabby Bertin [DC adviser], thought Jeremy H and Sue Gray were tops. Felt that what we had that they lacked was a basic agreed approach to a big project that we all supported. He was thinking about moving on and was really keen to be Brighton mayor. He clearly preferred campaigns to government, I think. Not lacking in charm or confidence. V indiscreet. Quite funny. Dave too tactical. He said the most brilliant thing I had ever said about DC was that he was my successor not TB's. 'It is so true. Can you believe he still chairs the main news management meetings, twice a day?' We agreed to keep in touch, but I had a feeling he wouldn't be there for that long. He said DC didn't rate Ed M at all, but George did a bit. Steve felt Balls was easily our best performer.

---

* Shortly after becoming an MP David Cameron had bought a strip of land near his constituency home from Lord Chadlington, the owner of a number of public affairs firms. It became known that at no time had Cameron disclosed the deal to either the Commons Register of Interests or the Register of Ministerial Interests.

Friday 25 November

Off to Retford reading the Leveson bundle which arrived this morning. I took out a swipe at Richard Desmond on the basis of his statement. Arrived at Mum's, practised the pipes a bit then to Doncaster for the Ed M CLP fundraiser. He was very nice to Mum, but could do with working on his working the tables technique. Nice bunch of people. He did a lovely intro to me, all about loyalty and values and how I was Labour to the core and I deserved a lot of the credit for all the changes for the better etc. Really warm. I did a thing about teamwork and why the press had it in for him, and how we needed to defend the record better, and also how he was right to wait on policy. Said the next election could be a big win for them or for us. Anything could happen. We had to make it happen. Books sold out, raffle tickets sold out and the auction did way better than they had ever done before. Then I pulled out the pipes, played really well and they seemed to love it. Photos then home. He seemed OK but there was definitely something missing and maybe it wasn't learnable. Mum thought he was much nicer than she expected but still felt his delivery poor.

Saturday 26 November

Rayan arrived at Mum's at eight and we set off for Glasgow for piping event. Practised a bit on the way, made a few calls, one stop and we arrived by lunchtime. Lunch at the hotel and it got a bit fractious because Mum and Liz were arguing about religion and I ended up saying Mum was narrow-minded. She had definitely got more judgemental and more dismissive of people not of her view but I felt bad for saying it. We sorted it later. Liz and she just had the same argument about heaven and hell, and why should she be damned and a killer or rapist not because of a late conversion. Anyway, it got a bit heavy. I had to peel off to do some filming, clocking up a few clichés in a cab, then to the dressing room at the Royal Concert Hall where I remained for most of the day. Lesson with Finlay, totally changing the way I played the reel. He didn't want me to overdo the practising now. Amazing comeback for Burnley at Hull. 2–0 down, 3–2 with winner in injury time.

Did a rehearsal on stage. Sounded good. Family arrived, bit of filming with the boys, Mum, Georgia and Donald, changed, then ate a salad and half-listened to the first half of the concert through the intercom, with Donald chantering away. Finlay watching at the side of the stage. Straight into it, though I was a bit confused about the spotlight, which came up slowly as I started to play. Spotted a nice-looking dad-type face in the bit of the crowd I could see and focused on him a fair bit. But for some reason I wandered on the lament and ballsed up a section of it. Really annoying, as I had been playing it brilliantly earlier, though I recovered OK. Finlay thought it was the best I had played it. So did Donald. But I was beating myself up a bit about messing the lament. They said nobody would have noticed unless they knew the tune and, in any event, I could say it was my interpretation. Had a really good laugh afterwards but though I had enjoyed it and felt everyone who had come with me was pretty proud of me, I really had felt the lament should have been perfect.

More interviews, more filming then a nice little drinks do in the VIP suite where all the relatives came. Everyone enjoyed it. Fiona and Grace both wishing they had come. George [Campbell] being great with the boys and Finlay very funny. We went out for a drink over the road, quite a few of the other performers and the crowd in there and several said they were pretty surprised how well I played. One guy said he was totally gobsmacked. We stayed for a couple of drinks then Finlay and I decided to head off but by now the weather was truly wild and awful. Howling gale, horizontal rain, no cabs, crowds of people outside clubs, soaked to the skin by the time I got back.

Sunday 27 November
I didn't sleep well and the tunes just kept going round and round in my head. I was also worried about the fact Mum felt we had been having a bit of a go at her. I was mugging up on Leveson on the train home when Matthew Doyle texted me to say that Guido Fawkes [political blogger] had published my submission to the inquiry. Bloody hell. I tried to call Robert Jay [inquiry counsel] but didn't get through so got David Sherborne [phone-hacking victims' barrister] instead. He said Leveson would go ape. He said he was really getting fed up with the way the media was behaving and last week's evidence had been bad for them. Fawkes had led on a misleading headline that I was saying the *Mirror* under Morgan hacked Cherie. I was not. I said I should tweet that I was shocked it had been leaked, unsurprised it had been misrepresented. Jay called back and he agreed I should send it. He said they would have to consider what action to take, perhaps summon Paul Staines [Guido Fawkes's real name]. I said I suspected he would love that. I said I imagined that one of the core participants had sent the thing to Fawkes to get the focus off the *Mirror* and on to them, but who knows?

Then out of the blue the phone goes and when I answer a voice says, 'My name is Brian Leveson.' I was a little taken aback but he went straight into his stride and said, 'I want to apologise.' I said it is not your fault. He said he was absolutely furious. He was minded to publish my evidence early. I said I would support that. I got the pretty clear sense that he was shocked by what he had heard and seen so far. He said, 'Do they not real-ise it is evidence when I see them jumping all over J. K. Rowling's car as she leaves?' Or when they twist the reporting of the day's events. He said it was very odd for a judge to talk to a witness but he felt he had to. He was remarkably open, said he didn't know what he would end up doing policy-wise, and also that he had not really wanted the job 'but the Lord Chief Justice has a way of getting you to do things you didn't want to'.

He also asked me if I thought the whole thing was a waste of time. I said I thought not provided he came up with good conclusions, that MPs then had the balls to take them through. He said there had clearly been too many last-chance saloons, and something had to happen. He just didn't know what. He said he was well out of his usual world in having to deal with these media issues. 'I certainly never imagined having this conversa-tion with you on this day.' He said he would welcome my advice on what to do. I said newspapers will be confused about whether they can report what Staines has done so he probably needed to say something today. He also said he was minded to publish my statement sooner than Wednesday. And he said if I had any ideas about what he might eventually come up with, he would welcome me dropping him a line.

He called me twice in total, first for a general chat to express his anger and say he intended to read the riot act, second to read me the statement he wanted to put on the website today re. the leak of my statement. He was summoning Staines and publishing my stuff tomorrow. Two long calls though and in both I had a bit of a sense of him not quite not know-ing what to do with all this. When I got home I had a proper look at what Staines had done and realised it was not the final submission which meant it was not from a core participant. It was weird. It meant he got it either by theft or hacking or through one of the people I sent it to for comments. I sent Piers a message saying I had NOT accused him of hacking, but he was really pissed off. Felt I had unfairly and with no evidence put him in the frame.

Leveson seemed fairly stressed to me, and felt the weight of it all, and also that maybe they would hear lots of stuff and then it would go nowhere. Long chat with Charlie who felt it was marginally helpful, also that we should take advantage of his offer to contribute ideas. He felt once it became clear the leak was not of the core participants, he would be less interested in a leak inquiry. I went through my emails to see who I had sent it to. TB and team, Charlie, Godric, Steve Morris, Martin Shee-han and David Bradshaw, Roy [Greenslade, media commentator], Harry Evans and Richard Peppiatt [former *Daily Star* reporter].

Sue Gray called. She had a few more comments to go through next week, mainly from the services 'and a few silly ones from the MoD'. She had been following all the stuff on my evidence leaking and said that she thought Leveson was OK. She felt that the Chilcot Inquiry would be autumn and difficult, so for me the key judgement remained the same – would it provoke a recall if I brought out Volume 4 now? She felt it impossible to tell, that even though we had seen that they could be really difficult and antsy, they must have known the book existed and yet hadn't gone for it. The cost was ratcheting up, maybe looking like £8 million by end of next year and on balance I felt they wouldn't be looking to re-open.

Monday 28 November

TB called from China. Long chat on Leveson first of all, and then on him. He agreed he needed to get a better grip of his diary and stop spending so much time on planes. He was going to be doing half a dozen countries in the next few days. He felt Leveson would be in an OK place and that he was going to see, as Hutton did, what it was like when the press spun stuff all their own way. Most of the papers covered the leak but, with one or two exceptions, not the contents of the evidence. I had a few exchanges with Robert Jay and sent an email just before they started saying it was now definite that the version Fawkes published was never sent to the inquiry. He was relieved at that. It came up when the inquiry opened. Leveson summoned Staines. He was challenged by Jonathan Caplan [barrister] for the *Mail* re. being rushed into publishing my evidence ahead of time. Caplan argued that the leak had been covered but most had been responsible and this would encourage others to leak.

Through the day Leveson changed his position. Carole Caplin [former adviser to the Blairs] called. She had seen the news last night and the line about me not knowing if she had been hacked. She told me she had been shown evidence she had been. She said she was in no doubt a lot of stuff got out via her phone. We had a nice warm chat and she said I should use whatever I wanted in my evidence. Spoke to Jay about it later. Mark came round to put my statement into a folder. I made one or two little changes, e.g. changing to take account of the fact that we did, three times related to the kids, have some success in winning PCC complaints. The evidence sessions were pretty box office stuff and getting loads of coverage.

Tuesday 29 November

I watched Leveson all day on and off, in between doing my own statement and getting in the zone. Richard Peppiatt. Nick Davies [*Guardian* journalist who initially uncovered phone hacking]. Paul McMullan. Three very different brands of journalism. McMullan was truly compelling. As it went on, you thought this can't get any worse, but it did, again and again. E.g. his being 'proud' at causing riots on the back of a paedophile campaign, and paediatricians being mistakenly attacked. Car chasing being 'fun' pre Diana. On and on. But at the end he seemed to say the Dowlers [missing child's parents] should be lucky we had brave fearless hacks who do whatever it takes to get a story. Peppiatt was good on the 'make it up' culture. Davies thoughtful and measured and very good on the failure of self-regulation (and his lack of fear of it).

I was feeling in OK nick. Also watched Osborne's economic statement to the House. Bad figures, poor presentation. It was potentially defining. Ed B did OK, but Labour were not landing blows as they should. Out later to a little fundraiser at [Ed Miliband friend] Juliet Soskice's flat for the (budget cut to zero) Camden Psychotherapy unit. They asked me to say a few words, David Sturgeon walking in halfway through. One of Juliet's friends was putting together a group for a dinner to discuss how Ed could be more strategic. Then told me Neil K was chairing. Decided against going. Also Ed still unable to decide whether to hire Tim Livesey. He needed to make bloody decisions for heaven's sake. Did my usual mental health stuff but also made a direct plea for cash. Fiona and I out to Fratelli la Bufala for dinner.

Wednesday 30 November

I couldn't really sleep so went out for a little run at 5.40 and got my head in gear. Felt OK about it all. One last read-through, then got a cab in with Calum, stopping for a coffee at the Costa I used to go to with PG pre his London School of Economics lectures. A fair bit of media at the court but the public sector strike was going to get wall-to-wall coverage. I walked to the court, to the same waiting room as for Hutton Inquiry. Feeling a lot more relaxed. The staff were all very friendly. Gerald Shamash came in with a text to the effect that Staines was saying I leaked the evidence. So I agreed with Jay that I should say something early on re. the process by which I wrote my statement and get in that three journalists were among those who saw the draft. Into court. I had to sit and listen to a fair bit of legal toing and froing, then took the stand and away we went.

Leveson said at the outset that he found my submission 'a formidable piece of work', which put me at ease. I sensed he was sympatico. Jay basically took me through my statement page by page and allowed me to get out most of my points. There were one or two objections from the *Mail* and the NI lawyers but I felt I held my own fine. Indeed, later Caplan said I did really well. I told him Alex had said he would only get reserve tickets for United games if he gave me a hard time. I had been expecting two hours but it was closer to three. I felt all the big points got out. I managed to avoid presenting myself as victim, and instead got things most of the time on to the bigger cultural changes and the need for reform and regulation. I sensed Leveson was definitely there but he clearly worried about the internet, and more generally how to balance freedom of the press with any change that was planned.

Put in submission and transcript. It was pretty tiring but I felt OK about it. Strikes [public sector pensions] meant it was fairly low down the news but it was getting loads of internet traffic and a lot of it positive. Jay had quite a nice manner, though the press will have thought he was too soft. Leveson didn't seem to interrupt others as much as he had me. Jay had said to me yesterday, when sending through the *Mail*'s (poor) questions, that he was up for any advice on how to deal with Murdoch *père et fils*. 'Cameron is a big one too,' he said, 'as I think he is in the frame a bit here.' I said so is Dacre, much more. I did OK in not going OTT re. Dacre. I think Leveson was treating it all as an education in the pattern of change and how it had impacted on the culture.

I walked out with Gerald S, and then through the pretty big strike march to LLR where they were having a strategy session run by Ideathon [charities facilitator]. Also allowed myself to be talked – fairly easily and happily – into playing next week at the Albert Hall. 5,500 people. Home to potter and watch the telly a bit then Tube to St Pancras for the not well organised Variety Club auction. Only made bearable by the banter with Cambridge Jones and his lovely wife Ondine. The thing started late, no food apart from ice cream, Robert Powell compèring, twenty-five different people introducing twenty-five different photos for auction. They all went pretty low. When I intro'd Cambridge and [portrait artist] Alexander Talbot Rice's 'Three Princes' [fanciful portrait of Princes William and Harry and AC] – really went at them for being tight – some had gone and ended up buying the bloody thing myself, for £2,250, much to Fiona's considerable annoyance.

The idea of us having it on the wall was a non-starter of course but I did wonder whether its value might not grow. That being said, Cambridge, who I sensed had not much enjoyed working with ATR, thought not. His wife was also very dry and funny. Both Labour despite some appearances. Both thought Ed – who had apparently been dire, as had Cameron, at PMQs – had no chance. The thing went on and on and we eventually sneaked out at half-ten. John and Pauline Anderton [actors] saying they had followed my evidence and they loved it. Fabulous message from Geldof. Said he had read my submission and it was 'finest hour … Think you may have nailed them.' *On verra*.

Thursday 1 December

Did a French radio interview ahead of my conference there next week. Did a blog on the coverage of yesterday which proved one of the points I was making. Nothing on reform of regulation. *Mail* the only one, bizarrely, to go on my general attack. Victor Blank [UK business ambassador] called to say well done and ask if Alex would do *Today* programme when he guest-edited. TB called from US (he had been to Korea in between), said it sounded like it went well. I said to him, and later to Charlie, that we needed to work out policy ideas the judge would take to. Couldn't get going exercise-wise. Pottering. Starting to think re. what I do for a submission for second half.

Nick Davies in touch saying he wanted to see me to let me know about some even worse stuff that was going to come out. Met Jonathan Jones [producer] to discuss booze film. Annie Robinson coming on board. Then saw Harriet Scott who was a former anorexic, bulimic, alcoholic and junkie and felt booze was the worst. Darren [Bentley, Burnley FC press officer] had the great idea of Clarke Carlisle. Sorted him too. Jay Williams [news agency journalist] getting sorted as well.

Friday 2 December

Cab to Euston. Bumped into Frank Field [Labour MP]. Civil but not friendly. Did a quick blog on the fact that Osborne preferred ideology to hard analysis and evidence. On the train read the latest briefing on the booze film. Alex taking the piss re. my latest charity gig at the Albert Hall. Picked up by Matt Parker, out to see Phil Burt [British Cycling physio] in Altrincham. Lovely big guy who very quickly put me through my paces. Felt I was in good shape subject to the flat feet being sorted, ankles improved, quads stretched and see off knee problems. But he really thought I was in good nick. Did some stretches, got a rollerfoam and then off to the Velodrome. Even better than last time I was there. Remarkable place and success story. Chat with Dave Brailsford re. the inquiry and he said the media reminded him of cycling when drugs was taking hold. People lived in denial of what was going on. They then started to tolerate and finally it was endemic. Dave on great form. Confident re. the Games.

Picked up and off to Swinton for filming of my cameo role in *The Accused* [BBC drama series]. Lunch on the dining bus with the director, producer and Jimmy McGovern [writer]. Nice guy. Changed with the costume guy, makeup then in to do my scene. Had a crib sheet of cue words on the camera. Eight or nine takes and they seemed pleased with it. Interesting. Anne-Marie Duff (the cute blonde in *Shameless*) was there. Nice atmosphere though weird it was all going on in a shed in Swinton. Grace really excited about it and keen to spend a day there.

To the station, met Burnley fans en route West Ham for the weekend. Trying to sort Highland gear to play the pipes at PG's internment. 5.15 train back. TB was on again re. football issues, wanting me to push one of the players Nicky [son] was representing – with CB apparently as the chairman of the company – to some of the managers I know. I tried Gus [Poyet], Sam [Allardyce] and Harry R. Gus was keen but then Nicky decided his Mexican was too good for Brighton. Did a bit of work on the booze film. Quite keen to get a politician in there somewhere.

Saturday 3 December

Off to Burford. Lunch with Gail and Georgia, later joined by Rory and Grace G. The girls seemed OK but Georgia looked vulnerable. I went off to Matthew Freud's amazing gaff – an old monastery turned into a kind of Chequers. We had a little chat with Liz then went off to the little cemetery garden to dig a grave for the time capsule and the token ashes. He had the PG funeral statue there which was nice. We had a good chat as we dug, a mix of banter and serious talk. It was harder than I thought it would be, and took longer but we got it done then I did a bit of practice on the pipes. I had done an adaptation of 'Lest We Forget'. I had the kilt with me and had a bet with Rory about how long it would take for CB to say something rude about the pipes and the kilt. It took two seconds from her entry. She just could not help herself. TB seemed a bit detached from it all.

We had a drink in the hall then went through to the service in the beautiful little chapel. Their chaplain and PG's sister sharing the service and prayers. It was a lovely setting and PG would have liked it but Gail and the girls had said they could have done without one more reminder right now. Grace had told me she was more worried about her emotions at this one and once we went over to the grave, me piping on the way, and the minister saying a few words, they both got upset. Gail focusing on Grace. Gail too said she was a convert. And CB apologised, said pipes 'sounded wonderful outside'!

Bob Dylan tape at the end and we hung around a bit. Just the three Gs, me, F and Rory, Matthew and Elizabeth M, TB–CB, PG sister and husband. I played several laments and had tears rolling down my face. Buffet dinner in one of the big lounges. Tessa and David now there too. I chatted mainly to David, a bit to TB. Matthew showed me his office and his amazing collection of letters written by some of history's biggest figures. Seemed to think he might be called to Leveson. We stayed till ten-ish then to Gail's and bed. Nice event. I had slightly been dreading it but Matthew made it work well. TB sent me a message saying it was nice to have been there and a reminder of who real friends were. I had said to him he needed to change his modus operandi next year. Burnley won 2–1 at West Ham.

Sunday 4 December

Nice chat with Gail before she headed off to the US. They were all three in their different ways going to find it so tough. Home then out for dinner with Tessa, David, Matt and Jessie. Nice enough but I was in a bad mood and lost it a bit with Tessa. I think I was dipping again.

Monday 5 December

Lunch with Natascha at the Wolseley. She was on great form. Wanted me to try an idea she had on Jimmy McGovern. Otherwise mainly all the usual family stuff etc. Sarko–Merkel Eurozone talks in Paris. Going to be a very interesting few days in Europe. Calum at the Labour Muslim dinner which he said had become a bit of a mess.

Tuesday 6 December

In to see TB and Catherine R, with JoP on the phone from Malaysia, re. Kaz. I still worried it was hard to get traction, but TB insisted his meetings had been good and that the President was up for change. JoP felt there was a battle going on and our job was to help the reformers. We also had a useful chat re. Leveson. Dan Franklin came over and we did the final tweaks to *The Happy Depressive*. Off to Eurostar and out to Lille. Car to Dunkirk and out for a quick run. Tripped on a step and worried I tore ligaments. Out to a long and rather odd public sector comms awards ceremony. No black people there. Speeches and citations all a bit long. A colleague of [French communications expert Jacques] Séguéla's presenting and she clearly didn't like him. Felt quite odd being there, at an event I would normally dominate and yet for now was a bit of an add-on.

Wednesday 7 December

Foot injury not good. Breakfast then over to the conference centre by the sea. Nice Dunkirk mayor Michel Delebarre – chatted with him and later enjoyed his speech without notes. My main event was a discussion chaired by film-maker Serge Moati, with a pollster and a strategist. It went fine. I'd written a speech which in the end I didn't deliver but it was useful to have it. My usual main points and it seemed to go pretty well. It was interesting to watch the clear respect for the public officials like the mayor. Definitely a less cynical culture politically. Charlie F did a note suggesting a third way re. Volume 4 publication, namely at the same time as the inquiry report. Not possible. United lost in Basel and were out of Champions League. Alex really down.

Thursday 8 December

My Rio Tinto meeting was cancelled so I could spend a bit of time with Mum and Rory in between pottering, doing another Europe blog and also practising the pipes for tonight. Looking forward to playing at the Albert Hall though it was clearly not totally gripped. Lots of the family coming, and Georgia. I had a nice dressing room, practised in there and after struggling to get into the kilt suit Sissy had hired for me, I was out there in front of 5,500 people. All mainly white, middle-class and getting on. Did a carol, a reel, happy birthday, then 'Scotland the Brave' and off. Went fine. Second half ended with a soap-star finale which just about worked. Reception in The Gallery with some of the stars. Good reception for the pipes. Tired. Foot sore. Interesting that people noticed the quality of the piping. Finlay's training had paid off.

Friday 9 December

Woke to the news that at 4 a.m. the EU summit had ended with Cameron vetoing the planned new Treaty. Huge moment for him and for Britain and Europe. Right-wingers would love it but medium and long term it could be a disaster. Off early with Rayan. Jonathan Jones with me for the day. Worked on my speech for lunchtime on the way up, in between chatting to Brendan – one of whose colleagues said I'd been great on the pipes. We arrived at the Variety Club do so all the usual MC in red coat, barker this and chief barker [members] that, but I had nice people on my table, and Louise Minchin [TV presenter] hosting it, who was really nice. Speech went down really well, a few jokes then a commentary on what had happened overnight in Brussels. Waited for the business awards and the charity stuff and a funny speech from Barry Cryer [writer, comedian], who had been really friendly, and was there for a lifetime achievement award. The line that went down best from my own speech was how many people made their best and biggest decisions at 4 a.m.? But Cameron was definitely going to get a lift out of this, until the reality kicked in.

Off to Ripponden for a really good chat for the booze film with Clarke Carlisle. Nice wife Gemma, from Leeds, two lovely little kids including a very polite son Marley who made me take my shoes off. Clarke was really candid about the drink stuff, said he saw it as a battle he would always have to fight, that he could never just have one, had to have another. Turning point was when Ian Holloway kicked him off the team bus, he watched the coverage in a pub, and when news of a QPR goal came in he was cheering then asking himself what the hell was he doing? Off to Riddlesden to see people in the Marquis of Granby, Dad's old local. Interviewed the land-lord and a few guys about their drinking habits. To Burnley and overnight in The Oaks where there was a hen night and a nurses' party. Straight to bed. Did a blog earlier suggesting Cameron genuinely didn't know how his decision was going to pan out. Could be making or breaking of him. The fact that it felt more tactical than strategic made me think breaking more likely than making, but Ed was just not well placed to capitalise.

Saturday 10 December

Out for a run, including through some really bad housing. Did make me wonder if we had delivered as much when in power as sometimes we claimed. Breakfast with Jonathan listening to all the usual breakfast minu-tiae of couples away for the weekend. Then filming at the club, loads of different shots doing the same thing, lots of stuff up looking down on town, then in the hospitality sections on both sides of the ground. Good interview with Chris Gibson [Burnley FC catering director] who said they sold £10,000 worth of beer last night, and that 90 per cent left pissed. Also said people tanked up at home first. The match was absolutely shocking. Beyond belief and we lost [one–nil to Portsmouth] in the last minute.

Sunday 11 December

Had a chat with Alex who was saying United were good to back for the title. Going out of the Champions League was the kick they needed. He said they were always best with their backs to the wall. Cameron was getting a lift in the polls from his Europe stance even thought a lot of the serious opinion-former comment was against him. Ed M sent me through his statement for tomorrow which I looked at while we were having din-ner. It was OK but lacked clarity and lacked a big point.

Monday 12 December

TB abroad, asked how the Europe stuff was going. He felt it was a disas-ter for Britain because though Cameron would get a short-term lift in the longer term we would see power and influence diminish. But the worst thing was that Britain was going back to traditional left–right politics, and the right would win. I asked for a few lines and wove them into Ed's statement, some of which he used for the ending. He did OK and Cameron was not quite as cocky as his people seemed to feel. Out to Lauderdale House [arts centre] to do an interview for PBS [American public broadcaster] re. Murdoch. I was involved in a bizarre car crash on the way back. The driver just careered up the kerb and into a set of traffic lights. Lunch Joe Hemani and Alan Donnelly [lobbyist] at the Rib Room. Alan trying to get work with him. Don't think he realised Joe and I were already good friends.

Tuesday 13 December
Catherine R had sent through book comments, so I worked on those before heading out for a long bike ride in the cold. I was low on the energy front. Out to see Michael Sheen's Hamlet at the Young Vic. Brilliant. Halfway through got an email from Kate Molloy, and a call from Alix, that Sandy [their mother] had died.

Wednesday 14 December
Spoke to Mike [former *Daily Mirror* editor] re. Sandy. The first time we had spoken since he wrote that awful piece for the *Mail* about why he was voting Tory. Nice chat. I was thinking a lot about losing friendships, and it wasn't sensible. Neil and Glenys after the 'We've got our party back' comment [after leadership election]. Maybe I just needed to forget it. David M distant probably because he had wanted me to do more in his leadership campaign. Peter M. Piers really hacked off with me because of my Leveson submission. Morning at Rio Tinto to chat with [chairman] Jan du Plessis re. the work we had been doing. Good chat re. the economy – he was really worried and felt global leadership was absent.

Nick Davies round for a chat re. where we were on Leveson and also for a book he was planning. He felt Leveson would come up with a good report and meaty recommendations but worried the government would not run with it. He was in a bit of a state because it had emerged it was not necessarily true that the *NotW* deleted Milly Dowler's messages. So some of the papers were going into kill mode on that and he was finding it hard. He was due to do *Newsnight* and I said he should say the main story was right, they got one detail possibly wrong, but when it came to it he floundered a bit until Jules Stenson, ex-features editor of *NotW*, came to his rescue by being so unpleasant. Briefly with Grace to Ed Victor's party.

Thursday 15 December

Blogged re. the OTT telly reaction to yesterday's PMQs. Ed had asked Cameron re. Clegg, 'Where did it all go wrong?', Clegg having stayed out of the chamber for the statement of Monday, and Cameron had said something like, 'At least we're not brothers,' and Nick Robinson et al. treated it like the end of the world for Ed. The by-election [Feltham and Heston] ought to settle things but there was a lot of negativity for Ed at the moment. The problem was it wasn't just the media. A lot of people were saying the same thing, that they couldn't see him as PM. That being said the PMQs reaction was OTT. Nick Robinson clearly read the blog because he came on to ask me a few questions about it. Maybe you needed to be there but he clearly felt it was a big moment.

Friday 16 December

OK result in the by-election though the turnout was poor.[*] All day home. Volume 4 mainly. Kip. Low energy levels. Had a row later with Fiona. Started with me saying how I missed PG and then got into how we didn't really listen to each other blah blah usual stuff. Really annoying. Bed early. Definitely on a dip.

Saturday 17 December

Row simmering. Blog re. Cameron making a speech on religion and saying he is a committed but vaguely practising Christian. Off to Brighton with the boys. Lunch with [Lord] Steve Bassam [Labour Chief Whip in Lords]. He voted for Ed but worried he had made a mistake. Brighton Stadium tour. Impressive. We won one–nil after they had two sent off in the first ten minutes. Stayed down for a drink with Eddie Howe and Gus Poyet. Loved reminiscing with Gus re. Soccer Aid, and Maradona.

Sunday 18 December

Out for a run then to Lemonia for the Gault reunion. I wanted Jack and Harry [sons of Mark Gault, who died in 2003] to meet his old friends from college. Sixteen of us in all, and they loved it. Hardly anyone got really pissed. Suzie seemed OK with it and the boys seemed really to enjoy it. Wondering which if any of them should be in the booze film. All nice and good and glad we did it.

---

[*] Labour candidate Seema Malhotra held the seat, caused by the death of Alan Keen, with an increased majority.

Monday 19 December

To Grosvenor Square for a meeting with Catherine and Steve Morris re. Leveson. TB popped in at one point, said the main point was the unaccountable political power, the fact that owners used their papers as instruments of power, that politicians had to go along with it to some extent because if they went into kill mode they could literally stop you getting your message through to the public. He said he intended to be very honest about it, to make clear he did indeed court them because he knew what damage they could do. He said the problem is no serving PM could really take them on because they have so much capacity to damage and they and your political opponents combine to do real damage under the cover of claiming you are trying to stop freedom. We chatted through what we needed – properly researched submissions, but above all policy proposals that we felt had some chance of being implemented. I was still not sure Cameron would go for anything too difficult for the press.

We all got a bit anecdotal and unfocused but at least we were beginning to think about it. I said to TB it was tricky for him because they would focus on Murdoch but important for any reputational rebuild. He said in terms of research we should not make it whingey but just show how e.g. he could not get any positive – or even non-hostile – coverage in the *Mail*, Ed in *The Sun*, GB in *The Sun* post switch, Cameron in the *Mirror*. It was about the bias and the abuse of power. I said we also needed stuff re. e.g. how that impacted on public services.

Saw Gail who looked shattered. She said she was very up and down. She said TB was thinking about doing a book on globalisation and faith. She said they were very excited about my e-book though I was still a bit unsure how to sell these things without doing lots of old media. Good meeting with Sue Gray, finally got sign-off from her. The MoD were asking for virtually every special forces reference to come out, which was a bit silly. The FCO wanted references to the Indians bugging us out, even though they had been in *The Blair Years*. Charlie had done a very good close read and concluded there was no problem publishing pre Chilcot. He felt the narrative was consistent with my and TB's evidence, even if it wasn't written in the same way, being a diary. He felt the issues which might arouse interest were not significant enough to merit any recall. Gail suggested we get the final copy to Chilcot before it was in the shops.

Sue said Gus O'Donnell was like a big kid over Alex being in his farewell video. TB and Clegg had been funny, DC less so. Saw Emma to plan mini publicity on *The Happy Depressive*, then off to Queen's Park to record the audiobook. Into No. 10 for Gus's farewell. Asked for identity at the gate by a policewoman who clearly didn't have a clue who I was. Some of the same crowd inside but a lot of fresh faces among the staff. I was at the door of the green room as Cameron came in and we had a brief chat re. happiness – I told him the sound engineer had been surprised how balanced I was about him. [Lord] Richard Layard [economist, active in 'happiness economics'] was there too and was trying to get him to go to the UNGA [United Nations General Assembly] well-being summit in the spring. Cameron rather deftly turned it into a discussion on PM travel and roped me in to explain how much travel there was in the diary and it was hard to add to it the whole time. Then on to 'Why do we take the press with us?' Then on to why do we do New Year messages, then let's maybe agree a list of things we ought to get rid of, and then he was off. Chatted for a while to John Scarlett re. his new life, mainly with Morgan Stanley. Richard Wilson complaining about being in the Lords. Robin Butler small talk, also rather bizarrely asking if I had got taller. Only a couple of non-whites, very much the male establishment. Fair few of the current Cabinet, and from our days Peter M, Jack S, Tessa. Jeremy Heywood telling me the Europe thing was not a problem.

Cameron did an OK speech. Major was the funniest by a mile. Cameron had said he and Gus had been with Lamont when Britain fell out of the ERM but it didn't seem to have damaged their careers. Major started by saying 'I'm glad the ERM did not damage YOUR careers'. He had a few good cracks about the civil service too. Clegg made an OK speech, but he and Cameron both seemed a bit tired and edgy. Tried to have a chat with Peter but he really wasn't up for it. I texted him to say the 'I'll try' reconciliation plan wasn't going well. He replied that I seemed to have no idea how grim I had been for how long, and the damage I had done. I said no, I didn't. Nuclear row F/Grace.

End of December to 6 January 2012

This must be the longest gap between recordings in the diary. Partly tired and a bit down. Partly bored. Partly holiday. Partly that I could feel myself going into a dip but it was the New Year before it finally became a big depression. I saw David S when we got back from Scotland, at his UCL office in Taviton St. He was sure there was a seasonal element to my depressions though like me he was pleased it had been such a while since the last bad one. He felt worry over the kids, my usual existential 'What is the point of all this?' and also aftershock-grief re. Philip were likely to be factors. I hadn't expected him to put me on anti-depressants because when I called him I said I was just a bit edgy. But he was convinced I was depressed and possibly en route to a big one. He put me on a new one which he said would also help with the sleep. Conaglen was such a wonderful place to sleep because it got dark early and light late in the morning, and was so, so quiet. Yet I was waking at four or five every morning and then just lying there fretting.

I did just two blogs during the holiday period, one on depression, one on tourism. I wasn't really following the political scene which was another source of down-ness. Ed was getting a pretty rough ride in the press, the sense being that he was just not making progress. I came across too many people from too many walks of life basically saying they could not see him as Prime Minister. When Tessa and David arrived in Scotland, I told her I didn't really want to talk politics. She did but I tended to avoid. Scotland was fine. Very wet, beautiful as ever and I was glad Gail and the girls came to Conaglen for Christmas. Fiona and I drove up, stopping at [TV presenter] Mariella Frostrup's and [husband] Jason McCue's on the way. His mum and dad, Terry and Jan, were there as last year. The boy Danny had a cold. I played the pipes outside and later we all got in the hot tub which was nice but a bit weird. But we had a nice time and as ever they were a good laugh.

The rain was unbelievable on the way up and pretty heavy the whole time we were there. Gail and the girls, Lindsay [Nicholson] and family, Audrey for Christmas, Tessa and David, Karen and Greg [Nugent] for New Year. The scenery and food wonderful as ever. Only got out three times on the bike, two runs, mainly walking. Decided to go back to zero on the drink front from New Year. We missed PG a lot but I got the feeling they preferred we didn't talk about him too much, let them take the lead on that. Grace G weepy on Christmas Day, Georgia smiley and happy as ever but I could tell she was hurting beneath. She was subtly filling the hole he left – making a holiday film, having ideas for trips etc. Rory and Calum were drinking a fair bit but Calum too decided at the end of the year he would knock it on the head for a while. Charles Kennedy came over for one night. He had had Sarah and Donald [wife and son] up for a week and they had gone back on the sleeper. He was drinking a bit, seemed fairly edgy but as ever was very good company.

Totally down on the coalition. He was keen to keep his seat but it was going to be a carve-up with Danny Alexander and they would move heaven and earth to keep DA in a winnable seat [following boundary changes that might pitch them against one another]. He felt the Libs would get routed but felt we were not yet making an impression. As for Scotland, Salmond was running away with it. So all in all a nice time. Fiona got me a fantastic new set of pipes as a present and as neither of mine for her – a bracelet which didn't fit and a bag I could tell she didn't like – really hit the mark, for once it was her present to me getting all the plaudits. I played every morning and they really were good-quality pipes. I was determined to keep playing now. Donald [brother] was obsessed with the idea that I should compete. He was sure I could win competitions at a certain level. F and I drove back with Calum on New Year's Day. Long day and I was definitely diving now.

I went with the boys the next day to Leeds–Burnley. Rayan took us and I did a bit of work on the Volume 4 intro on the way. Amazing match. Kieran Trippier sent off in the first half so we were a man short most of the match but played well, took the lead, only to go down to an own goal and a 97th-minute goalkeeping error. Out for dinner with Fiona on her birthday 2 January and she seemed to enjoy herself. She and I were getting on better than for a long time. Both of us worrying re. our next steps. She talked about going for a seat but – partly after talking to Tessa – talked herself out of it. She wanted a new mission yet was also torn, feeling we ought to spend more time in France and generally think about slowing down. Once I was back in the swing, the main thing was trying to break the back of the film on alcohol.

A morning at the BBC to meet people from Clouds [rehab clinic] to go over what we might film there and talk to some of the people who had been through the place. Claire and Kirby the counsellors, Jack, Edwina and Mark (Ann Keen's long-lost son)* the ones happy to be on camera, another guy who had some great insights but said he couldn't be on film. The thesis developing was that it was all-pervasive and very hard to resist. Edwina said her family and colleagues both felt there was something a bit abnormal about not drinking. Mark said it was all dressed up in sophisticated language. The third guy did Ironman challenges and so had clearly switched obsessions.

Saw TB on the first day back for a meeting on Kazakhstan and Kuwait. He seemed a bit distracted and had an appointment with a personal trainer and wanted to get out for that. Catherine said she was fascinated to read in Volume 4 the tensions he and I had when I was disagreeing and he was insisting he was always right. 'I think in that regard I have filled your gap,' she said. She had a few more comments on the book. Re. Kaz, there had been protests and violence over the holiday and they had not handled it well. We had tried to give them the right advice but they took bits but not all of it. TB felt they were genuinely in two minds. There was a real debate going on. What we could do was keep giving the advice and hope that eventually they moved and would realise we had been giving good advice all the time, and a tipping point would come and we would be on the right side of it.

Second day back spent being filmed running on Hampstead Heath for

---

* Labour MP Ann Keen had become pregnant when seventeen and put the baby up for adoption. In 1997 she became reunited with her son.

the booze film. Nice way to spend a depressed morning. Then in the afternoon interviewing Harriet, one of our middle-class alcoholics. Lovely girl and with a pretty harrowing story though she had come good. Saw Nicola Howson and collected my portrait of PG – there had been ten printed of him standing on his burial spot. We didn't quite know where to put it. France maybe. I felt it was a bit ghoulish to have such a big picture in the house. Gail had not even been able to look at hers. She and I kept in touch and she was clearly very up and down. I was in there a fair bit dealing with the launch of *The Happy Depressive*.

The only other meeting I had in the first few days was in Ed's office with his team. James Morris from [pollster] Stan Greenberg's place went through the polling. It was not as bad as I feared but I think it understated the negativity re. Ed. He said that as things stood it would be easier for us to get a majority than the Tories. I didn't buy that. I felt a lot of the Lib collapse would go their way. Also people would give Cameron the benefit of the doubt in a way they wouldn't give it to us. We had pretty much flatlined and then Cameron got a boost out of Europe. And we were still copping the blame for the economy and the cuts. I did my stuck record about the need for an audit of what we did well and what we did badly and though there was some agreement they also felt it was probably too late. There were a few interesting ideas but generally it all felt tired and lacking in energy (which I certainly was).

Tim Livesey, who Ed had finally chosen and appointed as chief of staff, would have his work cut out. They really had to get a new and clear economic narrative and they had to get some oomph and energy into the shadow Cabinet. Finally did first blog of the new year on the 6th. Explaining that I had had the Black Dog, hence no blog. Also helping disabled campaigner Sue Marsh with her press activity re. the government covering up the extent of opposition to DLA [disability living allowance] changes.* Had to watch out politically though – Matthew Taylor had made the point we must not just be seen as being on the side of the victims and the vulnerable but on those who really were surviving the bad times too.

Saturday 7 January
I had bought [former campaigning Labour MP] Chris Mullin's diaries and was enjoying them. They were very different in tone and style to mine. Particularly when he became a minister he saw himself more as observer

---

* The government's controversial welfare reform proposals included more rigorous assessment of applicants and a new costs-saving system, personal independence payment, replacing DLA.

than player. He clearly liked and admired Tony, disliked and didn't respect or admire GB. Like mine he had certain themes which kept coming back again and again – Murdoch, freemasons, the pointlessness of his career. He said at one point he will probably be remembered as the diarist of the regime more than anything he did as a minister and that may well be true. The depression was still kicking in and I forced myself to do a session on the exercise bike. I got a lot of good responses to yesterday's blog admitting I had not been blogging because of my depression, and also to the *Guardian* piece from *The Happy Depressive* which ran today.

Fiona and I set off for Norwich. Delia and Michael had invited us when we saw them at Sandy Molloy's funeral but for various reasons it had not worked out, getting there to stay over, so we went for the day trip option. That was fraught too. The train we were booked on was cancelled. The next one was late. A young Norwegian reporter came to talk to me, which passed the time. Spent the rest of the journey chatting to Fiona, and reading Chris Mullin. He really had a nice style and the diaries a nice feel. TB was 'The Man'. He clearly didn't like Peter M or GB. We were late and Delia sent her driver to get us to the ground for lunch. Charles Clarke [now visiting professor at University of East Anglia] and Carole Pearson [wife], Phil Webster [*The Times*], Delia's lovely mum Ettie (now ninety-two) and an old farmer who used to have Dad as his vet. Charles seemed fairly chilled. He and Carole both felt we had pretty much had it with Ed. He was trying to get me to do a session at UEA.

The match was not as bad as the result sounds – we lost 4–1. I went in the directors' box for once and quite enjoyed it. Cup games didn't seem to matter as much as they used to. Stayed for a chat with Delia and co., her mum telling me I had to run and oust Ed. Train back with Phil. He said *The Times* were trying to keep a distance from phone hacking, but that the mood in there had not been great. Murdoch was not as evident as he used to be.

Sunday 8 January

There was a lot of interesting stuff coming up on the well-being agenda. Children's Society doing a big report this week. Freddie Flintoff has a programme on Wednesday on depression in sport. So plenty of depression and well-being stuff around. Out early and off to Chelwood with the film crew. Stopped for coffee near Reading and a guy came over to encourage me to keep going on the depression agenda. He said he was married to a psychiatrist who was currently off sick with it. Down to Syd Young's. He was looking pretty well though said his arthritis was not great. The film guys decided we should do the chat in the garden. Syd funny as ever, lots of stories about drink and Fleet St amid the recollections of my visit there when I was recovering from my breakdown. Jay Williams was good on how much he just enjoyed drinking and did it to get blotto. Also good on how he stopped.

Jackie [Young] had made some lasagne for lunch and after all the faffing and shooting from different angles, we sat down with a plate in front of the telly for the United–City game. United three up at half-time so, sure it was all over, we headed for London. After which City got two back and almost nicked an equaliser. We got to Kensington and went to a pub to kill time before going to see Annie Robinson. Then to her nice little townhouse. Lithuanian housekeeper. Annie was in a good mood, very nice to the crew and when it came to the interview, after a slow start she came up with some good answers. Good on how she drank alone, to deal with fear. Good on being a woman in a man's world. She said she had forgotten most of what had happened. She said it didn't mean as much to her as it still seemed to mean to me. Nice chat re. the culture of Fleet Street etc. She had given up *The Weakest Link* [TV quiz show] but was doing the book show again. Keen for us to get Gail down to her Burford place for lunch soon enough. Spoke to Gail later. She had had a really bad weekend. Said she felt pretty bereft.

Monday 9 January

Sue Marsh [disabled campaigner] had done a good job with her team of fellow campaigners in preparing their paper on how the government had effectively covered up the scale of opposition to benefit reforms revealed by their own consultation. I gave over my blog to their press release. Within an hour or so of the launch it was trending on Twitter though needless to say the mainstream media were not doing that much on it. Kelvin MacKenzie [former editor, *The Sun*] made a tit of himself at Leveson, not least with his (admittedly quite good) impersonation of John Major. My sense was Leveson was not impressed. Did a little run then to Waterloo for a meeting with Gerald Shamash and Jeremy the QC. He said News International were taking a much more aggressive stance on settlements and mine was not the likeliest to get a decent settlement. I totally understood that, had never really believed I would. Jeremy said that News wanted to be able to say they had settled a whole load more before a trial which would involve just one or two.

We went through all the calls that came via the hub – i.e. calls to me from News – and they related either to the time I was doing the sport series, or the time I was advising Tessa and David on their separation. So it was entirely possible I was being hacked then. Later to Portcullis

House to see Andrew Mitchell. He seemed fairly happy with his lot. He had been offered Defence after Liam Fox left but he really wanted to stay at International Development. He was trying to turn it into a real department of State and felt he was having some success. Re. Ed, who had had another rough weekend in the media, he felt it was unlikely he would be able to turn it around. The party didn't know its instincts any more and they didn't feel led. He was raving about how much he had enjoyed Charlie's party. Told me a story of a chat he had with GB when he was in New York announcing a new education initiative. As GB was also there he decided to call him as a courtesy. All he got for his pains was a lecture from GB (without listening to the arguments) that he was messing it up and doing the wrong thing. He said his staff had told him to be polite but he ended up losing it with him.

Tuesday 10 January

Blogged on the overdone Ed negativity which was dominating a lot of the media. John Humphrys apparently asked him if he was worried that ugly politicians didn't make it. Ed's speech wasn't too bad but the media had just decided on a narrative that said he was failing and losing. Meeting with Tom Albanese. We agreed a number of plans for the future. He basically wanted me to work more on his speeches.

Salmond took the government by surprise by announcing autumn 2014 as the date for a [Scottish independence] referendum. Cameron had upped the ante and this was his response. High-wire game was beginning. HS2 rail link to get the go-ahead. Good.

Wednesday 11 January

I finally went to see Ron Marx about the pains in my arms. He felt it might be the bike, did not scoff at Fiona's thought that it was to do with playing the pipes, and maybe that it was to do with desk posture. Definitely not arthritis or RSI. He came round later and said I needed to get a new chair. A few other ergo-tips. Did a blog on Seumas Milne's column claiming 'Blairite zombies' – Jim Murphy [former Scotland Secretary] and [Lord] Maurice Glasman for God's sake – were taking Ed in the wrong direction. Usual problem – Tory press negativity reflected in broadcast echo chamber, left-wing press deciding to focus on invented internal divisions rather than the real enemy. Worked at home most of the day. Nice piece in the *Indy* on *The Happy Depressive*. I did an interview for an Albanian mag as a favour to Edi's team because one of their mates had tried suicide and was getting hammered in their media. They needed someone to put the case for a different approach.

Watched PMQs. Ed OK. Salmond really driving the agenda at the moment. I finally sent my note about a new Department for Sport to Jeremy Heywood, now Cabinet Secretary, and Steve Hilton. Keith Mills felt now was the right time, the Cabinet having gone to the Olympics site yesterday. My basic pitch was that at least for a decade or so have Sport and Olympic Legacy as its own department, in Cabinet, and use it to drive change across health, education, communities etc. Jeremy was totally up for it, worried that there would be some opposition because it was me, also not sure that Cameron and Osborne got sport. Out on the bike for an hour or so. John Bercow called to try to unpick the cock-up re. our next dinner in Speaker's House. Later watched the Freddie Flintoff programme on depression in sport.

Thursday 12 January

Out all day at Clouds filming for the alcohol film. Unfortunately Edwina, who had been terrific when we had the pre-meeting at the BBC, had decided against being on camera. She had been especially good on the idea that in her family – military, upper-middle-class – and in her profession – media and marketing – you were considered very odd if you didn't drink. But we had Mark, Ann Keen's son, plus James, who was now an Ironman regular, and a couple of new ones, Ben from an upper-class background who was very good on the depths he reached, and a nice woman called Teresa who lost her son as a result of her drinking, and now had him back as a result of her staying sober. Clouds itself was a lovely old house set in fabulous Wiltshire countryside. Lots of filming of me just walking in and out of the place, which was annoying, though the crew was a lot quicker and less faffy at this kind of thing than most.

The main filming session was me, Claire and Kirby from Clouds, and our four ex-residents talking about their experiences. Some common themes, but they were all surprised when I said that I could have the odd drink and not go crazy with it. Perhaps these guys were real alcoholics whereas I was someone who had a drink-induced breakdown. Some strong stories though and Mark came up with a great line when he talked about Britain facing a boozequake and being on the verge of an alcohol tsunami. I did separate chats with Ben, who was funny about the 'drinking career', and yet quite moving in his description of his last few days, in a Travelodge-type hotel drinking round the clock and smashing stuff. Then calling his mother (also an alcoholic) to say he had a drink problem. The problem with the film was going to be knowing what to use and what to cut. Yet *Panorama* needless to say were pushing for more big names. They were hoping we might be able to involve Kate Middleton [Duchess of Cambridge], who had chosen Action on Addiction as one of her first four charities. I was torn. It would definitely help publicity-wise. But what really would she have to say? Yet Kirby made the point it would be a real boost for the charity that ran Clouds.

We chatted over a sandwich lunch and I could tell Kirby and some of the alcoholics were very dubious about my controlled drinking. I made the point that I liked to have the sense of challenging myself and that included both having a couple of drinks and then stopping, but also looking at a bottle in the fridge and leaving it alone. I did wonder though whether even the occasional drink was sending the wrong signal to Calum, who once or twice had said that he felt I was more of an alcoholic than he was. I know he was doing that thing I used to do, looking around for excuses to keep on drinking and making favourable comparisons, but even if I thought I had it under control, and the kids had never seen me worse for wear, a big part of me wished I was back in those thirteen years of total sobriety. At least I could say I had had a totally dry 2012 so far.

I met several of the current residents. A mixed bunch. A couple of very posh women, one of whom asked me if I was David Cameron. The other was having her stay funded by her husband. Quite a few were funded by the NHS. One or two very wired drug addicts. I definitely left with the feeling there should be more places like this. The journey home was longer than it should have been. Sean misread the map and we ended up near Southampton. It was when I read the road sign to Exeter I realised we were in trouble.

Friday 13 January
Out early again, this time filming in Fleet St. Cheshire Cheese, Old Bell, El Vino's, old Mirror building, now Sainsbury's. Pretty painless. Did phone interview with *The Big Issue*, a nice Scottish girl on what advice I would give to the sixteen-year-old me. Drink featured fairly heavily. We also had a little chat about independence. I don't know why Cameron and Ed M had not even considered votes for the rest of the UK, or at the least Scots living elsewhere in the UK. If Scotland went on its own, that would affect the whole of the country, not just Scotland. Catherine MacLeod called to say Johann Lamont and co. wanted me to tweet re. SNP MSP Joan McAlpine suggesting anti-independence voices were anti-Scottish. I did so though it turned out she didn't exactly say that, and I ended up getting a fair bit of abuse. The debate was really taking over though, and Alistair Darling was getting really stuck in, and quite effectively.

After Fleet St, to Queen Mary's University to do an interview with Cathy, the very nice head of anatomy there. She showed me into the mortuary and the lines of embalmed bodies in white body bags. I managed to look at one for a while but warned her I was likely to faint. Filming, then interviewed her while explaining to me the difference between a healthy and a sick liver. The sick one was twice the size and covered in what looked like spots. Home for a fairly long bike ride but then felt like I was going down with a cold.

Saturday 14 January

Woke up feeling really grim. Head cold. Temperature. Glad I had decided not to go to the Middlesbrough match, though as it turned out I missed a great performance. 2–0 win. Stayed in bed till two, then pottered round a bit feeling like death warmed up. The boys away for a boozy weekend in Germany. F and G looking after me. Ed M called just as I was about to go back to bed. He was on *Marr* tomorrow, and he wanted to talk it through. He was getting a lot of bad press. He said it had been pretty horrific. The right-wing papers just battered him the whole time, said he was hopeless, then ran polls to say the public agreed, then ran more stories and so it went on and on. He said he was finding it tough 'but I don't need to tell you what it was like'. He said Marr was planning to wait to the end to do 'the me question'. I said he should raise it first.

He should say he would worry if it was all about personality, but that 'we are winning the battle of ideas', which is why Cameron and Clegg were coming on to his ground e.g. in talking of the need to rebalance the economy, and deal with croney capitalism. Ed Balls had done a speech today making clear that Labour could not promise to reverse Tory cuts, and that we would not reverse pay freeze etc. It was whacked by the left, but Ed M intended to carry on with it. I suggested also that he articulate what was happening re. the media take on him. He felt it was too defensive which may be right. I said in which case just say it is part of the territory for people in positions of leadership, and he had to show he could get through it.

Sunday 15 January

I thought Ed did OK, didn't get pushed around, energetic and pretty clear in his message. But when I tweeted to say so, a lot of negativity came back. He had a long way to go and maybe he didn't know how to get there. Blogged on [footballer] Dean Windass's interview on depression and suicide attempts, weaving in Time to Change and *The Happy Depressive* and trailing the Clegg event on Tuesday. The Twitter reviews for *The Happy Depressive* were good. I was feeling pretty shitty, possibly a chest infection.

I slept badly but stayed in bed till late. I had a feeling this depression was deeper than the last one. I was finding it hard to drag myself out of bed. When I did I found myself doing a blog on Blue Monday, supposedly the most unhappy day of the year. It was a silly but rather effective PR stunt dreamed up for a travel company seven years ago, but at least it got us talking about mental health again. The Sky Arts team was back for a last interview and filming in what they called 'my other life'. We did the interview upstairs but I wasn't really up for it. I just patted back questions or took the piss about jeopardy journalism, and their obsession with 'the journey' concept. After a while we headed to Random House to film me in a faux meeting re. *THD*. There was much excitement in the building because Rod Stewart was due in. I bumped into him in the entrance. I was surprised how short he was, but also how fit and well and young he looked for sixty-seven. His face was well lined so I'm not sure it was all surgery, if at all. He was very friendly and we chatted a bit about Scotland and bagpipes before he headed to the lift with Susan Sandon who had been waiting for him, all dressed and made up to the nines.

Then another faux scene with Joanna Taylor to go through the pix for Volume 4. Then to the Work Foundation [work advice consultancy] for a Blue Monday event. First an interview re. *THD* with Radio Monocle. Then a photo and interview session with Andrea Tyrimos [artist] who had a relative with bipolar and was doing an art exhibition of celebs and ordinary people with bipolar. I introducer her to Emma from Mind so that she could get help with the 'real people'. The event was Emma speaking, then me interviewed by Stefan Stern [work and leadership journalist], whose wife was organising the do, then a guy from the Work Foundation, then a Q&A. It was all fairly relaxed and I found *THD* a useful thing to have by way of pointing to the arguments I was making – mainly on the need for parity between mental and physical health. We were a long way off it but going in the right direction.

All the questions fairly standard but had a woman ex-Beeb pushing me on whether I had been sensitive enough to the mental well-being of others when in the job. Maybe not but the caricature was totally overblown and I felt it was not journos but maybe one or two MPs I had been harsh on. Nice event. Mingled afterwards then home.

Called Jane Clark [widow of late Tory MP Alan Clark] on the way home, prompted by watching *My Week with Marilyn* last night, a film on [late film-maker brother of Alan] Colin Clark's relationship with Marilyn Monroe. Jane said Alan (or Al as she invariably referred to him) thought Col made it all up after she had died. He did work on the film and she did take a bit of a shine. But it was nonsense they had an affair or even the kind of relationship shown. Jane sounded OK though said she still got really angry at Alan sometimes and went out to shout at him where he was buried. We chatted away for half an hour or so, mainly reminiscing about him. Half a dozen times she said that she sometimes hated him for the way he gallivanted. But she did say 'Yes I know' when I said he did love her. She didn't think he would have taken to Cameron or Osborne.

Tuesday 17 January

Still feeling rough. I cancelled morning stuff but had lunch with Victor Blank at The George private dining club. He was in good form. He was very solicitous and interested in what I was doing. He felt I probably had the balance right and felt that I would never have another experience like the one with TB – 'Most people never get to get that close to the sun and come away relatively unscathed'. He felt I maybe should go for one more big thing but he didn't know what. He was worried re. TB, felt he maybe underestimated the reputational hits he had taken. He was still a big supporter but he felt himself in a minority. He felt I had got myself into a better place, TB worse. He thought Piers had been a disaster at Leveson and that the whole newspaper industry was coming out badly. He was not sure where it was going but we yacked away about that for a fair while.

Bumped into Jonathan Luff [adviser] from No. 10 on the way out and we walked over to Whitehall. I had met him in Paris with Tom Fletcher who had hired him when Tom was doing the foreign policy job for GB. Very similar guy. Really liked Tom. He wondered if I might get involved in the GREAT [global communications] campaign he was helping to run. I said I would though I doubted Cameron etc. would wear it. He said they all liked and respected us but they were wary and of course DC in so many ways modelled himself on TB. Anyway he was hopeful of getting me involved, possibly in Beirut with Tom. We had a nice chat then I peeled off to Admiralty Arch and in for the Time to Change reception hosted by Nick Clegg. I always felt a bit weird going back into these kind of dos. It got off to an odd start when a woman, elegant in a bright sari, came up and asked me if I was Nick Clegg. I felt a cross between a politician, a celeb and a spare prick at events like these.

Some people lobbied me on government spending! A few wanted pictures or an autograph or to tell me how much they appreciated what I did. And some wanted a proper chat. Fiona Phillips and Trisha Goddard [television presenter] were there. Lovely chat with Fiona as ever though I was a bit surprised how much she liked Clegg. Nice chat with Marcus Trescothick [cricketer]. Clegg and Paul Burstow the health minister arrived late. Clegg seemed fairly relaxed, not at all fazed at the snappers trying to get him and me in the same shot. I told him about the woman who had mixed us up. He said he wasn't sure who that was worse for. 'On balance probably just you,' he said. He looked pretty good, still had a good manner with people. Knew how to work a room. And when he spoke, he did so without a note and hit all the right messages. Not to be underestimated. The mood in there was of course pretty good and as he pointed out, he was in the rare position these days of giving money rather than taking it away.

The Time to Change people were chuffed with the way it was going. Jonathan Naess from Stand to Reason [mental health charity] was there and clearly going through a hyper phase on the bipolar scale. He was wearing an Arsenal shirt and making lots of low-level noise through the speeches. Clegg spoke well. In fact, all the speeches were pretty good – Peter Wanless who was now head of The Big Lottery and used to come to my morning meetings. Also Peter Bennett-Jones representing Comic Relief [TV charity] who was asking me to think of a creative idea for it and mental illness. Then a young girl called Bryony who was bipolar, had been badly bullied at school, and spoke from the patient's perspective.

Off to the Courthouse Hotel near Carnaby Street where I was speaking at an event organised by Speed Communications. The main theme was about how the concept of control had changed. I was the main speaker, along with Will Whitehorn, ex-Virgin Galactic [space tourism company], who started his speech by saying he agreed with every word I had said – I had basically been saying the old command and control systems were fine for then but not for now, that the internet had changed everything but it was an opportunity not a threat if used properly. Will was a good speaker and we dovetailed well. Then a panel discussion, then home. I had managed to get myself up for the event but crashed on the way home. Combination of the depression and the cold really were getting me down.

Wednesday 18 January

Gerald Shamash called as I was getting out of the shower to say he and Jeremy the QC had managed to get £20k out of News Group Newspapers for the phone hacking and they felt I should settle. I agreed we should go for it. I wondered if News knew there was other stuff elsewhere and so were settling on that basis. Gerald and Jeremy said NGN were really trying to settle as many as they could now. Met Tim Allan for a breakfast with the Moroccan ambassador, a princess who was the King's cousin. One of Tim's former pals at business school, Rajaa, had scoped out the possibility of some work either with the Palace or with the new Islamist government. It was an interesting place and the politics had certainly got more interesting. These were two power zones and it was not clear how they would operate alongside each other. The ambassador was a cross between the Queen of Jordan and Thatcher. She was dressed in a twin set and pearls. She spoke in good English. We were served tea by a man in a fez. She was with two guys, one of them wearing an expensive pinstripe suit.

She said the French and the Spanish really made efforts there – e.g. through a network of Spanish schools. She felt the Brits didn't realise what a player Morocco could be in terms of a new economic and business target. I told her about Rayan and how he was always praising his own country.

Lunch with Chris Boffey [journalist friend] who arrived at the Camden Brasserie wearing a black cloth cap hiding a significantly balder head than the last time I saw him. We talked about Leveson. He said he knew for a fact some of the evidence had been lies but he didn't want to go up front. What would it do? I said we all had the chance to get back to some decent standards. He wasn't up for it, but it was good to see him. He was worried about Syd's health, but I called Syd who said he was fine, and sounded it.

I was finding too many bits and pieces being thrown at me that were making the diary a bit piecemeal. Needed to get back to more strategy for myself. Ed had been getting a bit of a battering. At PMQs the general feeling was Cameron hit him pretty effectively again. Another high in unemployment but still no sense things were moving Labour's way. The two Eds had been getting a fair bit of play because of a seeming shift in the stance on government cuts. It wasn't clear to me if it really was but it risked ending up as a muddle. They seemed to be saying they oppose the cuts but we wouldn't be able to reverse them. The unions were coming out against him. Ed was doing a 'if they don't like it, it is tough' routine but it wasn't terribly convincing. In any event the main thing out of PMQs seemed to be Cameron saying he told his kids they didn't need to go the natural history museums because [veteran left-wing Labour MP Dennis] Skinner was in the House. Cheap and didn't go down well. I did a blog comparing and contrasting Dennis with Gove, in the news in recent days for proposing a new royal yacht as a Diamond Jubilee gift to the Queen.

Out for dinner at Ben and Amanda Evans's place in Richmond Avenue. Ben and D-J [Collins] had had the idea of getting the Blairites together, not to plot but to see if there was anything we could do to help the party right now. There was little love lost for Ed, nor much respect in the room, but there was an understanding that we had something to offer and rather than whinge we should try to offer it. Once the drinks and small talk were over – we sat down and Ben put forward a suggestion from Peter Hyman, that we all write one idea to help Labour, give it to the person on our right, who would read it out and that would act as a spark for discussion.

So who was there? Going anti-clockwise from where I sat – Ben, Amanda, the guy who runs Progress [think tank], James Purnell, Sally M, Jo Gibbons [former TB director of corporate affairs], Matthew Doyle, Ben Wegg-Prosser [former TB director of strategic communications], John Newbiggin [former Neil Kinnock aide], Andrew Adonis, me, Pete H, Lisa Tremble [former special adviser], Kate Garvey. So some decent brains and even if we did keep coming back to the Ed question, some interesting ideas and arguments. Quite a few – Kate, Sally, Jo – were in the area of reducing or getting rid of the union link. But what about money? I asked. Amanda said that was the worst possible reason. Maybe it was. Andrew was suggesting a French-style primary to endorse the leader. He admitted it was a cheat re. Ben's strictures that 'getting rid of Ed' could not be the idea put forward. But it was a good idea nonetheless. Ben WP said we could maybe defend the ditching of New Labour and the attempt to distance himself from the past. But what was unforgivable was the ditching of the professionalism, the organisation, the determination to do what it takes to win. Several were in the area of needing a new approach to the economy and I did another presentation of my Great Economic Audit idea, saying we needed to audit the past as a process that allowed us to move to a new economic policy for the future.

There was an acceptance that Ed had at least made something of a mark in going for a new approach to capitalism. Having been derided as a left-wing maniac when he did, now Cameron and Clegg were both making speeches about responsible capitalism. In terms of reaching any conclusions, we agreed to do some work on my idea and perhaps set up something on the lines of John Smith's Social Justice Commission [former leader's 1992 body to develop new ideas]. I wanted Nobel Prize-winners, economists, experts to do a major report and inquiry into the economy of the last decade plus. We should be open and honest and use it as a platform to a future policy programme. They all saw merit in it but felt that Balls wouldn't allow it. Those closer to current activities than I said he was very much focused on gearing the party to a post-Ed existence in which he took over. And then we really were fucked was the general view.

My proposal at least spoke to several of the others who had been arguing in the 'new economy' space. John Newbiggin said nobody was talking about growth and we had to look for a new growth plan. I said that could emerge from this process. Incremental strategy was not going to work. We needed big process, big politics. Kate and Lisa both felt Ed was unelectable. Peter and Lisa said they were really shocked at the way he had conducted the campaign against David. But I said that if we were there to help, I suspect Ed would hire every single person at that table if he could.

PH said he only hired Blairites to help with positioning. I said I didn't agree. I told him privately that Ed had even asked me if I thought he

– Peter H – might go as his chief of staff. Anyway it was a pleasant enough evening even if my chest and my depression were a pretty toxic mix at the moment. Andrew A was interesting – he had little time or respect for Ed but was adamant none of us should walk away, and all try to help. James said maybe some of those at the table should stand as MPs. He felt that with GB it was very much are you with him or not? With Ed there was a middle way. Help the party but not directly work for Ed. E.g. Progress could take more ownership of some of the policymaking stuff.

Thursday 19 January

Some of the papers reported that I was among several phone-hacking victims who had settled, with quotes from Gerald. I was out early for a conference at the National Liberal Club run by OpenText [information software company] for software supply companies. A pretty dry, almost exclusively male and white bunch. I was one of two keynote speakers. The first was Jonathan Portes, an economist who used to work for Gus O'Donnell but now ran the National Institute of Economic and Social Research. Pre speech he seemed rather diffident and lacking in presence but he did OK, setting out an economic overview and showing a few graphs which made him a bit more optimistic than most. One of them screamed out at me, because it showed that during the Labour years the UK had on most measurements done better than the US, France and Germany. How the fuck had Labour lost that part of the argument? We really were paying a price for taking our eyes off the ball when the leadership election was going on.

He also said the sustainability of politicians redistributing through the tax and benefits system was not there any more. I argued against that in my speech and quoted the research from *The Happy Depressive*. Portes said he did not think the Euro would break up. He said even if Greek defaulted it wouldn't break up. 'If California goes bust, it is not going to stop using the dollar,' he said. If Swindon council went bust and stopped paying suppliers it was not going to be forced to have a currency for Swindon. Good point I thought. Interesting guy, and we had a good discussion at a roundtable of CEOs. Home, and I was feeling shattered and a bit low again.

Charles Kennedy texted and asked me to call him ASAP. I had a sense it would be about drink. It was. We did a bit of small talk, then coalition bashing, but I could sense he wanted to talk personally and after a few minutes he said, 'I wanted to tell you things I have not told you before.' 'Drink?' 'Huh-huh,' he said. He was like Mum in how he never said the word 'Yes' just 'Huh-huh.' He said he needed advice, political and personal. I sensed when he was at Conaglen with us that he had been drinking more than he let on, and he admitted he had. He said that after he had left us he had gone a few days drinking the kind of quantities that were manageable, but then he had a bit of a crash. Really hitting it. Bottles of the stuff. Pretty much all day on and off. Now he was staying with friends in Glasgow who knew about his whole story and one of them, after Charles had mentioned he had seen me and that we had always talked about drinking, had suggested he call me, and tell me what had been going on. I said I wasn't surprised. I said the fact he had called me showed that he realised he has a problem. The question was what he did about it. I told him about some of the people I had seen at Clouds, and how all of them said they lived in denial for a long time. He said he was trying to work it all through. We had talked last time not just about my time with a drink problem but also the depression, and he wondered whether maybe that was his problem too. I said I was certainly of the view that I made a mistake for years thinking drink was my only problem, and that not drinking was all I had to do. Maybe I drank to cover up depression. Maybe he was doing the same. I said that I had noticed his hands shaking a little when we last saw each other, and his skin was bad. Both probably related to the drink, but also maybe depression and anxiety. He said up to now he had only really been treated for drink – 'I've been in and out of the Priory in Glasgow,' he said. I said it was heartening that he had been in there and it had never got out into the papers, because I knew that had been one of his worries. I said there was nobody who would be surprised if he were to say he had a booze problem, and maybe it was time. He said he had been surprised too, that his spells in the Priory had never got out, maybe less surprised that he had been to plenty of AA meetings and nobody had ever told the papers. He had seen two Labour MSPs at AA meetings.

I said he really needed to think whether it was time not to treat it all a bit piecemeal but to go for treatment that was several weeks at a go, even if it meant people knowing. Fiona and I were due to go out and I felt bad trying to bring the call to an end but it was obvious he really wanted to keep talking, and he later sent a series of messages saying how grateful he was. I said he could call whenever he liked. He said he wouldn't abuse that but he did feel he was able to talk to me in a way he couldn't talk to others.

We talked again later, and I said I really felt he should think of a residential course. We both had a laugh about the thing George Best said about AA. 'How can you be George Best and stay anonymous?' He said he quite enjoyed the AA meetings when he did them, but he had never really got past Step 1, and he regularly drank straight after the meeting. He said he was getting into a bit of bother in his own backyard having missed a couple of surgeries. 'I'm not daft, I know people can tell.' It was probably all pointing to Danny Alexander getting the new seat in the carve-up, and this would not be helping, so why would he bother

January '12: Is Charles drinking to cover up depression?

keeping on keeping on? The political question he wanted advice on was whether he should succumb to the pressure to join Alistair Darling, who had been very active in the independence debate, and Annabel Goldie [MSP], as one of the tripartite team making the pro-union case ahead of any referendum. He was in two minds. On the one hand, he believed in the cause; on the other, was he up for it? I said the two issues were maybe linked. If he didn't sort the drink, he would not be able to handle it. I said I really think he has reached the point where he knows, everyone who cares about him knows, that there is no halfway house re. drink with him. As with Calum, I worried that my occasional drink sent him the wrong signal, though I had not been drinking at all last time at Conaglen. I said he should park the political question and focus on the personal one. 'Do you have a problem? Do you accept that you have to stop drinking truly to get on top of it? If yes, how?'

Fiona and I went out to the South Bank for a party reception hosted at his flat by Paul Gambaccini [radio and TV presenter]. In terms of new people there, Brian May [rock guitarist] was a surprise in a way. Ben Elton who apparently had come back [to Labour]. Lorraine Chase who had said she hated TB. Paul spoke for too long and made it all about Murdoch and Neil K. Great cheers when Neil was described as the man who made Labour electable. Similar when Harriet said he was the best PM Britain never had. Paul said his views of TB varied from contempt to admiration but that 'even he' delivered on social justice. And his two standout achievements so far as Paul was concerned were Ireland and gay rights. It really was remarkable though that Neil who lost two elections was treated by this kind of event as some kind of Mandela whereas TB who won three elections was somewhere between AIDS and leprosy.

It was all echoed in Harriet and Ed's speeches. In her intro they were still going on about Ed standing up to Murdoch as his leadership achievement. And now his getting 'the big C – capitalism – yes we're allowed to challenge it again' back on the agenda. She was strong when talking about people harmed by a Tory government, as was Ed, but it was all very much the politics of protest and the soft left. Ed was quite good in being self-deprecating about all the talk he was ugly, going through the Sky trump card fanciability ratings in which he was only one ahead of Gove. He said he was making the argument about the need for responsible capitalism, also tried to explain the cuts/no cuts strategy and they seemed to buy it OK. The only intervention I made during the leadership election was to say Ed would make the party feel good about losing, and that was what I felt tonight.

He had made a big thing of Ben Elton being back in the fold. Said it felt a bit like Red Wedge [1980s Labour-supporting collective] and that all that was missing was Billy Bragg [musician and left-wing activist]. 'We'll get him too,' said Neil. Also, seeing Ed I wondered if Peter Hyman hadn't been right last night when he said that Ed wanted the Blairites around him purely for positioning purposes. I kept trying to give Ed the benefit of the doubt but this didn't look or sound like a government-in-waiting event. We also had Harriet proclaiming on the back of a poll showing Ken two points ahead that he was going to beat Boris. Maybe it was my depression but I was desperate to get out.

I had to leave straight away because I was doing *Iain Dale's Book Club* on LBC. But I was glad to get away. I had a good laugh en route, tweeting I was stuck in traffic and might not make it, and then that I couldn't get in the building. Iain took it well enough but the producer said he had been panicking. Iain was a good radio interviewer, relaxed but informed. We focused mainly on *THD* but also the diaries. They were really pleased with the response to the mental illness element and even Iain said he was surprised how open I was. He said it had made him cry at several points. The TV news on in the studio was leading on more phone-hacking settlements and, thinking I was among them, I confirmed I had settled. Then it turned out I was in the next batch and not this one. No worry said the lawyers. Went to meet Fiona and Calum at a restaurant in Haymarket. But by now I had the usual crash that came when I had to get myself up to do something during a depression. By the time we were home I was not just monosyllabic but non-syllabic. Major plunge within a plunge I fear. Fuck fuck fuck.

Friday 20 January

Woke up feeling like death. Chest still dire. Head absolutely dead. Awful. Fiona was asking the usual 'why?' and 'what happened?' but I couldn't answer. I don't know. I don't like talking about it when I am. I wrote to her, on the basis of what I might say to Sturgeon if I saw him – that it is probably a dip within a dip. I was feeling myself going down between Xmas and New Year. I usually do. I was OK on the surface but struggling underneath. Charles K coming probably both helped and exacerbated. Maybe him calling yesterday for a major unburden – more than he has done before – was another blip. In other circumstances being able to help him might have lifted me. It went the other way. I had seen DS to get medication when I felt the dip dipping further and it seemed to help for a bit. But it probably only staved it off. When the peak of the depression came – which I hope was last night – the mood-changing stuff was overwhelmed.

So what are the things that go around the mind? Often, numbness. No desire to speak, think, feel, eat, taste, nothing. Then I manage to get myself up – to do a speech, a meeting, last night's radio show – and most people would not even know there was a problem. Then a crash down a few gears afterwards. I definitely crashed in the restaurant.

Then there's the whole existential thing? What is the fucking point of all this? (Be it the major or the micro things that I do.) Then there's politics. Last night's event definitely plunged me. Put to one side the personal slight I take at a party now happier treating people who lost elections well, and people who won them as lepers (a point I shall make to Ed when he next calls for advice) – the politics of it were so depressing, and weak. So on the one hand – as per from Ed down them all wanting me to give them help – they want advice and support. But they don't take the hard stuff and they don't recognise what hard yards are. I gave them a political strategy for the economy a year ago. They have just taken the first step and are already now rowing back.

Then there's me and Fiona. I actually think we have been getting on better and more consistently than for ages but when it comes to depression, I feel she doesn't get it. Being lectured about how much more I have going for me than Philip does is about as unwanted and unhelpful a thing to say as could be imagined. Depression has nothing to do with material, professional or any other comforts or opportunities. It just is. Philip's death has hit me hard. And being in the politics zone exacerbates that. I hated it latterly being dragged back in. I will hate it more without him there.

I actually do feel at times like a workhorse, doing all sorts of things but in a vacuum because neither Fiona nor the kids are really that much interested. One example – I've been struck by how many people – Lindsay, Gail, Greg, Godric, Peter Hyman, loads of people on Twitter and Amazon etc. – have sent me really thoughtful and moved responses to my e-book. Fiona's only response 'It's not what I expected.' No engagement on its substance at all. Or the diaries – the only point is why on earth would you want to read about things you already know? Without PG around, I am continuing to flail around, doing this weird mix of stuff, mainly happy with it – I actually am in general more happy than depressed – but when depressed feeling very isolated and unsure. And every time it is like the first time.

I also felt with Calum, a brick wall has grown up between us and I don't know how to break it down. It hurts to think I meant it when I said I left full-time work to spend more time with the family but I sometimes wonder if we didn't get on better when I was here less. I suppose that during the course of their upbringing the main fracture has been Fiona–me, the scars of which remain, and that has probably influenced them. I think on balance doing the happiness book, talking about it, doing the alcohol film, raking up my past with the bagpipe film too, has been a good thing.

But when I feel like this, it hasn't. Like all the people who ask me for help because they think I am strong and a hero and blah-di-blah. And every one of them takes me down a bit more. I sent Fiona an email, a very good line from Stephen Fry on the Depression Alliance website.

> If you know someone who's depressed please resolve never to ask them why. Depression isn't a straightforward response to a bad situation, depression just is, like the weather. Try to understand the blackness, lethargy, hopelessness and loneliness they're going through. Be there for them when they come through the other side. It's hard to be a friend to someone who's depressed, but it is one of the kindest, noblest and best things you will ever do.

Ben Wright [BBC journalist] came round for a chat about the book he was writing about politics and drink. It was an interesting subject, and I sensed he was torn about whether to make it serious/heavy, or light-hearted and anecdotal. He is [former Labour MP] Tony Wright's son, so from a good Labour family, but had been going out with Poppy Mitchell-Rose, a special adviser to George Osborne, for three years. She was from a posh Scots Tory family, and I said maybe his next book could be about cross-party marriages and friendships. I said there was no way I could live with a Tory. As for the drink chat it was fairly meandering. My own story. Tory ministers I used to drink with. Alan Clark and Nick Soames. We agreed that whereas MPs used to drink more than the public now they drank less. Told him some Bush and Putin drinking stories. He seemed happy enough.

Lunch with Tim Livesey at Chez Bob in Belsize Park. It was like a creche for the first ten minutes, half a dozen screaming babies and toddlers with coffee morning yummy mummies who thankfully left as our food arrived. He said his first priority was going to be sorting out the office where there were no proper management structures. He didn't know any of the key people and was clearly having to get to know them fast. Ed wanted him to meet Ed B and Douglas A, both of whom gave him cause for occasional anxiety. He needed to get a team going. He said he was shocked by how much relied on Ed in terms of public profile. The shadow Cabinet was pretty useless. Very few had a profile or made an impact. I said lack of strategy was the problem. Lack of clarity. Lack of big hitters. Yes the media were a pain and totally biased but there was no point him thinking that was the reason things were bad. Things were bad because they were bad.

I gave him too my economic audit plan, said it would have three tracks – audit of the past, running commentary allowing interventions and policy floating, then a clear process leading to an economic policy for the future. I went through how it might work in detail. He seemed quite keen on it but said he could see how Ed might feel a bit daunted by the scale of it. But I said incremental strategy just was not going to work. There had to be big bold steps. I said he needed to become a presence or else Balls and others would run all over him. We went through the current staff and agreed he needed more good people. And if the ones who were there were not good enough they had to be got rid of. My worry was if he was strong enough and whether he would be able to understand the ways of the party. I was also talking to a Russian-Armenian mag who wanted to interview me, and fixing my trip to Albania next week. Call from AF. He had changed his number again after someone was constantly prank calling. He was feeling pretty chipper, felt Manchester City were not flying as high as before and he had a few players coming back. He said Scotland would never vote for independence. He said Salmond did not know how to answer the questions on oil money, banks, currency, Army, nuclear weapons. He said he had met Nicola Sturgeon [Deputy First Minister] and felt she was pretty bright and switched on. I said I didn't share his view that independence was a never. Salmond was hoping for more time and I felt he did think he could do it.

I was really down now. Total depressive state despite the pills. Maybe need to up the dose. Not speaking to Fiona. She took the Stephen Fry quote as the go-ahead to be as silent as me. I did the captions for Volume 4 pictures, during which an email came in from Sue Gray saying 1. FCO are insisting we take out the passages re. the Indians bugging us even though it was in *TBY*. 2. Could I let John Scarlett see the passages about him and 3. They were reaching difficult situation with regard to the FoI claims for TB notes to Bush and Cabinet minutes. I asked Charlie for advice and he felt it would be OK.

He said it had been referred to, extensively, in my and TB's evidence in Chilcot. If I say nothing beyond what is disclosed by that evidence as to the content of the letter (as opposed to comment on the relationship) referring to the letter should not weaken the ability of the government to resist disclosure if that is their position. He thought an exchange of emails between me and the Cabinet Office saying I have carefully ensured no disclosure beyond that which is already in public domain and CO agreeing should give them the cover they need. He said on Cabinet minutes, the pass has already been well and truly sold in previous diaries, and in many other people's.

Saturday 21 January

Totally depressed. Chest awful. I stayed in bed till 10.30 and then called Harmoni [on-call NHS services] as it was now called. I got an appointment for St Pancras Clinic at one and headed off there. Half-hour delay but a very nice Pakistani lady doctor, Dr Tariq, whose daughter worked for *The Guardian* in Lisbon. She said she knew all about patient confidentiality but was it OK if she told her family I had been in? Fine, I said, I would tweet about her anyway. She cheered me up. The whole Twitter thing meant if you were reasonably well known you got spotted and someone somewhere tweeted it. It had happened virtually every time I had gone out this week. She gave me antibiotics and steroids.

I went to get something to eat at one of the new fancy cafés in St Pancras Station, then took my food to the car and just stayed there for a couple of hours. God knows why I thought it might just pass but I felt it was better on my own than making everyone at home feel miserable too. I was also getting into a row with some silly fucking magazine from Armenia called *Luxury* who wanted me to do an email interview. Agreed thinking it would be same old same old life and times. Six out of the ten questions were about David Kelly so I told them no, happy to answer one or two but not half the interview. So they changed it. Worked on that, but another sign I was plunging a bit. Rory was creating over me getting a ticket for Grace for the Arsenal–Man U game. I hated rowing with Rory – he didn't want Grace to go to the football, he wanted a 'proper fan'. I told Grace I might write a play called How Three Tickets Caused the Third World War. I told the kids it really upset me that trying to organise something for all of us to do had created a row.

Maybe I was using them to try to lift me out of the depression. Didn't work. I said I was well aware of the impact that has on the rest of the family, especially Mum, which is why I tend to become more absent and withdrawn. I said it was important to understand the difference between depression and being fed up. Grace telling me to cheer up, while well meant, is not as easy as it sounds. By Thursday night, after sort of lifting myself for a Labour event and a radio show, I crashed and went from mono-syllabic to non-syllabic and except when I have really had to force myself – e.g. speech, lunch, interview, doctor's appt – I have pretty much stayed there. I was normally on the same page as the boys about tickets for games like this going to 'real fans', but if for example Mum takes me to the opera, even if I don't want to go that much and am not a 'proper fan', it is not an over-riding reason for me not to go. You might equally argue that 'real fans' have season tickets, go to every game, save and scrimp to travel and beg steal borrow to get tickets for away games, and they should take precedence over people who get tickets because their dad knows the manager. They are part of the same argument and neither stand up to much scrutiny. If you get a ticket, you get a ticket.

Rory said he didn't like being made to feel guilty for my depression because he thought tickets for big matches should go to real fans and he didn't want to go if I was going to accuse him of being horrible to Grace or because he wanted to go to a pub to watch the City–Spurs match and all the rest. It is true I said I wished I had never bothered getting the tickets, and 'no wonder I was on the happy pills'. But I also said I was not blaming him for my depression but I would like him to take a ticket and do whatever he wanted with the day. I also hoped he would hope Grace might enjoy going whether she was a football fan or not. So there it is. Storm in a teacup. Totally avoidable if I had not bothered trying to please everyone and end up pissing off everyone.

Sunday 22 January

Out early for *The Big Questions* [TV moral and religious debates] in Peckham. The programme was being recorded at the Harris Academy, fantastic new building and the place had a great feel to it. I had a chat with Nicky Campbell [presenter] and was then joined by George, one of the Occupy London [social justice and democracy movement] protesters. We found ourselves agreeing with each other more than we expected to. Then a woman came up, said Hi and kissed me. I assumed I must have met her before but when someone told me she was the Tory MP Nadine Dorries, I knew I hadn't. The kiss quite took me aback. But with her too, e.g. on sexualisation of youth via the media, I found myself agreeing more than I expected to.

There were three subjects for the programme – Are we eroding the right to protest? Should governments care about happiness? And does sex education cause kids to have more sex? I was obviously there for the middle bit, prompted by the e-book, but I had plenty to say across the show. The Occupy people were OK, apart from a Northern Irishwoman who was too shouty. But I agreed with a lot of the substance of what they said and told them they should focus on that, rather than moaning about police tactics when to most people they were pretty well treated and got a pretty good press. Generally the feedback was good though, particularly on the happiness stuff where they had found two very right-wing robots who were opposed, said governments should only care about economic growth.

I had a chat with the Occupy people at the end. They invited me down to their tented village outside St Paul's which was about to be moved on. I did a blog on all the weird agreements which had broken out, e.g. me and George, me and Nadine.

It had been interesting how much George from Occupy and I, even if we expressed ourselves differently, were in deep agreement. He talked about the failure of neoliberalism and the need to hasten the collapse of a failed capitalist system. I talked about the need to recognise that if we are serious about the extension of happiness and well-being to the majority, then the prime focus has to be closing the inequality gap between top and bottom, with our energies focused on the bottom.

We agreed David Cameron was right to add happiness to the list of factors government policy-makers should address when devising policy. And we agreed he was talking the talk without walking the walk. In fact I would go so far as to say that if you distilled the very different words we were using, we had something close to a seven and a half out of ten agreement. He clearly sees Parliament as something of a failure. I don't.

But then – weirder and weirder – when it came to the programme's discussion on the right to protest, I said I agreed with a lot of their arguments and they were having an impact – for example all three party leaders were last week making speeches about responsible capitalism, and Occupy might be able to take some credit for that. But I felt they were making a mistake in going on about the way they felt they were being harassed by the authorities, because in comparison say to the miners under Thatcher, or the civil rights protest movement in the US, they were getting a pretty good press and fairly soft policing.

Then Mark Littlewood, a right-wing free marketeer from the Institute of Economic Affairs think tank, who pre programme was extolling the benefits of abortion clinic ads on telly, said, 'I never thought I'd say this but I agree with everything Alastair Campbell said.' Meanwhile Nicky said I was 'with the government' on the happiness agenda (which I am up to the point of the somewhat important question of policy proposals) and after a pretty lively debate on that – this time with the free market fundamentalists arguing that wealth creation was the route to happiness, me arguing that it was not the be-all and end-all – we moved on to sex education. And I found myself agreeing with Nadine Dorries rather more than I had expected.

She is the Tory MP who has carved out a niche in Parliament speaking out about issues like abortion, sex education, the sexualisation of youth. Once she persuaded me that she was not saying her call to talk of the benefits of abstinence in schools applied only to girls not boys, but the girls were the ones who had to live longest and hardest with the consequences of unwanted pregnancies, and once I realised she was not saying abstinence should be taught at the expense of teaching about relationships, love and sex, then I found myself nodding more than shaking my head as she spoke. Again, about seven out of ten. Afterwards, I had three members of the audience come up to me and say they had expected to disagree with everything I said (because they opposed the war in Iraq) and ended up agreeing with almost all of it.

So why did I enjoy the programme more than most that I do? Well, so much of media debate does not really have the time and space for *real* debate. News for example tends to have a headline, a proposition, a point in favour, a point against, then a glib conclusion from a reporter. Most chat shows skate over surfaces. In an hour it is impossible to cover three big debates in huge detail. But I thought Nicky and his *Big Questions* team did a pretty good job. I usually come away from telly feeling there had not been enough time, there was more heat than light and people just had a fixed position and stuck to it whatever subject came up. I sensed people in today's programme – myself included – feeling their own conventional wisdoms and paradigms shift a little. A programme which has Occupy protesters tweeting afterwards that I talked sense, me saying so did they, Mark Littlewood agreeing with me more than he expected to, me agreeing more with Nadine Dorries than I expected to may sound like dull telly – but when the agreements are all unexpected, it is actually quite refreshing. And interesting.

Off to Arsenal with R and G. OK match. 2–1 to United. Email from Sue Gray saying she was worried about Scarlett. She felt SIS were not looking out for him and I might let him see the book. She also worried that the government was resisting Freedom of Information and Chilcot re. publishing TB letters to Bush and Cabinet minutes re. Iraq but I was writing about them freely.

Monday 23 January

Out filming for the alcohol documentary from 12–3, first running shots, then an interview with Professor Gerard Hastings, Ilkley-born Scottish-based academic expert on alcohol marketing. We went through some of the papers the alcohol industry had drawn up to advise on ads and marketing strategy. He was pretty convincing in his argument that they spent £800 million because they knew it worked. He felt we were sitting on a bombshell. I was beginning to agree with him. The marketing tools were all about drinking to get pissed as quickly and cheaply as possible.

We spent ages talking about it, though it would probably make only two clips. Alex called, pretty chirpy after the win yesterday [2–1 at Arsenal]. However, he did say for the first time that he worried City might win the League. *The Happy Depressive* was No. 6 in iTunes biography chart which was pretty good. Watched *The Artist* [mostly no dialogue film]. Brilliant. Could be the Oscar-winner I think. I tweeted it would be brilliant if a French actor won for a role with only two words. Paul Mason of the Beeb was one of many to accuse me of ruining the ending of the film. They had a point. Deleted tweet!

Tuesday 24 January

The Lords had beaten the government on welfare reform last night. But what was interesting was how now they just used the *Mail* and *Express* headlines as part of the story on the Beeb. There was so much dishonesty in the reporting. I said Leveson should take a look. Worked on the *Panorama* script, then did a piece on safe standing for the Burnley v Peterborough programme. Called Helle to discuss Emma Tucker of *The Times*'s bid for an interview. Emma was obsessed with *Borgen* [Danish political TV series] and hoped Helle would do a big piece on the back of it. Helle said she was loving being Prime Minister though there was too much travel. She said she was following things here and felt Ed was looking too leftist. So was Hollande. It was the wrong response at the wrong time. I told her about the Gambaccini event and Neil's basic message. She said the left was too much in the comfort zone of defeat.

Nice lunch with Ed Victor in Fino, a Spanish restaurant where Ed was pushing me to do a political novel again, also pushing re. Alex and winning. He felt the e-book was fine but maybe I should also do a big book on alcohol, which he agreed was Britain's disease. Round to Carlton Gardens for the Institute for Government event with me and Chris Mullin being interviewed by Peter Riddell [TfG director] on diaries. Chris and I had a very friendly pre-chat and pointed out how much we tended to agree about things – e.g. TB–GB, Murdoch, Bruce Grocott being a top bloke. He was still living up north, still keeping a diary, still had a very keen mind. The discussion went pretty well. Lovely venue, funded by Sainsbury. Chris and I were able to make the most of the points we wanted to – we agreed broadly about what needed to come from Leveson. Peter said he shared my view that the government would water it down for their own political reasons. Q&A was fine – Andrew Cahn, Alun Evans [both TfG] (who said the stuff re. politicisation under me was nonsense), Ivor Gaber [academic], Ivor Crewe [master, University College, Oxford], and a guy who just couldn't ask a question and ended up testing Peter's patience (and mine later when he just wouldn't leave me alone at the book signing).

Wednesday 25 January

Up at 5.30. Two Malev [Hungarian airline] flights, Budapest and then Tirana and on both I was the only person in business class. I worked on the Radio 3 essay on doubt I had been commissioned to do. Met in Tirana by Endri. He was, as was Edi later, full of 21 January and the shootings of opposition protesters [three dead]. They clearly felt they could pin it on [Sali] Berisha [Prime Minister]. I couldn't work out if it was real and could be of lasting significance or whether it was one of those things that was huge at the time but would blow over. I checked in then went round to the Socialist Party HQ. Nice offices, and though there were only about twenty people working there, it had a good feel. Edi's office had an oval table with the SP symbol of the fist and the rose in the middle. We chatted away then he got in the polling guy. It confirmed my view that they needed to focus on the economy and leadership. They had to show they could govern. They had to develop better ideas for policy.

Edi was pretty relaxed though he felt the Jan 21 issue needed to be kept to the forefront even if it was slightly off-strategy. He said it was important I realised that in Albania winning is all, and even if Berisha cheated, people were expressing disappointment with him for not beating him. But there were some pretty amazing things going on – e.g. the family of one of the people shot had been offered money to say they blamed Edi's people. Edi also had me in hysterics at one point telling stories about ex-PM Fatos Nano, who was clearly a big character. He had been ousted in a coup but then returned to power, then lost to Berisha, then went off to live in Vienna but was now looking to come back as President (chosen by the Parliament). The pollster was sure Berisha couldn't win. But the section of the population likely to switch was very small. And the fear of cheating was real.

We went over the possible coalition deals that might be done. My money was on Edi linking up with the centre-right parties being formed who hated Berisha. The Red and Black Party may end up as kingmakers. 'If there are fair elections,' we win. But Berisha had done a good job persuading people change for the better was not possible. In stealing Tirana he was seen as strong. Some of the poorest people liked him best. Edi said when he visited a region hit by floods where people had lost everything they told him to get lost because they said they owed everything to Berisha. He was confident his progressive tax idea was working. They needed to make a big deal of it, reaching out to new territory. We worked on message. Renaissance as the umbrella. Policy development in twenty-one different areas. But he also needed to be out there as the agent of change all the time. Talked about his membership drive and how he could use social media on that.

Edi wanted me to think re. Nano. Nano had been in prison – put there by Berisha – but still could get back to him. I said Nano ought to write a novel. Edi described the scenes when Nano was being forced out with guns and hired thugs – the pollster said if Nano had stayed in office he would be dead. Gangs took control of state TV and left a bullet on Nano's desk. They'd have killed him for sure. He fled to Skopje.

Edi told a stack of stories that just would not happen in the UK. He said you have to remember this is a very different place. There is no real separation of powers. He said people like Berisha and Nano would be finished if they were UK politicians. But here they are seen as big characters. You cannot ignore them. Briefed me on tribalism and the way that the head of the family can decide the votes of the family. We had dinner with eight MPs, including one who he had brought in but who was something of a permanent rebel.

They were all a bit reticent at first but warmed up as I went on. I was basically telling them stories of our campaigns and emphasising the importance of teamship and co-ordination. Back to the hotel for a swim. Edi sent a message to say I had had a big impact on them.

Thursday 26 January

Out for a quick run through the park at the back of the hotel. Nice apart from too many dogs running around. Breakfast with Fiona McIlwham who sadly was due to leave as ambassador in six weeks. She felt that the 21 January stuff was serious and potentially a problem for Berisha. The US had got involved as a way of signalling some serious concern and activity about it. She said because there were deaths and some connections to forces close to Berisha it focused on them. She said the international community was definitely moving against Berisha. I told her I was helping Edi a bit more. We had a laugh about what added fun her successor would have if TB got involved on the other side. She sensed that Berisha would struggle. But they needed to work up a sense of what was needed to ensure a fair and free election.

She was very well informed, took it seriously and knew that outsiders made a difference. The poll was OK on the surface, but it required more visibility for the SP and more cohesion. They also needed to persuade people their vote might actually count. Off with Endri to the SP HQ, where young militants were giving blood, and another long meeting with Edi. I said the poll convinced me it had to be all about having solutions on the economy, and showing leadership. Renaissance worked as a theme. But the policies had to hit home. He had time, but they needed to be working on it soon. I did a session on how to turn tactical moves into expressions of strategy. I said I had felt a lack of cohesion with the MPs. They had to be brought into systems organised and run from the centre. He was eating it up. He also wanted media training.

I watched a couple of his speeches. I said he needed more energy, particularly in the face. He needed to switch on a light behind his eyes and make the lips smile a bit more. He had presence but needed more empathy. Even Ben, the MP who had been rebellious and difficult, said after I left that he had been glad to have been there last night, and he now realised why this co-ordination mattered. I did a session with Endri's staff, again emphasising pretty basic stuff, then headed for the airport, narrowly missing Hachim Thaçi, who was coming in for a visit. Slept on the plane. Audrey's birthday, ruined at the end by her leaving her handbag on the bus, but the bus driver tracked her down when Fiona went back to the stop and so all ended fine.

Friday 27 January

Blogged on the bus driver restoring faith. Booze film crew round for main interview with me in the morning, then with Fiona but she wasn't very keen, and it didn't go too well. Then Grace forgot to take her driving licence with her for her test. Nightmare. Out doing more running shots in town. Running past three pubs closed down on one road between us and Camden. Filming in Soho. Pretty good response from people at the moment.

Saturday 28 January

Cold sunny day so got out on the bike. New thermal socks were brilliant. We set off for Brighton and the surprise birthday dinner for Roy Greenslade at [writer and broadcaster] Simon Fanshawe's. Roy and Noreen, us, Simon, Natascha, an Algerian turned Brit, Jean-Luc, who was a friend of Roy's, and also his first girlfriend now married to a Scottish guy with whom I argued about the value of politics. Natascha was looking fabulous. F and I went to see Natascha's boys who were down the road at Roy and Noreen's flat then back for a very jolly dinner. Did a fair bit of politics – a lot of despair re. Ed but Natascha was on the line that it was all about the media stopping people from thinking about themselves. Simon said he was at a loss what to do about the political scene. He found it hard to defend Ed. There was no clear strategy and he had no cut-through. Natascha said she would help Ed in any way she could. Played the bagpipes which went down well. Roy really chuffed we went, I think. We had the same line on Leveson – the inquiry would come up with big change but Cameron would bottle it.

Sunday 29 January

Out early to pre-record a Radio 2 interview with Aled Jones [singer, presenter]. He had a faith programme so although we did *The Happy Depressive*, there was a lot of 'We don't do God' and whether I might find God, and so on. Talked about Philip a lot. Out on the bike then did a quick blog on the fact that finally EU leaders were saying they intended to put youth unemployment on top of the agenda for the Summit tomorrow. Off to Heathrow for the (absolutely packed) plane to Berlin. I was met by Orkan, one of the conference organisers, off to the rather splendid Regent Hotel then to dinner with a mix of think tank people, film-makers and political experts. I was sitting between two very interesting guys, one who was an entrepreneur currently doing something with Richard Branson [business magnate] on global warming. He had worked in Brussels and come to the conclusion the EU institutions were impossible. He was interested in my booze film but couldn't believe *Panorama* expected me to do it in half an hour.

The other guy was Lutz Hachmeister who also made films. He had done a fly-on-the-wall on the SDP and was currently working on a feature film re. spy wars between the US and Europe. I was tweeting in German and getting a lot back including JP tweeting by using Google translator. I was surprised how much my German was coming back but still felt my mind go into French when I tried to join in a conversation. Edi was texting me from Greece where he said he was practising some of my mental exercises re. speaking and interviews. He was also using the message that even if people did not believe him because of all the lies and smears, they believe each other, so join the campaign etc.

Monday 30 January

I did a quick blog about Merkel saying she would campaign for Sarkozy. The fact that both saw it as a bonus suggested both were a bit out of touch. All of these leaders were struggling in part because people feared a loss of national power. So the image of a German Chancellor riding to the rescue didn't strike me as a good one. Off with Leonard Novy [Institute for Media and Communications Policy] to the conference event. It was small but high-powered, a mix of top comms people, business people, academics and media. They all spoke good English, prompting me to do one of my regular tweets about how lame we are at languages. Pathetic.

I had done a new speech specifically for the event, on language and politics. Lutz was chairing it, introduced me as a mythical figure but said having dined with me last night he felt the reality was more interesting. The Q&A was pretty good, nothing too difficult, lots that allowed me to tell decent stories, then a few books to sell and sign and off to the airport.

Tuesday 31 January

Packed day. Out for breakfast with Petrit Selimi and Alan Donnelly to try finally to pin down the Kosovo contract. I wasn't sure about this one, but I couldn't back out now. The company that had been going for it before, and was now out, contacted me to ask if we could work together. Not so sure about that. Alan was very much the networkers' type, much more than me, but Petrit kept emphasising that Thaçi had wanted me out there. Did a phone interview with Nicky Campbell on men and depression on the back of the Gary Speed [footballer and manager found hanged] inquest. The coroner had given a narrative verdict, saying that there was no evidence he intended to take his life. To Pimlico for the Google staff conference. Half of them had been at the last one but when I asked them to go through my ten points from last year, hardly any could. I did a variation on the theme – fifteen points for campaigners.

Good Q&A and then off to the Centre for Social Justice where I was speaking at a mental health event alongside Andy Burnham [shadow Health Secretary]. Andy arrived with a bit of an entourage but I imagined it must be hard for these guys. So far as I could see there was no major media there even though he had billed this as his first major policy speech since getting the health job again. I did a ten-minute slot on stigma and discrimination, and called for more public figures to speak out. Andy spoke fine, but Labour lacked political energy just now. Ed M did well against Cameron on Europe today though. 'A veto is not for life, just for Christmas'. Off to Rio Tinto to see Tom Albanese.

But first Jan [du Plessis, chairman] wanted to have a chat. He told me the results on Tuesday were going to be good – record underlying earnings – but that they were writing off billions from the Alcan [packaging food division] sale which would land a very large blot on an otherwise strong picture. As a result he had spoken to Tom and they agreed Tom would forego a £1.4 million bonus. Tom seemed pretty chipper for someone who had just lost over a million.

Off to Forest with Greg [Nugent]. The big news now was that Fred Goodwin [former CEO RBS] had been stripped of his knighthood. What a silly country we must look like to others. Greg on the phone almost like I used to be. Enjoying himself though. I was working on the statement to be read in court on Friday for the phone-hacking case. I was trying to get in the point that I could reopen if more evidence emerged. We arrived in Nottingham with half-hour to spare, first half in the directors' box, second half in the away end. We played really well. A goal in each half. Jay Rodriguez [Burnley] scored twice but had the most amazing penalty miss – it almost hit the corner flag.

Wednesday 1 February

Did the Kazakhstan conference call, then off to the Moroccan ambassador's residence. She showed me a couple of bad stories they had had to deal with and I said they showed the lack of systems. She was heading back again and said she would be in touch.

The hacking settlement was sorted, pretty much totally as I had asked for. Substantial damages. Apology and also making clear that if more emerged it could be revisited. Home for a bit then out to the Thousand Club reception for former spads at the County Hall Hotel. Good turnout and a fair few old friends there. Sue Nye spoke about the importance of spads and teamwork – Catherine MacLeod whispered, 'It'd mean more if I'd ever seen her utter a civil word.' Peter M spoke of how hard opposition was, teamwork, said 'relics like us three' would do our bit but they the younger ones should do more. I spoke last and basically said it was a fundraiser, we were all richer and healthier than when we were spads, so it's about time people started putting back in. Left to meet Grace as F was out at a dinner.

Thursday 2 February
I'd agreed to do *This Week* tonight and persuaded them to do something on mental health so they came round first thing and I did a package on the need for more MPs to 'come out' as having mental health problems. Richard Bacon's editors refused to have me on, despite his efforts, because I had been on Stephen Nolan. Ridiculous. They imagine everyone is sitting there listening to every programme. But did *Steve Wright in the Afternoon*. Fun as ever, as when we were talking about bagpipes and I said it was about fingering, blowing and squeezing all at the same time. 'Like sex then,' he said. I tweeted a challenge for them to use it when they broadcast it on Monday. Then off to ITV to do the Alan Titchmarsh show live. Nice crowd and he was always very easy-going. Again a mix of the e-book and the bagpipes and a bit of David M and Ed, David having written a big piece in the *New Statesman* which I thought was OK. News came through that the hacking judge was off sick so my settlement for tomorrow was postponed. Annoying. Home – watched the *Panorama* rough cut. It was annoying that so much of what we had done had not been kept in, but they had done a pretty good job with what they had. Out for *This Week*. Gillian Tett [financial journalist] on the bankers where, as per my blog yesterday, I said the Goodwin knighthood was irrelevant and that we really needed a full-on inquiry into the banking crisis. I don't know why so few people were calling for one. The idea that one man's silly bauble was the only reckoning was ridiculous. Then a chat on Europe, in which Portillo and I got quite snappy with each other, then the mental health bit with Ruby Wax [comedian, mental health campaigner], and I played out the titles on the pipes, with Michael playing the triangle and Ruby dancing.

Friday 3 February

Did another blog on the banking inquiry idea then set off for Wheatley to see Mum for the day. Lunch with Mum and Auntie Chrissie at the Hop Pole. Watched the film with them later. Chatted away. Alzheimer's moment when I got to Retford station and realised I had booked the return train for the wrong day. Idiot. Bought new ticket.

Saturday 4 February

Off to Leicester very early, working on my Radio 3 essay on self-doubt in the car. Quite enjoying it even if I was having to force one or two parts of the thesis. Arrived at Radio Leicester where Radio 4 was recording *Saturday Live* presented by Rev. Richard Coles [musician turned priest]. Nice guy, very vicary. Did lots on Leicester and also *THD*. Finding the stuff on depression easy to communicate. Played the pipes at the end. I did the Leicester Mercury then Stuart Bolton, a student from Bath Uni who was doing a dissertation on the read-across from football, politics and business by interviewing one from each. Nice lad. He also gave me a good line for the self-doubt essay, Paul Arden [former creative director] of Saatchis saying, 'Only the paranoid survive.'

Arrived to snow in Burnley. Up to see Stan [Ternent] and the family. A couple of his SAS pals there. Currently working on the Olympics. Said they were sealing up the Olympic village. Said the organisers were obsessed with how much sex was going to be going on as the athletes fell out of the competition. Had a little chat re. Afghanistan. Down for lunch at the club. Sonia [Kilby, wife of club chairman Barry] had brought a young girl called Hannah who told me she wanted to be PM and how did she go about it? Match [v Peterborough] poor, one down, pulled it back. Sonia also told me Barry had cancer and might be stepping down as chairman. Wrote to him later. Took six and a half hours to get back as the snow and ice came in. Skids all over the place. Rory called to say Nigel Doughty [Nottingham Forest chairman] had died. Couldn't believe it. I'd spoken to him on Tuesday after the Forest match. He was fit as a fiddle. What with him and Barry, football was losing two good ones. Also a huge loss to Labour.

Sunday 5 February

The chest still bad. The weight coming back on because I wasn't exercising. Off to Natascha's with Calum to collect Otis [her son] and head to Stamford Bridge for the Chelsea–United match. Usual nice lunch with Joe Hemani, raging as ever against anything and everything but in a very amusing way. Ed M, Israel, the FA and refs particularly getting it today.

Seb Coe there looking very calm and relaxed but said there was lots going on inside. The United board but no Bobby [Charlton, former star player]. Amazing match. United on top but went one down in the first half, then three down early second half before United pulled it back to three–all.

Monday 6 February

Alex texted at 4.41 a.m. to say he felt they could win the title on the back of that. So clearly the adrenaline was keeping him awake. He said it was. Amazing it still got him at his age but it is what makes him better than the rest. Round with Rory and Calum to play with Natascha's boys for a bit, and talk to her re. the drink film. She was still at me re. the madness of drinking anything at all. All up to Rory's flat then out for dinner. Chat with Jamie Redknapp re. [father] Harry's [tax evasion] trial. He said it was a total nightmare. Their lawyers were confident but if it went the wrong way he was going down. Said his mum was not holding up that well. Really tough.

Started to think about *Question Time* and later watched Dacre at Leveson. He was uncomfortable and at one point his hands shook. I was tweeting away madly. E.g. when he said he would die in a ditch for Jan Moir's freedom to say what she did re. Stephen Gateley, I started a contest to find a ditch.* Jay was pretty good and did not let him just shut things down. Dacre had lots of examples of the badness of other papers to show he was not so bad. Also clearly testy about being there to be asked questions at all. Cathy Gilman called to say Beefy [Ian] Botham was going off the wall because LLR were refusing a 50k sponsorship from Burger King. She went through the arguments, in particular about the way we were trying to step up contact and influence with health policy-makers etc. I backed her but Ian was talking about doing no more walks. I suggested we invite him to the Speaker's dinner.

The Steve Wright R2 interview went out and got a big spike for *THD* on Amazon. To Wild Pictures to interview Gavin Partington [communications director, Wine and Spirit Trade Association] for the drinks industry for *Panorama*. He did OK. Overall drink was down but drink problems were up. Syria was raging across the news after Putin vetoed a fairly mild resolution calling for the violence to stop, and Assad to make way for his deputy. Putin a real shit but of course as always he was just promoting and protecting Russian interests. The NHS was also back and big in the

* Gateley, a gay member of pop group Boyzone, had died of a congenital heart defect in 2009. In the *Daily Mail* Jan Moir had suggested drugs and 'a dangerous lifestyle' were responsible for his death, prompting 25,000 complaints to the Press Complaints Commission.

news with Lansley really getting hung out to dry. *Guardian* called asking for an obit of Nigel Doughty so I worked on that till late.

Tuesday 7 February

Sent off the Nigel tribute. I think it caught him OK but I just couldn't believe he was dead. He was my age to the month. Blogged on how the NHS could be the end for Cameron, that it was about him and the promises he made re. 'no top-down reorganisation' and 'no cuts' not just Lansley. Also *10 O'Clock Live* wanted me for a discussion on Wednesday with David Mitchell and a pro footballer so asked me to chase Clarke Carlisle again. Did so and he was up for it.

Lunch with Kate Garvey who was worried her mum wasn't getting the right cancer care and what to do. I suggested getting David Cunningham [Philip Gould's consultant oncologist] on the case. Lovely to see her. I think she was getting a bit fed up and ready for a move. Also more happening at the High Court with JP getting his apology from the police [for failing to inform him his phone had been hacked]. Gerald Shamash called and said my phone-hacking case was definitely being settled tomorrow. I worked on a draft statement with some of my usual lines plus the causes I would be giving money to. Emailed TB, Charlie, Godric and Greg who all agreed just tweet, don't go to the court if there is no need.

Then to Directors Cut Films to record voiceover. I still wish it was an hour not half an hour but they had managed to get a lot in there. It was now 'The Hidden' not 'Secret' Alcoholics. Tweeted and said maybe do a series on addiction more generally. Interesting email from a Tory councillor in Wandsworth who said her colleagues were forcing her to resign because of depression. Lots of people coming forward right now.

Wednesday 8 February

Harry R's not-guilty verdict came through. The hacking settlements broke around eleven so I hit send on the blog and the tweets saying I was pleased the door was open for more action and naming the seven causes I would be making donations to. Coogan was also in my batch so he would get big play and along with Simon Hughes was down at the court. I decided to stay out of it but do stuff later.

Into the Commons to sign books at the Parly bookshop and then present an award to Campaigner of the Year at Whizz-Kidz [mobility for disabled charity]. Ed was there and spoke OK. Apparently he had won hands down at PMQs, even the Tory bloggers saying so. George Fielding won the award Ed was presenting. He was the one who interviewed me for Ouch a while back and we had a lovely chat about how he might have a political career. Lovely kid. Severely disabled but with an amazing optimism and positivity. The hacking stuff was running fine though Harry was now the big story. Bumped into Dominic Grieve in the gents and said I was pleased he was holding papers to the mark re. contempt, and also that he was not listening to the Tory right re. the ECHR.* There was a shout to ignore the ruling on Abu Qatada, an immigration judge having ordered he could not be held longer than the six and a half years so far, and the ECHR having already said he should not go to Jordan because of their use of torture.

Off to Millbank to do Bacon re. hacking. Also got in my criticism of 5 Live junking PMQs for a chat re. Harry. To Victoria St for *Question Time* briefing. We reckoned Syria, NHS, Abu Qatada, Leveson because Coogan and I were both on. [Dame] Ann Leslie [*Daily Mail* writer] lined up instead of Kirstie Allsop [TV presenter].

Back to do more telly then home to change before heading to Channel 4 for an interview re. hacking. Off to Roux restaurant for a dinner organised by Alan Donnelly. Max Mosley, Donnelly, David Puttnam [film producer], Arlene McCarthy [Labour MEP], Stephen Barnett [academic], Margaret McD and Horatio Lawson who worked with Alan. Taking stock re. Leveson but also discussing how to get Google on to the EU agenda in a bigger way. Nice enough do and there was something I liked about Max who was a man with a mission. MMD telling me about all the Tories who were becoming rebels at the moment. *Ten O'Clock Live*. Met up with Clarke Carlisle. Jimmy Carr and Mitchell the friendliest. Charlie Brooker [presenter] didn't much like me, I sensed. Lauren Laverne [singer, comedian] not so sure. The show was still not quite right. Clarke said he was way out of his comfort zone. Clarke did fine and then also got asked on to *Newsnight* so he was chuffed. Said he was buzzing on the way home. Took a hundred quid off Victoria Coren [writer, poker player] who was there as DM's girlfriend. She didn't know David had been to a Labour do, and I bet her first a million, then a hundred. Earlier long interview with Canal Plus re. hacking.

Thursday 9 February
Someone sent me a great blog from an Aussie sports commentator, Glenn Mitchell, on depression, so I posted as a guest blog. Fair bit in the papers on hacking. Dentist then into Victoria St. Added football to the list of

---

* The Attorney General had warned newspapers to be mindful of contempt of court laws. He also stated there was 'no question' of the UK leaving the European Convention on Human Rights.

expected questions and I think we were there. Home to have a bath and try to get my head in gear. Good chat with Douglas and then TB re. Syria. Both made really good points and I decided just to try to explain the region. I was going to be liberal on Abu Qatada [Salafi cleric and hate preacher], really steam in on health, dump on FA and England re. football, and do my usual stuff re. Leveson. I watched Dacre's Leveson recall. It was about the Hugh Grant stuff. He wasn't convincing but David Sherborne [barrister] overdid the ham acting and it didn't really go anywhere. Heather Mills [former wife of Sir Paul McCartney] dropped Piers in it, making clear she did not let him hear her voicemails. Also Max Clifford was up saying I let power go to my head. All OK and well set for *QT*.

It was being held at the business school in Regent's Park. David Dimbleby friendly as ever. [Baroness] Shirley Williams [Liberal Democrat politician] arrived with four people. Philip Hammond [Defence Secretary] friendly enough. Steve Coogan and I swapping notes about how heavy to go re. the *Mail*. We both managed to get good lines in. Ann Leslie just there to wind me up, Alex thought afterwards. In fact they had tried Littlejohn and others but they wouldn't come on. Abu Qatada up first. Then Leveson. Leslie talked about the damage Coogan and I were doing and I got a good hit in 'forty years on the *Mail* and you talk about damage to Britain'.

Syria was good I felt. Hammond and I in broad agreement about how hard the choices were. Then football, and then the NHS where I got in most of my points and also got in that Shirl talked the talk but didn't vote as she should. Nice mood after but I felt it hadn't really worked. Ann Leslie had just rambled and though she and I sparred it was lacking in substance. I got in my line on my worry that the Tories would backtrack on Leveson and interestingly Olly Grender [Lib Dem head of communications] got in touch to say Clegg would like to have a meeting about it. Watched it with Fiona later. Seemed OK. Good response on Twitter including too many saying I had to go back and sort them out.

Friday 10 February

Nigel Doughty's funeral, at Farm St [Mayfair] Church. Beautiful church, and the priest had a wonderful voice. I couldn't work out whether Nigel was a deep believer. It was a nice service and so sad to see both his dad but also the young boys running about. His older son Michael did a little speech but broke down. The reception was at the big hotel round the corner. Ed M was at the service but headed off. GB and Sarah were there and stayed a good hour or so. He still found these social small-talk situations difficult. Eventually he and I settled with a couple of the Forest people I had seen at the match the other night and talked mainly football. I waited for the widow, Lucy, to come back from the crematorium, then chatted to her for a bit before leaving. Off to record new bits for the *Panorama* to take into account new *Lancet* [medical journal] stuff.

Lovely singing blind busker in the Tube, whistling 'Over the Rainbow'. Home. Long chat with Alex re. *QT*, Harry, politics, football, usual stuff. He felt Harry was a shoo-in for the England job. He felt I had done well to hold my temper with Ann Leslie. Talked over Syria and how on the tough stuff Cameron was not bad at articulating difficult arguments. But boy he didn't like him. 'Would love to thump that baby face.' Got a message from Rachel that Ed M was in the same Southampton Hotel as the Burnley team. Arranged via Twitter to pop in tomorrow as the party south-east conference was on there.

Saturday 11 February

Off with Grace to Southampton, the aim being to do some French in the car. As ever we ended up rowing because of her lack of attention to detail and my obsession with it. Popped into the party conference, did a book signing then a little speech on how hard opposition was and some of the lessons from last time. Went down fine. To the match. Poor game. Lost 2–0. Just never got going.

Week from Sunday 12 February

Off to France, just Fiona, me and Molly. I was determined to finish the edit of Volume 4 and read it when F was driving. We stayed at the Château de Barive at Saint Preuve but had a big flare-up. Usual stuff. Me hating the logistics of travel, niggling away and eventually F building it up into a big thing and then all over the same old ground, what is the point etc.? She was also saying she wanted a quiet life and I said she was never going to get it with me. We sort of got over it within a day or two but Day 2 I had a massive plunge. Death stuff.

Picked up a bit but getting down with a problem with the fire, the heating, lots of stuff going wrong at the house. The view was amazing though and the scenery though bare in its own way even more beautiful than summer. I was out on the bike every day but one. I was doing a fair bit of media build-up to the booze film on Monday. I did a piece for *Times* 2 for Monday but Cameron made a big speech on the need to tackle alcohol abuse so Emma Tucker wanted to bring it forward. Good piece. Annoyingly I couldn't put on my own site because of the paywall. Phil Webster said it was most read online and had a massive response, usual mix of supportive and hating.

We watched a few episodes of *Borgen*. It was nowhere near as good as *The Killing*. I was thinking about next steps re. telly including maybe a film in Iraq. Also [writer and TV producer] Jimmy McGovern sent me a lovely note about *All in the Mind*. He said he would love to do it as a four-parter but he didn't have any time for several years. Gave me a list of possible others. Alex in Amsterdam for the Ajax match. We were texting in French for some reason. Cameron was doing loads of stuff. Tuesday car insurance, Wednesday booze, Thursday meeting Salmond, Friday Sarko in France. Two unexpected calls while away. One from Harriet Harman's office asking for a meeting. The second from Olly Grender saying Clegg would like to see me re. Leveson. Good. Hacked Off also sent me a note saying they were worried a new beefed-up PCC was the way this would go.

Monday 20 February
Money in from Murdoch. Sent off a few cheques. All morning and part of afternoon doing media for the *Panorama* programme. Breakfast telly. Then loads of local radio, News Channel, off to *This Morning*. Usual surreal morning telly stuff. Off to Beeb again, Mishal Husain [news presenter] really nice – BBC World. A few more local, then home and off out on the bike. Pottering. Good meeting with Adrian Warr from Portland re. strategy group. Also constant feedback from Kaz where TB was seeing Nazarbayev. Re. the *Panorama*, everyone else was out so watched on my own. Good response. A few AA people angry that I talked of having the odd drink. I felt I had to though, as it was important to be honest. I did say though that I accepted it was a bad message. But generally the reaction to the programme was good I would say.

Tuesday 21 February
Blogged on Greece – again – and the need for a banking crisis inquiry – again – on the back of *Newsnight* last night reporting on how Goldman Sachs [investment bank] had helped Greece hide billions of debts. Good stuff on Twitter re. *Panorama* but I was also using it to promote the pipes film tonight, said Adele [pop star] was refusing to go to the Brits till nine so she saw the film, and Petr Čech [Chelsea goalkeeper] was insisting on a TV in the goalmouth. Out for lunch with Paul Hamann and Tom Anstiss. They were really pleased with the film. Also the ratings were good. 4.1 million which was 700k up on usual *Panorama* when up against *Coronation Street*. Getting dozens of emails from drinkers and causes related to booze. This was both the joy and the problem of openness

and accessibility. Talked over a few ideas for more films. I was keen on doing one on schizophrenia. Into town to see Keith Blackmore re. book on PG. He said Georgia's piece on the last few days was amazing. It was too. Had me in tears at several points. He wanted a few insights from me that would add grit so we chatted over some stuff over Starbucks. Ran home. Pottered a bit then watched the pipes film [Sky Arts' *First Love*].

Wednesday 22 February

I did a blog on Gove's ridiculous speech to the press gallery yesterday in which he said that Leveson was having a chilling effect on freedom of speech. Quite an incredible thing to do with the inquiry still going on. It all fitted with my line – reported again in the *FT* today – that they had a strategy to get on the side of the press v Labour on the side of Leveson. I made sure Robert Jay and Leveson saw the blog. I also texted Ed to say someone should ask Cameron at PMQs if Gove was speaking for the government. Tom Blenkinsop [Labour MP] did so and though Cameron was shifty his basic answer was yes.

Out and about lots of people raising the *Panorama* film. Did a blog – which got the biggest number of hits for ages – on Gove's attack on Leveson yesterday. Clearly a strategy at work.

Thursday 23 February

TB meeting first thing with him, Pat, Sally, Catherine R and Ciaran Ward. He was seeing *The Guardian* for lunch so wanted a bit of a re-entry programme advice-wise. He felt he could be broadly supportive of Ed, and was broadly behind Balls on the economy, though he was off the pace on health. We kicked around a few thoughts. Pat and Catherine had seen the booze film. Said it made them think. TB said why was I determined to make everyone feel miserable? Lunch with Martin Townsend [*Sunday Express* editor]. He wanted to see me about their planned mental health campaign. Had some good ideas and lots of experience because of his manic-depressive dad. Gave me his book, *The Father I Had*, which I read very quickly. Terrific. Dealing with Desmond a nightmare because he is so quirky.

Friday 24 February

Off to Birmingham with Rayan. Hauliers event. Went really well. Good bunch. Did it all as Q&A. Interesting guy who had some great facts including Apple capital market valuation being £70 billion bigger than top six car companies combined. Tweeted it to big response. They also had some good facts about their industry but were not organised in putting them over.

Saturday 25 February
Off to Burford, collected Gail and the girls and off to lunch at Annie Robinson's. She was charming, really loved Calum. Rory arrived later from training at Barnet. Mike Molloy there too and it was a really nice do. Mike seemed to be doing OK. Went to his house to look at some of his paintings then back to Burford. Popped into Matthew's to see the PG statue. Dinner at Gail's. She was in OK form considering. The girls doing well. I had read their pieces for the book which were superb.

Sunday 26 February
First issue of *Sun on Sunday* getting massive coverage and sales to match. Problem in the end is the people in Britain. It is what they want and they don't care too much about the damage.

Monday 27 February
Blogged on wind turbines, lots of deals on hold. So clearly another of Cameron's top priorities down the pan. DAC [deputy assistant commissioner] Sue Akers's at Leveson – big stuff on the extent of police corruption at *The Sun*. Bike then back to watch JP. He did OK but Akers was the story today plus Charlotte Church £600k settlement [phone-hacking damages and legal costs] and big attack on News.

Tuesday 28 February
Tired. Not sleeping well. Annoying because I am off the medication again, totally off the drink, and feeling OK most of the time during the day. But I am waking up three or four times a night, and my mind is whirring. The next book. Chilcot. The kids. Travel. It is weird how I can lie there obsessing about details of a trip in three weeks' time – what time to call a cab, how many shirts, what to say in the speech. Blogged on Gove again, suggesting someone should go back to his attack on Leveson at PMQs tomorrow. Ed called later saying he was thinking about doing two on Leveson and four on health. I thought it was important to pin Cameron

back behind Leveson. I was in no doubt there was a strategy at play here. Ed agreed the goal had to be to get them in a position where they could not resile from any radical measures from Leveson without paying a price.

Then a nice lunch with Emma Tucker and Janice Turner [*The Times*] who wanted to thank me for fixing the Helle interview which came out as a *T2* cover yesterday. Helle a bit pissed off because they quoted her as saying her bodyguards carried her shopping, which she said she never said. Emma blamed the press man, said they sent him all the quotes on Friday. Anyway it looked good and she came over well. Both were pretty gossipy about *The Times*. James [Murdoch] had taken a hit with his evidence to Leveson. Then Janice arrived to tell us it had just emerged at Leveson that the Yard lent a retired police horse to Rebekah Brooks. This would be one of those details that really stuck.

Then off to meet Fiona at St James's Palace where for some reason I had been asked to present the Duke of Edinburgh awards. I was doing 100 or so young people from Northern Ireland, the biggest group of the day. There was a little reception for the presenters and some of the sponsors where a young black girl from London made a little speech about how much the DofE scheme had meant to her. We then had a tour of the building. 'This is Charles's old sitting room where he did his fightback interview against she who must not be mentioned … This is the window where the Duke of Windsor and Mrs Wallis Simpson were papped … This is the balcony where Charles will be proclaimed as King…' We then went to the big room where all the NI winners and their parents were gathered. All very well organised but a lot of hanging around. A briefing for them on how to talk to the Duke when he came in – no need to curtsey, only shake hand if he offers, volunteer information about what you've done.

I wandered around talking to them, all a bit forced. Actually made me think there is something of an art to small talk with groups. When Philip came in he had one or two set lines and questions – what did you do, did you go abroad, and one or two jokey lines about the food, or paying rent. The whole room was quiet when he moved from group to group. There were three German students here on scholarships and he asked them if they were being well fed – 'Doesn't look like it,' he said to a thin guy. He seemed quite surprised to see me there, said thanks for presenting, and asked if I had any DofE experience. He seemed a bit taken aback when I said I had been given an award for my involvement with kids in Burnley, but hadn't done the scheme myself. I then did photos with the groups, then awards and then a speech. Told them a few NI stories and finally a few maxims. Fail to prepare and you are preparing to fail – Franklin. Believe you can and you're halfway there – Roosevelt.

Interesting enough event and the kids were good, though overwhelmingly middle-class and Protestant I would say. Home briefly then set off with the boys for Barnet v Bradford. Four–nil to Bradford. Standing next to a Down's Syndrome lad who had a great line in abuse of referees and also kept asking Rory the scores of other matches and checking them against the longest betting slip I had ever seen.

Wednesday 29 February

Walked to Random House, met Ed V who was nagging me again about doing a political thriller. OK meeting on Volume 4. Had to decide whether to do big events. Gail thought it would be asking for trouble. She also thought I would be crazy to go to Iraq. Then to Victoria St to see Calum and watch PMQs. Ed did OK. Cameron sort of put Gove in his place. The problem with Ed right now was that so many people were saying he didn't cut it. Lunch with Calum and Martin Angus [Labour official] then to Portland for a meeting with Steve Morris to work out a plan for what I did for them. James Murdoch resigned as head of News International UK. Home to meet Grace and Anna and off to head to Wembley for England v Holland. 3–2 Holland. Nice chat with Danny Welbeck's mum and dad.

Thursday 1 March

Out for a little run, back to watch Yates up at twelve at Leveson. I went into Twitter overdrive, probably over the top, but it was hard not to. Robert Jay did a good job, focused on his relations with [Neil] Wallis [former deputy editor, *News of the World*] – Nick Candy [property developer] also emerged as a lunch companion. He was oily and smug and couldn't see the grave he was digging. He was doing it from Bahrain where he was seemingly an adviser on policing. The tenor of my tweets was that it was incredible he had got to a senior position.

David Miliband came round for a cup of tea. He seemed in better shape. He had decided he was not going to pack it in. He felt there was no chance of us getting back in under Ed, he was going to do nothing to undermine him, but he felt that he was the only one with a chance with the public and he had to be in the right place at the right time. He felt it was possible but unlikely that Ed would walk. He felt Balls was now totally focused on taking over, that he really would prefer power in a Labour opposition to a lower position in a Labour government. DM felt the real problem was that New Labour was now being attacked from left and right. Unite was almost a party within a party. Len McCluskey [general secretary], who had recently called for civil disobedience at the Olympics, was not far off Militant [Tendency, Trotskyist group]. The candidates being installed tended to be to the left of the party. Meanwhile Ed had given the party machine to the old right who hated New Labour for different reasons – Tom Watson, Michael Dugher [party vice-chair].

He wanted my ideas for how it could all be challenged. The best I could think of was a TV documentary. He said that when he did his *New Statesman* piece recently, the worst thing was not the kneejerk opposition of the left of the party, it was the lack of any real intellectual engagement at all. We had lost the art of building our politics through argument. It was all factional. This made it impossible to have proper debate, and Ed was being very tactical. Cameron was coasting but he had clearly decided that was all he needed to do.

Friday 2 March
Out on the bike with Rory, then a few conference calls re. speeches in the future. Also started working on the piece for the PG legacy book. Kate [Naish, AC niece] got selected to run in the Olympic stadium.

Saturday 3 March
To Regent's Park with Fiona for a short run. Watford with Calum. Weird match – we went two up but lost 3–2. Crap.

Sunday 4 March
Another sleepless night. Just lying there feeling flat and lethargic. Got up early to head for the Gatwick Express then the direct Tirana flight. Interesting little scene through the gate. Sniffer dogs going through bags. The cops told me the dogs were trained in currency searching. Three guys with wads of £50 notes were taken aside. Met by Endri who took me to a little hotel, the Padam. The city looking a bit happier with the sun out. It felt at times like they were expecting me to deliver magic bullets. In the end I asked them to come up with their own top three lines or arguments and we agreed to brainstorm it in the morning.

Also discussed whether to support Nano for President. I felt if he was seen as corrupt old politics they should not do it. It would hurt their own strategy. They did not have much appetite for leading on corruption because they felt Berisha would just use it to say they were all as bad as each other. Dinner with Edi and his wife Linda at Gusto, with Endri. Small-talky with a bit of politics.

Monday 5 March

Out for a run then to party HQ for a meeting of the Big Four. They were all vaguely in the same place re. what ideas they wanted to push on so we managed that into a postcard of five OK dividing lines. Then half-hour or so with Ilva Tare who did a pretty tough interview with Edi. I felt he needed more tone and energy and big points. She felt he was not nearly out there enough and Berisha (on the TV as we spoke addressing his MPs) was dangerous and not to be underestimated.

On the plane out I was sitting next to the foreign minister, from the small centre-left party run by [Ilir] Meta [former Prime Minister]. He recognised me and started up a chat re. what I was doing, then on to their politics and ours. He was en route Singapore. His wife and daughter were with him but sitting back a bit. He felt Edi lacked the connection to the left and lacked strength. He clearly thought Berisha would win again. I said Edi had asked me out but didn't say I was working with him. In Vienna bumped into [Sayeeda] Warsi and a load of Tories who had been to Bosnia. She was a lot smaller than I expected. Nice enough chat.

Tuesday 6 March

The Budget coverage was picking up. Lots of different tax ideas kicking around, and Clegg at the centre of them. Blogged asking if he was becoming JP to Cameron–Osborne's TB–GB, to which JP tweeted it was a QTWTAIN, a new one on me which seemingly meant 'question to which the answer is no'. But I certainly got the sense Clegg was moving between the two. Annoying trip to Burnley today in that I had built a few visits and meetings around the home match v Birmingham, but they had a Cup replay with Chelsea. With one of the meetings the UCFB [University College of Football Business] advisory board I felt I had to go. First stop Burnley College, to record a video for them. Then a run on the canal. UCFB meeting was fine though Philip Wilson took too long to go through the report.

The news was the Queen coming in May and a bunfight already about who should be there. Sky Andrew [sports agent] did a session with the students which seemed to go down well. Two of the students came to talk to us and were full of praise and enthusiasm. It was definitely having an impact on them. Then into town to see David Fishwick [Burnley FC sponsor] who was running his bank, doing a TV programme [*The Bank of Dave*] on how hard it was to set up a bank. Good idea and he was totally evangelical about it. I said he needed to resolve the tension between the programme and the mission. The effort to change things would be helped by publicity, but the programme might not be.

Wednesday 7 March

Out for a meeting with Paul Hamaan, psychiatrist Trevor Turner and a film-maker to discuss schizophrenia film. Wondered about setting the challenge of trying to change the name. It is not split personality but a disordered mind in which the bits do not hang together and the emotional parts do not relate to what the sufferer sees and hears around him. Lunch with Tim Hincks [TV producer] in Notting Hill. He was still keen to work with me and felt I should decide the kind of TV I wanted to do. He reckoned I could do pretty much what I wanted but had to decide. Then to see Richard Desmond [media mogul, owner Channel 5]. I thought it was just going to be for a catch-up but the meeting was in his tenth-floor office overlooking the Thames, with him, Paul Ashford [editorial director] and Jeff Ford, head of Channel 5. They wanted me to do a daily half-hour slot, 'Newsday', as a double act with Nick Ferrari. He was very hard sell, with his usual abundance of swear words, and seemed a bit deflated when I didn't jump at it. I said I had lots of other stuff on and this was virtually a full-time job if done properly. We went round in circles on it.

He did a big patriotic call to arms on how the country was shit and Cameron was shit and Miliband was shit and someone had to save it and we could do that. Then a bit of an argument on Big Brother to which he said I could say what I wanted on 'Newsday', then a tour of the newsrooms, which was a bit annoying because it was straight out on Twitter I was there. I said I would think about it but later emailed to say why it was not for me. He replied it was the wrong call, and 'You don't want to end up a has-been'. Off to LLR to see Cathy before heading for the [charity] dinner at Speaker's House. The second time John Bercow had given us the rooms. One or two of the medics went on a bit. Sally kept signalling we should try to get it on to more general stuff but the medics kept wrestling it back. Cathy was pleased though.

Thursday 8 March

Met up with Martin Sheehan for a pre-meeting before seeing Google – Rachel Whetstone, D-J Collins [communications director] and another guy. They were wanting advice for a strategy re. Microsoft, which they felt were engaged in a pretty major assault. We kicked a few ideas around which I later wrote up, basically advising that they get it into a bigger strategic space. Rachel was clearly bright but I got the feeling they were all a bit overwhelmed by the scale of their growth and the new challenges that brought. She was clearly pleased they were heading to the US. Murdoch something of a hate figure for them all.

Off to surgery for health check. Free for over-fifties. The nurse said it tended to be the healthy people who were taking up the offer. I was fine on pulse, blood pressure and cholesterol. A bit overweight. Annoyingly it seemed our bathroom scales were wrong so I was still over fifteen stone.

Friday 9 March
Blogged on Cameron failing to tell Mario Monti [Prime Minister of Italy] about the failed attempt to rescue a British and an Italian hostage in Nigeria.* I was broadly sympathetic.

Saturday 10 March
Good and by recent standards fairly long run with Greg Nugent. Bumped into a head hunter as we stopped in Primrose Hill who offered me 'opportunities' with banks.

Sunday 11 March
Long bike ride. Lovely day. Blog on crime – cuts to the frontline beginning to bite. Lib Dems making tits of themselves re. NHS at their spring conference.

Monday 12 March
Brian Cathcart did a good piece on the Hacked Off website on why the Operation Motorman files should be published, which I posted.† Leveson later indicated he might do so. Then to a meeting with Harriet Harman and Ayesha. Nice office on the corner of the building overlooking Parliament Sq. She wanted to talk about Leveson. She had my statement and evidence there and had clearly read them. She said I was uniquely placed because I was neither politics nor media and yet I was also both politics and media. She was pretty clear that there would have to be change and it would probably require statutory underpinning. But to say that was to provoke the whole of the press into a frenzy.

Ed had stuck his neck out but as I pointed out he had paid a price. But

---

* Italian politicians accused Britain of delivering 'a slap in the face' to Italy by not informing it of a rescue attempt that ended with a British construction worker and an Italian colleague being murdered by terrorists in north-west Nigeria.

† A cache of documents obtained by the Information Commissioners' Office in a 2003 raid on the office and home of private investigator Steve Whittamore had remained closed on official secrecy grounds. Whittamore was convicted in 2005 of illegally accessing data and passing it to journalists.

we had to do what we thought was right. The problem was I was in no doubt Cameron had a strategy to get the press totally onside for the next election and that meant that he was planning not to go for heavy regulation and not to have any Parliamentary involvement if he could get away with it. Harriet had been speaking to editors and felt they were all over the place in that they didn't all want the same thing, but they all agreed no statutory underpinning. She pointed to the solicitors' tribunal as a good example of a body set up by statute but independent when set up. I suggested she might make a submission to Leveson and use that to set out some ideas.

It was a perfectly friendly chat. We didn't really go into the old days at all. As Fiona was always saying, she was a real survivor. She was also an optimist, for example thinking she could persuade the editors to go for the kind of thing she was proposing. To Marsham St and an Italian restaurant I didn't know to meet Andy Grice and Michael Savage [journalists]. I didn't have much to say, and I am not sure they will have thought it worth their while. I was never much of a luncher when I had a big role and now I didn't it felt a bit like a waste of time. They were both nice guys and it was moderately interesting to get their take but it reminded me I was glad to be out of it. They felt Labour just weren't really at the races. The papers had reverted to type. Ed was behaving like government and the government like opposition.

DS at six. Back on the pills. He felt I was still depressed. Also that I needed to embrace my anxieties. Said yes to *Have I Got News for You*. Low-level depression been going on for weeks. Maybe needed a few big things. Fiona thought do less. Go to France more. Stop being so active. I felt inactive!

Tuesday 13 March

Rebekah Brooks and husband arrested for perverting the course of justice by Operation Weeting [phone-hacking investigation] cops. Popped in to see the guys at Portland. Suggesting to Tim and Steve they have a strategy for sport. Then to the Commons to see Nick Clegg. He was in the office I last went to when Paddy Ashdown was there. Photos of all the old leaders up the wall. He bounded in, said 'Buongiorno', bit of small talk then to the point. He said he had seen me on TV saying I was worried Leveson would come up with good ideas and the government would make sure they went nowhere. He said there was very little happening in government and he wondered why I said that. I said I sensed the Tories were looking for ways out of it and ways of getting the press even more onside by Labour being pro-Leveson and them against. I was sure Gove was a strategy. I felt others were at it. Cameron had apparently assured the Barlcays [*Telegraph*] nothing would happen. NC said Cameron was certainly pleased that Ed raised it. DC did not really want to do much if anything.

He was alarmed the extent to which editors from Dacre to Rusbridger felt that anything which went near Parliament was a vicious assault on free speech. He said they were all in a frenzy. He said he basically hated them all – he used the f word a fair bit, I noticed – but how did we keep that argument alive, that regulation underpinned by statute did not mean political control of the press? He had to go out to vote at one point and I said to Olly Grender and Tim Colbourne [deputy chief of staff] that I felt NC was the one who might have to get up there with a 'what's right?' argument. Nick had said he didn't want to be the one standing up alone for Parliament getting involved – much as Harriet had said – but if he had to he would. He felt he had nothing to lose as they all whacked him all over the place anyway. He was clearly very wary of Cameron on this. He felt the Lib Dems would be in quite a good place on it.

He felt he and Ed would not be far apart. But he felt if all the media were saying the same thing it would not be easy. He said Cameron really was not keen to do anything about the press. He really did buy the line that the inquiry was having a chilling effect on the press. He said Cameron had said to him he liked to get the *Mail on Sunday* and see which MPs were up to no good but they had gone tame. I said that was purely tactical and short term, hoping to get through the inquiry and have one more last-chance saloon, to which he agreed. I suggested that if he was going to be called to Leveson he should use a submission to set out how Parliament could do this without it being 'state or political control of the press'. He seemed quite up for that.

It was the first time I had been able to study him close up for a fair period of time, just shy of an hour. Nice open eyes and a warm expression. Little evidence of political side. Clear and articulate. Listened to answers. A bit careworn when the division bells rang and he had a little rant at his own party. He asked me if I enjoyed my life. 'It looks to me like an idyllic form of existence.' I pushed back on that, said when this was all over for him he would find out! He said he thought I was in a good position. He had said earlier he thought I should see Cameron re. Leveson. I said I felt the Tories still saw me as tribal and baggage. He thought not. Nice chat. Good he was thinking about it. I said to Olly he should think of this maybe as one of his big points of difference. I was starting on some new pills, Sertraline, which DS felt would be less numbing than the last lot.

Wednesday 14 March
Met up with Daniel Korski [foreign policy adviser] near King's Cross. He had been approached to head up a strategic comms role for Cathy Ashton and wanted my take. Her profile was low with the public, and she was

not yet seen as top rank by a lot of the decision-makers so he had a tough task. He said it was hard for her to develop a profile on the issue of Europe because of the domestic sensitivities. Even though she was not in the same league e.g. as Hillary, he said Cameron had seen off an attempt by Sarko to move against her. He realised she was not seen as a big player but she was very able, competent, incredibly nice, and learning. I recommended a 'two years in' strategy in which she reflected on what indeed she had learned and how she had developed, and used a series of speeches to frame some big arguments.

Off to Newcastle. Cock up because I got on the wrong train and had to get off and wait half an hour in Peterborough, in the buffet where I ended up once, pissed and with no idea how I got there, after a Cambridge May Ball. Met by Mia of GirlGeeks [online community for women interested in technology] who had booked me for the 'Science of Decision Making' event at Newcastle Library, as part of a Northumbria University event. An academic called Kenny Coventry [Northumbria University] was on before me. He seemed quite dull when I first met him but he came alive when he did his presentation. Interesting on the way the mind worked in decision-making. Two types of process – intuitive and analytical. I argued you could do both. We worked quite well as a double act I think and the event as a whole got very good feedback on Twitter. I'm not sure if decision-making is a science or an art, but he made me think about it in a slightly different way.

Thursday 15 March

Met Joanna Berry from Newcastle University Business College. Tall and good-looking and oozing a sense of confidence. It made such a difference at these events to have someone who looked and sounded in control. The set-up was that Chris Mullin was interviewing me in front of academics and students, then Q&A. I had always got on well with Chris and it licked along well, and seemed to go down OK. Did a book signing, then Chris and I were taken to meet a group of academics who were doing New Labour in various guises. The main guy, Chris Carter, knew my diaries better than I did. He was really happy to be meeting up and chatting, took it all very seriously. Off then to York for a meeting of headteachers at a hotel just outside the City. A Burnley fan was working there and wanted photos etc., which had his colleagues in hysterics. Met the council leader, James Alexander, who was the youngest leader in England and Wales, just thirty. I did a basic leadership and strategy speech, good Q&A then headed for the station and home. Pills kicking in. Watched David Frost's programme on interviews, which was excellent, especially on how the interview had changed down the years.

Friday 16 March

All day at Portland, doing two sessions with groups of staff on strategy. Some bright young things among them. Tim [Smith], tall and posh and 'I'm a big fan of Ken Clarke which is why I wear suede shoes', said, 'Strategy is God and tactics the way the earth is made up', when we did the strategy definition exercise. Liked it. Was getting a fair bit of public interaction going around the place today. A young guy thanking me for the mental health stuff and telling me, close to tears, about his sister's struggles with bipolar. A couple of people on the Tube asking me to go back and help Ed, one said 'Save Ed.' And I was still getting people coming up and mentioning the *Panorama* on booze.

Saturday 17 March

Out on the bike, tied up a few loose ends re. Volume 4 then out to see *In Darkness* at the cinema with Grace. A Polish film about a petty thief who looked after Jews in the sewers of a Polish town under occupation. Incredibly powerful and moving. I wondered just how I would be able to deal with that kind of fear, and endure that kind of deprivation. Later I was watching the Spurs v Bolton match when Fabrice Muamba [Bolton] collapsed, seemingly dead. Pretty shocking and the crowd sensed it straight away. Really sad. At first everyone seemed to think he was dead, and later it turned out his heart had failed for more than an hour, but then he was stable, then critically ill, then it would depend on the next twenty-four hours.

Sunday 18 March

Out for a walk with Fiona, then watched *Marr* because both Osborne and Balls were on. Balls did OK. Osborne seemed to be avoiding anything of substance, and halfway through I tweeted that all he had to say was there was a coalition government and the Budget was this week. But then he leapt on the back of the *Sunday Times* splash – probably put there by them – on how rock stars were avoiding tax by putting their properties into offshore companies. Ran to Primrose Hill to meet Peter M. He had finally suggested meeting up and we met in Regent's Park by the fountain. He was perfectly friendly, and we went for a long walk, well over an hour. Mainly he talked first about Global Counsel [strategic advisory firm], what he was doing there, who he was working with, the bits that interested him, the bits that didn't. He was full of praise for Ben Wegg-Prosser [managing partner], Geoffrey Norris [senior adviser] and the team, and for Maree Glass [office manager], whose husband had been ill but who insisted on keeping Peter's show on the road.

I asked where his house was and he pointed in a general direction, then said Reinaldo [PM's partner] was not quite ready for forgiveness in the way he was, so I was not yet ready to be welcomed. He said he was able to forgive me only on the basis that I had 'only been obeying orders, on the lines of the Waffen-SS!' He said he found it hard to forgive TB. He should have been loyal and supported him. Instead he sacrificed him when the going got tough. I saw little reason in going over it all in detail. He later said he had no idea that I had hated him to the extent I did. I said I had never hated him, but I hated having been the one who had to deal with everyone else's baggage the whole time. He said but there had been a rivalry when there didn't need to be. I said I was not responsible for that. We should have worked together better, and that was down to both of us. I tried.

He said that the reason PG got on with everyone was because he avoided confrontation whereas we did not. He for example had made lots of enemies when he was trying to help Neil make change and then he underestimated how much he alienated people by promoting Gordon and Tony and making people feel the party became a vehicle for their advance 'which to some extent it did'. We had both seen Balls on *Marr*. He said Ed B was in a similar situation to Peter when he first stepped out on his own. He had baggage and enemies and he had to try to distance himself just a little. Ed had done an interview in *The Times* – 'Mainly about cooking as it happens' – in which he had effectively said GB was a bit mad 'which he may well have been'. The point was that he was totally associated with GB and now needed to break from him a little. I asked if Reinaldo ever reflected that it was because of the second resignation that he went on to become an EU commissioner and then back as GB's (effectively) No. 2. 'Yes, but it is not what I wanted or how I planned it.' Which was... 'to be Foreign Secretary'... which might not have happened... 'indeed'. Anyway, he said, let's not dwell on the past.

He quizzed me on what I was doing, which bits I liked, which bits I didn't and though he wondered if I was challenging myself enough at the intellectual level he said, 'You seem to have found an equilibrium of sorts.' I felt I had, though I said I still had 'head problems'. But I wasn't terribly interested in building up a business and I was not keen to lose the freedom I now had. We talked a fair bit about TB. He said Tony kept asking to see him, and discuss various things with a view to tying up in some way, but nothing came of it and he wasn't sure he wanted it to. He said he had decided early on not to do government work. He said Kissinger had advised him not to do government work because 'you get tarred with whatever they do'. He said you can work around governments but not for them. He also said it would take a year or two to work out what you did well, so don't do too much during that period, and build up gradually. He really was sharp on TB, and even sharper re. CB. He said he had bumped into her at a John Birt dinner in the Lords and she had been seriously rude to him. He said he was quite taken aback. Anyway, a perfectly nice chat.

We ended at his house, on the Outer Circle and Reinaldo was outside, but Peter decided not to take me over. He said he was really not happy with any of us. I said to Fiona, and later to Gail when we met for dinner, that I sensed he was up for some kind of reconciliation, and it was a good chat and I was glad it had happened. Watched Kilmarnock beat Celtic before we headed out for a Mother's Day dinner with all the kids, Gail and the girls.

Tuesday 20 March

Budget hype really building and a lot of the big tickets already out there, including a cut in the top income tax rate, which the Eds were attacking big-time. Polly Toynbee had an interesting piece which included the line that the head of the OECD [Organisation for Economic Co-operation and Development] had warned China not to follow the US–UK route on inequality. Off to East Finchley for meetings at McDonald's, who had asked me via Portland to do an interview to be shown in a film at their big conference in Florida. Met by public affairs head Allison Bartlett, a bit edgy but a Labour supporter and interesting on how the business worked – via franchises – and how the company was not always as slick as its image.

Then met CEO Jill McDonald, pretty, blonde, looked like Fiona, so it was funny when she said she felt she knew me because she had seen me down the years on TV and I was the double of an ex-boyfriend. Clegg had been there recently re. apprenticeships and she said he was great. Bit of political chat then through with Nick Hindle, head of comms, to do the interview. Tried to do big themes – the conference was about boldness – without getting too McD specific. Nice enough crowd though.

Called Andy McCann [psychologist] to book an appointment to try to address all this anxiety in the night I had been having.

Wednesday 21 March

Budget Day. Out to film by Lambeth Palace for a Time to Change film. Lovely crew which made up for the lateness and hanging around. Home, run, then settled down to watch the Budget. I thought Osborne was doing quite well with bad figures but he half-announced a hit on pensioners which would take off. Ed did well, focused on the cut to the top rate and taunted the government front bench about whether they were better off.

It was his best performance to date. Sent him a message. He called later, said thanks for the help though all I really did was tighten and order a bit. I did a blog focusing on some of the things that looked like they would unravel. Also the borrowing figures were much higher than expected. Ed seemed comfortable with the politics of it. So did the Tories with theirs. So did the Lib Dems with the raising of the tax threshold.

TB called, just for a chat, family stuff mainly, but also keen to know how things had gone with Peter. 5.30 train to Ipswich v Burnley. Train out with Mike Lownes [friend], dinner with Simon Clegg [former CEO British Olympic Association. Clegg vicious re. [Lord] Colin Moynihan [Clegg's successor at the BOA]. Really loathed him. Got escorted round to the away end. Small turnout and we had very little to shout about. Lost one–nil. Should have been more.

Thursday 22 March

[Lord] David Hunt [Tory peer, chairman of Press Complaints Commission] had asked to see me re. the PCC and Leveson. I had always got on well with him when I was a journalist and, as he reminded me early on, I had stuck up for him when the right wing had gone for him. He was waiting with his right-hand man, Michael McManus [former Tory parliamentary candidate], who I vaguely remembered from when he worked for David H in government. They were at the PCC offices in Holborn, nice offices but felt a bit flat in there. He said that he had effectively abolished the PCC and the people who were most upset were the commissioners. He said he still saw me as a journalist in many ways and he wanted me to be happy with whatever he came up with by way of a new PCC. I said I didn't see myself as a journalist and my concern in this area was as a citizen who had been on both sides of the fence and felt the press had damaged both.

He said he was a passionate believer in freedom of speech and freedom of the press, and he felt it would be bad all round if Parliament was involved. I said there was a difference between parliamentary control of press regulation, and parliamentary underpinning. My problem was that I didn't trust the current leadership of the press to self-regulate. They were on their best behaviour through Leveson but if they got away with one last last-chance saloon, they would know they could get away with anything, and revert to type. His answer was to bind them all in with commercial contracts in support of a regulator which would have real teeth, including powers to investigate, powers to fine, powers to order corrections etc.

He said he had managed to get most of the owners signed up to that. Murdoch told him to go and get on with it. Barclays OK. Desmond OK. Having trouble with *Mail* because he couldn't get to see [Lord] Rothermere [chairman, Associated Newspapers], doubtless because Dacre wanted to call the shots there. He said at least in talking about an ombudsman, Dacre had signalled the need for change. I asked him how he got the job and when he said he had applied and then been interviewed by [Lord] Guy Black [former director, PCC], I said that made me even more suspicious. Black was part of the bad old system and should not be allowed anywhere near this. The funding mechanism for his new body would essentially be the same, namely the press would fund it. Better than state money, he said. I asked if he envisaged current media interests being involved in the actual regulation. He said maybe distinguished former editors. I said I had been worried when I first saw him because I felt the one message that came through was his belief in the freedom of the press, and while that was fine, it came over to me as though this was going to be one more Tory placeman singing the songs the press wanted to hear.

He said he also wanted to change the culture of the press. He wanted a robust independent regulator with teeth. He had been keeping Leveson in touch with what he was doing. They had gone to the same school, knew each other well, and he felt Leveson would come up with something sensible. What he wanted to do was devise a system that might be got up and running quickly and without legislation. He sensed none of the party leaders wanted a big role for Parliament. Harriet maybe. Clegg maybe. But he said he had far less faith than I did in Parliament not to go too far and to interfere with basic freedoms. He agreed with the idea of an annual report on each paper, and said that the Commission and editors and owners could be called to an overseeing select committee. But he was very strong in his view that it was all best done without Parliament. He said regulation should be proportionate, consistent, accountable, targeted and transparent. There were existing regulatory bodies able to do their job without government or Parliament being involved.

He felt that the new body would not be able to deal with compensation cases. Re. the name, they both felt it was best not to have any of the three words from the PCC in there. The favourite at the moment seemed to be Independent Editorial Standards Authority. As well as newspapers, they would be asking freelances and agencies to sign up to it as well. They were opposed to licensing however. He said he was disappointed to hear that I didn't think it could be done without legislation. I said I didn't say that. I said I did not trust the current leadership of the industry. I also said I believed both Leveson and large sections of the public had been pretty appalled by what they had heard, and something had to give. He asked if I was willing to trust him to give it a go, and try to make it work. I said fine, but I would be sceptical. He was hoping to come up with something fairly soon. Nice to see him though, good reminiscing re. his government days.

Had a call with Michael Aron, our ambassador in Baghdad. I had asked for his advice about an invitation to speak at a conference for the Camp Ashraf [headquarters of the exiled People's Mujahedin of Iran] people in Iraq. They were Iranians who had fought for Saddam against Iran. He said they were well-funded (they were offering quite a lot of money for me to speak) but they were a bit of a cult, the MEK, and if he were me, he would not touch it with a bargepole. They ran a very good PR campaign but it was fraught. That had been my suspicion and he confirmed it, so I said No. He said Iraq was definitely improving. Still real problems. Maliki not perfect but better than his reputation. Kurds doing well. BP and Shell doing good work there. On Iran and Syria, the Iraqis were being pretty sensible.

Home for dinner and then out to do *This Week* with Andrew Neil and Michael Portillo. Owen Jones [writer, left-wing activist] did the Budget but Andrew rather took him apart. Portillo a bit grumpy, Neil very caustic re. coalition and even more so about Bercow who had done a really odd speech when the Queen addressed both Houses of Parliament when he talked of her being a kaleidoscope Queen in a kaleidoscope country in a kaleidoscope world.* Queen looked bemused, Cameron looked fit to kill.

Friday 23 March

Calum had gone to the Blackburn–Burnley youth match, got pissed and ended up being mugged in Manchester. He had been calling but my phone was upstairs in my study, Fiona's was on mute and he ended up sleeping out. He admitted he had had too much to drink but also felt I was too harsh in the way I approached things with him. I was due to go into Portland for a morning session, so I sorted him a hotel and then fixed for Rayan to collect me and go and get him in the afternoon. The traffic as usual was dire. Saw the Queen on the other side of the M60 in Manchester, where she had been opening the new BBC centre. I did a blog on the way up on the government bringing forward plans for minimum pricing on alcohol. They had been getting battered with the granny tax [removal of higher tax allowances enjoyed by those aged sixty-five and over] backlash and no doubt rushed this forward to get them out of a hole. But I was reasonably supportive, saying it had to be part of a broader strategy to get Britain to face up to its drink problem.

Calum and I didn't talk much, and I could tell he felt I was too harsh, given he had just been mugged at knifepoint. But in a way he put himself in that position by being drunk and vulnerable. Off to Liverpool for

---

* The Commons Speaker was also president of the Kaleidoscope Trust, campaigners for human rights of lesbian, gay, bisexual and transexual people.

March '12: Another Calum drinking crisis

the fundraiser for mayoral candidate Joe Anderson. 500 people, among them Derek Hatton [former deputy leader of Liverpool City Council and member of Trotskyist militant group], which gave me some good material. Book signing, small talk, chit chat. Very white audience. One of the organisers told me Ed's leadership was coming up on the doorstep a fair bit now. Re. Hatton, he tweeted that it was his first Labour event since 1986 and that he was going because he supported Joe and 'to hear my old mate @campbellclaret'. I said he was the first person I met coming in, and he kissed me. Last time we brushed past each other in a hotel corridor he spat at me. Said we had also met in the gents. 'Look at me,' he said, 'I'm way to the right of you these days.' Went down well enough and he didn't seem to mind too much. Speech went OK, then played the pipes and marched out so that we could get off and head back through the night as Calum wanted to get home.

Saturday 24 March

Bike. Worried re. not sleeping. Constantly waking up, and have been for a couple of weeks now, worrying about the book and about Chilcot. Worried about Calum. He and I had another fairly tough heart-to-heart. He knew he needed help but didn't know how to go about it. Kip p.m. Burnley two up against West Ham but then blew it [2–2].

Sunday 25 March

Lovely warm day and managed a nice run. Also had a heart-to-heart with Calum, then we went to the Farthings [Alison and Michael, friends] for their little garden party. Usual mix of medics, academics and neighbours. DS there. Told him I was still waking up every night and fretting. He insisted the pills would kick in after a week or so. Out for dinner with Edi and the team. They had had a good trip to the States and he was now over for a speech but also to see EM, DM and Douglas A. He was with his usual team and we went over a few ideas and thoughts. He wanted me to step up involvement if I could. He was on a protein-only diet so just had two slabs of meat.

Monday 26 March

Edi 9.30–11 at Paddington Hilton. I had watched an interview he did and gave him a bit of feedback. The stuff we did last time was beginning to work though so he felt more strategic and wanted me to do more. He went off for his meetings. Said he found DM much more impressive than

Ed. Out on the bike then to Ernst and Young for a Time to Change event. 6,000 people in the building, mainly hot-desking. Couple of hundred came. Did my usual then Q&A. Mark Davies there from Rethink [mental health charity]. He said to them that when he first experienced mental health problems when working for Jack Straw I was the first person he told. He said it had been a huge thing for him.

Tuesday 27 March

Blogged on the news agenda still favouring the Tories. Terrific meeting with Roxy Spencer [script editor, RSJ Films] and Sita Williams [producer] who really liked *AITM*, and were really keen to do a four-parter for TV, with Jimmy McGovern. They stayed for ages, chatting over which characters and which plotlines they liked. Liked them both. They had read it carefully and they really got it so I was pretty chuffed.

Wednesday 28 March

Breakfast with Matthew [Freud] in Primrose Hill. I hadn't realised they had had a fire in the new house so they had moved out to Claridge's. He had also basically been taking a sabbatical. Not been in for weeks. He was definitely really still moved by PG's death. He was scathing re. the Murdochs, who were all over the *FT* as being in trouble for one of their companies hacking. Then off for a day with hedge funds. Lunch awards for services, dinner awards for the funds themselves. The people were not as bad as I expected but I still played it for laughs by going for them. Called them comrades, asked for money for Labour, took the piss out of the *Hedge Fund Journal* re. the budget and their stuff re. tax avoidance. Got a good line from a woman at my table, asked her who was the most unpopular person in the room and she said, 'Probably you.' Some seriously rich people in there. Some of them shifting currencies on their phones as we spoke. TB got his Leveson letter which was pretty tough. He wanted me to go in tomorrow.

Thursday 29 March

Off to Grosvenor Square to see TB, Catherine and Ciaran. CR felt the Leveson letter was pretty tough. TB felt it was the work of a junior counsel. But it was long and detailed and he was going to have to think through the answers, while Catherine was going to have to get a lot of research work done. His basic pitch was going to be that yes, he and I argued about this but in his mind it would have been crazy to take the press on. They were like a Mafia. If you wanted to get the job done – win, and then govern – you needed them onside to some extent. If they weren't they could kill you. So yes he wooed Murdoch and others because not to do so would have diminished his chances. Not killed maybe but certainly diminished. He said that under Thatcher there were five papers that were slavish and they were rewarded with knighthoods. They did real damage to Neil, just as other Labour leaders had been damaged. Re. Murdoch he reckoned he saw him less than GB did. He liked him a lot more since leaving. The godfather thing would never have happened when he was in office.* I said, but these are basically transactional relationships. These are not friends. He said that is the problem with Rupert, ultimately he is all about himself and whatever he thinks at the time is what he thinks to be right. Matthew had said this morning that whenever he bangs his hand on the table, you know he is lying. TB said he didn't want CR obsessing about this. But he did need to get his head in gear for it. He said he would but he was not going to obsess. He intended to set out the reality – that these people have huge and unaccountable power. To check it would be to risk having them en masse trying to kill you. So you keep them tame.

He did not feel that he had given on policy but I think he would find it hard to make that case. I filled him in on the chat I had had with Clegg, and also with Harriet. It was pretty obvious that if Leveson went for tough new regulation, Cameron would resist as a way of keeping the right-wing press on board, and set it up as a dividing line against Ed and Clegg. Caroline was telling me some of the phone number fees TB was getting offered for speeches. He was at least putting money into the charities. Gail called to say Peter M had written to her to say he couldn't come to the interment and that it was such a lovely letter that she burst into tears. He had said that I still underestimated the hurt I caused but PG was right – that it was silly to lose friends and what did it all matter now anyway?

Meeting with Andy McCann at the Royal Society of Medicine. He was the Welsh rugby team's sports psychologist. I told him all the mental anguish that had been waking me up. He said this was the chimp inside me, explained the way the different parts of the brain worked, and that this bit was the part that was alerting me to danger and calling up survival instincts. It is not good or bad. It just is. We went through peaks and troughs, times I felt confident and times I didn't. We talked about this hollowing-out feeling I sometimes got before an interview and we agreed we would think of a few strategies to deal with it. I needed to learn to switch off – be a human being not a human doing. He said PG's death will have made me feel more isolated. Adrenaline can be good. Doubt can be good. Put the two together and the result can be anxiety.

The chimp thing was all about the limbic system and the different ways different parts of the mind worked. Fight, flight, freeze, faint was the kind

---

* In 2011 Blair had become godfather to one of Murdoch's young daughters, Grace.

of process I went through on *Marr*. Fear – false expectations appearing real. I was definitely in that mode. The limbic was five times faster than the thinking part at the front. It also stayed awake while we slept. It was a predictor of how we will feel. He said it was putting me on alert for dangerous or difficult situations. We went through 'the needs of the chimp'. He emphasised that everything was a choice we made. I should ask why I did the things that made me anxious. I should seek real truths not just positive thinking. I should also be thinking about emotional painkillers – friends and time with them, exercise, switching off.

We talked about mental toughness and the need for turnaround strategy. Critical-moment toughness – doing what you are trained to do whatever the circumstances. Decision-making toughness. Endurance toughness. I said my personal mission on the book and the inquiry was to be absolutely confident of my case and my abilities. Also wanted to be mellower and wiser, more reasonable. He had a lot of experience with sport, military, all sorts and I felt he would be a help. Off to Random House to sign advance copies of *The Happy Depressive*. Looked really good.

Friday 30 March

Woke up to the grim, grim news that George Galloway [Respect Party] had won the Bradford East by-election with a massive 10k majority. Landslide. Disaster for Ed and for us. Nobody saw it coming. And him of all people! He was milking for all it was worth, said he failed to save the people of Iraq but he would save the people of Britain. Off with the family to PG's interment at Highgate Cemetery. Lovely sunny day. Gail and the girls OK. Lindsay took some flowers to John and Ellie's graves. Nice little service. I played 'Lest We Forget', which went down well. Nicola and Matthew in tears. TB and GB towards the back. Still missing him a lot. He'd have loved the whole thing though – the Christian bits by his sister and [Sir] Alan Moses [Appeal Court judge], the Jewish bits from [Baroness] Julia Neuberger [rabbi], the pipes, the PMs, the friends and family. Fiona and Grace rushed off to get the tunnel train to France while I went back to the do at Park Square East. Gail made a nice little speech. Lovely mood in the place. PG still there. Steve Hilton popped in. Sensed he and Andrew Cooper not too close. Both complaining at the handling of the Budget and the tanker drivers' dispute. Rory took me to the Eurostar and I set off for Rennes via Paris. Managed all the trains with help and got to Rennes by midnight.

Saturday 31 March

Théatre National de Bretagne for my session at the Liberation Forum with

Anne Lauvergeon, who worked for Mitterrand. Madeleine Bunting there to study the festival for *The Guardian*. Thousand-seater theatre near full, ninety-minute event. French held up well. The moderator got asthma and I had to lend him my pump. Good atmosphere. Sensed Sarko on the move a bit. Had to rush off to get train to Paris, then change for Lyon-Orange. Burnley won 5–1 at Pompey.

Sunday 1 April

The house and the view were looking great. Out for a run with Grace. Call from David Davis who was stirring. I reflected some of his comments in a blog I did on their current woes. We were back to lack of clarity of strategy. But also, as DD said, the fact that DC and GO didn't know any real people or get their lives.

Monday 2 April

The letter from Leveson on what they wanted me to cover in my statement came through. Worked on it for most of the day. Annoying being a professional witness again but got to be done.

Tuesday 3 April

Got Sam Nurding [AC's researcher] working on Leveson research and did my own draft. James Murdoch gone as BSkyB chairman. Ed V getting a bit more money from Sita for *AITM* but deal done. Sam and Charlie F on case re. Leveson draft.

Wednesday 4 April

Blog re. Cameron lack of strategy again. Left for Marseille at lunchtime. Private jet to Slovenia. Nice. Four-seater, very comfortable apart from when turbulence hit. Met by US Chamber of Commerce. Good laugh on long drive. Signed books, shower, speech on leadership which went down really well. Saw some of [former Slovenic PM] Borut Pahor's old team. Good Q&A then straight off, back to the plane, home by two.

Rest of holiday to 13 April

Did a few blogs, a bit of reading, lots on Leveson, lots of revision with Grace. Also a fair bit of socialising. Working with Georgia on her piece for the Dennis Kavanagh [academic] PG tribute book. Fair bit of cycling with Rory. Lots of football. Puymeras in local Cup final. We came back home via Colombey-les-Deux-Églises to take in the [General Charles] de Gaulle [former President of France] museum. Lovely museum, and resting place. Also saw his house La Boisserie, which they had bought for its seclusion when they had a Down's Syndrome daughter. Amazed nobody has made a feature film on his relationship with Churchill, about which I had been reading in Aidan Crawley's brilliant autobiography of de Gaulle.

Weekend off to Burnley v Coventry. Poor game. One–all. Season fizzling out. Back via Mum's who was in great form. Still honing Leveson. PG book arrived and Georgia and I did clips for a *One Show* package. Missing him a lot. DS. OK but upped the dose.

Monday 16 April
Dr Mark Hamilton, the gastroenterologist at the Royal Free, had booked me in for an appointment which turned out to be a follow-up to the colonoscopy all-clear. But there were something called hypoplastic polyps in there which might need attention later so I needed another colonoscopy some time in the future. To Gail's later to record the interview for *The One Show*, Georgia and I talking about Philip. She spoke really nicely about him. She was doing brilliantly but every now and then I caught a real sadness in her eyes.

Tuesday 17 April
Paul Veitch [community liaison] at the Jesus Centre in Northampton had worn me down and I gave up several hours to do a talk and a lunch with their business network. A pretty straight life-and-times interview, fair bit on Iraq, loads on we don't do God, no real problems. Nice enough crowd though a bit too much of the evangelical sympathy for the non-believer.

Thursday 19 April
Nice lunch in the Aldwych for PG's book with the Little, Brown [publishers] people, Ed, Gail and the girls, Matthew, Keith [Blackmore, editor]. Good happy mood. Home to work on Leveson.

Friday 20 April
Dublin day trip for an Irish accountants' conference. More fun than it sounds. Good chat with Brendan Foley, one of the other speakers, who was reading *THD* and said he was getting stuff out of it for his work too.

Good speaker. Did my usual leadership rap which went well, nice Q&A, lunch and home. TB fine re. my Leveson draft.

Saturday 21 April

Went out on the bike, got the bug and ended up going to Harold's Farm to see George [Mackie] and Catherine [MacLeod]. Lovely to see them. Sort of missed Grace's horse stuff though it was brilliant that she was finally getting into revision. Was absolutely knackered when I got back. Dinner with Tessa at the Bull. Lots of Ken and Boris talk. She was really up for it in the sense of motivating activists, but really found it hard to like Ken. In fact she hated him and could only keep going by thinking of the party more generally. The tragedy was that Johnson was beatable. Both he and Cameron had the gloss coming off at the same time.

Sunday 22 April

Did a quick blog saying that the choice was Ken v Boris and for all his faults it had to be Ken. Tessa felt the problem was going to be Labour voters backing Johnson. Ken had certainly given them plenty of ammunition to do so. Off to Heathrow via Al Jazeera, doing a spot on the French presidential elections today. Looking OK for Hollande. Off to Edinburgh, met by Donald [brother], booked into Radisson Blu and got set for the party fundraiser. Alistair Darling hosting it. Good to see him and he was almost embarrassingly nice about me when it came to the introductions. It was sincere too, about how I was able always to help him navigate the media waters but more than that that I was a team player and never stopped believing in Labour and the power of political change. I was sitting with him, his agent Andrew Burns, Donald, Anas Sarwar [member of Scottish Parliament] and next to me Johann Lamont [leader, Scottish Labour Party]. I had been expecting a bit of a dullard because of the media image but I was impressed. Very warm and engaging and when she spoke, very funny as well as speaking in a language redolent with values.

Alistair D was on good form, said the party was in a total mess and I needed to give them a bit of confidence and belief. He said he was looking forward to the referendum and he believed it could be won. Salmond was not good on the detail, not good with women, and not good at dealing with criticism. He said he had not spoken to GB since the election. He felt that Gordon had to make some kind of honest assessment of his own leadership, but that he was not yet ready for it and probably never would be because he believed his own denials and sense of victimhood. What he had found really hard was the open lying that he did.

Alistair was talking to Osborne because they realised the Tories were still neuralgic up here. He was pretty scathing on the Budget. The mood was pretty good. Loads of books being sold. Set Johann a word test – the longest word made up from a single line on a qwerty keypad and she got it – typewriter. I did a ra-ra speech without notes, lots re. how it had always been tough, leading change etc., and it seemed to go down well. Late night but a good crowd and always good to talk to Alistair. His book had sold 45,000. Hollande won the first round in France but Marine le Pen [leader, right-wing National Rally Party] got almost one in five of the votes cast. Smart money on Hollande obviously but not over.

Monday 23 April
Out for a run. Bloody hilly. Did a quick blog on the appeal of Johann, and also the fact that she 'got' typewriter. I reckon if they could get her real personality out there she would be a good foil to Salmond. I was opening the MacKay Hannah [conference organisers] leadership conference. Good event. Some good speakers after me including a very smart Army Brigadier who now ran the Edinburgh tattoo. O2 [telecommunications services company] sponsored a lunch I spoke at for some of the bigger fish from public and private sectors. I was sometimes amazed the extent to which people listened to what I said, not just about the past but the future as well. These guys were literally hanging on every word and I couldn't quite understand why. Flew back, met by Fiona. Cameron all over the news with another media blitz fightback. He should shut the fuck up.

Tuesday 24 April
Off to the Moroccan embassy with Tim Allan for a meeting with the ambassador. Tim was very good in these situations. Off to the airport and caught bits and bobs of James Murdoch at Leveson and he looked very uncomfortable, both about hacking and what he knew when, and about lobbying on the BSkyB bid. He really did come over as shifty. Too much 'can't recall' going on. But then he divulged a stack of private correspondence with [minister for the Olympics] Jeremy Hunt's special adviser and Fred Michel [James Murdoch lobbyist] which was going to be a big thing because it looked like Hunt had set up a back channel to help BSkyB. Out to the airport and had loads to eat before the first flight to Frankfurt, knowing I would want to sleep on the second one.

[Lord] Alexander Hesketh [businessman] got on and we ended up talking a fair bit. Pretty right-wing. Drinking a fair bit. I had forgotten he had left the Tories and defected to UKIP. He was on the board of Air Astana

[Kazakhstan airline] and though he didn't really press on what I was doing there, he assumed I was working with TB and said I ought to advise him to be very careful. He felt the regime was not as secure as we might think. He reckoned the Zhanaozen shootings were all about killing people who had just been complaining about the price of travel out of the place.* We talked a bit about UK politics. He was not impressed with Cameron, felt the Tories were losing their way. I managed to get a bit of sleep before landing around 5 a.m. local time.

Wednesday 25 April

Staying at the Rixos, bumped into the ex-Armenian PM at breakfast who came over and asked what I was doing there. He said the last time he was there he bumped into TB. First meeting Yermukhamet Yertysbayev [culture and information minister], who was in his usual pretty robust form, not giving much on reform. Drawing on a huge cigar the whole time. Then off to the Parliament building to meet Dariga Nazarbayeva, the President's daughter and apparently quite a big player. Her ex-husband [Rakhat Aliyev] was in exile, she was close to her dad and also a mover and shaker in the party. Quite edgy at first but we ended up getting on OK, though again I was not sure whether she felt the reform message we were constantly highlighting was the one to go for.

Lunch with Altay Abibullayev, acting head of MFA [Ministry of Foreign Affairs] comms, who was pretty downbeat about everything, then to the other end of the scale with Yerzhan Babakumarov, PM's deputy head, who was really up for the proposed new Government Communications Office, and clearly wanted to run it. Then a good meeting with the foreign minister, who got what we were trying to do and wanted to push it. He was keen for a top diplomat to be the new spokesman in the new system we were advocating. He was also keen for more support re. some of the bigger geo-themes – Iran, energy, China/Russia. They were keen to get a foreign policy image that moved them away from just being seen as part of Russia. He had done an interview saying *Borat* [mockumentary film made by British comedian Sacha Baron Cohen] had helped with tourism, but though it got OK coverage, some of the old hardliners hadn't liked it. Grace getting her tongue pierced.

---

* In December 2011 at least fourteen protestors, complaining about low wages and poor working conditions, were killed by police in the town of Zhanaozen on Kazakhstan's Independence Day.

Thursday 26 April

Meeting with Dauren Abayev, the President's new press secretary, who was very much on message re. reform and the new GCO [Government Communications Officer]. We would see if it made much difference. Then to Nazarbayev Uni to meet Anne Lonsdale, the Cambridge don who was Provost here, to sort TB's visit. Then to the meeting with the PM. Massimov was very up for the GCO and wanted Babakumarov to set it up, so he wanted me to spend some time with him. He said that he felt our work was beginning to bear fruit, but he knew they had a long way to go. I felt in general that the project was moving in the right direction but slowly.

The big news back home was the fallout from Leveson, with Hunt under real pressure. Murdoch himself up today, and back tomorrow. Seemed to have done better than at the select committee. A rather irritating American woman next to me on the flight to Frankfurt, and then Hesketh for the second leg. He had been pretty pissed on the flight out, literally bouncing off the walls when we got off the plane, and was a lot more interesting sober. We had a really good chat about all sorts of stuff, including de Gaulle. On the political side of things he reckoned UKIP were on for big gains in the locals, and that Cameron was in quite a lot of trouble. The Leveson stuff was adding to the sense of his being a gilded set looking after their mates.

Friday 27 April

I had sent a draft of my Leveson statement last week but wanted to update a little in the light of the Murdochs' evidence, which was totally dominating the media agenda right now. TB felt my regulation stuff was strong, and was happy enough for me to keep in the stuff on the differences of opinion we had over what to do about the way the press was changing.

Sunday 29 April

Peter M and Illtyd [Harrington, Labour politician, former deputy leader of Greater London Council] for lunch. It had arisen out of our walk and he seemed in OK form, though Illtyd felt he was subdued, asked him what was wrong and Peter said, 'Alastair has this capacity to trouble me.' He bought some nice books about his grandfather [Herbert Morrison, former Labour Cabinet minister] for Illtyd who was touched that it was all happening and physically better than the last time we saw him. We avoided politics in the main, just reminiscing and generally having an OK time. Glad we did it.

Monday 30 April

Grace eighteen. Unbelievable. First vote coming up. Working hard too. Getting into politics. Really doing well. Meeting with Steve Holliday CEO of National Grid. Nice enough guy, a bit defensive at first but I think by the end of it he had got the point about the need for a more strategic approach. I was a bit knackered after a fair bit of travel recently but decided I just had to put the Leveson statement behind me today, get it done and off. Nice exchange of emails with Jackie Ashley [broadcaster] re. her dad [Jack Ashley, former Labour MP] who had died recently. She talked of the way the Labour family came together at times like this, which was nice. United lost at City. Alex felt let down. He was talking as if the title race was over.

Tuesday 1 May

Fifteen years since our first election win. Tories in a lot of trouble at the moment and Ed doing pretty well. Tim Livesey and Francis Campbell [diplomat] round for dinner. Tim had definitely made a difference in getting Ed more organised and the office more efficient though I think he realised there was still a lot more to do, though I think they sensed Cameron was in a very bad place right now, and not really facing up to it. The general feeling seemed to be that Ken [Livingstone] had had it but that the council results would not be so bad and might be good. Tim said he liked Balls but that he was very tricky. Francis was full of the usual gossip and blarney and all in all quite a nice evening.

Wednesday 2 May

Interesting speaking event today. South Bank Purcell Room, Planets Collide, Jeremy Gilley of *Peace One Day* [documentary], [General] Mike Jackson, David Droga from advertising, me from politics, all speaking on the theme of how to win if losing is not an option. There was a vote at the end and we all had to sit there as they voted for who was the best and most useful speaker. I won, with Jacko second. He was a very engaging speaker. Had a good natter with him and with some of the advertising planners who made up the audience. I did my basic spiel and my ten points re. winning. Off to Battersea for the Sports Industry Awards. Sitting with Vic Wakeling [head of Sky TV sports] and Gareth Southgate [football manager]. Liked Vic a lot. Gareth was genuinely nice, and smart too. Met Gabe Turner and [scientist Lord] Robert Winston's son Ben who make films – including the Flintoff film on depression – and want to do one with me re. mental illness too. Good guys. Really good laugh. I reckoned it would be good to work with them.

Thursday 3 May

Breakfast with Tessa, David and Jessie for Grace's birthday. Tessa saying Ken had no chance, and a good candidate would have walked it. I had to leave early for a very good session with Andy McCann. I went through the recent panic attacks in detail and coming up with a few exercises on stress and panic. Nice guy. Liked him a lot. He was using some of the PTSD [post-traumatic stress disorder] stuff. Jonathan [Powell] round to do an interview for a radio programme he was doing on summits. As ever he was in a rush. Off to North Korea soon for his peace charity work. Francis Campbell had made an interesting point re. JoP and me, that it would have been easy for two poles of official power to have developed but we were both team players and made sure it never happened and also both confident enough of our own abilities and positions not to worry too much. We had the local party committee rooms set up downstairs with Calum directing. Grace and pals out knocking on doors. Tessa thought Boris would win by 6 per cent or more.

Friday 4 May

Blog on the elections, as it was clear fairly early on the Tories were in a lot of trouble. Long chat with Alex who called en route to training. He was chuffed re. Glasgow going Labour after all the talk of the SNP winning it, and thought people had really seen through Cameron now, even if they hadn't before. Worked a.m. then lunch with Richard Layard to talk about a report he was preparing on mental health losing out in the NHS. Wanted help with publicising it. Ed getting the tone right on the reaction to the elections – doing well but still more to do. Then off to *Newsnight* to do the panel with Danny Finkelstein and Miranda Green [political journalist]. I said the Nadine Dorries [Tory MP] jibe re. two posh boys [Cameron and Osborne] who didn't know the price of milk had connected, also that the CV problem was big – competence, values and vision all gone. Home to watch Boris win. For the Tories it was the only sliver of good news and of course it would move to Boris being a challenger to Cameron.

Saturday 5 May

Really struggling with the new iPhone. Totally hate the keypad. Also having a few teething problems with the new Apple computer. I was not quite as sold on the Steve Jobs [chairman, Apple Inc.] sanctification as so many other people seemed to be.

Sunday 6 May

City won at Newcastle so that was about it really. United beat Swansea at home afterwards but the non-celebration when they scored showed that they had basically assumed City would beat QPR next week and the title was lost. It was hard to disagree with the notion that City were the better team. I left the United game at half-time and went up to do a bit more on the Leveson stuff.

Monday 7 May

Bank Holiday. Did the Kazakh call. There was definitely a bit of progress in the right direction and the team were producing loads of good work, even if the media briefs were a bit depressing. Out on the bike then out for dinner with Mick Hucknall and Gabriella at Locatelli's. Mick doing the usual mega expensive wine and champagne. A bit down on United but like me felt they had not deserved it over the whole season. Politically he was thinking Cameron was shit but that Ed wasn't really up to it. There was too much of that kind of talk around. Fiona had spoken to Justine [EM's wife] and said she seemed really panicked when F mentioned – as had others to us – that Ed's nose seemed if anything worse after the operation, and that it was kind of receding into his face. She spoke later to Iain Hutchinson and agreed he could do something about it.

Tuesday 8 May

With Fiona to [*Daily Mirror* royal correspondent] James Whitaker's memorial at St Bride's. It was terrific. Good turnout, good speeches, especially Annie Robinson, and a fantastic rendition of 'Bohemian Rhapsody' from the choir. Nice to see so many old *Mirror* colleagues, loads and loads of them, lots of the snappers too. Lovely atmosphere at the do as well. Arthur Edwards [*Sun* photographer] asked me to give John Kay [*Sun* reporter] a call as he was struggling. I hadn't realised Arthur's son John [picture editor] had also been lifted re. police payments.* Arthur said the truth was there were very few bad apples, and he was pissed off at the way John had been dropped in it. I talked to John Kay later and he seemed genuinely touched I had called him. I said he had a lot of friends rooting for him. I said I had never forgotten his kindness when I was a young reporter. I said I did not think he would be a main target but I could tell he was really worried.

---

* John Edwards was later acquitted of two counts of conspiracy to commit misconduct in public office.

Meeting with Diane Goslar about the event in Brussels re. alcohol dependence report. She was an alcoholic who was part of the seminar we were doing on Thursday. She was nervous about it and wanted to talk through the whole thing. Tim Allan called to say did I want to go to the 30 Club dinner where Prince William and Kate were going, and he was due to make a speech and do Q&A. Sounded like fun. Big posh black-tie job, lots of the comms industry there. Nice chat with Andrew Knight [director, News Corporation] who felt the select committee had been ridiculous to say Rupert was not a fit and proper person. He said he had told Rupert in terms he had to take the rest of it on the chin and the whole board had said so. He felt Rupert was damaged and knew it, but did not think we should go down the regulation route.

Had to do the whole room standing bit when William and Kate arrived. He spoke reasonably well. A couple of OK funny lines. Said what he was passionate about – young unemployed, veterans, wildlife – but then talked mainly about great ordinary people he had met, and what made him tick. It was a bit formulaic but OK. He made a big defence of his dad which may have been part of the purpose of the event. William said his dad was used to the brickbats but he and Harry were proud of him and the way he really tried to make a difference. Bigged up the Queen. Talked about the values he believed in – courage, humility, selflessness, duty, sacrifice, good manners – fairly traditional stuff but he said he preferred to call it timeless. Then he did a Q&A which felt all a bit planted, but then when I was called I realised it was a mix. They were getting some tame ones but it was definitely genuinely open. A bit of a frisson titter when I was called, and then a laugh when I couldn't say what my organisation was.

I asked if, when Charles and then he were King, they would follow the Queen's brilliant media management strategy of never ever giving an interview? And also would he ever think of going on Twitter? I'm not sure he realised she had never done an interview. He said maybe it could be different. He certainly felt there should be a bit of mystique. Said he had looked at Twitter and didn't like it. He was pretty open, fairly relaxed, definitely easier in himself than Charles. Other questions – what would he make programmes on, what did he hope for the Jubilee, nothing too tricky. She looked pretty good and together they went down well. The pre and post speeches about them were way too cloying and, afterwards, Tom Bradby, who was sitting next to Kate, said they didn't really like all the OTT stuff. Texted Paddy [Harverson] later to say he did well. Tim very helpful re. Sky and how in truth the Murdoch political profile may have worked against him when it came to policy decisions.

Wednesday 9 May

Queen's Speech day. I was invited to the Speaker's reception but had too much stuff on, not least since I got my reading list from Leveson. Portland partners meeting. Tim chaired well. Some good young people there. Tony Ball [chairman] and I chipping in with thoughts and advice. Home to do a bit of work, rest up and then out to Dorchester for the Intellect [financial technology] dinner. Vince Cable pre-dinner speaker, me post-dinner. He told a very funny story about when canvassing a woman whose husband had just died but she said don't worry he had a postal vote. He did a fairly bog standard 'where we are on the economy' speech, managed to avoid being too political. I had a little chat with him and he had definitely lost a fair bit of his sparkle. I had a nice crowd at my table and for once totally enjoyed the dinner. Nice food, nice company and when it came to the speech I was really on form. Played mainly for laughs and then a bit about negativity and their importance to the economy. Then into the back of a car and off to the tunnel and Brussels.

Thursday 10 May

Arrived 4.30 a.m. I took a pill and slept the whole way, including through passport control and the train. Managed to get a couple of hours in the Radisson then out to meet the Lundbeck [pharmaceutical company] team who took me to the Parliament. Back in a place that had always produced a fair bit of stress. Crazy all the mobile catering, the lovely paintings etc. What a waste. Pretty good event. Video from Danish health minister. A couple of MEPs, including a very spiky Bulgarian, Antonyia Parvanova, who was saying alcohol was worse than tobacco, Glenis Willmott [leader European Parliamentary Labour Party] chairing, a guy from the WHO, an NGO, an academic, OK Q&A then book signing and off for lunch. I really felt this was an area I could make a difference, in terms of influencing policy on e.g. marketing and advertising but also just drawing attention to the scale of the problem. Diane Goslar spoke really well and I asked for her speech so I could put it on my website at the weekend.

On the train back I was following Coulson at Leveson via Twitter. He was clearly playing a very straight bat, but as they couldn't do phone hacking there was a bit of an odd feel to it. Stefan Stern emailed to say Toby Young [*Sun on Sunday* columnist] had said on Twitter that I had leaked my statement. I got Gerald [Shamash] on the case after I demanded an apology and he was pretty grudging. Met a guy from Deutsche Bank who felt we could win next time. He said Cameron was not taken seriously in Europe, and that Plan A was not working. I was feeling pretty knackered after last night's drive through the night.

Friday 11 May

Tim collected me and we headed to Heathrow to do a pitch to BAA. They wanted support both for the Olympics, which would give them their busiest day ever, and with the third runway. A team of four to greet and grill us, but I sensed it went well. Their first question after we did a basic presentation was what they called the 'Here today gone tomorrow' problem, so both Tim and I tried to persuade them I would stay involved. I said I only got involved in the issues I cared about. I had been blogging about third runway ever since Cameron made his opportunist move in opposition, and I was passionate about the Olympics. I think they liked the feel of what we were saying. Tim did well at these events, very urbane and charming, not too pushy or showy.

Martin Sheehan said the Brunswick [rival business advisory firm] team looked shell-shocked when they saw me arriving, so still had the reputation, I guess. Rebekah Brooks was at Leveson and was pretty defensive but felt by most of the commentators to have done OK. Not so sure. I dipped in and out of it in between trying to get my own preparation right. Fiona was going down with a bad dose of the flu and I was terrified of being ill on Monday.

Saturday 12 May

Pottered around for hours just going over all the stuff again and again. Good chats with Godric and then Charlie F who both felt the statement was fine and I just had to keep focused on those big arguments. Charlie said he thought Leveson would be mainly interested in my ideas for the future. I felt they would give me a hard time over TB/Murdoch. Early evening out to the Emirates to meet Jan Åge Fjørtoft who had roped me in for a charity football match with the German TV firm he worked with. Nice bunch. We had to play two games of forty-five minutes and I did both in full, and we won easily. Mind you it helped that we had the only ex-pros. Nice atmosphere and good fun.

The dressing rooms were terrific though the towels ran red ink over everyone who used them. I played pretty well and didn't feel too much off the pace. Jan really nice. Martin Keown [former player, TV pundit] there to watch and I had a good chat with him. He was quite interested in politics, but above all was taking the piss out of Alan Shearer [former player, TV pundit] for being dull, predictable and always saying 'But' and 'I have to say'. He said Alan Hansen [fellow pundit] earned forty times more per show than himself. Nice little do afterwards.

Sunday 13 May

Had a chat with Robert Jay re. tomorrow. He said he had not been terribly impressed by Brooks. He asked what I thought of how it was all going. I said fine, but there was a danger it was becoming a chattering class soap opera. That being said I was amazed how many people seemed to be following it quite closely. He said he was loving it, having a great time. I said I felt they were on the right track and that untough regulation was a non-starter. Watched the end of the Premier League p.m. City scored winner against United in injury time to clinch the title. United had had a few minutes thinking they had won it, but then it all evaporated. Alex gutted but was pretty gracious in his interviews.

Back to the office to work on tomorrow. Then an email came in saying one of the core participants, presumably the *Mail*, had asked me to be asked about the Black Rod episode.* Odd. So I had to read up on that, as well as get the papers from the Cabinet Office. Spoke to Catherine Rimmer and Clare Sumner who remembered it better than I did.

Monday 14 May

Gus O'Donnell at Leveson first. Dipped in and out. He was a bit over satisfied with himself and trying to joke a fair bit with Leveson. Managed to get the Black Rod papers and get my head round that. I went in in the pouring rain, and felt totally confident. I had a meeting with Jay and his team first and once he had gone through a few things ended up just chatting. He was clearly not very fond of the Murdoch lot. He told me in confidence that John Major would also be coming. I didn't feel as nervous as the last time. He warmed up fairly gently, reading out TB's book on how he hired me, how I was a 'genius' with 'clanking great balls'. Move on, said Leveson. He did it fairly thematically and the only time I felt under any pressure at all was when Leveson clearly felt it was odd that TB spoke to Murdoch three times in the days before the war in Iraq. I was able to say something about the call but only from my diary not memory, though to be fair I did not do nearly as much 'cannot recall' as the News lot.

Jay did not really press me hard. I kind of knew I had won when Quentin Letts [*Daily Mail* sketch writer] sloped out, looking a bit disappointed. The gallery not nearly as busy as last time. I fucked up when I said the euro referendum was one of the five party pledges on the 1997 'pledge

---

* In 2000 *The Spectator* had claimed 'a Downing Street aide' had contacted Black Rod, a senior House of Lords officer, and asked if Tony Blair would be able to greet the Queen and the coffin of the Queen Mother as it arrived at Westminster Hall for lying-in-state prior to her funeral. Amid press accusations that the Prime Minister was trying to 'muscle in' in the arrangements, Downing Street lodged a complaint with the Press Complaints Commission, only for AC later to inform the PCC that Downing Street saw no reason to take the matter further unless the allegations were repeated.

card', but Mark Bennett texted me to say it wasn't so I corrected that. Leveson appeared to nod off at one point. It certainly lacked the electricity of say Hutton [Hutton Inquiry into the death of Dr David Kelly], though I suppose I was somewhat the meat in the big sandwich bits of the News people and later the PMs. TB due in two weeks, Cameron 14 June. GB also going and likely to be interesting! I did put the boot into Charlie Whelan a bit, though not GB. I had a read of the transcript later and really felt it went fine. Jay seemed to enjoy it. Also had a chat with Elinor Goodman [former political editor, *Channel 4 News*], George Jones [political journalist, member of the inquiry] and the assessors. George said that Leveson was definitely leaning to the hard end of the market. A fair few snappers and cameras as I left but I was smiling and chilled and there was a fair bit of comment to that effect.

Fiona said the website went down at one point. Trending on Twitter and on balance fairly positive. Popped into Portland to wind down a bit, cup of tea with Bradders, then home. Saw DS and he felt stay on the pills for now, though I was actually feeling not too bad. Meanwhile news emerged that Rebekah Brooks was to find out tomorrow if she was to be charged, so that took the news, though the Beeb did a fair chunk on my evidence and it was pretty fair. Out to Union Club with Grace for a dinner for Axelle Lemaire, the Parti Socialiste candidate for the National Assembly Constituency of Northern Europe, ten countries, with London her base.

She introduced me, I spoke about her campaign and also what Hollande's win might mean for the rest of Europe, where the mood was changing already, and even Cameron was beginning to join in the pressure on Merkel to move from such strict austerity towards growth. Hypocrisy but a sign of the times. The Q&A was fairly straightforward. Axelle suggested that in relation to some of Hollande's ideas, he didn't intend to put them into practice. She was pretty impressive, clearly to the left of us I would say, but sharp. I chatted to her about the logistics of a campaign covering ten countries where she was limited re. fundraising. Agreed to do an event in Ireland together. TB called later, seemed to think today had gone fine. I think re. him Leveson would be interested in the relationships and also the extent to which he had not done the right thing because of a sense of the power they had. Pretty good feedback on website about the second submission.

Tuesday 15 May
In for a meeting with Dick Caborn and lots of PR firms re. the Labour fundraiser. Tim and Matt Carter both saying there needed to be a policy element

to make it work. Dick could be infuriating with his OTT claims of what we would be able to do with the dinner and Margaret M infuriating with her manner of talking to everyone as though they were three, but their hearts were in the right place. Off to see Nicola [Howson]. Matthew still hardly in work, and she wasn't sure why. Just that he was going through a change. Rebekah was charged and she and her husband were lashing out at the CPS [Crown Prosecution Service]. Out later to do CNN with Christiane Amanpour. Felt OK on all the big arguments on this stuff at the moment.

Wednesday 16 May

The Queen was in Burnley, including lunch at Turf Moor. Blogged on why Cameron had lots of reasons to be nervous about Hollande winning. Hollande was looking the part already and though he had been soaked to the skin, and his plane struck by lightning, and there was an odd moment where he and Merkel bumped into each other on the red carpet, he looked confident. Ed did OK at PMQs. Cameron had another dig at me, suggesting that Coulson and others didn't get DV status [Developed Vetting, required for access to secret documents] because of me. I wrote to Jeremy [Heywood] to complain. Out for dinner at [mental health campaigner Lord] Dennis Stevenson's. Nice bloke though a bit Tiggerish, but really sound on mental health and wanted to brief me both on stuff he was doing via a private members' Bill but also in relation to research.

He said Eliza Manningham-Buller said DS's job was to keep Jonathan alive. He had a lot of respect for what he was doing. Dennis claimed to be non-political, didn't rate the Tories but felt Ed was not a leader. His wife, who came in late on from a dinner with Russians, was posh Labour. More left-wing than I was, he said. It was a nice enough evening, a mix of gossip and chat and a bit of work re. mental health. He was worried about TB's profile and reputation. Remained an unadulterated fan but not sure why he had slipped so much in the public's eyes.

Thursday 17 May

GQ magazine round to do an interview re. the party leaders, my review of the year past and the year ahead. The mood was definitely getting more negative re. DC, a bit more positive re. Ed, and fairly static re. Clegg. Meanwhile I did a blog on the extent to which Cameron and Osborne blamed others all the time. So did Lansley, who had been slow-handclapped by nurses this week, and [Teresa] May [Home Secretary] who copped it from the cops. Now Hague was saying we didn't work hard enough, Gove was constantly slagging off the teachers. It was a very unappealing trait. A day at the cricket, first day of the first Test v West Indies as a guest of Mark Dransfield [property developer]. His wife Debs gave me a hard time all day, saying I was one of the few people in politics who could make a point, stand up for myself, knew what I believed, and I had a duty to become an MP. Geoff Thomas also a guest as Mark had been a big supporter of LLR, and chatted to him a fair bit. Nice day though cricket is definitely a sport you can watch better on TV, like cycling and golf.

Friday 18 May

Ran to the Trafalgar Hotel, taking twenty minutes longer than I was doing ten years ago. Met Craig Oliver. Jeremy still hadn't replied to my complaint re. Cameron, though he had promised to yesterday. Craig said he had not meant it to come out like it did. Yeah right. Jeremy meanwhile had said last night, when I suggested he try to stop Cameron being so nasty and silly, that he did not buy the line re. Craig being the new me. 'He is stuck in a groove.' Craig talked mainly Leveson at first. He said Cameron was doing a lot of preparation. He picked my brains on where I thought Leveson was heading. I felt he was going for statutory then independent regulation. He felt that Rebekah had not been impressive, that Jay had tied her up in relation to this idea that she only reflected what readers wanted. He thought GB would be the PM most worried, but I felt that was wishful thinking. Cameron Leveson witness on 14 June apparently. He was finding the new mood quite tough. The negativity and the difficulty to get things on their agenda. I said Cameron did too much and he was too day to day. Had to build up ministers.

He reckoned Ed was doing better but that Cameron still won on the 'prime ministerial sniff test'. He had wondered whether Geordie Greig [London *Evening Standard* editor] to edit the *MoS* was a move to make the *Mail* less vile. I felt it was tactical pre Leveson. I guess I did most of the talking and he just let off a bit of steam re. the job and how it was getting harder, said he liked having someone he could talk to who had been there. I sensed he did the job very differently to me though, for example not being with Cameron in the States where he was about to meet Hollande and then head to Camp David for the G8. Big stuff and he wasn't there. Did a few errands then to the Royal Free for an ultrasound check-up on my stomach. Two nice nurses who then called in first a doctor and then a consultant because they had spotted two cysts on my liver. The consultant said they were probably nothing to worry about but I should have an MRI. I had not been able to eat all day so went for a huge meal in Dominique's.

Saturday 19 May

Alex taken to hospital last night, with a nosebleed that just wouldn't stop. He had been due to speak at a Rangers dinner in Glasgow but could not stop the bleed. They staunched it and he headed home but by this morning it had started again. Better later on but he sounded a bit woozy. Catherine sent through a few TB ideas for Leveson which I sent on to Charlie F who did an excellent job on them, broadening and deepening and analysing where he thought Leveson's mind was. Edi called, chatted re. Meta. The other big drama recently was a Democratic Party MP who owned a football club seemingly going into the dressing room of the opposing team with a bunch of thugs firing at the ceiling as a warning. Cameron at the G8 and also meeting Hollande, Eurozone crisis back on full steam so he was dominating the news again, but it came over very oddly that he was backing austerity for the UK but criticising Merkel for her approach out there.

Monday 21 May

Portland for a meeting with Tim/Adrian re. selling strategy sessions, then photos and an interview with Danny Rogers for *PR Week*. Lunch with Nicola at a nice Spanish restaurant in Goodge St. Matthew still not in working much. Indeed, Danny had told me he felt MF still hugely affected by PG's death. I felt OK with Danny setting out why I was taking on the role with Portland but still wanted to keep the freedoms I had. Later agreed letters to staff and clients and also a statement for the website where I kept in references to all the other stuff I do. In to town again p.m. to do an interview for the ITV documentary on *Chariots of Fire*. I had watched it again over the weekend and one of the odd things was how much I empathised with people I would not normally empathise with, e.g. the posh boys. Emphasised the power of sport and of the human spirit. Played the Vangelis theme tune on the pipes. I was still chasing Jeremy Heywood for a response to the Cameron slur of last PMQs.

Tuesday 22 May

Finally got a response from Jeremy and I replied that I didn't intend to take it further but I was not very happy with it as I was the only 'specific individual' named by Cameron and the reply largely echoed his comments.

I wrote back pointing out that it was the second time he had slurred me in this way and if he did so outside the House I would not hesitate to take further action. Really low politics.

Anyway that was that. Out for coffee with David Millar [Scottish road racing cyclist] at Café Nero opposite the Ritz. He was in between races in Norway and Bavaria and had been over for a book awards (which he didn't win). He was taller and thinner than I expected. He was a good talker, very open about himself and what he thought of cycling. A little bit torn re. whether to ride in the Olympics if chosen. I felt he should. He reckoned Bradley Wiggins [multi-medal-winning cyclist] could win the Tour and that [Mark] Cavendish [British cyclist] could win the gold and Cav would definitely want him in the team. Later to PwC for a meeting with David Newton and team re. the event I was doing in Barcelona next month. Went through clips to use for the seminar on how not to do crisis management. Did a blog saying this could be a one-term government and we needed to raise the cash to fight them.

Wednesday 23 May

Churchill Hotel for speech to the conference of Australian pension funds industry. I was fairly measured, thinking there would be a fair few Murdoch supporters in there but they were more violent than I was. One of them said Murdoch was so toxic he was 'uninvestable'. Speech, Q&A then a panel debate including with David Pitt-Watson [financial adviser] of Hermes, who was also of the view Murdoch was toxic and the whole thing had been badly handled. But he and I were also both saying it was odd they were looking at this re. Murdoch but not, e.g., arms, tobacco, China, Saudi or whatever. The *PR Week* story about me and Portland went out, pretty big online, OK on most of the broadsheet websites, only the *Mail* really sniffing around to cause trouble.

Out later for the drinks at the Portland dinner for Lionel Barber. Lots of people saying congratulations re. the Portland 'job' and I was saying you should be congratulating them! Lionel on good form, said he was going to be doing the TB profile, also that he was planning to stay in UK more (like TB!). He didn't buy my line that pension funds would pull the plug on Murdoch. Off to the Hilton for a quick speech to the BMJ [*British Medical Journal*] Awards. Mind were the charity of choice so I did my usual spiel which went down OK. Paul Farmer told me demand for Mind services was up 20 per cent. Home via quick meeting with Andy McCann at his hotel. Felt he was a good influence. But anxiety picking up again.

Thursday 24 May

Off to Stamford Bridge in searing heat for the Cystic Fibrosis v MPs match. No ex-pros but we still beat them 9–1. Only Andy Burnham up to much. I played OK and was the only one to play the whole game. Nice little do after. To the Landmark for the Recruitment and Employment Council dinner. Nice crowd, very international, Gyles Brandreth [writer, former Tory MP] very funny compère, I did OK and best of all signed up a few people for the Labour dinner. Fred Michel and Adam Smith at Leveson. More pressure on Hunt and also big questions re. Cameron judgement in giving him the BSkyB brief. He had taken it from Cable because of an a priori position, but given it to Hunt who had expressed the opposing view publicly. Gyles Brandreth gave me a massive build-up, virtually said I had single-handedly destroyed his party for a decade!

The REC boss Kevin Green and his wife Sharon were huge Labour supporters and she was so keen for TB and me to get back in the frontline. The mood generally re. the government was negative. David Arkless, president of Manpower, felt they were clueless re. strategy. Lots of foreign companies there and I was on pretty good form so got a few inquiries re. other events. Earlier good chat with Edward [Campbell, son of AC cousin Lachie] re. his dad, and why he killed himself. Drink the big thing but Edward said both he and John thought depression.

Friday 25 May

Birthday. Presents all sorted earlier when F and I agreed to buy two amazing paintings from the Catto Gallery in Hampstead. Really nice. Catherine Rimmer called re. Nick Cohen [Observer] going for TB over Kazakhstan. Conference call to agree an approach. Off to Burnley for the Barry Kilby dinner. Traffic crap as ever. Five hours to Fletch's. To Turf Moor to do some filming then the event. Good mood. Old players there. Highlight the video of Barry's time and then I did an interview with him. He was very open and relaxed. The Fergie video clip was well received. Owen Coyle got booed a few times when he came on. The players seemed a bit disappointed by that, but hey-ho. Played the pipes, also got a massive cake from the club. God knows what I would do with it. I think Barry enjoyed the evening and he got a fantastic reception all night.

Saturday 26 May

Tired. Slept really badly. I texted DS to ask whether the acidic excessive saliva production might be a reaction to the pills. He thought not, but it was odd that three times now, immediately after taking the pills, I had this reaction, mouth filling with saliva, then tightness in chest. Not panicky but not nice. Good chat with Fletch re. friendship. He had been reading The Happy Depressive, and we did our analysis re. happiness. He said he once heard a happiness speaker who said the three biggest decisions we ever make are – who we live with (relationships), what we live in (house, car, clothes, environment), and what we live for (values). Good one. Set off but was yawning the whole time. Five hours home. Out on the bike then later out to Kingston for Fiona Ferguson's 40th. I knew Mark had done well for himself but no idea how well. The house, which used to be Ronnie Wood's, was astonishing. Fifteen bathrooms. Virtually a football pitch in the garden. Huge indoor pool. We arrived at the same time as Alex who was looking OK but said he had had a terrible week and still felt a bit ropy, if much, much better. 'It was a warning, that's for sure.' He had been shaving at the hotel in Glasgow before leaving for a dinner and suddenly noticed a drop of blood. Then it flooded out and didn't stop. By the time he was in hospital there were whole towels covered in blood. He was off the booze and looked better for it but said the problem was one of the drugs he was taking related to the heart and blood had thinned. He was on good form though.

He and I and one or two others were the only ones who didn't obey the edict to dress as gypsies. Certainly the bulk of people there were well-heeled, either his financial services pals or yummy mummies from the neighbourhood in Kingston. No expense spared on the booze or disco front either. I like him and Fiona though, both a good laugh. Mick and Gabriella arrived so Fiona and Gabriella were off round the house while we talked football, politics etc. Nick Clegg's house had been targeted by UK Uncut [protest groups network] protesters which would get him sympathy. Idiots. Not nice. Alex pretty much over the disappointment of the end of the season. He said the thing is we threw it away, you cannot say we were cheated. I played Happy Birthday on the pipes, then a few reels and jigs and got a fair few of them up dancing. Fiona said she felt a bit out of the comfort zone but for all their wealth Alex and Cathy, Bridget [Cathy's sister] and John [her husband] were all pretty down to earth still. Home by twelve.

Sunday 27 May

Pretty vicious piece in *The Observer* from Nick Cohen, saying TB's work in Kazakhstan is proof that he has lost all morality. Tim and I thrown in there of course. Not good and I suggested they get a rebuttal, not least to get some of the reform messages out from TB's speech in Kazakhstan on Thursday. Meanwhile he was preparing most of the day for Leveson tomorrow, though the bulk of advance coverage focused on Hunt who was going on Thursday. Did a quick blog on Osborne whose star was falling. Mentioned the Nadine Dorries whack at them as posh boys who don't know the price of milk, which was definitely working its way through.

May '12: Piping at Fergie's son's birthday party

Monday 18 June

Wow, several weeks since I put anything in here. I drafted something when we had a week in France but lost it when switching to a new phone. iPhone. Hate the keypad. Hate the iMac too, and tweeted a real slug at Apple, forgetting that they were one of Portland's biggest clients. Portland stuff going OK generally though. Helped win the BAA [British Airports Authority] pitch and also Funding Circle [small business investment], after stopping in to see them on the way back from France. Interesting how I was so slacking on the diary front though. It wasn't as if I was doing nothing or not being involved in a few interesting things. E.g. during the holiday Craig Oliver calling to pick my brains about how Cameron should pitch himself at Leveson. Ed called a few times too, wanting the same kind of advice.

TB was easily the best of the former PMs at Leveson, really showed an understanding of the issues, and good tone. GB was all smouldering and really unbelievable when it came to claiming he never used the press to undermine TB, or to do others. Major was Major, Cameron was Cameron, hated being challenged. Wonderful tweet – he hasn't been talked to like this since he was at school. Fiona and I went to see *Posh* at one point, a satire on the Bullingdon Club, and pretty stomach-churning. There are people like this and they run the country. I also chaired a debate on the play with Luciana Berger [Labour MP], Rachel Johnson [journalist sister of Boris], the producer and an Oxford don. Went well, and Rachel no less came out and said class in Britain would not change until private schools were gone. Audience was pretty posh though, and it was only when this became a film that it would have a major political impact I think.

The government were really struggling at the moment, loads of mistakes, no big strategy and now trying to use the Eurozone crisis as the fall guy for the double dip recession. Euro and Syria overhanging everything though Leveson was attracting massive coverage, with the papers trying to shape it away from statutory regulation, and Cameron clearly wanting to help them.

France was good. I flew out with John Mills [Labour-supporting businessman] the morning after recording *Have I Got News For You*, which I enjoyed and which seemed to go down well. Mixed views on Twitter, lots thinking Hislop really did me on Iraq but I felt he was not that harsh and, as the comedian Ross Noble tweeted, I showed I could take it as well as give it out, and 'fair play'. He was brilliant and somewhat put Merton in the shade, who later told me he was not a depressive, that he once had a reaction to anti-malarial tablets and it all came from that. I liked him though. Felt Hislop really did have a bit of an animus but I nonetheless persuaded him to do an LLR event in the autumn. One of the writers told me Hislop had not wanted to have me on at all, and they had never known that before.

It was an interesting process. Full-time gag writers, though I did some of my own. Recorded loads and loads and basically the ones that got the best laughs stayed in. Got into another satire row when the honours came out mid-June and Armando Iannucci [writer of *The Thick of It*] had accepted an OBE. I tweeted that Tucker and I did not approve of honours, he tweeted back re. Iraq/WMD and all his supporters went wild. Tessa Damehood!

David Muir checked out GB who said he was feeling a bit like a football. But the truth is he did not have a strategy for getting himself to a better place, and his Leveson appearance played to all his bad bits. TB was doing a bit more on the media front. Ed was doing OK, still looking a bit insubstantial but he was definitely in a better position. Osborne's star was falling. Gove was the key man on Leveson I sensed, but Leveson really put him down when he was there.

The other highlight in France was a day with David Millar in the Garmin-Sharp team car. Blogged on it, trying to convey the sense of closeness and also what you miss as well as what you see. Rory starting at Barnet full-time as part of the youth coaching staff which was good. Helping Calum with the sports fundraiser though not with the same level of commitment I did previously. We had our usual day at Queen's tennis, the final, and David Nalbandian [Argentinian player] had a rush of blood and kicked a hoarding, injured a linesman, and got disqualified. Nice chat with John Bercow. He felt Ed was getting stronger and Cameron weaker. He was getting a fair bit of grief from Tories for inviting Aung San Suu Kyi [leader of the Burmese Assembly opposition] to address both Houses next week, but said he had told Lord [Tom] Strathclyde [hereditary peer] he didn't think he was very well placed to lecture on democracy, and reeled off his half-dozen posh middle names. We were Roger Draper's guests but surrounded by the usual Old Etonian types. Seemingly 65 per cent of members were ex-Eton. They couldn't make speeches to save their life either.

My usual pre-publication angst, and a new illness, GERD [gastroesophageal reflux disease], which was like an acid reflux thing and a bit of a nightmare, causing me to lose sleep on several nights. Andy McCann was a real help calming things down at the psychological end. And Emma [Mitchell] was pretty good at making sure the programme wasn't too ridiculous. I ended up doing a fair few live interviews on Day 1 of the *Guardian* serialisation, which seemed to go OK. Speech circuit still rumbling on. I guess at the moment books, speeches, Portland, international consultancy and charity the main planks of what I was doing.

TB stepping up his domestic profile a bit. Lionel Barber in the Middle East with him. Olympics really picking up. Amazing crowds for the torch as it travelled the country. Diamond Jubilee also getting massive and very positive play. David Mills, arch Republican, told me he had given up. Queen fantastic, Charles improving, Kate and William stitched up for a generation. 'Not happening in our lifetime.' For sure. There was definitely something that was taking the country backwards in this regard, but equally it was clearly what people wanted. Stability when there was so much of the opposite to contend with. The Euros were going OK. England dull but doing all right.

The Craig Oliver calls were quite interesting, even if Cameron couldn't resist having a pop at me when he gave his evidence, saying I was more political than Coulson and that I overstepped the mark. Oliver had been pressing me on how in practice anything could be done about the fusion of news and comment, and we went round and round for ages, just as I did with Ed M when we were staying overnight in Langres, and he called re. whether he should steer clear of that area. In the end he did, though he went pretty far on ownership and regulation. According to Nick Watt, who was handling the *Guardian* serialisation stuff, Ed was coming into his own, really getting the bigger calls right. Also, Balls was picking up ratings-wise on the economy, and Osborne really looked like he had lost whatever touch he had.

Part 2 of the serial focused on 'brilliant but bonkers' re. GB so I did a blog to try to recalibrate a bit. I got David Muir to speak to him. He said he was pretty sore and feeling a bit like a football but he acknowledged it could have been worse. I sent GB an email to say I was sorry it was resurrected but also to say that it was his Leveson evidence that had decided them on that course. In truth he just about got away with his claim that he didn't do in TB, brief against etc., but I was worried re. how I was going to answer questions about it. I did the Kaz call, then revision with Grace and a call from Dr Stewart re. my GERD – he called it GORD, oesophagus v enterological – then out to do an hour with Richard Bacon. Good interview as ever. Really liked him, but he did press hard on GB. He had a really nice style though and as ever had clearly read the book.

Later to King's Place for [political commentator] Steve Richards's 'Rock 'n' Roll politics'. Nice interview with him and then a really good and varied Q&A which I ended up blogging about for the Huffington Post, and in particular the question about whether we were flattered or annoyed that Cameron and co. secretly hero-worshipped TB and team. Really good range of questions though and in so far as any were hostile it was directed at TB or politics more generally rather than me. Rory Bremner called to say he was totally with me re. Iannucci and that he had turned an OBE down. He said he was really surprised and agreed with my line that people like them should not take honours when so much of their work is taking the piss out of politicians and royals.

Tuesday 19 June

Loose Women the main media thing of the day. On with Gareth Gates [singer-songwriter] so a fair bit of Twitter piss taking re. that. I met him in makeup, where I was having a haircut and he introduced me to his 'speech coach'. I said I could do that. He said no, it was a different kind of speech coach. I had no idea – to Emma's astonishment – that he had a really bad stammer. We chatted away about nerves and how to deal with them and he seemed OK but once he got out there it all fell apart a bit. Stammered quite badly. Really felt for him. I was on after a break, during which the warm-up man told some of the filthiest jokes I had ever heard and the all-women audience seemed to love it. Carol Vorderman [media personality] chaired the interview with [actress] Denise Welch (fellow depressive and said *All in the Mind* was her favourite book).

It went fine, lots of people tweeting they were fawning all over me, though CV sneaked in a nasty one, namely would I give any money from the book to soldiers' charities as TB did. Lunch with Emma then meeting at LLR and home. Emma had set the week up pretty well, not doing too much, but enough to build up gently. I was writing a fair bit too, as well as helping Grace as much as I could with her French and politics, and watching loads of the Euros. England doing better than expected but Germany easily the best team there.

Wednesday 20 June

Out early for *Midweek* [radio show]. Really excited about meeting Frank Ifield [country music singer] who turned out to be a really nice bloke. I persuaded him and magician Romany that they should both be on Twitter. The other guest fashion designer Tommy Roberts so an eclectic mix. The chat whizzed by. Can't really remember what Libby Purves asked me, but I loved the stuff from Ifield on how he once had The Beatles as a warm-up act and showed them how to do makeup. He also made a record with them, but didn't have a copy of it. Would be worth a lot. Nice programme.

Off to Southwark St for a meeting to brainstorm with Funding Circle. I think we were all in roughly the same place – taking the pain out of finance, doing better than the banks, growth the big theme. My best idea was getting ordinary people called Fred Goodwin, Stephen Hester, Bob Diamond [former CEO, Barclays Bank] and having posters saying 'Meet your bank manager.'* Though Tim would have a problem with Diamond as Portland were helping him now.

* Diamond had resigned his post in April following controversy over manipulation of Libor (London Inter-Bank Offered Rate) interest rates by Barclays' traders.

Home for a bit, potter, then to Queen Mary's Uni. Sally M and Tessa there so I used both as foils, Sally pulling faces and Tessa being late and then looking at her BlackBerry the whole time. Tessa called later and said it just showed how it was still possible to persuade people if you had an argument and built it with confidence. Nice event and glad I did it. Few interviews then to the Italian in South End Green to meet Fiona. *Mail* broke the story that Gove wanted to bring back O Levels. Idiot. He was totally setting himself up as the darling of the right and the media.

Thursday 21 June

Publication day. Out early for Sky. Eamonn Holmes hadn't read the book and didn't even know I was on until minutes before but he busked it really well. Lovely guy. I got a bit panicky at the Kelly section though not as bad as before and recovered OK. Into town via 'Limobike', a motorbike taxi which took less than half the time of a car and got me to LBC just in time. Really enjoyed it. I was due to do an hour with Nick Ferrari but they cut to half an hour because Jimmy Carr had apologised for his tax arrangements, revealed in *The Times*, who were doing a huge thing on tax avoidance. Cameron had weighed in from Mexico where he had said Carr's scheme was 'morally wrong'. Typically idiotic because it meant that all their big donors – not to mention Gary Barlow [musician] who was using a similar scheme – would now come under scrutiny.

Off to Fred MacAulay [Scots comedian] down the line for BBC Scotland, funny as ever. Toing and froing re. Channel 5, but in the end I decided not to in case I missed the surprise 60th for Bradders. He didn't have a clue. Verity at Portland had done a great *This Is Your Life* [biographical TV show] which I presented from birth to Portland, then Tim took over. The staff loved it not least because DB [David Bradshaw] was so popular. Really nice do. Played Happy Birthday on the pipes, then off to the train for Durham. Late to bed, watching a good discussion on Gove, Adonis on form, a grammar school headteacher vituperative about the O Level idea, twat Toby Young as ever sticking up for his fellow twat.

Friday 22 June

Swim at the Radisson, breakfast, met a group who had been to the Bruce Springsteen concert at The Stadium of Light. Three and a half hours aged sixty-two. Lost my notes but one of the heads at the conference – it was a leadership conference for Durham headteachers – found them. Speech went really well, as warm as response as I could remember, followed by books getting sold out. I whacked Gove a bit, Q&A all nice and easy. On to *Sunday Politics London* for a discussion on Tory MP Gavin Barwell's private members' Bill re. mental health discrimination. He didn't look much but he spoke really well. Chatted with him afterwards. He told me Andrew Pelling ex-Tory had defected via independent to Labour and they were going to be up against each other at the election. Yet it had been Pelling's breakdown which had got him interested in the first place. Home afterwards, to learn Calum had been in meltdown last night, so I got really heavy with him. Fiona at a school event. I watched Germany batter Greece, tweeting happily in German about how good they were. As the week ended I felt that I had got through it OK. No massive dramas. Only the *Mail* really nasty – 'Dancing on David Kelly's grave' – good broadcast stuff, no real pressure on Iraq. Also feeling as I went round the place that people were pretty warm right now.

Saturday 23 June

Blogged re. Gove, and the fact that his beloved Murdoch was more responsible for dumbing down than the education system, and that he [Gove] was using the whole thing for his own personal and political ambitions and did not give a toss about kids. The reviews were OK. Excellent by Mullin – printed in *The Guardian* today. Aaronovitch in *The Times* really good. Phil Stephens a bit sniffy but not bad. Good online stuff too. Doing OK on Amazon.

Sunday 24 June

I spent most of yesterday late afternoon and evening dealing with the *Independent on Sunday*. Jane Merrick [political editor] having first said she was doing a short piece on the line that we were worried Goldsmith might resign, later I discovered that they were splashing on something else. I called Jane who said yes, they felt that the line about TB saying he did not want the Attorney General to present to Cabinet on 11 March was inconsistent with their evidence to Chilcot. I pointed out that Goldsmith duly went to Cabinet and was also able to point out from a later entry that he was challenged on his view and admitted to doubts. It felt like a non-story but with TB on *Marr* I had to get on top of it. Catherine R was helpful in going through Goldsmith's evidence and finding plenty of places where it helped support what I was saying. I started to tweet out that it was agenda-based journalism and also worked on a blog consisting mainly of quotes from Chilcot evidence.

Catherine had done a good rebuttal job – hardly anyone followed it up – and she had said to him to make sure he read my blog with all the quotes but when it came to that part of the interview he just looked irritable and did not really answer it as clearly as he could. It was a pain having to deal with all this again and of course there was still the outside chance of Chilcot deciding – as he was being asked to by Ming Campbell [former Lib Dem leader], [Peter] Kilfoyle [former Labour MP] and others – to recall. Happily it didn't make the morning news and the story being taken out of TB's interview was what he said about the euro and the continuing crisis. He was still saying one day we could be in it. It wasn't a bad interview and he got a fair bit of online traffic, broadly negative but with a fair bit of positive mixed in.

Monday 25 June

Early start, out to do *Daybreak* with Lorraine Kelly. Alistair Darling was launching the Better Together campaign against Scottish independence so I asked Lorraine if I could ask her her view. She said she wasn't allowed to say anything political. Nice enough interview and it went fine. Off with Emma Mitchell to Hatchards to sign stock, then a couple of calls before heading home, out on the bike in searing heat, doing a bit of radio and telly then to the 1000 Club summer reception at Ozer near the Beeb. Ed M spoke fine but it wasn't inspiring and we needed to be a lot further ahead given how shambolic the Tories were at the moment. Ed Balls there and quite chilly probably because of the book, though Yvette [Cooper] was quite warm. Chatted to Harriet a bit re. Leveson. I was more convinced than ever that Cameron was going to try to park it. I sensed at the do that there was a fair bit of coasting going on. Not enough bite and forward energy.

Tuesday 26 June

Another early start for *The Wright Stuff* [Channel 5 talk show]. Good stuff on the book, also stuff on mental health and public figures and a good discussion on literary hit *Fifty Shades of Grey* phenomenon. Fastest ever book to reach a million in the UK. I cracked a joke re. renaming the diaries *Fifty Shades of Power*. I was reading out tweets as they came in, including one asking me to replace Matthew W [presenter]. At the end I got a message from C5 they agreed – at least as a stand-in. Off to Waterloo to Gerald Shamash office for a meeting with police from Operation Weeting with Michelle Roycroft. Very nice woman. I greeted her with banter re. Yates and his work in Bahrain. She took it pretty well but said he was a really good boss. On hacking she just wanted to pick my brains on my time as a journalist and also my relationship with some of the key people she was looking into, especially Rebekah and Coulson.

I confirmed that Paul McMullan had said Coulson listened to voice-mail messages when I interviewed him but the lawyer wouldn't let us use it. I wasn't terribly sure of the purpose of the interview but she said she wanted to draft a statement for me based in part on Leveson. She had read my statements and transcripts and was also giving me a sense of the scale of the investigation. Gerald was trying to find out a bit more about where it was heading but she was pretty discreet. She did say, however, that they expected quite a lot of charges.

To a meeting of the Bible Society, Brian Mawhinney having asked me along. After the talk he said to the assembled, 'You have heard a master-class,' which was a bit over the top. The questions were all the fairly obvious ones – we don't do God, TB and faith, where I defended why I felt it was a mistake for UK politicians to go on too much about religion, and then more general stuff. They seemed a bit worn down and belea-guered but as ever it was because of media negativity.

Wednesday 27 June

The media was full of the Queen meeting Martin McGuinness though needless to say next to no mention of TB and his role getting there. Spain beat Portugal on penalties in a semi-final. Annoying as I was predicting Germany v Portugal final and had been right about a lot of games so far.

Thursday 28 June

Everything Everywhere [mobile network operator] event in Berkshire. Searingly hot. Lots of bright young things in a tent. Quite lively bunch though the poor things were having to stay in tents hence the event was called Brandstock. Back to see *Posh* with the girls. Second time around I was able to enjoy the jokes more though it was still pretty shocking and the girls were pretty horrified especially Anna [Sirius, Grace friend]. Meanwhile Italy beat Germany easily so that was both semis I got wrong.

Friday 29 June

DS. All a bit tame and in truth my main worries right now were not re. me but Calum. Went to see Liz and the kids at King's Cross, sorted them with centre court tickets.

Saturday 30 June

Freud Museum for a session on sport and psychotherapy! Mike Brearley [former England cricket captain] and I in conversation. I enjoyed talking to him. He kicked off interviewing me on the diaries and then broadening out to me asking him more about leadership in sport. Very Hampstead audience. Nice atmosphere. The Lionel Barber profile of TB appeared. A lot more snide than I expected. Even serious journos felt they had to slip in all the usual bollocks about him. TB called later. He said it was OK in that the scope of his activities got over, but it was all a bit snide and tabloidy for the *FT*.

Sunday 1 July to Thursday 30 August

That must be the longest period outside holidays when I have kind of given up doing the day-to-day diary recording, and as each day passes you just think I will give it another day and then I started to think whether actually, with the fourth volume out, I should just stop. But actually the post-No. 10 stuff in its own way is just as if not more interesting in that I kept in touch with the key players, and also I was beginning to develop a slightly different perspective. But the truth is what I do now matters less than what I did to a large extent, and that is beginning to weigh on me. I am starting to think too that I should now, aged fifty-five, start to think about doing one more big thing, and possibly get a seat at the next election. I was starting to think about it most days, and also talk about it to one or two people.

On the speaking circuit some pretty regular themes were coming up – Tories being exposed as pretty useless and possibly one-term; but Ed not credible as a PM; and, more and more, why don't you stand for Parliament, followed by, if Labour lost, you'd be well placed to go to the top and if you won, you'd be straight into pretty much any job you wanted. On 13 July, I went to see TB to discuss. He had been to the Labour sports dinner Calum and I and others had organised on the 11th, spoke well, Ed wasn't bad, and the mood was pretty good. He said Ed had definitely improved and Cameron had gone backwards. A while back the jury was not in on the question – DC won – but now the jury was out again. It all depended on policy. He was sceptical about Jon Cruddas [MP, former deputy leader candidate] being in charge of policy, but willing to give him the benefit of the doubt for now. His worry was that Jon would come up with a mélange that made little sense to the public.

When people talk about 'moving on' from e.g. New Labour, what they really mean – and this is classic GB – is let's not have the argument, let's avoid it. Their line was that New Labour was great in the first few years, then lost its way and we need to recapture the voters we lost over Iraq and public service reform. But TB was adamant if we lost the reform agenda, and a really radical approach, we were in trouble. He also felt Ed ultimately could not take the country with him. He still saw David as the more natural leader but also felt that he lacked the killer instinct. He felt deep down he was ambivalent. Ed might grow but the next phase was important and he would need to raise the game.

The dinner at The Emirates had gone well. We made about £300k and got £37k for the TB speech notes I found from 1995, £10k for the Fergie notes. Annoyingly he couldn't come because he was signing Shinji Kagawa [Japanese midfielder], and Tommy Godwin [former Olympic cyclist] had to drop out too because he was taken ill. He was amazing for ninety-one and people loved the little film Mark Lucas had made but it would have been even better if he had then wheeled in with his bike and his bronze medal. An award from TB to Tessa. Me interviewing Brendan, David Moorcroft [former distance runner] and Dalton Grant [former high jumper]. Big Sam [Allardyce] was at my table and I asked him at the end of the evening if he was political. 'I am now,' he said. 'I loved this. Really made me think differently about things.' Rory and his mates at next table. Lots of comments that it was the old team that brought the energy to the room and the new lot just didn't fill the space. They were low profile to the point of invisibility. Annoying.

TB, on the Friday, said there had to be a sense of big ideas to meet the scale of the challenges facing the country and the world. He felt Cameron was beginning to realise how tough it was and that maybe he didn't have what it took, and that explained the temper. TB got a great reception, really genuine warmth apart from some of the GB lot. I also heard from [Lord] Iain McNicol [Labour general secretary] that when he called GB and Sarah to invite them, Sarah said why would they come and hear me talk to Alex Ferguson after all the stuff I had put in my last book about GB? God, to think what I could have said. Tessa saying Danny Boyle [director Olympics opening ceremony] was insisting on Labour voices in the programme for the opening. I was in a total quandary on what to do about the Games. Fiona was adamant she was in France the whole time and I really felt I should be there for some if not all of it.

Back to the TB meeting. I asked his view about what I should do. I felt I was at a crossroads. I loved the freedom I currently had but part of me felt I was wasting myself. 'Do you want to be leader of the Labour Party?' he asked. I said when he had done the job as leader and PM I always felt I could pretty much do any other job but his, and maybe Chancellor, but now I was not so sure. In any event if we were going to win the next election, I knew I would have to be involved and I would make a big difference. I could make more of a difference if I was going for a seat and took over the whole campaign planning. He said he was sure Ed would want me to do that. He said ability-wise he had no doubt I could do the leader's job, and better than Ed, and probably better than David too. He said you can think deeply and on your feet, you speak well, you inspire people, you love building teams, you know what you think and you have a profile. He said it is different to what I did before though because then I always had his authority.

He felt I should not make a decision until 'lastminute.com' and meantime work out if I really felt I could manage and change the politics. At the moment he felt I had the best of both worlds – they wanted my input and advice, and my support and public profile, but I could do it on my terms. If I was in there as a real player as opposed to half-player / half-spectator, the politics became all-consuming. The tragedy is that the party has been sub-contracted to the wrong people with the wrong politics. He said of GB, I can forgive him a lot, even the awful things he did to him. What is totally unforgivable is the spite that was used to stop e.g. Liz Lloyd getting a seat, or that puts Tom Watson in such an important place, and above all which gets in Ed and Harriet Harman instead of David and say Alan Johnson. Absolute madness and the reason why we probably won't win. He said he felt Ed had improved but not enough. The banker-bashing, Murdoch-bashing stuff only took you so far. There had to be more interesting policy stuff coming through.

He didn't think the Lib Dems would be kingmakers again. It would be Tory or Labour and he couldn't see us doing it under Ed. The only exception to that was if Cameron did not realise the scale of the problem and failed to face up to it. He felt I should get more and more involved in helping Ed and in planning the campaign, and work out if I really wanted to spend the next years of my life involved in internal struggle. 'You are the best there is at taking on the Tories but you will find you are doing that and taking on the Ballses and the Watsons and the rest of them. So you get a seat, you make a difference but we don't win and then you are into a massive internal fight, and you are locked into it for seven years.'

He asked what Fiona thought. I said we were in a much better place and she was up for me doing whatever I decided to do. He said just be careful, having done so well in repositioning yourself after years locked in the tunnel that you don't get locked in again. He said we should both mull. 'I really don't rule it out. I have often thought you should have done this and could lead the party, but you have to be really sure, and you need to be clear you don't mind giving up everything else.' We chatted about the kids. He was really nice about Calum, having chatted to him the other night. His own kids were in great shape. He felt the re-entry stuff via the *FT*, *Evening Standard* etc. had been OK and he did intend to do more. Catherine Rimmer was a bit pissed off they had allowed the thing about him being a sports legacy adviser to dominate the coverage of the event but it was generally OK.

He still had a big appeal and a broader reach than any of them. He said mull over the summer, then spend the next year just dipping in deeper and seeing if you really can be arsed letting it take over your whole life again. He said they do not have the strength in depth we had and that would mean more and more falling on me. I raised it with a few other people as varied as the kids, Nancy, Natascha, and everyone seemed to think Go For It. He was right though that I didn't need to rush it.

I wasn't blogging much at the moment but when I did it was mainly on the theme of the government being all tactics no strategy. They were also fucking up Olympic planning. The M4 was shut for five days outside Heathrow. G4S [security company] hadn't recruited enough people so the troops were called in – a week after ten thousand service cuts were announced. The economy was not recovering and Osborne got himself into bother making wild accusations against Balls about Libor rate rigging. Omnishambles was sticking to them. Posh and arrogant were already settled. Incompetent was joining it.

Early July a few days in Albania with Edi. Good visit on one level in that I felt I could make a difference and he appreciated the really clear and blunt advice. But I wondered if they were all up for the fight. I liked him though. Watched Euros final, Spain beating Italy 4–0.

So what else – 4 July presented the mental health award for the Centre for Social Justice, [former Tory leader] Iain Duncan Smith's outfit. All a bit Tory but I liked the winners – a group from Birmingham run by a Bosnian woman and a former copper who lost his job through depression. William Reed [media company] dinner which was fun. 150th anniversary and they had had only five chief execs, all members of the family. 5 July meeting with Bahraini opposition leader Sheikh Ali Salman. Portland work rolled on a bit, one or two clients and also a pitch for a *PR Week* award. 6 July Halton council employment day at The Heath, Widnes. Again lots of people saying I should stand.

9 July health day. MRI to check out spots on the liver. Colonoscopy p.m. Heavily sedated and I was knocked out for a couple of days. Not doing much exercise not helped by dire weather. 10 July, David Frost's party. David tired and Carina [wife] not visible. Seb Coe cool as anything and confident Olympics was all going to go OK. He wanted me to go to loads of stuff, as did Tessa, but I was really torn because of Fiona wanting to go to France. 12 July, Direct Mail Association lunch. Totally off-cuff speech which went down really well though in the Q&A a guy said he was with me at school and I was a complete bastard. Beat him up once. We made up after! In the evening really nice event with Chris Mullin whose diaries had

been adapted into a play, *A Walk-on Part*. It was a pretty good job and the Q&A went really well. Chris's take on TB interesting and so much more mature than the usual leftist view. Home to see the brilliant *Bank of Dave* with Burnley's own David Fishwick [businessman]. Best telly I had seen in yonks, him taking on the establishment and trying to set up his own bank. It was legend-making material. I was tweeting wildly in support and later emailed him to say he should get involved with us politically. He said he was keeping his powder dry to see what he could get policy-wise out of the three parties who were suddenly all over him. I was annoyed neither of the Eds had taken up my idea of meeting him when he was in London.

Really pleased to learn Calum had told Gail, Charlie and others that he was going to try the rehab place in Ireland. Lunch with Nancy [Dell'Olio] who was going on about how loved she was, and how we should use her more as the most loved Labour supporter. Flirty as ever. Home to meet Georgia and advise re. her book. Also discussing with Gail whether I should take part in a documentary on the phenomenon of *Fifty Shades of Grey*, which was outselling all books of all time.

Long chat with Ian Holloway re. general stuff. Hilarious re. Rory doing his coaching badges – 'eh we don't want no clever people coming into football.' Great on pundits too. 'I love it when Shearer sits there and says what he would be telling the German team at half-time ... he tried at Newcastle and nothing fucking happened.'

Faucon August, working on getting Volume 4 done and dusted, and published without any of the problems I had worried about – up to and including a media frenzy which led Chilcot to think he had to re-open his inquiry, which was stretching out further and further into the future – actually happening. Fiona had decided to head off to the house in France for six weeks, and part of me felt like doing the same, but the Olympics was upon us so we compromised – out for a week with our mums, which was nice, and covered the start of the Games, and then I came back for a full immersion week at the Games. Back for the 100m final won by Usain Bolt. Great stadium, nice atmosphere, fantastic volunteers and organisation. The opening ceremony by Danny Boyle was superb, and in many ways a hymn to progressive values. It certainly celebrated British history in a way that did not immediately go down well with the right, and MP Aidan Burley tweeted about him overdoing the multiracial stuff and had a great storm crashing down on him. I was tweeting away merrily about how great it was, as were thousands of others, and pointed out that he was 'explaining the Big Society to David Cameron.'

Calum was working at the Games, Grace was working at the reggae festival, Rory at Barnet FC, but the boys came to one night's athletics and Rory came to a daytime session too. I had tickets for several athletics sessions, including Bolt's two wins, and [Kenyan middle-distance runner] David Rudisha's world record, and also for two sessions at the Velodrome, including [Scottish track cyclist] Chris Hoy's latest gold. Had lunch with Dave Brailsford [British cycling performance director] out in the park, and a really good chat about his future. He thought he would stick with cycling but felt it would be great to take on something like the challenge of England winning the World Cup and then trying to shape the game all to the direction. He said he wanted to make decent money for a few years, set up the family for good, then find new challenges. We had a chat in a neat empty Velodrome for an hour or so before the last session, and he was pretty philosophical. This is the environment I love, he said. This is what I know best. But he also felt at his best when he forced himself out of his comfort zone. He had contempt for a lot of people in sport, including Sport UK, BOA, because they did not really have the drive and focus on winning.

He said what really mattered to him was recognition by other coaches. I felt he had that, but he was not so sure. Around the park, a few people asking for his autograph and photo, but nothing like the recognition he ought to get. Kate Garvey joined us for a bit and we discussed politics. He felt the government was useless but nobody thought Ed could win. If your business is winning, you have to change him. He was essentially advocating a men in grey suits approach. I tried to explain it was not so simple, but to him, applying sports winning principles, it was.

Also had a long session with Brendan [Foster] and Georgia. Reminded Brendan how against it all he had been. I was wrong, he said. It has been fantastic. He said, as we watched thousands of people milling around in the sunshine, 'These are your people, this is your Games, surely Labour can get back on the pitch with this.' But the more successful the Games became – and by now they were already a roaring success, in terms of organisation, crowds (apart from too many empty corporate seats early on), volunteers and above all GB medal success – the more non-political it felt. The only politician getting a bounce from it was Boris Johnson. Cameron looked a bit out of it, Ed was nowhere. TB was around but written out of the script. Major got a lot of credit for the lottery as the medals came in, TB for getting the Games, but Boris was the only one successfully milking the whole thing and becoming a bit of a problem for Cameron.

Brendan felt I should get involved in the legacy stuff. I did surface the idea I had been discussing with Keith Mills re. sport as a Cabinet position. It said something for the government's current incompetence that something as good as this was giving them no bounce at all. Cameron kept turning up at events we were expected to do well in, and got known as a jinx. The mood in London was fantastic, helped by the weather, with just a couple of bad days. Bumped into a guy from Belize who sorted Rory a ticket for [British distance runner] Mo Farah's second gold-medal race. The buzz was fantastic. Toured the housing, truly fantastic that it had gone up so quickly and was of such good quality. The same went for the stadia, beautiful and efficient. Lots of space so that I can barely remember queuing. The whole thing was giving a sense of possibility for the future, really changing the mood about what we could achieve. It would be interesting to see how long it lasted.

Towards the end of the Games, as I headed back to France with John Mills, I wrote a piece for CNN which got a huge response, which pretty much captured what I had felt about it all. Really great to be British right now, and loving that sport was the key to this sense of what Britishness meant.

I always thought the Games would be a success, but never imagined it would be quite the triumph it has turned out to be, and Tessa was beaming with pride the whole time. Brilliant opening ceremony, festival of music closing it, epoch-making athletic events, and a home team performance that exceeded even the most optimistic expectations, the Games have given London two of the most remarkable weeks in its history. So where now? Onwards and upwards? Or, like the Aussies and the Greeks, great games but then a sense of decline?

I said to Georgia, remember the mood in Athens eight years ago, the public and politicians saying this was the starting point for a new and better Greece. A lot has gone wrong since. And Mervyn King, even as the Brits were celebrating more gold, was giving one of the gloomiest gubernatorial assessments of the future I have ever heard. So maybe it will be a hangover time. Maybe sport has been filling the gap left by the fall in reputation of politics, banking, the media, the church. I had another go at pushing No. 10 to raise sport to the Cabinet table, not least for the economic and social opportunities it brings. I got a big response to the tweet that Danny Boyle had to explain the Big Society to David Cameron. OK, a bit of a cheap shot. But for me the genius of the ceremony lay in capturing not just the greatness of our past, but the insight that, provided we recognise we are now a very different country to what we were, we have the chance for a great future too.

Fast forward several days to the greatest night of all when in less than an hour, Mo Farah, a black Somali asylum seeker, a mixed-race northerner Jess Ennis and a tall, good-looking ginger man, Greg Rutherford, won athletics golds, and you could almost hear the nation saying: 'This is who we are.' The problem with the Big Society was not the idea but its execution. Danny Boyle did give a more coherent vision of it than the politicians have done, and the Games gave a sense of what it could mean in practice. When I think of all the stadia I have left after a sporting event, the atmosphere coming out of the Olympic Park was like no atmosphere I have ever experienced before.

Brilliant volunteers. They are everywhere. And they are nice. And they are just having a good time helping others to have a good time. A positivity that comes not just from sporting success but the scale of the project and the fact Britain pulled it off; the superb venues and the smoothness of the movement of big crowds through them; the transport system working well; the phenomenal support the British public has given at every single venue – the Games Makers: Mr and Mrs Britain. These are the real Middle Englanders, and they are the antithesis of the negativity of those newspapers which claim to be the voice of the British people. It is also why Labour need to make more of the Tories constant refrain about Broken Britain, and the relentless negativity.

Blog-wise, did a few on Olympics legacy – Gove had gone missing – and on Mitt Romney's new running mate Paul Ryan [Republican candidates for President and Vice-President in the US election], who had enlivened things much as Sarah Palin did. But this really was a holiday. Lots of sleep, exercise, reading, eating, and apart from re. the kids, not that much worrying about the future. And for some reason that worried me. I was still pondering about standing for Parliament. I discussed it more with TB. He said the question is whether you want to be leader of the Labour Party. He said it was not impossible. I said I enjoyed my life in many ways, the variety and the freedom, but politics and campaigns were what I did best, and I really disliked this government and wanted to see the back of them.

I also told Tessa I was thinking about it. She felt I would hate it, that it would make me a huge target again, and there would be a lot of people aiming for me. TB said both the family and I needed to be clear we could take the pressure cranked up again. Part of him felt I had the best of both worlds but he could see why I was tempted. Tessa was much clearer that I would hate it. She felt I had gone from being big political figure to big national figure and I would go crazy dealing with the shadow Cabinet and the party more generally. She felt I could do as much outside but do it on my terms. She was thinking about her own future too. She loved the whole 2012 thing and felt nothing would ever be as good again, so she was definitely standing down.

I did bits and bobs on Lance Armstrong, after he announced he had decided not to contest further the doping allegations made against him. Did I like Armstrong when I met him? Yes, I did. Was I impressed by his strength of his character, his humour and intelligence? Yes, I was. Was I chuffed that he gave me one of his Tour-winning shoes to raise funds for Leukaemia and Lymphoma Research? Certainly. Was I inclined to believe the passionate denials that he made for the nth time when I asked him about the swirl of allegations that have surrounded him for years? Yes, I was. Was that possibly because a part of me wanted the denials to be true; because I wanted to believe the legend of a man who could come back from cancer to become the seven-times winner of the toughest sporting event in the calendar? I am sure that it was.

What came over in his statement was the sense that he is being persecuted and so he is throwing in the towel. But this time, it is not the French out to get him, but the Americans. And it is not a new piece of evidence that has emerged as the final straw, but the sense that he has just had enough of it all. The reaction on social networks underlined his divisiveness. To critics and detractors, it was 'the proof', a tactical retreat which reveals a hidden guilt. To supporters, the culmination of a witch-hunt against not just a great cyclist, but a tireless campaigner against cancer. I doubt he will go away quietly. Dropped him a couple of messages, but got very non-committal replies. Chatted to David Millar who was telling me Lance was an alpha male, ruthless and attractive and a man like him and me. But he was a cheat and he was still cheating by not admitting it.

Blogged on Romney and Ryan as a Palin-style move and *Time* asked for a piece which got a big response. It felt a bit too much like an appeal to the base, and could undermine Romney as Palin did for John McCain [Republican nominee for President in 2008]. He had hardline views on abortion, guns and government spending. Romney has also screwed up by attacking our preparations for the London Olympics. Palin electrified the base, excited the media, and for a while discomfited the Democrats, much as Ryan is doing now. But McCain's strategy was rooted in experience and distancing himself from George W. Bush. The appointment of the unpredictable, right-wing Palin fired a double-barrelled shotgun through both planks of his then even-keeled campaign. Ryan is a more substantial figure than Palin. But similarly Romney might be alienating voters whose support he needs to win.

Clegg pulled the plug on the electoral boundaries review in retaliation for the Tories pulling the plug on Lords reform and the sense now is very much of the coalition as a source of struggle and tension rather than co-operation. The economic figures were pretty bad too, and Osborne still tanking. So it was definitely game on. I had a couple of long chats with Ed, who had loved the Olympics, said he had been getting a positive response, and that he felt there was a real possibility of Labour harnessing this new energy because it was in part about government working with business and people. I had been picking up a lot of negativity but I didn't say so, instead said he needed to show at conference that we had moved beyond criticism to a clear plan for the future. He went through some of the arguments he was intending to deploy, which sounded OK, but lacked the big-picture vision as yet. But he was definitely in a more positive place than a few months ago, though he knew it was as much about the other lot failing as us doing well. He also needed to put a bolt up the backsides of the shadow Cabinet, most of whom were invisible.

Accused [Jimmy McGovern series on TV] started on 14 August, to good reviews, and I stated tweeting up my 'acting debut'. But in France both of us were pretty lazy for most of the time. Calum off to Ireland, which was important. Rory not enjoying his job. Grace got the grades for Paris, which was great. She was out for a week, Gail and Georgia for a long weekend, but otherwise it was just Fiona, me and Molly. Fiona and I getting on really well, which was terrific, but I was a bit worried we were slowing down too much. We had a couple of dinner parties for some of our old and new friends and Fiona was definitely moving to a position of seeing more of our life here than in London. I would need to reshape work if that were to happen. It was great getting on with her so well again, and I was finally understanding the merit of some of the things she had said about me in the past, and the impact it all had on her and the kids.

I was still on anti-depressants/anxiety pills, the longest I had been on them for ages and maybe that was also slowing me down. I was probably more depressed than I realised, and Calum had said a few very blunt things which made me low for a few days after the Skype sessions with Miriam Finnegan [counsellor] in Ireland. I sensed he saw me as the source of a lot of his problems which was harsh in a way but he maybe had a point. Out on the bike every day. Tried Mont Ventoux by moonlight, but the Vaison doctor, Dr Lopez, had given me a new inhaler when I went to see him with a bad chest. I had a massive asthma attack a few k up, and Fiona had a sixth sense and drove up to get me. It turned out that on the notes of the inhaler he had given me it said do not give to asthmatics. I managed Ventoux a couple of weeks later at the height of the heat wave, but slow, 2:45. Meanwhile Dave B was sorting me a new bike. Needed it!

I tried to get back for Burnley v Bolton for the start of the season but the planes didn't work out. Missed a good one. 2–0, big crowd, and Judas banners being flown across the ground [Burnley then manager had defected to Bolton in 2010]. Email traffic fairly light, mainly speeches and charity bids, which were slightly wearing me down as so many of them were essentially either asking me 'as a celeb' or asking me to get other celebs. Ear infection. Pain like I have never known. Long chat with Alex re. Calum and also re. his landing of van Persie. He was losing it with Rooney, who was drinking and smoking and losing pace, so maybe opponents don't fear him like they did. He loved Kagawa. Berbatov on the way out. He also got me involved in a campaign to get Aberdeen council to reverse a decision to block a new training complex at Calder Park. Got him in return to help the Pedal for Petrov ride.* Football's response has been pathetic.

On my future I was hoping things would clarify once I got home, but in the end it was the trip to see Calum at Toranfield House [Co. Wicklow, Ireland] that clarified things. I flew back from Nimes to Luton, got a lift in so back in time for my meeting with Edi Rama. He, Endri and Adia had come over to see Mark Lucas on making films and doing branding, and also Greg Cook re. polling. We had a session in the garden to go over the plans for the autumn. Mainly economy and building up the policy agenda. Then watched my *Accused* episode with Grace, Rory and Audrey. Having to sleep downstairs because the water tank had flooded our top two floors.

Next day off to Ireland. Met by a driver, off in the sunshine, chatting re. football mainly. Met Miriam who was in charge at Toranfield for a debrief – she said he was engaging – then with Cam and we went over lots of small talk before settling down to a long and fairly harrowing session. He said some pretty harsh things, felt that I had not always been there when I should have been, expected too much of the kids to cope with the life I had led and the pressures I brought into the house. He was making progress I felt though, and also I realised I had to make changes in my attitude too.

A lot of what he said echoed with what Fiona has said down the years. That I can be good and loving but also hard and angry and self-obsessed. That I underestimate the force of my moods which can be scary. I remember when she first said that he and Rory sometimes were scared to say what they thought to me, or worried about upsetting me, I just saw it as part of her having a go for not being there, or for taking on a job she was opposed to. I didn't actually listen and hear and think. And because it is true that I tried hard to be there for them all when I wasn't working, I thought that was enough. Well clearly sometimes it wasn't and I said I was sorry for that too.

I thought well it might be a pain but one day they will be proud of all this. They'll read the diaries and they'll see why I had to do it. But today I came away realising if I were them I'd probably read the diaries and think, 'How the hell did we fit into that?' I realised more clearly that Fiona had a point, much bigger than I ever accepted, and also that part of his anger with me was that I wasn't fair to her and maybe part of his anger with her is that she let me get away with it a lot of the time. I said he should be very proud that he spoke up for her the way he did, and being upset when she is upset is a good thing not a bad thing.

It had become an annual joke on holiday – 'There's the place you dumped

---

* A 400-mile charity cycle ride to raise money for leukaemia research in response to Aston Villa captain Stiliyan Petrov's diagnosis of the disease in March 2012.

me and the kids and headed off to your new glamorous life with Tony.' And I never felt like that. But I now realise why she did and it is only natural that the children would have felt some of the same. There is no doubt that doing the job I did for Tony and Labour added to the hurt and the blame. But when Fiona made the criticisms it sometimes made me harder and angrier. And Calum admitted sometimes he drank more if we nagged him not to. When what I should have said is, I understand and I really do hear what you say and let's try to change things. I kidded myself I did but it tended to be on my terms and Fiona had to pick up the pieces.

I said it is only in the last few years that I have even begun to get a proper handle on it at all. We are now in such a better place. We had a great time together in France and in a way it was like falling in love starting all over again and I sometimes wake up and wonder how the hell did I keep putting this at risk? But I said there has still been something big missing in our lives and our relationship and that is your happiness. The truth is we are never happier than our least happy child. I said that is not because we want to control. But because we love you so much. We want you to learn from our lives, what we have done well, what we have done less well, in building your own, making the most of the real talent and character you have to do your own thing. Mum and I had managed to start all over again in a way, forgiven if not forgotten, and I wanted to do the same with him. I said a lot of couples would have cracked under the pressures we – especially I – brought into the home. The divorce courts are full of people who put the need of the moment ahead of the insight that love can be hard. That we didn't is partly down to the fact neither of us are quitters. But also at a deeper level because I knew Mum cared more about the family than anything. So did I, at a deeper level, but my whole life was absorbed with work, other people's problems and weaknesses – and I just expected everything to roll on behind me. She did pick up the pieces. Miriam said that when that kind of thing happens it is clear kids can get left behind. Rory I think tended to deal with it by immersing himself in his own activities, perhaps a more developed innate self-confidence. Grace perhaps by making sure she was always heard. The truth is with them too I probably never took enough time to ask, to find out what was really going on. I said if Fiona and I had been separated from them all at birth and met them now, we would know which was which. Part of their characters and personalities were on full display from the word go. So kids are all different. But we maybe expect them all to be the same, don't see – especially when parents are caught up in themselves – how things are affecting kids as individuals, not just as a family.

I started to write to him on the flight back. By the time I got home I felt totally drained, exhausted, and I cried for half an hour. It was just the build-up of the last few days, and the sense of failure. He was in pain, and I guess he wanted me to share that pain, which I had tried to do. I hoped though that it might be a turning point. I was actually very proud of him for the way, for example, he took me to task for the way I sometimes spoke to and treated Fiona. I said if we can get back to a sense of love and respect but also honesty, I would feel happier and more confident about the future, his and mine.

I then watched the end of the Paralympics opening ceremony, which was also incredibly emotional, the most fantastic, life-affirming thing I have seen in years. At a greater level I think I was celebrating the insight I got during the day in Ireland that Calum's problems, and mine, and all of our problems in a way, are not only about individual impairments and difficulties any of us may have now or may have had in the past. They are about impairments in relationships. And relationships are never about one person, but two, three, a dozen as friends and family, 100 as workmates, millions as fellow countrymen, billions as fellow citizens. Of all of those it is family and friends that matter most. I said in the letter I had started to write that it is only when we interact at that level that we get meaning and love in our lives. It is only when we allow the power of the human spirit to act positively not negatively that we make progress and deal with problems. It is only when we actually decide to change a relationship that we can.

When relationships go wrong hurt and anger move in. Where there is hurt and anger then there is blame. Where there is blame there are set patterns and ruts which develop, and so change can't come. And that is what happened with me and Calum. I kind of knew it and it seems obvious now after all that he said today. I had heard the words before, I guess – not least from Fiona over many years – but it is possible to hear without listening and maybe I hadn't listened as much as I should have done. Today I listened and I heard. I heard it not just from Calum but I heard an echo of so many of the things Fiona has said down the years to which I have listened but – truthfully – not heard. Because sometimes we choose to hear what suits us rather than what honesty demands. Calum had taken a big step in saying honesty has to be the way forward and I think that must go for all of us. No more assuming we know what we think and how we feel and why, but saying and accepting not undermining.

The night I got back from Ireland, I couldn't sleep, and at five gave up and went out for a run, stopping just before six, on Regent's Park Canal, to pick up the letter I was writing to Calum, which I then decided to send to Fiona, Rory and Grace. I felt in yesterday's heart-to-heart we got somewhere, in that I felt there was at last a bit more openness and honesty, him saying at times he did find it difficult me being his dad, me saying I could see that, but also that he needed to understand his, Rory's and Grace's happiness meant more to us both than anything. I accepted too that I had not always been as kind as I should have been to Fiona, and that he had always rightly stood up for her.

In many ways the past decade for me – all the books, all the weird and wonderful try this, try that, see what happens – has been trying to make sense of a period that was politically and personally so important to me that I only now fully realise the risks I was taking with, and the damage I might have been doing to, the people I really love and who will be with me to the end. I can defend how I was and how I am. But I can also take blame, shoulder responsibility, try to learn. And one thing I have learned, and DS has been a great help in this, is that we can't change other people. We can only change ourselves.

I got the feeling Calum did accept he had to make change, and that we would always support him, always try to be non-judgemental – not always succeed – and always act in what we thought were his best interests regarding his relationship with alcohol. He was almost certainly right that a lot of my concern for him on this may be rooted in what I have known and feared in myself. Had it not been for Mum, friends and family, a good boss, good colleagues, I would have gone under. I know that. It is why I give daft money to people living on the streets, as I had twice on the run down to the canal, because I think but for all the good fortune I had it could have been me. It is why I still dream about the crazy bad things I did. It is why I have worked to get a better relationship with drink, but feel a little tingle of fear and panic and self-destruct every time a drop passes my lips. But I know that nagging drinkers gets nowhere. Everyone told me I was drinking too much. I heard all that too but I didn't listen. Until the right person came along. Dr Bennie – the duty psychiatrist in Paisley. I said to him I really hoped that Miriam at Toranfield would become to him what he became to me. The catalyst that moved me from whatever hurt and anger I felt, and the blame games I played, to responsibility. Only you can do this, I said. You need the help and support of others but every choice you make is yours. Every word we say. Every thought we have. Every slight we feel. Every purchase we make. We make choices every minute of every day. We make them with the influence and help of others, dead and alive, but ultimately we make them with the one person with whom we have no choice but to face every waking and sleeping second of every day – ourselves.

Miriam had pointed out that what had come over in the Skype sessions we had done when we were in France, and Calum in Ireland, is that when people do get into hurt and blame and anger, they turn in on themselves. We both became brooding and introspective. It is a shield. A way of dealing

August '12: Trying to process Toranfield rehab trip

with the hurt and the anger. But in the end it adds to the hurt. Makes us more isolated, more angry, more depressed. And so the spiral goes on.

I guess why I felt more hopeful after yesterday was that we were both moving maybe to a place where we saw a better side of blame, namely responsibility. I took responsibility for a lot of the things we talked about. I also felt Calum at least had an understanding that we were always trying to do our best for him.

So the two big revelations to me yesterday should not have been revelations at all. When Bob died, and when Ellie died, we all tried our best. But it was only in seeing the pain on his face yesterday that I fully realised the impact, and realised that at the time we were so busy dealing with our own grief, our own issues, willing things to heal rather than helping them to heal and giving them time to heal. So the scars of unresolved grief are there. They are painful. Fiona has them because though Bob had been ill they never really had those final conversations and because she knows how much more he had to give to us all. I have unresolved grief with John because I never wanted to admit he would die and so never really discussed it – a mistake I learned from when Philip died, which is why I wrote the letter I did, and I said it gives me comfort now because I miss him just as I still miss John and wonder how all our lives would be if he was still here. I have it with Ellie because the last thing John said to me was 'Look after her if I go' and every time I see Lindsay and Hope a little part of me feels – I know it is irrational – that I let them down, because she died. I have it with my dad because for various reasons I felt I never let my own parents and siblings into my life at my lowest point. I hope this was for good reasons not bad as I had Fiona by then, and Bob and Audrey, and didn't want to upset my own parents still dealing with the life-changing fallout from Donald's illness. But that feeling that I shut them out, essentially lied about how I was feeling and how bad things were, the fact I didn't want them to feel blame but also I didn't want to have to explain myself, was never resolved for me. I said it is why I am so keen that our children always feel they can come to us and say anything and we will be there to help. I'd said yesterday that I don't want a relationship just focused on football and logistics and small talk, but want to feel the walls that had sprung up between us can be taken down and we can discuss anything without fear or suspicion. But feelings as deep as those both of us showed yesterday cannot be locked away and suppressed, they have to be brought out, embraced as a big and important part of who you are.

One thing for sure is that he showed real maturity at times yesterday, and a lot of insight. It was also helping me think more clearly about my own future. I said to Fiona out walking the day before I flew to Ireland that I felt the holiday had been wasted. I'd been worried about Calum.

Worried about whether Grace would get her grades and when she did whether she would find stuff to do to keep her active and busy. Worried that Rory seemed a bit fed up with work. Worried about politics. Worried that yet again I was thinking about my own future and could feel her thinking, 'Here we go again, something is brewing,' and asking herself whether she hadn't already sacrificed too much of her own career and life chances to me. Worried about Mum and Audrey who are both great but getting on and we all have that to face too when they go. And worried that I hadn't resolved any of the professional issues I have been thinking about. But yesterday things fell into place more.

I said I had been talking to Mum about maybe getting a seat and standing for Parliament. I know I can help beat the Tories. I might not be able to do the very top job but I could get close and make a big difference again.

But I realise that however well intentioned it is not where I need to be, for all of us. I have had a dream all my life of having both personal freedom and political and cultural impact and I have it. But parents will always live part of their dreams through their children. It is not a bad thing unless it leads them to make them do things not for the kids but for themselves. On Manchester, I said I hope he understood where I was coming from. But the truth is I was hearing but not listening again. I wasn't thinking *of* myself. But I was thinking *as* myself. Not as Calum. And that was a mistake.

I said that when I wrote in *The Happy Depressive*, all I really wanted was for my parents to think I was a good son, Fiona to feel glad we spent most of a life together and all three kids loving me to the end, and thinking on balance I did OK by them, and changed the world a bit on the way, and had some great friends and some amazing experiences: it was all true.

I told him that when I woke up this morning, I felt tired and still drained but I also felt like I had been living with toothache and a load of bad teeth had been removed. I ran up to Highgate Cemetery, first to Philip's grave, then John's, then Ellie's, and asked them whether I should hit the send button. And I did, and felt better. I imagined telling Philip about the other Toranfield clients, and the banter, and reminding him he was the one who had always said Calum would be fine in the end.

Friday 31 August

Couldn't sleep again. Thinking about Calum all the time. Two ideas for novels in my mind at the moment. Father–son stuff. Or a set of alcohol stories which end in a Toranfield-type place. Calum being more communicative, e.g. asking me to help Toranfield promote a Run for Recovery.

He was still saying he would drink though, even if in general attitudes seemed to be improving. Out for an early run, then stopped at the café as F was setting off from Faucon. To Rio Tinto to see Tom Albanese. Good chat re. Europe (he thought five bad years ahead).

Lunch with Jill McDonald at Gaucho Hampstead. Quite liked her though pretty Tory, even if in common with most business people she was not too impressed with this lot right now. We talked a lot about her kids, and I suggested one thing I had learned was that busy parents kid themselves their lifestyles are not affecting their kids. Later Tessa came round and we had a pretty profound chat about our own lives, especially in relation to the kids. She said she cried lots when she read my diaries because it reminded her how she had varnished the truth to herself about the effect her career had on the kids. David was brilliant with them which is why they got through. But the truth is inevitably there had been times when she put her career first, and though they loved her to bits and were proud of her, she would always feel a bit of guilt, a sense that she must have let them down. I said I saw nothing but closeness when they were together. We talked about Calum, and the Ireland trip, at length and she felt, as Philip had, that Calum would be fine in the end because he had such a good heart, a lot of good qualities, and he needed to find the right vocation to let them shine. She was adamant I would hate it going back into the fray full-time, and that if I felt I should genuinely spend more time with the family, even though they were grown up, I should follow my instinct.

She said she knew I disapproved of the honours thing but her dame-hood had been a really important piece of validation for her. It gave her a real sense of who she was as a person, of being something of a success. She said that a lot of her career, she had felt almost like an imposter, that she was not really up to the things she was doing, and thought she would be found out. A lot of it was clearly about her dad never validating her. She said she wanted to have the same kind of transition I had done, and felt she had to cut down on the political side of things. It was the first time I had heard her speaking so honestly about how she had been as a parent with political ambitions, and also about how her dad's disapproval had made her so much in need of validation. It was a nice chat, and I felt better for it. I was really starting to worry about my insomnia.

Saturday 1 September

Again couldn't sleep. Out for a run. Chat to Alex. Reading on the train north. How could I be so tired when I had just had a long holiday? The Irish trip had taken it out of me. The football was dire. Burnley's first shot on target was a headed own goal by Brighton. Lost 3–1. Worked on train back then met Rory and Fiona for dinner. Rory was pushing back a bit on my decision to take a lot of the responsibility for how Calum felt. He said they had a good childhood and I should not beat myself up so much. But I was determined to have a new relationship with Calum, and I felt this could help. Grace a bit of a nightmare flying off the handle at the moment.

Sunday 2 September

Watched Osborne on *Marr*. I tweeted very merrily as he trotted out a load of old crap. He had nothing to say. He kept mentioning the Olympics as though somehow that would create growth. They had billed a big thing on changes to get growth going and there was nothing there. Total crap. Rest of the day working to get back on track and watching loads of Paralympics and football. C4 doing a really good job on the Paras. It had been such a success, right from the off. I actually liked the ending of the opening ceremony as much as Danny Boyle's.

Monday 3 September

Blog urging Cameron once more to put sport in the Cabinet. Then out to Pall Mall to record a tribute for a film on Nigel Doughty, home, bit of work, but was so tired I fell asleep at my desk and missed a meeting with David S. Bad. Then out for dinner with Fiona, who had been to see Justine [Thornton, wife of EM] with Tom Baldwin to discuss her 'wife of' profile. Build-up to reshuffle. God knows what it is about. Osborne got booed at the Paralympics which was quite a moment. As Marr had said to him, 'You really are not very popular are you?' There was something nauseating about the way they talked up the Paras while cutting benefits etc.

Tuesday 4 September

Reshuffle day. Out to the Olympic Park with Sissy. Great day. Swimming first, including Ellie Simmonds. Off to the goalball, then wheelchair tennis, blind five-a-side football, lunch with Grace and later with F to the athletics and another David Weir gold. Saw Caroline Daniel and her bloke, otherwise fairly quiet on the meetings front, though had one amazing exchange with a cop who came up and said, 'Can I ask you for a favour – please go back and get these cunts out!' Hated Cameron especially. Said he had a close protection friend who had been looking after him once and he was just rude and arrogant.

The reshuffle was awful. Chris Grayling for Ken Clarke [as Lord Chancellor]. Hunt to Health. Owen Paterson to Environment. Cable doughnutted, surrounded by Tories in his own department. Maria Miller DCMS. No sport. Not one move I would support. Bumped into Hugh Robertson [sports minister] who admitted Cameron never even really considered doing the sports thing. Nice chat with Godric and Greg Nugent who were loving the whole thing. Going to be hard for them after. Home late, another tricky one on the sleep front.

Wednesday 5 September

Tweeted last night re. the paucity of US athletes in Paralympics c.f. with Olympics and got massive response so blogged on it, bringing in the dreadful rightward reshuffle of yesterday. It did seem odd that the US, so dominant in Olympic sport, was so relatively marginal in the Paralympics. Distilling the answers, the general view from both sides of the Atlantic was that it was down to the absence of an NHS-style healthcare system, poor welfare and poor appreciation of its importance, a governing philosophy that puts the individual ahead of the community, media attitudes that value mythical perfect looks, sponsors who do not want to be associated with impairment, and the paltry coverage of Paralympic sport are among the main factors.

The worst thing is that every single move in the reshuffle is moving Britain in that direction. Rightward on health with Hunt, one of whose last acts as Culture Secretary was to try to remove the NHS section from Danny Boyle's 2012 opening ceremony. Rightward on justice with Chris Grayling as far removed as it is possible to be in the same party from Ken Clarke's decent-minded approach to issues of crime and punishment, and the need to understand we need a new approach on prisons. Rightward on the environment and Europe with Owen Paterson whose appointment will have thrilled the climate change deniers and the 'all European legislation is bad' brigade. Rightward at BIS [Business, Innovation and Skills] with Michael Fallon in there to spy on Vince Cable and keep him off the telly. Rightward at transport with Patrick McLoughlin. As for DCMS – what a mess, and what a mass of wasted opportunities. Not even a token Lib Dem to check Maria Miller, who has been a poor disabilities minister and now takes on her new job with sport, equalities and disability effectively downgraded by lumping them all in under culture.

I wrote a piece about the chat with Hugh Robertson last night – he still hadn't heard if he was still sports minister – and asked him why Cameron had not even considered making sport a fully fledged Cabinet post to build on the amazing success of recent weeks. I like Robertson, think he has done a good job on the Olympics, he is a loyal minister and said nothing to undermine his leader. But it was pretty clear that it was not even remotely on the agenda. A huge wasted opportunity. The message of the Games was meant to be 'inspire a generation'. With their austerity obsession, their failure to tackle youth unemployment, their attacks on the poor, their undermining of the NHS, their cuts to universities and the things that help disadvantaged kids get there, their failure to face up to climate change, this is a government heading to lay a generation to waste.

There was a real risk this amazing spirit was just going to evaporate and die. Yesterday – massive queues to watch blind men play football; a packed stadium watch disabled women from Sweden and Australia hurl a ball at each other; a wheelchair tennis match as skilful and exciting as anything I have ever seen at Wimbledon; a man with no arms swimming faster than most of us could even dream of swimming; and of course David Weir careering round the track with the force and power that only great athleticism and human endeavour can bring. And I really do wonder if any other country in the world would have so many of its citizens clamouring to be part of it. But I reckon the government has missed the point of the Games, and missed the moment. The reshuffle takes the country backwards not forwards. It takes us closer to the America we don't like and away from the America we do like.

Thursday 6 September

Calum back today but I had to go to Scotland and so Fiona went out to meet him. Felt he was OK but he was clear from the off that he was still going to drink. Miriam was not going to be his Dr Bennie equivalent, it would seem. Rory felt he was a bit subdued. It was probably going to be a bit of a struggle. Fiona texted me to say he had had a couple of beers but seemed reasonably OK. But I had a sense it had not really worked, maybe even that the fact he had managed a spell in rehab without booze, and not had a lot of the side effects that some of the others had, meant he felt he had less to worry about than they did. To the Travellers' Club for a TV discussion with Hezza, Gus O'Donnell, Alan Johnson and Simon Hughes on *Yes, Prime Minister*, which was being remade for the coalition. I suppose it took me firmly into the territory of old fartism but it was quite good fun. It got a bit spiky between me and Hezza when he did his line on our supposed politicisation of the civil service and also had a go over Iraq but it was quite good fun. Alan Johnson was very funny when he was recalling how TB wanted to rename DTI the department of productivity, enterprise, innovation and skills and Alan said on balance he

did not want to be Secretary of State for Penis. We all had our little anecdotes and they seemed happy enough. Gus said it was not the case he
was going for the Bank of England job. He seemed to be putting together
quite a good portfolio.

To City airport and off to Edinburgh. Calum called to say one of the
patients at Toranfield had called him to say that just after he left all the
staff were called in and told they were not making enough and they were
going to have to shut down. I called Miriam F and it was true. She sounded
fairly philosophical. At least Calum had got to the end of the course but it
was a bit of a blow. Arrived at Gleneagles, worked a bit then to the dinner
at the end of which Lucy Kellaway of the *FT* did a little speech and Q&A
on dilemmas. It was hard-going and afterwards she said it was the hardest audience she had ever had. Did the *Observer* debate on the booing of
George Osborne, Danny Kelly [broadcaster] defending the booing; me not.

Friday 7 September
TalkSPORT with Keys and Andy Gray on the Petrov bike ride, then into
my two sessions for Pinsent Masons [law firm]. When we did the crisis-
management scenarios, they did extremely well. I felt very deflated that
Calum had had a couple of beers when he was out with Fiona and Rory last
night. Plane delayed, slept for the whole flight. Dinner at Ed Miliband's.
Perfectly nice but bit of an odd evening. The other guests were Tessa and
David, and Charlie. Ed said very little, and quite often he would chip
in halfway through with a question about something that had already
passed. Tessa was clearly on a high again about the Games. Ed didn't
really get sport. He was very relaxed about Boris, felt that his rise was all
good for us, whereas I felt it made it OK for some people to vote Tory and
he also took the 'interesting-politician' space. There was a general feeling
Cameron was in trouble, and details were emerging of the reshuffle – e.g.
he told Caroline Spelman she was too old, he sacked Cheryl Gillan while
sipping red wine, he was showering sacked ministers with Ks – that were
doing him in further.

David and I were both on the rampage on the continuing dither re.
the third Heathrow runway. Charlie was very funny re. the different TB
and GB styles when sacking, but both involved not being wholly frank.
Charlie has such a wonderful analytical mind and is so good at giving an
assessment of people's basic character, including all his, our and TB's kids.
Charlie was very fond of Calum but felt that it was a mistake for him to
be at the party because my shadow was so large there. Ed was very subdued, so Charlie chatted away – re. Leveson, re. Balls, re. the statement
due next week on Hillsborough, with 400,000 documents being released

for the first time.* Ed had a slight look of panic on his face all the time. He was in a better place but it was hard to imagine him as PM. We slept in our own room for the first time since getting back from France after the water tank drama, when it came through the roof and into my office and then into the bedroom. The room was still a total mess though and Fiona was wishing we were back in France.

Saturday 8 September

Decent enough chat with Calum after he got up. He looked a lot better, though I was disappointed he had had a few beers when he went out on both nights back. He also said he would not be going to the pub for the Scotland v Serbia match but he did. A bit alarming. I went off to Osterley where I was doing *Soccer AM* to promote the Pedal for Petrov bike ride. Usual mayhem but good fun. The interview was fine and I was able to get loads in, saying lots of footballers did stuff for charity but that the response to the Petrov appeal had been poor. Then a bit of politics, and a question about Boris, after which they showed his rugby tackle at Reading, and yet again it was obvious a lot of people really liked him.†

Watched Scotland v Serbia 0–0 – then off to Euston and the train to Manchester. Did a blog on how sad I felt that the Games were ending but saying we could keep the spirit going through legacy, joining in and celebrating the volunteers, e.g. by saying thank you when they wore their uniforms on Monday, Parade Day. Arrived at the Marriott. The two Aston Villa masseurs doing the ride were there, so I had a massage on my calf then up to watch the last night of the Paralympics, in between channel-hopping to a very disappointing *Thick of It*, now changed to take account of the coalition. Couldn't sleep. Worrying about Calum.

Sunday 9 September

The Observer did a nice spread on my debate with Danny Kelly on whether the crowd had been right to boo Osborne at the Paralympics. On Twitter there was more support for him than me but I still felt it was right to defend politics and politicians in general. Breakfast then off early to Albert Sq where Mike Summerbee, Paul Lake [former footballers], Paul Goggins

---

* The Hillsborough disaster in April 1989 saw ninety-six football fans die at the FA Cup semi-final match between Liverpool and Nottingham Forest at the Sheffield Wednesday Stadium.

† Johnson had rugby-tackled an opponent in a charity football match, prompting a *Daily Telegraph* headline, 'Great tackle, Boris – but it's football, not rugby'.

[Labour MP], the mayor and Sir Richard Leese [City Council leader] had turned out to cheer us off. Summerbee [former Burnley player] good fun as ever. Reminiscing about the time he tried to pull Maxine Sugden [AC ex-girlfriend] when our match v Notts County was called off. The ride was good, long and with some mean hills, including one near Congleton of 25 per cent, where I came off when my foot just went through the pedal.

Nice scenery through Cheshire and Staffs and a good welcoming party of the lads' families, players and club officials at Villa Park [football ground]. Pictures with the players pitch side, shower in the home dressing room, then the dinner. Loads of current and former players and yet when it came to the auction it was a struggle, even though this was for one of their own [Lilian Petrov, former player, leukaemia sufferer]. We were on LLR's table. Talking to Cathy Gilman about people she was going to have to move. I was pretty tired after the ride and didn't mix much. Speeches OK, auction crap, silent auction dire. At one point the top bid for a day's training with Celtic was seventy-five quid, which I drove up to a thousand using Twitter. Lift home with Cathy. Bed at one, knackered.

Monday 10 September

Breakfast with Ed Victor. He felt I should get on with the next volumes of the diaries. Also still pushing me re. *Winning*, and a political novel. I was back, but not motoring, partly because of the house being in such a mess after the flooding, and partly because I still couldn't decide – again – about the political role. Saw DS and mainly discussed Calum, and he felt we had to be far tougher if he came back drunk. He felt we laid down rules but let him break them, which was only going to make things worse in the long run. On me, he was far less opposed to the political idea than I thought he would be.

Andreas Baumgartner [Portland adviser] round for chat re. Kaz. He felt the bigger question was what did TB plan to do with the business more generally? He had been there to do Middle East but had essentially been diverted. Out to do a session with Norma Percy [film-maker] for her documentary on Iraq. I had decided against an interview but had agreed to read my diaries. She was desperate for me to put a word in with TB.

Tuesday 11 September

Eleventh anniversary 9/11. Out to BGC [global brokers] for their charity day, when all the profits from the trades were shared among lots of charities. I had got a decent team together, me, Gary Lineker, Dani King [cyclist] and Greg Rutherford [long-jumper], plus Geoff Thomas. Dani was good

September '12: AC psychiatrist urges tough love re. Calum

399

fun and Greg showed he could take a message when I gave him one fact about research and survival rates and he took it and used it like a pro. Mo Farah and Lewis Hamilton probably the biggest hit. Lineker friendly, and we were definitely over the spat of a few years ago when I criticised their World Cup coverage.

Peter Capaldi [actor, *The Thick of It*] there for Barnardo's [children's charity] and he and I did a few trades together. Warm and friendly. Then we had a swear-off, where we were trying to get as much bad language into a sentence as we could. Went down well but then the mics got cut and we realised it was being watched in other parts of the building, including the crèche. Oops. We did well out of the day though. Home to potter amid the builders, then Rory round to watch Scotland draw with Macedonia. Calum was out till late, back pissed again, and quite truculent with me. Really depressing. Toranfield had not worked. Another sleepless night.

Wednesday 12 September

Train to Birmingham for The Energy Event at the NEC [National Exhibition Centre]. Went to the wrong station but just made it in time for the first of two talks I was doing. Huge event, thousands of people, hundreds of exhibitors and I tried to make it relevant to their issues. I was amazed how angry people were that Charles Hendry had been sacked as energy and climate change minister. He seemed to have a lot of support across the sector. It was a bit alarming how far down the agenda climate change had gone. Obama's crusade on saving the planet was now seen as fair game for jokes. We cancelled the theatre to have a chat with Calum but it was same old same old and he was falling back into all the old patterns. He was fine, could do it on his own, they hadn't really understood him etc. etc. etc. Same old same old, too familiar. I asked him what he had thought of the things I had written to him and he just shrugged his shoulders. Felt like one step forward, several steps back. I felt he had taken a big step when he said honesty has to be the way forward and how I thought that must go for all of us. But now he was not really engaging again. Tessa called after stepping down from shadow Cabinet.

Thursday 13 September

Breakfast at Asia House with NHS chief executives from London. Nice bunch, all feeling a bit beleaguered. I was advising on how to engage with a new Secretary of State, and how to focus on a small number of key arguments rather than the kitchen sink. They agreed the three priorities were reconfiguration – they reckoned there were ten too many hospitals in London and would get better care with bigger and fewer – nurses' pay and the impact on morale, and alcohol. I suggested a letter setting that out to Hunt, saying they were developing their own strategy paper they would like to discuss with him, and also play in Boris, even if he had no real focus. Boris Johnson was probably the most talked-about politician in the country right now, and more and more people seemed to be seeing him as a serious prospect for power. Cameron seemed to be ballsing up the whole time, and more and more MPs were suggesting he wasn't really up to it. The Boris factor was becoming real, like or not.

Friday 14 September
Calum in a real state again. Hungover. Openly talking about drinking as much as he likes. Has it under control. Doesn't need all this outside help. Only went to Toranfield because it made me and Fiona feel better. I spoke to Miriam and Rory O'Connor and I said we were minded to ask him to leave, felt we had tried everything and also DS was clearly of the view he had to know there were limits, and if he crossed them we would not tolerate it. I said but what if he ends up getting hit by a bus or falling in the canal and freezing to death? David said he might, and there is nothing you can do to stop it because you cannot be with him 24/7. Miriam and Rory O'C agreed that we should give him a deadline and say it can be brought forward if he does it again. Have to hold firm. Fiona said we had to harden our hearts. I told him we had done everything we could, it hadn't worked and he had to move out. He was making our lives intolerable and we were not helping, because we didn't know how. The whole thing was grim beyond belief. He had come home late after a night of changing stories about where he had been, then Fiona discovering him drunk, rude and aggressive. Fiona was saying Toranfield had failed but what had failed was his ability to take any ownership or responsibility for his actions. Miriam said that this was nothing to do with the past, and we must not take the blame, this was him making choices mindful of the consequences.

I asked him to show me the prescription he said he had and clearly it didn't exist. I said we had tried our best, we had been as supportive as we could be, but now he had to face up to all of this himself. He was back to all the old patterns, holes in socks, sleeping in clothes, lying, stealing, not home when he said he would be, not doing the things he said he would like a new CV, training and so forth. It was pretty much impossible to believe him, and yet he went on about trust. Fiona weepy. Then off to Retford, met Mum and Liz, and on to South Shields.

The last time I had been at David M's place in South Shields was when

I started my theatre tour at the Custom House. The house hadn't changed much, very much MP's second home, not as homely as London, but it was a nice sunny day and we sat out in the garden, and David was more relaxed than the last few times I had seen him. I told him I had seen Ed a few times, and that I was helping him with his speech for conference. David said he intuited that it was going to be a One Nation pitch and I was able to confirm that, having seen the latest not-bad draft on the way up. He felt it would not work because while the message was fine, the policy direction was not, and he could not lead the party to the right place on policy because he had subcontracted policy to the wrong people, organisation to the wrong people, and also there was a reason the Tories went on about the unions having too powerful a hold – they do.

He felt that with the Tories in such trouble we should be way ahead but people did not feel we had been punished enough, and even aiming off for people being nice to him because he lost, he picked up a lot of negativity about Ed. He said he tried to be dispassionate, though he knew it was difficult. For himself, he could not really see a way back to the top table with Ed as leader. The people around him saw DM as a problem, and they did not want him in. He said he and Ed only really spoke at family events and it was very strained and they did not really talk politics. He took care not to rock the boat, so that if he made any input into the political debate, he would always leave enough leeway for them to be able to say he was echoing Ed's strategy but in truth there was not much clarity there.

He did not think Ed could win. He lacked leadership skills, the team was weak and the policy agenda incoherent. He felt Jon Cruddas [Labour MP] would take us to the wrong place on policy, just a different wrong place to the one Balls would go to. He was busy, doing lots of different things, but I could tell he found it frustrating, and the strained family relations cannot be helping on any level. He felt the Boris phenomenon was real and that he could be seen as a credible PM, which surprised me. We chatted a bit about TB, his reputation, his inability to seem to re-engage properly at the domestic level. It was warm and friendly though, a mix of reminiscing and talking about now and the future, here and in the States.

Off to the Sea Hotel where Alan Donnelly had organised the dinner. Nice enough crowd. I decided to forego a speech and instead took in loads of written questions which worked well, and Alan bought a book for everyone who asked a question. Went down well.

Really nice vote of thanks from David. I had been asked about my 'unique contribution' and had talked it down, said I had been one of the small inner team TB could trust, a friend as well as adviser. David said it had been monumental, that much of what we did would never have happened, that I made good ideas better and bad ideas redundant, that I worked round the clock to meld the team and to make sure we were heard, that he had never known anyone who could work twenty-four hours a day, even when asleep thinking of ways to tackle the Tories because I knew how tough they could be, but for the first time we could match them. He also spoke well on what we needed to do, and how, and did a very strong anti-government blast. We were away by eleven then stayed up fairly late, mainly talking about family stuff. They had lost some of the anger of the past but politics was still very difficult for them. I wonder if also the boys [two adopted sons] had taken them in a very different direction and part of them was relieved he was not at the very top.

Saturday 15 September

Breakfast with David and Louise. Lift to Newcastle, David giving me the guided tour. Amazingly clean and tidy around the place. Train down to York then over to Burnley, lunch with the board and then a good 5–2 win v Peterborough. Cab to Preston, home reasonably early, Calum flat hunting.

Sunday 16 September

Cab early to Ham with the bike for my nth LLR bikeathon. Eighty-five miles round Surrey, including for part of it the Olympic route. Nice ride, and with Geoff Thomas doing a lot of the heavy lifting, hit some good speeds.

Monday 17 September

To Freuds where Matthew, Georgia and I were judging Gould Global, four teams putting forward ideas for them to travel and learn stuff to bring back. Two were trips to Silicon Valley, one a project to raise awareness of albinos through Albino Utd FC in Tanzania, and then three guys who could get on to the Obama campaign team. They won, though Georgia and I loved the Albino project so we gave that the go-ahead in lesser form too. Train to Oxford, for the first meeting of the Healthtalkonline [health database] depression advisory group. All a bit *Guardian*-esque and earnest but it got better when the discussion got going. It was run jointly by Nottingham and Oxford Universities and was focused on interviews with depressives on the side effects of anti-depressants. The group was a mix of academics, depressives – one guy had been on anti-depressants since 1966 – pharma experts, medics, a journo. Our role was to read and advise and also try to get other interviewees.

Tuesday 18 September

Total balls up. I had arranged visits in Leicester all day, based on seeing the match v Burnley tonight, but it was moved because City had been on telly on Sunday. I offered to do the visits anyway but it turned out the university, who had invited 600 people, always thought it was Wednesday because they knew about the shift. And I could not do Weds. Bit of a nightmare. Had to postpone. So a bit of a nothing day, working a bit but not easy with the builders and all the dust etc. *Telegraph* called, asking me to do a piece on Romney, a secret video of a speech he made in May dismissing 47 per cent of the US population as being government-dependent, having been published by Mother Jones investigative website. Dave Brailsford yes to Labour conference event 'so long as I don't see your leader who is a muppet, and nobody says I am backing them.'

Wednesday 19 September

To Portland for meeting with NSPCC re. their idea of a new campaign on the theme of aggression today leading to child abuse tomorrow. I suggested documentary ideas but also using the tender process to get some creative juices flowing and really hone down the idea. Slight TB Hillsborough [stadium] problem, a note from Liz Lloyd published in which she had said Jack Straw wanted a new inquiry and TB scribbled, 'Why, what is the point?' He was obviously asking for factual answer and the fact the inquiry went ahead was good, but it was the latest negative thing around.

AnaCap [private equity firm] dinner at Scott's, small and select, and quite enjoyable. All hedge fund guys and it was odd advising them how to get a better profile, and get their heads above the parapet. Hugely depressing discussion re. Ed. They really didn't rate him on any level. All the negatives came flooding out. Doing in David, the voice, the nose, the look, the lack of sincerity said one, the lack of insight, the unions. They were scathing re. Cameron but just felt he was better.

Thursday 20 September

Did a line-by-line on Ed's speech. OK without being great. One Nation needed more policy edge. I sent him a note, saying it was a lot stronger, but still weakest when it came to policy agenda going forward. He didn't need to set out every spit and fart of a manifesto, but give a sense of process at least, and general direction. One Nation is a perfectly good idea, and a contrast with the current lot, but it lacked policy edge. There was a case for publishing a background pamphlet (or at least a briefing note) which built on the theme in a more discursive and policy-rich way than is possible in a speech. I could see he did not want to clunk everything up with a string of announcements, but 'What would you do?' remains a legitimate question at the end. I set out the questions he has to be answering at this stage of the parliament.

1. Who are you?
2. Are you the right leader for Labour at this time?
3. Could you lead the country?
4. Why are the other lot wrong for the country at this time?
5. What would be different?

The easiest is 4. The hardest right now are 3 and 5. I said he should re-read the speech with the above in mind and see if it took him to a different place. He had some strong lines, but there was too much 'tell not show' about being ready to lead. I did lots of desk clearing, and sorting out papers, then out on the bike. Clegg apology for tuition fees turned into a song ['Nick Clegg Says I'm Sorry (The Autotune Remix)'], going viral, and cleverly he agreed to it being released provided proceeds went to local hospital.

Friday 21 September
Blog re. the cops, Andrew Mitchell having had a huge row with police at No. 10 because they wouldn't open the gate for him to cycle out. Not good. Would fly. I used it to tell the story of the cop at the Olympics who said, 'Get these fucking cunts out.'

Monday 24 September
I had a good session with Steve Broome of the Royal Society of Arts, who with his wife was writing a book on depression. He had done a fair bit of research and actually for once I quite enjoyed it as an interview. Lunch with [Lord] Jonathan Sumption [historian and Hutton Inquiry government barrister] at his favourite restaurant in Shoreditch. He arrived carrying a book on the history of Scotland, saying it was a gap in his knowledge. He was on his fourth volume of his great medieval history and loving it. His new role in the Supreme Court was clearly quite interesting but, I sensed, not quite as challenging as perhaps he had hoped. He was not terribly impressed by the government, felt that neither Cameron nor Osborne were really on top of the job, but was not terribly impressed by Ed, feeling 'everyone knows' they picked the wrong brother. He was pretty sure Chilcot would be scathing.

He felt Hutton had been right in his judgment but underestimated the extent to which he made things worse for us by being so clear. He was one of those judges who, once he had decided where right and wrong lay, would go for 100 per cent right and wrong. A lighter moment when he said that because of my line in the diaries that he owned a whole village – figure of speech – the *Sunday Times* had been down looking at every home sale record. In fact he had one house, though admittedly a large one. He hadn't changed much, still oddly dressed, very precise in what he said, but also quirky and with flashes of good humour. He had had a long holiday, was working away on the book, reading loads, clearly enormous scope and intellect. He felt TB had slightly lost his way, and didn't quite know why. He was sure Chilcot would go for him but the longer he waited the less the impact. He said Robin Butler had essentially gone for him but did it in such mandarin language nobody noticed.

Tuesday 25 September

Prime Performers [speakers' agency] event at Soft Drinks Association lunch, Mandarin Oriental. Nice bunch. On form, great reaction. Can't remember a thing I said though.

Wednesday 26 September

Terrific event first thing down near Tower Bridge, Rocket to Recovery organised by Equinox [care homes] who look after addicts and the homeless. I kicked it off after a nice chat with a group who were down from a similar group in Birmingham. Then stories from survivors – drugs, drink, gambling, several of them in and out of prison – and good crowd. Just the kind of people Cameron and Osborne just do not get on any level. The cuts were beginning to bite. Met up with Matt Parker of British Cycling, lunch then off to UK Sport to meet Graham Taylor and his colleague who were putting together a strategy for an elite football coaching course. Matt was hoping to get me involved. Interesting concept, amazing that we didn't have it already.

To the Savoy for dinner – WACL, Women in Advertising and Communications London – hosted by Camilla Harrisson of Saatchis. Really nice woman and in part because of an OCD relative she was keen to do more for Mind which they had adopted as their chosen charity. Fiona came which was nice. Lovely atmosphere, nice crowd and impossible to fail. But it really went down well, as good as I could remember. Mix of politics and personal re. mental health and then an appeal to them to apply their creativity to what we were trying to do.

Call from doctor on the growth in my groin. It was going down but she felt it sensible that I still go for an ultrasound. Ed sent through another draft of the speech which I had a go at. It was much better than last year's at the same stage. He was really hammering One Nation but still worried whether it was clear and credible. I said well, at least it is a strategic line and allows you then to shape the policy in that direction. He was still too keen to distance himself from Old and New Labour, and though this was clearly closer to New, it allowed him the space he felt he needed. I wrote a few new lines including one re. the incompetence of the Tories based on the old Coke ad, lip smacking, thirst quenching etc.

Lunch at The Cube on top of Festival Hall. It was a great venue, a temporary restaurant which could be transported around the place. It was an event for the Bobby Moore [former England captain] Fund for Cancer Research, so Stephanie Moore [widow] was hosting and used it to tell us about their next campaign and pick brains for ideas. Stephanie was really impressive, had all the facts and figures at her fingertips and was really nice too. Posher than I imagined. Had a good chat with Roy Hodgson. He was waiting to hear the outcome of the FA hearing on [England captain] John Terry's racist blast at [Anton] Ferdinand [Queens Park Rangers player].* Four matches and a fine. He seemed to think that was what had been expected. He struck me as being a little bit jaded with the job, made a couple of cracks on how hard it was to get the players together, where power lay, how much time he had on his hands etc. Nice do, and gave them some ideas for fundraising. Fiona enjoyed it and she and I were getting on so much better, though still worrying the whole time re. the kids.

Bike, then train north for Burnley v Millwall. Did a quick blog en route setting up a few thoughts re. Labour conference. Ed said he was pretty much settled on the speech now, which we never had been by the Saturday. Drew the match, throwing away a lead again. 2–2. Ray Ingleby [Burnley chairman] had called the other day asking if I could do the after-dinner speech at the end of an all-day sales conference for a pal of his in the software industry in Blackpool. I asked them to send me a car to take me there, via a planned trip to the Football Museum in Manchester, and they sent a bloody Bentley, to the amusement and/or irritation of Burnley fans

---

* Terry was cleared in magistrate's court of racially abusing Ferdinand in a match between Chelsea and QPR but disciplined by the Football Association and removed from the England captaincy.

streaming out after the match. The museum was excellent and it was a shame I had to rush. Then to Blackpool and a nice enough crowd, and both speech and Q&A went down well. Got to Manchester by about twelve.

Sunday 30 September

I missed Ed M on *Marr* but by all accounts, including Georgia, he did well, and the mood around conference was actually pretty good, as much because the Tories kept shooting themselves in the foot because we were offering much. I did a last short note to Ed, saying that the speech was in good shape, but he should read through it one more time from the point of view of whether it says enough about him, about values, about what we would do differently. But it was much, much better than last year's. Len McCluskey was all over the papers saying that he would pull the plug financially unless etc... Tosser. They were going to become a big problem at some point, for sure. I went out for a run in the drizzle, then met up with Georgia who was worrying about whether there would be enough people coming to the fringe event I was doing tomorrow, with Peter M and Danny Finkelstein about the Denis Kavanagh book on Philip G. She was worrying needlessly but we talked through a few things we could do to promote it.

My only actual event was a stage interview with disc jockey Dave Haslam at the Royal Exchange theatre, which had sold out, and was a terrific venue. His wife and daughter came up to see us before and both were fans, but he gave me anything but an easy time. It was good though, really pushing me on Iraq and people's sense of powerlessness in politics and I think it brought out the best of me in terms of passionate debating. Met up with Gail and the girls, Theo, Calum and Rory for dinner at Don Giovanni's. Again the issue of why I did not stand had come up, and one of the Manchester seats had been there asking me to think about standing for them, and I discussed it with Gail who warmed to it as we went on. I just was not sure. And I was not sure why I wasn't sure.

Calum a bit distant but OK. Rory staying with me and going to Everton for a couple of days. Fiona up tomorrow. We went to the *New Statesman* party at the town hall, which was fine but I just got inundated at these events with a combination of political starfuckers, MPs and candidates and charities wanting advice, and journos. At one point it was like there was a little queue there and I just wanted to get away. A really weird guy who to my amazement said he was a candidate, presumably for a very safe Tory seat. Rory made the observation that politics did appear to attract an excessive share of oddballs.

September '12: Rory points out 'politics attracts oddballs'

Monday 1 October

Up to the Velodrome to meet up with Fran Millar [Team Sky] and get sized up for a Pinarello bike with two of their top mechanics. Back to the flat to change then to conference. A lot smaller than usual, fewer people and stands, but OK mood. Watched Douglas A who did OK, and also Balls who got a good response but said very little. I watched it with Gail and Peter M, who looked like he would rather be anywhere else. Our event went well though, packed out with people standing outside trying to get in, and though Danny's interviewing was a bit odd at times – e.g. getting bogged down re. CND at one point – it went well. Neil was there, commentating as he went along. Peter was a little subdued though insightful. I managed to get them going a bit with attacks on the Tories and defence of our record.

Signed loads of the PG book at the end, then went off to do media, Sky, Beeb (slapped James Landale [deputy political editor] gently when he kept asking the same questions, and they bloody used it). Had a little dig at Kay Burley on Sky re. her saying unions were the problem, then off to Iain Dale who asked me why I didn't stand and when I said I thought about it it went pretty big around the place, and led to loads of people telling me I should. Tea with Peter Reid [football manager] and Eddie Izzard who both said go for it. Fiona not sure. We had dinner together which was nice, then hung around the hotel a bit before I did *Newsnight* down the line on whether voters did not like clever people. At least it meant they were promoting the line Ed was clever. Fiona had come up mainly for the PG event and her own fringe meeting tomorrow but in truth we were staying pretty distant from things. In the hotel we bumped into Iain Dale and co., and also had a civilised chat with Nick Robinson. My line re. intellectuals was that we had to get away from the idea it was possible to be 'too clever by half' and also that politicians had to combine being clever with human skills of empathy etc., and the ability to explain complex arguments in simple language. Not always easy.

Tuesday 2 October

Over to the Midland for breakfast with Endri Fuga, Mark Lucas and Greg Cook to go over what Mark and Greg could do for the Albanian elections. Endri very excited because they had just heard Edi would be meeting Obama when he was in the States next week. Dave Fishwick in town for his latest bank [Bank of Dave] push. Met him for a filmed chat on the steps of the hotel in which he told me the FSA had threatened him with prosecution if he did not desist. He was his usual defiant self though.

He said he wanted to keep the idea quiet for now, but my advice was that he should go for it. He was at conference for the day and wanted to meet some Labour faces. I tried Balls who was in the foyer, but he was too calculating, would not take on trust the idea it might be worth doing. Then Neil K, who had the good idea of getting Arlene McCarthy, who in addition to being plugged in to the financial world was also Dave's MEP.

Dave Brailsford arrived and we went to Starbucks for a coffee and a chat prior to the Olympics session we were planning. Quite a lot in the papers on me becoming an MP and Dave was sure I should. He said either I will be a big thing in the next government, or we lose and I am a big thing in the next leadership, even leader. He said that I was way cleverer than Ed or Cameron so why not? Stop seeing the reasons not to and go for it. He wanted some advice on his and the team's positioning re. drugs. He had set up the idea that they were totally clean but some of the older technical hands were known to have worked with teams that doped. I said he needed to have a message that said it will take a generation and he will lead that. Maybe have an element of truth and reconciliation, let people admit any wrongdoing and then move on. He wanted me to come up for a brainstorm at some point and really work it through. Agreed to do it. He was still really negative on Ed.

Over to the conference centre and several people were saying 'Go for it' re. becoming an MP. Calum was meeting Seb Coe and Paul Deighton [CEO Olympics organising committee] and their team, and once everyone had arrived – Jonathan Edwards [former long-jumper, committee member], Tessa, some of the athletes and families – Tessa did a run-through for everyone. The mood was terrific, Tessa spoke OK, though I had Dick Caborn next to me chuntering about her, also saying there was no way a Tory audience would have welcomed a Labour equivalent of Seb. Seb had picked up on the rumours re. me and Parliament and he said, 'Just don't, I beg you, you will hate it.' Chatted with Deighton re. his ministerial job [Commercial Secretary to the Treasury], which he would be taking up in the New Year. I sensed he would get frustrated pretty quickly. Walked out with Dave who had another go at me, then I was off and heading for the train. I was sorry to miss Ed's speech but had to get back for the National Grid executive board dinner. It meant following the speech on Twitter on the train. He was doing it without notes, and as the speech went on, it was clear he was doing really well. By the end it was something of a triumph. Certainly there was the sense that it was game on and that the Tories could not be so dismissive. Fair play to him. Fair to say he had never had any kind of honeymoon, not even with the party, let alone the media and the Tories, who thought they could kill him from the off. He was definitely back on the pitch.

Wednesday 3 October

All day at the National Grid strategy powwow. I had been a bit sceptical but actually found the process really good, and the preparation they had done excellent. I had thrown out a few ideas in one of our earlier brainstorms – e.g. analyse other energy companies' messaging and perceived strategies. We were at it all day, including through lunch. Very early on, in part through the huge variations in their descriptions of the message and strategy, and in part through looking at the jumble they currently had, they went for the idea of change without any trouble, and then it became a discussion of exactly what they would go for as a new message framework.

I was fairly impressed. It was remarkable how much they all saw the New Labour New Britain prism as a good one to view through, including the Americans who really made a good contribution.

Thursday 4 October

Nice message from Ed, saying thanks for help and support on the speech, and thanks for some of the best lines. Also got a letter from David M saying thanks for the South Shields dinner, and also that he had been too dismissive of the idea of me getting a seat, and actually he felt it was a good idea.

Friday 5 October

Off to Dublin for a trip sponsored by Lundbeck, the drugs company who were developing new drugs to combat alcohol addiction. Photocall in a park in the city, them off to the Royal College of Physicians, one of the bodies that kept the royal title. Lunch with John Bowman [broadcaster], who was going to be interviewing me, Eithne Boyan, the Lundbeck boss in Dublin, and a GP specialising in alcohol, Dr Garrett McGovern. Lots of TDs [Irish MPs] at the session, good interview, mixing my own story with new figures they had about the extent of alcohol abuse in Ireland. Good Q&A, nice comments from Garrett and others, then a stack of interviews before I went over to join a group who would be sharing stories of addiction and recovery. Really good event, enjoyed it.

Popped in to Twitter's office and got shown a bit how it works and how they make money, e.g. promoted tweets and trends. Showed me I had a seventy-two reputation, whatever that meant. But they said it was very high. To the Merrion for dinner and then out to *The Late Late Show*. Alan Quinlan [retired rugby player] there and took me to one side to say thanks for the work on depression. He was trying to do the same in Ireland. The interview went fine. Novelist Joe O'Connor already on the sofa, so after my bit we mixed it up a bit and then did the same with the Canadian immigration minister who was over pitching for skilled labour. There were several people in the audience who said they were planning to emigrate, including one woman who looked very scared, heartbroken even.

Saturday 6 October

Blogged on the immigration debate last night. Canada's approach showing on so many fronts the wrongheaded approach of our government.* Also showing some economies recovering better than others. Out to the airport and off for home, quick turnaround to get out for Kate Garvey–Jimmy Wales [co-founder, Wikipedia] wedding. Kate had wanted to get married in church but of course it was his third time, and in the end [Baroness] Jan Royall [Labour leader in the Lords] had found a Labour peer who agreed to do the ceremony. Packed church, lots of the old TB team, including TB, Cherie, David M and Anji (who last week had done an interview I hadn't seen, in which she complained JoP and I minimised her role). Neil and Glenys there and G said Anji had every right to be peed off that Jan and Sue [Nye] had ended up in the Lords, having been maybe less important to Neil and GB than she had been to TB.

The service was fine, then I had to nip out to play the pipes and lead them over to the reception. Pipes going OK. There was a lot of hanging around outside with drinks and canapés before going inside. I was happier playing than snatching all those five-minute chats. Peter M there but didn't see him to talk to, Juliet Soskice and her ex-husband – though apparently she was currently seeing Andrew Rosenfeld [property developer, Labour supporter]. Inside, and another delay before food, with a band playing and Kate insisting there was dancing before dinner. Eventually through to three beautifully laid out long tables where 300 were to sit down for dinner. We were with Neil and Glenys, Nicola H and Gail. Neil on good form, and giving quite sound advice on Parliament. He felt it was a great idea for the party, but not so sure for me. He also thought I might be 'too big', and he refuted the idea I could be PPC [prospective parliamentary candidate] and run the campaign at the centre. A constituency would expect me to be there. Jan concurred.

TB came over at one point and we had a little chat re. this and that, including Obama's bizarre performance in the first presidential TV debate with Romney. All sorts of theories were going round – altitude sickness, flu, complacency, deliberately being low-key to go for a no-score draw – but whatever it was, he was dire and Romney had probably got himself

---

* Canada's liberal immigration policy included the humanitarian consideration of refugees and other persecuted people.

back into the game. The polls were moving a bit, and though Obama was still ahead in the swing states it had definitely gone from all over to back on. I said that we maybe underestimated how much better at debating regular PMQs made British leaders. Or maybe Obama's arrogance was kicking in. Odd. Had a little chat re. Kaz. TB said he was really proud of what we were doing there.

Sunday 7 October

Out on the bike, missed Cameron on *Marr* but reading the media brief it looked like they did not have a clear strategy, also that they were a bit wrongfooted by Ed seeming to have done better than expected. Mum was down, long chat with her before Audrey arrived and we all headed to the Albert Hall for a celebration of the Calendar Girls. First to a reception for *Good Housekeeping* magazine, then to a LLR drinks do in the Prince of Wales room. The girls had announced there were to be no more calendars. All six there and on great form as ever, and blown away by the stage show, which was a mix of stories, music and history of their own story, ending with them on stage winning the inaugural John Baker [late husband of CG girl Angela, whose death from cancer was the inspiration for the calendar] award.

Monday 8 October

Mum off early and I headed to the Royal Free for an ultrasound on my groin. All fine. To Freuds for a chat with Nicola, who was clearly finding Matthew difficult at the moment, and then the guys who were off to the US to work on the Obama campaign. Osborne's speech was average. I did a blog on his observation that they were making difficult changes now because Cameron did not want to be like TB and discover after ten years he had achieved nothing. Pointed out some of the many historic changes and compared it with the lack of anything comparable from this lot. Went down well with Labour people, not least those asking why we never defended the record. I did a little run but my cold was grim now. Went to bed at six with a couple of sleeping pills.

Tuesday 9 October

India Knight had done a silly piece in the *Sunday Times* essentially saying 'everyone got depression' and criticising the idea that there was still stigma. Time to Change asked me to respond which I did, really taking it on. Huffington Post also ran my piece, plus good response on my website. Rushanara Ali [Labour MP for Bethnal Green and Bow] came in for a chat about her own profile and future. She was clearly struggling to break out of the slight ghetto that the media wanted to put non-white MPs into. I couldn't really work out if I was able to help. I was feeling like death warmed up, so rested up, apart from a call with Ed's Irish publisher friend Kathy Gilfillan, who was keen on doing the Irish version of my diaries. Dinner with Chris Lennie to go over the possibilities if I did decide to stand. He felt Keighley and Burnley were the best bets, though both marginal. He thought Falkirk might be a safer option. He said he was not sure I would enjoy it but the party and leader's office would both back it. He felt I would need to work out how to handle the Respect [far-left firm] circus as Galloway would not be able to resist.

Wednesday 10 October

Met Mark Lucas at the airport and off to Tirana via Vienna. We were due to meet Edi and Endri, en route back from the States, in Vienna, but they got delayed. So when we got there we had meetings with Erion, Arbi who did branding stuff, and a mathematician who used to work for Edi in the mayor's office and did my head in with a presentation on how to put together a strategy. Edi wanted me to work on a one-page strategy note he could show to his party exec so I got working on that too. Mark enjoying the place and got on with Arbi. Erion felt things were OK but Berisha was really stepping things up and getting more and more aggressive. He felt Edi was in OK shape but needed to move up another gear.

Thursday 11 October

Met Edi for a long chat and went over strategy, how to handle the coalition question, how to play the idea of the team. He had been reading the updated *Unfinished Revolution* and was raving about both the book and the scale of the political operation we ran. He wanted more of the same. He was more confident. He felt Berisha was a bit rattled. The latest EU candidate status report was more positive and Berisha was really trying to milk it. Edi felt things were moving his way but he knew that to win, and have the win accepted, he would have to win big. It was clear Berisha would stop at nothing. The big news was a hunger strike of former political prisoners, two of whom had set fire to themselves, and Berisha was pretty scathing of them.

I worked on the strategy paper for him, then he set off for Fier, and we later joined him for a meeting of a women's conference. Gave his team a few ideas on how to improve outside events. They needed more music, atmospherics. Interesting drive. So many houses only half built, and ugly. Planning a mess. Drove back with Edi and went over the whole feel of the campaign. Renaissance was working. He wanted a new look. Said he loved the London 2012 Olympics colours so we decided to work on purple with Mark and Arbi. Stopped halfway for dinner and Endri lost it a bit when Edi kept saying they needed to do all the things I was recommending, because he said they had no money and nobody ever took responsibility for fundraising. Nice chat with Edi on the drive back. Went for a late swim. Cameron's conference speech seemed to go down pretty well. Most of his ministers had lurched to the right but he was centrist in tone at least. Not sure the speech would have much enduring impact though.

Friday 12 October

Worked through all the various notes on strategy. Chatted to Edi about how to handle his team when he presented it next week. Re. Meta we agreed he should just let him carry on whacking Berisha. Henri Çili [business-man] had been interesting re. strong leadership. He said because of their history Albanians were suspicious of strong leadership and they wanted these other players to keep Edi in check. He also felt that they had yet to put policy flesh on the renaissance theme. So it sounded OK but did not add up. Gave a few more ideas – e.g. real people as backdrop, who emerged as the people behind the stories he told. Addressing an old man who says nothing changes and going through the changes in his lifetime. That kind of thing.

Edi was really up for ideas for new ways of doing stuff. Also wanted one of our people to advise on layout of the office and how to integrate the campaign team. He liked Mark who was adding a lot. Signed off a draft new logo with Arbi. Off to the airport with Mark and Adia, and home two airline dinners later. Edi felt the trip had been great. I felt a bit ill still, and knackered.

Saturday 13 October

Off to the Cotswolds to stay with Annie Robinson. She, Fiona and Calum went off to the Cheltenham Literature Festival for a talk about Philip by Gail. I opted to go out on the bike, which was fantastic. Cold but sharp and nice and amazing scenery. I was still not 100 per cent but I was glad to get out. Later they all came back and we had a very nice dinner, lots of *Mirror* and Robert Maxwell [late *Mirror* proprietor] reminiscing, a bit of politics, lots of [deceased radio and TV personality] Jimmy Savile, with more and more stuff emerging about how much of a sex abuser he was.

Annie was on great form. Calum really liked her. Georgia also surprised I think by how nice she was.

Sunday 14 October

Another long bike ride, back to skim the papers then lunch. Left after a terrific lunch then pottered all afternoon, trying to get on top of all the work coming up. Dave Brailsford called. The USADA [anti-doping agency] report on Lance [Armstrong] had been pretty devastating and the fallout was continuing. Dave said he wanted a bit of advice on how to handle. He was confident in his past statements re. building a clean team, but clearly some of the backroom team had been involved with dirty teams. He was obviously minded to move them on.

15 to 27 October

Another long period during which I just could not be arsed to keep my usual kind of diary, day after day thinking I might and then thinking oh sod it, who cares? So here we are, back in Faucon, back thinking about whether to get a seat, back thinking about another book, back thinking about whether the consultancy and speaking stuff I was doing added up to a row of beans. It was still pouring in, and Fiona said we had a huge tax bill coming in soon. Since the summer, the speaking market paid and unpaid had picked up and for some periods I was out speaking pretty much every day. BNP Paribas [French banking group] was interesting, another bank keen to do stuff on mental health, so I spoke there as part of their Diversity Week. It was interesting how the audience, nice though they were, and dozens of *The Happy Depressive* though they bought, had not expected mental health to figure alongside gays, women, race and physical disability issues.

Did another one for a mental health service users group in Croydon, Hear Us, where Sue Baker and Gavin Barwell [local MP] were also speaking. Also Ed M had decided to make his first big speech post conference about mental health, the One Nation case for a new approach, and he sent me various drafts which I was pleased to help with. It would make a difference having both him and Clegg out there on this. The pre-Leveson skirmishing was stepping up and I was meeting from time to time with the Hacked Off campaign team to advise on strategy. They had picked up worrying signals from Harriet's office that Labour was looking to back a deal with the editors, and when I texted Ed about it later, he indicated that they worried Hacked Off were too inflexible. Not a good sign. But when Harriet went on *Marr* she remained firm – whereas Eric Pickles on

[Dermot] Murnaghan [Sky News] and Boris Johnson in the *Telegraph* were out with the anti-statutory regulation arguments on the same day.

The other campaign I had got drawn into was No More Page 3 [topless female glamour feature in *The Sun*], and I had a meeting with them, including Stella Creasy, shortly before we left for France. It was important for them not to be part of the Leveson debate. We went over the kind of names that would be good on a letter to Dominic Mohan [editor] to try to draw him into a debate. He needed to feel it was actually a bit old-fashioned. Lots of involvement in the Burnley manager's job, Eddie Howe having gone back to Bournemouth. Alex recommended we take a look at Steven Pressley [Falkirk FC manager] so I fixed up for him to come down and he did pretty well, got a second interview but in the end the board felt he lacked experience at our level. They went for Sean Dyche [former Watford manager] in the end, again leaving the fans a bit underwhelmed, especially as there had been a buzz about Ian Holloway being interested at one point.

I did a good session for Portland at Barclays, did a Chatham House gig on social media with Chris Mullin, was presumably at least part of the reason for them winning medium-sized agency at the PR week awards, went to a reception at which I enjoyed meeting a very flirty, and funnier than I expected, Sophie Wessex [Countess of Wessex, wife of Prince Edward], and also chatted to Paul Mylrea [director of public affairs] of the Beeb amid the growing Jimmy Savile sex abuse scandal. Pretty amazing stuff, clearly a serial abuser, so my thought when I met him that he was gay because all he did was talk about shagging women was clearly wrong. Hiding in plain sight. Nice to see lots of people who used to work for me there, as it seemed to be a gathering of comms directors.

Did a Credit Suisse [financial services company] dinner and sat next to Ivan Glasenberg, CEO of Glencore, who was a lot nicer and funnier than I anticipated from the profile. He was very funny about TB's role in the Xstrata [mining company] merger talks. The papers were full of the idea TB made £1 million for a few minutes in a meeting, but Ivan told me he had paid him nothing and he would only get paid if the deal came off. Also said that at one point be had asked TB to go back with another proposal, TB had protested that there was a limit to what his dignity would allow, to which Ivan said, 'You have no dignity, you're a politician.'

Peter M was speaking at the main dinner – the biggest black-tie dinner in Europe – and we sent each other a few mutually abusive messages both to amuse Ivan and give us lines for speeches. Ivan asked me to talk about qualities of different leaders I had worked with, which went fine. Q&A went fine too. Was on top form at these speeches these days, and was getting into the habit of not writing anything till I got there, and mixing hardy annuals with assessment of current affairs. Cameron and Osborne not going down well but despite the conference there were still too many people saying that they could not see Ed in charge of the country. Also, as I said to Ed a couple of times, there had been next to no follow-through post conference. I wondered frankly what most of the shadow Cabinet did all day.

On the decision to go for a seat or not, Mum, Seb, Syd [Young] and Fiona were broadly against. Mum and Seb violently so. He had taken to texting me, 'Just don't do it.' Charlie F was hugely in favour, but said he felt Ed would be worried by it because the media would immediately find me a more interesting character. He felt I would like it more than I thought, as did Sally. They both felt I would turn it into something bigger than it was. Charlie felt I had to be honest about whether I wanted to be leader. He felt I could do it. If we won, I would be straight into a top job. If we lost, I would be a key player in the direction of the party, and possibly a contender for the top job. He was wildly enthusiastic. Ditto David Mills. Alex more balanced. Rory on balance in favour. Fiona worried about the impact on life and lifestyle.

We had a dinner with Chris Lennie who felt Burnley was there for the taking, Keighley also possible, and Falkirk if I wanted a safer option. He and Sally both warned that I would become a big target not just for the media but Respect, so maybe not go for a Muslim area. Tom Baldwin told me that when Ed called Dacre when doing his post conference speech ring-round, Dacre's first words were, 'It had better not be true AC is getting a seat.' So that went down in the reasons to do it list. Everyone seemed to see so clearly that I would do it well and enjoy it but I had nagging doubts. Gail away in China and news broke of possible merger between Random House and Penguin. Big deal. Not sure immediately what it meant for her. Nice dinner for Rory's 25th.

A lot of the time I was thinking about, and talking to friends about, the seat idea. Rory very positive. Calum felt it would be OK if I was doing it for the right reasons, but also that it would undermine Ed more than I realised. Peter M thought part of me would love it but part of me would hate it. And I would find the PLP a total pain. Added to which he felt EM was incapable of delivering strategy. Did a few blogs from France, one or two in Kazakhstan where I spent early November. Mainly working with Massimov and Yerzhan Kazykhanov on the President's speech next month. Start of winter and I tried and failed to get a coat in Paris Charles de Gaulle – no shops anywhere to be found, but did in Frankfurt.

Usual horror overnight short flight, snowing on landing, packed round of meetings the key of which was with Massimov. His new role at the Akorda [President's residence], he said, made our project better and stronger. There

October '12: Taking soundings on getting a seat

was definitely a chance to make themselves more relevant with power and wealth shifting from West to East. If this was to be the Asian century, they were well-placed geographically and strategically. They could become a bridge between East and West. Not a time to be inward-looking, but outward-looking. Continue down the path of openness. Also said they had to address Zhanaozen.* Why did it happen? What lessons have been learned? What changes have been made? How to repair damage done to image at home and abroad. Need to make sure the world knows how the country is changing.

Nice long email from Calum. He said he was totally on board with the idea to go into frontline politics 'as long as you are doing it for the right reasons'. He said when he discussed it with Fiona the other night, the main thing that came out of it was that she was not sure whether I was doing it just because I was bored and want a new challenge, or whether it is because I actually really feel like I want to make a difference to the Labour Party or politics in general. He said if it is because I want a new challenge and am bored in life on the outside, 'who's to say that you won't be bored of being an MP in a few years' time and want to move onto something else?' He also said he would be 'incredibly anxious' about the impact this could have on Ed's leadership if you go for it. He felt the media would start a frenzy on the basis of 'Campbell looking to replace Miliband'. He was also unsure I would enjoy not being able to go to France when we felt like it. I was pleased though that he had thought it through and sent such a nice mail on it.

Sean Dyche was off to a great start at Burnley. 2–0 v Wolves then one–nil v Leeds. Had a few friendly text exchanges with him about it. Seemed like a really good bloke, very clear and strong-minded. The players were buzzing. Edi called after the Hillary visit last week and said she had been saying I was the difference between winning and losing the Albanian election.

Wednesday 7 November

Obama won. He had been up and down since the first TV debate, where he was dreadful, but in the end it was an OK result. I did a blog based in part on reading Robert Caro's latest book on Lyndon Johnson, showing how Obama needed some of that raw political skill now and less of the showbiz glam look.

---

* The massacre of Zhanaozen, in western Kazakhstan, took place in December 2011, with fourteen protestors being killed by police during civil unrest on the country's Independence Day.

Thursday 8 November

Hugh Grant round first thing to interview me for his documentary on the press, pre Leveson. Fiona and Grace keen to meet. We went up to the study and it was really just a chat, but I pointed out, as I had done to the Hacked Off lot, that they needed to do a better job of understanding where others were coming from, not to compromise as such but to understand how to beat them in argument. He had a fairly cut-and-dried view about it all. We chatted for an hour or so, pretty much all my usual stuff, then a bit with him trying to press me re. our role in it all, after which he apologised for being a bit Paxmanesque. I said he really didn't need to and he really wasn't that tough in his questioning. Off to Which?, meeting for Portland, to persuade the chairman to be more strategic and less day to day. Interesting set-up, I had no idea they were into so much more than just the consumer watchdog stuff. It wasn't difficult to persuade them to operate according to a more strategic framework.

Then off to Dublin via City and the Advertising Industry Awards. *The Times* called asking for a piece on cycle safety after Bradley Wiggins was knocked off his bike up north. Did a bit of media, photos for the event, then a reception. Nice bunch as ever. The speech was pre dinner and it was a paean to advertising which went down pretty well. The other speaker had a nice line: 'Unforgettable brands advertise.' One firm won a stack of awards and I had a chat with one of the team, Margaret Barron, who said she loved my speech, that everyone there saw a genius communicator and she would love it if I put that to the use of Ireland by offering to work for Enda Kenny [Taoiseach], who really needed that now. Margaret was really forceful and made a big impact, telling me I probably underestimated how I was seen by people like those in the room and I needed to set my mind to doing more and really going for it.

Friday 9 November

Breakfast with Kathy Gilfillan to discuss the Irish edition of diaries. Nice woman, clever, would do a good job. Flew home. Donald down for a piping tournament, agreed to meet at Grill at 424 with Calum, Jamie [Naish, nephew] and others, but C came back a bit worse for wear and we ended up in another bad scene with him.

Saturday 10 November

Getting close to giving Calum an ultimatum, that he could only stay with us if sober. Donald persuaded him to try an AA meeting, but he said he was only doing it for us, not for himself. Went to Ipswich with Mike Lownes.

Stayed in directors' box. Chatting with Simon Clegg whose loathing of Colin Moynihan was even greater than Seb's. [Manager] Mick McCarthy's first home game and they were really up for it and we lost 2–1.

Sunday 11 November

Lovely sunny day. Speaking at BLP law firm conference in Watford. Did my usual strategy speech and it went down pretty well, plus a book signing that went on for ages, and had an artist there taking photos for a portrait he wanted to enter in the BP awards at the National Portrait Gallery.

Monday 12 November

Lots of talk re. the BBC, with Entwhistle now gone and Tim Davie acting DG. I did a blog for CNN.com which was broadly supportive and said the important thing was not to panic and steer a course back to clearer strategy. Also suggesting [BBC Trust chairman Lord] Chris Patten's role of cheerleader plus part regulator had to be looked at. Amazing how he swanned from one establishment job to another.

Tuesday 13 November

Portland strategy session with some of the newer and younger ones. Met by Rayan and off to Bishop's Stortford High School. Nice place, disciplined, quite a political audience. Did a speech and Q&A and a book signing, plus interview with the school paper. Rayan said they had been given a lecture beforehand about how they had to be polite etc., no rudeness in the questions, so maybe it was a bit flat but the basic pro-politics message seemed to go down OK. Dinner at Mossiman's, an event organised by Nationwide. OK crowd, and was on form, especially in the Q&A with a guy there who everyone else seemed to hate, so when he started to have a bit of a pop, I was popping back pretty well. Another business audience very down on Cameron, Osborne and Cable, but not up on Ed M and Ed B.

Wednesday 14 November

Writing speech stuff and also generally trying to shape next few weeks. HSBC for Mind event at the private bank. Robin Janvrin [bank chairman, former Buckingham Palace adviser] introduced me and said some very nice things not just on the mental health campaign, where he said I was 'moving the dial', but re. the work I did 'working with me when my previous organisation was going through tricky times.' Did my usual anti-stigma talk, with a fair bit of the backstory. Good event. Definitely something stirring too as the Schizophrenia Commission Report on 'The Abandoned Illness' was getting a lot of media attention.

Thursday 15 November

Set off early, drive to Burnley to check in, then to Nelson for a 'Speakers for Schools' charity event at Marsden Heights. Terrific facilities, two schools merged on new premises, mainly non-white, good teachers I sensed. Chatted with the pupils and the local paper, then a speech, Q&A and then a 'University Challenge' quiz, my team against the head's team, which we won. Good bunch. The Speakers for Schools scheme was [broadcaster] Robert Peston's brainchild and seemed to be going well. Teachers broadly hated Gove. Drove over to Manchester to collect my new Pinarello Kobh [custom-built bicycle]. Fantastic. Love it. Ollie from the Sky Team fitted me, watched me have a little spin round the car park, chatted with Fran [Millar, head of business operations] then we had dinner. Agreed that I should do a strategy presentation to the team with a view to doing an audit and then having a centralised system in place. Wiggins and Froome both quite difficult to manage, and their antagonism and that of partners didn't help. Fran was clever and a team player and clearly Dave B trusted her. She said the problem was Dave didn't like getting new people in so those who had tried had been pushed out because they didn't meet his expectations. He trusted me and I needed to get him to move to a different approach, e.g. he wasted a lot of his own time talking to media because he didn't trust others to do it for him.

I worried Sky might oppose me being involved because of the Murdoch stuff, but she felt that was manageable. They basically needed a strategic approach to comms, not reactive and then I could work with Dave and have a couple of juniors doing the doing. Dave called while we were in the restaurant so we chatted a bit. He had been more impressed than he expected to be when he went to the Velodrome and looked around. He had had his own views challenged.

Friday 16 November

Burnley Bondholders meeting. Me, Kevin Keith and Steve Rumbelow from the council, a guy starting a new spa, PR company looking after them, and Mike Tomlinson re. a Burnley 10k race but raising money for other causes. 150 or so people there and there were some bright people. Sky had done a very negative report on Burnley earlier in the week when the jobless figures came out and both Steve and I had hit back on that. Off to a junior school just outside town. 100 per cent English second language. No white kids at all, yet some walked past the school to go to all-white schools elsewhere. Head teacher said it might be too late to address. It was like apartheid. She was angry though they were marked in the same way as leafy lane schools in the south.

Met the Pupil Management Team, two per class who liaised with the teachers re. curriculum etc. Nice kids. But the head said some of them worked at school all day, plus homework, but also two hours at the Mosque after school. Being in Burnley meant I was thinking more closely re. the MP or not MP situation. Moving against, but feeling bad about it. So much to do for places like this, but there was something holding me back.

Out to Whalley and a nice restaurant where I met Sean Dyche, Ian Woan [assistant manager] and Tony Loughlan [coach] for dinner. I was impressed. Very sharp, really thought about the game and had worked out our strengths and weaknesses quickly. Sean felt our basic problem was one of mental weakness, flabbiness, the sense we were a soft touch. He rated a few of our players, said they were training hard, basically up for it. He was clearly about changing the culture, giving them time to change and if not they would be off. Ian Woan in particular asking about my life in politics and whether there were things they could learn, e.g. dealing with big egos, getting people to do things they didn't want to, etc.

Saturday 17 November

Out on the new bike in the cold and the frost, beautiful scenery, some amazing hills. Did a blog on the low turnout in the police commissioner elections and saying it was too easy to blame politicians and media but the public had to take a look at themselves too. Off for bacon sandwiches at Stan [Ternent] and Kath's. Long chat re. the kids before Stan went off to Birmingham v Hull to see Steve Bruce [Hull manager]. He was heading up his scouting operation. Game v Charlton was not bad but ruined by the ref sending off Kieran Trippier for handball on the line after ten minutes. Lee Grant saved the penalty and we didn't do badly with ten men but went down one–nil. Drove home and was knackered so missed Tim Allan's party.

Monday 19 November

Breakfast at Belsize Park with Geoff McDonald and Becky from Unilever. He had read my books and wanted to do something to help on mental illness. He was a depressive himself. Liked them both and we worked up the idea of a 'Time to Change employer', which I later put to Sue Baker. Out to the Mind Awards at the British Film Institute. Sat with Camilla

Harrisson from WACL [Women in Advertising and Communications]. Stephen Fry MCing an event bigger than ever. He seemed very down and admitted halfway through he had recently been in hospital. Piers Morgan won an award, Iain Dale (sitting in front of me) didn't, which was a shame because he had done a lot of good stuff.

Tuesday 20 November

Pottered around writing bits and pieces then later out to the Portland media quiz. Damian McBride* in Phil Webster's team so made sure they didn't win. Still had to present a prize to them – my book for all the team – so had to kind of communicate to McBride. Nice event, Café de Paris a good venue for it, won by legal correspondents, McDonalds bottom. Good laugh, and played the pipes for a musical round, a few tunes with questions attached.

Wednesday 21 November

Train out to Dagenham for a speech at the Sanofi/Businesseast event based on The Heath business park in Runcorn. John Lewis from The Heath said he had always wanted to get me and Steve Norris [former twice Tory London mayoralty candidate] on the same platform so he was thrilled we were there. We both did ra-ra speeches for the project [science park], praised Sanofi for not just walking away. Did a good Q&A then a long lunch. I was on the table with the unions, one of whom stood up and thanked Sanofi for their handling of the closure [of site in Newcastle], and called on Ford [plant closures in Dagenham and Southampton] to do the same. Later out to another speaking engagement at the RSA [Royal Society of Arts], as part of the National Freelancers' Day. Apparently there had been a bit of hostility to the idea of me doing it but I won them over, helped by a flirty Q&A with Sue Lawley [broadcaster] after my speech, which was advice on how they should influence government.

Thursday 22 November

Did an hour or so tweeting responses to young people as part of a European Parliament youth event, then off by train to Kew to meet Stephen Jones [rugby international] and off to Cardiff for the launch of his testimonial year. However, just an hour earlier they had learned that the Welsh Rugby

---

* Former Gordon Brown adviser who in 2011 resigned his position when it emerged he had sent emails discussing the possibility of spreading rumours about leading Conservatives that he had fabricated.

Union, having said they were backing this as their first ever testimonial for a player, now said they were supporting it but not giving it official backing. It threw the organising committee, chaired by the charmingly bonkers Adrian Davies, into a real spin, still going on by the time we got there for an emergency meeting. Adrian was all for wading in and killing a few people but we agreed in the end best to carry on as if nothing had happened, get the president of the WRU to talk tonight about how great Stephen was, get one of his earlier clubs to stand by as a backstop offerer of the testimonial, but essentially put the onus on the WRU to announce a U-turn rather than create a fuss.

Stephen such a nice guy. Good chat re. all sorts of things on the way down, family, sport, politics, his future, my future. He reckoned he had a couple of years left and then maybe coaching. Didn't fancy punditry. His restaurant was going well, winning awards already. I went for a swim at the hotel and found the pool full of All Blacks [touring New Zealand squad], which was all a bit masculinity-challenging. Did a bit of work then down to the reception and the dinner. Adrian was compèring and I was the butt of a lot of his jokes which went down well, and set me up for a little ten-minute speech about the [British and Irish] Lions and why I liked Stephen. Went to bed 11.30 thank God because the singsong in the bar lasted till 3 a.m.

Friday 23 November

Breakfast with Stephen and family. Stephen had been up till three but he seemed pretty fit. Had to be back training this afternoon though he was still injured. Still no clarity re. the testimonial situation. Got home and did a bit of work setting up next week before heading off to Lincoln for the CLP fundraiser. Lucy Rigby the candidate, bright and attractive, and pretty clever I think. Straightforward event with dinner, speech, Q&A and books and then off. I was on the 'no complacency' end of the market, saying I did not think we had yet connected in a way that suggested protest against the government would come our way. Got to Mum's about 11.30.

Saturday 24 November

Out on the bike then took Mum to the village hall where Liz and Rob were hosting a sports talk/God talk with Henry Olonga [former Zimbabwean cricketer]. He had been there the night before and Mum had said he talked far too much. He was shorter this time but a bit too preachy and a bit too much on the 'I am right everyone else is wrong' message. Liz and I had a little chat about it after. Off to Hull v Burnley. Bumped into Steve Bruce and we had a laugh about Stan, said he had given him the job to get him out of Kath's hair. Good chat with JP who seemed OK at having lost the PCC [police and crime commissioner] election. He won on first past the post but lost on second preferences. Lunch with the KC people and Alan Johnson who was with the new woman in his life, from Carlisle, boss of a translation service. Had lunch with them then went to watch the match in the chairman's box with JP, Jonathan [son], Pauline [Prescott]. JP was fascinated by the Burnley fans who were on good form today, mainly getting geared up for Blackburn next week. Left on the whistle, good away win, one–nil, and the team definitely getting stronger.

Sunday 25 November

Hamish Jenkinson, one of Kevin Spacey's team, had talked me into doing the first SundayWise, a monthly arts-themed event at the Ivy Club for people to gather and talk about whatever. All a bit winky wanky woo, lots of tweed and Prada bags and cashmere jumpers and what's in the papers. Not really our types at all. First up an arts writer from *The Independent* on her favourite book. Then Craig Murray who was very strong on his own story as ambassador in Uzbekistan, and his battles with Jack Straw, but slightly lost it when he broadened things to defend Julian Assange. Then me, and I made a joke of not agreeing with him about everything and instead did my main pitch re. mental health. All interspersed with poems from Lisa Tempest who was strong.

Lunch with the other speakers, Kevin and Aussie billionaire Michael Hintze [businessman], who tore into Craig a bit re. Assange. Nice enough time, and I got on better with Craig than I thought I would, had a good laugh with Kevin before he headed off to what he thought was Chelsea v Man United, when in fact it was City. I watched it in a bar before heading to the Criterion for our sixth LLR night with a name from the arts, Alan Yentob, having secured Miranda Hart [actress and comedian]. Really really popular and it went well.

Monday 26 November

Into Portland for a session on the LTA [Law Tennis Association], who were looking for a new PR partner on some aspects of their strategy. I had spoken to Roger Draper [CEO] and got an indication as to the kind of thing they wanted so I did a note as the basis of a brainstorm. Kaz call, then went to see Calum for lunch in Victoria Street before a meeting with AFP TV re. backgrounder on Leveson etc. Worked on a speech for Edi Rama and the Albanian independence celebrations. He was doing the 'dream' theme we had talked about before. Lots of media build-up to Leveson, the papers in their usual dishonest way making the issue of any statutory role the equivalent of a state regulator on content. Bunch of lying bastards. The worry was either that it would influence Leveson to water down, or influence Cameron not to go for it. Clegg and Ed seemed pretty solid on it all, sticking to the line that if it was not bonkers they would go for it.

Tuesday 27 November

Worked on my programme notes for the Rovers match. Albania trip cancelled because so much was going on re. the independence stuff. So I had a day to get on top of other stuff but failed miserably, ended up just frittering time, doing a bit of writing, a few calls, a bike ride, a kip, musing uselessly about the kind of thing I ought to be doing. Long chat with Euan Blair re. his political ambitions. He was keen to be an MP, had been building a bit of a base and reputation having quit banking to work on youth unemployment in Coventry. By the end of the chat we both agreed it might be better to wait till 2020. Later out to Midtown Business Club dinner in the big tent in Bloomsbury, which I was doing for LLR. They were trying to create Midtown as a label to match The City or the West End. Did an OK speech on positivity, weaved around a few jokes, as well as my LLR pitch. Seemed to go OK.

Wednesday 28 November

Ran into Grosvenor Square, conference call with the Kaz team re. their draft paper on Iran, then waited for TB to come back from his Europe speech which had had a bit of attention. New office look and furniture which CB had put together, including sofas on which it was impossible to sit without sliding into a heap. TB looking fit and well, had lost a bit of weight – unlike me, over 15 stone again – and was fizzing with stuff. Now working in ten countries, and wanting to double that so he had ten African projects on the go, and ten outside Africa. Mongolia and Vietnam the latest to look likely. He had raised £3 million for the Faith Foundation in the US and was looking for someone to toughen up the operation.

On Leveson he said the coverage of the build-up underlined why the papers needed tougher regulation. The basic dishonesties ran through them the whole time. He said he was still in this remarkable position where we were seen as the best example of modern political operation by most political operators around the world, but battered here. Re. GB, he said he wrote to him when Leo [TB father] died, but apart from that there had been no contact. Said he had been more upset by Leo's death than he thought he would be, as it had been on the cards for so long. Re. me, he said he felt I would be a good MP and could go very high but was I really up for it if, as was possible, we lost, or for the fact that 60 per cent of the life of most MPs is drudgery.

He felt on Ed M that though he was doing better, the basic strategy was wrong. He had spoken to him, said he was happy to help but he felt Ed had the view that the country had essentially moved to the left because of the austerity programme etc., and he didn't agree. Also business was there for the taking because of Cameron's drift and dither on Europe, but the top rate of tax pushed them back. He felt Ed was not making the impact he could be but ultimately it was because he had the wrong politics and the wrong strategy. He felt on balance I should go for it but be aware of how shitty it can be especially if we don't get a majority and despite everything that is entirely possible. No idea when the Iraq inquiry was coming. Amazing that Leveson had started and finished after Chilcot started and before he finished.

I had a few chats with both Ed M and Charlie about Leveson. Ed was clear he would go along with it, including statutory underpinning, provided it was clear that was not the same as state regulation. Charlie believed Cameron would sign up to Leveson and take the hit from the media. He said on Hillsborough, and Bloody Sunday, Cameron showed he was capable of doing the right thing. Yes, but that was for stuff with no political impact on himself other than positive. It is easy to apologise for the mistakes of predecessors. I was sure he would try to get Ed on the side of regulation, and himself on the side of the press and press freedom. Even by their standards, the papers had set it up totally on their terms, but I was confident the public would and could see through it. I sent Jeremy Heywood a note saying how DC should go for it and create a narrative on himself that he does the right thing when it comes to difficult choices posed by major inquiries. The media would go mad but it would pass. Cameron and Clegg had been studying the report today and clearly Cameron was not going to go for it, as they announced they would make separate statements tomorrow.

Thursday 29 November
The media wall-to-wall Leveson. I had a stack of bids and headed down to the QE2 to meet the Hacked Off people before Leveson was published. The core participants were in there reading it, and came out a bit disappointed, feeling that though he has called for statutory underpinning, there was enough in there for Cameron to wriggle out of. Brian Cathcart [co-founder] thought 6/10, maybe 7. Hugh Grant ditto. Some of the others

more optimistic but I felt there was enough in there for Cameron to say this was last last-chance saloon. I was surprised that Ed and Charlie both felt it was brilliant and that Cameron would find it impossible to turn down. They felt it was really clever, in that the statutory underpinning would be in part to guarantee free speech and self-regulation.

I went over to Millbank and did a round of interviews saying I could not understand why Cameron and Clegg could disagree. It was measured, sensible and proportionate and given he set up the inquiry, he could not really reject the main proposal immediately. But he did. I was in the 5 Live studio for his and Ed's responses and he suddenly came out all man of principle re. any statute – for the first time. Did about ten interviews then back to QE2. Zac Goldsmith [Tory MP] was there and saying he still felt it could happen because there were a lot of Tories determined to press ahead on this. I stayed for the Hacked Off press conference and the tone was disappointment and a sense of betrayal that Cameron had led them up the garden path. My main points were similar to those made giving evidence but also making clear that the other parties had to keep this on the agenda as the papers would do all they could to get it off the agenda.

Did *The One Show* then motorbike taxi for Channel 4 News with Carl Bernstein down the line arguing against any role for the state. Ended the day though feeling that because Cameron was a tit on the issue, the once-in-a-lifetime opportunity to reform the press was not going to be taken. Spoke to Ed a few times during the day. He felt he did OK and also that it was still possible to get Cameron to change his mind. Yet when he met with DC and Clegg, Cameron was pretty clear statute was a step too far.

Friday 30 November
Still getting a lot of bids re. Leveson but decided to stick to a piece for *The Guardian*. [Lords] Hunt and [Guy] Black [former director PCC] were still out there talking up self-regulation and their role in it. Some of the victims were out criticising Cameron's speed in rejecting it. J. K. Rowling asked what was the point of her giving evidence? Gerry McCann [father of missing three-year-old Madeleine] launched a petition to get all the party leaders to sign up. Long bike ride and later out for dinner with Fiona at Ravel's.

Saturday 1 December
Last minute I called Alex and got a ticket for Reading v Man Utd. Good match but Alex must be really worrying about his defence. Two soft goals. Won it 4–3 but not good performance. Met an ex-manager of Swindon,

Iffy Onuora, now working as referee assessor, who said he had heard me on 5 Live and agreed with everything I said re. Leveson.

Sunday 2 December

Up early and off with the boys to Burnley v Blackburn. Security more ridiculous than ever. Breakfast with Stan and Kath then down to meet Alex and Mike Phelan. Both on great form. Alex was sure we would win but though we battered them first half his loanee Josh King came on, turned the game and they took the lead. Sam Vokes got a late equaliser which was something but if ever we were going to beat them this had to be the time because they were so poor. Fergie confident re. the title but having problems with several of the players.

Monday 3 December

Out to meet Chuka Umunna [shadow Business Secretary] and his spad at Delauney's. I gave him an honest assessment of his and the party's position. I wasn't sure he had thought through too many policy or strategy positions. I just went through a few simple things we were not doing e.g. re. the record, teamship, attack and so on. He tended to bring most items round to his own profile, which was a bit worrying. Lunch with Harry Evans at the Garrick. God I hate these clubs but I like Harry and we had a good old natter about old times and about the current scene. He was showing his age a bit, sometimes answering questions I hadn't asked, a bit stooped, but he was sharp on the media and political scene and he was spot on re. the media and how they would try to wriggle out again. Lots of old fogeys and all too private school dining room for me. But great to talk to Harry. Off to Random House to sign a stack of new books for lunches and dinners then to see DS. Keen to get off the pills but we agreed to keep going till the New Year.

Tuesday 4 December

Up to Preston and over to the UCFB advisory board meeting. We were due to be named as part of the 2012 legacy plans tomorrow but the likelier option was going to be a campus at Wembley. The UCFB seemed to be going OK though there were problems with accommodation and also some of the students' attendance was poor. But definitely going in the right direction. Train back and straight to another PWC event at the hotel near Tower Bridge. Tax massive in the news with Margaret Hodge [Labour MP] doing a brilliant high-profile job as chair of the PAC, and Starbucks coughing up £20 million to try to calm public hostility. Spoke OK, short Q&A, books then home. Calum in a bad way again.

Wednesday 5 December

Autumn Statement. The build-up had all been pointing to disaster area, and the figures weren't great but Ed Balls had a bit of a nightmare. His stammer kicked in and then didn't really recover, added to which Osborne had done a sleight of hand so it looked like the deficit was coming down. Only later that the truth showed he was wrong. The cuts to benefits emerged as the main issue and the Tories deliberately presented it as a trap for Labour but when it emerged six out of ten of those facing cuts were the working poor it looked less clever and easier for us to vote against.

Meeting at LinkedIn who wanted me to become an 'influencer'. Then to the BMA HQ for my interview on God with Delia Smith as part of the Lancaster University 'Religion and Public Life' series. Good event and enjoyed it, though I felt she did a lot to communicate her own faith but not why a sceptic should agree.

Dinner at Langan's with her and Michael, Charles and Carole Clarke, David and Debbie [agent wife] Owen. Michael an atheist. David a believer. He had read I was thinking of getting a seat and he said only do it if there is clarity I will get one of the big jobs if we win and don't do Burnley because it is too far from London! Charles felt I would hate it. Ditto Margaret Hodge who I had texted earlier and who said the place was full of self-obsessed tossers I would hate and I had influence and a name without the letters so why not stick with that?

Thursday 6 December

Donald not well. He had had a chest and urinary infection and had stopped taking the medication. He had been taken to A and E and was now at Gartnavel [Glasgow hospital], and was going to have to withdraw from clozapine before going back on it. Really sad about it. Need to get there soon.

Friday 7 December

To Barclays to meet up with Tim, Oliver Pauley, Martin Sheehan and Mark Flanagan to do the pitch for the strategy advice job. I did the big picture and the rest the detail and it seemed to go OK. Tim and I from there to a meeting with the Moroccan ambassador and the finance minister who was looking for advice on country branding.

Saturday 8 December

Nottingham Forest away with Greg and Calum. Good to talk to Greg Nugent re. his Obama campaign experience. Definitely stuff Labour can learn. Poor game and we lost 2–0. Did a radio interview re. Nigel Doughty. Last time I spoke to him was from here.

Sunday 9 December

Off to Rome for Enel [Italian energy group] conference. Lovely hotel in the suburbs. Had a run, then a swim and watched the end of the City–United derby. Good win for United, 3–2. Rome cold and wet but still such a lovely place. The news dominated by Berlusconi announcing he would go for PM again, Monti signalling election would be earlier. Not yet clear if he would stand.

Monday 10 December

Really well-organised event. Four hundred of their comms teams from around the world. Gianluca Comin [external relations director] the guy in charge of the event, did a brilliant presentation. The CEO [Fulvio Conti] a bit more CEO-ish but both set up mine well in that I could talk re. big strategy, energy/environment/global change. Went down really well. Antonio Politi [physics academic] also speaking and he was pretty good too, and the Brazilian strategist for Lula and Chavez and others. Good event. Shame to leave early. Blogged re. Silvio being crazy but who knows. Home late p.m. Catching up on stuff pre Scotland and Fiona also trying to sort me a visit to see Donald ASAP.

Tuesday 11 December

Another paid speaking gig to a veterinary conference. Did a decent job weaving in loads of Dad stuff. Nice crowd. Cameron getting into a mess re. gay marriage, with the CofE now exempt to such an extent it would be illegal for them to do it.

Wednesday 12 December

Peter Chadlington breakfast of his Wallbrook Club [private members' City club] at the Mansion House. Good and influential crowd in fabulous setting. *All in the Mind* on all tables for all guests. I spoke re. mental health and did a bit of politics in the Q&A. Nice event, and he was a very good laugh. Off to LHR but the fog was causing cancellations and I narrowly missed getting the delayed 8.55 because of a jobsworth at the gate. 11.25 flight finally took off at one, and I made the hospital by 2.30. Donald really not well. Knew me some of the time but not all. Often confused and slow. Some pretty bad other cases in there. Nurses OK without being inspiring.

We went for a walk to the hospital café but he would stop every few yards and ask something about something we had discussed earlier. Didn't recognise pictures of Fiona and Grace. Didn't know Dad was dead. He was like he had been when first diagnosed years ago. Had to get him back on the medication soon. One or two of the other patients latched on to me trying to get me to help them get out, but between the guy who kept praying to Allah (a working-class Glaswegian) and the psychotic in full paranoid mode, the nurses had their hands full. Stayed a few hours and headed back to the airport, a lovely BA guy getting me on to the City flight so home earlier than expected. Very drained though. Worried about Mum going up and seeing him like that. Worried re. him, Calum, Graeme [unwell brother], a lot going on at the moment.

Thursday 13 December

Spoke to Donald's doctor, Dr McKeever, who sounded really nice and believed that the drugs would kick in soon. But she did admit she was alarmed by how he had been in the last few days. Portland filming for a web advert thing. *Any Questions* briefing at party HQ, tea with Calum, home then out to Tessa CLP Xmas party. OK, but I was getting tired of saying the same old things, especially on our inability to defend the record properly, and fight the Tories with real vigour.

Friday 14 December

Lots of AQs prep. Ed M immigration speech. Angry he did the usual we made mistakes stuff. Also a bit dog whistle on no jobs in public service for no English speakers etc. but all OK. Nice run in the rain. Dinner with the panel and Jonathan Dimbleby [presenter] at Leyland. Good event. I was definitely feeling a lot more warmth towards me, less hostility. My attack on Gove went down well. His main success, so far as I can tell, is in persuading the media and the Tory Party that he is a success. Tim Montgomerie [ConservativeHome website editor] looked somewhat shocked to see a Middle England audience, in a non-Labour area, loudly clapping the line that far from being a success, Gove is a disaster for our children.

Saturday 15 December

I did a blog on Gove based on the reaction last night, referring to Frankie Boyle on the radio yesterday echoing one of my favourite lines – never confuse media opinion with public opinion. Not least because he is essentially the media's man in Cabinet, as his outrageous undermining of the Leveson Inquiry showed, and because he is a journalist close to Rupert Murdoch, Gove tends to get a very good press. But never forget that virtually all national newspaper editors, and a majority of the commentariat, use private schools for their own kids, and as a result not only know next to nothing about state schools, but have a vested interest in running them down. Gove is the same. Instead of supporting schools, he undermines. Instead of building up, he knocks down.

Sunday 16 December

Out to Edgware Road for dinner with Edi, Endri and co. Home to see Bradley Wiggins win Sports Personality of the Year and Dave [Brailsford] get Coach of the Year.

Monday 17 December

Started making notes about a new novel. Did the Kaz call then met Edi and Endri for lunch and on the way I was jotting down thoughts. I had read a book, *The Spinning Heart*, from Lilliput Press's Kathy Gilfillan, and it had the format of each chapter as someone's name. I felt something like that, with only one person per chapter, might work. Decided to make it a young woman. Didn't really have a plot, just the idea of telling the story of a young girl's life from birth to alcoholism. Good chat with Edi who seemed to think things were OK, who loved the speech stuff I did and wanted more.

Tuesday 18 December

Starting to put pen to paper. Decided to call her Helen. Only left the house once, for an interview with the BBC. But I could feel the writing bug beginning to bite.

Wednesday 19 December

Heavy rain all day, writing at home, out for TB 94 [TB leadership] party at Kate and Jimmy Wales's place. Nice enough do. TB, Anji, Liz L (about to go to Tanzania to run a bank there), Tim A, Pete H (loving his school), Sally, Mike Craven [former adviser], Pat, Jonathan. Nice food, good laugh,

TB on OK form. Not as much bitching as before re. Ed etc. David M had been there for a bit at the start but left because he was flying somewhere with the Sunderland FC crew.

Thursday 20 December
Out to Pinner for a school prizegiving. Matt Chataway, teacher at a private school, has collared me in the park and asked if I would go to his former school, where his girlfriend taught, Haydon school. Drive out, did Q&A with politics student, great crowd, then the main prizegiving and did a good speech for fifteen minutes or so and then sold dozens and dozens of books. Yet another top state school full of good kids and staff.

Friday 21 December
Early train to Glasgow, writing en route, picked up by John and Edward Campbell [sons of AC cousin], and on to get Mum then to see Donald at Henderson ward, Gartnavel Royal. Not great but better than last time I saw him. Dazed and confused, some sad souls wandering around. Fiona collected me later and off we went for Conaglen. Couple of nice days.

22 December to 4 January 2013
Conaglen was fabulous as ever. Very wet but I still got out on the new bike every day. Kids arrived two days after us, plus Audrey and Lindsay and Mark [Johannsen, Lindsay's husband] and Hope came with Lindsay's mum. Charles Kennedy a guest for one night, on the wagon which was good and we had a good time with him. The best thing for me though was the total unplug of the writer's block and I did 80,000 words in eleven days, finishing the first draft by the time we got home. Fiona took me to Preston en route and I stayed at the Tickled Trout and did three really good chapters. Also did an ending though I changed that once or twice. James Macintyre [political journalist and friend] taken ill and was in Lambeth Psychiatric Hospital. He was in a bad way but the visit there helped me because I interviewed some of the nurses about their work in the PICU [paediatric intensive care unit], where one of my characters was based.

Football up and down. Kids up and down. Donald out by Jan 3. Saw him a couple of times and I was determined to make this mental health stuff my main thing. Fiona agonising re. whether to stand for Hampstead and Kilburn. I think I was moving away from doing the same in Burnley despite getting a lot of pressure. Rory was promoted to head of recruitment at Barnet, including first team but the manager got sacked and Edgar

Davids [Dutch player-manager] was now in sole charge. The book was my main thing, working on it obsessively and once I had the draft then spending hours wandering around Holloway, Highbury etc. to find the places where it was set. Work-wise things ticking over fine. Less sure re. politics and I wrote a note to Ed which might have been a bit OTT but I felt there was a lot of denial out there.

I said that this year, and particularly the first half, would be crucial for the outcome of the election. The Tories had a very bad year, but they are not down and out, far from it. Given how bad it was, Labour should be much further ahead. The Lib Dems are in trouble but showing more resilience than many expected. UKIP have replaced them as the mid-term protest party, but because of their Europe salience they may hold on to more of their current vote from by-elections than the LDs used to hold on to theirs. The SNP are still doing well as a party of government but losing the independence argument. As for Labour, he personally had done better than was widely expected, and shown good resilience, but the party as a whole has not. The Tories are banking on the doubts people have about him, Balls, Labour's role in the crash etc., to play alongside a sense of recovery in the economy and the fact Cameron still looks the part and will have experience. The main points I made:

1. The shadow Cabinet need a massive kick up the arse. Most could walk down any street in the country unrecognised. By 1995/96, we had eight to ten near-household names in the shadow Cabinet, and a host of others jockeying for position and attention, and that was after a long period in opposition rather than, as now, a time when several of ours have been Cabinet ministers in recent years. Honestly, what do they do all day? How on earth have we allowed e.g. Gove and IDS – disasters for the country – to be identified as successes? How has Jeremy Hunt been allowed to settle in nicely at Health? Where have we gone on climate change, or anti-social behaviour, or cuts, or women?

2. In so far as they are visible, they are almost always reactive. Chuka is at least more visible than most but it tends to be popping up as a commentator on a running issue, not driving an agenda. I assume they are all making speeches but why are none of them connecting? Why are we not creating the talking points and the points of connection with the public that drive political debate forward? They seem scared of their own shadow, terrified of risk, unimaginative, lacking in empathy or political/emotional intelligence.

3. The One Nation speech he made has not been given any real policy flesh at all. It was a good speech, gave a moment of opportunity, but it has not been taken. Point me to examples where colleagues have picked up on it and made it part of a bigger picture. Or tell me what a member

of the public is meant to say One Nation Labour means? It was a good message which has not been developed.

4. Energy and activity. There is a sense of managerialism rather than politics to the operation. Government fucks up, Labour says something. Government announces something, Labour responds. But where is the energy and activity that drives through a positive, proactive message that answers the questions a) where are we different? and b) what would we do?

5. Living in the bubble. Too many shadow ministers and MPs are frankly in denial about our lack of visibility. It is as though we are not relevant to the main debates taking place. I dipped in and out of SW1 and am alarmed the extent to which people think the public are following every twist and turn. They are not. They are following the government because they are the government. They are not following us with anything like the interest there needs to be right now. Equally, too many of your people still judge success or failure according to press profile and press reception. The only question is whether what they say and do connects with the public and helps frame the debate for the election and for a place in the manifesto. The rest is for the birds.

6. The record… I apologised for being a stuck record on this but said it was the one part of the strategic jigsaw he was getting badly wrong. We have totally played into the Tories' hands in allowing New Labour, the TB–GB years, to be defined negatively. With all the doubts people always have about change, 'At least the last government delivered abc' would take him a long way forward in getting people over those doubts. Instead of which we have totally capitulated to the 'mess we inherited' mantra. It is an act of strategic suicide. Both on the economy and on everything else we must reclaim the sense of progress the country made from '97 to 2007, and the extent to which that is being put at risk. There has been so little defending of the record, so much emphasis on the 'What we did wrong' that one of the most successful governments ever is defined negatively.

I think sometimes he – as Gordon did before him – thinks that when I bang on about this it is because of my own involvement in that time and through that period, and anger that a leader who won three elections is seen as something of a pariah in his own party. Perhaps a bit. But it is mainly because I know that for doubters to come over to us, they have to feel basic confidence in these things – what we represent, what we are promising, the leadership. But we have so much to look back on and say, 'That is what we did when we were given an extended period in power … c.f. what little this lot have done.' I am absolutely convinced if this part is not fixed, he has no chance.

7. Cultural space. They needed to break out of the policy-area-by-policy-area approach, and instead focus on big themes. Shift of power from West

to East. Europe as good thing not bad. Sport as driver of national success. Jobs for life thing of the past ... whatever, you can think of loads of these. Break out of the 'five-point plan' approach. Think big themes and big topics.

8. Social media. We were still not at the races.

9. Political language. It needs refreshing. He should think about bringing in outsiders for brainstorms, also think seriously – though they would hate it – of doing awaydays in a totally different way, e.g. the way sporting organisations or businesses do, role playing, written exercises etc.

10. His own profile. There were still basic things that could be done better, re. delivery, demeanour. Also I said he should not underestimate how much the 'knifed his brother' thing is still the first thing that comes up. Getting David back in some kind of policy role would be worth doing, though I knew things were not great between them.

I apologised for it being negative but it needed saying. I said we can win the next election, but only if there is rapid moving through gears, and he cannot do it all. He needed to decide which of the shadow Cabinet are capable, and get them motoring. Freshen the operation. Redefine the past. Have a process for policy development that is more visible and more exciting. Take a few more risks. I had partly sent it because Tom Baldwin had sent me a draft of another Ed M speech which was full of distancing from New Labour and I honestly felt it was a strategic error unless there was clarity of strategy and policy with regard to what he was putting in its place. Tom was pretty exasperated I think, said in a note to Ed and his speech team, 'I sometimes wonder why I voted Labour when I see the way you tell me how terrible everything was.'

Ed came round on the Monday evening, 7 January, while I was watching Everton demolish Cheltenham, a couple of days after I sent it. He wanted to go through it line by line. He agreed with most of it, for example the shadow Cabinet's performance, the lack of creativity and energy, and the failure to land blows on the Tories, but he did not agree about my message on his approach to the past. He felt he has to have distance between himself and the TB–GB records. I felt we had to have in people's minds a sense that at least when Labour was in power, we got stuff done, but he was not buying it. I felt we had conceded way too much, that we had played into the Tories' line of attack on the whole financial mess being of our making, and that we had lost any sense that the country had got better as a result of a long term of Labour in office.

He felt he had to be seen as change. I said you are making the same mistake as GB, thinking change has to be matched against our past rather than the current Tory vision. We were up against a bunch of incompetent ideologues and yet we were only a few points ahead. He said he understood a lot more needed to be done but I was not much clearer how he was going to do it. Balls was clearly a problem, not really on the same page, tricky, and he made no effort to disguise that. There was no real agreement on how to message the past, and no real agreement on policy for the future. Balls quite obstructive and low profile. Yvette cautious. All of them a bit careful and scared of their own shadows. It was a nice enough chat but as he left – forgetting his coat so he had to come back later – I didn't feel overly enthused.

We had discussed my and Fiona's dilemma. Re. Fiona going for Hampstead, he felt she could win and would be an asset and was happy to talk to her. Re. me, he was amazed I was even interested as he felt in a way it would be a backward step but if I went for it he said he felt it would be good for him as he was short of big hitters and if we won, he would imagine me going in early as a Cabinet minister. Happy to discuss etc. He ended up staying a couple of hours or so. He and Justine had been away for a few days without the kids over the New Year and had enjoyed it. He was looking OK despite the black shadows under his eyes. He said the situation with David was still not good, that he did not think he would come back under him.

On Leveson, I had seen Brian Cathcart and Evan Harris and they had said they were a bit worried that Labour was going down the Royal Charter route which did not give the victims everything they wanted. They wanted to know where he was on it. My sense was that he did think the charter went a fair way towards what was needed. It was still not clear if the editors could agree on anything at all. I still found it hard to imagine him as PM but Cameron was doing badly, economy not good, Europe a mess. We had dinner with Neil and Glenys. They were still a bit starry-eyed about Ed and felt we would get a majority. We just were not landing blows though. Nor did we have an alternative agenda. Ed said the policy stuff was coming together fine and from the summer onwards they would step things up.

Tuesday 8 January

I signed off *My Name Is…* [novel] draft and Ed sent it to Susan at RH. She read it within a couple of days and came back with very encouraging noises. Went to the screening of *Lincoln* with Calum. Really good. Blogged on Cameron and his ludicrous mid-term review with Clegg where he said they were like Ronseal, did what it said on the tin. Everyone who was reading *My Name Is…* was liking it, including Calum.

Wednesday 9 January

Comic Relief wanted me to go to Ghana so was needing to sort jabs, new passport etc., because it had to have six months validity for a visa. Visiting James Macintyre at Lambeth. A little bit better, but still struggling to separate what was real and what wasn't.

Friday 11 January

Passport collection. Tom Albanese [RTZ] session. Under real pressure because of a deal that went wrong. Some talk of a coup against him, which he doubted. We talked about his own profile which was pretty good but I felt he needed a bit more on the big picture geostrategic side of things. Still agonising re. MP-ery as was Fiona. Totally torn both of us.

Saturday 12 January

Dinner at the Sumptions. Liked his wife. Less so a judge, [Sir Andrew] Popplewell, real Tory type though his wife, a doctor, seemed OK. Telling me about her obsession with tango. All a bit permanent establishment for my taste though. Lovely house, beautiful paintings, including a Gainsborough. Sumption told Fiona he was against the war but in no doubt we were not guilty of the charges made against us on the preparations for war. I enjoyed talking to him.

Sunday 13 January

Met Godric at Great Dunmow and did two hours bike to Saffron Walden and looped back, mainly chatting about the novel, MP or not MP, the lack of strategy in government, and his future setting up a comms, strategy and marketing firm with Greg [Nugent]. Back to watch United beat Liverpool, then to the Emirates with Calum as guests of Frank Warren.

Tuesday 15 January

Met Paul Hamaan and team at Kentish canteen to discuss the idea of a documentary about alcohol and women. They liked the novel and also thought there was a film in it. Lunch with Jan Åge Fjørtoft at what used to be Chez Gerard. He was interesting on the failure of English football to influence world football. Portland for a couple of meetings, then tea with Bruce G who as ever was sound on just about everything. He thought it would be great if Fiona and I got seats but said only do it if you really want to do it.

Wednesday 16 January

To Leicester, tour of Glenfield hospital children's unit, threatened with closure, who had got in touch when they realised I was going to Leicester University. Given a tour by Peter Barry who introduced me to most of the doctors who sensed they were being eased towards an already made decision on closure.* They were adamant the facts flew in the face of the decision and they did seem to have a point when looking at the population figures for Southampton, which was being kept open at Leicester's expense. Picked up by the university driver then taken there to meet the Labour students group before signing books and then doing what was billed as a lecture, though I just spoke off the cuff. Q&A fine, reception, train back.

Thursday 17 January

Tom Albanese sacked from Rio Tinto. I sent him a nice message and he replied almost immediately saying these things happen, thanks for help, he will resurface etc. Later out to *This Week*. With the Algerian hostage crisis dominant, and having forced Cameron to ditch his Europe speech tomorrow yet again, they had Kofi Annan [Ghanaian former Secretary-General, United Nations] on and so it was all a bit more serious than usual.† Nice chat with Kofi who asked me to get in touch to let him know how I found Ghana. Interesting how respectful Andrew Neil was to Kofi.

Friday 18 January

Rather odd media training session with Princess Cristina of Spain [daughter of King Juan Carlos and Queen Sofia]. She was nice enough, much more personable and down to earth than most royals, but there was something a bit odd about how these people couldn't really read speeches in public. She was doing work for Gavi the vaccines global programme and just wanted very basic coaching which I think went OK. I left early to collect Mum from King's Cross, then home for a meeting with Kevin Nicholson, head of tax at PWC, in advance of his select committee appearance on tax where he expected to get hammered. He was up with others and I suggested he submit a serious paper and pursue a differentiation strategy of not being like the others. He was not your usual City type at all and would be able to carry it off if he had good arguments and confidence in them. Out for

---

* In July it had been announced that the East Midlands Congenital Heart Centre, which had been in operation for twenty years, would close. A petition to save it attracted 100,000 signatures.

† Al-Qaeda-linked terrorists took ex-pat hostages at the Tigantourine gas facility in Amenas.

dinner with most of the family. Mum on good form. Algeria situation was pretty grim and what with the French troops in Mali, now the hostages at the energy plant, there was a sense of North Africa being a new front.

Saturday 19 January

Freezing cold, but Millwall v Burnley on. Took Mum and though we had a car park space right by the door, I was still part-surrounded by a bunch of Millwall yobs going on about 'the fucking cunts who let all the foreigners in'. How 'you and that poof Mendelson destroyed the country'. One said, 'If the old lady wasn't there I would fucking do you.' Real tossers. We played really well, won 2–0, then off to Reading for cousin Lachie Brown's 60th birthday. Some of his colleagues at the airport where he worked on logistics had never believed I was his cousin and so he was desperate for me to go. Nice enough do and they were really glad we went.

Sunday 20 January

Did a blog on Lance Armstrong after his Oprah confessions, basically saying David Walsh [sportswriter] got it right.[*] I was getting a bit of flak for the 2004 interviews [with Armstrong] but not much. It was sad as much as anything. I only saw parts of the interviews and he seemed less than contrite to me. Also interesting that when he was in denial mode it was with exactly the same tone and formulations as he had denied doping at all to me. Met Judith McNeil [Comic Relief charity] at the airport, then flew to Accra, but only after a four-hour delay, sitting on the tarmac and waiting for the plane to be de-iced. Arrived after midnight, met and taken to the High Commission. HC Peter Jones up to say hello. Nice guy and really pleased we were there.

Monday 21 January

Out with the Basic Needs [mental health organisation] team to a self-help group of mentally ill women. In a mosque so introduced by a young disabled iman, then the guy in charge started on a long spiel before Abdulai, our host, interrupted and said we wanted to hear from the women. They opened up slowly and it was clear there was everything from depression to schizophrenia. Unfortunately they also included epilepsy as a mental illness which confused things a little. Polygamy and witchcraft were much bigger issues than I expected. Only twelve trained psychiatrists in the

* Walsh revealed details of Armstrong's doping history in the *Sunday Times*.

country – 45,000 traditional healers. They spoke and we had translators and then I went around getting names etc. Then a tour of the very poor district. Back to a briefing, getting all the facts and figures, off for a drink by a beach somewhere, back for dinner with the HC.

Tuesday 22 January

Visit to Maamobi Polyclinic, also interviewing some of the women who had been there yesterday. It was proving difficult to get proper access to Accra psychiatric hospital but eventually we did. The hospital was worse than I had expected. Almost medieval. Comic Relief were keen for me to emphasise progress not just doom and gloom. But it was grim. Women running around naked. People lying in the dust. Mute children. Prisoners mixed with patients. Staff over-stretched. Observation of patients minimal. Really tough.

Comic Relief's support for Basic Needs Ghana was funding 193 self-help groups across the country. Met Leyla Suraka, schizophrenic. A bad enough condition anywhere. But even worse in a country where many think mental illness is caused by witchcraft, or punishment from God for sins committed in a past life. Where there are 46,000 'traditional healers', but only a dozen trained psychiatrists. Where the mentally ill are often sent not to hospitals but to unregulated 'prayer camps' where herbs, fasting, beatings and exorcisms are considered the right way to treat someone hearing voices. Through the interpreter she told me, 'People sometimes run away from you when they know you are mentally ill. Or they abuse you, call you a mad person, throw stones.' She was fifty-three, looked older. 'I was hearing voices, thought I was being told to wander, to walk away on my own. It was ten years before I got treatment.' In and out of Accra's psychiatric hospital, spending a total of three years there, but since attending the Nima 441 self-help group, she has not been back for several years.

Some of the women in the self-help group didn't speak. Adama Amad has had severe depression most of her life, and speaks only when encouraged by her sister and carer, Fuseina Amadu. They both look desperately sad, and Adama tends mainly to stare into the middle distance. Suddenly, after a call from one of the volunteers, the room exploded into activity as another mentally ill woman, Abiba Sulemana, took hold of a younger woman, Awusatu Sulemana, and together they enacted an improvised play about getting help for someone who is ill. 'Many people in Ghana think mental illnesses are contagious,' explained co-ordinator Mariama Salifu, who said they have eight drama groups now. 'We go out and show people they are not contagious, explain what the illnesses are, show through drama that it is possible to be ill, but recover.'

Maamobi polyclinic was also supported by Basic Needs. Basic indeed, but at least it is there, and the need clear from the long queue of patients waiting in the heat. The first patient, lottery agent Dickson Dorcoo, in his sixties, became suicidally depressed after the lottery boss absconded with the takings, leaving twenty-three angry winners chasing Mr Dorcoo for their money. This is his fifth visit and the nurses review his medication. His wife, Victoria Adika, says she has seen some improvement. But the pain and fear are clear in his eyes and the stigma clear in her voice when she says, 'We hide him away. We don't want him to be seen as a mad person.' Next a young schizophrenic woman, Sahara Jubrila, thirty, who like some psychiatric patients the world over has been failing to take her medication. Nurse Winfred Darko pleads with her to understand why she must, warns that her husband might leave her if she doesn't recover to help look after their eight children.

The challenges to medical staff can hardly be overstated. A country of 25 million people in which psychiatrists on duty today in the three psychiatric hospitals can be counted on the fingers of one hand; in which an estimated 4,000 psychiatric nurses are needed to deliver minimum basic care – 3,300 more than they have. It is genuinely shocking to a British eye. The day we arrived, the local paper reported a murder by one female patient – or 'inmate' as the paper called her – of another. Ninety-two men in a shed made for thirty. Sheetless beds that are mats or foam. In another ward, which has more the feel of a prison exercise yard, three nurses looking overnight after 140 men, sixty-four of them sent by the courts for observation, among them alleged murderers. A children's ward including children dumped and left by parents on the doorstep. A busy ECT (electroconvulsive therapy) unit operating three mornings a week. Outpatients queuing to see Dr Akwasi Osei who is chief psychiatrist, government adviser, and in addition tries to see up to seventy patients a day.

When I phoned home and tried to describe to Grace what it was like, I realised the gap between our conception of a hospital and this reality is too wide. There is progress on the political front. The issue of mental health even came up in the election TV debates (more than can be said for the UK!). Back to the HC residence and met the new minister for social protection before a quick bite and off to the airport. Just before we left, I got a text from Ed re. Cameron. 'Any thoughts re. PMQs tomorrow. Cameron announcing in/out EU referendum by 2017.' Wow. Big stuff. I did a note suggesting he hold firm and whack him for doing it out of weakness not strength but I could tell he was a bit worried about it. My hunch was Cameron would get a lift, also get the press back on board a bit more, but over time it would unravel. Off to the airport, sleeping pill, six-hour flight, home.

Wednesday 23 January

Watched Cameron's Europe speech. He delivered it well and it was better argued than I expected but it was still a big risk and in all likelihood a terrible mistake. I wasn't sure he needed to do it [a referendum], and it was obviously all about internal politics, not any real demand from the country. Also, as was clear from the press conference and PMQs, he could not say whether he would definitely be voting that we stay in, as it would depend on the outcome of negotiations for a new settlement. A lot was now going to depend as well on how the other EU leaders reacted. Most were being reasonably polite, but that would not necessarily translate into progress. Laurent Fabius [foreign affairs minister of France] was pretty heavy, said they would roll out the red carpet for businesses who wanted to move to Paris, that it was like playing football and suddenly deciding you wanted to change to rugby.

Ed did OK, but Cameron got him to make an explicit commitment against a referendum which looked like Ed going further than he wanted to. He seemed a bit discombobulated which was no doubt partly why DC was doing it, though his big thing was internal politics, dealing with the Tory right and the rise of UKIP. I came back with a bad cold and the MP-or-not-MP thing was hanging over both of us. Glenda Jackson was about to announce she was standing down soon as MP in Hampstead & Highgate so Fiona was going to have to decide very soon as it would spark a stampede. Conference call re. Afghanistan paper. Andreas, JoP and I all saying it was a long way from where it needed to be. Out to the Arlington centre to do a Skype conference with Irish GPs on alcohol and addiction issues for Lundbeck. Good stuff. Felt confident talking about the issues in the novel too.

Thursday 24 January

To Bob Edwards's [former Mirror Group senior editor] memorial at St Bride's. OK turnout though I thought there would have been more old faces. Fiona pointed out a lot of the people we might have expected were dead. Chatted to Bill H about the diaries, to Chris Buckland [non-drinking political journalist] about drinking. Unlike me, he was totally teetotal.

Friday 25 January

Feeling rough as hell, but felt I had to go to Tessa's investiture lunch or else she would think it was a snub. She knew my views about the honours but to be fair to her she was one of the few I didn't begrudge it. I just couldn't understand why it meant so much to people. The lunch was at

Roux. Mainly family and closest friends. Cameron's Europe gambit was yet to pan out clearly. I got the sense nobody thought, if it happened, that he would lose.

Seb and his wife there. Speech by Tessa's brother-in-law from first marriage, nice enough do. Margaret thought Fiona should definitely go for Hampstead and on balance I should not go for Burnley. She felt my baggage and my size as a figure would combine to make me not enjoy it. She might be right. Fiona was definitely warming to it, and everyone was telling her she would be the best candidate, which she would be. Almost certain to be an all-women's shortlist and she was moving to a position that if it was she would go for it and if it wasn't, she would support Mike Katz [Labour councillor]. We all trooped over to the Commons for the reception for constituents and other friends. Nice crowd, lots of the good people from the party, a few MPs and peers, Lindsay, Gail and the girls, Greg N, Olympics people. Speeches from Seb, TB and Ed, all good, and Tessa was clearly loving it all. One of her elderly constituents collapsed and they had to get paramedics in but apart from that it went really well for her. The Olympics had definitely given her a different edge and a fixed and positive profile.

Home for a bit then Fiona and I out for dinner at Ed and Justine's, with Tim and Katie Livesey, and Conor Gearty. Chatted about Cherie, who had been spectacularly nice to Fiona earlier, and less so to me. Ed said that after the sports dinner she said, 'I will take your speech as an apology to my husband.' Conor, who had worked with her for years, spoke up for her. Fiona said Cherie had taken a lot of crap, and was basically a good person.

Fiona and my political situation was discussed a fair bit. They all thought Fiona should go for Hampstead, and were not terribly swayed by any of her arguments against. I think Ed was still quite keen for me to do Burnley but he also said Margaret might have a point and that it was unfair but he could see why I might hold back. But he said there was a real problem with lack of talent and lack of big figures. He said he worried if I went there I would really not be able to hide what I thought of most of them. 'It'll be like a whale arriving in a goldfish bowl.' But he was keen for both of us not to rule it out and determined Hampstead should be all-women shortlist if Fiona wanted to do it. Conor on good form. Justine also very good fun, and Tim seemed to be relaxed and settled in. Ed seemed more comfortable in himself too. I could sense in myself that I was 80 per cent against doing it, and Fiona moving the other way. It was probably the best outcome.

The others left and then we had a really quite honest session on strengths and weaknesses, whether DM would come back – Ed felt he was in no-man's land but still not ready for it – whether Balls was a problem, generally yes, who else was doing OK, a few but all a bit lacking in strength in depth. He felt the Cameron Europe speech would give him a lift but then backfire. He felt Labour had to hold firm. On Leveson, I suggested he meet Brian Cathcart to find out just what their position was, because he was moving towards accepting Royal Charter plus statute. Cameron just wasn't going to go the other way so this was probably the best way to get close to it, but he realised Hacked Off might not like it. Otherwise all nice and chatty and relaxed and he said to me he felt we were on course to be the biggest single party 'unless we really screwed up'. Today's bad growth figures, and some nonsense about DC, Osborne and Boris all having a laugh eating pizzas in Davos, were not good for them.

Sunday 27 January

The Lundbeck board meeting in Denmark was cancelled because the CEO had to travel but by then I had fixed up to do a piece on *Borgen* [TV political series] for *The Times* so went ahead anyway. Weather all a bit grim and the plane was late out but made it to the hotel Skt Petri – nice, very chic – in time to get settled and then head out to Helle's. Steve [Kinnock] and the girls were there and they all seemed happy and getting on well. Helle on terrific form though the polls were a bit grim and the politics quite tough now. Lots of talk of the kids, lots on whether Fiona and I should go for seats – they basically felt yes but understood the doubts.

The girls had grown into really nice young women. Camilla loves football. Johanna doing a project on New Labour. So we talked a bit about that. Talked re. *Borgen*. She felt the storylines got a bit near the knuckle but we agreed a quote for the *Times* piece. Johanna very bright on the political front. Interesting that she said she found herself disagreeing with Neil's analysis a lot of the time. We were at a lovely restaurant with a very flirty waitress who kept stroking me and Steve. All a bit odd. Steve very keen to get a seat next time too. They gave me a lift back to the hotel and we chatted in the car. Neil a really doting grandfather. Probably found her politics a bit tricky. She and Steve seemed to be getting on really well. She was so chilled and unchanged. A bit too fond of Cameron's charm for my liking though.

Monday 28 January

Out to Lundbeck, which was like a little town on its own, a couple of thousand people working there. Good meeting to plan my speech in Dubai in March. Nice team. A bit naïve about politics and the way it worked. Back into town and met up with the photographer Paul Rogers from *The*

Times at the Phoenix Hotel and waited for Sidse Babett Knudsen and Pilou Asbæk, aka Birgitte and Kasper from *Borgen*. Really liked them both. He was probably the more political. He has certainly learned a thing or two about spin doctoring. He bows on meeting, and within a minute has said he is 'honoured' and 'thrilled', only agreed to the interview because it was with me, enjoyed researching my 'amazing' life, and asked if I minded that he sees me and a US Republican – Karl Rove – as the top exponents of what he calls our 'art'. She was very pretty and charismatic though less so shorn of all the TV PM stuff. But the interview and the pictures both worked and I was sure I would get a good piece from it.

He loved all the spin stuff. She knew about the mental health campaigning too and confided there had been alcoholism in her family. Both of them had had issues with some of the storylines but they realised it was quality stuff. She was big on how good it was for Denmark that they had first *The Killing* [TV crime series], now *Borgen*, and both with strong women as the lead characters. Also said it was good for politics that *Borgen* doesn't just do the easy cynical thing but shows politics as human beings trying to do their best according to what they believe. She said the longer it went on the more she liked Birgitte, she was a real heroine because she was fighting for things she believed in. She has never met Helle, and said she was worried she would start to copy her so took an active decision not to look at her.

It was when she listed 'the room' and 'the car' among her key relationships that I was reminded she is an actor above all else. But surely there is an added responsibility, I asked, because you have the chance to impact on the reputation of politics for good or bad? 'That is not my job. I feel responsibility with every part I play, whether it is this or a love story.' Pilou said something similar: 'The more we let people take their own choice or meaning, the more people we influence. If we say "This is what it means" we narrow it down.' Both said they learned a lot, especially about the media. She said she thought the media was there as a witness, not as a player, but it's not so. Pilou's takeout was that politics is much more difficult than people imagine it to be – right again – that the 'taxi driver view that "I could sort it out" shows a lack of respect' – right again – and that 'there is no black and white in politics, it is not a perfect square.' *Borgen*'s success has taken them by surprise. When she got the part, they were talking about maybe selling to Sweden, and now it is in fifty-seven countries.

I told them that Helle gave François Hollande a box set, and his partner Valerie Trierweiler tweeted when they were watching it. She said, 'Wow, that's kind of amazing.' Pilou said he spent time with a few real spin doctors in Danish politics, like a fly on the wall. 'It was awesome.'

One had worked for the same guy for eight years and they were clearly a team, but the guy had never visited her home. Sidse said she wanted to work in English, and her dream was to play Hamlet. I broke the back of the piece on the plane and finished it at home. The flight home was a bit snowy and turbulent but just about on time. Sidse asked for my books and because of the alcohol discussion I sent her the new novel too.

Tuesday 29 January

Finished and filed the *Borgen* piece which Nicola Jeal [*Times* weekend editor] really liked. Pictures good too. Off to Canary Wharf for a Portland meeting with Barclays.

From there to RTZ. Tom Albanese had been sacked because of another massive write down and his replacement Sam Walsh wanted me to help with his speeches.

Wednesday 30 January

Half-day coaching with the Portland guys for Virgin Media. It was another example of a big and successful company that did not really seem to get its own strategy terribly well. Lunch at seventy4, the addiction charity in Westminster. Thomas Boal at Portland had introduced me to it via his dad who was a recovering alcoholic and patron.

Thursday 31 January

Ernst and Young [professional services firm] conference. I opened it and speech and Q&A went well despite a bad throat. Then had to sit through [Lord] Andrew Mawson, social entrepreneur, who was so full of himself it was embarrassing. Even said, 'When I first had the idea we should go for the Olympics.' Constant use of his own name and speaking in the third person. There was someone bright and delivering under it but the sense of self-importance was almost comic.

Friday 1 February

Ran to Vauxhall to meet Jocasta Hamilton who was going to be editing *My Name Is…* She really liked it but had a few points. She felt I should cut Helen's direct speech so that the impact of her letter at the end was stronger. My worry was I liked the dialogue and some of the best bits were her talking. We agreed to take a look though. She was a nice and clever character though. Knew a bit about addiction. Like the others at RH, she said she loved the way I told the story through a succession of different people speaking about Helen in their own voices. She was unaware of it having been done before.

From there to Cleveland Sq. to see Jeremy Slaughter, CBT [cognitive behavioural therapy] psychologist recommended by David S. A bit like a priest, tended to talk in running commentary. But he was cerebral and it was good to go over this stuff with someone new. I had sent him the long read I did when I first saw David and he had gone through it in detail. He made up a grid of thoughts and consequences. His big idea was that everyone should have a mental health plan. He felt I was someone who needed to be constantly reaching out and up for big challenges and at the moment I did not know what it was. He also felt I was someone who was neither an insider nor an outsider and whichever I seemed to be at any one time I wanted to be the other. There was something in that. Interview for *History* magazine in which I had to select a historical hero – I went for Lincoln. Party at home for Grace farewell. Going to miss her. Fiona crying a lot.

Saturday 2 February

Up at half-four and out to Heathrow to see off Grace to Jamaica. Not sure about her being on her own but she would hopefully get a lot out of it. Her blog was looking good. More problems with C. Off to Peterborough. Met up with Darren Ferguson [football manager, son of AF] for a chat. Telling him about Rory's stuff and picking his brains on how he should proceed. He said at Peterborough he had very little infrastructure and it sounded like he could benefit from the kind of thing Rory did and wanted to develop. I was doing the commentary for Radio Lancs, sitting on wooden chairs at the back of the stand in among the fans. Good game but very different watching it and talking. Burnley one-up, 2–1 down, two–all. Off to David and Tessa's. Main focus of the chat was Fiona and whether she should go for it.

Sunday 3 February

Out for a run. So slow. Past the gypsy camp which was now like a little village. Fiona back late from her walk and we headed to Heathrow for my flight to Astana via Frankfurt. We were delayed though because the fucking first officer was late and we missed the connection by minutes so I did the Abu Dhabi flight instead and got to Astana twelve hours later than planned. It meant that the meeting with Massimov was cancelled because he was off to Spain with the President. Instead had dinner with the team.

February '13: Fiona in tears as Grace off to Jamaica

It was interesting to note in the media brief the comments of Kaz foreign minister [Erlan] Idrissov in Brussels, to the effect that Kazakhstan is an evolving democracy and looking to the EU as a role model and also as a support in its drive towards a more modern form of democracy and a better approach to governance and human rights. It confirmed me in the view that there is a need and opportunity to reposition the TB narrative in relation to this whole project. There was a problem with the broadly defensive posture so far. The comments of Idrissov opened the possibility of a different approach. It's an important country, faces important choices in debates which will have an impact well beyond its own borders.

I told TB he needs to make more of such a thing as 'post-power politics' as leaders who reached the top positions relatively young now leave office relatively young but still have an enormous amount to offer. It argues for a strategy that does not actively seek coverage but does not shy from the opportunities that come. That we are advising them on issues as varied as Afghanistan, Iran, rule of law, regional development, economic modernisation. Up to now, any comment TB's team has made has tended to be in the 'Kaz not as bad as you think' frame and 'here are a few things they have done to show that'. I think a better frame is one that says the TB operation is engaged in important work in an important country and here is where we are making a difference. Nor should we shy away from saying that improved comms are part of that though the main focus should be related to policy.

Tuesday 5 February

Woke up with a really sore throat and my voice fast vanishing. It was clear that without Massimov support the CCS [central communications service] would be in trouble even though it was doing a lot of good stuff. All young and bright and the outputs were not bad but the embedding across government was still a problem. Then the main meeting at the Diplomat Hotel with Yerzhan Kazykhanov [former ambassador to the UK] and Bakhyt Sultanov [presidential aide]. General overview. Then to the regional development stuff and comms. Lunch then off to the airport. Left a bit late but made the connection and slept a fair bit of both flights. The voice almost totally gone now and whacking down loads of stuff for it. Home and did a bit of work then bed.

Wednesday 6 February

Cancelled everything apart from going to see the doctor and the Political Book Awards at the IMAX in the evening. Felt grim. Not blogging but doing a fair bit of Twitter banter with @toryeducation, *The Observer* having been pushing that it was run by Gove spads Dominic Cummings and Henry de Zoete.

Thursday 7 February

To Labour HQ for meeting with Iain McNicol. He was pressing re. me and F re. seats. Said they could hold Burnley for a while yet. Also re. lack of strategy in Ed team. Gove U-turn on English Baccalaureate but [Stephen] Twigg [shadow Education Secretary] failed to land a blow.

Friday 8 February

Out with Rory on the bike. Then Jeremy Slaughter. Showed me his word grid. Also drew mountain with me pushing up load, then coming off the mountain and now trying to make a mountain out of all the various things I did today. It was all very different. Tea with Camilla H at Rapha café. Amazing place with hooks for bikes etc. Dinner with F at Fratelli. All the kids worrying us for differing reasons. And she was totally torn re. the MP thing.

Saturday 9 February

Bike for an hour or so. Wet and cold. Work on novel. Warming to some of Jocasta's ideas. Watched Scotland beat Italy. Burnley threw away the lead to lose at Bolton 2–1. Cameron getting good press from Brussels summit. Gove spads getting more grief but still going for it on @toryeducation.

Sunday 10 February

Out to Neil's and Glenys's where Helle, Steve and Camilla were over. Helle had been part of the Cameron team that had managed to get the EU budget down. Joe [Bentham, son of Rachel Kinnock and Stuart Bentham] and Camilla very excited as I'd got them tickets for the United–Everton game. The kids were great. Edi Rama round p.m. We took Edi and Endri with Mark Lucas to the Gaucho in NW3. We worked on plans for a new approach to the manifesto programme and at a meeting at the house, and later over dinner with the family, we worked out how to maximise its potential. Fiona still in mixed mode re. whether to stand. My sense was that deep down she did not want to because of the loss of freedom, but I did not want to push her against. She had to decide. There is no doubt it would change our lives a lot, and mine probably for the worse, but I was determined that should not be a, let alone *the*, reason against. Rory and Grace in particular were keen she should do it.

Week from Monday 11 February

Off to France, in my case via the Bank of England where I was doing a talk for their mental health network in the main events room. It was the first time I had been to the Bank and the power of the building and the environment was strong. In its own way greater than the Palace and certainly greater than No. 10. Nice courtyard on to which Mervyn King and the other main bods looked out. The mental health scene was not bad, good network, also a resident shrink, good young staff. Did an off-the-cuff speech then Q&A, book signing and lunch then off to meet Fiona and off to France. I was planning to use the week to do a major edit and rewrite on *My Name Is...* Worked on it for at least part of every day and I was happier with it by the time I had finished.

We stayed in most nights, had Leighton Andrews [Labour member of Welsh Assembly] and Ann [wife] round one morning, otherwise the only out-of-ordinary social event was a trip to Marseille to see Joey Barton play for Olympique Marseille v Valenciennes and then have dinner with him. Took Calum and Craig but also Zizi and Julien [local friends], who were in raptures. Barton was so different to what I expected. He was brilliant with Zizi and Julien, showed them the dressing rooms then took them out on the pitch at midnight to take penalties. I was getting regularly stuck into Gove's special advisers, who seemed out of control. Fiona exasperated at what was happening. Headteachers at the end of their tether at the political nature of the change, and the sense that Cummings was running amok.

Tuesday 19 February

Cab to Marignane with Calum then flight to Heathrow. Had to be back for JCORE [Jewish Council for Racial Equality] event in the evening, with Fiona driving home. Charity was a Jewish charity for asylum seekers and refugees, and also looking outwards. Raised a few bob. Dave Brailsford sounding me out re. ghosting his book.

Wednesday 20 February

Ian Burrell from *The Indy* round for a chat about the BBC. Lots of bids on Iraq ten years on coming in. Lunch with Victor Blank. Keen to go to the Lords I think. Felt we were going to win. Ed improved etc. Popped in to see Rachel Grant [director of communications] at TB's office who felt the pictures of TB at some posh do with shirt unbuttoned at top and medallion on display had set them back. She wanted him to do more pre Iraq anniversary.

Thursday 21 February
Kent Gavin [photographer] documentary interview, retelling some of the stories about the arguments we had about the ease with which he got royal pictures on the front of the *Mirror*. Then to a meeting in the Strand re. French translation of new book. Fran Millar keen for me to ghost Dave B.

Friday 22 February
To the British Library to do an interview for their upcoming exhibition on propaganda. The idea was that visitors would put on headphones and listen to different chats amid all the exhibits. Session with Jeremy Slaughter, the new shrink David had asked me to see. He was saying I should model myself on Dalai Lama! 'Be wise, offer sage advice to others.' He was putting my previous mental health stuff into a weird kind of chart. Long chat with Dave B about the book idea. He was not totally persuaded it was the right time, and I was not totally persuaded I was the right person to ghost it. He was sure that if he did it, I was, but even talking about the idea, I could tell there would be a hell of a lot of work attached to it. Out with Fiona to *Macbeth* with James McAvoy. Brilliant. Dinner at Prezzo, where the Kosovan waiter refused to let me pay. 'We never forget what you did,' he said. Nice.

Saturday 23 February
Met Alex F for coffee at the Corinthia Hotel. He said even if Wenger had lost it a bit, he hated the way fans were disrespecting him. He was very short with a young kid who came over for an autograph. Then Alex suddenly said, 'Right, worst part of the day – telling the ones who aren't playing.' To Brighton for the Burnley game. Lost one–nil. Should have got something out of it.

Sunday 24 February
Gail round for a chat re. F and my positions re. seats. She could not see why we would give up our freedom and equilibrium. Watched Scotland

beat Ireland at rugby then off to Heathrow for flights to Vienna then Tirana. Feeling rough though. Donald called as I was on the way to the airport, said he just wanted to say how grateful he was for the fact that we all worried about him so much! He was back on an even keel.

Monday 25 February

Late flight to Tirana via Albania. Not for the first time, Sali Berisha's son was on the flight from Vienna, with a few luxury bags. On landing, I had heard the stewardess say, 'One special services,' which turned out to be him, but he spotted me coming down the steps and indicated I should get in the VIP minibus. 'Is someone meeting you? Tell them to come round to VIP.' I couldn't work out if it was friendly or threatening. Erion collected me and we headed into town. He felt things were in good shape. The Italian election was looking grim, with no clear winner and Beppe Grillo [comedian, leader Five Star Movement] getting a quarter of the vote and the other clown Berlusconi even more.

Into the SP HQ. The building had been rebranded to take account of the new look Mark, Arbi and I had devised. The mood in there was pretty good, though there was still the fear Berisha would just steal it. The 'road to the programme', based on our old Road to the Manifesto, seemed to be going OK. Edi was thrilled with how the two-day convention event I had suggested and planned with Endri had gone. He and I had a session to go over how to fill the space between now and the start of the campaign proper. A series of draft chapters of the manifesto with each designed to dominate a week. Ben, the guy on the strategy group who he was keen to keep on board, had broken his leg, and Edi was keen we go to visit him at home. Nice flat, nice wife who was fussing around him. Both smoking which was annoying. I was suggesting he be put to the task of writing some of the manifesto draft chapters.

The other purpose of the trip was to launch the Albanian translation of my diaries. Did a few interviews to go with that. Good turnout at the official launch, where first Henri Çili from the European Tirana University and then Ilva Tare [TV news presenter], who had written a foreword, spoke, then me. Ten TV crews, some doing it live. Did a big pro-politics thing, plugged Edi a bit. Most of them went on the idea I was advising him. Did a signing then to TV studio for a very long interview. Mainly Kosovo, but also a bit of life and times. This was the guy who was close to Berisha who I had met at the dinner Fiona McIlwham hosted for me ages ago. I had advised Edi to do more with him and it seemed to be bearing fruit as he was quite down on Berisha.

Tuesday 26 February

Raining. The place looked so different when wet. Really gloomy. Good session with Edi after Endri and I had worked out a plan. Also met a couple of the policy group guys who felt things were going OK, then all the heads of the teams in charge of the different manifesto sections. A bit of an eye-opener re. justice though, someone saying he doubts there is not a single non-corrupt judge in the country. Edi said there was one case where clearly the verdict went against all the evidence, he challenged the judge at a dinner and the guy said, 'I invested half a million euros to become a judge.' It was like a business. Edi was convinced they were going to win on the votes but they could not rule out theft and they could not rule out the people not being too concerned. Late flight back.

Wednesday 27 February

Portland for meetings then with Idil Oyman to a law firm to do a sales pitch. Also talked about Hutton – a fair bit on Iraq at the moment as the ten-year anniversary was soon – and how the legal strategy was right but in vacating the PR field we had maybe made a mistake. Fiona was moving towards saying yes to standing for Hampstead and Kilburn. I was moving to No re. Burnley. It ought to be an obvious thing to want to do but I was feeling divorced from the whole politics scene just now. Fiona and I were getting on fine, Grace seemed happy enough on her travels and her blog was good, Rory was frustrated at Barnet but was at least developing, but Calum was drinking badly again and distancing himself while being unable to move out. It was a nightmare at times. DS was adamant we had to move him out, but it was hard when push came to shove. We did it a few times, including once not letting him in when he was back late and drunk and had lost his keys, but somehow he always got back within a day or two.

Friday 1 March

Fiona went to see Ed Miliband and Justine. She was blowing hot and cold re. the MP thing and they were keen for her to do it. She said Ed said he would not persuade her against her will but he was clearly worried about the quality of candidates coming through. I had said No to Burnley and he wanted to talk to me about it.

Saturday 2 March

Charlton–Burnley. Didn't go because of Calum disappearing allegedly to

456   *February '13: Ed M persuading Fiona to stand*

watch the rugby which wasn't even on. Came back later and we didn't let him in. Next day I asked him to leave but he worked on first Audrey then Fiona and was back in again. I felt we had to do the tough love thing, but whenever I felt able to Fiona wasn't, and vice versa. We never seemed to be totally aligned on the best way to handle him, and of course he sensed the differences and played us.

Radio 4 did an hour-long play on the WMD dossier, which Aud said was the usual crap. Nick Robinson's documentary on the row with the Beeb was not so bad and indeed had Kevin Marsh [former editor, the *Today* programme] saying Gilligan was journalistically criminal.[*] Tweeted 'if only you had said that ten years ago.'

Sunday 3 March

Ed M called. He said he had heard I had ruled out Burnley but Fiona seemed to think I was still torn and he just wanted another chat about it. He said if I wanted to get a seat at the last minute it could happen. He was keen for me to do it, felt I had a big role to play and he was sure he could help me get anything I wanted in there. And in any event he wanted me to do more on strategy and if we won there were lots of things I could do. I had been reading Al Gore's *The Future* and suggested he read it, to show that it is possible to make big themes interesting. One of the themes was the gap between the scale of challenges facing the world and the quality of leadership, and he should be focusing much more on big themes. The Eastleigh election and particularly the UKIP vote had shown up the anti-politics vote, as did Beppe Grillo in Italy. He sounded like he got that but it was not clear what he intended to do.

For example his next PPB [party political broadcast] was on immigration and would doubtless be another mea culpa on behalf of the last government. I said his strategy of distancing from Labour was not doing him any good, it was helping the Tories. He felt he had to get that bit of distance. I said it only worked if he had a clear policy agenda and it did not seem to be emerging. Fiona was definitely moving towards standing and worried that my 'support you whatever' was actually a desire for her not to. Truth is I was ambivalent but did not want to push her either way. We both needed change in our lives and it might be the best thing for her. I had to keep thinking and decide whether to go for a new mountain or chill.

---

[*] Andrew Gilligan had stated on *Today* that the government had 'probably known' that a dossier detailing Iraq's WMDs was wrong.

Monday 4 March

Appointment at the Royal Free – I got the wrong bloody day. Chat with Bounceback, painting and decorating firm employing ex-prisoners. Drift feelings growing. Then a long chat with Dave Brailsford about the book plan. Penguin said they were worried I was too big a name to be a second-fiddle character. Ed V also had a long chat with Joel Rickett [non-fiction publisher] at Penguin and confirmed they were worried whether I realised just what ghost writing entailed.

Tuesday 5 March

Judging the Sport Industry Awards. Entries not as good as they should have been considering the year we had had. Channel 4 did well. I suggested Danny Boyle as Outstanding Achievement. Someone suggested David Walsh for lifetime achievement and the support for it was overwhelming. Left early for a housing conference in Brighton. Lovely sunny day, and the event was OK. I did my best to give them advice on how to influence policy debate but I felt I was going through the motions.

Wednesday 6 March

Iraq interview with Norma Percy [award-winning film-maker] for her documentary. She was back from seeing [Dick] Cheney [former US Vice-President]. She said he was charming!

Thursday 7 March

Covent Garden to sit for a portrait for charity fundraiser. Then to LLR to plan the John Bercow event, he having given us Speaker's House for a dinner. Portland, see Bradders who was totally opposed to me getting a seat, said he was sure I would regret it, and go mad. Ditto Nicola when I saw her at Freuds. She reckoned my greatest success was rebuilding myself and regaining balance in my life and why did I want to put it all at risk? Freuds to do the Gould Global judging. A project in Egypt won it. To the Liberal Club for Random House authors' party. Ed V keener on me becoming an MP than before. Gail felt it would be terrible if Fiona did it and I didn't. Rory round to talk re. work, and his problems with Edgar Davids.

Friday 8 March

Meeting with TB. I saw Rachel Grant first who felt he was doing OK, but still not political enough. She felt I should do more on Iraq. He was doing another round today. He was looking a bit gaunt. It was worrying that Martin Gilbert [historian and author] was in a bad way and effectively off the Chilcot team, as he had always seemed supportive. I told TB though of the text I got after I gave evidence: 'Absolutely brilliant today. Word perfect – Martin Gilbert.' And I stared at it in disbelief until I realised it was Martin Gilbert, the boss at Aberdeen Asset Management! Chilcot media stories were tending to suggest he would take a hard line. TB ever the optimist said it might be Chilcot was taking time in part to let Syria develop. Optimist indeed, but TB felt the Syria civil war changed the picture. His basic message was that Iraq was improving in parts, that there was democracy, that the insurgents were always going to try their worst. My line was that controversy for leaders about Iraq was making leaders not do what they should with regard to Syria and other challenges.

He was going to the GWB [George W. Bush] library opening. As for his own position, he was keen to do more domestically. He had seen Ed yesterday and was not at all sure he had a strategy. In so far as he did, he felt it was the wrong one. He felt the Tories would get a majority because floaters would look at the two Eds and say they were not having it. Douglas, Jim Murphy [shadow Defence Secretary], JP and David M had all done a bit of Iraq distancing recently – 'I told Douglas it gave them nothing. At least Ed was always opposed but shifting now gives them nothing.'

Off to Jeremy Slaughter. We chatted away perfectly well, and some of it felt both relevant and interesting but I wasn't sure how much it was helping me either to make decisions or to feel better in myself. On the latter point, I was finally off the anti-depressants, and maybe it was that which had caused the feelings of lethargy, indecision and drift. I was even from time to time feeling suicidal, not in a way that meant I would do it, but just feeling that it wouldn't overly bother me if it was all over. Also saw David Sturgeon later, mainly talking about Calum and how sad I felt about it all, and hopeless too, that no matter what we did it didn't seem to get through to him when it came to drinking. He was clear that we had to take a harder line. Tough love. The only way.

To the Hospital Club, Covent Garden, for a rather odd International Women's Day event, which June Sarpong and her friend Sofia had persuaded me to do. All-men panel, a couple of businessmen, including one who turned weapons into jewellery, a violinist, a DJ, and a very vapid male model, David Gandy, who really got on my tits. [Former Labour adviser] Sam White's wife came up at the end and said I had rescued the thing by at least being a bit serious and making a few feminist points! Partly Grace's blog had helped as she had made the point women's rights in law did not mean the same as equality. Did a couple of interviews then sloped off to meet Fran Millar to talk about the Dave Brailsford book project. She said she was not 100 per cent sure he was 100 per cent sure he wanted to do it but she was sure if anyone could get the best out of him, it was me. She said he was someone who had to like people he worked with, and also had to be committed. She said Penguin were worried I was too big a figure and it would become more about me than him which was bollocks. But anyway we agreed he needed to be sure he wanted to do it, and that he would give it the time and attention it needed.

Home via DS then out for dinner at C London [restaurant] with F, Melanne Verveer and Phil. Both out of government post Hillary but both going into big jobs. Melanne convinced both Fiona and I should go for it. She said Hillary had shown what was possible post mid-fifties, and I had to aim high. I could not work out why I was so reluctant. Maybe I was worried about the head. She was also keen for Fiona to do it. I had told Anna Yearley in Ed's office I was not going for Burnley so they could go ahead and make it an all-woman shortlist. Both she and Ed felt I should go for a last-minute seat.

Melanne and Phil were keen on our take on the British scene. She felt TB was not in a good place. They seemed a bit down on Obama. I said I would love to help Hillary if she went for it. Clearly her fall and the subsequent illness was quite serious so she was resting a fair bit as well as making money, speeches, book, and deciding whether to go for President. Bill was keen. Melanne said he was just a happy character who was loving his life at the moment. C London clearly one of the happening places. Lots of money in there. She and I agreed inequality the coming issue, possibly with civil disorder, also 'too much democracy', and making it too hard to make change. Car broke down. Had to leave it.

Saturday 9 March
Ran in to Brook St to meet the RAC man. He was a nice guy, quite well informed, but riddled with conspiracy theories. Later a heavy session with Calum on the choices he was making. Problem was I sensed he was listening, but not ready to change. To QPR with Georgia. Paul Collingwood and Steve Harmison [England cricketers] in the bar, so had a chat with them. Good laugh both of them. Harmison's football knowledge impressive. Collingwood interested in politics I sensed. QPR won 3–1, giving the fans the idea they could still stay up. Saw Harry and Jamie Redknapp for a chat after, then Steve Cotterill [ex-Burnley manager]. Steve on good form.

Sunday 10 March

Out on the bike, freezing cold. Fiona had the local Fabians [Labour society] around. Calum another dire weekend on the drink front. Very depressed.

Monday 11 March

Out early and off with Rayan to the airport. Pretty good. Did loads of work, then read *Night* by Elie Wiesel, which was fantastic. The story of his love for his father and how it kept him going was so moving. The concentration camp inhumanity was at times overwhelming but so was the power that saw it off. Watched *Hitchcock*. Tony Hopkins brilliant. Touching portrayal of a marriage. Made me realise how important longevity with Fiona was to me. Arrived and got whisked through and off to the JW Marriott Marquis [Dubai]. Met the conference team and talked through the plan for tomorrow. Dinner at the Lundbeck welcome chatting with one of the guys involved in the Selincro [drug to curb desire for alcohol] trials who said they had been inundated with volunteers based on two small ads in the *Standard* and the *Metro*. Out for a run, nice heat. Got Burnley v Hull [0–1] on Al Jazeera. Having to lobby to get Edi invited to the Labour arts dinner. Ridiculous. They just don't get this kind of stuff.

Tuesday 12 March

Work on the speech, meeting with Lundbeck CEO, Ulf Wiinberg, going over the need for a new campaign. Mental health going down the agenda again, had to get it up. They were relatively small, and he said when they did a big drug, it cost £800 million or so, so it was like betting the farm every time. They were the only mental health specialist firm left. NICE [National Institute for Health and Care Excellence, advisers to NHS] had been a good idea but there were unintended consequences, and the UK was now a hard place to get new drugs in. I was speaking at the session on Selincro which was aimed at reducing drink consumption rather than total abstinence as the only option.

Lunch then the event. They showed a clip from my *Panorama* film on drink, and I did my usual spiel without notes, three hats, patient, government creature, current campaigner, and urged them to be less defensive and understand the need to take it on as an issue and in a different way.

Wednesday 13 March

I'd decided after Dubai to jazz up my speeches and other presentations so went in for a meeting with Mark Lucas and team re. doing new films and presentation for speeches, website campaigns etc. In addition to doing stuff for speeches, I wanted to build a video library for schools and colleges and also to develop a different way of doing political speeches which Ed and others could use, e.g. iPad voting for speech subject. Instead of quoting people, use video clips of them speaking. And for my speeches, use clips and stills of the main themes etc. A lot of the day talking to Fiona about her going for Hampstead and Kilburn. She was moving to it.

Out to St James's Palace [Duke of Edinburgh gold awards presentation] with Mum and Audrey p.m. They enjoyed it. Mum loved all the royal stuff still. I think the Palace people saw me as a bit of a guilty pleasure. They were certainly aware of some of the things I had said in the past. Same organisers as before but this time the kid who spoke to the presenters and guests was a young guy who had done his Duke of Edinburgh scheme in Reading jail. I was in the main room again with kids from the NW, including a fair few from Burnley. Still very white and middle-class but maybe a bit better than last year. The Duke was exactly as a year ago, same small talk, same beelining for pretty girls and at one point turning to the parents and saying, 'What a dreary bunch.' He was still remarkably fit for his age though, walked well. He gave me almost the exact same 'What are you doing here?' look as last time. Nick Witchell [BBC royal correspondent] was there because his daughter was getting one. I was impressed he remembered meeting Mum in '94 at my farewell do from *Today*.

Got Rayan to take Mum to Dorking then met Liz [sister] and Ania [sister-in-law] in Oxford St. To the Commons for the Speaker's LLR dinner. Much more focused this time on politicians and looking to next steps. Great turnout and Bercow superb as ever in his welcome and in his commitment. He was also saying we should definitely go for seats. He said I was too big a fish to be swimming outside and felt I would be able to make of it whatever I wanted. Iraq ten years on was bubbling away the whole time and I was being thrown into it a fair bit but it could have been a lot worse. TB out there making the comparisons with Syria etc.

I enjoyed the evening but part of me was thinking could I really see myself as Stephen Dorrell [Tory MP], who was one of the guests – he had been a minister, now select committee chair but was he really making the difference he could, or that I could in my half-out, half-in way? Fiona definitely going for it and I had reconciled myself in a positive way. She should not hold back because of any fears about Calum. Nor re. me. Earlier Cameron's U-turn on alcohol pricing led to Ed's best PMQ line yet – Is there anything in a brewery he could organise?

Thursday 14 March

Gospel Oak [Camden council] by-election team took over the kitchen to run the 'get out the vote' campaign. Low turnout but good win for Labour. Both Sally Gimson and Tulip Siddiq [councillors], likely to be Fiona's opponents if she went for the seat, were around. Fiona ought to beat them both but Tulip was definitely operating. Out on the bike and thinking mainly about Calum. I was at a loss to know what to do. He seemed to be getting worse not better, both the drinking and also the treatment of us. Out for dinner with Rory to discuss his problems with Edgar Davids. Advised him to hang in and learn from how not to do it. He was still young, had made his mark at the Academy sufficiently to be brought in to help with first team recruitment and now was really doing OK but Davids wasn't having him and had 'warned' him about an email Rory sent about the dysfunctional way they were working. My advice was to hang in for now and look around.

Dinner at Lemonia then in for *This Week*. Got quite spiky with Michael Portillo on benefits.

Friday 15 March

I was due to go into work at Portland when Fiona called. Calum had called her. It looked like the situation was finally reaching crisis point. People at work said they had started to notice the effects of his drinking and they felt he had to address it. He called us and said he was worried about it. I felt sick to my stomach but also that maybe this was the low point that David S and Rory O'C both said we might need to get to before things got better. I spoke to his boss, one of his colleagues and got the picture that though they loved him to bits and felt when he was good he was great things had definitely deteriorated and they felt he might need help. More importantly he had reached that point too. I said I felt almost relieved in a way that they knew and were being sympathetic but we had to get it sorted once and for all. We had to go out for dinner but I had nothing on my mind but Calum.

Saturday 16 March

I had written yet another note to Calum last night and asked to see him first thing. We had all reached the same position – he should resign his party job and get help. I called Gavin [Millar] who agreed we should get him out of there and into help. He was terrific as ever. I contacted Stepping Stones [rehab centre] in South Africa but later C said he would prefer maybe Scotland so we got Rory O'C to make contact with Castle Craig. The website looked perfect. As Fiona said, it was like Conaglen with nurses and doctors. We went to see his boss and he gave her a resignation letter. She was taken aback I think but we were all clear this was the way to go. It was all very sad and emotional and she was very nice, as were the others.

The truth was he had decided he had to get help and could not do it while worrying about getting back to work. It had to be for as long as it takes. We met at the Old Vic pit bar then I took him to Brewer Street to clear his desk. He was very down now. I talked to Alex F, said we were reaching the low point I think, and he surprised me when he said he had a deep belief in God and would pray for Calum every night.

Sunday 17 March

I had two box tickets for Blackburn v Burnley. Calum decided to stay home, probably to avoid me, but also he said to decide where he was going to go of the various rehab places we had looked at. The Scottish place looked the best bet. I set off really early with the bike and after fixing up to meet Mike Phelan at the Dunkenhalgh Hotel, went for a little ride around the place. Even there, the security for the match was in evidence as it was one of the pick-up points. Totally OTT. Mike was a top bloke, clearly a No. 2 in many ways, but a very good one.

Off to the match, a bit of abuse on the way in, but nothing too serious. We were easily the better team and one up at half-time thanks to Jason Shackell. Ben Mee sent off second half and even then we never looked in danger. Six fucking minutes of extra time. I was filming our fans ready to get them going crazy at the end and David Dunn pops up to score the equaliser. Felt like a defeat. We stayed around till the cops had cleared the place. Puddles with broken glass all over the roads. Really disappointing but hey-ho. Home and out for dinner with David and Tessa on their anniversary. Calum was in bed by the time I was home. Scotland sorted for Tuesday.

Monday 18 March

Woke to news that the main parties had done a deal on Leveson. Not helpful that Hacked Off were in the room till the early hours as the press would claim bias but it did look like Cameron had caved because he knew he would lose the vote. Ed called before leaving his house for a chat re. what he should say as he left, and how he should handle the statement in the House. No gloating, and don't just focus on the victims but what had happened before re. change of culture. The press continuing to mislead and distort and lie and exaggerate, as I said in a 5 Live debate with Neil Wallis [former *News of the World* executive]. Did a few calls, then sorting out things for Calum – returning his stuff to the party, and sorting admission to Castle Craig. Hospital appointment re. gut. Blood tests all good. Back for chat with the Castle Craig people and Calum spoke to the shrink. He was fairly open with him – a German guy – which was good.

Only went out later to do a Time to Change media event. I was chairing it with a panel of Mary O'Hara [journalist and author], Fiona Phillips and three people open about illness. Good event but still a bit preaching to the converted. Not ideal that it was happening as the Leveson debate was going on in the House, but a good turnout and a good debate. At one point in the Q&A I realised I was not concentrating at all, I was thinking about Calum, and whether rehab would work, whether he would always have this unhappy side that made him want to drink to excess, and I suddenly realised that they were looking at me, I had been asked a question and I hadn't listened to a word of it. 'I'm sorry,' I said. 'I have an issue right now and to be honest I was away with the fairies just now.'

Tuesday 19 March

Out early with Fiona and Calum and off to City for the flight to Edinburgh. It felt like this was a bit make or break. Maybe the party was the worst possible place for him to have worked, and anyway now he was out there would be no false timetables to meet. Rory O'C had been clear that Castle Craig was one of those places where you really needed to commit to the time. So if it took months, it took months. Calum was OK en route, a bit subdued maybe, but slumped on arrival. Nice enough looking place, lovely grounds. A gaggle of smokers outside. F and I met Mr Peter McCann the owner, therapist Mark Abrami and the psychiatrist Florian Kaplick we had spoken to yesterday. It felt more thorough and professional than Toranfield had done when we first went there. They spent an hour or so with us setting out the background while Calum had medical tests. Fiona was getting very teary and also when he came back he was getting resistant to some of the rules, for example no phone or laptop and limited access to the gym because of the worries about cross-addiction.

He said rather snappily he would 'give it three weeks max'. I said try to go with the flow. The staff seemed good and included people who had started there as patients. There were a fair few Dutch people there, mainly heroin addicts funded by the Dutch government. The Brits were a mix of well-off and working class. Calum's room seemed fine. The food seemed OK. We had a little tour, said goodbye and headed back to the airport. Fiona and I were getting on a lot better and we had quite a nice time on the way back, just chatting, but we were both still worried sick. We told a few people who all felt 'what a breakthrough' but we thought that re. Ireland. Emailed Mark Abrami to sort out visits and was meanwhile a bit inundated with bids for travel which I would have to watch. Home then out to Sainsbury's for a thank-you dinner for their £11 million this year for Comic Relief. The dinner itself raised £105k. Nice bunch. Economic mood not so gloomy as expected. General mood re. politics very low though. Fiona very weepy about Molly, who wasn't at all well.

Wednesday 20 March

Budget Day. Ed had sent me through the speech at several stages but I had not engaged. Partly because of Calum. Also because post Leveson I needed to signal I did not want to be sucked in as though a member of staff. He did OK, though mixed views on Twitter. Osborne did reasonably well with a dreadful hand. Cyprus economic collapse also part of the backdrop. I actually missed the Budget live because I was first in a meeting with Katherine Fry re. copy-editing *My Name Is...*, and then a video conference with Portland. I decided to press for a trip to Astana next week as Mark Abrami had said we could not go up to see Calum until after Easter.

I went to see Ron Marx [osteopath] about my back and told him about Calum. He felt it was for the best. Katharine loved the book. Grace meanwhile was loving her time in Jamaica, and working on a novel, the first part of which she sent through. She can write, for sure. Mark Abrami called, said Calum had settled OK. There would be no further contact till Monday. We were pinning all our hopes on this place now. I just hoped he could embrace it and go with the flow. They had a pretty good success rate according to R O'C, but the truth is unless Calum wants to stop, he won't.

Thursday 21 March

Molly not been well and had been kept in overnight at the vet's. Fiona really weepy. It was all getting on top of her. To Silverfish [film-makers] to interview students for my video library project. Then to an *Economist* event where I was making a speech on 'the big rethink'. Did it from a few postcards, and it went well. I gave the Labour arts dinner a miss and instead met Fiona at the vet's, where Molly was being kept in again, then dinner at the Indian. I was meanwhile writing a long piece on Calum to send to Mark A. Rory called and said for the first time Davids had been nice to him and he later learned why – because he had learned I was his dad and was asking if I would meet him to advise him on media and strategy. What a tosser. But I was speaking to Nicola Howson who was saying go along with it and do anything that will help Rory.

Friday 22 March

Chris Underhill from Basic Needs around for a chat. Liked him, and agreed to do stuff with them under my Time to Change umbrella. Out on the bike with Rory for an hour and then off to Euston. Broke the back of the Calum piece on the train to Manchester. Met by Paul Lake [former player, now with Man City Community], up to the Velodrome. Man City in the community doing a 24-hour non-stop ride, with me and Patrick Vieira [former Man City player] in the first group. Loved it. Lapped him five times, and only the City physio beat me so far as I could work out. Nice crowd and nice atmosphere. Amazing negativity towards [Roberto] Mancini [club manager]. One of the physios, who I had never met, said that he could not go soon enough. Shower then off to the station, did a bit more work on the Calum statement and then home late. Fiona up looking at her pictures for the website. Definitely going for seat now. Also working a bit on her basic pitch.

Saturday 23 March

I spent all morning going through tons of photos of Calum's childhood and deciding which to take or send to Mark before we went. Feeling sad but also hopeful. This had to work. Off then with Rory to see Barnet's 0–0 draw with Cheltenham. Bloody snowing. March! Edgar Davids had finally had a civilised conversation with Rory, and it turned out it was because he had learned who his dad was. Rory pissed off at the idea he could treat him like shit and then suddenly behave differently because he thought I might be useful. I said you can learn a lot from crap leaders and bosses as well as good ones, but go with the flow. I just don't want him to get anything good out of it, he said. Rory clearly rated by most of the people there and got on with most of his colleagues.

Davids came up forty minutes or so after the match and was straight into talking mode. Smaller and thinner than I expected. Very direct. Not hugely intelligent I don't think. He said, 'You are the great manipulator, how do I manipulate the media?' I said that was not the best way to think of it, that it was far better to work out a strategy and pursue it, blah blah. I said he needed to be clear what his purpose was in having a comms strategy. He said he wanted to be an icon, and be seen as an icon. He said Beckham was the only player icon and there was only one of him.

He asked how I saw him. I was tempted to say I only had what Rory tells me to go on and he says you're a jerk. I said I still saw him as a player, but that I liked the fact he had decided to go to a club like Barnet. But it was pretty clear that he saw it as a stepping stone, not something really important to him. He talked about his clothing label a lot. I talked a bit about how Alex runs United, how he knows everyone, how he goes to more funerals than anyone I know… 'What is the point of going to funerals?' Oh dear. I said it was about showing respect and being out there as a symbol of something decent and good. I might as well have been talking a different language. Definitely not my kind of guy. Dismissive of too many people, arrogant, which is the word everyone seems to apply to Dutch footballers. Gave him what advice I could but I was not sure he would learn much from it.

Tuesday 26 March

David M called when I was at the airport waiting to get the flight to Vienna then Kaz. He said he had some news – he was announcing tomorrow he was stepping down from Parliament and heading to New York to head up a charity that dealt with victims of conflict. Big job, global reach, good staff. He said he felt he had tried to work out a proper role but it was not possible, and that he just helped to fuel a soap/psychodrama. He also felt Ed was pursuing the wrong strategy but that he could not really influence it because there was no real private dialogue and any public statement just caused a rift. He felt we were unlikely to win. We chatted for half an hour or so, told him what was going on with us. He was clearly disappointed on many levels but really felt this would free him to do a proper job in a different way. He still thought I should go for it and was pleased Fiona was too. Flew to Vienna, then switched to the overnight plane for Astana. Never again Austrian Airlines. Little seats, impossible to sleep.

Wednesday 27 March

We – as in Portland – were meant to be doing a country branding project but there was a bit of a split in the government. Some of them clearly wanted the work, or had promised it to someone else. Our timelines were very tight, but we just had to keep on keeping on. To the Akorda, first to see Kazykhanov and then Marat Tazhin, State Secretary and something of a mythical figure. Physically he was big and imposing. I went through what we were trying to do, emphasised the timelines and the contrasts with others who had done big projects like this. He wanted a report by 1 June to give to all the government, said he needed results. Pretty clear political support for the project is strong.

Tazhin made it clear that despite his security background, he was now overseeing this project, and the overall comms, at the strategic level. He did not hide his view that we were not the most suitable team for this kind of work, as our expertise was comms not branding. He said we got the work because the CCS had been a good idea and had done good work, and because they assumed I would lead the branding work. But he did not hide that others were opposed. The reason he was in charge was that he was the only one capable of ensuring others followed whatever approach is agreed.

He was looking for really detailed work in two areas: core reputation of Kaz and investment – ideas likely to attract business: culture, mythology, geography (not least as part of a tourism strategy). He had one or two doubts about the purpose of research focused on media, signalling he was much more interested in the views of what he called expert opinion, by which I think he meant in particular diplomats, think tanks, businessmen trying to work there.

Kazykhanov was at pains to explain that Tazhin did not want some branding idea rooted in politics, strategic positioning re. Russia, China, East–West or some of the other things we had discussed during the brainstorm earlier but something 'poetic and creative, something that can build on and develop a sense of mythology about Kazakhstan'. He was thinking folklore, fairy tales, history etc. I pointed out this didn't sit well with the dominant idea from the workshop – which was that they want to be seen as modern, free, independent. I think they are looking for ideas and images which link past, present and future.

Tazhin wanted a paper within seven to ten days on 'what worked, what didn't and what kind of creative ideas we will be seeking to develop'. He was particularly interested in the rebranding of Malaysia, Brazil, South Africa, the Baltic states and Romania.

I pointed out that the Malaysia campaign cost a fortune. He said if we got the right idea they would spend on it. What they are looking for is a strong creative idea that can act as a strategic umbrella.* Tazhin was pretty clear that so long as the quality of the work was high he would be our strongest supporter inside the government.

The most interesting thing at the workshop was that they do not wish to be seen in the context of their relationships with others but as themselves. They do not welcome comparison with the other -stans. Unique. Tolerant. Free (they really seem to believe they are much, much freer than most other countries). Fast growing and fast developing. Modern came

* 'Umbrella branding' – the use of a single brand name for two or more related entities or products.

up again and again. A desire to attract more business and more tourism. A desire to educate about what the country has to offer. When it came to asking them to devise their own branding message, young country was the dominant theme.

They were big on the theme of undiscovered beauty and mystery. They have a grand canyon bigger than the Grand Canyon! Ecotourism. Adventure holidays. Bird life. Amazing journeys. I asked if they were ready for *Top Gear* thinking they would reject it but they were keen. *Borat* is still in the air, upsetting for some, but an opportunity in the eyes of others who felt he can still be used in some way. One of the Akorda guys suggested a new town called Boratville. I suggested 'A country too good for Borat' as a possible theme. Kazykhanov thinks the general public still find the whole *Borat* thing insulting but they are fully aware that for some *Borat* is all they know re. Kaz. 'Asian roots, Islamic past, Western outlook' was another theme they wanted to develop.

Week to Friday 5 April

To France via Moscow. Grace sending me lots of stuff she was writing. Calum doing OK so far as we could tell. Working on the Irish diaries. Got it done and sent to TB, Clinton and Bertie A, to ask them for forewords. Long chat with TB re. Kaz, after sending note to the team following chat with Tazhin. TB was travelling all over the place, talking a lot of sense re. world stuff and domestic but clearly frustrated that he couldn't find the right way to use it publicly. Biked most days. Really bad depression for couple of days. Saw it off OK but one of the days really bad. Leighton Andrews and Ann for dinner. Gove refusing to see him, even though he was Welsh education minister. Ludicrous. We had an OK time but I didn't feel rested. We drove back in a day, rewriting Grace's novel.

Saturday 6 April

Set off early with bike for the north. Did The Rake hill in Ramsbottom and Nick of Pendle hill climb at Sabden. So beautiful. Burnley for lunch. Ladies Day. Took John and Tracy [Banaskiewicz, Burnley director and wife]. Both shocked I think at the way the women behaved. Good win 3–1 [v Bristol City]. Then another ride later around Dunkenhaulgh before meeting Fiona and Rory at Preston station. Long drive to Macdonald Cardrona Hotel in Peebles. Knackered again. Slept well though and woke in fabulous Borders countryside. Calum's therapist had said it would be good to have a session with the family. Grace wasn't up for it but Rory was.

Sunday 7 April

Long bike ride with Rory. Failed to find many decent hills. To Castle Craig. Liked the therapist in charge with Mark away. She did the talk for families. The three of us went to that. She had a nice manner. Really just explaining what they did, the issues they were dealing with, the role of family support. We also went to an AA meeting, just sat and listened. We had a chat with Calum, the three of us and Mark the therapist. I was still feeling a lot of resentment from Calum, and at one point Rory said, 'I don't get what the problem is. We had a good childhood, we have great parents and you can't keep this anger up all the time.' Calum looked a bit hurt. I said it is possible for kids growing up in the same circumstances to feel very different about them. Rory headed off later by cab to the airport, and Fiona and I stayed over again after a nice dinner in a little hotel in Innerleithen. I felt today had been OK and it was nice that Rory was so concerned for him and supportive but also able to defend me a bit when I was taking a few hits.

Monday 8 April

Swim, breakfast, row with Fiona. I was flaring up a lot at the moment. Apologised. It was hard for both of us and we had to try to stay on the same page. To Castle Craig. Good session with Alex and Mark. Liked his style. Tough at times, in that I felt I was taking the brunt of the blame, without really knowing why, but I felt these sessions were better than Toranfield. More intense in a way. We all held it together pretty well. Fiona did seem on the edge of tears quite a lot. I could feel the intensity of Calum's feelings, and I still didn't feel we were getting to the bottom of the drinking becoming a problem, but I sensed we were making progress. The three of us went for a walk, and when we were out in the little wood behind the house, I got a call from Irish radio asking for an interview on the news that Margaret Thatcher was dead. Then a torrent of bids. I turned the phone off, decided to stay out if it apart from a tweet saying she was amazing to cover as a PM, that I disagreed with a lot of what she did but she was one of the few real change PMs.

Back in for another less intense session. Calum's resistance to the rules seemed to be softening, and he seemed up for staying a bit longer. We said our goodbyes again and set off, listening all the way to 5 Live, clearly going massive on Thatcher's death. Cameron was cutting short a trip to Europe, which seemed OTT. Then a buzz there might be a recall of Parliament. Ed M sent through draft comments which were pretty good. No point playing politics with this but equally lots of people did not want to show her any respect at all. Cameron looked like he was milking it.

Fergie sorted a ticket for the United–City match so Fiona dropped me at Wigan and I got a train to Manchester. People on the tram to Old Trafford were trying to get me to laugh about Thatcher. 'Go on, mate, go on, you know you want to.' 'Now, now,' I said. I did not get the feeling the media mood matched the public mood. Bumped into Mike Summerbee [former Man City player] and had a good chat about Burnley. Paddy Crerand [former Man United player and assistant manager] making no effort to disguise his hatred of Thatcher. After the match – City deservedly won 2–1 – to Alex's office for the usual after-match drink and eat. I mainly chatted to Martin Ferguson [AF's brother]. Very down on the club, the game, coaches, methods. Felt City better team. AF looking a bit tired. Mainly talking Thatcher and Burnley. Stayed till midnight.

Tuesday 9 April

We got a good note from Mark Abrami. He had asked us to write down what we felt about what had happened. He said he had shown Calum our notes and he had been emotional. 'He is beginning to FEEL,' he said. Fiona said she felt more optimistic. She felt Calum was beginning to engage.

Wednesday 10 April

I wrote a long Thatcher blog, basically saying that it would be wrong only to have glowing tributes and not to debate her legacy in the round. It got a fair bit of pick-up. I was asked on by *Newsnight* with Eleanor Laing [Tory MP] and Ronnie Campbell [Labour MP]. It was as though because she had died, people now had to give a totally one-sided and positive portrait of who and what she was. Yet if there is one thing Margaret Thatcher liked it was a good argument; and if there was one place where she felt those arguments should be held, it was in the House of Commons. So it was right and proper that MPs pay genuine respect to her strengths and achievements in Parliament today, and express sadness at her passing, but wrong if MPs who disagreed with her policies and the impact of them upon their constituents and the wider world felt unable to say so.

It was odd listening to people I knew could not stand her queueing to say how marvellous she was. Those who helped bring her down because she had become hugely unpopular with the public – the fact she was forced from office seems to have been little mentioned in the last two days – were rushing to tell us how amazingly popular and in tune with public opinion she had been. I made the point that nobody should speak ill of the dead, and the parties and dancing in the streets were offensive and misplaced.

April '13: Lively debate over Thatcher legacy

But nor should anyone condone hypocrisy, and hypocrisy comes when people say not what they believe, but what they believe they ought to say.

It was hard for MPs to get the balance right. Ed Miliband – who got the tone right on the day her death was announced – has perhaps a trickier task. He has to do the praise but also the reality that she was a divisive figure, and her legacy far from being an unalloyed success. She was elected as I sat my finals at university. By the time she was gone I was political editor of the *Daily Mirror* and, in between times, I had followed her around the world, written about her with all the passion I could muster. She was one hell of a story to work on, and she was also one of the few real change Prime Ministers. I was also keen to make the point that the Tories were so much better than us in the politics of death and historical legacy. Tories never tire of talking up their past. It is not an act of vanity, but strategy. To have a generation unborn at the time of the Winter of Discontent still vaguely aware of it speaks volumes for the Conservative Party's disciplined use of history as a political tool.

To have a young generation today being bombarded with messages about how marvellous she was is good for the Conservative Party tomorrow; and they know it. Labour, by contrast, has a habit of running down its own past and its own history. We have seen too much of that in recent years re. TB – won three elections, presided over the peace process in Northern Ireland, helped rid the world of murderous dictators like Saddam Hussein and Slobodan Milošević, saved our schools and hospitals from remorseless decline under the Tories, delivered devolution, the minimum wage, ten years of growth and prosperity, Bank of England independence, Sure Start, I could go on and on. Yet to hear a lot of Labour figures, and the media echo chamber, his record was a negative one. I also talked of the sense of unease at the scale of the funeral arrangements, and, following on from the snub to Labour Prime Ministers at the wedding of William and Kate, the royal presence.

The royals represent and embody the state. The case for a state funeral for Winston Churchill did not even need to be made. There is not a person alive who does not believe he helped to save the UK. But Margaret Thatcher's role and record is not so clear. Cameron says she 'saved the economy'. But for many parts of Britain, people and communities feel she destroyed it, and abandoned families in her wake. Yes, she can point to a historic role in saving the Falklands from Argentina, and even more significantly in working with Ronald Reagan and Mikhail Gorbachev to end the Cold War and bring down the Berlin Wall. But her role in defending dictators like Pinochet, and her support for the apartheid regime in South Africa, deny her the right to be free from criticism on the foreign policy front. And for all the Tories liked to say that TB was her achievement, a lot of what Labour did was to repair the impact of Thatcherism, not build upon it. I liked reminding Tories Cameron felt he had to run not as the heir to Thatcher, but the heir to Blair, and indeed felt he had to invent the idea of The Big Society as a direct antidote to her – admittedly misquoted – line that there is 'no such thing as a society'.

I could respect Thatcher enormously as someone who knew what she believed and fought tirelessly to put those beliefs into action, through a life of public service. But it does her memory no good for any of us, least of all the MPs speaking today, to pretend there is only one side to the Thatcher story. I had a long chat with Bercow who told me Cameron had steamrollered the recall of Parliament, that the agreed plans in the event of her death during recess were no recall, but he had suggested it, Ed felt he had to agree and so JB felt had to go along with it. Tories and right-wing media were milking it ludicrously. Blog said they would pay a price. Cameron or [Lynton] Crosby [political strategist] had clearly decided there was an opportunity for strategic repositioning on the back of it. I sensed Jeremy Paxman was more with me than them on this one.

Thursday 11 April

Ed M called first thing, really angry at a piece TB had done in the *New Statesman*. Essentially saying the country had not moved left, there was a real need to bring policy forward, and also that progressives risked being in the comfort zone. No mention of Ed but he must have known where it was heading. The front pages. TB had sent me the piece but I had not really focused. I could understand why Ed was pissed off. For a TB piece, it was not very well written, argued or structured. Ed said he had really tried with TB but was of a mind to go out and say he was a figure of the past and he should define himself and his leadership against him. I had never heard him quite so angry.

TB was broadly right in the analysis, wrong in how he did it. I talked to him, conveyed how pissed off Ed was and I sensed TB rather regretted it. I sent a note to Ed saying I could see it was annoying but no good would come of flaring it up further. I saw clips later and he seemed to agree. I said I had communicated how angry he was, TB had taken it on board and also accepted he should have forewarned him. I urged him not to go over the top. I said 'engage but broadly dismiss' was the best approach, and suggested a line to take on these lines – TB a huge political figure, of vast experience, always worth listening to. Right to point out the crash was not Labour's fault. Welcome the focus on growth and jobs as key challenge. Also the questions he poses are in the right area, and they are the questions being asked and answered by the policy review underway. But if there is one thing TB and Margaret Thatcher showed, it is that in a world of change, leaders must adapt to the change. If there are leaders of progressive parties around the world living in a post-crash comfort zone, EM is not one of them. But just as TB and MT changed their parties according to their beliefs and the world around them, so he is doing the same.

Neil decided he was not going to Thatcher's funeral. I sent him a text 'Are you sure?' and the one he sent back was funny but also made clear, yes, he was. Did *This Week*. Will Self [political commentator and author] and I agreeing a fair bit re. Thatcher. Portillo defending all of it. I was making the point re. politicisation all the time. The Tories saw a real opportunity.

Friday 12 April

To Albania early via Vienna. Met by Endri. Meeting with Edi, and the strategy group. He was feeling pretty good about things, felt that Berisha was on the defensive, and also trying to copy some of the stuff we were doing. Trying to work out a shape to the campaign from now on. The new press office was up and running. The whole office had been revamped in the colours of the campaign. Good enough meeting, then chat to Edi re. his Balkans policy speech tomorrow. It was all about trying to show leadership not just for the country but for the region. Late p.m. I drove with Endri and events colleague to Pristina. Quality of road much better in Kosovo than Albania. Nice scenery. Crossed the border at the point where years before I had seen hundreds of refugees trying to get out. Staying at the Swiss Diamond. Had a drink with Vlora Çitaku, EU integration minister, who feared the Serbs' pulling of the plug on the talks was a really bad blow and it was not clear what the plan B was going to be.[*] She adored TB, as did a lot of people here. Even had a picture of him in her wallet. Dinner with Endri and his girlfriend who worked as a lawyer there.

Saturday 13 April

Did a few TV and press interviews, and after one of them, with the *Express* website, the editor cum MP Berat Buzhala asked me to help a guy called Behgjet Pacolli with a campaign to become mayor of Pristina. Wealthy former President, richest Albanian in the world. Had two meetings with him, Berat and Mimoza Kusari-Lila, Deputy PM. They were in the new Kosovo party – his – but he was friendly with [Hashim] Thaçi [Prime

---

* EU-mediated talks between Serbia and Kosovo in Brussels, designed to resolve the status of Serb-dominated northern Kosovo, had broken up without agreement.

Minister] who was keen for him to do it, possibly to get him off the scene, also because the current mayor Isa Mustafa was leader of the main opposition party who would run against Thaçi in the general election. Behgjet oozed wealth, but I liked the way Mimoza talked to him, telling him he had to listen!

Edi, Linda [wife] and colleagues arrived and then we headed off to a restaurant called Pinochio's to meet Thaçi for dinner. Vlora and Petrit Selimi [Kosovo politician] also there. Thaçi was feeling more confident re. the Serbia situation than Vlora. He felt they had to come round and move eventually. The north was an outstanding problem. No real rule of law. He was pretty keen on me helping Pacolli so long as afterwards I helped him. He felt he would win.

He was clearly fond of Edi, very keen for him to win, but said Berisha was not to be underestimated because he would do anything to hold on. He said all of Edi's comms were intercepted. Edi seemed pretty relaxed about it. Nice enough chat with both of them, then Edi and team and I headed out to Pacolli's place. Like a Middle East palace. Something a bit [Robert] Maxwellian about him, loved the trappings and the talk of closeness to Putin and others, but also something a bit vulnerable about him.

Sunday 14 April

Had breakfast with Thaçi, partly with Petrit as translator, then just the two of us. Thaçi wanted me to send a message to Cathy Ashton that she should get them straight back into talks again, that he felt the Serbs would move because they had to. We spent half the time talking about that, and work he wanted me to do, and the rest about Serbia. He was pretty sure that the Serbs, or at least the PM, knew they had to do something about the situation in the north. I sent a note to Cathy, told her, truthfully, that Thaçi had been singing her praises. He said she had handled the talks brilliantly and could not have done more. But he said though he knew people were feeling disappointed he felt there was a case for her trying to get people back into talks straight away.

He had been reading my diaries and said they needed something like we did for the Good Friday Agreement, get her to force the parties into a dingy room and make clear 'We are not leaving till it is done … we are all too close to a deal to let it founder now, has to be worth the effort, create a sense of momentum through urgency etc.' He said he felt the deal was the right one but ultimately the Serbs felt they would lose too much face in being seen to agree to anything. But he thought at least two of the three out of the PM, Deputy PM and President would be up for going back into it again. He was worried if it did not work now it would not work again

April '13: Meeting in Kosovo with Thaçi and Rama

for some time. He felt she should really make this issue her main thing, that it was there for the taking if everyone shows the same commitment and determination she had. He was clearly quite a fan.

Off to the book event at Sheshi 21 [restaurant], good media turnout though not so many people as the Tirana launch. Spoke re. NI and the need to keep going, also how far Kosovo had come. Edi was on really good form at the moment. He said he intended to use my line about the difference between this time and the last time I crossed the Kosovo–Albania border in his speech later today.

Off to the airport. Glad I was away from all the Thatcher stuff which was going way over the top. I had a chat with TB, who was feeling a bit chastened at the way the thing with Ed had gone. But he felt he was right on substance. I met Kevin McDonald on the second flight, to Edinburgh, manager of the Red Hot Chilli Pipers [Celtic bagpipe rock band]. There were now two full bands and soon they would be simultaneously in China and the USA. He dropped me off at my hotel.

Monday 15 April

Went for a run, did a bit of work then went to meet Fiona at the airport. Castle Craig sent a car for us. Calum seemed OK, or at least seeming to be engaging more. In the therapy session we discussed letters he had written to us and also one he wrote 'To alcohol'. Hard pounding but cathartic. His main points about me were about me not being there enough when he was young, and him feeling I did not believe in him. Some of the stuff he said felt harsh and hard to take. But I think we all felt a bit better at the end of it. Some fascinating characters there among the Dutch drug addict contingent. Today felt a bit more rushed. Also I sensed Calum was getting more involved in the way they wanted and intended even if he was overdoing the anti-authority thing a bit. Maybe.

Fiona was really finding it hard to decide re. Hampstead and Kilburn. She was wondering if the campaign for selection side of things was really her. Tulip starting to fight dirty, e.g. re. Iraq, bringing me into the equation, and also saying Fiona really knew only about education. I think hearing Calum talking about me having been taken away by politics might be weighing on her too.

Tuesday 16 April

I did a few lines for Fiona on the attacks Tulip was starting up. Meeting with Clive Tulloh [producer] and team who wanted to turn *The Happy Depressive* into a three-part series. To airport for the flight to Denmark.

Staying at Marriott on the waterfront. Nice run, then ate in, working on the speech for tomorrow.

Wednesday 17 April

Denmark. Best place to be on the day of the [Thatcher] funeral. So OTT. Run round the front again, meeting with the Danish Mental Health Fund, interview with *Berlingske*, all re. mental health, then out of town to the conference centre. The interviewer was a guy called Jens, who said he had experience of depression. The whole interview was mental health related. Cab out to somewhere half-hour out of Copenhagen which the taxi driver said was the most expensive real estate in the world. Very Scandinavian conference centre, felt like a mix of a university campus and a four-star hotel. The manager came up to me and said, 'Mr Mandelson, I am a big fan of your work.' Tweeted it and told Peter, and we got into an exchange about how ludicrous it was that Thatcher was having this quasi state funeral. Attlee had 150 people at his funeral. It was partly about the way the right always defended their history and the left attacked it. Good enough event and the Lundbeck people really seemed to appreciate the stuff I did with them. Caught bits and bobs of Thatcher stuff. Osborne crying. Big crowds.

Thursday 18 April

Calum was starting to reject the idea of visitors and said it made him feel controlled from afar. I saw David S, and we discussed whether I should suggest to Calum that we do AA together. He thought it might be a good idea, but felt we should wait to see what happened. He felt yes to saying to Calum we stop drinking for good together but do for me not for him.

Friday 19 April

Did first longish run in ages. JoP emailed me saying he was in Belfast and [Peter] Robinson [First Minister] and [Martin] McGuinness needed my help on comms, and could I get there soon!

Monday 22 April

Freuds' leadership event, Q&A with Nicola. Really good crowd in there. Quick lunch then off to the airport for a flight to Belfast. I was picked up on landing and straight for a long session with Robinson and team, including one of McG's spads, up at Stormont. First in his office, then an early dinner.

We chatted a bit about JoP who had done a radio programme in which he had said the Unionists did not look after their working-class support the way that Sinn Féin looked after theirs. They were both at the end of their tether re. the EIS, Executive Information Service, which sounded like the GIS [Government Information Service] when we took over, reactive, not understanding etc. He wanted me to do a review but as we talked I sensed that was a bad idea and they would be far better off working out what they wanted and just going for it. Partly I did not want to be going back and forth the whole time, but also I think I would become a controversy in it and it would stop them doing the things they wanted to.

We talked through all the various things they would need for a proper strat comms plan and agreed I should write a note for them after seeing McGuinness in the morning. He was scathing re. the government, said Cameron and co. just did not care. 'I've seen Obama five times and Cameron once.' He seemed to be getting on OK with McG, but was a bit jaded generally. Very down about the media negativity. I tried to get him to raise his head up above it but he kept coming back with stories of woe. Stephen Nolan's phone-in was just an incitement to whinge. I said he should engage with him.

Tuesday 23 April

Out for a run along the Falls Rd then met McGuinness and Vincent Parker [special adviser] at the hotel. He echoed Robinson and also agreed with my strategy – no to review, yes to decide and do and take the hit. He asked after TB, shared my sense that it was crazy as well as sad he could not make a contribution without being seen as PNG [*persona non grata*]. Asked me about the election, was clearly desperate for us to get back in because 'this lot just do not get it'. He felt DC saw it all as Blair territory and only engaged when he really had to. Certainly didn't feel it. He asked me to get a message to Clegg which later I did. He said, as Robinson had last night, that they had been taken aback by the flags controversy, but they had more or less stuck together.* It was a problem though for Robinson to be seen as being too close to McG, who was a hate figure for a lot of Unionists and for the dissident Republicans. We chatted a bit about old times, and he seemed to me genuinely to be on a different tack, in terms of how he pursued his objectives. He was even warm in the way he spoke

---

* Belfast City Council's decision to limit the days that the Union Flag was flown from City Hall led to street protests throughout the Province by Ulster loyalists, who saw it as a move to dilute 'Britishness'.

of some of the Unionists. Both he and Robinson both seemed to think the need for sharpening the comms was urgent.

I worked on a shared position paper which could easily be adapted to a speech, consultation paper, briefing paper, or whatever. I tried to base it around the flow of what they were saying. The context was the pace of change in the media landscape. Social media – Facebook, Twitter, now one of the fastest and most important primary news sources, YouTube, which in any given month now sees more video content uploaded than was broadcast by the three main US networks in the first sixty years of their existence. An explosion in TV channels. The blogosphere. Citizen's journalism. Newspapers finding it hard to adapt to this world of technological change, yet still major political players. They were struggling to adapt to it. And they were still using systems and ways of thinking from a very dissimilar era, one where the very system of government was different.

We were now in an era in which the public feel they have an absolute right to know what is being done in their name. So that put on leaders the absolute democratic duty to communicate effectively, about purpose, objectives, the strategy to meet them. Both admitted they had not been doing that and I said it would do no harm to admit it. They were maybe too focused on the bubble, not the world outside. But the research done recently underlined the extent to which many people are frankly unaware of what the Assembly's functions are, and unaware of what the Executive does.

McG said it was possible to see that as a good thing, a sign of progress, and normalisation. People were certainly aware of the politics when night after night the news bulletins were filled with stories about bombs and violence and death and destruction and hatreds that felt like they were going to be with us for ever. But it meant decisions were now being made without proper understanding. And there was insufficient public debate. My paper, which I worked on as soon as we said goodbye, set out how they could take greater responsibility for ensuring that the public properly understand, and engage with, the systems of government, the decisions taken, the thinking behind them, the debate about the impact which inevitably follows. Also, I said they needed to engage properly with critics. People like to see and hear their leaders tested, not just in Stormont but they should also do town hall and village hall meetings, regular press briefings and press conferences, radio phone-ins, Q&A sessions on Twitter and other social media sites. It was clear they needed to modernise the systems that currently operate within the Executive. Current systems were essentially inherited from an era when Northern Ireland waited to be told what it had and what it should say about it. But now less reactive and more strategic approach was called for. Far from needing more money, it could be done with fewer people.

I recommended a new body, the Executive Communications and Information Service, headed by a director of strategy and communications, with two deputies who should, in addition to their general roles as deputies, be the official spokespersons for the First Minister and his deputy respectively, based in their private offices. Both Peter and McG had said that far too often they have had to rely on press spokesmen for their parties to deal with legitimate media enquiries and stories relating to their work as ministers. I said the director of strategy should have working to him an official with responsibility for co-ordinating all government announcements and events.

Each government department should have someone appointed, either full-time or as part of other functions, to liaising with this person so that all of government can be properly informed about what the rest of the government is doing. Also recommended a head of digital comms, building on the work of NI online, who will take responsibility for ensuring Northern Ireland is maximising the potential of the digital revolution in relation not just to media but also public services and inward investment; proper professional systems of media monitoring, rebuttal, the routine preparation of handling notes and so-called 'lines to take' on contentious or newsworthy issues.

Flight back then out for a debate on Europe with John Redwood [Eurosceptic Tory MP] in front of a load of asset-fund managers. I did OK but was not really on top form. Redwood felt Ed M was doing a lot better than the Tories thought. My main point was that Cameron's strategy was driven by the threat of UKIP and the Tory right. He accepted the second part not the first and also did not accept my notion that Cameron had put at risk UK influence e.g. on the Single Market. Q&A was OK.

Wednesday 24 April
Off to Leeds for the 'Yorkshire Mafia' [business network] event. Speech was supposed to be mainly about mental health and in fact every question in the Q&A had a MH element. Did a couple of student interviews, but was on the first train back after the event, in and off to the Institute of Directors Portland event. Odd crowd.

Thursday 25 April
Off to Scotland with Fiona and Rory. Saw the boss guy, Mr McCann, who clearly knew a lot about the issues. Calum was not great. He seemed pretty cast down. I sensed from the therapists too that things had gone backwards again, that he was not engaging, not going with the flow, not

believing it was the right place to be. He was a bit truculent with us, and I could tell Fiona's fussing and my wanting to find out what was bugging him were getting to him. He seemed to be getting on with some of the other residents, especially the Dutch guys. I couldn't put my finger on it, but I left feeling a bit despondent, and Fiona was too. It was definitely feeling like one step forward, two steps back.

Back to London and I was speaking at a small dinner organised by Jimmy Worrall [CEO, Executive Sport Limited] and Mike Forde [leadership specialist]. Small and select, mainly designed for top sports people to share ideas and experience. Dave Brailsford, which gave us the chance for us to have a chat about the book project, but I sensed his heart was not going to be in it while he was still so focused on the cycling; the head engineer from McLaren, who seemed a really smart guy; Andy Flower from England cricket – had a nice chat about mental health; Damien Comolli [former coach, director of football, who was really friendly and warm; Steve McClaren [former England team manager], good guy; and a mix of business guys. I was asked to speak to dealing with the unknown and the main point was that too many defined their reality according to the media, also that people exaggerated their problems because the media did. Good Q&A in which they seemed interested above all in what happened to team and mindset whenever real crisis hit.

Friday 26 April
Met Greg Nugent at the airport, chatted over Calum and also the Pacolli brief. He was just up for doing new stuff and didn't even seem that bothered about getting paid. The plane to Munich was on time until we were about to land, when the pilot spotted a flock of birds getting hit by a plane taking off and he decided to head up again, and we had to wait for a new slot. So we were late and already had a massively tight connection. Had to chat up the bus driver taking us to the terminal to step on it, then run like fuck through the terminal, queue-jumping on security, all the time joking about the need to set a new world record for terminal transfer, and we just made it as they were calling our names. Luckily everything went according to plan and we made it from one terminal to another through new security etc. with no time to spare.

Adria [Airways] to Pristina, met by the hotel and straight into a meeting with Behgjet, Berat, Mimoza and Valon. Behgjet looking very low. Polls not good. Tried to persuade him that it was like a German footballer being in the list for Spanish player of the year – his name was not in the mix, nobody knew he was thinking of it. The main thing was the fact that people were saying they wanted change and they were tired of the old ways. We went round and round for a couple of hours then headed to his house which I had said to Greg was a Dubai version of Buck House. Chatted away for a while on the balcony and then after a while a group of guys arrived and Behgjet said we needed to ask them what they thought.

Goatee-beard guy who was close to Thaçi but felt BP should go for it. Bald guy who didn't say much but thought it was going to be tough. Big guy who ran telecoms who was really pushing him to go for it. Former Kosovo Liberation Army guy who ditto. Another guy who was probably going to be the spokesman. Really frank discussion of his strengths and weaknesses. Some of them thought he should really go for Thaçi as a way of signalling that he was distancing himself from the government but some of us felt that if he was going to present himself as a new kind of politician it felt a bit old-style stuff.

He was coming under pressure from these guys but they were also giving conflicting messages on the substance etc.

Saturday 27 April

Tired after a late night. Greg and I did an OK run taking in bits of the city, past the Clinton statute, stopping at an open-air bookstore that had me next to Hitler! We were mulling over what to do for a strategy. Lunch with Berat. Behgjet was nervous about losing and about having to distance himself from Thaçi. He was clearly quite a loyal sort of bloke and did not seem to want to damage Thaçi or create chaos. We headed back for a meeting first with him, Mimoza and Berat trying to get a proper fix on whether he was up for it and then with the broader team.

Worked out a few policy lines and then a campaign structure. Had to plead with them at times not to talk at the same time but we made more progress today than yesterday. The Kosovans were not convinced Edi would win.

Sunday 28 April

Swim, breakfast, off to Tirana. Straight to SP HQ to see Edi who was in one of his grumpy disengaged modes. I sent him a note later on the terrible impression he made on Greg. The policy development stuff was largely at an end and now they had fifty days to fill which they were struggling with. I said they needed to go for talking points and we had a bit of a brainstorm on that. Greg good at this stuff. Long lunch then back to HQ to go over ideas and then to a betting shop to watch Arsenal v United. Dinner and airport. Black singer Low Deep T telling me how big he was in this part of the world when a truly stunning American Albanian woman called Kristale came over and said I was her hero. Greg was open-mouthed in jealousy. We had a good laugh with her. Been fun travelling with him, he had a very good mind, and I reckoned he and Godric could be a good team [in new agency].

Monday 29 April
TB had delivered a good draft foreword for the NI book. Later to TBWA [advertising agency] for chat re. Labour strategy, then talk to staff and book signing.

Wednesday 1 May
Potter. Bike. Lunch Charlie F at Delauneys. He had lost loads of weight. Endlessly drinking Diet Coke. He was worried about TB's profile. David M called later, and said much the same. Charlie felt I should get more involved with Ed. He liked him and felt with proper support he could win.

Thursday 2 May
Up early and off to Horewood House Hotel for another Lundbeck event, this time their UK team. Did my usual re. the need for governments to take curbing alcohol abuse more seriously. Discussed with Andy Hockey and Steve Turley [Lundbeck staff] the idea of doing events at the party conferences related to the new novel about alcoholism. They definitely seemed up for doing more stuff up front to try to shift the dial on the agenda. Car to Heathrow en route to Faucon. Loads of French school trip kids on the plane. Met by Grace back from Jamaica.

Some Time During May…
For whatever reason, I've not really been bothering to keep a diary for a while. Nor blogging or tweeting so often. Not exercising so often. Depressed? Definitely. Older? Fact. Not doing so much that was interesting? Maybe. Yet in this period, several meetings and chats with TB, Alex's retirement, lots of travel to Albania, Kosovo, Kaz and two breaks in Faucon and the usual mix of speaking, media, charity, consultancy etc. Grace was back from travelling. Calum was now set to be in rehab for up to twelve weeks. It was nice to have Grace back but big scene one night at hotel en route home from France when I went into a major dip. Calum was up and down. One visit from me that went OK but he was agitating to leave and

creating lots of battles to fight. TB – he had received an incredible 'period of silence would be welcome' letter from Neil, saying he has broken the unwritten rule of a trade-off between total access and total support.

TB was right in what he was saying, namely that the party seemed to think the public had moved to the left, it was wishful thinking. If anything, the rise of UKIP, and the relatively small Labour lead – considering how badly the government was doing, and how poorly the economy was recovering – suggested anything but. It was pretty remarkable though that TB was in such a bad place with the party and the party's centre of gravity so clearly in an anti-TB place. TB and I had a couple of meetings on his place and his positioning. He wanted to intervene more but he was not in a good place with the party and media in particular. I said to him that before he just popped up and down saying what he thought, he needed to ask why he was where he was with the party, whereas Clinton was seen as the guy who could rescue Obama at his convention.

Partly it was because TB had vacated the field, but also because so much of the coverage of him today was either negative via the party, or Iraq, or about money. Clinton made loads of money but his profile had stayed political. We agreed with Sally M and others that he should start to do more in the north-east as a way of showing he was still engaged and as a vehicle to show his beliefs and views in a context that was not just intervening in a way that would be seen as anti-Ed. Good TB meeting with Edi in London, and while the cameras were in he totally delivered in saying he would help if he won, which ran big in Albania but the *Telegraph* ran it as another cashing in story, needless to say followed up by the *Mail*. Not easy for him, given so much of what he did was for free. Edi going well. Mark Lucas doing a great job for them. Bertie Ahern came up with a good piece for the Irish book, different to TB's, but it would complement it well.

Alex wrote a wonderful letter to Calum, long, handwritten, urging him to stay with it, talking of some of the setbacks in his own life. Alex's retirement was absolutely massive. It leaked out early and the first confirmation I got was a text he sent to all friends saying he was sorry not to have been able to tell people individually, family, friends, colleagues, but it had leaked. It broke on the same day as the Queen's Speech and yet was leading the news. I did a couple of pieces for *The Times* and the *Mirror*, plus a bit of telly. I had a little chat with him on the day and he was sounding tired. Couple of days later Tim Livesey called and said Ed wanted to sound Alex out about a seat in the Lords. He had been asked to put in five names next week and they thought both for publicity and for the possible contribution he could make, it would be a good name. I said I doubted he would go for it but I would ask. I called, and he said no way, as I expected he would. Nonetheless he then pretended to be saying yes in front of Cathy, who totally fell for it, was saying, 'You are not,' him saying, 'Yes I am,' then falling about laughing.

I went with Rory to his last home match against Swansea, seeing Mum on the way. With friends and family etc. Crowd did him proud. Guard of honour. Sea of red. Families on the pitch. David Moyes was going to be his successor. I saw him at the LMA [League Managers Association] dinner. Said he was shitting himself, but excited and in a way amazed it had happened. He had already felt the scale of the step up, with his daughter for example getting targeted on Twitter. Not sure re. who he was keeping on from the coaching staff. Nice chat with Malky Mackay [Cardiff City manager], Rory having applied for a job there. Another chat with Alex re. his future. He picked up a couple of awards. He said he had got a nice letter from Calum in reply to his. He felt Calum was getting there slowly.

Kaz nation branding was moving on. The work from Marksteen Adamson [creative strategist] at Asha [branding agency] was good. He did a presentation to me on FaceTime and I was blown away. In Kosovo Pacolli had decided against standing. No word when Chilcot was due. Iraq hanging over TB I felt. John Scarlett doing loads of stuff. Strategy company with Alex Carlile. Advising Qataris. Board of Statoil. Board of *The Times*. Said he enjoyed seeing the media from the other side. Recalled a lunch with Dacre who clearly hated me. Ed M not doing great in face of serial crapness from government. Up to see Mum a couple of times. Worried about Graeme. Definitely depressed I would say. I was doing some good events with Time to Change.

Bosnian social democrats wanting me to do for them what I had done for Edi. Gave Edi a great idea for his convention, getting films done in advance of doubters saying why they had doubts, and him answering. Went really well. Also an idea to do a film on Berisha's obsession with roads – he was constantly announcing the same road opening, and clearly felt it was working for him. Edi keen for me to stay involved afterwards if he won, helping to build a comms machine in govt, doing country branding, and also the idea he had discussed with TB of trying to get a Balkan-wide co-operation re. their EU discussions.

Nice event 17 May, interviewed by Steve Richards at the British Library to help launch their propaganda exhibition. Grace and Audrey came and enjoyed it. My favourite exhibits were the Norman Rockwell [American illustrator] 'Buy bonds' posters in the war for Americans, and the chart showing how the UK government measured public morale during the war.

21 May, Cystic Fibrosis charity match v MPs at QPR. Euan Blair in goal. I played OK, but we lost for the first time in ten years. *Telegraph* ran pix of me flooring Gregg McClymont, and looking obese! Got to lose a bit of weight. Then off to Chelsea Flower Show with Rory to meet the Welcome to

May '13: Ed M asks AC to sound out AF re. peerage

Yorkshire team for next year's Tour, and Christian Prudhomme [director, Tour de France] and Bernard Hinault [French former professional cyclist]. I liked them both, and arranged to meet up when next year's Tour was in Vaison.

Thursday 23 May

Off to Albania again. In to meet Edi and the team, in the middle of making a broadcast. Edi was on OK form and laughing and smiling more than usual, while Endri was working well too. I was worried though that too much was going to fall on a small number of people. Mark Lucas already there, going down really well. Edi talked about how humble he was, and how committed. We had a couple of meals together, including with Linda, who did seem to have a good calming effect on Edi. Mark's little biog film had worked well and Edi's mum had become something of a hit. Berisha was out and about the whole time, banging on about how many roads he had built so we did a bit of a funny on how roads was the answer to any difficult question. Edi had really gone for the idea of putting critical voices into his speeches via video and it had worked well.

One of the nice things about working with him was that he took new ideas and just went with them. In fact his entire strategy – road to the manifesto, renaissance, taking in the critics, the foreign trips etc. – had been based on our occasional meetings, and he seemed confident there could only be one result, unless Berisha somehow managed to steal it. The latest poll had Edi and co. between ten and twelve ahead. The rallies were getting bigger and we drove past one at one point. Impressive. Also had the idea of him doing two rallies on the last day, in which half the speech was delivered in the south, half in the north. He was beginning to do more in Berisha stronghold areas and was getting a pretty good reception. I was hoping maybe I would get back for one more trip.

Saturday 25 May

Fifty-six today. Feeling it a bit in the limbs. Flew back from Tirana to Marseille, into a cab, and then back to a disaster. Fiona had gone into Vaison-la-Romaine with the two new Sky bikes still on the roof, forgotten they were there, and both the bikes were written off when she smashed into a barrier on the way in. Nightmare. She handled telling me reasonably well, phoning and saying, 'Are you sitting down, because something terrible has happened.' My immediate thought was Calum, and so when she said it was 'just the bikes' I was relieved. Some bloody birthday present though. Two top-range bikes smashed to smithereens. Jean Cristophe at Ventoux Bikes lent me and Rory a couple of decent bikes. Just Fiona and me for a few days then Rory. Nice chat with Calum on my birthday. He seemed to be engaging with it all more, and for the first time I sensed he was saying he could see a life without booze.

Wednesday 29 May to Friday 31 May

Set off from Avignon by train for Paris CDG, Frankfurt then the overnight flight to Astana. TB was already there. Marksteen and his small team had done a brilliant job, but it was still going to be a tricky meeting. I arrived 5.30 a.m. and decided to go for a long run down the river rather than try to get any more sleep. Then a few meetings before heading to the CCS with Justin Stevens. Dan Timms [Portland] there from London along with Marksteen and his colleague.

Yerzhan Babakumarov the usual warm welcome. Good chat with Kazykhanov before Tazhin arrived. It was clear they all feared Tazhin a little. In fact probably a lot. Endless fussing and fretting re. where to put the coffee and snacks etc. TB arrived. We all sat down, Tazhin welcomed, TB spoke – a bit too long. I did my thing, then Marksteen who did pretty well, though Tazhin was not really following it. He was scribbling at what I assumed to be pre-prepared speaking notes.

The rest of the room seemed OK with things but Tazhin only really came alive when Marksteen played a two-/three-minute video. I had seen it several times now and it did get better and better with each viewing. Tazhin immediately said he would like to use it for Astana Day which totally missed the point about it being the culmination of a branding strategy. When Marksteen was done, Tazhin basically whacked the research paper we had done. He left me an open door though in saying, 'No umbrella brand ever worked,' because I was able to say 1, yes they do and 2, that was what they asked for. By the time we took him into a side room to show all the materials on the walls, as opposed to on the screen, he was in a much better mood, but then we had an incident with the Swedish guy who they had wanted us to work with, and who had been filming when we were presenting. First he denied it, then said he was entitled to as he was involved in the project, then asked me if I was police or military to 'dare to talk to me like that'. Yerzhan said he had been there as his adviser and he was entitled to have a second opinion there, but he accepted we should have been told and also that he should not have filmed.

After TB left I asked if we could fix one-on-one meetings with the key members of the Inter Agency Commission into nation branding so that we could take them through it, and not have the presentation done second-hand by people who were not that keen on it. So Marksteen and I did the culture minister and the environment minister, and both liked it, and then I did the tourism minister with Justin. Again he liked it, and said the sooner they could get going on it the better. It was not going to be easy though to hold the politics of this together.

Then we had a problem in that Tazhin was asking for the video so that he could show it to the President and we were holding back, making the point that it was not copyright cleared, and was simply the kind of thing they could do visually if they went for this concept. Eventually I saw him and – I think – smoothed things over, by making clear it was about copyright issues and not that they did not own it.

I think we just about turned it round, but it was hairy at times. I was also in a position of becoming too central to the whole thing. Andreas and Kazykhanov in their different ways made it clear I would have to be there for all the main moments of the presentations. The weather was at least nice and I had a couple of good runs. I set off for the airport, Astana – Almaty, Almaty – Bangkok, Bangkok to Singapore. Loved Thai Airlines.

Saturday 1 June
Arrived Singapore, staying at the Fairmont, overlooking two giant round swimming pools and in the middle distance a town centre cricket pitch near the church I remembered TB used when here many moons ago. Such an interesting place. In the days of Lee Kuan Yew [former Prime Minister], the issue was one of survival. They were building from scratch. The challenges now were less dramatic but the expectations were high. The sense of their identity being eroded by foreigners was real and even though people knew success was in part because of them, it remained a problem. Housing issues in particular. Gap between rich and poor. Wage erosion. Even a broken-down train was a problem. My sense was they were becoming a more normal democracy, in which the public were not cutting the ministers – among the best paid in the world – much slack. The PM [Lee Hsien Loong, son of Lee Kuan Yew] was in many ways as popular as his father, but with fewer heavyweights around him.

Sunday 2 June
Breakfast at the Shangri-La Hotel, where there was massive security for the defence conference going on, with the US Defence Secretary in town. Interesting chat with a group of Singaporean politicians, one of whom said, 'No other state has had to put up with a quarter of its population becoming foreign in such a short time.' The conspicuous consumption of some of the foreigners was really creating tensions.

The power of the Lee Kuan Yew legend still strong and had a big hold on debate. He had been an instinctive communicator, whereas a lot of the current class of politicians were maybe more technocratic. Interesting, in the museum for example, to get the sense of the scale of transformation. Quite a success story. It meant though that the public had incredibly high expectations. 'Perfection is the enemy of the good.' I couldn't believe how big a story it was that a train – yes, a train, as in one train – had broken down!

Got an interesting take too on their view of India and China. The threat less cheap labour than middle managers. Paternalism had worked for Singapore, few ever questioned LKY authority because he and the system delivered. But now, as one of them put it, bored rich people in their fifties tweeted a lot and thought that was opposition. The people had had their hands held so tightly they could not let go but that is what needed to happen. The government saw globalisation as an opportunity not a threat but many of the people saw it as a threat.

Monday 3 June

Fascinating series of meetings with policy experts. Health area was trickiest as they were wrestling with the same issues we were – older population, more people with chronic disease, more and better drugs, social care. 'No such thing as a free lunch', but a free lunch is pretty much what their people expected. How to move from individual responsibility to shared responsibility? In housing, there was the paradox of an open market liberal economy and the government as the main provider. Foreigners were distorting the market and the next generation was feeling squeezed. Education took 15–20 per cent of their budget yet people spent lots on extra tuition. Only defence took more of the budget (still had national service). Interesting how often, whenever I was discussing public service delivery abroad, the name of Michael Barber [educationalist, former adviser to TB] would come up. There was also a tension I sensed between saying there must be change and yet not wanting to admit failure.

Tuesday 4 June

Breakfast then set off for the airport. It had been interesting to see the paradox: Singapore by any definition a hugely successful and respected country, people well fed, clothed, housed, educated, cared for, employed, and with plenty of opportunities in work and leisure; and by any normal political standards, the government with satisfaction ratings, generally and in specific policy areas, that most governments would give their right arm for. Yet real worries too. I was surprised by how little issues like the Eurozone crisis, US gridlock and stagnation, even the rise of China, were viewed as relevant.

In a way Singapore's success story has been so remarkable, and so much driven by government, that two linked things have happened. The first is that the public have grown to take for granted success, delivery, and rapid improvement in their lives and living standards, and so are excessively – unreasonably even – spooked and unhappy when they think things go wrong. There is also the paradox that they complain a lot, but when change is made to address the complaint, they complain about the change. The second is that the politicians are not really used to being criticised and attacked and ministers are not sure how to handle them.

Wednesday 5 June

Long chat with TB about his own role and profile. He was keen to re-engage more systematically in the national debate, felt he had something to say, cares deeply about the country, can see that at present it is taking a poor direction for its future. He also felt there were reasons beyond ego for re-defending his government and the record, and challenge the wholly prejudicial view of what we did and why, which he saw as being driven by the fact that the UK media largely still divides into an old-fashioned left/right pattern. 'The one thing they have in common, is that they both hate New Labour.' I said the problem up to now was that his interventions have seemed both random and those of a passer-by. We went through his note on how to get re-engagement that feels both genuine and sustained.

Sally had suggested re-connection with doing more in the north-east, such as building the Sports Foundation into something significant. Support local business, do national events and speeches from the region. Sally and I were also pressing him to do more Labour Party work, especially fundraising and putting money into local campaigns. Meet more MPs, moderate union leaders. He said he needed to work out a political critique of the Tories that can help the Labour Party – a kind of stump speech but also a proper intellectual case against them. But also do the big speeches on issues that concern the country. He said the obvious subject was Europe, but he was worried making that the main or first point of entry.

So he wanted to start with a big economic speech, laying out the reasons why Third Way progressive politics remains the way forward.* Wanted to go big on how technology could revolutionise government's workings. He was clearly frustrated that his Foundations were not making news other than as being about him. He said he felt he needed to be out there explaining why only now he had decided to speak up, namely that for the last six years, he has been building an organisation and needed time out from UK politics, just as UK politics needed a break from him. But as the

---

* Centrist amalgamation of right- and left-wing politics.

centre ground had been vacated, he now wanted to speak. He wanted a plan written up and activated in the autumn.

Thursday 6 June

I felt bad that for various diary reasons I had pulled out of the London-to-Paris ride for LLR, so went down to Greenwich to help see them off, and do the first hour or two. Nice day and good atmosphere, though as ever with these things very white and middle-class. Ian Wright and Mitchell Thomas [former footballers] the only black guys I saw. Did a couple of interviews and a little spiel at the start then off we went. Mainly talking to John Salako [former footballer] who was fine but then revealed he was a major Tory, had even thought about getting a seat. Nice route through Kent but eventually I had to peel off and head home.

Friday 7 June

Off early to Sky for the first of a stack of mainly radio interviews about Abraham Lincoln. Very tartish, as I had to keep mentioning the 'survey' on the greatest orators and speeches of all time, and say it was done to coincide with the 'launch of the Blu-ray/DVD of the film *Lincoln*.' I had watched *Lincoln* the film again last night and to be fair the Blu-ray did have extra material including good interviews with cast and crew that I could refer to. But for all that, it was pretty tarty.

Saturday 8 June

Out for drinks and dinner with Mark and Fiona Ferguson. Enjoyed it. Mark clearly now totally rolling in it and his investment firm seemed to be going from strength to strength. He admitted he voted Tory last time, mainly because he believed Zac Goldsmith was committed to the environment. But he thought we would win next time, purely because the government was so crap. Nice evening and she is a really good laugh.

Sunday 9 June

Off early to Matlock to do a couple of the hills in my cycling book. Really beautiful round there and they were both tough. Then cock-up time. Locked myself out of the car while putting the bike on the roof. Saved by a brilliantly patient RAC guy who wedged open one of the doors and eventually managed to switch on the ignition and then ping down the window. Tweeted RAC how brilliant he was.

Tuesday 11 June

Breakfast with Richard Glynn, CEO of Ladbrokes, who was nice enough but a bit too rugby fan for my taste, northern lad made good and everything was common sense. Then a session with Richard Hytner – interview for his book re. the case for being No. 2s. Liked him and an interesting theme.

Wednesday 12 June

Train to Brighton for a speech on crisis management to AIRMIC. Was on form and good Q&A, though I was a bit troubled by a question about TB. Someone said he had had power, success, fame, wealth, 'but every time I see him he just doesn't seem happy'. It struck a chord and though I could answer at an intellectual level, and waffled on about him being essentially private, and finding it difficult in the UK, and how he vacated the field for GB blah, I felt it struck a chord with the audience too. I dropped Catherine R an email and said I felt if he thought about his happiness and well-being first and foremost, he would re-order his priorities.

Thursday 13 June

In to JLA [business speakers agency] to do a filmed interview for KPMG on tax and publicity/politics. Then to Portland before a nice lunch with Paul Henderson, who was still toiling away as associate editor at the *Mirror*. He said Ed M had been in to talk to the staff and people were deeply underwhelmed. Then to Grosvenor Square to see Catherine. TB just never stood still. Had done a day trip to the US to see Kerry. Then wanted to go to Paris for a day and then wanted them to fix Abu Dhabi for the weekend. Partly because of the *persona non grata* feeling politically, he was running and never standing still. I said if he sat down and asked what made him happy, or feel good about what he did, he would probably end up with MEPP, Africa, and the rest was stuff he felt he had to do to make the money to run the place. So let the business take care of itself and focus on what mattered. But at least redraw the map. Really analyse what mattered and what didn't. I said he went through this kind of phase when leader too. People forget he once tried to get rid of JoP, also lost it with David M, and probably with me. He had also played the 'You're indispensable' card and I said Anji H and I used to get that, but we both went. I felt the best thing to do was to sit him down before the summer and ask him to rethink for himself what his priorities were. He always came back from the summer in better form.

Meanwhile Murdoch had announced his divorce from Wendi Deng yesterday and almost as soon as I got home, the *New York Times* called and said the rumour was he had said it was because of an affair with TB, and what had I heard? I could truthfully say I had never heard anything to that effect. Eventually TB called and I said is there any truth in it, and he said absolutely not. I said then sleep on it and decide in the morning whether you need to say something. That would depend on the extent to which it started to spread virally.

Friday 14 June

The TB/Wendi Deng rumours were still flying around though none of the papers here had run anything. *The Hollywood Reporter* ran a story with a denial but then it was being said the denial only referred to the present tense so that sparked more stuff on Twitter. Catherine and Rachel called, and then TB and I said I felt they had to say something on the lines of 'untrue and actionable' which would give them the chance to run the story as a denial but at the same time signal intentions re. legal action without being specific. That is what they did and it seemed to work. The problem was the word was that it was coming from Murdoch's people though when Catherine spoke to his lawyer they denied that. In the end it just about worked. One or two biggish pieces but nothing massive.

Syria meanwhile rising up the agenda again pre G8. Cameron looked like he really wanted to do something but the world was probably two years too late. Short speech at the Guildhall at a Legal and General [financial services company] event for Rethink so sat with Paul Jenkins, charity CEO. Comedian Stephen Amos doing the awards and he was very near the mark. Out for dinner with Rory and Calum. Rory been very helpful and supportive on all the stuff we had been going through with Calum.

Monday 17 June

I went to an Al-Anon meeting up in Hampstead. Not my scene. Too much about the families being the victims. Maybe some truth in that, but I couldn't see myself going regularly. Tom Baldwin asked me to meet up, and I met him in a café near the Beeb. He was totally fed up, and thinking of leaving. The team was not a real team, Ed was indecisive, there was no grip, the politics was in the wrong place.

Tuesday 18 June

Interview for an Irish TV documentary on Sinn Féin. Aussie diplomats round ahead of my trip, saying Julia Gillard [Prime Minister, Labour Party leader] could be out next week.

Thursday 20 June

Another round of Gould Global, the thing at Freuds, where groups bid to do trips and projects in PG's memory. Georgia was tied up with her book, but Grace came and we had quite a good laugh with Matthew. The usual holiday bids – e.g. Google and one to New York fashion week. The only two that interested me were a group of four guys who wanted to do something with technology in parts of Africa, and my favourite was a guy and a woman who had an idea about fair trade supply chains and also rebranding Ghana. That was probably my favourite though actually we were both, MF and I, a bit underwhelmed. Off to the airport for another Kaz visit. The sleeping pill didn't work as well as usual so I didn't get much sleep overnight. Amazingly, Behgjet Pacolli was on the flight. A bit embarrassing given the work with him had not exactly led to a great political triumph. But we had a nice chat mainly about Kaz. He was very well plugged in.

Friday 21 June

Met at the airport, off to the Diplomat Hotel, pre-meeting with Dan Timms and Justin Stevens, meeting with the interpreter, and then I took the planned presentation to the Akorda. Chat with guys from the team preparing for the Cameron visit. There was going to be an energy and business focus but clearly they were a bit worried about what our press would get up to, and wanted guidance on how to deal with them. Tazhin was in a better place, and that became clear when we went to the Inter Agency Commission later. The most important thing was that Tazhin said that it was going to happen.

Saturday 22 June

Good meeting with Kazykhanov, who felt it had gone well. He said Tazhin seemed pretty happy and soon would do a presentation to the President whose support would be needed to give the next steps a green light. They were clearly worried re. the UK press on Cameron's visit, so we chatted about that. I said do not be defensive. Decide the three positive points you want to make, and make them. Run, change, out to the airport, and off to Almaty.

Long chat with Calum, who sounded OK. Somehow managed to kill the time then off to Kuala Lumpur on Air Astana. Aussie woman next to me said the town where Cameron was going was getting a total makeover. In KL I had a shower, read lots about the smog from Indonesia falling on Singapore, killed more time, then off on Malaysia Airlines to Sydney.

Worked on the various speeches and events, slept a bit and arrived bang on time mid-evening, met and off to the Shangri-La Hotel. Love Sydney. It was a bit cold but still buzzy and welcoming. Up on the 36th floor with a fantastic view on to the bridge and the Opera House.

It was clear the Gillard–Kevin Rudd [former PM and Labour Party leader] division was, and had been for ages, the only show in town. When I had seen the guys from the Aussie High Commission last week I had thought they were exaggerating when they said there might be a change of PM while I was there but it was looking entirely possible. What was bizarre was that the economic numbers were good, but the polls were terrible and people were talking about a total meltdown. There did not seem to be much difference in policy between Gillard [Rudd's deputy] and Rudd, but she had knifed him (by challenging his leadership) in 2012 and he was clearly hell-bent on getting her back. He was saying he was not going to challenge her, but he was clearly building up the numbers.

Monday 24 June

Sent Edi a good-luck message on the Sunday. He sent one back saying it was the best campaign they could have done, and thank you. Off to the (amazingly efficient) airport, bought PG book in the shop (two rows below mine so tweeted a picture) then off to Canberra. Could be quite a day. The plane was a bit late, horrible weather, straight from the airport to the Parliament to meet John McTernan [former TB's director of political operations], who was working for Gillard. I had never been that close to him, but he was friendly, showed me round the place a bit, met some of the key people, then sat down and talked it over with him. He said Rudd was a total egomaniac, only cared about himself, had been useless, had to go, and ever since had done nothing but undermine Julia with a destabilisation campaign.

He was suspected of doing it during the election which is probably why they ended up with a hung parliament and the need to do a deal with the Greens, who were not that popular. They did a deal to make him foreign minister but then he was accused of leaking from Cabinet. So she sacked him. Then a vote, and she beat him, then the threat of another one, and he bottled it, and now it is building up again. He did say that he felt their objective had to be to avoid a ballot, while saying that if Rudd had the numbers he would do it. But I sensed they worried he did have the numbers. He said he had been working in various Oz campaigns for a while and Alan Milburn among others had suggested he go for this job. He had been getting a pretty bad press for it, but he did point out he could walk down any street without anyone knowing who he was.

I was due to do interviews and asked if it was helpful to say that it was time for Rudd to piss or get off the pot. He thought it was. What I found remarkable was the disjunction between the economic numbers and the political mood. Also Tony Abbott, the opposition leader, was getting away with murder because he was used as an attack dog to make hay re. the divisions, but did not seem to have any policies beyond 'stop the boats, cut the carbon and mining tax, and grown-up government'. He was also a much more negative, talking-down Australia force than they were used to. John said re. Rudd, 'All you need to know is that GB was his favourite other PM and the feeling is mutual.' He said it was a psychodrama, not about politics or policy.

Did a couple of interviews with *The Australian* and *The Age*, Joanna Bennett from Random House having sent them my diaries, and of course lots of the questions were on Oz not UK, though the *Age* guy, Michael Smith, had read the books and was pretty insightful. The *Australian* guy, Christian Kerr, said, 'My editor must have a sense of humour … I am a depressive recovering alcoholic ex-press secretary.' And he was. But he asked good questions and we had a good chat. Gillard was doing PMQs, which she had to do every bloody day when Parliament was sitting, with Rudd sitting there looking miserable. John had said that her calm and her niceness were her best qualities and they did come through. But just as the economy did not translate to polls at the moment, these qualities didn't seem to get through to the public.

Her chief of staff, Ben Hubbard, who I had met when I had been here last time with Helen Liddell [former British High Commissioner to Australia], said she wanted to see me after PMQs, so John and I went round to meet her in her office the minute she came out of the chamber. She was calm, poised, charming, but, I sensed, totally at a loss to know what to do with Rudd. I asked why she didn't call him in and say look, you know this is killing us, now either bring it to a head or stop. She said he would immediately go out and give a totally different account to the media. He was a narcissist. He saw everything through the Kevin lens. She said that if people knew the truth about what he had been like, they would not be asking for him to come back as PM, they would be wondering how on earth he ever got there in the first place.

She said he had been incapable of leading a team, incapable of making decisions, and everyone knew it. I said if she could get out from the noise, they had a good record, better policies for the future and they could start going for Abbott. But they had to resolve the soap opera. I said if they did she would need game-changers. Told her of some of the stuff we did with Edi and she was interested. The debates would be important, but she needed to make sure they were as much about Abbott's policies as hers.

I liked her, felt she had a warmth and a charm that I had never sensed in him, and every time I spoke to Fiona she just reminded me how awful she thought Rudd was when we met him at Chevening [Foreign Secretary's official residence]. David M and I were exchanging texts. He felt Rudd should not have been ousted. I said I felt it was all about Kevin and ego. He said he had learned.

She asked me to think a bit of what other game-changers there might be, and how she could emerge stronger, but I really had a strong sense of her vulnerability. Brief meeting with the High Commissioner, Paul Madden, who was picking my brains about what she said. I passed on that they had said they did not want a vote, which meant they did not have the numbers. He said Hague was very pro-Oz, whereas we had never had a Foreign Secretary out there. Jack went once but had to turn around because his dad died. He said it was not possible to call what would happen, but he was pretty sure Abbott would win whatever happened and also, that Abbott was not as bad as people thought. He had stopped saying stupid things and he had started to be a bit more measured. Julia had said though he really did have a problem with women.

Flew back to Sydney, then out to do Emma Alberici at *Lateline* [current affairs show]. Half Oz, half UK, and the 'piss or get off the pot' line about Rudd had a good reaction on Twitter. Getting updates from Endri, and it was looking good, though Berisha was signalling he felt he had won. Edi said it could be a landslide. He had definitely won.

Tuesday 25 June

Up really early, still dark, and went for a fantastic run around the Botanical Gardens and then the Harbour. Chat to Fiona and Calum, who was in the home straight at Castle Craig and seemed fine with it, then breakfast with Douglas Alexander. We were up in the Horizon Club with fabulous views. Talked a bit re. the Oz scene and then inevitably re. us in the UK. Balls a problem. Ed's office not functional, nothing ever written down, Stewart Wood always the last one in the room telling Ed he was marvellous, no agreed strategy. He said what was unforgivable was that they distanced from New Labour not just on policy but on running a competent ship. He asked if I thought Tom B would go. I didn't let on I had discussed it but said I felt he thought he was not making a difference. I said I had unplugged a fair bit because I did not think they had the right approach and I could not see why I should work my balls off for people who essentially undermined our record.

He said he felt Ed had dipped since David M left. He felt that he was not sure of his bearings. He won by distancing himself from TB, and because he beat David he had to pretend that there was some kind of big political difference between them. What was actually just a sibling thing had taken on political connotations, but deep down Ed had never really been New Labour and he genuinely believed the country had moved in its politics since the crash. And yet, I said in some ways they have moved right, e.g. on immigration, or welfare, or Europe. He felt Ed had many qualities but he was not crossing the basic threshold for leadership. I told him some of the stuff from Albania and he said I should tell Ed, but I doubted he would ever do, e.g. getting critical voices into the mix. He had to give a political justification for why he won.

Re. TB, I asked why they all thought he was such a negative, when I went round the place and was able to win people round. He said people knew I was Labour in my DNA. Maybe they were not so sure re. TB. He said he had watched the three Norma Percy films on Iraq and the first showed we did well in the build-up. But then we were irrelevant and I feel people just think Tony let us all down by surrendering our interests to the Americans, he said. He felt Fiona and I would have been great assets as MPs but he felt we were right not to do it, for our sake. I said Ed had to be confronted with the reality because if things went on like this, I could see Cameron back in. Nice chat, and he was bright and sharp as ever. He was seeing Paul Keating, who told him that the two greatest qualities in politics were courage and imagination. PK had been the first to say Oz was part of Asia, got criticised for it, but had been proven right.

I did a photo session for *The Age*, then off to Guardian Australia [online edition], which Kath Viner was heading, and was already getting 1.5 million users. Q&A with the staff then a quick interview. Trailed the speech a bit, gave them a few lines re. Oz. Melbourne radio down the line, mainly on the books, nice interview. Then saw Andrew Sholl [ex-UK Labour official] who was working for National Broadband rollout. Nice to see him. Married to author Nikki Gemmell who preceded Erica James with erotic novels. Like most people I had met, not at all impressed with Rudd.

Edi called in the middle of the night saying Berisha had still not conceded, and should he go out. Yes. Nearly all the votes were counted. It was a clear win. He was going to be PM. I had written him a speech for the acceptance, very humble and measured, even generous to Berisha, and he said it was 'very beautiful. It will be like so much of this campaign, not what people expect.' Endri called me afterwards and said it was incredible. The crowds were wild. Even Democratic Party supporters were telling Edi they liked the speech and the way he set himself out as the leader for everyone, not just those who voted for him. It sounded a bit like '97, in that the win was even bigger than they had dared imagine, and Edi was handling it well. Another night interrupted loads. Getting bids to write tributes to Mandela. He was on life support and possibly dead already.

Wednesday 26 June

Another nice run, then out for books and arts radio interview which was good, in-depth and ranging far and wide. Said goodbye to Joanna from Random House, who had been really efficient and was arranging more for Melbourne, then to do a speech for the firm that had sponsored the trip. They were warm, I was on form, really good crowd. Off to the airport. Gillard had announced she was calling a leadership vote in the caucus and that whoever lost should leave politics. I assumed that meant she felt she had the numbers but the buzz was not so. What was remarkable was that in the lounge, with PMQs on live, and a 'breaking news' banner saying there was going to be a vote, hardly anyone was paying any attention at all. Talk about shouting in an empty stadium. I watched it a bit, before writing some mental health stuff then getting the plane to Melbourne.

Arrived, quick change and out for dinner with BHP Billiton. Geoff Walsh, ex-Labour senior official, was there and he was keeping in touch with what was happening in the vote. Rudd clear win. Bill Shorten had jumped. Julia was out. McTernan sent me a message saying simply, 'We're gone.' Pretty brutal stuff and most people at the dinner did not think Rudd would be able to turn it around. There was a sense though that the public liked him. But so much on record of his colleagues hating him. I talked about some of the themes in my speech tomorrow, and the social media/strategy thing and how they needed to get into the engagement business more, and also that only companies with values did well.

At AMP I had asked people whether Murdoch had a good or bad reputation and everyone said bad. I reckoned that was because people felt it was only about power and wealth and there was no social good. He would die an unhappy man. News at home was all spending review but I felt totally cut off from it and in any event this was more interesting. Everyone kept saying I could not have picked a more dramatic week and it was true – almost three years to the day they went for her as PM to replace him.

Thursday 27 June

Most of the papers focusing on 'revenge' but there was a poll showing a quick bounce. Polls were definitely too much a part of the landscape here. Out to Melbourne Business School for the Centre for Corporate Public Affairs speech with 'students', those on a week-long course from their jobs, pretty bright bunch. Q&A a fair bit re. social media, [Princess] Diana, my image, Malcolm Tucker – who came up in a lot of interviews. Really good crowd, big rush to the book signing at the end. Then had a few hours to play with so went for a run, had lunch, chat to TB re. Albania – he felt it would be good as a place where he could show there was a sensible Muslim country, also that they could help with capacity for the building of a new government machine. Edi said next week he would like me to go out alone and work things through.

Did the R4 *Today* programme from ABC, used the line re. Julia and Kevin making TB–GB look like Mills & Boon [romance publishers]. Pushed back a bit on the idea it was all about macho politics, and a macho culture, also starting to develop a line that at least now they could do the three things you need for a campaign – own the record, promote agenda for the future, and attack the other side. Abbott had got away with murder by not being subject to the kind of scrutiny a would-be Prime Minister should be. To the Hyatt to meet up with Paul O'Connell [Irish rugby player]. He had played a blinder in the first test but had a broken arm and was out for the rest of the [British & Irish Lions] tour. Top bloke. He came to my speech at the dinner of the Centre for Corporate Public Affairs.

Some pretty big corporates there, also a guy called Terry who had worked for both Rudd and Gillard. Clearly had doubts about them both. Good crowd and the speech, which got a bit of pick-up after being posted on the Huffington Post, went down really well. Felt there was a pretty strong argument, and good colour. Book signing, brief drink with some of the students from earlier, and bed. Spoke to Rory who was out in Vegas, telling me again that poker was skill, not gambling. 'I'm winning, Dad. Relax.' Mandela was on life support. His death is going to be such a big moment for so many people. Fixing trip to Albania.

Friday 28 June
Finally managed to sleep through, then out to meet Mark Souster [sports journalist] for breakfast. Joined by Lawrence Dallaglio [former England Rugby Union captain] and a guy from Land Rover, who were sponsoring Lawrence's trip. Chatting re. the media and how it was changing. Long interview at the hotel with TVNZ re. the Oz scene, *Australian Financial Review*, more of the same. Sue Baker had put me in touch with BeyondBlue, which was a mental health campaign doing some great work, and I went out for a meeting. They had a fair bit of funding from government and in addition to awareness stuff were about to spend £15 million on providing improved access to talking therapies based on what we did. They were also very good at using humour, e.g. with a character for ads called Dr

Brian Ironwood who was a fake doctor telling people to man up but then putting the other side as part of an online site called mantherapy.org.au.

Five times more women than men went for help for a mental health problem. They had some good ambassadors but not enough. The chief exec had read *The Happy Depressive* and rightly said I was too kind to Cameron. I was. Good feel to the place, out in Hawthorn, felt calm and well run and with really motivated people. They had done a good anxiety film. Like everyone, chewing over the Rudd situation, feeling he could make a difference but might not win. I felt Abbott was vulnerable.

Running late for an interview with Scott Carson on Sky News Business channel where they went over not just Oz, but stuff from my diaries and other books, including one minute reading out TB saying I was a genius, the next I was a mad axeman. I felt I was on form on the Oz scene and setting out the shape of a strategy they could actually go for. It was not clear if Rudd could change his ways though. Photo session for AFR then that was me done work-wise.

Went for a long run round all the stadia, tried to get Lleyton Hewitt [tennis player] stuff for Calum at the tennis centre, took pictures of the statues at the MCG [Melbourne Cricket Ground], bit of shopping, a bite to eat and then off to the airport. Been away a bit long, but Kaz had gone OK, and as ever I just loved being in Australia. Not just that the timing was so interesting, but they are lively, not chippy, non-classist in the main, know lots re. the UK, and love a good intelligent conversation. I felt they were becoming a bit less confident, considering they had done pretty well in the GFC, and it might be to do with further negativisation of media – still not as bad as ours – and Abbott talking everything down. Rudd could maybe change both. The first flight was fourteen hours with a lovely Indian stewardess looking after me. Took a pill, slept for almost ten hours.

Wednesday 3 July

Edi was keen for me to get out to Albania as soon as possible after the win, and to start to advise on systems and personnel. Got the morning flight from Gatwick, met by Endri and straight into a meeting with Edi at HQ. Hot and sunny, and there did seem to be a pretty good atmosphere around the place. Edi OK, his voice a bit weak, at times maybe a bit daunted by the scale of the challenge, but he was up for it. Meta to be Speaker of the Parliament. Edi had still not decided key appointments. Focused on main priorities, EU (possibly with a vice premier for integration to signal the importance of the issue), another Deputy PM for key projects. Deloitte were up for doing an audit of the economy at cost. Crown Agents were in there advising on a new customs system. The campaign pledges had been pretty big but the hard work really did begin now.

Chatted on how to use TB. Edi did want a Kaz-style major project. What he wanted was TB support for greater EU support for the Balkans as a whole, and maybe advice on systems. I had spoken to JoP and he had agreed to go out for a couple of days and advise on the setting up of the PM's office. What we all agreed on was the importance of scheduling, priorities and comms. Of those three, only the third was really in place and of course once into government – early September – the need for greater stuff on that would become apparent.

Berisha had still not had any communication with Edi, and when finally he had thrown in the towel, he had presented it almost as a resignation rather than a defeat. He had become obsessed with the attack that he was old and tired. He had said he was retiring but then a day later said he would lead the attack in Parliament. Edi was more relaxed than of late, but it was clearly dawning on him how hard it was going to be. All of the big projects were going to require a huge amount of focus and discipline, and with a lot of inbuilt resistance. For example the deputy head of police had said on Facebook that the police could not allow their leader – Berisha – to be defeated like this. Most top civil servants, most ambassadors, were totally political. Edi seemed up for the job of chopping a lot of people but it meant he was going to be starting by creating a lot of enemies.

Thursday 4 July

Out for a run through the park. I tripped on a piece of wood, fell and rolled on the ground a bit, cut my knee and thigh and later discovered I had broken a rib. It only really hurt when I sneezed, coughed or laughed, but hurt it did. Endri suggested we go to the American hospital, which was a private hospital set up by a guy who was Albanian but had worked in the UK and elsewhere. Turkish doctor, efficient X-ray guy, said it was definitely a break, but all he could do was strap it. I was impressed by the service.

Back to the office to discuss the idea of an appeal for Team Albania – asking people who had never thought of public service to do just that. The idea was to launch a new website with it next week. Some of the party guys were worried, felt that they had to give jobs to people who had helped in the campaign, said the idea that Edi did not look after his own was out there, but he was pretty robust, said they had to trawl for the brightest and the best at home and abroad, not just jobs for the boys. Lunch with Edi and Endri where we talked in more detail on systems and personnel.

UK ambassador [Nicholas Cannon] was at the same restaurant having lunch with other EU ambassadors. I popped in to see him. He said, 'Great campaign, now it gets hard,' and he said Berisha would operate a scorched-earth policy. He felt the economy was probably worse than we thought.

My Melbourne speech had had a fair bit of play online and now the *Mail / Telegraph* including Max Hastings were trying to get a thing going that I had insulted Churchill. I had made the point that TB was routinely called a liar, yet both Churchill and de Gaulle had admitted lying in war-time, whereas TB had not lied at all, whatever people said. Left for the airport, late flight home.

Friday 5 July

Meeting with TB on Albania. Also discussed his own work and image. Catherine had passed on to him what I had said about my sense that he was not happy. He said he was reasonably happy, and he would be more so if he could focus more on those things he really wanted to. But he was not up for much of the kind of analysis she and I had done. I sensed he was just going through a bit of a rough patch and needed a holiday. On Albania I sensed he was pretty much on the idea of the same model as Kaz, and I was not sure that would work. The Wendi Deng thing was still around. He took me aside at the end and said it was total crap but Murdoch clearly did not think so, and he had a real problem there. But he said he also felt better in some ways having nothing to do with them.

Met up with Fiona and off to Clive Tyldesley's wedding at Stoke Poges. Nice hot day. Nice do.

Saturday 6 July

Lions won the final test, easily. Grace had been working for Rob Hallett [music promoter] on the Hyde Park concert so we went to see the Rolling Stones. Bumped into Boris Johnson in hospitality, recalled our Miley Cyrus experience, and then on to politics. He said Ed M was dying on his feet. Felt we should be hammering the government but no blows were landing. It was true. Fiona mentioned she thought I should go for mayor, and he said I would love it. Great job. I said yes but you had owned it in a way I wouldn't as a non-Londoner. 'I was born in New York,' he said. Grace commenting on how scruffy he was. Concert was OK, Mick Jagger amazingly fit, but also a bit machine-like and the crowd was not what I expected, very white, middle-class, probably down to the pricing.

Sunday 7 July

Andy Murray won Wimbledon. Novak Djokovic not really at his best. Cue OTT political reaction. Cameron front row royal box, Salmond behind him getting out a Saltire despite the rules on flags, and Murray all set tomorrow for a No. 10 visit and all the leaders being there and Cameron talking about a knighthood.

Monday 8 July

Saw David S. Not feeling great and I worried there would be a plunge on holiday. He felt Diazepam. I felt not. I had a speaking engagement at the Dorchester, small group of retailers. Lively bunch. Was sitting with the boss of Waitrose. Not much respect for the government but Ed not improving either.

Tuesday 9 July

Dentist to get crown fitted. Later to Cardiff with Rayan. Met up with Andy McCann [sports psychologist] at the hotel, walked down to a café on the waterfront. He was on great form. Sam Warburton [Lions captain] a bit down at missing the final Test, but felt he had answered all the critics. Clive [Woodward, former Lions coach] had apparently said that Sam's second Test performance was the best he had ever seen. Talked over our various projects, then up to the hotel, did a photocall for Wales Time to Change, then the dinner Leighton Andrews had asked me to do. Good turnout from business, and the format of half Labour, half mental health, worked pretty well. Very good reaction. Several of the ministers there, plus Chris Bryant who said that the evidence in the phone-hacking trials would reveal the Rebekah Brooks Andy Coulson affair.

Did the speech, plus Q&A, and a good response when answering the guy who asked if it was too late to hit back on the 'mess we inherited' line. No, but the longer they waited, and stuck with the wrong strategic decision, the harder it would be. Ed did his big unions speech today which seemed to go OK. The Tories have been attacking him for weeks now over links to the unions, Unite in particular, and he was now talking about changing the relationship with unions in a way TB probably wanted to but didn't do. They got TB to back it, saying Ed was showing real leadership. It was certainly ballsy, but I felt he had to be careful not to look like he was dancing to the tune of others. We had conceded the Tory attack on the economy. We were getting hit hard on the NHS, and now there was a danger that the idea of being a member of a trades union was a problem. He would never be able to satisfy those on the right who hated unions full stop and I sent him and Tom a message that he should not end up looking like he was trying to meet them halfway. Home early hours.

Wednesday 10 July

To Notting Hill for an interview with Alan Yentob for his film on Machiavelli. To Rethink for a presentation by a music company who had done an anti-gun campaign and wanted to do something similar on mental illness. Sue Baker arrived late and stressed out because she had just had a meeting with donors and was getting a hard time from the Department of Health in particular because discrimination was going up not down. Clearly to do with welfare reform, and some of the other Time to Change indicators were good but she was clearly worried.

Went home via a restaurant near Leicester Square where the Albanian Socialist Party was holding a celebration. Edi called just before to discuss planned TB meeting. JoP had been in Albania for the last two days. He liked them, and did a good note on what they needed and how to get it. We were going to have to look for good people, mix of public and private. I did a little speech and book signing and there is no doubt they felt we had made a big difference to the campaign.

Thursday 11 July

Met up with Grace and went to the National Portrait Gallery to see the BP portraits, including mine which was OK but not one of the best. They placed it alongside the winner, so plenty of traffic. Off to Oxford for dinner at Magdalen with Richard Layard, [Baroness] Molly Meacher [Lady Layard, former social worker] and some of the experts and academics who had been at their conference for the day. I did a talk on the politics of mental health, after which Layard and Molly asked if I would start up and front a new mental health lobbying organisation. Quite an interesting bunch and they liked my argument that we needed to take a much more strategic approach.

Friday 12 July

Flew out from Luton to Nimes with the boys. Good to be with them both. Rory had been supportive to both of us, in different ways, and Calum now having left rehab in Scotland, he seemed in a better place than he did when he first came out of Toranfield in Ireland. It had been a long haul, but he was not drinking, whereas after Toranfield he had gone straight back on it. Tweet re. Ryanair being like childbirth – if you remembered you would never do it again – picked up as tweet of day in the *Standard*. They definitely seemed to get a kick out of the cattle truck feel, and the sell-sell-sell atmosphere was oppressive. It was true, though, that they had extended air travel to millions. Calum was on OK form as we went out and I was OK until we got in the hire car and for whatever reason I felt a bit of a plunge coming on. I think I had worried myself into these holiday plunges becoming almost automatic because they had happened before when I tried and failed to unwind. I was worried there would be too many people around which made me a bit edgy at the start of a holiday. By the time we got to the house, I felt a plunge coming on. I felt bad about it, but I knew it was one of those I wouldn't be able to stop.

Saturday 13 July

Worked on dedication and acknowledgments for the new novel about my teenage alcoholic. Included a tribute to the founders of AA. Out on the bike. Chilling. Or trying to.

Sunday 14 July

Tour de France. Cyrille Tricart from ASO [Amaury Sport Organisation] had sorted a car pass for the Ventoux stage. We had to drive to Vacquey-ras to get it, then head slowly up the Ventoux from the Malaucène side, then parked 4k down the other side and got a great spot just before Chris Froome left Quintana having already broken from the pack. Froome was out of this world, amazing to see him close up firing on all cylinders hav-ing been at it all day. The French were starting to murmur quite openly about doping, and he was getting a bit of abuse en route. I sent Dave B a message of congratulations but they were clearly worried that the rumour mill was so strong and that it was going to be very hard to prove a negative.

We spent a bit of time at the Rapha Sky bus. The guys from Rapha [Sky's clothing partners] saying just how fast they were growing. The whole UK cycling thing really was an enormous success story. It took us a while to get down from the mountain, with very French chaos around Chalet Reynard [restaurant], but we made it to Crillon-Le-Brave, and a very nice evening with Peter [Chittick] and Carolyn [Fairbairn] and some of their friends. Carolyn and I had our usual discussion about relevance. We both needed it.

Monday 15 July

I had arranged to meet Dave B and some of his team at the top of Ventoux at

1.30, so I set out early, Rory an hour later. My new Pinarello hadn't arrived so was on my old bike and struggled up in 2.38. The Sky guys were held up and so we had a bit of a wait before Dario Cioni [PR adviser], then Tim Kerrison [coach], then Dave. Chatted up Tim on how they were handling all the doping rumours. I had not realised the French media and the Dutch fans had been so in their faces about it. But they had. I said winning was the most important thing, plus it was impossible to prove a negative, and all the moves had been tried by Lance [Armstrong], e.g. legal action, libel writs etc. but they should not be pushed on to their enemies' agenda. I liked David Millar's line, that people believed in Lance when they knew they shouldn't, and didn't believe in Chris when they knew they should. Dave had a few admirers up at the top of Ventoux and when I said he might get mobbed when we stopped for coffee in Malaucène, Tim said rather drily, 'Don't worry, he loves it.'

We raced down to Malaucène, sat for a good chat on the various things they might try, e.g. more openness, more published data, but do not lose competitive advantage. Dave in his element. Home briefly then out to Radisson Orange for drinks and dinner with David Millar and the Garmin-Barracuda team guys. Charly Wegelius's book was going well, *Domestique*, about his life as a lower-order rider. Now the manager, he was picking my brains about speaking, saying he sometimes felt he lost the riders' attention in team talks. Chatting to David re. retirement and post plans. Nice dinner with all the riders, good bunch, great food. Surprised a few of them drank, both beer and wine. Bumped into Dave B in the car park on the way out, had a chat, prompting DM to text me, 'How sweet, and how typical, he wanted the last word.' Liked them both, but clearly there were tensions there.

Tuesday 16 July

To Puymeras to watch the Tour going through. God, PG would have loved it. Out for a longish ride. Finalised dedication and acknowledgements for *My Name Is…*, adding Dr Bennie who had helped me so much in 1986, Fiona, and the French woman in Peterborough who looked after me when I was out of it in the railway buffet.

Wednesday 17 July

Edi and Endri were in London for *HARDtalk* and a meeting with TB. I talked to both, then joined the meeting by phone and we got to an OK position. But my depression was getting worse. Anxiety too. I'd arranged for medication to be sent out but it got lost in transit somewhere. England were battering the Aussies in the cricket, which was good, but I knew I was watching it just to pass time and hope this mood shifted. I was getting a load of new bids for work, e.g. to present *Fighting Talk* on 5 Live, also a programme on negotiation, and as a guest on *Room 101* [talk show]. But I was in a mood where nothing appealed, nothing at all.

Sunday 21 July

Last day of the Tour. A few exchanges with Michelle Cound on Froome's victory speech, which he used. Paris did a great job, and I tweeted they should get the Olympic Games one day. David Millar was out on his own for a fair bit up and down the Champs Élysées. Froome went over the line with the whole team. Dave B looking happy hanging out of the car.

Monday 22 July

Greg and Godric out from Luton. I had arranged for them to meet the Albanian team here. Long ride with Godric, but we both had a massive energy crash. Chatted re. his agency stuff which seemed to be going OK. Royal baby finally came, amid hours of TV babble.

Tuesday 23 July

Ventoux with Godric. 2.23 up, he did 2.20, but took seven minutes off him on the descent so I was claiming victory. He was using Rory's bike and hit the brakes so hard and so often the wheels were practically burned through.

Wednesday 24 July

Endri and Arbi's flight had been delayed yesterday but we got underway late morning with an agenda re. Inauguration, UN, personnel, country branding. Mark Lucas arrived p.m. for the country branding piece. Endri spoke to Linda and put her on. She said I had become Edi's guardian angel and was always in his mind, as whenever anyone suggested anything he said, 'What would Alastair say?' Going to be tough though. I did a long note to Edi after the main session. Greg good on ideas, Godric good on systems. Could see they were complimentary. Good laugh having them both around. And I was endlessly sending messages to Edi saying his guys were swimming, sleeping, sightseeing etc.

Endri was clear that the public do not want too much heated political debate during August, but they do need to realise the nature of the game Berisha is playing. I said another part of the messaging should be an appeal to everyone, in politics, public service, judiciary, every walk of life, to try to put the brutal politics of recent years behind you and work together for the new Albania. Edi's inauguration speech and UN speech were going to be important events. There was also his visit to Turkey.

He should have an outline agreement with Erdoğan to announce, while also being aware of the dangers of placing too many eggs in this one basket. So within the Turkey visit there was also scope to begin to talk about the message for the UN. The need for much outside help. Broader Balkan strategy (though the UN was the best place to announce that he intended to be the first Albanian PM to go to Serbia).

On the inauguration, given Berisha's refusal to be involved, and the politics of the President etc., there was a case for him keeping the protocol to a minimum. Recommended doing a few smallish events in the immediate build-up, perhaps something at party HQ to say farewell (kind of), something with public servants maybe, then as the main event... Possibly in main square, or maybe in the space between PM office and Parliament... Backdrop an arc of several rows of young people. The message is Next Generation Albania. Then Edi looking out with them behind him, to an audience mixed of those who have to be there, MPs, ambassadors, key people, plus people from every part of the country, perhaps chosen by mayors or some other system.

For the UN, I thought something on the lines of asking the world to take a fresh look at Albania. I set out a plan for comms based on an assumption Endri would be to Edi what I was to TB, and with a writ across the system, the central co-ordinator of all government communications. He had seen how this could work in a campaign covering all those core functions. It was up to him to make sure they understand this is in all of their interests, theirs included. Then each ministry should have its own small media and comms team, but the heads must understand his director of comms can instruct and direct them. Later I filmed them all in the pool, sent it to Edi who sent back a very funny line re. using [artist] David Hockney's pool as a logo.

Saturday 27 July

Call with TB to go over Albania, agreed what we needed, and he needed to approach Jim Yong Kim [President] at the World Bank, and the Kuwaitis for funding. We chatted a bit re. Richard Dearlove who was clearly on manoeuvres, having been in the *Mail on Sunday* last week saying he had written his account on Iraq and if criticised at the Chilcot Inquiry he might bring it forward. TB said Dearlove had been emphatic on the intelligence, but was positioning and it was gearing up to be nasty. TB said it would be whatever it would be and we just had to get through it. But what with the depression and the anxiety, I was not feeling as rested as I ought to be considering we were not doing much.

Sunday 28 July

Grace was in tears over the pain in her ankle. Took her to see Thierry and Olivia Judet, surgeon and radiographer who lived nearby, who were really nice, put her at ease, also agreed to do weight-bearing X-rays when she was in France. Took Grace to Avignon then round to see John Mills. Marjorie Wallace [CEO SANE, mental health charity] there, ditto Lizzy [sister] and family. Usual mix of politics, France and mental health. Everyone pretty down on Ed. He had had a bad few weeks and the Tories were getting their act together. Long chat with Gail who had been to David Miliband's family farewell last night. Nice but sad, she said. Sent DM a message saying how sorry I was I missed it, and how we needed to do a better job of staying in touch.

Monday 29 July

Grace in Paris trying to sort a flat. I had major anxiety for a week or so. Just on edge all the time. Sick feeling inside. Catastrophising rather than sleeping. Andy McCann sent some exercises. Ed was getting a hard time back home. I did a blog on them paying the price for not defending our record. *The Observer* asked me to expand it for them, which I wrote, but then I didn't send after Charlie and Peter M advised against. I did tell Tim Livesey though that I was going to sit out if they kept on the distancing strategy. The Tories were doing well at getting the media to cheerlead on the economy. Liz and Rob and their friends Dave and Sue over for a night. Good bike ride with Rob [Naish, Liz's husband]. I was sorting getting Jamie Naish [nephew, consultant] out to help Edi. Mike Stephens [university friend, singer] over for dinner with the new love of his life. Part of me regretted not sending the *Obs* piece because I really felt it needed to be said. In the end, I did a version of it along these lines which I sent to Ed and some of his team:

> There are three main parts to any election campaign narrative – a story about yourself, a story about your opponents, and a story about the future. The third of these is the most important, because what a government will do in the future to deal with the challenges of the present is more important to a voter today than what may have happened in the past. It's why Bill Clinton used Fleetwood Mac as his campaign backing: 'Don't stop

thinking about tomorrow.' However, arguments about the past have to be won before people will hear you about the future; and that is especially important when your opponents are drowning out the truth about the past with a series of very big lies, delivered so often, so consistently and with such force that the media now act as an echo chamber for them.

Of those three campaign planks, Labour should be well ahead on the first two – its own strong record in government, the coalition's patchy, often omnishambolically incompetent record three years in; and on the third, with big policy proposals still to be unveiled, they are in with a shouting chance of winning on that too. Unfortunately, however, the Tory mantra about 'the mess we inherited' has become part of the political landscape, and it has to be shifted if Labour are to win the battle about the past, which then becomes relevant to exposing the truth about the weakness of the Tory record, and thus being listened to when it comes to setting out the all-important policy agenda for the future.

The Tory strategy is pretty clear. Establish in the public mind the idea that the economy was a basket case when they took over, so that the slightest sign of recovery can be presented as a triumph for Cameron and Osborne, the right-wing cheerleaders in the media hyperventilating in their favour. Then portray Cameron as someone who now has a bit of experience behind him, looks the part, and meanwhile target Ed M, again with the help of the right-wing press, as viciously as they can. Ed has shown he has the calmness and resilience needed to deal with that. Added to which it is hard to see what Cameron has done to win over doubters who couldn't quite bring themselves to vote for him last time, amid plenty of reasons why people who did vote for him might have second thoughts. But that first part of the battle of the big arguments – about the past – has to be engaged in, and it is never too late.

The only way to counter the Tory Big Lies is by fighting back with the truth, even if it means doing so belatedly, and at the risk of the Tories screeching 'mess we inherited' ever more loudly. We see the same in their approach to the NHS. Another 'mess we inherited', they say, to justify changes for which nobody voted and for which they have no mandate. The Britain the coalition inherited after a decade of Labour in power was fairer, better off, with improved and improving public services, stronger regions, a vibrant culture. It was not a mess. The mess is happening now, with living standards falling, NHS crises returning, unprecedentedly low morale among teachers and police, power shifting back to a few at the top. Britain, far from booming, as the cheerleaders would have you believe, is recovering more slowly than had they followed the Brown–Darling approach that was beginning to deliver the jobs and growth we needed.

That is a message Labour must take into the political debate with the same vigour as the Tories took 'the mess we inherited'. It has the merit of truth, and though it means looking at the past, it is an essential part of winning the argument about the future. The Tories are planning to run the line that the country should not give back the keys to the people who crashed the car. The truth is the car ran a lot better under Labour, and can do so again, provided those three areas of argument are engaged in, and won.

Sent to TB, Charlie and Peter, asking whether to do as article or advice, and their reactions were interesting. Peter M said in response that he thought the argument was right. But that we have to be aware that – for all the 'zeal with which EM chose to attack New Labour and our overall record' – the problem we have now in fact started before we left government. The seeds were sown by Gordon's refusal to accept that once we had accelerated out of the storm of the banking crisis (burning up a lot of very expensive fuel as we did so, pushing up borrowing and widening the deficit even more than the recession would have done) we needed to accept that deficit reduction was an issue and that a debt/GDP ratio of the sort we were facing (even greater now by the way) was totally unsustainable.

He said the second aspect of the problem is that, in truth, Labour's growth record was based more on the credit boom than we chose to acknowledge and that the economy was not transformed in the way we like to promote. We were banking on rates of growth continuing to support a level of public spending and borrowing that in reality could not be sustained and, indeed, was in danger of crashing. Tony started to recognise this in 2005 with his fundamental savings review which was about sustaining expenditure on a more solid/sustainable footing than Gordon would ever admit to needing.

He said whenever he was speaking in private about all this that he accepted some critique of our record in order to win the bigger argument, which is that we saved the economy from going into the abyss, we were carefully rebuilding confidence and growth and that, following the election, the coalition did in fact go too far, too fast in their policies, failing to realise the risk that private demand/investment would not replace the public rug they were pulling away from under the economy.

Charlie was against me doing an article. He said it defined me as a commentator rather than a player within the Labour Party, would be damaging for the party, and lessen the chances of me being seriously engaged in fighting the next election. He said my recent blog has been characterised by the press as part of the chorus of voices attacking Ed M, and this would be seen in that light. Me being understood to be continuing to attack Ed is damaging for Ed. And contributes to a picture of Ed being regarded as hopeless, particularly by Blairites, and the people who know how to win elections. He said he sensed he was feeling very embattled and friendless. 'If he is wise, he would get your help to fight the election. The article would make that less likely. So I wouldn't do it. It will be more incendiary in England than it might appear from France.'

TB had a different take entirely, perhaps unsurprisingly focused on his belief about the need to defend the record. 'Definitely a good idea! You should add some of the economic stats which show that in 2007 Labour had cut the deficit from 1997 and had lower spending as a percentage of GDP than under Tories. And figures on waiting lists. And London schools report that came out in *FT*.' Then he got Ciaran in his office to send them through.

In the end I decided against publication but sent a few copies around. Tom Baldwin said he agreed with every word. Tim Livesey said, 'Ed not wild about this simply because it feeds the current frenzy. The media is gunning for us. It will pass. Anyway, that's his reaction. You must do what you think is right.' I replied that the question was not whether it feeds frenzy, but whether there was any substance in what I say. I felt a large part of the party wants and needs to hear it, and the Tories need to know they are vulnerable to attack across the board for their strategy of running everything down as a way of justifying misguided policy. I said I had warned Ed at the outset that without us owning the good side of the economic record, the Tories would not need much of a recovery to win the economic debate. They do not deserve to, but they are, and we had let them. I said I was determined not to be one of those people who goes into print at the drop of a hat to carp and criticise but it is incredibly frustrating to see this unfold as it has.

Then Ed got in touch asking to meet up when I was back. I said I was happy to, but said I wasn't sure I could face getting involved in endless strategic discussion which then, in my view, takes the wrong turn. I said it might be easier in those circumstances just to sit it out. I said I could understand why Ed felt he needs to distance in some way from TB–GB era, but the calibration on it is wrong. I also felt they responded too much to the negative messages coming through focus groups. They are coming through because the Tories have recovered their discipline and are being heard. The response had to be our own set of very clear messages, taken forward with similar vigour and discipline. Looking in, I was hard pressed to see what they are.

I went out for a ride and had a bad fall when my pedal sheared and I ended up in a ditch and had to go one-legged to local bike shop owner Jean-Christophe's to get patched up and get some new gear. Fiona was definitely wanting to shift the balance of our life out here. With a bit of coming and going, we were near enough seven weeks total. I came back only for the Yeovil match, poor game but won two–nil.

Catherine called re. Chilcot, asking if I had had my warning letter, because clearly TB had. I hadn't, but was still anxious though, felt maybe they were working their way through the people they intended to criticise, rather than all at once. She felt if JoP and I were not to be criticised, at least it meant they were not on the politics, but the substance and probably the aftermath. It had definitely hung over me over the holiday though. I wondered if TB was more worried than he was letting on. He was also getting hit a bit reputationally. Had a couple of chats with Peter M, who sounded down. He also suggested he and I work together on some things, said he would enjoy it, I would, and so would any clients. Reinaldo still viewed me as PNG, went ballistic when Peter said he might see us in France. Peter making good money, travelling a fair bit, but said this was not the life he would choose. Said he could not get the Labour Party out of his system, but Ed patronised him, they did not really want us around, etc. I called him also to get advice on whether to take up all of the many bids I was getting on Syria and Iraq. He felt not, ditto Gail and Fiona, Ed V and Emma more ambivalent. Between a rock and a hard place, said Ed. I had a good book to promote but these foreign policy issues always seemed to be top of the agenda when I did. George Galloway crowd-sourcing a film *The Killings of Tony Blair*, and in the promo said Peter and I were also in his sights.

We came back on the August Bank Holiday, and I went up to Burnley on the Tuesday for the Preston match [2–0] but also to do media for the announcement that Burnley won the Most Enterprising Area in the UK Award. It came as the talk of military action in Syria was cranking up and with the media saying it looked like Labour would support and Cameron would win the vote, I was very supportive when asked on TV. Within forty-eight hours the whole thing had unravelled though. England won the Ashes.

The disagreement with Ed on the failure to defend the record became a running argument. But Ed was able to park it and simply send me various drafts of his speech for conference, on which I would comment before he would send another with a few changes. His main line seemed to be 'Britain can be better than this', which I said was a comment not an argument, and it lacked the how. Once we were back from holiday, the Syrian crisis blew up after Assad used chemical weapons. Obama had called it a red line so now what? He wanted to take action. Cameron recalled Parliament, thought he had support from Labour, claimed Ed went back on his word. Bottom line was that both sides voted for military action in some circumstances but the government motion was defeated, and Cameron stood up and immediately ruled out trying to bring the issue back for another vote.

Ed was being hailed for strength but I felt it was a disaster for him, for Cameron and for Britain. He had been leading the calls for action and now we were irrelevant. Putin was behaving in the most appalling way, pouring in the weapons, and also buying the Syrian line that it wasn't them. It all looked like Cameron had screwed up his management, and Ed had played it for politics, and of course we, because of the Iraq/trust issue, were getting a lot of the blame, though in this case the fact of WMD was clear and nobody seriously in doubt where they came from.

Horrible stuff, but the politics of it was a mess. Labour meanwhile still failing to surge ahead and on the economy my point to Ed was being proven with a rash of average news being hailed as great. I had a few chats with TB, who felt Ed's slim election chances had gone, but was also being asked to take part in a 'leadership' PEB [party election broadcast]. He said that the problem was people just did not get the reality of what was happening in the Middle East, and how dangerous it was for us. Also, as my Bosnian friends said on a conference call, it is happening as Britain feels like it is divorcing from Europe and from America.

Friday 29 August

Out to Prague to meet Jasenko [Selimović] from the Bosnian SDP, and then Zlatko Lagumdžija. Liked him, though the scene was even more complicated than I imagined and they admitted no party would get more than 20 per cent share of the vote. The SDP had slipped from first to third in the polls, currently led by a guy who had left them to set up his own party, Democratic Front, and who was one of the three rotating presidents. The Dayton Accords really had set up a nightmare scenario for political campaigns, making it virtually impossible for any party to win, but I guess it was inevitable.* We agreed they should play to their strengths as the only multi-ethnic party and build the argument that that is what a multi-ethnic country needed. The Serb population equation was always complicated but they felt they could get to 20 per cent, no more. The other parties tended to be ethnic, tribal.

Some very basic things were going to have to be done, though. First meeting all p.m., then we headed off to the Chelsea v Bayern Munich

---

* The General Framework Agreement for Peace in Bosnia and Herzegovina, known as the Dayton Accords or Dayton Agreement, had reached agreement in Dayton, Ohio, in 1995, when a single sovereign state was established and the Bosnian War came to an end.

SuperCup [annual UEFA fixture contested by champions of the Champions League and the Europa League] match which, unusually for this kind of game, was really good, finally settled on penalties in Bayern's favour. Great fans, so much better than Chelsea who at one point had [José] Mourinho [manager] trying to rouse them as they hung on through extra time, Bayern equalising in the last minute before winning the shoot-out. We were a few rows away from the Sky box so I texted [Sky panellists] Ben Shephard to tell Jamie Carragher he is eating too much chocolate and Niall Quinn too many biscuits. They turned round waving a box of biscuits at me. Back to the hotel, yet another room with over-loud air conditioning.

Saturday 30 August

Syria fallout from the Parliament vote [rejecting possible UK military action against Assad to deter the use of chemical weapons] was pretty grim all round. TB was doing a piece for the *Sunday Times* and not really holding back. I felt the whole thing was shameful. Good long meeting with Zlatko and Jasenko where we went through some very basic stuff re. organisation of message etc., and how they should operate strategically. I felt they would be OK to work with but rather than go all out for the election campaign from now on in, we agreed to try out for three months and see how it went for all concerned. They wanted me to do for them what I had done for Edi, though the politics were much, much more complicated. I had called Paddy Ashdown – the morning after the Syria vote, so first we had half an hour on that, him saying he was ashamed to be British – and re. me doing Bosnia, he said I would love it and I would hate it.

He said there was a famous Bosnian saying – 'Fight a thorn bush with someone else's prick.' They would definitely want to fight with your prick, he said. Zlatko laughed out loud when I told him and said, 'Paddy understands Bosnia.' He said he had been like a bulldozer, really good, especially at first, and fairly popular. Like Edi, they could not understand why TB's reputation was so low in the UK. Lunch with Zlatko's family and his schoolfriend, now a businessman, who used to play pro football. Then off to Tirana via Vienna and arrived at the hotel just after midnight. Wrote long note to Zlatko re. next steps. I watched Obama's speech announcing he wanted to take the chemical weapons issue to Congress. Big gamble.

Sunday 1 September

Endri collected me and we headed to party HQ for a meeting with the strategy team. I pressed them on some of the policy positions and we ended up in hysterics when the policy guy from the opposition – now the health minister – talked about the policy of artificial insemination for family cows, with male offspring owned by government and female back to the family. He just ploughed on. Off with Endri to the coast because Ilir Meta had asked to meet me.

En route Grace texted me to say David Frost had died. Checked it out, and he had had a heart attack on the *Queen Elizabeth* cruise ship. Awful. I tweeted a series of tributes and then did a BBC phoner from Meta's garden. Really sad about David. Awful for [Lady] Carina [wife] and the boys that he was alone and nobody with him. As I did tributes down the line, so many strong memories came back. He was such a life force. Hard to believe he was gone.

Meta was not as I expected him. He seemed very calm, intelligent, he knew British politics inside out. He had read my diaries and was asking a lot about both the systems and the personalities. He felt Edi should not go for Berisha personally, also that the two or three priorities should be absolutely clear and Edi should not get too distracted. His wife, also an MP, was there but did not take part in the discussion over lunch, just me and Endri, Meta and his head of office. He seemed happy enough with his Parliament Speaker position. Nice enough chat, and though Edi said he could be tricky, clearly he could, he struck me as someone they ought to be able to get on with. Berisha had not spoken to him since the coalition was formed.

Back into town and we interviewed for the shadow chief of staff role. Edi and I agreed Jamie N as an assistant to Vali Bizhga [chief of staff] and Endri would be better. Edi really lost it on the phone with a minister who had done a silly interview with a hostile paper and, in front of several ministers, completely tore her apart. In the meetings though he was good. A rather odd evening as it was his mum's birthday and I was there with Vali and Endri, but not really able to get much work done. Linda as ever telling me to go there as often as I could, as it always calmed him and got him focused.

Monday 2 September

To HQ and an interview with Edi for the inauguration film Silverfish were making. First in English, and he was on good form, then me in English, him in Albanian. We were moving from Renaissance to Next Generation Albania. Still no access to government though word came via a third party that Berisha would not take part in the handover. Crazy stuff. Long meeting with Edi on the message for the first speech to Parliament. Made it back via Vienna, just. Worked on speech plus Bosnia note.

Edi sending me on lots of good notes being done e.g. by the Turkish development ministry who had analysed the programme, some of the

Clinton team who had set up the Clinton–Gore office, and some of the internal analysis. He seemed pretty confident, but everyone was making the point about just how big the challenges would be.

Tuesday 3 September

I was getting inundated with Syria bids, and also still getting a bit of grief on the idea that the No vote by MPs came because of lack of trust on Iraq. Ed V had got *Newsnight* to suggest a film on booze to go with the novel as a *quid pro quo* for a first interview on Syria, but I was not so sure. Ditto Fiona, Gail, Peter M, Tim, all of whom felt I would drown out coverage for the book, and that people who were against action would go against the book. We went round and round it and eventually decided to wait until I had done planned interviews with Decca Aitkenhead [*Guardian*] and Celia Walden. The novel was getting a fair bit of media interest pre publication, so I was starting to get my head into gear on the drink stuff.

Wednesday 4 September

Decca loved the book. The interview was two thirds book and booze, then a third politics and Syria and she could tell I was uncomfortable. I felt both Cameron and Ed had fucked up but did not really want to say so. I felt strong on the book, and she said it felt to her I had become a proper novelist. Good interview and then out for pictures. Back for Grace who interviewed Decca for the No More Page 3 campaign. Mutual love-in. Pottering about, sorting Bosnia, doing more on Albania, blog on alcohol and drugs figures. Dinner with Jamie to brief him on Albania. He was totally up for it.

Thursday 5 September

Celia Walden for the *Telegraph*. She loved the book too. She said I should give up on politics and just write novels. I said Piers [Morgan, husband] said the opposite, that I should stop fannying around and get into politics. She was funny about him claiming he could change nappies with one hand while phoning with the other. Never changed a nappy in his life. Quite a languid interviewing style. Nice though. Weird life now. Beverley Hills most of the time while he was flying all over the place. She said she felt Piers and I were quite similar. I told her of the time Mary Parkinson [wife of Michael] told me I must get a chat show 'to stop Piers being the next Parky'. She was asking me mainly about my relationship with booze, and the book, with a half-hearted chat on Syria and Iraq. They all had to do it, I guess.

TB was doing an interview for a documentary which was going to get big play as it would essentially be seen as a whack at Ed. I just about avoided it though I had said to Decca Labour had fucked up on the economy and gifted Cameron strategically, Cameron was putting on a brave face at the G20. I then recorded a David Frost tribute interview. The more you thought of his life the more extraordinary it was. Out for dinner with F and Rory to discuss flats. Grace's Paris accommodation was still not sorted and she was off to a bloody festival.

Friday 6 September
Meeting with TBWA [ad agency] to discuss Labour. They wanted to hire me as a consultant to advise them on how to deal with the Labour account. I was very frank with them, said I did not think we could win, unless there was a real change in approach. Cameron could win, and it was our fault. They were good guys and felt maybe if advice came via them with my input it would have more chance. They were pretty down on Ed too but desperate for Labour to get back. I ran home, getting back into it. Calum was doing well which made us all feel better. The Decca piece was good, but crap headline focused on military action. Dinner at Ben Evans's birthday party. Sitting between Amanda and a really nice woman called Harriet, German, wife of V&A boss who shared our views on class and education. Played pipes, nice do, Ben as down about Labour as we were. No chance, he felt, yet it was hard to see who replaced Ed.

Saturday 7 September
Set off by train for Retford. Mum met me and we went for lunch at the Hop Pole. She was on really good form though unable to raise her arms very high. She felt I was doing too much and looked tired which was a bit odd after such a long break. Later off to an event in Nottingham where the BBC guy John Hess [East Midlands political editor] did a rather good interview about the book, and politics, and then opened up to a really friendly Q&A. He said he felt it was like Dante's Inferno with a double vodka. Q&A really good, though Mum was upset when I said I thought I probably always had depression.

Monday 9 September
Independent interview with Paul Gallagher, really nice guy. Then PTA magazine. *The House* magazine crisis comms event with Tim Bell. Good guy, really hated Cameron. I think the audience felt I was maybe a bit more

modern and up to speed but he had some great stories. Dinner at Charlie and Marianna's. They were worried about TB, felt he had not really sat down and focused on what his post-PM life should be.

Tuesday 10 September

I was working in the morning at home then had a meeting in the Strand. I was walking through Covent Garden area behind the Strand and suddenly felt very shivery. I staggered into a hotel and sat down in an armchair. Now feeling faint as well. The hotel doorman came over, said I looked very pale, was I OK? He got me a glass of water and helped me to a cab. I was now feeling like death warmed up. Lying across the back seat. The driver asked if I wanted to go to hospital. I said No, but when I got home, I could tell Grace was really worried, Fiona was laughing which she later said was panic! I was now shivering so much my teeth were also chattering.

We called out the paramedics who arrived about an hour or so later, did loads of tests and said all fine apart from a temperature of 42.8. Pulse and heart and blood pressure OK. He thought I should go to hospital but I had been invited to Frostie's funeral which I knew was a small private affair, and I really did not want to let them down. So I stayed home with Grace looking after me, Fiona out at some do with Tessa. Slightly delirious but they gave me drugs to lower the fever.

Wednesday 11 September

Bad night. I should probably have taken the paramedics' advice and gone to hospital but felt maybe I could go later. So we set off for Frostie's funeral with Rayan. Really feeling grim. It was at Nuffield village church, lovely setting, star-studded attendance. Carina and the boys did readings and they used the Queen's quote I had used in my letter – 'Grief is the price we pay for love' – on the cover. Back to their house. A photo of TB/Bill C/David when he did the joint interview at the G8 was in pride of place. Zac Goldsmith felt Leveson was moving in the right direction. Had a chat with Parky and Mary about his cancer and also again about Piers, and Mary's warning to me he would be the next big thing unless I did it. Nice do, but sad of course, and I was still feeling rough so left fairly early to get home and get to bed.

Thursday 12 September

Another day, another funeral. I did a Frost tribute interview for the BBC, then Richard Bacon and Steve Wright interviews, both good, then off to [former *Mirror* industrial editor] Geoffrey Goodman's funeral. Mainly union people rather than *Mirror*. I was feeling very rough though, and running to the loo the whole time, at one time in real pain. Nice service, but not easy when I was worrying about how ill I felt. We stayed for the burial, chatting to Rodney Bickerstaffe, but I was desperate to get back to bed. Nice send-off, good turnout.

Friday 13 September

I went to see the GP who said I should take stools and get bloods done at the Royal Free as I had a routine appointment with Dr Hamilton on Tuesday. Did all that then set off with Emma Mitchell for the north. I had agreed to go up to do *BBC Breakfast* on the book, Emma saying it was one of the best to shift books. We stopped off to see Alex and Cathy in Wilmslow. We sat at the kitchen table drinking tea and eating those caramel biscuits you only see in Scotland. He said he was not missing the football at all since retirement. Hilarious re. Rooney. Can't take Liverpool out of the man etc. Very down re. politics, OK re. David Moyes, but I sensed he worried it may have been a mistake. His book was clearly going to be massive. He intended to do one big media launch, then four follow up-talks, plus one signing where he would stay till all were done.

Emma was surprised the house not a lot bigger or more excluded. He proudly showed off his library. Good photos, tartan carpet. Cathy loved the photo album the players gave him and he took us through it, talking about the pictures as he went. Nice to see them so relaxed, but I was really worrying about losing control of my guts. By the time we got to the Holiday Inn Salford, I was really struggling, feeling really bad. Went to the toilet seventeen times in the night. Something was really not right at all.

Saturday 14 September

Up early and I managed a couple of bites of toast, a cup of tea, but that was enough to set me off. I felt like death, and of course Breakfast telly was all about being chirpy and upbeat. I did my best, but God I felt bad. I liked the feel of Media City. I somehow managed to hold things together for the interview with presenters Charlie [Stayt] and Naga [Munchetty], and it led to an instant massive rise on Amazon from number 1,100 to 40. Off to Burnley to do *Soccer AM* pitchside. Big game. We were the better team, took the lead but then gave away a dire sloppy equaliser. Again. Agony. What do we have to do to beat Blackburn? I headed home feeling like death.

522   *September '13: Visiting Fergie, falling ill*

Sunday 15 September

Bed all day. Just dying.

Monday 16 September

At 11 a.m. I saw Dr Hamilton at the Royal Free with Fiona. I had been terrible all night. He said the blood tests were not great and the colon was probably infected. My obvious worry was the return of colitis. He felt I should stay in hospital, get more tests and have a colonoscopy ASAP. It all happened very quickly, and I sensed both he and Fiona were a bit worried. I had the tests and then went back at 1 p.m. for the colonoscopy. I fainted with the enema, then sedated and by the time I came round they had done it all, and they had me in a very large, well-furnished private room. He said it was partly because it was me, and they assumed I wouldn't want it widely known I was there, but also because they were worried about infection of others.

Grace looked really worried when she came to see me. Rory was great, coming round a lot, doing his work on the sofa. Calum popped in then went off to the gym. Hamilton was very solicitous and keeping me informed as we went. His initial assessment was that it was not colitis but an infection. The food was good, the nurses fantastic. I was still running to the loo the whole time and at one point I was doubled up in agony.

Tuesday 17 September

Hamilton was at my bedside first thing, as I woke up. Christ he works long hours. He said they were still not totally sure what was wrong. But then he came back later and said it was definitely not colitis. The boys came in, Fiona a couple of times. I was on a drip which was helping but I was still going to the loo every few minutes and most of the time it was like draft Guinness. Through the day X-rays, scans, endless tests, and even though I was managing to eat, I felt very weak a lot of the time.

Wednesday 18 September

They reckoned it was definitely dysentery, shigella sonnei bacteria, and gave me a massive dose of antibiotics to get through it. They said it could have come from food here, or maybe Kaz or Albania, hard to tell, but it had been a very bad dose of it. Had lost a fair bit of weight. Then Fiona and Calum started to go down with something. Hoping to Christ they don't get it. I watched Charlie F on Breakfast TV re. assisted dying, texted him to say it was a good interview, he called and on hearing where I was he came round. Then while he was there Neil K popped in. Lots of joking about the socialist room next to the Kuwaiti prince. They were both down on Ed. I stopped myself having a row with Neil who had been such a supporter. Ed had sent me another draft which was better but still not brilliant.

I had new doctors seeing me now, Dr Murray and Gautam Mehta. Dr Mehta had actually tweeted me after my interview on Saturday, saying how much of a problem alcohol was for the NHS. They saw me and said as long as I took it easy, and kept taking the drugs, I could go home later in the day. I had had to cancel loads of media on the book but had had time to think through the alcohol campaign I wanted to develop around it. Dr Mehta said alcohol was the single biggest factor in virtually every single ward. He said if I took you to any ward in the hospital, I can show you people, whatever the ward specialism may be, who are really there because of drink. They said I should stay in until the end of the day, so I got home in time for the football. They said I could definitely not go to Bosnia.

Thursday 19 September

The drugs were beginning to work and bizarrely I had loads of energy. I was catching up, also writing lots, and using social media to promote the book which was going well. Ed Victor was pissed off with Random House because we were getting the usual feedback about not enough books being in shops, including NW3 where Waterstones were asking if I could lend some to them for signing! Gail said the good news was it showed it was selling well, Ed replied the bad news is we could be selling a lot more. I was still having to be very careful to be near a toilet, and also had chest infection. Started to tweet re. Damian McBride selling his book [*Power Trip: A Decade of Policy, Plots and Spin*] to the *Mail*.

Friday 20 September

Chest was still bad. Stomach settling again. Fiona seeming a bit better. The media going wild with the McBride poison. Bit of pick-up from my tweets last night asking if the *Mail* money was going to the party, and suggesting he was utter poison. Out to take a book to David S who was on his way to a depression conference and thought I looked better 'with a bit of weight off'. I had lost almost a stone. The hospital had had some calls and also the *Standard* knew an ambulance had been out a few days ago, so I called Syd Young and we agreed to get the dysentery story out via Andrew [Syd's son] at South West News Service who wanted to catchline it 'weapons of arse destruction'! Actually quite a good story and would help set up another wave of stuff on the book which was doing fine.

I went for a haircut and chatted to my Albanian barber, Alex Palushi, re. Edi who was en route to the UN. He felt things were going OK and his family were happy. Also there was a Kosovan in there who shook me by the hand and said Jamie Shea [NATO spokesperson] and I would never be forgotten and could I say thanks to Tony when I saw him. JP called for a rant about McBride and also Wegg-Prosser who had released a load of emails about the TB operation to stop the GB coup in 2006. All ghastly. JP said the problem was it was all toytown. We didn't have a serious policy message, did not make big arguments so this history tittle-tattle stuff could easily fill the gap.

He said he had warned Ed re. the unions he had to be sure he could win this battle because he was in trouble if he didn't.[*] He also said, 'He hasn't got a chance,' and he said re. GB, 'The mistake I made was thinking he would change as leader. I believed he had a plan and he didn't.' He had challenged him over McBride's briefing many times and GB of course just denied it, as he did with me. JP went through the shadow Cabinet and was pretty scathing about all of them.

I was working on the press release and articles for the Alcohol Concern launch on the Monday of Labour's conference and called Andy Burnham to get him to come along on the 5k run. He didn't want to sign up specifically to a 50p minimum unit pricing on alcohol but he was up for doing the run and generally being more on board for our approach. He said he had no idea what Ed would be talking about. But he sounded like he was engaged and gung-ho but added, 'If we do not get going this week I think we have had it, people have just made up their minds he is not good enough and we are not good enough and the Tories don't have to do that much.'

Saturday 21 September

Working a bit, then watching the football all day. Finally a win against Leeds [2–1].

Sunday 22 September

The McBride book was getting a lot of play so I agreed to do *Sunday Politics*

---

[*] The Unite union had been accused of trying to sign up members to vote for its favoured candidate for a general election candidacy and although a Labour internal inquiry found no rules were broken Ed Miliband proposed widespread changes to the party's links with the trades union movement.

September '13: JP down on GB, furious re. McBride

525

and Channel 4 before heading off to Brighton. I was starting to do deals with the broadcasters about doing half McBride and half alcohol campaign and the book, which Andrew Neil went along with, and allowed me a fair slab of time to make the point that this blew once and for all the idea that it was six of one and half a dozen of the other between TB and GB teams. The real tragedy was that if we had stayed together and Gordon had not had these truly awful people around, we might still be there. Grant Shapps [Conservative Party chairman, Minister Without Portfolio] was on the programme and I asked him if he could cut through the crap and sort my accreditation for the Tory conference so I could do the Alcohol Concern fringe stuff. To be fair, someone was messing around and he did sort it. I liked his spad who told me she was not even born when Neil made his attack on Militant [Tendency] at the 1985 conference. Wow.

Ed seemed to have settled on his speech and was now memorising it. He was trying to make the economic debate less about the big numbers than about living standards, and was having a bit of traction on it. I still felt strongly he needed to reframe the argument about the record but he didn't agree about that. Off to Brighton with Lundbeck driver.

Monday 23 September
Up early, met Rakhee Shah [PR] at the hotel and off to do a round of interviews both on the conference and mainly on Alcohol Concern, then a 5k run with Eddie Izzard and Andy Burnham and others. I was not fully fit yet so just did bits and bobs of it before a breakfast and speeches where we sort of got Andy to commit to minimum unit pricing 'in principle'. Andy had been a bit on manoeuvres of late, but there seemed little chance of Ed being challenged. Eric Appleby [Alcohol Concern] spoke well, pointing out how disappointed he was with Cameron's U-turn on pricing, also that we needed a much bigger strategy. We had pledge cards with a call for minimum unit pricing and also to raise the proportion of dependent drinkers getting treatment from 6 per cent to 15. I also did a pretty big focus on sports marketing and sponsorship, e.g. 'Carlsberg, official beer of the England team'. Nice event, OK turnout, also getting loads of bids now re. McBride. Followed Kevin Maguire [*Daily Mirror* political journalist] on *Daily Politics* and pointed out people like him drank this poison the whole time. Book signing went OK, then more media, and a tour of the stands.

Went in for Balls's speech which was OK without being great. It was classic GB as well, going well beyond his brief and with loads of name checks. He was diddling on HS2 [high-speed railway], which was pretty stupid, as Andrew Adonis said when I bumped into him later. Fringe meeting went fine, speeches from Eric Appleby and me, then Diane Abbott who committed even more than Andy had to MUP. Then off to the Grand for the Thousand Club dinner. I was sitting opposite and ended up having a massive row with an actor, Larry Lamb, who said that we should not be spending money on aid for foreigners when we had so many children starving in the UK. I gave him the chance to rephrase but he didn't so I ended up asking why he didn't donate to the BNP instead. He was really taken aback. I probably was a bit OTT, but I gave him a few facts on aid, and why it was of benefit here as well as there, and how these populist arguments were a menace. It kicked off in style before Tessa moved in and calmed it down. But I was furious. Charlie asked me to do a little speech at the dinner, which went down fine and in which I said what I had been saying a bit in the media, on the need for more fight and strategy and energy and grip. But it was all winnable. Did STV – really good interview – then out to Steve Coogan's house where he was having a party for Hacked Off supporters and MPs. Beautiful girlfriend Loretta who was half his age, and Gloria De Piero. Coogan a good lad, JP there a bit pissed, but as always good fun. Conference was generally feeling a bit flat though.

Tuesday 24 September

Went out for a walk, bumped into Stephan Rousseau [Press Association photographer] who was complaining about how useless the party was at pictures 'since your day'. Breakfast with Steve Kinnock, who was still looking for a seat, and hopeful. Talked a lot re. Calum and also Helle, who was being suggested by Merkel and others as the next European Commission President. Merkel was clearly going to win again, though it was not yet clear who the coalition would be with. Helle was worried about leaving Denmark. The polls were not good and she was unlikely to win, but she did not feel she could just jump ship. Steve felt also that it was possible to make an argument it was good for Denmark, which it was. But how they would live their lives, heaven knows. Then later I sent Helle a text and said I was on the side of doing it.

I got driven home after a couple of interviews and watched Ed's speech while tidying my desk. He delivered it well and the message was strong, living standards, and endlessly repeated, 'this is Britain, we can do better than this'. The Tories and the media were straight out with 'lurch to the left' because of the freeze on energy prices, and our defence was not robust enough. Then later Peter M gave out some quotes critical of it, suggesting it was reversing his approach to industrial policy. I tweeted 'it is more New Deal than Old Labour' and he went mad, saying I was being wound up by Baldwin, this was an attack on him blah, and then a rather unpleasant, 'At least I know you think it is fine for us to attack each other.' I said you are being ridiculous and he said, 'You are back to your old self' and it all got a bit silly. I said I really did not want to fall out but I felt we should at least let Ed get his arguments across without us making it harder for him.

Wednesday 25 September

I was trying to get good people for the Alcohol Concern run next Monday. Texted Joey Barton who said he was up for it if Harry Redknapp let him off training. I called Harry who said, 'Yeah, no problem, Al, he don't do much in training anyway!' Joe Hemani meanwhile wanted a hundred of the books to give to staff. Schools also asking, so it was going well. So far all five-star reviews on Amazon too.

In to do Iain Dale who was at the centre of a bit of a storm re. a fight on live TV with Stuart Holmes [anti-nuclear protestor] who had gate-crashed a photo op with McBride. Iain was McBride's publisher and trying to persuade me that it was worth reading. We did a newsy bit, when I ruled out standing in Burnley, as I had done with *The Times*, and then re. the book. But I could tell he was distracted and eventually I sat down and gave him a bit of calm down advice. Later he would have to go to the cops and get a caution and I rewrote his statements as he drafted them. He was too close to it all.

Up to Milton Keynes, collected by Sean Dyche, met Rory and off to a pub for lunch. Really liked Dyche and could see why he was doing well. Interesting that he never made personal criticisms of the players. Good on psychology. Clearly well organised. Filled him in on Harry Redknapp's assessment of us being good front to back, but the problem was if we had injuries we were in trouble. He was really good with Rory who could definitely hold his own in terms of football discussion. He was good fun and clearly heading for manager of the month. *Der Spiegel* called for an interview re. Merkel win. Then I started to get messages about Asda and Tesco selling 'mental patient' psycho Halloween fancy dress costumes. That they did showed how far we have still got to go. Sick. Tweeted, 'What on earth possesses these people?' Then started to get bids for the morning.

Thursday 26 September

Meeting at Portland then loads of interviews on the Asda–Tesco–Amazon story. Really easy target and thanks to social media and the pressure of the arguments we were making across radio and TV, local and national, they pulled them within hours. Real win for social media and also the Time to Change campaign. Watched *Question Time* where the two politicians,

Douglas A and Michael Gove, really outclassed the rest of the panel. Gove toasted Will Self. I even tweeted a moderately favourable tweet re. Gove destroying him. Gove also exposed the Tory worry about the Ed energy plan to freeze prices, as he did not go for it in a big way, and later he virtually love-bombed Douglas.

Friday 27 September

Meeting at home with Paul Mace, a Midlands-based PR who was working for the NFL in the UK and wanted a pre meeting before I had a meeting with NFL comms vice-president Paul Hicks and three senior Brits who were involved in the sport. There were two matches in London in the coming weeks, the first one this weekend, and they wanted a discussion about how to get London as a base for one of the thirty-two teams. Basically they had hit saturation point with the US market, which was at $9 billion a year, and wanted to get into Europe, with UK and Germany the obvious places. The London games had always gone well but clearly getting a team based here was a much bigger thing and there would be resistance because of jetlag.

The new Fulham chairman [Shahid Kahn] was an NFL owner and there was a feeling he might be the one. I felt politically and economically and PR-wise they would be able to make the argument and win it, but their problems would be over there. Paul [Mace], Rory and I went to the Landmark where the NFL big shots were staying. They were very open, said they wanted to bring a team here and needed big-picture strategic advice on how to do it. Hicks said the commissioner was keen and saw it as a big piece of his legacy. I said they needed to understand the UK was fanatical about sport in a way no other country was. That was good, but there was massive competition precisely because we had so many major sporting events and clubs every week. More big sporting events in London most weekends than perhaps any city in the world. But I was sure they could build a massive fan base though they might need to do more community activity and discounting than they did in the US where it was a money machine and where a lot of poorer people were totally priced out of it.

I also said that they would need to develop talent in the UK and in schools, and they would have to have UK connections that were meaningful. Suggested they also got into sports journalism colleges to develop Brits who would write about it. Important too to bring the best of broadcasters and help drive up standards of broadcasts in other sports too e.g. use of in-play analytics. They wanted me to try to meet the commissioner when he was over for the game next month. They said every team who had been over had liked the experience and been amazed at how knowledgeable the British fans were.

Saturday 28 September

Off to Burnley, taking Marion Van Renterghem from *Le Monde* having suggested that she get out of London for a better perspective on the so-called
economic recovery. Also meant that I could share the driving as I was
feeling pretty tired. Peter Reid [football manager] came as my guest and
saw us at our best, playing well front to back and easily beating Charlton
3–0. At this rate we were heading for promotion. Marion felt the trip had
been worthwhile though wanted to come back to do a bigger piece and
also to do something on Scotland and the referendum debate. My sense
was that she was not too impressed by Cameron or our politics more
generally.

Ed M called as we were driving up re. how to respond to a *Mail* piece
about his dad [Ralph, New Left sociologist] headlined: 'The man who
hated Britain', which was so over the top and could easily backfire on
the *Mail*. I said the minimum should be a right of reply. He spoke to the
deputy editor – Dacre clearly being too grand – and they came back and
said they would give him right of reply but Dacre was away and wanted
to oversee it and could they wait to Tuesday? I said just tell them you
would therefore announce on Monday you would be getting right of
reply, otherwise they would try to string you along and wriggle out of it.
He did sound very wound up about it, said these people are total cunts,
but he had already taken on Murdoch and now the *Mail*, so it was a big
decision. Tom Baldwin and I were both arguing that it was a total waste
of time, that they were always going to try to kill him and he could get
good strength and definition out of this.

Took Marion to Manchester airport then into town for the Tory conference where Kate G's friend Ameet Gill met me and helped me get
accredited. He was one of Cameron's speechwriters but said the speech
was virtually done so we ended up going for dinner with Thea Rogers
[special adviser], who despite being basically Labour had been hired by
Osborne. Getting lots of funny looks from Tories alongside locals coming up and saying it was great to see me there and they hoped I gave the
Tories hell. Ameet amused. We had a chat about the different way we
did speeches – sounded similar in some ways, e.g. meet before holiday,
write argument and key sections, then hone and heavy lift in the last few
weeks. But they seemed to keep it tighter than we did, also definitely got
it finished before we did. Chatted to Thea about some of Osborne's odd
mannerisms on TV, especially the way that his face started to answer the
question in a rather smug way before the questioner had finished. They
agreed they were never going to shed the posh boy image but that in fact
Cameron was much less of a people person than George.

Sunday 29 September

Staying at the Hilton, thankfully not one of the main conference hotels. Did *C4 News* on Eric Pickles telling a woman to 'change her medication' though later Pickles persuaded me there was more to it than meets the eye, and C4 dropped it. Spent a fair bit of time with *Daily Politics* working on a piece for them about me being at conference but also the Alcohol Concern campaign which was getting good play and a lot of interest. Watched Cameron on *Marr* and felt Marr got the better of him. He seemed a bit tetchy and clearly didn't like the fact that Ed was making the weather after his speech. They were well into the 'lurch to the left' line. The *Mail* attack was running on the news and Cameron broadly supported Ed's response without going for the *Mail*. But this was definitely going to go big and could help Ed get definition. Could also overshadow the Tories.

I was out and about pushing my usual line that it was a poison and Dacre the biggest debaser of public life. Ameet fixed me a good meeting with Arminka Helic, Hague's Bosnian spad, who I really liked. She had come from Bosnia in the '90s, hated the Major government handling on the issue, loved what we did re. Kosovo but rather than joining us decided to join the Tories to try to get them to change tack and ended up working for Hague. She was very bright, also told me that she was thrilled I was working for Zlatko in Bosnia because she had recommended it. She felt the SDP was the best hope and the only serious party. She was thrilled too that in Kosovo Edi was planning to develop a pan Balkan strategy and was sure she could get political support though she said the official FCO line was less warm. But she was sure we could develop the cohesion of the seven – Albania, Serbia, Kosovo, Macedonia, Montenegro, Bosnia, Croatia – and Edi felt maybe Slovenia were warming too even though they did not like to be seen as Balkan. She was really excited at the idea we might be able to take this forward and wanted to be kept in touch the whole way through.

Daily Politics was interesting in that I reckon eight out of ten of the people I spoke to supported our line on minimum unit pricing and treatment and some of them were pretty strong in their view that Cameron had done the wrong thing in his U-turn. Managed to get Michael Fallon [Energy Secretary] and Patrick McLaughlin [Transport Secretary] squirming on it on camera – not my department kind of thing. Nice chat with Grant Shapps who seemed a little bit shallow but nicer than I had been led to believe. One of his people said the only people anyone seemed too interested in at the conference were me, Boris Johnson and Nigel Farage [leader UK Independence Party].

Dinner with Danny Finkelstein, Andrew Cooper and a polling friend of theirs. They all felt Ed had moved to the left and would pay a price. I was defending the speech. Also got the sense that Cameron had not really worked out a response. Danny said that the battle line was all about the recovery, that Ed had tried to make it about 'for all' and he claimed that whereas the Tories claimed 'recovery' but without the 'for all,' in part because they were out of touch but also because the recovery was not really touching so many parts of the country e.g. the north. Lovely chat with Rakhee who was terrific, just what you needed for this kind of operation, calm and always looking out for me re. food and water and rest, and good with the media. Gave her a reference, high marks out of ten.

Monday 30 September

Breakfast with Peter Reid, Joey Barton and Mark Covell then off with them, Andy Gregory [rugby league player] and Lou Macari [former footballer] to Albert Square for the Alcohol Concern run. Good media turnout, waited for Jill Scott [footballer] then set off. It felt a lot longer than 5k. Lou Macari struggling with really bad knees. Barton was good as gold, chatted to everyone, did all the media he was asked to. Eric Appleby of Alcohol Concern and I spoke at the breakfast and also got Jill Scott and Joey to speak. Both terrific. Jill really good on how hard it is to resist peer pressure when other girls are trying to get you to go on the piss and you want to choose the sporting route. She was really nice, bright too. Joey spoke of his own past and also how we needed to act as ambassadors within sport. I was pushing the line not just about pricing and treatment but also availability and sports marketing.

5 Live had figures released via FoI [Freedom of Information Act] about the number of teenagers as young as ten and eleven in hospital through drink so I pushed that too, and the book, and the campaign more generally, in two hours of radio interviews at Media City [Manchester]. Lovely place, great atmosphere and energy there. Back for book signing which went well, them ended abruptly when Ann Widdecombe [former Tory minister] came over and said it was her slot now. The bookseller said she was like a machine. Then finished the *Daily Politics* film, hung around then more media, then LBC fixed a meeting in George Best's favourite pub, the Circus Tavern, which had one of the smallest bars in Europe, for a debate with Farage on booze. He had a couple of rather odd-looking bods with him. I found him more intelligent than I expected to, and very personable, but the Europe obsession kept coming through. He accepted there was a booze crisis but did not want to operate lower price controls.

He had been prevented from attending conference so I used the line it must mean he is a threat and I am a has-been. Back to the hotel for more media and then the fringe meeting, which went well. Better attended than the one at Labour, and we did a proper Q&A, including with the health services minister Dan Poulter when he arrived, and he got quite a hard time, not least from two liver specialists who described the kind of thing they were dealing with and said they did not need to wait for evidence of how minimum pricing in Scotland worked because the evidence was clear. The minister was nice and reasonable, met his wife later who was Labour! But when a woman said she had been this morning at her son's inquest – he had died of alcohol-related illnesses – there was hardly a dry eye in the house.

Dr Kieran Moriarty from Bolton was really passionate about the damage it was doing to people as individuals and to the NHS as an institution. Another doctor looked like he was going to explode when Poulter defended their inaction. The two fringes had gone really well, charity happy, Lundbeck happy, media happy, and I had bumped into Jeremy Hunt who said they had 'definitively not ruled out' MUP. Ameet told me Cameron was just not going to revisit it because this was all part of Lynton Crosby paring down the campaign to bare essentials, but I felt we could definitely get Labour to the right place.

The mood around the conference was quite flat and lacking in energy. More lobbyists than activists and it was much more stage-managed than in the old days. Portland dinner – I was at Tim Allan's table with a No. 10 policy guy called Alex who like most of them was obsessed with the Blair machine and how I operated in No. 10 – they were all pretty vile about the civil service – and Danny Finkelstein, a guy from Heathrow, Kamal Ahmed [*Telegraph* business editor], a minister from Guernsey, and Emma Reynolds of InBev. I went off on one to their amusement but actually she did also want a serious discussion. When Tim spoke he did a very funny thing about what my Britain would be like – no drinking, no gambling, all work apart from everyone is allowed to watch Burnley and attend party and AA meetings. Danny spoke well, entertaining.

I worked the tables a bit, including Shapps's and Owen Paterson's spads, a few of their clients but all got a bit dramatic when one of the Tory Party rebuttal team – a rather attractive woman in a slit dress – fainted and crashed to the ground. George Pascoe-Watson [Portland] and I helped her up as someone went for help. Nice enough do, then gate-crashed the *Telegraph*. Long chat with Osborne, half humorous half serious. He felt his speech had gone OK but I had not sensed that around the place. He also kept saying Ed had buried New Labour. Daniel Korski there with Laura Trott [David Cameron spad]. He was now in No. 10 so I filled him in, and later got over David Lidington [minister of state for Europe], to talk about the Balkans stuff. Crosby's wife [Dawn] seemed quite nice. Clearly a power in the home I would say, and in the office. They were now over full-time. He was quite funny just saying to everyone who came over that I was using them as a book promotion tool.

Tuesday 1 October

Off to collect Rory at Retford – he was going to see Burnley at Doncaster – lunch with Mum, Liz and Graeme – then back for a kip before heading off to Trent College in Long Eaton where I was doing a speech and a dinner. Meanwhile it emerged Jon Staefel, deputy editor of the *Mail*, had agreed to do *Newsnight* who were desperate for me to debate with him. So was I but I kept them on tenterhooks both via logistics and also re. whether I would. Did a no-notes speech on my life and also the importance of politics, book signing then the dinner which I turned into a debate on whether I should do *Newsnight*. I was sitting next to a fantastically clever girl from Moldova, Victoria, who spoke six languages and had learned French – which she spoke beautifully – in three months. Nice kids all of them, but as ever in these private schools I was struck by the thought that everyone could do this well if they just had the proper support and opportunities. I said in the speech that I passionately opposed private education for that reason, because 7 per cent got 70 per cent of the top jobs etc.

The vote was 100 per cent to do *Newsnight* so I did. Drove to BBC Nottingham, where a nice old guy looked after me. I had emailed round TB, Tim and a few others and got a general line about being calm and dissecting. I certainly dissected, maybe went OTT once or twice but just did not let go of him and forced an admission that the use of the picture of Ed's dad's grave with the caption 'grave socialist' was an error of judgement. Got massive response on Twitter, apparently their second most tweeted interview ever. Overwhelmingly positive and saying that it was about time someone stood up to them. 'Where is Dacre?' was my most repeated line.

The radio station greeter said he could not believe I had managed to do that down the line like that without even being able to see the people. Felt totally on top of the arguments and felt this was a real opportunity to get them on the back foot. Ed, who had really wanted me to do it, called and said, 'Fucking brilliant, you nailed them.' Finally managed to get up my line about the *Mail* being the worst of British values posing as the best. Wired and tired and no way I could drive home, so I stayed in a hotel opposite the Beeb. Meanwhile we beat Doncaster 2–0 to go top of the league. Incredible.

Wednesday 2 October

Really hammering the *Mail* on Twitter now. Having called Dacre a coward and a bully, I was encouraging the media to doorstep him and started to hint at his address, which Roy Greenslade got for me. Also talking up the Scottish estate and the business of his wealth. It was really taking off against him and the *Mail*. 5 Live replaying our exchanges from last night. Today much more focused on the error of judgement acceptance. Took hours to get home. To Canary Wharf for a nice event – Light the Night – sponsored by Barclays, Morgan Stanley and Thomson Reuters – for LLR and the US equivalent. Little speech, then the walk, all holding lanterns. Raised good money. *Mail* still running big and Dacre's only sighting was being driven away hiding behind the *FT*. Alex Thomson at *C4 News* really going for it.

Then Ed M called to tell me that he had been at his uncle's memorial at Guy's Hospital today, and after he left, relatives were approached by a woman who offered condolences and then started asking them about the 'grave socialist' row with the *Mail*. She said she was from the *Mail on Sunday*. 'Fuckers. Fucking, fucking fuckers.' I said he should first ask Geordie Greig [editor] if true or not – which he did, and it was, and Greig told Bob Roberts he was mortified – then write to [Lord] Rothermere demanding a proper inquiry into this. He was first reluctant to go to Rothermere but eventually came round to it, but he said he would sleep on it. A statement did the rounds and we all chipped in. They did far too much round-robin stuff.

Meanwhile someone from the party had got me in touch with change.org who helped me launch a petition to do a TV debate with Dacre which was instantly into the thousands. Still raging massively on Twitter, getting a bit nasty though with someone publishing pictures of the house and also our full address. I was probably tweeting too much but was determined to flush him out and to get the bully and coward and hypocrite line to stick. Others were now piling in behind me as well, which meant the momentum was growing and with both Dacre and Rothermere going to ground, they were totally on the back foot.

Thursday 3 October

Fiona off early to Paris to sort out Grace's accommodation, which she did by agreeing to [French friend] Emily Senes's studio. Ed M had asked to see me and I wandered round there for 8.30. Geordie Greig having said last night he was appalled and would apologise had clearly been got at and was saying now he would not. We had a conference call of Ed's main people and though he was initially reluctant agreed he should write to Rothermere about it and ask for an inquiry into their practices etc. Tom B was really the only one instinctively in the same place as I was. Bob Roberts seeming to think it would be possible to draw some kind of improved relationship with them. They did have a tendency to go round in circles but I suppose we did at times too.

Ed made some coffee, we sat down in the front room, and he asked me pretty much straight out whether I would go back and run his campaign. I said I was reluctant. I was happy to help, as I had been doing, but I did not want all that strain and the pain in the arse of endless meetings. He said that he was having a reshuffle next week – Stephen Twigg [shadow Education Secretary] and Liam Byrne [shadow Work and Pensions Secretary] out for Tristram Hunt and Rachel Reeves – with Gloria [De Piero] and maybe one or two others. The choice for campaign co-ordinator was Douglas A or Michael Dugher [shadow Minister Without Portfolio]. I said I could work with Douglas, didn't know Dugher but felt he was pretty GB-ish. He said neither was perfect, and he was worried about Douglas's ability to work with Balls – who was staying but who might still move later – and also what he called 'paralysis of analysis'.

He laid on the flattery, said the last few days had shown, re. alcohol and the *Mail*, that there was nobody who could campaign and drive a message like I could, and he would like me in there as much as possible. I said I felt it went OK as it was, and I did not yet want to get sucked in more. He seemed to accept that but did keep coming back to it. He felt strengthened by the last week or two, felt he had done well at conference and the Tories less so. Certainly, as I had seen in Manchester, he was making the weather on policy and strategy perhaps for the first time. He wanted Charlie back in too, but not Peter, said he did not feel he could trust him totally. He said what he had learned in recent months was that the people to value were the ones who were plain decent. He was very down on Jim Murphy. He had called him in to try to read the Riot Act and he had gone straight to Rosie Winterton [Labour MP] and said, 'I don't mind taking it from a strong leader, but not a weak one.' He was thinking of moving him to NI, knowing he would probably not take it.

We talked a bit about policy, and I was pressing him again to seize this mental health agenda, and he seemed vaguely to get it. He was not sure what to do about Andy Burnham, who he said was obsessed by social care to the exclusion of other areas. Justine popped in and out, looked OK, less tired than at conference. He was in OK shape, but I emphasised he must win this battle with the *Mail*, but constantly emphasise that the public have better and bigger things to worry about. He said he was confident he could win but he needed me in there. It was clear there was no chance of David [brother] being involved. Sad.

Pottered at home a bit then off to the Royal Society of Arts for a discussion on mental health with Ruby Wax. She was quite a livewire. We just about managed to make it work as a double act, her on mindfulness, me on sort of accepting depression. She had not had a bad bout for seven years so maybe there was something in what was she saying. Q&A all fine, a few good laughs, short book signing then I was doing interviews re. the *Mail on Sunday*, Greig having apologised but, keeping the focus on Dacre and now Rothermere. Police were keeping an eye on the house after a few threatening tweets including with pictures of the house and reference to the alarm system. Did a bit of a schmooze around the Portland office, Bradders loving the *Mail* stuff, then to Millbank first for a disco with John Whittingdale who felt the *Mail* attack was OK – comment if in bad taste – but the *MoS* was not, and then Sky where I was pretty much on full-frontal attack.

Also tweeting now re. Dacre, where is Wally, *Wo ist Wally*, *Où est Wally* etc. getting T-shirts made, usual stuff. To the Fleming Collection, event for Scottish landowners. Mix of Hoorays, public-school Tories, rich Anglo Scots. Mainly spoke on devolution and the referendum and warned them it could still be lost and they should get their hands in their pockets. The economic case was strong. Emphasised the power case too – could we seriously stay on UN Permanent 5 if we lost Scotland? One of them met Charlie on a train later and said it was the most persuasive argument for the union yet and I ought to go up there. The Dacre petition had reached 40k plus.

Friday 4 October
Off early with Rayan for the flight to Vienna. Did more than usual covering up of the *Mail* in the freebie bins. CNN asked for a blog which I worked on and sent from Vienna, sparking four days of lawyers trying to get me to tone it down. Sat next to a very nice guy, a retired cardiac surgeon Ken Taylor who had overseen TB's heart fixing at the Hammersmith. Off to a conference in Vienna. His wife had died three years ago and not long after us meeting he was showing me the framed picture of her he took everywhere. I really did not want Fiona to predecease me. I could not cope. He said lots of friends tried to fix him up with another woman from time to time but he was not interested. I thought he would make an interesting addition to my grief book.

I landed at Tirana and I was not on the VIP list for the bus out. Hilariously, Berisha's son came out and came to my rescue, again. He was just back from Stockholm, was warm and charming, introduced me to a businessman as 'the man who helped Rama beat us' but did it with a smile. Jamie was there to meet me and said he worried Vali, Endri and all of them were being overwhelmed. Edi was in his vast office, where I had first met Berisha. Tidy, seemed calm, and we went over a poll which showed two things – a boost for him, with real relief at change, but also massively high expectations.

Ricardo Hausmann [Venezuelan economist] had said to Edi that his big challenge was going to be how to communicate the scale of the economic challenge and keep the people with him. He said that was why he needed me. My own visit got bogged down in a ridiculous and extraordinary row about office space. Edi's office was half the size of a football pitch. Endri's office across the way was the size of a tennis court. Vali's round the corner was the size of a squash court.

I suggested Edi move to where Endri was, and Edi's office become a private office with key people – maybe up to six or eight. Endri and Vali were resistant, and though they claimed it was not about status etc. I was not so sure. They said they needed space to think and speak privately. I said you could have meeting rooms for that. Edi said that he would go crazy with it as it was, having to wander around the place trying to find them, and also the building totally lacked energy.

We barely discussed policy or speeches or priorities. Ridiculous. Dinner with Edi, Meta, Endri and Jamie. Meta was very well informed about UK politics. They had both seen snatches of our conferences. We agreed expectations were too high, also that they had to emphasise how bad things were. They were going to have to do a version of the Tories' 'mess we inherited' plus 'only just begun, don't go back' at next election. He saw that. He felt Berisha had lost the plot which was going to help Edi, but that was why they really needed to press on now. He thought the team was OK, right mix of younger and older. Edi on good form, worried re. Endri and Vali who was exhausted. Susan from USAID good.

Saturday 5 October

Swim first thing, then wrote a note to them all on the need for change, and why they would get energy and direction from positioning themselves closer to Edi, all in the same space.

I enlisted Jonathan who started by saying, 'Endri and Vali have a point' but concluded, 'Alastair is right.' I sent that bit round, Endri alighted on the other bit, much to Edi's annoyance. He had been making a joke of it all but said, 'I am sick of this.'

Jamie was doing well and sent a note round immediately on the meetings structure I had recommended. Ultimately Edi was going to have to grip this, but I was also going to have to go back soon.

Driver brought his fourteen-year-old English-speaking son with him and we set off on a near-eight-hour journey through Albania, Montenegro, Republika Srpska [part of Federation of Bosnia and Herzegovina] then

Bosnia–Srpska. Slept a bit, wrote a bit, admired the scenery a lot, in parts, as I texted to Fiona, like a cross between Conaglen and Provence. Stopped at a café on the Montenegro RS border, a bit *Borat*, but good news came through, Burnley 2 Reading 0. On fire. Toby Helm [*Observer*] and Tom Baldwin called asking for my help in getting third parties to whack the *Mail*. Eventually they went with Anthony Seldon [educator and writer] and a bishop.

Tired on arrival, booked into Europe Hotel, then dinner with Zlatko and Jasenko. Chat re. other countries in the region. Filled them in on Arminka Helic, who he knew all about, Daniel Sorski and David Liddington. Then planned tomorrow. He went through all the people who would be there. First the main strategy group for the morning, then a broader group, then a Q&A. We reprised some of our earlier discussions, e.g. the only serious party, only multi-ethnic party, and also started to explain how we had done the road to the manifesto process, and also taking on the critical voices. Zlatko had decided to do a big interview with a TV commentator critic on Monday based on that. He was a major note-taker with two books, constantly flicking through them, and also a major process-talker. I said I had watched some of his speeches and interviews and he must become sharper, clearer, briefer, more political, less professorial. Didn't sleep too well. Lots of weddings and parties and noise down below.

Sunday 6 October

Out for a run then Jasenko picked me up and we headed for the SDP HQ, a fairly old-style building shared with a government department. I did my usual strategy workshop stuff and got them working on objectives and strategy and they were pretty good. All also more or less in the same place – win and be the biggest party with a big role in government, and all based around future, change and team.

Most of them spoke some English but we had interpreters who occasionally had to stop and slow us down. I tried to avoid getting sucked in to too much of the political system, also banned 'the problem is', which became a bit of a running joke. We spent the morning with the inner group which included Zlatko, Jasenko, Sasa, Lydia, Dino who I had met in Prague, a couple of ministers and the very impressive PM of Herzegovina. Later did a version of the same thing with a bigger group.

Charlie called and so did Gail about the impending shadow Cabinet reshuffle. Ed wanted Charlie in as shadow Attorney General and wanted to say something about me going back. Gail felt no. She felt I was in a good place and don't risk it as I could easily tip back and I did not need to do full-time. I could still help. Dinner with Zlatko and our ambassador

Nigel Casey. Liked him. He clearly liked Zlatko. Was interested in the pan-Balkan stuff from Edi. Was clear that SDP probably best bet but the politics was so complicated. Ed M called later. Clearly Tristram Hunt to education and Rachel Reeves to work and pensions would be the news. I did not want to be in the mix for now but said I was happy to keep helping him.

Monday 7 October

To the foreign ministry for a session with Zlatko. He was going into a Lion's Den interview and we went over how to deal with it – big point at the top on new politics, clarity and brevity. We had agreed on a road to the manifesto process yesterday so we agreed we would trail that too. I had to leave before he did it but according to Jasenko it was recognised as the best he has done. Zlatko seemed to think he had got a lot out of it and so did Jasenko. Flew to Munich and then home. I got a text from Osborne saying thanks for book and what would an alcohol strategy look like. I worked on a note and later emailed him.

Tuesday 8 October

Grace was not settling in well so I went off to Paris. Met the Senes with her for lunch. Nice lunch in an old-fashioned French restaurant and then she and I just walked around and talked. She was very up and down and later when talking to Fiona just started crying. Bad anxiety and feeling like maybe the whole thing had been a mistake. Eric Appleby sent through some good thoughts re. a note for Osborne. Jeremy Hunt's people also on saying he would like to discuss MUP. No doubt he had heard Osborne was talking to me and so wanted to make sure if it turned into a big cause he would be engaged from the health angle, and not undone by George.

Wednesday 9 October

Really worried about Grace. Never seen her as upset as she was last night. Had to go back for meetings at Portland. Then a speech to a conference for *The Economist*. John Scarlett and Stephen Page [digital security adviser] on first re. cybercrime. John quite impressive as a speaker though neither of them really left me much better informed. Chinese clearly a nightmare for everyone. They both said the Edward Snowden revelations in *The Guardian* had done enormous damage to intelligence gathering.* Scarlett was

---

* Central Intelligence Agency employee Edward Snowden had turned whistleblower with disclosures revealing numerous US global surveillance programmes.

October '13: Working on alcohol note for Osborne

shocked that an outside contractor had such access. Idil Oyman [Portland] and I did a double act on crisis comms. Ed M was on *Watchdog* re. energy prices. Did OK though Annie [Robinson] called me later and said he had a few mannerisms and verbal tics that got on people's nerves and she was happy to see him and advise. The best thing at the moment was that at least people were talking about policy, and he was making a few waves.

Thursday 10 October

World Mental Health Day. Did a blog on that then off to Portland, then talk-SPORT supposedly to talk about the book but it was mainly sport. Colin Murray interviewing with Kelly Sotherton [former heptathlete] and Danny Murphy [ex-footballer]. She was a good laugh, he was bright. Off to the Commons terrace for WMHD Time to Change event. Had a good chat with Clegg, gave him a copy of the novel and said I hoped he could push on alcohol as he had on mental health. He said his secret desire was to write a novel. He looked pretty tired but spoke well. I sensed the Liberals were doing some of the better stuff in government, at least trying to. I doubt there was that much Clegg and I would disagree on if he had a free hand.

Meanwhile we had the Bank of England, Unilever and Legal and General all signing up today to Time to Change. The Bank said the presentation I had done had been the thing that swung them. *Total Politics* had decided to do my interview as front cover so they wanted more pictures. Did them at Portcullis House plus a bit more chat with Sam Macrory [editor *Total Politics*]. Nice guy. Liked him. Then to Euston Rd, Royal College of GPs to meet Martin Baggaley [psychiatrist], medical director of the Maudsley to chat about the series for the *Radio Times* piece. Liked him too.

Friday 11 October

Chatted to Annie about tonight, when she was going to be interviewing me on the novel and life and times at Cheltenham Literature Festival. Did a bit of telly then two events. First me and Annie which was good. Nice intro from Gail. Good chemistry with Annie. Shifted a few books. Later did a session with Pilou Asbæk, the Danish actor from *Borgen*, Martin Dobbs [writer, former Margaret Thatcher spad] and Emily Maitlis [TV presenter] re. political drama. Couple of signings then home.

Sunday 13 October

Tristram Hunt's first outing as shadow Education Secretary in the *MoS* of all places, followed up on *Marr*, and all a bit too much on the Tory agenda, saying he wasn't going to shut free schools. Also Rachel Reeves first outing at welfare saying we would be as tough as the Tories. Spoke to Ed who said it was not deliberate, and he was confident both were going to be good.

Monday 14 October
LBC meeting to discuss programme next week. Lunch with Zlatko at the National Portrait Gallery. He felt progress was being made. The big constitutional stuff was difficult though. He was happy his interviews had gone better. To Mumsnet for a session on booze, taking questions submitted by their followers, which went fine.

Tuesday 15 October
Mum down for a few days, met her with Rory, then to his flat. In the evening I had to do a driving speed awareness course to get out of more points on my licence. Angel. Chinese guy taking the course who spotted me straight away. Interesting mix of people. It was actually quite an interesting course and might make me slow down in future. COAST – concentration, observation, anticipation, space and time.

Thursday 17 October
Madrid, to the Danish ambassador's residence for the Lundbeck event. Sixty or so medics and experts. I spoke OK but wasn't terribly motivated. Tweeted about the Danes saying they were worried they were adopting an Anglo-Saxon drinking model. We really did have a booze reputation. The ambassador was a very nice woman. She was born with only one arm and only wore a prosthetic because her son wanted her to. She was very fond of Helle, and though it was difficult she thought the opposition were beginning to make mistakes and there might be a chance yet. Helle was still being chased re. EU job by Merkel. Speech and short Q&A, lunch then off to the airport. Lundbeck really good to work with. Flew to Brussels then Birmingham and off to Hinckley Island for tomorrow's event.

Friday 18 October
Society of Local Council Clerks. Good bunch. Just did a flipboard presentation half on strategy and half played for laughs. Book signing then home. Potter. To the hospital for blood tests as I was still feeling crap. Round to Rachel and Stuart's then out for dinner with them, Neil and Glenys. Neil raging re. Tristram. Glenys seemed a bit subdued. Rachel funny but

also telling us Tim Livesey was a nightmare, totally obsessed about status. She said Ed was improving but it still sounded like the office was a bit dysfunctional.

Saturday 19 October

Ipswich away with Calum. Boardroom for lunch – lots of posh sorts – then to the away end. Good win [one–nil].

Sunday 20 October

Still feeling rough. Ed M came round later to discuss stuff. Still pressing for me to do more. Preferably full-time. Balls clearly a problem. Not totally sure re. Douglas etc. I suggested working back from five big talking points policies. He seemed more confident and had realised that when you make the weather on policy, you have a chance. He was pressing for me either to come back and do the campaign or to take a seat late on. Still quite confident, and aware of his issues. He said there was no chance of David coming back, and I sensed things had got worse rather than better.

Monday 21 October

To LBC, standing in for Iain Dale. First hour on addiction with Addaction [drug, alcohol and mental health charity] CEO Simon Antrobus, Amy Winehouse's stepmum and a recovering alcoholic called Hannah! How weird that she should have the same name as the self-harming addict in my novel. Her arms were covered the whole length in scars. Russell Brand joined us for a bit. Good value. He really was a bright guy, and funny, but also knew his stuff. Then did living standards, police and then the impact of alcohol on the NHS with Dr Mehta, who had looked after me in the Royal Free. LBC were keen for me to do more, maybe a regular show. I enjoyed it OK but not enough to want to do all the time.

I got a nice email from George Osborne re. *My Name Is...* said he had addiction issues in the family, also that he felt it really brought home just how pervasive alcohol is in UK society. He was slightly ducking MUP, but said the availability of rehab, education and court directions were all things they should be looking at. He asked me what I thought happened to Hannah in the future. I also thought it was a good sign if someone saw the fictional character as real, with a future beyond the book. 'I'd like to believe Hannah gets through it all,' he said. It was good that he had read it and I felt a door had opened re. policy. Also Hunt's office was in touch to meet up re. the same.

Tuesday 22 October

Jonathan Heaf from *GQ* came round, asking me to do the main interview slot. They said they had the idea when seeing me taking apart Staefel on the *Mail*. He was really keen. He said Dylan [Jones, editor] was desperate for me to do it, and I would have a lot of fun. *Total Politics* published. Good piece. The bits that were picked up were re. me still havering about being a candidate MP and my criticism of our move to 24-hour licensing. Huge coverage for AF book launch. He called me later, said he really didn't like the non-football journos. I said you never liked the football ones that much either!

Wednesday 23 October

Fiona off to Paris to collect Grace before we headed off to Faucon. I had to do a few interviews first for the book next week, the Irish Diaries. *Guardian*, Nick Watt and Patrick Wintour, Irish book the peg but they were more interested in Labour stuff. Then *Irish Examiner*. Andy Burnham call re. whether to sue Hunt over his claims Andy had wanted things covered up.[*] Gavin M thought he had a case. Andy wanted my view. I agreed but said be clear how far you might have to go. Don't sue unless prepared to see it through. He cannot be sure that Crosby/Hunt might want to have a legal battle, to keep it up in lights. Do not lose sight of the main battles.

Thursday 24 October

Out 5.30. Fly to Marseille. Hire car. Send my draft Cambridge Uni speeches on the media to John Lloyd [journalist, media commentator], Roy Greenslade. Good feedback and ideas for change. Fiona had a bit of a nightmare journey driving down. Unseasonably hot. Incredibly beautiful. Fiona arrived with Grace and Emily [Summers, friend]. Anxiety kicking in again. Both me and G.

Friday 25 October

First proper exercise in ages. Three hours on the bike. Trying to rest up work-wise. Still not feeling totally right. Also struggling to work out what I really wanted to say at times. Head not good.

---

[*] Around 7,000 more deaths than expected occurred in fourteen NHS trusts in the four years before Labour left power, when Burnham was latterly Health Secretary. Up to 2,800 of the deaths came after alarms were sounded about the Mid Staffordshire Hospital and reports criticised the quality of care there.

Saturday 26 October

Another OK ride. Edi called. TB had been there and Edi had said it was fine but he was still unsure how to use TB other than as voice and introducer. The reason for his call was chemical weapons. US and Russia seemed to have got the Syrians to disarm and were asking Albania, Norway and Belgium to act as hosts for dismantling. Belgium and Norway had said no. TB had said they needed to drive a hard bargain which I echoed. Compensation, and support for clean up more generally, but more importantly political support for their plans for EU integration/IMF/World Bank etc. A visit not just from John Kerry [US Secretary of State] but Obama. He said it was very tricky. Indeed it was but it was also a big opportunity. He wanted Albania to be seen as a player and taking a new approach and this did both.

He was worried about noises he was picking up about the Brits going cold on their EU candidate status plans. I wrote him a note. I also said assume everything you say and write on this is being tapped so take care. The Americans were getting a lot of grief for the allegations of tapping Merkel and others. It didn't mean it would stop. Spoke to TB and we agreed an approach re. Edi/US. My worry was the US not moving quickly enough and Edi was not pressing them hard enough. This was one of those things that had to have everything properly in place before it was announced – Obama and Edi to meet, big historic step, others lined up to be supportive, especially Merkel, nice noises from financial institutions, plus pledges of environmental and political support and a worked-through plan on the disarmament itself. He would need all of that to deal with the obvious negatives that would come with it.

There was still no word on Chilcot. Andy Burnham called for advice about his spat with Jeremy Hunt. The more he thought about it, the angrier he got and the more he wanted to sue for the allegation he covered up abuse as Health Secretary. It was clearly a Crosby thing to undermine the record. He had seen Gavin and Charlie and both felt he had a case. He said Ed was worried about it but he felt if he did not get a clear win on this we would not be heard. We beat QPR two–nil.

Sunday 27 October

Another chat with Edi on Syria/chemical weapons. He was pretty confident he could win support for the argument but agreed everything had to be in place. Dinner Senes etc. after I took Grace and Emily back to Avignon. I said yes to *GQ* but not starting till the New Year.

Monday 28 October

Doing lots on the speeches for Cambridge, taking in John Lloyd stuff.

Nice last day, chatting to Fiona re. how to make my time work better for me. I was spreading thin again and also not sleeping well. Then drove to Marseille, nice chat with a Burnley lad who had seen my tweet on our record being better than Barcelona. Flight a bit delayed then to Heathrow.

Tuesday 29 October

I couldn't sleep so went out for a run, sent a photo to F of my view – a plane flying over Starbucks. Then she sent hers – the sun rising over Mont Ventoux. Met Ed Victor at the gate and off we headed for our road trip to launch the Irish diaries. He seemed good, very good shape for seventy-five and we were going to have a good laugh. He was still pressing me re. Fergie collaboration on winning but I doubted it was going to happen. Fergie's book [*My Autobiography*] now the bestselling first week non-fiction ever. Ed was telling me the story of how he fell out with Peter Chadlington over the Andrew Marr collaboration on a novel [*Head of State*]. Peter had the idea – a leader who dies with a week to go to the election and they cover it up – but then going sour and hiring [author] J. K. Rowling's agent when publishers said it could only have Marr on cover. Lots of good stories and banter. Met by driver and taken to home of judge [Sir] Donnell Deeny and wife Alison, friends of Paul McGuinness and Kathy Gilfillan [wife]. She was very good fun. He told me, as did others, that the security situation was going backwards a bit. Letter bombs, extremes making more noise etc.

Into Belfast to do radio, then UTV, then the Belfast launch. Noel Hamilton [journalist] did the on-stage interview, Q&A then books. Long conference call with Endri and Vali on Syria. They sounded a bit panicky. The media were asking and they were holding back because they feared they were being manipulated into it by the Americans. They had made clear to the ambassador that they were pressing for Obama to endorse in person but he was pushing back a bit. I said have a line ready that does not commit but does make clear they are discussing. Out for dinner at the Ox then drive down to Dublin. Staying with Paul McGuinness and Kathy Gilfillan.

Wednesday 30 October

Wall to wall day. Out before seven and off to Breakfast TV. Two slots, review of news with a panel and then solo on the book. I did a big defence of Bertie Ahern, also warning on complacency about the peace process.* Phoners in

---

* Ahern experienced hostility following his resignation in the wake of the Mahon Tribunal into planning and payments to politicians. The Tribunal found that while not judged corrupt, Ahern received money from developers and disbelieved his explanations regarding the payments.

the car then to RTÉ and a really good interview. Then a mental health talk to students. Fantastic campus, nice students, good event in a lovely theatre. Also sold a fair few books considering a student audience. Questions very varied, only one on Iraq, fair few personal. Lunch with them and Ed then to the event at the Royal Hibernia Academy. Really good apart from a slightly dodgy sound system. Bertie came and said he was grateful for all the nice things I had been saying about him. When I defended him to the students, there had been a sense of genuine shock. It was better at the event and got a round of applause for defending him. I also made Jonathan – who was there for another event – stand up and take a bow. Miriam O'Callaghan, who is lovely, did the interview – tough but fair – and then a pretty good Q&A somewhat slowed by not one but two speeches by PJ Mara [ex-spokesmen to Charlie Haughey]. Dinner at Guibaud with Paul and Kathy, their daughter Alexandra, Ed – having a good time and sorting books for UK – John Banville [novelist and screenwriter] and friend. Good time, good trip, good press. Running second on the RTÉ news after doing clips.

Thursday 31 October

Breakfast, to the airport with Paul McG and Ed, Ed doing that thing he does of talking over what we did and then putting in new anecdotes on other people based on that. Paul a good guy, talked in much the same style. Another Twitter spat with Louise Mensch on the same thing as last time – was I being sexist retweeting a tweet suggesting she go on Page 3 and telling Murdoch to 'sort it out'. Got a bit nasty and personal and Grace called me and said cool it. Out with Mete Coban [social entrepreneur] to Greenwich Uni for talk to his all-party pro-politics group MyLifeMySay. Again good mood and good mix of politics and persona. Briefly to Soho for Portland Q3 results party. A bit loud and drunken for me but they seemed glad I went.

Friday 1 November

Into Portland to do a training session. Guy from Wonga [loans provider] was in and he came in and did an impromptu session. Good crowd. Lunch with Richard Layard on the mental health policy campaign. He was really pushing me into it. Sunday stuff then out with Rory to the Alex F book event at the Festival Hall. Packed of course. Terrific production values. Huge backdrop of the book, lights music etc. Eamonn Holmes did a great job as interviewer. It was a bit rowdy at times, very male. Some good laughs and Eamonn playing it for both serious and fun.

Bit of an incident on the way out when I was being stopped for photos and a guy came by shouting AC is a prick. Could see Rory bristling but he disappeared when some of the people around us pushed him on. After-party nice. Big Sam [Allardyce] who I pressed re. Rory and who agreed to see him Wednesday. He was knocking back the Moët like nobody's business. Fergie little speech. Nice chat.

Saturday 2 November

Donald was down for a piping contest, went to see him, so did Rory. But he didn't play well and was disappointed. Called our ambassador in Sofia who gave me a useful briefing about all the protests following the new government appointing a gangster to a senior intelligence position. To Millwall with Rayan – two–all after two–nil down – then to Burford for the Matthew Freud party. Totally OTT of course. Booze, all sorts of cuisine, tattoo parlour, four quality films on Bono and Geldof performing. Had a chat with George Osborne re. booze. He said he was interested in developing a strategy but he felt MUP was not possible because of pressure on living standards. It was a second term thing. I said so can we press re. the manifesto? Mainly talking to Jamie [Rubin] and Christiane [Amanpour]. Jamie and Jimmy Carr both saying how much they loved the fact News [International] were in such trouble. Jimmy Carr said, 'So there are two press secretaries called AC. One did a great job and isn't going to jail. You must be loving it.'

Played the pipes after a near disaster when a reed fell into the bag. Gail and the girls there. TB and Queen Rania. TB looked stressed. Chat to Nat Rothschild re. addiction. Good speech by Matthew and a great film by the kids and his daughter sang a lovely song. We stayed till about one. Nigella [Lawson] and the Hardings [James and wife Kate] also staying chez Gail.

Sunday 3 November

Burford. Out for a run, chat to the Hardings over breakfast – James clearly glad to be out of *The Times* and into the BBC – then off with Rory to Cardiff. In Malky Mackay's box with wife Pamela, kids Calum and Francesca. Nice day out. Good atmos though tense. Malky showed me around the set-up after. Impressive, especially the half-time technology zone. Pamela lovely and so were the kids.

Monday 4 November

The Louise Mensch Twitter row kicked off again and I wrote to her saying I really had not intended to be sexist. She sent back a long email saying why she took offence. I accepted it and apologised. Good response for doing so. To be fair it had been a bit of a lapse. I had retweeted a tweet by someone asking her to go on P3 and I thought I was supporting No More P3, but I could see why she took offence and we had been snarling and snapping at each other pretty stupidly.

Lunch with Tom Fletcher at the National Portrait Gallery who wanted to write a book on new diplomacy. He had not told the FCO yet but sounded like a good idea. He was a good gossip. Felt Hague was OK but not sure re. Cameron. His main idea was about totally changing the structures of diplomacy e.g. to have regional rather than nation state. Also to modernise the approach at every level. Put him in touch with Ed V, who thought there would be a market for it. Tom said I had become a national treasure whereas TB had gone the other way. Not sure it was quite like that but he had a point in that I seemed to be getting less grief, TB more.

Meanwhile more delay to Chilcot. To the DoH [Department of Health] for a meeting with alcohol policy people from Health England, before I saw Hunt. The woman in charge had never met Hunt. 'He wouldn't know who I was.' So we just chatted around what we might do together. They were interested in what Osborne said to me but I sensed they were not that dynamic or empowered. Up to see Hunt. The private office was a bit moribund. He was reasonably charming though a bit stilted and I quickly realised he knew next to nothing about all this. He even said at one point 'It is really interesting – I see you talking on TV and things and I can't help asking why would someone like you be depressed?' I reacted calmly but said if he said that publicly he would be dead, and I would lead the charge. I said it is an illness not a choice. 'Would you say to someone you could not believe they were asthmatic or diabetic or had cancer.' I think the officials in the room were pretty shocked both at what he said and the strength of my reaction.

He asked about MUP and said he was not against it in principle but then went off on one about alternative therapies and stuff. I didn't get the impression he had looked into alcohol and mental health much at all. He said he wanted to learn from people like me. The novel was on his desk, perhaps for show though he said he was a third of the way through. He was not terribly flattering about the NHS. Not responsive enough, lots of waste. I was in there for an hour, half with officials, half private. In the first session I really just went through familiar arguments. He has not read the paper I sent through, unlike Osborne. He was not that well informed. And a bit cold while trying to be warm. Grace could not believe it when I told her what he had said about depression and thought I should say publicly what he had said. I felt not, though it definitely coloured my sense of his grasp of the issue or likelihood to do much about it.

To Pizza East to meet F, Rory, Grace, Andrew Rosenfeld – who had just been done over by the *MoS* – and Juliet. Ed M called in a real tizz re. Falkirk because Alistair Darling had responded to a *Mail* story by saying there should be a new inquiry.* Ed sounded very het up because he was making a speech on living standards tomorrow. I said he had to make it and just push the other thing aside. I sensed he was getting it out of perspective. Long chat earlier with Alistair about Scotland. He was his usual rather understated self. He felt things were OK but I sensed he was a bit worried. There were a hell of a lot of don't knows and they were basically mid-age-range working-class people who in the past would certainly have backed Labour and what Labour recommended and were now less sure.

Tuesday 5 November

Flew to Sofia, finished speech then worked on the Cambridge lectures on the plane. Out for a run, narrowly avoiding stray dogs. Did a few interviews, including – this on the anniversary of PG death – with the main TV guy I had been meant to see the day he died. Good interview. The guy was very well informed. To the Military Club for the launch of *The Happy Depressive* translation. Looked great and there was a lot of interest in it. Great cover. Did a talk mixing tomorrow's speech and mental health. Shifted loads of books, including for a very sweet barmaid who asked me to sign it to 'a future Prime Minister of Bulgaria'. She was involved in the protest movement against the government over the intelligence job appointment. Ambo Jonathan Allen came along. Very helpful in insight re. government and the protests – one of which came by as we were talking. He felt the Balkans was totally on the Hague agenda but they never quite knew what Cameron's interests were. He said mental health services were awful. People were basically just locked away. Nobody talked about it. Out for dinner with the main sponsors and movers and shakers at a nice restaurant, Moskva17, with the most incredible chocolate dessert, and a waiter setting fire to drinks. Nice do. Interrupted a couple of times by Edi and TB re. chemical weapons. Getting tougher for Edi. Word [about Albania hosting dismantling chemical weapons] had leaked out, they were saying nothing and the press and politicians were getting jumpy.

Wednesday 6 November

Email from Edi to TB who was urging him, as was I, to try to win support

---

* The Labour Party had cleared the Unite trades union of trying to rig the selection process for a parliamentary candidate in Falkirk after 'key evidence' had been withdrawn.

for the chemical weapons decision and to see the opportunities as well as the threats. He said it was a very tricky moment and he felt all the burden of such a responsibility – 'No one can understand it as you and Alastair can.' So he definitely didn't want to pull back, but the hostility was growing daily and the risk that Albania looked like a trash bin internationally and also inside is more and more obvious. Russia saying, 'We will give $2 million' or Germany adding €2 million only fuelled the hostility and increased the amount of public dissent! Edi said the Americans had to help substantially with a real programme of co-operation. Telling people that thanks to this they will clean up Albanian waste which is harming the country's image and touristic potential, would be great. He was also asking for help with the World Bank and IMF and getting a White House meeting.

Thursday 7 November

Lunch with Emma Reynolds of InBev at Home House. Tory. Wore blue. I had met her at Tim's dinner at the Tory conference and she was keen to discuss the alcohol scene. She was OK in terms of knowing the issues but I don't think she really bought my argument that the industry was not capable of sorting all this itself. Met Ed Richards for coffee over near the Tower. He was on good form and seemed to be enjoying Ofcom after getting through the *Mail* trying to kill him. He said he had made a comment which was barely an attack which Dacre took as such and he said it led to the most brutal language he had ever heard. He was keen for me to keep going with the campaign against Dacre, felt he was a truly awful man who had done real damage. He said until the *Mail* went for him he had always thought I had been exaggerating it.

Edi called and then Endri pre the call with Kerry re. Syria CW. Edi had essentially been positive at the start but was making clear that he had to have certain guarantees on safety and the environment, and economic and political support. The Americans clearly felt it was a done deal which it wasn't. TB and I were both saying it could be a good thing for Albania. But he needed to own the choreography and the presentation of it and Obama had to be involved to signal how big a deal it was and how they would give ongoing support.

Sean Dyche was seeing Alex. Said he was terrific. Really warm. He took a bottle of plonk and pretended that was his gift before he gave the right one. Grace back in Paris. She wrote an amazing piece on anxiety but Fiona was worried about publishing it because of the reference to me and whether Grace would become identified for mental health first off as it were, before establishing herself on her own terms. But it was one of the best things I had ever read about anxiety.

Friday 8 November

A lot of the day on Edi and the CW issue. TB involved at various stages. He told Edi he had both a great challenge and a great opportunity. If they turn it down someone else will emerge to do it, but right now Albania is the only game in town. He said to Edi that gives you leverage but it must be handled with care and also with speed. He felt they were entitled to demand a lot. Being publicly congratulated for this by the USA President at a meeting in the White House. Help with all the environmental aspects so he can say justifiably to the Albanian people that Albania will be cleaner and better after. IMF support and acknowledgment of reform. EU candidate status granted in December. He said prior to the meeting in the UK a minister should be sent to London to tell them what they need in order to say yes to the chemical weapons issue. Then insist on seeing the UK PM to make the same case when you come in November.

TB and I had both assessed the UK government understood how difficult this was. Then send someone to DC to speak to senior officials and WH people and explain the situation. Make clear to the Americans that he needs their specific intervention on the EU in respect of candidate status especially with UK/Germany. He also recommended trips to Berlin and Paris, and a briefing to the EU plus the European Parliament on the measures taken re. organised crime. 'Don't give your leverage up until you know firmly what you're getting!'

Edi was up for most of it but said he could not countenance candidate status being postponed. Inside government it would be unmanageable and the opposition would go crazy.

Edi sent through a note on Syria later and we did a call. I said he needed to be tough but make clear in principle he was prepared to take the hits.

Hugh Grant and Evan Harris [campaigner for press reform] came round to discuss Hacked Off. They were worried Labour was going a bit flaky. Maria Miller [Tory MP] had said that the charter could be irrelevant if IPSO [Independent Press Standards Organisation], the rival press body, met the demands of Leveson. Harriet Harman had echoed that. Hugh seemed tougher than last time. Quite spiky with Evan. I said they should have a major series of events to build up to the anniversary of Leveson and get more of the victims writing to the party leaders. They stayed for an hour and I didn't think there was a reason to be as down as they were. I called Ed M who said there was no backsliding and they were just reflecting the realty that IF the rival body was Leveson-compliant it would be fine. But everyone knows it won't be.

We had a chat on the general scene. He felt he had made real inroads on living standards. Also that the Tories were discomfited. He said Osborne had warned the Tories not to fall into the trap of making the debate all about living standards. *Hot Press* [music and politics magazine] did a really good piece on the interview I did in Dublin. Ed Llewellyn [Downing Street chief of staff] confirmed that Edi could go to No. 10 and Cameron would do a drop-by.

Saturday 9 November

Set off with Calum for Burnley–Doncaster. One–all, poor game. I saw Stan [Ternent] who told me I needed to lose some weight, which I did. Met up with Sean for a chat. He has a lot to him. The more I see of him, the more I like him. I'd fixed for him to meet Fergie, and he had loved it. Really felt he learned a lot just from talking about how he handled players, how he managed his time, ordered priorities. Off to the Peak District and Dick Caborn's 70th. Vile weather. Sat nav took us to the wrong place, eventually found it and the thing was in full swing. Slightly chaotic but nice do. Blunkett with his son William who was really sweet. Played the pipes with the cakes and then Dick wanted me to play again and again.

After Edi's Kerry call John Kerry had got Obama to send a letter to Edi, which was helpful in some ways, unhelpful in others. It seemed to take the decision for granted and also it suggested they would meet next year, rather than at the start of the process. I said probably cock-up not conspiracy and suggested he send a letter back via Kerry – who was up to his eyes in Iran negotiations – spelling everything out in black and white. The US ambassador said it was not a good idea, but Edi agreed to do it but then they just took too long.

It was not perfect but it was also a step in the right direction, but the Americans did not seem to understand the politics of this. Edi was under pressure from them to sign off within days, and it was being set as a clear deadline, but as they were the only country in the game at the moment, they could take longer. Trouble was that protest was growing and it was happening in a vacuum because Edi could not explain the choices or the benefits. All that was being said publicly was coming from opponents and NGOs saying Albania was to be used as the world's dustbin and it was humiliating.

Sunday 10 November

Run. Home. Harriet on *Pienaar's Politics*. Not sure what she was saying but clearly she was prepared to give IPSO a go. Another day spent on the Albanian issue. The US willing to construct an incinerator and landfill. If the Albanians would rather hydrolyse them, the US either build a top-of-the-line storage facility that could be used for all of Albania's toxic waste or export the waste water to another country. Funding negotiable. US willing to offer help cleaning up existing toxic waste, advocating for candidate status with the EU; additional aid for things like civil service reform and crime; political cover for the decision to accept the waste. The 15 November deadline not set in stone. 30 June 2014 deadline for destroying the weapons is 'fungible'.

The heat was rising on all this and it was clear to me from Endri's calls that they were panicking a bit. I said the fundamentals had not changed and they needed to make their choice one way or the other and frame tactics accordingly. Both yes and no were explicable but they needed to decide. At the moment they were leaning towards yes internationally but no domestically and it was not sustainable. The Americans lacked urgency and they were not squaring everything off quickly enough, and the opposition and misinformation were growing.

Monday 11 November

Very nice handwritten letter from Jeremy Hunt about *My Name Is...* Said it had really moved him, felt very real and made him realise we had failed so many girls like Hannah. But he didn't believe MUP was the answer. It was more about education, councils, courts, culture. Met Douglas Alexander who like Ed was trying to get me more involved. He worried the Better Together campaign was stalling. Re. Labour campaign he felt Ed had cut through on living standards but they were still very weak in terms of strength in depth and Balls was a problem. He felt on the economy we were still not in the right place. Osborne making it all about growth, us making it all living standards but the debt/deficit issue still there. Lunch with Owen Jenkins, head of Western Balkans at the FCO. He was mainly focused on Serbia and Kosovo, where he felt progress was being made, but also very well informed on Albania and Bosnia. He felt Edi was taking too big a risk with the CW issue, that he could get through the problems now but that if something went wrong it would destroy him. Also he did not think helping the US would be seen as a great thing by the EU. I passed that on, though I didn't wholly agree with it.

Launch of my Irish diary at their embassy. Good crowd, nice to see ex-ministers like Hain and Paul Murphy [Dublin MEP], officials like JoP. Spoke basically re. NI and defending politics etc. Then out to Koha bar for a meeting with Albanian Youth Forum. They were worried re. the CW issue. Spoke to Edi a couple of times and got TB to speak to Kerry and emphasise the need for support and speed. Bumped into [Baroness] Olly Grender [former Lib Dems head of communications] who said Clegg was holding firm re. Leveson/Charter etc. Lovely letter from Harry Evans about my Cambridge University speeches on the media. 'Brilliant. Need to get wide circulation.' Though we both agreed most of the press would ignore them on account of them criticising the culture.

Tuesday 12 November

Finished and sent off my Cambridge University speeches and started to hype via *The Guardian*, *Indy*, *FT*, HuffPo. Lunch with Jamie Rubin and Christiane. Jamie seemed quite down, demotivated. She was a bundle of knowledge and energy as always. He felt TB just had not moved on or developed in the way that e.g. Clinton and Gore had. I got verbally attacked in the Post Office by anti-war yummy mummy. Placing articles re. the speeches, then to Speaker's House for the launch of the National Youth Arts Trust which Fiona was chairing. Good turnout, Ewan McGregor [actor], Alistair McGowan [impressionist], Grayson Perry [cross-dressing artist] dressed as a woman. John Bercow terrific as ever, but no sign of Sally.

Edi had been sent an insider account of the candidate status discussion in Berlin. It said the decision was not yet made. December was the time for the final decision on the level of the council. The general view was that Albania was not yet ready. They recommended that the Albanian government should suggest itself a postponing of the decision for six months to avoid a NO. They were not ready for YES.

Edi was definitely getting more and more nervous. There were now protests outside the office, and his son and some of his ministers' kids were part of the protests.

Wednesday 13 November

Good pieces on the lectures in *Guardian*, *FT* and HuffPo: right-wing Twitterati getting stuck in against. Debbie Dye [photographer] round to do a portrait for an exhibition re. recovery. *Feminist Times* round to pick my brains. Charlotte Raven [editor]. I sensed they had not really thought through their positioning properly and gave them a few ideas to do so – charter, events, agreed written strategy. I liked the idea of mixing the feel of the *FT* and *Private Eye*. I did a call with Endri and Vali. They were getting more worried. There were protests not just in Tirana but other towns too now. The media was in full cry and social media was full of the idea it was all a humiliation for Albania, the poor kid told by the rich kid to eat shit and enjoy it. I sent an email saying the basic arguments had not changed, but they needed to decide. The opposition was growing because they were not shaping the debate.

Edi called and said, 'Why do you drive me crazy with this? How can I decide when I do not know if we can get all we want?' I said OK, maybe decision is the wrong word but you need a clear judgement – yes if, or no but. You need to own the call with Kerry and be totally clear that you cannot do it without the environmental, political and economic guarantees we have been talking about. Also you cannot do it without Obama owning it with you from the top. He calmed down a bit but I could sense him feeling the heat. He said Berisha was out saying he was betraying the people whereas other countries stood up for their people.

He told Kerry he wanted to do it but there was a Cameron Syria risk – say yes but then have to say no because of Parliament and public opinion. Kerry said let's not talk about that! He was friendly and polite, almost begging Edi to do it. He said three times, 'Will you not take my word?' Edi said he trusted his word but he needed more. The US were asking him to sign a letter to the CW body within two days. He said he needed more commitment and guarantee before he could do that. Kerry admitted they had not yet secured Obama. TB and I both said he had to hold out for that. He said the next step was Kerry going off to see what he could do and another call tomorrow. I sensed that the team was getting very jumpy but Edi felt if he could get the arguments out he could persuade people. He said he was not bothered about having a meeting with Obama for the sake of it. If they did it, he would want Obama to speak directly to the Albanian people, to explain why it was good for the world to do this, and to pledge their support for the environment and ecology of Albania.

Cambridge lecture went well, though I found these academic types quite weird. They took an age to say not much. Good Q&A after the speech. Security quite tight but no real problems. Dinner at King's with John Thompson and Sally Lewis, a couple of the sponsors including [Sir] Michael Pakenham [diplomat]. He and his wife were a good laugh, seemed supportive, if a bit pro-establishment for my taste, and he did after all have a pinkie ring! But they all seemed to like the speech. Edi sent me a message to say the call with Kerry had been postponed. 'Things here getting nasty. Two basic question become more and more obsessive: Why Albania alone? How Albania can recover its tourism potential after it? And the main word being used all over the social network is: Humiliation!' I said hold firm. He owed it to Kerry to have another call.

Thursday 14 November

I went out early for a Portland meeting with Barclays public affairs team. Came out to several missed calls from Edi and an email which said, 'Very bad! Met the EU ambassadors about the CW and they simply said, "It's not our job, it's your problem, it's nothing to do with Albania's EU path!"'

He said he was shocked by the cynicism. I called. He also said that the NATO spokesman came out and said: NATO has nothing to do with it! It's a bilateral issue between Albania and US!!! He said kids were leaving high schools to protest in front of the Parliament. He could not see any way forward. 'Our American friends' were too slow in understanding the points we put together. We lost a month and now the country is overwhelmed by hysteria and fear.

He said he felt totally alone but fortunately had a way out, namely to say to the people: 'I tried hard for the good of the country and for the good of every one of you but the needs to make it happen weren't met so Albania is not part of it.' I still felt it was salvageable but the next time I tried to call him – he was en route to Montenegro – I eventually got hold of Endri and said I felt he needed to take a deep breath, but Endri was sure Edi had already called the US ambassador to say no. I said he owed it to Kerry to see what he had managed to secure and he should not be rash. We were talking about a few thousand people protesting – they could be beaten in argument once people knew what was happening as opposed to all the rumours. But Endri and Vali both sounded very down and tired.

I contacted Ed Llewellyn, in India with the PM, and he immediately got on to the Americans and also got DC lined up – reluctantly, he admitted – to speak to Edi or if it could not be arranged for Ed to pass on a message direct that the ambassadors' view did not matter, that this would be a political decision taken by leaders. He said this was Commission theology – of course there was no direct connection with the EU candidate process, and yes some Europeans were anti-American but clearly if Albania did this there would be a positive political benefit.

Edi's point to me when finally he called was that it was all happening too late. He had protests all over the country, his own MPs causing trouble, Berisha whipping it up – although he was chased when he went out to try to whip up the crowds, so it was not an anti-government thing, it was all about the issue. I said he needed to keep the door slightly open but I could tell he was not going to do that. I said he must speak to Kerry before he does anything. I got TB to call Kerry and make sure he understood how close he was to losing this – they came back and said yes to White House visit and also $100 million help for clean-up.

I spoke again to Ed Livesey, and also Cathy Ashton suggesting she get a grip of the message out of Europe. I told Edi I was getting Cameron to call him. He said, 'Too late! The Americans screwed it up – one long month of no strategy.' I said I didn't think he should make the decision based on protest/what an ambassador says. It is bigger than that. Yes, the Americans have screwed up, but the fundamentals have not changed. He said yes, but even the NATO spokesman came out and said it was just a bilateral issue between Albania and US. For God's sake.

Martin Moore of the Media Standards Trust sent through an analysis of IPSO showing how far it was from being Leveson-compliant so I wrote a bit of that into the next Cambridge speech, including a prediction there would be a news blackout on it. Edi called as I was leaving and I could tell it was over. He said he hated the people who had lied about it. I said if they were lying you would be able to expose that. If the arguments were the same you could win them. He said it was too late. They should have had all this tied up before we got to this stage.

Ed Llewellyn called a couple of times from India and later Sri Lanka, and he was really pressing DC to help. The speech went well, Q&A ditto. Went for dinner and a real Oxbridge twat at the next table. Took me back. Chinless wonder. Loud and dim. Would be a bus driver if he was not from the pinkie-ring brigade.

Earlier popped into TB's office and spoke to him – he was getting on a plane in Hong Kong. He said the White House had moved, and I should get Edi to hold off. I said I feared it was too late but I would try. Saw Catherine who said there were ever stronger rumours that Chilcot was going to go hard for TB. But they were still delaying because of the inability to publish the TB–Bush letters, and there were reports too – denied – that it was the White House who were preventing publication. Catherine said re. Murdoch that – privately – the divorce settlement was done. They had a near miss with the *MoS* at the weekend because they were going to run a story that TB was the cause of the divorce. TB had denied to her absolutely they ever had an affair. She felt he could not do much pre Chilcot, but I did not agree. Also agreed with JoP that he should be out with a pre-message on that too.

Friday 15 November

I had the Bosnians over – Jasenko now joined by Damir [Marjanović], education minister. Arranged to meet them at party HQ and show them around, especially MMU [Media Monitoring Unit], and also introduce them properly to Mark Lucas and show them the work we did in Albania, which they liked a lot. Meanwhile I was having to deal with the fallout from Albania. Edi was about to announce the firm No following his call with Kerry. I emailed Ed L and said so and he said yes, they had heard the same, a clear No, so no point having the call. I told Cathy Ashton, who was in Myanmar – as was TB.

I had a long chat with Endri and said I felt it was the wrong decision for the wrong reasons and even though it is true that the Americans fucked it up, it was still possible they would have been able to win support. He felt not.

I emailed Cathy Ashton after Edi said no to Kerry. I think Edi could have won the arguments. But there were conflicting signals from State/WH and Obama sent a letter to Edi which suggested they were taking the yes for granted without any real understanding of the politics, and as Kerry sought to deliver on the things Edi needed, they took too long and the protests grew, including within his own MPs. But both she and Cameron had been lining up to speak to him last night/today and make clear political support, and we had also got the White House to agree, finally, to an early meeting.

The EU ambassadors saying the decision would have no impact on candidate status (technically correct but politically stupid and insensitive) and the NATO spokeswoman saying it was a bilateral issue not a NATO one (again stupid) really had not helped.

The Bosnians seemed to think they got a lot out of the trip. I had to leave for Windsor and a speech to a kitchen catering trade organisation – what a crazy life – did my usual spiel without notes, went down fine. Back for dinner with Fiona and the Bosnians at Mimmo's. They were unsure how to set up MMU Bosnia style. Agreed I would go out 11–13th. Giving Fiona lesson in Balkans politics and history. Complicated or what.

Saturday 16 November

OK reaction to speeches. Needless to say zero coverage of Media Standards Trust analysis of IPSO not being Leveson-compliant. Out with F, then into town for European Bank for Reconstruction and Development/CB meeting in Strand re. Albania etc. Brief email exchange with Edi but basically setting up for next week. Grace not feeling great in Paris, not happy, anxious all the time, so got her to come back for the weekend.

Tuesday 19 November

Grace back to Paris. Into town for various things then a speech at Alcohol Concern conference. To the Goring to meet Edi, Deputy PM, economic minister, Endri and Ina pre their meeting with Cameron. Ed Llewellyn had come back to me yesterday, as I always expected him to, to say that it was best I didn't go. So we had a chat about what they should discuss and off they went. Came back and it seemed to have gone OK without being spectacular. They had maybe fifteen minutes with DC – which was more than most of a small country would get – and Edi felt the discussion was OK though none of them were very impressed. Felt he was 'miles from being Tony', thought he was very tactical and quite superficial. But Ed had delivered in terms of the overall presentation and they had Ed, Craig Oliver, events person and one or two others all go through how No. 10 worked. They felt it was useful though they knew candidate status was going backwards.

Wednesday 20 November
Albanians at the EBRD. Off to Cambridge for the 'symposium' on my lectures. All fine if too long. Three hours. Basically four people saying what they thought of my main points then a discussion. Back with a postgrad from King's to do an interview. Then to the Hilton where I was double booked. Doing Haymarket awards but also dinner with Edi and co. He was a bit late after seeing Home Office people re. a customs and crime thing. Endri looked exhausted.

The main problems were the same as last time but worse because time had passed and they were still unable to fire and hire. The courts would be clogged up if they did. Down to the awards dinner I was doing which was just a case of getting through it.

Thursday 21 November
Sign books at Waterstones. Bought the new Merkel biography which was excellent. Read it en route to Bristol for CBI dinner. Signed 540 books, hotel to change, down for drinks with big wigs and Syd [Young] and his boys. Nice event. Well organised. Was at top table with Graham Cole, Labour-supporting SW chairman of CBI, [Avon and Somerset] chief constable Nick Gargan and Neil Bentley-Gockmann, deputy director of CBI London. Did speech based on Qs from the audience plus bagpipes which all went down well. Syd loved it, doing lots of 'I knew 'im when he were nowt' with everyone who came over.

Friday 22 November
Gym, breakfast then train to Durham, working on speech for housing conference and finishing Merkel book. TB called a couple of times because the *MoS* were trying another go at doing the Wendi Deng story.

Stayed at the Ramside Hall, did speech, book signing then Alan Pardew [manager, Newcastle United] came round. He wanted to discuss the possibility of getting involved in a discussion about strategy. He felt if by the time he was near sixty he had not landed one of the really big clubs he would go into something different and it might be politics. He didn't rate Ed. Felt we were thin on the ground. Correct. Felt I should get back in. Brendan Foster joined us after a while and we chatted mainly sport after that. Dinner with Brendan in Durham. Very down on Ed. Said if I went in I would be leader after election defeat. Not sure.

Saturday 23 November

Asthmatic run. Then to Nottingham via Newark then met Greg and Calum. Burnley lucky to get a point, 1–1. Dinner at the Rubins. John and Shelley Sawers. Terje Rød-Larsen [Norwegian diplomat] and Mona Juul [wife, diplomat]. John and Shelley both on great form. He was still a total enthusiast, Tiggerish. He was fifty-eight, due to end his term at MI6 in two years, but said Cameron wanted him to stay on at least through the election. Seemed to quite like DC and Hague. He said Hague was a strong supporter of MI6 and calm when things went wrong, but he was mainly managerial, did not really have his own ideas and agenda, beyond easy stuff like women's issues with Angelina Jolie [actress].

He was scathing about Dearlove, said he had done immense damage to the Service – not just because of Iraq, and getting too close to Downing Street. He did not run the place managerially in the way he should have done. He was obsessed by the idea he had this special relationship with George Tenet [former director, CIA]. He was a terrible mistake. Scarlett stabilised things well. He said he was not sure what the Chilcot report would say or when though he felt it could be even further delayed. His sense was that it would go mainly for TB, maybe Goldsmith but also others in the system for not ensuring proper procedures were followed etc.

Terje said he was a massive fan of mine, had read everything. He said as far as he was concerned 'you made Tony' and that is why he is not in such good shape now. His wife was currently deputy foreign minister hoping to become London ambassador any time and they were over looking at schools. So we had a chat about that, trying unsuccessfully to persuade them to use a state school. Christiane and Jamie on form as ever, both down on Obama, though Kerry was doing OK.

Sunday 24 November

Called Arminka re. Kosovo, as Hague was due to see Kerry today, but she couldn't really grip it as they were tied up with what looked like it was going to be an Iran deal. Came good later. Cathy Ashton getting a great press.

Monday 25 November

Felt really tired and was basically just at my desk all day pottering. Tired. Depressed. Never left house.

Tuesday 26 November

Watched Salmond launch his independence white paper. He did OK but too many of the big questions went unanswered and so the length of the document rather played against him. Lunch with Stephen Castle and Steven Erlanger of the *New York Times* at Bradley's. Steven was back as bureau chief and wanted to do a big number on booze partly focused on my story and the novel. Then to Royal Society for the launch of the Health Talk Online anti-depressants section. I did a little speech which went fine. Hugh Grant there for a chat re. Leveson. He seemed quite pessimistic. To the Ritz for a speaking engagement, fairly small dinner, organised by Scandinavian Airlines, Victor Blank the only one I knew personally. Rather offputting when I saw him dozing off during my speech.

Thursday 28 November

Berenberg Bank for a speech for GLG [consultancy] – first one for them. Lunch with Emily Maitlis who was going to stand in for maternity leave political editor on *Newsnight*. Really good company.

Friday 29 November

The *MoS* were planning to do something on TB and Wendi Deng, and the buzz was that they had emails and texts that could be seen as incriminating. It turned out it was her saying to her shrink that she felt a real fondness for TB. We agreed that whoever said 'ramblings of a sad old man' re. Rupert – probably Matthew Freud – was not exactly helpful. Then Ed M on re. energy and how to take forward. Blog re. Cameron all over the shop on so many issues.

Saturday 30 November

Blog on Osborne shares rising as DC and Boris fall. Off to Huddersfield. Two QPR fans on the booze big-style at the next table – four bottles of cider, twelve cans of lager. Bottle of vodka. TB story not so bad. Splash but thin.

Tuesday 3 December

Nominated for political fiction award for *My Name Is...* 7 a.m. flight. Sleep on plane to Tirana. Hotel. Lunch with Edi. He was on OK form. Edi was rightly mainly worrying about candidate status. He felt they had come out OK from the CW issue. Americans were blaming Democratic Party as much as anything. Meta in Brussels as was Ditmir [Bushati, foreign minister]. Doing lobbying and they were getting messages Germany better but worried re. UK Holland and Denmark. Meeting with UK ambassador. He felt they were doing OK in terms of the measures on crime and corruption. But he did not feel that they would get candidate status because the EU was used to bursts of action and they needed to know it would be sustained. Also the politics of Bulgaria and Romania had become more difficult.

Dinner at PM residence. Edi, Endri, Jamie and me. Detailed work on the Budget strategy and also the first hundred days. Need to change tone. Under promise, over deliver. Gave Edi idea of 'Your PM' town halls inside the PM's office. He sort of knew what needed to be done but was struggling to get the systems needed and struggling to get people working well together, though said Jamie was making a difference.

Wednesday 4 December
Edi asked me to draft a letter to DC re. candidate status, and the insight that yes would not be a big deal, but no would be a big setback. He wanted to thank Cameron for the meeting and thank Hague who had been good in Brussels recently. He went through some of the changes they had made, especially on corruption and organised crime, early arrests and the crackdown on illegal gambling dens, drugs etc. He said he was aware of the sensitivities of the immigration debate, and also of the current focus on the expected arrival of Bulgarians and Romanians next year.* He knew that the issue of more countries from the eastern side of Europe coming in would be a source of further political sensitivity. But he hoped the UK would continue to look favourably upon them. He said the awarding of candidate status would be a major boost to efforts to make the changes needed. However, I sensed DC was definitely moving against. Edi came in with news of a school shooting.† These types of things could really get him down. He looked sad for the rest of the day. Edi had decided I should speak to the Cabinet and all their comms guys so they were all brought over to the Cabinet room. Seemed to go down OK though no Qs which

---

* Following restrictions on working abroad, citizens of Romania and Bulgaria could work without restrictions across the EU from January 2014.

† Police arrested a fifteen-year-old boy in Shkozet, near Tirana, after the shooting of a seventeen-year-old suspect armed with an automatic rifle.

was always unsettling. Later they told me it was because they saw it as disrespectful.

Edi underlined the message. They looked a bright bunch but they seemed slightly cowed. Met the comms people separately and gave them a pep talk. Edi had said to the ministers they had to take the comms people seriously. This was their chance. Off to the airport. Deputy foreign minister and comms guy there. Wrote to Edi with a few ideas and observations. He had delivered the right message but there had to be a determination now to make sure it happens, at the centre and within the ministries.

I suggested a new meeting structure for his day, and also warned against the long hours culture becoming endemic.

He had asked me for a shorthand version of the ten points on my strategy card that I had used with the ministers:

- OST objective then strategy then tactics (strategy is not strategy until it is written down)
- TLTP best team leaders are best team players
- YSTA you set the agenda
- BB be bold
- BA be adaptable
- CC stay calm in a crisis
- LBL listen but lead
- HAP head above parapet
- GGOOB get good out of bad
- VTV visualise the victory

Fiona was speaking at Eton. And she had a fainting spell.

Thursday 5 December

Watched Autumn Statement. Osborne did pretty well. Balls barracked. More and more red-faced as he tried to shout down the noise. The issue of 'mess we inherited' coming to haunt. Mark Lucas re. Bosnia. Trying to get me to stand again. Rumours started to swirl that Mandela was dead. Finally it was confirmed by [Jacob] Zuma [President of South Africa]. Wall to wall. Tweet and pics. Really sad. Going to be a news blackout for days on anything else. Pretty vile to see the Tories out saying what an inspiration he had been to them given their role in keeping apartheid going.

Friday 6 December

Sam Delaney [author and editor] came round to do an interview for his book on political advertising, then I wrote a blog re. Mandela. We had all had such a long time to get used to the idea it might happen, but that does not minimise the sadness, nor the sense of loss. Both are reflections of the fact that Mandela was one of the small number of historical figures from our lifetime whose name will resonate through history for eternity. Lincoln of our age in some ways. Many historical figures endure because they were forces of badness. He will do so because he was a force for such good, a byword for values, courage, resilience, endurance, humanity, forgiveness, reconciliation, the politics of protest, the politics of hope. I said it was a great human being we are mourning, not just a great leader.

So some memories. When he was finally freed, he wanted to come to London fairly soon afterwards to thank the British people, particularly on the left, who had campaigned so hard for his release, and for the anti-apartheid movement more generally. I was at the *Mirror* and Labour MP Dick Caborn asked if I could get publisher Robert Maxwell to sponsor the planned tribute concert for Mandela. Maxwell said he would – though I am not sure he ever paid – and part of the deal was that Mandela would come to the *Mirror* for a meeting and a meal with the then owner.

Mandela was very gracious, everyone feeling they were in the presence of someone special. A picture from that meeting is one of the few pictures of my meetings with public figures that I have kept, and have on display in my office. Maxwell could not resist, however, giving him 'advice' about the art of negotiation, even pointing out that as Mandela had been locked up for so long, he would 'need to learn' from people like him, experienced as he was in dealings with Eastern European dictators. To the embarrassment of everyone else in the room, he said, 'Nelson, one of the most important qualities a negotiator requires is patience.' To which the saintly Mandela, perhaps reflecting on twenty-seven years in prison, replied gently: 'Bob, I think I know a thing or two about patience.' My memory of him from the concert is of him 'dad dancing' with rather more grace, style and rhythm than anyone else in the royal box.

I remember when he came to the EU summit in Cardiff, though some of the big names of world diplomacy were there, he was very much the first among equals, his presence, charisma and grace of a scale and quality that others could only dream of, and admire. I think it was when he came to Labour conference to thank the party for the role it had played in the fight to free him that TB said Nelson uniquely managed to make every other politician feel they had something lacking.

There was another time, in an argument about Libya, when Mandela said something TB totally disagreed with, but he knew enough about the power of the Mandela legend to admit 'the trouble with you, Nelson, is that you are such a saint you can come out with any old nonsense and nobody can challenge you.' Mandela laughed, slapped his thigh, and nodded in agreement.

Whenever we went to South Africa people were always asking me to take books for him to sign, and I remember on a visit to Pretoria asking him to sign one for Monica Prentice, [Downing Street messenger] one of the few black people working in No. 10. She adored Mandela. Of all those who asked me to take a book on that visit, I decided just to take her copy of his *Long Walk to Freedom*, and after the meeting ended I asked if he would dedicate it to Monica. He was very slow and deliberate in his actions, had classically old-fashioned and neat handwriting. He took a while to get the top off the pen, open the book at the right page, and start to write. He was halfway through 'to Monica' when he looked up and said, 'Hold on, it's not THAT Monica, is it?' And then the smile, and then the laugh.

I said in the blog I hoped that in the millions of words the media will devote to Mandela in the coming days, some will go on explaining the role played by a number of Labour MPs in particular in the creation of the Anti-Apartheid Movement, and its constant struggle in the face of often huge opposition. Neil Kinnock, Dick Caborn and Peter Hain were among them, and should feel a real pride in the role they played. But if there is one man whose role must never be forgotten it is Bob Hughes, a man who sums up that wonderful statement by Harry Truman that it is remarkable what a small group of people can achieve, provided nobody cares who gets the credit.[*] Bob is one of those people.

I set off for Bolton. 5 Live great coverage of Mandela, non-stop. Bolton hospital. Stephen Hodgson the Burnley-supporting medical director, Tommy Banks, ex-Bolton player. Kieran Moriarty, liver specialist who had fixed the visit. Met the alcohol support staff then three patients. Linda whose husband was dead through drink and she was on the same track. Kids offside. Went two years dry but tipped back. Zoe, twenty-eight, on the streets. Distended liver so couldn't eat. 'Paul' tattooed on her neck. Sean, forty-six, in withdrawal. Lives with mum. Slight brain damage. Liver recovering. Spoke to us and then came back in tears wanting to go home.

Nurses Sharon and Rebecca fantastic. But my God what sad stories, all of them. Hotel for a swim. Dinner with Kieran Stephen and Banks. Cameron was barely challenged on the Tory record on apartheid. Edi and Meta called. Said 'Your PM' idea got great reaction. They were worried about Denmark being strongly opposed to accession candidate status. Emailed Helle. Wrote a letter to DC via Edi. The hotel was full of Xmas party

---

[*] Labour politician Bob Hughes, later Baron Hughes, was chair of the British Anti-Apartheid Movement from 1976 until it was dissolved in 1995 after the end of South Africa's apartheid policies.

boozing, which after the earlier visit was all a bit odd. Wondered how many would end up in the state of the woman with the distended liver.

Saturday 7 December

Ditmir called to chat before his call with William Hague on candidate status. He wanted advice on how to use Hague's genuine support for the Balkans. *Bolton Evening Post* called re. a tweet I did on the alcohol team. Quick interview. Off to the match. One–nil v Barnsley. Tom Baldwin called saying *The Observer* had [Labour adviser, wife of MP Pat McFadden] Marianna McFadden's memo on election structures and there might be a load of 'AC back' stuff because there was a reference to monthly meetings with Ed and Douglas. Mandela was applauded at every match.

Monday 9 December

Spoke at the Alcohol Alliance conference in Regent's Park and later at Graveney School in Wandsworth. Great kids. One or two tough Qs on Iraq but OK. Black girl came up at the end and said could I give her some advice – she had an interview at Caius tomorrow. Good turnout and nice mood for a pro-politics message. I asked them all if they were basically pro- or anti-politics and I would say five to one pro.

Tuesday 10 December

Mandela memorial so I stayed in and watched on TV. All a bit of a shambles. Thousands of empty seats. Fiasco over the sign language guy who wasn't. Turned out he had just blagged his way there. The speeches over-running. Zuma booed every time he was seen or mentioned. Stadium near empty by the end. Helle did a selfie with Cameron and Obama which got massive coverage around the world. I tried not to be too political, but it was annoying the way people like Bob Hughes were barely mentioned in the UK coverage. Zlatko call to plan my next visit to Sarajevo. Then to Ed Victor party at his flat in Regent's Park. Fiona loved the place. Mainly talking to Celia Walden and sending a picture to wind up Piers. Will Hutton [*Observer*] said he had given his son my book on depression and would I talk to him? Ed funny as ever. Freddie Forsyth cut me dead. Sort of chatted to Matthew Parris. Dylan Jones. Nice do then off to Lemonia with F and Rory.

Wednesday 11 December

Off to Bosnia to get Mark Lucas working with them, but the fog was dire and after several hours of hanging around I gave up and went home. TB spoke to Cameron re. Albania candidate status and clearly they were moving against. Edi getting nervy about it.

Thursday 12 December

Finally got away. Met up with Mark Lucas. Yesterday there were lots of Wigan fans heading to Maribor, Slovenia. Today lots of shooters heading to Croatia for some big event. Changed at Zagreb with Mark. Met from plane. Hotel then a couple of hours with Zlatko and Jasenko to go over the latest poll. Some OK stuff in there but a fair bit of bad stuff too. The opposition was going for Zlatko personally over his property portfolio and he didn't know how to defend.

Friday 13 December

Call from Massimov in Kaz first thing. All-day strategy session up and down. First polls. Then strategy and there was not much engagement going on. Zlatko read the Riot Act to them and after a while things picked up and we managed to get some decent work done on messaging and planning of it.

Had a long chat with Helle on Albania but also re. the fallout from the selfie photo with DC and Obama at Mandela memorial service. She said the fallout was OK in Denmark, because it showed her as a big figure, but awful in Britain, where people were saying it was showing off and looked disrespectful, and Neil was none too happy. Also it might be a problem for Steve going for Aberavon seat, her being seen as close to DC. I said she should not worry, that it was fine for her and good for Denmark. There was a lot of talk as well of Michelle giving Obama a dirty look for the way he was flirting with Helle. She and later TB and Ed M said the whole thing had been pretty shambolic. TB said it was alas a metaphor for the country. It just felt like it was going backwards.

I had been there a couple of years ago with the government comms team and suggested they get a grip of the funeral events as a key moment, not just about Mandela but about the future of the country, but they didn't grip it at all. In the afternoon we had another strategy session which went better. Then dinner with Zlatko and Amina. He felt we made progress today and now needed to take next steps.

Saturday 14 December

Couldn't sleep. Up at five. Run. Early pick-up for the airport. Note to

Zlatko. A group of English private-school kids at Zagreb, behaving like tossers. Home. Leicester–Burnley match on TV. One–all. Edi called. Holland had come out with a clear no, the government having given the decision to Parliament. It sounded bad but in fact he said it helped because it was so obviously about their politics rather than about them not knowing what they were doing or doing the wrong things. So it was more saleable. However, it would also lead to other countries to come out against.

To Tim Allan's party. He wanted me to talk to Osborne who seemed to want to stay despite being due at a dinner with Gove. He was a lot warmer in this kind of setting and also quite frank. As in his letter about *My Name Is...* he had told me about there being drugs issues in his family. He said again that the book had really got him thinking a lot. Ed and Justine there, didn't really have time to talk to Ed. Justine said she loved the Mandela funeral. Surreal. Being with the other UK leaders in a minibus. Changing clothes on the way. Sent Tim an email saying he had done well in his life and business and deservedly so.

Monday 16 December
Off to Paris, part work, part media, but mainly to see Grace. Still getting panic attacks.

Tuesday 17 December
Grace not in a great way. We had clearly underestimated how she had been feeling. We had a long chat, then went for a walk but had another row because I called Fiona. I said of course I had to talk to Mum, and eventually she got that, but was just very edgy and anxious. I said we would do anything, and if she felt she would be able to deal with it all better at home, not a problem. Rory home. Malky Mackay on the edge of getting the chop from Cardiff, big row with Vincent Tan, the owner. Spoke to Malky. He sounded really worried, felt there might be no way out, but he had the fans behind him big time.

Wednesday 18 December
Neil on re. Cardiff, said he had been trying to get the chairman more involved in keeping Malky on. But he had been sent a mad seven-page email that was full of libels. Malky felt it had now gone way too far but he was not going to go.

Thursday 19 December

Long heart-to-heart with Grace. She was weepy but also amazingly mature in how she was so determined to address it all. TB office event p.m. His various teams from around the world. Did a Q&A with Jonathan and me. Saw Jackie Ashley for a chat.

Friday 20 December

Around all day talking to Grace. I had to go to the doctor, bad asthma and also to get more anti-depressants. DS felt I should stay on them through to the New Year.

Saturday 21 December

Drove up with Calum for Burnley–Blackpool. Good win [2–1] after going behind. Then to Lancaster to pick up Fiona and stay over. Major drunkenness around the hotel.

Monday 22 December

Swim then long Conaglen drive. Weather pretty wild over Glencoe. TB called re. Albania and also re. himself. Still getting hassle re. Wendi. Still not sure re. Chilcot. Said his away-day thing went really well. Felt he had built something good. Ed V called and pressed me to do the Winning book we had been discussing. Really felt it would go well.

Tuesday 23 December to Sunday 29 December

Weather not great but got out on the bike most days. Mark and Lindsay and Hope there throughout. Kids plus Aud till the 27th. Others coming and going. Mum and Donald Boxing Day. Usual three massive meals a day, exercise, football on telly and yak. Grace up and down. Calum distant. Rory keen to do the research on the Winning book. We chatted re. that a fair bit, and by the end had a really good outline structure and plan. Read the new Hillary C. The publisher wanted me to give a quote. Went for 'Makes you sure she will run and hope she does' kind of thing. Bike on good form. Body less so.

Malky still there. Hanging on. Asked me to give him various lines at various times. Working a bit re. Bosnia. Zlatko asked for help re. his end-of-year press conference. Edi asked for help re. New Year message. Gave him a structure and some half-decent lines. Worked on Winning outline with Rory. Did intro for Ed V to take to publishers.

Tuesday 31 December to Wednesday 15 January 2014

Great night at Conaglen with the singing and Donald and I piping. He loved being with the kids, and they loved being with him. First week back I did the first of my *GQ* interviews with Farage, which went OK. He was in what felt a bit like a shell office operation. Very hail fellow well met. Bluff, quite funny, but edgy. Also chasing some of the people we had decided to try to get for the Winners book. Lance Armstrong who said yes then went quiet. Usain Bolt. Lined up Salmond for *GQ*. Enjoying working with Rory who was digging up good stuff and having good ideas. I was not doing enough exercise and though not drinking weight going on. Not good. Need to get back into hard exercise. Nick Clegg's office came on asking me to do a mental health visit with him to help push something he was doing. I was not sure but spoke to Charlie and he said do it. He felt I could not be out there campaigning on mental health and not engage with government publicly, added to which I had said plenty of times Clegg got this stuff way more than the Tories. Harris Goodberg [Canadian film writer and director] was on wanting to do TV series based on my character. Advising TB re. how to change perception. [Ariel] Sharon [former Israel Prime Minister] dead. TB spoke at funeral.

Thursday 16 January

Saw TB with Anji [Hunter]. She and I had discussed how we might help him get to a better position with his own profile which was still not great. Obviously Chilcot was still a problem and we still had no idea when it was coming. TB admitted there were times when he felt like an exile in his own land. He felt he had to come back into the domestic scene and also that he had to be out there making the case for better engagement in the Middle East even though it could mean criticising Obama. He accepted that he could not just go out and say he had done the right thing again and again. But he did feel he had to make the case that we were losing the battle against extremism because we were learning the wrong lessons.

Libya – we went in but then left them to sort it out and it is a mess. Egypt – he said he was actually welcomed there now because he had been saying for some time that he saw the problems emerging from the uprising. We saw it through Western eyes rather than through those of the region. Syria was a total disaster because we had made a threat and then not seen it through. The deal with Iran was far from secure. TB had spoken at Ariel Sharon's funeral yesterday – he said he had no real choice once he was asked – but it was hardly making the Arabs feel warmer towards him. There was always this push to portray him as one-sided, but he said he did so much on the Palestinian economy side the leaders knew it was nonsense. He did seem open to ideas – e.g. to do a more thorough and deeper media engagement up to and including full major documentary about his operation – but he did not yet feel right for it.

He said that his goal on leaving office had been to set up this big operation and he was doing so and he wanted to get that properly established before he made a change of tack. He wondered about putting his sports foundation at the heart of it all. Neither of us thought that was big enough. Anji thought maybe Europe which she felt was crying out for leadership to counter all the negative stuff and bolster Cameron et al., because the scepticism was really taking hold. We both said the conventional wisdom that a referendum was unloseable could be tested. Cameron had launched the idea but there was no follow-through. He said he would be keener on doing immigration because he hated the way the argument was going and wanted to challenge it. We had our usual argument about how we had not done enough to tackle the right-wing media who had just got away with relentless mythmaking and lying on Europe and it was taking things to a bad place.

I felt his own strategy had to be more about moving to make his experience relevant by engaging on what was happening today rather than seeming to justify the past. He said that is what he was trying to do. He said Clinton had a few tough years and it was only after he got the Global Initiative up and running that he really started to turn things around. He was a bit down but at the same time open to doing something to change things. He was worried about Chilcot, I could tell. I know I have to go out and take the heat, he said. But when he saw what was already happening on both front benches in foreign policy, he worried that the wrong lessons were being learned, he said. Lack of engagement is creating real problems for the long term.

Off to get the train to Orpington to meet up with Nick Clegg at a psychiatric unit at Princess Royal Hospital. He was planning to host a big conference on it next week and this was for pre-filming. A chat with doctors, and some service users who had helped make films for staff and others to show how it felt at their end – a depressive woman called Anne and a schizophrenic called Peter who said he was really nervous. Clegg had a nice manner, a bit politician-y at times but he was genuinely into the issue and his questions weren't daft. Then to the ward and a sit-down chat with current patients who were doing some kind of art therapy.

Funny moment when a woman called Caroline was explaining her design of stuff taken from magazines and there was a gap for a slogan at the bottom. Clegg asked what she was going to write there. Vote Labour, I said. Yes, vote Labour, she said, laughing, and the snappers got some terrific pictures, they said, of the three of us laughing. Also chatted to an alcoholic called Richard who said he had been there fourteen times and nine times in rehab, and he was terrified about leaving on Monday. They were discharging him because he did not have a mental illness. He said he had lots of mental illnesses and was terrified because he had no support and was almost certain to go back on the drink.

Down with Clegg to a round table with the medical staff. They felt things were changing a bit in terms of attitudes, but very slowly, not least inside the NHS. Again he was good with them in terms of listening etc. Chatted a fair bit one on one but mainly on the mental health stuff rather than the Lib–Lab momentum which had been given a bit of a push by Balls saying he could work with Clegg. Also my interview with the *Fabian Review* of ages ago came out and I was predicting a Lib–Lab coalition. Saw Ed M later. He seemed OK but seemed to me to have settled on the view that winning meant being PM. In other words, a majority was not likely though he didn't say that. He was clear that he had to keep the focus on living standards. I said he needed more emblems of that. He said he was going for the banks next.

I said he should be careful not to alienate all business. He agreed but also said that to get clarity of message he did have to be clear and maybe pay a bit of a price. Just don't get painted as anti-business, I said. He said he was trying to get the shadow Cabinet more active but it was a struggle. They had to be liberated a bit, I said. Tristram [Hunt, shadow education minister] was going well and Ed said he had that public-school confidence which meant when people said he fucked up on something he just got straight back up and went for it again. On Peter M, he said he knew he had ability but felt he couldn't trust him to take him into the inner circle because there was always another agenda.

He felt Clegg was in real trouble and that there was still a chance he wouldn't be there at the election. He was more confident than the last time I saw him but I still felt there were things he needed to do that he wasn't. Fiona and I were spending a bit of time with Andrew Rosenfeld [businessman and Labour Party donor] and Juliet Soskice [partner] because he had been told he had cancer and didn't want many people to know. Weird going to see him next door to PG's. *GQ* liked the Farage piece and wanted Salmond next. Yeovil away good [1–2]. Like going back in time. Roy Hattersley and David Blunkett came to the home game v Sheff Wed. Did a cancer thing half-time with some mild-mannered booing which was a laugh. One–all. OK game.

On 3 January a good meeting with Norman Lamb [Lib Dem MP] and Andrew Adonis re. a mental health equivalent of Teach First [educational disadvantage enterprise]. Norman good on policy, Andrew fizzing with energy. Fixing a few trips and speeches. Calum moved out. We had another heart-to-heart, and I made the point that as parents we made mistakes and that we maybe did more damage than we realised by the way we lived our lives.

Wednesday 22 January

Writing this weeks after the event – a mix of depression and also being busy with the Winning book and too much other stuff going on – so no doubt I have forgotten lots. Off to Berlin today for a conference of an American law firm. Richard Susskind [author and legal adviser] had been there on day one and called to fill me in. He said he was working on a book with his son which felt like fate sending me a message, given Rory and I were thinking through whether to do the Winning book. It was going to be a lot of work, but Richard's call definitely pushed me in that direction.

I bumped into [Lord] Jim O'Neill on the plane. He was very down re. United. Also felt that Alex's book had not done him justice. I filled him in on the Winners book and he liked the idea. Later agreed to do an interview for it. Said he had left Goldman Sacha because the culture was basically that they spat you out and he wanted to go before that happened. Now doing a mix of backing enterprises and also speaking, consulting etc. Going to Davos tomorrow. Was a non-exec at the department of education. Said he found Gove a bit odd. He just loved to argue. Everything was just a debating game, like he was still at university. Like most people in business he felt that Ed was not cutting it. Got a lift to the hotel, did a bit of work and then off to the British embassy to see Simon McDonald, who was now ambassador there.

Reminiscing re. the GB period. Re. Merkel he had set me up to see Steffen Seibert [head of German government's press and information office] tomorrow. He said Merkel was surrounded by an incredibly bright team. Beate Baumann [office manager] was the main one. He said she was like me, Peter and Cherie combined, but had next to no profile and the German media by and large let her. Merkel liked Cameron. Cameron had to get on with her because she was the only one who could help him deliver any of the things he wanted post an election and pre a referendum. They really wanted the UK to stay in. She liked him personally though they felt he had made a few missteps along the way. Difficult relationship with Putin. Told me the story – confirmed by Steffen later – of her being scared of dogs and so Putin brought a dog to a bilateral to sit and stare at her.

Thursday 23 January

Out for a run in the freezing cold. Beautiful. Up the Brandenburg Gate and then found a lovely snowy park. The conference event was fine. Did my usual stuff re. reputation and strategy but was starting to use some of the material I was gathering for the book which was good. Rory was mainly at the British Library and doing some good stuff. Crunchier than my stream of consciousness. Meeting with Steffen at the federal press office. Nice guy. Perfect, flawless English, even on technical stuff. Left books for him and Dorothee who was the brilliant interpreter from Kohl's time and still going strong. Merkel actually speaks good English but felt she had to speak German publicly. Dorothee only there for the really difficult stuff. I was trying to persuade her to do *GQ* which might be a stretch as she was sometimes criticised for not doing enough German interviews and that had to be priority.

Steffen said she had always got on with TB, liked him, felt he understood Europe. He then said, 'She will get on with Ed Miliband if he wins. It is what she does.' She was clearly a real pragmatist. He was clearly important to Merkel. Lovely office. Had maybe an hour just chatting, different things in politics and comms, how fast things were changing. He said she really tried with Putin because she felt she had to, but it was difficult. Putin was mid his big build-up to the Sochi Winter Olympics, milking it. He was getting worse. The dog story was true. They knew she was scared of dogs, and he brought this hulking thing into the meeting, and sat there smirking. 'A wrong man with wrong values.' He said he lowers his voice when talking to her, which he would know she would know was a KGB interrogation thing.

She quite likes Cameron and wants to help. She worried about the Europe debate in the UK, felt EU without UK would not be good. Really does not want Britain out. Germany does not have anything like our media, and people were baffled by the nature of the debate. So much of it was based on myths and falsehoods. I told him what Gerhard Schröder had once said to me: 'There is something very weird about a country with a press like yours.' Steffen said Merkel's strength is that she knows what she is good at. She is serious, into detail, good at reading people. She watches Obama's soaring oratory and she knows she can't do that. She thinks, 'Great speech.' But then she sees the way he struggles with Congress and thinks, 'I could have handled that better.' He said she had wanted to be an ice skater but had lacked elegance. Real work ethic. Tough, but with a very nice side. Always on top of detail. He told me the latest book on her, which I really liked, had not sold well. Another wonderful detail, that she had a stylist, whose job was to make sure nobody talked about her looks. Same hair, same clothes. Impressive guy, liked him.

Car to the airport and home. Tired and my nose was agony. Spent the weekend working on the book. It was sort of coming together but we were going to need to internationalise it and businessify it a lot. Fiona and

I getting into *The Bridge,* half-Swedish half-Danish crime series. United struggling. I was feeling sorry for Moyes. They just lacked something at the moment.

Monday 27 January

Grace back permanently from Paris. Definitely the right thing. She had called me and said, 'Would it be terrible if I gave up the course?' I said no, if you are not happy, then why worry? It means it is not the right thing. She was much more interested in film than French. She said when I said come back, she felt so relieved. I took her to meet Kim Cattrall [actress], who was making a film on Shakespeare and wanted to interview me about political oratory, looking at different famous speeches in a Millbank studio and discussing how Shakespeare oratory worked. I liked her. She was very nice to Grace and encouraging her to go for film and drama if that was really what she liked. To a dinner for Andy Marr and Jackie at Ed Victor's. With Ben Macintyre [author, historian] and Kate Muir [author, critic] and Gail [Rebuck] and an actor friend of Ed's. Nice enough evening but a bit odd. Andy seemed to be worse health-wise than he let on, I think. Jackie finding it all very difficult.

Tuesday 28 January

Met Nigel Wilcockson at Random House, who was going to edit the book. Not a sport fan but I liked him and he had some good thoughts. Good mental health event with Geoff McDonald [global vice-president] at Unilever. Paul Polman [CEO] not there but sent me a nice message. I think these guys could really be good for the Time to Change campaign. Off to *King Lear* which was brilliant. Simon Russell Beale stunning. Very white audience of course. Robin Butler there. Little chat re. power and madness!

Wednesday 29 January

Worked a bit then off to Parliament for an Alcohol Concern Dry January meeting. Lou Macari was there doing a package for MUTV. Tessa. A few others. Going OK. To *Newsnight* to talk about [philosopher and author] Alain de Botton's book [*The News: A User's Manual*] re. the news. Paxman telling me in the makeup room he was thinking of moving on.

Thursday 30 January

A meeting with the top two guys at Berenberg Bank. They wanted advice on how to strategise and communicate a plan both to grow and push for a new banking model. They said the banking system had not changed. Interesting challenge and we agreed I would do a scoping report and see where it led. A lot of it was above my head but we would be able to do something together. Bumped into Mark Ferguson, chatted about United. He said business was not buying Ed. Portland party then dinner with Jonathan Yeo [artist] and his wife Shebah [Ronay]. They had no contact with Rebekah [Wade] at all, having been so close.

Friday 31 January
To Mum's with Rayan. Mikey [Campbell, nephew] over from Poland. Off to York Uni. Interviews then the union. Anthony Seldon's son chairing. Whacked him re. private education. Mainly doing mental health and a bit of politics.

Saturday 1 February
QPR away. Three–all. Amazing match. Deserved to win. Philip Beard telling me he had never met anyone like Harry Redknapp. Like a kid in a toy shop in the transfer market. We were the cheaper but better team and had kept all our players through the transfer window. Jamie Redknapp there with his kids, had a good chat.

Sunday 2 February
To the 'Being a Man' (BAM) festival at the South Bank. Interesting talk from a hip-hop artist re. black male sexuality or more accurately white men's interpretation of it. My talk was with a music business guy re. depression and addiction. All fine. One or two wanker questions but I got a bit too aerated probably.

Tuesday 4 February
A business trust meeting at KPMG for ICAS [Institute of Chartered Accountants]. One guy asked why I couldn't fix TB reputation like I had my own. It was becoming a given that he was in a bad place just now. To Watford for a gig for Greg Nugent with the Co-op leadership team. Off to National Theatre, where we were seeing *King Lear* again, and beforehand I was doing a talk for theatre supporters with American psychiatrist Nassir Ghaemi. Met Simon Russell Beale [lead actor]. Ghaemi was very interesting and agreed to meet up for an interview for the book. Fascinating about the positive effects of mania. Also that Martin Luther King was a manic

depressive. Mania – leadership, charisma, innovation, drive, inspiration. Depression – empathy, the human soul, suffering. F and G there, seemed to enjoy it. Evan Davis [BBC broadcaster] chairing. Charles Clarke in the audience, which was made up mainly of lots of rich targets for fundraising for the theatre.

Then got a message to call Margaret McDonagh urgently. Mark Bennett had dropped dead of a heart attack. Fucking unbelievable. Had he been drinking again I wonder? I could hardly take it in. Was he that unhealthy? A bit overweight maybe, but no, not really. We had been through a lot, he had always been a total support. Funny too. Everyone in the family liked him. So fucking sad. I got home feeling really down. Called round a few people. TB and others put out nice words. I then sat down and wrote a blog. I wanted to add my voice to the tributes that have been paid. Virtually everyone who called or emailed has said the same thing. 'I just can't believe he has gone.'

A lot of memories. When I first met him, he was a civil servant, the only 'Garden Room Girl' who wasn't a woman. Then working with Alison [Blackshaw], the two of them sitting outside my office, gatekeepers, support staff, advisers and friends. They basically ran my professional life for me and I trusted them totally to do so.

And then as the 2001 election neared, he did something that few civil servants do. He resigned his position so that he could continue to support us in the election and effectively became my right-hand man for the duration of the campaign. This despite the fact that it meant an inevitable end to his civil service career. Then all those efforts to get selected as a parliamentary candidate, finally becoming a councillor in Lambeth, and a brilliant one at that. Then Mayor of Lambeth, loving the status – and the regalia!

Right-hand man on the diaries. Sitting here now, writing this where usually he sat, day after day up here at the top of the house. In the cast list in *The Blair Years* he is down as my 'researcher'. That does not get close. Tough times too, always there. The last time he worked for me on a big project was preparing for the Chilcot Inquiry. He and Rory accompanied me to the inquiry hearing. He always knew when I might need him around, didn't have to be asked. Like when he had been helping me prepare for BBC *Question Time* in Burnley with George Galloway and as I got ready to head north, he just turned up and got into the car without being asked. 'Are you coming?' 'I think I'd better ... I'll step in if it gets to fisticuffs.' Great guy, team player, too young.

Wednesday 5 February
Tube strike. Rayan picked me up and took me to the Treasury. I was in the

waiting room and the little guy who had been there for years came in with my coffee. 'This is not right. You are a tea man!' he said. 'Ah, I've changed.' Said he had done nine chancellors and was leaving after ten. I got the strong sense he preferred us to this lot. I was there for a Time to Change event to sign the pledge with Osborne, Nicky Morgan and Sue Baker [Time to Change director]. Met Osborne in his office. Couldn't resist saying that he felt Ed had totally dumped the centre ground. 'Who was that guy who kept winning elections, you know, that Blair guy?' He felt Ed had no chance of winning, and that they had at least some. He spoke well at the event. He was nice about me, if barbed, and seemed genuinely to get the importance, not least the fact that he was the one giving the message to the staff, not just about mental health policy, but as an employer, that they needed to feel supported and that we all did what we could to end the stigma.

Huge turnout. Sue and I spoke then Q&A and book signing. Good event. A woman afterward in tears because she was living with an alcoholic husband. Off to Liverpool St to meet Brendan Foster for lunch. He had penned an attack for the *Mirror* on Gove, who had said running round the football field should be a punishment. Crazy speech yesterday. Brendan in great form and had good ideas re. the Winning book. To Norwich for the UAE literary festival. Met by Special Branch because there was a demo planned and there were some dangerous elements involved, they said. They decided to move the venue of the meeting with [novelist, lecturer] Henry Sutton's students, because they were worried protestors had found out where I was to be before the main event which would be easier to secure. Liz [sister] and Nina [Parker, student, friend of Grace] joined us. Liz was coming to Albania with me tomorrow so she could see Jamie. Good enough session with the students, bright bunch, most of it on the process of writing then to the festival. Sold out.

Henry did a good job chairing. I had not had so much security for years. It felt a bit over the top, but the Special Branch guy said they had a genuine concern. I sensed they wanted me to say did they want me to call it off. They sat me down and talked through what they had in place. They even made us change the set-up on the stage so that I was nearer a door for evacuation. Henry seemed a bit alarmed. 'Does this happen often?' 'Now and then.' 'I don't understand it. Everyone I talk to likes you.' 'There are definitely some who don't.' There were a couple of people in the fourth row whose looks on their faces made me think, but then one of them asked a question, and it was one of the warmest of the night, suggesting I was doing better on the reputation front than TB, and why didn't I go back and help him. Sad that he was seen like that. Liz drove me to Gatwick Sofitel and I managed to get a few hours' sleep. Henry said he couldn't believe how much I packed in.

Thursday 6 February

Met Liz for coffee, got her upgraded and off we went. Laughing at the time we went on holiday to Tiree and Mum made us wear our school uniform. What the hell was that about? Met by Endri's driver and to the hotel then office but hanging around a lot because Edi was trapped in Parliament. Berisha was the first face I saw on TV as we arrived. Raining. Good meeting with Endri and Vali to work out a more thematic approach to strategy based on security, progress and innovation. Chatted for hours and eventually had to give up on Edi. Dinner with Liz and Jamie at Gusto. Erion Veliaj [Albanian politician] joined us. He was still loving it as Mayor of Tirana.

Friday 7 February

Good meeting with Edi, really felt he was listening and more strategic. Proud of his new wallpaper made up of his desk doodles, which included a drawing he did of an *FT* cartoon of me. Meeting with Meta, who also felt things were OK-ish but that Berisha was not going to stop. [Sir] Suma Chakrabarti [president European Bank for Reconstruction and Development] who had been in Moldova was on the second leg of the flight. Good chat re. Edi, and Bosnia, and also reminiscing re. GB and looking forward – or not – to Chilcot. He felt we were all likely to get whacked. Rory had done some good stuff for the book from Nassir Ghaemi about the link between mental illness and elite performance.

Saturday 8 February

Burnley 3 Millwall 1. Worked on the mania and depression section for the book most of the day.

Sunday 9 February

Sent an email round people with money for Rory's run for Philip [Gould]. Man U held by Fulham at home. Mike Phelan sent a message saying it was not a happy place. Reading [businessman Sir Richard] Branson's books ahead of our interview with him for the book.

Monday 10 February

Jim O'Neill [economist] interview for the book. Smart guy. Lunch with Eric Baker of Viagogo [online tickets agency]. Interesting on innovation. A talk at City Uni for Roy Greenslade. I was doing too many of these kinds of bitty events for pals.

Tuesday 11 February

Saw Dr Shilpa Patel to try to sort nose. Savoy dinner for Lloyds Bank. Futurologist Mark Stevenson quite interesting. He had a great line on Gove – preparing us for the last century rather than the next one. Andy Brough from Schroders [global investment managers] backing UKIP. Lloyds economist very optimistic.

Thursday 13 February

Worked on an *Indy* obit for Mark Bennett. To Plasterers Hall for awards for Euromoney. I had done enough of these sell-out events for a while thank you.

Friday 14 February

Off to France. Mainly working on the book. Did the *FT* crisis management piece on the back of Cameron's piss-poor floods management and safe standing debate in *The Observer*. I was starting to crunch down the book argument to being one about politics needing to learn from sport and business. Going to be a lot more work to get good. Reading Warren Buffett [American business magnate and philanthropist] books which were excellent. Lovely time with Fiona but Molly getting ill again. We got into *The Bridge*, a new Danish-Swedish police series which was fantastic. Good mental health portrayal too, loved the Saga Norén character.

Saturday 22 February

We stayed overnight two hours from Paris at one of Fiona's posh hotels and she dropped me off at Charles de Gaulle, heading to Dubai for a conference. Mainly working and reading Obama book. Arrived late. Chaos at Dubai airport because of earlier fog. Got VIP'd through with a woman who was holding up a card for Mrs Alaister Campbel and so didn't believe it was me. Driven to Hilton Sharjah and bed just after midnight. Burnley beat Forest 3–1.

Sunday 23 February

Rory won his half-marathon, Fiona and Georgia keeping me updated through the race. Wish I had been there. Breakfast then out for start of the Forum. Really high budget event. All a bit OTT. Audience mainly male and government. Chat Nik Gowing [foreign affairs journalist], who was keeping me up to speed with events in Ukraine – [Victor] Yanukovich

[President] on the way out. Met Mikhail Gorbachev who was guest of honour and who did a very good speech. Also chatted to him a bit for the book. He was pretty down about where Russia was but fascinating on how he made change. Looked his age but sharp as ever. He had the same interpreter as when he had been in power, who told me how much he had enjoyed the meetings with Thatcher. Good time with Bill Daley [former Obama chief of staff], who said he did 'a fair bit of this sort of shit', which I could add to my collection of descriptions of post-politics speaking circuit life. Simon Anholt [independent policy adviser] also there. Interesting on Putin. Said that he went up in standing around the world not just Russia when he did what we considered illiberal things because most countries have a morally conservative majority. Worked and ran then official dinner work at the hotel. Met Rana Nejem from Jordan, who I had met when helping Portland. Sat with her, Daley and Tim Allan. Tired.

Monday 24 February
Went to the Simon Anholt [independent policy adviser]–John Kao [American author and strategic adviser] talk and also Bill Daley on cities. The event as a whole somewhat lacking in energy. Decided for my own event just to stand up and talk and try to get them interacting a bit. Meeting with Tim Allan and a Bahraini contact. Lunch with Anholt etc. Amazed that he basically worked on his own. Speech no notes went well. Good feedback. Good Q&A but it was cut short by a very un-Arab time stickler.

We all got a kind of award. Interesting music etc. Plane not till 3 a.m. so had to decide whether to go to bed or wait up. Ended up going to Dubai for a couple of hours. So different to conservative Sharjah. Twinkling palm trees. Went for a walk to kill time. Amazing atmos around the place. Emirates first class fantastic.

Tuesday 25 February
Landed on time. Rayan collected me and off to meet Edi Rama and team at the Goring. Then to the Lords where he was speaking to a mix of peers and MPs. He felt things were going OK, but that candidate status was not looking great. Grace really upset post a row with F about one of her friends sleeping in our bed when we were away. Home. Airport. Fly to Berlin.

Thursday 27 February
Pottered at home then out to see Hilary Coffman and David Hill [former TB communications staff] pre Walthamstow CLP dinner. Chatted re. TB.

Awful *G2* cover with TOXIC in red across his face. Really hit a kind of tipping point. I had protests outside the venue so in the back with Yousaff the Bollywood bodyguard. Did a postcard Q&A and book signing which kicked off when one of Galloway's film people tried to do a citizen's arrest on me. I stayed pretty calm, playing for laughs, though it was pretty obvious they were trying to provoke me into doing something physical so they could scream violence. The guy was pretty determined and it took police ages to restrain him, the whole thing being filmed. Arrested then Galloway announced he was off to the station to demand his release. Stella Creasy [Walthamstow Labour MP] very apologetic but hey-ho.

Friday 28 February

Portland training session. Galloway at Chingford police station trying to get the film director released. Blogged on it to get the line over that I would pre-empt it. Also kids at Portland had good idea to film it myself next time it happened.

Saturday 1 March

Burnley with the boys. Reading on Salmond. Loved the line from his grandad – if you are saying something radical, wear a suit. The Winning book is coming on fine and is up to 170,000 words even without most of the interviews to fit in which is way too much. Enjoying it though. Rory digging up good stuff. Working through the holy trinity of strategy, teamship and leadership. Getting good insights, I think. Looking forward to April and France when I would have a good slab of time but too much stuff coming into the diary. I need to start saying no to more CLPs and colleges. Fiona and I getting on really well though she thought I was manic again. The longest I have ever been on anti-depressants and certainly I felt quite chirpy most of the time. Feeling pretty creative. Not sleeping well. Definitely on the manic side of life at the moment.

Talking a fair bit to the Jordanians about the possibility of a tie-up there and also TB wanting me to help in Egypt. And Kosovo pushing me to get out there too. Jordan was the most interesting in a way. Really mattered. The huge thing going on at the moment was Crimea and Ukraine and Putin finally deciding to go for it. The weak leadership in the West was really being exposed now. Obama a disappointment, Cameron an embarrassment, Hollande weak, only Merkel strong and of course the Germans worried about their own power. Putin looking like a classic case of power-crazed but he was strong. Face-lifted and Botoxed. Labour special conference went OK. A few weeks ago it had looked bad for Ed but he has got his reforms through. Another banana skin avoided.

Monday 3 March

Off to City for a flight to Dublin. Bumped into Dominic Grieve [Attorney General]. Nice chat. To Buswells Hotel and then to do a bit of media with Suzanne Costello of Alcohol Ireland. Good event in the evening with me and a doctor. Good turnout. Had to push Suzanne to be a bit more aggressive with the industry. Like a lot of these NGOs their heart was in the right place but they were slightly cowed by the industry. Guinness a powerful brand but actually didn't do much for the community in the way the family did pre Diageo.*

Tuesday 4 March

More media including the main radio and a few papers and then the main event at the Dáil. All-party group on alcohol abuse. All fine. Good nurse from Galway and a paramedic. Totally on the right side of the argument but not going to be easy to turn it around. Finding good stretches of down time to write book stuff.

Wednesday 5 March

Worked a.m. then Bath Festival on the novel with Richard Kilgarriff [producer and host of literary events]. Good chat to huge audience though one of the sponsors had a pop. Doing too many of these kinds of events, though. Really need to slow down and focus. People were starting to say how tired I looked.

Thursday 6 March

Work on book, too many words already! KPMG dinner. One of those instantly forgettable ones though the Metrobank CEO was interesting, about how he had essentially taken all the things people disliked about their banks and done the opposite. No big salaries etc. Nice guy from Waitrose who seemed sympatico but like a lot of people was not buying Ed. Cameron down at the moment too. Osborne the one on the move.

---

* In 1997 Guinness became part of Diageo, a British company formed from the merger with Grand Metropolitan. Draught Guinness remained the company's No. 1 product.

Gove on manoeuvres. Agreed to do the Metrobank guy, Craig Donaldson [co-founder], for the innovation section of the book.

Friday 7 March
Good interview with Matthew Benham [gambler, owner Brentford FC] for the book. No shoes. Took a while to look in the eye. But really interesting on football. Felt we were up and would stay up. Good on conventional wisdoms almost always being wrong. Biggest bet 6 million on Spain Euro 2012 because the market was marking them down.

Sunday 9 March
And finally after thirty-five years we beat Blackburn Rovers [2–1]. Chat with Mike Phelan [former Man United player and coach]. Said United not a happy place. Moyes – who was also there – changing too much. Players not happy. Rooney taking the piss. Joking re. Fergie being at the Oscars etc. Good game. Down one–nil. Amazing comeback. Buzzing all the way home. Surely going up now.

Monday 10 March
David S. He said he sensed the demon was out. Probably right. Another conference call re. Jordan. Martin S scoping Egypt. PR Academy speech and awards.

Tuesday 11 March
Long chat with Gail and then OK meeting with Nigel Wilcockson. He seemed to be on the right page. Saw TB re. Egypt. Also to discuss him. He was not in good shape reputationally. He was determined to do Egypt and though it was important and right it would be another reputational hit for all of us.

Wednesday 12 March
Ed M has done his big speech on Europe. He trailed it in a good bylined piece in the *FT* making clear an in/out referendum is unlikely, all slightly marred by Nick Robinson saying on the Beeb that policy was confused with a promise to have a referendum after all if more sovereignty is transferred. I told Tom B it was OK but needed clarity on whether he meant 'yes, but' or 'no, but'. He said they had got to the right place on the policy

– 'no, but' – but it had all got a bit muddied by the usual internal bollocks of too many people, too many views. It meant that the edges were taken off maybe. Ed could have got a lot more strength from this speech than he did. It was tricky stuff though.

Thursday 13 March

David Frost memorial. What an event. Lovely day. Westminster Abbey packed. We were out just behind the front row opposite Prince Charles and Camilla and the family. David Mellor behind me said it was like one of Frostie's parties without the booze. Greg Dyke did a good eulogy. Parky a reading, looking a bit frail. Major and Cherie there. Jamie and Christiane. Seb. Everywhere you looked. Lovely tributes to him on film and some of his clips. Really top man. Unique. Loved him. Didn't get chance to speak to Carina but she seemed OK. Off to Oxford Union. Good turnout. All on mental health. Told them why I didn't like Oxbridge. Crimea getting worse. Putin not stopping. Destabilising left right and centre. Planning Egypt.

Oxford Labour fundraiser for Andrew Smith [MP]. Lovely guy. Nice tribute to me in intro. Fairly typical party audience. Did a postcard Q&A, and was clear about the need to do more to challenge the Tories blaming us over the 'mess we inherited' and also praised Ed for standing up in a serious way on Europe. But it was never quite good enough. Neither his new party reforms nor the Europe speech really cut through to the public. Doing all this work on winning, and analysing so many winners, it was becoming clear to me that he was almost certainly going to lose. Not going to happen. Or if it does it will be only because of default. Good book signing. Andrew a real team player. Loving being a backbencher. His wife had cancer. Back home late and slightly stressed.

Friday 14 March

Off to Aberdeen. Melissa [daughter] called Fiona to say Tony Benn had died. Got to Aberdeen and met up with Alex Salmond at the Marcliffe. Both getting bids for Benn tributes so we did those in between an interview lasting several hours. More impressed than I wanted to be. He was very friendly and warm and also less sneery and narky than usual. He was interesting for the book as well on winning and how he had changed his mindset from one of opposition to one of government. He had read my blogs, knew about my family, talked up my being Scottish, asked me to stay for a long lunch and then most surprisingly of all asked me to be part of the negotiating team with the rest of the UK, Europe etc. if he won.

He seemed quite serious too. He said if they got independence he would want to reach out to people like me, and use the skills I had in government, and also nation branding.

He clearly didn't rate Cameron. Loathed Osborne. Not impressed by Ed. My sense was he really thought he could win. Good strong interview, *GQ* would be happy. Not sure he meant to be so warm re. Putin, which would be a story, and he was loose with his words on Scotland's reputation on booze. Rory doing data stuff. Off to Durham. Collected by a guy who took me to the wrong hotel. Very annoying. Fundraiser good though. All the old Sedgefield folk there. Iain McNicol [Labour general secretary] and I had a bagpipe play-off. He plays well. Did the postcard Q&A again. Goes down really well. Chat Lee Sherriff and some of the other candidates. She seemed confident about Carlisle. Ed not going down well though. Bed late.

Saturday 15 March
Driven to Burnley by a party guy. Worked on leadership. Went to see Stan. Good form as ever. Felt Moyes changing too much. Leeds match – their fans were great and they played pretty well too but we turned it around [2–1] after going one down.

Sunday 16 March
Crimea referendum.* Putin running rings round everyone. Obama weak. Cameron nowhere.

Monday 17 March
Briefing at EBRD with their Balkan guys. Impressed by Edi, worried about Bosnia. Possible existential crisis re. Russia/Ukraine, because they were their biggest clients. Putin basically trying to resurrect the Cold War and clear that he did not fear the reactions. Lunch with Suma Chakrabarti and Jonathan Charles [ex-BBC, now EBRD spokesman]. Wanting me to help with Moldova, another one Putin would be destabilising. With Grace to Hacked Off party at Millbank Tower. Great chat with Gerry McCann who thanked me for saying what I did at the time it was all going wrong for

---

* The Crimean status referendum, held by the Ukraine subdivisions of the Autonomous Republic of Crimea and the local government of Sevastopol, asked local populations if they wanted to join Russia as federal subjects. In each locality 97 per cent of a high turnout voted to integrate into the Russian Federation.

them. I said I had wanted to get in touch when it all happened, and he said that is weird because a BBC guy said, 'You should get hold of Alastair Campbell.' Liked him. John Bishop [comedian] hilarious. Very funny re. how he had to do a sex scene on his own in *Accused* [TV series] because it was just for sound only! Good guy. High Grant good speech, ditto Anne Diamond and her very posh sons.

Tuesday 18 March

Off to Barnes to interview Lineker in a nice yummy mummy café cum restaurant. He is smart, thinks, and a lot friendlier than when we met on the golf course a while back. He was trying to be positive about England winning the World Cup while also realistic, and going through some of the deeper issues – poor coaching for kids, big pitches, parents. Spain and Germany changed their whole thinking about how to coach young players. England so far half-hearted about it. I said Spain's B team would beat England and he didn't demur. Champions League champions better than World Cup winners. Messi better than Ronaldo. Good on alcohol in sport. Just don't have it. Also strong on all the betting advertising and sponsorship in sport. 'Crisps are fine. They do no harm at all.'

Not happy re. FIFA. Defended Shearer as pundit. Agreed too many replays on *Match of the Day*. Hasn't played any charity games. 'Can you imagine the horror of being embarrassed on the football field by Alastair Campbell? I'm not risking it.' Said his dream panel of pundits, dead or alive, would be Andy Gray, Alan Hansen, Gary Neville. If allowed a manager, Cloughie [the late Brian Clough].

Told me he once got a bollocking for saying in the trailer that you'd be better off going to bed. His best manager – Bobby Robson; best coach Terry Venables, runner up Johan Cruyff. Into Shakespeare! After the interview we chatted over a nice lunch and I sensed he was a lot more political than he admitted in the interview.

Thursday 20 March

Work on Winners book. Great lunch with Guillem Balagué re. [Lionel] Messi [Barcelona player], Pep [Guardiola, Bayern Munich manager] etc. He said Pep and Messi hadn't spoken since Pep left for Bayern because Messi only focuses on his own football. Never read a book. Ronaldo much deeper. Pep fallen out with [José] Mourinho [Chelsea manager]. Not what he is cracked up to be. Takes mind games too far. Not sure Fergie likes him.

Friday 21 March

Off to Streatham for Mark's memorial with Fiona and Grace. Lovely sunny day. Fantastic turnout. Great that TB came. Mark would have loved that. Church [St Leonard's, Streatham] packed top and bottom. Lib and Imogen, two of his friends, spoke beautifully. They were close to tears but got through it. So did I with a large quantity of Diazepam. Good turnout from No. 10. I wore a red not black tie, as I know he would have preferred that. I started the eulogy with his own words from his website, his comical account of his own life as measured against observations by music hall comedian – 'Dan Leno said, a former resident of Lambeth by the way (Akerman Road, SW9 since you ask)' – and Shakespeare's ages of man – puking infant, whining schoolboy, sighing lover, then 'a soldier, full of strange oaths and bearded like the pard, jealous in honour, sudden and quick in quarrel'.

I told stories mainly that showed his humanity and his dedication to the team. TB laughed out loud when I recalled Mark's comment on the slow-handclapped Women's Institute speech. 'All wool, no thread.' Loved being mayor [of Lambeth]. Loved the chains. Loved meeting the Queen. Good laugh when I told the story of the diary preparation, explaining that was why his dog was called Index. His help on Chilcot, big TV moments. The whole event was really sad but also moving and he would have loved it. People commented on how great it was that TB just turned up as an ordinary mourner. All the speeches went fine. Nice to see so many of the old No. 10 people there. Anne Marie O'Brien [No. 10 Garden Room] in tears, one or two others and his mum looked in bits. Had a chat with his sister – hadn't realised that his passion for the campaign on hearing aids was because she had a profoundly deaf daughter.

Saturday 22 March

Did a blog on Mark and then off to Charlton. John Banaszkiewicz [Burnley director] was holding court and buying drinks in a pub near where he lived. Great mood, lovely day and we battered them 3–0.

Sunday 23 March

Working on book. Coming together well. Evening with the Kennedys [academic lawyer Sir Ian and sons Tom and Jack]. New flat at the top of Jack Straw's castle. Nice evening. Went out for something to eat but then back to watch Barca win at Real Madrid. He was reading [New Zealand rugby player] Richie McCaw's book. Said McCaw had a pop at me over the handling of the O'Driscoll spear tackle incident.

Tuesday 25 March

A call with TB re. Egypt. I was a bit worried about it, but TB was adamant that Sisi [Abdel Fattah el-Sisi, Deputy Prime Minister] was the only guy who could hold things together and he would need support. The idea was that he and I went together. At first he was pushing hard but then said that it might be better if he went without me. I said why him who had more to lose than me? He said because he had the MEPP locus, and Egypt was an important player. The Murdochs thing, his name being dragged into the Brooks trial – though Gavin thought she might get off – and all this focus on money were not great. He was aware but also so driven by the desire to build his organisation, which needed money for salaries, and the projects he funded himself, and also being engaged in these big issues. I was getting it raised more and more when I was out and about, and people we're asking about the contrast in the way our reputations had gone.

Met Dave Brailsford at the Renaissance with Rory for the book. First the usual of him telling me Ed M had no chance and that if I got a seat I would be leader in no time and win an election. He was adamant about it. I said it is not so simple. He said it is. Like when he said they would win the Tour. Was it possible he asked? Yes. Then got scared. You need a bit of fear, he said. Definitely the Ed mood was down – there had been another public shift. Great interview, really good. He was so clear about the way he did things. Rory said after he was a total genius.

Some great stuff on working back from an objective. Tim Kerrison [coach] on how they used data to do it. Very down on Bradley Wiggins. Probably not going to ride him in the Tour. He had got too Billy Big Bollocks. He was still wondering about his next career. Maybe giving up British cycling just to concentrate on Sky. He said he got bored between big events but then it all kicked in and that was where he was now. Massive BRAILSFORD down his suitcase and phone. Off to Spain for a race. We were talking about Clive Woodward when who should walk in? Clive! He was doing a Deloitte event next door. Got him over for a chat. The two of them very similar and with a lot of empathy for each other.

To Browns for lunch with Victor Blank. He too very down on Labour. He thought the huge house at the top of the Heath taking years to build was Putin's. Reminiscing re. Frost and his amazing memorial. Jim Murphy there and we walked to the Tube together. He was writing a book on football. Said that the shadow Cabinet that morning would have made me want to shoot myself. Total denial and complacency. Laziness. Arrogance. All telling each other how good they were. Awful.

Out to Surrey with Rory for the UK sport elite coaching group. Top coaches from different sports, gymnastics, netball, rowing, synchronised swimming. Did my usual stuff and seemed to go down OK, Q&A, a lot of it focused on GB and teamship. Stayed for a part of the dinner mainly talking about the Putin situation. Watched the United City debacle. United lost 3–0 at home to Man City. Before David Moyes had called me and asked if I could have a chat with him about his media handling. He felt it was not quite crisis point but getting close. He sounded a bit panicky.

Wednesday 26 March

Long chat with Tom Baldwin. I said I was getting close to saying something public. There was just no sense of the gears being shifted. Ed was in the wrong place on so many issues. Tom said the problem was that Ed genuinely believed that he was into something with this idea that he was standing up for the ordinary man against the toffs. It was not a winning strategy. Also the public were not buying either of the Eds. The shadow Cabinet was piss-weak, Osborne had done OK. I could see us losing to an overall majority. The public were just kind of becalmed about the whole thing. He talked me out of doing anything public. He said I had a near unique brand as a loyal supporter of the party who could say privately what I wanted and still manage to support in public. I said Ed's Budget response showed he only listened to the bits he wanted. I was pushing the same stuff on the failure to challenge the Tory line on 'mess we inherited' and Germany and leadership on the Putin situation.

Writing a speech for Edi to give in Germany. Evening out to St James's Theatre for an evening with Matt Forde [comedian and writer]. He did half-hour stand up and then me – good interview. Both of us funny. Got a bit heavy when we got on to depression etc. Then in the Q&A I slightly lost it with a guy who called TB a hypocrite. Got very feisty. Went for a drink with them after. It was yet another crowd that was OK with me but had real issues with TB.

David Moyes called and asked if I could maybe go up and see him. I was heading up anyway so agreed that I would see him when up seeing Alex. He sounded pretty nervy and said all manner of stuff was getting out which wasn't true like he and [Ryan] Giggs had fallen out. But both Alex and Phil Townsend [communications director] had said there was something in it. Phil said he had got off to a bad start with him and it had not got better. He was too blamey about the press. He had not really had the same kind of big club experience at Everton and was finding it hard to step up. Fergie said to tell him to stop talking so much to the press and stop letting them drive the agenda. Moyes said he accepted that. He was not controlling the agenda at press conferences etc. He was firing off thought after thought and sounding very defensive.

Thursday 27 March

Tony Benn funeral. Lovely day. Nice crowd outside. Red flags, union banners and the like. Queue to get in. Down by the front opposite the family. Melissa really worried about holding it together, but all the kids spoke brilliantly. Hilary was rehearsing his words during the hymns. Melissa was having to look after Josh who didn't want to speak so she did it for both. Applause outside when they were mentioned by Stephen who spoke really well. Bercow in tears. Ed OK but I sensed he and Justine were both really tense. I felt a mood of negativity around him. Good turnout. Hezza. Lots of the unions. Cherie. Lots of MPs. Nice chat with Melissa and Hilary on exit. They seemed really relieved though she wrote to us later to say they felt desolate when they got back.

Off to Manchester with Rory, working on bits and bobs. Dire traffic. Talked to Phil and then Alex en route. Both very down on the situation. I sensed Phil thought he [Moyes] wouldn't last. Eventually made it 5.15 p.m. I had an hour with Moyes. Not in great shape I would say. A bit hyper and worryingly said at one point did I think he needed his own PR guy? When I probed it turned out that Paul Stretford [football agent] had recommended it and had suggested one of his own people. Alex was gobsmacked when I told him that. Added to which, according to Alex, Rooney was pissing off the other players by trying to take control, telling them when they could have days off etc. He could not see how several of them would stay.

Moyes was definitely blaming the media too much. I said he had to grip the reality. If players were not happy that would get out. He said that he had not heard a peep from the club or the board to suggest there was a problem and maybe he should get that out there, but I said he should be careful with that, as it could be taken as a sign they were not behind him. I repeated endlessly that he needed to have a long-term plan and messages and just keep them going. Say interesting things. Make the same points again and again in different ways. Make better use of e.g. the programme notes or the MUTV channel or the club photographer. Control your own message. Do not let them set your agenda.

He kept coming back to 'What shall I say tomorrow at the Villa press conference?' kind of question. He had always seemed OK on this stuff, but it was such a big leap up I guess that he had underestimated just how big a leap it was from Everton to Man U. I spoke to Phil after. He was very down on him. I said he had to support him while he was there, but I sensed Phil felt he wouldn't be there for long. I noticed there was a prayer book on Moyes's desk. 'You wouldn't believe the things people are sending me.'

Friday 28 March

Fergie over to the hotel for breakfast. Good chat. Couple of hours with him first to go over last night with David Moyes. He had seen him at the Darren Fletcher charity event last night and David had said we had met. I said I felt he didn't come over as being in control. I could never quite get to the bottom of how much David had been Alex's choice, and how much the board's that it would be easier to have someone follow AF of whom it would be clear he approved, in same image kind of thing. He said at one point that 'it'll be interesting to see what the Glazers [American owners of the club] do', almost as though he was a bit detached from it. He said he knew that DM had pissed off Chicharito, Ashley Young and one or two other players. He didn't like Hernandez because he had a poor first touch. He always had – but he would get you a good number of goals. 'Squads win titles.'

We had a good chat for the book, Rory having worked out the questions, and would definitely be enough for the foreword and bits more. He was quite helpful on a few ideas of others to talk to e.g. Jorge Mendes [Portuguese 'super-agent']. Good enough chat I would say. Good on teamship/resilience/mindset.

Off to the Dunkenhalgh [Blackburn hotel] for an event for Every Action has Consequences, which was born from the death by a single punch of a guy called Adam Rogers who was trying to break up a fight. Did a little talk then off to do something similar at Sir John Thursby Community College in Burnley. Good kids basically. It was the same place where I had done *Question Time* with Galloway, with Mark B. Went to see Sean and Ian Woan [assistant manager] at the training ground. They were totally owning the place. Great mood there. Impressive how he was running things. Off to the bond-holder dinner – John B doing his presentation re. the world changing. Good night then later with Marlon Beresford, Liam Robinson and Paul Weller [former players] back at the hotel. Liam a tree surgeon and going on about how much he loved it. Marlon an accountant still. Paul had lost his job at Bury, unemployed.

Saturday 29 March

Run. Up to Stan Ternent's for breakfast. Kath's world-class bacon sarnies. Match v Leicester. They were too strong. Lost 2–0. Gary Lineker winding me up on Twitter. I was meant to be going to Cairo tonight but agreed with TB that it was better he went with the Portland guys.

Sunday 30 March
Edi seeing Merkel. Chatted over his strategy for the meeting. So important to have her making supportive noises about Balkan enlargement. The Farage interview for *GQ* was out, getting a fair bit of coverage for his seeming warmth towards Putin.

Monday 31 March
Lebedev [owner *Evening Standard*] party at his place in Portland Place. Tessa, Cameron, long chat with Vince Cable and his spad. Andrew Neil winding him up about the unnamed minister – thought to be [Defence Secretary] Hammond – who had said there could be currency union. The papers had done stuff on Farage from the interview saying he admired Putin. Farage there and he seemed fine with it. Great laugh with Geordie Greig [*Mail on Sunday* editor] on how best to get rid of Dacre. He said that he hardly spoke to him. Also that when he left the *Mail* for *Today* as a reporter Dacre had accused him of unforgivable betrayal. Harriet H there and chatted re. Leveson. Ditto Hugh Grant. Kind of odd do. Lebedev launching his new London Live TV station. Young presenters. Kay Burley [Sky News] saying I ought to help Ed. He was going nowhere.

Tuesday 1 April
Lots of April Fools. Lineker suckered me with one about *MotD* having celeb presenters and was I interested? Edi called on a high after seeing Merkel. He said it could not have gone better. They went in feeling like schoolboys going to see the headteacher and not sure what to expect. By the time they came out they were flying high. She was intelligent, informed, constructive, serious but also good fun. In the meeting he asked her to visit Tirana and she was non-committal but in the press conference she said she would within a year, and also that she was supportive of Albanian candidate status. It was all so different to the way Cameron dealt with these issues. He said she was very much a detail person, said at one point she didn't really like the showy side of politics, she was all about doing and she loved strategy and she loved to take change forward in a very clear and organised way.

I had never heard Edi quite so high about someone, and Endri was the same when he called later. He too said it had been at the outer end of expectations. Steffen had been great with him and offered him a visit to see how their press service worked. He was so chuffed. Edi said he had given my letter, asking for an interview for the Winning book, to one of her advisers as she went to take a call and when he said what it was about, Steffen said I was obviously coming in at all angles. He told them the story of how I had bet him that when she went to the UK Parliament she would say that she would neither satisfy those who said she would have big news to announce to help Cameron, nor that she was going to change her basic position, nor that she was going to be overly critical of scepticism. They were laughing when she came back in and she asked what they were laughing about.

Edi said that he had given her team my letter and explained the project I was trying to do. He then told her about the bet and said I was a great admirer and obviously on the same wavelength because I accurately predicted what she would say. Later she took him to one side as they were walking to the car and she said, 'Say this to Alastair, but to nobody else – it was quite easy to win that bet, because David gave me no choice as to what to say.' Basically she felt Cameron had screwed up by pandering to the right, and there was no way she was going to go too far in helping if it meant going against the basic European project. He said she got quite skittish when he said I saw her as the great political winner of our time, and that she would be in with Ferguson and Guardiola and so forth. Steffen didn't seem too pissed off that I had gone direct. Edi was so chuffed about the whole meeting, one on one, with the team, lunch and then a press conference and said she could not have been warmer or friendlier.

Wednesday 3 April

Edi on to say their health minister had been stopped from coming in because of visa difficulties. So after the high of yesterday with Merkel, back to this shit. Also having a nightmare with Jason Ferguson, who was clearly trying to block anything good from Fergie in the interview because he was doing his own book on leadership with Mike Moritz [businessman]. I think it was a power kick with him. We had a few testy emails and eventually I asked Alex if he could sort it out. It seemed odd to sit down and do a long interview with a tape recorder on the table, and then have Jason come on and say you can't use it. Flew to Glasgow. Chatted to Douglas and we agreed things were pretty dire. He said that Scottish conference had been poor. People used to like Neil because he was one of theirs, and Tony because he was a winner. Ed had come over as neither of those things.

Douglas said he was meant to have a weekly face-to-face but it never happened. He worried that in general his office was neither professional nor honest, just told Ed what he wanted to hear. BAe [security and aerospace company] event at Blair House in Ayrshire. Good Q&A. Interesting ex-spooks there explaining to me what they were all doing re. cyber security, and explaining just how serious the stuff hitting us from China was.

Friday 5 April

Christine Graeff round. ECB [European Central Bank]. Wanted me to be a bit of a mentor, advise her on how to shake up the comms side of stuff. Sounded a bit nightmarish in terms of bureaucracy. She was bright and feisty and there could definitely be a project in it. Train later to Derby, for the Margaret Beckett fundraiser. Leo [husband] in charge, a bit unsteady on his feet which was hardly surprising given his age, but he was still sharp. Margaret was standing again. Good turnout, good mood, shifted lots of books, did the 'Ask Alastair anything' event again which went really well. Was pretty frank re. our difficulties. Pipes. Jazz singer. Driven to Luton airport, staying there overnight.

Saturday 6 April to Saturday 13 April

Crack of dawn flight to Nimes. Started a daily letter to Dacre, one question per day, because he wouldn't do the *GQ* interview. Matthew [Freud] trying to broker an interview for *GQ* with me and TB which seemed pretty ludicrous at first blush, on so many levels. He seemed to have persuaded TB, but I checked with the team who all thought it was barmy. Mainly working on the book and cycling. Tired. Book much harder than I expected but enjoying it.

Tuesday 9 April

I was due to do Mario Balotelli [Italian footballer] for *GQ*, so off to Milan by train via Geneva. Loads of work on the train, dinner in Geneva, then arrived late. Joking loads with Fiona re. the fact that I was 'in the box', struggling for relevance, and Manuel Valls, who used to ask me for advice the whole time, was now Prime Minister of France. Coulda woulda shoulda. Also getting more and more people saying Ed could not win and I had to try to knock him out. Dave B on at me again.

Wednesday 10 April

Out for a run then to the studio where I was doing Balotelli. All a bit of a circus. He was doing a shoot for Puma whose people were there warning he was always a bit hit and miss, that he would definitely be late, could be a nightmare etc. Sitting around for a while but then he just pitched up in his red Ferrari. Interesting to watch him. Smiled a lot. Joked around, quite chatty. His agent and lawyer, Mino Raiola and his wife, were both there, plus a lawyer who sat in on the interview later. Shared the interview time with *GQ* Italia and it was very strong. To the airport, Al Italia, transcribed on the plane, home for United losing to Bayern then dinner with Calum who seemed in good form.

Thursday 11 April

Rayan picked me up, off to the University of Essex for an OK mental health event, then back into town to see Paddy Harveson for a chat on royal image transformation. Interesting. Could be a chapter on the way they turned things around. Royal brand strong, opposite to every other. To the pharma industry dinner at Westminster Plaza Hotel. JLA said it was black tie so had to rush around getting clothes from M&S. Turned out it wasn't. Nice crowd and again did Q&A from cards. Nice woman at next table with her husband who both came and thanked me, said she had had chronic depression and my book *The Happy Depressive* had really helped her.

Friday 12 April

Lunch with Charlie F at Delauney. He'd lost five stone. Great to see him as ever. Just a good old gossip really. Then to Metrobank with Rory to interview Craig Donaldson for the book. TB – on/off re. me going to Egypt with him, eventually off and then it got really complicated because Portland, who were to be sending an on-the-ground team to Cairo as part of the TB/Sisi deal, got offered a huge contract with Qatar but one of the conditions would be not to work in Egypt. Tim (Friday) said he felt sick about the idea of telling TB. I said, 'What would TB do?' He said that was the only comfort he took from any of it.

Saturday 13 April

Out to Cecconi's with Rayan to meet Mike Forde [sports management consultant], Damien Comolli, Rory and the legend that is Billy Beane. Lovely, lovely man. Really engaged about the book, talking loads to Rory, and with some terrific insights. He must have been asked the same questions so many times, but he was really into the whole thing, also keen on TB (though he said he was basically a republican). Mike and I gently piss-taking as ever, Comolli good fun, definitely a good session for the book. Agreed Rory should do the data chapter. Out to the airport and off to Marseille, cab up to Faucon, hoping to get loads done re. the book. Lost at home to Middlesbrough, one–nil. Tim in a certain amount of agony having gone with the Qataris at the expense of working with TB on Egypt. TB furious for a while but came down pretty quickly and they had a perfectly civilised email exchange. One of the best things about him, that he doesn't bear grudges.

Wednesday 17 April

Maggie, and then Alistair Darling, called to say they were getting worried about the Scottish independence scene. As a result, I sent a message to Osborne, saying that for the first time I actually thought it was loseable. We talked it over. He said he agreed that the momentum was with Salmond but the poll lead remained substantial, and inevitably the No campaign will by its nature be more negative and rationalist. He said his job was to be the tough cop setting out the home truths. Meanwhile he was trying to bolster the No campaign with money, polling and professional advice. He said he was not passing the buck, but there was a limit to what they can do from London. Tory reach in Scotland was very limited, and their main contribution has been cash (no one else seems to have any up there).

The Lib Dems were even less popular than the Tories, he said, while Scottish Labour had provided almost no practical support, was riven by division and left Darling without campaigning support. He said GB, though he still has purchase there, refused to co-ordinate or co-operate with the campaign. He said Alistair was an excellent spokesman but not a campaign organiser. The feud between Douglas Alexander and Jim Murphy was complicating things. He said DC and Ed were meeting to discuss, next week. I said I felt it was serious. I had been up there last week and was going up next week again to do a fundraiser and go to see the Better Together team. I had also been talking to Alistair, Helen Liddell and Margaret Curran [shadow Secretary for Scotland]. AD is excellent in many ways but too much of a safe pair of hands for what is needed now. Scottish Labour seem to believe their own propaganda and have seriously underestimated Salmond's appeal and skills throughout.

I said it was when I interviewed him for *GQ* a month ago that my alarm bells started ringing. He definitely has the scent of victory in his nostrils. He has also got the media eating out of his hand and has disabled people from feeling they can make attacks without being dismissed as 'project fear'. I said Osborne's recent interventions on business and the economy made a difference and business started to move. But it has not been followed through and because Salmond is up there every day, day in day out focused on what he needs to do to win, there is insufficient firepower against him. I agreed the Labour big names seem more concerned with each other than a common enemy. Gordon does his own thing but has to be harnessed.

I recommended a bit of the panic button pressing so that people are made aware of what needs to be done. I felt someone – him, Cameron or Ed M – has to make the point that this is loseable unless we do what is needed to win. For Labour in particular that meant engaging in a debate about what a constitutional settlement might look like post a No vote. For the Tories I think it means ignoring the stuff about not being popular up there and find new ways of being heard on the arguments. He said he felt the way to outsmart Salmond was on the ground. But we were miles away from that. He said we were definitely underestimating how smart and how effective Salmond was. Tories were not the answer to any question there, he said. Labour had to do more heavy lifting.

Monday 21 April

Up for the match v Wigan, won 2–0, promoted. Amazing success story. Rumours starting to circulate about Moyes going from Man U. The players were clearly not buying him. Moyes's view that because he had heard nothing meant he was probably safe was clearly naïve.

Tuesday 22 April

Moyes out. Pretty horrible how it was done. In the press before he knew. I called him. He said he was gutted and how they did it was disgusting. He understood the results were not good enough and he had to take the rap for that, but clearly pissed off at some of the players, and Giggs among them I sensed. He said he was talking to the LMA [League Managers Association] and putting out a statement tomorrow and he asked me to help with that. I worked on a draft and sent it through. A really sad story but the truth is he had looked haunted for a while.

Alex F had agreed to do a foreword for the book, but Jason was clearly against it and when it finally came I sensed Jason had deliberately made it unusable. The whole episode was a bit strange. Alex had asked me to draft based on our chats but then when Jason saw it he felt it would cut across what he was planning to do with his project. Mike Phelan [football coach] had said too that Jason could be tricky and was determined to have his moment in the sun with his dad, but this all seemed so petty.

Chatted to TB again re. Egypt. His speech was excellent content-wise but the reaction showed some people just cannot get beyond him as the speaker. It underlined the need for him to have a bigger strategy on his reputation, but he seemed unable or unwilling really to put the hard graft in. Kept coming back to positions about the past rather than relevance about the future. Met Ailsa Anderson [former press secretary to the Queen] re. the Queen chapter for the book. Now working for the Archbishop of Canterbury. Had some good insights. Then Sam Trickett [poker player]. He and Rory sounded like they were speaking a different language at times, but he was definitely a winner and would be good in data. Also John Browne who was excellent.

Friday 25 April

Really good meeting with Robin Janvrin to discuss the Queen chapter. Some fantastic stuff. He was such a nice guy. He had thought it through and had set out his thoughts in a note to himself and just went through it. What I sensed was that when he and others got involved under [Lord] David Airlie [former Lord Chamberlain], there was a strategy by stealth but actually the Queen knew exactly what was going on. He was getting involved in education too now, albeit some of it private. Off to City for the flight to Scotland. Jack Irvine [management PR, former newspaper editor] on the plane saying the Better Together campaign just wasn't firing. I had been asked to go in and see them, so I did, met the whole team – didn't take long – in a rather odd office above a shopping centre. Blair McDougall [Better Together strategist] OK, and a few bright young things, but I didn't have a sense of strategy and there was a lot of – doubtless true – talk about how difficult it was to get the politicians off their arse. Everyone liked Alistair but felt he was lacking that killer instinct needed for Salmond.

GB was doing good stuff but slightly on his own. The whole shadow Cabinet was up today which was fine I guess but they basically said Ed did not really resonate, the Scots were not working hard enough up there and the rest were not known. I had felt a few weeks ago that it was unloseable but having spent time with Salmond and now with the BT people, I was not so sure. At the fundraiser in Helensburgh, I made the point that they needed to start fighting it like we could lose, rather than coasting. Johann Lamont [leader Scottish Labour Party] was there and she was very nice and a good speaker but I wasn't sure she had the fire in the belly needed for this. The *FT* were chasing a story about TB and my involvement in Egypt.

Saturday 26 April

Breakfast with Helen Liddell and Margaret Curran. Helen said even her kids were voting Yes. Margaret was asking for advice about how to get herself more active. It all lacked co-ordination and drive. They both said it would be great if I could go up there full-time. I really didn't want them to lose but I knew if I went I would become too much the focus of it all and I just was not up for taking on the responsibility others should have shouldered long ago. Helen nice as ever, and Margaret seemed great, but they were all, from Ed down, seeming to lack basic campaign skills.

Train to Preston. One–nil Ipswich. Great season. Back for dinner at the Blackburns [David and Janice, family friends] with David's daughter and son-in-law. Usual political and cultural chat. They told me [author] Tom Bower's next target was TB. Mind you, his Richard Branson book went nowhere. Been discussing Branson lots with Nick Fox [Virgin chief communications officer] trying to get him for the book. Anna Wintour [editor-in-chief US *Vogue*] had said yes to an interview for the book. Call from Salmond's office. They were worried about the *GQ* quotes re. Putin, trying to get me to finesse them.

Sunday 27 April

Anxious. Worked on Queen chapter. The *FT* were on to the story re. TB and me and Egypt. Chatted to Alistair re. Scotland, gave him my impressions, above all lack of strategy and oomph. They just needed a clearer sense of where they were heading. Flew out to Cairo with Catherine Rimmer [TB chief of staff], Darren Murphy and Chris McShane [former adviser to TB]. Spent much of the flight talking to Catherine about how to get TB in a better place. She said we underestimated how much I, JoP, Sally and Anji were able to act as checks. I felt TB's whole modus operandi had to change so that media and public could be educated more to get a sense of what he did and why, post-power politics. I had been saying it for ages. It was what Clinton did. It was no good just thinking that the Yanks didn't have our press. They had different issues but BC had worked them out.

Monday 28 April

Salmond interview was going really big, and bad for him. Leading the news in Scotland, politicians in Westminster and later the US piling in, suggesting he was an ally of Putin. I did a couple of clarifying tweets, to give a context, but when I spoke to Aileen in his office she said he seemed OK with it and reminded me of 'the mair they talk, I'm kent the better'

[Robert Burns]. Meetings all day. First a Brit working for an American outfit inside the transitional government. He seemed pretty amazed to see us.

Saw Abdel-Latif [former sport minister] p.m. who was the guy we had seen in London and his team. Did a workshop at the military hotel where Sisi lived. Fairly bright bunch but starting from scratch in some ways.

Tuesday 29 April

More meetings with the key Sisi people and trying to get them to understand 1. how to do a campaign – really fairly basic stuff; 2. how they were not going to get a better understanding in the international media while courts were sentencing hundreds to death and Al Jazeera journalists were in jail. The team seemed enthusiastic but fairly inexperienced and of course as far as the media were concerned it was not an election so much as a procession and Sisi was going to walk it. Added to which it was hard to get people to see a distinction between courts and politicians. When finally I met him, after a drive on a golf buggy around the grounds of the main military hotel, to a bungalow where he was holed up without his family, and unable to make proper campaign visits, he said that the pressure he was under was to be harder on the Muslim Brotherhood, not weaker.

Gerard Russell had done a report on the MB with [Sir] William Patey [former diplomat] and we had met Dr Abdel-Latif, who was close to Sisi, in London, to discuss how much of it was new and how much to put in public domain and when. It was certainly an eye-opener for me, the scale of the terror networks everywhere. There were even one or two moments when I wondered whether this was not all a bit dangerous. TB was totally persuaded Sisi was the only guy who could do this, and he needed support, as he had said in his speech. I met him with Darren M, Abdel-Latif, his spokesman, a former officer, and an interpreter with beautiful mesmeric eyes. Sisi was in civilian clothes but still looked military. Short dark hair, very erect bearing, polished black shoes, incredibly smart blue suit. Certainly had presence.

He started in listening mode, especially on the need for them to change perceptions for international media, but quickly was asking about TB's speech, and whether he should have made it. He said the argument was definitely right but he wondered about the timing. I think it was a polite way maybe of saying 'right message, wrong messenger'. He was quite inscrutable, and I couldn't work out whether he was pissed off or not. But he then got on to the task ahead for him, and really wanted to drill down on how you get a message over when it is complicated.

We were strongly suggesting that he had to give some indication of the difficult things that were going to have to be done – the economy was struggling and the levels of subsidies to all levels were unsustainable, but they were pretty sniffy with the IMF, and it was not clear what reforms he was planning. He was pretty low-key on that, but we emphasised he had a real opportunity to signal change, because everyone knew he would win, whereas if he waited until he was in power, he would merely sew more disappointment and rebellion. Like several of the people we met, he emphasised that the MB threat was real. A lot of our discussion was campaign-focused but I kept coming back to the point about the need to signal the direction and use the campaign to set out the steps.

He seemed to get it, was clearly bright, listened in English but spoke in Arabic. If there was one thing he kept coming back to, it was what do you do if it is complicated and the message doesn't get through or doesn't work, and if there was one thing I kept coming back to, it was my usual line about the need for strategy and clarity etc. Sisi was not really what I expected. Softly spoken. Very calm. Impressive in his own way. He wanted to know some pretty basic things about messaging and campaigning. The fact everyone knew he was going to win put an added onus on the need to campaign well and with real energy. There was a problem though in that he could not travel freely or safely. He was having to organise his own protection, very little from the state at this stage. I also said that as it was clear he was going to win, he had the opportunity to lay down some difficult messages at this stage about reforms that would need to happen to the economy and curbing handouts etc. I had no idea just how many subsidies were paid out, including to the well-off. His big problem was going to be the middle classes as much as the poor. He asked me a number of 'What if?' media-type scenarios, like how would you explain this, that or the other. We talked a bit about whether media training was effective.

We were there over an hour. I emphasised that the Al Jazeera journalists being locked up, plus the huge number of mass death penalties without real trials, made it virtually impossible for him to get a proper hearing in the West. He seemed to accept that, but also said that on the one hand we press them to have an independent judiciary, then ask the politicians to step in when we don't like the judgment. And re. the death sentences passed on Muslim Brotherhood people, he said several times the pressures were all to kill more. Tricky, tricky stuff.

The plan TB had been discussing with the UAE was essentially to work towards a major international donor conference, but it would not get off the ground with this as a backdrop. It was hard to overstate how bad, difficult and dangerous things were. The economic numbers were dire. The security situation was not great. The expectations of Sisi, both from the people and from the international community, were sky high. One of his advisers told me there was a worry the whole place would go up like

Syria. They were really worried about the extent to which the Western powers did not really get how bad it was and didn't really want to engage.

Phoned Mum from the hotel and it would turn out to be the last time we spoke. She had had a bit of a turn at the weekend so I just wanted to check in. She sounded OK, if a bit frail, but at one point she did say – as she had many times – when I go, I want to go quickly. Dinner with the team, early night, trip to Jordan tomorrow.

Wednesday 30 April

Started the day calling Grace to say happy birthday, and ended it flying home ASAP because Mum had collapsed and was clearly dying. By the time I got back to London, she was dead. I went to the airport crack of dawn with Catherine Rimmer who was heading back to London. She was really keen for me to head up a new SCU [System Control Unit]-type operation in TBO to bring all his activities together and to try to repair his reputation. I was pretty frank, said that I was always happy to help but I had really moved on, and I just felt he needed good outsiders to come in and work with our support. She went off to her flight and I to mine, needing three bribes to get through baggage check and customs.

Worked on the book on the flight [to Amman], landed, met, then driven into town. Lovely sunny day. Starbucks for first meeting! Then to a meeting in town, and we were chatting when I could see my phone ringing where I had left it on a charger in the corner of the room. Then ringing again, then again. I went to check and it was missed calls from Fiona and Liz. I feared the worst. I left the meeting and called Fiona who said Mum had been taken ill. Then called Liz who was in an ambulance with her. Graeme had found her half in half out of the bed and called 999. Looked like a stroke. By the time she got to the hospital she was alive but when I asked a doctor if she thought I should come back she said yes, I would come as soon as you can, she is not well. I said is she going to die? She said I think you should try to get here as soon as you can. Wishing I had got on the same flight as Catherine now. Called Gavin Mackay [TB travel adviser] who worked wonders and while I was heading to the airport, he sorted me a flight back via Beirut. I was being driven to the airport and just before we got there I burst into tears, asked the driver to pull over and just sat there for ages, crying. It was partly thinking about telling Donald that hit me. He didn't know yet, though later Liz told me he took it fine.

I was calling the kids from the airport, all saying the right things, but all upset, and also Liz who told me they had said she probably wouldn't wake up. That was just as I got on the flight Amman–Beirut, called on take-off, still the same. The connection in Beirut was really tight, just made it, thought I was last on, as the plane seemed full. Seat 5A, and the seat next to me about the only empty one. Then they announce we are waiting for one more passenger, and a minute or so later in comes a totally ripped guy who sits down next to me, doesn't look at me or anyone else, spends the whole flight reading the Koran or praying. I was not holding out much hope, and I started to write a eulogy. I had arranged for Rayan to meet me, texted when I landed and texted back to say Fiona was waiting for me in arrivals, which pretty much told me she was dead. In a way I would have been surprised if she hadn't been. She looked quite panicky as I came out, and just said, 'You've heard, yeah?' I nodded, even though I hadn't. I just knew from that last call from Liz that it was only a matter of time. But she had always said when she went she wanted to go quickly. We set off for Wheatley, Rory and Calum having gone ahead, and Liz, [son] Graeme, Rob [Liz's husband] and Kate [daughter] all there. I guess it was the best way to go. Totally had her marbles. Busy to the end. A quick stroke and then never really came round. But it was such a shock because she had never really been ill. Rory said he had no memory of her not laughing, smiling or singing. One of the hardest bits was calling Grace from the car. She was on holiday in Morocco, and I could tell just wanted to be back with us.

Thursday 1 May
Didn't sleep well. All a bit in a daze. Liz came across a poem Mum had left for us all. We were just sitting around chatting, dealing with the usual that comes from a death, lots of people phoning and calling in. I had to head back to London p.m. for tomorrow's interview with Steve Coogan.

Friday 2 May
Interview Coogan for *GQ*. Then trying to help Liz sort stuff for the funeral.

Saturday 3 May
Last game of the season at Reading [2–2]. Then head north with Calum.

Sunday 4 May
Grace, Audrey and Fiona up. White House for lunch. Donald on good form and had taken it all in his stride. We were talking about maybe doing a film on his schizophrenia. Mum had always been worried about it but he was keen.

May '14: Dealing with aftermath of Betty Campbell's death   605

Monday 5 May

Met the people who were doing the service to go over all the details. Back with Grace. The political scene was getting me down a lot. Ed just not motoring. When he did policy it ran for a day and fizzled out and there was no big linking theme at all. He was really looking a bit lost. Cameron all tactics as ever. Scotland going wrong. My Salmond interview had gone massive. I felt a bit bad because it was actually a really good interview, rich and with some engaging insights from him, but the furore over his sort of praise for Putin was pretty intense. Also his line about Scotland not being able to promote whisky properly 'from a nation of drunks' ran big too, once the Putin remarks calmed down a bit. Someone sent me a note saying the first FMQs after the interview appeared took up twenty-three out of thirty minutes with stuff directly from the interview.

He was clearly worried, because his office had called me, when *GQ* put out some quotes, to say the Putin words were not quite accurate and it risked being a problem. It is true that there was a bit of an inaccuracy in transcription when we had been speaking at the same time, but it didn't change the sense and if anything the full tape made it worse not better for him. Once the row had been going for a few days – Cameron did it at PMQs, Hague had a go in the Commons too, then some American Congressmen got involved, and Ukrainians were piling in up north. Meanwhile Labour and the Better Together people were loving it because it had him on the back foot for the first time in ages. He had asked me to be part of his negotiation team if he won, and one of his people told me that was a serious proposition, and the furore did not change that. 'If anything it makes him keener, because it shows you can still get a message up, even at his expense.'

Thursday 8 May

At the Sport Industry Awards Dan Walker sought me out and said how sorry he was re. Mum. He clearly remembered her from when they met in Wheatley and he was genuinely nice about it. Sitting with Ade Adepitan [TV presenter, wheelchair basketball player] who I later got to come to the house to do an interview for the book. Lovely guy and he was a great story of resilience. His attitude to setbacks was not to acknowledge them as such.

Weekend at first Burford with Gail and the girls (and our Grace), then to Annie Robinson's. Emma [daughter] and her family there. Annie on fine form as ever. Not doing much work-wise, working on Mum's eulogy but it was pretty much sorted, I think. Couple of runs. Must get back into it. Feeling very tired, which I hadn't been aware was a product of grief, very common. Certainly felt different to when Dad died, partly because there had been no real build-up this time, couldn't quite believe it still, also because it was the final part of that older generation in the direct family. Fiona worried about Audrey more now of course. Auntie Mattie the only one of Mum's left. Gail seemed on OK form, more relaxed than usual. Georgia getting way behind with her book on young people. Grace doing really well at work but still lots of issues. Ditto our Gracie who was moving back in with us. I had been to her loft in Stoke Newington and really didn't like the feel of it.

Monday 12 May

Russell Brand for an interview for his series. Clever guy if only we could get him off this 'don't vote' kick. We did it at his house in Shoreditch, pretty funky as you would expect, 'Messiah complex' in neon red letters on the wall, lovely roof garden, and though he was off the booze and off the drugs, he nonetheless was pretty wired all the time. Talked loads of football, loads of politics, and after the interview had a discussion about him and his positioning. I said he needed to move on to the next stage, which was not just say how terrible things were, and how disconnected people were, but have some answers. It was too easy at the moment and precisely because he was clever – which he definitely is – he could do a lot better. He was a real character though, funny, serious, very likeable. He was clearly down on us re. Iraq but nonetheless did feel that at least we seemed to get the public better than the current lot. Wouldn't be hard. Gave me a hard time over Iraq but listened to the arguments as well.

LMA dinner. Mainly chatting to Sean [Dyche] and the Burnley guys, Brian McDermott [manager Leeds United], who was a funny guy. Tony Pulis PL manager of the year [Crystal Palace], Brendan Rodgers [Liverpool] overall winner, Nigel Pearson [Leicester City] won best Championship manager – so Sean got nothing despite being in for that and for overall award. Achievement award for Russ Wilcox [Scunthorpe United], presented by Fergie who called him Bruce throughout the citation. Chatted to Moyes a bit, to Malky about the nightmare he was having with the owner, really gunning for him, and to [Chris] Hughton [former Norwich City manager], all three in very different circumstances to this time last year. Moyes looked a bit more relaxed but was clearly still hurting. I had been talking to Malky on and off, and to Raymond his agent and they had finally done quite a big climb-down to get out of the whole thing at Cardiff. In the end a statement released a few days ago was pretty much a win for Vincent Tan, who was now blaming Malky for relegation. Nice evening. Chatted to Roy Hodgson who was pretty clear he didn't expect miracles with England.

Tuesday 13 May

Working on book and then to Gatwick for a session with Nestle re. strategy and social media mainly. Seemed to go OK. Then to Parliament for one of our John Bercow dinners for LLR. Usual mix of charity, politics and science. Fixing meeting with Arsenal who had proposed a £5 million sponsorship partnership with Albania. Edi quite keen but hard to justify the money. Did a bit of research and sent a note before agreeing to meet their main people at the Emirates stadium.

Wednesday 14 May

Cathy [Gilman] called and said that they had been presented with the chance, through Geoff Thomas [ex-footballer, amateur cyclist], to get Lance [Armstrong] involved in London to Paris, and maybe the full Tour de France pre-route next year. Geoff's journalist pal had set up the reconciliation of sorts with Lance and the whistleblower physio and said he was now up for doing a big piece with Geoff. I said to Cathy it was one of those decisions we were likely to regret either way. Suggested she sit down with her team and work out how they would explain 1. Announcing we have said yes and he is taking part; and 2. We have turned him away. She felt if it went to the trustees it would be a straight no. She had spoken to Pelham Allen the new chair who had not ruled it out of hand but wanted to know what people in the sport felt about Lance right now. I called Dave B, Fran Millar [Team Sky executive] and David Millar [professional cyclist, Fran's brother] and all three said don't touch it with a bargepole.

They felt it would be seen as a publicity stunt by us and an act of exploitation by him. David said the feeling was that he had not really accepted he had done wrong, he was still playing games, refusing to deal with the authorities etc. Fran thought David might have been a bit more sympathetic than her and Dave B, but far from it. Rory felt yes. Virtually everyone else felt no. We agreed to sleep on it and make a few more calls. Went north with Calum, nice time, big numbers expected for the funeral tomorrow.

Thursday 15 May

Went out for a run to clear my head and rehearse the speech to a field and then to Grace on the phone. It was a nice eulogy, got her character and above all her positivity, and I felt OK, provided I took some Diazepam. Big drama when Grace was late and they missed the train from London, so all stressed about that, but they made it in time to do lots of pictures and then rehearse the poem they were all doing. Donald remarkably composed considering. Hearse came around one. Liz cracked up, then me and Rory in the car, Graeme Naish [AC nephew] inconsolable as he carried the coffin at the crematorium. Family only there and lots of relatives down from Scotland. Then to the Sally Army church in Doncaster. Nice venue, good service, all went as well as it could considering. Maybe 300–400 there. To the hotel for the do after and nice enough mood, lots of the Scots, bridge players, locals, fair few from London which was nice. Aud of course – more pictures of her than anyone else in the montage! Piped with Donald then off we headed. Still a lot for Liz to sort out, possessions, will etc. Slept on train back, really tired now.

Monday 19 May

Work on book then Royal Free for check-up. All fine. [Dr Mark] Hamilton terrific in terms of knowledge. He was even wondering if my first case years back was not colitis but an infection like the recent one.

Tuesday 20 May

Clive Woodward came round p.m. Terrific interview. He and Dave were a cut above in terms of how they thought about their work. Really into his new software idea too. Convinced it was going to be a very big thing. Put me in touch with the backer who also owned an IPL [Indian Premier cricket League] team so maybe could get a chapter out of that too. Manoj Badale [businessman]. I was pleased with the way the Queen chapter was developing and could maybe get Michael Peat [former principal private secretary to the Prince of Wales] too.

Fiona had lunch with Cherie. We had been invited to her surprise 60th party. Fiona said she had been saying that she was much more left-wing these days. F felt CB not taking the Wendi Deng thing seriously. I went round to see Charlie F and he was even thinner than last time. Doing a big case and losing it at the moment, something to do with banks, fraud, prostitutes involved, sounded all very sordid. Felt Ed was nice, not at all useless but not top level. He felt TB was not in a good place overall but he was not sure what we could do about it pre Chilcot. Of course that could get even worse. Final decision re. Lance and had a few calls to make on that. Geoff very upset, thought it was a huge opportunity and we were silly not to take it. Cathy torn but convinced it was the right decision.

We left for France on 22 May, the day of the local and European elections.

UKIP had been the big story the whole way through. They did well, won the Europeans, caused havoc in the locals, and it was bad news all round for the three other parties. LDs looking like wipeout time. Ed just not breaking through. Worrying for Cameron but still winning on economy and leadership/prime ministerial. Worrying for his referendum gambit. The tragedy of TB's position was underlined when social media started pumping out his exchanges with Farage in the European Parliament, when he demolished him.* But the other three couldn't handle it. Douglas called me the day after the locals. He said that Ed was refusing to do *Marr* at the weekend, which was OK in and of itself but part of a bigger problem of preferring to hide from questions rather than confront them. The campaign was clearly pretty dysfunctional.

Douglas said he and Spencer worked well together but Michael Dugher was pissed off not to be the main man, and they didn't get on. Balls and Cooper were on the sidelines. Burnham was plotting for his own position post defeat. The party was functioning OK, but the Tories had money and drive, and we didn't. Meanwhile similar story in Scotland, where there were too many egos and too many divisions and it wasn't working out as it should. He sounded pretty down. I said I didn't see how we could win when so many of our own people were behaving like we had already lost. Then when the Europeans came through, the Front National was the big winner in France, People's Party in Denmark, and UKIP at home. The populist anti-politics thing was growing all the time.

I worked pretty hard on mindset chapters, re-did data with Rory. Great stuff from Garry Kasparov [Russian chess grandmaster] on strategy. Genius mindset, and interesting on politics too. Hates Putin so much. Also thanks to Jonathan Prince I made good contact with David Plouffe [American political strategist]. Got hold of David Axelrod [former Obama chief election strategist]. Good chat. Peter M sending messages re. whether I was helping Sisi. I was a bit guarded but he came back saying the Army were part of the problem, big resisters to economic reform etc. He was in Milan. Last weekend there was a bit of a flurry when the *Mail on Sunday* came on saying that they had been informed I was advising Sisi. I said I was not part of the campaign. But they ran a story anyway, didn't fly.

TB very nice re. Mum, asking me how I was etc. Maybe feeling bad because he knew she had never wanted me in the frontline. Liz upset before we left because she came over some old notes 'not to be read until

---

* In 2005 Farage had challenged Blair, then chairman of the European Council, over the amount of money paid by the UK to the European Union. Blair's withering response was considered to have demolished the UKIP leader.

I am gone', which were about her disappointments in life – Donald going in the Army, me being obsessed with politics and her being made ill when I was in the firing line. Quite an odd thing. Session with DS who wanted me to get *The Big Book* [Alcoholics Anonymous basic text] – which I did – and go to AA – which I didn't, not yet. A few conference calls and speech stuff while away but basically just a nice time. Breakfast, work, exercise, eat, watch films, the odd night out, Fiona and I getting on well the week it was just the two of us, though the kids still had the capacity to bring us down a bit.

Thursday 29 May

The Chilcot row over the TB–Bush papers finally got settled, so there was another splurge of that and of course it meant the whole thing was coming closer. Filled me with dread, less for me, though I doubted I would come out unscathed, than for TB, who was still getting absolutely battered. I don't know why it had taken such a dip – Wendi, Rebekah and the fact he was one of the few to stand by her, and that to come out in court, money definitely, plus his big Middle East speech, though he said a lot of the right things, I am not sure he was the right person or this the right time. Lib Dems in meltdown. Edi doing well, Merkel had got the Dutch to see him and they had shifted.

Sunday 1 June

Early start. Flight to Glasgow, really busy. Met by a driver called Mandy who gave me her whole life story, like a lot of people not a happy one. Drumtochty Castle absolutely beautiful. Run. Fab room. Speak after the dinner. Dana Petroleum [Aberdeen-based oil and gas production company]. Fairly right-wing group but some really nice people, including a couple of ex-spooks. UKIP win Euros.

Monday 2 June

Run with one of the Dana people. Turned out her dad was an alcoholic and we talked a lot about that. Aberdeen airport, fly to Birmingham. Burton-on-Trent. FA HQ at St Georges Park. Great set-up but was it too late? Tour of pitches, gym, sport science, hotel. I was doing a talk to some of the guys taking their coaching diploma. Celtic guys. Hope Powell [England women's football coach]. Sat with her at dinner. Good bunch. Excellent Q&A. Stayed for dinner then off with Rayan. Enjoyed it and good set-up but couldn't help thinking the FA had got to this approach too late.

Tuesday 3 June

Train to Exeter. Rory doing innovation section for the book. Mental health lecture Exeter uni. Q&A, row with a woman after re. Iraq. Car back. Tired.

Thursday 5 June

Interviewed Arianna Huffington [author, businesswoman, co-founder Huffington Post] for the book. Great line – 'Innovation is the mindset that says everything we do is work in progress.' Then Charles Dunstone [co-founder Carphone Warehouse] re. book, excellent. Told me I must see [Sir] Ben Ainslie [Olympic champion sailor] and put me in touch. Research Wintour.

Friday 6 June

I had been feeling a plunge coming on and today it came. Gradual build-up, then when it came, bang. Very down. Later dinner with Fiona, Evan Harris [executive director, Hacked Off] and Steve Coogan at The Ivy but I was not feeling great. The hardest part was trying to be engaged and energetic when inside feeling the opposite.

Saturday 7 June

[Calum's friend] Charlie Watts's wedding. Calum was his best man and spoke really well. Gove–May row.* Bed as soon as home. I had spent a lot of time talking to Adem's parents [a friend of Calum and Charlie who had died] about grief. So sad.

Sunday 8 June

Home most of day, very, very down, working on the speech for the US. My mood not helped by having agreed to a meeting at Ed's, pre his team meeting which Tom B said was awful. Ed better than before but still it was hard to see him winning. I just wish the steel he showed with David was on show again. I felt we were going over the same old ground. I asked what happened to my Germany idea, of him going there and actually

---

* An acrimonious public quarrel between the Home Office and education ministers over responsibility for alleged extremism in Birmingham schools ended with the intervention of the Prime Minister, the sacking of special adviser Fiona Cunningham by Home Secretary Theresa May, and Education Secretary Michael Gove apologising to Home Office head of security Charles Farr for alleged uncomplimentary briefings.

spending a decent amount of time looking at how things were done differently? Not a lot. He had been keen, but it never happened. What about getting a proper attack squad? Not happened. Had he decided re. Balls? Etc. etc. Everything a problem, few solutions, lots of bubble.

Monday 9 June

Work on speech for US then innovation chapter. Off to the airport and my first transatlantic Virgin flight to NY. Pretty good, definitely a different kind of feel. F convinced my plunge was bereavement plus lack of status/ relevance. Met at JFK and off to the Grand Hyatt. Dinner with Jonathan Prince [political strategist and communicator]. On good form and gave me some good leads for the book. No doubt Hillary was going to run and probably win. Not sure if he would work with her. He was writing a book for someone corporate plus had some decent PR clients but clearly wanted back into politics I think. The TB image issue had crossed his radar too, said that a lot of the US coverage now tended to focus on the negativity set by ours. Hillary in good shape, Bill behaving reasonably well.

Tuesday 10 June

Out for a run. One of those moments where new and old lives collide. George Stephanopolous [former Clinton spokesman now TV presenter] and Hillary down there at ABC, lots of rubber-neckers watching them do the interview through the window. HC book was out and she was totally on manoeuvres. Met Louise Shackleton [David Miliband's wife] for breakfast. She was fine but still very angry about Ed. DM was OK with his new job but going to be hard. To Condé Nast and up to be met by a stunning, beautifully dressed young woman who took me into a room where I waited for Hildy Kuryk [*Vogue* director of communications], ex-Obama fundraiser, and we chatted before I was taken to see Anna Wintour. All in red. Lovely office, tastefully done. Enjoyed the interview. She was partly what I expected and partly not. Decided maybe do her in the leadership section of the book, rather than innovation. She took a while to warm up but when I listened back to her answers they were pretty frank, and gave a good insight into how she operated. She definitely has a sense of vision and purpose and strategy.

Lunch with Tim, who was overseeing the Omnicom [media group] people and agonising over the fact he sold majority stake in Portland too soon. Potter and work, then met Nick Keller after he came back from a Beyond Sport soccer event. Later off to the Beyond Sport United dinner which included people from all the US major leagues. Speech on leadership went down well, good Q&A but one of the questions kept me awake most of the night. A woman asked how I had managed to make such a smooth transition from having a full-on, close-to-power existence, to something very different where I seemed much more in control of my own destiny. She hit a bullseye on the dilemma that is swilling around my head all the time – carry on with this rather odd, varied, mostly enjoyable but ultimately less intense life, or get back stuck into something full-on. That means politics I guess and right now I can't face it.

I was at a table with Jean Afterman, assistant general manager of the NY Yankees, who did a mean UK accent, and loved my speech to the point of raving. Speech after dinner re. leadership, the great question re. making the transition from one life to another turned out to be from Kelly Swanson, Floyd Mayweather [undefeated multi-world championship boxer] right-hand woman. Walk back. Didn't sleep well, was thinking a lot about what Kelly Swanson said, she got right to the heart of my never-ending dilemma, re. a life of ease or a life in politics. But the fact is that though people like Ashcroft were still saying Labour would win, I couldn't really see it happening.

Wednesday 11 June

Up for gym, off to the Yankee Stadium, great venue, good event, well organised and I opened the session on social media. I spoke to Kelly afterwards. I asked if she was asking for a particular reason to do with herself. She said no, not me, but the guy I work for – has a full-on life but one day will have to retire. Floyd Mayweather. Wow. I told her about the book on winners and said given he has never lost a fight, I would love to talk to him, she said she would try to make it happen. Trip definitely worthwhile if that comes off. Off to airport, slept all the way. Nice trip, glad I went.

Thursday 12 June

Arrive 6.50, two cock-ups, Rayan there when I thought he wasn't, and then wrong day for Michael Peat. World Cup start. Brazil Croatia, dodgy penalty. ISIS Iraq crises really big. Chat with TB re. whether he should say something. I felt yes because there would be lots of people saying 2003 caused this, added to which I just felt he needed to be in the debate.

Friday 13 June

More abuse on Twitter re. Iraq. I saw Michael Peat, who was fantastic re. the Queen. He had a good historical take on her success, also was almost convincing about the way that the hereditary principle worked, pointing out that the Queen and Charles never for one moment forgot they were only there because of birth, not talent. Then joined Rory to do Joe Rospars [political strategist], recommended by Hildy. He had done the Obama digital campaign and would be good for innovation.

Thursday 19 June

Call from Ed on how to deal with all the negativity. Peter M damned him with faint praise on Paxo's last *Newsnight*. I said he needed to embrace the problems, not pretend they don't exist. Out of blue I took a call from Advani people in India about doing a book on [recently elected Prime Minister of India] Narendra Modi's campaign in India. It sounded a lot like the one I was doing but focused on the Modi campaign. Slight problem was that they wanted it done within three months and there was no way I was going to be able to do it in that time frame. Flurry with Ed and Gail about whether to explore and I decided it would be fun. England lost to Uruguay. Fran called asking for media support for Dave. Clearly the Sky support operation just was not adequate. I suggested we meet Greg and Godric.

Friday 20 June

Saw José Mourinho for the book at Chelsea. Not as I expected in some ways but a great interview, I think. He was late, and not warm, but very open and frank, to the point that at the end Steve Atkins [Chelsea head of comms] asked me not to use certain things. He had a totally different analysis to mine re. strategy but thinking about it maybe not. He was essentially saying that his strategy was tactical dominance, and he saw strategy as the art of making a change to suit the circumstances. He said he was not keen to be playing Burnley first game of the season. Didn't seem too bothered re. Fergie not being around, not very sympathetic re. Moyes. Had a long chat with Steve when waiting for him, and he was clearly quite a bundle to deal with, not really controllable, full of conspiracy theories e.g. re. the fixtures etc. Listened back on the train, a lot of really interesting insights.

Then to see Dave Brailsford with Godric at John St. I felt he was a bit spooked by 19 [Wiggins's new agents], who were advising [Sir] Bradley Wiggins, and he was losing focus. My sense was that he felt they were not likely to win, and he would cop it. So we needed to build some big messages around him, that looked back on the remarkable success of the last decade and positioned him as the architect. He had definitely decided Wiggins was not going and so we needed to plan around that too, again with big message on teamwork. I already knew from him and Fran how bad things were between Chris Froome and Wiggins but Dave said it was worse. He said that both of them were as bad as each other at times but in the frenzied atmosphere of the Tour there was no way they were going to be able to live together on that bus and on the road. The wives were a part of the problem, he said.

He said Sky media support was limited and he felt exposed. He was not going to pick Wiggins and that would bring a lot of shit on his head so how should he deal with it? We agreed we would do a note and come up with a package for the Tour period. GS and I started to work on that. Then with Grace to [*Guardian* writer] Decca Aitkenhead's husband's funeral [Decca's partner Tony Wilkinson had drowned in Jamaica]. So sad to see their two boys. Fiona was doing a thing at Wellington College, where she said Jimmy Mulville [comedian and writer] said I was a war criminal, and it had not gone down well.

Monday 23 June

Albania. Early flight to Vienna, writing up José. Meeting with Vali and Endri to plan the coverage around candidate status which was likely but still needed to be pinned down. Dinner with Edi. He said the Italians had said they found Cameron like something from another age. Edi on good form. To a local bar to watch the football. Then we did a last bit of ringing round on candidate status. Looking good.

Tuesday 24 June

Layne Beachley [Australian surfer] interview by phone. She was fantastic, and would make a great profile on how to use setbacks. Coulson guilty Brooks not.[*] Meeting with Endri's comms team and as we were meeting, candidate status came through, all good. Edi ecstatic, taking selfies and stuff. Lunch with Meta, but he was a bit subdued. Health minister Ilir Beqaj peed off, felt that Edi was not devoting as much time as he should to the kind of strategic discussion they used to have in opposition. Swim/run. Work. Pub with Edi etc. to watch Italy and England both go out. He was very popular when we went out, but it was hard to know if it was a celeb thing or a political thing. A few Brits in the pub but apart from them nobody was even watching the England match.

---

[*] Andy Coulson was found guilty of one charge of conspiracy to hack phones, but the jury failed to agree a verdict on two charges of conspiring to cause misconduct in public office. Rebekah Brooks was found not guilty on five charges, one of conspiracy to hack voicemails and four of conspiracy.

Thursday 26 June

Willie Walsh [CEO, International Airlines Group] at the Arts Club [Dover Street]. Wanted to talk to him for the crisis management section of the book, especially Terminal 5 launch. John Smith trust. [Baroness] Elizabeth Smith [widow] asking me to get involved in Glasgow on a campaign to get young people to see public life as being a good thing. *FT* party. Lionel Barber [editor], Fred Studemann [*FT* literary editor] and I talking in German. *FT* Middle East correspondent asking me why I hadn't replied to her emails re. work in Egypt, which was still bumbling along.

Friday 27 June

Lido. Then all day working on book. Also two fucking hours trying to sort an Indian visa, without success. 11 a.m. Dave Brailsford did the team announcement which went well, despite the blah re. Wiggins.

Saturday 28 June

Lido. Potter. Victor Blank called asking if I would play instead of Flintoff at his match tomorrow. The one he used to do with Frostie. Carina and the boys were going to be there so said yes.

Sunday 29 June

Drove down to Victor Blank's amazing country gaff complete with cricket pitch. Useful to interview a few stars for the book – Brian Lara, Sachin Tendulkar, Wasim Akram, Shane Warne [international players]. Stunning knock though I say so, 26no. I hit both Wasim Akram and Kevin Pietersen [England all-rounder] for 4. Nice chat with Lara and his lovely Scottish girlfriend. Tendulkar good. Sat with Lara and Jonathan Crystal [barrister]. Warne agreed to an interview for the book. Carina seemed a bit subdued, which was understandable, her boys on good form.

Monday 30 June

Lunch with Brendan. Such a good guy. Had read and liked stuff so far but felt the main OST point needed to be hammered through. Went to see Brian Cox [physicist] who was good on data. Rory back from Brazil. Germany through.

Tuesday 1 July

Branson interview with Rory. It was OK, though Rory was shocked at how inarticulate he was at times. Great for boldness though. We had breakfast at the old County Hall which started with him asking his PA to sit somewhere else because he said he didn't like being surrounded. Also when we got breakfast he would sometimes takes ages to eat something before answering, but he got warmed up. Nick Fox had to chivvy him a bit every now and then. After a bit we went back to the event he was at, for young entrepreneurs, and he did a pretty good little speech and then got them to tell their stories.

Off to the HoC for the Richard Layard book launch [*Thrive: The Power of Evidence-Based Psychological Therapies*]. Tracey Crouch MP and two people in the audience both said they basically came out as having mental health problems after hearing me speak. Alan Howarth [Tory defector, former Labour minister] came out at the meeting. To the Indian High Commission. Got my visa at last after three trips but then decided against going because they were saying it had to be done in months and also that when we met Modi on the 12th it was when not if.

Wednesday 2 July

To Wembley for the UCFB board meeting. Going well. Popped into Portland and walked with Tim to the Shard for their party. Nice do. Dinner with Margaret Hodge. Definitely thinking of going for mayor. She said she was avoiding Tessa all she could, as she didn't want to confront her over it. She was totally down on Ed, as everyone seemed to be right now.

Thursday 3 July

To Harrogate with Rayan for Team Sky meetings, writing new visualisation chapter en route. Arrived Rudding Park Hotel, saw Godric, then Dave, then Froome. GS, Dave and I worked out a few key messages for his press conference later, and the need to focus on the success of the past as a bridge to developing the future. He was worried about Froome though, felt his mind was not in the right place, also that he was getting a bit distant. He wanted me to talk to him not least to explain that they had to get their minds out of the bubble. These guys rode all day and then spent too much time looking at what people were saying about them on social media. The riders were out on a training ride but when they came back Dave got Froome in and I gave him the basic spiel that they were a big and positive story, and they should not allow themselves to get dragged down.

I told them about the visualisation work that Andy McCann [psychologist] did with the Welsh rugby guys, and especially the idea of visualising what kind of person was tweeting about you, like the guys calling me a war criminal every day, I saw them as fat and ugly, spotty, in their bedrooms, no friends or girlfriend. Told him I got abuse on there every day but it only mattered if you let it. You were a top rider, a winner, and that was the mindset you had to have all the time. DB was up for taking big points for the presser, also we were doing a series of profile interviews. Godric needed to get a bit more in his face. What Dave needed was people just to tell him. Lunch then set off for Liverpool. Stopped for a run, then arrived for the dinner, black-tie Trinity Mirror event. Did speech totally off-the-cuff mainly on mental health. Peter Sissons [broadcaster] said best after-dinner speech he had heard. OK reaction. Back early hours.

Friday 4 July

Swim, work, then off to Oxfordshire and the Juliet Soskice–Andrew Rosenfeld [businessman, political donor] wedding in Manoir aux Quatre Saisons. Took Justine and we chatted a bit to her en route. Very hot day, nice event, nice dinner, good speeches. Saw a bit of France–Germany [World Cup, 0–1] on TV with Stewart Wood [Ed M adviser]. Discussed Ed M. It was like talking to a commentator though rather than someone tasked with trying to make it all come together. Ed had a real problem with having surrounded himself with people who were academically bright but just not tough enough when it came to politics.

Saturday 5 July

Working on the book. The Dave B piece we had done for the *FT* worked well. He was bad on *Today* though, and I could tell why. The moment I heard his first answer it was obvious he was in a semi-public place and was therefore keeping his voice down. We had told them to make sure he was in his own space. Godric kicking himself for not staying up there to oversee it. The fact of doing DB meant that they co-presented the programme from there, plus we had given them the *FT* early and Evan Davis gave him a total full-toss question on it, but he just wasn't on form. I sent him a note bollocking him, and he replied saying that was exactly the kind of feedback he needed.

Out on the bike for a bit, then down to Wales, write up Branson. Aberavon. Met by Steve Kinnock at Port Talbot, he filled me in on the party, off to the mayor's parlour, very Welsh, then a Young Labour Q&A, which went well. Steve had to write out the postcards for questions because his CLP secretary had not done it even though it was the one thing he was meant to. He had some really lively people and some deadbeats. Told me his dad did a CLP dinner in Cardiff last week and spoke for ninety minutes. Steve did the vote of thanks and spoke OK. He had definitely gone down well there after a tough struggle.

Sunday 6 July

DB in *The Observer*. Run on beach. Back with Steve K on the train. Worked on a new mini-chapter on the team and individual section. Steve told me a bit about their life together. They had had an agreement that Helle would do her thing and he would travel and commute and then they would go to where he was posted for work. The girls seemed to handle it all OK but it was clearly a very odd life in some ways. Back then to Rachel's for Glenys's surprise 70th. Helle on great form. She loved the Edi idea of having critics beamed into speeches and couldn't believe Ed hadn't fancied it.

Monday 7 July

Excel for auditors' conference. Beatles tribute band warm-up, then video message from Prince Charles. Went fine. Shifted loads of books. Met Frank Luntz [US pollster and strategist], who was picking my brains because he wanted to set himself up as a UK politics pundit for the election. Into town. Then went to the Team Sky bus to wait for Dave and the guys. Andy Murray there to see him. Afterwards chatted with Dave re. stuff. Still seemed quite nervous about it all. Ditto Froome. The riders were saying the crowds in Yorkshire had been beyond anything they had experienced or expected. Took a look at the way the media operation worked, all a bit chaotic. Dave and I had a chat round the back of the bus and agreed to keep in touch daily and I would come out at various points. The Team Sky PR people seemed fine with it, or didn't realise where these ideas were coming from.

Tuesday 8 July

Transcribe Branson, then off to see Ben Ainslie. What a guy. Also his colleague Jono Macbeth, a New Zealander who was helping hire the team. Ainslie great on mindset and teamship. Also saying that I would love the mind games and the black arts that were involved in the America's Cup.[*] Fixed F1 [Formula 1 motor racing] for tomorrow. Froome crash.

---

[*] Ainslie had formed a team, Ben Ainslie Racing, to compete in the 2011–13 America's Cup.

Germany–Brazil. 7–1. Unbelievable stuff. Germany definitely best team there. I was making the most of having predicted them from the start.

Wednesday 9 July

In to see TB, to talk over Egypt, and his profile more generally. Said he felt fine overseas but in the UK was surrounded by this media mood that was definitely getting to him. He was still not really facing up though to the things he might do. Not wanting to do major TV projects, and I had a hunch it was because he just didn't feel comfortable with outsiders getting in too close. I headed off to Silverstone to see the Mercedes team practising. Good interviews with Paddy Lowe [engineer] and Bradley Lord [Mercedes communications manager]. Different class when it comes to innovation and data.

Thursday 10 July

Tanni Grey-Thompson at Benchmark [global company developing sport for social change]. Good interview, mainly mindset and setbacks, and also the Ade Adepitan mindset that did not see setbacks as setbacks at all. Tanni clearly loved the Lords. Nick Keller [Benchmark CEO] a bit down because of his girlfriend having to go back and not yet getting work permit etc. He had signed Michael Johnson [businessman and broadcaster, retired athlete] and I was talking re. DB getting involved with him too. Later did a dinner for Delyth Evans [former member Welsh Assembly] who really had something about her. Good turnout, Anji, Peter Hyman, whose school had just got outstanding in all areas Ofsted report. Lift home with Peter H whose car was still a total mess but was clearly doing brilliantly at school. Interesting too on leadership and how he felt we had made a lot of mistakes in terms of the culture, and that he operated much flatter structures.

Friday 11 July

Senior moment. Meant to be having breakfast with US ambassador and totally forgot!

Sunday 13 July

DB on *Sportsweek*. Did a call beforehand and it was so much better than the *Today* programme. Briefing system that worked was definitely written note week before and chat on the day, literally just as he did it. *Sun on Sunday* chasing about my work in Albania so did a pre-emptive blog before the inevitable 'hordes of immigrants/organised crime' etc. World Cup final, Germany worthy winners.

Monday 14 July

To the Trafalgar Hotel for the Chuka Umunna interview for *GQ*. There was more to him than I expected, bright and engaging, yes a bit too smooth maybe, but a good brain. He struggled a bit when trying to talk up Ed and the chances of winning, but he came over fine. I stayed in the hotel and just worked on the book for hours after he left. Also did a good phone interview with Martha Lane Fox [businesswoman].

Tuesday 15 July

Having screwed up by forgetting the breakfast, today had lunch with Matthew Barzun, US ambassador, at Wingfield House. Nice guy. Pretty young, close to Obama. We talked a lot about the book, and he had some interesting insights. He loved the story about how Kelly Swanson asked me that killer question and as a result was going to get me Mayweather. Loved his sport. He was really getting out and about in the country. He was keen to come to a Burnley game and it turned out an old college mate was coming over and wanted to come to the first game of the season, so we agreed to fix that.

He seemed a little taken aback when I said that a lot of people, left as well as right, felt Obama was a disappointment, and had not really done world leadership as he could and should have done. He was not impressed by Cameron, especially on Europe. He felt there was a leadership role there to be taken but he didn't seem to want to, or know how to if he did. He said he felt TB was still the most credible political voice in the UK, but he had allowed his reputation to get to a bad place. He said TB was still a huge star and a big hit in the US. Putin off the scale at the moment, he said, in terms of his enmity to the US. Definitely a guy to keep close to. He did some terrific stuff in schools, and had some great materials for interaction with kids on what they know about the US. Nice time.

Into town for Bear Grylls [TV presenter, survivalist] interview for *GQ*. I had forgotten I had met him before, and of course I knew his dad [Sir Michael Grylls], ex-Tory MP who died a while back, and who had always been very friendly when I was in the lobby. Grylls a very interesting guy, big God man, interesting views on all sorts of stuff, and a nice manner. I didn't want to like him what with being Old Etonian etc. but he was very likeable and had an amazing story to tell too. Good interview.

Wednesday 16 July

Off to do Tristram Hunt for *GQ*, really knocking them off now, though Osborne finally said no. Lunch with Calum, later to Twitter HQ to do a talk at their new offices, first with the media team, then some of their clients and business partners. They were strangely defensive considering how of the moment they were. Not growing fast enough they felt. 'The Radio 4 of social media.'

Thursday 17 July to Sunday 17 August

Flew to Lyon, and via her tweeting about me being on the plane ended up chatting with a woman called Steph Brown. She was ex-NHS facial surgeon turned director of aesthetics for a Botox firm! Interesting world, about which I knew nothing. Huge growth market. Picked up by Fiona and off to Faucon. Ed sent me the speech he was intending to make about his own image which I felt was way OTT, and made it look like the bacon sandwich thing had really got to him. He changed it a fair bit after I sent a note, but it was still a bit too much 'poor me'. There was a danger it made him look really defensive, rather than play to the strengths he had been showing, e.g. over Murdoch/hacking etc., referendum, unions. He does have qualities and he probably deserves more credit than he has had for some of the bold steps, but the speech feels a bit late.

The real issue remained lack of really hard strategy, teamwork, fight, all the things I was writing about. The winning book was definitely becoming a form of therapy, also becoming very sport-centric. I said to Ed it was 'almost a good speech' but as it stood I felt it would backfire badly. Too defensive. Leadership is not about saying it's not fair but how you are going to fix things. He was also far too kind to the media. Far better to make the point leaders are having to adapt to a new world and that is part of what leadership is about. There was also a casual pop at New Labour in the same breath as Cameron – a mistake he keeps making. I said if we play into this idea that we were all about presentation rather than good substance strategy and policy delivery we just pile another layer on 'the mess we inherited', 'What was the point of voting Labour then so what is the point now?' narrative. Why play their game for them?

He said I was a stuck record on this, but I said it was the single biggest strategic error he has made and I knew from speaking to CLPs I was not alone in thinking that. Far better to start from the standpoint that communication is a fundamental part of politics. All you can control is what you do and what you say about it. It has to be authentic. I said Merkel was no Clinton or Obama, but in her own way is a great communicator – because she is a good leader. People don't bother taking pictures of her eating because they have so much else to write about what she says and does. I told him what Clinton had once said about TB – that he felt Tony thought he should get a blue ribbon for doing the job 'but the job is the blue ribbon'. Less complaining, I said. Less about you and more about people. All people will take out of the draft is another excuse to use that picture, 'bacon sandwich politics' will enter the language and people will think it weird you talk about 'moobs' ['man-boobs'], as he had a reference in there to that too.

He was on stronger ground saying that Cameron does great photos but shit policy. There was also the risk he was making himself the issue not on his terms but those of Cameron and Osborne. They would think they and their media friends had got to him. When I put it down in a note, Tom B replied, 'Spot on.' Marc Stears [EM's chief speechwriter] said he would change it and did. Ed still felt this was the issue though and when I saw him at CB's party he said it all had to be said. He felt the public saw him as principled and serious in contrast to Cameron being all over the place and a showman. But in the last few days I had had several people tell me they just saw him as a bit weak, and Cameron as strong by comparison.

I did a phone interview with Shane Warne [former Australian spin bowler] for the book and decided to do a special Australia-only chapter. There was something about them that made a disproportionate number of people with extreme winning mindset. I was reading [Australian Rules football star] Leigh Matthews's book and managed to track him down and fix an interview. What a bloke. Rory was writing the stuff on data and F1, and new innovation. I was redoing setbacks and boldness and also sent off first three fifths of whole book to Ed and Gail. Gail liked it a lot. Ed was violently opposed to the Anna Wintour chapter, feeling I gave her too much, but I sensed it was personal, some long-forgotten enmity.

Malky called asking if I would speak at the SFA [Scottish Football Association] leadership course and after working out one of the dates coincided with Chelsea at home fixed for that meeting. Also went down to Nimes when the Tour de France was there, and saw Dave B on the team bus. Froome was out of it, Richie Porte [Australian road racer] had a bad bug and was not firing so it was all a bit downbeat. He said he was going to make big changes, though probably keep Froome. He was talking to agents a lot trying to work out whether to buy one really top guy or spread it more. He was getting sensitive about the accusation that there was a lack of Brits in the team, so I emphasised he just had to keep saying they came with a British rider who would have won it had it not been for injury etc.

The Commonwealth Games opening ceremony was low-budget but OK. Salmond did a minute's silence for the victims of the Malaysia Airlines attack over Ukraine. Putin totally out of control. That and Gaza under attack from Israel the big news over the summer. Cameron seemed irrelevant to a lot of it. I was doing the book several hours a day. Nigel

Wilcockson was up to his neck in a John Cleese [comic actor] book so he was not quite giving it full attention but he did send through a good redraft of innovation. I was motoring mainly on Australia, new setbacks and new boldness, and also trying to improve general shape and think through an end chapter.

I was fretting a fair bit about Alex's foreword. It was in my view unusable, so the question was whether just to tell Alex that, say that it would have to change, or spike it; or just accept that his name on the cover was more important than the content. But if it was the first thing people saw in the book I would feel it was bad for the book, bad for him and bad for me. Far better to have nothing than what he sent over. Georgia read it and said there is no way he wrote that, he would be ashamed of it. It made me wonder if Jason had just taken it off him. Dave B would be better. Also if the designers go for my idea of all the names from the book being inside a gold medal on the front, then it would not matter so much anyway. I was thinking I would see him at the Burnley United match and we would resolve then, one way or the other.

Grace came back with us after we went back for Cherie's surprise 60th party. It was at their place in the country. Rayan took us down there, all set up in the garden. Marquee. Entertainment by singing chefs, *Strictly Come Dancing* dancers and Bobby Davro who was funny but near the mark at times. Amazing impersonator of singers. Mainly talking to Bill Blair [judge, TB's brother], a bit to TB, a lot to his team, [hotelier Sir] Rocco Forte's wife who was effusive re. my mental health work, and I was effusive about his triathlon work. Charlie and Marianna, Charlie who liked the book but also had some good thoughts about improving it. He said he found it helpful more as a barrister than a politician and thought maybe it needed more about how Labour won. Nice chat with the Levys, Michael looking good considering he had not been well. The Blair kids all in good form. Nicky getting married next.

We went back to France with Grace Gould and she was on great form, as was Georgia when she came out a few days later. Our Grace back home and doing some amazing stuff, now signed up by *Cosmo* [*Cosmopolitan* magazine] for a blog. She was great on one level, but needed to build resilience when things went a bit wrong. Calum came out after his big Inc [strategy and marketing firm] presentation to the Co-op.

I was not sleeping that well, but it worked out as I tended to get up between 6 and 6.30, work flat-out till lunch, bike after lunch, more work, dinner and then Fiona and I were watching *True Detective* [TV crime series]. Dave B seemed happy with our work and we now needed to agree next steps. He was sticking with Froome and looking to build a new team around him. He felt that losing had been good for them in a way. We fixed for Matthew Syed [*The Times*] to go out to the Tour and he did a brilliant piece albeit with a headline that didn't quite fit with the whole piece, all about how he felt humiliated. But generally it was a really good piece and Matthew loved it.

Also doing pieces for the Scottish media on the referendum and doing a bit of work with Alistair D around the Salmond debates. He won the first one pretty well and was much more confident afterwards. I felt he could have been less shouty and less feeling the need not to dump on the Tories, but AS was poor, and it got a bit silly. Salmond ended well but overall AD won. I spoke to him next day and he clearly felt relieved and was buzzing, or at least as buzzing as Alistair gets. He said GB was back 'and would doubtless want revenge for me doing well and being called the leader of the campaign!' He said Salmond blanked him totally, also that Sturgeon's people were now briefing against him.

I felt he could go harder next time. No plan B on the currency had been his best attack, but I felt he could also make it about Salmond seeing this as *his* destiny not Scotland's. Someone on Twitter suggested to me we should change Salmond's name on publicity materials to A£EX and I got them to do poster van re. same. Also gave Alistair a nice line about the penny dropping about the pound. Margaret McD was doing a nice little sideline campaign re. Let's Stay Together, and she roped me in for a bit of work on that. Cameron had a reshuffle – Gove and Hague demoted. A few sacked.

TB was sending me drafts of a speech he was planning to make on ISIS, which was excellent, though would lead to the usual man-not-ball problem. I suggested he wind back some of the Saddam stuff, because his last intervention was dominated by the idea it was all about him not being to blame. The scale of ISIS horror was getting worse, US journalist James Foley beheaded, lots of Syrian soldiers likewise. Hard to know at this stage if this was a serious political force or a bunch of *Clockwork Orange* hooligans. In any event they were on the march, with by end August territory in Iraq and Syria bigger than the UK. Kelly Swanson finally came good with my Q&A session with Floyd Mayweather so I worked on a chapter for mindset. Alex had definitely gone cold generally, no idea why, but possibly to do with me suggesting to Jason the foreword was not up to scratch.

When I went to Glasgow for the SFA Pro Licence course, thank God I did, because I saw Donald and he clearly wasn't well, and ended up in hospital for a long spell. Not the mind but the body, a chest thing which they took ages to work out. But my heavens thank God for the NHS. I flew Marseille to Edinburgh 16 August with Ryanair, met by Jim Fleeting [SFA director of development], lovely guy, though voting Yes, then off to Motherwell v Inverness. Gordon Strachan [Scotland team manager] there, nice guy, very warm. Poor game, ICT [Inverness Caledonian Thistle] won, but the money in Scottish football was peanuts compared with England, and they were struggling. Dinner with Donald and Jim, I was worried about him though, and not surprised when he called later to say he was in hospital. I got Jim to bring forward my session at the Pro Licence so I could go and see him.

I was staying at the Seamill Hydro, where Celtic used to stay before big games under Jock Stein [European Cup-winning manager]. I was picked up first thing and off to the sports centre where the SFA course was held. About twenty on it, fairly lively bunch. Walter Smith [former Rangers manager] did an analysis of the World Cup, and I wound him up a bit by saying I had predicted Germany to win and he didn't. His main conclusion was that there was less focus on the art of defence. The teams that defended well did best. He barely mentioned England, as though they were irrelevant. My session was really a mix of my usual stuff and the book, probably more sport-focused than I had planned. Jim had said not to go on about strategy because it was above some of their heads and a difficult concept in football, but I did anyway. Q&A was fine, then a quick lunch with Walter, Jim and one or two others before Darryl Broadfoot of the SFA drove me to Glasgow.

I did an interview with a paper from the Gulf who were doing the campaign and also a piece on the Premier League. In between times I saw Donald several times. Oxygen mask. Mentally seemed OK, but I was worrying the drugs would be clashing. The Western Hospital seemed OK if a bit run-down.

Malky was up for the Crystal Palace job, but at the last moment the *Mail* ran a story about his offensive texts found on [sporting director] Iain Moody's phone, and he was out. The LMA made it worse by putting out an otherwise OK statement with the word 'banter' and suggesting it was two colleagues under pressure letting off steam. I recommended he get on TV, admit he was wrong, big mistake, need to learn from it, but make clear he was not walking away from football etc.

Monday 18 August

From Glasgow down to Preston, met by a BBC driver and taken to the Dunkenhaugh Hotel for an interview with Steve Hewlett [broadcast journalist] for his documentary on the royals. Hung around till Dave B and Fran Millar came over and we talked over how we might build on what we had done working together during the Tour. Dave wanted to come to a Burnley game so we met up before the Chelsea match and chatted it all over. He had spoken to Team Sky and had raised the idea of me being integrated through Inc, and seemed like it was on. He was driving a Bentley, very smart suit, trendy glasses. Off with Dave to Burnley, he and I in to have dinner with the US ambassador, Matthew Barzun, and his mates. Obama was going to be the first US President to visit Wales when he went to the NATO summit, so I got Dave to teach him a bit of Welsh. We took the lead, but Chelsea were just too strong [3–1]. Looked like contenders to me; going to be a hard season for us.

Back to France the next morning. Holiday then flew by too fast and in fact I didn't really feel I had had one, though Fiona and I were getting on really well. Tessa had been full-on when she came. She was definitely going for mayor and was very absorbed with it the whole time. Fiona and I both felt she would not win it, that people would think let's go younger, and not TB–GB era, but she was totally determined to do it. We drove back over two days and I took ill as we arrived at the Château De Barive [Sainte-Preuve], clearly flu or some such and the second night I was drenched in sweat all night. Yet when we got back I stupidly went to the Burnley–Man U game, with David Davies. Fergie was there, and so far from his usual friendly self, and I didn't really know why. It must be something to do with the interview and the foreword, but it was such a trivial thing to fall out over. Fiona was convinced Jason had always resented me being close to Alex. I remember though Roy Keane once saying to me, 'One day he will fall out with you, and you will not have a clue why.' I had tried to talk to him a couple of times, but he said there was no problem. I could tell there was. United were poor, Burnley organised well and we drew nil–nil, first point of season.

31 August still struggling with flu but off to Singapore for a speech and a couple of meetings. Mike Garlick [Burnley director] on same plane. I slept most of the flight, two pills, but I was feeling a bit weak and after a day went to see a doctor. Possible urinary infection. Hospital for X-ray. Superb facilities. On the return flight I left my laptop and other stuff on the plane. Singapore Airlines brilliant, not only found it but someone came to the house with it.

Friday 5 September

To Newcastle with Rory to interview Haile Gebrselassie. Great talk. A possible end chapter. Had to get back to Gatwick and off to Tirana, partly to see Edi, also because Erion Veliaj had invited me to his wedding.

Saturday 6 September

Breakfast, run, then with Endri to Durres, to Edi's place by the beach. He said Cameron and Obama were both 'terrible' at the NATO summit in Wales. Full of words but no strategy. He said to them that the one great success NATO had was Kosovo because TB and Clinton led with bombs and it led to peace. And now the Muslims in those countries in the region are basically loyal to NATO, EU and the West. But what are they getting back? He had said to Cameron that he had taken just half an hour to persuade the Pope to come to Tirana because of the broader Balkan significance but 'they really want to see you'. Cameron said yes, he understood we had to keep the supportive Muslims on board, but it would have to be after the election. Edi asked him, 'Will you win? Alastair says you might not win.' He said Dave went bright red and said he hoped so, and also 'your friend is not right about everything, sometimes he can be wrong'.

At one point Edi had said in the plenary that it was all very well to react to what was happening, but Putin had a strategy, ISIS had a strategy, and we did not have a strategy to deal with them. What happens if Putin goes on to Kiev? He can and he probably will. The whole NATO thing felt like it had also been, organisationally, a bit of a shambles, Endri saying they had focused on Obama at the Celtic Manor venue to the exclusion of others. Edi said Merkel as ever had been good.

Due to see IMF guys after we saw him. Beach house Durres. Nightmare situation with the President who was basically just doing everything he could to fuck them up. Sending back legislation etc. Need two-thirds majority to get rid of him though. Problems too with the mayor who was accusing him of blocking job plans (to do with illegal buildings). Lots of Falimanderit [thank-you] posters around, part of the campaign Mark Lucas and I had suggested, to give the credit for progress to the public. The wedding was a long drive south to Gjirokastër, and I stayed in a nice little hotel at the bottom of a hill and did some half-decent hill running. Edi decided against going to the wedding and was perhaps right. It was all very grand. I was with Meta and also Edi's son Greg who I liked. Artist. He said his parents split before he was born. Lots of music and dancing but I sloped off fairly early by their standards, late by mine.

Sunday 7 September

Out for a run round the town, breakfast with Endri and Besa [wife] and then back to Tirana. The polls narrowed right down in Scotland and in one which broke late today, Yes was ahead, so meltdown time up there. Finally though it meant there was some proper galvanising of the politicians and businesses, and a steady drumbeat about real risk began.

Wednesday 10 September

Meetings all day then off with Grace on the sleeper north. First Douglas came round though – he was on the same train – and we chatted about

Scotland and what if anything I could do. At least GB was now motoring, Cameron had agreed there should be new powers etc., so we were going to end up with the devo max [full fiscal autonomy] position Salmond had asked for in the first place. They had really not put together a proper campaign. It sounded fairly chaotic. Slept OK on the sleeper, as did Grace next door.

Thursday 11 September

Arrived Glasgow, then out to see Donald. I went to the Malmaison for breakfast with Alistair D. He was pretty down. He had been taking a bit of a hammering and of course now GB was moving in. I said the most important thing was just to get his mind focused on the idea it would be over in a week. Do the big interviews well. Rest and eat well. He said he was finding it hard to sleep. I have never known an event that was causing so many people not to sleep well. He told me in confidence that he was definitely quitting politics after this. He did not want to screw over Ed at his party conference so wouldn't do it then, but of course there was a danger that the Tories would then say that he heard Miliband and realised he couldn't win. It didn't really matter when he did it, I said. Just get this out of the way first.

Talking to the Labour guys I was reminded of Alan Clark [AC friend, late Tory Secretary for Defence] saying, 'We're fucked, because we hate each other more than we hate you.' The Labour Party was not in good shape. Julian Braithwaite took a few days out from Brussels and sent me some interesting thoughts. Torsten Bell [Resolution Foundation think tank CEO] was slowly getting a grip. Greg Nugent felt he had been excluded by Blair McDougall, even though his stuff was exactly what was needed, and had been for ages. He said he had seen Alistair with Catherine MacLeod six months ago, went through what they needed, and then nothing happened because Blair etc. didn't follow up. Meet with Torsten (who swore incessantly), Greg and Grace then we went to see Donald in the hospital. Saw him a couple of times, hoping to get out soon. Grace doing interviews in town, me working on book, dinner at The Grill. Interviewed a Yes in there who said she was doing it because of the illegal wars.

I got to bed about eleven. Grace was going out to see a friend. I fell asleep and then suddenly the door opens and there is Grace, saying, 'There is someone here who wants to see you.' Ed M! Roused myself and sat up in bed chatting to him. 'How do you think it is going?' I said I thought OK but a lot of anxiety. It was as much a rejection of Westminster as anything else. He said he had just been abused in the lobby. Stayed for half an hour or so. Truth is he didn't have much locus in this, but he had to get involved, I guess. Grace told me later he had really insisted he had to see me, even though she kept telling him I was asleep.

Friday 12 September

Had to get back first thing. Met Torsten on the concourse at the station, talked through a plan for the last few days, main focus unanswered questions. Train back working on the book, final chapter.

Saturday 13 September

I was writing messaging for Scotland, also off to Palace v Burnley with Rory. Nil–nil. Good game though. Then to Greenwich for an after-dinner speech for a Norwegian shipping firm. MC Myleene Klass [singer and model], very sexy. Scotland polls came through, No in the lead in three, behind in one, which would allow them to keep going with a neck-and-neck narrative. Chatted to Alistair on the need to get up unanswered questions on the Marr show. He admitted he was exhausted. I was keen for John Reid to do *Marr*, but Alistair felt with Salmond also on it would become a bad process story if he didn't do it.

Sunday 14 September

AD was poor on *Marr*, and knew it. He called me afterwards and said he had felt really tired. Salmond was given an easy ride. Also John Reid fucked up. Main line: 'If you don't know, vote no,' and he said, 'If you don't know, don't vote.' Annoying but we would get through it. Alistair looked exhausted, grimaced rather oddly at times. Douglas said that the GB constitutional changes idea had been the usual mad toing and froing. But Cameron was desperate and so happy to let him do whatever he wanted to. No. 10 and others had been badgering me for ages about getting Alex involved. I had really tried, and Fiona thought my persistence might be the reason he had seemed so chilly of late, though he had still been taking my calls, talking away, but definitely not as warm. He had been saying how desperate he was for No to win, but when I said he could do something to help, he pulled back. He said he didn't want to get involved because the people putting their heads above the parapet were getting shot at. He saw the abuse that J. K. Rowling and others had been getting, and he was not up for it. It was lose-lose. Unsure that an intervention would help, but sure that he would get dog's abuse. I said he had had a lot worse, and it had never stopped him before. I was really a bit surprised that he would not even allow us to put out a few words, but when I discussed it with

Fiona, she said just leave it, stop pushing him so hard. So I did, though I did point out the one thing everyone knew about Alex was that he pushed as hard as you had to get to what he wanted. The whole thing was really strange. Maybe Fiona was right, that Jason had stirred it, I don't know. Jeremy Heywood said Alex had been one of his heroes, he had been thrilled when I had taken him into No. 10 and introduced him, but he had sunk in his estimation. He asked if I thought a call from Cameron would help. I said definitely not. He could not stand Cameron. In fact that might be the other thing holding him back. He had a couple of times asked me why I was helping Cameron. I said I wasn't; I was helping the campaign to stop Salmond breaking up the UK. Train up to Glasgow, working on the book.

Met by Liz and off to Donald's to help clear out a load of old stuff, then Liz took me back into town to meet Pat McFadden [Scottish Labour MP] and Catherine MacLeod. Pat very worried that working-class Catholics were moving to Yes. Catherine was worried about the organisation, or lack of it. I said it was not possible to help sort it now. I would just try to help AD and Douglas Alexander, GB if he would take it, have ideas and generally motor a bit. Catherine said Alistair was exhausted and I needed to help him. Torsten joined us in an Indian restaurant and we worked up a few ideas. Got banjaxed by an anti-New Labour bearded guy on the way out and ended up having a long conversation with him and a few others who joined in. Pretty amazing the extent to which people were talking about it. The Yes demo at the BBC had been a mistake, I think, and the intimidation was beginning to backfire on them a bit.[*] But they just ploughed on.

Monday 15 September

Alistair and Douglas came round for a meeting and we planned out a few things. GB out again today which was helpful. Douglas said Alistair was a bit shot and I had to try to bolster him just to get him through the last few days. Douglas told me that he was definitely getting out of politics after this, that he no longer enjoyed it and he needed to get himself sorted with something. I asked if he had enjoyed any of it. He said not really. 'Campaigning is not really my thing because you're endlessly having to turn it all on for people.' Every time I suggested Jim Murphy for something, Douglas baulked. Jim told me later the campaign had been a shambles.

We had a real problem with working-class Catholics so I was trying Neil Lennon, Scott Brown [Celtic player], also Joe Miller [agent] who looked after former Celtic players. Lennon was friendly and onside but said he got

---

[*] A large crowd had gathered outside the BBC's Glasgow headquarters to protest that coverage of the referendum had been biased against independence.

enough shit in Glasgow without adding to it. Brown was really friendly, wished me well and all that, but said he was contractually not allowed to get involved. We had a good chat, not least about Burnley and Celtic, recalling the night he and half the Celtic team joined us at the BFC promotion celebrations. Trying to get up the story that English Premier League would shut the door on Scottish clubs if Yes won. I tried Fergie again, promised it was the last time I would ask, but it was clearly not happening. He said he was off to Russia for a couple of days. I worked a lot on words for Alistair for the last few days. Also general message and then started to work on his words for after the event. Need to heal and reconcile. Things getting quite edgy on the streets. Out to see Donald who was doing OK, amazing attitude.

Tuesday 16 September

I went to my first Better Together morning meeting. Not as bad as I was led to believe but Catherine said afterwards that was because I was there and they were trying to be grown-up. Paul Sinclair [adviser to Scottish Labour] had got up a good story on the NHS and planned cuts post referendum which was going big and which Alistair pushed well. I was worried tomorrow's events were not big and booster-rocket enough. We worked on a final rally with GB, Alistair, Scottish leaders and five real people. Also trying to get No projected on to landmark buildings, which they managed to do fine, if a bit late. Also late, Clinton finally delivered really good words thanks to TB's constant badgering. TB called several times. It must have hurt that they so clearly didn't want him involved. He would have been able to make the case better than most, but it was clear that Iraq was one of the issues in the background.

TB – seeing GWB of all people today, so I said get him to come out for YES fast – was confident the Scots would see sense but couldn't understand how it had been allowed to go so close. He thought Salmond had stuffed Cameron on the negotiations, but also that it was 'evil' the way he was using these nationalist and divisive tactics. The NHS SNP bandwagon was stalled a little, but Salmond was amazing for the way he would just bat away inconvenient truths. The NHS tactic had been highly effective, even though it was simply not true that independence was the only way to guarantee no privatisation etc. Paul Sinclair was the main GB point man and he said – as did Douglas – that he was as difficult as ever.

Today for example, he demanded the David Dimbleby interview was pre-recorded, then wanted an earlier time, then said it was too early. Douglas said that at one point GB had said, 'Danny Alexander is a total fucking madman!' I had my first sense of Danny A, as he took part in the meeting and was very calm, very affable. Also had a sense of humour about himself, as when I said he needed to cover the Cairngorms with a No banner. Later he called in and said he was. Alistair got a bit hot under the collar with Torsten because he was pushing for GB tomorrow at the final rally and Alistair was worried it was becoming too Labour. Torsten was pretty firm and didn't mind upsetting people, but Alistair said he was not taking lectures on divisions. He clearly felt that a lot of people had just let him do the heavy lifting, without really helping, and spent the whole time criticising. Blair McDougall and Rob Shorthouse [director of communications, Better Together] struck me as a lot better than I had been told.

Interesting to see how well the different parties got on. I had a private chat with Danny Alexander who said he thought in the end it would be a ten-point lead for No. We talked about the next election. He said that he did not think either the Tories or Labour could win, so 'provided we do not get obliterated, I think we will be holding the balance of power again'. He felt Ed M was just not cutting through but if we got the numbers the Libs would go with them again. He felt part of the problem with politics was that everyone pretended there were these huge differences between them but actually there weren't. There were fairly small differences, and a pretence. He said, 'I probably agree with someone like Douglas on 90 per cent of issues.' He said Clegg was definitely staying and actually still enjoyed it and was looking forward to the campaign.

Lunch with Alistair, Catherine and Torsten, chatting over his next media interviews. Quite a good reception as we walked to the restaurant and back, though Alistair always looked fearful when anyone came near him. Torsten wanted me to talk him into accepting GB at the final rally. I did a motivational call for the staff re. last few days, just ignore the noise, focus and remember winning was the best feeling of all. Back with Alistair, met to sort last day then I headed off to see Donald in Faifley [Clydebank]. Clinton words came through, so I sorted that from there, was then driven down to Moffat for *Newsnight*. In a tent in a churchyard with David Mundell, local Tory MP [Parliamentary Under-Secretary of State for Scotland], about Tories in Scotland.

Simon Schama [historian] on with Neal Ascherson [journalist]. Schama was good, and very warm and friendly. Isabel Hardman [*The Spectator*] and the *Sunday Herald* guy, the only paper to back Yes. Murdoch still sitting on fence, probably to the end. I was actually quite gentle with a Scots Nat, but still Twitter full of stuff saying I had been arrogant and boorish. They had such a big social media operation. Used the 'case for separation not proven, but the risks are' line. Got out Clinton messages. Had a bit of a pop at Cameron re. the negotiations etc. Starting to think there could be a lot of trouble after the event. Going to get a bit sectarian. Chatted with Emily Maitlis, who said Mundell had said he wouldn't debate with me but then did. Driven back by a No-voting Pole. Bed by one.

Wednesday 17 September

Alistair excellent on *Today*. Salmond was given an easy ride by [James] Naughtie [presenter], e.g. when he swatted away Spanish PM quotes in the Parliament today that they could get automatically into the EU. Greg Nugent and Eddie Izzard came over for breakfast at Catherine MacLeod's. I was giving Eddie lines for his introduction role at the final rally at Maryhill. E.g. No is not a negative word if you are stopping something negative. No to apartheid was a positive message. Reminded him that Glasgow was the first city to give Mandela its freedom. Also the lines from the Clinton statement about Scotland showing we can co-exist in unity despite differences. Round to the morning meeting. Douglas was very edgy. All focused on the final rally, at which in the end GB did brilliantly, passionate and full of great argument. The whole event went pretty well but we still looked a bit weak in the afternoon which meant Salmond had the last big event, Perth, good words and pictures.

Their people definitely looked like they felt they could win. [Scottish Labour MP] Frank Roy's son Brian took me through the numbers and because of the lead in the postal votes he was clear that Yes would really have to get all their support out, and have the undecideds fall to them, if they were to win. They would need to win big in Dundee and win in Glasgow. He felt it was unlikely. Annoyingly, Cameron did clips on good jobs figures so was on the news, which was the last thing we needed. I did AD final words for the rally, which he memorised and delivered well, but GB stole the show. It was going to be galling for Alistair to have GB portrayed as the man who saved the union, but there you go. He really found his voice today. Absolutely at his best.

Before I headed back, I had a long chat with Douglas who felt that Ed M just did not get how he was seen. Ed had said to him this morning he was popular in Scotland, not realising that when he got a warm reception it was usually when he met people the party had put there. He had been given a rough ride yesterday in Edinburgh. He wanted to be out again today, and Douglas A had had to tell him there must only be Scottish voices involved on the final day, and including a lot of real people. He said that the party machine had just about responded but it was not there as before. He could not see the public electing Ed, other than maybe as part of a Liberal coalition. But the Tories would not find it hard to kill him during the campaign. He said they had always intended to start going for him properly after the referendum.

Nice chat with Catherine and Frank who also said the party machine was broken in many ways but that they had just about held it together. But the divisions and the hatreds were too strong and too negative. Ego a real problem as ever. Not just the UK guys but the guys in Scotland. Left on the 12.40 train and worked mainly on the book, also writing a few lines for tomorrow. Alex having said no, Jason called to make sure I wouldn't be putting anything out. He had really gone down in my estimation. Paddy Crerand [former Man U footballer, MUTV commentator] had been calling me, asking why I couldn't get Alex out saying something, sure it could have an impact. When I told him he had said he saw how J. K. Rowling etc. were treated, he said there were little old ladies standing up to intimidation, we all have to. Paddy really passionate against the Nats.

Thursday 18 September

Bit of a wasted day, just constantly trying to find out what was happening, and scanning social media. Out on the bike. Did a blog on lessons for politics more broadly, to post when polls close. Had an exchange with Kevin Pringle [adviser, SNP] who felt they were on for 51.5 per cent. But Frank Roy was sending me updates suggesting we were winning in Glasgow, which Yes had to win to win overall. Andy Murray [Scots tennis star] came out for Yes. Texted Alex, who said, 'Won't make a difference; he doesn't have a vote.'

Was keeping in touch with Frank and Brian Roy who despite one or two worries were confident it was going to be OK. Turnout was huge which some saw as good for Yes, thinking it was people who had never voted coming out to vote for change, and others felt was a sign of the silent majority coming out as expected. Danny Alexander had said to me he felt it would be a ten-point win for No and that is what happened. 45 per cent wanting the country to leave the UK though was not to be messed with or misunderstood. I wrote a blog saying politics had to learn the lessons, and some of them offered real hope, but there was little sign either of the main parties really got what was happening. Stayed up most of the night as the results came in.

Friday 19 September

Cameron out at 7 a.m. in Downing Street, and he came up with his nonsense about English votes for English laws. Talk about not heeding the lessons. Straight into his own tactics rather than heeding the message of change. Depressing. Likely to trouble Ed though which was largely the point. Salmond announced he would be stepping down and Nicola Sturgeon

September '14: Scotland referendum day

would be a shoo-in. She had had a good campaign, as had Ruth David-son [Tory leader in Scotland]. Talked to Jim Murphy, who was thinking about standing up there. Going to be difficult for Labour. SNP would get a big boost and they would carry on portraying Labour as the same as the Tories, which was why Cameron's move was so annoying and stupid. Saving the union and his job by the skin of his teeth, and he dives straight into another constitutional mess, short-termist nonsense.

Saturday 20 September to Tuesday 23 September

To Sharjah, working flat-out on editing the book on the flights and in spare moments. I slept a bit on the plane and again on arrival before being picked up and taken for a meeting with the Sheikh i/c the Media Centre, one of the younger ministers, some of the team. Talking through the days ahead and the need for them to get signed up to a more strategic approach. Good to get their sense of where the power lay. I was due to meet the Crown Prince [Sheikh Mohammed bin Zayed Al Nahyan] Sunday and they were clear that if I could get him on board, he would get the ruler on board and it would all become a lot easier. Some of the agencies were signing up to more co-ordination, others were not, and they were in any event purely driven by events and press releases and did the ruler notice? All in need of cultural change.

The Crown Prince was smart, and he seemed to get what the Sharjah Media Centre was trying to do. It was also clear that they saw culture as their stand-out point and they wanted to develop that. They needed to get a sense of their own identity and culture past present and future was the key. The main meetings were with the Crown Prince, who was asking a fair bit re. Scotland, and later a training session with the Sharjah Media Cen-tre team. Some of the women in particular were bright and on it, but they were clearly struggling to get buy-in across the board for a new approach and they didn't really have the tools they needed, or the authority.

Hotel fine, gym OK, also did a couple of slow runs in the ridiculous heat. Don't know if I managed to achieve what they wanted me to, but the feedback on the training session was good, and the Crown Prince was clear I should see the ruler next time, and also that I should speak at the Sharjah International Book Fair which they said was one of the biggest in the world. Got back on the Tuesday so that I could go to the No. 10 LLR reception.

Tuesday 23 September

LLR reception in Downing Street was all a bit grim. Nice to see some of the old No. 10 team, but the LLR money people via Charlie Metcalfe [charity supporter] were all real Tory types. Samantha Cameron made a little speech. DC was in NY at UNGA [United Nations General Assembly] where the whole ISIS scene was top of the agenda and he was planning to recall Parliament on Friday to have MPs vote for air strikes. Ed was signalling that fine for Iraq because the government wanted support but not for Syria. All becoming a real quagmire. I missed the entire Labour conference. Ed's speech not great. He insisted doing without notes again and he completely forgot the economic section allowing the Tories to run rampant with the idea that he didn't even mention the deficit. Andrew Neil pressed Douglas immediately afterwards and he struggled possibly because he knew what had happened. Even without that rather big error, the whole speech was not likely to cut through.

He had too many accounts of random encounters with people, all supporting his view of the world or whatever issue he was addressing. He had sent me the draft at various points, and I had said to him, please don't use the story about a woman saying she was hoping he was Benedict Cumberbatch [actor]. I had given him a really good anti-Tory passage exploiting the fact that Cameron had told Scots they could get rid of the effing Tories, and he said he thought it was brilliant but the team was worried it would overshadow everything else. Nonsense. Overthinking. He used a line I gave him re. UKIP and Cameron worrying more about them than the UK, but he couldn't deliver these attack lines with real venom. The Tories seemed stuck and UKIP were making the weather. Cameron was not dealing with it as he should, and if he ran as bad a campaign on Europe as they had in Scotland, he would struggle.

Wednesday 24 September

I went down to deepest south London for [former *Mirror* colleague and novelist] Murray Davies's funeral. Brilliant eulogy by Mike McCarthy [former *Mirror* colleague]. Welsh male voice choir. Lots of Dylan Thomas. Nice service for a crematorium. Fair few old names from the *Mirror* there. McQueen telling me about his son's struggles post military injury. He said Headley Court [Defence Medical Rehabilitation Centre] were brilliant. Nice chat with Bill Hagerty. Donald called, still struggling with his breathing. He wanted me to go up next week when he goes to the doctor at Gartnavel [Glasgow hospital].

Thursday 25 September

Lunch with Nicola Howson at Freuds. She was leaving, had had enough. Said Matthew/Liz all over really. Out later to Bertelsmann [media conglomerate] reception at St Pancras. Grayson Perry, very interesting on masculinity. [BBC political journalist] Ben Wright's girlfriend Poppy, ex-Osborne now Freuds, was there, Ben came along and I introduced him to Ed V so he could get a take on the book he was writing about alcohol and politics. Ben said Ed M speech had pretty much bombed, big coverage but no cut-through, and the big take-out that he forgot the deficit.

Friday 26 September

To St Pancras Renaissance again for my stint at Gail's creativity and innovation conference. I was doing a short talk followed by interview with Clive W. Watched Arianna Huffington do a bit on her Thrive [Global, well-being and productivity initiative] agenda, then me and Clive. Good production values. Clive on form, some of the same stuff we had in the book. I had been chasing Joachim Löw [German team coach] and he came good with a date, which annoyingly I couldn't do because of a thing I was committed to do in Malta. I tried to get them to take Rory but they wouldn't. Really annoying. My effing diary. Calum was starting to sort his move to Scotland. Definitely on for it and probably going to get a three-day-a-week deal to carry on the Co-op work. Left with Rory for Woking, to interview Ron Dennis [CEO, chairman and founder] at McLaren.

We did a tour of McLaren, impressive outfit, then interviewed Dennis. He had aged since I last saw him. Amazing set-up. Lovely building, Norman Foster, sparkling and clean. Hundreds of trophies around.

Sunday 28 September

Down to Oxfordshire, lunch at Carina Frost's. The boys there, Chadlingtons, (Peter taking the mick re. Ed speech, on which Carina was fulminating too), other friends, nice enough do though we left early to get back for West Brom's 4–0 battering of Burnley. First time this season we really didn't turn up.

Monday 29 September

Labour's conference having been poor, Tories started out in a grim situation, an MP [Mark Reckless] defecting to UKIP, and a minister resigning because of sending pictures of his privates to an undercover reporter.* Cameron pretty good on *Marr* though and through the week they managed to get

---

* Braintree MP and civil society minister Brooks Newmark resigned his ministerial role after *Sunday Mirror* allegations that he shared sexually explicit images with a reporter over social media.

up a message at least. Osborne doing more austerity, Cameron promising tax cuts some day whenever. But they were going to lose the [Clacton MP] Douglas Carswell by-election [following Carswell's defection to UKIP]. UKIP also eating into us though. Labour attack was absolutely hopeless. Lots of people on Twitter, and in trains etc., asking me to go back and sort them out. I couldn't face it. I had pretty much done the book. Going to be way too long so a lot of cuts to come.

Wednesday 1 October

Pre-recorded an interview with Victoria Derbyshire [BBC] on the Diaries, then lunch with Tom Baldwin. Ed wanted me to get involved in the launch of their football policy. Fans on boards and able to buy shares the main things. Tom realised conference was a disaster in some ways, but he felt they did at least have some meat out there they could campaign on now. Also that the Tories seemed stuck. Cameron speech today though seemed to go down pretty well. Tom going to stay till election then go come what may. Clearly not a great sense of cohesion in the team, I would say.

Thursday 2 October

Early train to Glasgow, working on the book, then Donald met me and off we went to the hospital. He was still far from right and the meeting with the consultant was not very satisfactory. I was really not sure what was happening and said he would not know more until he came off the steroids. Wondering whether we needed a second opinion. Donald was realising that there was a chance he would have to give up both work and piping, the two things that gave him some identity and meaning to his life. His attitude generally was amazing though, totally positive and upbeat.

Fiona sent a message with a picture showing that our car had been smashed in by a hit-and-run driver, probably a truck. ISIS stuff getting worse and worse, but there was so much other bad news too, Ebola [virus disease], a really bad murder, massive protests in Hong Kong, Ukraine. Took Donald out for lunch and he had asked earlier when did I last see Ally McCoist [ex-Rangers and Scotland footballer] and who should walk by but Ally? Lovely guy, good chat. Worked more on the book on the way back, felt I had totally broken it now, wanted it off my plate.

Saturday 3 October

Leicester–Burnley, great day out, fans good and rewarded with 96th-minute equaliser. 2–2, first goals since opening day of the season. Over the weekend we learned that TB had had a letter from Chilcot warning him Maxwellisation letters were to follow and the thinking was the report would be published by February or after the election.[*] Sue Gray and Jeremy H felt February was likely. It meant I would probably have to delay publication of the book. Annoying but hey-ho. It was my fourth book since the inquiry started.

Monday 5 October

Work a.m., swim, then to Random House for planning meeting on book publicity. Saw Nigel briefly. Then to Soho House for screening of *Rosewater* with Grace. Jon Stewart [TV host, writer, producer, activist] political drama film as I was to be interviewing him at the weekend for *GQ*. Dinner at Juliet and Andrew's, his health not good again.

Tuesday 6 October

Out with Rayan to the airport, heading to Malta. Bumped into Shane Warne, brief chat re. the book, thanked him for his contribution. He looked exhausted. Mind you people said the same to me. Call from Malta PM office, Kurt Farrugia [head of communications] re. possible traps in my interview on TV later. Three-hour flight, met by Ronald Attard of EY [advisory services agency], and we went over some of the content of their attractiveness to invest report which was the ostensible reason for the conference. It was all very different in the sunshine. The last time I was there was for the Bush–Gorbachev summit in 1998, which I had written into the nation branding speech. The weather had been biblically awful, but the place looked totally different in nice weather.

Hotel, swim, meet up with Barbara Nestor who had been the link fixing it up. Off to the press launch at the Chamber of Commerce, where the turnout made it dawn on me that this was quite a big deal. Though the Polish ex-PM was there all the focus seemed to be on me and what I felt about the issue of Malta branding. Small business minister Chris Cardona was there, nice guy, bright, though I advised him not to wear such an expensive watch. (Later he had a cheaper one.) It was a good job I had done a proper speech with some real substance which I was able to draw on for the interviews, and my little talk at the launch. Off to *TimesTalk* at Malta TV, two TV journalists 'grilling' me and alongside me Godfrey Grima [PR]

---

[*] Maxwellisation is a legal practice in England and Scotland where persons who are to be criticised in an official report can respond prior to publication, based on details of the criticism that are received in advance.

chipping in. Usual bollocks, spin, Iraq, Diana, a bit of mental health, but it was clear they wanted to try to be Paxman types.

Lots of the Maltese afterwards thought it had been really tough. It wasn't really, though I did get a bit spiky with them at times. Back to the hotel and a dinner for EY partners, clients and some ministers and others. Very masculine society. The dinner was fine, Cardona an interesting guy who ran the Gaming Commission, and filled me in on the extent to which gaming was now a huge part of the economy, maybe 8 per cent; Grima an ex-journalist turned events manager and PR who was running the event, and Phyllis Muscat [task force head] who was in charge of the team preparing for CHOGM [Commonwealth Heads of Government Meeting]. She and I were talking about the relevance of CHOGM (they were intending to call it the Commonwealth Summit) and also the difficulty for women to reach the top in Malta. Nice enough evening, though I was a bit knackered.

Wednesday 7 October

Swim, finish speech, which was in good shape and I was pleased when I realised how much of a deal the conference was. PM Joe Muscat was in London and he did a video message. Ronald and then the Chamber of Commerce guy opened it, then an EY guy presented the largely favourable report, then me. Air conditioning had broken so it was brutally hot, but I had a proper message – the need for them to co-ordinate their branding, and general messages of how, and both speech and Q&A went well. One of the media reports said I had upstaged the PM and the opposition leader, whose speech was poor. He had led the EU referendum campaign to victory ten years ago, but he did not strike me as a winner.

Labour had won the last election by a landslide though the electorate was so small they were already worrying about how many they had lost from some of the early difficult decisions. Kurt Farrugia and his team were all there, and we arranged for me to meet them all tomorrow. Did a fair few interviews, then a panel. Muscat was now in Milan for an EU summit (largely a favour to Renzi) and so dinner was delayed till he got back. We were driven, Ronald, Barbara and I, out to the official residence half an hour out of town. Formerly home to the Inquisitors,* beautiful place.

The wife, Michelle, was nice, and very sharp, clearly committed to him and to the party. She was a lot quieter once he arrived. Smaller than I expected, a bit pudgy, but sharp. He arrived with his chief of staff, and

---

* The first General Inquisitor and apostolic delegate of the Maltese Islands arrived in Malta in 1574 and was offered an unused palace as an official residence.

a press guy, Kurt and two or three others already there, including Johann Grech [head of marketing] who said Peter M and I were his all-time heroes. He had worked in Millbank 2001. They were all unbelievably well informed about UK politics. Muscat clearly not much of a fan of Cameron. He was reasonably diplomatic, but his chief of staff kept using the word 'shallow'. Muscat felt Cameron had resilience and he was energetic but lacked strategy. He felt he was mishandling the EU issue pretty badly. But they were not impressed by Ed either. The PM said he had met him a couple of times and he could not detect hunger for winning, and the fight needed. He had seen him at the Commonwealth Games opening ceremony and whereas Cameron and Salmond were operating and working the room, Ed sat in the corner having a cup of tea.

He felt Osborne had managed to outmanoeuvre them on the economy – true – and that they at least had a plan. Yet he felt that we would win, just. He said if Labour could only find the fight to look like they believed they could win, then it was there for the taking. We agreed another coalition of some sort was likeliest. After dinner he took me aside and said he would like me to work with them. He had been asked by a journalist if he was hiring me and he said, 'I doubt we could afford him,' but he seemed pretty keen, whether from government or party perspective. Nice evening, very late, lots of photos and all that stuff. Definitely a nice guy with a good team though I told them they needed more women. I had said the same at the conference, when I said it did not say much good about their image that they had a panel of eight men and no women. Back to the hotel and had a drink with Barbara. Jan Åge Fjørtoft was in town with the Norway team v Malta and we arranged to meet tomorrow. Lots of media coverage for the speech, front pages two days running, loads on the news, EY happy.

Thursday 8 October

Meeting with the Richmond Foundation mental health charity, who wanted me to do an event at the presidential palace. Nice group and seemed to know what they were doing. One psychiatric hospital on the island. Lots of stigma. Off to the OPM [office of the Prime Minister] in Valletta to speak to ministers, comms directors and others. Maybe sixty in the room and I did some pretty basic stuff on teamwork and co-ordination. Q&A then back to the hotel and off to see Jan Åge and his colleagues at the Radisson Golden Sands on the other side of the island. Per-Mathias Høgmo the manager was a big Labour guy and very intelligent. Had a good political chat. He felt that the problem for leaders was lack of power not too much. Jan Åge and his comms guy both raving re. the Diaries so Per-Mathias asked me to send. Nice lunch with them, good bunch. Felt English football in a bit of a mess. Back, then Norway team hotel, and fly back after a two-hour delay at the airport. UKIP win Clacton and run Labour close in Heywood. Grimsville. Donald not good.

Friday 9 October

Catching up then out for a lunch event with Paxman at Corrigan's. Pretty standard stuff and they were clearly keen on us disagreeing on bits, which we did. Jeremy totally playing into the idea that the political class had lost it. Bright bunch, but there was definitely a problem with the huge and uncheckable power a lot of these business types had. Later to Admiralty Arch for the Clegg event for World Mental Health Day. He had made mental health the centrepiece of his conference speech, which was good, though there was something unconvincing about the way the Lib Dems suddenly turned nasty against the Tories. Nice event, and definitely felt things on the move. Frank Bruno [retired boxer] there too.

Sunday 11 October

Jon Stewart all day, interview in the morning, transcribe and write in the afternoon. Very bright guy and we had a good chat. 'I could sit and talk to you all day,' he said. Likewise, I said. I sensed he was fairly sympatico but really couldn't understand why TB had got involved as he had with Iraq/Bush. Excellent on media but also on how politicians were not really facing people up to the reality of decisions they had to take, e.g. re. ISIS. Bright and easy to see why he was such a cultural voice. He was not wisecracking at all, wanted to be serious, I think. Also not pushing his film too hard, which was nice. Told him re. the book and said we should do a rematch.

Monday 13 October

Off to KPMG for the Business Disability Forum. Good event. Police from Wales and the Met there saying they were really struggling with mental health, both in terms of it being a cause of discrimination in the service, but also that so much of the police's work was now mental health-related. They had taken so long to get even near where they needed to be on gender and race, and they were worried they would be way too far behind on this. I had a lovely chat with a girl called Pru, who told me she had heard me talk about my breakdown and had been in exactly the same boat as me re. psychosis, that it had been worst thing ever to happen to her but now she saw it as the best.

Tuesday 14 October

Up really early and off with Calum and Rayan to the horror that is Luton airport early in the morning, heading to Poland for the Scotland match. I was always stunned at how much drink was going down first thing. Wizz Air was fine, sitting with a Scotland fan so Calum and he just talked football while I did some work on the book. Nice time with Calum, lunch in Warsaw old town, dinner near the ground. I had a run which was fine. Over to the Intercontinental p.m. to meet Darryl Broadfoot and collect tickets. He introduced me to Stewart Regan, SFA CEO, and we chatted away for an hour or so. I later discovered they were going to approach me to be SFA non-exec independent director. Tempting.

Good atmosphere around the city, nice weather, we walked out to the stadium and it was a fantastic match in a great ground. Scotland fans terrific as ever. Calum worried I would get grief because of the referendum but they were fine, pretty warm. Poland took lead, Scotland equalised, then took lead, then 2–2. Really good game. Glad I went. The big story of the night was Serbia v Albania. Someone sent in a drone with a Greater Albania flag, the Serbs tried to take it off the pitch, a massive brawl ensued and eventually the game was abandoned as the Albanians came under attack from the crowd. The Serbs were saying Edi's brother was behind it.

Wednesday 15 October

Woke to several missed calls from Edi and Endri. Horrific stuff. The Serbs claimed it was Edi's brother – which was untrue – but the story had gone round the world. I wrote a strategy note basically making sure he stood up for the Albanian players, but kept the focus on the big picture, and the importance of his planned meeting with Aleksandar Vučić [Prime Minister of Serbia] next week. I helped Edi put together a statement with Vučić. Lots of pressure on them to cancel their meeting, but they were both determined to keep going, and go ahead with the meeting, and Merkel was keen too. They agreed to meet in Belgrade on 10/11 November. The timing of the incident couldn't have been worse, and then the Serbs started to spread rumours that Edi's brother was involved, and the more they were denied, the more they spread.

Got back, then out with Fiona, Grace, Ines [Nebi, Grace schoolfriend], Georgia, Gail, Melissa Benn [writer and campaigner] and Juliet [Soskice] to the Labour women's dinner. Natashca and Noreen there too. Ed M was the main speaker but had a dreadful cold, so he was more adenoidal than ever. He spoke OK, but there was a lack of energy in the room. Harriet spoke fine, very Harriet, Gloria [De Piero, shadow minister for women] OK, Lucy Rigby [parliamentary candidate] good. Nice enough evening but it didn't feel like a winning environment, it really didn't. The UKIP thing was real and deep and though a lot of it was about immigration it wasn't just that. My sense was people needed leadership and nobody was showing it.

Thursday 16 October

Gordon Strachan [Scotland manager] called for a chat. He was happy with the performance in Warsaw. He had told Darren Fletcher he wouldn't get in the team if he didn't get regular club football. With Daley Blind [Dutch midfielder] the latest arrival at United he was falling further down the pecking order. Off with Fiona to the Lords for Gail taking her seat. Our idea of hell but as Fiona said it would have made Philip happy. Margaret McD and Clive Hollick [Labour peers] introducing. Lots of hanging around then into the gallery. Like looking down on our past lives. All the old Tories who were ministers when we were journos, then on the other side, Peter M, Derry Irvine, Hilary Armstrong, Helen Liddell, loads of them. Gail looked quite moved by it.

I bumped into Peter on the way out with Clive Soley, who said Peter and I had to save Ed. Peter was also at the lunch and he and I had a long chat about the general scene and about his life. He felt Ed was lacking in so many respects. So was Cameron but Cameron would do whatever it took to win. Gave Ed V and Carol [wife] a lift back. Carol very funny. Having started out saying I was an imbecile not to want to take a seat in the Lords, she ended up saying it was the worst place in the world and I was absolutely right. Talking to Tom B re. the football policy launch tomorrow with Clive Efford [shadow minister for sport]. Boards representation for supporters' trusts, and share availability when clubs change hands. Stewart Regan pressing me re. SFA. Called Alex to brief him on the football policy and pick his brains re. the SFA, who were sounding me out for the board. He was in Boston, at Harvard, but very cool again. Really odd.

Friday 17 October

Keir Kennedy Mitchell [fitness trainer] came round for our first training session. Really good. Had a nice manner and a lot of expertise. To Random House for a planning meeting for *Winners*. I explained that Chilcot was likely to be February or after the election. We chatted around it for a while and finally decided to stick with 18 February as the launch date, unless it absolutely coincided with Chilcot. My sense was that TB was going to be in the firing line, but I wasn't. But it would be difficult promoting the book if the inquiry was around then. The new cover was good, taking on my idea of different-sized names according to where they were in the book, inside a big No. 1 rather than a gold medal. Lunch with Ed V at the new Jeremy King restaurant. We agreed next steps. But he seemed a bit ill to me, and I said he needed to take care. To the Shard for a Portland event, then off to the BBC to do a clip for the Beeb's farewell to Paxman, then a few interviews on the Labour football policy.

Saturday 18 October

Calum and I off to Burnley, rewriting the teamship chapters en route. David Moyes was at the match and we ended up sitting together. He said he was trying hard not to be bitter, but his record at this stage was better than Louis van Gaal [new Man United manager] on a far smaller transfer budget. He was also worrying about Alex and the papers as there was stuff in the press that he would blame Moyes for. He said he had a pretty tight gagging clause, still hadn't got all the money owed. He felt he was treated really shabbily but that was life. He wanted to get back in the game soon. Had been in for Schalke but Di Matteo spoke German. Looked a lot better, but his anger was pretty clear. He was pissed off that Alex had not picked up the phone. He said the players had been pretty good and they told him it was chaos now.

Good game, we battered them first half but couldn't score then they came out second half and scored two headers. Lost 3–1. Loads of West Ham fans at Manchester Road station, started singing a few songs. Reasonably good-natured, but I was glad the cops were there. Met some of their directors and a media lawyer who had been part of Rebekah's legal team. He said she got off because she was a perfect witness, absolutely brilliant and they never got near her, whereas with Coulson he was damned by the paper.

Sunday 19 October

Up early and I was working on the Edi chapter rewrite when he called re. the Serbs. Basically Vučić was under a lot of pressure to call off the meeting. Edi less so. Merkel had called them both and said that it must go ahead. The most that was acceptable was a short delay. Edi was due to speak to Vučić at 4 p.m., and he asked me to send a note setting out what would be an ideal outcome. He said the last few days had been weird. Edi's brother was being hailed as a hero for something he didn't do. The celebrations had spread to Kosovo and Macedonia which was feeding the Serb paranoia. Also Vučić was known to be pretty volatile. The call seemed to go fine.

Monday 20 October

Alan Johnson interview for *GQ*. On good form, loving his new life as a writer/politician. No desire to go back. Totally agreed with me re. strategic failure over the politics of the economy. Lovely bloke, good chat, would work well. Gave him my novels as he was planning to write one. Flu jab. Greg Beales [former Downing Street adviser, Labour Party executive director] asking if I would do debates strategy.

Tuesday 21 October

Stan Greenberg [pollster] was flying in for a few days and wanted to meet up, so he came in from the airport. Vile weather. US going crazy because of Ebola. They could be a ridiculous country at times. He said the Tories could not win and we could. But we agreed at the moment both Ed and the party were too becalmed. There was no fight or energy, and it was all about coasting and playing safe. I felt the whole issue came down to leadership. He had to find three or four strong leadership positions and just hammer them, and let the shadow Cabinet do their stuff more. Ed clearly worried about them getting too high a profile. But the reality is he had to address the weaknesses and get out there on the big things, not everything. The groups were pretty unrelentingly negative. Also frankly we had lost the politics of the economy and it was hard to see how they were going to win it back unless they admitted they had gone on the wrong course. Stan lively and sharp but I was never totally sure about his analysis, for example his adamant view the Tories couldn't win a majority.

To Clerkenwell for a speech to Cancer Research UK, for which they were making a donation to LLR. Then cab to Tooting for the BBC *Free Speech* programme. Jon Ronson [journalist], Zoe Hardman [TV presenter] and Sarah Wollaston [MP] – fast becoming my favourite Tory – were the other panellists. The audience was all young people with mental health conditions, including Rebecca who told her self-harm story in a film at the start. I was getting huge applause for all the mental health stuff and said to Sarah she could no longer defend the government on this, but I got a negative response re. Ched Evans, the rape case footballer when I said he was not a role model, footballers are not role models, and he should be allowed to play again.[*]

It got quite heated. But the show as a whole was brilliant, especially the contributions from young people talking about their conditions and their

---

[*] The Welsh-born footballer, then with Sheffield United, was convicted of rape in 2012 and served two and a half years in prison before being found not guilty at a retrial. He subsequently resumed his career at Chesterfield.

struggles. Grace was with me and when I was talking about Evans she was yelling at me to shut up when I said teachers and doctors and vicars should be role models – 'Dad, stop embarrassing yourself' – and eventually I did. But I did think it was ludicrous how we called anyone who was famous a role model. Off at the end to Lemonia for Rory's birthday with the family.

Wednesday 22 October

First blog in over a month, on *Free Speech*, and the energy it created. I also tried to contact Oli Regan [actor and mental health activist], the one who had said he had tried to kill himself twice while waiting for CBT. Grace had said she would only forgive me for my non-PC Ched Evans comments if I got him help. A lot of reaction online to me saying Jeremy Hunt had said he couldn't understand why I was depressed. I had said to myself at the time he said it I wouldn't use it but when I heard the Tories talking the talk on mental health, I thought sod it. Breakfast with Neil Blair and Dan Marks, who were J. K. Rowling's agents, and also now acting for the Class of '92 over the Salford City project. They told me the BBC were doing a major series on it and they wanted a book to go with it, which they wanted me to write.[*] It sounded a lot of fun, could also be quite important socially, but I had to weigh up all the different projects on the go.

Portland was taking up a fair bit of time, LLR and Time to Change, the book, Labour would get more demanding as the election neared, still mulling re. the SFA, Albania would become more time-consuming, off to Sharjah again soon, projects in Asia, *GQ*. So I had to take stock a bit. Diary was just about manageable, but it might not stay that way. I liked Marks and Neil, though they admitted they had fallen out with Ed V over the Marr/Chadlington book. Anyway we agreed we would wait till I got back and the next step was see Gary Neville who was clearly the leader in terms of commitment to the project. They said when they first met his first words were: 'I fucking hate agents.'

They said there were some fantastic characters involved in the club. Crowds of 160. GNev etc. determined to do it properly and get them into the football league. Would certainly be interesting. Quick run then headed off to France, Fiona driving, me finishing the Alan Johnson piece for *GQ*, then work on innovation chapter. Stayed in nice hotel in Épernay. People at the next table at dinner slagging off TB, didn't see me and when they

---

[*] Earlier in the year the club was taken over by former Manchester United players Ryan Giggs, Gary Neville, Phil Neville, Paul Scholes and Nicky Butt, later selling 50 per cent to Singapore billionaire Peter Lin. At the start of the 2014–15 season the five players were in a 'Class of '92' team that lost 5–1 to Salford in the 'showcase' match.

did later were all over me. I said I listened to your rubbish at the dinner table and the guy said, 'Oh, I talk rubbish all the time, lovely to meet you.'

Thursday 23 October

We drove down to Faucon listening to Grayson Perry's Reith lectures. Brilliant and funny. Ed V not well, and I called and told him he must get to see a doctor and insist on being checked out. Later he called to say he was in hospital. I dropped a note to Ed M after Tom B sent me through an OK though not brilliant note they had agreed on the next 200 days. Douglas called and said he would like to try to revive the idea of a three-way meeting. He was clearly worried about the whole operation. He said Ed's confidence had been knocked sideways. Since last year's conference speech, whenever there was criticism, at least he could say he could do a tour de force conference speech without notes. That had gone.

Douglas was mildly suspicious that Ed had forgotten the deficit section on purpose because he didn't want to tell the hall something it didn't want to hear. Terrible if true, but I didn't believe it because of the way Ed looked after the event. But Douglas said he had been there when he was told and he didn't seem shocked. Anyway, Douglas A was of the view there had to be a fiscal piece to the strategy, deal with immigration, win on the NHS. The *Mail* were running a vicious campaign, which was being used by the Tories from Cameron down, against the NHS in Wales. Burnham was fighting back for England, but Ed's team were worried Burnham was all about positioning for after the event. I said to Douglas that if we lost Ed was done for anyway, so he had to fight like his life depended on it. The trouble is they had set their sights on winning with 33 per cent. They felt the Tories could not win and we could.

He and I both agreed if the economy did improve – as opposed to the current mirage – then the Tories could pull ahead. So there had to be more campaigning, more strategy, more aggression. We agreed Torsten was the best in there and had to be brought centre stage. DA thought it odd that Ed was not helping Torsten to find a seat, which is what he wanted. His general analysis of conference was that people were exhausted post Scotland, and also a bit complacent. Everyone said it was flat.

Once I got to France, I worked on a long note. I said he had to use the tough phase as an opportunity to show fight and leadership. There is no merit in just letting the other side screw up. He has to make more of the weather between now and the campaign. I felt he was coasting on the belief that the Tories can't win and 33-ish will be enough. But I said if he thought he could get 33 with this approach he can get more than that by boldness. There are Greens to be won back, floating UKIP and Lib Dem supporters who can be won over. There are Tory business voices who can be got right over. I gave him a list of things I felt he could do:

- Reclaim the politics of the economy. I said he not Ed Balls needs to take this on as a central act of leadership, that winning the political argument is the essential precondition for being listened to.
- Revisit the deficit as part of this, with humour, humility and a plan.
- Europe. I said there was a big opportunity. Cameron will sacrifice any national interest as part of Operation Pander to UKIP. Ed should get out there and make the case for Europe as a force for good. It was the key to the business voice coming back, and a way to show strength. Cameron had gone down the referendum route out of weakness. Make the principled case.
- Immigration. I said he must not follow them down the UKIP line or anywhere near it. UKIP can only be beaten by taking on their arguments.
- Scotland. He has to take the lead on the constitution where again Cameron is doing the political rather than the national interest thing.
- NHS. There was a need for real old-fashioned campaigning. The Tories were in government and yet campaigning against Labour – e.g. Wales, attacks on Ed M personally, Europe – more than we were against them.
- State of politics. It could be another good area for Ed if he went for it properly.
- Shadow Cabinet. I said they had to become more visible. It seemed at times like he felt he had to do everything. He should be there for big things, big themes, big moments.
- Leadership the key. I suggested he use the fact he has had a few rough weeks to go down to come up again. He had to be tested and be seen to be tested.
- Economy – we fight back on the record and show there is a different way for the future.

I said he also needed to attack the miserabilism of media and Tories with a stronger message of hope. Young people crying out to be engaged. He had to lead in bringing them into the debate. On climate change, it had been so much his issue, but it had gone down the agenda again. It was another leadership position. I was talking to Tom and Greg and others about the debates, but I said there was absolutely no point thinking of a debates strategy out of context of real strategy. I was keen not to depress him, though, so said he was still very much in the game, but the game has to be upped. More fight. More confidence. More campaigning. More clarity.

Friday 24 October

Posted Oli Regan guest blog after a bit of toing and froing with him. Also persuaded *Free Speech* they should get him in for the Clegg programme next week. I said the important thing was to get in front of Clegg and get him to commit to sorting out his CBT treatment. I had to do an interview for UBS [bank and financial services company] to set up the instability conference and found myself devising what I thought was a pretty good line of attack on Cameron for lack of leadership over Europe, UKIP, Scotland etc. But if only Labour would step up, they could get something out of it.

Kevin Spacey [American actor] sent a message that he was on for the *GQ* interview in Boston on the 14th. Long swim, later out on the bike. Then playing with the book cover. Edi and Endri called after UEFA gave the game to Serbia, fined Albania, docked the Serb points and fined the Serbs too. They were trying to please everyone and ended up pleasing nobody. I emphasised to Edi he must keep on the meeting with Vučić strategy. It was more important than football.

Saturday 25 October

Fabulous sunny day, fresh and cold in the morning then warm and fabulous. Out on the bike for almost three hours. I was getting a few calls from the press on the *Telegraph* splash saying TB had said at a dinner party that Ed couldn't win. Tories were being hit hard by a Europe demand for almost £2 billion because of improved economy though if they had the nous to handle it properly, it could play to their advantage. It seemed Osborne knew about it two days before telling Cameron. [José Manuel] Barroso [president of the European Commission] was definitely gearing up against UK. Labour just seemed invisible just now, though because of Johann Lamont's resignation as Scottish leader yesterday, and her barbed comments about London Labour not understanding Scotland, it was really just seen as another blow to Ed.

Nice week, just the two of us and Molly. Weather good. Feeling fitter as a result of the work I was doing with Charlie and Keir, though still not able to get into running. Mainly bike and swim and some of the exercises they had shown me. I was reading Brian O'Driscoll's book which was pretty good, and I was still keen to get him in the book if I could. Something had definitely gone on with Fergie that had made him cool and distant. When I called him to ask about the SFA approach asking me to be on the board I sensed he couldn't wait to hang up.

Wednesday 28 October

I did a day (and overnight) trip home to do a Thames Water session with

October '14: Tories hit by Europe demand

Portland, and also a rather odd meeting with two investment bankers from Norway who were picking my brains for GLG. The Thames guys were better, and the CEO was quite a rough diamond sort and I liked him. I had no idea the underground sewage tunnel was such a huge project. It was interesting too how they were keen to know what Tessa's view was on things. She was definitely going for mayor, no doubt about it, and it was being seen as likely she would win. F and I seemed to get on better than ever when it was just the two of us down here.

Saturday 1 November

Fiona was driving back, and I flew back for the Arsenal–Burnley match. I went with Calum, met Keir, Roland, also Godric and Jude [son] and had an odd lunch at a slow service café on the Holloway Road, then to the ground. We actually did OK for over an hour, but we ended up losing 3–0. Home alone, I did a bit of work, book almost done. Rowing about Oz and the last chapter, which Nigel was not sure worked. I felt they did but could still improve them a bit.

Sunday 2 November

I took Calum to Euston and off he went to Glasgow. I was sad on one level, but I felt he was doing what he wanted to do, and doing it in his way, and that was a good thing. He had always been strong on the Scotland connection, and he was sure it was right to move away from us and make his own way.

Monday 3 November

Meredith Kennedy of Washington Speakers Bureau came round for a meeting to discuss possible work with them. The truth is I could take or leave the speechifying but she was pretty clued up. I went to Random House to sign some books and also finalise the cover and have a catch-up with Nigel. I also met Graham Walpole and Ian Stafford who wanted to sign me up as a 'star' on Kicca, a sports social media site. It sounded moderately interesting though I couldn't quite see why I would get followers compared with the real sports stars.

Tuesday 4 November

Out to the airport and off to Dubai, working on speech and reading a brilliant book about the relationship between the US military psychiatrist at Nuremberg jail, Douglas Kelley, and the Nazi defendants, especially Göring. Arrived, met, hotel and prepared for tomorrow. Lovely weather, went for a run.

Wednesday 5 November

Started day with the book fair, a huge event, much bigger than I expected, where I had a brief meeting with the ruler [Sheikh Mohammed bin Rashid al-Maktoum] as he wandered around, Crown Prince also there, Dan Brown [American author] as the star guest wandering behind them. Introduced by Sheikh Sultan, whose wife was also there (daughter of ruler), and then a lot of hanging around meeting various people. I went back to the hotel p.m., working on a couple more chapters of Nigel's edits. We were definitely getting there and the 220,000 words had lost about 60k. Ed V struggling a bit with the US because it was UK-centric on the political front. Actually it wasn't but I could see he might struggle. He was approaching a small publishing house called Pegasus. Also with a Middle East journo who used to come to my briefings who had done a book on ISIL [Islamic State of Iraq and the Levant]. His thesis was that the whole thing was a creation of TB and Bush, that the key people were Saddam's ex-generals, also that there was no point talking to them because their real purpose was to kill anyone who didn't agree with them. Scary stuff. I did a signing, also a Sharjah TV interview, but skipped the dinner to get more work done on the book.

Thursday 6 November

To the Media Centre and did a long workshop with the media team. Lift to Dubai and booked into the Palm at Atlantis. Ghastly. Gaudy. Full of Russians. Nice gym, though, worked out there then off to meet Trevor Pereira and Tamanna who were putting together the Maritime Standard Awards. Royalty there, Sheikh Maktoum. The awards were straightforward, plus I had to do a little speech and I played the pipes as well. Nice enough event. Standing ovation for the pipes.

Meanwhile John Woodcock [shadow transport minister] was calling me. He said that there was a real mood now of despair. People had gone from disillusion and discontent to a real sense that Ed could not win, and there had to be a move. He said that if Alan J was up for it, there would be 200 who would back him. I said I didn't think he would and later I spoke to him and he said it just wasn't going to happen. He felt that it was not the right thing, for him or the party. I had definitely moved to the view that anything was better than this. The polls were dire, the Tories were winning the battle of the airwaves, and all we had was this message that we needed to unite – but around what?

I sent Ed a couple of notes saying what I felt he needed to do, especially with regard to the politics of the economy – Alan and I had agreed 'Labour caused the crash, we created the recovery' had to be rebutted – and also the need for the team to be out there. John said there was a lot of manoeuvring going on, and Yvette and Burnham were waiting for a dam to break. But the reality was the dearth of political talent was beginning to hit home. Sad but true. And of course as the pressure grew, the more people felt they had to express public support and that cemented him in. The whole thing was dire.

Saturday 7 November

Up at five, off to the airport, flight to Glasgow. Sitting opposite a guy clearly pissed from the night before. Working, finishing the book, listening to music. Arrived and straight to the Thistle Hotel, nice guy in the gym, who ran the Red Onion restaurant, telling me I should have a shot at Scotland. The Ed M story was growing, and there were clearly moves afoot to move him. It may be the right thing to do, but replace with who? Calum came up and we went to see Donald, still not right. He was going to come to the Spinal Injuries Dinner I was piping at, but wasn't up for it. Good event. Kevin Bridges the after-dinner comic. He was funny but not friendly. Had a few pops at me during his spot. Lots of dancing on tables. Late night. Knackered. I sensed the referendum had calmed down. Solicitors Digby Brown were the firm hosting it and they were very Labour for a law firm but were saying we were in a lot of trouble up there.

Saturday 8 November

I collected the hire car then set off for Burnley. Through that wonderful scenery north and south of the border. Lunch at Burnley with Lee Hoos [chief executive] and a couple of Irish agents. Good game, our first win of the season, 1–0 v Hull. Had cocked up my diary and forgotten I was meant to be doing a dinner for Hilary Benn [former Labour Secretary of State] in Leeds, while also meant to be in Burford with Fiona and Gail, and a dinner party with Will [*Observer* columnist] and Jane Hutton, Juliet and Andrew Rosenfeld, and Annie Robinson. So I did the speech pre dinner and then set off. The mood at Leeds was OK, and Hilary his ever-optimistic self, but I spoke to several of the activists who felt we were in deep shit. I did a pretty blunt speech saying what we needed to do, especially vis-à-vis the economy but I was not sure they had the capacity. It felt like a slow death at the moment. Left at eight-ish and I was at Burford after eleven. I was saying I felt Ed could not win and anything would be better. The tragedy was that Cameron was so crap; well, if not totally crap, certainly beatable.

Sunday 9 November

A typical dire consumer experience to kick off the day. Europcar were supposed to collect the hire car at nine, and nobody showed up. Gail was giving me a hard time about my diary, as was Fiona, but actually yesterday's double-booking cock-up was relatively rare. The Sundays were full of Ed M crisis, but clearly he was soldiering on. He sent me his speech for Thursday which was another fightback. Tom B sent me a note saying what he thought was wrong with it and asked me to press Ed – for example, saying that he had the same views since aged seventeen, which I think a lot of people would think was a bit weird – because 'he might listen to you'. It also had too much of an anti-wealth rhetoric and nothing you could call an economic policy.

Tom said EM was in denial, that Lucy Powell was now the person he listened to because she told him how marvellous he was, and if only the world saw more of him, the better it would be. We headed to the Rosenfelds' country gaff, which was nice enough, more EM talk, went for a walk, then to Annie Robinson's for lunch. Neil K was all over the radio defending Ed. He did it fine, but I am not sure he was the right voice at the right time. Charlie out there too 'because Ed asked me to and it was hard to say no.' But he agreed things were grim and getting grimmer.

Monday 10 November

Sky News with Mitch Winehouse [Amy Winehouse's father] on addiction. It was fine, and we got on well. Needless to say they slipped in a question about Ed. I tried my best to be supportive but I was beginning to feel angry, because he was not doing what was needed to persuade the unpersuaded he was the right man. To 9GS to see TB, JoP and Catherine Rimmer to discuss Chilcot. They had sent potential criticisms for three-fifths of the report, with the legal issues to come. JoP was to be criticised for telling the Attorney General not to go through his views with Cabinet, and keeping [Lord] Andrew Turnbull [former head of civil service and Cabinet Secretary] out of the inner circle. JoP said it was definitely going to be the revenge of the establishment. Though TB blamed GB partly, it was Robin Butler [Wilson's predecessor] and Richard Wilson [Turnbull's predecessor] who had led the charge for this kind of full inquiry. The main criticism was that TB drove the policy – would have been odd if he didn't

– but also that he shaped it to the end of supporting the US. Also that we were not prepared enough and he ignored advice. It would be a lot worse if they said it was illegal. That might be something they were holding back. I could not imagine that they would have held that back for TB.

The first issue was timing. They wanted to get it done before the election, and TB was given a 5 January deadline, JoP some time later this month. So it was OK for them to take fucking years to write it, I said, and then they expect people to respond in no time at all. Charlie felt that if someone were to go for judicial review on that basis, they would win, but he felt it would be unwise for TB to do that. Sue Gray was indicating it was the Tory spads pushing for it, seeing political advantage, but I was not convinced it would help them. We all agreed it was pretty grim, and could get worse.

The only good news was that I was not being criticised, which, as TB said, suggested they were not getting into the whole WMD dossier bit. It also meant I could go out and defend him. TB seemed OK, but I could tell he was worried. We agreed he needed to set up a team, with a lawyer and also rebuttal people, and I said he needed to prepare something that could be published alongside the report itself. We agreed it was in his interests to have more time, even if that meant it going the other side of the election. But it was not in his interests to push for it. Others were likely to do that anyway, as seemingly thirty named individuals were going to be criticised. They would not all take kindly to being given no time at all. He said he would need to reshape his diary to get more time to focus on it. Charlie F said afterwards it was such a difference to be with a group of people who could analyse and give clear advice, and felt Ed M could be so much better if he had the kind of team TB had built.

TB said he was going to have to defend himself and he would. I worried it could lead to all sorts of people going after him, so it might not bring closure. Charlie felt that was only possible if they said it was illegal. But even with what they had sent – e.g. the extent to which he drove the policy, with the sense he kept decision-making from others, and also that he didn't listen to advice about the aftermath, was bad enough. The mood was not exactly gallows but it wasn't great. Catherine R felt it could have been a lot worse. JoP felt that it was bad but a lot of it was discounted.

I asked TB why he didn't ask Cameron what he was thinking about timing, but he wasn't sure. We knew Cameron would be worried about the way Libya was panning out. Brief discussion re. the political scene. He felt David M returning was the only possible game-changer but it was not going to happen. David and I had an email exchange and he said it was 'predictable and dire'. He said he was trying to stay out of it. John Woodcock called me again and asked if I would speak to Alan J again. I did. He said John Reid and Peter M had also been on to him. But he had definitively decided – not happening.

Wednesday 12 November

Worked a.m., then out for a business event. Ghastly bunch of right-wing moneymen (one woman). Their only real concerns came through the idea that any kind of progressive government was bad for them. Then to the Landmark for a financial services panel on risk with [Lord] Michael Forsyth, Vernon Bogdanor [academic], and an economist. It was OK but I was glad when it was all over. One of those days when I felt pretty tartish as I would not have done either event without getting decent money to talk mainly to audiences I would normally avoid. The extent to which these people saw anything progressive as a problem, and themselves as a solution when they had helped create the mess in the first place was annoying in the extreme.

I actually felt, and Forsyth seemed to agree, that if only leaders led, and stood up for difficult choices and complicated issues, things would not be such a mess. On Europe, Farage was making inroads because of the weakness of others not because of his strength. To LLR and off with Cathy to pick up a cheque from the Worshipful Livery of Cordwainers. Pinkie rings and Tories galore, though the people I was with were OK. I always feel I don't really understand Britain when I go to this kind of event though. Toasts all night. School dinners etc. I did a little speech then legged it for David Millar's farewell bash at Shoreditch House. Much more my scene, talking bikes with proper cyclists. Nice do, David really chuffed I was there.

Thursday 13 November

Ed's fightback speech. He had sent me a draft and I had sent over a few points. He took one on board so far as I could tell. Douglas had suggested to me amid the flurry that Ed actually felt because he won the leadership when nobody felt he could, so he could do the same with the election. But the party is not the public, and as things stood we were treading water with the potential to sink. Only the crapness of the Tories and their own problems with UKIP, which Cameron had helped with his referendum, were holding Labour up. Ed's ratings were diving even lower. The speech was average and for all that they complained about the media he actually got a fair hearing for it. There was no argument on the economy, no real clear set of policies we wanted the public to know about.

With Rayan to Tobacco Docks, Festival of Marketing. Bradley Wiggins had done yesterday and I was main event today. I had written a new speech on the theme of 'Is spin dead in the era of social media?' Loads of good Qs at the end, held back for ages for selfies and books. Off to Watford, The Grove Hotel, for a speech to an investment firm re. risk. Rather offputting guy in the front row who was picking his nose the whole time. Off to Heathrow and on the flight to Boston I finished the edit on the book intro and conclusion. British Airways feeling really tired after flying Emirates recently.

Friday 14 November

I was staying in W Hotel, nice enough but it was clearly a cool hang-out place and the noise downstairs was a bit much when sleeping. Also the room either too hot or cold. But good sleep, didn't get jet lag and did a bit of work before meeting up with Suzanne [Kahn, family friend]. Used Twitter to find a Scottish bar to watch Scotland v Ireland and was recommended a place called The Haven in Jamaica Plain, decided to walk out there so as to see more of the city, about an hour or so. A guy called Jason pretty stunned when I walked in, had been there sixteen years and had started it because there were so many Irish bars and no Scottish. Also a few students tracked me down and it ended up being quite a nice session. A good place to watch a great 1–0 win.

Calum and Rory were both at the match so I was keeping in touch with them through the game. I walked back and then to the Fairmont Copley Plaza to meet Kevin Spacey who had been filming in Baltimore and was now heading to North Eastern University to speak at their Homecoming. He had three guys with him, driver/fixer, manager type and a makeup guy constantly padding his forehead. We had a little chat at the bar in the hotel, and he was telling me something of the background to how the Netflix/*House of Cards* [political TV drama series] thing happened which would make a piece for data and innovation in the book. He had been a star for a long time but I sensed *HoC* had taken him to new heights, lots of people coming over and he seemed to love it. Lots just saying they loved his work.

We chatted a bit re. the UK, the arts there, how shit politics was, Clinton and how well he was doing – Kevin was going tomorrow to compère the 10th anniversary of his library – then we set off for the university. 5,000 students there. He had done a proper speech with slides and autocue and a lot of humour and he went down a storm. He actually performed a lot like a politician but it was clear he didn't want to be one. He was definitely operating on a different level even to how he had been at the Old Vic. The kids loved him, and everyone seemed to be watching *House of*

Cards. Afterwards we headed to a restaurant to have dinner with some of the people involved in the 2013 Boston Marathon. I hadn't realised that after the bomb attacks Kevin had gone there just to visit and spend time with survivors and others and he had got close to the cops, the organisers, survivors, so we had a really nice evening just letting people relive their memories of that.

Again he was intensely political and empathetic in how he dealt with them. I finally checked out about eleven feeling the tiredness a bit. Peter M called out of the blue, said that he felt things were desperate, and that Neil was the key to persuading Ed to go. I had spoken several times to Alan Johnson who just wasn't up for it. Nobody else really made it, but I felt that maybe a contest would at least give us the chance to be back making the weather. At the moment it was all UKIP and the Tories. Peter felt Ed was not lazy in that he was putting in the hours, but they were not doing the work that needed to be done. And he had convinced himself people had to see more of him when in fact they needed to see more of the team.

Saturday 15 November

I went for a run around a pretty grim area of Boston, realised it was where Nassir Ghaemi [academic psychiatrist] was based and arranged to meet him. He was still pressing on with his Martin Luther King book. I walked to the Fairmont, breakfast across the road, noticed a fair few people begging on the way. Met Kevin, hat on and sweatshirt, and sat down for the interview proper, a lot of it going over the stuff we had talked about yesterday. Good talker, good stories and anecdotes, but a little elusive at times. Almost two hours on tape so there was going to be a need to cut it down but it felt like a good talk, and all the better for the fact we knew each other and had spent time together earlier.

It would make for a good interview though. Interesting on LBJ and Lincoln as rounded characters, not just one thing. Fascinating on how they had used analytics to help shape *HoC* casting, plotting, style. Loves tradition like Shakespeare, theatre etc. but also modern. I transcribed it p.m. and Jonathan Heaf loved it. Met Nassir for a nice chat about the mental health stuff. I had read a brilliant book, *The Nazi and the Psychiatrist*, about the relationship between the Nuremberg US military psychiatrist, Douglas Kelley, and the defendants, especially Goering. Nassir put me in touch with the author, Jack El-Hai, and we exchanged a few emails and arranged to meet. To the airport, sleeping pill, slept whole way, despite a woman in next seat reading a Jimmy Kimmel [TV host and comedian] book and laughing loads.

Sunday 16 November

Papers still full of Labour in trouble, even if Ed had managed to survive the last storm. John Woodcock telling me his marriage was over and wanting help with an open letter to his constituents.

Monday 17 November

Charlie round for a boxing session. Working on book events. Round to Random House to sign some. Tea with Jim Murphy. He said he was confident of winning the leadership election but the party in Scotland was a total shell. Ed was 'a liability'. Sturgeon cold and hard, he said, and would not be a pushover. He felt he had money but nothing else. Asked HQ for e.g. housing policy and it was 'we will build 65,000 houses'. Why not 75? 100? 20? Random. No overall economic message. He was desperate for a few outside names with which to develop policy. Mental Health Media awards. Chatted with the team who had made *Bedlam*, brilliant mental health documentary. Stayed for a bit then dinner with Peter [Chittick] and Carolyn [Fairbairn, personal friends].

Tuesday 18 November

Lunch with Alpha (City) at the Gherkin. Usual stuff, good crowd though. All down on all parties. All worried on Europe. Meeting with Godric and Fran Millar. Dave B seeing James Murdoch [son of Rupert, supporter of Sky cycling] and wanting some strategic input. We worked on a paper, which Dave loved, a chapter-by-chapter unveiling of the Team Sky story.

Wednesday 19 November

Meeting with a guy about our wills. He was keen for me to sort literary estate questions. Then Ian Stafford round to do some films re. Kicca, the new social media sports thing. Not sure this was going to work for me but they seemed to think it would. Would need Grace's help though. She came round to see how it worked. Really starting to motor on events for the book. I talked to Neil to ask if he thought we could get Ed to go. He felt not but agreed there had to be a major shake-up or else we were heading for disaster. We had a long chat, agreed about a lot of the problems, and agreed to fix a meeting with him together. Neil went mad when he emailed Tim Livesey who said he would try his best to sort a meeting. They were running round in circles.

Thursday 20 November

Out early and off to Liverpool for the North West Alcohol Conference. Going down with a cold but I managed to get through it OK, went down well. The problem with these events was the constant preaching to the converted. [Sir] Ian Gilmore [hepatology professor], a guy from Sheffield University etc., nobody from the industry. But probably worth going even if I felt like death warmed up.

I wrote a note to Ed but after discussing it with Fiona decided not to send it. It basically said I would not help in the forthcoming campaign. I said I had tried since he became leader to feed in strategic thinking, both of a general nature and of a specific nature when asked to. He had asked me to get more deeply involved, but I have been reluctant both for personal and political reasons. I said the main political reason was that I can only operate when I have a clear sense of an agreed strategy. It was very hard to discern what that is, and in so far as I can discern one, it is not one that I believe can lead to the kind of win that is there for the taking against this useless, awful, totally beatable government with a PM whom history will judge as one of the worst we have ever known.

I felt I was just making the same points again and again but getting nowhere. If I compare the level and scale of political, organisational, intellectual and campaigning activity going on at this stage pre 1997, with what is happening now, it was scary in terms of the difference. I said it felt tired, lacklustre, lacking in cohesion, and open goals were being missed. Horrible to watch and I had to stop watching. I think Douglas was right that Ed thought having won the leadership when everyone said he wouldn't, he could do the same with the country. But the public are not the Labour Party. I was hearing the same message everywhere – and anyone telling him this was a winning position was lying to him. Maybe he could limp over the line as leader of the biggest party in a coalition propped up by Libs, Greens, nationalists or whatever, but it could be so much better.

Of course he deserved credit for holding the party together after defeat but I kept hearing the calls for unity and wondering what exactly we are uniting around. Fiona said it would only damage his confidence, and burn bridges if I sent it, but I wasn't sure. The combination of watching so many mistakes being made, the shambles in Scotland, the weakness of the shadow Cabinet, it was dementing. In the end I binned it, but it was hard to see a party winning that I didn't really think on current performance deserved it, and that against these useless toerags.

Friday 21 November

Bad cold and slightly dreading having to travel. Grace round to do a video for the website re. *Winners*, which we put up later, alongside a blog I did on UKIP's win in Rochester, and what the book said about the need for strategy, teamship, leadership, data, innovation etc. It was fairly coded, with Cameron in sight, who was definitely failing on strategy and would be worried that having thought he had neutralised Europe, as soon as it goes to an electoral test he seems to cop it. But the truth is it was largely about Labour. How the fuck had we managed to turn a UKIP win over the Tories into a story about Labour, and Emily Thornberry [shadow Attorney General] resigning over a tweet about a white van man house covered in England flags?* It could easily have been toughed out, but they turned it into a huge thing, even had Ed saying he had never been angrier – what? Compared with the bedroom tax, the cuts, the lies about the economy? So annoying. It was stupid, but honestly, ultimately it would have blown over and people would have focused on UKIP and the Tories. It might have stuck, it might not, but it sure has now.

To Stoke, met by Carrie from Tristram Hunt's office, to the Upper House Hotel then to the Britannia Stadium for the Labour fundraiser. They had organised every table to be named after a former Labour leader. Fairly good turnout, unions main sponsors and a local law firm. Tristram took me around though I could feel my voice going. We did the Ask Alastair Anything thing, with questions pre-submitted on postcards, and Tristram's wife Juliet was saying she could not see how I could get through them all. By the end she – and Peter Coates, Stoke City chairman – was asking me to get parachuted into a safe seat and become leader before the election. The frustrating thing was that at all these events, when you made the case against UKIP, for the Labour record, for Europe, against Cameron, for the politics of the economy, they would respond provided there was a proper argument. When you tried, as Tristram did, to make the case for Ed as PM, nobody bought it.

I reckon a good tenth of questions were on the lines of 'what the hell do we do about Ed?' Though I was losing my voice, I think I made the case for how we could win, but – though I did not articulate it as such – nobody felt it possible with Ed. The brother thing was still huge. Energy prices was the only policy move he had made and that was almost forgotten. The public were unaware of anything we were promising. Yet the election was there for the taking. Tristram agreed with my analysis but felt without Alan J coming along and saying he would do it, nothing was

---

* Thornberry resigned her shadow Cabinet position after being criticised for tweeting a picture of a house in the Rochester and Strood constituency adorned with three flags of St George. A white van was parked outside. Mark Reckless, who had defected from the Conservatives to UKIP, retained his seat at a by-election on 20 November.

going to change. Nice crowd, and he had some good people there, but I left feeling we were heading for a fucking car crash.

Saturday 22 November

The news still going with Ed M/Thornberry tweet. Talk about making a crisis out of a minor fuck-up via a silly tweet. Off with Tristram to Staffs Uni to talk to media students and do a few interviews for them. Good kids but just lacking in confidence. Questions good in the series of interviews I did with them after. To Tristram's office, more chat re. the need for Ed to shape up or ship out. He felt Andy Burnham and Yvette Cooper were just biding their time, Chuka was developing, nobody wanted to make a move. He thought if Balls pulled the plug then maybe something would happen, but not without it. So the truth was we were limping on as we had with GB.

At the football, Peter Coates over lunch saying much the same thing as people at the dinner last night, namely that we just could not expect to win with Ed. The football was terrific, we were two up after thirteen minutes, then Stoke pulled one back and we hung on for dear life. Great atmosphere and I did some good stuff for Kicca, including a chat with Dave Burnley [avid fan who changed his name to the club's]. Good atmosphere, club looked after me well, back to say goodbye to Coates and his very funny wife. Train back with Calum, feeling rough, dinner then watch us third on *MotD*, team and fans looking good.

Sunday 23 November

Man flu. Work on diary. Pat McF asking what Ed should have done re. Thornberry. Dismiss as a silly mistake and get focused on the bigger picture re. Cameron and UKIP. I advised Pat to make a big pro-EU/pro-immigration speech and say the need is to challenge not pander.

Monday 24 November

Ed M cancelled meeting with me and Neil K tomorrow because of a Lee Rigby statement.[*] He was avoiding us I would say. GP/antibiotics.

---

[*] Off-duty British soldier Rigby had been attacked and killed by two men near the Royal Artillery barracks in Woolwich in May 2013. The assailants were tried and sentenced to life imprisonment. A parliamentary inquiry, which found Rigby's death could not have been prevented, was concluded on 25 November 2014.

Tuesday 25 November

Worked on a speech for the *Economist* depression summit, then off to King's Place for that. Great they were doing it and they had some decent speakers and panels. Kofi Annan [former Secretary-General of the United Nations] opened, OK but I felt he was slightly going through the motions. It gave it a big international name and gravitas though, and some of what he said was good. Listened to Norman Lamb [Lib Dem MP], who did his usual heart in the right place stuff, then I spent several hours going through the book with Kathy and Rory. Getting there.

Some good Aussies at the conference, one of them Jack Heath [CEO] of Sane [mental health charity] Australia who used to work with Paul Keating [former Australian PM] and was also looking for a seat. He was around the same age as me and was saying I should do it too. If I thought we could win, I might, but the more I thought of the election, the more I could see it becoming a disaster area. I put Jack in touch with Nassir as he wanted someone to go and talk to the MPs and get them to understand mental well-being and therapy etc. A German professor of depression who spoke too much. Medics were interesting. At times in the panels the questions were longer than the answers.

Wednesday 26 November

Work at home on the editing, also doing bits and bobs for Kicca. Then out to LLR for the Mark Johansen Channel swim charity reception. Very emotional speech. Not a dry eye etc. Hard to work out just why it was so emotional for him. Cathy on form. Out for dinner with F and Georgia who had finally delivered her MS (of book on young people in politics). She said she had not had much support, certainly nothing like I had, but they had finally got a better cover and she was getting a lot of interest. Meanwhile Ed sold *Winners* to Pegasus in the US.

Thursday 27 November

Portland training. Set one group the task of projecting Ed as PM material. They laughed. This was not good. Tim was hiring a lot of young people and there were some good ones there. Tristram H fundraiser at Ben and Amanda's [Evans and Levete, friends]. Jim O'Neill surprised to be there, had no idea it was a fundraiser. Saying that re. his Cities work, Osborne had gone for it, 'These guys' (Labour) had been asleep at the wheel. Met Ed recently and felt there was not much there. Peter M said he had seen Roy Hattersley who said Ed had told him he was Croslandite [former Labour socialist intellectual], but he felt it was not at all clear what he stood for.

Peter said polls showed people want Labour not Tory, but they want Cameron not Miliband. Ed Balls there to make a little speech, and afterwards I asked him why we were not defending the record and not rebutting the 'Labour car crash/Tory recovery'. He said it was all down to Ed.

He actually spoke OK, so did Tristram, but there was a general sense that despite the Tories having yet another shit week we could not win. Tom said the whole operation was a shambles. I told Tom I was getting angry which he said he understood, because he was too, but we had to make the best of a bad job.

Jim O'Neill told me he had seen Alex at the City match and he had told him he was worried he didn't seem very well. Later I texted Alex to ask if he was OK, got a very terse message saying he was fine and going to Aberdeen for the weekend. I asked if I had offended him because he had been very cool the last few times we met/spoke. No reply. Might be the book, might be the referendum, might be ill. All very odd.

Friday 28 November

Cameron immigration speech. Talk about a pathetic pandering journey from his own actual position towards UKIP-lite, though under pressure from Merkel he pulled back from any suggestion of change on basic freedom of movement. But my God why were we not killing him? To South Ken, meet Najma Finlay [Hutchinson's publicity director] to discuss book publicity. Liked her and it was slowly coming together around the events and media. Met up with Godric re. Sky, chatted over our objectives for the day, then to Ampersand Hotel for Team Sky brainstorming on next few years. 19 guys, marketers, Hugh Chapman ex-Olympic marketing, Rapha [sportswear] guy Simon, 21st Century Fox people, new Sky press person from 19, good bunch.

Dave wanted a new moon landing, winning the Tour being the last one. Where do we want to be 2020? We had sent him a paper 'Believe in best'. At the end of day he called and he wanted me, Hugh and Fran as an advisory board, with Godric serving it. Wanted big goals. Did a big thing round objectives. He sometimes could be repetitive and slow in discussion, but it was his way. I think it was his version of TB's circular conversation. He wanted to explain not just who everyone was but why they were there. He admitted the meeting was too big but he said he just wanted these brains to fire off each other, and to get him thinking in a different way.

He could be too open at times, for example going into some of the detail on the row between Bradley and Chris Froome. Wiggins had been there earlier talking with Dave and the 19 guys, and Dave was, as I told him later, far too open with people basically working for Bradley not him. One of the 19 guys at one point seemed to suggest he should have picked the team at the last Tour for media not cycling reasons and we had a bit of a to-do.

Dave floated his idea of the knowledge hub. I took it to the UCFB [sports higher education institution] concept, and maybe a university of human performance, a physical building attached to the Team, but more real than the Sky Academy. The Sky guy seemed OK, though not overwhelming. They were more corporate than I imagined, less creative. His eyes did light up at the university idea though. He could see a positive legacy maybe. Lunch with Godric Smith, Simon from Rapha and a guy who had come in from Hong Kong before we went back in for more of the same. Dave said afterwards he was really happy with how it went. Wanted us to go out to Majorca next. Godric asking – Are they happy? Do they know what they want? What more should we do?

Saturday 29 November

Still feeling ill but set off for BFC v Villa [1–1]. Fletch gave us a lift to and from Preston and we went over plans for a book event at Turf Moor. They were totally up for it.

Sunday 30 November

After a fair bit of toing and froing we finally had the meeting, me, Ed and Neil, at Neil's place. Glenys said she was going round to Rachel's. 'Don't be too hard on him,' she said. But I said he was destroying any chances we had of winning against a totally beatable and useless government. I just felt it was the same as some people couldn't run fast or some people couldn't learn languages, there was something missing, and the public clocked it. When he arrived he was clearly a bit nervous. Fiona had bumped into Rachel at a party last night and she had said that he was worried we were going to tell him to go. The closest I got was to say that he had to be really honest with himself about whether he thought he could do this.

We had a coffee and a bit of small talk and then Neil sat us down at the kitchen table. He said that we would not have asked for this meeting if we didn't think it was important, serious and urgent. We were both loyal, would never do or say nothing to undermine him or be anything but loyal but that meant we had to tell him things as we saw them. He felt this was a useless and beatable government and we could win. But we were not winning the arguments on the economy, and there was little sense of winning within the campaign. I said they had a simple message

– 'Labour caused the crash, we created the recovery and who do you think looks more like a Prime Minister?'

I had no sense of what our main campaigns were or even what they saw as how to do a campaign. No rebuttal. Not enough energy. Cameron had made his speech on Friday and on Saturday it had died. No attack. No follow-through. The shadow Cabinet was invisible. He didn't say much at first, just the occasional 'Sure, sure,' took a few notes but he was defensive. I said I didn't think there was a clear strategy. Neil said if we two couldn't discern a strategy it meant it was not clear. Ed said it was about inequality and the recovery not being for all, focused on living standards, energy prices, NHS etc., with immigration squared off. Is it written down? I asked. Is it disseminated to everyone in the party? Do they know what they are meant to be saying and doing?

I said the reason the Thornberry thing happened was because she didn't really know what she was meant to say re. the by-election and UKIP, and also they overreacted. He said Lucy Powell was already making a difference and bringing more order and discipline. He felt Douglas was always constrained by 'the paralysis of analysis', and that Lucy would get things done. He said at one point he couldn't micro-manage. I said you don't need to and if there was clear leadership and strategy you wouldn't need to. The strategy point we came back to again and again. I revisited the argument about the record, Neil seemed to agree with me but he also knew Ed would not shift on this. Eventually he said, 'Look, David was the continuity candidate and I was the discontinuity candidate, so I have to do things differently.'

Not if they are the wrong things, I said. Not if they are damaging us. He felt his argument about inequality was getting through. I said compared with '97 the public did not have a clue what we were planning. In so far as they knew anything it was just the sense of being a bit more left-wing. We didn't really talk about David but at one point, half an hour into the argument about the politics of the economy, I said this was not some psychodrama about the past, it was about framing politics for the future, based upon the idea that if the public associated Labour with all bad, why would they trust us again? He said, 'This is not about my brother.' I wasn't saying that, I said. I am saying in failing to defend what a Labour government did, and in failing to rebut the 'mess we inherited' attacks, we have played right into the Tory hands and given them a priceless strategic gift. I'd been arguing that he was not defending the Labour record properly but he wrongly assumed I meant in order to differentiate from David. He said re. the record that in the end we had an honest disagreement. We disagree, that's it.

I said to him that the polls were dire, for this stage of the parliament.

If you asked people do they want Labour or Tory government, they say Labour. If they say DC or EM, they say Cameron. He said, 'not so much'. I said yes and you must not let yourself be surrounded by people not prepared to tell you the truth. I said we hear more than you do because people are more honest with us. I hear it all the time. 'I don't like this government but I can't see him as PM.' He grimaced a bit. Ed, you have to face up to this. It is not a winning position. Now, you have seen off that flurry and it is probably not coming back, but you are not going to win unless you up your game, the party ups its game and we have a compelling set of arguments that relate to people's lives. You are all in a bubble. Messages are not getting through.

He said a lot was because of the media. I said do not make the mistake of blaming the media for everything. They were tough but Neil had it worse. Neil said on some issues yes, on others not. Neil said Ed had to try to turn strengths to weaknesses, and brains and guts were the two qualities to pick upon. Others should be saying that all the time. Ed said the shadow Cabinet didn't like to talk him up and also that he had to be careful not to look like they were propping him up on the lines of 'he is not as bad as you think'. On the discontinuity candidate point, I said in many ways the public didn't think he was that different, not just to TB, GB or David but to Cameron and Clegg. There was no real sense of what the differences were. He seized on that as a way of saying he needed to be more progressive.

I felt on immigration though that we were pandering. Also that on Europe he was missing a trick in terms of the leadership position he could get from this. Cameron had made a massive tactical gamble, to which he should reply with a clear strategy. But both sides were moving in the wrong direction. Neil probably softened as we went on, I if anything got a little bit harder. Then Ed did what he always did which was ask, 'What more can we do to bring you in?' I said I am not attending hundreds of meetings. Also I cannot work on strategies I do not support. I was happy to help up to a point re. strategy, debates etc., but I did not want to get sucked in even as much as when GB was fighting 2010. I said for all his faults I did at least feel I knew what he was about and what he was fighting for.

We left on fairly reasonable terms, he said thanks, Neil repeated we were only trying to help, then off he went. I asked Neil what he thought he would take away. My sense was just relief that we didn't say straight out you should just make way for someone else. Neil said Stewart Wood had said Ed was his own main adviser and Neil said that was the problem. He only really listens to what he wants to hear. In which case he will probably have gone away thinking he got away with it. But one thing he will definitely have taken away is the shared idea that there is no strategy.

If we didn't know what it was, how was a member of the public not rooted in politics expected to?

Monday 1 December

Still feeling rough, went to see the doctor, more antibiotics plus steroids. Cancelled a prison visit I was meant to do. Good meeting with Matthew Syed re. his book, which was essentially about making progress through error I guess. Lots of the same themes as *Winners* so in the end I sent him the MS.

Tuesday 2 December

GB had announced yesterday he was standing down from Parliament, and I had turned down lots of bids yesterday but did the *Today* programme and it got a terrific reception. I didn't over-varnish, did the whole brilliant but impossible thing, but I did at least say he was a politician who believed in big things, unlike Cameron. Was very frank about the difficulties, and about TB thinking of getting rid of him, but also emphasised his strengths. I used the line Mum used to say about him being more suited to an earlier era in history.

Up with Rory to Bury. Working on edit. I drove so Rory could prepare for the Brendan Foster interview at UCFB. To Bury – nice little town centre – and did the recording of 'Silent Night' on the pipes for Sean Ruane, Burnley-supporting opera singer, who was doing a project for the National Football Museum on the truce football match in the First World War.

To UCFB, chat with Phil Wilson [chief executive]. Rory down on him but I felt he was having to cope with a fair bit and they were very stretched. Brendan arrived, on great form as ever, really good with the students, who were a bit unenergetic, and I don't think quite appreciated just how big a figure he was for the things they were studying. I stayed in for the start then to the advisory board meeting. Lots to get through. Change name to make it more generally about sport not football. I was the only one who was arguing for. Fletch fixing up the UCFB launch of *Winners*. Also there were a fair few mental health issues, including a couple of suicide attempts. The staff at both ends were totally stretched and needed more people. Rory had a good chat with Brendan. Fletch then took us on a tour of the ground, did some hilarious Kicca videos with him.

Went to see Sean [Dyche] who was on great form in his new office. The match was OK, though Newcastle were poor and we should have won in the first half. One–all. Douglas called and said Ed had told him about our discussion but it was clear that he had given a totally sanitised version. He said I had said I was willing to help. I said I was willing to help by working with people I could work with but I was not wasting my time and I was clear we could not win if he did not up his game. Douglas talked me through some of the recent horror stories.

Then Greg Beales came on and said would I do the TV debate planning next week, and also Marianna – would I see Axelrod when he came over? Getting sucked in. But I was going to give two or three goes watching him up close and if I concluded there was no chance, I would say so, have one last go and then have nothing to do with it. Calum was organising a fans' meeting with some of the board. End of match to Leeds Bradford airport Travelodge for the nightmare journey tomorrow.

Wednesday 3 December

I was up at 4.45 and off for the first of three flights to get me to Tirana, tweeting on the way about the totally mad things we do to watch football matches. At least it meant I had time to go through the last edit before sending through final changes to Nigel. Nice friendly women running the Leeds Bradford lounge. Amsterdam airport buzzy and also noticeable for the extraordinary almost X-rated lingerie ads. I met Andreas Baumgartner in Vienna and we flew on to Tirana. He felt the team was bedding in OK. He also thought the TB operation generally was improving more. Endri seemed very down, felt that the priorities were not clear and they were losing the sunny uplands from the campaign.

To a bad meeting with comms directors, where Endri explained they had not brought forward what they were meant to for the diary for the next two months. I said this will only work if the whole lot of them bind in, but what became clear was that with one or two exceptions they were not really plugged in at the top, and also that they did not have the capacity to do much better.

Endri said the focus groups were showing that people liked Edi, felt he was really trying, that they had done a lot of good things but did not yet feel the link through to their lives. Also, they were actually absorbing a lot of the negative messages from Berisha and the DP, e.g. that taxes had gone up when for most they had come down. I saw Edi immediately afterwards and he felt better about things. The big thing at the moment was energy, dealing with the theft of energy from the system by both business and individuals. He had an amazing picture of a house where the guy had built a stick-out extension around the top of a lamp post to take the energy from it. Others were more sophisticated but the bottom line was the loss of over a billion dollars.

He reckoned as much as 6 per cent of GDP was taken in this way. He actually felt things were going OK. The Serbia visit was difficult but he had big positive approval for the way it went. He said Vučić was really hurt when Edi mentioned Kosovo at the press conference. Hard to imagine how he wouldn't. He said he spoke constantly of his honour being attacked by the drone at the football match – they clearly weren't buying the idea it was not Edi's brother – and then by the mention of Kosovo. He was worried about Putin who had gone there for a full-on state visit with armed guards and the rest, then basically said he wanted their massive bills for energy paid off, and then when he got home called and gave him seventy-two hours to pay – even though Vučić said it would be calamitous for the economy – and he said, 'You don't think I would be impressed by all those guards of honour, do you?'

Putin was definitely playing hard ball everywhere. The story was doing the rounds that he had turned on the other G20 leaders in Brisbane, saying he was the only one with a strategy, and they were all tactical, that they thought they would bring him to his knees but he would outlast them all, and they would end up going to him on their knees. Putin was clearly now thinking he could do whatever he wanted, and that though the sanctions were a pain, they were not as crippling as the oil price, which was doing the real damage to the economy. We went on foot to the PM's residence to wait for TB. Edi told a funny story from a summit where Cameron had been talking to him, and Edi took the chance to say that he was really trying to make a lot of change and needed support and it would be great if he came, because it would showcase a country that was Muslim and able to be peaceful and co-exist with others. He said that if it flared up in the Balkans you had similar tensions that were exploited by ISIS and they needed the support. Cameron said he would try to do it but it would have to be after the election. Edi said, 'Alastair tells me you might not win it though,' and he replied, quite funny for him, that Alastair was wrong because he had got the right Edi in Albania and the wrong Edi in Britain.

Cameron had also said to someone in a recent meeting with someone TB had seen since, 'I cannot lose against Ed. David would have given me a problem.' TB said he had seen Ed a bit. He felt we could actually lose quite badly, because the economy was picking up finally, better than most, and because Ed was struggling. Cameron had vacated the centre ground but now we had gone further left. Even the SNP and UKIP, he felt, were actually doing well only because we were doing badly, and because we had no credibility on the big issues facing the country. Ed had apparently done OK at PMQs today, but Osborne did a seemingly good political job with the Autumn Statement. They definitely had a message, with weight, and he had also been dominating the media for days with e.g. roadbuilding, tax cuts (admittedly unfunded) and other stuff. We were not really at the races.

TB was in OK form, seemed not too knackered though it did drive me a bit bonkers the way he felt he had to keep saying he had never ever been so busy. Good chat on the delivery unit, the need to focus on a small number of key priorities – the first were energy, water, FDI [foreign direct investment] – but also he wanted the team to act as a kind of mid- and long-term policy unit for Edi. For example he would need and want to do something about judicial reform, but what options were there? The Georgians had made the judges re-apply for their jobs. Edi felt that would be difficult because people would think they were just trying to politicise. But the EU ambassadors could lead on this maybe, and demand more be done to deal with corrupt judges. There had been a bad report by Transparency International [anti-corruption NGO] today, but Edi insisted that was all about the judges and that on the doing business indicators they had done a lot better, and risen up the table. The corruption issue they just had to keep plugging away.

TB was interesting in these meetings, part politician, part adviser, part consultant. He had seen Netanyahu the night before – he felt he might lose the election he had just called, and we agreed that he was never going to deliver a peace deal – and was also full of advice for Edi e.g. on how to deal with the Chinese, the Gulf guys etc. OK food, some good laughs, especially me saying how right-wing Tony was and him telling Edi I had always been Old Labour. Edi was getting more confident and comfortable in telling stories. Nice evening, part social, part work.

On the work side he wanted TB to get more involved under the Merkel umbrella on the Balkans situation. He felt that if he, Barroso and others like that were involved with her it would give him the chance to push a bit more on the reform programme and the EU route. Back to the Sheraton with TB. Still a lot of security for him. He said he was pretty much settled on the business and felt it was well established and would need less of his attention in terms of travel. He wanted to spend more time at home, partly because of the family. He also wanted to rebuild his UK reputation. *On verra.*

He had had the second letter from Chilcot and this time it was about the Chirac *'quelques soient les circonstances'*, suggesting TB had deliberately exploited what Chirac said by misinterpreting it. Jack Straw had sent the inquiry a stinging letter saying it was a totally shoddy piece of work. He was pretty clear they could not do it before the election. He also felt Cameron would not go too heavy, partly because of Libya, but also because Iraq was actually beginning to improve under the new PM.

When I saw Matthew Syed the other day we discussed Iraq – which he supported at the time and on which he was now not so sure – and we had an interesting discussion about doubt. I was always grey not black and white, but at the inquiry I was determined not to let anyone say I was distancing myself. But I did sometimes have real doubts, whether we had just followed the US line, whereas even now, TB said he didn't and that he would do the same thing again. He said he found it repugnant the way Labour leaders were claiming some kind of victory for stopping action in Syria when what was happening there now was worse than ever.

Thursday 4 December

Up for a swim. In to see TB. On Labour, he said it was just not going to happen and the tragedy was that if David M had won, or even if he had just stayed around, he would be in there. He had seen a fair few MPs who were basically panicking now. It had gone beyond. He said it was only salvageable from a sensible centrist position and Ed just wasn't going to do it. Re. himself he said he just did not know what to do. He felt part of the problem was that he had just lost any real constituency in the media. The right hated him because he won. The left because he was not left enough and ultimately they did feel more comfortable with losing than winning.

The Murdoch papers had always been fair but now he had lost that too. He felt he could do more to engage in the UK but he didn't know how. He was also wondering about putting all of his earnings into his foundation. But would that help? I again said he needed a big-picture rationale for this weird post-power politics, and he needed to engage in a totally different way. He said I guess I had shown it was possible but he was under such sustained attack in certain quarters. Added to which, I said, he had been PM.

I felt Edi had been in good form, the rest less so. Bumped into Vali at the airport so filled her in too. She looked exhausted. Met a nice guy on the plane, James something, a Manc living in Wiltshire who had been out there for Vodafone. He loved the place, had never encountered corruption and wanted to help. Asked him to write a piece which I would get placed. Turned out he was leaving Vodafone for Metrobank and was going on about how much he loved the culture and the energy. I showed him the bits of the book about Metrobank. Both he and the BA stewardess were desperate to get rid of the Tories but felt Ed wasn't going to win. Home, light session with Keir. Book all done, off to the typesetters. Not bad work in less than a year.

Friday 5 December

Up early and off with Rayan to Hopton Hall in the Derbyshire countryside. Arrived a little late because of the traffic but Ed M and Douglas were even later. A big house and a number of smaller cottages and in Card House some of the team had already arrived. Michael Sheehan was over from the US, the same two nice guys who had done the debate prep with GB in 2010, Ayesha and later Lucy Powell and Stewart Wood. Torsten came for a bit but then disappeared for a funeral. The whole day was pretty grim. It was not just that Ed was so slow on his feet but also that they had so clearly not thought through the big strategic questions and so too often just dived down into the weeds.

What was the economic plan he kept talking about? It turned out to be minimum wage, zero hours contracts, energy prices, NHS and vague notions re. deficit. Greg Beales reported that the Tories under Craig Oliver were definitely trying to stop the debates happening. God knows why. However, Greg's view was that they knew there were limited opportunities for Ed to 'disrupt his own narrative' and the debates was one of them. Cameron would kill him if he was like he had been today. I think he knew he was off form, and my demeanour probably hadn't helped. He said he found it useful and wanted to do more. He knew it was important and he knew he had to work at it.

Sheehan laid out a few general notions e.g. only try to do two or three things and be clear what they are. Understand that most people hear about the debate rather than watch it. Social media important. Tone and body language. Do not agree to applause – he was particularly firm on that re. the Farage debate. We watched a brilliant Clinton clip from his first campaign v Bush senior. Different class. Empathy and policy and message rolled into one. TB had told me Obama had said to him, 'Why did Labour pick that Ed guy over David?' I wondered at times if Sheehan was thinking the same, though he was quite hard to read.

I was playing Cameron in the rehearsals and basically used a frame – Labour created the crash, we created a recovery and he was not up to it. In so far as he had a frame it was that the Tories were for the rich and the recovery was not working for all. But whenever you pressed down on policy it was too flimsy. They could take for ever to decide what a good line was, with his team chipping in. Douglas at least had a sense of strategy – or the need for one – Greg a bit, Torsten was clever but seemed down, Ayesha was at least frank, as when telling him that his body language made him look weak and he needed to fill the space as I did.

I was probably being more aggressive than Cameron would be in part to show where his arguments were weak. But their response was usually to talk about whether Cameron would do that, not whether the argument was weak. When he did an OK answer – as on immigration – they told him it was brilliant when in fact it was OK. Michael S rightly said he was talking too much as though it was a radio phone-in show not a debate. Too much throat clearing. Not getting to the point. I suspected – and Douglas confirmed later this is exactly what Ed had thought – that to some extent he felt I was just beating up on him. I certainly went for him over Syria, not defending the record and not having an economic plan. But I was actually fairly mild. Also I had not really done that much proper research. A bit of that and he would be flat on his back.

The whole thing felt a bit amateur. None of them took notes. The discussion was not focused enough. At lunch it reminded me of an '80s by-election. Crisps, snowballs, Kit Kats, awful sandwiches. When I talked about the need for good diet and exercise I might as well have been talking Swahili. He had been doing PMQs for four years yet there was no clear driving narrative that had emerged, whereas I worried Cameron had one, all focused on the economy and leadership. It was also possible to discern the points Cameron would attack on – constant mention of tax, the rich, nothing good to say about business, no sense of plan. One of the questions was: 'What was the most difficult decision you ever had to make?' As Cameron I wanged on about sending troops into action, then whacked Ed over flaking on Syria. He said the most difficult decisions were about what are the right policies for the country blah blah, and I cut in and said the only difficult decision he ever faced was how deep to stick the knife into his brother. I saw Douglas wince. Ed looked shocked. 'He wouldn't do that, would he?' Greg said, 'I suspect he might.' 'Do you think I should bring it up before he does? Do you think he will do that line?' Oh my God.

Fiona asked me later if there had been any good parts to it. Only by reference to the average being so low. Yet they constantly talked to him as though it was fine. I got the thing about not wanting to smash his confidence, but they were so far off where they needed to be. Douglas said to me afterwards there was a massive gap between where the public was on him and where he thought they were. Also they had convinced themselves that Osborne's Autumn Statement had bombed but it hasn't. Douglas said with me as Cameron it had felt like Eden Hazard [Chelsea and Belgium football star] going on loan to Rangers. When I thought who would have been in that room for us – Peter M, Peter H, Jonathan, Sally Morgan and Anji Hunter, Charlie and Derry, and then a whole other lot like Bruce and Tim Allan and Liz Lloyd and Pat McFadden and so on. Really quality people with brains and with a leader who wanted to be challenged.

I did a big thing at one point re. Osborne's northern economic power-house. Ed said it was like Dracula in charge of the blood bank. Groan. 'That was brilliant,' said Lucy. God help us. It was raining when I left, Rayan was late and I was in a foul mood all the way back. Rayan had said earlier if he saw him he would tell him he had to go. We were going to limp on and lose, possibly quite badly. Grim grim grim. No power, no passion, not enough energy. Just a vague collection of policies that did not add up to a plan, economic or political. Glad to get home. I found an excuse to have an email exchange with Osborne. I said I was only just catching up on his statement because I had been in the New Labour landslide haven that is Albania. I said though that it was impossible to miss the makeover! 'A haircut is not a policy. A suit is not a strategy!'

Anyway 1. How did it go? 2. What is your prediction for May?

George Osborne reply:

I'm not sure I agree – the haircut and the suit have been one of the more effective strategic policies I've seen. To your questions:

1. It went well – 4 days of coverage on long-term economic plan in advance as per grid (NHS, roads etc.); then serious reforming manoeuvre on the day (stamp duty); then row with BBC next day takes the news rather than row with an opposition on verge of government – look back at the Autumn Statement equivalent in 1996 and the coverage Blair and Brown would have received setting the agenda then compared with coverage Miliband and Balls received. Above all, subject of debate now back to the economy where we have a 25-point lead.

2. I think we will win. I am a child of the Clinton/Blair era. Back then you taught us that you had to be trusted on the economy, have the more leader-like leader and hold the centre. We've got all three. We've also got Clinton's devastating argument from the last Convention that our opponents' main charge is that we're not clearing up their mess fast enough. They've done absolutely nothing to cover the bases you need to cover as a Labour opposition – be trusted with the money and show you understand there's such a thing as aspiration. They're still stuck arguing the toss about the decisions they took in government six years ago. And I think Ed Miliband's pain is just beginning – if you've not established by now you're a leader, then you're not going to manage to do so in the next 5 months. Our challenge at the moment comes from a Poujadiste force on the right. Provided we stick to the centre, I am confident we will be OK as the squeeze is applied.

Why? What's your view?'

Depressing, because it showed the gulf in understanding between him and Ed and his team. I didn't say so.

I spoke to Neil about the debate prep. Said it was not great. Even worse, that apart from Douglas, the American who was over moderating/

coaching, and the two guys operating the equipment, nobody in the room really seemed to realise it.

Saturday 6 December

Long chat with Douglas. He said it had been both better and worse on Day 2. Ed did some things reasonably well. He said he felt cold fury at Neil and co. who had put him where he is knowing there was a better alternative. He also felt he could not push too hard because the minute anyone did so Ed saw it as disloyalty. I said I was minded to tell him that I did not think he could win and I did not think I could help him. He said he would just dismiss that as disaffected Blairites wanting him to lose.

Neil felt I should just withdraw if I felt so demotivated or that ultimately he couldn't do it. I pinged an email to Axelrod asking for a chat before he came over. If there was nothing there to grab onto by Wednesday I was out of it. QPR away. Went with Georgia to Westfield, Greek outdoor café for lunch, then to the game, where we outplayed them and lost [2–0]. Bad sign at this stage of the season.

Monday 8 December

Charlie Watts round for a decent session. Feeling 80 per cent. Lunch with Matthew Mills [son of Tessa Jowell and David Mills]. He had swung totally behind Tessa doing the mayoral campaign, and felt she could win. I was staying out of it. Walked through town trying to do a bit of Christmas shopping. I skipped Andrew Neil's do. Definitely anti-social at the moment.

Tuesday 9 December

GQ lunch, Quaglino's. Ed Victor there, Paul McGuinness, also good to meet Maggie Draycott [manager, highest value customers] finally after all the help she had given me at BA. Sitting next to Heather Kerzner, ex-wife of Sun City [luxury South African resort] guy Sol, who was unbelievably flirtatious, as Ed had warned me she would be. We did though end up talking mental health. One of those old-style media lunches that went on and on, and I was off by 2.20.

Did a call with David Axelrod pre his flight overnight to London. I had sent him a note saying I was worried 1, that things were really bad and getting worse and 2, that he would get a glossed view of things. He said he was a massive admirer, both re. my political work but also mental health and we agreed to collaborate on that. I told him how bad things had been in Derbyshire. He said he was aware we were dealing with a struggling candidate, and we were in a weak strategic position. He said he liked Ed, but both of us had a curse and a blessing – we had worked with truly exceptional men in TB and Obama. He felt that within what he said and thought there was a strategy struggling to form but it was not clear and it was not well articulated. We probably spoke for half an hour or so before he boarded his flight.

I was probably too negative. But immediately afterwards I was doing a training session with Portland account managers, and I gave them four challenges in the post-spiel tests, one of which was 'prepare a plan to turn EM's negatives into strengths, and make him electable'. As before, they laughed. When I told David by email he said 'that makes me want to cry'. The Portland session showed me how many bright young people were out there, how many of them were basically wanting us to win but could not see Ed doing it.

Chatted with Tim who was sure we would lose, and also sure that it would tip back to a New Labour candidate, and even Tristram maybe. Then again we could get wiped out. Not impossible. Axelrod felt that there was at least a clear choice. The issue was whether it was one we could win, and also how we were affected by the slide to UKIP/Greens/SNP, which itself in my view was a product of our weakness rather than their strengths. It would be good to work with him maybe but I think we both felt things were not great.

Wednesday 10 December

To Norman Shaw North for the Axelrod and a member of the US team planning meeting. As usual, most people arrived late and wandered in rather aimlessly. I had a frank chat with Greg Beales about what I really felt about the TV debate situation. He said it did get better on Day 2. He also said Ed had said that it was hard with me because I was a big character, to which Greg had said for fuck's sake, in the real thing you are up against a PM with experience under a massive and intense spotlight, so get real. Greg felt that at least we had teased out the main difficulties and challenges, which enabled them to devise the strategic answers. But why so late? And could they do it?

When Axelrod arrived, Douglas went through the plan for their two days, then James Morris did a polling presentation which showed pretty clearly that momentum was with the Tories, that leadership and the economy were where they would frame the election choice, that Ed was falling, Labour as a brand holding up sufficient for us to think it was still winnable if... I did say at one point if this was any other type of organisation it would be obvious what we did. There was a bit of a sharp intake but nobody seemed to want to engage. They were a curious team. Douglas was quite managerial, but spent much of the time making notes to himself about his own campaign in Paisley, which he said was far from a walkover, and he was wishing he could spend more time there and less time here.

At one point, when Axelrod said that it was important Ed spoke to who and what he was, Douglas said that when he had said that to Ed on his last visit, what Ed took out of it was a message that has made him 'authentically out of touch'. Everyone laughed but it was a serious point. Ed had this belief that he was somehow more in touch with 'ordinary people' than most. He spoke in terms of concepts not people. And he truly believed the world would follow him if only they could hear him as Lucy Powell did. Axelrod said what the public probably felt was that people like us were sitting in a room trying to decide what Ed ought to feel and think and say. Greg had a few half-decent things to say, Torsten likewise, Spencer [Livermore] said little, ditto Tim Livesey when he came in.

When Spencer did speak it was usually to say they were already doing things we were suggesting and then get defensive when I said they didn't seem to be working. Later he said to me privately that he agreed with everything I said, but they could not get Ed to do the things they needed to. I revisited for the nth time the argument about the record and the economy. Axelrod said he was worried about relitigating the record because it was too late. My point exactly. Should have been done years ago. Likewise we would only get heard on the future if we won arguments about the past and the present and despite the Tories' appalling record we had conceded on both. I was banging my head against a wall on this one but I said, again for the nth time, that they were in this position because of that basic strategic failing.

Ed was planning to do a speech on the economy and the deficit tomorrow and they were running in and out on that. Plus there was a discussion re. the rollout of the pledges and again I said they would not connect without the strategic framing. I said they needed to stop thinking day to day and instead frame their planning around what they wanted people to be thinking of, focusing upon front of mind when the campaign started. Neutralise economy and leadership, focus and fight on NHS. Big message about a new and different sort of economy. Chapter by chapter through the new year, then big document re. us and a big attack document re. them. I felt exhausted by the end of it because apart from Axelrod giving a bit of insight and his team a bit of analysis I felt I was having to lift it the whole time. Douglas said to me afterwards, and so did Marianna, it was the best meeting of its kind that they had had. God help us.

Charlie F came in at the break and I told him how bad I thought things were. He was hosting an Axelrod dinner for donors later, Gail was at it, and she said it was all very backward-looking. She felt Axelrod had little to say about the campaign. It was all about how they won for Obama, and even on that nothing about Obama as President, all about him as campaigner. Charlie, who had lost even more weight, said to Axelrod, 'Listen to Alastair,

I have never known him to be wrong on political strategy.' Axelrod – this was the closest he got to saying openly what I knew he thought – said we agreed on a way forward, but we feared we did not have the capacity to deliver. He went off to see Ed Balls. Greg said he would be defensive and wanting to explain nothing was his fault. He came back saying he felt he wanted to be used more. Raised eyebrows from the Ed team.

Marianna kept looking at me and rolling her eyes. When Rachel [Kinnock] came in to talk about visits, she said to me it was interesting how they talked Ed up at times, but at others were brutally frank on his weaknesses. It was also fascinating, incredible in fact, that though we were having a break at the time, nobody watched PMQs. Axelrod sent me a nice message saying he felt we were kindred spirits, but in terms of future collaboration, he mentioned me going to Chicago to do a talk on the book, and working together on mental illness. Off to Renaissance Hotel for the first long-form interview re. the book, with India Knight for *Red* magazine. She was quite bumptious – for example didn't want Najma to listen in – but also very pro-me, and spent as much time trying to persuade me to get a seat or run for mayor as doing the interview.

I felt I was in OK shape in terms of messaging on the book but it was going to be hard not to make it all about Ed M and could Labour win? Or, as she put it, 'Why are Labour so totally useless?' The photocall was hilarious, a photographer called Amelia saying she had been told to 'think Clooney and Denzel Washington' photos, not politician. Half a dozen assistants. Some good photos but I needed new shirts that fitted better, especially now that I was losing weight.

Thursday 11 December

Goring Hotel for breakfast with D-J Collins and Paddy Harveson [partners in PR company]. Both impressive in their own different ways.

Met Godric on the train to Gatwick. Did Fred Macauley [Radio Scotland] interview on depression at the airport then we headed off to Palma de Majorca. EasyJet slightly better than Ryanair. Working out a plan based around what we thought we needed. Met at the airport and then off to the Sky team hotel. They had taken over the whole place and, moderately, kitted it out with Sky memorabilia. Lunch with Fran and Dave B. He was very much in his environment, but it must be odd for these guys to be away from home so long, together so much, and often having the same kind of conversations again and again.

Quite hard to get a handle on what they needed and what they wanted, and Dave didn't help, in that he tended to bounce around a bit too much. Went for a walk along the beach with him later, and he said that he was expecting more problems with Chris Froome. Wiggins was going to be with them till Paris–Roubaix early April, then starting his own team. Chris F and Brad relations irreparable, but also they felt Chris was becoming more difficult to manage, partly because of Michelle. Maybe it was inevitable. DB said that if it came to it, he would just get rid, but the truth is he did not have a deep squad right now. Interesting to see his manner in the end-of-day team meeting. Quite methodical, deferred to others quite a lot, allowed people to speak if they wanted to. He introduced Godric and me as having 'worked for Prime Ministers and started wars so they ought to be able to help a bike team'. Riders all fairly welcoming. Nico Roche there in his last team kit because still technically tied to them. Pete Kennaugh good laugh. Some of the younger and also the foreign ones quite shy. Cold was back with a vengeance so I saw the team doc and he gave me my third round of antibiotics.

Friday 12 December
Breakfast, showed Dave the OST bits of the book, then a long brainstorm with Godric, Fran and Rich. Joined by Dave, Rod, Tim K and Carsten [Jeppesen, Team Sky]. We presented what we did and how we would do it for them. Major buy-in. Tim said it was the first time he felt there could be a link between comms strategy and performance. Rod definitely up for it too. Main idea was to have a five-year plan based on the goal of being seen indisputably as the best team in the world; with it broken down into phases, the first being the road to Paris–Roubaix which was going to be their No. 2 target after the TdeF. Explained how a grid system works and suggested we built it around races, people, innovation and data (once I had explained this did not need to mean state secrets), long-form content and short-form content including trivia, quizzes and the like. It went down well, and Dave seemed to think I should go back early in New Year and get CF signed up for it too. Agreed to do another one with riders and others New Year. Quick lunch then we headed off to the airport and an overly eventful return flight. GS lost iPad. Then we got diverted to Paris because there had been a glitch in the NATS computer system and the whole of London airspace was shut for a while. Very irritating pilot overdoing the light touch, making jokes about a cleaner taking out the wrong plug.

Peter M called asking if I had seen the TB/*Vanity Fair* piece which he thought was dire.

Saturday 13 December
Rory off to LA. To Burnley with Calum. Almost a month now feeling shit, or at least below par. Good on train, guy saying had heard re. book

on Breakfast telly. Fletch met us, off to the ground to record a video for the launch of the book at Turf Moor in March. Good match and we beat Southampton one–nil. Starting to think we could stay up. Missed the connection because first train was delayed, took ages to get a cab to Preston, got soaked. Shared a cab back with Mike Garlick and the editor of an Ipswich football website en route back from Bolton. To Tim's party. Tristram tipsy, and asking me in front of Ameet from Cameron's team: 'How awful was debate camp in Derbyshire then?'

Friday 19 December

Peter M called having seen TB yesterday. He said something remarkable has just happened. 'Ed Miliband has asked you to run his campaign comms,' I said. Something far more remarkable, he said. He said that he had had a 'very raw' discussion yesterday, and at the end as he was leaving Peter had noticed one of the paintings on the way out and how much he liked it. 'And guess what just happened? The painting arrived with a note from TB.' I said he should embrace it, and embrace the sentiment. I pointed out I had never had such a gift from him. 'And arguably you did more for him than I ever did,' said Peter. He was clearly thinking about how TB could rescue his reputation. We chatted for the second time this week, at some length. Another of those spells when we were all trying to resurrect old relationships.

Sunday 21 December

Workout, work, then a day watching football, Tyne–Wear derby and then Liverpool v Arsenal. Dinner with Tessa and David and Matthew. David had read and loved the *Winners* proofs.

Monday 22 Saturday

Conference call with GS, Fran and Rob to sort out Majorca and the training camp media day. DB's *Times* interview came out well, back-page lead and the headline on the warpath re. UCI weak leadership re. drugs stance. Off to Scotland. We got caught up in a dreadful jam following an accident on the M74 and then the news broke of a horrible incident in Glasgow city centre, a bin lorry careering out of control and killing several people out Christmas shopping. I was supposed to be seeing Stewart Regan of the SFA for dinner but we were late getting to Glasgow and so we postponed. Then news that Clarke Carlisle had been hit by a lorry. Sounded like he may have tried to kill himself. I sent a message to him and to Gemma.

On the road up was tweeting lots of beautiful Scotland pictures which took off, Nicola Sturgeon asking me to 'keep up the good work', Martin McGuinness tweeting pix of Ireland to say it was more beautiful etc. The more we went there the more I believed this part of Scotland was as beautiful as anywhere in the world. Kate Gross [former TB aide] died. She sent me her book just before. Beautifully written and so sad.

Christmas and week to New Year's Eve
Conaglen was unchanged, though we didn't have the whole house as they were refurbishing part of it. I was doing less than usual, working out for an hour a day in the hot room, walks now and then, a bit of work on the proofs, a bit of political stuff but not doing nearly as much as usual. Also napping a fair bit. Charles Kennedy and Donald [son] came round one night. Charles was anxious about his seat. He was determined to fight it as himself, not the party. Felt the outcome generally was totally unclear but probably a Labour narrow win. His brother had been involved in a freak accident and had become quadriplegic.

Politically he seemed strangely detached and also even on things to do with the constituency he was fairly unplugged. Donald [AC brother] was up for a few days and was in good form, despite still needing the oxygen twenty-four hours a day. Agreed to buy him out of the Retford flat left to us in four shares by Mum so that he could buy a wardened place for himself. Mental health-wise he was OK. Grace was keen to do a film with him and was doing some nice interviews with him about what schizophrenia was like. Later I spoke to Paddy Wivell [director and producer] to get him teed up maybe to take it on. He was keen but busy with Ethiopia.

Had a few chats with Gemma Carlisle [wife] re. Clarke [depressive former Burnley footballer]. He had been depressed again, had stopped taking the medication, and had gone AWOL. He was seen for several hours walking up and down a busy road in York and eventually jumped in front of a lorry. Amazingly injuries were not as severe as they might be, but it was going to be a long, long haul to get back. I helped her a bit with press stuff, e.g. journalists approaching family. In fact they were reasonably restrained given that they would have assumed possible suicide.

Team Sky were taking up more work than Godric and I had envisaged. We were putting together a list of people for us to interview before whittling down to a couple to see Dave and the team in Majorca.

Thursday 1 January 2015
Drove to Newcastle where Fiona dropped me and I went to the Burnley

match. Great game. We went down three times and came back three times, and actually should have won. Following on from coming back from two down to draw at City on the 28th, we were getting great reviews right now. Sean doing well.

Friday 2 January

I was OK up top but started to get anxious and a bit down after we came back. Partly seasonal probably. Also I wondered if I was maybe very depressed but the medication was keeping me artificially higher so I just felt bad but not wretched. It was a new feeling, not full-on – as I was through most of December – and not crushed down, just not right. Also the pressure was cranking up to get me to go back to help Ed. I had him on the phone a couple of times, and he asked me straight out if I would go and run the campaign. He said I had a lot of weight in the party and was respected by all the team and I would make a big difference. At different times I had Charlie, Douglas, Tom Baldwin all on at me to do it. I said to Charlie that I did not feel up to it, or up for it. I felt bad not wanting to help more but I did not feel ownership of the strategy or the team, and I knew it was too late to change much. Ed listened to what he wanted to hear. That is his prerogative. The approach he takes to strategy is his choice and he was elected leader and so was entitled to go down the road he chose. But I could only operate if I felt motivated and felt that I really believed in what I was doing.

Of course I wanted Labour to win but I was more driven by the hatred of the Tories and what they were doing, less by a great positive belief. Also though of course I could make a difference I think the cost–benefit analysis in terms of how much I would have to put in in order to get some modest change and improvement was something else I had to think about it. Added to which the diary for March was already full.

Monday 5 January

In Hampstead and as I walked down Perrin's Lane some guy came towards me shouting abuse: 'You are the biggest piece of shit, you should be in jail etc.' I walked by and put out my arm to keep him away. Then I carried on but he came after me, aimed a kick and spat at me. Not nice. Galloway later tweeted about it, the guy having contacted him, asked for witnesses, said I had spat at the guy and assaulted him, and I started to get media calls about it. Ignored them.

The political season had kicked off properly with a sense now that we were into the long campaign. Cameron on *Marr* yesterday, Ed big speech today. He had sent it to me last night and I had had a read. It was OK without being great. But the fact that it said 'seventh draft' at the top made it highly unlikely I could change it much so I didn't. He had called me on Saturday and I said I had been at the football. 'What league are Burnley in?' It wasn't a joke or a piss-take either. He genuinely didn't know. I remembered Douglas's 'authentically out of touch' line. He also never quite came out with what he wanted. E.g. would I like to go and work at party HQ? Doing what? Well, it would be good for people if they saw you around? But doing what. Well. Whatever you like really. I guess he didn't want to come straight out in case I rejected. As Tom B told me, he could sense there was negative energy and he knew that I felt they had screwed up on several strategic points.

Tuesday 6 January

Most of the day Team Sky interviews with Godric and Fran. Ben Hurley and Darryl Broadfoot top two. Ben ex Olympics and was good. Darryl a bit more corporate but good and asked a lot of the right questions. Tom Baldwin came round and was following up on Ed's call at the weekend. He said they really felt they needed me in there more, and wanted to know how much I could face doing. We agreed I would do more media, help with debates and engage publicly on issues they wanted help with, also help maybe on speeches etc. But I said I had found the TV debate rehearsal day and the Axelrod day a bit dispiriting. I also felt I had gone beyond in terms of thinking I could really influence the strategy. He said the fact is he still listens to you more than most people, and he reeled off a series of past speeches and moments where he said I had made a material difference just by engaging and giving advice, e.g. a couple of conference speeches, party reform, Murdoch and Leveson. So I said I would do more but the minute I got on the bus to go home – reading Johann Hari's excellent book on the war on drugs – I felt down about it.

Wednesday 7 January

Paris horror, gunmen going into *Charlie Hebdo* [satirical newspaper] office and just wiping out twelve people because they continued to do cartoons of the Prophet and generally be at the outer end of free speech re. Islam. I had breakfast with Miles Protter, mainly talking family and books and Oz, then lunch with Jan Åge Fjørtoft. He was over to see the Norwegian chess world champ in action against eighteen people at once. Also had been doing some work with Erling Haaland, the wonderkid footballer all the big clubs were trying to get. Pep Guardiola had almost got down on his knees, said he could make him the greatest player ever. He was there also to ask me on behalf of the Norwegian Labour Party if I would help them. Re. the UK Labour situation, I exchanged emails with TB who felt I should help but not run it because it was not my team or strategy and I would not be happy doing it. The kids felt much the same. Edi Rama felt it was odd for him to want one of the 'New Labour stars to polish Old Labour', which is how he saw Ed. He could not get over how Ed had managed to lose any sense of the Labour legacy. Gail was also of the view that it would drive me crazy. She said you have got a better life back, don't lose it again.

The whole afternoon was taken up with sorting out the index for the book. Some bad mistakes. Like having Tony Sinclair (Floyd Mayweather's uncle) as 'footballer'.

Thursday 8 January

To RH meeting with Susan, Nigel, Najma, Pippa (serial still not fixed) and Chloe re. social media planning. *Ham&High* sent another email saying they now had CCTV which, they said, appeared to corroborate the guy's version. Yesterday Gavin, Gerald, Tim and Fiona had all basically said sit tight, they couldn't run a story without putting it to me so wait and meanwhile have something ready. I had done a long note for the file, which Gavin had advised, especially as George Galloway has become involved. It turned out Ron McKay, one of Galloway's pals, had been in contact with the guy. The allegations put to me were the opposite of the truth – I was abused, kicked and spat at in the street, and was being told it was the other way round. I think they got there was a political agenda at play here. Gav and Gerald suggested I ask to see the CCTV and the reporter, Tim Lamden, agreed, so we arranged to meet in the morning. Fiona was saying I brought all this stress on myself. I was at a loss to know how I could be accused of some guy spitting at me in the street.

NHS dinner for a dozen or so senior people. Clearly pressed and not greatly keen on Tories, felt Jeremy Hunt weird and hated the way he seemed to attack staff morale. But also a bit down on Burnham because he had gone 'too NHS England'. Some of them a bit down on New Labour, but also that another five years of this lot would be grim. Nice group of people, enjoyed it. Cameron trying to duck TV debates. Lance [Armstrong] back on for March so 1, had to change diary for book tour and 2, had to change book slightly re. Lance bits.

Friday 9 January

Tim Lamden came round at eight and showed us the CCTV he had seen.

From Villa Bianca, but very limited, just the first part. The moment of contact by me was even thinner than I thought. I wanted to speak to Gavin first but I made clear the truth was the opposite of what was being said, and I would set that out. Tim said, 'There is no way we are going to say it is assault but there was some sort of contact.' I must say, if you did not know the background you'd interpret it as a rather friendly greeting to a known passer-by. Tim said the guy had said he didn't wish to be identified. That weakened the story as well. Tim was also aware that there had been another incident with me and Galloway pals at Walthamstow.[*] Fiona told him this was the first time in ages I had had trouble like this. I spoke to Gavin etc. and then did a short statement, just sticking to the facts. They were bound to run it but having seen the CCTV I felt it supported my story not his and the fact he wouldn't put his name to it was pretty weak.

On the way to Gatwick I worked on a speech that Edi was planning to do at a gathering of all the religious leaders, post *Charlie Hebdo* killings. There was also a plan for lots of leaders to descend on Paris for a march of solidarity. I felt the thing was going OTT, that when 20,000 people had just been wiped out by Boko Haram [jihadist terrorism organisation] in Nigeria, to little fanfare or outrage, why this mega outpouring for twelve people, some of whose work was frankly borderline racist. Had a good chat with Calum on his football community ideas. Met Godric at Gatwick, and picked their brains on the Hampstead incident, also working on the vision statement for Dave B.

Going to be quite an odd couple of days because we had both Darryl Broadfoot and Ben Hurley, the two shortlisted for the comms job, on the plane with us. I made light of it, doing *Apprentice*-style TV voiceover. I felt Darryl would be good, Ben probably favoured by the others. Hugh Chambers [Team Sky commercial director] also at the airport. Felt he was too political for his own good. He was a bit bitchy about Fran, for example, also running down others. Plus he was far too keen to get into the press stuff and the words. He felt our vision statement was too long, and was clearly dying to get his hands on it. Greg very unsure about him. Godric getting that way too. Godric and I worked on it on the easyJet flight out to Majorca.

Landed, waited for the chef, minibus with a pissed driver wandering all over the road. The hotel, Vanity, seemed better than the other one. First a long meeting with Dave, Fran, Godric and Hugh to go over plans for the media day, and the statement. Ben and Darryl in odd interview situation,

---

[*] The previous year Galloway had been involved in an incident when people working on a film he was making were sent to try to carry out a citizen's arrest of Campbell at a Labour dinner. One of the group was subsequently charged with assault of a police officer.

hanging around talking to the others. Dave's priority for my limited time was to spend some time with Chris Froome, so after an hour or so Chris F, Dave B, Godric and I went to a small room away from the rest and had a good chat. Dave said he felt CF needed more support, he explained how we worked and how we tried to plan and strategise.

Chris said he didn't like or enjoy doing media much. He had been very open when he first was big time, but felt they turned against him. I said he had to see them as being there for him, not the other way round, decide what he wanted to communicate and how, and then do it. He was a remarkable guy to look at. Painfully thin, a little pin head and a nervous smile. But we had two long sessions with him, the first one me mainly doing the talking, the second one more him and what his long-term plans were. He said he wanted to stay as a competitive cyclist well into his thirties. He wanted to be seen as the best clean rider ever.

He came over as a team player, and that was echoed by stuff Dave and others said. The hatred for Wiggins was clear. When we went through the questions planned for the Sky Sports interview tomorrow, one was about Wiggins, and I said all he needed to say was he was a great servant to the sport and he wished him well. He smiled, shook his head and said, 'But I don't think that.' I had just been talking about the importance of authenticity! He felt he had been totally selfish and actually not that great a servant of the sport or the team. He said there was no love lost between them or between their wives. The best he could say was that they were now going separate paths. He told Dave and others afterwards he had really enjoyed it and also that he felt he understood better how to deal with this stuff. Dinner then another Chris F meeting then Dave etc. to finalise the statement. We agreed it would be good to let the media attend a team briefing and also to go on a ride with the riders. Dave to do a short intro on the what, the how, the why of the next stages. All about looking back five years and forward to the next five. We definitely had a strategy for comms, but needed the person to come in and deliver it. Godric might end up doing more. Chris said that he felt Dave B had been a lot better and more focused since we were involved. I had an early start in the morning and so went to bed saying it was time to do it and stop talking.

Saturday 10 January

Up at five, off to the airport, to fly Majorca to Barcelona then Liverpool. Working on statement for *Ham&High*. Ben Hurley dropped an email re. same, suggesting without being heavy we should question whether they even have a story. Ben was clearly favourite but later I got a message from Dave that he felt Darryl had something about him. He had finally had a chat with the candidates separately, going for a walk down the beach and just chatting. Darryl had said, 'Why are you guys seen as being hard to work with?' and Dave liked that.

Picked up by Fletch and Morgan [grandson] at windy John Lennon airport, off to the match, and a great win against QPR. I was beginning to think we could stay up. *MoS* doing a story re. my role in TV debates and the headline was me telling Ed he is unfit to run Britain, without making clear I was speaking as Cameron not me. How the fuck did this stuff get out from something so private with only the inner team?

Sunday 11 January

Work on Serbia, thinking through the plans for the next couple of days. Flight out via LHR, Zurich, then arrived Belgrade fairly late and got a car to Metropol Palace. Godric was calling me to update me on the media day with Team Sky which seemed to be going really well. Dave and Chris were on good form. Chris much more relaxed, did his intro, was engaged etc. Also the hacks loved riding out with the team, plus the coffee stop. Godric still going on though re. how odd the working environment was. Still no clarity re. Darryl or Ben.

Monday 12 January

Nice hotel, very quiet. Meeting with Andreas and team. First meeting was with PM's right-hand woman who went through some of the policy issues, and also the weaknesses in operation. She was pretty hyper and seemed a bit stressed. I got the sense from some of his team that Vučić was hard to handle, had a temper, also the ministers said they had to stress constantly how good he was and how he was the only one capable of getting anything done.

In to meet him. Very tall. He had really bad flu, closed his eyes when he spoke. I went through the basics, the need for a clear strategy, the need for proper co-ordination, the need for it to be run as a team. He did quite a lot of 'the problem is', but he also felt as the opposition were useless, he would do well again. He wanted to join us for the dinner later, but clear he shouldn't because he was so ill. Gave him the *Burden of Power* [Volume 4 of Diaries] and he seemed quite touched by it. Joking about how he and I had been opposed when he was the [Slobodan] Milošević voice [former President of Serbia, died in war crimes detention centre in 2006] and I was TB's.

He talked about UK politics, said Cameron was viewed as a bit of a lightweight but he felt he would beat Ed. He said re. the EU membership drive, for a lot of people it was less about being in the EU than a process to drive change. I said there were countries that definitely wanted to join and he said name one. I could see Andreas prickling in case I started talking about Albania, which given recent events he had asked me not to talk about too much. I decided at this stage to ignore the cynicism and press on. Back to the main points re. strategy.

After lunch a meeting with about ten or a dozen ministers, and a strategy workshop. Mixed quality, two or three good, one or two genuinely useless. One or two, health or defence for example, saw their job as to defend the PM whatever. I was told that the defence guy and a couple of others literally went out and defended him about everything. Health and Labour ministers were sending each other texts and cynical looks, being a bit dismissive, but the others seemed up for it.

They realised they had no strategy, that they were siloed, not co-ordinated, and they relied too much on the PM. It was not enough to say the PM's speech was the strategy. There was too much in it, and it had to be brought down to the level of messages and slogans, and a single-page graphic. I think by the end they were up for it. I went to the pool, then out for dinner with our team plus Ivica, chief of staff. Good discussion, and I ended up drawing a message map on the Iguana table mat (like the old days in the Camden Brasserie). Essentially a top message, three boxes on economy, trust/reform, and empowering youth, with a separate box for foreign policy and positioning. Policy strands and messages below that. We mapped it out pretty quickly and it would work.

Vučić had wanted to join us but was really not on good form. He was a bit old-school on the media, felt he could demand stories were not run etc. It was so odd to be there at all really, he having been Milošević's information minister, me having done the NATO job during Kosovo. Ivica said that they would never recognise Kosovo but they would manage it. Nice food, good chat, they were much friendlier and welcoming than I expected. Edi stole the show at the Paris march with red white blue crayons in his breast pocket.* Edi sent me a message that he had said to Cameron that TB said the economy was recovering and AC said it wasn't. Cameron said this was the difference between statesmanship and Old Labour immaturity! Helle sent a message apologising for being next to Cameron on the march. 'It was him or Netanyahu.'

Tuesday 13 January
Gym, breakfast, meeting with the team in their office in the PM's building, which looked out over bombed-out buildings. They had been kept not as

---

* Millions took part in Unity marches across France to demonstrate against the attacks on the *Charlie Hebdo* magazine, police officers and a kosher supermarket.

a reminder but because of the reparation cost and also protests because some of them were historic buildings. Meeting with the comms and media guys from all the ministries who were OK, probably better quality than ministers in terms of their own jobs, but the usual story in terms of not having access, not being taken seriously, lots of 'the problem is'. One or two of them felt their ministers got it, but most did not. The girl from the economy department was almost in tears, she said afterwards it was far worse than anyone had said. With a bit of leadership they would do OK.

Then to a meeting with the PM and our team. I gave him my assessment, mixed quality, some goodwill but no clarity and no real sense of team. He had to build that. I mentioned the girl who was almost in tears, he asked who it was and when the aide couldn't answer, he turned on her really. I had been through the rules of strategy with the press people and the ministers and I said to him he had to do more to lead and inspire the team. I went through the one-pager and he loved it. 'I like this a lot, this is what we need.' He said he wanted to do a big thing, launch it as a major event. I said yes but get the team bought into it first. Take this as the end process and work towards it from now. He seemed to get that, but I worried he was going to jump in too soon.

He asked me to come back again, and I said OK, but let's see how this goes forward first. He went all Serb on me towards the end, said that nothing in the region could happen without Serbia, not just Serbia, but then he ran through all the percentages of Serb population in Balkan countries. His other big point was that Germany were all over the region, and Britain was nowhere. I said I wondered if that was because of the Kosovo legacy. He said people had moved on. 'Have you had a bad word from anyone? No. We have moved on. But Germany is winning everything here, and Britain is nowhere.' Out to the airport with Andreas, Zurich to London. Ed was chasing me re. tomorrow's PMQs, wanting lines re. Cameron clearly trying to duck TV debates. Also getting dates for TV debate camp and feeling I just didn't want to be there. Home late.

Wednesday 14 January

Lunch chez Bob [restaurant], major diet lapse when I went into Everyman Cinema and got a big bag of chocolate-covered honeycomb balls. Tying up loose ends then off to the Spurs–Burnley Cup replay with Rory. Two up, four down. Bit of abuse re. blood on hands at half-time. Then also an email from *The Times* who had the *Ham&High* story. They had my statement but it meant it would go big tomorrow. After getting home, dealing with that, talking to the paper, also with Dave B, long chat. Dave said he had shaken things up and people were finding their way a bit. Darryl was offered the job but was thinking about it – had a bad vibe re. Hugh, he told me – and though I was trying to get Dave to woo him, he seemed reluctant. The press stuff from the other day had gone really well. Jeremy Darroch [Sky CEO] had said to DB unprompted that they seemed to be getting much better PR. 'I didn't tell them it was your work. They still don't know you've been around.' Also had a really nice chat with Grace in the early hours re. her analysis and her course.

I loved her openness and determination to get to where she needs to be professionally and personally. It will take time and there will be lots of bumps on the road but so long as we all keep learning from them it is all good experience. Major death fear and the abandonment issues are probably linked.

Thursday 15 January

The *Ham&High* were doing the story on the front, and *The Times* had it too. I got loads of calls following up. I sensed most of the papers saw it for what it was, and I went into overdrive on Twitter against Galloway, and also the fact that this guy could say all this stuff without even being identified. Geoff Martin [*Ham&High* editor] had a weird defence, said he decided to run it without naming the other party because 'from a news point of view, no one really cares who that person is'. But he said he was not comfortable about not naming him. Tim did a good job getting some of the more lurid headlines in the nationals changed, e.g. 'Campbell "punched and spat" at elderly man' (sixty-one ffs). Galloway had over-reached on it. Geoff Martin's editorial was very supportive of me. Even Mail Online comments broadly on my side. Kelly Swanson [Mayweather team] must have seen it because she did a tweet that I needed to get down to Floyd's gym to learn how to punch properly!

I sent a note to Dave B and Fran re. the need to sort modus operandi. I think Darryl and Ben had found the whole interview experience a bit weird. I got a rash of calls following up *The Times* and the *Ham&High*. Put full statement on blog.

Saw David S. We were talking about me maybe doing full-on analysis, but he felt that my lifestyle would make it difficult. He said he had done it twice, and it was very painful sometimes. He seemed to think I was OK, keep on the Sertraline, record dreams etc. Talked a lot about Grace. Also re. Ed M wanting me back, and he said I should think about what I want, and push the demands of others to one side. Trouble is I felt guilty.

Dinner with Edi and Endri at the Goring. He was over for an art event tomorrow night but wanted to start discussion about the local elections campaign, which we agreed should not be too shouty or over-claiming.

Something fairly prosaic and 'next steps' focused. He was on good form, relaxed and seemed pretty pleased with the way things were going. The opposition were all noise without too much real pressure on them. We had a long chat with Vučić. I said he nearly screwed up the whole thing because he had said to Vučić he heard I was going there, and that was before Vučić knew. They'd had to cover up a bit. Edi was really keen to build relations, felt that an Albania–Serbia partnership could really be a big thing, a real change in the region after centuries of bloody conflict, and he wanted me to play a role in it.

I had felt that the first meeting with Vučić was not the place to raise it but I was pretty sure we would get there. I passed on what Vučić had said re. nothing being possible without Serbia, and he said 'they certainly help'. He agreed with Vučić that the Germans were winning the power and economic battles in the region. He said he had seen Cameron close up again in Paris and yet again been struck by how lightweight he was compared with TB or Merkel. He agreed that the *Je suis Charlie* thing had gone a bit far. Agreed I would go out next week and plan the local elections, and come back with him when he went to Vienna.

Friday 16 January

Long chat with Dave. We had still not sorted the comms job. Papers quieter and broadly OK re. the spitting guy. Did my first Skype conference, speaking to an audience in Wales hosted by Andy McCann [performance coach]. Good questions based on the fact he had clearly read the book. Good response down the line. Cameron in Washington getting fairly big licks from Obama. Sorting out Donald flat situation.

Saturday 17 January

Gavin sent me a message saying Edi had been terrific last night at the art event, relaxed and charismatic and very un-Balkan, and I forwarded it to Edi who sent me a really nice email, saying how far he felt he had come since I told him about the energy lightbulb and the need to switch it on before entering a room. It was a really warm and effusive message. He said I know you don't cope well with compliments but this is heartfelt.

Up to Burnley, lunch, chat with Brendan who said they had all been laughing at the UCFB [University College of Football Business] board meeting re. my 'fight'. Two up, but lost 3–2 to Crystal Palace, very disappointing. Home for our second first on *MotD* [*Match of the Day*] of the season.

Sunday 18 January

Slept till 10.30. Tired. India Knight [*Sunday Times*] was very supportive in her column about the altercation, and generally it had come out fine, I think. Off to Heathrow, and set off for Tirana via Vienna. Worked on plane, arrived after midnight.

Monday 19 January

Strategy meeting. Everyone seemed to have a cold, including Edi. They were planning for the local elections and we were working out the best way to balance the positive claims of change and improvement and the need to emphasise what more needed to be done. The strategy group was a mix of those involved last time, and one or two new ones. They had a fair bit of energy going for them but Endri seemed quite down again. He didn't feel that they were really getting the best out of what they had. I went down with yet another cold – Fiona was convinced it was all the flying, and maybe she was right. But everyone in Tirana seemed to be ill.

Friday 23 January

Working at home and then off to record an interview with Alex Brooker for *The Last Leg* [Channel 4 news show]. I had never seen it before, but it seemed to be doing well with younger people. I was advising them on how to interview Clegg next week, e.g. first question 'Boris Johnson – statesman or twat?' Gave them the idea of a bullshit buzzer, whenever he didn't answer the question, hit the buzzer and move on. Then they were trying to grill me on what I had for breakfast, but needless to say they switched to Chilcot, which was back in the headlines because of yet another delay. Stuck to my line that I was not saying anything until it was out. Part of me was tempted to say I had not had a fucking letter.

Saturday 24 January

F and I out for dinner with [Sir] Keir Starmer [prospective Labour MP, former director of public prosecutions] and wife, Vicky. Both very likeable. I was probably a little too frank about how bad Ed was at the debate camp, and also re. how I felt about our prospects. He seemed pretty switched on. Too early to say he had what it took to go all the way but he was a cut above the average candidate, for sure. Maybe a bit too lawyerly, not instinct-driven, but smart and sorted. I liked her too. Quirky sense of humour.

Sunday 25 January

Audrey's 90th. Gavin and family, most of her old friends. Nice day and Audrey enjoyed it. Fiona spoke well, Calum announced the plan to take her to Hull, and all good.

Monday 26 January

Working at home, out in the evening for a speech at a BearingPoint [business management consultants] conference in the RAC club. Going through the themes of the book, which worked well. Former Labour candidate there who was saying how tragic it was TB was being branded as toxic, and how hard he felt it was to get motivated by Ed. Sense I got though was that neither party was giving out any sense of passion or generating real enthusiasm.

Tuesday 27 January

Meeting with Stewart Regan, SFA CEO, and Barrie Walker, the independent non-exec. They were trying very hard to persuade me to join the board. They had someone else lined up but they would prefer it if it was me. I mentioned my stance on alcohol and gambling which I suspected could become a problem for both of us down the track. Clearly there were issues with relations with SPFL [Scottish Professional Football League], and the clubs tended to represent their own interests in the SFA, but they did at least have an understanding of the need for a community role which could become a USP for Scotland.

Celtic basically wanted to play in England. Rangers was a basket case and a law unto itself, and the SFA had very little clout there as it was a PLC. But they were keeping tabs on the Mike Ashley situation as he was driving coach and horses through some of the rules re. player and board control.* I was keen, but worried it would take a lot more time than they were suggesting.

Wednesday 28 January

To Gatwick for an all-day strategy session with the CEO and the key advisers of Jersey Telecom. I think they got a lot out of it – they certainly said they did. Gatwick Hotel was the place we met because they were worried if I landed in Jersey it would become a big thing and everything

---

* Controversial owner of Newcastle United Ashley had seen his attempt to raise his shareholding in Rangers to 29.9 per cent rejected by the SFA.

they did got in the news there, often negatively. But I made the case all day that if they had their own strategy, they would be able to worry less and drive it more.

Back for an Alcohol Concern dinner in the Lords. Dry January had gone well, their idea. Bumped into Michael Farthing who was going to another dinner, which was weird because Calum had sent us an email showing there was a petition to oust him [as Vice-Chancellor] from Sussex University. I did my usual spiel on the booze stuff, then a good roundtable, but they needed more voices and they were too quick to say that because it was alcohol it was just hard. A *Telegraph* journo who was dry now and kept telling me – and later tweeted – how young I looked. A photographer who had done whole books on Britain and booze. Nice enough evening but they needed more oomph.

Thursday 29 January

In for a meeting with Godric, still trying to make sense of the Sky set-up. Round the corner to David Bailey's studio for a shoot for *GQ* for the planned book on fathers and sons. He chatted away the whole time, some of it interesting, some of it a lot of shit, but he was likeable enough. He said last time he did me – it was with Joe Haines [former *Mirror* colleague] – he found me a bit aloof. He liked my tweeds but not my trousers! He was banging on about politicians like a lot of people do. Doesn't like TB. Loved Maggie. Doesn't rate Cameron. Bailey's son was working as his assistant. To Millbank to see Jonathan Powell who was doing a radio programme on politicians' language.

Friday 30 January

Interview re. the *Winners* book for *FHM* [magazine]. We went through chapter by chapter, and it felt easy and straightforward. Then I set off for Kent by car, for the first of a three-day debate camp with Ed M and team. Axelrod was over, with his team, plus Douglas, Greg Beales, Spencer Livermore, Marc Sears [EM adviser], Ayesha and the crowd. It was at [media entrepreneur Lord] Waheed Ali's place, lovely house, which I remembered from the time we went there for a planning meeting before one of our party conferences. I had been feeling very down about our ability to win, but Waheed was convinced we would win.

His basic point was that the Tories and the media had thrown loads at Ed and he was still standing, and qualities would come through. Also, Cameron's strengths were becoming his weaknesses, and he felt the public were looking for reasons not to vote for him, and we had enough time still to provide them. He was absolutely sure, and almost convincing. But I still felt we lacked clarity of strategy, a real sense of teamship, and there was a lack of energy too, across the shadow Cabinet especially. Also we still did not have the big washing line that Peter M used to talk about, from which everything else could be hung. I felt it was probably in the inequality area but interestingly when I raised that in the main meeting later, Ed said he felt that if our main message, as authored by Douglas and Axelrod, was 'Britain works best when working families succeed' then we had to stick with that.

I didn't feel it was sharp enough. I also had my usual – failed again – attempt to explain why there was still time to mount and win the politics of the economy by focusing on the record as a signal of how life and the country were better under Labour than under Tory governments. It was a battle I had lost four years ago, yet I would keep going on it because it was so obvious and frankly a terrible blind spot that Ed and co. couldn't see it. Tom Baldwin told me later the reality was even worse. Not only did they not want to defend the record, they would actually like to attack it, and he had at least won the battle to stop that from happening. When I arrived, up at the barn where they were looking at Ed's stump speech, there was the usual chatty stuff and then a discussion. Ed was good at bringing people in and taking their view.

Axelrod was fairly languid, clever and smart, but like me he had a book out soon – and his was the big one, his main autobiography – and I wondered both how engaged he was with everything else he had on, and how much he really got the differences between UK and US politics and campaigning. I liked him though, smart, warm, and a lovely manner. Larry was more streetfighty in a way, and Mike was good at spotting things when we went through actual debate. The mood was a lot better than the last time, and so was Ed's performance. That was a good sign, that he had maybe reflected on why the previous session had been so poor and changed things. Cameron's shenanigans meant it looked like we were heading to a couple of seven-way debates which would be absurd, and one one-to-one, so that was our main focus for the first session. Ed was wearing a suit this time, and also standing and looking better. He was definitely more confident.

Greg and Douglas had both taken me to one side and said that re. the last time Ed felt I had been channelling me as much as Cameron and maybe I should tone down a bit. He felt any aggression when playing Cameron in debate prep was as much about my own anger as thinking what Cameron might do or say. I probably toned down too much though, because I was pretty sure Cameron would play fairly hardball. But the bottom line was that he was a lot better. He didn't let me run over him as I had the last time. The US contingent had flown in overnight and at one point I could see all of them struggling to keep their eyes open. I did feel he was still lacking a really clear and powerful argument on a par with the Tories. Economy plus leadership. He was quite good at turning all my positive messages on the economy into an out-of-touch 'everything is fixed' place.

Had a chat with Axelrod on his book, and his planned tour, and he said he was hoping there would be no screaming headlines. I sensed he had the same attitude to Obama as I did to TB, that there were enough people out there ready to attack him and point up any weaknesses without him adding to his woes. I went for a run then down for dinner in the main house, where Waheed was pouring drinks and they were chatting over US politics. Dinner was a pretty jolly event, but the Yanks were tired and so was I so we went without the movie screening Waheed had set up. The Ed team definitely felt they were in a stronger position than before and to some extent they were. But some pretty big fundamentals remained unaddressed I would say.

Saturday 31 January

Sat with Axelrod at breakfast and we talked book tours a bit and then had a pretty frank chat about the whole operation. We both felt Ed was improving but a long way short of what and where he needed to be to knock over Cameron, and to win over waverers. Waheed was absolutely sure we were on course, and it was always good to have someone being so positive. Axelrod and I were due to be there for the morning only so we had a bit of a debrief re. yesterday then another full round of head-to-head, me as Cameron, Ed as Ed. I asked the camera guys to say what they thought of yesterday and they basically said that they felt Ed talked a lot about a plan but it didn't really come over what it was. Also that too often when I was speaking he looked almost lifeless. Axelrod put a note on his lectern saying, 'You can smile, you are not a detainee.'

It's true that his resting face had a tendency to drain itself of energy, as though literally he was resting, and we had a chat about the need to understand there was a camera on him the whole time, and even when he was not speaking people were making judgements about body language, energy, facial reaction. But he was definitely getting to a clearer and sharper message and having been so down on him last time, I made a point of talking up the positives when we had a bit of a wash up. We did all the obvious policy stuff, Tom slipping me notes to keep me up to speed with what Cameron had said on things, and I was framing everything with economy plus leadership, whereas he was rather going point to point. During a break, I told Ed I was doing the *Sunday Times* next week, who were serialising *Winners*, and they would be desperate for a 'Campbell Whacks Loser Miliband' headline. I talked about the one-word OST section and asked what his one-word S for Strategy would be. It was very revealing, in that he said 'people' and then 'better' and I explained that neither of those were strategy. I suggested inequality and discontinuity, but neither quite worked.

But it was alarming that they did not have the answer to such a simple question. Likewise what were our top three policy priorities? What were our strategic rebuttal lines? The clarity they needed was not there. I did feel it went a lot better nonetheless. Off to meet Rory to watch Sunderland v Burnley. Poor game, lost two–nil.

Sunday 1 February

Watched Andy Murray lose to Novak Djokovic in Melbourne [Australian Open final], then Celtic Rangers. Lots of hype but poor game on a poor pitch, Celtic never in danger. Went to see *The Theory of Everything*. Probable Oscar for Eddie Redmayne. But why did today's top performers seem to be from such a narrow class background?

Monday 2 February

Another bloody cold or something. Bumped into Alan Rusbridger [retiring editor, *The Guardian*] and talked a little about the election – he hoped I was getting involved – and his succession plan. Probably Kath Viner. Home to play the pipes for BBC Creative [culture archive], an [Alan] Yentob [executive and presenter] request. The guy they sent said he sometimes got depression and was keen to make mental health films. To St Pancras Renaissance for a meeting with Dave B, Fran, Hugh Chambers and Godric. Hugh had done quite a good paper on overall strategy, which sort of dovetailed with what we had done.

We had not gone into nearly as much detail on the comms side and I sensed Dave was a bit underwhelmed. I later emailed him and Fran and said they were difficult to work with, because we never quite pinned down the clarity about who was doing what, and so the goalposts tended to move the whole time. Later talked to Walter Smith and Gordon Strachan re. SFA. Walter felt I should do it, and that they did have plans for change. Gordon was a funny guy – told me Phil Bardlsey [Scotland international] would never play again 'because his wife is on that Cheshire Housewives thing'. Said he didn't do politics but I sensed he worked his way round the SFA pretty well.

Tuesday 3 February

Went to see Matthew Freud in his fantastic new office. Really stunning. Not just the great art, but the energy in the main working space. He had refound some of his energy, I think. But the marriage break-up [from Elisabeth Murdoch] was really still front of mind. She had another guy, and was very much back in the Murdoch family bosom. I was doing the *Sunday Times* interview later and picked his and other brains re. how to avoid the headline they would most want, namely 'Campbell blasts loser Miliband'. He felt to take it to the one real leadership test before – beating his brother. Not a bad line. I felt I could also talk up recent improvements. On the way out we bumped into a Burnley fan complaining that we hadn't bought anyone in the transfer window which ended yesterday.

Lunch with Allegra Stratton [political editor, *Newsnight*]. She felt Ed was doing better but that he was still not punching through. The sense in the lobby was that Cameron was not that great, Ed was better than the public perception, but neither was he setting the world on fire. She said she was a supporter, and though constrained by where she was, more than at *The Guardian*, keen to help. Planning meeting at Random House then the interview with Tim Shipman of the *Sunday Times*. Went pretty well. Felt OK pushing the book and felt the argument re. sport teaching politics and business was a good one. He didn't push me too hard either on Chilcot or on Ed and in so far as he had a story I think it was in the area of me saying MPs should have psychological support.

Long chat with Stewart Regan. I asked if he was there [SFA] for the long haul. He said he was interested in the FA job but not convinced he would get it. If he did not get that he was there for the long haul. I said my concerns were whether I could really make a difference without too much work, and also I said I would not stop speaking out re. alcohol in sport.

Wednesday 4 February

Train with Rory to Manchester. Worked on speech for the Premier League event I was doing for Paul Lake. Lots of the academy managers there. I did a talk through the various chapters of the book, trying to make relevant to them. OK Q&A. Good session, though it did make me think Rory was probably too bright for this scene. We met Fran Millar and Brendan Flood to discuss the UCFB idea. Dave B had this idea of the human performance knowledge hub and I had said at the away day brainstorm they should think of it being a physical building and I thought a tie-up with Brendan might be good for both.

Good chat, then Fran and I had a session re. Sky. Later Dave called and said he really wanted us to stick with it because already we were making a difference. I was sure we could but it needed to work better than it was. Long chat on the phone with Rod Petrie about the SFA. Stewart was trying to get people to push me towards it but I sensed the alcohol issue would become a problem. Train back then to a dinner for Aberdeen Asset. [Dame] Katherine Grainger was on stage as I arrived. She spoke well and I liked her.

Good chat over dinner. I was between [Sir] Martin Gilbert [Aberdeen Asset boss], who was to interview me on stage, and Geoff Aberdein, who had been Alex Salmond's chief of staff and was now with Martin. So we had a great chat re. Salmond and the campaign. He said Alex 'really likes you' and has said so in his book. He said they really had felt one week or so out from the referendum they thought they were going to win and that poll which shocked the system was a real blow. I said I felt it would always have been No but because Cameron had fucked it up since if there was another one Yes would win. He said Nicola [Sturgeon] would be having mixed feelings re. Alex being in Westminster. But as the evening wore on – and he mentioned a couple of times that he had been speaking to Alex today – he raised directly the idea of Salmond as DPM in a Labour coalition government. After the Q&A with Martin, during which I said I felt Labour could win, and said why, Geoff said you don't believe that, you know he can't win a majority, but he might do it with Alex in there as No. 2. I said I would try to sus it out.

Thursday 5 February

Off to Essex with Najma to sign 4,000 books in Colchester. Just under 1,000 an hour. Did some interviews on the way re. Clarke Carlisle in *The Sun*. He had admitted he had tried to kill himself when he jumped in front of the lorry. John Browne called asking if I could help Cuadrilla [oil and gas company] who were trying to get fracking going in Lancs, but they were being stymied by the council. Then Tom Baldwin called, saying George Parker, who had done a big profile of Ed for the *FT* magazine this weekend, was running a story that Peter and I had approached Alan Johnson and asked him to say he would go for the leadership. There was of course a grain of truth in it, but I had to square the circle so it did not damage Ed.

I called George and said it was not me asking Alan to do it, but me calling from overseas to ask if there was anything in the rumours, and Alan had been adamant from the word go it was a non-starter. True. Ish. Tom said he had been heavy about it, said that I was known as Mr Loyalty in the party, and I just would not do something like this… Peter on the other hand! Home and then out to do a dinner for Sarah Sackman in

Finchley. Keir S there, also a few bods from Gibraltar as Sarah's mum was from there. Sarah spoke really well. Lance A interview off. He had now been charged with a driving offence, having said his girlfriend had been driving when in fact it was him.

Friday 6 February

Off to Clarke Carlisle's place a few miles outside Harrogate. He was at the doctor's and I spent a bit of time with Gemma, who seemed pretty stressed. She told me a bit about the day Clarke tried to kill himself. He had gone off sleeping rough, nobody knowing where he was, and he had jumped in front of the lorry going at 58mph. Amazing he lived. He had jumped in arm and shoulder first and didn't even break them. But he had internal bleeding, a massive scar across the top of his head, and obviously it was going to take time to get his head sorted. He came in, wearing shorts and flip flops despite the cold. Big hug, and he said thanks for being so supportive. He said he had read *All in the Mind* and he just could not believe how much it spoke to him.

I said when I heard the news, I worried he got the idea from the suicide scene in the book. He said he had already decided that was the way. He said when he realised he was still alive, he felt devastated. But now, having survived, he felt it had been a message from above that he had to see it out. He was sure he wouldn't do it again. He talked a lot about the other people at the place where he recovered and said he wanted to write a book called 'The Suicide Fantasy'. He said they all spoke of this feeling that suicide would make everything better. He seemed pretty good considering, and was due back doing radio tomorrow. But he had been sacked by ITV and that may have been a factor.

I stayed for an hour or two. He said he wanted to start a charity or trust and would I chair it? Off to Darwen for the fundraiser for Will Straw [prospective parliamentary candidate]. Jack [Will's father, former Foreign Secretary] there looking quite old and worn. He said he had got his Chilcot letter, was shocked I hadn't had one. He was fighting hard because he felt the whole thing was ludicrous. It was a good turnout, lots of Burnley–Blackburn banter. The loudest applause, as so often, when I said we needed to do a better job of defending the record.

Saturday 7 February

Out for a run, breakfast, chat with Tom B who seemed to have done pretty well with the *FT*. The story wasn't really running far and Peter M did a good job on the radio. They had been furious he was going on, Ed had spoken to him but in the end it was probably helpful. I spoke to Alan J, who was in Paris, to make sure we were on the same page. Long chat with Tessa re. the general scene. She said she understood I did not want to get too involved re. mayoralty but if ever I did she would love it if I would. Drove to Birmingham, met Kelly Sotherton [former heptathlete] and she asked me to help her and a colleague get going with an events company. I liked her. She said long term she wanted to get into a sports politics role.

Chelsea were at Villa so I sorted a ticket with Steve Atkins [Chelsea head of comms] and sat with him and Michael Emenalo [technical director]. Not a great game, Villa poor, and Chelsea won 2–1. To [Labour organiser] Fiona Gordon's for a bath, then out to the Labour Finance and Industry Group. Bishop of Brum there, liked him a lot. Q&A good again. F in Glasgow with Calum.

Sunday 8 February

Breakfast with Fiona Gordon and Steve McCabe [Labour MP] going over the political scene. They felt we were unlikely to win. Just too much negativity about Ed. They felt that his people just didn't get it. Steve was very astute, and of course Fiona was second to none at what she did. Set off for Burnley. Two–nil up v West Brom and then blew it again. Long drive back. Ed called re. message narrative. He had been speaking to Peter who had emphasised the need for some kind of overall message. Christ!

Monday 9 February

Into Mayfair to see John Browne who briefed me re. Cuadrilla and the politics of the fracking issue in Lancs. He wanted a more aggressive approach and wanted me to help. Not sure it was my scene. To LLR to see Cathy and go through a presentation on the new name, Bloodwise, and the way they would present it. Home to do *Sunday Times* pix on the Heath. Another shout of 'war criminal'. Then to Soho for Labour pub quiz. Great turnout and good evening, even if we lost. [Former GB aide, Baroness] Sue Nye's team with Rachel [Kinnock], Patrick Loughran [former PM aide] and Anna Yearley [Ed M's political secretary] winning. Neil runner-up, did 'we're all riiiight' as he accepted his prize, a box of Celebrations. Chat with Carol Linforth who felt things were improving but that the Ed M team was way short of what it needed to be.

My team was pretty hopeless. Ed called for a chat. He was fine about the *FT*, seemed to accept our explanation even if he knew we had big doubts. He was not a big blamer, and had a calm and resilience. He was, however, still behind the curve. He had been struck by Peter saying there was no clear narrative, but why was that only clear now?

Tuesday 10 February

Guardian and international media doing a big number on HSBC [bank] tax avoidance. They had got stacks of emails and other papers showing the extent of it. I tweeted merrily all day. Ed M out on it. Important moment to get up his 'whose side are you on?' message. It also went to Cameron's judgement in getting [Lord] Stephen Green [former HSBC chairman, trade and investment minister] into the government. Usual Coulson-style non-diligence. To the RNIB [Royal National Institute of Blind People radio] studios to record the intro and the last chapter of the book. Still not decided who was reading the whole thing.

Home for a bit then out to the Treasury for a talk to civil servants re. mental health. Good turnout and response. One of them from Keighley, and Dad had been their vet. Dinner with Grace and her friend from film school then to the Almeida for *The Merchant of Venice* with an Elvis touch. Lou Macari and Paddy Crerand both called me re. tomorrow and we arranged to meet up. Efforts to contact Fergie went nowhere. I had no idea what had happened but he was definitely offside about something. Paddy raging about the Tories and why we were not killing them over the hedge fund ball.

Wednesday 11 February

FHM guy round to do an interview re. the book. Chat Lionel Barber re. the 25 Feb event. *FT* were keen for me to do an op-ed piece to coincide. Train to Manchester, working on bits and bobs, booked into hotel, then walked out to Old Trafford. Met Lou Macari who was with Neil Baldwin, who had been his kitman at Stoke and had become famous through the brilliant film *Marvellous*. Just as nice as the film suggested. Labour. Asking re. TB. Saying the country had gone backwards with this lot. MUTV interview saying United not what they were, then to the away end, met up with Calum. Battered them first half but conceded a set piece, equalised, then conceded another just before half-time. Eventually lost 3–1 but God United were poor. Got a cab back, dinner in an Indian near the hotel, watch *MotD*, bed. Paddy Crerand really really hated Cameron. Hilarious on the subject.

Thursday 12 February

Bad night. Catarrh and wheeze. I had seen the doctor yesterday and got another batch of antibiotics. Up and off at 5.30 to get the train to Birmingham. Good hour or so to hang around. Did a bit of work then off on Flybe to Lyon. Bought some Valentine's Day presents then waited for Fiona to collect me. Fixing to see Chris Froome in Monaco on Sunday.

Friday 13 February

Starting to blog again and being much more positive re. Ed. Partly because Cameron was so awful, but also because Labour were starting to get a bit more energy and life into the campaign.

Saturday 14 February

Cameron had come out with some utter drivel about stopping benefits for fat people and alcoholics. I tweeted a comparison with Merkel, busy dealing with Ukraine and Greece. Then blogged on that, HSBC, also defending Harriet re. her pink bus that she was taking round the country. Cameron was a total no-go, he really was. All about the PR stunt, no strategy, just photocalls and shit ideas. We really needed to hit him harder. I felt Labour should welcome and embrace these attacks as sign of their fear. The papers also becoming more and more ridiculous. Saw that tonight when the *Sunday Times* take on the book/interview was 'Every MP should have a shrink – AC', which the *Telegraph* immediately lifted as 'Ed Miliband needs a shrink – AC'.

We set off p.m. for Nice, took ages to get to the hotel, because a big festival was on and the Promenade des Anglais was not allowing traffic. Dreadful rain though and the first two days had been washed out. We had a nice time wandering around the pedestrian precinct and then the old town. Hadn't changed that much. Jack Straw called me. He had been the victim of a sting by *Dispatches* who had done to him what they did a while back to Geoff Hoon, Pat Hewitt and Steve Byers [ex-Labour ministers], a fake company trying to hire him. He sent me all the correspondence and I felt, as did Godric to whom I sent the papers, that he was on strong ground. I had been a bit slow to pick up on the '5k a day' line in their questions though. I said I felt his aim should be to try to get them not to include him in the programme. That required a really strong lawyer's letter alongside a plan to pre-empt if they did decide to go ahead.

He seemed relieved at what I was saying. 'So you don't think I am a crook?' Certainly not. He had looked really tired at the Darwen fundraiser and I guess a combination of this, Chilcot and the torture inquiry must be really grim, and feel like a terrible end to his career.* It also meant, and he said as much, that the Lords would not happen. If this was swilling around him his appointment would get blocked, especially if he had said, as they were suggesting, that he was definitely going there, and his work

---

* Documents found in Libya after the fall of the Gaddafi regime claimed an operation, conducted by MI6 alongside the CIA, saw a Libyan dissident and his pregnant wife kidnapped, tortured and imprisoned in 2004, when Jack Straw was the UK's Foreign Secretary.

for them would be easier. I worked on various lines he could take, but did say that it needed to be consistent with what he said, and it was never easy to recall exactly. Be careful not to get caught saying something misleading.

Sunday 15 February

Sunday Times ran the section on the Queen from the book. There was a fun run along the seafront at Nice. Nice atmosphere. We walked around the port and then around the old town, breakfast in the flower market, gym, potter, blog – I wrote re. the *Sunday Times* serial and in particular took the *Telegraph* to task for their 'Ed needs a shrink' line. The *ST* news story was fine apart from the headline, and the News Review coverage was terrific, over three pages, with a huge graphic of the Queen in three of four stamps and me in the other. Getting lots of bids for radio and telly. The line re. politicians needing psychological support not a bad one. Set off for Monaco. Chris and Michelle Froome had booked Amici Miei, a very nice Italian restaurant in Fontvieille. We had a really good chat with them. Godric arrived half an hour in and we worked our way towards a decent strategy, and later I sent them a long paper, ideas for broadening and deepening his profile, also trying to develop his popularity in the UK, especially through long-form media stuff.

Michelle was not as I expected. Not as pushy as I had been led to believe she would be. Savvier than Chris in many ways, definitely watching his back, but open and welcoming. They were both very frank. He was naïve in some ways but thoughtful and intelligent about himself and the sport. Totally in the cycling bubble though. I asked him who the UK PM was and it took him a bit to get it. He admitted he was obsessed re. cycling.

Fiona asked about Bradley Wiggins, innocently, and actually they were reasonably polite, though I had been reading Chris's book – fascinating re. his background – and he clearly hated Brad as a self-obsessed charlatan, not a team player. Dave B had said the team actually preferred Chris. He had clearly put up with a lot. We talked through a few ideas that we could get going, e.g. *Sports Illustrated* etc. He was keen to get a profile in the US but we figured that would require him to go for Lance. He had been out on the bike for five hours alone this morning.

We agreed to do a note for him and also I would do him for *GQ* as part of the long-form strategy. Liked them both, so did Fiona. She was South African but Welsh-born. I said to him he should not hide his African roots. He would never be seen as a Brit like Brad and he should just be who he is. Cup of tea with Godders to work out next steps then we set off for home through dreadful rain. Random House were tweeting out quotes from the book and Mayweather retweeted one re. him which got a lot of traction. Thanks Kelly.

Monday 16 February

Massage in Malaucène, work on Froome note, and also a piece for the *FT* re. mental health/politics. Andrew Mitchell had sent me a nice text re. the Queen piece – as had many others, including Charles Anson [ex-Buckingham Palace press secretary], who said it was the best analysis of her he had read in a long time, which was nice. Andrew and I had been talking about putting together a mental health campaign, but we had put it on the backburner while he dealt with his 'Plebgate' problems. But as he had got in touch, I sent him a message saying he should call for a chat any time. He called back, and said he wanted to pick my brains. He was going to have to pay the copper £80k.* It was cheaper than trying to defend himself again. He was £2 million down and was having to borrow from friends as well as sell homes. Sharon [wife] had been great but both of them were being treated for depression. He wanted to stay as an MP. He even felt if he could get out from under he could return as a minister. He talked a lot about what people would think and I said he should not worry about it. He should decide what he wants, write down why he wants to do it all again, and then write down the advantages of not doing it.

His wife wanted them to start a new life somewhere, maybe the US with Bill Gates foundation. I could tell he felt the pull of the Commons still. We talked for an hour or so and he was effusive in thanks. He said he didn't know who to talk to and he felt I had real wisdom at this kind of thing. I talked to Charlie about it and said he should talk to him too, and maybe steer him away from thinking he could resurrect a Cabinet career. It had clearly been a terrible period for him, and I still felt he had been hard done by, but the judgement was done and he had to move on. Charlie felt the Jack situation was not good.

Tuesday 17 February

Jack S and Rosie [Winterton, Labour MP] called me again re. the *Dispatches* thing. Rosie told me that there was a problem because when Hewitt, Hoon, Byers did it, Jack went on the *Today* programme to defend their suspension from the PLP. Rosie felt it would be hard not to suspend Jack. For a start,

---

* On the evening of 19 September 2012, Mitchell, then the government's Chief Whip, was cycling out of Downing Street. A policeman, PC Toby Rowland, asked him to dismount and walk the cycle through the pedestrian entrance. Mitchell argued and, according to the officer, said, 'You don't run the f***ing government – you're f***ing plebs.' *The Sun* broke the story and although Mitchell denied using the word 'plebs' it became a major talking point and bad publicity led the politician to resign. Mitchell then sued *The Sun* for libel and PC Rowland sued Mitchell for calling him a liar. The judge found against Mitchell, who faced an enormous bill for costs.

he was in breach for using his office for a meeting like this. Also, she said he had apparently boasted about changes he had made and contacts he had, and 'my name', and also talked about 5k per day. She felt it would be grisly. So did Charlie.

Ed M called during the PSG–Chelsea match (1–1), I thought re. Jack but actually he wanted to pick my brains on story development. Re. Jack he said it was pretty open and shut so far as he was concerned. He had a policy line on no second jobs, and he would have to use this to put that over. Jack had been foolish, he felt, but he couldn't see how he could avoid suspension à la Hoon etc., especially in light of the *Today* interview. All sad for Jack. Re. the general scene, he felt he had had a good week re. HSBC and nailing the Tories as friends of the hedge fund guys. I said he still needed to watch the anti-business tone. Should do more to talk up business. He sounded a lot chirpier. I said he seemed to have more oomph. He said, 'It was since I beat you in the second debate.' I said I did it deliberately.

After another chat with Godric, I emailed Jack Straw. Horrible stuff for him. It was hardly surprising he couldn't remember every detail. But it meant being absolutely sure not to say anything that might be disproved by film material. I advised against trying to stop broadcast. The only actual wrongdoing might relate to the use of a parliamentary office, so pre-empt with a self-referral. I felt the best approach was to say that this was a classic sting operation and he regretted being caught up in it and lulled into saying some of the things he did. I said he should work out where he thought it would end and get there first.

Wednesday 18 February

I had been toing and froing with *GQ* re. a FOI request from Tom Gordon of the *Herald* [Scotland] – both Douglas and Aileen Easton [Scotland First Minister spokesperson] said he was a total snake – who wanted the unpublished parts of the Salmond interview. I told *GQ* to resist. Ludicrous demand. Aileen said Gordon was a total wanker. She said she was settling in with Nicola. Clearly a bit worried re. Salmond going to Westminster. He was obviously thinking he could be DPM. *Guardian* had video of Chelsea racist scum stopping a black guy getting on the Metro in Paris.

Thursday 19 February

Did a strong blog re. the Chelsea racists and what the club could do. Mike White called re. TB. There was a piece in *The Guardian* re. his Serbia contract and he wanted to do a piece defending what TB did. I gave him my usual lines. Sent through a note to Jack Straw following his sending me his latest note on the matter last night. Rosie called and said she, Charlie and Patrick Hennessy were seeing him later. I said to Jack he should work out where it would end and get there first. Rosie said later he had gone for that, but looked broken. Also, his lawyers were now advising him against a pre-emptive media strike.

I sent off a letter to IPSO re. the *Telegraph* story – 'Ed Miliband needs a shrink, says Alastair Campbell'. They had taken the *Sunday Times* interview about *Winners*, when I had said MPs could benefit from the kind of psychological support that sports stars take for granted, and headlined it, 'Every MP needs a shrink – Alastair Campbell'. OK, a distortion, but not worth a complaint. The *Telegraph* made it about Ed. I said I hardly ever complained, don't think I ever had about something related to myself, but I was keen to see if IPSO was as toothless and useless as its predecessors.

Saturday 21 February

Chelsea v Burnley. I took the book signed for José Mourinho and Steve Atkins and there was some talk of seeing him after the match, but a 1–1 draw and a 'tackle' by [Ashley] Barnes [Burnley striker] on [Nemanja] Matić [Chelsea], which led to Matić exploding and getting a red card, led to José throwing toys out and really going for us. I had lunch with Joe Hemani and a couple of American banker-type friends. Over to the press side to share the Clarets Player commentary with Phil Bird. It was OK, but not the best way to watch a match. Also, I got excited by a Barnes shot which led to the corner that led to our goal, a header by Ben Mee. I accidentally unplugged the whole box so that we were off air when the goal went in! Looked like the Lance visit to Texas was off again. *Sunday Times* Part 2 on the book did José, which looked pretty good. Liz called to say Graeme was not well, and they had taken him to hospital.

Sunday 22 February

Up early and off into *Marr* show. He was walking in an even more laboured fashion following his stroke, but still sharp and bright up top. We sat around and agreed which stories to pick, with Christiane Amanpour who as ever was fun and feisty and clever. She and I had a chat and agreed Cameron had just vacated the field on foreign policy. TV debates skirmishing still going on. Danny Alexander was also on, as was William Hague, who was friendly as ever. I actually quite liked Danny. I reminded him he had been spot on about 55–45 [referendum result] in Scotland, and he said, 'Ah yes, those last few days when you came up to get the credit!' Breakfast with him and Andy and then I set off to see Graeme. Rob and Kate picked me up at Retford, over to Bassetlaw Hospital. Graeme didn't look good.

Liz had said when she found him he had collapsed, breathless, and she had a sense he had given up. The nurses seemed a bit dopey but we found one who seemed a bit more clued up. Pneumonia, blood clots. His feet were freezing which was presumably the blood not flowing. I stayed for two or three hours and a part of me wanted to shake him, make him face up to responsibility, and shake off his cynicism. He was even now complaining about nurses and doctors who were working hard to work out what he had and what he needed to do, though I felt maybe it was a lot more serious than he realised. Added to which, in addition to the obvious physical problems, he had severe mental problems too. I felt he was zoning out. Back to London and out for dinner with Rory.

Monday 23 February

To RH, to do a mix of signing books and interviews. Naomi Ackerman for PA, the one who had asked me for the interview when she was at the Finchley fundraiser. Pushed the line that sport had psychological support though it was primarily physical whereas politicians and business people did not when their work was mainly mental. Zoe Williams of *The Guardian*. Unfortunately Decca [Aitkenhead] couldn't do it. Zoe was OK but I think pretty determined to dislike me, but I just about won her round. I sensed quite a lot of intellectual snobbery re. the idea of sport being seen as anything other than, well, sport. John O'Malley, Irish guy who did stuff for *Spectator* and also a civil service magazine. He seemed to have the words civil service in virtually every sentence. They all went pretty well. Najma happy enough, signed a few books then home.

Tuesday 24 February

Breakfast Kevin Cahill, CEO Comic Relief, at some club in Soho. I liked Kevin, wondered if he was coming to pick my brains re. next steps for the mental health campaign, but it turned out he wanted to tell me he was stepping down and pick my brains about what he might do with the rest of his life, feeling I had done pretty well rebuilding life after a full-on existence into something a bit more. He thought Greg [Nugent] might be a runner to take over. Pictures for *Guardian* at Corinthia, with the Scottish guy, Graeme Robertson, who had done me last tine with Decca.

I went along with Jonathan McLory [Portland] to an EY Malta event. Lots of the people from my trip there, Ronald Attard, the CHOGM team (still trying to change it to Commonwealth Summit), the gaming commission guy, Chris Cardona looking good having given up the booze, and Joe Muscat making a pretty good speech. In the Q&A I asked him about the refugees dying at sea and whether we had a strategy for Putin. He had a pretty good set of answers. In a way all linked. People escaping poverty, coming to a region close to Libya, Putin exploiting the weakness of the West.

Wednesday 25 February

CNBC [business news TV channel] with Wilfred Frost and his co-presenter. Finding good arguments for business from the book. They did a brilliant graphics job on the set, with quotes from some of the big names in the book. I felt Wilf had it, real presence and authority. Then to Bloomberg, similar interview. Michael Noonan [Ireland finance minister] and the Irish ambassador in for an interview and lunch so chatted to them not least re. the upcoming Ireland v England rugby match. To Kicca and Sportsvibe [sports online magazine] to record some videos re. the books. Nice guy from *Sunday Business Post*, didn't really press me on the political stuff.

FT event had sold out, mainly male professional I guess. John Browne and Andy McCann also with me as winners in the book and from very different backgrounds, both excellent in different ways. I wasn't sure about Tim Harford as chair. I didn't feel he had a sense either of the book or of me. He was also one of those 'obviously I have to do Iraq' types. As an event it was good though. I struggled – especially with F, G and Decca in the front row – with the question about whether men and women won in different ways. Sales and signings went well. Dinner with G, F and Andy McCann who really had something special about him. The Mills there throughout, Tessa just at the end.

Thursday 26 February

Publication date. Car with Rory to Sky after six. The producer desperate for a signed copy. Eamonn Holmes hadn't read it, but it was a good interview. Developing an answer re. Ed that he had won the only battle that really tested him, also that he focused on big things. Bookomi [business management consultants] event at Shoreditch House with Richard Kilgarriff [literary events producer]. Interview with him, then Q&A, bit of filming, then leave for the Ivy and a lunch sponsored by MSL [global public relations]. Anders Kempe, their boss, chaired it, and was absolutely effusive re. the book, said that it was the best of its kind he had ever read. Then BBC, then over to do CNN with Christiane Amanpour. They had done the set-up beautifully, pictures on the walls, and a cover of the book in giant form at an angle from the desk. She was a terrific interviewer and I felt on form.

Off to Hult International Business School. René Carayol [executive coach] loved the book, and was also effusive. Standing room only, two overflow rooms, he said they had been worried they would not necessarily know who I was but in fact the interest was huge. Later Sadiq Khan [Labour MP] dinner. Pretty grim affair. Owen Jones [Labour activist], who sees himself as a latter-day Dennis Skinner, but who strikes me as a bit phoney, was making a classic 1983-style speech, all attack and how we missed Tony Benn [former MP and Cabinet minister] and if a floating voter had heard it they would be straight off to the Tories. I focused on winning, and said there was no point talking to and about ourselves, it was about reaching out to the undecided. Was developing an OK line re. Ed – namely that it was odd people saw him as weak when he did what he did to David, and also that he stood up for big things not little things. Tessa texting and calling the whole time, worried about Ukraine and Greece and Libya – all grim. Cameron talking about Tim fucking Sherwood and pretending he supported Villa. Graeme was getting worse, and they were worried he might lose a leg, and was being moved to Doncaster. Piece came out OK in *Standard*. Headline saying I would have kneed the guy who spat at me in the bollocks and headbutted him twenty years ago.

Friday 27 February to Saturday 28 February
To Paddington to meet Najma and head off to Bristol. John Hartson [former footballer] was on the train having been commentating last night. So was Graham Cole [businessman], so we chatted a bit, about the commission report on business he was writing for the party. Hartson a nice guy. Tattooed up his arms. Keen to talk re. his cancer fight. Gave him the book. Did a Bloomberg online interview. Met and taken to University of West England. Local BBC interview, then lunch Q&A with Dave Harvey [BBC business correspondent] and then Andy McCann joined us on stage. I felt that the combination of my old stories, and the new ones flowing from the book, was pretty good.

Off to Bath for a book signing at Toppings, fabulous store, then to the Bath festival, did a Skype interview with Richard Keys and Andy Gray re. Burnley/Chelsea, José still going on about 'criminal' Barnes, though Sean had dealt with it really well, done a very good straight rebuttal of the key moments and the Chelsea claims. *Indy* interview, then the main event with Gavin Esler [presenter]. Lovely guy, good chat, sold a fair few at the end. I was due to stay over but decided to get driven through the night by Graham Cole's driver so I could see Graeme in the morning. Nice email that Anna Wintour was happy with the profile of her in the book.

Arrived at Liz's about one. Graeme now at Doncaster Royal Infirmary, went in with Liz who was brilliant with him, and he seemed responsive some times, others not. Pneumonia not really improving. Nor was the clotting. His legs might have to come off. Hideous to see the people outside in wheelchairs and on drips still smoking. Nurses seemed a bit more clued up and Liz had a Christian friend who was a doctor who was popping in to make sure he was getting decent care. I stayed a couple of hours then was picked up by taxi to take me to Burnley. Crap reviews in *FT* and *Times*. Taxi driver raging re. immigration. Lunch in the boardroom, chatting to Clive Holt [Burnley director] re. whether he was the only director to have been to ninety-two grounds as a director. Poor game, lost one–nil.

Monday 2 March

I did a note to Ed, mainly written in his constituency, as I was visiting Graeme in hospital in Doncaster. I suggested he develop a much deeper profile on foreign policy; it was not about garnering votes, but showing depth and leadership. Cameron had an inbuilt advantage as he was already PM and it suited the Tories to have the debate focused on campaign process, what Matthew Parris called 'a scattergun of trivialities'. Ed's economy speech had not really landed and, though it should be revisited, I felt he also needed to do something bigger and bolder on foreign policy. People find the world scary right now and need to know their fears are understood by him, if they are going to elect him.

Also, there is a greater than ever understanding of the link to domestic policy and priorities. He needed to show he got all the issues, did an event with a high-profile, serious audience, showed leadership underpinned by values and principles, an analysis of the world and an honest assessment of the role we can play in meeting its current challenges. Cameron is stymied on it because of Europe. Because he has let tactics beat strategy, with his referendum and his games with UKIP. I said we should kill him on it. Then there was climate change, developing markets, immigration – tricky but there is a business and economic angle too.

Train to Coventry but there was a body on the line after Rugby so I jumped off there and Fiona Gordon and a Jaguar guy picked me up. She was no more optimistic re. the election than the last time I saw her. Back later to interview Clegg. Clegg on form, I found it hard not to like him. Best line was his big attack on Osborne and also ruling out all but Tory or Lib coalitions. Said SNP as bad as UKIP. Also that Labour could not possibly do a deal with a party that wants to break up the UK. Off to meet Najma and off to Euston and up to Manchester, sorting diary ahead. Holiday Inn fine, but felt another bloody cold coming on.

Tuesday 3 March

Breakfast telly was excellent. It drove the Amazon ranking for the book from 122 to eleven over the course of the day, really good feedback on Twitter too. Did Radio Manchester with a real working-class guy who told me he hated Cameron, bits and bobs, then a good interview with Dan Walker and friend for 5 Live – really liked Dan – and then off with Fletch to Burnley for the *Winners* event. The club had really done me proud. Clarke Carlisle there along with half a dozen or so former players. Great do, with Fletch compèring in his own inimitable style. Alan Kennedy [former football star] was excellent once he realised it was an interview not an after-dinner speech. Sean came in halfway through me and I got him over and we had a good chat. Something very impressive about him. Teamship, leadership, working within means etc.

Did the *Observer* friendship piece and then back to Preston and off to London, Gloria De Piero and Luciana Berger [Labour MP] fundraiser. Mood actually not bad. Alistair D spoke before the dinner, mainly re. the crash and also re. how to attack the Tories on the economy. I did a pretty good tub thump after dinner. Fiona Phillips [TV presenter] a bit tipsy, and still glad she didn't go for a seat but also guilty. Same as me. Rumours started early that *Winners* might be No. 1 and by four it was confirmed so lots of congrats and a bit of tweeting and bonuses for Rory and Kevin Keith for all their brilliant research work.

Wednesday 4 March

Doing lots of bits and bobs of media, regions etc., then Steve Wright, usual top stuff. Such a good guy, as is his sidekick Tim [Smith]. Gave me some pills for the cold, but they seemed to make it worse. Danny Rogers for *PR Week* with Tim, re. the New Labour campaign, then with them to Kettner's for the Portland book event, interviewed by Matt Forde [comedian, radio presenter]. Was meant to be at the LLR dinner at Speaker's House but felt rough and went home.

Thursday 5 March

Cameron had effectively ruled out head-to-head debates with Ed. Tom B called me last night and asked if I would do the media on it, so I did a blog saying he was morally cowardly and democratically wrong, also that he was going right back on his word of 2010. They all threw 'You didn't want TB to do it' at me but the reality is since then we had had them and he had said they were now part of democracy. Did *Today*, 5 Live, Sky and Beeb in the street, later C4 live. I was off to Ally Pally [Alexandra Palace] for the first of several events, for Joe Hemani/Westcoast [marketing], good do, and again feeling the book lent itself to top-quality speaking. Next to Excel for the Ecobuild (construction and energy) conference, huge event, good crowd. All good. Green people clearly preferring us to Tories. Louise Minchin chairing. Used the line re. her show pushing the book highest.

Spoke at the BVRLA [British Vehicle Rental and Leasing Association] dinner at the Hilton, 900 people, shifted loads of books. Stayed late, so did Najma who was really doing well. Wish I could say the same for trade more generally. Getting the usual tweets from people who couldn't get it, none in WHSmith [retailers] in stations, though OK in airports, and getting a fair few good pix and comments from UK and elsewhere. Good to be able to use 'No. 1' in interviews too. Home twelve. Earlier popped in to see Greg and Godric, collect books, but also tell Greg that Calum was coming back from Glasgow to live in London. He was pleased and felt he could get him engaged in big stuff on the community front.

Friday 6 March

Write democracy piece for *Bristol Evening Post*, women and winning for CNN.com – do men and women win in the same way? – and a mental health piece for HuffPo which Arianna loved. Off to Doncaster to see Graeme, Liz having decided to stick to her plans to go away for the weekend with Rob. On one hand Graeme seemed a bit better but one of the better nurses told me he was in a bad way, and that the pneumonia was not improving fast enough, and they could not risk operating on the legs yet. Also he was not eating and the nasal drip for nutrition kept jumping out. So sad to see him like that. Also I had to persuade him he should see Mike [son in Poland] but Mike's passport had expired and we had to go through rigmaroles to try to speed that up.

Later I spoke to Mike and I could tell he was a bit scared. He said he is not a great dad but he is still my dad and I do love him. He was clearly quite emotional, wanted to keep talking and when he hung up I was in floods of tears. Couldn't believe how Graeme had wasted his life, just so so sad. He flitted in and out – was on fair amount of morphine – but I found it easier to talk to him than other days. Belinda Scarett from intensive care came through and at last I felt I got a real picture of what was happening, and it wasn't good.

Saturday 7 March

Eurostar, out early, F following later. Checked into Hôtel des Grands Hommes at the Pantheon, long run, then a brief signing at WHS where it was No. 1, interview with Marion Mertens *Paris Match*, who had read it and liked it, then back to get Fiona before the Irish Cultural Centre gig for Kathy Gilfillan [publisher], husband Paul [McGuinness, music manager] with her son, Max, a few friends, Irish ambassador Geraldine Byrne Nason intro'd me and Ryan Tubridy [Irish broadcaster] who Fiona thought was the best interviewer of me she had ever seen. Very relaxed and flowing and he also clearly had a love of the issues and was on it re. the detail. One woman went off on one re. Iraq and I probably overreacted but these people made me sick. I didn't mind the disagreement on the issue; it was the conspiracy theorising etc. Otherwise very Irish and really good. Dinner with Geraldine, Ryan, still asking questions, also Kara from the UK embassy who I met in Hong Kong years ago and had written to because she was brilliant, and was now deputy chief of mission. Nice Lebanese restaurant, good craic. *ST* ran third extract of book, Anna W, and we had our first 'top' position in *ST* list. Bonuses all round.

Sunday 8 March

Out for a walk, then to see Marion from *Le Monde* who wanted to do a portrait. Liz sending messages saying Graeme still not improving fast enough. She sounded quite worried. Train back, kip, football, bit of work, then Keir [trainer]. Tired.

Monday 9 March

Loads of media. BBC Belfast. *Telegraph* with Matt Stadlen, good interviewer I thought. Talked to Jim Murphy re. Scotland. He said they had more energy and activism but they were not really making inroads. SNP still managing to be challenger brand. Winners behaving like losers, losers like winners. Lots of talk re. Labour–SNP coalition which was tricky, because there was a lot of support for it, and yet now the Tories were gunning for it, e.g. poster of Ed in Salmond's pocket. Nicola doing well. Salmond's book coming soon, the buzz was pretty poor and very self-indulgent.

Jim sounded down, felt he had done all he could but that there had been a shift and it was not coming back any time soon. *Last Word* [current affairs show] Dublin, then train to Glasgow. Liz sending ever worsening messages about Graeme. Working with Godric re. setting up Sky for the CIRC [Cycling Independent Reform Commission] report etc. Arrived

Glasgow, cab to Crowne Plaza in unbelievably strong winds. To the BBC for Sarah Smith interview re. the election. Did OK.

Tuesday 10 March

Breakfast with Paul Sinclair who was looking for new work after quitting with Johann Lamont. Not close to Jim Murphy, who he said was GB-like in his 'for me or against me' approach to life. To the Blythswood for interviews with Radio Clyde. *Daily Record*, then to the SFA. Barrie [Walker] chairing it, with Stewart Regan to his right, Peter Lawwell [CEO Celtic FC], Alan McRae [president]. I was totally upfront re. not changing my stance on booze and gambling but said I would not openly attack, would go for other sponsors but accept in the current climate it was hard to get them. Peter L was frank re. the financial mess Scottish football was in. He said the Premier League was killing the game. Diehard Scots moving to English teams.

I emphasised the community role especially of the smaller clubs. Felt it went fine, that they saw both the downsides and the upsides of me being involved. Wanted to use my profile in some ways, but also worried I would be too political, and make enemies. All the questions were fair and fine, and I sensed they wanted me, but the drink issue might become a problem. They said they had someone else lined up to do it and were seeing him 2 April and would then decide. The finances of the TV world were pretty dire. Two EPL [English Premier League] games amounted to the whole TV deal for Scotland. Donald collected me at the hotel and we headed south for the hospital. Graeme seemed much worse.

Wednesday 11 March

Spent the morning at the hospital, trying to see his doctors and find out exactly what was going on. The cold feet issue, which at Bassetlaw they had tried to deal with by putting on socks and blankets, turned out to be so serious they were going to have to remove at least one leg, possibly two. One for booze, one for fags. Twenty per cent liver function. Clot in aorta had embolised and impacted kidney and spleen too. They were worried though he would not survive anaesthetic because the pneumonia was so bad, and had decided it would have to be epidural. He seemed quite calm about it all but I didn't sense a real fighting spirit. He seemed scared at times, but also the cynicism came through from time to time too. Liz was brilliant with him, and thank God we had her friend Peter popping in because the general care was not great. They were just too pushed all the time.

Also my God was obesity an issue. One of the nurses admitted there was a drug addict up the ward who they all hated because she was so rude and aggressive. Hard to care for people like that. Graeme was pretty snappy with the nurses at times and asked us to apologise to one of them. The op was now definitely going to be tomorrow and when they came to talk about it they were pretty clear that without it he had no chance but there was a risk that with it he would still not get through, and he was so weak he might not survive. But the choice was definite death or possible death so there was really no choice at all. I had a car to collect me and take me to Warwick for a speech to OPTIX, a conference of opticians! Johnny Phillips there from Sky Sports to do a piece on the book for *Gillette Soccer Saturday*. Liked him. Speech fine, book sale and signing, then back to Liz's.

Thursday 12 March

To the hospital with Liz, and see Graeme for a couple of hours before his op. Definitely a bit scared and the doctors and anaesthetists very clear that it was a dangerous procedure. Liz had been holding it together well and was brilliant with Graeme but as he was wheeled off to the theatre she broke down. I think we both thought he wouldn't come out alive. We went for a walk then the canteen and waited for Rory, and later Mike to arrive from Poland. Talked a bit about his life, where it had gone wrong.

We waited four hours or so and eventually heard he was in the acute care ward. Op went fine, one leg off to the thigh, the other the foot. He looked better, was in less pain and except when he was a bit panicky his breathing seemed more settled. Mike arrived and tried to give him a big hug but of course the tubes were all there, and the oxygen mask. But they did seem pleased to see each other. The doctors came and explained it had gone well but they had not sealed the wounds because he was too weak and they would just reopen so there would have to be another op another day, also made clear that the health problems were still as severe re. liver, lungs, aorta etc. But he had got over one big hurdle when we feared he might not.

Heaven knows what life lay ahead though. Calum sent a nice letter urging him to seize this as the opportunity for real change etc., which we agreed Liz would show to him when he was more compos mentis. I had been keeping the various events tonight and tomorrow, unsure re. whether I would go but once I knew he was fine, and Mike settled, I headed off to Newcastle for the Prince's Trust dinner. Julia Hartley-Brewer [political writer and broadcaster] had been sent up as a stand-in in case I didn't make it, and was by all accounts good as warm up. Zoe Mulvenna [fundraising manager] really nice – the main organiser. Best of all Emma Black, daughter of Jonny Wilkinson's guy Steve Black [fitness coach and mentor]. She told me she was reading *Winners* because Joey Barton's mate had told her to. Joey reading it too. She bought twenty for staff and colleagues. I did my usual Ask Alastair Anything but I was not on top form, a few old war stories, some serious stuff in between but probably because of what had been happening with Graeme I didn't feel totally on my game.

Friday 13 March

Car collected me after breakfast and we set off for Lancaster Uni. Event hosted by [Sir] Cary Cooper [psychologist]. Fantastic place and a good crowd. He was such a good guy and a great enthusiast. I did a straight talk then Q&A, all fine, then off to Cattal near Harrogate to interview Clarke Carlisle for *GQ*. I had spoken to him last night and he admitted that he and Gemma were separating for a while. He was still scarred and bruised but said he was getting himself together. Very frank interview, really strong. Set off for Salford, to another business school talk, this time with Chris Brady [sports business professor] in the chair. To Wheatley and everyone still up, chatting away for a bit, Graeme seemingly a bit better today. Going to be a very long haul though.

Saturday 14 March

To the hospital with Liz, try to see all the consultants. Some pretty heavy cases in there but everyone got one-on-one nursing. The longer he could stay there the better. He was in not-bad spirits considering but what it must be like to be lying there hour after hour reflecting on all that has gone wrong. Bedsores becoming a problem. Toilet issues difficult too. All pretty humiliating. Not eating much at all. Teeth terrible. Had the occasional good laugh but it was all pretty grim. I had booked Rayan for the day and we set off for Burnley, stopped by at Fletch's, Chris Brady and wife popped in too, so carried on from last night. They were happy with it. Off to Burnley and one of the highlights of the season, beating City one–nil. Drove home and by the time we got back I had transcribed and written the Clarke C interview which was very strong.

Monday 16 March

Breakfast with London correspondents of the main EU papers. I found I was just about able to make the case for Labour winning but it wasn't easy. Also I was trying to get Ed to do something big re. foreign policy pre campaign but he was not really up for it. He had an infuriating habit of saying he agreed but then not quite doing it. For example, he said yes great idea, I will do it in the campaign and I said No, signal now that you will do it in the campaign and you get two hits out of it, and what is more you get the foreign policy establishment behind you. I spoke to Tom and Douglas and they were in the same place as me. He was very focused on domestic messages, but missing a trick re. leadership. Tom virtually admitted he didn't want to do e.g. Christiane on CNN, because 'she knows more about foreign policy than he does'. Not a ringing endorsement of leadership credentials. The EU guys were not impressed by Cameron but felt Ed just could not break through. I said we should make Europe a big thing in the campaign, not least because that was the way to get business less hostile, but I knew he wouldn't. Met Fiona for lunch before we went to the bank to meet Fiona Gibson to plan new wills. All very real in a way with Graeme lying on what might be his deathbed. Will quite simple, literary estate less so. AFP interview p.m., then off with Najma and Millie to the Rose Theatre, Kingston. Books sold as part of ticket price so shifted a fair few.

Tuesday 17 March

Into Millbank to do Aussie TV and radio, then to King's Cross and off to Doncaster. Was there for three hours or so and Graeme seemed not bad, and later they came and said they were moving him back to a ward. But it was obvious that they were doing it for reasons of bed space not his interests and Liz and I kicked up a bit of a fuss later. Still not eating. Panicky in his breathing. Ed called for a chat about his Budget speech again. He said he had had something of a Eureka moment because Osborne had been talking about a national recovery and he didn't feel they could ever be the party of the whole country in a way that we could be. It didn't feel very Eureka to me, but we chatted long enough for him to take out of it that I was agreeing by saying Many not Few was a good place to be. But we still had a basic problem on business credibility and the notion of him being anti-business, or at least not understanding business, was embedded and we were doing little to shift it.

Wednesday 18 March

Budget day and the Tories had it set up pretty well. The press were totally reverting to type. For example, Ed's so called 'two kitchens' were getting massive coverage where a clear example of Grant Shapps lying again about having two jobs under two identities was barely covered. What would it be like if it was a Labour chairman or some such? Hard for Ed right now but by all accounts he did OK in the response. I saw some of Osborne and he certainly adds a lot of brio to it. He was overdoing the sense of economic recovery maybe, and in the end it was going to come down to who people felt they could believe and trust. The Tories had clearer and stronger messages. It was not a headline-grabbing budget though he had a few decent smaller items in there.

It was on the big message he was strong – road to recovery, plan for the long term – and Labour by comparison were neither clear not strong. Ria Higgins from *Sunday Times* round to do me and Rory for Relative Values. Hoped it would be good for him. Still deciding whether to do the West Ham analytics team job he'd been offered. The Ed kitchen thing has got out of control. Jenni Russell had said – 'as a friend' blah – that it was not their real kitchen, this after Sarah Vine [*Daily Mail* columnist, wife of Michael Gove] had gone for them over how unhomely it was. So 'two kitchens' became a campaign theme. What a ludicrous country we live in because of our wretched fucking media. Liz agitating re. Graeme who was out in a ward and not happy and starting to panic a bit.

Thursday 19 March

Got the train up to Nottingham early on, met by a cab driver who was so thick it was truly breathtaking. He thought UKIP was the SNP. He thought voting was compulsory. He thought the Tories wanted to bring back hanging. Frightening. Dropped me at the Belfry Hotel for a speaking event on the book.

Another driver, Archie, drove me to Oswestry, which was a couple of hours away, including through parts of Wales. Checked into the hotel, went for a lovely run down the canal. Did Downtown Radio Liverpool then Najma arrived and we did the book festival. Organised by an excellent bookshop, the Q&A pretty good. A bit of friendly heckling but all good-natured. A bit alarming that when someone talked of TB reputation being at rock bottom, and there was no demurring. I was able to push back as usual but it got harder and harder.

Friday 20 March

Breakfast, train from Crewe to Glasgow. Near total eclipse en route, people trying to see it as we travelled through the darkening Scottish borders. Cab to BBC Scotland, interview with Johnny Beattie. He hadn't read the book but I managed to get in some of the key themes in between him essentially pressing me on me and my head, especially around the time of David Kelly's death. Donald collected me and we set off for Edinburgh to see Auntie Mattie [Barr, sister of AC mother] on her 94th. Cousin Evelyn there – cannot believe she is a granny. Moira [cousin] – interesting chat re. how easily she cried, and how she and her mum hated farewells. Liz Barr [cousin] arrived too, said I was too thin – couldn't wait to tell Keir. Nice to see them all.

Donald took me to the Sheraton, met with Malcolm Robertson and colleagues from Charlotte Street Partners [strategic consultancy] to see whether we could do an event for the book or other speaking gigs. Malcolm Labour (though anti-Ed) clear the mood and culture had just shifted and though Jim M was active and energetic he was not really cutting through. Nicola was popular and doing well. They felt independence was likelier than a year ago. They also felt things were as bad for Labour as the polls suggested. Some MPs even giving up on Glasgow.

Swam before the oil club dinner. Over to the EICC. Andrew Mackenzie, CEO of BHP Billiton did the talk before me. A Labour member, as was his wife. Felt we were not going to win largely because of Ed. Also a Dutch guy who knew Putin well, having built one of the main pipelines, still defending him, and also saying he never saw corruption of Putin himself. I did the usual Q&A postcard format and all about Ed – about a dozen – were negative. What would he be like with Putin? How can you save him? etc. Some very funny questions. How many kitchens does a Labour leader need? Is the Dyson Blade the fastest and most hygienic hand drier in the world? (from the gents) Malcolm Tucker the most common question. Rosie asked, 'You have given lots of advice, what is the best advice received?' I said Ernest Bennie [psychiatrist] after my breakdown and 'Know your own mind.' Works on a lot of levels.

Saturday 21 March

Walked to Waverley St. Selfies with joggers and Irish rugby fans. *Scotsman* magazine interview appeared, and was really good, words and pictures. Tweeted it out. Rab Perry [photographer] had done pretty well getting what he called my 'Cromwell look'. Writing thoughts for the EM debate prep tomorrow. Cameron doing loads of personal media at the moment. Salmond book was getting panned. Paddy Ashdown called it literary masturbation. Reviewers saying bitter and vain and vindictive.

Train to Doncaster, off to see Graeme. In a bed now opposite a guy called Carl who was morbidly obese and whose parents brought in oodles of junk food and sweets. Awful. Graeme doing a bit better but not really improving as fast as he should. Liz and Kate in. I stayed a couple of hours then off and back to the station. Stayed in with Fiona and watched *House of Cards*.

Salmond on *Marr* basically saying that they would hold the balance of power and use it. If you have the balance you have the power. I think he was over-reaching a bit. Ed's driver, Sid, collected me and we headed off for Waheed's place in Kent. Sid was convinced Ed would win. He had driven Shaun Woodward, John Reid, Alan Johnson. Clearly liked Ed, said he thought the Tories were liars and snobs and people knew it. Ed was actually a decent bloke, said he really liked working for him. So that was good to hear.

Arrived to find they had spent yesterday largely working on the seven-way debate, which was going to be ridiculous, and he was not happy with it but knew it had to happen. Cameron had basically got what he wanted – Paxman with each individually, town hall with each individually, a seven-way and a five-way without him. Stan Greenberg, Michael Sheehan, Kezia Dugdale [MSP] (impressive, who had been Nicola S yesterday), Chris Leslie [Labour MP] as Clegg, Greg, Torsten leaving to work on manifesto, Tom B arriving, the usual others, Tom Hamilton etc. We chatted a bit and then I did Paxman sessions a couple of times, first pressing him on 'Are you weird?' and second on the economy and foreign. Ed was ranting about Paxman being a tosser, a cynic and an egomaniac. Said he once bumped into him on holiday and usually when you met people on holiday you ended with a better sense of them, but he had ended with a much worse sense. Cynical and pompous and self-obsessed. I still felt we did not have clarity on priorities or what the main elements of 'the plan' we were talking about were. Also I had been pressing again for him to do something major and serious on foreign policy before the campaign but as with the Merkel strategy of a few months, or even a year, ago now, it didn't happen. He was better on tone, but he still lacked a presence that I feared he needed, and that Cameron had.

The qualities I felt he did have which would be important in a campaign were a sense of calm and also resilience. Both were impressive. He sometimes took too long to think about things though. I remembered the Jack Welch [US businessman] 'don't overbrain' message. Ed overbrained, but not always to great effect. I think the Yanks were a bit taken aback by how Paxmanesque I was on the 'weirdness' questioning. Ed said he would not be like that. Maybe not, but worth preparing for the worst. He didn't really engage when I told him some of the things wrong in the Doncaster hospital. Stan G just back from Israel, and genuinely seemed shocked Netanyahu had done as well as he did. Train back with Tom B, Tom H and James Morris who had been doing groups and said there was no desire for the Tories back but massive resistance to us. The problem with that scenario was 'better the devil you know'.

Monday 23 March

Out to St James's Church Piccadilly to do Adweek Europe [event for advertising and marketing professionals] with Richard Kilgarriff. A giant wooden cross in the background. Getting questions now about how well I had managed my post-No. 10 profile compared with TB. Then off to Liverpool St and then to the book warehouse. Did a record 1,360 books signed in one hour. Meanwhile started to get calls to do media on Cameron telling James Landale [deputy political editor] in the BBC series of behind-the-scenes leaders' profiles that he would not do a third term. Was exercising but felt it was both a political opportunity and a book opportunity. It struck me as a silly thing to do. Massive distraction. He had even named Johnson, Osborne and May as possible successors. It suggested non-winning mindset and also that it was all about him.

The Tory line was that it was an honest answer to a straight question (compare Blair–Campbell spin etc.) but I don't think it washed. It was a mistake. Not one that would cost votes per se, but because it would create a whole different mood and momentum around him, and create a distraction he would not be able to shake off. Jon Snow quite spiky, e.g. saying that he was only doing what I don't like politicians to do – tell the truth. But I managed I think to get over various lines, e.g. that it suggested he felt he had already won – presumptuous – but above all that it suggested he was not on it, not focused totally on winning, and Osborne and Lynton Crosby [DC political strategist] would be tearing their hair out. Meanwhile, however, Rory told me that there was a steady shortening of the odds on both Tory most seats and a Tory majority. This was so winnable if only we had a decent fucking campaign.

Home, then back in for *The World Tonight* and *Newsnight* with Gove. No. 10 had said he would not do a debate, and it was meant to be first me, then him, then me again, but it was clear he was up for it and we ended up doing a disco which was fine. Great response on Twitter because we kept it pretty light and good-natured and because he didn't seem to believe what he was saying. Said I was a brilliant spin doctor for a different age but now politicians didn't spin and told the truth and answered questions etc. Also he plugged my book which was kind of him! Allowed me to do it more. I asked him off camera how he thought the election would go. He said he felt it was still too close to call, but he felt their strengths would come through more as it neared, along with Ed's weaknesses. I couldn't tell whether he genuinely thought Cameron's Landale move was anything other than an error.

Tuesday 24 March

Breakfast event at the beautifully refurbished Canadian High Commission where I was chairing a Portland session on 'digital diplomacy' with Jimmy Leach and Scott Nolan Smith from Portland, Tom Fletcher, Facebook's Elizabeth Linder, and Aussie High Commissioner Alexander Downer. He was actually very thoughtful, clearly not that taken with social media, and absolutely scathing about our media and the state of political debate. Another line I was deploying re. Cameron's move yesterday was that it was hard enough to get debate focused on policy without adding to the nonsense yet another Cameron psychodrama, first TV debates now this. The debate was pretty good, essentially focused on the fact people were still obsessed with the platforms not the content and also not as good and fast as e.g. Russia or ISIS. Tom also made the point that we still applied e.g. purdah during elections, but ambassadors should in his view still be putting out positive British messages. Same if there was a hung parliament, he said. Downer was comically undiplomatic both about his own view of Twitter – who cares that I hosted a cultural event at Australia House? – and also about Ban Ki Moon [Secretary-General UN], taking the piss out of his 'Met with xxx, met with yyy' Twitter feed. Tom and he were at different ends of the generational spectrum. Facebook woman pretty good, though it must have been galling most of the talk was of Twitter.

Off upstairs to do Oz radio on the book – while NZ were batting their way to the cricket World Cup final – and then Singapore TV re. Lee Kuan Yew [first Prime Minister of Singapore] who had died two days ago. To RH to re-sign a load of books for Oz interviewees. Nigel said the book was holding up really well. The interviews re. Cameron would help that. News dominated by French plane crash, Germanwings plane in the Alps. Cameron heckled at Age UK but doubtless would not be covered like TB's slow handclap at the WI [Women's Institute].

Wednesday 25 March

Lovely sunny day. Work on diary on train north. Almost fainted seeing the ends of Graeme's legs for the first time as they were patching the wounds. PMQs apparently a disaster. Only there for an hour or so then back south for Ed debate prep at Labour HQ. They all seemed a bit down with PMQs having gone so badly. He had asked Cameron to rule out VAT rise. DC did so but Ed ploughed on with prepared questions. I stayed three hours or so, and we were just going over the same ground really, assuming economy, NHS, immigration, devolution, foreign.

Tom B was a very good Paxman. They felt he would be fine at the town hall event with Kay Burley, less good with Paxman. Ed was getting into a bit of a state re. the idea that Paxman would make it all about him. I said so what, all you can control is the answers. Imagine it is someone else.

Later to Ed's for the end of his session with Andy McCann. Andy was trying to get him to a Personal Statement relishing the chance to show who he was. Ed said the Eureka moment was when I had said he should stop seeing this as an ordeal and more as an opportunity. He got to that eventually. Andy came back to collect some books for his mates and he said he felt he had not really been able to help because the engagement was so piecemeal.

Thursday 26 March

Ed final run-through, all OK, Tom on form. I had to go to a school, Evelyn Grace Academy, to do a talk for the end of their sports week before heading to Oxford. Nice school, some great kids, especially Dominic who was twelve, looking after me, saying he wanted to read my book 'because you have been successful and you have talked to successful people and I want to learn from them.' Told me off when I jokingly suggested he nick a book. 'Sir, you cannot be a winner and a stealer.' Lovely kid. Signing then off to Oxford watching the debates in the car. Cameron pretty nervy. Ed did OK, especially with Paxman. Would be good for his and party morale.

Friday 27 March

Reaction to debate OK. Lot of focus on Paxman saying at end, 'Are you OK, Ed?' and Ed saying, 'Yeah. Are you?' He more than held his own. Paxo gave Cameron an easy ride. I had hundreds of Qs to sift, did so, did the event, played it for laughs but also played up the idea of challenging negativity. Newton Europe [consultants] staff, good bunch, good event.

Saturday 28 March to Sunday 29 March

Really nice weekend, taking Audrey back to Hull, Calum's idea for her 90th. Train up, me, F, Aud, Rory and Cam. Nice little hotel near the theatre, Wilberforce House Museum, walk to her old house. People in but nobody answered at her old house. Curtains drawn, video game noises inside. Tried the neighbour, door a bit open and a woman came charging out asking why I kicked the door. Aud oblivious saying, 'We are on a reminiscence trip.' Something very sad about the place. Other parts better but it did feel a bit neglected and left behind. Dinner at Cerutti's on Alan J recommendation. Long walk Sunday – Oz winning Cricket World Cup and players being tweeted with the cover of *Winners*, then to Doncaster to see Graeme. Pleased we went but a bit out of it, and Aud was surprised how weak he was and also shocked when she saw the legs beneath the blankets.

Monday 30 March

Blog on Aussie cricket win. [Stuart] Prebble [TV producer] meeting re. book film ideas and also whether to do Team Sky/schools re. marginal gains. To Labour HQ for another long session with Ed M. Several hours. The Yanks there and Mike Donilon [American election advisers]. Growing on me. Sheehan a bit too American, Stan G a bit too playing into Ed's instinctive leftism. Did OK though. Needed to make this him v Dave.

Tuesday 31 March

To Soho to record a voiceover for LLR film. Millbank for a *Media Show* interview with Steve Hewlett. To party HQ, chatted to Rosie re. Doncaster hospital and maybe the need to get her involved. Did pep talk to the staff, mainly focused on teamship, also staying calm when things went wrong. Also invoked PG memory re. optimism. Went down well, great response, book signing, tour and then went for a tea with Andrew Adonis [former Labour minister]. He felt things were going OK. Tessa ought to win. He was shaping policy for her. He saw housing as his next big thing. Off to Hilton Edgware for a speech, hundreds of books, all went. Email from Mark Lucas saying working with Labour a nightmare at the moment.

The strategy for the ads changed again this morning for the fourth time. They cut the budget last week to 1/10th of last time. Also, 'a party that brings out mugs about immigration is not really the message of a party I would be proud to support.' I told Ed but he was strangely detached, asked me to speak to Douglas. I was talking to Gerald Shamash and Gavin re. suing authors of *Blair Inc.* for saying I asked for a free piano from Chappells for Kathryn Blair.[*] Total nonsense. I was doing lots of media on media coverage of Andreas Lubitz [German co-pilot] who had flown a passenger plane into a mountainside killing 150 people. 'Madman in cockpit. Why was he allowed to fly?' This kind of stuff when it was not yet known if mental illness was the issue.

Wednesday 1 April

Off to Doncaster, and having seen Rosie yesterday I got her to call the hospital CEO and raise the fact that there had been no counselling. Indeed Liz had been told there was only one counsellor and 1, she was on holiday and 2, Graeme probably wouldn't qualify because she did near-death and anxiety. FFS. So why did they say four weeks ago he should get it? Anyway a COO [chief operating officer] bloke arrived, looking nervy, and a

---

[*] *Blair Inc.: The Man Behind the Mask* by Francis Beckett, David Hencke and Nick Kochan.

April '15: Andrew Adonis tips Tessa for mayoralty

senior sister, and said it would be sorted. Liz had had a big up and down with the sister yesterday.

Train to Manchester, waited for Ed and then we went into several hours of preparation. First though hours of round-and-round conversation about his strategy for it. Greg was advising against really going for Cameron. I was advising that he did. Andy [McCann] was upstairs from four waiting to see him for a final session and finally saw him at half ten. He was finding it quite frustrating I think, felt that they were playing catch-up, also that they were hopeless at sticking to a schedule.

In the debate prep, Ed had apparently not been great yesterday but Ayesha was keen not to emphasise that. He was clearly getting quite nervous, especially re. foreign and devolution. On immigration, James [Morris] was pushing him not to budge from a fairly hard line. He seemed comfortable with that. I didn't. I played Julie Etchingham and tried to get the others to gang up on him. Also gave him a hard time over 'weaponise the NHS' and during a break Douglas suggested that we say yes, people should use their vote as a weapon to save the NHS. In other words admit to saying it and make that a big part of the debate. He went for it and in the next session it went OK.

There was a danger he was becoming over-rehearsed though and he needed to be relaxed and confident. For example, in the first one, if we had said 'say hell yeah', nobody would have gone for it, but in the moment it kind of worked. We worked at it till gone ten, talked through the substance but also how to handle Farage and Sturgeon. He was very reluctant to have a go at Nicola. I felt he could not give her an easy run. Up to see Andy McCann and Ed was now slightly in head-in-hands mode. It was the same room where GB collapsed in a moaning heap after seeing Mrs Duffy in Rochdale five years ago.* Tom Baldwin was worrying re. TB speech next week in Sedgefield. Spoke to TB and got him and Julie Crowley to agree to joint briefing operation. Meanwhile, Aussie businessman Neil Jenman, who had read *Winners* on a flight home after buying at the airport, placed an order for thousands for all his staff.

Thursday 2 April

Up early and off to Piccadilly. Nice woman from Public Health England got on at Stafford. Said the cuts were really eating in now. I got a good response to my *Guardian* piece on the need for mental health to go centre stage in the campaign. At the airport in Birmingham, a couple came up

---

* During the 2010 election campaign Gordon Brown was forced to apologise when overheard to refer to Rochdale pensioner Mrs Duffy as 'a bigoted woman'.

to me in WHS to say they had read it and it was the best thing they had ever read re. mental health. Signed books – they were on pretty good display though in two shops had sold out, which underlined how crap it was there were none in stations. Sent a note to Ed after a chat with Andy, emphasising the need to enjoy it and relish the chance to go head-to-head with DC. He was overbraining last night, and he needed to get his nerves in a better place, use them to drive performance not stultify it.

I did a note to Ed about the debate. Important to learn from the Pax-man experience, when he suddenly realised it was not an ordeal but an opportunity. It was important to focus on the things that only he could control; what he says, how he says it, how he looks in between. I felt that his having the central position was a bonus. Cameron would hate the whole thing, Ed would get a big advantage if he looked like he was enjoying it, enjoying the interaction with the audience.

I said it was good to be worried, or at least anxious, but at some point he had to take that anxiety and build it into something positive, look in a mirror and say, 'There is nowhere I would rather be than here. My whole life has been a preparation for this moment. I relish the fact people have underestimated me. I love that Cameron thinks I am not up to it. I am happy that Sturgeon has me in her sights. Because I have the values and the decency and the *passion* to show I can beat any of them.' The only risk was that he overbrained things. He needed to get some down time today.

Flew out to Lyon, met by Fiona, arrived Faucon about five. Stewart Regan called. The SFA board had met and had decided to go with 'the safe option'. He said there was a feeling that my stance on alcohol and gambling, and my close identification with Labour, was a problem. He hoped we could work together on some projects, but he felt for now they wanted to play safe. It was annoying on one level – to get headhunted and to have them pursue me the way they did, and then go safe – but in a way it was perhaps for the best. The booze issue would have been difficult at some stage. Added to which I felt they didn't quite have the dynamism to turn things round.

Dinner, then watched the debates. The format, as we anticipated, wasn't great, but Julie Etchingham did a good job making it flow along. Ed did OK, nervy start but got going better later, and landed a couple of good blows on Cameron. Sturgeon was probably best, strong and clear and articulate and landed blows on all of them. Leanne Wood [leader Plaid Cymru] a bit Little Britain but got the first applause when she went for Farage over saying non-Brits should not get HIV treatment. Ed best when going for Dave over NHS. He used the weapon line, saying use your vote as a weapon to save the NHS, but it didn't quite land. The polls were a bit all over the place, but my impression was Sturgeon good, Cameron detached and nervy and pissed off to be there, Clegg not really in the game, though resilient, Farage a bit below par, Ed good in parts, Natalie Bennett [Green Party] poor, Wood a poor version of Nicola.

Ed called afterwards and I could sense he felt fairly pumped up. The polls were putting him on a par with Cameron and he said remember their hope was he would trounce me and the general message via the media was I am a twat. Certainly the combination of the two debates so far had him in the game. He definitely needed to find a way to take some of the shine off Sturgeon though. She was the anti-austerity campaigner, and she was pro-NHS but he let her away on that one. But she was good, without a doubt, and the five-way debate required a different approach.

Osborne and I had had an exchange of emails after the first one and I had said Cameron was not match fit. He had said, 'Your boy never will be.' He sent me an email tonight: 'See what I mean about him not being match fit?' He might be right. There was a basic level and when Ed met it, people felt an improvement in morale, but he was not top drawer. He said he had been nervous but got into it. Didn't like the format inevitably. He was also weak in just taking the hits on the economic record. Fought back better on the NHS but the five-year failure to stand up to 'mess we inherited' was coming back to hurt him, as it was always going to.

Friday 3 April to Saturday 11 April

France. Speaking to Ed most days, and Jim Murphy, with Nicola still making a lot of the weather. Was talking to Jim at the Girocedre [restaurant] when story broke of a HMG note re. a chat between Sturgeon and the French ambassador suggesting NS had said she preferred Cameron as PM which went totally against her public-facing messages. She and the Ambo denied it so it ran big for a while but died quickly. I did sense, however, she might be in danger of over-reach. They had two debates on consecutive days in Edinburgh and Aberdeen, with Jim doing OK in the first and better in the second, when he was more aggressive with Sturgeon. Kezia Dugdale [deputy leader, Scottish Labour] was emailing me from time to time for thoughts and she said the problem was that NS had a Princess Nicola touch, and also was beginning to come over a bit like Merkel, if feistier.

The problem with the seven-way debate was that it showed her getting away with stuff, in that Cameron didn't want to attack her because he needed her to do well in Scotland, and Ed didn't want to lose sight of this being the only time he and DC went head-to-head. But it had meant she went back to 'hero's welcome' headlines and the sense of an unstoppable momentum that had to be stopped. Douglas was arguing, to be fair, that we needed to start landing blows, but Greg and James were both on the Ed–DC contest, and also the idea that if we re-ran arguments from the referendum we pushed Labour Yes voters towards her. But it was one of those cases where the groups said what they were hearing, but could be moved by what they heard. I sent Ed the Wayne Gretzky [ice hockey player and coach] quote re. skating to where the puck is going, not where it has been.

I did a note to Ed saying three things needed to be fixed. Economy. Foreign policy/leadership. Puncturing the Sturgeon balloon. On the economy, I went stuck-record mode on the failure to rebut 'mess we inherited'. It was becoming a given that 1. We caused the crash, and 2. They are fixing things. 'An economy that works for all' is fine as a message but it's not clear what it means in practice. He had to win the argument that Labour governments make you better off than Tory governments. It was lethal for them to own this territory. Past, present and future. On foreign policy, I said the campaign was coming over as very parochial. People are genuinely worried about terrorism, Putin, climate change, Brexit. He needed a speech taking head-on worries people have about his leadership on the heavy stuff.

On the SNP balloon, the trouble was they were buying into the notion that to go for Sturgeon is to go for Scotland. The attack should be that she is not as progressive as she would have people believe. And she is Cameron's secret weapon.

Later in the week, we had a rather odd exchange based on him saying I was 'going around saying he had done badly' in the debate. I hadn't said anything outside his own circle. As I said on the call we had after the event, it was good, he did well, but we have to be able to have frank discussions and I felt Nicola did better than we wish to acknowledge and we have to learn from that. I had only said it to him and Greg because I was aware of the need for camp morale and confidence. But even that was taken as 'going around saying he had done badly'.

I said there was no point hearing only what you want to. He said, 'Please stop saying she won the seven-way when three out of four polls say I won it. It isn't helpful!' I watched the Nicola S–Jim Murphy debate and felt she had been poor when she was under pressure and there were times she lost the audience. If we play into the English new conventional wisdom that she is some kind of Scottish Merkel, we play her game. She has one big goal – independence – and the current hypocritical support of the idea of a Labour government is a tactic towards that. She has to destroy Labour in Scotland to take the next step towards it. She is more vulnerable than we think, and Ruth Davidson and Jim exposed it.

After the Scottish leaders' debate, when Sturgeon said SNP MPs would vote for full fiscal autonomy next year, I got the two Eds to agree to go up there together on the Friday and do a full-on press conference with Jim on full fiscal austerity. It was an opening. What does it mean, for Scotland, for the UK? It was interesting how she lost the audience when she resiled from detail and instead went for confident assertion. We had to puncture this idea that an SNP vote was a guarantee against austerity. After the second debate, when she said Trident was a 'red line', the Tories revisited their 'Ed in the SNP pocket' attack, and Michael Fallon [Defence Secretary] went further, likening his 'backstabbing of his brother' to the idea he would stab Britain in the back to do a deal with Nicola. The general feeling was it went too far, and I did a note to Ed saying get out and say Fallon is a decent man being driven to desperate things by Cameron and Crosby because the campaign is going wrong.

I sent a note saying he should use this as an opportunity to show he is nicer and more decent than them, but also has real steel. I drafted a speech on why the Tories were making the SNP the issue, on why Nicola Sturgeon was their secret weapon, on how they had given up on the idea of winning a majority, given up on putting forward a positive vision for the future. He could use it to reframe the presentation of a positive agenda against what was becoming an ever more shrill negative campaign. Labour had to use it, not least to boost morale.

Ed's Scotland visit went fine. Laughing before he went re. the *Mail*, which did a two-page thing on his 'tangled love life', which was just an account of former girlfriends. Juliet was one of them and it appeared on the day she was coming out to France with Grace. He was very good though at not getting fazed by this kind of stuff. Always wanted to get focused on the question in hand. Loved to say there was a strategic problem. We did have a post-mortem meeting/conference call, but he called me afterwards to say he had cut it short because there were too many people in the room. Actually though I think he didn't like that Michael Sheehan and I both said that we felt Nicola had clearly won the seven-way. I replied that I needed to be able to be frank and we needed to base strategy on what was real not what Douglas called 'the happy talk' around him. We were getting on fine though.

I sent David M a couple of emails re. a Nick Keller idea and also to say I was thinking of him, saying it was hard enough for me seeing some of the mistakes made, so heaven knows what it was like for him. He said that he was angry at the bad politics and the bad positioning. When I said I was advising Ed on the debates, he didn't come back. I did feel though that even if I would not go in full-time I wanted to help because I really felt Cameron was dire. He was focusing too much on family rather than policy, and also seemed to me to be very becalmed and lacking in energy and drive. The sense was developing their campaign was pretty poor.

Maybe it would be like 1992 and make no difference, but I felt there was no real appetite for the Tories if Ed could break through.

The other thing I was dealing with was TB speech on Europe on the Monday I was away. Tom Baldwin said there was a lot of nervousness and we had to make sure it was a clean landing. He wrote a terrific draft but there was some pretty strong stuff re. SNP and UKIP – e.g. as cavemen blaming the other from their caves – so we toned down a bit wanting it to be TB slams DC on Europe and unequivocally backs Ed to win. Some at Labour HQ wanted all the SNP stuff out but I emailed saying he would water down caveman to make it about Farage, and tone down some of the SNP stuff.

TB led the news all day, on the day Cameron was flying around all four UK countries. Lots of messages saying it was good to see him back on the trail. He and I had talked a few times, and he felt Ed was doing OK. But he didn't buy my analysis that Cameron was not really on it. He felt he was trying to stay above the fray and hope that the two main messages broke through as the campaign neared the end. He was still getting panned in most of our press, and all the right-wing papers did him as a toxic force that would not help Ed. But it did, as did TB visit to party HQ, where he went down really well according to Tom B. So the mood at the end of the week was pretty good. That being said the polls in Scotland were not shifting and both Tessa and Rosie called me to say they thought we were short of a win in England and Wales, even without the SNP problem.

Greg Beales called me a few times, and on one occasion said he had shifted to my view that we had to go for Sturgeon, otherwise Ed just looked weak and she could say whatever the hell she liked. He told me Cameron media were saying it was a totally controlled campaign and also that Samantha and the kids had been to the last PMQs which was a bit odd. Like a footballer taking his kids on the pitch for his last game at home. Occasional pitches from Steve Coogan and Evan Harris, pissed off that we were not going to commit to the 'L word', legislation, on Leveson. I spoke to Ed about it and at greater length to Ayesha. They said they had to see if the Royal Charter worked, but there would be no doubt of their commitment to honour what they said to the victims. Hacked Off very hacked off though that we would not go as far as the Lib Dems.

Brendan Foster called with a good idea on the day Ed announced changing the rules on non-doms. He said most people would support it, but to counter the anti-business charge have a 'fair tax fair wage' company award or Kitemark.

Book still doing OK. Also, fixing more speeches with book deals. One of them standing in for Seb again. Rory heard John McDermott of Spurs Academy was sending out quotes from book to everyone. Got in touch and offered a deal for all staff. Note from Scottish government that Scottish Information Commissioner was overruling the decision not to release the full transcript of my Salmond interview. Annoying but hey-ho.

Bits and bobs with Godric on Sky. Clegg *GQ* fine but he was struggling to get noticed in the debate. Marion Van Renterghem [French journalist] said François Hollande had suggested we meet, which we fixed for 4 May. Two-hour bike minimum most days. One spill when I was on the phone to Douglas up Col d'Ey and got hit by a Belgian car overtaking as a motorbike came the other way. I landed in the ditch and the biker sped off and caught up the guy and brought him back. All ended fine. Grace would have loved the biker.

Saturday 11 April

Met by Ed Victor and Rayan at Heathrow, off to Burnley for the Arsenal match. Nice to spend a day with Ed, and to give him a bit of a northern education. The book was definitely connecting. When we arrived, we got out of the car, passed bags to Fletch who was taking us on to Manchester later, and the first people we saw were four young Arsenal fans. One said, 'I have just finished your book. Loved it, especially the Albanian PM chapter!' Then met Gareth Southgate who said he was halfway through it. Spurs Academy manager John McDermott had been raving about it to him, and was asking me to go in to talk to them about it. David O'Leary [former Arsenal player] was raving about the Mourinho section, asking me what he was really like etc.

I liked O'Leary, warm and friendly and telling me if ever I was up north I could stay with him. Interesting re. Arsène Wenger, said he had nothing else, had maybe been to four London restaurants, just obsessed with football, nothing else. He was not keen on Ed but there was a general view we were doing better. Off with Ed and Fletch to Manchester after the one–nil defeat. Not a great game, but Wenger was really positive about us. Artisan restaurant extraordinary and as I expected Fletch and Ed got on really well. Lots of piss-taking of me, also some serious stuff re. their respective work. Ed couldn't quite believe how popular I was when we were going round Burnley. He was joining the 'You must stand' club. Nice dinner then Fletch gave me a lift to the Crowne Plaza.

I had a chat with Ed M, said the key to the next week/ten days is that the public are making a reassessment of him. So lots of things said and done before can be said and done again. Depth and texture. Someone should be set to go over old speeches, events and interviews and find talking points that worked at the time but didn't fly because of the context.

Sunday 12 April

Train to Doncaster to see Graeme. He was a bit chirpier. He said Ian Botham had been on the ward yesterday which I thought might be one of the tricks his mind was playing on him, but then I saw [Ian's wife] Kath Botham's mum and sister and it turned out Kath's dad was in there. Had a nice chat with all of them. Train back p.m., then off to party HQ. Ed had spent the weekend with Michael Sheehan, Mike and Stan, plus the usual UK crowd, preparing for the five-way debates. Tom Hamilton as Farage, Kezia Dugdale as Sturgeon, [Baroness] Eluned Morgan [Welsh former MEP] as Lianne Wood, another woman who I didn't know as Natalie Bennett. Well I did know her but had forgotten her name and nobody said. Ed was mainly worrying about Farage, and the free hit he would get, especially with three PC women, as he would see them, between him and Ed.

Immigration tricky as ever, and I felt as with the economic mess non-rebuttal he was not keen to go with my line, so there we go. We agreed that he should not let any one of them get away with anything. But equally he did need to show that he was the only one who could be Prime Minister and prime ministerial. Sturgeon had meanwhile gone to a whole new level in Scotland. She was also a very good communicator. She espoused policies others would chew out but somehow got away with it. Kezia said that it was hideous up there, a real rerun of the mood of the referendum but worse. We also discussed how to bring Cameron into the room even though he wasn't there, and agreed that at some point there should be a direct message to him down the camera. We ended up agreeing it should be a challenge to debate. Sundays pretty good for Labour, sense Ed was doing OK, but SNP rampant. Jim Murphy asked me to go up there.

Monday 13 April

Keir round for a workout then I watched the manifesto launch in Manchester. It went well and Ed had real energy and passion. The benefit of these hours of preparation for the debates was that he was generally improving. He really looked and sounded confident. They had gone for fiscal responsibility as the main pitch, largely I think because there was not really a big policy offer that had not already been put out there. But the mood was good, the Q&A with hacks went well. There were rumblings in the Tory camp that they had no Plan B.

Met Jessica Case from Pegasus, who was over for the London Book Fair, to discuss the US launch of *Winners*. We were still top ten. She wanted me to sort speaking gigs and go from there. Debate prep all p.m., usual crowd, two complete run-throughs. Ed was OK but today lacking in energy a bit. Kezia was doing well as Sturgeon. I said to Stan, and he thought I was joking, that Scots are just more eloquent than the English. But they are. Worked a bit on his opening and closing statements. Out for dinner with Calum at Chez Bob. He was in OK shape. I was missing Fiona and Grace who had stayed in France a few more days.

Tuesday 14 April

I did an interview with the *Stoke Sentinel* about my plans for their book festival, giving free tickets and books to people who do not normally go to book festivals. To Ibis to meet Marion VR for her profile of me in *Le Monde*. She was pushing hard re. Kaz, and also why TB's profile was so bad. She had seen him for the piece and really liked him, and liked what he said about me, but he was still getting hammered. Had a meeting at Strand Palace Hotel, then into Brewer's Green [Labour HQ] for another Ed preparation session. Better than yesterday but still quite jumpy. He was also putting on weight and I told them they had to get a grip of his diet and exercise etc. I think sometimes he felt I was a bit harsh, but the trouble was he was too surrounded, as Douglas put it, by 'happy talk'. He had too many people telling him all was OK, and too few people coming up with genuinely strategic ideas.

Greg Beales was pretty down because his plans to replace Geoffrey Robinson [Labour MP for Coventry NW] had come to nothing, and he was not keen to stay around after 7 May. Ed asked me to see Charlie re. post-7 May planning. He was worrying that if he didn't win – e.g. get more seats than the Tories – there would be a few of the older ones coming out saying we did not have legitimacy, and there would be a move against him. Charlie had done an awful lot of research re. precedence and also process. There was no clear system. Basically the Queen sat there, and waited till someone said they thought they could form a government. Charlie said as things stood, all the numbers having been crunched, then the Tories would win more seats than us, they would have maybe a million plus more votes than us in England, but the Lib Dems would lose seats, as would the Tories, and between them, even with DUP and UKIP, they would not get over the 323 line.

We would be second in all probability but if you added us to the Lib Dems we could form a minority government which the SNP would not want to bring down. This was the best possible outcome, but far from perfect and it was not at all clear if the LDs would want to support us. It was difficult to make approaches, though Andrew Adonis was in contact with some of them and Ed spoke to Cable from time to time (he did not have a very good relationship with Clegg). Charlie felt Ed was doing well enough not to be immediately toppled but there was no doubt that e.g. Yvette Cooper and Andy Burnham were on manoeuvres. The truth is Ed's team had been working on every scenario, except one where we lose seats, and when I asked why, I was told they thought it would have been 'bad for morale'. We chatted for an hour or so, usual good-humoured and well-informed Charlie stuff, while we waited for Douglas. Douglas was up and down in his worry about his seat. At the moment he was down. Jim Murphy had told me the numbers and the groups were going backwards not forwards. He felt even his own seat was in danger.

Douglas said Ed's status in Scotland was really hurting them. Also Sturgeon was terrific at what she did. But we had to remember that she existed to destroy us because the SNP saw Labour as the only party that could stop the march to independence. The holding out of the hand of friendship was a ploy to make Ed's life more difficult, and for the Tories to exploit, as they were doing. He felt Ed had shaped up pretty well, and had some good moments, but he was not helping in Scotland. Also Jim M had said no more cuts and he would have control of that and Ed had said yes there would have to be more cuts, and Chuka had slapped Jim down by saying he would not dictate the budget.

We worked out a line for the debate that Jim would be part of the Budget team and also that Alex S and Nicola S most certainly would not. It was fine as a debating point, but as Douglas said there were forces here stronger than all of us. We were starting to plan how to handle the moment of polls closing, exit polls etc. We had to buy time. I said we should be immediately talking up some of the big themes – is the political system fucked? Is PR inevitable? Is independence inevitable? We also had to win the argument that a minority government could work.

There had been a precedence in the early 1920s when a Lab–Lib government was formed even though the Tories had more seats. It lasted seven months. The Fixed-term Parliaments Act was a complicating factor and Charlie talked me through what that meant for the possibility of a second election. Jeremy Heywood [Cabinet Secretary] had said to Charlie that if there was the slightest sign that it was going to be messy, or Cameron might get pushed, then he would resign. He was not going to fight. The forces would be out if he did not win. He might try to stay a while as the party decided whether to go for Boris Johnson. Labour meanwhile would face a massive onslaught from the establishment, money and the media, to hand over.

Sturgeon meanwhile was saying that she was giving Ed the chance to win and he should take it – thereby playing into the Tories' hands. It was all very very tricky. I felt it would be hard to sustain. But as Charlie said the Fixed-term Act gave us more leeway than people might realise. If a government was defeated it did not automatically mean another election.

There had to be two. The SNP would not want to be seen to usher in a Tory government. Charlie said that he thought I should be Scottish Secretary from the Lords! No chance. Stayed there till gone eleven, and at the end of it had moved a little. I had started out thinking there was no chance if we were not the biggest party but ended thinking maybe there is.

Ahead of the five-way debate, I did another note for Ed. He had to take it to Cameron, Farage and Sturgeon from the get-go, and emphasise that only he or DC could be PM, and it was an outrage Cameron was not there. Just use it as another opportunity to highlight the choice between the only two possible PMs and governments. 'He can run but he can't hide' kind of thing.

Wednesday 15 April

To Bafta in Piccadilly for the London Business Forum event on the 150th anniversary of Abraham Lincoln's death. A Lincoln lookalike, whose day job was as a John Cleese lookalike, added to the fun and did the Gettysburg Address to introduce me. 150 or so business guys, liked it I think, then a good Q&A, more topical, and a signing. Chatted to Jim Murphy en route to my next thing, a McKinsey seminar on a new approach to mental health care in NW London. Good event.

Then to HQ, chatted with Iain McNicol re. the numbers coming in moneywise to party coffers. Doing OK. £2 million online, £19 million total. But the cost would be a nightmare if we had a second election. The key had to be to get in there and see if we could stay there. He felt Ed was doing fine but he would be very vulnerable 8 May and they wanted me around. There was already a bit of moving by the Balls lot, e.g. briefing about all the old GB lot should be in charge of negotiations etc. re. coalition. Planning some messaging with Tom B and Torsten at Leon's, in between going back for another session with Ed. We had become perhaps a little too fixated on Sturgeon and needed to think a bit more about Farage who had actually broken through pretty well last time. The three women in the leaders' debate [Nicola S, Leanne Wood, Caroline Lucas] had met to plot their joint approach, and that was going to include challenging him over what he said re. foreigners should not get HIV care, and I worked hard with Ed on how he could empathise without losing the Stan/James shtick.

Americans had gone back apart from Stan. There was a danger now he was over-braining. Tried to get him to go home early. Failed. But I left and had dinner with Rory, then Andy McCann saw Ed and then came round to Estelle Road, after Ed had called me. Ed was obsessing re. what he called the whole time his 'line of sight' issue, e.g. on Sturgeon we agreed we should give her principle, and real belief, but say we disagreed fundamentally because she wanted to break up a country at a time the world needed us to be strong. For Farage that he exploited rather than sought to resolve problems.

He called when I was with Rory, and Andy with him, and was going over much of the same ground we had been going over all day. He was in circular mode. How did we get Cameron in the room? What did we do if the three women ganged up? Immigration? Devolution? etc. etc. etc., round and round. Andy was finding it quite frustrating but he felt Ed was better and stronger, just worrying about tomorrow for obvious reasons. I felt so long as Ed was focused and was clear about the main goals he would be fine. We would see.

Thursday 16 April

Keir round for a workout, then telly, then a phone interview for *The Herald*, all about sport and the book. Into Brewer's Green and had a light-hearted black humour session with Douglas and Tom Baldwin before we had a final run-through, but without all the camera stuff. This time I was Dimbleby, and Ed was definitely stronger in his presence, but it was not going to be easy. The whole thing was set up for Nicola and Farage to do well. They went off to the Methodist Hall a couple of times and had to lean on the BBC to agree to Ed having a taller lectern. He then came back and we were just honing and rehoning lines on the SNP. Final session was to be honest just comfort stuff, then eventually I said we should just stop. He needed to get into his own head.

Kezia said Scotland was getting worse, ditto Jim. Even her dad had joined the SNP. I chatted for a bit with Marianna and Rachel and then slipped off to the School of Life,* Alain [philosopher] and Charlotte de Botton's outfit, where Jemima Khan was interviewing me about the book. Good audience, packed out, and we shifted a fair few books. Jemima wanting to get me going re. Iraq, but I was managing to steer it both to the book and to life lessons. Afterwards Alain said that I could and should turn it into a theory of consultancy. The book was ticking away well, definitely connecting with people. Grace and Gail were there, plus our Grace and Rory. Grace said to me afterwards that she had said to Rory, when I was talking, 'It is quite cool having him as our dad, don't you think?' When I was asked my worst quality and I asked them, they said none. Proud of them!

Another question on whether men and women won differently. Really interesting subject. Maybe a different book. Grace's little film getting Anne Robinson to watch porn for the first time had gone on the *Guardian* website

---

* Global organisation helping people to live more fulfilled lives.

yesterday and was trending on the top of Facebook all day. Brilliant. Peter Morgan who wrote *The Queen* [film] was there and we chatted a bit about that. Angus Deayton [broadcaster] also there, who loved my onslaught v Dacre. Zac Goldsmith [MP for Richmond Park] called Jemima and we ended up having a chat. He said he loved his Labour opponent, Sachin Patel [Labour PPC], and wished him the best.

Fiona back from France but with a bad back. She said Ed did really well in the debate and that seemed to be the general view. The others were all turning to him as the PM-type figure on the stage. He did his challenge to Cameron well. Sturgeon warm and friendly most of the time, all about locking out the Tories, but then at the end did another appeal and said the country would not forgive Ed M if he turned down this chance and let them back in.

Friday 17 April

TB sent me a note saying he felt Cameron had made a mistake in abandoning economic credibility and the centre, that Ed did well, had been good at resisting Nicola last night, right to focus on inequality but also came over as sensible and we needed more of the latter. I still felt he had to up the heavyweight interventions on foreign policy, Europe, the union, education and skills, political and media culture, optimism. But I did a note saying in each of the three big telly moments people had reassessed him upwards. He was at the threshold of 'not what we thought'; next stage has to be 'definitely PM material'. I reminded him that in '97 TB's six big speeches were important. His [Ed's] planned immigration speech should be more than a bit of focus-group-tested positioning.

Spoke later and emphasised again the need to be out on big themes. Foreign policy was not getting a look-in. Another dire poll in Scotland, even worse, Jim and Douglas in trouble. I set off for Euston, Liverpool-bound. Philip Hammond [Foreign Secretary] was in the first-class lounge on the way to Chester and we had a chat. He had not seen the debate but felt from the reaction that Sturgeon had made life difficult for Ed. The Tories were going to push even harder on the Lab–SNP link. I said Cameron did not appear energised and unsurprisingly he disagreed. He felt that the economic message would get through. I said it was remarkable the extent to which foreign policy was just not in the debate. He said it hardly ever was, but I am not so sure that is true.

To the Hilton and finally met Carolyn Hughes [PR] who had put together the lunch for the book. A real livewire. Good production values, fantastic attention to detail, e.g. the book in marzipan on cakes, an Instagram board for people to take pictures and upload them. Loads and loads of

Liverpool ladies who lunch including some who were very forward and later very pissed. Ex-footballer Mark Wright's wife said that she would vote Labour if I was leader and there was a lot of applause. Someone else said none of the current lot could speak to all sorts, and I could. Another that I was trustworthy in a way most weren't. Quite an eye-opener for Marion from *Le Monde,* who was tracking me for her portrait piece, after all the shit in the press.

There was a piper and I played by popular demand, then a Sinatra impersonator who was pretty good. Carolyn said she had never known a reaction like it, felt it was real pin-drop territory. One woman had a pop over Iraq, I dealt with it fine but the other women at the table said they were going to kill her! I was being inundated at the end with people saying I should stand, so would be heading for a big guilt trip. The Burnley team arrived and Ian Woan [assistant manager] and Tony Loughran [coaching staff] had eyes on stalks as all these women came staggering down from the dinner.

Later had dinner with Sean after seeing the end of the team talk. Still confident. We had a terrific chat. He was always really interested in how I lived, how I operated, a real hoover of other people's stories and methods. Not sure what he was looking for next season. Would obviously depend on what happened.

Alex F had been to Gawthorpe recently, and I asked how he was. It was really quite weird that our friendship had just evaporated without clear reason. I had tried a couple of times to make contact, but nothing back. Usual chat and gossip and then we went to the bar to meet the other coaches. Weird for a Hilton but basically it became a night club. Quite a scene. I got to bed about half eleven. Liverpool definitely a buzzing place. Liam Smith [champion light-middleweight boxer] fighting tomorrow but he came for a picture at the lunch and also he was around getting pizzas for all his mates upstairs.*

Saturday 18 April

Carolyn had sorted me a driver, a very nice chap called Tony, to take me to Doncaster to see Graeme before coming back for the match. I started to read the Max Moseley [former president Federation Internationale du Sport Automobile] book, as I was interviewing him next week for *GQ.* Not a bad read, but too much F1 for me. Got Graeme some weights to build up his arms. He was on pretty good form, much better than last time. Seemed to see a future. Liz feeling the strain, I think. Jan, Ian Botham's

---

* Smith won the WBO Inter-Continental light-middleweight title the following evening.

mother- in-law, came in. Ian's all-time wicket-taking record had been beaten by Jimmy Anderson yesterday. Off back to Liverpool, Goodison Park. Bill Kenwright [chairman Everton FC] had invited me for lunch but he was ill and didn't make it. Lovely old club. Another good performance but which yielded nothing. One down, Ashley Barnes sent off for two yellows, and then though we battled away, didn't really threaten.

Carolyn lift to station, then train back with John B who told me in confidence that he was going to step from Burnley co-chairman to normal director. Basically Mike Garlick had got more shares, just short of fifty, because John had given as loans not share transfers. He was pretty angry about it, especially as Mike made his move when he was having his cancer treatment. But he was settled now and had decided it was probably for the best. He wanted me to help him with the announcement. Some Everton fans on the train had been talking to him and were raving to me about what a top bloke he was. He really was a different sort of chairman. Fiona met me, Greek restaurant, nice chat then I headed for Gatwick Hilton and a few hours' sleep. John Blake [publisher] accepted story re. piano wrong in *Blair Inc.*

Sunday 19 April

Did another blog taking apart the Cameron campaign which was now moving much more on to the Labour/SNP theme. He was basically talking up Sturgeon rather than himself. Up at five and off to North Terminal, signed stock in the three shops and picked up *Sunday Times*, Relative Values piece good. Rory came over well, though he did say I had thought about going back into politics but only if I thought I could be leader. Arrived at Tirana, off to the Sheraton and had a quick swim to try to wake up a bit. Lunch with Erion and Endri.

After a bit of a struggle to push aside another candidate, Edi had asked Erion to go for Mayor of Tirana. SP way ahead in the polls and the DP candidate – the current mayor was stepping down – was a 61-year-old gynaecologist who seemingly didn't fancy doing media. But we agreed it was important to put together a strong campaign and fight for every piece of support. Young, dynamic, action man, fixer. They were thinking 'the right direction' as a slogan (had to go for all of the mayoral campaigns on 21 June, municipal election day) but it felt too staid and static to me. They went through the polling with me, which all looked OK, and we then had a meeting with his key people where I went through some of the basics for a campaign and suggested they work back from 21 June, and plan big bold stuff. Two weeks still to go as minister. Then two weeks to consult party and public, then launch, then build-up to the day with three big things per week. Mark Lucas coming out to help.

Tirana had 'grown' in the reorganisation and it meant almost one third of the country was involved, so it was a big deal but also important for the next election if he did well. He would. A lot of interest in our election of course. Back to the hotel and I had a massage. Hoped it would get me a bit of energy back but in fact I was pretty knackered. Out with Endri to Edi and Linda's new house. Remarkable place about half an hour from Tirana. As you arrived, up some very windy hills, there was a big metal gate, down a steep incline and past what looked like two giant dark stone vats. Nice house, lots of character. Edi greeted us, Linda brought through the baby.

Nice meal, ate way too much. Cherie the only other guest they had had for dinner. Edi had said he was pleased my book had done well and she said yes, Alastair was very lucky to have worked with a winner. Lots of chat re. our election and at one point Ed M called to discuss Scotland. He said the Tories were really starting to crank up the idea of a Labour–SNP coalition, and with the SNP doing the same, it meant we were being squeezed. He and Douglas were both talking to GB who wanted to get involved. Jim reluctant but it was going to need big stuff to turn it around. Ed was beginning to see that the whole Tory and media establishment would cry foul if he got in with SNP support. And he was worried that some of our lot would move against him before he had even tried to get through the door.

He said they had a positive message – social justice, a squeeze message re. 'If you wanted a Labour government you had to vote for it, not take the risk.' But the Tories and the SNP were both pushing the message that a vote for the SNP would help deliver a Labour government so we were being squeezed. Chatted with Edi both about the Serb project – he was seeing Vučić and the other Balkan leaders in Brussels tomorrow – and also Erion and how to make the campaign the platform for his next one. He was in good shape. Lost a bit of weight. Getting tired later and eventually bed by twelve. Ed M called again just as I was falling asleep. Same chat re. Scotland. Said he really wanted me to think about how we could get some of this Scottish stuff back.

Monday 20 April

Liz called first thing to say Donald was in hospital again. The pneumonia was back. Sorted a trip to Glasgow tomorrow to see him and arranged to see Jim Murphy too. Liz quite upset. She was having to deal with a lot right now. Breakfast then a meeting with Erion to go over his backstory – son of military couple, dad died when he was ten, off to Greece with an uncle, educated US, lots of charity and volunteering stuff, real sense of being a fixer. Also widely seen as best of the ministers. Said we needed to get Mark to film him through the week. Edi showed me around the new media centre, which was excellent. Lunch in the new lunch place. Nice food as ever. Talking about sport, the book – I could tell he was chuffed it was going well – our election, and his next steps. Off to the airport with him, met the EU ambassador [Romana Vlahutin], a Croatian woman, and chatted to her re. what more we could do.

I was in business not realising Edi always travelled economy, which clearly went down well with the selfie hunters. I worked on a note for Ed re. Scotland, then for Erion/Mark re. what they might do together. HuffPo posted the mental health blog I had done a while back, good reaction. Vienna, quick connection, then Heathrow, bought new suit, Paul Smith, dinner. Ed called to tell me Michael Forsyth had done an interview for *The Guardian* attacking the Cameron tactics on the SNP, saying he was playing a dangerous game with the union. He was convinced this was a game-changer if we could get more out.

The Tories were wheeling out Major tomorrow to trot out the line and we had to go hell for leather in saying that if they played England v Scotland, down that road lay disaster. We agreed that there was no avoiding this as a big thing. It had to be played out as such. If the Tories can prevent making the election a vote on them, and instead make it about Lab/SNP deals, they get the upper hand back. We had to make this backfire the same way we had made other tactics backfire. I started to put feelers out to other Tories. Fly to Glasgow. Hilton at the airport. Douglas called to say I should 1, speak to Alistair Darling who was doing the *Today* programme and 2, get Jim to get more organised and strategic and to get GB into the game. I was happy to do both.

Tuesday 21 April

Douglas called asking if I could call Alistair Darling to 'put some steel in him' pre the *Today* programme. He was worried that Alistair would be a bit commentariatish rather than political and really go for the Tories over the way they were pitting England v Scotland. To be fair he did well. He said he was glad he wasn't standing, that Scotland was a mess, and the minute the interview was over he texted me to say, 'Back to retirement.' He said to me earlier that he felt I needed to talk to Kezia 'because the reality is she could be Scottish leader quite soon, and she needs to be ready.' He was not being disloyal, but it showed up how had things were that we were thinking both Jim and Douglas might lose.

I went for a run, then got picked up and driven over to Jim Murphy's place. We took a cup of tea out to the garden. I found him strangely becalmed, obviously aware how bad things were, but not really on it in terms of how to get on top of it all. As in when I asked if he had a grid and he said yes, 'well, someone does'. He didn't really have a strategy, or a sense of one. I said we had to get up the line that the Tories were playing with fire on the union and he said he knew a guy who was a fire eater and they could use him! He had also been playing in a charity football match yesterday, which seemed an odd thing to do on the day of the SNP's rather effective manifesto launch. Nicola was becoming quite irritating for the English, which may have been part of her plan.

Ed had called and asked me to go up for a couple of days. Douglas had called asking me to get Jim out of the mindset that said if GB or others came into the campaign, somehow that was undermining of him. I said these small incremental initiative-type things would not cut through. He had to be on big themes and big message. He had to have bold ideas and we had to start taking the fight to them more aggressively. I felt with the two to three weeks left he needed e.g. GB out a couple of times, Ed and Ed Balls up a couple of times, even wheel out TB if we wanted to make noise. But he had to have a plan. I said Jim should go into the office, review the forward agenda and just make sure it had bigness.

He said his wife actively wanted him to lose because she hated the whole thing, felt politics had ruined their lives, and she could not understand why he wanted to do it. They did not even have a Labour poster up because she said it just attracted abuse. Spent about an hour with him, and he seemed OK but aware of how bad it was going to be. I went off to the hospital to see Donald who was not as bad as I expected him to be. The hospital was pretty dingy, being run down to close. A dementia patient in the next bed who kept trying to grope the doctors and nurses.

Into the BBC to do Adrian Chiles, partly about rivals but also about the current campaign. Back to the hospital, had a quick bite to eat then back to see Donald before heading off to the station and back home by train. Did a couple of notes to Ed and Douglas re. Scotland – suggested maybe saying we would go all out to stop a second referendum – and also trying to get hold of Ed's speech on foreign policy which he was making on Friday. Was hammering Cameron for his playing fire with the union. Ed called later and asked if I could spend more time up there, said he felt Jim appreciated the visit and would benefit from having me around a bit more.

Jim seemed up for GB doing his thing tomorrow so we should seize that. He is inevitably a little worried that it will be spun against him but I explained that Major coming into the campaign – both the fact of it and the message – was a perfect pivot for GB. I said that this argument has to be played out to the max over the next day or two to prevent it becoming the Tory staple for the rest of the campaign.

April '15: Jim Murphy's wife wants him to lose

I said he should build into the grid two or three big set speeches from himself plus events with Ed M, Ed Balls, maybe Alistair.

I told Ed Jim is clearly a bit besieged and a little becalmed in terms of the rest of the campaign. Clearly he worries that none of the attacks on the SNP are sticking.

I said he needs to take the fact that Scotland has become such a big thing for the whole election and embrace it.

Wednesday 22 April

Another note to Ed. Again, I was trying to be honest without hitting his confidence. I felt there had definitely been a shift in his favour, but it was still catch-up. He had at least opened the door to the possibility of a re-evaluation from some who had ruled him out. Also, Cameron was not campaigning well, which provided an opportunity too. But the media narrative of choice, as so often the one the Tories wanted, was about the SNP as Labour's only route to power, and so a risk. Tom B and I had a mutual rant about the way the media, despite such a proliferation of space and outlets, would always get fixated on one narrative, and because the right-wing media shouted louder, and the broadcasters followed them, it was so often the one the Tories wanted. They had become totally fixated on Scotland as the story of this election. It felt most days like BBC and other broadcast journalists were taking it in turns to go up and do big pieces on 'what it means' which usually ended up with them reinforcing Tory attack ads about Ed being propped up by SNP. Getting harder to cut through with any other message. However, the opportunity it presented to Ed was that it took the Tories away from where they had initially wanted to be – economy and leadership. They were looking weak on both.

Ed kept hammering zero-hours contracts, but it was not an economic message. He needed more reassurance for business, especially as the Tories would be winding up the message about run on the pounds, market mayhem etc. He had to inoculate against that. I said again he needed to show more on foreign policy, again in part because Cameron was vacating on leadership. He needed a bit more world view. And the union debate was another leadership opportunity, accepted difficult because of Scotland, but a route into seriousness on the economy too. My final point was that we needed to see more of the team.

Major had a pretty big hit with his speech. Definitely need GB up. I set off for Knightsbridge, long chat with Ed about his foreign policy speech. I was trying to inject bigness into it, leadership around Europe and the union. Douglas was agitated because Ed did not want to roll the union into it – felt it just meant another day playing on the Tories' turf – and also he seemed determined to do Iraq as a big thing – differentiation. I said he had to make sure this was PM not NUS [National Union of Students] speech. He would have Stewart Wood whispering in his ear.

As Douglas said, Wood was a courtier, but he also sought constantly to persuade Ed that 1, he had a real meaningful project and 2, his instincts on policy positions were right when it was pretty clear they did not really strike a chord with a lot of people. I felt I could defend him to most reasonable people, but on the economy non-rebuttal and on his failure to have a message on foreign policy – Douglas said the problem was he was not really interested and he did not really get it! – I couldn't. Interviewed Max Mosley for *GQ*. I had read and liked his book and we had a nice chat. Him, his background, F1, the media, it all flowed pretty well and he gave a lot of himself.

Thursday 23 April

Write Mosley, flowed really well. Worked on Ed speech before I headed out to Excel for Motivate Europe event [leadership showcase]. Douglas called re. the draft I had done and said, 'Wow, if only he delivers that speech he will get himself to a different place. It is elevating and it is the speech of a leader.' But though he took some of it on board he didn't take it all and it was not that brilliant. Definitely missed opportunity. He called me a couple of times and he said I had to understand that most people did not know he was against Iraq. He was doing quite a lot of 'This is who I am', and had also said to Tom B, 'You have to trust my judgement.' According to Iain McNicol and Douglas, Tom was playing a blinder but still did not get on with Bob Roberts [Labour Party director of communications]. Had a long chat with Tim Livesey, who was mainly working on planning for government. Asked me if either Fiona and I were interested in the Lords. No and no. He said he felt the best hope was Lib–Lab. We had not made approaches to Clegg. He and Ed did not get on great, also they could not be trusted. We were pretty sure Clegg would prefer a deal with Cameron. Also unless there was a real push towards Cameron, and the UKIP vote fell, hard to see how they would get the numbers.

He said there would be no discussions with the SNP. The coalition team would be Charlie, Balls, Harriet H, Douglas and Rosie W. Tim scathing re. Wood and his constant briefing of his own importance. They were not a terribly cohesive team. The Scotland situation was still dominating. As Jim had said we were actually getting hit up there by both SNP and Tories saying that if you voted SNP you effectively voted for a Labour government. Good chat with Torsten who I liked and who had a bit of weight and also was a good laugh.

Sent Ed speech to TB who felt we should tone down the volume of attack on Cameron and talk up hard power/soft power. It was OK but not brilliant. Scotland not moving. Tories really pushing it now in England. Cameron has gone to an EU summit on the migrants who died in the Med, and was doing his usual bollocks. Helle texted to say he looked nervous and needed a haircut.

Douglas was emphasising to Ed that the redraft of the foreign policy speech I had done was really strong, and what we should do. But he was talked back into the comfort zone by Wood and others. Worse, some of them had been arguing for Ed to turn the speech into a full-scale whack at TB over Iraq. I asked Ed, 'Am I writing into the ether?' I said an elevated foreign policy/leadership speech is exactly the right place to locate an argument about the union being an important foreign as well as domestic issue. The union strong. British strong in Europe. Sturgeon wrong. Cameron and Farage wrong. I said if I turn on the telly tomorrow and hear people blathering about New Labour and Iraq 2003 rather than Miliband and Cameron and foreign policy now, I will react as I have done over the past five years re. economy. Only more violently.

Friday 24 April

Lift to Euston with Rory and on the way Ed called twice because the Tories had seized on a line in the briefing and were saying that Ed was accusing Cameron of being responsible for the deaths of the migrants who had drowned in the Med. In a way he was but he felt it meant he was in danger of losing the moral high ground. He was sounding a bit panicky and it took me three calls to get him to calm down and we worked a position that was basically, nobody was accusing DC of drowning people and the people responsible were the traffickers. But a combination of weak leadership, EU failure and failure of post-conflict planning meant that these were all contributory factors. Tom felt a bit under pressure because of the briefing being blamed on him. But I said to Ed bear in mind yesterday we were worried we would not get the speech up, but we did, and we had to embrace that.

The only people pushing this as a row were the Tories. He held his nerve. More disappointing though, as Douglas said, was that he did not really embrace the bigger and more elevated speech. Train to Preston, lift to Gawthorpe to make the profile of Sean and BFC for *Football Focus*. Good fun. Saw Big Sam Vokes [striker] who said he was injured which was a bit of a blow. Lunch with Sean and his team – they love to talk – then the interview out on the artificial turf, good chat, obvious stuff but I do think he was more open etc. because we knew each other well.

Had a cup of tea, then off to Rossendale and Darwen, school gate with Will Straw then canvassing. Lots of undecided. It was also as though Cameron was not really in the debate. SNP starting to come through as a problem for us. Ed still a problem though people did say they thought he had been doing better. Later at Bury North a woman called Pam really pressed me to stand. I did a little pep talk and a book signing. James [Frith, Labour PPC] definitely had something I would say. I said that to us the idea of being undecided is anathema but lots are and they are the ones we have to get, mix of ground and air war but above all face-to-face etc.

In the Q&A, even though they were all party activists and canvassers in a campaign, a good half of the questions were about mental health. Did *MEN* interview. They said Tories were avoiding local media so I said Osborne was hiding in his northern economic cowardhouse. Twitter stuff was going well though I was probably too negative. But we did have to keep whacking them. I also found it easier to be negative about them than positive about us. To Manchester, train via Sheffield to Retford.

Saturday 25 April

Out for a run, sat and chatted with Liz. Got the train to Doncaster to see Graeme, tweeting madly re. Cameron confusing West Ham and Villa, what a total phoney.* If that was Ed we would never hear the end of it. Villagate starting trending. Graeme struggling mentally and physically. To Burnley v Leicester, yet another one–nil defeat we should have got something from.

Sunday 26 April

Blog on Villagate, trying to make it more serious – re. phoneyness – than the media wanted to. Ed on *Marr*, did OK, especially a little head-to-head with Boris Johnson re. non-doms [people living in the UK with non-domiciled status for tax purposes] at the end. Main thing today was Rory and the London Marathon. Drove him to Charing Cross and said it was going to be one of the best days of his life, but ended up a bit of a disaster. Went with Georgia and Grace Gould first to Canada Water then Canary Wharf, where he was looking OK, and doing around 3.31–3.33 per kilometre, and then to Big Ben. But suddenly on the app he stopped moving and it turned out his hamstring had gone and he had been lying in an ambulance for eight minutes but then decided to walk to the end, and just missed out

---

* The Prime Minister claimed he supported West Ham United during a speech in south London, despite previously saying he was an Aston Villa fan. Later he claimed 'brain fade' for forgetting his favoured side.

on three hours. He would have been in top fifty or so non-elite sub 2.40 having got to twenty miles in 1.55. He was totally gutted at the end, and took a while to get over it.

He had prepared so hard. Also Brendan had given him a shout-out as promised and said he was on for 2.40 so word went round that is what he had done. Got Brendan, Dave B and Andy McCann to speak to him. I went back to party HQ after we all went to the Albert for lunch, the Goulds, Greg and Karan [girlfriend]. Meeting at Labour re. *Question Time* strategy. I had missed yesterday's where Ed had apparently been OK, but today, whether too tired or just not up for it, it was not so good. Getting in a bit of a muddle about how to deal with SNP and also the economy. I worried re. the SNP that we were allowing ourselves to be bullied into a position where any kind of contact with them pre or even post-campaign was seen as some kind of betrayal.

Ed stayed till about seven, round and round we went re. some of the key arguments. He felt he had had no choice but to have a really hard position on the SNP, but it had gone from no coalition to no anything really, yet the reality was we were likely to need them to survive. The Tories clearly felt they were on to something in their attack re. Labour–SNP chaos, Ed being controlled by Nicola, who was continuing to be the star of the campaign really.

Monday 27 April

Suggested to Ed he announce appointing Margaret Hodge to examine how best to implement the tax avoidance policy? She has cut through on the issue. Also, fresh campaign re. students on new housing stuff with tuition fees. Suggested 'bring an undecided' party events, where he is seen to persuade. The message that our core support is solid, but there are a lot of undecideds and they are the key. So rather than just preach to the converted, get the converted to bring the non-converted to events. I said the media will see it as new form of engagement. Small risk of course that loads of people come out and say undecided still or he made them decide the other way, but unlikely if they come with party members.

I was also getting more worried re. the economy, that the failure to rebut over the last five years was really hurting and that was coming through via doorstep reports too. I did a blog to do a bit of thinking in ink, then off to Stratford by train. Literary festival fine. Lovely hotel, the Arden. Interviewed by Viv Groskop [journalist and comedian], all good, though a guy collapsed halfway through and we had to delay. Good applause for saying Cameron should have done the debates and also for defending TB record.

TB asked me what I thought was happening. Lots of undecideds. Will either fold to 'stick with Tories cos of economic risk' or 'I think on balance Miliband can do it'.

Have to make Cameron 'the risk'. I told Ed about the Stratford Literary Festival last night. Very Middle England audience. Loudest applause – in order:

1. Saying media coverage to blame for political disengagement
2. Attacking Cameron for not sticking to a strategy and for ducking the debates
3. Defending TB record as a winner

Swim, train back, lunch with Rory at Marylebone. He was not really over the marathon. Most people just impressed he had finished. To Labour HQ and another long session, this time with me as Dimbleby. The Americans were over. Sheehan getting a bit frustrated at times, but actually I found his demeanour pretty good and I found his answers more confident and more commanding. Axelrod back, and he had a good calming effect on Ed. When we were doing the audience Q&A the Americans were at times taken aback by how rough the questions were, also by my sarcasm and interruptions but the reality is that is what Dimbleby would do. This was going to be the one where the public were given the chance to hit them all pretty hard.

We were focusing on immigration, economy / deficit, SNP, and in terms of stock arguments it was fine, but he needed a bit more energy and cut-through. I was trying to get him to row back a little on the no talks, no deals, no truck with the SNP – we were making them sound like Sinn Féin during the Troubles – but he had persuaded himself he had to. He said even if we did not win a majority, the SNP had made clear they would not support a Tory Queen's Speech whereas they might support ours and he was confident they would. I was talking more and more to Charlie and Tim about what would happen after 7 May. Nice late lunch with Axelrod. I did a note suggesting how he could turn up the idea that Cameron was the risk. Again Ed said he liked it but then didn't particularly want to commit to it.

Stayed till about nine, he was pretty tired at the end, and also I could tell that Douglas was starting to worry even more about losing Paisley, where his SNP opponent was a feisty twenty-year-old woman. Most of Ed's team starting to think they would definitely get to No. 10. Tim asking again if F or I would reconsider re. the Lords. Charlie asking if I would do Scotland or sport, or both. The Ed / Russell Brand interview had emerged and was clearly going to be a big thing. Usual suspects condemning it but actually it was a good thing to do. The book slipped out of the top ten, just ninety more books would have kept it in there.

Wednesday 29 April

Blog re. Brand, defending him and Ed for doing it. Meeting with BBC Scotland and film-maker Wendy Rattray, who wanted me to make a film with her husband the wildlife guy Gordon Buchanan about wildlife in the Hebrides. There would be a focus on seals, so I checked out that Lachie's nearest and dearest were OK with it. [AC cousin Lachie Campbell had killed himself in 2000. He had been a child star in a film about a seal.] Liked her and her colleague and felt it would be a good film. To Labour HQ and debate prep for several hours. Me as Dimbleby again. Not bad, struggling a bit on when he last spoke to David – clearly a while ago – handling of SNP, and immigration depending on whether attacked from the right or the left. Dinner with F at Lemonia. Andy McCann round at Ed's later on. He felt he was OK but still work to do. They watched the Kay Burley interview with the audience and agreed it worked because he was relaxed and conversational.

Thursday 30 April

Grace's 21st. Breakfast with her then out to Hackney with Dave B and Godric, for a visit to a school that did marginal gains, City Academy. Jeremy Wilson of the *Telegraph* with us. Went well. Dave in an amazingly sharp suit. Meeting with GS to plan pre-Tour. Sent a final note to Ed, who had headed up to Leeds for the *Question Time*. I was going to miss it because of Gracie's dinner at the Soho House but I managed to watch most of Ed and follow DC getting a hard time on Twitter. But the audience was tough on all of them and the feeling was that Ed screwed up a bit on spending, denying we had overspent. It was in a sense five years too late.

This was always going to hurt us because we had allowed the negative assessment of our economic stewardship to stick. It turned out that Tory plants were behind the tough questioning but that didn't matter. The truth is he should have done a better job on the substance over the past few years. Really annoying. He had a bit of a stumble at the end and called me as soon as he was out, saying, 'How can they say I fell off the stage?' He was working himself up into a rage about it. I stressed it didn't really matter, it was not worth worrying about and I felt in general he had been OK. But his team were more worried, maybe because they had been there.

I had missed the worst of it, but I didn't see the point of getting him down on it. The reality though was that it was a bit of a no-score draw. Cameron won the instant poll. Clegg did OK but was seen as largely irrelevant and he got hit hard because of the early betrayal stuff. Axelrod asked me what I thought. I said fine but not a breakthrough moment. He also felt I was too down on Cameron, that he had done better than I said. I was becoming too biased re. DC possibly. Ed had looked and sounded better in some of the rehearsals. Not a good sign.

Friday 1 May

General feeling that Ed had not won the debate. Torsten blaming me for getting Ed to feel he had to defend the record – as if – Charlie and Greg feeling it was OK but not a step up, which was what we needed. Steve Coogan recording with Mark Lucas for a PEB [party political broadcast] in Brighton. Party HQ. Charlie and Andrew A. I was worried we had no real feelers out for intelligence on SNP and Clegg and how they were going to handle election night. Charlie was confident we could claim victory on the basis that Cameron could not win a majority in the Commons for his Queen's Speech.

The Tories were throwing everything now at the Labour–SNP chaos line. Lunch with Greg Beales. He was still hoping to get a seat next time. He also thought I should. We had quite a personal chat about it all. Good guy. Saw Marianna on whether she was up to doing the Paul Brown [No. 10 official in charge of events grid] job in government – she was not so sure and I needed to assure. Talking to Charlie re. some of the research needed on precedent etc. pre the 7 May fallout. To the V&A for Alan Edwards's PR exhibition where I was doing two talks interviewed by him.

Saturday 2 May

Glowing profile in *Le Monde*. Plus Marion doing media on it. 5.30 pick-up and off to Sandbanks in Dorset. Kate [Duchess of Cambridge] into labour for second royal baby so had a bit of fun with that while waiting for Gazza [Paul Gascoigne, former football star] to turn up. His manager Terry Baker had assured me he would be on time and he was. Looked OK, smoking too much, twitching a little, a bit thin, and his voice occasionally disappearing. But it was a terrific interview, really open and frank and with some pretty stark stuff re. what went on inside his head. Terry and his wife Freda were looking after him as well as Terry being his agent and trying to get him work. Also Jimmy Greaves's manager. He said Gazza had been in a really bad way recently, far worse than the press were saying, even though he railed against them. Also the family were a nightmare. He said he was working out of pocket for him, keeping him afloat.

Did the interview quickly and Dylan [Jones] and Jonathan Heaf both loved it, especially for some reason the bit where Gazza talked about wine gums staring at him and his watch listening to his brain. He had some great stories – Ostrich prank, when he took an ostrich to training, an argument with José Mourinho about who the special one was. Lovable but in a bit of a mess. Nice to see him again though and we agreed to keep in touch. He had changed his number again because of the hacking etc.

Cab to Parkstone, breakfast then train to West Ham via Waterloo. Another fucking one–nil defeat. Another crap ref decision, sending off [Michael] Duff. When Sean texted me re. Ed Miliband's two kitchens, I said you worry about nine points and getting your No. 10's head in shape and leave the other No. 10 to me. Cab to Battersea to do a members' motivation event for Will Martindale. They were spooked by an Ashcroft poll and I gave them a pep talk re. the air war no longer counting. Also will to win, fruit and water, usual stuff. Book signing then off to Grafton pub for Grace party. Pipes, speeches, Rasta friends, plus all her usual pals. Good event, she loved it. I liked the idea of playing the pipes with the Suns of Dub, her reggae friends. Royal baby news sponge, probably good for us as it kept the right-wing papers busy.

Sunday 3 May

Train to Doncaster, trains in chaos because of failure at Hatfield. Wrote the Gazza interview there and back, strong stuff, moving and funny. Graeme in not-bad shape. Took him out in the wheelchair. Nice chat. Didn't feel like the election was just days away. Mayweather had won and Kelly was worrying about a fuss re. two women hacks who had been excluded and were kicking up a stink.* Told her not to worry, really didn't matter. Edi had a big speech planned on Europe and the importance of accession and I worked on that for a while, making the case for why foreign policy matters to domestic strategies. Talking up Merkel visit and support.

I then had a final go at persuading Ed to rebut mess we inherited. Axelrod said he agreed too, felt we were straying too far from the core message. I felt we could marry rebuttal on mess we inherited to his core message re. Britain doing best when working families do best. I sent him a note headed 'My final final final go!'

The combination of 'the mess we inherited', the Liam Byrne letter, the claims of overspending, the 'car crash' analogy – all now underpinned by 'chaos' re. SNP – were hurting him. It was still not too late to push back

* A unanimous points decision saw five-division world champion Floyd Mayweather beat eight-division world champion Manny Pacquiao in Las Vegas.

and turn them to his advantage. Link rebuttal of 'mess we inherited' to the mess they are making now. I know it was late, but it was not enough to win on values, he had to win on competence.

I wrote a possible line of attack, but even as I did so, I knew it was too late, also that he would not do it. It was one of those arguments where we had just got stuck. But it was quite a thing that you had people believing we caused the crash by investing too much in schools and hospitals. And still they were standing up for the bankers, the hedge funds, the privatisers. I sent him the recent headline 'Poll blow for Labour' – a survey showing that investment bankers are massively in favour of the return of David Cameron, alongside the *Mirror* headline on a poll of nurses who by a massive majority want a return of a Labour government. That was how to link the crash to now – in everything the Tories say about the past, the present and the future, they show themselves to be on the side of those who caused the crash not those who paid the price.

There was a really powerful 'Whose side are you on?' pitch to be made still. I remembered Bill Clinton's line about compassionate conservatism. Two words. But only one that they understand. Conservatism. Keep things the same. Protect the status quo. Fight against change. Finally, on Scotland, I understood why he had to take a tough line on deals with the SNP, but there was a danger we were making them sound like Sinn Féin in the bad old days, and so helping the Tories and the media build an illegitimacy argument in the event the numbers do suggest some kind of Labour–SNP arrangement.

Monday 4 May

Out with Grace, kilted and all, to some industrial estate out east, to record the bagpipes with Suns of Dub. Tiny little studio, had to perch on a speaker to record it, at times just doing my own stuff, then with headphones listening to their stuff and trying to jam along. Grace in her element of course. Charlie called me and said he had been at a meeting with Ed and his inner team re. transition, and handling of 7 May, and at one point Ed slammed his hand on the table and said why isn't AC involved in all this? Charlie asked if I could go in and be part of all the planning meetings. Agreed to, though I had arranged all manner of out-of-town stuff which I might have to cancel. I also said I was worried that he was locking himself too hard against the SNP. The line we would not even talk to them was treating them like the Tories used to treat Sinn Féin.

He said he agreed with that too. It was always hard to get him to change tack on anything. He said that he felt he had no alternative on the *Marr* programme, but he had hardened his line even more. I had sent Kevin

May '15: New line of attack, but too late

Pringle a copy of the book and asked him by email if he had received it. I said – joking – we had to decide whether emailing re. a book represented 'talks'. Nicola was still making clear she would not support a Tory government. Not ruling out us but she would demand certain things. Tories ramping it for all it was worth. I was really worried we were locking ourselves out. Ed confident we could sit tight and watch Cameron fail to put together a majority and then we could do it. Charlie said we were struggling to make progress because of two major strategic errors – the economy and non-rebuttal, and the handling of Scotland.

Tuesday 5 May

I was on the bike when Charlie called. I had sent him and Ed a note on the idea of Ed sending Cameron a letter as soon as it became clear, if it did, that he could not form a government. Ed had responded by saying to Charlie he had to get me in, so I headed into HQ. I said if it is unclear, he has to play tough immediately. Write to Cameron, say neither has got a majority but both have to make sense of the result and it is clear from all that was said in the campaign DC would not be able to build support for a Queen's Speech. Rebut the idea that in the event of no clear winner it would be about number of overall votes or most seats in England. The constitutional experts were united in seeing this as nonsense. So basically it would be asking him to accept he had lost, whereas he felt he – Ed – would be able to form a majority for a Queen's Speech. Of course it all depended on the numbers.

TB unsure. He said it would depend on the numbers. We would have to be close. Meeting with Charlie, Spencer, James Morris, Tim, Tom, Torsten and Greg. Generally accepted now that the Tories would be the biggest party, but even with the Libs and the DUP they were unlikely to be able to get over the 323 mark. We were heading for fewer seats but possibly being in a better position to be able to form a government that could command a majority, with the SNP not part of a coalition but with them not bringing us down and going through stuff on Bill-by-Bill basis. Charlie said it was possible to have a QS that was full of things we had promised but not so contentious and we could avoid the really tricky stuff now. They agreed the letter seemed the best way to frame the argument and get people talking around that.

We had papers on historical and constitutional precedent but politically it was going to be tough, not least because the right-wing papers would go into meltdown. They had so overshot themselves though. There were no more heights – depths – for their hysteria. I asked whether we should not at least be trying to tease out intelligence from SNP and Libs, but they felt we could not trust any of them, also that the SNP would use anything we said. I felt we had locked ourselves in too hard. They all liked the letter idea but wanted it to be harder on the idea of us saying that the Tories had lost and Cameron had to go.

I sent a draft to TB – we were lining him up possibly to call on DC to go when it became clear he could not form a majority. But he said that the English would react very badly if the SNP decided who the government and the PM was. But Tom B was beginning to get out the lines that we would need to deploy re. the constitutional position. Cameron trying to move to the 'largest party gets to form government' rather than constitutional reality. He was too early with it. Allowed constitutionalists to get out there.

Train to Burnley for Julie Cooper [Labour candidate]. Hilarious on the train. Sitting opposite a Lancaster Uni student doing politics who didn't know who I was, and was embarrassed when I told her. Met at Preston, over to Burnley. Julie told me it was TB who inspired her to go for a seat, and though she felt Ed had done well, she still had doubts. Did some pretty tough streets close to Turf Moor, a few UKIP lads roaming around abusing but otherwise mainly OK. Then an Asian street where we seemed to be doing better.

Out to Manchester Business School. Speech, interview Andrew Bounds *FT*, good Q&A, asked again why I did not stand. Good feedback re. book and politics. Punted Peter M candidacy re. Manchester University chancellorship. Read out his text on why he would be the right person. Networking, authority, support for Vice-Chancellor. Good event, nicely organised, dinner then back to meet Calum at hotel. He was up for the Co-op. As usual making some very astute observations.

Wednesday 6 May

Out briefly for a run, filmed some of the huge numbers of people sleeping rough, then the *FT* front page about some of the remarkable salaries of hedge fund guys 'despite a mediocre year'. Got the train back south after breakfast, lots of people saying they hoped it went well. Into OBG to see Tom, Torsten and Charlie, who felt that we were on for being second party but able to stop Cameron getting a Queen's Speech through. We had four scenarios to go over: Tory majority, Labour majority, and two forms of minority. We actually stopped talking about the majority idea, and everyone seemed to believe that was the reality, that nobody was going to get a majority. Charlie was convinced based on all the numbers that Ed would win. The Tories and the Libs would not between them get anywhere near the 323 they needed, even with the DUP, and we would be able to get through a Queen's Speech by the SNP and others not bringing it down. It felt odd, mind you, because the other numbers – economy, leadership, direction – were not that good for us. Lunch with Tom and Torsten and we were talking about who would do what in Downing Street. It was almost like it was a given. Tom had said no, he was definitely not going in. Torsten still wanted a seat, as did Greg. Tim chief of staff. It all felt a little unreal. I went off to the Savoy for a speech to Axa insurance re. Europe and I was allowing myself to get a bit carried away too maybe, saying I felt Cameron was on the way out. I did the same later at the British Media Awards. I had with me paragraph 2.12 of the Cabinet manual, which set out what happened in a hung parliament, that Cameron was entitled to stay to see if he could win a majority for a QS, but expected to resign once he realised he couldn't, and then the Queen would ask Ed M as 'a clear alternative'. We sat around, Charlie and I, virtually memorising the line so that we could use. We had TB coming back from overseas as we felt there might be a point at which he would be needed to call on Cameron to go rather than cling on. There was a part of me that thought we were deluding ourselves but who knows? The polls were all saying hung parliament. The last eleven had given nobody a clear lead. Only in Scotland was there any sense of clarity. But even there both Douglas and Jim felt they were going to hold on. And if we got a few more seats either way in Scotland and the Tory-held marginal in England we could definitely get close to being viable. The media was already starting to crank up the idea of legitimacy. How could Ed take power as second party propped up by a separatist party we had so opposed? It was a fair point but we just had to hang on to the point about the constitution. I was tweeting madly but the reality was the arguments had been pretty well laid out and it was now all about the people, especially the undecided, making up their minds. The BMA awards was fine, nice enough people, but it was probably not the best speech for that kind of event. I was home by nine and watched Barca v Bayern. Messi out of this world. A bit of a to and fro with Tessa who claimed she was up first for the live coverage tomorrow night, BBC election special. Charlie et al., and Ed, said they wanted me up because if we were second party, the party needed a strong message that constitutionally we were on for it if the Tories could not command a majority. TB called and said he still felt that the Tories would win, that he felt we had not built a majority argument, that we were too narrowly focused on ideas that were based at a minority and without a big economic argument. The Tory campaign had been shit but could still get over the line. Nice message from Douglas re. how much he and Ed had appreciated support and advice. Ed called a couple of times, and the tone was very much about what he could do as PM, how he held things together. Could he ask for Clegg to go? How much room for manoeuvre did he have with his own team? What to do re. Scotland? I was worried that we had made the SNP MPs sound like Sinn Féin or the North Korean Communist Party. We had to have language and tone to get closer. Gus O'Donnell [former Cabinet Secretary] was out doing a good job on pointing out the constitutional reality, but Robin Butler had bumped into someone on our side and said that we had played into the delegitimisation of SNP MPs and that would make it difficult when we then needed them to get through our programme. Scotland was going to be such a big part of the picture for the next five years.

Thursday 7 May

Woke up feeling fairly up, weather good, sense around the place that we had done OK and even if we could not get a majority we might be able to stop them again. Was talking to Peter M, as Charlie was worried what he would say. Keir came round and really worked me hard even though I was probably going to have to go a couple of days without sleep. I did a long blog saying why I thought Ed would win and why he deserved to. The question of the campaign was does DC deserve another five years? I was not quite able to bring myself to believe it but the numbers were indeed pointing to the answer being no.

I went in to see Charlie and Tom. Charlie was briefing the media one-on-one about the Cabinet manual. We were pointing everyone to 2.12. They were more or less buying it though James Landale pushed back quite hard. As the afternoon wore on a few more people came in and we went through all the various scripts. Tessa saying the mood out there was great. Harriet saying she had never seen such enthusiasm. It was becoming a given that Ed was PM. We had a seemingly never-ending discussion about all the possible lines to take. Torsten did make me laugh the way he talked everyone down. Harriet didn't seem terribly pleased to see me, but she did say, when she heard Peter M and Andrew Adonis were taking up two of the main Beeb slots, that 'at least if Alastair is on, the party likes to see and hear him, Peter and Andrew send the wrong message'.

I was still banging on about the need for better tone and language re. the SNP. I was also worried about resting the legitimacy argument purely on technicality of constitution. We had to be into the language of healing and accepting this was not a ringing endorsement. Tessa and Harriet seemed to compete to see who could keep a discussion going longest. I texted Charlie across the table to say that this was the reason I had not wanted to come in full-time and be constantly in endless meetings that went round and round in circles. Charlie was hoping to be Lord Chancellor again but Greg Nugent had told me Cabinet Office. Torsten told me that when Lucy had been talking to the Cabinet Office they had said it might not be a Cabinet position. I was hoping to get home for a bit but all of a sudden it was 8.30 and time to head to Elstree.

Peter M was due to follow me on telly – and in fact he was first up on ITV – and he said to me he was totally alarmed by the chat he had with Charlie. He said the constitutional stuff was easy but there was no sense of how we were going to build momentum for a process that got us an argument about why we deserved to be the government and how. He was clearly totally incredulous about the whole thing.

Ed had called earlier before he went to vote. He said he felt things had moved to us a bit in the last couple of days. The buzz around the place was good, high turnout, good returns and so forth. He felt it was possible we would be the largest party. I said why do you think that? He said just a sense that they have thrown everything and it has not quite landed. We had a conference call with him and Douglas and Lucy before I left for Elstree. He sounded a little bit stressed and panicky. We talked about whether, if it looked like we were winning, or the Tories losing, he staked a claim ASAP at the count – I felt so – or wait till back to London. I felt a little vulnerable that we did not really have proper intelligence either on the SNP or on the Libs and what they planned to do in reaction to an outcome where we would depend on them.

YouGov has revisited a lot of their polled people and were saying still neck and neck. Word also coming through that we were doing really well in Tory-held marginal. I headed out to Elstree, into makeup, and there was Michael Gove. He thanked me for the book I had sent after we had been on *Newsnight* together, said he had not read it all yet, but had read about teamship and totally agreed. Then Paddy [Ashdown] arrived. He and I had chatted before. He felt things were going to be fairly bad for the Libs. He started to make noises about the need for the progressive left to come together at the end of all this. That sounded a little bit like the language of defeat to me.

There was a massive operation at Elstree. David Dimbleby, Laura Kuenssberg [*Newsnight* presenter], Nick Robinson and Peter Kellner [polling specialist] down in the main bit, Andrew Neil chairing the panel which was meant to be me, Paddy and Gove. But I was put to one side at the start, and once the exit poll emerged I realised why. I asked Andrew Neil for the numbers. He said no, I can't, but then added: 'I will tell you this – you are going to be shocked, all of you.' A part of me thought, 'My God, have we won? Are we the biggest party? Or is the shock that the SNP have won every seat?' As the bong came and Dimbleby announced it, I was sitting next to Robert Peston. 'Shit,' he said. 'Nobody saw that coming.'

The Tories were the biggest party by some margin. Bad for us, even worse for the Libs, which is why they wanted Paddy on first. He said he would eat his hat if the exit poll was right. I said I would eat my kilt if the SNP got 58 out of 59 as the poll was suggesting. But clearly it was a bad bad result. Harriet was first up for us, and was OK, basically saying let's wait and see, and not how it felt out and about. I did much the same, said that it didn't feel right. Gove was cautious, so was Sturgeon, but it was going to have to be very very wrong for us to be in the game. Then as the results came in a few things became clear. UKIP were taking votes from us in working-class areas. Massive swings to SNP. Tories wiping out Lib Dems. And the Tories holding up in marginals.

Gove said to me that if the poll was right, it was at the top end of their expectations. He seemed genuinely surprised, loads of caveats. Michael Fallon, on later, said he had expected a small majority even. Paddy seemed pretty shell-shocked, said he knew it would be bad, but not this bad. Ed Balls came on and was basically spouting the line we had been talking about all afternoon, namely Ed M could be PM. I managed to defend him without looking totally stupid. Torsten and Charlie sending ever more pessimistic texts.

Chatted to Paddy, off into Millbank to do Channel 4, ITV down the line, CNN and LBC on College Green, and then to join Fiona, Rory, Calum, Georgia and Grace – just missed our Grace – at the Marriott County Hall bash. Sad affair. We didn't stay too long. Paddy called to say we should discuss way forward. Ditto Alistair D. He said Scotland was a total disaster, there was no other way of describing it. We were being wiped out systematically. It was existential. Got home, watched till four, then went to bed.

Friday 8 May

Woke around seven to find that not only were the Tories the biggest party, but they had a majority, and the scale of Lib Dem wipeout was such that it was going to grow as the day wore on. I was getting loads of bids and felt I should do them as I wanted to say that we should not rush the leadership decision. Ed called early on though to say he was planning to quit, and that frankly he could not really face staying on, so would go immediately, with Harriet as interim. He sounded pretty shell-shocked. He felt the polls had misled them all along and had allowed the election to become a referendum on us/SNP rather than on five years of the Tories. I said he had fought a good campaign and maybe that blinded us to the reality that the fundamentals were never right for us.

Godric made an interesting observation later – he said to me that if there had been no polls, and you looked at the fundamentals – Tories ahead on

May '15: Ed calls to say he was planning to quit

economy and leadership, Ed seen as not up to it, nothing moving in the campaign – why would we think he could win? Dave B sent me a long message saying it was all about assessing what happened to people psychologically when they saw a leader. He was still banging on at me to stand and to get in and do it, but I just could not see it. Maybe ten years ago but not now. Ed called a couple of times re. his words, what and when to say. Rachel told me that Justine seemed almost relieved.

I did a short blog to think in ink, re. the fact that we believed our own propaganda and now we had to have the debate we had been avoiding for too long. Into town to do a huge media round basically trying to be reflective and follow that line. Andrew Neil on the Green, with John Reid, Kate Hoey [former Labour minister] and Daniel Hannan [Tory MEP]. John R and I on same page – not about the leader now but about direction. We were already talking about Ed in the past tense. He was due to resign at midday. Tom B had asked me to talk to him to ask him to stay on for a bit. His argument was that if there was a three-month hiatus, in which Ed just steadied the ship, it might stop the party going mad in the aftermath. I could see that, but after speaking to Ed, and talking it over, he was pretty mind-made-up, and not up for it. I said he had put a lot into it and he deserved to go when and how he liked. I had always worried Ed would really struggle against Cameron, and I did feel there had been some pretty major errors of strategy and politics, but he had shown a lot of guts, a lot of commitment, and if he had decided it was time to go, and go straight away, he was entitled to that decision. Added to which it is just a fact of life that when a party loses like this, a leadership contest effectively starts immediately anyway. I said that on the media too, and did my best to talk him up, and not rub it in. He must be feeling pretty wretched, given how even on the day he and his team had felt he was a lot closer than people thought, and certainly a lot closer than the final outcome. Did loads of bids – CNN, CNBC, Sky, foreign stuff. 5 Live – a producer grabbed me and asked if I would do Peter Allen. Fine.

Went to the tent and Jeremy Corbyn was already there. Allen asked if we minded doing a discussion. No problem. Corbyn neither friendly nor unfriendly. Wearing a really scruffy coat. We agreed this was about direction not just the face at the top. Ken Livingstone already out saying we had to go more left and Corbyn was echoing that. I said we must learn from losing, of course, but had we lost in part because we had already forgotten too many lessons about how we won. Back to OBG to watch Ed's resignation statement, which was a bit comfort zone, then he came back with Rachel and he and I had a chat in his office.

He was very warm, said he had really appreciated all I had tried to do for him, that it had been a massive help. I said maybe we kidded ourselves that the fundamentals had shifted when they hadn't. But the Tories, most of them, definitely thought they were in trouble. So did the civil service, whose expected scenario was a Labour minority government not a Tory majority government. I told him about Gove's reaction. He said Cameron, when he conceded, had said he had defied the polls and the pundits, said he had defied himself too, so maybe he was also surprised. Ed seemed pretty together considering. We went through the runners and riders to replace him and agreed it was pretty grim as choices go. I sensed he favoured Burnham. He said, 'Leaders have to have big thoughts and big things to say and Andy does at least have big thoughts.'

Harriet came in and she too was pretty together. She would now be interim leader. She told Ed he should get away for some sunshine and peace. She said, 'When I was sacked from the Cabinet I did that and after a couple of days I had forgotten why I felt so bad.' I said a few farewells and then headed off home with Rachel who said she was looking forward to seeing the kids. At least Steve [Kinnock, Aberavon] won, as did Julie in Burnley, and Keir Starmer won a huge majority [in AC seat, Holborn and St Pancras]. Not many other good moments to be honest. I had a bit of a kip, did a piece for the *Mirror* and then out to Old Street with Grace for *Question Time*.

Chatted to TB en route. Had to be about the future. He said he had been worrying he had totally lost his sense of the country when people like me and Charlie were saying we might do it because to be fair to him he had been saying a small Tory majority the whole way through. He felt I had to say nice things about Ed but emphasise the importance of the centre ground and the necessity always to focus on the future. Both were a state of mind. The programme was in an old church. First did a clip for Lucy Manning [BBC special correspondent] package then in to see first of all Paddy, who had not slept at all, then John Swinney [Deputy Scotland First Minister] and Kevin Pringle who was looking after him. Kevin not as I imagined him. Very mild and unassuming, specs, tidy, quiet.

John Swinney had a lot of natural charm. Loves Tiree. Had me and Grace in hysterics describing a John Harris [*Guardian*] film of Tom Clarke [Labour MP until 15 May] campaigning in Coatbridge, essentially asking large crowds of Catholics to shout they were voting Labour, followed by people saying no they weren't when Tom and the cameras left. He was interesting on Nicola, how she had changed, become stronger, escaped the shadow of Alex. Clearly they were a bit down on him, felt he had used his book to get in on the act when in fact they had been hoping he would keep his head down. Nicola had always been in his shadow but having escaped it she had really emerged in a stronger light.

I told John S that in my only real meeting with her, when she was health minister, she had come over as quite cold. He said a lot of people said that but she had developed; also that back then she was a lot shyer than now, and probably 'a bit petrified as to how to handle you.' He said she was very analytical, liked solving problems, good with the team. I asked what we should do. He said Jim [Murphy] just had to go. He said as leader, he failed first time in the elections and he never recovered.* Once you get a sense of being a loser it is hard to shake off in the same role.

We chatted about the SFA role re. MUP and he said he would look into it, said he was sure the government would welcome it because they knew it needed direction and drive. He said no way would he or anyone else in the SNP have blocked it and as far as he was concerned, a strong stance on alcohol was a good thing. He and Kevin both said they were genuinely shocked by how well they did. They had not really dared to believe the polls. The exit poll came as a shock. Grace was with me and she said afterwards that the SNP guys were just so much nicer than everyone else. She said she found Paddy a bit pompous and emotional. She didn't take to Julia Hartley-Brewer, who was standing in for the UKIP No. 2, who had pulled out.

Three leaders had left during the day, Farage, Clegg and Ed. I gave [Francis] Maude [paymaster general, panellist] and Swinney a copy of *Winners*, pointing out they had won. I was pretty tired but felt on form and all the interviews earlier had got me into my mode re. the need for a proper debate about Labour's future, not just a change at the top. The warm-up question was about alcohol and cannabis so that allowed me to get a good nice line in re. SNP leading the way on MUP, and a round of applause re. my general line.

Once we got going on the programme proper, it was: is Scottish independence inevitable (no but likelier)?; is Labour too right-wing for England and too left-wing for Scotland (more complicated)?; why did Libs get punished and Tories rewarded for the coalition (because they are ruthless bastards)?; is the voting system fair (no but we had the chance to change it and didn't take it)?; and can Cameron keep us in Europe (no, but the people will)?; I got owned at the end. Having said to a young woman – Hannah, who it turned out I knew from BFC – that she should stop complaining re. not being represented and get involved, I then said having a referendum on EU was damaging and a guy in the audience pointed out the contradiction. Fair enough. But I did pretty well, especially tonally re. Scotland and message-wise re. Labour. Best laugh was when Julia [HB]

---

* Elected leader of Scottish Labour in 2014, Murphy announced he was standing down following Labour's loss of forty of its forty-one seats in the election.

was telling Swinney to stop interrupting her and he did and I said, 'That's how Nicola shuts him up.' I liked him a lot.

Trouble was we painted them as awful and even though nationalism might be, they are not. He said to me afterwards my *GQ* interview with Salmond was a nightmare for them. Alex on back foot. Maude's spads telling me how awful Sue Gray was when given she is the least awful person imaginable said a lot about them. Also that she had said 'let's keep in touch' as though she was sure the Tories had lost. I stayed for the dinner. They had started the show by presenting Paddy and me with chocolate hat and chocolate kilt which we ate for pix. I was pretty knacked by the end. Home and watched a bit of telly late on. Shagged out.

Russell Brand called. He wanted to meet up to discuss him becoming mayor! Meanwhile I was being inundated with lots of messages saying it was a vindication of TB/New Labour/'you guys'. But I suspected the next steps were going to be fraught. TB was in one of his 'I know I am right' modes on the various calls through the day. Maybe he was. But I said we had moved a bit left from TB to GB, a bit more left from GB to Ed, and even if it seemed obvious to us what needed to happen, I'm not sure it will.

I chatted on and off through the day with Axelrod. We had enjoyed working together and had arranged to do stuff in the autumn. 'How the hell did we all miss this?' he said. 'Not one poll forecast this result. What happened? And what could we have done?' I said I was not sure we could have done anything. The polls were wrong and that meant the election framed much more around the question of what we/SNP would be like rather than what five more years of Cameron meant for the country. I told him what TB had been saying, and said I feared I underestimated Cameron's appeal. Ed outperformed expectations for sure, and showed some real qualities en route, but we had started from such a low base that we had started to kid ourselves. I felt there had to be a rethink and a change of direction because what we were offering has been rejected. David said he was sure the focus on working people had been the right frame, and that it would increasingly be an issue if people don't start to see real gains. But you have to offer your prescriptions here as part of a broader vision of how to achieve lasting economic growth. He said Ed was resistant to elements of that because it strayed too closely to the New Labour message, and so we lost some lift. But he performed admirably, he said, and you're right, we probably started thinking with our hearts and not our heads, deluding ourselves a little about the obstacles. 'Not the worse shortcoming, though!'

He said the problem of being squeezed by nationalism on both ends intensified at the end, and in truth we were unable to communicate Ed as a plausible PM. That much was pretty clear from the polling. Ed's performance and his personal appeal improved. But his 'ready to be PM' numbers didn't.

I sent David M a message: 'How you feeling?' And back came reply: 'Gloomy, angry, sorry.' He said it had worked out as he feared it would, and that nobody could say we modernisers had been the problem. Just as Neil had shocked him with 'we got our party back', he shocked him again last night when the poll came in and he had said it was the result of false consciousness on the part of an electorate brainwashed by the media. The media were indeed awful, said DM, but that was not the reason we lost.

Index

Alastair Campbell is AC throughout.

7/7 [London bombing] 71, 188
9/11 victims 215
10 O'Clock Live [Ch4] 120, 323, 324

Aaronovitch, David 53, 186, 219, 374
Abayev, Dauren 354
Abbas, Mahmoud 46
Abbott, Diane 20, 30, 526–7
Abbott, Tony 497, 498, 501, 502
D'Abbro, John 76
Abdel-Latif, Hatem 602
Abdullah, King of Jordan 169, 193
Abell, Stephen 189
Aberdein, Geoff 702
Abibullayev, Altay 353
Abrami, Mark 465, 466, 467, 471, 472
Abramovich, Roman 106
Abu Qatada 324, 325
Accused, The [BBC] 280–81, 386, 387, 588
Ackerman, Naomi 711
Ackerman, Roy 145
Adamson, Marksteen 486, 488–9
Adele 327
Adem [CC friend] 612
Adepitan, Ade 606, 621
Adonis, Andrew 9, 302, 303, 373, 526, 573, 728, 737, 754, 760
Afghanistan 445
Africa 441–2
Afterman, Jean 614
Afwerki, Isaias 123

Agnew, Jonathan 221
Ahern, Bertie 6, 102, 124, 127, 470, 485, 546, 547
Ahmed, Kamal 533
Ainslie, Ben 612, 620
Airlie, David 600
Aitkenhead, Decca 519, 520, 616, 711, 712
Akers, Sue 329
Akram, Wasim 617
Alan Titchmarsh Show, The [ITV] 320
Albanese, Tom 70, 90, 294, 319, 393, 440, 441
Albania 249–51, 314–17, 332–3, 414–15, 455–6, 475–6, 483–4, 502–4, 509–10, 517–19, 537–8, 550–58, 628–9, 671–4, 743–5
Alberici, Emma 498
Alexander, Danny 6, 14, 18, 20, 105, 289, 304, 633–4, 636, 710
Alexander, Douglas 145–6, 238–9, 529, 595–6, 629–30, 674–8, 679–80, 697–8, 737–8, 745–9, 747–8
    AC hit by car while talking to 735
    as campaign co-ordinator 536
    coalition team 748
    conference speech 409
    election day 761
    on EM 498, 554, 610, 635, 638, 650, 658, 721
    EM and 173, 308, 670–71, 728
    EM debate preparation 729, 740
    EM foreign policy speech 749
    EM on 668

holding on to seat 759
    Iraq distancing 459
    Labour fundraiser 144
    Murphy and 598
    Question Time 208
    Saatchi Gallery party 50
    Scottish independence campaign 631, 632, 633
    Scottish polls 741
    Syria 325
    talking to GB 744
    on TB–GB 709
    worried about losing seat 752
Alexander, James 338
Ali, Rushanara 414
Ali, Waheed 697, 699, 724
Aliyev, Rakhat 353
All in the Mind [AC novel] 16, 87, 92, 112, 142, 346, 349, 372, 432, 703
Allan, Tim
    AC and 618, 693
    Assad and 183
    BAA pitch 360
    EM and 569
    Labour and 362, 679
    meetings with AC 112, 582
    Morocco 300, 352, 431
    on Murdoch 358
    Omnicom 613
    Portland 81, 119, 359, 365, 533, 665, 715
    sport strategy 336
    TB and 142, 368, 597, 598
Allardyce, Sam 281, 378, 548
Allen, Jonathan 550
Allen, Paul 6, 47, 102, 113, 125–7, 169, 201, 265–6

Blair, Tony (TB) *cont.*
 interviews 328, 374–5, 596
 and Iraq 614, 644
 and Ireland 175, 179
 Irish Diaries, The 470, 484
 on ISIS 626
 Jerusalem and 200
 and Kazakhstan 282, 290,
  354, 367, 368, 413, 488
 and Kosovo 525, 628–9
 on Labour Party 474–5
 leak of AC statement 276
 'leaving do' dream 60
 legacy of 473
 letter from Neil K. 485
 Leveson Inquiry 248, 277,
  280, 287, 346–7, 351, 354,
  368, 369, 427
 Libya and 140
 London 2012 382
 and Mandela 565–6
 Mandelson on 340–41
 meeting with AC 378–80
 meets Nazarbayev 155
 memoirs 7–10, 13, 26, 36,
  41–5, 47, 48–9, 126, 185
 memorials attended 282, 589
 Merkel and 575
 the Middle East and 370, 516
 Murdoch and 204, 234, 347, 361
 and N. Ireland 479
 Obama visit 177
 office event 570
 peace-keeping envoy 31
 and PG 69, 106, 263, 264
 PG funeral and interment
  269, 348
 as PM ix
 position in Labour Party 485
 'pre Chilcot' work 178, 186
 press and 120–21, 211
 Prince Charles and 192,
  196–7, 202–3
 Progress pressure group
  204–5, 209
 projects on the go 427
 Qatar 2022 WC bid and 91
 Rebekah Brooks and 204
 religion and 52, 111, 258
 reputation 253, 266, 287, 577,
  579, 585, 591, 609, 611,
  622, 673, 696, 699, 722
 Robinson on 127
 role and profile 491–2, 571–2,
  601, 621, 674, 737
 royal wedding snub 157,
  164, 178

 royalties 39–40
 and savings review 513
 Scottish independence
  campaign 633
 Sharon and 571
 speeches 347, 378, 427, 729,
  734, 741
 strategy and leadership 93,
  178, 252
 stressed and worried 242,
  347, 548
 and Syria 325, 517, 674
 TB–Bush papers 109, 112,
  113, 114, 309, 313, 611,
  654
 US Liberty medal 52
 visit to Kazakhstan 244, 245
 Wendi D. and 494, 504, 558,
  560, 562
 working on MEPP 20, 24, 46,
  220, 234
 and Xstrata merger 417
Blair Years, The [AC] 13, 72, 118,
 168, 248, 287
Blairites 6, 77, 85, 99, 216, 301–2
Blake, John 743
Blake, Nick and Clio 223
Blank, Victor 280, 299, 453, 562,
 590, 617
Blatter, Sepp 179, 181
Bleakley, Christine 15
Blekinsop, Tom 328
Blind, Daley 646
Blunkett, David 553, 573
Boal, Thomas 449
Boffey, Chris 301
Bogdanor, Vernon 658
Bolland, Mark 197, 200
Bolt, Usain 381, 382, 571
Bolton, Stuart 321
Boonen family 229, 254, 255
Boothroyd, Betty 44
Borat [mockumentary] 353, 470
Borgen [TV series] 314, 327,
 447–8
Bosnia 486, 516, 517, 531,
 539–40, 559, 567–8, 570
Boston, USA 659–60
Botham, Ian 168, 218, 221, 322,
 736, 742–3
Botham, Kath 736
Botham, Liam 221
Botting, Anna 62
de Botton, Alain and Charlotte
 576, 740
Boulton, Adam 3, 217
Bounds, Andrew 758

Bower, Tom 601
Bowman, John 411
Boyan, Eithne 411
Boycott, Geoffrey 148, 221
Boyle, Danny xiv, 378, 381,
 383–4, 458
Boyle, Frankie 434
Bradby, Tom 45, 358
Bradshaw, Ben 13
Bradshaw, David 276, 362, 373, 458
Brady, Chris 720
Bragg, Billy 306
Bragg, Melvyn 62
Brailsford, Dave 507–9, 615–16,
 618–19, 625–8, 666–7, 681–2,
 688–90, 692–3, 701–2
 on AC as MP 410
 AC 'ghosting' book 453–4,
  458, 460, 482
 Armstrong and 416, 608
 Campbell sons and 23, 751
 chats with AC 382, 694
 on election result 763
 on EM 404
 Fran Millar on 422
 on Froome 707
 and J. Murdoch 661
 media and 280, 620, 621
 sorting new bike for AC 386
 Sports Personality of the
  Year 434
 way of working 609, 624
 Wiggins and 617
 and *Winners* 590, 625
 working with AC 753
Braithwaite, Julian 147, 630
Brand, Jo 83, 114
Brand, Russell 543, 607, 752–3,
 766
Brandreth, Gyles 367
Branson, Richard 318, 580, 601,
 617–18
Brearley, Mike 376–7
Bremner, Rory 371
Brexit xi, xv
Bridge family 106, 161
Bridge, Sissy 36, 230, 283, 394
Bridge, The [TV series] 576, 581
Bridge, Victoria 161
Bridges, Kevin 655
British & Irish Lions 64, 181,
 501, 504
Britton, Fern 33
Brivati, Brian 83
Broadbent, Jim 164
Broadfoot, Darryl 627, 645, 686,
 688–90, 692–3

advertising 146, 505
employers and 423
events for 299–300, 346, 465, 486, 541, 579
films 341
funding 164, 506
work of 55, 81, 528, 576
Timms, Dan 488, 495
Today [R4] 501, 670
Tomlinson, Mike 422
Top Gear [BBC] 21, 26–7, 29, 470
Total Politics [magazine] 541, 544
Tour de France 23, 66, 366, 384, 487, 507–9
Townsend, Martin 328
Townsend, Phil 28, 591, 592–3
Tremble, Lisa 302
Trescothick, Marcus 299
Tricart, Cyrille 507
Trickett, Sam 600
Tricycle Theatre 35
Trierweiler, Valerie 448
Triesman, David 8
Trimble, Daphne 126
Trimble, David 126
Trott, Laura 533
Trousset, Nathalie 233
Tubridy, Ryan 221, 717
TUC [Trades Union Congress] 51–2
Tucker, Emma 314, 326, 330
Tufnell, Phil 57
tuition fees 70, 78, 80, 82, 91, 97, 99
Tulloh, Clive 477
Turley, Steve 484
Turnbull, Andrew 656
Turner, Gabe 355
Turner, Janice 330
Turner, Nikki 11
Turner, Ruth 169
Turner, Trevor 334
Twigg, Stephen 452, 536
Tyldesley, Clive and Susan 144, 172, 504
Tyrimos, Andrea 298

Ukraine 583, 624
Umunna, Chuka 212, 430, 436, 622, 738
Underhill, Chris 467
United States 613–14
University College of Football Business [UCFB] 42, 82, 91, 144, 188, 207–8, 215, 259, 333, 430, 670, 694, 701
Ussher, Kitty 213

Valls, Manuel 596
Vassilenko, Roman 243
Van Renterghem, Marion 530, 735, 737, 742, 754
Vaz, Keith 50
Veitch, Paul 350
Veliaj, Erion 18, 255, 257, 414, 455, 580, 628, 743, 744–5
Verveer, Melanne and Phil 224–5, 460
Victor, Carol 646
Victor, Ed
AC as MP 458
and *Head of State* 649
literary agent 12, 16, 314, 331, 349, 549, 639
meetings with AC 49, 62, 107, 144, 399, 678, 735
parties at 101, 285, 567, 576
PG and 233, 264, 350
and publishers 26, 458, 524
road trip with 546, 547
unwell 650
in US 271, 665
Winners:... and 570, 624, 647, 654
Victoria Derbyshire [BBC] 640
Vieira, Patrick 467
Vine, Sarah 722
Viner, Kath 499, 700
Vlahutin, Romana 745
Vokes, Sam 430, 749
Vorderman, Carol 372
Vovk, Špela 198, 200
Vučić, Aleksandar 645, 647, 672, 690–92, 694, 744

Wakeling, Vic 355
Walden, Celia 31, 101, 142, 206, 519, 567
Wales, Jimmy 412, 434
Walker, Barrie 696, 718
Walker, Dan 173, 271, 606, 715
Wall, Stephen 113
Wallace, Marjorie 511
Wallace, Ross 85
Wallis, Neil 331, 465
Walpole, Graham 653
Walsh, David 442, 458
Walsh, Geoff 500
Walsh, Willie 617
Wanless, Peter 300
Wanted, The 182, 183, 186
Warburton, Sam 505
Ward, Ciaran 185, 204, 242, 328, 346, 514
Warne, Shane 617, 624, 641

Warr, Adrian 327, 365
Warren, Frank 262, 440
Warsi, Sayeeda 52, 333
Waters, John 29
Watson, John 135
Watson, Roland 112
Watson, Tom 43, 48, 186, 217, 219, 247, 272, 332, 379
Watt, Nick 95, 109, 169, 192, 196, 197, 200, 201, 371, 544
Watts family 106
Wax, Ruby 320, 536–7
Webb, Howard 32
Webb, Justin 67
Webster, John 142–3
Webster, Phil 82, 292, 326–7, 424
Wegelius, Charly 508
Wegg-Prosser, Ben 68, 69, 77, 109, 187, 302, 339, 525
Weir, David 394, 396
Welbeck, Danny 331
Welch, Denise 372
Welch, Jack 724
Weller, Paul 593
Wen Jiabao 196
Wenger, Arsène 60, 65–6, 70, 102, 230, 454, 735
Werritty, Adam 249
West, Alan 17
West, Dominic 63
Westmacott, Peter 159
Wheeler, Charles and Pip 186
Wheen, Francis 83
Whelan, Charlie 217, 362
Whetstone, Rachel 123, 334
Whitaker, James 357
White, Kate 55
White, Mike 156, 214, 709
Whitehorn, Will 300
Whittamore, Steve 335
Whittingdale, John 120
Whitton, David 90
Widdecombe, Ann 532
Wiesel, Elie 461
Wiggins, Bradley 23, 366, 420, 422, 434, 590, 615–16, 617, 658, 666–7, 682, 689, 707
Wiinberg, Ulf 461
WikiLeaks 94, 96, 98, 103, 131
Wilcockson, Nigel 576, 585, 625, 641, 653, 654, 671, 726
Wilcox, Russ 607
Wilkinson, Joy 17–18
Wilkinson, Tony 616
Willetts, David 171, 215
William, Prince 86, 97, 157, 160, 197, 200, 358